THE HERITAGE OF
WORLD
CIVILIZATIONS

TEACHING AND LEARNING CLASSROOM EDITION

BRIEF THIRD EDITION

COMBINED VOLUME

Albert M. Craig
HARVARD UNIVERSITY

William A. Graham
HARVARD UNIVERSITY

Donald Kagan
YALE UNIVERSITY

Steven Ozment
HARVARD UNIVERSITY

Frank M. Turner
YALE UNIVERSITY

PEARSON

Prentice
Hall

Upper Saddle River, New Jersey 07458

Library of Congress Cataloging-in-Publication Data

The heritage of world civilizations / Albert M. Craig ... [et al].- Brief 3rd ed., combined volume
    p. cm.
    Includes bibliographical references and index.
    ISBN 0-13-219682-4
      1. Civilizations–History–Textbooks.   I. Craig, Albert M.
    CB69.H45 2005

VP, Editorial Director: Charlyce Jones Owen
Executive Editor: Charles Cavaliere
Associate Editor: Emsal Hasan
Editorial Assistant: Maria Guarascio
Senior Media Editor: Deborah O'Connell
Editor-in-Chief, Development: Rochelle Diogenes
**AVP, Director of Production
  and Manufacturing:** Barbara Kittle
Senior Managing Editor: Joanne Riker
Production Liaison: Randy Pettit
Prepress and Manufacturing Manager: Nick Sklitsis
Prepress and Manufacturing Buyer: Ben Smith
Director of Marketing: Brandy Dawson
Marketing Manager: Emily Cleary
Creative Design Director: Leslie Osher
Interior and Cover Designer: Laura Gardner

Cartographer: CartoGraphics
Electronic Artists: Maria Piper, Mirella Signoretto,
  Bruce Killmer, Carey Davies
Director, Image Resource Center: Melinda Reo
Interior Image Specialist: Beth Brenzel
Cover Image Specialist: Karen Sanatar
Image Permission Coordinator: Michelina Viscusi
Photo Researcher: Elaine Soares
Color Scanning Services: Joe Conti, Greg Harrison, Cory
  Skidds, Rob Uibelhoer, Ron Walko
Editorial Production and Composition: GEX Publishing
  Services
Printer/Binder: The Courier Companies
Cover Printer: The Lehigh Press, Inc.

Wracked by wars and civil strife since the Soviet invasion of 1979, nearly three-million refugees from Afghanistan live in neighboring Pakistan, such as this woman from the Khairab camp in Baluchistan province.

Credits and acknowledgments borrowed from other sources and reproduced, with permission, in this textbook appear on appropriate page within text or on page C-1

Pearson Education Ltd., London
Pearson Education Australia Pty., Limited, Sydney
Pearson Education Singapore, Pte., Ltd.
Pearson Education North Asia Ltd., Hong Kong

Pearson Education Canada, Ltd., Toronto
Pearson Educación de Mexico, S.A. de C.V.
Pearson Education — Japan, Tokyo
Pearson Education Malaysia, Pte., Ltd.Pearson Education

10 9 8 7 6 5 4 3 2 1

ISBN 0-13-219682-4

Visualizing The Past

Goddesses and the Female Form in Ancient Art 102

5

Africa, Early History to 1000 C.E. 104

6

Republican and Imperial Rome 122

7

*China's First Empire
221 B.C.E.– 589 C.E.*   152

Visualizing The Past

PART 3
CONSOLIDATION AND INTERACTION OF WORLD CIVILIZATIONS 172

Visualizing The Past

The Divine in the Middle Ages 308

14

Visualizing The Past

Mapping the World before 1500 334

15

PART 4
THE WORLD IN TRANSITION   370

Europe 1500–1650: Expansion, Reformation and Religious Wars   372

Religions of the World

Africa, ca. 1000–1800   414

18

Conquest and Exploitation: The Development of the Transatlantic Economy 434

19

East Asia in the Late Traditional Era 456

20

*State Building and Society
in Early Modern Europe* 484

21

The Last Great Islamic Empires 1500–1800 514

Visualizing The Past

PART 5
ENLIGHTENMENT AND REVOLUTION IN THE WEST 534

22

The Age of European Enlightenment 536

23

Revolutions in the Transatlantic World   556

24

Political Consolidation in Nineteenth-Century Europe and North America, 1815–1880   582

Visualizing The Past

PART 6

INTO THE MODERN WORLD 616

Northern Transatlantic Economy and Society, 1815–1914 618

26

Latin America from Independence to the 1940s 652

27

India, the Islamic Heartlands, and Africa: The Challenge of Modernity (1800–1945) 672

Religions of the World

PART 7
GLOBAL CONFLICT AND CHANGE 726

29

Imperialism and World War I 728

30

Depression, European Dictators, and the American New Deal 750

31

World War II 772

32

The West Since World War II   794

33

East Asia, The Recent Decades   818

34

Postcolonialism and Beyond: Latin America, Africa, Asia, and the Middle East 836

Visualizing The Past

Imperialism and Race in Modern Art 862

History's Voices

SPECIAL FEATURES

Maps

SPECIAL FEATURES

SPECIAL FEATURES

Visualizing the Past

Religions of the World

PREFACE

The response of the United States to the events of September 11, 2001, including the war in Iraq and Afghanistan, have brought upon the world a new awareness of human history in a global context. Prior to the attacks on New York and Washington and the subsequent U.S. intervention in the Middle East, readers in North America generally understood world history and globalism as academic concepts. They now understand them as realities shaping their daily lives and experience. The immediate pressures of the present and of the foreseeable future draw us to seek a more certain and extensive understanding of the past.

The idea of globalization is now a pressing reality on the lives of nations, affecting the domestic security of their citizens, the deployment of armed forces, their standard of living, and the environment. Whether, as Samuel Huntington, the distinguished Harvard political scientist, contends, we are witnessing a clash of civilizations, we have certainly entered a new era in which no active citizen or educated person can escape the necessity of understanding the past in global terms. Both the historical experience and the moral, political, and religious values of the different world civilizations now demand our attention and our understanding. It is our hope that in these new, challenging times *The Heritage of World Civilizations* will provide one path to such knowledge.

THE ROOTS OF GLOBALIZATION

Globalization—that is, the increasing interaction and interdependency of the various regions of the world—has resulted from two major historical developments: the closing of the European era of world history and the rise of technology.

From approximately 1500 C.E. to the middle of the twentieth century, Europeans gradually came to dominate the world through colonization (most particularly in North and South America), state-building, economic productivity, and military power. That era of European dominance ended during the third quarter of the twentieth century after Europe had brought unprecedented destruction on itself during World War II and as the nations of Asia, the Near East, and Africa achieved new positions on the world scene. Their new political independence, their control over strategic natural resources, and the expansion of their economies (especially those of

the nations of the Pacific rim of Asia), and in some cases their access to nuclear weapons have changed the shape of world affairs.

Further changing the world political and social situation has been a growing discrepancy in the economic development of different regions that is often portrayed as a problem between the northern and southern hemispheres. Beyond the emergence of this economic disparity has been the remarkable advance of radical political Islamism during the past forty years. In the midst of all these developments, as a result of the political collapse of the former Soviet Union, the United States has emerged as the single major world power.

The second historical development that continues to fuel the pace of globalization is the advance of technology, associated most importantly with transportation, military weapons, and electronic communication. The advances in transportation over the past two centuries including ships, railways, and airplanes have made more parts of the world and its resources accessible to more people in ever shorter spans of time. Over the past century and a half, military weapons of increasingly destructive power enabled Europeans and then later the United States to dominate other regions of the globe. Now, the spread of these weapons means that any nation with sophisticated military technology can threaten other nations, no matter how far away. Furthermore, technologies that originated in the West from the early twentieth century to the present have been turned against the West. More recently, the electronic revolution associated with computer technology and most particularly the internet has sparked unprecedented speed and complexity in global communications. It is astonishing to recall that personal computers have been generally available for less than twenty-five years and the rapid personal communication associated with them has existed for less than fifteen years.

Why not, then, focus only on new factors in the modern world, such as the impact of technology and the end of the European era? To do so would ignore the very deep roots that these developments have in the past. More important, the events of recent years demonstrate, as the authors of this book have long contended, that the major religious traditions continue to shape and drive the modern world as well as the world of the past. The religious traditions link today's civilizations to their most ancient roots. We believe this emphasis on the great religious traditions recognizes not only a factor that has shaped the past, but one that is profoundly and dynamically alive in our world today.

STRENGTHS OF THE TEXT

Balanced and Flexible Presentation   In this edition, as in past editions, we have sought to present world history fairly, accurately, and in a way that does justice to its great variety. History has many facets, no one of which can account for the others. Any attempt to tell the story of civilization from a single perspective, no matter how timely, is bound to neglect or suppress some important part of that story.

Historians have recently brought a vast array of new tools and concepts to bear on the study of history. Our coverage introduces students to various aspects of social and intellectual history as well as to the more traditional political, diplomatic, and military coverage. We firmly believe that only through an appreciation of all pathways to understanding of the past can the real heritage of world civilizations be claimed.

The Heritage of World Civilizations, TLC Edition, is designed to accommodate a variety of approaches to a course in world history, allowing teachers to stress what is most important to them. Some teachers will ask students to read all the chapters. Others will select among them to reinforce assigned readings and lectures.

Clarity and Accessibility   Good narrative history requires clear, vigorous prose. Our goal has been to make our presentation fully accessible to students without compromising on vocabulary or conceptual level. We hope this effort will benefit both teachers and students.

Current Scholarship   As in previous editions, changes in this edition reflect our determination to incorporate the most recent developments in historical scholarship and the expanding concerns of professional historians. To better highlight the dynamic processes of world history, significant new coverage of the Silk Road, Byzantium, the Crusades, Southeast Asia, women in Islam, nineteenth-century European science, the homefront during World War II, and recent events in the Middle East has been added.

Pedagogical Features   This edition retains many of the pedagogical features of previous editions, while providing increased assessment opportunities.

- NEW • **Chapter Highlights** begin each chapter and provide a preview of the key developments and themes that are to follow.

- **Part Timelines** show the major events in five regions—Europe, the Near East and India, East Asia, Africa, and the Americas—side by side. Appropriate photographs enrich each timeline.

- **Chapter-Opening Questions**, organized by the main subtopics of each chapter, encourage careful consideration of important themes and developments. Each question is repeated at the appropriate place in the margin of the text.

- **Chronologies** within each chapter help students organize a time sequence for key events.

- **History's Voices**, including selections from sacred books, poems, philosophy, political manifestos, letters, and travel accounts, introduce students to the raw material of history, providing an intimate contact with the people of the past and their concerns. Questions accompanying the source documents direct students toward important, thought-provoking issues and help them relate the documents to the material in the text. They can be used to stimulate class discussion or as topics for essays and study groups.

- **Map Explorations** and **Critical-Thinking Questions** prompt students to engage with maps, often in an interactive fashion. Each Map Exploration is found on the Companion Website for the text.

- NEW • **Religions of the World** essays examine the historical impact of each of the world's great religious traditions: Judaism, Christianity, Islam, Buddhism, and Hinduism.

- **Visualizing the Past** essays, found at the end of selected chapters, analyze important aspects of world history through photographs, fine art, sculpture, and woodcuts. Focus questions and a running narrative guide students though a careful examination of the historical issues raised by each topic in question. Four new Visualizing the Past essays have been added to this edition: "Humans and Nature in the Ancient World," "The Silk Road," "Mapping the World before 1500," and "Imagining Women in the 18th and 19th Centuries."

- **Chapter Review** Questions help students focus on and interpret the broad themes of a chapter. These questions can be used for class discussion and essay topics.

- **Overview Tables** in each chapter summarize complex issues.

- **Quick Reviews**, found at key places in the margins of each chapter, encourage students to review important concepts.

- **Key Terms**, boldfaced in the text, are listed (with page reference) at the end of each chapter, and defined in the book's glossary.

- **Documents CD-ROM**, containing over 200 documents in world history, is bound with all new copies of the text. Relevant documents are listed at appropriate places in the margin of the text and at the end of each chapter.

- NEW **Study in Time**, a laminated six-panel timeline of world history, provides a succinct overview of key developments in social, political, and cultural history in global history from earliest times to the present.

- NEW **Online Essays**, located on the companion website for *The Heritage of World Civilizations*, provide additional learning opportunities. One set of essays examines technology and civilization from a cross-cultural perspective, while a second set introduces each chapter's content from a wider global viewpoint.

Content and Organization The many changes in content and organization in this edition of *The Heritage of World Civilizations* reflect our ongoing effort to present a truly global survey of world civilizations that at the same time gives a rich picture of the history of individual regions:

- **Strengthened Global Approach.** This new TLC edition more explicitly highlights the connections and parallels in global history among regions of the world.

Greater emphasis is now placed on cultural exchange, trade, encounter, and the diffusion of ideas.

- **Expanded and Improved Map Program.** The entire map program has been completely clarified and expanded. Several new maps graphically illustrate key global developments, such as trade in the classical world, the spread of Buddhism, the Islamicization of Southeast Asia, the Columbian exchange, world slavery, European global conflicts in the eighteenth century, global migration, and the Holocaust. Every single map in the text has been redesigned for greater visual appeal and accuracy. A listing of all the maps in the text can be found on pp. xxiv–xxvi.

- **Improved, Streamlined Organization.** To better accommodate typical teaching sequences, the number of chapters has been reduced to 34, with coverage of European society and state-building in the seventeenth and eighteenth centuries now treated in a single chapter. In addition, coverage of Han China (chapter 7) now immediately succeeds coverage of the Rome (chapter 6) making it easier to draw connections and parallels between these two empires. The final chapter has been exensively reorganized to better examine important recent events in the Middle East.

- **New Design and Photo Program.** The entire text has been set in a lively and engaging new design. Each of the 34 chapters includes photos never before included in previous editions of the text, the total number of illustrations in the text has been increased.

A Note on Dates and Transliteration We have used B.C.E. (before the common era) and C.E. (common era) instead of B.C. (before Christ) and A.D. (anno domini, the year of our Lord) to designate dates.

Until recently, most scholarship on China used the Wade-Giles system of romanization for Chinese names and terms. China, today, however, uses another system known as pinyin. Virtually all Western newspapers have adopted it. In order that students may move easily from the present text to the existing body of advanced scholarship on Chinese history, we now use the pinyin system throughout the text.

Also, we have followed the currently accepted English transliterations of Arabic words. For example, today Koran is being replaced by the more accurate Qur'an; similarly Muhammad is preferable to Mohammed and Muslim to Moslem. We have not tried to distinguish the letters 'ayn and hamza; both are rendered by a simple apostrophe (') as in shi'ite.

With regard to Sanskritic transliteration, we have not distinguished linguals and dentals, and both palatal and lingual s are rendered sh, as in Shiva and Upanishad.

ANCILLARY INSTRUCTIONAL MATERIALS

The Heritage of World Civilizations, TLC Edition, comes with an extensive package of ancillary materials.

For the Instructor

- **Instructor's Resource Binder** This innovative, all-in-one resource organizes the instructor's manual, the Test-Item File, and the transparency pack by each chapter of *The Heritage of World Civilizations* to facilitate class preparation. The Instructor's Resource Binder also includes an **Instructor's Resource CD-ROM**, which contains all of the maps, graphs, and many of the illustrations from the text in easily downloadable electronic files.

- The *Instructor Resource CD-ROM*, compatible with both Windows and Macintosh environments, provides instructors with such essential teaching tools as hundreds of digitized images and maps for classroom presentations, PowerPoint lectures, and other Instructional material. The assets on the IRCD-ROM can be easily exported into online courses, such as WebCT and Blackboard.

- *Test Manager* is a computerized test management program for Windows and Macintosh environments. The program allows instructors to select items from the test-item file to create tests. It also allows online testing.

- The *Transparency Package* provides instructors with full color transparency acetates of all the maps, charts, and graphs in the text for use in the classroom.

For the Student

- *History Notes* (Volumes I and II) provides practice tests, essay questions, and map exercise to help reinforce key concepts.

- *Documents in World History* (Volumes I and II) is a collection of 200 primary source documents in global history. Questions accompanying the documents can be used for discussion or as writing assignments.

- **DK** • Produced in collaboration with Dorling Kindersley, the world's most respected cartography publisher, *The Prentice Hall Atlas of World History* includes approximately 100 maps fundamental to the study of world history—from early hominids to the twenty-first century.

- *Reading Critically About History* is a brief guide to reading effectively that provides students with helpful strategies for reading a history textbook.

- *Understanding and Answering Essay Questions* suggest helpful analytical tools for understanding different types of essay questions, and provides precise guidelines for preparing well-crafted essay answers.

- • Prentice Hall is pleased to provide adopters of *The Heritage of World Civilizations* with an opportunity to receive significant discounts when copies of the text are bundled with Penguin Classics titles in world history. Contact your local Prentice Hall representative for details.

Media Resources

OneKey Prentice Hall's Online Resource, **OneKey** lets instructors and students in to the best teaching and learning resources–all in one place. This all-inclusive online resource is designed to help you minimize class preparation and maximize teaching time. Conveniently organized by chapter, OneKey for *The Heritage of World Civilizations*, TLC Edition, reinforces what students have learned in class and from the text. Among the student resources available for each chapter are: a complete, media-rich e-book version of *The Heritage of World Civilizations* TLC Edition; quizzes organized by the main subtopics of each chapter; over 200 primary-source documents; and interactive map quizzes.

For instructors, OneKey includes images and maps from *The Heritage of World Civilizations* TLC Edition, instructional material, hundreds of primary-source documents, and PowerPoint presentations.

ResearchNavigator.com *Prentice Hall One Search with Research Navigator: History 2005* This brief guide focuses on developing critical-thinking skills necessary for evaluating and using online sources. It provides a brief introduction to navigating the Internet with specific references to History web sites. It also provides an access code and instruction on using Research Navigator, a powerful research tool that provides entry to three exclusive databases of reliable source material: ContentSelect Academic Journal Database, the *New York Times* Search by Subject Archive, and Link Library.

The *Companion Website with Grade Tracker*™ (*www.prenhall.com/craig*) works in tandem with the text and features objectives, study questions, web links to related Internet resources, document exercises, interactive maps, online essays on technology and global history, and map labelling exercises.

World History Document CD-ROM Bound into every new copy of this textbook is a free World History Documents CD-ROM. This is a powerful resource for research and additional reading that contains more than 200 primary source documents central to World History. Each document provides essay questions that are linked directly to a website where short-essay answers can be submitted oline or printed out. A complete list of documents on the CD-ROM is found at the end of the text.

Pearson Prentice Hall is pleased to serve as a sponsor of the **The World History Association Teaching Prize** and **The World History Association and Phi Alpha Theta Student Paper Prize** (undergraduate and graduate divisions). Both of these prizes are awarded annually. For more information, contact *thewha@hawaii.edu*

Acknowledgments

We are grateful to the many scholars and teachers whose thoughtful and often detailed comments helped shape this as well as previous editions of *The Heritage of World Civilizations.* The advice and guidance provided by Magnus T. Bernhardsson of Williams College in the revision of the coverage of Islam is especially appreciated. We also thank Tianyuan Tan of Harvard University, who helped with conversion of Chinese words to the pinyin system and Gayle K. Brunelle, California State University (Fullerton), who provided invaluable input on strengthening the book's global approach.

Special thanks to A. Dan Frankforter of Pennsylvania State University who helped edit this new TLC edition.

Wayne Ackerson, *Salisbury State University*

Jack Martin Balcer, *Ohio State University*

Charmarie J. Blaisdell, *Northeastern University*

Deborah Buffton, *University of Wisconsin at La Crosse*

Loretta Burns, *Mankato State University*

Gayle K. Brunelle, *California State University, Fullerton*

Chun-shu Chang, *University of Michigan, Ann Arbor*

Mark Chavalas, *University of Wisconsin at La Crosse*

Anthony Cheeseboro, *Southern Illinois University at Edwardsville*

William J. Courteney, *University of Wisconsin*

Samuel Willard Crompton, *Holyoke Community College*

James B. Crowley, *Yale University*

Bruce Cummings, *The University of Chicago*

Stephen F. Dale, *Ohio State University, Columbus*

Clarence B. Davis, *Marian College*

Raymond Van Dam, *University of Michigan, Ann Arbor*

Bill Donovan, *Loyola University of Maryland*

Jaime Dunlap, *Olivet College*

Wayne Farris, *University of Tennessee*

Anita Fisher, *Clark College*

Suzanne Gay, *Oberlin College*

Katrina A. Glass, *United States Military Academy*

Robert Gerlich, *Loyola University*

Samuel Robert Goldberger, *Capital Community-Technical College*

Andrew Gow, *University of Alberta*

Katheryn L. Green, *University of Wisconsin, Madison*

David Griffiths, *University of North Carolina, Chapel Hill*

Louis Haas, *Duquesne University*

Joseph T. Hapak, *Moraine Valley Community College*

Kenneth E. Hendrickson, *Sam Houston State University*

Hue-Tam Ho Tai, *Harvard University*

David Kieft, *University of Minnesota*

Frederick Krome, *Northern Kentucky University*

Lisa M. Lane, *Mira Costa College*

Richard Law, *Washington State University*

David Lelyveld, *Columbia University*

Jan Lewis, *Rutgers University, Newark*

James C. Livingston, *College of William and Mary*

Moira Maguire, *University of Arkansas, Little Rock*

Richard L. Moore Jr., *St. Augustine's College*

Beth Nachison, *Southern Connecticut State University*

Robin S. Oggins, *Binghamton University*

Louis A. Perez Jr., *University of South Florida*

Jonathan Perry, *University of Central Florida*

Cora Ann Presley, *Tulane University*

Norman Raiford, *Greenville Technical College*

Norman Ravitch, *University of California, Riverside*

Thomas M. Ricks, *University of Pennsylvania*

Philip F. Riley, *James Madison University*

Thomas Robisheaux, *Duke University*

William S. Rodner, *Tidewater Community College*

David Ruffley, *United States Air Force Academy*

Dankwart A. Rustow, *The City University of New York*

James J. Sack, *University of Illinois at Chicago*

William Schell, *Murray State University*

Marvin Slind, *Washington State University*

Daniel Scavone, *University of Southern Indiana*

Roger Schlesinger, *Washington State University*

Charles C. Stewart, *University of Illinois*

Nancy L. Stockdale, *University of Central Florida*

Carson Tavenner, *United States Air Force Academy*

Truong-buu Lam, *University of Hawaii*

Harry L. Watson, *Loyola College of Maryland*

William B. Whisenhunt, *College of DuPage*

Paul Varley, *Columbia University*

Finally, we would like to thank the dedicated people who helped produce this revision: our acquisitions editor, Charles Cavaliere; Laura Gardner who created the handsome new design for this edition; Randy Pettit, our production Liaison; and Ben Smith our manufacturing buyer.

A.M.C.
W.A.G.
D.K.
S.O.
F.M.T.

ANNOUNCING A NEW SERIES IN WORLD HISTORY

✳ CONNECTIONS: KEY THEMES IN WORLD HISTORY
Series Editor: Alfred J. Andrea

The increasing pace and specialization of historical inquiry has caused an ever-widening gap between professional research and general surveys of world history. The titles in the Connections series are designed to bridge that gap by placing the latest research on selected topics of global significance, such as disease, trade, slavery, imperialism, decolonization, holy war, and revolution, into an easily accessible context for students. Brief and tightly focused, each Connections title examines cross-cultural themes by employing a combination of narrative, documents, and analysis to show students connections in world history.

PUBLISHED

- TRADING TASTES: *Commodity and Cultural Exchange to 1750*
  Erik Gilbert, *Arkansas State University*
  Jonathan Reynolds, *Northern Kentucky University*

- THE FIRST HORSEMAN: *Disease in Human History*
  John Aberth, *Castleton State College*

FORTHCOMING TITLES

- THE GLOBE ENCOMPASSED: *The Age of European Discovery*
  Glen Ames, *University of Toledo*

- JIHAD AND CRUSADE: *Islamic and Christian Holy Wars Through the Ages*
  Alfred J. Andrea, *University of Vermont*

- GENDER AND POWER: *Women and Nationalism, 1880–1960*
  Nupur Chaudhuri, *Texas Southern University*

- CHANGING THE COURSE OF HISTORY: *Revolutions Past and Present*
  Jack Goldstone, *George Mason University*

- CAPTIVES AS COMMODITIES: *The Trans-Atlantic Slave Trade*
  Lisa Lindsay, *University of North Carolina, Chapel Hill*

- AN IMPERIAL WORLD: *Empires and Colonies, 1750–1945*
  Douglas Northrop, *University of Michigan*

- CONFRONTING THE WEST: *Modernization in the Developing World, 1877–1936*
  Cyrus Veeser, *Bentley College*

Contact your local Prentice Hall representative for additional information regarding the Connections series.

ALBERT M. CRAIG is the Harvard-Yenching Research Professor of History at Harvard University, where he has taught since 1959. A graduate of Northwestern University, he took his Ph.D. at Harvard University. He has studied at Strasbourg University and at Kyoto, Keio, and Tokyo universities in Japan. He is the author of *Choshu in the Meiji Restoration* (1961), *The Heritage of Chinese Civilization* (2001), and, with others, of *East Asia, Tradition and Transformation* (1989). He is the editor of *Japan, A Comparative View* (1973) and co-editor of *Personality in Japanese History* (1970). At present he is engaged in research on the thought of Fukuzawa Yukichi. For eleven years (1976–1987) he was the director of the Harvard-Yenching Institute. He has also been a visiting professor at Kyoto and Tokyo Universities. He has received Guggenheim, Fulbright, and Japan Foundation Fellowships. In 1988 he was awarded the Order of the Rising Sun by the Japanese government.

WILLIAM A. GRAHAM is Albertson Professor of Middle Eastern Studies and Professor of the History of Religion at Harvard University, and Master of Currier House at Harvard University. From 1990–1996 he directed Harvard's Center for Middle Eastern Studies. He has taught for twenty-six years at Harvard, where he received the A.M. and Ph.D. degrees. He also studied in Göttingen, Tübingen, and Lebanon. He is the author of *Divine World and Prophetic World in Early Islam* (1977), awarded the American Council of Learned Societies History of Religions book prize in 1978, and of *Beyond the Written Word: Oral Aspects of Scripture in the History of Religion* (1987). He has published a variety of articles in both Islamic studies and the general history of religion and is one of the editors of the *Encyclopedia of the Qur'an*. He serves currently on the editorial board of several journals and has held John Simon Guggenheim and Alexander von Humboldt research fellowships. *Three Faiths, One God*, co-authored with Jacob Neusner and Bruce Chilton, published in January 2003.

DONALD KAGAN is Sterling Professor of History and Classics at Yale University, where he has taught since 1969. He received the A.B. degree in history from Brooklyn College, the M.A. in classics from Brown University, and the Ph.D. in history from Ohio State University. During 1958–1959 he studied at the American School of Classical Studies as a Fulbright Scholar. He has received three awards for undergraduate teaching at Cornell and Yale. He is the author of a history of Greek political thought, *The Great Dialogue* (1965); a four-volume history of the Peloponnesian war, *The Origins of the Peloponnesian War* (1969); *The Archidamian War* (1974); *The Peace of Nicias and the Sicilian Expedition* (1981); *The Fall of the Athenian Empire* (1987); and a biography of Pericles, *Pericles of Athens and the Birth of Democracy* (1991); *On the Origins of War* (1995), and *The Peloponnesian War* (2003). He is coauthor, with Frederick W. Kagan of *While America Sleeps* (2000). With Brian Tierney and L. Pearce Williams, he is the editor of *Great Issues in Western Civilization*, a collection of readings. He was awarded the National Humanities Medal for 2002.

STEVEN OZMENT is McLean Professor of Ancient and Modern History at Harvard University. He has taught Western Civilization at Yale, Stanford, and Harvard. He is the author of eleven books. *The Age of Reform, 1250–1550* (1980) won the Schaff Prize and was nominated for the 1981 National Book Award. Five of his books have been selections of the History Book Club: *Magdalena and Balthasar: An Intimate Portrait of Life in Sixteenth Century Europe* (1986), *Three Behaim Boys: Growing Up in Early Modern Germany* (1990), *Protestants: The Birth of A Revolution* (1992), *The Burgermeister's Daughter: Scandal in a Sixteenth Century German Town* (1996), and *Flesh and Spirit: Private Life in Early Modern Germany* (1999). His most recent publications are *Ancestors: The Loving Family of Old Europe* (2001), *A Mighty Fortress: A New History of the German People* (2004), and "Why We Study Western Civ," *The Public Interest* 158 (2005).

FRANK M. TURNER is John Hay Whitney Professor of History at Yale University, where he served as University Provost from 1988 to 1992. He received his B.A. degree at the College of William and Mary and his Ph.D. from Yale. He has received the Yale College Award for Distinguished Undergraduate Teaching. He has directed a National Endowment for the Humanities Summer Institute. His scholarly research has received the support of fellowships from the National Endowment for the Humanities and the Guggenheim Foundation and the Woodrow Wilson Center. He is the author of *Between Science and Religion: The Reaction to Scientific Naturalism in Late Victorian England* (1974), *The Greek Heritage in Victorian Britain* (1981), which received the British Council Prize of the Conference on British Studies and the Yale Press Governors Award, *Contesting Cultural Authority: Essays in Victorian Intellectual Life* (1993), and *John Henry Newman: The Challenge to Evangelical Religion* (2002). He has also contributed numerous articles to journals and has served on the editorial advisory boards of *The Journal of Modern History, Isis,* and *Victorian Studies.* He edited *The Idea of a University,* by John Henry Newman (1996). Since 1996 he has served as a Trustee of Connecticut College. In 2003, Professor Turner was appointed Director of the Beinecke Rare Book and Manuscript Library at Yale University.

When writing history, historians use maps, tables, graphs, and visuals to help their readers understand the past. What follows is an explanation of how to use the historian's tools that are contained in this book.

TEXT

Whether it is a biography of Gandhi, an article on the Ottoman Empire, or a survey of world history such as this one, the text is the historian's basic tool for discussing the past. Historians write about the past using narration and analysis. Narration is the story line of history. It describes what happened in the past, who did it, and where and when it occurred. Narration is also used to describe how people in the past lived, how they passed their daily lives and even, when the historical evidence makes it possible for us to know, what they thought, felt, feared, or desired. Using analysis, historians explain why they think events in the past happened the way they did and offer an explanation for the story of history. In this book, narration and analysis are interwoven in each chapter.

STUDY AIDS

A number of features in this book are designed to aid in the study of history. Each chapter begins with **Chapter Highlights**, mini-summaries that preview key themes and developments, and **Questions**, organized by the main subtopics of each chapter, which encourage careful consideration of important themes and developments. Each question is repeated at the appropriate place in the margin of the text.

CHAPTER HIGHLIGHTS

North Africa Developments in African history from 1000 to 1800 varied from region to region. In North Africa, the key new factor was the imperial expansion of the Ottoman Empire as far west as Morocco. But regionalism soon rendered Ottoman authority in North Africa purely nominal.

Empires of the Sudan Several substantial states arose south of the Sahara: Ghana, Mali, Songhai, and Kanem. The ruling elites of these states converted to or were heavily influenced by Islam, although most of their populations clung to their older traditions. Much of the wealth of these states was tied to their control of the trans-Saharan trade routes. Farther south, in Central Africa, another substantial kingdom arose in Benin, famous for its brass sculptures.

East Africa On the east coast, Islam influenced the development of the distinctive Swahili culture and language, and Islamic traders linked the region to India and East Asia.

The Coming of the Europeans The key development of the fifteenth century was the arrival of European traders, missionaries, and warships. The Portuguese and later Europeans came in search of commerce, converts to Christianity, and spheres of influence. Their arrival disrupted indigenous African culture and political relations and presaged Africa's involvement in a new, expanding global trading system dominated by Europeans.

WHICH ECONOMIC factors led to the spread of slavery in the New World?

SLAVERY IN THE AMERICAS

Black slavery was the final mode of forced or subservient labor in the New World. It extended throughout the Americas.

ESTABLISHMENT OF SLAVERY

As the numbers of Native Americans in South America declined, the Spanish and Portuguese turned to African slaves. By the late 1500s, in the West Indies and the cities of South America, black slaves surpassed the white population.

On much of the South American continent dominated by Spain, slavery declined during the late 17th century, but it continued to thrive in Brazil and in the Caribbean. In British North America, it began with the importation of slaves to Jamestown in 1619, and quickly became a fundamental institution.

The spread of slavery in Brazil and the West Indies was promoted by the market for sugar. Only slave labor could provide enough workers for the sugar

MAPS

Maps are important historical tools. They show how geography has affected history and concisely summarize complex relationships and events. Knowing how to read and interpret a map is important to understanding history. Map 11–1 from Chapter 11 shows Muslim conquests from 622–750 C.E. It has three features to help you read it: a **caption**, a **legend**, and a **scale**. The caption explains the rapid rise of Islam from its beginnings in Arabia to its domination of much of the Mediterranean and Persia.

The legend is situated on the bottom left corner of the map. The legend provides information for what each colored area of the map represents. The purple region is the Byzantine Empire. The dark orange represents Muhammad's conquests from 622–632. The areas in light orange were conquered in 632–661. The territories in brown were conquered between 661–750.

The scale, located on the top of the map, informs us that three-quarters of an inch equals 1000 miles (or about 1600 kilometers). With this information, estimates of distance between points on the map are easily made.

The map also shows the topography of the region—its mountains, rivers, and seas. This helps us understand the interplay between geography and history. For example, note how the spead of Islam stops at the Caucasus Mountains. Do you think the topography of this region played a role in limiting the Muslim advance?

Finally, a **critical-thinking question** asks for careful consideration of the spatial connections between geography and history.

MAP EXPLORATION

Interactive map: To explore this map further, go to **http://www.prenhall.com/craig/map11.1**

Legend:
- Byzantine Empire
- Conquests of Muhammad, 622-632
- Conquests, 632-661
- Conquests, 661-750

MAP 11–1

Muslim Conquests and Domination of the Mediterranean to about 750 C.E. The rapid spread of Islam (both religion and political-military power) is shown here. Within 125 years of Muhammad's rise, Muslims came to dominate Spain and all areas south and east of the Mediterranean.

WHY DID so many subject peoples welcome Islamic rule?

MAP EXPLORATIONS

Many of the maps in each chapter are provided in a useful interactive version on the text's Companion Website. These maps are easily identified by a bar along the top (see example above) that reads "**Map Exploration**." An interactive version of Map 11.1 can be found at **www.prenhall.com/craig/map11.1**. The interactive version of this particular map provides an opportunity to move a timeline from left to right to see the progress of Muslim conquests.

ANALYZING VISUALS

Visual images embedded thoughout the text can provide as much insight into world history as the written word. Within photographs and pieces of fine art lies emotional and historical meaning. Captions also provide valuable information, such as in the example below. When studying the image, consider questions such as: "Who are these people?"; "What are their relationships to each other?"; "What are they doing?"; and "What can we learn from the way the people are dressed?" Such analysis allows for a fuller understanding of the way people lived in the past.

VISUALIZING THE PAST

These essays, found at the end of selected chapters, analyze important aspects of world history through photographs, fine art, sculpture, maps, and woodcuts. Focus questions and a running narrative guide the reader though a careful examination of the historical implications of each topic in question.

Plantation. In the American South, the islands of the Caribbean, and in Brazil, slaves labored on sugar plantations under the authority of overseers.

The Granger Collection.

Visualizing The Past...

Industrialization

HOW DID the advent of industrialization in the 19th and early 20th centuries shape the art of those countries that industrialized? Did artists view industrialization as a negative or a positive force?

The Industrial Revolution began in Britain in the 18th century. By the mid-19th century factories, coal-fired machines, and railroads had spread throughout Western Europe, and also the eastern portion of the United States. By the later 19th-century industrialization and railroad building advanced in the United States, and also in Japan, which had become the most industrialized non-Western power in the world by the 1930s. Industry was understood to be about power, not only the power machines generated and artists celebrated, but also the power of political and military domination.

◄ **Power Loom Weaving of cotton cloth in a textile mill; colored engraving, 1834.** Industrialization began in the cloth industry because cloth was the most important manufactured product in the world from ancient times to the dawn of the modern era. Early factory owners often employed women, whose labor came cheaper than that of men. Factory women worked long hours and were subject to close supervision designed to ensure that their morals would not suffer in the factory setting.
The Granger Collection.

724

Religions of the World

JUDAISM

Monotheism, the belief in a unique God who is the creator of the universe and its all-powerful ruler, first became a central and lasting element in religion among the Hebrews, later called Israelites and also Jews. Their religion, more than the many forms of polytheistic worship that characterized the ancient world, demanded moral rectitude and placed ethical responsibilities both on individuals and on the community as a whole. Their God had a divine plan for human history, which was linked to the behavior of his chosen people. This vision of the exclusive worship of the true God, obedience to the laws governing the community that derive from him, and a strong ethical responsibility was connected to humanity's historical experience in this world. Ultimately it gave rise to three great religions: Judaism, Christianity, and Islam.

At the beginning of this tradition stands Abraham, whom all three religions recognize as their founder. According to the Torah (the first five books of the Hebrew Bible or the Christian Old Testament), Abraham entered into a covenant with God in which he promised to worship only this God, who in turn promised to make Abraham's descendants his own chosen people—chosen to worship him, to obey his laws, and to undertake a special set of

Jonah Eaten by the Whale, from a Hebrew Bible, 1299. Like the Christian illuminated manuscripts they closely resembled, Jewish medieval manuscripts were filled with images of scenes from the Torah and Jewish history. Hebrew writing also developed into an elaborately beautiful calligraphy. Many of these Jewish medieval illuminated manuscripts were, like their Christian counterparts, commissioned by wealthy and influential leaders of Jewish communities in Europe.
Instituto da Biblioteca Nacional, Lisbon, Portugal/Bridgeman Art Library.

moral responsibilities. God renewed the covenant with Moses at Mount Sinai when he freed the Israelites from Egyptian bondage. He promised them the land of Canaan (later called Palestine and part of which is now the state of Israel) and gave them the law (the Torah), including the Ten Commandments, by which they were to guide their lives. As long as they lived by his law, God would give them his guidance and protection.

In time the Israelites formed themselves into a kingdom which remained unified from about 1000 to 922 B.C.E. In the period after its division, prophets emerged. Thought to be inspired by God, the prophets chastised the Israelites for their lapses into idolatry and immorality. Even as the kingdom was disintegrating and the Israelites falling under the control of alien empires, the prophets preached social reform and a return to God's laws. They saw Israel's misfortune as punishment for failing to keep the covenant and predicted disaster if the Israelites did not change their ways. When disasters came—the Jewish kingdoms captured, the people enslaved and exiled—the prophets interpreted Israel's status as a chosen people to mean that their sufferings would make them "a light unto the nations," leading other nations to the true worship of one God

The prophets also preached that God was righteous and demanded righteousness from his people. But he was also a God of justice. Although he might need to punish his people for their sins, he would one day reward them with divine favor. Traditional Jewish belief expects that the Messiah, or Anointed One, will someday come and establish God's kingdom on earth. He will introduce an age of universal brotherhood in which all nations will acknowledge the one true God.

The Jews are "people of the Book," and foremost among their sacred texts is the Hebrew Bible, consisting of the Five Books of Moses (the Torah), the books of the prophets, and other writings. The Torah is the source of Jewish law. Over the centuries new experiences required new interpretation of the law, which was accomplished by the oral law, no less sacred than the written law. Compilations of interpretation and commentary by rabbis (wise and learned teachers) were brought together to form the Talmud.

50

RELIGIONS OF THE WORLD

Each of these special, two-page essays examines one of the world's great religions and the impact it has had on history.

OVERVIEWS

The **Overview** tables in this text are a special feature designed to highlight and summarize important topics within a chapter. The Overview table shown here, for example, summarizes the Columbian exchange.

OVERVIEW   THE COLUMBIAN EXCHANGE

The same ships that carried Europeans and Africans to the Americas also transported animals, plants, and diseases that had never before appeared in the New World. There was a similar transport back to Europe and Africa. Historians call this cross-continental flow "the Columbian exchange." The overall result was an ecological transformation that continues to shape the world.

To the Americas

Animals:	cattle, chickens, goats, horses, pigs, and sheep
Plants:	almonds, apples, apricots, bananas, barley, cabbage, cherries, dandelions, grapes, lemons, mangos, melons, oats, okra, olives, onions, oranges, peaches, pears, plums, radishes, rice, sugar cane, wheat, and other green vegetables
Diseases:	bubonic plague, chicken pox, diphtheria, influenza, malaria, measles, smallpox, typhoid, and typhus

From the Americas

Animals:	turkeys
Plants:	avocados, beans, blueberries, chilis, cocoa, guavas, maize, manioc (tapioca), peanuts, pecans, pineapples, potatoes, pumpkins, squash, sweet peppers, sweet potatoes, tobacco, and tomatoes
Diseases:	syphilis

QUICK REVIEWS

Quick reviews, placed at key locations in the margins of each chapter, provide pinpoint summaries of important concepts.

> **QUICK REVIEW**
>
> **Women Under the Qing and Ming**
> - Confucian family ideals changed little during the Ming and Qing eras
> - Footbinding spread among the upper classes and some commoners
> - As population grew, more women worked at home

Church and Empire

910	Monastery of Cluny founded
918	Henry I becomes King of Germany
951	Otto I invades Italy
955	Otto I defeats the Hungarians at Lechfeld
962	Otto I crowned emperor by Pope John XII
1077	Gregory VII pardons Henry IV at Canossa
1122	Concordat of Worms settles the investiture controversy
1152–1190	Reign of Frederick Barbarossa
1198–1215	Reign of Innocent III
1214	Collapse of the claims of Otto IV
1220	Frederick II crowned emperor
1232	Frederick II devolves authority to the German princes
1257	The German monarchy becomes elective

CHRONOLOGIES

Each chapter includes **Chronologies** that list, in chronological order, key events discussed in the chapter. The chronology shown here from Chapter 12, lists the dates of key events in the history of the Holy Roman Empire. Chronologies provide a review of important events and their relationship to one another.

WORLD HISTORY DOCUMENT CD-ROM

Bound into every new copy of this textbook is a free world. History Document CD-ROM. This is a powerful resource for research and additional reading that contains more than 200 primary source documents central to world History. Each document provides essay questions that are linked directly to a website where short-essay answers can be submitted online or printed out. Particularly relevant or interesting documents are called out at appropriate places in the margin of each chapter (see example). A complete list of documents on the CD-ROM is found at the end of the text.

11.1
Mansa Musa: The "King Who Sits on a Mountain of Gold"

PRIMARY SOURCE DOCUMENTS

Historians find most of their information in written records, original documents that have survived from the past. These include government publications, letters, diaries, newspapers—whatever people wrote or printed, including many private documents never intended for publication. Each chapter in the book contains a feature called **History's Voices**—a selection from a primary source document. The example shown here is a description by a Chinese traveler of India. Each **History's Voices** begins with a brief introduction followed by questions on what the document reveals.

HISTORY'S VOICES

A CHINESE TRAVELER'S REPORT ON THE GUPTA REALM

Fa-Hsien, *a Chinese Buddhist monk, was the first of several Chinese known for traveling to India to study and bring back Buddhist scriptures from the intellectual centers of Buddhist thought there. He wrote an account of his travels, first through Central Asia, then all over India, and finally through Ceylon and Indonesia again to China (399–414 C.E.).*

WHAT THINGS about India seem most to surprise Fa-Hsien? Is his image of Indian rule a positive one? What do his remarks say about the prestige of the Buddhist tradition and its monks in the Indian state? What does he tell us about Indian society?

On the sides of the river, both right and left, are twenty san ghârâmas [monasteries], with perhaps 3,000 priests. The law of the Buddha is progressing and flourishing. Beyond the deserts are the countries of Western India. The kings of these countries are all firm believers in the law of Buddha. They remove their caps of state when they make offerings to the priests. The members of the royal household and the chief ministers personally direct the food-giving; when the distribution of food is over, they spread a carpet on the ground opposite the chief seat (the president's seat) and sit down before it. They dare not sit on couches in the presence of the priests. The rules relating to the almsgiving of kings have been handed down from the time of Buddha till now. Southward from this is the so-called middle-country (Mâdhyadeśa). The climate of this country is warm and equable, without frost or snow. The people are very well off, without poll tax or official restrictions. Only those who till the royal lands return a portion of profit of the land. If they desire to go, they go; if they like to stop, they

stop. The kings govern without corporal punishment; criminals are fined, according to circumstances, lightly or heavily. Even in cases of repeated rebellion they only cut off the right hand. The king's personal attendants, who guard him on the right and left, have fixed salaries. Throughout the country the people kill no living thing nor drink wine, nor do they eat garlic or onions, with the exception of Chandâlas [outcasts] only. The Chandâlas are named "evil men" and dwell apart from others; if they enter a town or market, they sound a piece of wood in order to separate themselves; then men, knowing who they are, avoid coming in contact with them. In this country they do not keep swine nor fowls, and do not deal in cattle; they have no shambles or wine-shops in their market places. In selling they use cowrie shells. The Chandâlas only hunt and sell flesh. Down from the time of Buddha's Nirvâna, the kings of these countries, the chief men and householders, have raised vihâras [monasteries] for the priests, and provided for their support by bestowing on them fields, houses, and gardens, with men and oxen. Engraved title-deeds were prepared and handed down from one reign to another; no one has ventured to withdraw them, so that till now there has been no interruption. All the resident priests having chambers (in these vihâras) have their beds, mats, food, drink, and clothes provided without stint; in all places this is the case. The priests ever engage themselves in doing meritorious works for the purpose of religious advancement (karma—building up their religious character), or in reciting the scriptures, or in meditation.

Source: "Buddhist Country Records," in Si-Yu-Ki, *Buddhist Records of the Western World*, trans. by Samuel Beal (London, 1884; reprint, Delhi: Oriental Books Reprint Corporation, 1969), pp. xxxvii–xxxviii. Reprinted by permission of Motilal Banarsidass Publishers Pvt. Ltd., Delhi, India.

Indigenous Reactions The vitality of so many of the cultures and traditions that bore the brunt of the Western onslaught has been striking. Arab, Iranian, Indian, African, and other encounters with Western material and intellectual domination produced different responses and initiatives. These have borne full fruit in political, economic, and intellectual independence only since 1945; however, most began much earlier, some even well before 1800.

One result of the imperial-colonial experience almost everywhere has been the sharpening of cultural self-consciousness and self-confidence among those peoples most negatively affected by Western dominance. The imperial-colonial experiences of the Third World nations may well prove to have been not only ones of misery and reversal, but also of transition to positive development and resurgence, despite the looming economic, educational, and demographic problems that plague many of them.

REVIEW QUESTIONS

1. What kind of policies did the British follow in India? What were the kinds of political activism against British rule were there in India after 1800?

2. How was the Islamic world internally divided after 1800? How did those divisions influence the coming of European powers?

3. How did nationalism affect European control in south Asia, Africa, and the Middle East?

4. What was the role of African nationalism in resisting foreign control?

IMAGE KEY
for pages 672–673

a. A fez.
b. Kemal Ataturk.
c. ivory for sale, congo.
d. An Imperial procession, or *durbar*.
e. Mahatma Ghandi.
f. Bungandan Kabaka Mutesa I and members of his court.
g. A page from a 19th-century Moroccan Koran.
h. Imam Shamil of Dagestan.
i. Sepoy cavalry attacking British infantry at the Battle of Cawpore in 1857.

KEY TERMS

bazaari (p. 681)
cantonments (p. 677)
Great Trek (p. 684)

mfecane (p. 684)
mujtahid (p. 680)
pan-Islamism (p. 682)

raj (p. 675)
scramble for Africa (p. 689)
Wahhabis (p. 679)

 For additional study resources for this chapter, go to:
www.prenhall.com/craig/chapter27

SUMMARIES, REVIEW QUESTIONS, AND ADDITIONAL STUDY RESOURCES

At the end of each chapter **summaries** and **review questions** reconsider the main topics. An Image Key provides information about the illustrations that appear at the beginning of the chapter. The URL for the Companion Website ™ is also found at the end of each chapter; this is an excellent resource for additional study aids. In addition, a laminated "Study in Time" chart is found at the front of the text and provides a succinct timeline of world history.

GLOSSARY/KEY TERMS

Significant historical terms are called out in heavy type throughout the text, defined in the margin, and listed at the end of each chapter with appropriate page numbers. These are listed alphabetically and defined in a glossary at the end of the book.

EXPLORE THE POWER OF ONEKEY

OneKey is Prentice Halls' premium exclusive online resource for instructors and students. **OneKey** gives you access to the best online teaching and learning tools—all available 24/7. Harnessing the power of WebCT **WebCT**, Blackboard **Bb**, and Course Compass **CourseCompass**, OneKey puts all of your resources in one place for maximum convenience, simplicity and success.

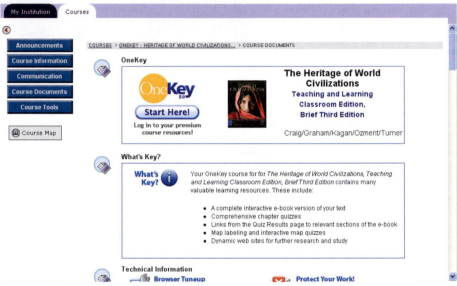

PRESENTATION RESOURCES FOR INSTRUCTORS

VISUALS

- Images
- Maps, Tables, Figures
- Map Outlines

PowerPoint™ Presentations

- Lecture Aids—Visuals
- Lecture Aids—Text
- Lecture Aids—Lecture Outline

Changing Religious Life

✹ Religion in fifteenth-century life
  - ◆ Clergy made up 6% to 8% of urban population
  - ◆ Considerable political and religious power
  - ◆ Monasteries were prominent and influential

✹ Religion in sixteenth-century life
  - ◆ Numbers of clergy fell by 2/3
  - ◆ Monasteries and nunneries nearly absent
  - ◆ Worship conducted in the vernacular
  - ◆ Clergy could marry, paid taxes

Animations and Activities

- Interactive Maps

Text

- Instructor's Manual

ASSESSMENT RESOURCES FOR STUDENTS

HOMEWORK

- Review Questions
- e-book

ADDITIONAL STUDENT RESOURCES

LINKS

- Companion Website
- e-themes in World History

ADDITIONAL RESOURCES

 • Research Navigator

Take a tour at www.prenhall.com/onekey

THE HERITAGE OF
WORLD
CIVILIZATIONS

EUROPE

◄ *Paleolithic sculpture*

*The Akkadian victory ►
stele of Naram-Sin
ca. 2230 B.C.E.*

NEAR EAST / INDIA

ca. 8000   Neolithic Revolution, Mesopotamia

ca. 3500	Development of Sumerian cities
ca. 3000	Development of writing in Mesopotamia
ca. 2800–2370	Early Dynastic period of Sumerian city-states
ca. 2370	Sargon establishes Akkadian dynasty and Empire
ca. 2250–1750	Indus (Harappan) civilization; writing first appears in India
ca. 2125–2027	Third Dynasty of Ur
ca. 2000–1800	Establishment of Amorites in Mesopotamia
ca. 1800–1500	Aryan peoples invade northwestern India
ca. 1792–1750	Reign of Hammurabi
ca. 1550	Establishment of Kassite dynasty at Babylon

▲ *Burial urn from China,
Neolithic period*

EAST ASIA

2205–1766	Traditional dates of Xia dynasty
1766	Bronze Age city-states, aristocratic charioteers, pictographic writing
1766–1050	Traditional dates of Shang dynasty; writing first appears in China

4000 B.C.E.   Neolithic Revolution

*Ceremonial food vessel, ►
Shang dynasty*

AFRICA

3100–2700	Early Dynastic period (I–II), Egypt
ca. 3000	Writing first appears in Egypt
2700–2200	Old Kingdom (III–VI)
2200–2025	First Intermediate period (VII–XI)
2025–1630	Middle Kingdom (XII–XIII)
1630–1550	Second Intermediate period (XIV–XVII)
1550–1075	New Kingdom (XVIII–XX)

*Neolithic statues from ►
Ain Ghazal, Jordan
ca. 8500–7000 B.C.E.*

*Seated Egyptian scribe ►
from the Fifth Dynasty*

THE AMERICAS

ca. 4000   Neolithic Revolution in Mexico

ca. 2750   Monumental architecture at Aspero

PART ONE   THE COMING OF CIVILIZATION

624–545	Thales of Miletus
ca. 611–546	Anaximander
ca. 546	Anaximenes

469–399	Socrates
429–347	Plato
384–322	Aristotle
435–404	Great Peloponnesian War
ca. 460–400	Thucydides
ca. 400	Hippocrates of Cos
384–322	Demosthenes

Thales ▶
of Miletus

▲ *Poseidon, Athena, Apollo, and Artemis, 5th century* B.C.E.

---

ca. 1500–1000	Rig-Vedic period, India
ca. 1400–1200	Hittite Empire
ca. 1100	Rise of Assyrian Power

ca. 1000–961	Reign of King David
ca. 961–922	Reign of King Solomon
ca. 1000–500	Late Vedic period, India
ca. 1000–800/600	Composition of Brahmanas
ca. 800–500	Composition of major Upanishads
ca. 700–500	Probable reintroduction of writing
732–722	Assyrian conquest of Syria-Palestine
722	Assyrian conquest of Israel (Northern Kingdom)
612	Destruction of Assyrian capital at Nineveh
612–539	Neo-Babylonian (Chaldean) Empire
586	Destruction of Jerusalem; fall of Judah (southern kingdom); Babylonian captivity
539	Restoration of Temple; return of exiles
540–ca. 468	Mahavira, the Jina/Vardamana
ca. 566–ca. 486	Siddhartha Gautama, the Buddha

ca. 400 B.C.E.–200 C.E.	Composition of great epics, the *Mahabharata* and *Ramayana*

Indus stone ▶
stamp seal

◀ *Ishtar Gate in Babylon*

1050–256	Traditional dates of Zhou dynasty

Confucius ▶

500	Age of philosophers
370–290	Mencius
Fourth century	Laozi
221	China is unified under the Qin

771	Iron Age territorial states
551–479	Confucius

Laozi ▶

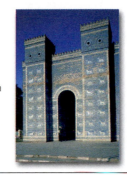

671	Assyrian conquest of Egypt

◀ *Babylonian map of the world, 612–539* B.C.E.

1500–400	The Olmec

800 B.C.E.–200 C.E.	Chavin (Early) Horizon

200 B.C.E.–750 C.E.	The Classic period in central Mexico
150 B.C.E.–900 C.E.	The Classic period of Mayan civilization in the Yucatán and Guatemala

◀ *Olmec head*

Temple of the Sun ▶

1

The Birth of Civilization

CHAPTER HIGHLIGHTS

The Emergence of Civilization Beginning in 10,000 B.C.E., human beings shifted from a hunter-gatherer way of life to one marked by settled agriculture and the domestication of animals. Between 4000 and 3000 B.C.E., civilization began to appear in the Tigris and Euphrates Valleys in Mesopotamia, then along the Nile River in Egypt, and somewhat later in the Indus Valley in India and the Yellow River Basin in China.

Mesopotamia The Sumerians founded the oldest Mesopotamian cities around 3000 B.C.E. Beginning around 2370 B.C.E., the Sumerian city states were conquered by the Akkadian, Babylonian, and Assyrian empires. The Sumerians passed much of their civilization down to their successors: a system of writing called *cuneiform*, the worship of gods based on natural forces, semi-divine kings, and a highly developed bureaucracy.

Egypt Watered by the Nile and protected by deserts and the sea, Egyptian civilization was more secure and peaceful than that of Mesopotamia. Religion dominated Egyptian life. The pharaohs were considered gods on whom the lives and prosperity of their people depended.

Indus Civilization By 2300 B.C.E. at least 70 Indus cities had developed a sophisticated urban culture. Indus civilization disappeared for unknown reasons between 1800 and 1700 B.C.E. In its place, Indo-European (or Aryan) invaders established the "Vedic" culture, named after the ritual writings known as the Vedas.

China The Shang dynasty and Zhou dynasty are the earliest known civilizations in China. By the fourth century B.C.E., as population and commerce expanded, many petty states clustered into a few large territorial units.

The Americas The first civilizations in the Americas arose in places that produced an agricultural surplus. In Mesoamerica, this was based on the cultivation of maize. In the Andes, it was based on a combination of agriculture and the rich marine resources of the Pacific. The Olmecs (1500–400 B.C.E.) established the first civilization in Mesoamerica, while the first monumental architecture appeared in the Andes around 2750 B.C.E.

CHAPTER QUESTIONS

WHY CAN humans be defined as *cultural beings*?

WHERE DID the first civilizations in the
Near East develop?

WHICH EMPIRES competed with Egypt to control
the ancient Near East?

HOW DID the first civilizations of the Indus Valley
develop the religious and social foundations
of Indian civilization?

WHY DID large territorial states arise
in ancient China?

HOW DID agriculture influence the
development of civilizations in Mesoamerica?

CHAPTER OUTLINE
- Early Humans and Their Culture
- Early Civilizations to About 1000 B.C.E.
- Ancient Near Eastern Empires
- Early Indian Civilization
- The Rise of Civilization in the Americas

The earliest humans lived by hunting, fishing, and collecting wild plants. They learned to cultivate plants, herd animals, and make pottery only about 10,000 years ago. These discoveries transformed them from food gatherers to producers and allowed them to grow in number and to lead settled lives. About 5,000 years ago, a far more complex way of life began to appear in some parts of the world. In these places, humans learned how to increase harvests through irrigation and other methods and to sustain much larger populations than ever before. As villages grew into cities, centers of industry and commerce appeared. Writing was invented. Specialized occupations emerged, complex religions took form, and social classes developed. These events marked the birth of civilization.

EARLY HUMAN BEINGS AND THEIR CULTURE

WHY CAN humans be defined as *cultural beings?*

Humans, unlike other animals, are cultural beings. **Culture** may be defined as the way of life built up by a group and passed on from generation to generation. Language, which appears to be a uniquely human trait, greatly facilitated the development and transmission of cultures.

THE PALEOLITHIC AGE

Anthropologists identify early human cultures by their tools. The earliest cultural period—the **Paleolithic Age** (from Greek, meaning "old stone")—dates from the first use of stone tools some 1 or 2 million years ago to about 10,000 B.C.E. During this long span of time, people survived by hunting, fishing, and gathering—but not by producing—food. They learned to make and control fire, to manufacture increasingly sophisticated tools, and to refine language.

Paleolithic technology could support only a thinly scattered population. If hunters became too numerous, game would not suffice. Paleolithic society was probably characterized by a division of labor by sex. Men most likely hunted, fished, and fought. Women, who were less mobile because of childbearing and nursing, probably gathered nuts, berries, and wild grains; wove baskets; and

culture The ways of living built up by a group and passed on from one generation to another.

Paleolithic Age The earliest period when stone tools were used, from about 1,000,000 to 10,000 B.C.E. From the Greek meaning "old stone."

Paleolithic Cave Drawings. Approximately 30,000 years ago in a Chauvet cave, near Avignon, France, Paleolithic artists decorated the walls with exquisite drawings of animals.

Jean Clottes/Corbis Sygma Photo News.

made clothing. By gathering food, women probably discovered how to plant and care for seeds, and they acquired the knowledge that eventually led to agriculture and the **Neolithic Revolution**.

THE NEOLITHIC AGE

However it happened, some 10,000 years ago people living in parts of what we now call the Middle East began to shift from the Paleolithic hunter-gatherer way of life to the settled agricultural lifestyle of the Neolithic Age ("new stone"). Neolithic people domesticated animal and plant species native to certain regions and then spread them to new lands. They invented pottery and learned to weave cloth from flax and wool. They nurtured crops from planting to harvest and built permanent buildings, usually in clusters near their richest fields. Everyone lived at much the same level. There was a little long-distance trade, but most villages were self-sufficient.

In the regions where agriculture and animal husbandry appeared, the number of human beings grew steadily. The Neolithic Revolution was a major step in human control of nature, and it was a vital precondition for the emergence of **civilization**. The earliest Neolithic societies appeared in the Middle East about 8000 B.C.E., in China about 4000 B.C.E., and in India about 5500 B.C.E. Settled agricultural societites began to become prevalent in Mesoamerica (modern Mexico and Central America) and in the Andean region of South America about 2500 B.C.E.

THE BRONZE AGE AND THE BIRTH OF CIVILIZATION

Between 4000 and 3000 B.C.E., civilization first appeared along the Tigris and Euphrates Rivers in the region called **Mesopotamia**. It developed a little later in the valley of the Nile River in Egypt, and somewhat later still in India's Indus Valley and China's Yellow River basin (see Map 1–1). Civilization was marked by the appearance of urban centers, monumental architecture, hierarchical societies, and the invention of writing. This period is called the **Bronze Age** because it coincided with the discovery of the technique for smelting tin and copper and combining them to make bronze, the first metal strong enough to be used for tools.

EARLY CIVILIZATIONS TO ABOUT 1000 B.C.E.

About 4000 B.C.E., people began to congregate in large numbers in the river-watered lowlands of Mesopotamia and Egypt. By about 3000 B.C.E., when the invention of writing signaled the transition from prehistory to history, urban life and centrally governed states appeared along the Tigris and Euphrates Rivers in Mesopotamia and the Nile in Egypt.

The concentration of people in cities created a new way of life. Many urban dwellers did not grow their own food, so urban life was possible only where farmers produced substantial surpluses and a method existed to collect and redistribute this resource. Organization was also encouraged by the need for intelligent management of water in the arid regions where civilization first appeared. Irrigation was essential in Mesopotamia, but it was difficult. Rivers flooded during the harvest season and water was in short supply at other times. Farmers had to build dikes and reservoirs to manage these challenges. Egypt's rivers flooded at a convenient time of year, making irrigation much simpler. Egypt's rivers were also confined to the floor of a valley, whereas Mesopotamia's rivers flowed through an open plain. Its rivers often changed their courses and forced people to relocate.

Venus of Willendorf. This famous statuette found near Willendorf, Austria, in 1908 may be 25,000 years old. It is only four and one-half inches tall.

Erich Lessing/Art Resource.

Neolithic Revolution The shift beginning 10,000 years ago from hunter-gatherer societies to settled communities.

civilization A form of human culture marked by urbanism, metallurgy, and writing.

Mesopotamia Modern Iraq. The land between the Tigris and Euphrates Rivers.

Bronze Age The name given to the earliest civilized era, ca. 4000 to 1000 B.C.E. The term reflects the importance of the metal bronze for the people of this age in making weapons and tools.

WHERE DID the first civilizations in the Near East develop?

MAP 1-1
The Four Great River Valley Civilizations to ca. 1000 B.C.E.   By ca. 2000 B.C.E., urban life was established along the Tigris and Euphrates Rivers in Mesopotamia, the Nile River in Egypt, the Indus and Ganges Rivers in India, and the Yellow River in China.

WHY DID the first civilizations in the Near East and Asia develop in river valleys?

MESOPOTAMIAN CIVILIZATION

The oldest Mesopotamian cities appear to be those founded by the Sumerians around 3000 B.C.E. in the southern half of Babylonia. From about 2800 to 2370 B.C.E., the Early Dynastic period, several Sumerian city-states arose in southern Mesopotamia. They formed leagues, fought among themselves incessantly, and, as stronger towns conquered weaker ones, kingdoms appeared.

The region immediately upstream from the principal Sumerian city-states was primarily occupied by people who spoke a language that belongs to the same family as modern Arabic and Hebrew (i.e., a Semitic language). These people established a kingdom with a capital at Akkad, near the site where the famous city of Babylon was later founded. The Akkadian king, Sargon, conquered the Sumerian cities and created an empire. The dynasty of Semitic kings he founded, about 2370 B.C.E., ruled Sumer and Akkad for two centuries. When it succumbed to internal weakness and external attack, smaller independent states appeared. About 2125 B.C.E. the city of Ur, under its Third Dynasty, restored unity to the region, and Sumerian civilization flowered for the final time. When it fell about 2027 B.C.E., the Sumerians disappeared as an identifiable group—though their language survived as a scholarly tongue preserved by subsequent Middle Eastern civilizations.

About 1900 B.C.E., a people called the Amorites gained control of the region and established a government with its seat at Babylon. The Amorite, or Old Babylonian, dynasty dominated Mesopotamia for about 300 years. Its high point was the reign of Hammurabi (r. ca. 1792–1750 B.C.E.), who is best known for

HISTORY'S VOICES

THE CODE OF HAMMURABI

The Code of Hammurabi (r. 1792–1750 B.C.E.) was only one of many collections of laws produced by Mesopotamian societies. Mesopotamian law codes, such as that of Hammurabi, seem unjust, in that they prescribed different rights, responsibilities, and punishments, depending on the gender, class, and slave or free status of the persons involved. But Hammurabi's code represents an enormous advance in legal thought because it organized and standardized laws and punishments, which made the legal process less dependent on the whims of rulers and judges. Hammurabi's code also provides invaluable information for historians about the social structures and culture of Babylonian society.

WHAT DO the passages suggest about Mesopotamians' views on the role of marriage in society and on the role of women in marriage? If you formed your judgment about the roles women played in Babylonian society from passages 129, 137, and 138 alone, you might assume that women primarily reared children and were confined to the home. What do the other passages reveal about other roles that women played in this culture? What does this difference suggest about the importance of evidence and the accidents of its survival in understanding the lives of women in history?

109. If rebels meet in the house of a wineseller and she does not seize them and take them to the palace, that wineseller shall be slain.

110. If a priestess who has not remained in the temple shall open a wine-shop, or enter a wine-shop for a drink, that woman shall be burned.

117. If a man has contracted a debt, and has given his wife, his son, his daughter for silver or for labor, three years shall they serve in the house of their purchaser or bondsmaster; in the fourth year they shall regain their original condition.

129. If the wife of a man is found lying with another male, they shall be bound and thrown into the water. If the husband lets his wife live, then the king shall let his servant live ...

137. If a man had decided to divorce ... a wife who has presented him with children, then he shall give back to that woman her dowry, and he shall give her the use of field, garden, and property, and she shall bring up her children. After she has brought up her children, she shall take a son's portion of all that is given to her children, and she marry the husband of her heart.

138. If a man divorces his spouse who has not borne him children, he shall give to her all the silver of the bride-price, and restore to her the dowry which she brought from the house of her father, and so he shall divorce her.

Source: *The Human Record*, vol. I, Afred J. Andrea, James H. Overfield, eds., pp. 14–15. Their source is Chilperic Edwards, *The Hammurabi Code* (1904), pp. 23–80.

---

the law code that bears his name. Hammurabi's laws document a society strictly divided into classes: nobles, commoners, and slaves. Punishments were harsh, but less so for privileged people than for the lower classes. Hammurabi claimed the king-mediated law and justice came from the gods to the people (see "The Code of Hammurabi"). Invaders from the north and east brought down the Babylonian kingdom about 1600 B.C.E.

Writing and Mathematics The Sumerians invented a writing system we call **cuneiform** (from *cuneus*, Latin for "wedge") because of the wedge-shaped marks

cuneiform A writing system invented by the Sumerians that used a wedge-shaped stylus, or pointed tool, to write on wet clay tablets that were then baked or dried (*cuneus* means "wedge" in Latin). The writing was also cut into stone.

Key Events and People in Mesopotamian History

ca. 3500 B.C.E.	Sumerians arrive
ca. 2800–2370 B.C.E.	Sumerian city-states
ca. 2370 B.C.E.	Sargon establishes Semitic dynasty at Akkad
ca. 2125–2027 B.C.E.	Third Dynasty of Ur
ca. 1900 B.C.E.	Amorites at Babylon
ca. 1792–1750 B.C.E.	Reign of Hammurabi
ca. 1600 B.C.E.	Invasion by Hittites and Kassites

QUICK REVIEW

Mesopotamian Religion

- Sumerians worshipped gods with human forms
- Babylonians sought evidence of divine action in movements of heavenly bodies
- Religion played an important part in Mesopotamian art and literature

1.4
The Epic of Gilgamesh

they made with reed styluses on clay tablets. The Sumerian writing system used several thousand characters, some of which stood for words and some for sounds. It was difficult to learn, and literacy was confined to a circle of highly educated scribes.

The Sumerians also began the development of mathematics. At first, people did not conceive of numbers apart from counting specific things. Therefore, they developed different numerals for counting different things. Once the abstract concept of number was grasped, however, mathematics developed rapidly. The Sumerian system was sexagesimal (based on the number 60), not decimal. The convention of the 60-minute hour and circle of 360 degrees still survives. Mathematics enabled the Sumerians to develop, by means of observation of the heavenly bodies, the first calendars.

Religion The Sumerians and their successors worshipped gods in human form, who were usually identified with the forces of nature. Priests flourished, for they alone commanded the knowledge needed to influence the gods. Armies of scribes compiled the many kinds of information that learned priests needed for their work. The Babylonians' belief that the movements of the heavenly bodies revealed the will of the gods led to the development of astrology.

Religious myths dominated the literature and art of Mesopotamia. The Mesopotamians believed that the human race was created to labor for the gods, who were imagined to need and enjoy the same kinds of things that human beings did. Mesopotamian temples were literally homes for gods. Their staffs provided banquets, changes of clothing, and entertainment for their deities. Human beings, on the other hand, did not anticipate much for themselves. There was no reward for virtuous living. All the dead were thought to descend to a gloomy netherworld where they suffered from hunger and thirst unless their needs were supplied by their living descendants.

The Babylonians believed in omens and developed elaborate means for divining the future. They also wrote epics to explain the creation of the world, and some of their stories (e.g., a great flood that almost destroyed human life, and an island paradise from which a god was expelled for eating forbidden plants) have entered the Western religious tradition through the Bible.

Society The many sections of the Code of Hammurabi that are devoted to debts, rates of interest, security, and default indicate how important commerce was to the ancient Babylonians. Other sections of the code deal with builders, surgeons, and various kinds of professionals; with land tenure; and with the family. Marriages were arranged by parents. A husband whose wife was childless or ill could take a second wife. Extramarital relations between a married man and concubines, slaves, and prostitutes were accepted.

The law appears to have protected wives as individuals with rights. Divorce was relatively easy, and women who were divorced by their husbands without good cause received their dowries back. A woman who sought a divorce could also recover her dowry if her husband could not convict her of wrongdoing. However, a woman's place was definitely thought to be in the home.

Slavery: Chattel Slaves and Debt Slaves Slavery in Mesopotamia usually arose from debt. Parents could sell their children into slavery or pledge themselves and their family members as surety for loans. Some slaves worked for the king and the state, others for the temple and the priests, and still others for private citizens. Slaves were property, were subject to their master's will, and had little legal protection. But slaves could engage in business and hold property. Those who acquired sufficient wealth could buy their freedom. Slaves could marry free men or women, and the children of these unions were free.

Egyptian Civilization

The center of Egyptian civilization was the Nile River. From its source in central Africa, the Nile runs in long navigable stretches broken by several cataracts north some 4,000 miles to the Mediterranean Sea. Ancient Egypt included the 750 miles of the valley from the First Cataract to the sea. The narrow valley of the Nile constituted Upper (southern) Egypt, and Lower (northern) Egypt occupied the river's broad delta, which fans out along 150 miles of the Mediterranean coast. The Nile alone made life possible in Egypt's almost rainless desert. Each year the river flooded and covered the land. When it receded, it left behind a fertile mud that renewed the land and produced two crops a year. The construction of irrigation ditches to utilize the river's water and careful planning and organization of agricultural work produced prosperity for Egypt that was unmatched in the ancient world.

The Nile served as a highway connecting the long, narrow country and encouraged its unification. By 3100 B.C.E., Upper and Lower Egypt were unified as a single kingdom. Nature helped protect and isolate the ancient Egyptians from outsiders. The cataracts, the sea, and the desert made it difficult for foreigners to reach Egypt for either friendly or hostile purposes. Egypt knew far more peace and security than Mesopotamia. This, along with the sunny, predictable climate, gave the Egyptians a more optimistic attitude toward life than that manifested by their Mesopotamian neighbors.

Events in the more than 3,000-year span of ancient Egyptian history are traditionally dated by reference to the reigns of 31 royal dynasties, which modern historians cluster into eight periods.

The Old Kingdom (2700–2200 B.C.E.) By the Third Dynasty, Egypt's kings had achieved absolute supremacy over their subjects. Ruling from Memphis in Upper Egypt, just above the entrance to the delta, they had the resources of a huge, prosperous nation at their disposal. Kings (the title **pharaoh**, meaning "great house" or "palace," was not used until later in Egyptian history) governed through their families, appointing and removing officials at their pleasure. Peasants were carefully regulated and heavily taxed.

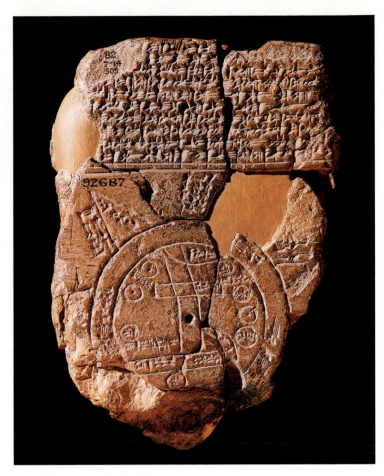

Babylonian World Map. This clay tablet from the Neo-Babylonian period (612–539 B.C.E.) shows a map of the world as seen by the Babylonians. The "Salt Sea" is shown as a circle. An arc inside it is labeled "Mountains." Below it is a rectangular box marked "Babylon," and to the right of the box is a small circle marked "Assyria."

Courtesy of the Trustees of the British Museum. ©The British Museum.

pharaoh The god-kings of ancient Egypt. The term originally meant "great house" or palace.

QUICK REVIEW

Egyptian Kingship
- Egyptian kings were considered gods
- Kings were the direct source of law and justice
- Egyptian government was an aspect of religion

Periods in Ancient Egyptian History (dynasties in Roman numerals)

ca. 3100–2700 B.C.E.	Early Dynastic period (I–II)
ca. 2700–2200 B.C.E.	Old Kingdom (III–VI)
ca. 2200–2052 B.C.E.	First Intermediate period (VII–X)
ca. 2052–1786 B.C.E.	Middle Kingdom (XI–XII)
ca. 1786–1575 B.C.E.	Second Intermediate period (XIII–XVII)
ca. 1700 B.C.E.	Hyksos invasion
ca. 1575–1087 B.C.E.	New Kingdom (or Empire) (XVIII–XX)
ca. 1087–30 B.C.E.	Post Empire (XXI–XXXI)

An Egyptian king was considered a god on whom the lives, safety, and prosperity of his people depended. The land was his personal possession, and the people his servants. Because his will defined justice for his people, Egypt published no law codes. Religion dominated Egyptian life and government. The gods appeared in many guises, as animals, humans, and natural forces. Elaborate conventions governed the burial of the dead and the equipment of graves with items the departed were believed to need for a pleasant life after death. Bodies were mummified to preserve them. Tombs were beautifully decorated with paintings, and offerings of food were regularly brought to the dead.

Nothing better illustrates the extent of royal power than the three great pyramids built as tombs by the kings of the Fourth Dynasty. They are remarkable not only for the great technical skill needed to erect them, but also for the concentration of power and resources they represent.

The First Intermediate Period and Middle Kingdom (2200–1786 B.C.E.)   About 2200 B.C.E. the Old Kingdom collapsed. After a period of confusion (the First Intermediate period, ca. 2200–2052 B.C.E.), the governors of Thebes in Upper Egypt established the Middle Kingdom. The Middle Kingdom's Twelfth Dynasty (2052–1786 B.C.E.) restored order, peace, and prosperity to Egypt. Its pharaohs were less absolute, distant god-kings than their predecessors and more directly concerned for the well-being of their subjects. They encouraged trade and extended Egyptian power and influence into Palestine and Ethiopia.

The Second Intermediate Period and New Kingdom (1786–1087 B.C.E.)   The resurgent power of the local nobility and the erosion of central authority mark the end of the Middle Kingdom and the beginning of the Second Intermediate period. A people called the Hyksos—Semitic peoples from the eastern Mediterranean—controlled the Nile Delta for about a century (beginning ca. 1700 B.C.E.). Then a dynasty from Thebes drove them out and reunited Egypt, marking the beginning of the New Kingdom or Empire.

The rulers of the New Kingdom (ca. 1575–1087 B.C.E.) built a powerful army that pushed out Egypt's frontiers up the Nile to the south and east across Palestine and Syria to the upper Euphrates. Egyptian expansion was finally checked by the powerful Hittite Empire of Asia Minor. Egypt survived, but its period of greatest glory came to an end. Throughout the Post–Empire period (1087–30 B.C.E.) it repeatedly fell to foreign invaders.

Language and Literature   The idea of writing may have come to Egypt from Mesopotamia, but the Egyptians independently invented a script that the Greeks later called **hieroglyphs** ("sacred carvings"). Although this writing script utilized hundreds of picture signs and was very difficult and complex, it remained relatively unchanged for more than 3,000 years. The Egyptian literature it recorded consisted of sacred hymns, myths, and magical formulas, as well as tales of secular business, letters, travel stories, and "wisdom literature" (bits of advice to help one get on well in the world).

hieroglyphics   The writing script of ancient Egypt. It combined picture writing with pictographs and sound signs. Hieroglyph means "sacred carvings" in Greek.

Religion: Gods and Temples   Egyptian religion encompassed concepts that appear inconsistent to the modern mind. There were, for instance, three separate explanations for the origin of the universe. The Egyptian gods also cannot be organized into an orderly pantheon, for their functions and natures combine and overlap. Worship of the sun took a variety of forms in this hot, arid land, and for a brief period the pharaoh Akhenaten elevated a new sun god over all Egypt's traditional deities. The gods, often represented as having animal heads on human bodies, were thought to inhabit their lavish temples. Ordinary people did not worship there, but the gods' images were occasionally carried out and paraded before the masses.

Worship and the Afterlife   Most Egyptians worshipped at small local shrines. Their homes also had niches for images of household deities. They worshipped their ancestors, and they believed strongly in magic, dreams, and oracles. They wore amulets to ward off evil. Magic, they assumed, was essential for escaping the dangers that confronted souls in the afterlife. Originally, only the pharaoh was thought to have a hope of immortality, but gradually this privilege extended to all who could make the necessary preparations. Preservation of the body was considered essential for survival in the afterlife.

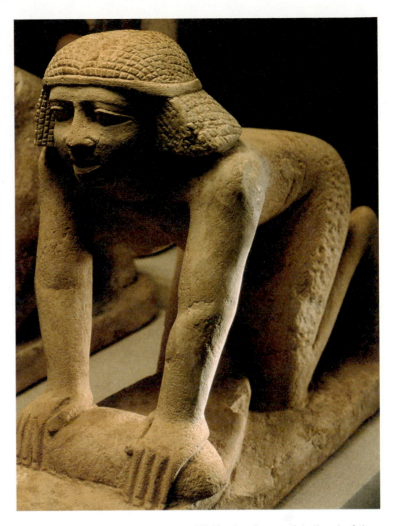

Old Kingdom Statue. A hallmark of the early river civilizations was the development of techniques to increase harvests. This statue from the Old Kingdom in Egypt (ca. 2700–2200 B.C.E.) shows a woman grinding wheat for bread.

Kenneth Garrettings/National Geographic Society.

Women in Egyptian Society   A woman's primary role was management of a household, but she was not confined to her home. Although women could not hold office or receive the kind of education that fit men for public functions and crafts, they could control their own property, sue for divorce, and enjoy equal legal protection. Royal women occasionally had great power. Hatshepsut, daughter of Thutmosis I, ruled as pharaoh for nearly 20 years.

Slaves   Slaves were not numerous in Egypt until the Middle Kingdom, when Egypt launched military campaigns that built its empire. Black Africans from Nubia and Asians from the East were taken captive, branded, and brought to Egypt as slaves. Slaves performed numerous tasks. Some were common laborers, while others served as policemen and soldiers. They could be freed, but that appears rarely to have been done.

ANCIENT MIDDLE EASTERN EMPIRES

W hile the Eighteenth Dynasty ruled Egypt, new groups of peoples established themselves in the Middle East. Among them were the Kassites in Babylonia and the Hittites in Asia Minor. These groups forged an empire that lasted 200 years (see Map 1–2).

WHICH EMPIRES competed with Egypt to control the ancient Near East?

THE HITTITES

By about 1500 B.C.E., the Hittites had established a strong, centralized kingdom with its seat near Ankara, the capital of modern Turkey. Between 1400 and 1200 B.C.E., they contested Egypt's control of Palestine and Syria, but about 1200 B.C.E., their kingdom fell to waves of migrants from Europe. The Hittites appear to have been responsible for a great technological advance—the smelting of iron. They also played an important role in transmitting the ancient cultures of Mesopotamia and Egypt to the Greeks, who lived on their western frontier.

THE KASSITES

A people of unknown origin, the Kassites succeeded the Amorites as the rulers of Babylon. Their dynasty survived for 500 years. They were organized into large tribal families and are particularly memorable for their contributions to Babylonian literature. Their power was maintained with the aid of the prestige weaponry of their age—an aristocratic corps of charioteers.

THE MITANNIANS

The Mitannians were part of a large group called the Hurrians, some of whom traced their roots in Mesopotamia and Syria back to the days of Akkad and Ur. The Mitannians were important mediators of Mesopotamian culture to Syria and Anatolia, and they developed the art of chariot warfare and horse training to a high degree. The Hittites eventually overthrew and absorbed them.

THE ASSYRIANS

The Assyrians inhabited the upper reaches of the Tigris River. Their language was related to Babylonian. Their capital, Assur, was an early trade center, but it emerged as a political power in the 14th century B.C.E. as the Mitannians declined. This First Assyrian Empire collapsed at the end of the second millennium and the Arameans, Semitic nomads, invaded Assyria. The Aramean language became one of the common tongues of the ancient Middle East.

Key Events in the History of Ancient Middle Eastern Empires

ca. 1400–1200 B.C.E.	Hittite Empire
ca. 1100 B.C.E.	Rise of Assyrian power
ca. 732–722 B.C.E.	Assyrian conquest of Palestine-Syria
ca. 671 B.C.E.	Assyrian conquest of Egypt
ca. 612 B.C.E.	Destruction of Assyrian capital at Nineveh
ca. 612–539 B.C.E.	Neo-Babylonian (Chaldean) Empire

THE SECOND ASSYRIAN EMPIRE

About 1000 B.C.E., the Assyrians began steadily to expand their territory, and by 665 B.C.E., they controlled all of Mesopotamia, and much of Asia Minor, Syria, Palestine, and Egypt. The Assyrians succeeded thanks to a large, well-disciplined army and a society that valued military virtues. Fierce and cruel, the Assyrians boasted of their brutality, which was a useful strategy for terrorizing opponents into submission.

Unlike earlier empires, the Assyrians systematically exploited the area they held, using various methods of control. They collected tribute from some regions, stationed garrisons in others, and sometimes pacified districts by deporting and scattering their native peoples.

The Assyrian Empire grew too large to be managed efficiently, but the precise reasons for its fall are unclear. A civil war may have divided the Assyrians and made them vulnerable to attack by the Medes, a powerful people from

MAP 1–2

The Near East and Greece ca. 1400 B.C.E.   About 1400 B.C.E., the Near East was divided among four empires. Egypt extended south to Nubia and north through Palestine and Phoenicia. Kassites ruled in Mesopotamia, Hittites in Asia Minor, and the Mitannians in Assyrian lands. In the Aegean, the Mycenaean kingdoms were at their height.

WHY WERE there so many empires during this period in the ancient Middle East?

Assyrian Palace Relief. This eighth-century B.C.E. relief of a hero gripping a lion formed part of the decoration of an Assyrian palace. The immense size of the figure and his powerful limbs and muscles may well have suggested the might of the Assyrian king.

Giraudon/Art Resource, N.Y.

western and central Iran. The Medes were assisted by the Babylonians, who had been restive subjects of Assyria's empire, and in 612 B.C.E. the great Assyrian cities were destroyed.

THE NEO-BABYLONIANS

The Medes did not follow up their conquests. This opened the way for the Babylonian king, Nebuchadnezzar, to take over much of the former Assyrian territory. Babylon, his capital, prospered as a center of world trade, although his dynasty did not long survive. Confusion and misman-agement by his successors cleared the way for Babylon to fall to Persian conquerors from Iran in 539 B.C.E. (see Chapter 4).

EARLY INDIAN CIVILIZATION

*T*he Indian subcontinent's earliest literate, urban civilization arose in the valley of the Indus River sometime after 2600 B.C.E. By about 2300 B.C.E., the people of this region were trading with Mesopotamia. Known as the **Harappan** or Indus culture, early Indian civilization lasted only a few centuries. The second identi-fiable contribution to the region's civilization came from the Vedic Aryans, named for an **Indo-European** (or "**Aryan**") immigrant people who composed influential holy texts, the **Vedas**. Their arrival dates to about 1500 B.C.E., and their power endured for nearly a millennium. They created no cities and no writing system, but commingled religious and social traditions with older cultures to shape the civilization that has flourished in India for the past two and a half millennia.

THE INDUS CIVILIZATION

No one knew of the Indus culture until archaeologists discovered its remains at the site of Harappa in the 1920s. Since then, some 70 cities, the largest being Harappa and Mohenjo-Daro, have been identified. The Indus civiliza-tion had a diversified social and economic organization. These early Indian people created cities, bronze tools, and writing, and engineered covered drainage systems. Indus life is the least understood of the early civilizations, but enough evidence remains to reconstruct something of its culture.

General Character The Indus culture was remarkably homogeneous. City layouts, building construction, a refined system of weights and measures, seal inscriptions, fine-patterned pottery and figurines, and even the kind of burnt brick used for buildings and floodwalls are unusually uniform throughout all Indus towns. This suggests an integrated economic system and good internal communications.

Indus culture was also remarkably constant over time. Because the main cities and towns lay in river lowlands subject to periodic flooding, they were rebuilt often. Each new level of construction closely followed its precursor's pattern. Similarly, the Indus script shows no evidence of change over time. This stability, regularity, and traditionalism have led scholars to speculate that this far-flung society was centrally governed, perhaps by a conservative priestly organization rather than a less stable royal dynasty.

Cities   Harappa and Mohenjo-Daro may each have had populations exceeding 35,000 people. They were meticulously laid out. To the west of each stood a large, walled citadel on a raised rectangular platform. The citadel contained the main public buildings. The town proper was laid out on a north-south, east-west grid of main avenues. The town "blocks" formed by the main avenues were crisscrossed by small, less rigidly planned lanes lined by private houses. The typical house was built around a central courtyard, and its walls facing the street were blank and windowless.

Perhaps the most striking features of these cities were their complex drainage systems. Private houses had wells, bathrooms, and latrines. The sewers that served these facilities were engineering feats unrivaled in the ancient world until the time of the Romans nearly 2,000 years later.

Economic Life   The Indus state or states were supported by a thriving agricultural economy. The Indus people wove cloth from cotton, made metal tools, and used the potter's wheel. Evidence shows that they traded with Mesopotamia. Metals and semiprecious stones were imported from present-day Iran, Afghanistan, and Central Asia, from the southern Indian peninsula, and perhaps from Arabia. Artistic styles suggest that trade contacts inspired the borrowing of ideas from other cultures.

Material Culture   Among the most striking accomplishments of the Indus culture are fine sculptures and artifacts, including copper and bronze tools and vessels, painted pottery, stonework, figurines and toys, jewelry, and dyed fabrics. Except for some decorative brickwork, no monumental friezes, mosaics, or sculpture have been found.

Religion   Elaborate bathing facilities suggest that the Indus religion may have utilized washing as an important purification ritual. The many images of male animals, such as the humped bull, that have been found imply that animals may have been worshipped as symbols of power and fertility. A recurring human male figure with leafy headdress and horns, often seated in a posture associated later in India with yogic meditation, suggests the Vedic Aryan "Lord of All Creatures" of the Indian god Shiva. Figurines of females, often pregnant or holding a child, resemble female images in several prehistoric cultures. They may represent an element of pre-Aryan religion that reemerged later to figure in Hindu culture.

The Passing of Indus Civilization   Between 1800 to 1700 B.C.E., Indus civilization faded away. Warlike Aryan invaders, abnormal flooding, and a long period of dessication may have contributed to its decline. Today, the Indus culture remains in the shadows of prehistory and its influence has yet to be accurately gauged.

Indus stone stamp seal. Note the familiar humped bull of India.
© Scala/Art Resource, N.Y.

3.1
Rig Veda

THE VEDIC ARYAN CIVILIZATION

The Aryan culture, which effectively "refounded" Indian civilization around 1500 B.C.E., is known primarily through the "winged words" of the Vedas, the Aryan sacred texts. For this reason, the culture is called Vedic. The Vedas are ritual, priestly, speculative works, not histories. The texts offer little about events but provide insight into the religion, society, values, and thought of early Aryan India.

Veda means "knowledge." The Vedas are the four major compilations of Vedic ritual texts. The Rig Veda, the oldest material, dates from ca. 1000 B.C.E. to perhaps 1700–1200 B.C.E. when the Aryans spread across the northern plains to the upper reaches of the Ganges. It recounts the history of the early Aryans through a collection of 1,028 religious hymns.

Aryan, a different kind of term, was apparently the name of a people who originated in the steppeland between Eastern Europe and Central Asia and emigrated to Europe, Greece, Anatolia, the Iranian plateau, and India during the second and first millennia B.C.E. Those who came to India are more precisely designated *Indo Aryans* or *Vedic Aryans*.

In the 19th century, Aryan was the term applied to the widespread language group known more commonly today as Indo-European. Greek, Latin, the Romance and Germanic languages, the Slavic tongues, and the Indo-Iranian languages, including Persian and Sanskrit and their derivatives, all belong to the Indo-European family. The Nazis perversely misused Aryan to refer to a white "master race." Today, Aryan usually refers to the Indo-European speakers who invaded India and the Iranian plateau in the second millennium B.C.E. It is also the name linguists use for the Indo-Iranian languages.

"Aryanizing" of North India The Vedic Aryans were seminomadic warriors who reached India through the mountain passes of the Hindu Kush. They probably entered India gradually in small tribal groups. The Vedic Aryans were horsemen and cattle herders rather than farmers and city builders. They left their mark not on material culture but in the languages, social organization, techniques of warfare, and religions of the regions they overran.

The Vedic Aryans first penetrated the Punjab and the Indus Valley (1800–1500 B.C.E.). Their horses, chariots, and copper-bronze weapons likely gave them military superiority. Echos of early conflicts can be heard in some Rigvedic hymns. The extent of their conquests during the Rigvedic age (ca. 1700–1000 B.C.E.) is not clear, but their main locus remained the Punjab and the plains west of the Yamuna River. From about 1000 to 500 B.C.E., the Later Vedic age, the Vedic Aryans spread across the plains between the Yamuna and the Ganges, northeast to the Himalayan foothills, and southeast along the Ganges, occupying what was to become the cradle of subsequent Indian civilization.

The Later Vedic period is also called the Brahmanic age because it was dominated by the priestly religion of the Brahman class, which is documented in commentaries called the *Brahmanas* (ca. 1000–800 or 600 B.C.E.). It was the setting for India's two classical epics, the ***Mahabhrarata*** and the ***Ramayana***, both of which reflect complex cultural and social mixing of Aryan and earlier subcontinent peoples.

By about 200 C.E., this mixing had spread a distinctive new "Indian" civilization over most of the subcontinent. Its basis was clearly Aryan, but its language, social organization, and religion incorporated many non-Aryan elements.

Mahabharata and Ramayana
Two classical Indian epics.

OVERVIEW   THE FIRST CIVILIZATIONS

Civilization is a form of human culture usually marked by the development of cities, the ability to make and use metal tools and instruments, and the invention of a system of writing. The first civilizations appeared in the Middle East between 4004 and 3000 B.C.E., and by the second millennium B.C.E., there were civilized societies in Eurasia, China, and the Americas.

Mesopotamia	Sumerians arrive in the Tigris-Euphrates River Valley, ca. 3500 B.C.E., and establish the first city-states ca. 2800 B.C.E.
Egypt	Egyptian civilization develops along the Nile River, ca. 3100 B.C.E. Egypt becomes a unified state ca. 2700 B.C.E.
Indus Valley	Flourishing urban civilization develops in northern India along the Indus River, ca. 2250 B.C.E.
China	City-states appear in the Yellow River basin ca. 1766 B.C.E.
Americas	Agricultural surplus gives rise to the first cities in Mesoamerica, ca. 1500 B.C.E., and to the first Andean civilization in South America, ca. 2750 B.C.E.

Vedic Aryan Society   Aryan society was apparently patrilineal; that is, succession and inheritance passed down in the male line. Gods were predominantly male. Marriage appears to have been monogamous, but widows could remarry. Related families belonged to larger kin groups, and the largest social grouping was the tribe, ruled by a chieftain or **raja** ("king" in Sanskrit). By the Brahmanic age, the power of the priestly class increased, along with that of the king, who, with the sanction of the priestly establishment, became a hereditary ruler claiming divine qualities.

Aryan society seems at first to have had only two basic divisions: noble and common. In time, the Dasas—the darker, conquered peoples—formed a third group of the socially excluded. Eventually, a rigid scheme of four social classes (excluding the non-Aryan Dasas) evolved: the priestly (Brahman), the warrior/noble (Kshatriya), the peasant/tradesman (Vaishya), and the servant (Shudra). By the late Rigvedic period, these four divisions, or *varnas*, had become so basic to society as to be sanctioned explicitly in religious theory. Only the members of the three upper classes participated fully in social, political, and religious life. This scheme underlies the rigid caste system that later became fundamental to Indian society.

Material Culture   The early, seminomadic Aryans had little impressive material culture. They lived simply in wood and thatch or, later, mud-walled dwellings. They measured wealth in cattle and were accomplished at carpentry and bronze work. They cultivated some crops, especially grains.

The Brahmanic age is poor in material remains. Mud-brick towns appeared, but urban culture was undeveloped. Established kingdoms with fixed capitals existed. Trade grew. Later texts mention artisans, such as goldsmiths, basketmakers, weavers, potters, and entertainers.

Writing had been reintroduced to India some time earlier, perhaps around 700 B.C.E., and its use became common about 500 B.C.E. The prestige of oral transmission for the Vedas remained so high among the Brahman class, however, that writing continued to be scorned for truly sacred texts.

raja   An Indian king.

Ancient India

ca. 2250–1750 B.C.E.	Indus (Harappan) civilization
(2500–1500?)	Written script still undeciphered
ca. 1800–1500 B.C.E.	Aryan peoples invade northwestern India
ca. 1500–1000 B.C.E.	Rigvedic period: composition of Rigvedic hymns; Punjab as center of Indo-Aryan civilization
ca. 1000–500 B.C.E.	Later Vedic period; Doab as center of Indo-Aryan civilization
ca. 1000–800/600 B.C.E.	Composition of *Brahmanas* and other Vedic texts
ca. 800–500 B.C.E.	Composition of major Upanishads
ca. 700–500 B.C.E.	Probable reintroduction of writing
ca. 400 B.C.E.–200 C.E.	Composition of great epics, the *Mahabharata* and *Ramayana*

Upanishads Vedic texts most concerned with speculation about the universe.

WHY DID large territorial states arise in ancient China?

Religion   The earliest Indo-Aryans probably worshipped numerous gods. The Rigvedic hymns address anthropomorphic deities linked to natural phenomena such as the sky, the clouds, and the sun. Chief among them was Indra, god of war and the storm.

Ritual sacrifice was the central focus of Vedic religion. Its goal apparently was to invoke the presence of the gods to whom the offering was made rather than to expiate sins or express thanksgiving. An intoxicant (soma juice) was drunk as a prominent feature of the sacrificial ritual. A recurring theme of the Vedic hymns that accompanied such religious ceremonies is the desire for the good things of this life: prosperity, health, and victory. Burnt offerings were particularly important and feature in both public and private worship.

By Brahmanic times, a considerable body of mystical speculation had developed around sacrificial ritual. The god, the offering, the sacrifice, and the sacrificer were all identified with one another. The word *Brahman*, which originally meant a ritual utterance or word of power, came to refer to the generalized divine power present in the sacrifice. In the **Upanishads**, some of the latest Vedic texts and the ones most concerned with speculation about the universe, *Brahman* was expanded to refer to the Absolute, the transcendent principle of reality. As the guardian of ritual and the master of the sacred word, the priest was known throughout the Vedic Aryan period by a related word, *Brahmana* (*Brahman* in English). Echoes of these associations lent force in later Hindu tradition to the special status of the Brahman caste groups as the highest social class (see Chapter 4).

EARLY CHINESE CIVILIZATION

NEOLITHIC ORIGINS IN THE YELLOW RIVER VALLEY

Agriculture began in China about 4000 B.C.E. in the basin of the southern bend of the Yellow River. The chief crop of China's agricultural revolution was millet. The early Chinese cleared land and burned its cover to plant millet and cabbage and, later, rice and soybeans. When the soil became exhausted, fields and sometimes villages were abandoned. The Chinese used stones to make a variety of tools (axes, hoes, spades, and sickle-shaped knives) and pottery to store grain. They domesticated pigs, sheep, cattle, dogs, and chickens.

The first Chinese cultivators lived in wattle-and-daub pit dwellings with wooden support posts and sunken, plastered floors. Their villages occupied isolated clearings along slopes of river valleys. They buried their dead in cemeteries with jars of food. Tribal leaders wore rings and beads of jade.

EARLY BRONZE AGE: THE SHANG

The traditional history of China postulates the existence of three ancient dynasties: Xia (2205–1766 B.C.E.), Shang (1766–1050 B.C.E.), and Zhou (1050–256 B.C.E.). Until early in the 20th century, modern historians believed the first two to be legendary. Then, in the 1920s, archaeological excavations near present-day An Yang uncovered the ruins of a walled city that had been a late Shang capital. More Shang cities have since been discovered. The archives of the department of divination of the Shang court, containing thousands of "oracle bones" incised with archaic Chinese writing, have been found in the ruins. The names of kings recovered from artifacts almost perfectly correspond to the names that feature in the traditional historical record. The discovery that the Shang existed increases the probability that there was also a real Hsia dynasty.

The city-state was the characteristic political institution of Bronze Age China. Cities were walled compounds containing public buildings, altars, and the residences of the aristocracy. They were surrounded by a sea of Neolithic tribal villages. By late Shang times, several such cities were scattered across the north China plain.

The military aristocracy rode to war in chariots, supported by levies of foot soldiers. The Shang fought against barbarian tribes and, occasionally, against Chinese city-states that rebelled against Shang rule. Captured prisoners were enslaved.

The three most notable features of Shang culture were writing, bronzes, and the appearance of social classes. Scribes at the Shang court kept records on strips of bamboo, few of which have survived. Large numbers of inscriptions on bronze artifacts and oracle bones, however, have survived. Some bones contain the question put to the oracle, the oracle's answer, and the outcome. Oracles were asked such questions as: Which ancestor is causing the king's earache? Will the king's child be a son? Was a particular sacrifice acceptable to ancestral deities?

Our knowledge of Shang religion derives from inscriptions on oracle bones. The Shang believed in a supreme "Deity Above," who had authority over the human world. There were lesser natural deities—the sun, moon, earth, rain, wind, and the six clouds—who served at the court of the Deity Above. Even the Shang king, however, did not presume to sacrifice to the Deity Above but only to his ancestors, who interceded with the Deity Above on the king's behalf. Kings, while alive at least, were not considered divine but were regarded as the high priests of the state.

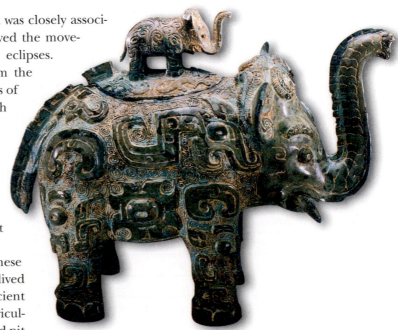

Bronze Vessel from the Shang Dynasty.
The little elephant on top forms the handle of the lid. Wine was poured through the spout formed by the big elephant's trunk.

The Freer Gallery of Art, Smithsonian Institution, Washington, D.C.

In Shang times, as later, religion in China was closely associated with cosmology. The Shang people observed the movements of the planets and stars and noted eclipses. Celestial happenings were seen as omens from the gods, and chief cosmologists maintained records of them at court. The Shang calendar had a month of 30 days and a year of 360 days. An extra month was inserted periodically to keep the solar and lunar years in sync. The king used the calendar to tell his people when to sow and reap.

Bronze, which appeared in China about 2000 B.C.E., was used for weapons, armor, chariot fittings, and ceremonial vessels.

A class hierarchy defined life in the Chinese city-state. The king and the officials of his court lived within the walled city. Their lifestyle was, for ancient times, opulent. A far larger population of agricultural workers lived hard, meager lives in cramped pit dwellings outside the city. Nowhere was the gulf between the royal lineage and the baseborn more apparent than in the Shang institution of human sacrifice. When a king died, hundreds of slaves or prisoners of war, sometimes together with people who had served the king during his lifetime, might be buried with him. Similar sacrifices were made when a palace or an altar was dedicated.

LATE BRONZE AGE: THE WESTERN ZHOU

To the west of the area of Shang rule lived the Zhou people. They were less civilized and more warlike than the Shang. By 1050 B.C.E., the last Shang kings had been debilitated by campaigns against nomads in the north and rebellious tribes in the east. Taking advantage of this opportunity, the Zhou swept in, conquering the Shang.

The Zhou continued the Shang pattern of life and rule. The agrarian-based city-state remained the basic unit of society, and by the 8th century B.C.E. there were about 200 urban centers. The Zhou also assimilated Shang culture and continued the development of China's ideographic writing.

The Zhou kept their primary capital in the west but set up a secondary capital at Loyang along the southern bend of the Yellow River. They appointed kinsmen or aristocratic allies as rulers of other city-states. Blood or lineage ties were fundamental to the organization of Zhou government. The Zhou king was the head of the senior branch of the family and performed sacrifices for the entire family. The rank of a lord of princely state depended on how closely he was related to the senior line of Zhou kings.

The Zhou, having conquered the Shang, needed a rationale for why they, and not the Shang, had become China's rightful rulers. Their argument was that heaven had withdrawn its mandate from the Shang, awarding it instead to the Zhou. The concept of the **Mandate of Heaven** was subsequently invoked by every dynasty in China down to the 20th century.

IRON AGE: THE EASTERN ZHOU

In 771 B.C.E., the Wei valley capital of the Western Zhou was overrun by barbarians. The heir to the throne escaped to the secondary capital at Loyang and inaugurated the Eastern Zhou period.

The first phase of the Eastern Zhou lasted until 481 B.C.E., but the Zhou kings were never able to reestablish their old authority. By the early seventh century B.C.E., kinship and religious ties to the Zhou house had worn thin, and its leaders no longer had the military strength to reimpose its rule. During the seventh and sixth centuries B.C.E., numerous small principalities maintained political equilibrium on the north-central plain. Larger, autonomous territorial states occupied the borders of the plain and gradually expanded by conquering the states on their peripheries.

The second phase of the Eastern Zhou is called the Warring States period. (It is named for a chronicle that treats the years from 401 to 256 B.C.E.) By the fifth century B.C.E., all defensive alliances had collapsed, and the stronger states had swallowed their weaker neighbors. As the border states grew in size and power, conflicts increased until the fourth century B.C.E., when only eight or nine great territorial states existed. It remained to be seen which one would defeat the others and unify China.

Mandate of Heaven The Chinese belief that heaven entrusts or withdraws a ruler's or a dynasty's right to govern.

Early China

4000 B.C.E.	Neolithic agricultural villages
1766 B.C.E.	Bronze Age city-states
771 B.C.E.	Iron Age territorial states
500 B.C.E.	Age of philosophers
221 B.C.E.	China is unified

Three basic changes in Chinese society contributed to the rise of large territorial states. One development was the expansion of population and agricultural lands. The walled cities of the Shang and Western Zhou had resembled oases in the wilds. They were bounded by plains, marshes, and forests. But in the Eastern Zhou, the wilds started to disappear as the population grew. States began to abut, and friction arose over boundaries. These changes accelerated after the start of the Iron Age in the late sixth century B.C.E. With iron tools, farmers expanded agricultural resources by clearing new lands and plowing deeper. Irrigation and drainage canals appeared. By the third century B.C.E., China had about 20 million people and was the most populous country in the world, a distinction it has never lost.

The second change that promoted the growth of large states was the rise of commerce. Roads built for war were used by merchants. Products of one region were traded for those of another. Copper coins joined bolts of silk and precious metals as media of exchange. Zhou tombs show that the material and artistic culture of China leaped ahead during this period despite endemic warfare.

2.3
Ch'u Yuan and Sung Yu: Individual Voices in a Chaotic Era

A third factor that encouraged the development of large city-states was the rise of a new kind of army. War chariots of the old aristocracy, which were effective only on level terrain, gave way to cavalry armed with crossbows. Most of the fighting was done by conscript foot soldiers, and professional commanders replaced the old nobility. Territorial states could field armies numbering in the hundreds of thousands. Military tactics were bloody and ruthless, and prisoners were often massacred.

Government also changed. Lords of the new territorial states began to call themselves kings, taking a title that previously only Zhou royalty had enjoyed. The hereditary nobility began to decline, supplanted by ministers appointed for their knowledge of statecraft. To survive, new states mobilized their agricultural and commercial wealth for support of their military, necessitating administration by a literate bureaucracy. Its members constituted a category of people called the *shih*, a term that came to mean "scholar-bureaucrat." The shih included petty nobility, warriors, landlords, merchants, and commoners. From this class, as we will see in Chapter 2, came the philosophers who transformed the culture of China.

THE RISE OF CIVILIZATION IN THE AMERICAS

During the last Ice Age, the Bering region between Siberia and Alaska was dry land. Perhaps as early as 30,000 years ago, humans crossed this land bridge. These Asian immigrants moved south and east until they reached the tip of South America and the eastern regions of North America.

HOW DID agriculture influence the development of civilization in Mesoamerica?

The earliest immigrants to the Americas, like all other Paleolithic peoples, lived by hunting, fishing, and gathering. However, many parts of North and South America were poor in animal resources when compared to Africa and Eurasia. Neither horses nor cattle were to be found on the American continents. Where fish or small game were insufficiently plentiful, people relied on protein from vegetable sources. In the exploitation of plants that provided protein, America far outpaced Europe. One of the most important early achievements was the development of useful species of maize. Wherever maize (corn) could be extensively grown, the food supply was essentially secured. Maize appears to have been cultivated in Mexico by 4000 B.C.E., as were other important foods such as potatoes, manioc, squash, beans, peppers, and tomatoes.

Early Civilizations of Mesoamerica

1500–400 B.C.E.	The Olmec
200 C.E.–750 C.E.	The Classic period in Central Mexico. Dominance of Teotihuacán in the Valley of Mexico and Monte Alban in the Valley of Oaxaca
150 C.E.–900 C.E.	The Classic period of Maya civilization in the Yucatán and Guatemala

Mesoamerica Region of North America that extends from the central part of modern Mexico to Central America.

Olmec Head. This colossal Olmec head, now in the Museo Nacional de Antropologia in Mexico City, was excavated at San Lorenzo. Carved of basalt, it may be a portrait of an Olmec ruler. Olmec civilization thrived between 1500 and 800 B.C.E.

Josephus Daniels/Photo Researchers, Inc.

Eventually, **Mesoamerica** and the Andean region of South America saw the emergence of strong, long-lasting states. In regions that lacked maize-based agriculture and settled village life—notably the North American Southwest—food supplies might have been too insecure to support the development of states.

Mesoamerica, which extends from the central part of modern Mexico into Central America, ranges from tropical rainforest to semiarid mountains (see Map 1–3). Archaeologists divide its preconquest history into three broad periods: Preclassic or Formative (2000 B.C.E.–150 C.E.), Classic (150–900 C.E.), and Post-Classic (900–1521). The earliest Mesoamerican civilization, that of the Olmecs, arose during the Preclassic on the Gulf Coast about 1500 B.C.E. The Olmec centers at San Lorenzo (ca. 1200–ca. 900 B.C.E.) and La Venta (ca. 900–ca. 400 B.C.E.) exhibit many of the characteristics of later Mesoamerican cities: symmetrical arrangement of large platforms, plazas, and monumental structures situated along a central axis. Writing developed in Mesoamerica during the late Formative period.

The Andes rise abruptly from the coastal plain and then descend gradually into the Amazon basin to the east. Agriculture is possible on the coast only in the valleys of the many rivers that flow from the Andes into the Pacific. The earliest monumental architecture in the Andean region was built on the coast at the site of Aspero by people who depended on a combination of agriculture and the Pacific's rich marine resources. It dates to about 2750 B.C.E. and is contemporary with the Great Pyramids of Egypt's Old Kingdom.

From 800 B.C.E. to 200 B.C.E., a civilization associated with the site of Chavín de Huantar in the highlands of Peru exerted great influence in the Andes. Artifacts in the distinctive Chavín style of this period can be found over a large area, which archaeologists call the Early Horizon. In many places this was a time of technical innovation with pottery, textiles, and metallurgy. The spread of the Chavín style may be due to political integration or the influence of a strong religious center. The period following the decline of Chavín, which archaeologists call the Early Intermediate period, saw the development of distinctive cultures in several regions. Most notable are the Moche culture on the northern coast of Peru and the Nazca culture on the southern coast. A second period of transregional integration, called the Middle Horizon, occurred around 600 C.E. and was probably caused by the rise of empires centered on the highland sites of Huari and Tiahuanaco. The Late Intermediate period was dominated on the northern coast of Peru by the Chimu successors of the Moche state. This era ended with the founding of the vast, tightly controlled empire of the Incas in the 14th and 15th centuries C.E.

MAP 1–3
Early Civilization in Mesoamerica and the Andean Region.   Both Mesoamerica and the Andean region of South America saw the development of a series of civilizations beginning between 1500 and 1000 B.C.E.

WHY DID the first civilizations in the Americas develop in Mesoamerica and the Andes?

SUMMARY

The Emergence of Civilization Beginning in 10,000 B.C.E., human beings shifted during the Neolithic Revolution from a hunter-gather way of life to one marked by settled agriculture and the domestication of animals. Between 4000 and 3000 B.C.E., civilization began to appear along the Tigris and Euphrates Rivers in Mesopotamia, then along the Nile River in Egypt, and somewhat later in the Indus Valley in India and the Yellow River basin in China. Each of these early civilizations developed urban centers, monumental architecture, a hierarchical society, and a system of writing. The period is known as the Bronze Age because it coincided with the discovery of the technique for making bronze tools and weapons.

Early Civilization of the Andes

ca. 2750 B.C.E.	Monumental architecture at Aspero
800–200 B.C.E.	Chavín (Early) Horizon
200 B.C.E.–600 C.E.	Early Intermediate period (Moche on the northern coast of Peru, Nazca on the southern coast)

IMAGE KEY

for pages 4–5

a. Bone from China
b. Sumerian stone with cuneiform writing
c. Theban tomb of Nebamum
d. Tablet with cuneiform writing
e. Neolithic stone figure
f. Venus of Willendorf
g. Votive statue of Sumerian priest
h. Hittite warrior
i. Indian stone stamp seal
j. Zhou dynasty ritual water vessel
k. Egyptian Old Kingdom statue
l. Paleolithic cave painting

Mesopotamia The Sumerians founded the oldest Mesopotamian cities around 3000 B.C.E. Beginning around 2370 B.C.E., the Sumerian city-states were conquered and absorbed in turn by the Akkadian, Babylonian, and Assyrian empires. The Sumerians passed down much of their civilization to their successors: a system of writing on clay tablets called cuneiform, the worship of gods based on natural forces, semi-divine kings, and a highly developed bureaucracy.

Egypt Watered by the Nile River and protected by deserts and the sea, Egyptian civilization was more secure and peaceful than that of Mesopotamia. Egypt became a unified kingdom around 2700 B.C.E. Religion dominated Egyptian life. The kings, or pharaohs, were considered gods on whom the lives and prosperity of their people depended. Egyptian history is divided into three main periods: Old Kingdom (2700–2200 B.C.E.), Middle Kingdom (2052–1786 B.C.E.), and New Kingdom (1575–1087 B.C.E.). Under the New Kingdom, Egypt contended for mastery of the Middle East with the Hittite Empire.

Indus Civilization By 2300 B.C.E. at least 70 Indus cities, the largest being Harappa and Mohenjo-Daro, had developed a sophisticated urban culture. Indus civilization disappeared for unknown reasons between 1800 and 1700 B.C.E. In its place, Indo-European (or Aryan) invaders established the Vedic culture, named after sacred texts called the Vedas. In turn, Vedic culture evolved into a "new" Indian civilization that spread over the whole subcontinent.

China The Shang dynasty (1766–1050 B.C.E.) founded the earliest known Bronze Age civilization in China. The Shang and their successors, the Zhou (1050–256 B.C.E.), ruled as warrior aristocrats from city-states that fought outsiders and each other. By the 4th century B.C.E., as population and commerce expanded, rulers needed bigger armies to defend their states and trained bureaucrats to administer them. The result was the consolidation of many petty states into a few large territorial units.

The Americas The first civilizations in the Americas arose in places that produced an agricultural surplus. In Mesoamerica (central Mexico and Central America), the civilization was based on the cultivation of maize; in the Andes valleys, it was based on a combination of agriculture and the rich marine resources of the Pacific. The Olmecs (1500–400 B.C.E.) established the first civilization in Mesoamerica, and the first monumental architecture appeared in the Andes region around 2750 B.C.E.

REVIEW QUESTIONS

1. How was life in the Paleolithic era different from that in the Neolithic period? Is it or is it not appropriate to speak of a Neolithic "revolution"?

2. What defines civilization? What are the similarities and differences among the world's earliest civilizations?

3. Why were the Assyrians so successful in establishing their Middle Eastern Empire? Did this empire advance the developoment of civilization in the Middle East? Did it have a weakness?

4. How does the early history of Indian civilization differ from that of the riverine civilizations of China, Mesopotamia, and Egypt?

5. What were the stages of early Chinese history?

6. What factors gave rise to civilization in the Americas?

KEY TERMS

Aryans (p. 17)

Bronze Age (p. 7)

civilization (p. 7)

culture (p. 6)

cuneiform (p. 9)

Harappan (p. 17)

hieroglyphics (p. 12)

Indo-European (p. 17)

Mahabharata and
    Ramayana (p. 18)

Mandate of Heaven (p. 22)

Mesoamerica (p. 24)

Mesopotamia (p. 7)

Neolithic Revolution (p. 7)

Paleolithic Age (p. 6)

pharaoh (p. 11)

raja (p. 19)

Upanishads (p. 20)

Vedas (p. 17)

 For additional study resources for this chapter, go to:
www.prenhall.com/craig/chapter1

2 The Four Great Revolutions in Thought and Religion

CHAPTER HIGHLIGHTS

The Four Great Philosophical and Religious Revolutions
Between 800 and 300 B.C.E., four philosophical and religious revolutions arose that were to shape the subsequent history of the world.

Chinese Philosophy Traditional Chinese philosophical thought, which took shape with the teachings of Confucius in the sixth century B.C.E., remained dominant in China until the early twentieth century. It was concerned with social and political issues and sought to teach human beings how to live harmoniously and ethically under Heaven. Other Chinese philosophies were Daoism, a mystical way of thought that offered a refuge from social responsibilities, and Legalism, which taught that a good society requires a strong state that enforces the law and punishes wrongdoers.

Indian Religion Hinduism took shape by 400 B.C.E. Indian religion saw existence as an endless alteration between life and death. The escape from this dilemma lay in the concept of *karma*, the idea that good actions (*dharma*) could lead to rebirth as a higher being. Another Indian religious tradition, the Jains, sought to liberate the soul from the bonds of the material world. Buddhism traces its origins to the teachings of an Indian, Siddhartha Gautama (b. ca. 566 B.C.E.). Buddhism holds that escape from *samsara* lies in following a moral path of right actions and in having compassion for all beings.

Hebrew Monotheism Monotheism is the faith in a single, all-powerful God. The Hebrews were the first people to emphasize the moral demands that the one God, Yahweh, placed on individual and community. The Hebrews, or Jews, were the first people in history to be defined by shared religious faith and practice. Through the Christian and Muslim traditions, Judaic monotheism would change the face of much of the world.

Greek Philosophy The Greeks were the first to initiate the unreservedly rational investigation of the universe. They thus became the forerunners of Western philosophy and science. Greek thinkers sought to explain natural phenomena without recourse to divine intervention. In the later fifth century and the fourth century B.C.E., philosophers such as Socrates, Plato, and Aristotle, applied the same rational, inquisitive approach to the study of moral and political issues.

CHAPTER QUESTIONS

WHAT WERE the four great revolutions in thought and religion that developed between 800 and 300 B.C.E.?

WHY WAS the Chinese revolution more akin to Greek thought than to Indian religion or Judaic monotheism?

WHAT fundamental institutions and ideas form the basis of Indian religion?

WHAT WAS distinctive about the Hebrew concept of God and religion?

WHY, BEGINNNG in the sixth century B.C.E., did Greek thinkers produce an intellectual revolution?

CHAPTER OUTLINE

• Comparing the Four Great Revolutions
• Philosophy in China
• Religion in India
• The Religion of the Israelites
• Greek Philosophy

All human cultures develop religious or philosophical systems. Some people have speculated that human beings may be biologically "hard-wired" for religious faith. Whatever the explanation, it is clear that religion and philosophy respond to profound human psychological needs. They address our curiosity about our ultimate origins, our final destiny, and the meaning of our lives.

COMPARING THE FOUR GREAT REVOLUTIONS

WHAT WERE the four great revolutions in thought and religion that developed between 800 and 300 B.C.E.?

The religious revolution that took place in China provides the clearest example of how philosophical breakthroughs emerged from the legacies of the earliest civilizations. Natural barriers isolated China and prevented outside forces from influencing its development. In India, by contrast, it was not until the culture of the Indo-Aryan immigrants replaced the original Indus civilization that the foundation was laid for the great tradition of Indian thought and religion. The situation in the Mediterranean world was even more complex. No direct ties have been traced from the early Mesopotamian and Egyptian civilizations to Greek philosophy and Judaic monotheism, but they drew on the complex amalgam of cultures that the early Middle Eastern civilizations inspired. The full impact of Greek and Hebrew thought was not felt in the West until centuries later when Christianity and Islam emerged as a second stage in their evolution.

PHILOSOPHY IN CHINA

WHY WAS the Chinese revolution more akin to Greek thought than to Indian religion or Judaic monotheism?

Of the four great intellectual revolutions of the first millennium B.C.E., China's was closer to Greece's than to India's or to Judaic monotheism. Greece produced many different philosophers, and Chinese tradition claimed "one hundred schools." But whereas Greek thought was speculative and interested in natural phenomena, Chinese thought was practical and sociopolitical. Chinese thought also had far greater staying power than Greek thought, which only a few centuries after the glory of Athens was submerged by Christianity. It became the handmaiden of theology and did not reemerge as an independent force until the Italian Renaissance. In contrast, Chinese philosophy, although challenged by Buddhism, remained dominant until the early 20th century. How were these early philosophies able to maintain such a grip on China when the cultures of every other part of the world fell under the sway of religions?

Part of the answer is that most Chinese philosophy had a religious dimension. But it was a different kind of religion, with assumptions unlike those derived from Judaic roots. In the Christian or Islamic worldview, there is a God who, however concerned with humankind, is not of this world. This worldview leads to dualism, the distinction between a supernatural other world and this world.

In the Chinese worldview, the two spheres are not separate: The cosmos is single, continuous, and nondualistic. It includes Heaven, Earth, and humanity. Heaven is above. Earth is below. Humanity, ideally guided by a wise and virtuous ruler, stands in between and harmonizes the cosmological forces of Heaven and Earth by virtuous living and ritual sacrifice.

CONFUCIANISM

Confucius was born in 551 B.C.E. in a minor state in northeastern China. Since he received an education in writing, music, and rituals, he probably belonged to the lower nobility or the knightly class. His father died when Confucius was young, so

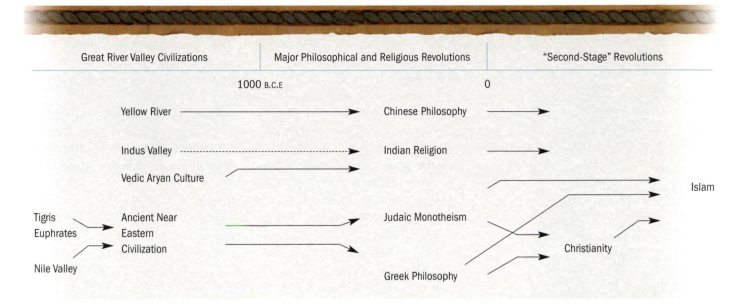

Great River Valley Civilizations	Major Philosophical and Religious Revolutions	"Second-Stage" Revolutions

1000 B.C.E   0

Yellow River ——————→ Chinese Philosophy ———→

Indus Valley - - - - - - - - - → Indian Religion ———→

Vedic Aryan Culture ————→

Tigris
Euphrates ↗→ Ancient Near ——————→ Judaic Monotheism   Islam
Eastern
Civilization   Christianity

Nile Valley ↗

Greek Philosophy

he may have known privation. He made his living by teaching, and he traveled with his disciples from state to state, seeking a ruler who would put his ideas into practice. Although he may once have obtained a minor post, his ideas were usually rejected as impractical. He died in 479 B.C.E., honored as a teacher and scholar but having failed to find a ruler who would implement his ideas. *Confucius* is the Latinized form of *K'ung Fu-tzu,* or *Master K'ung,* as he is known in China.

The only records of Confucius's teachings are the *Analects,* collections of his sayings made by his disciples. The picture that emerges from them is of a man of moderation, propriety, optimism, good sense, and wisdom. In an age of cruelty and superstition, he was humane, rational, and upright, demanding much of others and more of himself. Characteristically, when asked about death, he turned the questioner's attention back to this life: "You do not understand even life. How can you understand death?"[1]

Confucius described himself as a transmitter and a conservator of tradition, not an innovator. He idealized the early Shang and Zhou kings as paragons of virtue and imagined early Zhou society as a golden age. He sought the secrets of its success in its writings, some of which became Confucian classics. Throughout most of Chinese history they have had an authority not unlike Scripture in the West.

Confucius proposed to resolve the turmoil of his own age by a return to the good old ways of the early Zhou. When asked about government, he said, "Let the ruler be a ruler, the subject a subject, the father a father, the son a son." His vision was of an unbroken social harmony (extending from the individual family member to the monarch) based on five categories of relationship: ruler-subject, father-son, husband-wife, older brother-younger brother, and friend-friend. China, however, was undergoing a dynamic transition, and it was not enough simply to stress basic human relationships.

The genius of Confucius was to transform the old aristocratic code into a new ethical system that any educated Chinese could practice. His reinterpretation of the early Zhou tradition can be seen in his concept of the **chun-tzu,** literally "the son of the ruler" (or of an aristocrat). Confucius redefined it as a person with the inner virtues of humanity, integrity, righteousness, altruism, and loyalty,

[1]Confucius, *The Analects,* trans. by D. C. Lau (Penguin Books, 1979).

QUICK REVIEW

Confucius
- Born in 551 B.C.E. in northeastern China
- Probably belonged to the lower nobility or knightly class
- Made his living as a teacher and a scholar

2.4
Confucius: *Analects*

chun-tzu The Confucian term for a person who behaves ethically, in harmony with the cosmic order.

Confucius. The philosopher is depicted here wearing the robes of a scholar of a later age.

Collection of the National Palace Museum, Taiwan, Republic of China.

Daoism A Chinese philosophy that teaches that wisdom lies in becoming one with the *Dao*, the "way," which is the creative principle of the universe.

matched by an outward demeanor of propriety. This redefinition was not unlike the change that has taken place in the meaning of *gentleman*, from "one who is gentle-born" to "one who is gentle-behaved." But whereas *gentleman* remained a fairly superficial category in the West, in China *chun-tzu* went deeper. Confucius saw ethics as grounded in nature. The true gentleman was in touch with his basic nature, and through it, with the cosmic order.

Confucius taught that good government depended on the appointment to office of good men, who would serve as models for the multitude: "The virtue of the gentleman is like wind; the virtue of the small man is like grass. Let the wind blow over the grass and it is sure to bend." Above the gentleman was the sage king, who possessed an almost mystical virtue and power.

Confucianism was not adopted as the official philosophy of China until the second century B.C.E., during the Han dynasty (202 B.C.E.–9 C.E.; see Chapter 7). But two other important Confucian philosophers had appeared in the meantime. Mencius (370–290 B.C.E.) is famous for his argument that humans tend toward the good just as water runs downward. The role of education, therefore, is to uncover and cultivate that innate goodness. Moreover, just as humans tend toward the good, so does Heaven possess a moral will. The will of Heaven is that a government should see to the education and well-being of its people. The rebellion of people against a government is the primary evidence that Heaven has withdrawn its mandate. At times in Chinese history, only lip service was paid toward concern for the people, but the idea that government should care for the people became a permanent part of the Confucian tradition.

The other influential Confucian philosopher was Xunzi (300–237 B.C.E.), who felt that Heaven was amoral and indifferent to whether China was ruled by a tyrant or a sage. He believed human nature was bad or at least that human desires and emotions, if unchecked and unrefined, caused conflict. He emphasized etiquette and education as restraints on unruly human nature, and good institutions, including punishments and rewards, as a means for shaping behavior. These ideas influenced the thinkers of the Legalist school.

DAOISM

Daoism (pronounced "Dah-oh-ism") offered a refuge from the burden of social responsibilities. The classics of the school are the *Lao-tzu*, dating from the fourth century B.C.E., and the *Chuang-tzu*, dating from about a century later.

The central concept of the religion is the *Dao*, or way. It is the mysterious, unnameable creator, the sustainer, and the process or flux of the universe. The Dao functions on a cosmic scale. As the *Lao-tzu* puts it, "Heaven and Earth are ruthless, and treat the myriad creatures as straw dogs; the sage (in accord with the Dao) is ruthless, and treats the people as straw dogs."[2] But the sage is also described as one who "excels in saving people." By realizing the Dao, he transcends disruptive action and allows nature to flourish.

The sage follows the rhythms of nature, the *Lao-tzu* says, by regaining or returning to an original simplicity. To attain this state, one must "learn to be without learning." Knowledge is bad because it creates distinctions and leads to a succession of ideas and images that interfere with participation in the Dao. One must also learn to be without desires beyond the immediate and simple needs of nature.

Along with the basic Daoist prescription of becoming one with the Dao are two other assumptions or principles. One is that any action pushed to an extreme

[2] *Tau Te Ching*, trans. by D. C. Lau (Penguin Books, 1963).

will initiate a countervailing reaction in the direction of the opposite extreme. The other is that too much government, even good government, can become oppressive by its very weight. As the *Lao-tzu* put it, "Govern a large state as you would cook small fish"; that is, without too much stirring.

LEGALISM

A third great current in classical Chinese thought was **Legalism**. Legalists were also concerned about ending the wars that plagued China. True peace, they felt, required a strong state. The Legalists did not seek a model in the distant past nor model their state on a heavenly order of values. They began with the assumption that human nature is selfish and in need of restraint by a strong state. Severe laws, rewards for service that strengthens the state, and punishment for acts that weaken it are the means to a good society.

Legalism was the philosophy of the state of Qin, which destroyed the Zhou in 256 B.C.E. and unified China in 221 B.C.E. Because Qin laws were cruel and severe, and because Legalism put human laws above an ethic modeled on Heaven, later generations of Chinese execrated its doctrines. Yet its legacy of administrative and criminal laws survived. Even Confucian statesmen could not do without them.

China	
551–479 B.C.E.	Confucius
370–290 B.C.E.	Mencius
300–237 B.C.E.	Xunzi
Fourth century B.C.E.	Lao-Tzu
221 B.C.E.	Qin unifies China

RELIGION IN INDIA

By 400 B.C.E., new social and religious forms took shape in the Indian subcontinent. A tradition was created whose fundamental institutions and ideas came to prevail virtually throughout the subcontinent. Despite staggering internal diversity and divisions and long periods of foreign rule, this Indian culture has survived for more than 2,000 years.

WHAT FUNDAMENTAL institutions and ideas form the basis of Indian religion?

"HINDU" AND "INDIAN"

The word **Hindu** lumps together an immense diversity of social, racial, linguistic, and religious groups. It is not a term for any single or uniform religious community. "Indian," on the other hand, commonly refers today to all native inhabitants of the subcontinent, including Muslims, Sikhs, and Christians. We, however, shall use *Indian* to refer to the distinctively Indian tradition of thought and culture that achieved its classical formulation in the Hindu society of the first millennium C.E. (before the arrival of Muslim culture ca. 1000 C.E.). The Jains of India and the Buddhists of wider Asia were also its heirs.

HISTORICAL BACKGROUND

We saw in Chapter 1 how, in the later Vedic or Brahmanic period, a priest-centered cult dominated the upper classes of Aryanized northern Indian society. By the sixth century B.C.E., this cult had apparently grown so extreme that most people had little or no access to it. Elaborate animal sacrifices on behalf of Aryan rulers imposed economic burdens on peasants whose religious concerns they did not address.

The latest Vedic texts themselves reflect a reaction against excessive emphasis on the power of sacrifice and ritual formulas, accumulation of worldly wealth and power, and hope for an afterlife in paradise. Treatises called the **Brahmanas** (ca. 1000–800 B.C.E.) dealt with the ritual applications of the old Vedic texts, the

Legalism Chinese philosophical school that argued that a strong state was necessary to have a good society.

Hindu Term applied to the diverse social, racial, linguistic, and religious groups of India.

Brahmanas Texts dealing with the ritual application of the Vedas.

explanation of Vedic rites and mythology, and the theory of the sacrifice. Initially they had focused on methods for controlling the sacred power (*Brahman*) of the sacrificial ritual, but they gradually came to emphasize the acquisition of this power through knowledge instead of ritual acts.

This tendency became central to the Upanishads (ca. 800–500 B.C.E.), and extended meditations on the meaning of ritual and the nature of *Brahman*. The Upanishadic sages and the early Jains and Buddhists shared certain revolutionary ideas and concerns. Their thinking and piety influenced not only all later Indian thought but, through the spread of the Buddhist tradition, much of the intellectual and religious life of East and Southeast Asia as well. Thus, the middle centuries of the first millennium B.C.E. in India began a religious and philosophical revolution that, like China's, marks a turning point in the history of civilization.

THE UPANISHADIC WORLDVIEW

The Upanishads emphasized two new ideas: that knowledge is more important than ritual, and that immortality is not an afterlife but escape from existence itself. An early Upanishadic prayer said, "From the unreal lead me to the Real. From death lead me to immortality." The first sentence suggests the Upanishadic focus on speculation about the nature of things, the quest for ultimate truth. Here ritual takes a backseat to meditation, and knowledge, not sacred words or acts, becomes the source of power. The second sentence reflects a novel belief that true immortality is liberation from existence in any earthly, heavenly, or other sense. These two Upanishadic beliefs changed the shape of Indian thought forever and provide the key to understanding its basic worldview.

The Nature of Reality   The Upanishadic quest for knowledge focused on discovering the nature of the individual self (*atman*) and the self's relation to ultimate reality (*Brahman*). The gods are seen as part of the total scheme of things, subject to the laws of existence, and not on the same plane with the transcendent Absolute. Prayer and sacrifice to particular gods for their help continues; but the higher goal is realization of *Brahman* through intellect alone, not ritual.

The culmination of Upanishadic speculation is the suggestion that the way to the Absolute is through the self. Through contemplation, ***Atman-Brahman*** is recognized not as a deity, but as the very principle of reality itself—the unborn, uncreated, unchanging infinite. Because the ultimate cannot be conceptualized or described in finite terms, all that can be said of this reality is that it is "neither this nor that." Beneath the impermanence of ordinary reality lies the changeless *Brahman*, to which every being's immortal self belongs. The difficulty is in recognizing this self (and with it the Absolute) while one is enmeshed in mortal existence.

A second, and related, focus of Upanishadic thought is inquiry into the nature of "normal" existence. The realm of life is seen to be ultimately impermanent and ever changing. Things that appear to be "substantial"—the physical world, our bodies and personalities, worldly success—are revealed in the Upanishads as ultimately ephemeral. Even happiness is transient. Existence, therefore, can never be satisfying in any fundamental sense. Only *Brahman* is enduring, eternal, unchanging, for it is the unmoved ground of being. Here we see the roots of the Buddhist belief that impermanence and suffering are the fundamental facts of existence as we know it.

Atman-Brahman The unchanging, infinite principle of reality in Indian religion.

Life After Death   The Upanishadic sages conceived of existence as a ceaseless cycle, a never-ending alternation between life and death. The concept of *samsara*, the endless cycle of existence, became the basic assumption of all Indian thought and the key to its understanding of reality. It regards the prospect of endless "redeath" as the dismal lot of all beings in this world

Karma   The concept of *karma* helped make sense of the cycle of *samsara*. It holds that every action has inevitable effects. Good deeds bring good results, perhaps even rebirth in a heaven or as a god, and evil deeds bring evil consequences, whether in this life or by rebirth in the next. Because of the fundamental impermanence of everything in existence, both good and evil are temporary. The flux of existence knows only movement, change, endless cause and effect far transcending a mere human life span.

Solutions   The Indian tradition developed two kinds of solutions to the problem of *samsara*. The first recommends a strategy of maximizing good actions and minimizing bad actions to achieve the best possible rebirth in one's next round of existence. The second, and more radical, solution seeks "liberation" (*moksha*) from existence: escaping all karmic effects by escaping action itself.

The first strategy has been characterized as the "ordinary norm," as opposed to the "extraordinary norm" (a path possible only for a select elite). Essentially, the ordinary norm aims at living in accordance with a code of social and moral responsibility. The most significant such codes in Indian history are those of the Hindus, Buddhists, and Jains. The seekers of the "extraordinary norm" usually follow an ascetic discipline aimed at helping them to withdrawal from the karmic cycle altogether and win release (*moksha*) from cause and effect, good and evil, birth and rebirth. These two responses to the problem posed by *samsara* underlie the fundamental forms of Indian thought and piety that took shape in the mid- to late-first millennium B.C.E.

Social Responsibility: *Dharma* as Ideal   The "ordinary norm" of life in the various traditions of Indian religiousness can be summarized as life lived according to *dharma*. *Dharma* has many meanings, but its most common is "the right (order of things)," "moral law," "right conduct," or "duty." It includes the cosmic order (comparable to the Chinese Dao) as well as individual moral responsibility and the right conduct of political, commercial, social, and religious affairs. For most people, life according to *dharma* is the life of moral action that will lead to a better birth in the next round of existence.

Life according to *dharma* accepts action in the world of *samsara* as necessary and legitimate. It demands acceptance of the responsibilities associated with one's sex, class and caste group, stage in life, and other circumstances. It allows for legitimate self-interest—the right to do whatever acquires merit for one's eternal *atman* and to avoid whatever brings evil consequences. Rebirth in heaven, in paradise, is the highest goal attainable through the life of *dharma*, but every achievement in the *dharma* realm (the world of *samsara*), even the attainment of Heaven, is ultimately impermanent and is subject to change.

Ascetic Discipline: *Moksha* as Ideal   Persons who have the mental and physical capacity to abandon the world of ordinary life and pursue freedom from *samsara* pursue a way of life in direct contrast to the "ordinary norm." First, any action, good or bad, is counterproductive, for action produces only more action,

samsara   The endless cycle of existence, of birth, and rebirth.

karma   Indian belief that every action has an inevitable effect. Good deeds bring good results; evil deeds have evil consequences.

dharma   Moral law or duty.

India

ca. 800–500 B.C.E.	The Upanishads
540–ca.468 B.C.E.	Mahavira, the Jina/Vardamana
ca. 566–ca. 486 B.C.E.	Siddhartha Gautama, the Buddha

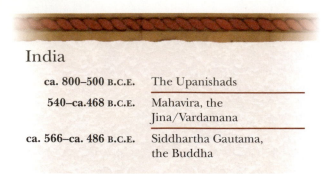

3.5

Mahavira: The "Great Hero" of the Jain Religion

more *karma*, more rebirth. Second, nonaction is achieved only by withdrawing from "normal" existence. The person seeking release from *samsara* has to move beyond the usual responsibilities of family and society. Most often, this involves becoming a "renouncer" (*sannyasi*)—whether a Hindu hermit, yogi, or wanderer, or a Jain or Buddhist monk. Third, true renunciation of the world demands selflessness, the elimination of ego. One must give up the desires and attachments that normally enable the self to function in the world. Fourth, the highest goal is not rebirth in Heaven, but liberation (*moksha*) from all rebirth. *Moksha* is permanent. Its realization means no more becoming, no more suffering in the realm of *samsara*. Eternity, transcendence, and freedom from suffering are its attributes.

Seekers of the Extraordinary Norm The ideas that inspired some people to live by what was called the extraordinary norm were first developed in the Upanishads. They appealed to individuals who wanted to abandon both ritualistic religious practices and the class distinctions and material concerns of their societies. Many of these were of warrior-noble (*Kshatriya*), not Brahmanic, birth. They lived as hermits and pursued spiritual power through yogic meditation and radical self-denial. They hoped to transcend bodily existence and experience the absolute.

In the sixth century B.C.E., teachers of new ideas appeared in the region of modern Bihar. They rejected traditional practices and the authority of the Vedas in favor of ascetic discipline. Two of these teachers founded lasting traditions of piety and faith: those of the Jains and Buddhists.

MAHAVIRA AND THE JAIN TRADITION

The **Jains** are an Indian community that traces its tradition to Vardhamana, known as Mahavira ("the great hero"), who is traditionally believed to have lived from about 540 to 468 B.C.E. Mahavira is hailed by the Jains as the final Jina ("victor" over *samsara*). The Jains (or *Jainas*, "adherents of the *Jina*") do not regard Mahavira as a god, but as a human teacher who found and taught the way to extricate the self, or soul, from the bonds of the material world and its karmic accretions. Mahavira's path to release focused on the elimination of evil thoughts and acts, especially those harmful to others. His radical ascetic practice aimed at destroying karmic defilements and, ultimately, all actions leading to karmic bondage.

In the Jain view, there are only innumerable, ceaseless cycles of generation and degeneration. The universe is alive with an infinite number of souls, all immortal, omniscient, and pure, but trapped in *samsara*. Any thought, word, or deed attracts karmic matter that encumbers the soul. The greatest quantity of such matter comes from evil acts, especially those done out of cruelty to another being. Jains are vegetarians and regard *ahimsa* ("noninjury") to any being as paramount. Compassion is the great virtue for them, as for Buddhists. Today, as in earlier centuries, there is a thriving lay community of perhaps three million Jains, mostly resident in western India.

THE BUDDHA'S "MIDDLE PATH"

The Buddhist tradition remains one of the great universalist forms of faith in the world today. Despite the fact that Buddhism originated in India, few of its people are now Buddhists. It did, however, leave its mark on Hindu and Jain religion and culture.

Jains Indian religious community that teaches compassion for all beings.

Like the two other great universalist traditions, Christianity and Islam, Buddhism traces its origins to a single figure who has loomed larger than life in the community of the faithful for centuries. He is Siddhartha Gautama, known as the Buddha, or "enlightened/awakened one." Like his contemporary, Mahavira, Gautama was born (ca. 566 B.C.E.) in apparently comfortable circumstances.

At the age of 29, Gautama was struck by the reality of human existence: aging, sickness, and death. He abandoned his home and family to seek a solution to the dilemma of the endless cycle of mortal existence. After this "Great Renunciation," he studied with renowned teachers. Then he adopted extreme ascetic disciplines and, still unsatisfied, turned finally to intense yogic meditation under a pipal tree near Varanasi (Banaras) known as Gaya. On one historic night, he moved through different levels of trance, during which he reviewed his past lives, grasped the nature of the cycle of existence that entraps all beings, and discovered how to stop the karmic outflows that fuel suffering. Thus he became the Buddha, the one fully enlightened by omniscient consciousness of reality as it truly is.

Gautama devoted the last of his earthly lives before his final release to teaching others his "middle path" between asceticism and indulgence. This path has been the core of Buddhist faith and practice ever since. It begins with acceptance of the "four noble truths": (1) all life is *dukkha*, or suffering; (2) the source of suffering is desiring; (3) the cessation of desiring is the way to end suffering; and (4) the path to this end is eightfold: right view, thought, speech, action, livelihood, effort, mindfulness, and concentration. The key idea of the Buddha's teaching, or *dharma*, is that everything in the world of existence is causally linked. The essential fact of existence is *dukkha*, suffering, for no pleasure—no matter how great—is permanent (the Buddhist endorsement of the fundamental Indian theme of *samsara*).

Dukkha comes from desire, from craving, from attachment to self, and Buddhism recommends the moral "eightfold path" and the cardinal virtue of compassion for all beings as the way to eliminate the selfish desiring that is the root of *samsara* and its unavoidable suffering. The Buddha himself attained this goal. When he died (ca. 486 B.C.E.) after a life of teaching others how to master desiring, he passed from the round of existence forever. In Buddhist terminology, he attained nirvana, the extinguishing of karmic bondage (see History's Voices: The "Turning of the Wheel of *Dharma*": Basic Teachings of the Buddha). The Buddhist movement, like the Jain, included not only those who were willing to renounce marriage and normal occupations to become part of the Buddha's communities of monks or nuns, but also laypersons who strove to live by the Buddha's high moral standards and support those who sought final release by becoming mendicants. Buddhist tradition enbraced seekers of both the extraordinary and the ordinary norms, and this dual community has remained characteristic of all forms of Buddhism.

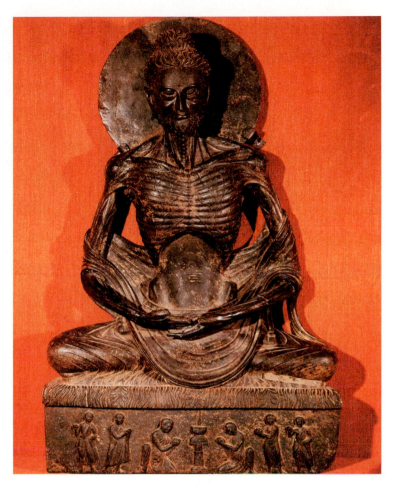

Fasting Buddha. Before Gautama arrived at the "Middle Path," he practiced severe austerities for six years. This fourth- to second-century B.C.E. statue of a fasting Buddha from Gandhara (in present-day Pakistan) reflects Greek influence on early Buddhist sculpture.

Borromeo, EPA/Art Resource, N.Y.

QUICK REVIEW

Siddhartha Gautama

- Great Renunciation: at 29 left home to seek answers to eternal questions
- Unsatisfied with study with renowned teachers
- Achieved status as the Buddha through yogic meditation

HISTORY'S VOICES

THE "TURNING OF THE WHEEL OF THE DHARMA": BASIC TEACHINGS OF THE BUDDHA

Following are selections from the sermon said to have been the first preached by the Buddha. It was directed at five former companions with whom he had practiced extreme austerities. When he abandoned asceticism to meditate under the Bodh tree, they had left him, but this sermon is said to have persuaded them to become his first followers. Because it set in motion the Buddha's teaching, or Dharma, it is described as "setting in motion the wheel of Dharma." The text is from the Dhammacakkappavattanasutta.

WHAT EXTREMES does the Middle Path try to avoid? What emotion drives the chain of suffering? How does the "knowledge" that brings salvation compare to the knowledge sought in the Hindu tradition?

Thus have I heard. The Blessed One was once living in the Deer Park at Isipatana (the Resort of Seers) near Baranasi (Benares). There he addressed the group of five bhikkhus.

"Bhikkhus, these two extremes ought not to be practiced by one who has gone forth from the household life. What are the two? There is devotion to the indulgence of sense-pleasures, which is low, common, the way of ordinary people, unworthy and unprofitable; and there is devotion to self-mortification, which is painful, unworthy and unprofitable.

"Avoiding both these extremes, the Tathagata has realized the Middle Path: it gives vision, it gives knowledge, and it leads to calm, to insight, to enlightenment, to Nibbana. And what is that Middle Path? It is simply the Noble Eightfold Path, namely, right view, right thought, right speech, right action, right livelihood, right effort, right mindfulness, right concentration. This is the Middle Path realized by the Tathagata, which gives vision, which gives knowledge,

and which leads to calm, to insight, to enlightenment, to Nibbana. . . .

"The Noble Truth of suffering (Dukkha) is this: Birth is suffering; aging is suffering; sickness is suffering; death is suffering; sorrow and lamentation, pain, grief and despair are suffering; association with the unpleasant is suffering; dissociation from the pleasant is suffering; not to get what one wants is suffering—in brief, the five aggregates of attachment are suffering.

"The Noble Truth of the origin of suffering is this: It is this thirst (craving) which produces re-existence and re-becoming, bound up with passionate greed. It finds fresh delight now here and now there, namely, thirst for nonexistence (self-annihilation).

"The Noble Truth of the Cessation of suffering is this: It is the complete cessation of that very thirst, giving it up, renouncing it, emancipating oneself from it, detaching oneself from it.

"The Noble Truth of the Path leading to the Cessation of suffering is this: It is simply the Noble Eightfold Path. . . .

"But when my vision of true knowledge was fully clear regarding the Four Noble Truths, then I claimed to have realized the perfect Enlightenment that is supreme in the world with its gods, in this world with its recluses and brahmanas, with its princes and men. And a vision of true knowledge arose in me thus: My heart's deliverance is unassailable. This is the last birth. Now there is no more re-becoming (rebirth)."

This the Blessed One said. The group of five bhikkhus was glad, and they rejoiced at his words.

—Samyutta-nikaya, LVI, II

Source: What the Buddha Taught by Walpola Rahula. Copyright © 1974 by W. Rahula, pp. 92–94. Used by permission of Grove Atlantic Inc.

THE RELIGION OF THE ISRAELITES

*T*he ancient Near East was a **polytheistic** world. Everywhere people worshiped local or regional gods and goddesses who were represented largely as capricious, amoral beings, no more affected by the actions of humans than were the natural forces that some of them represented. Out of this polytheistic world came the great tradition of ethical monotheistic faith represented historically in the Jewish, Christian, and Islamic communities. This tradition traces its origin to the small nation of the Israelites, or Hebrews.

Monotheism, faith in a single, all-powerful God as the sole creator, sustainer, and ruler of the universe, may be older than the Hebrews, but its first clear historical manifestation was with them. It was among the Hebrew tribes that emphasis on the moral demands and responsibilities that the one God placed on individual and community was first definitively linked to human history itself, and that history to a divine plan.

FROM HEBREW NOMADS TO THE ISRAELITE NATION

The history of the Hebrews, later known as Israelites, is pieced together from various sources. The Hebrews are mentioned only rarely in the records of their ancient Middle Eastern neighbors, so we must rely on their own accounts as compiled in the Hebrew Bible (the "Old Testament" in Christian terminology). Scholars once tended to dismiss the Bible as a reliable source of history, but the trend today is to use it cautiously and critically.

Tradition maintains that Abraham, the ancestor of the Hebrews, came from Ur in southern Mesopotamia and wandered west with his clan to the land later known as Palestine. Precise dating of the arrival of the Hebrews in Palestine is impossible, but it was likely between 1900 and 1600 B.C.E.

It was Moses, however, early in the 13th century B.C.E., who led the Hebrews clearly onto the stage of history. Some of Abraham's people had settled in the Palestinian region, but others wandered into Egypt. As the biblical narrative tells it, there they had become a settled but subjected, even enslaved, people. Under Moses, part of the Egyptian Israelites fled Egypt to find a new homeland in Canaan, the province of Palestine that is described in the Bible as the homeland God promised them. This is the key event in the sacred history of the Hebrews or Israelites: the forging of the covenant, or mutual pact, between God *(Yahweh)* and His people. In secular terms, the Exodus marked the emergence of the Israelites as a nation, a people with a sense of community and a common faith.

By about 1200 B.C.E., the Israelites had displaced the Canaanite inhabitants of ancient Palestine. About two centuries later, the now-settled people reached the peak of their power under their kings David (r. ca. 1000–961 B.C.E.) and Solomon (r. ca. 961–922 B.C.E.). But their nation split into two parts in the ninth century B.C.E.: Israel in the north and Judah, with its capital at Jerusalem, in the south (see Map 2–1).

The rise of great empires in the Middle East spelled disaster for the Israelites. The northern kingdom fell to the Assyrians in 722 B.C.E., and its people were scattered.

WHAT WAS distinctive about the Hebrew concept of God and religion?

polytheism The worship of many gods.

monotheism The worship of one universal God.

The Israelites

ca. 1000–961 B.C.E.	Reign of King David
ca. 961–922 B.C.E.	Reign of King Solomon
722 B.C.E.	Assyrian conquest of Israel (northern kingdom)
586 B.C.E.	Destruction of Jerusalem; fall of Judah (southern kingdom); Babylonian captivity
539 B.C.E.	Restoration of temple; return of exiles

MAP EXPLORATION

Interactive map: To explore this map further, go to
http://www.prenhall.com/craig/map2.1

MAP 2–1

Ancient Palestine.   The Hebrews established a unified kingdom under Kings David and Solomon in the 10th century B.C.E. After Solomon, the kingdom was divided into Israel in the north and Judah, with its capital, Jerusalem, in the south. North of Israel were the great commercial cities of Phoenicia.

WHICH NEAR Eastern empire was responsible for the destruction of the Hebrew kingdoms?

1.9
Hebrew Scriptures

Only the residents of Judah remained, the Jews. In 586 B.C.E., Judah was conquered by the Neo-Babylonian king Nebuchadnezzar II (d. 562 B.C.E.). He destroyed the great temple built by Solomon and sent the Jewish nation into exile in Babylon. There, in the "Babylonian captivity" of the Exile, without a temple, the Jews clung to their traditions and faith. After the Persians defeated the Babylonians in 539 B.C.E., the Jews were allowed to return to Jerusalem, and by about 516 B.C.E., a second temple had been erected.

The new Judaic state continued for centuries to be dominated by other nations, but its people maintained their religious and political identity. However, Judah was again destroyed and its people dispersed after the Romans sacked Jerusalem in 70 C.E. and again in 132 C.E. By then, however, the Jews had developed a religious worldview that could thrive without the support of a Judaic state.

THE MONOTHEISTIC REVOLUTION

This small nation developed a tradition of faith that amounted to a revolution in ways of thinking about the human condition, the meaning of life and history, and the nature of the Divine. The revolutionary character of the faith lay in its uniquely moralistic understanding of human life and history and the uncompromising monotheism on which it was based.

At the root of this monotheistic tradition stands Abraham, whom Jews, Christians, and Muslims honor as the symbolic founder of their faith. Abraham probably conceived of his Lord as one deity among many other divinities whom he might have worshiped. But the biblical account recognizes him as the "Father of the Faithful," for Abraham promised exclusive loyalty to God. Abraham was the first Hebrew patriarch to make a covenant with God. He pledged to serve only God, and God promised in exchange that Abraham's descendants would become His special people.

When Moses renewed the covenant at Mount Sinai, he and his followers may not yet have conceived of a purely monotheistic faith. The covenant united the Israelites as a people with a special relationship to God, and at Sinai they received both God's holy law (the Torah) and God's promise of protection so as long as they kept the law. This pivotal moment launched the monotheistic revolution that came to fruition several hundred years later. Exclusive loyalty to one God became belief in only one God.

The monotheistic revolution might be said to have begun with Abraham or Moses. Historically, we can trace it to the period when the Israelite kingdom divided (922 B.C.E.). At this time, *prophets*—inspired messengers of God—appeared to call their people back from false gods to faith in the one true God and to obedience to God's commandments. The prophets' concerns with purifying Jewish faith and with morality, focused on two ideas that are central to Judaic monotheism.

The first is the significance of history in the divine plan. The prophets saw in Israel's troubles God's punishment for the people's failure to fulfill their covenant duties. But they also saw Israel as the "suffering servant" of God, as the instrument God would use to purify other nations and bring them to knowledge of God. The prophets transcended the nationalistic focus of earlier Israelite religion and proclaimed a universalist monotheism: Yahweh was God of all.

The second idea fundamental to monotheism centered on the nature of Yahweh. God was a righteous God who expected righteousness from human beings. He was a moral God who demanded goodness, not blood offerings or empty prayers.

The crux of the breakthrough to ethical monotheism lay in linking the Lord of the Universe to history and morality. The Almighty Creator was seen as concerned with the actions and fates of His human creatures (as exemplified by Israel). History thus took on transcendent meaning. God had created humankind for a good purpose; people were called to be just and good like their Creator, for they were involved in the fulfillment of His divine purpose. The prophets promised that this fulfillment would come for the Israelites in their restoration as a people purifed of sins.

Although the Exile came to an end, however, the prophesied days of peace and blessedness under God's rule still did not come. This sparked the idea that history would culminate in a future Messianic age. The faith and morality that the Jews had long seen as keys to human destiny became in later Jewish teaching a prediction of a day of judgment that would cap the golden age of the **Messiah**. These ideas played a key role in the later formation of Christian and Muslim expectations for a Messianic deliverer, a resurrection of the body, and a life after death.

The other key element in the monotheistic revolution of the Jews was the role accorded to the law embodied in the five books of Torah (Genesis, Exodus, Leviticus, Numbers, and Deuteronomy). The law enabled Jews who lived in exile to survive the loss of their Temple and its priestly cult. Observation of the Torah,

Messiah   The redeemer whose coming, Jews believed, would establish the kingdom of God on earth. Christians considered Jesus to be the Messiah (Christ means Messiah in Greek).

Scroll from the Dead Sea.   This photograph shows part of one of the ancient scrolls found in 1947 in a remote cave at Khirbat near the Dead Sea in Jordan. The passage from the Hebrew Bible contains part of the Ten Commandments in the Book of Deuteronomy. The scrolls were written sometime between 200 B.C.E. and 68 C.E. They contain documents that suggest they belonged to a monastic sect of Jews called Essenes whose beliefs bear some similarity to those of John the Baptist and Jesus.

ASAP/David Harris.

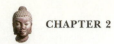

OVERVIEW   FOUR GREAT SYSTEMS OF THOUGHT AND RELIGION

Between 800 B.C.E. and 300 B.C.E., four philosophical or religious revolutions occurred that shaped the subsequent history of the world. These revolutions, which were attempts to answer universal questions about the human condition, established cultural patterns that have endured to the present day.

Chinese Philosophy	Three principal schools: Confucianism, Daoism, Legalism. Each school was concerned with social and political issues, with how individuals interact with each other and the state, and with the question of how to lead an ethical life that was in harmony with nature and the cosmos.
Indian Religion	Hinduism, Jains, Buddhism. Indian religion saw existence as an endless cycle of birth and rebirth (*samsara*). *Karma*, the concept that every action has good or evil effects, was the key to resolving the dilemma of *samsara*. Good actions could result in a person's being reborn in a higher state, even as a god. Complete withdrawal from the world could lead to escape from *samsara* into nonexistence.
Hebrew Monotheism	The Hebrews, or Israelites, were the first people in history to base their identity as a nation faithful to a single, all-powerful God who made ethical demands and placed responsibilities on them as individuals and as a community. History, itself, was the unfolding of a divine plan for human beings. Through the Christian and Muslim traditions, Hebrew monotheism would profoundly influence much of the world.
Greek Philosophy	Beginning in the sixth century B.C.E., Greek thinkers were the first to try to explain the natural world without reference to supernatural powers. Later Greek thinkers used rational analysis to investigate ethical, political, and social problems: how human beings should govern themselves, live in society, and act toward each other. The Greek tradition of rational inquiry lies at the root of all subsequent Western science and philosophy.

the earthly focus of their faith, enabled them to preserve their special identity as God's people.

In the second century B.C.E., the role of Torah was ensured by its compilation, together with the books of the prophets and other writings, as the Holy Scriptures or Bible (from Greek *bibloi*, "books"). A holy, authoritative, divinely revealed scripture put the seal on the monotheistic revolution that had made the sovereignty and righteousness of God the foci of faith.

GREEK PHILOSOPHY

WHY, BEGINNING in the sixth century B.C.E., did Greek thinkers produce an intellectual revolution?

Many, if not most, Greeks in the ancient world must have lived with assumptions about life and the universe similar to those held by people in other ancient cultures. But some Greeks innovated ideas that set a part of humankind on a new path. As early as the sixth century B.C.E., Greeks began to raise questions about the natural world and proposed explanation for its processes that made no reference to supernatural powers. A historian has explained the originality of Thales of Miletus (624–545 B.C.E.), the first Greek philosopher, in this way:

> In one of the Babylonian legends it says: "All the lands were sea. Marduk bound a rush mat upon the face of the waters, he made dirt and piled it beside the rush mat." What Thales did was to leave Marduk out. He, too,

said that everything was once water. But he thought that earth and everything else had been formed out of water by a natural process, like the silting up of the Delta of the Nile. It is an admirable beginning, the whole point of which is that it gathers together into a coherent picture a number of observed facts without letting Marduk in.[3]

By looking for an explanation for the world's origin in nature, Thales may have initiated the rational investigation of the universe and both Western philosophy and Western science. The same rational approach was applied to questions about the gods. In the same century as Thales, Xenophanes of Colophon expressed the opinion that humans think of gods as resembling themselves. Thus, Africans believed in flat-nosed, black-faced gods, and Thracians in gods with blue eyes and red hair.[4] In the fifth century B.C.E., Protagoras of Abdera (ca. 490–ca. 420 B.C.E.) verged on agnosticism, saying: "About the gods I can have no knowledge either that they are or that they are not or what is their nature."[5]

This rationalistic, skeptical attitude also affected thinking about practical matters. Hippocrates of Cos (ca. 400 B.C.E.) attempted to understand and cure disease without recourse to supernatural forces, and by the fifth century B.C.E., the historian Thucydides (ca. 460–ca. 400 B.C.E.) was analyzing and explaining events completely in terms of human nature and chance, leaving no place for the gods. The relative unimportance of divine or supernatural forces also characterized Greek views of law and justice. Greeks believed that laws were made by humans and derived their authority from the fact that they represented the consent of the citizens they governed.

Ideas of this kind contrasted dramatically with earlier approaches to understanding the world and inaugurated discussions of issues that remain major concerns for modern thinkers: What is the nature of the universe? How can it be controlled? Are there divine powers? If there are, what is humanity's relationship to them? Are law and justice human, divine, or both? How should human societies balance freedom and obedience to authority?

Thales of Miletus, the First Greek Philosopher. His explanation for the origin of the world was based on reason and the observation of nature without any need for the supernatural.

Corbis-Bettmann.

REASON AND THE SCIENTIFIC SPIRIT

The rational spirit characteristic of Greek culture blossomed in the sixth century B.C.E. into the methods for seeking an understanding of the physical world and humanity's place in it that we call *philosophy*. The first steps along this path were taken in Ionia on the coast of Asia Minor, which was in touch with the learning of the East.

Thales (mentioned above) believed that the Earth floated on water and that water was the primary substance from which all things originated. Thales noted that water exists in all the states found in nature: liquid, solid, and gas. He believed that it "created" land by alluvial deposit, and he knew that it was necessary for all life. It seemed to him, therefore, that water could account for the phenomena of nature without the need to postulate any supernatural activity.

[3]Benjamin Farrington, *Greek Science* (London: Penguin Books, 1953) p. 37.
[4]H. Frankfort et al., *Before Philosophy* (1949), pp. 14–16.
[5]Hermann Diels, *Fragmente der Vorsokratiker*, 5th ed., ed. by Walther Kranz (Berlin: Weidmann, 1934–1938), Frg. 4.

Later Greek philosophers accepted his assumption that the world was knowable, rational, and simple.

Another native of Miletus, Anaximander (ca. 611–546 B.C.E.), suggested that the primal element was the "unlimited," something combining all attributes. The world emerged from this basic element as the result of an interaction of opposite forces—wet and dry, hot and cold. Anaximander pictured the universe as eternally fluctuating, with all things emerging from the "unlimited," then decaying and returning to it. He also theorized that human beings originated in water and had evolved to their present state through several stages, including that of fish.

Heraclitus of Ephesus, who lived near the end of the sixth century B.C.E., carried the dialogue further. His fundamental hypothesis was: "All is motion." This raised important questions, for if all is constantly in motion, nothing ever really exists. Heraclitus argued, however, that the world had order, for it was governed by a guiding principle, the *logos* ("word," "language," "speech," and "reason"). Phenomena changed, but the *logos* did not. Heraclitus's point was that the physical world obeyed rational laws that could be comprehended by rational minds. The study of nature, therefore, necessitated speculation about language, the essence of human thought and knowledge itself.

Parmenides of Elea and his pupil Zeno disagreed with Heraclitus. They argued that change was an illusion. Reality had to be unchanging, for if something new (i.e., a change) appeared, it would have to originate from nothing—and it was rationally impossible for nothing to create something. Empedocles of Acragas (flourished ca. 450 B.C.E.) postulated the existence of four basic elements (fire, water, earth, and air) as a compromise between Heraclitus and Parmenides. He argued that reality was permanent but not unchanging. The elements did not change, but they were constantly recombined by two primary forces, Love and Strife, or, as we might say, attraction and repulsion.

Leucippus of Miletus (flourished fifth century B.C.E.) and Democritus of Abdera (ca. 460–370 B.C.E.) proposed something similar. They believed that the world consisted of tiny, solid particles (atoms, "indivisibles") that could not be divided or modified. Atoms moved about in the void, and their size and combinations produced the things that our senses perceive. Anaxagoras of Clazomenae (ca. 500–428 B.C.E.) had previously postulated the existence of tiny fundamental particles called *seeds* that were arranged in rational ways by a force called *nous* ("mind"). He assumed that mind was distinct from matter, but the **atomists** regarded "mind" as material. They believed that everything was guided by purely physical laws. These debates began the continuing dialogue between materialism and idealism.

A separate category of philosophers did not speculate about the physical universe but applied reasoned analysis to human beliefs and institutions. They were professional teachers in the mid-fifth century B.C.E. called **Sophists**. They traveled about and were paid to teach practical techniques of persuasion, such as rhetoric. The Sophists explored the tension, perhaps contradiction, between nature and custom or law. The more traditional among them argued that law was in accord with nature. This view strengthened traditional beliefs about the ***polis***, the Greek city-state (see Chapter 3). Others argued that laws were based in nature, and were merely agreements among people aimed at preventing them from harming one another. The most extreme Sophists even insisted that law was contrary to nature, and that laws were a strategy the strong used to dominate the weak.

Atomists School of ancient Greek philosophy founded in the fifth century B.C.E. by Leucippus of Miletus and Democritus of Abdera. It held that the world consists of innumerable, tiny, solid, indivisible, and unchangeable particles called atoms.

Sophists Professional teachers who emerged in Greece in the mid-fifth century B.C.E. who were paid to teach techniques of rhetoric, dialectic, and argumentation.

polis The basic Greek political unit. Usually, but incompletely, translated as "city-state," the Greeks thought of the polis as a community of citizens theoretically descended from a common ancestor.

POLITICAL AND MORAL PHILOSOPHY

Like thinkers in other parts of the world in the mid-first millennium B.C.E., some Greeks were vitally concerned with the formulation of moral principles for the governance of the state and the regulation of individual lives, as well as with abstract problems of the nature of existence and transcendence. Nowhere is the Greek concern with ethical, political, and religious issues clearer than in the philosophical tradition that began with Socrates in the latter half of the fifth century B.C.E. That tradition continued with Socrates' pupil Plato and with Plato's pupil Aristotle. Aristotle also made major contributions to the scientific understanding of the physical world and to later Western and Islamic metaphysics.

The starting point for all three was the social and political reality of the Greek city-state, the polis. The greatest crisis for the polis was the Great Peloponnesian War (435–404 B.C.E.; see Chapter 3). The life and teachings of Socrates (469–399 B.C.E.) should be viewed in this political context. Our knowledge of him comes chiefly from his disciples Plato and Xenophon (ca. 435–354 B.C.E.) and from later tradition.

Socrates was committed to the search for truth and for the understanding of human affairs that he believed reason could uncover. His strategy was to question and cross-examine his fellow Greeks. The result of these encounters was always the same. He demonstrated that those whom he questioned might have some technical information and skill, but they seldom demonstrated any knowledge of the fundamental principles of human behavior. Athenians understandably were disturbed by Socrates' unrelenting intellectual challenges, and they concluded that he was undermining the beliefs and values of the polis. Socrates' unconcealed contempt for democracy, a political system that he said allowed ignorant amateurs to make important political decisions, also angered them. His insistence on pursuing his individual philosophical agenda even against the wishes of his fellow citizens further prejudiced them against him.

But Socrates, unlike the Sophists, did not accept pay for his teaching. It was not wealth or pleasure or power that motivated him, but he insisted that he sought "the greatest improvement of the soul." Also, despite his criticism of democracy, he did not question the legitimacy of the polis' claim on its citizens. He proved that in 399 B.C.E., after he was condemned to death by an Athenian jury. Given a chance to escape, he refused because of his respect for the laws that had condemned him.

Socrates' career set the stage for later approaches to dealing with the problems raised by the polis as a system of government and a way of life. Although he refused to play an active role in politics, he did not reject the idea of the polis. He fought as a soldier in its defense, obeyed its laws, and tried to find rational justifications for its fundamental values.

The Cynics Socrates' concern with personal morality and the soul, disdain for worldly pleasure and wealth, and withdrawal from political life became, in exaggerated form, the basis for the teachings of the Cynics. Antisthenes (ca. 455–360 B.C.E.), one of Socrates' followers, was said to be their founder, but their most famous representative was Diogenes of Sinope (ca. 400–325 B.C.E.). To show his contempt for convention, he performed shameful acts in public, dressed in rags, and lived in a tub. He taught that happiness lay in satisfying natural needs in the simplest, most direct way. The Cynics also ridiculed all religious observances. Plato described Diogenes as Socrates gone mad.

Major Greek Philosophers

469–399 B.C.E.	Socrates
429–347 B.C.E.	Plato
384–322 B.C.E.	Aristotle

Plato Plato (429–347 B.C.E.) was the most important of Socrates' associates. He was the first systematic philosopher and, therefore, the first thinker to situate political ideas in a broader philosophical context. He was also a writer of genius, who composed 26 philosophical discussions in the form of dramatic dialogues. In 386 B.C.E., Plato founded the Academy, a center of philosophical investigation and a school for training statesmen and citizens. It survived into the sixth century C.E.

Like Socrates, Plato firmly believed in the polis and its values of order, harmony, and justice. One of its goals was to produce good people. He accepted Socrates' argument that virtue was a form of knowledge, and he believed that knowledge was *episteme*, science, a body of true and unchanging wisdom obtained by only a few philosophers whose training, character, and intellect allowed them to comprehend truth. They were the only people qualified to rule. Although they would prefer lives devoted to contemplation, they would accept the responsibility entailed by their gifts and serve society as philosopher-kings. The training of these people required specialization and subordination of individual to community interests. Plato claimed that true justice lay in each person doing only that one thing to which his nature was best suited.

The polis in Plato's day suffered from terrible internal stress, class struggle, and factional divisions. Plato, however, believed that harmony could be restored by moral and political reforms that would eliminate the causes of strife. Among these causes were private property and the family—things that individuals were tempted to put before their devotion to the common good represented by the polis.

Plato asked the traditional questions: What is a good man, and how is he made? Given that doing the good necessitated knowing the good, a theory of knowledge and an investigation into the nature of knowledge was where Plato believed the discussion had to begin. The search for an understanding of what made ideas true led Plato into metaphysics. Once the nature of the good was established, however, the question remained: How could the state bring its citizens to knowledge of the good? This issue forced Plato to develop a theory of education. Purely logical and metaphysical questions were pursued as part of the quest for solutions to political challenges. Plato's need to polster the beleaguered polis thus contributed to the birth of systematic philosophy.

Aristotle Aristotle (384–322 B.C.E.) was a pupil of Plato whose different experience and cast of mind led him in new directions. In 336, he founded his own school at Athens, the Lyceum. The Lyceum's mission differed from that of the Academy. Its members concentrated on gathering, ordering, and analyzing the data that was the basis for all human knowledge. Aristotle and his students prepared collections of information that advanced scientific studies of logic, physics, astronomy, biology, ethics, rhetoric, literary criticism, and politics.

In each field, Aristotle's method was the same. He began with observation of empirical evidence, which in some cases was physical and in others was common opinion. He then rationally examined this body of information to uncover inconsistencies or other difficulties. To deal with these, he developed metaphysical models. His approach to metaphysics, like Plato's, was teleological; that is, he believed in goals apart from and greater than the wills of individual human beings. Plato characterized those goals as ideas or forms—transcendental concepts beyond human experience. But for Aristotle, they could be inferred by observing the behavior of things in our world.

The most striking characteristics of Aristotle's thought are moderation and common sense. His epistemology (i.e., theory of knowledge) acknowledges the importance of both reason and experience. His metaphysics honors both mind and body. His ethical system envisions a good life that is contemplative and humane—acknowledging as legitimate concerns moderate wealth, comfort, and pleasure.

4.8b
Aristotle, Virtue and Redemption: The Doctrine of the Mean

In politics Aristotle, like Plato, opposed the Sophists' assertion that the polis was contrary to human nature and the result of mere convention. The teleology that he saw in all nature also gave him an explanation for politics. Matter, he claimed, existed to achieve an end, and it developed until it fully realized its end, its form or potential. The primitive instincts of the individual could be seen as the matter out of which the human's potential as a political being could be realized. As the culmination of a series of institutions (marriage, household, village, and finally, polis) that brought human beings together, it served the natural end of enabling them to continue their species. For Aristotle, the purpose of the polis was neither economic nor military, but moral: "The end of the state is the good life," the life lived "for the sake of noble actions," a life of virtue and morality. [6]

Characteristically, Aristotle was less interested in the best state—a utopia ruled by idealized philosopher kings—than in the best state practically possible, one that enabled ordinary people to enjoy both justice and stability. He characterized the constitution for such a state as a *politeia*, not the best system, but the next best—the one most possible for most states. Its quality was moderation. It empowered neither the extremes of the rich or the poor, but the middle class. For the health of the state, he claimed that the middle class should be the largest class. It possessed essential virtues. Because its wealth was moderate, the middle class was not tempted to the arrogance of the rich, and it did not excite the malice of the poor. It fostered stability, a condition that was also promoted by what Aristotle called a mixed constitution (a combination of democracy and oligarchy). Aristotle was both a visionary and a policial realist.

The desire to understand nature in a purely rational, scientific way remained strong through the fifth century B.C.E. It culminated in the work of the atomic theorists, Democritus and Leucippus, and in the medical school founded by Hippocrates of Cos. In the mid-fifth century B.C.E., however, men like the Sophists and Socrates turned their attention to humankind and to ethical, political, and religious questions. This latter tradition of inquiry led, by way of Plato, Aristotle (in his metaphysical thought), and the Stoics, to Christianity, and it had a substantial impact on Judaic and Islamic thought. The former tradition of thought, following a line from the natural philosophers, the Sophists, Aristotle (in his scientific work), and the Epicureans, had to wait until the Renaissance in western Europe to exert influence. Since the 18th century, however, it has been the more influential force in Western civilization. The other tradition has, however, never been forgotten, and since the Enlightenment of the 18th century, the Western world has been engaged in a dialogue between the two intellectual communities the Greeks founded. As Western influence has spread throughout the world, that dialogue has assumed new importance, for other societies have not separated the religious and philosophical from the scientific and physical realms as radically as has the modern West.

[6]Aristotle, *Politics*, 1280b, 1281a.

IMAGE KEY

for pages 28–29

a. The dead sea scrolls in Washington D.C.

b. Confucius

c. School of Plato

d. Mathura sculpture head of Buddha

e. Shiva sculpture carved into a granite wall niche

f. Painting of Confucius

g. An early carving showing the *chakra* or wheel of *Dharma*

h. Aristotle

i. Thales of Miletus, the first Greek philosopher

j. Assyrian wall carving depicting the Jews with their cattle and baggage going into exile.

SUMMARY

The Four Great Philosophical and Religious Revolutions Between 800 and 300 B.C.E., four philosophical and religious revolutions arose that shaped the subsequent history of the world. These were Chinese philosophy, Indian religion, Hebrew monotheism, and Greek philosophy.

Chinese Philosophy Traditional Chinese philosophical thought, which took shape with the teachings of Confucius in the sixth century B.C.E., remained dominant in China until the early 20th century. It was concerned with social and political issues and sought to teach human beings how to live harmoniously and ethically under Heaven by prescribing the correct relationships between ruler-subject, father-son, husband-wife, older brother-younger brother, and friend-friend. Confucianism became the official philosophy of China in the second century B.C.E. Other Chinese philosophies were Daoism, a mystical way of thought that offered a refuge from social responsibilities, and Legalism, which taught that a good society requires a strong state that enforces the law and punishes wrongdoers.

Indian Religion Hinduism, the dominant Indian religious tradition, took shape by 400 B.C.E. Indian religion saw existence as an endless alteration between life and death (*samsara*). The escape from this dilemma lay in the concept of *karma*, the idea that good actions (*dharma*) could lead to rebirth as a higher being, even a god, or to escape the cycle entirely and cease to exist entirely (*moksha*).

Another Indian religious tradition, the Jains, sought to liberate the soul from the bonds of the material world by eliminating evil acts. Although there are few Indian Buddhists today, Buddhism traces its origins to the teachings of an Indian, Siddhartha Gautama (b. ca. 566 B.C.E.). Buddhism holds that escape from *samsara* lies in following a moral path of right understanding and actions and in having compassion for all beings.

Hebrew Monotheism Monotheism is the faith in a single, all-powerful God as the sole creator, sustainer, and ruler of the universe. The Hebrews were the first people to emphasize the moral demands that the one God, Yahweh, placed on the individual and community and to see history as the unfolding of a divine plan. The Hebrews, or Jews, were the first people to be defined by shared religious faith and practice. Through the Christian and Muslim traditions, Judaic monotheism was to change the face of much of the world.

Greek Philosophy The Greeks were the first to initiate the unreservedly rational investigation of the universe. They became the forerunners of Western philosophy and science. In the sixth and fifth centuries B.C.E., Greek thinkers, such as Thales of Miletus and Heraclitus, sought to explain natural phenomena without recourse to divine intervention. In the later fifth century and the fourth century B.C.E., philosophers, such as Socrates, Plato, and Aristotle, applied the same rational, inquisitive approach to the study of moral and political issues in the life of the Greek city-state, or polis.

REVIEW QUESTIONS

1. What are the differences and similarities among Confucianism, Daoism, and Legalism?

2. What fundamental assumptions about the world, the individual, and reality do the Jain, Hindu, and Buddhist traditions share?

3. How did the concept of monotheism develop? Why was is it regarded as a radical innovation in the context of ancient Middle-Eastern civilization?

4. How did the approach to understanding the world taken by the Greeks differ from that of other ancient peoples? What did Socrates contribute to philosophy? How do Aristotle's political and ethical ideas compare with those of Confucius?

KEY TERMS

Atman-Brahman (p. 34)
atomists (p. 44)
Brahmanas (p. 33)
Chun-tzu (p. 31)
dharma (p. 35)
Daoism (p. 32)

Hindu (p. 33)
Jains (p. 36)
karma (p. 35)
Legalism (p. 33)
Messiah (p. 41)

monotheism (p. 39)
polis (p. 44)
polytheism (p. 39)
samsara (p. 35)
Sophists (p. 44)

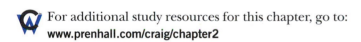 For additional study resources for this chapter, go to:
www.prenhall.com/craig/chapter2

JUDAISM

Monotheism, the belief in a unique God who is the creator of the universe and its all-powerful ruler, first became a central and lasting element in religion among the Hebrews, later called Israelites and also Jews. Their religion, more than the many forms of polytheistic worship that characterized the ancient world, demanded moral rectitude and placed ethical responsibilities both on individuals and on the community as a whole. Their God had a divine plan for human history, which was linked to the behavior of his chosen people. This vision of the exclusive worship of the true God, obedience to the laws governing the community that derive from him, and a strong ethical responsibility was connected to humanity's historical experience in this world. Ultimately it gave rise to three great religions: Judaism, Christianity, and Islam.

At the beginning of this tradition stands Abraham, whom all three religions recognize as their founder. According to the Torah (the first five books of the Hebrew Bible or the Christian Old Testament), Abraham entered into a covenant with God in which he promised to worship only this God, who in turn promised to make Abraham's descendants his own chosen people—chosen to worship him, to obey his laws, and to undertake a special set of moral responsibilities. God renewed the covenant with Moses at Mount Sinai when he freed the Israelites from Egyptian bondage. He promised them the land of Canaan (later called Palestine and part of which is now the state of Israel) and gave them the law (the Torah), including the Ten Commandments, by which they were to guide their lives. As long as they lived by his law, God would give them his guidance and protection.

In time the Israelites formed themselves into a kingdom which remained unified from about 1000 to 922 B.C.E. In the period after its division, prophets emerged. Thought to be inspired by God, the prophets chastised the Israelites for their lapses into idolatry and immorality. Even as the kingdom was disintegrating and the Israelites falling under the control of alien empires, the prophets preached social reform and a return to God's laws. They saw Israel's misfortune as punishment for failing to keep the covenant and predicted disaster if the Israelites did not change their ways. When disasters came—the Jewish kingdoms captured, the people enslaved and exiled—the prophets interpreted Israel's status as a chosen people to mean that their sufferings would make them "a light unto the nations," leading other nations to the true worship of one God

The prophets also preached that God was righteous and demanded righteousness from his people. But he was also a God of justice. Although he might need to punish his people for their sins, he would one day reward them with divine favor. Traditional Jewish belief expects that the Messiah, or Anointed One, will someday come and establish God's kingdom on earth. He will introduce an age of universal brotherhood in which all nations will acknowledge the one true God.

The Jews are "people of the Book," and foremost among their sacred texts is the Hebrew Bible, consisting of the Five Books of Moses (the Torah), the books of the prophets, and other writings. The Torah is the source of Jewish law. Over the centuries new experiences required new interpretation of the law, which was accomplished by the oral law, no less sacred than the written law. Compilations of interpretation and commentary by rabbis (wise and learned teachers) were brought together to form the Talmud.

▲ **Jonah Eaten by the Whale, from a Hebrew Bible, 1299.** Like the Christian illuminated manuscripts they closely resembled, Jewish medieval manuscripts were filled with images of scenes from the Torah and Jewish history. Hebrew writing also developed into an elaborately beautiful calligraphy. Many of these Jewish medieval illuminated manuscripts were, like their Christian counterparts, commissioned by wealthy and influential leaders of Jewish communities in Europe.
Instituto da Biblioteca Nacional, Lisbon, Portugal/Bridgeman Art Library.

The destruction of their temple in Jerusalem by the Romans in 70 C.E. hastened the scattering of the Jews throughout the empire. Thereafter almost all Jews lived in the Diaspora (dispersion), without a homeland, a political community, or a national or religious center. In the fifth and sixth centuries the decline of the Sassanid Empire in Iran and the collapse of the Western Roman Empire undermined the institutions in which the Jews had found a stable way of life. In the seventh and eighth centuries, the missionary zeal of the Christian church also brought hard times for the Jews in Western Europe and in the Byzantine East. In the West, their condition improved in the ninth century under Charlemagne and his successors.

Under Islam, Jews, like Christians, were tolerated as people of the Book. Jewish settlements flourished throughout the Islamic world. After the Islamic conquest of Spain in 711, the Jews there enjoyed an almost 300-year-long golden age. During this period of extraordinary intellectual and cultural accomplishment, Jews practiced their religion openly and flourished economically.

The beginning of the Crusades in the 11th century brought renewed persecution of the Jews in both the Christian and Islamic worlds. In the wake of the Christian reconquest of Spain, Jews were persecuted, killed, forced to convert, and finally expelled in 1492.

By the Middle Ages, Jews had divided into two distinct branches: those who lived in Christian Europe, called *Ashkenazim,* and those in the Muslim world, particularly Spain, called *Sephardim.* The Sephardim, with greater opportunities, developed a more secular lifestyle. Their language, Ladino, combined Hebrew and Spanish elements. The Ashkenazim, scattered in tiny communities, were forced to turn inward. Centered in German lands, they developed Yiddish, a combination of Hebrew and German. In time, Yiddish became the language of most Jews in northern Europe, although the Torah was always read and studied in Hebrew.

Two of the dominant influences on modern Judaism have been Zionism—the effort to found a Jewish nation—and the death of some 6 million Jews in the Holocaust of World War II. Bolstered by the determination of Jews never again to find themselves victimized by the forces of anti-Semitism, the Zionist movement culminated in the founding of the state of Israel in 1948.

Adherents of Judaism are divided into several groups—Reform, Reconstruction, Conservative, and Orthodox—each holding significantly different views about the place of tradition and traditional law in the modern world. All, however, would give assent to the saying of Hillel, the great Talmudic teacher of the first century B.C.E.: "What is distasteful to you do not to your fellow man. This is the Law, all the rest is commentary. Now go and study."

- In what ways did Judaism differ from the polytheistic religions?
- What elements of the religion helped it persist through the ages?

Visualizing The Past

Humans and Nature in Antiquity

WHY DID the natural world figure so prominently in the culture and religions of ancient peoples? What does this tell us about the relationship between humans and the natural world in antiquity?

Animism—the idea that everything in the natural world, from inanimate objects to humans, is in some way alive and sentient, part of single connected cosmos—describes the belief systems of many ancient peoples. Animals, in particular, were integral to ancient religions. They were admired for their strength, wisdom and other virtues, and were either worshipped as gods or played central roles in the religious ceremonies of ancient peoples across the world.

Shaman. A reproduction of a ▶ 20,000-year-old cave painting, from the Grotto of Les Trois Freres in the French Pyrenees, of a barefooted **shaman**, or sorcerer, dressed in a deerskin costume. Shamans often dressed fantastically, clothing themselves in deer or bear skins, antlers or claws. The shaman depicted here may be performing a dance as part of a healing ritual. Shamans still form an important part of many non-sedentary societies across the world today.

Sheila Terry/Photo Researchers, Inc.

◀ **Images of Animals.** These 4,250-year old seals from the ancient Harappan civilization of the Indus valley in present-day Pakistan show various animals, including a rhinoceros, an elephant, and a bull. Images of bulls are widespread in the ancient world and the depiction of one here suggests that the sacred status of cows and bulls in Hinduism has its roots in the first civilization of the Indus valley.

Seals from Mohenjo Doro (Indus Valley culture). National Museum of Pakistan, Karachi, Pakistan. Copyright Scala/Art Resource, N.Y.

Pharoahs and Gods. The pharoah Ramses I kneels between the jackal-headed god of the underworld Anubis and the falcon-headed god Horus, from a painted limestone relief in the Ramses's tomb, circa 1292–1290 B.C.E., from the Valley of the Kings in Egypt. Anubis and Horus were one of many Egyptian gods who were imagined as part human, part animal. The Art Archive/Dagli Orti

Lamassus. This human-headed, winged ▶ lion is from the palace of the Assryian ruler Ashurnasirpal II (r.883–859 B.C.E.) at Nimrud, present-day Iraq. It demonstrates the admiration of the warlike Assyrians for powerful animals, which are combined into a fanciful creature, a *lamassus*—divine guardian protectors of palaces and throne rooms.

Human-headed winged bull and winged lion (lamassu). Alabaster (ypsum); Gateway support from the Palace of Ashurnasirpal II (ruled 883–859 B.C.E.). Limestone. H: 10'3½". L: 9'1". W: 2"½". The Metropolitan Museum of Art, Gift of John D. Rockefeller, Jr., 1932. (32.143.2) Photography © 1981 The Metropolitian Museum of Art.

PART TWO   EMPIRES AND CULTURES OF THE ANCIENT WORLD

EUROPE

ca. 2500–1100	Minoan civilization on Crete
ca. 1600–1100	Mycenaean civilization on Greek mainland

ca. 1100–800	Greek "dark ages"
800	Etruscan civilization begins in Italy
ca. 750–550	Rise of the polis
594	Solon's legislation at Athens
509	Foundation of the Roman Republic
508	Democracy established in Athens

Sixth-century B.C.E. Attic jar ▶

NEAR EAST / INDIA

ca. 3500–3000	Emergence of Sumerian city-states
ca. 3000	Emergence of civilization along the Nile River
ca. 2300	Emergence of Harappan civilization in Indus valley
2276–2221	Sargon of Akkad creates the first Mesopotamian Empire
ca. 2000	*Epic of Gilgamesh*
1750	Hammurabi's code

ca. 1500	Aryan peoples migrate into northwestern India
960–933	Rule of Hebrew king Solomon
ca. 628–551	Traditional dates of Zarathushtra
ca. 537–486	Siddhartha Gautama
559–529	Cyrus the Great creates the Persian Empire

◀ *Ruins of pyramids in Ancient Kingdom of Kush-Sudan*

EAST ASIA

ca. 4000	Neolithic cultures in China
ca. 8000–300	Jōmon culture in Japan
ca. 1766–1050	Shang dynasty in China with city-states and writing

1027–771	Western Chou dynasty, China
771–256	Eastern Chou dynasty in China
ca. 771	Iron Age territorial states in China
551–479	Confucius in China

◀ *Homo habilis skull*

AFRICA

ca. 3000	Practice of agriculture spreads from Nile River Valley to the Sudan
ca. 2000	Ivory and gold trade between Kush (Nubia) and Egypt
ca. 1500	Practice of agriculture spreads from the Sudan to Abyssinia and the savanna region

750	Kushite king Kashta conquers Upper Egypt; founds 25th Egyptian dynasty
ca. 720	Kushite king Piankhy completes conquest of Egypt and reigns as king of Kush and Egypt
ca. 600	Meroitic period of Kushan civilization begins

THE AMERICAS

ca. 4000	Maize already domesticated in Mexico

ca. 1500–800	Olmec civilization in Mesoamerica
ca. 800–200	Chavín (Early) Horizon in Andean South America

◀ *Olmec monument, La Venta*

480–479	Persian invasion of Greece
478	Foundation of Delian League/Athenian Empire
431–404	Peloponnesian Wars
338	Battle of Chaeronia; Macedonian conquest of Greece
336–323	Career of Alexander the Great

◄ *The Charioteer of Delphi,*
ca. 470 B.C.E.

264	Rome rules all of Italy
146	Rome destroys Carthage; rules all of western Mediterranean
44–31	Civil wars destroy Roman Republic
31	Rome rules Mediterranean
31 B.C.E.–14 C.E.	Principate of Augustus

96–180	The good emperors rule Rome
180–284	Breakdown of the *Pax Romana*
306–337	Constantine reigns
313	Edict of Milan
325	Council of Nicaea
391	Theodosius makes Christianity the official imperial religion
ca. 400–500	The Germanic invasions
426	*The City of God,* by Augustine
476	The last Western emperor is deposed

▲ *Arch of Constantine*

---

ca. 540–468	Vardhamana Mahavira, founder of Jain tradition
334	Alexander begins conquest of the Near East; invades India in 327
321–181	Mauryan Empire in India

◄ *The Great Stupa at Sanchi*

ca. 300	Foundation of Seleucid dynasty in Anatolia, Syria, and Mesopotamia; Ptolemaic dynasty in Egypt
269–232	Mauryan emperor Ashoka patronizes Buddhism
247 B.C.E.–224 C.E.	Parthian dynasty controls Persia
180 B.C.E.–320 C.E.	India politically divided

▲ *The Lion Capital of Sarnath*

30	Crucifixion of Jesus
70	Romans destroy the Temple at Jerusalem
216–277	Mani
ca. 224	Fall of Parthians, rise of Sasanids, in Persia
ca. 320–500	Gupta Dynasty in India
ca. 400	Chandra Gupta (r. 375–415) conquers western India; increases trade with Near East and China
ca. 450	The Huns invade India

---

ca. 500–200	Rise of Mohist, Taoist, and Legalist schools of thought in China
401–256	Period of the Warring States in China
ca. 300	Old Stone Age Jōmon culture in Japan replaced by Yayoi culture

256–206	Ch'in dynasty in China
221	Ch'in emperor unites all of China
206 B.C.E.–8 C.E.	Former Han dynasty in China
179–104	Han philosopher Tung Chung-shu
145–90	Han historian Ssu-ma Chien
141–187	Emperor Wu Ti of China reigns

Standing attendant, ►
Han dynasty

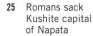

Han dynasty ►
sculpture

25–220	The Later Han dynasty, China
ca. 220–590	Spread of Buddhism in China
220–589	Six Dynasties period in China
ca. 300–500	Barbarian invasions of China
ca. 300–680	Archaic Yamato state in Japan

Terra-cotta head ►
from the Nok culture

25	Romans sack Kushite capital of Napata
100 B.C.E.–1 C.E.	Probable first Indonesian migrations to east African coast

ca. 200	Camel first used for trans-Saharan transport
ca. 200–900	Expansion of Bantu people
ca. 250	Aksum (Ethiopia) controls the Red Sea trade
ca. 300–400	Rise of kingdom of Ghana
ca. 350	Kush ceases to exist

---

ca. 200–600	Early Intermediate period in Andean South America; Moche and Nazca cultures
ca. 150–900	Classic period; dominance of Teotihuacán in central Mexico, Tikal in southern Yucatán

ca. 500–200	Founding of Monte Alban

3 Greek and Hellenistic Civilization

CHAPTER HIGHLIGHTS

Early Greece   Greek civilization is divided into several periods. In the Minoan and Mycenaean ages, the Greek states were ruled by powerful kings. By 750 B.C.E., during the archaic period, Greek society took its characteristic form: the *polis* (plural *poleis*), a self-governing city-state. The most important *poleis* were Athens and Sparta. At first governed by land-owning aristocrats, then by tyrants, many *poleis* evolved more democratic forms of government by 500 B.C.E. In an effort to avoid the pressures of overpopulation and land hunger, the Greeks established colonies around the shores of the Mediterranean and Black Seas.

Classical Greece   After defeating two Persian attempts to conquer them in the early fifth century B.C.E., the Greeks entered their golden age. The greatest achievements in art, literature, and philosophy of Classical Greece took place in Athens, where the government was the most democratic seen until modern times. Among the accomplishments of Greek artists, writers, and thinkers were naturalistic sculpture, tragedy and comedy, secular history, and systematic logic, all of which still influence Western art and thought.

Hellenistic Greece   The *polis* went into political and cultural decline after Sparta defeated Athens in the Great Peloponnesian War (435–404 B.C.E.). Alexander the Great's (r. 336–323 B.C.E.) conquest of the Persian Empire spread Greek culture over a wide area and ushered in the Hellenistic era. Hellenistic Greek culture, which was fostered by the kingdoms that succeeded Alexander's empire, was more accessible to outsiders than that of classical Greece. Hellenistic scholars made Greek literature and science available to many different peoples who adopted it as their own. The Romans were particularly impressed. They spread Hellenistic culture across the Mediterranean world and transmitted it to later generations in the West.

CHAPTER QUESTIONS

HOW WERE the Greek states organized during the Mycenaean period?

WHY WAS the *polis* the most characteristic Greek instition?

WHAT FEATURES distinguished archaic Greek society?

WHY WERE the Greeks able to defeat the Persians?

WHAT WERE the causes and results of the Peloponnesian War?

WHAT WERE the main cultural achievements of Classical Greece?

CHAPTER OUTLINE

- Bronze Age on Crete and on the Mainland to ca. 1150 B.C.E.
- Greek "Middle Age" to ca. 750 B.C.E.
- The *Polis*
- Expansion of the Greek World
- Life in Archaic Greece
- Major City-States
- The Persian Wars
- Classical Greece
- Culture of Classical Greece
- Emergence of the Hellenistic World
- Hellenistic Culture

About 2000 B.C.E., Greek-speaking peoples settled the lands surrounding the Aegean Sea, where they came in contact with the more advanced and earlier civilizations of the Middle East. Adapting from these predecessors, the Greeks forged their own way of life, forming a set of ideas, values, and institutions that would spread far beyond their homeland. The foundation of this way of life was the independent city-state, or polis (plural poleis).

BRONZE AGE ON CRETE AND ON THE MAINLAND TO CA. 1150 B.C.E.

HOW WERE the Greek states organized during the Mycenaean period?

*T*he large island of Crete provided a cultural bridge between the older civilizations of the Middle East and the new ones of the Greeks.

THE MINOANS

In the third and second millennia B.C.E., a Bronze Age civilization arose on Crete that powerfully influenced the islands of the Aegean and the mainland of Greece. This civilization is called **Minoan**, after Minos, the legendary king of Crete. Scholars have divided Minoan history into three periods—Early, Middle, and Late Minoan.

The civilization of the Middle and Late Minoan periods in eastern and central Crete centered on a few great palaces. The distinctive and striking art and architecture of these palaces reflect the influence of Syria, Asia Minor, and Egypt, but they have a uniquely Cretan style and quality. Minoan cities lacked strong defensive walls, suggesting that they were not built with defense in mind.

Excavations at Minoan sites have revealed clay writing tablets like those found in Mesopotamia. Tablets found at the royal palace at Cnossus, accidentally preserved when a great fire that destroyed the palace hardened them, have three distinct kinds of writing on them. The Minoans were not Greeks, but one of these writing systems was an early form of Greek. The contents of the tablets reveal an organization centered on the palace and ruled by a king who was supported by an extensive bureaucracy. This sort of organization is typical of early civilizations in the Middle East but is nothing like that of the Greeks after the Bronze Age. The development of Greek civilization on the mainland was encouraged by contacts between Crete and the mainland's Helladic culture during the Bronze Age.

THE MYCENAEANS

In the third millennium B.C.E., most of the Greek mainland, including many of the sites of later Greek cities, was settled by people who used metal, built some impressive houses, and traded with Crete and the islands of the Aegean. The names they gave to places make it clear that they were not Greeks and that they spoke a language that was not Indo-European (the language family to which Greek belongs). Not long after 2000 B.C.E., many of the Early Helladic sites were destroyed, abandoned, or yielded to an invading people. These signs of invasion probably signal the arrival of the Greeks.

The shaft graves cut into the rock at the royal palace-fortress of Mycenae show

Minoan Bronze Age civilization that arose in Crete in the third and second millennium B.C.E.

Minoan Fresco. Acrobats leaping over a charging bull, from the east wing of the Minoan-period palace at Cnossus on the island of Crete. It is not known whether such acrobatic displays were for entertainment or for part of some religious ritual.

Scala/Art Resource, N.Y.

that by the Late Helladic, the conquerors had prospered. At Mycenae the richest finds come from the period after 1600 B.C.E. The city's wealth and power reached their peak at this time, and the culture of the whole mainland during this period goes by the name **Mycenaean**. Greek invaders also established themselves in Crete, and at the height of Mycenaean power (1400–1200 B.C.E.), Crete was part of the Mycenaean world.

Excavations at Mycenaean sites reveal a culture influenced by, but different from, Minoan culture. Mycenaean cities were built on hills commanding the neighboring territory. The Mycenaean people were warriors led by strong kings who, with their retainers, lived in palaces protected by defensive walls while most of the population lived outside the walls. Like the palaces of Crete, Mycenaean palaces were adorned with murals, but instead of the peaceful pursuits and games depicted on the Cretan murals, the Mycenaean murals depicted scenes of war and boar hunting.

About 1500 B.C.E., *tholos* tombs—large, beehivelike chambers cut into hillsides—replaced the shaft graves. The tholos tombs, built of enormous cut and fitted stones, were approached through unroofed passages carved into the sides of the hills that enclosed them. Only a strong king could undertake such a project. His wealth probably came from plundering raids, piracy, and trade. Some of this trade went to Italy and Sicily, but most was with the Aegean islands, Asia Minor, Syria, Egypt, and Crete. The Mycenaeans exchanged pottery, olive oil, and animal hides for jewels and other luxuries.

Further evidence that the Mycenaean world was made up of a number of independent, powerful, and well-organized monarchies comes from the many clay tablets with Mycenaean writing found throughout the mainland. These reveal a society similar to that of Cnossus on Crete. A king, whose title was *wanax*, held a royal domain, appointed officials, commanded servants, and kept a close record of what he owned and what was owed to him.

The Fall of Mycenaean Power   At the height of their power (1400–1200 B.C.E.), the Mycenaeans enlarged their cities, expanded their trade, and even established commercial colonies in the east. Sometime about 1250 B.C.E. they probably sacked Troy, found on the coast of northwestern Asia Minor, an event memorialized in the epic poems of Homer, the ***Iliad*** and the ***Odyssey***. Around the year 1200 B.C.E., however, the Mycenaean world showed signs of trouble. By 1100 B.C.E., it was gone. Reasons for the collapse of Mycenaean civilization are unclear. Greek legends attribute the fall to a new wave of Greek invaders, the Dorians, from the north—a rude people who spoke a Greek dialect unlike that of the Mycenaeans.

GREEK "MIDDLE AGE" TO CA. 750 B.C.E.

*T*he immediate effects of the Mycenaean collapse were disastrous. Palaces were destroyed, kings and bureaucrats were swept away, and wealth and organization evaporated. Greece entered a dark "Middle Age" about which little is known.

The turmoil surrounding the Mycenaean collapse launched a migration of Greek-speaking people eastward from the mainland to the Aegean islands and the coast of Asia Minor (Ionia). This turned the Aegean into a Greek lake. Trade, however, diminished, and each community was left largely to its own devices. However, because the Middle East was also in disarray, no great power arose to

Mycenaean Bronze Age civilization of mainland Greece that was centered at Mycenae.

The *Iliad* and the *Odyssey*
Epic poems by Homer about the "Dark Age" heroes of Greece who fought at Troy. The poems were written down in the eighth century B.C.E. after centuries of being sung by bards.

WHAT KIND of society does Homer depict in the *Iliad* and the *Odyssey*?

The "Trojan Horse." The legend of the Trojan horse is depicted on this seventh-century B.C.E. Greek vase. According to legend, the Greeks finally defeated Troy by pretending to abandon their siege of the city, leaving a giant wooden horse behind. Soldiers hidden in the horse opened the gates of the city to their compatriots after the Trojans had brought it within their walls. Note the wheels on the horse and the Greek soldiers who are hiding inside it.

Deutsches Archäologisches Institut, Athens.

4.1
Homer: *The Iliad*

impose its ways on the helpless people who lived around the Aegean, and the Greeks were free to create a unique style of life.

AGE OF HOMER

Homer provides the best picture of society in these poorly documented "dark ages." His epic poems, the *Iliad* and the *Odyssey*, emerged from a tradition of oral poetry whose roots reached back to the Mycenaean Age. Through the centuries bards had sung tales of the heroes who had fought at Troy, and in this way preserved some very old material. In the eighth century B.C.E., the oral poetry was reworked as the poems attributed to Homer. Although the poems tell of the deeds of Mycenaean heroes, the world they describe resembles that of the 10th and ninth centuries B.C.E. more than Mycenaean.

Government Kings in the Homeric poems have much less power than Mycenaean rulers had. Homeric kings were expected to make important decisions in consultation with a council of their followers. The right to speak in this council was limited to noblemen, but common people could not be ignored. If a king planned a major change of policy, he would call the common soldiers to an assembly. They could not take part in debate, but they could express their feelings by acclamation. Homer shows that even in these early times Greeks practiced a form of constitutional government.

Society Homeric society was aristocratic. Noble status was hereditary and usually associated with wealth. Below the nobles were two other classes: *thetes* and slaves. Thetes were landless laborers. They endured the worst conditions in Homeric society. In a world where membership in a settled group provided the only security, free laborers were desperately vulnerable. Slaves were attached to family households, so they were at least protected and fed. Slaves were few in number and were mostly women who served as maids and concubines. Agriculture mostly utilized free labor throughout Greek history.

Homeric Values Homer's poems became the schoolbooks of the Greeks, who memorized his texts and emulated the behavior and cherished the values displayed in them. The values of the Homeric poems—physical prowess, courage, and fierce protection of family, friends, property—reflected an aristocratic code that influenced all future Greek thought. Defense of personal honor and reputation was of supreme importance. The great hero of the *Iliad*, Achilles, withdraws from the field of battle at Troy and allows his fellow Greeks to be almost defeated, when Agamemnon wounds his honor. He returns to the army not out of a sense of duty but to avenge the death of his friend Patroclus.

The highest virtue in Homeric society was *arete*—manliness, the excellence proper to a hero. Arete was best demonstrated by competing in a contest, an *agon*. Homeric battles are primarily individual matches between champions, and the major entertainment for Homer's heroes are athletic contests. The central ethical idea in Homer's epics is found in the instructions that fathers of heroes give to their sons: "Always be the best and distinguished above others"; "Do not bring shame on the family of your fathers." The chief aristocratic values of Homer's world—to vie for individual supremacy in *arete* and to defend and increase the honor of the family—would remain as prominent Greek values long after Homeric society was only a memory.

THE POLIS

The characteristic Greek institution was the *polis*. The common translation of that word as "city-state" says both too much and too little. Because all Greek poleis began as agricultural villages or towns and many stayed small, the word "city" does not accurately describe them. All of them were states in the sense of being independent political units, but they were much more than that. The polis was thought of as a community of relatives; all its citizens were theoretically descended from a common ancestor. They were organized into subgroups on the basis of presumed blood relationships: fighting brotherhoods (*phratries*), clans, and tribes. They worshipped the same ancestral gods with the same traditional rituals.

Aristotle (see Chapter 2) claimed that the human being is by nature "an animal who lives in a polis." Humans alone have the power of speech—a social attribute—and from it derive the ability to distinguish good from bad and right from wrong, "and the sharing of these things is what makes a household and a polis." Without law and justice, humans are the worst and most dangerous of the animals. With them, they can be the best, but justice can be maintained only with the aid of the institutions of a polis.

DEVELOPMENT OF THE POLIS

Originally the word *polis* referred to a citadel, an elevated, defensible rock to which the farmers of the neighboring area could retreat when attacked. The **Acropolis** in Athens and the hill called Acrocorinth in Corinth are examples. For some time such high places and the adjacent farms made up the polis. Towns grew up around these fortresses gradually and without planning. For centuries they had no walls. The availability of farmland and of a natural fortress determined where poleis sprang up. They were usually situated well inland or at least far enough away from the sea to avoid raids by pirates. Only later and gradually did an **agora**—a marketplace and civic center—appear within the polis. The agora provided the setting for development of the Greeks' unique fascination with conversation and public debate.

Some poleis probably appeared early in the eighth century B.C.E., and all the colonies established by the Greeks after 750 B.C.E. took the form of poleis. Once the new institution had been fully established, true monarchy disappeared. The original form of the polis was an aristocratic republic dominated by a council of nobles who also monopolized all political offices.

THE HOPLITE PHALANX

A new military strategy promoted development of the polis. In earlier times the brunt of fighting had been carried on by small troops of cavalry and individual "champions." Toward the end of the eighth century B.C.E., however, the **hoplite phalanx** came into being and remained the basis of Greek warfare thereafter.

WHY WAS the *polis* the most characteristic Greek institution?

Acropolis Religious and civic center of Athens. It is the site of the Parthenon.

agora Greek marketplace and civic center. It was the heart of the social life of the polis.

hoplite phalanx Basic unit of Greek warfare in which infantrymen fought in close order, shield to shield, usually eight ranks deep.

WHY DID the Greeks establish colonies?

A hoplite was a heavily armed infantryman who fought with a spear and a large shield. Hoplites were arrayed in close order in a formation called a phalanx that was at least eight ranks deep. The success of a hoplite army depended on the discipline, strength, and courage of its individual soldiers. At its best, the phalanx could withstand cavalry charges and defeat less disciplined infantries. Until the Roman legion appeared, it was the dominant military force in the Mediterranean.

The usual hoplite battle in Greece involved the armies of two poleis quarreling over a piece of land. One army invaded the territory of the other when its crops were almost ready for harvest. The defending army had to protect the fields. If the defenders were beaten, the fields were captured or destroyed. The farmer-soldier-citizen, who defended the polis, usually hoped to settle a dispute quickly by a single decisive battle and then get back to work. It was to the advantage of an agriculturally based society to keep wars short and limit their cost.

Service in the phalanx created a bond between the aristocrats and the family farmers who fought side by side. This may explain why class conflicts were slow to develop, but it also meant that aristocratic monopolies of political power within a poleis would eventually be challenged.

EXPANSION OF THE GREEK WORLD

From the mid-eighth century B.C.E. until well into the sixth, a burst of colonizing activity planted poleis from Spain to the Black Sea. A century earlier a few Greeks had established trading posts in Syria, and about 750 B.C.E., they borrowed a writing system from one of the local Semitic scripts. By adding vowels to it, they created the first true alphabet. The Greek alphabet, which was easier to learn than any earlier writing system, enabled literacy to spread widely in Greek communities.

GREEK COLONIES

Syria and its neighboring territory were too strong to penetrate, so the Greeks sought out less populated regions for their colonies. Before long, there were so many Greek colonies in southern Italy and Sicily that the Romans began to call those lands **Magna Graecia** ("Great Greece"). The Greeks also established colonies in Spain, southern France, around the Black Sea, and on the north African coast. Most colonies were independent, but they maintained a special relationship with their mother cities (see Map 3–1).

Colonization relieved the pressure of a growing population on the Greek mainland, and confrontations between Greek colonists and diverse peoples made the Greeks acutely aware of their own cultural identity. They cultivated a **Panhellenic** ("all-Greek") spirit through the establishment of common religious festivals, the most important of which were at Olympia, Delphi, Corinth, and Nemea.

Colonization also encouraged trade and industry. The influx of new wealth and the increased demand for goods stimulated a more intensive use of land. Crops were rasied for export, chiefly olives and wine grapes. Craftsmen also manufactured pottery, tools, weapons, fine metalwork, and perfumed oil (the soap of the ancient Mediterranean) for a world market. The opportunities created by the growing economy made some men, who were not nobles, wealthy. They constituted a troublesome element in the aristocratically dominated poleis, for they resented being barred from political power, religious privileges, and social acceptance by the nobility. This led to crises in the many states that culminated, between 700 and 500 B.C.E., in the establishment of tyrannies.

Magna Graecia Meaning "Great Greece" in Latin. The name given by the Romans to southern Italy and Sicily because there were so many Greek colonies in the region.

Panhellenic Meaning "all-Greek." The sense of cultural identity that all Greeks felt in common with each other.

MAP EXPLORATION

Interactive map: To explore this map further, go to **http://www.prenhall.com/craig/map3.1**

MAP 3–1

Phoenician and Greek Colonization. Most of the coastline of the Mediterranean and Black Seas was populated by Greek or Phoenician colonies. The Phoenicians were a commercial people who planted their colonies in North Africa, Spain, Sicily, and Sardinia, chiefly in the ninth century B.C.E. The height of Greek colonization came later, between ca. 750 and 550 B.C.E.

WHAT IMPACT did colonization have on Phoenician and Greek societies?

Rise of Greece

ca. 2900–1150 B.C.E.	Minoan period
ca. 1900 B.C.E.	Probable date of the arrival of the Greeks on the mainland
ca. 1600–1150 B.C.E.	Mycenaean period
ca. 1250 B.C.E.	Sack of Troy (?)
ca. 1200–1150 B.C.E.	Destruction of Mycenaean centers in Greece
ca. 1100–750 B.C.E.	Dark Ages
ca. 750–500 B.C.E.	Major period of Greek colonization
ca. 725 B.C.E.	Probable date of Homer
ca. 700 B.C.E.	Probable date of Hesiod
ca. 700–500 B.C.E.	Major period of Greek tyranny

THE TYRANTS (CA. 700–500 B.C.E.)

A tyrant was a monarch who had gained power in an unorthodox but not necessarily wicked way and who exercised a strong one-man rule that might be both beneficent and popular.

The Rise of Tyranny   The founding tyrant was usually a member of the ruling aristocracy who either had a personal grievance against members of his own class or who led an ambitious faction. He sought the support of disgruntled elements within the polis: the politically powerless, newly wealthy, and poor farmers. He often expelled his aristocratic opponents, terminated the privileges of the aristocrats, and divided their land among his supporters. Tyrants presided over a period of population growth in the Greek world, and to maintain popular support they fostered trade and colonization. They sponsored programs of public works, founded new festivals, and provided patronage for the arts.

The End of the Tyrants   Tyranny, however, could turn oppressive, and there was something about the concept of tyranny that was inimical to the idea of the polis. The notion of the polis as a community for which each of its members was responsible, the connection of justice with that community, and the natural aristocratic hatred of monarchy all made tyranny seem alien and offensive to the Greeks. By the end of the sixth century B.C.E., tyranny had disappeared from the Greek world, and the last tyrants were remembered with bitterness. The tyrants had, however, helped secure the prosperity of Greece and had cultivated technology, the arts, and literature. Most importantly, they had broken the grip of the aristocracy on Greek society.

LIFE IN ARCHAIC GREECE

SOCIETY

WHAT FEATURES distinguished archaic Greek society?

As the "dark ages" came to an end, the features that would distinguish Greek society took shape. Most people farmed the land, but the role of the artisan and the merchant grew increasingly important.

Farmers   The poet Hesiod (ca. 700 B.C.E.) described himself as a small farmer, and his *Works and Days* gives us an idea of the life of a Greek farmer. His crops included grain (chiefly barley but some wheat), grapes for wine, olives for oil (used for cooking, lighting, and washing), green vegetables, and fruit. Sheep and goats provided milk and cheese, but ordinary farmers usually ate meat only when animals were sacrificied at religious festivals. Life was continual toil under the burning sun and in the freezing cold, and pleasures were few.

symposion   Carefully organized drinking party that was the center of Greek aristocratic social life. It featured games, songs, poetry, and even philosophical disputation.

Aristocrats   Most aristocrats employed hired laborers, sharecroppers, and some slaves, to work their lands. This gave them leisure for other activities. Aristocratic social life revolved around the drinking party, or *symposion*, a carefully organized activity for men only. Symposium guests might play games, enjoy professional entertainment, or amuse themselves with songs, poetry, or even philosophical disputes. Often, their activities took the form of contests, with a prize for the winner. Aristocratic values emphasized competition, the need to excel, and the desire to be recognized for one's achievements.

This aspect of aristocratic life explains the popularity of the athletic contests that became widespread early in the sixth century B.C.E. The games included running events, boxing, wrestling, and the chariot race. Only the rich could afford racehorses, so the chariot race was a special preserve of aristocracy. Wrestling, however, was also favored by the nobility, and the *palaestra* where they practiced became an important social center for nobles and men of leisure. The contrast between the hard, drab life of the peasant and the leisured and lively one of the aristocrat could hardly be greater.

RELIGION

Like most ancient peoples, the Greeks were polytheists, and religion played an important part in their lives.

The Greek pantheon consisted of the 12 gods who lived on Mount Olympus. They were

- Zeus, the father of the gods
- Hera, his wife
- Zeus's siblings:
  Poseidon, his brother, god of the seas and earthquakes
  Hestia, his sister, goddess of the hearth
  Demeter, his sister, goddess of agriculture and marriage
- Zeus's children:
  Aphrodite, goddess of love and beauty
  Apollo, god of the sun, music, poetry, and prophecy
  Ares, god of war
  Artemis, goddess of the moon and the hunt
  Athena, goddess of wisdom and the arts
  Hephaestus, god of fire and metallurgy
  Hermes, messenger of the gods, connected with commerce and cunning

Attic Jar. From late in the sixth century B.C.E., this jar shows how olives, one of Athens's most important crops, were harvested.
Courtesy of the Trustees of the British Museum.

The gods were assumed to behave like humans, from whom they differed primarily in strength and immortality. Also, like humans, the Olympians were believed to be subordinate to the Fates. Zeus, however, was not an arbitrary ruler but a defender of justice. Each polis honored one of the Olympians as its guardian deity, but all the gods were Panhellenic. In the eighth and seventh centuries B.C.E., common shrines were established at Olympia for the worship of Zeus, at Delphi for Apollo, and at Corinth for Poseidon. Each shrine held athletic contests in honor of its deity, to which all Greeks were invited and for which a sacred truce was declared.

The worship of the Olympian deities did not inspire intense emotion. Worshippers offered a god prayer, libations, and gifts in hope of currying protection and favors. Greek religion offered little moral teaching. Most Greeks seem to have thought that civic virtue consisted of worshipping the state deities in the traditional way, performing required public services, and fighting in defense of the state. Private ethics required only that one do good to one's friends and harm to one's enemies.

In the sixth century B.C.E., the cult and oracle of Apollo at Delphi began to exercise great influence. The priests of Apollo preached moderation. They urged self-control and warned that arrogance (*hubris*) caused moral blindness and invited divine vengeance. Famous mottos summed up their advice: "Know thyself," and "Nothing in excess."

To assuage human fears, hopes, and passions, the Greeks turned to deities who were worshipped with more emotional rites. Of these, the most popular was Dionysus, a god of nature and fertility, of the grape and drunkenness, and of ecstacy and sexual abandon.

POETRY

The great changes that swept through the Greek world were reflected in a new genre of poetry, the lyric. Sappho of Lesbos, Anacreon of Teos, and Simonides of Cous treated personal themes, often describing the pleasure and agony of love. Alcaeus of Mytilene, an aristocrat driven from his city by a tyrant, wrote bitter invective. But the most interesting poet from a political point of view was Theognis of Megara, the spokesman for the old, defeated aristocracy of birth. He divided Greeks into two classes—the noble and the base. The former were good and the latter bad. Only nobles could aspire to virtue, for he said that only they possessed critical moral and intellectual qualities. These things could not be taught. They were innate and were lost if a noble wed a commoner. These prejudices remained strong in aristocratic circles throughout the next century and greatly influenced later thinkers, Plato among them.

MAJOR CITY-STATES

Generalization about the poleis is difficult, for although the states had much in common, some of them developed in unique ways. Sparta and Athens became the two most powerful Greek states.

SPARTA

About 725 B.C.E., population pressure and land hunger led the Spartans to conquer their western neighbor, Messenia. The Spartans now had as much land as they would ever need, and because they reduced the Messenians to serfs, or **Helots**, they no longer had to work this land themselves. About 650 B.C.E., the Helots rebelled, and the Spartans faced a turning point. To keep down the Helots, who outnumbered them perhaps 10 to 1, they turned their city into a permanent military academy and camp.

Society The new system exerted control over each Spartan from birth, when officials of the state decided which infants, male and female, were sufficiently strong to be raised. At age 7, the Spartan boy was taken from his mother and turned over to young instructors who trained him in athletics and the military arts. The Spartan youth was enrolled in the army at age 20 and lived in barracks until he was 30. He could marry, but could visit his wife only by stealth. At age 30 he became a full citizen, an "equal," and was allowed to live in his own house with his wife, although he took his meals at a public mess in the company of 15 comrades. His food, a simple diet without much meat or wine, was provided by his own plot of land, which was worked for him by Helots. Only when he reached 60 could the Spartan retire from military service to his home and family.

HOW DID Spartan society and government differ from that of Athens?

QUICK REVIEW

Spartan Society
- Spartan system controlled Spartan life from birth
- At age 7 Spartan boys began military training
- Spartan girls were also indoctrinated with idea of service to state

4.5
The City-State of Sparta

Helots Hereditary Spartan serfs.

Spartan girls were permitted greater freedom than other Greek females and were, like their brothers, indoctrinated with the idea of service to Sparta. The entire system was designed to subordinate the natural feelings of devotion to family to a more powerful commitment to the polis. Privacy, luxury, and even comfort were sacrificed to produce the best soldiers in the world. Nothing that might turn the mind away from duty was permitted.

Government   Sparta was governed by two kings, a council of elders, and an assembly. The power of the kings was limited. The council of elders—28 men over age 60 who were elected for life—was consulted before any proposal was put before the assembly. The assembly, which consisted of all males over age 30, could only ratify, not debate, the decisions of magistrates, elders, and kings. Sparta also had a board of ephors, five men elected annually by the assembly. The ephors controlled foreign policy, oversaw the generalship of the kings, presided at the assembly, and guarded against rebellion by the Helots.

Suppression of the Helots required all the Spartans' effort and energy. They did not try to expand their borders, but they did force their neighbors to follow their lead in foreign affairs and supply them with troops on demand. This formed an alliance known as the Peloponnesian League, which made Sparta the most powerful polis in Greece.

ATHENS

In the seventh century B.C.E., Athens and the region of Attica constituted a typical aristocratic polis. The state was governed by the **Areopagus**, a council of nobles. Annually the council elected nine magistrates, called *archons*, who became members of the council after their year in office. A broad-based citizens' assembly, the Areopagus had little power. It represented the four tribes into which Attica's inhabitants were divided.

Pressure for Change   In the seventh century B.C.E., quarrels within the nobility and the beginnings of an agrarian crisis disturbed the peaceful life of Athens. A shift to more intensive agricultural techniques forced the less successful farmers to borrow from wealthy neighbors. Many defaulted and were enslaved for their debts. Some were sold abroad. The poor began to demand the abolition of debt and a redistribution of the land.

Reforms of Solon   In 594 B.C.E., as tradition has it, the Athenians elected Solon (ca. 639–559 B.C.E.) to revise Athens' governing institutions. Solon immediately canceled debts, forbade debt slavery, and brought back Athenians enslaved abroad. He forbade the export of wheat, a food staple, but encouraged production of olive oil and wine for sale abroad. This nudged the Athenians toward a commercially based economy that utilized their land most efficiently for cash crops, such as olives and grapes.

Solon changed the way Athens was governed. He expanded citizenship to include immigrant artisans and merchants, and divided the citizenry into four classes on the basis of wealth. Only men of the wealthiest two classes could be archons and sit on the Areopagus. Men of the third class could be hoplites and serve on a council of 400 chosen by the assembly of all male citizens.

The Charioteer of Delphi, ca. 470. B.C.E. This freestanding statue, the *Charioteer of Delphi*, is one of the few full-scale bronze sculptures that survive from the fifth century B.C.E. Polyzalus, the tyrant of the Greek city of Gela in Sicily, dedicated it after winning a victory in the chariot race in the Pythian games, either in 478 or 474. The games were held at the sacred shrine of the god Apollo at Delphi, and the statue was placed within the god's sanctuary, not far from Apollo's temple. Greek (Classical). Bronze, H: 180 cm. Archaelogical Museum, Delphi, Greece. Photograph © Nimatallah/Art Resource, N.Y.

Areopagus Governing council of Athens, originally open only to the nobility. Named after the hill on which it met.

Key Events in the Early History of Sparta and Athens

ca. 725–710 B.C.E.	First Messenian War
ca. 650–625 B.C.E.	Second Messenian War; Solon institutes reforms at Athens
ca. 560–550 B.C.E.	Sparta defeats Tegea; beginning of Peloponnesian League
ca. 546–527 B.C.E.	Pisistratus reigns as tyrant at Athens (main period)
ca. 510 B.C.E.	Hippias, son of Pisistratus, deposed as tyrant of Athens
ca. 508–501 B.C.E.	Clisthenes institutes reforms at Athens

Pisistratus the Tyrant Despite Solon's reforms, Pisistratus (605?–527 B.C.E.), a nobleman and military hero, seized power in 546 B.C.E. and made himself the city's first tyrant. Pisistratus sought to increase the power of the central government at the expense of the nobles. He made no formal change in the institutions of government, but saw to it that his supporters filled key offices. The unintended effect was to give more Athenians more experience with participatory government and a growing taste for it. The tyranny ended with Pisistratus's son, Hippias (r. 527–510 B.C.E.). When his rule became harsh and unpopular, his aristocratic opponents, with Sparta's help, rallied and drove him into exile (510 B.C.E.).

Clisthenes, the Founder of Democracy Some factions in the Athenian aristocracy tried to restore the aristocracy to the position of dominance it held before Solon. Their plans were upset by Clisthenes, an aristocrat who proposed a program that won him the backing of the masses. A central aim of Clisthenes' reforms was to diminish the political influence of the tribal territories into which Attica was divided, for these territories were the power bases of the noble families. Clisthenes replaced Attica's traditional four tribes with 10 new tribes composed of units drawn from all parts of Attica, rather than each tribe representing a single locale. The new organization increased devotion to the polis by weakening regional loyalties.

Clisthenes vested final authority in all things in the assembly of all adult male Athenian citizens. Debate in the assembly was free and open; any Athenian could submit legislation, offer amendments, or argue the merits of any question.

THE PERSIAN WARS

WHY WERE the Greeks able to defeat the Persians?

The Greeks' period of isolation and freedom from interference by the outside world ended in the sixth century B.C.E. The first to be threatened were the Greek cities on the coast of Asia Minor, which came under the control of the rapidly expanding Persian Empire (see Chapter 4).

IONIAN REBELLION

At first, the cities of Ionia (the central part of the west coast of Asia Minor and nearby islands) prospered under Persian rule and did not resist Persian domination. The private troubles of an ambitious tyrant of Miletus named Aristagoras, however, ended this calm. Aristagoras had urged a Persian expedition against the island of Naxos. When it failed, he tried to avoid punishment from Persia by raising a rebellion in Ionia (499 B.C.E.). When he turned to the mainland Greeks for help, Athens agreed to send a fleet. In 498 B.C.E., the Athenians and their allies burned Sardis, the seat of the Persian governor. The revolt spread. But after the Athenians withdrew, the Persians reimposed their will. In 494 B.C.E. they wiped out Miletus and put down the Ionian rebellion.

THE WAR IN GREECE

In 490 B.C.E. the Persian king, Darius (r. 521–486 B.C.E.), sent an expedition to punish Athens. Miltiades (d. 489 B.C.E.), an Athenian who had fled from Persian service, led the city's army to a confrontation with the invaders at Marathon, a plain north of Athens, and won a decisive victory.

The Great Invasion For the Persians, however, Marathon was only a temporary defeat. In 481 B.C.E., Darius's successor, Xerxes (r. 486–465 B.C.E.), gathered an army of at least 150,000 men and a navy of more than 600 ships for the conquest of Greece. By then, Themistocles (ca. 525–462 B.C.E.) had become Athens' leading politician. His policies were aimed at making Athens a major naval power, and by 480 B.C.E., when Xerxes invaded, Athens had more than 200 ships. It was the Athenian navy that defeated the Persians.

Darius had launched a naval attack on the Greek mainland, but Xerxes invaded by land. His huge army had to keep in touch with its fleet for supplies. Themistocles reasoned that if the Greeks could defeat the Persian navy, the Persian army would have to retreat. His strategy was to try to delay the advance of the Persian army until he could fight the kind of naval battle he might hope to win.

The Spartans led a Greek army that made a famous, but futile, attempt to block the Persian invasion at a place called Thermopylae. The fate of Greece was subsequently decided by the Athenians in a sea battle in the narrow straits to the east of the island of Salamis. When they destroyed more than half of Xerxes' fleet, he retreated to Asia with a good part of his army.

The Persian general Mardonius was left behind to continue the fight. The Spartan regent, Pausanias (d. ca. 470 B.C.E.), amassed the largest army of Greek allies yet assembled, and at Plataea, in the summer of 479 B.C.E., it killed Mardonius and routed the remaining Persian forces. Meanwhile, the Ionian Greeks urged King Leotychidas, the Spartan commander of the fleet, to fight the Persian fleet. At Mycale, near Samos, he destroyed the Persian camp and fleet, and the Persians withdrew from the Aegean and Ionia.

Greek Hoplite Attacking a Persian Soldier. The contrast between the Greek's metal body armor, large shield, and long spear and the Persian's cloth and leather garments indicates one reason why the Greeks won.

Greek. Vase, Red-figured. Attic. ca. 480–470 B.C. Neck amphora, Nolan type. SIDE 1: "Greek warrior attacking a Persian." Said to be from Rhodes. Terracotta. H. 13-11/16 in. The Metropolitan Museum of Art, Rogers Fund, 1906 (Acc. # 06.1021.117) Photograph © The Metropolitan Museum of Art.

CLASSICAL GREECE

The repulse of the Persians marks the beginning of the Classical period in Greece, 150 years of intense cultural achievement that has rarely if ever been matched (see Map 3–2). Although it was an era of progress for civilization, the Classical period was not a time of peace and stability for the Greeks. It was plagued by destructive conflicts among the poleis that left them weakened and vulnerable.

WHAT WERE the causes and results of the Peloponnesian War?

THE DELIAN LEAGUE

Greek unity gave way within two years of the Persian retreat. Two spheres of influence emerged—one dominated by Sparta, the other by Athens. The developments that led to the split were motivated by a need to protect the Ionian Greeks and make sure that the Persians did not return to the Aegean. Athens, Greece's largest naval power, was best equipped to direct this campaign.

In the winter of 478–477 B.C.E., the Aegean islanders, the Greeks from the coast of Asia Minor, and some from other Greek cities met with the Athenians on the sacred island of Delos to swear a permanent alliance under Athenian leadership. Known as the **Delian League**, the alliance kept the Persians at bay and cleared the Aegean of pirates. To create a workable system, some Greek states were forced into the league, and some who wished to resign were prevented from doing so. The Delian League and Athens were led at this time by a statesman and soldier named Cimon (d. 449 B.C.E.). His policy was to aggressively attack Persia while maintaining friendly relations with Sparta. He worked

Delian League Alliance of Greek states under the leadership of Athens that was formed in 478–477 B.C.E. to resist the Persians.

MAP 3–2

Classical Greece. Greece in the Classical period (ca. 480–338 B.C.E.) centered on the Aegean Sea. Although there were important Greek settlements in Italy, Sicily, and all around the Black Sea, the area shown in this general reference map embraced the vast majority of Greek states.

WHY WERE most Greek cities located close to the sea?

within the constraints of the popular democratic constitution that Clisthenes had given Athens.

THE FIRST PELOPONNESIAN WAR

The Fall of Cimon In 465 B.C.E., the island of Thasos rebelled against the league. Cimon's suppression of this rebellion began the transformation of the league into an Athenian empire. Despite his success abroad, at home Cimon faced challenges from a faction led by Pericles (ca. 495–429 B.C.E.). Although Pericles was a member of a distinguished Athenian family, he wanted to increase the power of ordinary Athenians and break with the Spartans, traditional allies of some Athenian aristocrats.

In 461 B.C.E. Cimon's opponent engineered his exile, and Athens allied with Argos, Sparta's enemy in the Peloponnese. Almost overnight, Cimon's domestic and foreign policies were overturned.

Outbreak of War The policies of Athens' new regime helped incite a conflict with Sparta known as the First **Peloponnesian War**. The Athenians made great gains during the war's early years. They seemed invulnerable, winning control of some neighboring states and dominating the sea.

In 454 B.C.E., however, the tide turned. An Athenian fleet, which was dispatched to help the Egyptians rebel against Persia, was destroyed, and revolts broke out within the Delian League. Athens moderated its behavior and agreed to a peace of 30 years with Sparta. Greece was divided into two blocs: Sparta and its allies on the mainland and Athens and what had become the Athenian Empire in the Aegean.

THE ATHENIAN EMPIRE

The Athenians moved the Delian League's treasury from Delos to Athens and began to keep one-sixtieth of the league's annual revenues for themselves. Athens gave up the pretext of being the leader of a free alliance.

Greek Wars Against Persia

ca. 560–546 B.C.E.	Greek cities of Asia Minor conquered by Croesus of Lydia
546 B.C.E.	Cyrus of Persia conquers Lydia and gains control of Greek cities
499–494 B.C.E.	Greek cities rebel (Ionian rebellion)
490 B.C.E.	Battle of Marathon
480–479 B.C.E.	Xerxes' invasion of Greece
480 B.C.E.	Battles of Thermopylae and Salamis
479 B.C.E.	Battles of Plataea and Mycale

Peloponnesian Wars
Protracted struggle between Athens and Sparta to dominate Greece between 465 and Athens' final defeat in 404 B.C.E.

WHAT WERE the main cultural achievements of classical Greece?

The Acropolis. It was both the religious and civic center of Athens. In its final form the Acropolis is the work of Pericles and his successors in the late fifth century B.C.E. This photograph shows the Parthenon and, to its left, the Erechtheum.

Meredith Pillon, Greek National Tourism Organization.

Key Events in Athenian History Between the Persian War and the Great Peloponnesian War

478–477 B.C.E.	Delian League founded
ca. 474–462 B.C.E.	Cimon leading politician
465–463 B.C.E.	Rebellion of Thasos
462 B.C.E.	Pericles rises to leadership
461 B.C.E.	Cimon ostracized
ca. 460 B.C.E.	First Peloponnesian War begins
454 B.C.E.	Athens defeated in Egypt; crisis in the Delian League
445 B.C.E.	Thirty Years' Peace ends First Peloponnesian War

The league had become an empire that was the key to Athens' prosperity and security.

ATHENIAN DEMOCRACY

While the Athenians tightened their control over their subjects, they expanded democracy for themselves at home. Under the leadership of Pericles they evolved the freest government the world had yet seen. Property qualifications for offices were removed, opening all offices to all adult male citizens. Pericles introduced pay for jury service, which allowed the poor to take time off from work to serve. Judges traveled circuits to provide swift impartial justice for the poor who were living in the countryside. As the privileges of Athenian citizenship grew, however, access to citizenship was sharply restricted. Only those who had two citizen parents could claim what had become a valuable commodity.

Athens was governed as a direct democracy. Every political decision had to be approved by the popular assembly— the people themselves, not their representatives. Every judicial decision was subject to appeal to a popular court chosen from the Athenian male population. Many officials were selected by lot, which made class irrelevant. Elected officials generally continued to be members of noble families and were almost always rich men, but the people were free to choose whomever they wanted. All public officials could be removed from office and were held to a compulsory accounting at the end of their terms. There was no standing army; no police force, open or secret; and no way to coerce the people.

Pericles was elected to the generalship (a military office with important political influence) 15 years in a row and 30 times in all. After the First Peloponnesian War, he instituted a conservative policy designed to preserve the empire in the Aegean and peace with Sparta.

WOMEN OF ATHENS

Subjection   Greek society was dominated by men, and democracry did nothing to challenge male supremacy in Athens. Women were excluded from most aspects of public life. They could not vote, take part in political assemblies, or hold office. Their only public function—an important one—was participation in certain rituals and festivals of the state religion.

In private life, women were always under the control of a male guardian— a father, husband, or relative. Women married young, usually between the ages of 12 and 18, whereas men typically did not marry until the age of 30. Marriages were arranged; the woman normally had no choice of husband, and her dowry was controlled by a male relative. To obtain a divorce, a woman needed the approval of a male relative.

The main function of an Athenian woman of a citizen family was to produce male heirs for her husband's household (*oikos*). Because the pure and legitimate lineage of offspring was important for ensuring transmission of rights to citizenship, women were segregated from men outside the family and confined to women's quarters in their homes. Respectable women stayed home, raised children, and oversaw their households. Their husbands spent most of their time outside the home and were free to seek whatever sexual gratification they wanted.

It may be that the role played by Athenian women was more complex than their legal status suggests, for myths, pictorial art, and the tragedies and comedies performed at Athenian religious festivals often feature women as central characters and powerful figures in both the public and the private spheres (see "Lysistrata Ends the War").

THE GREAT PELOPONNESIAN WAR

The Thirty Years' Peace of 445 B.C.E. endured little more than 10 years. About 435 B.C.E., Athens and Sparta plunged back into conflict. This new war shook the foundations of Greek civilization.

The Spartan strategy was traditional: to invade the enemy's country and threaten the crops, forcing the enemy to defend them in a hoplite battle. The Athenian strategy was to retreat to their impregnable city, allow the devastation of their land, and raid the Peloponnesian coast to put pressure on Sparta by harrassing its allies. The Athenian plan required restraint, and it was abandoned after Pericles died in 429 B.C.E. After 10 years of fruitless fighting, the war ended in stalemate.

In 415 B.C.E., Alcibiades (ca. 450–404 B.C.E.), a young and ambitious kinsman of Pericles, persuaded the Athenians to invade Sicily. When the entire expedition was destroyed, Athens' power and prestige were greatly diminished. Subjects of Athens' empire rebelled, and Sparta reopened the war—with Persian aid.

The Athenians fought on and won several important victories at sea, but their resources steadily diminished. When their fleet was destroyed at Aegospotami in 405 B.C.E., they could not rebuild it. The Spartans, under Lysander (d. 395 B.C.E.) blockaded Athens and cut off its food supply. In 404 B.C.E. Athens surrendered unconditionally.

STRUGGLE FOR GREEK LEADERSHIP

The Hegemony of Sparta   The collapse of the Athenian empire opened the way for Spartan dominance of the Aegean. Lysander installed boards of 10 local oligarchs loyal to him and supported by Spartan garrisons in most of the cities along the European coast and the islands of the Aegean. These tributaries brought Sparta almost as much revenue as the Athenians had collected.

Some of Sparta's allies, especially Thebes and Corinth, were alienated by Sparta's increasingly arrogant policies. The oligarchic government that Lysander installed in Athens in 404 B.C.E. came to be called the "Thirty Tyrants" by Athenians who resented its heavy-handed policies. When supporters of democracy fled to Thebes and Corinth and recruited an army to challenge the oligarchs' hold on Athens, Sparta's conservative king, Pausanias, arranged a peaceful settlement and the restoration of democracy. Thereafter, Athenian foreign policy remained under Spartan control, but otherwise Athens was free.

Theban Hegemony   Sparta's actions grew increasingly arrogant and lawless. In 382 B.C.E., Sparta seized Thebes during peacetime without warning or pretext. In 379 B.C.E., a Spartan army made a similar attempt on Athens. This move persuaded the Athenians to join with Thebes, which had rebelled from Sparta. In 371 B.C.E. the Thebans defeated the Spartans at Leuctra. They helped

The Great Peloponnesian War

432 B.C.E.	Sparta declares war on Athens
431 B.C.E.	Peloponnesian invasion of Athens
421 B.C.E.	Peace of Nicias
415–413 B.C.E.	Athenian invasion of Sicily
405 B.C.E.	Battle of Aegospotami
404 B.C.E.	Athens surrenders

HISTORY'S VOICES

LYSISTRATA ENDS THE WAR

ristophanes, the greatest of the Athenian comic poets, presented the play Lysistrata *in 411* B.C.E., *two decades into the Great Pelopennesian War. The plot's central idea is that the women of Athens, led by* Lysistrata, *tire of the privations imposed by the war and decide to take matters into their own hands to bring the war to an end. Their plan is to get the women on both sides to deny their marital favors to their husbands until the men agree to make peace. Their sexual strike quickly succeeds. Before the following passage, Lysistrata has set the terms the Spartans must accept. Next she turns to the Athenians. The play is a masterful example of Athenian Old Comedy, which was almost always full of contemporary and historical political satirical references and sexual and erotic puns and jokes. The references to "Peace" in the stage directions are to an actor playing the goddess Peace.*

WHAT WAS the real role of women in Athenian political life, and what does the play tell us about it?

LYSISTRATA

(*Turning to the Athenians*)

—Men of Athens, do you think I'll let you off?
Have you forgotten the Tyrant's days, when you wore the smock of slavery, when the Spartans turned to the spear, cut down the pride of Thessaly, despatched the friends of tyranny, and dispossessed your oppressors?

Recall:

On that great day, your only allies were Spartans; your liberty came at their hands, which stripped away your servile garb and clothed you again in Freedom!

SPARTAN

(*Indicating Lysistrata*)

Hain't never seed no higher type of woman.

KINESIAS

(*Indicating Peace*)

Never saw one I wanted so much to top.

LYSISTRATA

(*Oblivious to the byplay, addressing both groups*)

With such a history of mutual benefits conferred and received, why are you fighting? Stop this wickedness! Come to terms with each other! What prevents you?

SPARTAN

We'd a heap sight druther make Peace, if we was indemnified with a plumb strategic location.
(*Pointing at Peace's rear*)

We'll take thet butte.

LYSISTRATA

Butte?

SPARTAN

The Promontory of Pylos—Sparta's Back Door.
We've missed it fer a turrible spell.
(*Reaching*)

Hev to keep our hand in.

KINESIAS

(*Pushing him away*)

The price is too high—you'll never take that!

LYSISTRATA

Oh, let them have it.

KINESIAS

What room will we have left for maneuvers?

LYSISTRATA

Demand another spot in exchange.

KINESIAS

(*Surveying Peace like a map as he addresses the Spartan*)

Then you hand over to us—uh, let me see—let's try Thessaly—
(*Indicating the relevant portions of Peace*)

First of all, Easy Mountain ...
then the Maniac Gulf behind it ...
and down to Megara for the legs ...

SPARTAN

You cain't take all of thet! Yore plumb out of yore mind!

LYSISTRATA

(*To Kinesias*)

Don't argue. Let the legs go.

(*Kinesias nods. A pause, general smiles of agreement*)

KINESIAS

(*Doffing his cloak*)

I feel an urgent desire to plow a few furrows.

SPARTAN

(*Doffing his cloak*)

Hit's time to work a few loads of fertilizer in.

LYSISTRATA

Conclude the treaty and the simple life is yours.
If such is your decision, convene your councils,
and then deliberate the matter with your allies.

KINESIAS

Deliberate? Allies?
We're over-extended already!

Wouldn't every ally approve of our position—
Union Now?

SPARTAN

I know I kin speak for ourn.

KINESIAS

And I for ours.

They're just a bunch of gigolos.

LYSISTRATA

I heartily approve. Now first attend to your purification, then we, the women, will welcome you to the Citadel and treat you to all the delights of a home-cooked banquet. Then you'll exchange your oaths and pledge your faith, and every man of you will take his wife and depart for home.

Source: Aristophanes, *Lysistrata* trans. by Douglass Parker in *Four Comedies by Aristophanes*, ed. by W. Arrowsmith (Ann Arbor: University of Michigan Press, 1969), pp. 79–81. Reprinted by permission of the University of Michigan Press.

the Arcadian cities of the central Peloponnesus to form a federal league and freed the Helots, who founded a city of their own. Sparta's population had shrunk, and hemmed in by hostile neighbors and deprived of much of its farmland and of the slaves who had worked it, Sparta ceased to be a first-rank power. Its aggressive policies had led to ruin.

The Second Athenian Empire   In 378 B.C.E. Athens organized a second confederation aimed at resisting Spartan aggression in the Aegean. Its constitution was designed to prevent the abuses that had turned the Delian League into an Athenian Empire, but the Athenians tried to revert to their old habits. This time, however, they did not have the power to dominate their allies, and when the threats posed by Sparta, Thebes, and Persia receded, their allies rebelled. After two centuries of almost continual warfare, the Greeks returned to the chaotic disorganization that had characterized the era before the founding of the Peloponnesian League.

CULTURE OF CLASSICAL GREECE

The term *classical* often suggests calm and serenity, but the word that best describes Greek life, thought, art, and literature during the Classical period is *tension*. Among the achievements of this era (discussed in Chapter 2) were the philosophical works of Socrates (469–399 B.C.E.), Plato (427?–347 B.C.E.), and Aristotle (384–322 B.C.E.). The same curiosity about the nature and place in the universe of human beings that motivated the philosophers also animated the arts of the period.

Spartan and Theban Hegemonies

404–403 B.C.E.	Thirty Tyrants rule at Athens
401 B.C.E.	Expedition of Cyrus, rebellious prince of Persia; Battle of Cunaxa
400–387 B.C.E.	Spartan War against Persia
398–360 B.C.E.	Reign of Agesilaus at Sparta
395–387 B.C.E.	Corinthian War
382 B.C.E.	Sparta seizes Thebes
378 B.C.E.	Second Athenian Confederation founded
371 B.C.E.	Thebans defeat Sparta at Leuctra; end of Spartan hegemony
362 B.C.E.	Battle of Mantinea; end of Theban hegemony

The Striding God from Artemisium.
This bronze statue, dating from ca.
460 B.C.E., was found in the sea near
Artemisium, the northern tip of the
large Greek Island of Euboea, and is
now on display in the National
Archaeological Museum in Athens.
Exactly whom this god represents is
not known. Some have thought him to
be Poseidon holding a trident; others
believe that he is Zeus hurling a thun-
derbolt. In either case he is a splendid
representative of the early classical
period of Greek sculpture.

National Archaeological Museum, Athens.

FIFTH CENTURY B.C.E.

Two sources of tension contributed to the artistic outpouring of fifth-century-B.C.E. Greece. One arose from the conflict between the Greeks' pride in their accomplishments and their concern that overreaching would bring retribution. The second was the conflict between the hopes and achievements of individuals and the claims and limits put on them by their fellow citizens in the polis. These tensions were felt throughout Greece. They had the most spectacular consequences, however, in Athens in its Golden Age, between the Persian and Peloponnesian Wars.

Attic Tragedy   Nothing reflects these concerns better than Attic (Athenian) tragedy, which emerged in the fifth century B.C.E. The tragedies were selected in a contest and presented as part of public religious observations in honor of the god Dionysus. Poets who wished to compete submitted their works to the archon. The three best competitors were each awarded three actors and a chorus. The actors were paid by the state and the chorus was provided by a wealthy citizen. Most of the tragedies were performed in the theater of Dionysus, which accommodated up to 30,000.

Attic tragedy raised vital issues. Until late in the century the tragedies, drawing mostly on mythological subjects, dealt solemnly with religion, politics, ethics, or morality. The plays of the dramatists Aeschylus (525–456 B.C.E.) and Sophocles (ca. 496–406 B.C.E.) follow this pattern. The plays of Euripides (ca. 480–406 B.C.E.) are more concerned with individual psychology.

Old Comedy   Comedy was introduced into the Dionysian festival early in the fifth century B.C.E. The great master of the genre called Old Comedy, Aristophanes (ca. 450–385 B.C.E.), wrote political comedies filled with scathing invective and political satire.

Architecture and Sculpture   Beginning in 448 B.C.E., Pericles undertook a great building program on the Acropolis with funds from the empire. The new buildings visually projected Athenian greatness, emphasizing the city's intellectual and artistic achievements and providing tangible proof that Athens was the intellectual center of Greece.

History   The first prose history ever written was a description of the Persian War by Herodotus (484?–425? B.C.E.), "the father of history." His account attempts to explain human actions and draw instruction from them. Herodotus sometimes treated legends and oracles as sources for history—although not uncritically—and often explained human events in terms of divine intervention. Yet his *History* also stresses the importance of human intelligence in guiding events. Herodotus recognized the significance of institutions. He claimed that the Greek polis inspired voluntary obedience to the law in its citizen soldiers whereas fear of punishment motivated the Persians.

Thucydides, the historian of the Peloponnesian War, was born about 460 B.C.E. and died about 400. He took great pains to achieve factual accuracy and tried to use his evidence to discover meaningful patterns of human behavior. He believed that human nature was essentially unchanging, so that a wise person, equipped with an understanding of history, might foresee events and guide them.

FOURTH CENTURY B.C.E.

The power of the poleis waned after the Great Peloponnesian War. Some Greeks tried to shore up its weakening institutions; others despaired and looked for radical alternatives; and still others turned their back on public life altogether. All these attitudes are reflected in the literature, philosophy, and art of the period.

Drama   The tendency to forsake the public for the private sphere is clear in a new genre that emerged in the fourth century B.C.E.: Middle Comedy. Old Comedy had dealt amusingly with serious subjects, but the themes of Middle Comedy were ordinary daily life, intrigue, and domestic satire. This tendency was magnified in New Comedy, which focused entirely on domestic scenes, the foibles of ordinary people, and the travails of lovers. The art of tragedy declined, but the great works of the previous century were revived, and Euripides, who had explored the psyches of individual characters, found his most appreciative audiences.

EMERGENCE OF THE HELLENISTIC WORLD

*T*he term *Hellenistic* was coined in the 19th century to describe a period of three centuries during which Greek culture spread from its homeland to Egypt and Asia. The result was a new civilization that combined Greek and Asian elements. The Hellenistic world was larger than the world of classical Greece, and its major political units were much larger than the poleis. Hellenistic civilization had its roots in the rise to power of a dynasty in Macedonia whose armies conquered Greece and the Persian Empire.

HOW DID the diffusion of Greek culture affect the cultures of Egypt and Asia?

MACEDONIAN CONQUEST

The kingdom of Macedon, north of Thessaly, had long served as a buffer between the Greek states and barbarian tribes farther to the north. The

OVERVIEW   GREEK CIVILIZATION

Historians divide ancient Greek civilization into periods marked by different forms of social and political organizations and by significant cultural achievements.

Minoan	Based on the island of Crete, ca. 2900–1150 B.C.E., sea-based power, probably ruled by kings. Palace architecture, vivid frescoes.
Mycenaean	Mainland Greece, ca. 1600–1150 B.C.E., city-states ruled by powerful kings assisted by an elaborate bureaucracy. Monumental architecture, gold, and bronzework.
Archaic	Colonization from Greece to Asia Minor, southern Italy, and the coasts of the Black Sea, 700–500 B.C.E.. Characteristic form of government was the polis, a city-state dominated by land-holding aristocrats or ruled tyrants. Lyric poetry, natural philosophy.
Classical	Golden age of Athenian civilization, fifth century B.C.E.. Athens and other poleis became much more democratic. Drama, sculpture in marble and bronze, architecture (the Acropolis), philosophy, history.
Hellenistic	Conquests of Alexander the Great (356–323 B.C.E.) spread Greek culture to Egypt and as far east as the Indus Valley. Decline of the polis. Domination of the Greek world by large monarchical states. Stoic and Epicurean philosophy, realistic sculpture, advances in mathematics and science.

Macedonians were of the same stock as the Greeks and spoke a Greek dialect. Macedon's kings sought to bring Greek culture to their court. By Greek standards, however, Macedon was semi-barbaric. It had no poleis. The king gained his throne through acclamation by the army, and a council of nobles checked his power. Constant internal conflict prevented Macedon from playing much of a part in Greek affairs up to the fourth century B.C.E., but once unified under a strong king, that changed.

Philip of Macedon   That king was Philip II (r. 359–336 B.C.E.). Like many of his predecessors, he admired Greek culture. His natural talents for war and diplomacy and his boundless ambition made him the ablest king in Macedonian history. After he won control of a lucrative gold and silver mining region, he used his resources to turn his army into the finest fighting force in the world.

4.6

The First Philippic: A Great Orator Warns of Macedonian Imperialism

Invasion of Greece   In 340 B.C.E., Philip besieged Perinthus and Byzantium, the lifeline of Athenian commerce. The Athenian fleet saved both cities, so Philip marched into Greece, and in 338 B.C.E., he defeated Athens and Thebes at Chaeronea in Boeotia. Chaeronea marked the end of the era of freedom and autonomy for the Greek polis. Poleis retained their institutions and control over their internal affairs for some time, but new political realities began to chart Greece's future.

ALEXANDER THE GREAT AND HIS SUCCESSORS

In 337 B.C.E., Philip announced his intention to invade Persia, but in the spring of 336 B.C.E., as he prepared to begin the campaign, he was assassinated. Philip's son, Alexander III (356–323 B.C.E.), later called Alexander the Great, succeeded his father at the age of 20, and inherited his plans for the conquest of Persia.

The Conquest of Persia   In 334 B.C.E., Alexander crossed into Asia. His army consisted of about 30,000 infantry and 5,000 cavalry; he had no navy and little money. Consequently, he needed a quick and decisive battle, and the Persianss obliged him. Alexander met them at the Granicus River (see Map 3–3), where he won a smashing victory. Alexander then captured the coastal cities, denying them access to the Persian fleet.

In 333 B.C.E., Alexander marched inland to Syria, meeting the main Persian army under King Darius III (r. 336–330 B.C.E.) at Issus, and sent Darius fleeing to the east. Marching on to Egypt, he was greeted as liberator and proclaimed pharaoh and son of the god Re.

In the spring of 331 B.C.E., Alexander left Egypt and marched east into Mesopotamia. At Gaugamela, near the ancient Assyrian city of Nineveh, he met Darius again. Alexander's tactical genius and personal leadership carried the day. The Persians fled, and Alexander moved on to occupy Babylon and burn Persepolis, the Persian capital.

Darius was murdered by his relative Bessus as he fled east to escape Alexander. Alexander pursued and captured Bessus and then continued east to the frontier of India. His strategy for consolidating the territories he conquered was to encourage an amalgamation of their people. To this end, he married a Bactrian princess, Roxane, and enrolled 30,000 young Bactrians in his army.

In 327 B.C.E., Alexander conquered the lands around the Indus River (modern Pakistan). He hoped to continue east to the river called Ocean that the Greeks believed encircled the world, but his weary men rebelled and refused to go any further. By the spring of 324 B.C.E., the army was back at the Persian Gulf.

MAP 3–3

Alexander's Campaigns. The route taken by Alexander the Great in his conquest of the Persian Empire, 334–323 B.C.E. Starting from the Macedonian capital at Pella, he reached the Indus Valley before being turned back by his own restive troops. He died of fever in Mesopotamia.

GIVEN THE extent of Alexander's conquests, why do you think his empire was divided after his death?

Rise of Macedon

359–336 B.C.E.	Reign of Philip II
338 B.C.E.	Battle of Chaeronea; Philip conquers Greece; founding of League of Corinth
336–323 B.C.E.	Reign of Alexander III, the Great
334 B.C.E.	Alexander invades Asia
333 B.C.E.	Battle of Issus
331 B.C.E.	Battle of Gaugamela
330 B.C.E.	Fall of Persepolis
327 B.C.E.	Alexander reaches Indus Valley
323 B.C.E.	Death of Alexander

Alexander's Death and His Successors   Alexander was filled with plans for the future, but in June 323 B.C.E., he took ill and died in Babylon at the age of 33. He quickly entered myth and legend, and a debate began about his goals, his personality, and his achievements that has continued to the present day.

Alexander had no child at the time of his death, and he made no arrangements for a successor. He left his enormous empire without an obvious heir. After prolonged warfare, three of his generals founded dynasties that continued the spread of Hellenistic culture:

- Ptolemy I, 367?–283 B.C.E.; founder of the 31st Dynasty in Egypt, the Ptolemies, of whom Cleopatra, who died in 30 B.C.E., was the last
- Seleucus I, 358?–280 B.C.E.; founder of the Seleucid dynasty in Mesopotamia
- Antigonus I, 382–301 B.C.E.; founder of the Antigonid dynasty in Asia Minor and Macedon

For the first 75 years or so after the death of Alexander, the world ruled by his successors enjoyed prosperity. The vast sums of money he and they had put into circulation increased economic activity. The opening of vast new territories to Greek trade, the increased demand for Greek products, and the greater availability of things Greeks wanted all helped stimulate commerce. The new prosperity, however, was not evenly distributed. The urban Greeks, the Macedonians, and the Hellenized natives who made up the upper and middle classes lived in comfort and even luxury, but native peasants did not.

Eventually, war and inflation produced economic crises. The kings bore down heavily, but the middle classes skillfully avoided their exactions, and peasants and city laborers reacted by slowing work and striking. In Greece, economic pressures caused clashes between rich and poor and civil wars.

These internal difficulties made the Hellenistic kingdoms vulnerable to attack, and by the middle of the second century B.C.E. Rome had absorbed all of them except for Egypt. The two centuries of Hellenistic rule had, however, promoted economic and cultural cohesion throughout the eastern Mediterranean coast, Greece, Egypt, Mesopotamia, and the old Persian Empire.

HELLENISTIC CULTURE

HOW DID Hellenistic culture differ from that of classical Greece?

Alexander's empire and its successor kingdoms ended the role the autonomous polis had played in Greek affairs, and this marked a turning point in Greek literature, philosophy, religion, and art. The Greek cities lost the kind of political freedom that was basic to the outlook of the Classical period. They became municipalities within military empires. Deprived of political influence, their citizens turned inward and focused on their private hopes and fears. The confident, sometimes arrogant, humanism of the fifth century B.C.E. gave way to a kind of resignation to fate, a recognition of helplessness before forces too great for humans to manage.

PHILOSOPHY

These developments explain the direction philosophy took during the Hellenistic era. Plato's Academy and Aristotle's Lyceum continued to operate, but changed their foci. The Academy drifted toward skepticism, and the Lyceum abandoned scientific work for literary and historical studies Two especially influential new schools appeared: the Epicureans and the Stoics.

Epicureans   Epicurus of Athens (342–271 B.C.E.) claimed that the highest good was happiness, a state achieved by living according to the dictates of reason. Reason, the **Epicureans** believed, indicates that reality is only a construct of atoms continually falling through the void. When combinations of atoms strike our sense organs, they create the things we perceive in the world. When we die, the atoms that compose our bodies disperse so that we have no further existence or perception. There is, therefore, nothing to fear after death. Epicurus also believed that gods took no interest in human affairs.

The purpose of Epicurean physics was to liberate people from the fear of death and the supernatural. Epicurean ethics identified happiness with pleasure, but a pleasure that was chiefly negative: the absence of pain. The goal was *ataraxia*, the condition of being undisturbed, without trouble, pain, or responsibility. To achieve it, one should ideally have sufficient means to withdraw from worldly affairs; Epicurus even advised against marriage and children. He preached a life of restrained selfishness, which might appeal to intellectuals of means but was not widely attractive.

Stoics   The Stoic school, established by Zeno of Citium (335–263 B.C.E.), took its name from the *Stoa Poikile*, or Painted Portico, in the Athenian Agora, where Zeno and his disciples met. The **Stoics** also sought the happiness of the individual, but Stoic philosophy was almost indistinguishable from religion. The Stoics believed that god and nature are the same and that humans must live in harmony within themselves and with nature. The guiding principle in nature is divine reason (*logos*), or fire. Every human has a spark of this divinity, and after death it returns to the eternal divine spirit. From time to time the world is destroyed by fire, from the ashes of which a new world arises.

Happiness, according to the Stoics, lies in living virtuously—that is, living in accordance with natural law. Wisdom is needed to distinguish good from evil and both from things that are "indifferent" (neutral). Good and evil are dispositions of the mind or soul. Prudence, justice, courage, and temperance are good; folly, injustice, and cowardice are evil. Life, health, pleasure, beauty, strength, and wealth are "indifferent" in that they have no innate moral worth. Morally indifferent things, such as these, become sources of misery when they inspire passion, an irrational mental response. The wise seek *apatheia*, or freedom from passion.

The Stoics viewed the world as a single large polis and all people as children of god. Many Stoics were politically active, but they were indifferent to many concerns that often produced political arguments. With their striving for inner harmony and a life lived in accordance with the divine will, their fatalistic attitude, and their pursuit of a form of apathy, the Stoics fit the post-Alexandrian world well. The spread of Stoicism eased the creation of a new political system that relied on the docile submission of the governed.

LITERATURE

The literary center of the Hellenistic world in the third and second centuries B.C.E. was Alexandria, Egypt, where the Ptolemies founded the museum—a great research institute that provided patronage for scientists and scholars and a library that included a comprehensive collection of the literature of the ancient world. Alexandrian scholars collected, copied, edited, and wrote commentaries on a vast

Epicureans School of philosophy founded by Epicurus of Athens (342–271 B.C.E.). It sought to liberate people from fear of death and the supernatural by teaching that the gods took no interest in human affairs and that true happiness consisted in pleasure, which was defined as the absence of pain.

Stoics Philosophical school founded by Zeno of Citium (335–263 B.C.E.) that taught that humans could only be happy with natural law.

logos Divine reason, or fire, which according to the Stoics, was the guiding principle in nature.

One of the masterpieces of Hellenistic sculpture, the _Laocoön_. This is a Roman copy. According to legend, Laocoön was a priest who warned the Trojans not to take the Greeks' wooden horse within their city. This sculpture depicts his punishment. Great serpents sent by the goddess Athena, who was on the side of the Greeks, devoured Laocoön and his sons before the horrified people of Troy.

Direzione Generale Musei Vaticani.

heliocentric theory The theory, now universally accepted, that the Earth and the other planets revolve around the sun. First proposed by Aristarchos of Samos (310–230 B.C.E.).

amount of material. To them we owe the preservation of most of what has survived of ancient literature.

ARCHITECTURE AND SCULPTURE

The Hellenistic monarchies lavishly funded the work of architects and sculptors as well as scholars, and they competed for the services of prominent artists. In general, Hellenistic art continued a drift that began in the fourth century B.C.E. toward the sentimental, emotional, and realistic.

MATHEMATICS AND SCIENCE

Among the most spectacular intellectual accomplishments of the Hellenistic age were those in mathematics and science. Indeed, Alexandrian scholars were responsible for most of the scientific knowledge available to the West until the Scientific Revolution of the 16th and 17th centuries C.E.

Euclid's Elements (written early in the third century B.C.E.) is still the foundation for courses in plane and solid geometry. Archimedes of Syracuse (ca. 287–212 B.C.E.), who also made advances in geometry, established the theory of the lever in mechanics and invented hydrostatics.

As early as the fourth century, Heraclides of Pontus (ca. 390–310 B.C.E.) argued that Mercury and Venus circulate around the sun and not the Earth. He made other suggestions leading in the direction of a **heliocentric theory** of the universe, but it was Aristarchus of Samos (ca. 310–230 B.C.E.) who clearly asserted that the sun, along with the other fixed stars, did not move and that the Earth rotated on its axis while revolving around the sun. The heliocentric theory, however, was not generally accepted. More popular was the geocentric model of the universe proposed by Hipparchus of Nicea (b. ca. 190 B.C.E.). It was complicated, but it did a good job of accounting for the movements of the sun, the moon, and the planets. Ptolemy of Alexandria (second century C.E.) adopted Hipparchus's system with a few improvements, and it remained dominant until the work of Copernicus, in the 16th century C.E.

Hellenistic scientists mapped the Earth as well as the sky. Eratosthenes of Cyrene (ca. 275–195 B.C.E.) accurately calculated the circumference of the Earth and wrote a treatise on geography based on mathematical and physical reasoning and the reports of travelers.

SUMMARY

Early Greece Greek civilization is divided into several periods. In the Minoan and Mycenaean ages, the Greek states were ruled by powerful kings supported by elaborate bureaucracies. Invaders from the north destroyed Mycenaean civilization around 1150 B.C.E. By 750 B.C.E., during the Archaic period, Greek society took its characteristic form: the polis (plural poleis), a self-governing city-state. The most important poleis were Athens and Sparta. At first governed by land-owning aristocrats, then by tyrants, many poleis evolved more democratic forms of government by 500 B.C.E. In an effort to avoid the pressures of overpopulation and land hunger, the Greeks established colonies around the shores of the Mediterranean and Black Seas.

Classical Greece After defeating two Persian attempts to conquer them in the early fifth century B.C.E., the Greeks entered their golden age. The greatest achievements in art, literature, and philosophy of Classical Greece took place in Athens, where the government was the most democratic seen until modern times. Among the accomplishments of Greek artists, writers, and thinkers were naturalistic sculpture, tragedy and comedy, secular history, and systematic logic, all of which still influence Western art and thought.

Hellenistic Greece The polis went into political and cultural decline after Sparta defeated Athens in the Great Peloponnesian War (435–404 B.C.E.). Macedon under Philip II (r. 359–336 B.C.E.) and Alexander the Great (r. 336–323 B.C.E.) came to dominate first Greece and then all the Middle East from Asia Minor to northern India. Alexander's conquest of the Persian Empire spread Greek culture over a wide area and ushered in the Hellenistic Era. Hellenistic Greek culture, which was fostered by the kingdoms that succeeded Alexander's empire, was more accessible to outsiders than that of Classical Greece. Hellenistic scholars made Greek literature and science available to many different peoples who adopted it as their own. The Romans were particularly impressed. They spread Hellenistic culture across the Mediterranean world and transmitted it to later generations in the West.

IMAGE KEY

for pages 56–57

a. A gold jewelry pendant with the shape of bees

b. Fifth century B.C.E. Greek vase

c. Column capital from Temple of Artemis at Ephesus

d. Lyre

e. The "Alexander Sarcophagus" from the Phoenician royal necropolis at Sidon

f. Ancient Greek Athenian Coin

g. Scene on an Attic jar showing how olives were harvested

h. Attic vase, 475 B.C.E.

i. Artemisian statue, 460 B.C.E.

j. The Acropolis

REVIEW QUESTIONS

1. How did the Greek world of the Minoan and Mycenaean period compare with the classical era?

2. What was a polis? How did it influence classical Greek civilization?

3. Why did Sparta develop its unique form of government? How did Athens become a democracy between 600 and 500 B.C.E.?

4. Why did the Greeks and Persians go to war in 490 and 480 B.C.E.? Why were the Greeks able to defeat the Persians? What were the consequences of their victory?

5. Why did Sparta win the Peloponnesian War?

6. How did Alexander's conquests change Greek civilization?

KEY TERMS

Acropolis (p. 61)
agora (p. 61)
Areopagus (p. 67)
Delian League (p. 69)
Epicureans (p. 81)
heliocentric theory (p. 82)

Helots (p. 66)
hoplite phalanx (p. 61)
The *Iliad* and the *Odyssey* (p. 59)
logos (p. 81)
Magna Graecia (p. 62)
Minoan (p. 58)

Mycenaean (p. 59)
Panhellenic (p. 62)
Peloponnesian War (p. 71)
Stoics (p. 81)
symposion (p. 64)

For additional study resources for this chapter, go to:
www.prenhall.com/craig/chapter3

4 Iran, India, and Inner Asia to 200 C.E.

CHAPTER HIGHLIGHTS

Indo-Iranian Empires Between 600 B.C.E. and 200 C.E., imperial governments arose in the Indo-Iranian world whose power and influence surpassed that of any before them. The Achaemenid Empire based in Iran, the Mauryan Empire in India, and the Hellenistic empire of the Seleucids provided the security and wealth that permitted trade and culture to flourish from the Mediterranean to India. The Achaemenid Empire established two centuries of tolerant, stable, prosperous rule from Egypt to the borders of India. The Mauryans created the first Indian empire, while Seleucid rule fostered the spread of Greek culture in Western Asia.

Cross-cultural Contacts In Asia these empires enabled widely influential, lasting religious traditions—Zoroastrianism, Buddhism, Hinduism—to come of age and spread. The empires also fostered an increase of cross-cultural contact, especially in Central Asia where Greek, Iranian, Indian, and steppe-people languages, ideas, arts, customs, and religious practices intermingled. These contacts and influences were manifested in new peoples, structures of government, technological innovations, specialized skills and arts, and ethical and religious ideas.

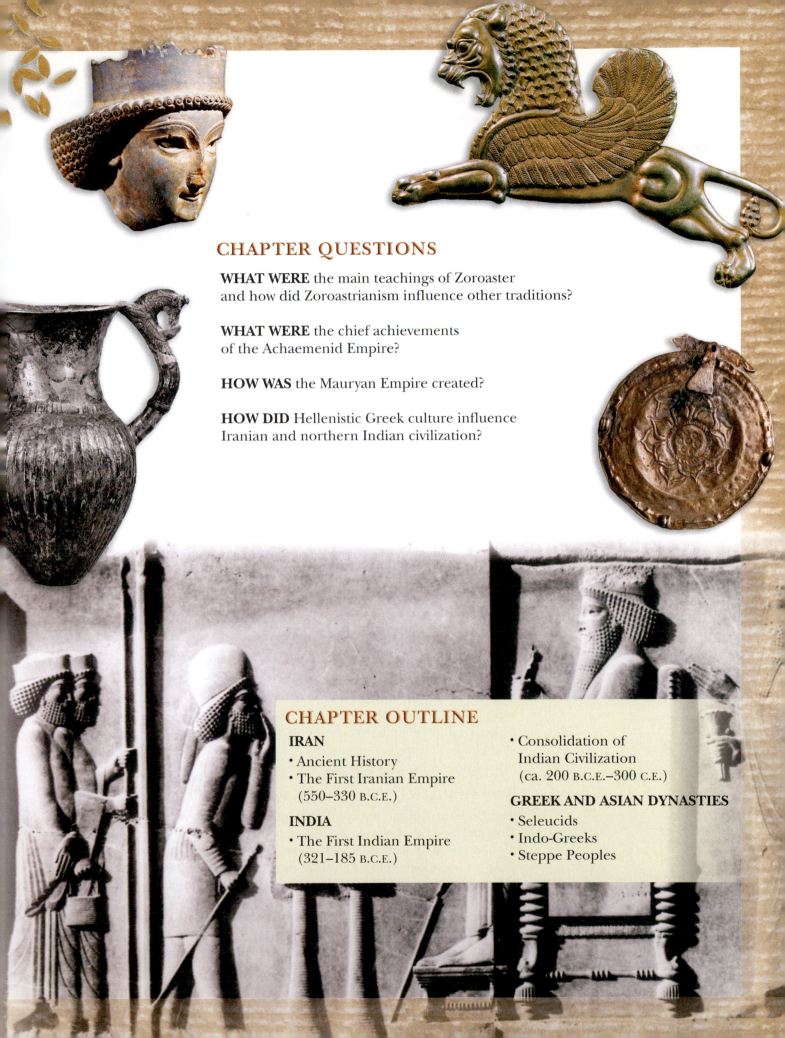

CHAPTER QUESTIONS

WHAT WERE the main teachings of Zoroaster
and how did Zoroastrianism influence other traditions?

WHAT WERE the chief achievements
of the Achaemenid Empire?

HOW WAS the Mauryan Empire created?

HOW DID Hellenistic Greek culture influence
Iranian and northern Indian civilization?

CHAPTER OUTLINE

IRAN
- Ancient History
- The First Iranian Empire
  (550–330 B.C.E.)

INDIA
- The First Indian Empire
  (321–185 B.C.E.)

- Consolidation of
  Indian Civilization
  (ca. 200 B.C.E.–300 C.E.)

GREEK AND ASIAN DYNASTIES
- Seleucids
- Indo-Greeks
- Steppe Peoples

From the Mediterranean to China, the period from about 600 B.C.E. to 200 C.E. saw the rise of centralized empires on an unprecedented scale. Well before the Qin unification (221–207 B.C.E.) or the Han dynasty (202 B.C.E.–9 C.E.) in China, and long before imperium replaced republic in Rome, imperial states flourished in Iran. The Achaemenids (ca. 539–330 B.C.E.), an Aryan dynasty from the mountains of southwestern Iran, created an empire based in Babylonia and Iran that was the greatest yet seen anywhere. Two centuries later the Mauryans, a northeast Indian dynasty centered in the Ganges basin, founded the first great Indian Empire (ca. 321–ca. 185 B.C.E.). Both of these empires, like their later Chinese and Roman counterparts, built sophisticated bureaucracies, professional armies, and strong communication systems. They also contributed to new cultural, political, and religious developments in their domains.

Another characteristic of this period was increased and sustained contact among the major centers of culture from the Mediterranean to China. Alexander the Great's conquest (334–323 B.C.E.) of the Persian Empire and the regions eastward to north India increased the growing contact among diverse cultures, races, and religious traditions.

A third characteristic of this period was the rise, spread, and consolidation of major religious traditions that would affect later history from Africa to China.

IRAN

"Iran" designates the vast expanse of southwest Asia bounded by the Caspian Sea and Jaxartes (Syr Darya) River to the north and northeast, the Indus Valley to the southeast, the Arabian Sea and Gulf to the south, the Tigris-Euphrates to the west, and the Caucasus to the northwest. The heart of this region is the vast Iranian plateau, bounded on all sides by mountains.

The great Asian trade routes put Iran at the heart of east–west interchange. Their location, as well as the locations of the cities and towns that flourished because of them, was determined largely by mountain passes, river fords, and plateau crossings.

ANCIENT HISTORY

WHAT WERE the main teachings of Zoroaster and how did Zoroastrianism influence other traditions?

THE ELAMITES

The Elamites were a non-Semitic people who built a flourishing civilization in the southwestern lowlands on the eastern frontier of Mesopotamia. They were repeatedly at war with the Sumerians, Babylonians, and Assyrians from around 2700 B.C.E. until their destruction by the Assyrian emperor Asshurbanipal in 639. The Elamite language long outlived the Elamite state and was one of the three official languages of the Persian Empire.

THE IRANIANS

The forefathers of the Iranian dynasts were Aryans. The oldest texts in ancient Persian dialects show that Aryan people settled on the Iranian plateau sometime around 1100 B.C.E. Like their Vedic or Indo-Aryan relations in North India, these people were evidently pastoralists—horse-breeders—from the Eurasian or Central Asian steppes. The most prominent of these ancient Iranians were the Medes and the Persians. By the eighth century B.C.E., they had spread around the deserts of the plateau to settle and control its western and southwestern reaches, which were named for them: Media and Persis (later Fars).

The Medes developed a tribal confederacy in western Iran. By 612 B.C.E., they and the Neo-Babylonians had defeated the mighty Assyrians. But by 550 B.C.E., their supremacy on the Iranian plateau had ended. The Achaemenid clan, led by Cyrus the Great, incorporated the region into the sprawling Persian Empire. Many of the institutions of his empire (such as the satrapy system of provincial administration) were based on Median practices, some of which had been drawn from Babylonian and Assyrian models. The Achaemenids' unparalleled success in building and ruling a far-flung empire owed much to the use of existing institutions.

ANCIENT IRANIAN RELIGION

We know more about religious traditions of ancient Iran than about other aspects of its culture because our only pre-Achaemenid texts are religious. These texts suggest that old Iranian culture and religion were similar to those of the Vedic Aryans. The emphasis was on moral order, or the "Right." The supreme heavenly deity was Ahura Mazda, the "Wise Lord."

ZOROASTER AND THE ZOROASTRIAN TRADITION

The first person who stands out in Iranian history was not Cyrus, the founder of the Achaemenid Empire, but the great prophet-reformer of Iranian religion, Zarathushtra, commonly known in the West as Zoroaster. It is clear from his hymns that, like the Hebrew prophets, the Buddha, and Confucius, Zoroaster urged moral reform on an age of materialism, political opportunism, and ethical indifference.

Zoroaster was evidently trained as a priest in the old Iranian tradition, but his hymns reflect a new religious vision. Zoroaster's personal religious experience inspired him to reinterpret the sacrificial fire of the old faith as a symbol of Ahura Mazda. He called on people to abandon worship of and sacrifice to all lesser deities, whom he dismissed as demons, not gods. He urged his people to reform their morality and warned of a "final reckoning," when the good would be rewarded with "future glory" but the wicked with "long-lasting darkness, ill food, and wailing."

By the mid-fourth century B.C.E., the Zoroastrian reform had spread into western as well as eastern Iran. The quasi-monotheistic worship of Ahura Mazda, the Wise Lord, was rapidly accommodated to the veneration of older Iranian gods. The old Iranian priestly clan of the *Magi*, as reforms, may have integrated Zoroastrian ideas and texts into their polytheistic tradition. The name "magi" was later used for the priests of the faith now called "Zoroastrian."

Zoroastrianism probably influenced not only Jewish, Christian, and Muslim ideas of angels, devils, the messiah, the last judgment, and the afterlife, but some important Buddhist concepts as well. Zoroastrianism was wiped out as a major force in Iran by the spread of Islam in the seventh and eighth centuries C.E. However, its tradition continues in the faith and practice of the Parsis, most of whom live in western India.

A Fifth-Century B.C.E. Achaemenid Amphora. This amphora from southwestern Iran has double tube-handles.

Gisela Croon/Bildarchiv Preussischer Kulturbesitz.

Zoroastrianism A quasi-monotheistic Iranian religion founded by Zoroaster (ca. 628–551 B.C.E.) who preached a message of moral reform and exhorted his followers to worship only Ahura Mazda, the Wise Lord.

THE FIRST IRANIAN EMPIRE (550–330 B.C.E.)

THE ACHAEMENIDS

Achaemenid regional power in southwestern Iran (Persis) went back at least to Cyrus I (d. 600 B.C.E.), but the rise of Iran as a major civilization and empire is usually dated from the reign of his famous grandson, Cyrus the Great (559–530 B.C.E.).

WHAT WERE the chief achievements of the Achaemenid Empire?

Iran to the Third Century C.E.

ca. 2000–1000 B.C.E.	Indo-Iranian (Aryan) tribes move south into the Punjab of India and the Iranian plateau
ca. 628–551 B.C.E. (or before 1000 B.C.E.?)	Traditional life of Zoroaster, probably in eastern/northeastern Iran (perhaps originally in Herat?)
559–530 B.C.E.	Reign of Cyrus the Great Persian Achaemenid ruler
539–330 B.C.E.	Achaemenid Empire
331–330 B.C.E.	Alexander (d. 323 B.C.E.) conquers Achaemenid Empire
312–ca. 125 B.C.E.	Seleucid rule in part of Achaemenid realm
ca. 248 B.C.E.–224 C.E.	Parthian Empire of the Arsacids in Iran, Babylonia

The empire founded by Cyrus the Great was anticipated in many ways by the large but loosely controlled empire of his predecessors, the Medes. Cyrus defeated the last Median king about 550 B.C.E. He then subdued northern Assyria, Cilicia, and the kingdom of Lydia, near the Aegean coast of Asia Minor. The Lydian capital, Sardis, became a provincial capital of the growing Persian state. Next, Cyrus defeated the last Babylonian king.

The conquest of Babylon, in 539 B.C.E., symbolically marks the beginning of the Achaemenid Empire, for it joined the Mesopotamian and Iranian spheres for the first time under one rule (see Map 4–1). Cyrus subsequently extended Achaemenid rule in the east where he died fighting steppe tribes. His readiness to utilize local elites and institutions rather than impose new political superstructures was perhaps his most notable legacy.

He and his successors ruled what was really a tribal confederation. They adopted so many Median administrative practices and employed so many Medes in their government that the Achaemenid rulers are referred to in the Bible and other sources as the "Medes and Persians." What the Medes had set in motion, Cyrus and his heirs consolidated and expanded to create an Iranian Empire that was the most extensive the world had ever seen. Among its beneficiaries were the Jews, whose Babylonian exile Cyrus brought to an end (see Chapter 2).

Cyrus's successor, Cambyses (r. 529–522 B.C.E.), added Egypt to the empire, but his brief reign was followed by a succession struggle. The winner, Darius I (521–486 B.C.E.), enjoyed a prosperous reign in which the Achaemenid Empire reached its greatest extent—from Egypt northeast to southern Russia and Sogdiana (Transoxiana) and east to the Indus Valley.

The next five rulers (486–359 B.C.E.) fared less well, and after 478 B.C.E., the Persians found the Greeks pulling ahead of them militarily. They utilized diplomacy to keep the Greeks divided and at bay, but Greek cultural influence steadily grew in Asia Minor. Egyptian rebellions, succession struggles, renewed conflict with Scythian steppe tribes, and poor leadership plagued the empire. The capable and energetic Artaxerxes III (r. 359–338 B.C.E.) might have solved these problems had he not been poisoned in a palace coup just as Philip of Macedon was unifying the Greeks. When Philip's son Alexander succeeded him, the days of Achaemenid rule were numbered.

THE ACHAEMENID STATE

Perhaps the greatest achievement of the Achaemenids was the relative stability of their empire. To justify their sovereignty—and the title of **Shahanshah**, "king of kings"—they claimed that Ahura Mazda had entrusted them with universal sovereignty. The emperor acted as priest and sacrificer in the court rituals; his role as cosmic ruler was symbolized by a special royal fire that burned throughout his reign. The Achaemenids were, however, tolerant of other cultural and religious traditions in ways earlier empires had not been.

The Achaemenids built a powerful army, but much of their success derived from their administrative abilities and willingness to learn and to borrow from

Shahanshah "King of kings," the title of the Persian ruler.

MAP EXPLORATION

Interactive map: To explore this map further, go to **http://www.prenhall.com/craig/map4.1**

MAP 4–1

The Achaemenid Persian Empire.   The empire created by Cyrus reached its fullest extent under Darius when Persia attacked Greece in 490 B.C.E. It extended from India to the Aegean, and even into Europe, encompassing the lands formerly ruled by Egyptians, Hittites, Babylonians, and Assyrians.

WHY WERE the Persians able to govern such a large empire for so long?

predecessors such as the Medes or Babylonians. Most of their leaders worked to maintain what has been termed a *pax Achaemenica*.[1] They preserved continuity as their state evolved from a tribal confederation into a sophisticated monarchy supported by a noble class, professional armies (led by Persian elite troops), provinces ruled by governors called *satraps*, and fixed-yield levies of revenue.

Communication and propaganda systems illustrated the excellence of Achaemenid administration. Couriers linked imperial outposts with the heartlands over a well-kept highway system. Herodotus called the greatest of these highways, which ran from Sardis to Susa, "the King's Road." A network of reporters and royal inspectors kept the court abreast of activities beyond the capital. An efficient chancery served administrative needs. The adoption of the Aramaic language by the bureaucracy helped link east and west, and Achaemenid inscriptions emphasized the provision of universal justice through the rule of law.

The Achaemenid court rotated among a series of palaces and never had a single, fixed capital. Whole states were incorporated intact into the empire as

satraps Governors of provinces in the Persian Empire.

[1]Richard N. Frye, *The Heritage of Persia* (New York: New American Library, 1966), p. 110.

Persepolis The ruins of the famous royal complex at Persepolis, begun ca. 518 B.C.E. The foundation of the treasury is in the foreground; part of the restored women's quarters is visible on the left; and the tall pillars of the main audience hall stand in the rear.

Giraudon/Art Resource, N.Y.

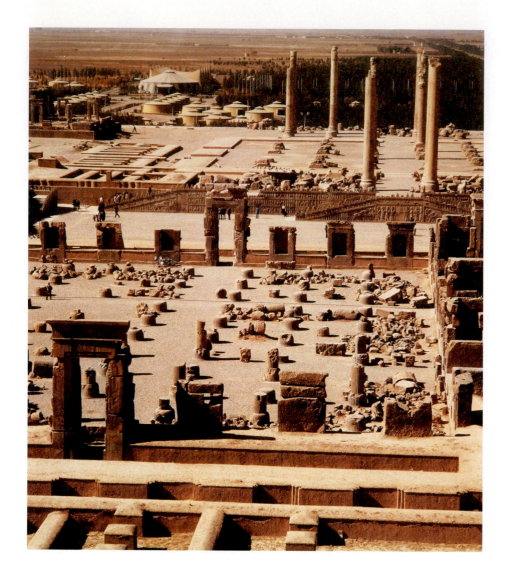

satrapies. This caused little disruption to local customs and encouraged conquered people to accept Achaemenid rule. Some satraps rebelled from time to time, but the centralized power of the "king of kings" succeeded remarkably at governing diverse provinces.

THE ACHAEMENID ECONOMY

The success of the Achaemenid government boosted economic activity from Greece to India. Coinage gradually displaced in-kind payments and stimulated banking operations. The Achaemenids levied taxes on estates, livestock, mines, trade, and production. Wages were regulated and monetary values for goods were published (e.g., the worth of a sheep might be set at three shekels). Agriculture remained the basic industry for most free men. Serfs and slaves provided much of the labor. Where water was scarce, the government created irrigation systems using both subterranean and surface canals.

The quality of life under the *pax Achaemenica* helps to explain why the empire was fairly stable for more than two centuries. Its stability and cosmopolitan culture facilitated the Hellenization of western Asia that flourish in the wake of Alexander's conquests.

IRANIAN AND INDIAN EMPIRES

From 600 B.C.E. to 200 C.E. a series of centralized empires arose on the Iranian plateau and in India. These states built sophisticated bureaucracies, professional armies, and effective communication systems. They also contributed to new cultural, religious, and social developments.

Achaemenid Empire, 539–330 B.C.E.	Founded by Cyrus the Great (r. 559–530 B.C.E.), the empire was based in Iran and ran from Egypt to northern India. It provided a tolerant, stable, and prosperous cosmopolitan environment that paved the way for the eventual Hellenization of western Asia under Alexander the Great and his successors.
Mauryan Empire, 321–185 B.C.E.	The first Indian empire, it stretched from northern India to the Deccan. Its greatest ruler was Ashoka (r. ca. 272–232 B.C.E.), who converted to Buddhism. The Mauryans helped spread Buddhism, developed strong administrative and communications systems that helped give India a sense of unity, established contact with the West, and fostered the growth of cities and the flourishing of art and literature.
Seleucid Empire, 312–125 B.C.E.	A successor state to Alexander's empire. The Seleucids controlled much of the Middle East from the Mediterranean to northern India. By fusing Greek and Persian cultural and political elements, the Seleucids helped to spread Hellenistic culture throughout western Asia.

INDIA

Large-scale imperial expansion came much later to the South Asian, or Indian, subcontinent than to Iran. A cultural and religious heritage going back to the Aryan invaders of North India left its mark on the subsequent history of this vast and diverse subcontinent. However, on only four occasions has a substantial part of the whole come under a single rule: in the Mauryan, Gupta, Mughal, and British imperial epochs.

THE FIRST INDIAN EMPIRE (321–185 B.C.E.)

HOW WAS the Mauryan Empire created?

Alexander the Great conquered the northwest Indian provinces of Gandhara and the Indus Valley in 327 B.C.E., but this had little or no impact on the Indian subcontinent. Only under the Mauryan emperors was much of North India incorporated into the first true Indian empire.

POLITICAL BACKGROUND

The basis for an empire in North India was the rise of regional states between the seventh and the fourth centuries B.C.E., the strongest of which were the monarchies of the Ganges plains. Farther north, tribal republics were more common. King Bimbisara (d. 493 B.C.E.) of Magadha built the first centralized state strong enough to attempt imperial expansion, but his successors fell behind in competition with the Mauryans.

The Lion Capital of Sarnath. This famous Ashokan column capital was taken by India as its state seal after independence in 1947. It reflects both Persian and Greek influences. Originally the capital stood atop a mighty pillar some 50 feet high; the lions supported a huge stone chakra, the Buddhist "Wheel of the *Dharma*," the symbol of universal law.

Bridgeman-Giraudon/Art Resource, N.Y.

THE MAURYANS

The first true Indian empire was established by Chandragupta Maurya (r. ca. 321–297 B.C.E.), an adventurer who made Pataliputra (modern Patna) his capital (see Map 4–2). He pushed westward into the vacuum that was created when Alexander the Great's army returned to Babylon (326 B.C.E.) and brought the Indus region and much of west-central India under his control. A treaty with Seleucus (ca. 358–280 B.C.E.), Alexander's successor in Bactria, added Gandhara and Arachosia to his empire.

Chandragupta's son and successor, Bindusara (r. ca. 297–272 B.C.E.), continued his father's imperial expansion. He moved swiftly to conquer the Deccan, the great plateau that covers central India and divides the far south (Tamilnad) from North India.

Ashoka   The third and greatest Mauryan, Ashoka (r. ca. 272–232 B.C.E.), commissioned numerous rock inscriptions that record information about his reign and character. He conquered Kalinga, the last independent kingdom in North India and the Deccan, and extended Mauryan control over the whole subcontinent except the far south.

The bloodship provoked by the Kalinga war revolted Ashoka and prompted his religious conversion. He devoted himself to the Buddhist "middle path" in both personal and public affairs. He abandoned hunting and meat eating and championed nonviolence. He eschewed aggression in favor of "conquest by righteousness" (*dharma*), winning others to humanitarian values by example. He looked on all his subjects as his "children." His edicts show that he pursued the layman's version of the Buddhist *dharma*, a striving to win heaven by the merit of good actions. He stressed tolerance for all traditions, but sent envoys abroad to spread Buddhist teaching. He appointed "dharma officials" to investigate public welfare problems and foster just government at the local level (see "The Edicts of Ashoka").

Ashoka eased burdens imposed on his people by earlier rulers and instituted beneficial public works. However, by the end of his reign, the empire's size hindered its administration, and under his successors, Mauryan rule fell apart. Ashoka's memory survived, however, to create the model for the ideal king in later Hindu and Buddhist thought. As a symbol of enlightened rule, he has few equals in the history of East or West.

The Mauryan State   Mauryan bureaucracy was marked by centralization, standardization, and efficiency in communications, civil and military organization, tax collection, and information gathering (by a secret service). The fundamental unit of government was the village, with its headman and council. Groups of villages formed districts within the larger provincial unit. The provinces were controlled by governors sent from the capital or by native rulers, like the Achaemenids' satraps (probably the model for the Mauryan imperial system).

The king directly administered the empire with the aid of an advisory council. Revenues came primarily from taxing the produce of the land, which was regarded as the king's property. Urban trade and production were also heavily taxed. Slavery existed, but most slaves did domestic labor.

The Mauryan Legacy   An imperial ideal, a strengthened Buddhist movement, and strong central administration were not the Mauryans' only gifts to Indian culture. They left behind new cosmopolitan traditions of external relations and internal communication that encouraged cultural development and discouraged provincialism. Their many contacts with the West reflect their international perspective, as do the Ashokan edicts, which were executed in various languages and scripts. Writing and reading must have been common by this time, or the edicts would have had no purpose. The Mauryans' excellent road system would later provide routes for Buddhism's spread to Central Asia and China, as well as corridors for successive invaders of the subcontinent.

QUICK REVIEW

The Mauryan State
- Government was centralized, standardized, and efficient
- Fundamental unit of government was the village
- Administration depended on the king

3.6
Ashoka: How a Life Was Turned Around

MAP 4–2

Southwest Asia and India ca. 250 B.C.E.   This map shows not only the major cities and regions of greater Iran and the Indian subcontinent, but also the neighboring eastern Mediterranean world. Although the Mediterranean was closely tied to Iran from Achaemenid times onward, its contacts with India in the wake of the conquests of Alexander the Great were many and varied.

WHICH STATES helped spread Greek culture from the Mediterranean to northern India?

HISTORY'S VOICES

THE EDICTS OF ASHOKA

I n the first of the two following excerpts from Ashokan edicts, the monarch explains his change of heart and conversion to nonviolence after the Kalinga war and states his determination to follow dharma. "The Beloved of the Gods" was the common royal epithet Ashoka used for himself. The second excerpt is from the end of Ashoka's reign and speaks of his efforts to better his and other people's lives by rule according to the dictates of dharma.

WHAT DOES Ashoka suggest is the role of the monarch? What is his concept of "conquest?" What does he think of those of other faiths and what does he want for them? What reforms does Ashoka propose, and why? Can you reconcile his expressed abhorrence of killing with his words to the forest tribes? How do these edicts compare to other approaches to law, leadership, and government? See, for example, "The Code of Hammurabi" (Chapter 1).

FROM THE THIRTEENTH ROCK EDICT

When the king, Beloved of the Gods and of Gracious Mien, had been consecrated eight years Kalinga was conquered, 150,000 people were deported, 100,000 were killed, and many times that number died. But after the conquest of Kalinga, the Beloved of the Gods began to follow Righteousness [*dharma*], to love Righteousness, and to give instruction in Righteousness. Now the Beloved of the Gods regrets the conquest of Kalinga, for when an independent country is conquered people are killed, they die, or are deported, and that the Beloved of the Gods finds very painful and grievous . . . The Beloved of the Gods will forgive as far as he can, and he even conciliates the forest tribes of his dominions; but he warns them that there is power even in the remorse of the Beloved of the Gods, and he tells them to reform, lest they be killed.

For all beings the Beloved of the Gods desires security, self-control, calm of mind, and gentleness. The Beloved of the Gods considers that the greatest victory is the victory of Righteousness; and this he has won here [in India] and even five hundred leagues beyond his frontiers in the realm of the Greek king Antiochus, and beyond Antiochus among the four kings Ptolemy, Antigonus, Magas, and Alexander. Even where the envoys of the Beloved of the Gods have not been sent, men hear of the way in which he follows and teaches Righteousness, and they too follow it and will follow it. Thus he achieves a universal conquest, and conquest always gives a feeling of pleasure; yet it is but a slight pleasure, for the Beloved of the Gods only looks on that which concerns the next life as of great importance . . . .

FROM THE SEVENTH PILLAR EDICT

In the past kings sought to make the people progress in Righteousness, but they did not progress ... And I asked myself how I might uplift them through progress in Righteousness . . . Thus I decided to have them instructed in Righteousness, and to issue ordinances of Righteousness, so that by hearing them the people might conform, advance in the progress of Righteousness, and themselves make great progress . . . For that purpose many officials are employed among the people to instruct them in Righteousness and to explain it to them. . . .

Moreover I have had banyan trees planted on the roads to give shade to man and beast; I have planted mango groves, and I have had ponds dug and shelters erected along the roads at every eight kos. Everywhere I have had wells dug for the benefit of man and beast. But this benefit is but small, for in many ways the kings of olden time have worked for the welfare of the world; but what I have done has been done that men may conform to Righteousness . . . .

I have enforced the law against killing certain animals and many others, but the greatest progress of Righteousness among men comes from exhortation in favor of noninjury to life and abstention from killing living beings.

I have done this that it may endure as long as the moon and sun, and that my sons and my great-grandsons may support it; for by supporting it they will gain both this world and the next.

From *Sources of Indian Tradition* by William Theodore de Bary. Copyright © 1988 by Columbia University Press. Reprinted with permission of the publisher.

This era also saw the flourishing of cities across the empire. They were centers for arts, crafts, industry, literature, and education. The stone buildings and sculpture of the Ashokan period reflect sophisticated aesthetics and technique, as well as strong Persian and Greek influence.

CONSOLIDATION OF INDIAN CIVILIZATION (CA. 200 B.C.E.–300 C.E.)

*I*n the post-Mauryan period, North India was dominated by the influx of various foreign peoples. In the rest of the subcontinent, indigenous Indian dynasties held sway. Autonomous regional and local governments continued unbroken until the rise of the empire built by the Guptas (320 C.E.–ca. 550; see Chapter 10). However, the centuries between the Mauryans and Guptas saw religious and cultural consolidation of transregional patterns and styles that helped to shape Indian and, through the diffusion of Buddhism, Asian civilization ever after.

THE ECONOMIC BASE

Although agriculture remained the basis of the economy, commerce flourished amid the post-Mauryan political fragmentation. The fine Mauryan road system facilitated trade throughout India(see Map 4–3). Chinese and Roman demand for Indian luxury goods made India a magnet for world trade, and wealth flowed in. Guild organizations provided technical education in crafts, and kings as well as merchants invested in guilds. Coin minting increased after Mauryan times, and banking flourished.[2]

HIGH CULTURE

During this era, the major achievements in the arts were inspired by Buddhism. Northwestern India saw the rise of the Gandharan school of Buddhist art. It joined Hellenistic naturalism with the more recent Indian tradition of Buddha images, and it created relief and freestanding sculptural figures with flowing, draped garments through which the muscular lines of the human body are discerned. In central India as early as the first century B.C.E., artists were producing stone-relief sculpture with the naturalistic, yet flowing, plastic human and animal forms that would become earmarks of the "classical" style of Indian art.

Language and literature during this period employed the sophisticated Sanskrit grammar of Panini (ca. 300 B.C.E.?). Two masterpieces of Sanskrit culture, the epics of the *Mahabharata* and the *Ramayana*, probably took general shape by 200 C.E. The first is a composite work concerned largely with the nature of dharma (see Chapter 2). Included in its earlier, narrative portions is the Bhagavad Gita, or "Song of the Blessed Lord," the most influential of all Indian religious texts.

HOW WAS the period between 200 B.C.E. and 300 C.E. formative in the development of Indian civilization?

India from the Sixth Century B.C.E. to the End of Mauryan Rule

ca. 600–400 B.C.E.	Late Upanishadic age: local/regional kingdoms and tribal republics along the Ganges and in Himalayan foothills, the Punjab, and northwestern India
ca. 540–ca. 468 B.C.E.	Vardhamana Mahavira, Jain founder
ca. 537–ca. 486 B.C.E.	Siddhartha Gautama, the Buddha
ca. 550–324 B.C.E.	Regional empire of Maghadan kings
330–325 B.C.E.	Alexander campaigns in Indus Valley, Soghdiana, Bactria, and Punjab
324–ca. 185 B.C.E.	Mauryan Empire controls most of northern India and the Deccan
ca. 272–232 B.C.E.	Reign of the Mauryan emperor Ashoka

[2]Romila Thapar, *A History of India*, vol. I (Harmondsworth, U.K.: Penguin Books, 1966), pp. 105–118.

MAP 4–3
Eurasian Trade Routes ca. 100 C.E.   An extensive network of overland and sea routes connected Eurasia from the Mediterranean to China.

HOW CENTRAL were Iran, India, and Inner Asia in the Eurasian trade networks of the ancient world?

RELIGION AND SOCIETY

The post-Mauryan period saw Buddhist monasticism and lay devotionalism thrive across the subcontinent. However, the Brahmans continued to dominate Vedic learning and ritual. Toward the end of this age, Buddhism in its Mahayana form began to spread from India to Central Asia and eventually to China and Japan.

Hindu Tradition   What is now called Hinduism emerged at this time. The major developments shaping Hindu tradition were: (1) the consolidation of the caste system, Brahman ascendancy, and the "high" culture of Sanskrit learning; (2) the increasing dominance of theistic devotionalism (especially the cults of Vishnu and Shiva); and (3) the intellectual reconciliation of these developments with older ascetic and speculative traditions deriving from the Upanishadic age.

Buddhist Tradition   Indian Buddhist monastic communities prospered under mercantile and royal patronage. Buddhist lay devotion figured prominently in Indian religious life, especially in the Ganges basin. The Buddha and

Buddhist saints were naturally identified with popular Indian deities, and popular Buddhist practice was indistinguishable from countless other devotional cults that began to dominate the Indian scene. One reason why Buddhist tradition remained only one among many Indian religious options was Buddhism's absorption into the religious variety that then and now typifies the Hindu religious scene.

GREEK AND ASIAN DYNASTIES

SELEUCIDS

Alexander's successors in the Achaemenid lands were the Greek general Seleucus and his heirs. They ruled most of the former Achaemenid realm from about 312 to 246 B.C.E. and lesser portions until about 125 B.C.E. Alexander's policies of Greco-Persian fusion helped make the Seleucid rule of many eastern areas viable. The new "cities" that Alexander founded provided bases for Seleucid control. As a foreign minority, the Seleucids relied on mercenary troops to hold their domain, but it was the leaders of these troops and of the Seleucid satrapies who gradually whittled away at Seleucid rule. Neither Seleucus (r. 311–281 B.C.E.; see Chapter 3) nor the strongest of his successors, Antiochus the Great (r. 223–187 B.C.E.), ever secured lasting dominion on the scale of the Achaemenids.

Alexander's strategy of joining Hellenes with Iranians in political power, marriage, and culture bore fruit more lasting than the empire. During the second century B.C.E., Hellenistic culture and law spread new ideals among the Seleucid elites, and the Seleucids welcomed into the ruling classes those non-Hellenes who were willing to be Hellenized.

Zoroastrian religious tradition declined with the loss of its imperial-cult status. The many syncretic cults of the Mediterranean Hellenistic world made inroads even in the East in Seleucid and Parthian times. Mystery and savior cults were becoming more popular. The new Hellenistic urban centers may have provided an environment in which the individual was less rooted in established traditions of culture and religious life. This would have enhanced the attractiveness of the focus on individual salvation common to many lesser Hellenistic cults and to emerging traditions such as the Christian, Mahayana Buddhist, Manichaean, and Hindu devotionalist that came to dominate Eurasia.

INDO-GREEKS

The farthest reach of Hellenization in the East came not under the Seleucids but with the **Indo-Greeks** of Bactria. About 246 B.C.E., Bactria's Greek satrap broke away from the Seleucids. His successor, Euthydemus (r. ca. 235–ca. 200 B.C.E.),

Indo-Greek, Iranian, Indian, and Steppe Dynasties After Alexander

312–ca. 125 B.C.E.	Seleucid rule in part of the old Achaemenid realm
ca. 247 B.C.E.–224 C.E.	Parthian Empire of the Arsacids in Iran, Babylonia
246–ca. 50 B.C.E.	Indo-Greek ("Graeco-Bactrian," "Euthydemid") rulers of region from modern Afghanistan to Oxus
ca. 171–138 B.C.E.	Reign of Arsacid king Mithradates I
ca. 130 B.C.E.–ca. 100 C.E.	Movements west and south of Yüeh Chih (including Kushans) and Sythians (Sakas) into Sogdiana, then Bactria, then northwestern India
ca. c.e. 50–ca. 250	Height of Kushan power in Oxus to Ganges region
ca. 100–150 C.E.	Accession of King Kanishka to Kushan throne in Taxila (ruled about 28 years)

3.7
"King Milinda": The Greek Worlds Incursion into India

HOW DID Hellenistic Greek culture influence Iranian and northern Indian civilizations?

Indo-Greeks Bactrian rulers who broke away from the Seleucid Empire to found a state that combined elements of Greek and Indian civilizations.

steppe peoples Nomadic tribespeople who dwelled on the Eurasian plains from eastern Europe to the borders of China and Iran. They frequently traded with or invaded more settled cultures.

WHAT IMPACT did nomadic steppe peoples have on Eurasian history in antiquity?

The Great Stupa at Sanchi is an outstanding example of early Buddhist relic mounds. The mound, seated on an Ashokan foundation, was added to over the centuries. Magnificent carvings adorn its stone railings and gateways, one of which is shown in the left foreground. Sanchi is located in north-central India.

Dale Williams.

extended his sway north and southwest. His son Demetrius exploited the growing Mauryan weakness to conquer Arachosia. Demetrius and his successor, Menander, made Taxila their capital. Most of the Indo-Greeks were Indian in language, culture, and religion, as their coins and inscriptions show.

Before their demise at the hands of invading steppe peoples (ca. 130–100 B.C.E.), these Indo-Greeks left their mark on civilization in all the areas around their Bactrian center. Bactria was a major source of the later Greco-Buddhist art of Gandhara, one of history's remarkable examples of cross-cultural influence. The Indo-Greeks also probably helped spread Buddhism from India to Central Asia.

STEPPE PEOPLES

The history of North India and the Iranian plateau was dominated from about 250 B.C.E. to 300 C.E. by incursions of Iranian tribal peoples originally from the Central Asian steppes. Although commonly ignored, the nomadic **steppe peoples** have been a major force in Eurasian history.

PARTHIANS

The Parni, said to be related to the Scythians, were probably the major group of Iranian steppe peoples who first settled the area south of the Aral

Sea and Oxus. In late Achaemenid times, they moved south into Parthia. Thenceforward we can call them Parthians. The independent control of Parthia by the dynastic family of the Arsacids dates from about 247 B.C.E. For decades they were only a regional power, but under Mithradates I (ca. 171–138 B.C.E.) they became a new Eurasian imperial force and the true successors to the Achaemenids.

The Parthian Empire stretched across the Iranian plateau from Mesopotamia to Arachosia. Its center was Ctesiphon, on the Tigris. From the time of their victory over the Romans at Carrhae in 53 B.C.E. (see Chapter 6) until their fall in 233 C.E., the Parthians were the major Eurasian power alongside Rome. Eventually, wars with Rome and the pressure of the Kushan Empire in the east weakened them sufficiently for a new Persian dynasty to replace them.

Parthian Warrior. The Parthians were superb fighters and were particularly noted for the "Parthian shot," firing arrows backward while mounted on a galloping horse. It is not difficult to imagine the fear that must have gripped sedentary peoples at the sight of such swift and mobile cavalrymen.

Werner Forman Archive.

Culturally, the Parthians were oriented toward the Hellenistic world of their Seleucid predecessors until the mid-first century C.E., when they experienced a kind of Iranian revival. Similarly, the magi preserved the worship of Ahura Mazda despite the success of other eastern and western cults and the tendency to assimilate Greek and Iranian gods. The Parthians, however, tolerated religious plurality.

SAKAS AND KUSHANS

The successors of the Indo-Greeks were steppe peoples who played a major political and cultural role in Asia for several centuries. They reflect the cosmopolitan nature of Central Asia, eastern Iran, and northwestern India at this time.

Beginning about 130 B.C.E., Scythian (Saka) tribes from beyond the Jaxartes (Syr Darya) overran northeastern Iran, conquering Sogdiana's Hellenic cities and then Bactria. One group of Sakas extended their domain into North India. Another went southwest into Herat and Sistan. In northwestern India the Sakas were, in turn, defeated by invading Iranians known as the Pahlavas.[3]

The Sakas had been displaced earlier in Sogdiana by another steppe people, known from Chinese sources as the Yüeh Chih. These peoples, led by the Kushan tribe, drove the Sakas out of Bactria in the mid-first century B.C.E. About a hundred years later, they swept over the mountains into northwestern India. Here they ended Pahlava rule and founded a long-lived Indian Kushan dynasty.

The Kushan kingdom of India was—along with Rome, China, and the weakened Parthian Empire of Iran—one of four major centers of civilization in Eurasia around 100 C.E. Its greatest ruler, Kanishka, reigned either around 100 or possibly 150 C.E. He was the greatest patron of Buddhism since Ashoka.

QUICK REVIEW

The Parthians
- Settled area south of the Aral Sea and Oxus
- Control of Parthia by Arsacids dates from 247 B.C.E.
- Empire stretched across the Iranian plateau from Mesopotamia to Arachosia

---

[3]Tradition gives one of their rulers, Gondophares, the role of host to Saint Thomas, who is said to have brought Christianity to India. But because Gondophares probably ruled in the early to mid-first century C.E., it may be a confused report. Even if traditions of Thomas's mission to India are correct, some connect him instead with southern India.

At its height in the first to third centuries C.E., Kushan power in Central Asia facilitated the missionary activity that carried Buddhism across the steppes into China. A lasting Kushan contribution was the school of Greco-Buddhist art fostered in Gandhara by Kanishka and his successors and supported by a later Kushan dynasty for another 500 years.

SUMMARY

IMAGE KEY
for pages 84–85

a. Barley seeds (Mai Ya)

b. Achaemenid Goldwork Winged Lion

c. Archaemenid Gold Chariot 5th-4th Century B.C.E., Persia Antiques

d. Wheat stalks

e. Gandharan gold pendant depicting Hariti

f. Coin of a Parthian monarch

g. Head of Achaemenid Prince

h. Gold winged lion set in a circle

i. The Lion Capital of Sarnath

j. Persepolis treasury relief of Darius I receiving tributes

k. A fifth-century B.C.E. Achaemenid amphora

Indo-Iranian Empires Between 600 B.C.E. and 200 C.E. imperial governments arose in the Indo-Iranian world whose power and influence surpassed that of any before them. The Achaemenid Empire based in Iran, the Mauryan Empire in India, and the Hellenistic Empire of the Seleucids provided the security and wealth that permitted trade and culture to flourish from the Mediterranean to India. The Achaemenid Empire established two centuries of tolerant, stable, prosperous rule from Egypt to the borders of India. The Mauryans created the first Indian empire, while Seleucid rule fostered the spread of Greek culture in Western Asia.

Cross-cultural Contacts In Asia these empires enabled widely influential, lasting religious traditions—Zoroastrianism, Buddhism, Hinduism—to come of age and spread. These empires also fostered an increase of cross-cultural contact, especially in Central Asia where Greek, Iranian, Indian, and steppe-people languages, ideas, arts, customs, and religious practices intermingled. These contacts and influences were manifested in new peoples, structures of government, technological innovations, specialized skills and arts, and ethical and religious ideas.

REVIEW QUESTIONS

1. What key factors contributed to the long survival of the Achaemenid Empire?

2. How did Ashoka develop Mauryan power and prestige?

3. How do Buddhism and Hinduism compare?

4. What roles did the Kushans, Sakas, and other inner-Asian groups play in world history?

KEY TERMS

Indo-Greeks (p. 97)   **Shahanshah** (p. 88)   **Zoroastrianism** (p. 87)
satraps (p. 89)   **steppe peoples** (p. 98)

For additional study resources for this chapter, go to:
www.prenhall.com/craig/chapter4

Visualizing The Past

Goddesses and the Female Form in Ancient Art

ANCIENT ARTISTS created images of women as often as men in their art, but there were key differences in how they depicted the female versus the male form. What were these differences, why did they come about, and what did they signify?

Artists celebrated male gods and human men alike for their roles in society as priests, warriors, or commoners. By contrast, from ancient times to the present, sexuality has been central to artistic conceptualizations of women and the female role in the divine and human realms. In most societies, earthly women and goddesses alike were usually drawn or sculpted nude, at least from the waist down, and, given the link between female sexuality and fertility, with breasts and hips prominent or even exaggerated. Goddesses in the ancient world tended to have a dual nature, of death and regeneration, and to be linked to symbols of earth, love, death, and war, and often also to mastery of snakes, a prominent symbol in many cultures of male fertility. Biology thus tended to be the primary factor in how artists conceived of women's role in ancient societies and how they depicted the female form in art.

Innana-Ishtar, ca. 2025–1763 B.C.E., ▶ Babylonian goddess of love and death.
Inanna-Ishtar has a lovely feminine form but taloned feet, denoting her dual nature. She stands upon her symbol, the lion; holds a rod and a ring, symbols of kingship; and is surrounded by two owls, symbols of her mastery over death.

"Snake Goddess," Minoan, c. 1650 B.C.E.

Strong cultural and economic ties linked Mediterranean and Near Eastern cultures, as can be seen in the similarities between this small statuette of a Minoan goddess and the preceding image of Innana-Ishtar. As was typical in Minoan and Greek art, this goddess is nude only to the waist. Like Innana-Ishtar, however, her arms are raised and she holds symbols of power, in this case snakes rather than a rod (although both are symbols of male sexual power).

Photograph ©Erich Lessing/Art Resource.

Fertility Goddess, India, Third Century B.C.E.

Even before Alexander the Great reached India in 327 B.C.E., trade brought Greek objects and artistic influences to India, where Indian artists assimilated them into Indian aesthetics and religion. This life-sized statue of a fertility goddess resembles Hellenistic statues such as the Venus de Milo (c. 150 B.C.E.) in that she is a free-standing figure and nude to the waist. Her prominent breasts, like those of the Minoan "Snake Goddess," symbolize female fertility. Hindu culture and religion have traditionally celebrated female beauty and sexual power more than most other world religions.

Dirk Bakker.

Coatlicue, Aztec mother goddess.

Although hailing from the New World, and depicted in a radically different artistic tradition, Coatlicue, the "goddess of the serpent skirt," shares with goddesses of the Old World an emphasis on mastery of male sexual power (her serpent skirt), fertility and motherhood (she was the mother of the powerful Aztec god Huitzilopochtli), and death (she craved human sacrifices).

Mexican National Tourist Council.

5 Africa
Early History to 1000 C.E.

CHAPTER HIGHLIGHTS

Geography and History The human species, *homo sapiens* (*sapiens*) probably originated in Africa. Africa's geography and climate, however, limited Africans' contact with peoples outside the continent. Nonetheless, Africa cannot be considered a dark continent without a history. Within Africa itself, archaeology reveals that there were extensive migrations of peoples across the continent from the earliest days of African history with widespread crosscultural influences.

Contact with Other Cultures In three parts of Africa, there was considerable contact with non-African civilizations. In the Nile River Valley, Egypt had extensive interaction with the Nubian peoples to its south. Nubian kingdoms— Kush, Napata, Meroe, and Axum (Ethiopia)— adopted many features of Egyptian civilization and sometimes dominated Egypt itself. Axum adopted Christianity in the fourth century C.E.

On the coast of East Africa, trade across the Red Sea and the Indian Ocean with Arabia and east Asia fostered a distinct and sophisticated culture. Extensive trade across the Sahara between North Africa and the western and central Sudan enabled products and ideas from the Mediterranean to reach the African interior in exchange for African products, such as gold, ivory, and salt.

CHAPTER QUESTIONS

ON WHAT continent did the modern human species (*homo sapiens*) originate?

WHAT EVIDENCE is there that early African cultures were in contact with each other?

HOW DID Egypt influence the various Nilotic civilizations, such as Kush, Meroe, and Axum?

WHAT ROLE did trade play in the rise of large political entities in the western and central Sudan?

WHY DID the coastal and inland regions of East Africa have different histories?

CHAPTER OUTLINE

- Problems of Interpretation and Sources
- Physical Description of the Continent
- African Peoples
- The Sahara and the Sudan to the Beginning of the Common Era
- Nilotic Africa and the Ethiopian Highlands
- Roman Imperialism
- The Western and Central Sudan
- Central, Southern, and East Africa

Africa, the world's second largest continent, forms the southern frontier of the Mediterranean world and connects to Asia through the Arabian peninsula and the Indian Ocean. Evidence suggests that the first humans emerged from eastern Africa, and the continent's subsequent history is one of ongoing interaction, both internally and with the rest of the world.

PROBLEMS OF INTERPRETATION AND SOURCES

THE QUESTION OF CIVILIZATION

The narrow definition of "civilization" emphasizes social complexity (e.g., cities) and technological developments (e.g., writing, metallurgy), but people may lack these and have a level of intellectual, cultural, and artistic sophistication that merits identifying them as civilized. Until recently, outside the Nile valley and the Ethiopian highlands, most African societies may not have been civilizations in the narrow sense, but they were hardly uncivilized in the broader sense of the term.

THE SOURCE PROBLEM

Stateless societies, such as those that characterized much of sub-Saharan Africa, leave few historical records. Surviving oral traditions and scattered reports by outside observers provide some insight into recent centuries, but there is much that is unknown. Archaeologists have recovered evidence of large, advanced societies whose existence had been forgotten. But the tropical climate of sub-Saharan Africa has destroyed many artifacts, and few traces remain of the continent's smaller communities. Beginning about 950 C.E., descriptions of Africa by outsiders become available, but these are often distorted by preconceptions and biases.

ON WHAT continent did the modern human species (*homo sapiens*) originate?

savannah An area of open woodlands and grassy plains.

Sahel An area of steppe and semi-desert that borders the Sahara.

Sahara The world's largest desert. It extends across Africa from the Atlantic to the eastern Sudan. Historically, the Sahara has hindered contact between the Mediterranean and sub-Saharan Africa.

Kalahari A large desert in southwestern Africa that partially isolates southern Africa from the rest of the continent.

PHYSICAL DESCRIPTION OF THE CONTINENT

Africa makes up over one-fifth of the Earth's landmass. It is geologically massive, with unusually high relief over virtually its entire expanse. The result is a dearth of natural harbors and islands and generally steep escarpments surmounting narrow coasts. This has made access to, as well as egress from, its interior difficult. All of Africa's major rivers (the Niger, Kongo [Zaïre], Nile, Zambezi, and Orange) lie largely in plateau basins and are navigable in their inland reaches. They are not, however, navigable across the cataracts they traverse before they reach the coastlands. (Only the Nile has a relatively long navigable stretch below its cataracts in upper Egypt.) The vast size and sharp physical variations—from high mountains to swamp lands, tropical forests, and deserts—have also made rapid long-distance communication and movement difficult.

The special character of various regions is due in considerable part to Africa's position astride the equator. As a whole, its climate is hot. North and south of the equator, dense rain forests dominate a west-east band of tropical woodland territory. North and south of this band, the lush rain forests give way to the **savannah**—open woodlands and grassy plains. This, in turn, passes into steppe and semidesert (the **Sahel**) and finally into true desert. Africa contains two of the world's greatest and driest deserts. The **Sahara** is the world's largest desert and historically has hindered contact between the Mediterranean world and sub-Saharan Africa. The **Kalahari** in southwestern Africa partially cuts off the southern plateau and coastal regions from central Africa.

Other natural factors are of importance to Africa's history. Its soils contain meager amounts of humus, or vegetable mold. Because they are easily leached of mineral and nutrient content, they are not highly productive for extended periods. Water shortage is another perennial problem for agriculture in most of Africa and a potent factor in its history. Crop pests and insects have also hampered both farming and pastoralism in Africa; the tsetse fly has blocked the spread of domesticated cattle and horses to the forested portions of the continent. However, in most regions Africa's abundant animal life has always been a major resource sustaining hunting and fishing.

Africa has great mineral wealth, and this has long stimulated trade. The market for salt, for example, was motivating merchants to cross the Sahara, linking the western Sudan with North Africa, as early as the first millennium C.E. Iron, copper, and gold were also traded in significant quantities.

The African continent contains seven distinct regions:

1. *North Africa*—the Mediterranean coastal regions from modern Morocco through modern Libya and the northern Sahara, including the Sahel that marks the transition from mountains to true desert.

2. **Nilotic Africa** (i.e., the lands of the Nile), roughly the area of modern Egypt and Sudan.

3. *The Sudan*, the broad belt of Sahel and savannah below the Sahara, stretching from the Atlantic east across the entire continent.

4. *West Africa*, including the woodland coastal regions and the desert, Sahel, and savannah of the western Sudan as far east as the Lake Chad basin.

5. *East Africa*, from the Ethiopian highlands south over modern Kenya and Tanzania.

6. *Central Africa*, the region north of the Kalahari, from the Chad basin across the Zaïre basin and southeast to Lake Tanganyika and south to the Zambezi River.

7. *Southern Africa*, from the Kalahari desert and Zambezi south to the Cape of Good Hope.

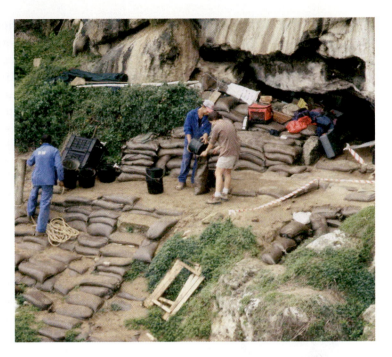

Excavation in Progress at Blombos Cave, South Africa. The recent discovery of bone tools, decorated ochre blocks, and polished spear points that have been dated to about 70,000 years ago indicate that earliest evidence of tools and artwork come from Africa.

National Science Foundation.

Nilotic Africa The lands along the Nile River.

WHAT EVIDENCE is there that early African cultures were in contact with each other?

AFRICAN PEOPLES

AFRICA AND EARLY HUMAN CULTURE

Archaeological research indicates that our ancestors evolved in the Great Rift region of highland East Africa at least 1.5 to 1.8 million years ago. It was probably also here that, sometime before 100,000 B.C.E., modern humans—the species *homo sapiens* (*sapiens*)—appeared and moved out to populate the rest of Africa and the world.

"Lucy." One of the most famous fossils found in the north end of the Great Rift Valley, an area rich in fossils of species ancestral to humans, Lucy represents one of the earliest species to walk upright.

Cleveland Museum of Natural History.

HOW DID the Sahara impact the early history of Africa?

The once popular view of sub-Saharan Africa as a vast region isolated from civilization until its "discovery" by Europeans distorts reality. Although its interior and southern reaches were isolated from direct contact with Eurasia until relatively recent times, African goods circulated for centuries through Indian Ocean and Mediterranean trade. Archaeological research documents the existence and substantial internal movements of peoples—and hence languages, cultures, and technologies—both north-south and east-west within the continent in ancient times.

DIFFUSION OF LANGUAGES AND PEOPLES

Despite continental barriers, Africans have not been separated from one another. As many as 3,000 languages or dialects are spoken in Africa. The precolonial tongues belong to four major families: Afro-Asiatic, Nilo-Saharan, Niger-Kongo, and "Khoisan." The first originated near the Red Sea and includes Arabic, Hebrew, Aramaic, Syriac, ancient Egyptian, and other tongues spoken in north and northeastern Africa. The second is found from the upper reaches of the Nile across the Sahara to Moroccan highlands. The third lie in a belt west and south of this region, and the fourth is found today in southern Africa. The Afro-Asiatic tongues probably began to spread from the Jordan and Nile valleys across North Africa about 8000 B.C.E. The Nilo-Saharan languages may have originated in the Nubian region and spread west about 5000 B.C.E. The Niger-Kongo family appeared in the forested districts of west and central Africa. Its largest subgroup, the Bantu speakers, spread southward through equatorial and rain forests to the savannahs. Khoisan at one time covered most of the southern half of the continent, but yielded much of its territory to the Bantu language.

RACIAL DISTINCTIONS

In recent times lighter-skinned Caucasoid Africans have predominated in the Sahara, North Africa, and Egypt and darker-skinned Negroid peoples have been the majority in the rest of the continent. The Greeks called Negroid people *Ethiopians,* "burnt skins," and the Arabs referred to sub-Saharan Africa as *Bilad al-Sudan,* "Land of the Blacks." Attempts have been made to link race with cultural and historical developments, but race itself is a problematic concept, and African populations are so mixed that most Africans are best seen as members of one race or none—regardless of color or physical attributes.

THE SAHARA AND THE SUDAN TO THE BEGINNING OF THE COMMON ERA

EARLY SAHARAN CULTURES

One of the most striking and imposing physical features of the African continent is the Sahara. Since the second millennium B.C.E., this vast arid wilderness has separated the North African and Egyptian worlds from the wide expanse of the Sudan and, farther south, West and central Africa. Still, this desert barrier never fully blocked north-south contact and exchange. The Nile valley and the Great Rift plateau provided one corridor for movement of ideas and peoples south to north and vice versa. Similarly, the Red Sea, the Atlantic and Indian Ocean coasts, and a few routes through the Sahara itself allowed people, goods, and ideas to breach the great Saharan barrier as far back as our evidence takes us.

What is hard to imagine, however, is that until about 2500 B.C.E. the Sahara was arable land with lakes and rivers, trees, grasses, and a reasonable climate.

Then climatic changes caused the Sahara to undergo a relatively rapid desiccation. By 1000 B.C.E., the drying-up process had made the Sahara an immense east-west expanse of largely uninhabitable desert, separating the greater part of the African continent from the Mediterranean coastal rim and the Middle Eastern centers of early civilization.

NEOLITHIC SUDANIC CULTURES

Most interesting to speculate about are the repercussions of the Saharan desiccation for later settled communities, especially those in the Sahel and savannah of the Sudan. From the first millennium B.C.E., preliterate, but complex agricultural communities with Neolithic and early Iron Age cultures dotted the central and western reaches of the great belt of the sub-Saharan Sudan. We may surmise that these peoples had once been spread farther north in the then-arable Saharan lands that they would then have shared with ancestors of the Berber-speaking peoples of contemporary west-Saharan and North Africa.

OVERVIEW   THE GEOGRAPHY OF AFRICA

Geography has played a large role in the history and culture of Africa, limiting its contacts with non-African peoples and influencing patterns of trade and settlement. Africa is divided into a number of geographical zones and cultural regions.

North Africa	The region along the Mediterranean coast, extending from Morocco in the west to Egypt in the east. This area has long had extensive contacts with Europe and the Near East and has been dominated by Islam since the seventh century C.E.
Sahara	The world's largest desert. It extends across Africa from the Atlantic to the eastern Sudan. Historically, the Sahara has hindered contact between the Mediterranean and sub-Saharan Africa.
Sahel	An area of steppe and semidesert that borders the Sahara.
Savannah	Areas of open woodlands and grassy plains that border the Sahel.
Rain forests	Large areas of dense vegetation along the equator and much of the West African coast.
Kalahari	A large desert in southwestern Africa that partially isolates southern Africa from the rest of the continent.
Nilotic Africa	The lands along the Nile River Valley. It extends from the Mediterranean coast of Egypt south to include the modern Republic of Sudan and Ethiopia. Historically, it has been one of the African regions most open to outside cultural, religious, and economic influences.
Sudan	The broad belt of savannah and Sahel below the Sahara that extends east across the continent from the Atlantic.
West Africa	The woodland coastal regions, savannah, Sahel, and desert that extends as far east as the Lake Chad basin. Many of the slaves caught up in the Atlantic slave trade from the 16th to the 19th centuries came from this region.
East Africa	Extends from Ethiopia south over modern Kenya and Tanzania. Historically, East Africa has had extensive trade and cultural contacts with Arabia and east Asia.
Central Africa	Extends from the Chad basin across the Congo to Lake Tanganyika and the Zambezi River.
Southern Africa	Extends from the Kalahari desert and the Zambesi River south to the Cape of Good Hope.

A Terra-cotta Head. This is from the Iron Age Nok culture, which occupied what is today northeastern Nigeria from about 900 B.C.E. to about 200 C.E.

© Werner Forman Archive/Art Resource, N.Y./ Jos Museum, Nigeria.

One theory proposes that the progressive desiccation of the second millennium B.C.E. forced these peoples farther south. Pottery found in the first-millennium settlements in places such as Jenne (in Mali) are clearly "offshoots of a Saharan pottery tradition."[1] These migrants carried with them both languages and techniques of settled agriculture utilizing cereal grains and animal husbandry. Assisted ultimately by knowledge of iron working (probably passed on from North Africa or the Nilotic kingdom of Kush), they were able to effect an agricultural revolution. This caused considerable population growth in the more fertile Sudanic regions, especially near the great river basins of the Niger and Senegal, and the Lake Chad basin. (A similar spread of agricultural techniques and cattle and sheep raising seems to have occurred down the Rift Valley of the East African highlands.) This agricultural revolution, completed during the first millennium B.C.E., paved the way for the growth of new cultural centers in the sub-Saharan regions.

Whatever their earlier history, we know that in the first millennium B.C.E. the Sudanic peoples developed and refined techniques of settled agriculture. They must have carried these together with their languages eastward through the savannahs and southward, largely along the rivers, into the tropical rain forests of central and West Africa. This changed the face of sub-Saharan Africa, which previously had been dominated by small groups of hunter-gatherers. Knowledge of iron smelting enabled these settled peoples to develop larger and more complex societies than their predecessors.

THE EARLY IRON AGE AND THE NOK CULTURE

Common features of the oldest iron-smelting furnaces found in widely scattered sites across Africa suggest that Africa's iron-working technology was invented within the continent, probably in Egypt and Nubia, or possibly in the central Saharan highlands of the Tibesti, Ahaggar, and Aïr. Thence it likely spread southward into western, central, and eastern regions. Some of the most significant Iron Age sites have been found in northeastern Nigeria. Near the village of Jos, archaeological digs have yielded evidence of an Iron Age people, the Nok culture, dating between 900 B.C.E. and 200 C.E. The Nok people cleared substantial woodlands from the plateau and practiced both agriculture and cattleherding.

The Nok culture is significant for two reasons. First, the Nok people, who mastered the relatively difficult art of smelting as early as 500 B.C.E., had the earliest Iron Age culture in West Africa, and their probable acquisition of this art by way of the Aïr Mountains to the north is evidence of early contacts among African cultures. Second, Nok culture offers extraordinary sculptural art, most vividly evident in magnificent burial or ritual masks. The apparent continuities of Nok sculptural traditions with those of other, later West African cultures to the south suggest that this culture had an important impact on later West and central African life. These continuities indicate that ancient communities of considerable sophistication laid a foundation for subsequent, better-known Sudanic civilizations. (See Map 5–1.)

[1]S. J. and R. J. McIntosh, *Prehistoric Investigations at Jenne, Mali* (Oxford, U.K.: B.A.R., 1980), p. 436.

MAP 5–1
Ancient African Kingdoms and Empires.

WHAT EFFECT did the migrations of people and the spread of technology have on early African history?

HOW DID Egypt influence the various Nilotic civilizations, such as Kush, Meroe, and Axum?

NILOTIC AFRICA AND THE ETHIOPIAN HIGHLANDS

THE KINGDOM OF KUSH

The land of Kush lies in the upper Nile basin, just above the first cataract. It was here that an Egyptianized segment of Nilo-Saharan-speaking Nubians built the earliest (except for Pharaonic Egypt) known literate and politically unified civilization in Africa. The Old Kingdom pharaohs subjugated and colonized Nubia, but in the early second millennium B.C.E., an independent kingdom arose in Kush just above the third cataract of the Nile. As early as 2000 B.C.E., its capital, Kerma, had become a major trading outpost for Middle Kingdom Egypt.

The early Kushite kingdom reached its zenith in the years between the Middle and New Kingdoms of Egypt about 1700–1500 B.C.E. It appears to have been wealthy and prosperous by any standard. Egypt's revival under the pharaohs of the New Kingdom restored Egyptian colonial rule in Nubia and hence stronger Egyptian influences. Then, sometime after 1000 B.C.E., as the New Kingdom floundered, a new Kushite state reasserted itself. By about 900 B.C.E. it had conquered lower as well as upper Nubia.

THE NAPATAN EMPIRE

This new Kushite empire, with its center first at Napata and then at Meroe, survived from the 10th century B.C.E. until the fourth century C.E., when the Ethiopian Aksumites replaced Kush as the dominant power in northeastern Africa. It was the true successor to Pharaonic Egypt. The kings who ruled at Napata saw themselves as Egyptian. They practiced the Pharaonic custom of marrying their sisters. They embalmed their royalty and buried them in pyramids in traditional Egyptian style. They used Egyptian protocol and titles. In the eighth century B.C.E., they conquered Egypt and ruled it for about a century as its Twenty-Fifth Dynasty. The Kushite pharaohs were driven out of Egypt proper by Assyria around the middle of the seventh century B.C.E. (see "Kushite Conquest of Memphis").

THE MEROITIC EMPIRE

Forced back above the lower cataracts of the Nile by the Assyrians and kept there by the Persians, the Napatan kingdom became increasingly isolated and evolved in distinctive ways. After Napata was sacked by an Egyptian army in 591 B.C.E., Meroe became the kingdom's political and cultural capital. In the sixth century B.C.E., it was the center of a flourishing iron industry, which may have spread knowledge of iron smelting west and south to the sub-Saharan world. Certainly the Kushites traded widely to the west across the Sudan as well as with the Hellenistic world and beyond. The Meroitic state maintained a wide network of internal African and external, intercontinental commercial relations. The empire survived until it was defeated and divided in the fourth century C.E. by Nuba peoples from west of the upper Nile. It was replaced as the dominant regional power by a rival trading state, Aksum on the Abyssinian plateau.

Culture and Economy   The heyday of Meroitic culture was from the mid-third century B.C.E. to the first century C.E. The kingdom mediated various African goods to the Mediterranean and Near East: animal skins, ebony

QUICK REVIEW

The Early Kushite Kingdom
- Located just above first cataract of the Nile
- Capital Kerma a major trading outpost as early as 2000 B.C.E.
- Reached its zenith between 1700 and 1500 B.C.E.

Meroitic Pottery. The people of Meroe produced many examples of fine pottery. This fired clay jar is decorated with giraffes and serpents.

University of Pennsylvania Museum of Archaelogy and Anthropology.

HISTORY'S VOICES

KUSHITE CONQUEST OF MEMPHIS

T he following text comes from a granite pillar, a victory stela that the Kushite king Piankhi had erected near Napata to commemorate his conquest of Egypt in the decade before 750 B.C.E. It describes the siege and capture of Memphis.

WHAT ELEMENTS in the description might be slight exaggerations or hyperbole rather than sober chronicling?

When day broke, at early morning, his majesty reached Memphis. When he had landed on the north of it, he found that the water had approached to the walls, the ships mooring at [the walls of] Memphis. Then his majesty saw that it was strong, and that the wall was raised by a new rampart, and battlements manned with mighty men. There was found no way of attacking it. Every man told his opinion among the army of his majesty, according to every rule of war. Every man said: "Let us besiege it—; lo, its troops are numerous." Others said: "Let a causeway be made against it; let us elevate the ground to its walls. Let us bind together a tower; let us erect masts and make the spars into a bridge to it. We will divide it on this [plan] on every side of it, on the high ground and on the north of it, in order to elevate the ground at its walls, that we may find a way for our feet."

Then his majesty was enraged against it like a panther; he said: "I swear, as Re loves me, as my father, Amon (who fashioned me), favors me, this shall befall it, according to the command of Amon . . . I will take it like a flood of water. I have commanded . . ." Then he sent forth his fleet and his army to assault the harbor of Memphis; they brought to him every ferryboat, every (cargo) boat, every (transport), and the ships, as many as there were, which had moored in the harbor of Memphis, with the bow-rope fastened among its houses. [There was not] a citizen who wept, among all the soldiers of his majesty.

His majesty himself came to line up the ships, as many as there were. His majesty commanded his army: "Forward against it! Mount the walls! Penetrate the houses over the river. If one of you gets through upon the wall, let him not halt before it (so that) the (hostile) troops may not repulse you . . ."

Then Memphis was taken as (by) a flood of water, a multitude of people were slain therein, and brought as living captives to the place where his majesty was.

Source: J. H. Breasted, *Ancient Records of Egypt* (Chicago: University of Chicago Press, 1906), Vol. 4, pars. 861 ff. Reprinted in Basil Davidson, *The African Past* (New York: Grosset and Dunlap, 1967), pp. 51–52.

and ivory, gold, oils and perfumes, and slaves. The Kushites traded with the Hellenistic-Roman world, southern Arabia, and India. They shipped high-quality iron to Aksum and the Red Sea, and the Kushite lands between the Nile and the Red Sea were a major source of gold for Egypt and the Mediterranean world. Cattle breeding, other animal husbandry, and agriculture were their economic mainstays. Cotton cultivation in Kush preceded that of Egypt and may have been an early export.

Many monuments were built, including royal pyramids and the storied palace and walls of the capital. Meroitic culture is especially renowned for two kinds of pottery: The first was wheel-turned by males and attuned apparently to market demands; the second was hand-thrown by women largely for domestic use. This latter pottery seems to have come from an older tradition of African pottery craft found well outside the region of Kush—an indication of ancient traditions shared among regions of Africa and of the antiquity of internal trade within Africa.

Early African Civilizations

ca. 7500–2500 B.C.E.	"Wet Holocene" period
ca. 2500 B.C.E.	Rapid desiccation of Saharan region begins
ca. 2000–1000 B.C.E.	Increasing Egyptian influence in Nubia
ca. 1000–900 B.C.E.	Kushite kingdom with capital at Napata becomes independent of Egypt
751–663 B.C.E.	Kushite kings Piankhi and Taharqa rule all Egypt
ca. 600–500 B.C.E.	Meroe becomes new Kushite capital
ca. 500 B.C.E.–330 C.E.	Meroitic kingdom of Kush (height of Meroitic Kushite power ca. 250 B.C.E.–50 C.E.)
ca. 500 B.C.E.–500 C.E.?	Nok culture flourishes on Jos plateau in western Sudan (modern central Nigeria)
First century C.E.	Rise of Aksum as trading power on Ethiopian (Abyssinian) plateau
ca. 330 C.E.	Aksumite conquest of Kush

Nilotic Africa and the Ethiopian Highlands

ca. 500 B.C.E.	Yemenites (southern Arabians) enter and settle the Ethiopian plateau
30 B.C.E.	Egypt becomes part of Roman Empire of Octavian
ca. 1–100 C.E.	Earliest mention (in Latin and Greek writers) of the kingdom of Aksum on Ethiopian plateau
ca. 330 B.C.E.	Fall of Kushite empire to Ezana of Aksum
ca. 200–400 C.E.	Heyday of Aksumite Ethiopia
ca. 500–600 C.E.	Christianizing of the major Nubian states of Maqurra and Alwa
652 C.E.	Maqurra and Alwa make peace with Arab Muslim armies from Egypt

Rule and Administration The political system of the Meroitic Empire, like the Pharaonic, was evidently stable over many centuries. Although the king was considered a living god—an idea found in both ancient Egypt and many other African societies—he seems to have ruled by customary law. According to Greek accounts, his actions were limited by firm taboos. Royal succession was not from father to son, but it stayed within the royal family, often passing through the maternal rather than the paternal line. (Evidence suggests that matrilineal succession was a widespread norm in ancient Africa.) Succession to the throne was by election. The priests presented several candidates for king, from whom the god would choose the heir. (We are not told how.) The role of the queen mother in the election appears to have been crucial—another parallel to African practices elsewhere. Indeed, the queen mother seems to have adopted her son's wife upon his succession. In the second century B.C.E., a woman became monarch and initiated a long line of queens.

We know very little about Meroitic administration. The empire seems to have been under the autocratic control of its sovereign, perhaps on the Egyptian model. He or she presided over a central administration run by numerous high officials. The provinces were delegated to princes.

Society and Religion Limited sources mean that we can only speculate about social groups outside the ruling class of monarch, royal relatives, priests, courtiers, and nobles. Slaves are mentioned, most commonly female domestics, but there were also male laborers taken as prisoners of war. Cattle breeders, farmers, traders, artisans, and minor government functionaries probably formed an intermediate class or classes between slaves and rulers.

Kushite religious practices followed Egyptian traditions for centuries. To judge from the great temples dedicated to him, Amon was the highest god for the earlier kings. By the third century B.C.E., however, gods unknown to Egypt rose in importance alongside Amon and the Egyptian gods. Most notable was Apedemak, a warrior god with a lion's head. The many lion temples associated with him reflect his importance. Such gods were likely local deities who grew increasingly popular.

THE AKSUMITE EMPIRE

A highland people who had developed their own commercially powerful trading state to the south of Kush delivered the final blow to the weakened Kushite Empire, apparently about 330 C.E. This was the newly Christianized state of Aksum, which centered in the northern Ethiopian, or Abyssinian, highlands where the Blue Nile rises. With the ascendancy of Aksum, our sources lapse into relative silence concerning the Nubian regions of the Nile. Not until the rise of Christian Nubian states in the mid-sixth century is there again much information about the heirs to the land of Kush.

The peoples of Aksum were the product of a linguistic, cultural, and genetic mixing of African Kushitic speakers with Semitic speakers from Yemenite southern Arabia. This mixing occurred after southern Arabians settled on the Ethiopian plateau around 500 B.C.E., giving Aksum, and later Ethiopia, Semitic speech and script closely related to South Arabian. Greek and Roman sources attest to the existence of an Aksumite kingdom from at least the first century C.E. By this time, the kingdom, through its chief port of Adulis, had already become the major ivory and elephant market of northeastern Africa.

In the first two centuries C.E., its location on the Red Sea made Aksum a strategic site on the increasingly important Indian Ocean trade routes that linked India and the East Indies, Iran, Arabia, and the East African coast with the Roman Mediterranean. Aksum also controlled trade between the African interior and the extra-African world, from Rome to Southeast Asia—notably exports of ivory, but also of elephants, obsidian, slaves, gold dust, and other inland products.

By the third century C.E., Aksum was one of the most impressive states of its age in the African or western Asian world, as the remains of its major cities—Aksum, Adulis, and Matara—attest. From the late second century onward, the Aksumites often held tributary territories across the Red Sea in southern Arabia. They also gained control of northern Ethiopia and conquered Meroitic Kush. Thus, by the third and fourth centuries they controlled some of the most fertile cultivated regions of the ancient world: their own plateau, the rich Yemenite highlands of southern Arabia, and much of the eastern Sudan across the upper Nile as far as the Sahara.

The resulting empire was ruled by a king of kings in Aksum through tribute-paying vassal kings in the other subject states. Aksum's minting of gold, silver, and copper coins (the first by a tropical African state) indicate its political and economic power. Goods from the Roman-Byzantine world and India and Sri Lanka, as well as of neighboring Meroe, flowed into Aksum, and its vast herds and good agricultural land helped to ensure its prosperity.

The pre-Christian paganism of Aksum resembled the pre-Islamic paganism of southern Arabia, with various gods and goddesses associated with natural phenomena such as the sun, moon, and stars. There is also evidence that Jewish, Meroitic, and even Buddhist minorities lived in the major cities of Aksum—an indication of its cosmopolitanism.

An inscription from the reign of the powerful fourth-century king, Ezana, records his conversion to Christianity, the start of the Christianizing of the kingdom

A Giant Stela at Aksum. Dating probably from the first century C.E., this giant carved monolith is the only one remaining of seven giant stelae—the tallest of which reached a height of 33 meters—that once stood in Aksum amid numerous smaller monoliths. Although the exact purpose of the stelae is not known, the generally accepted explanation is that they were commemorative funerary monuments. Erecting them required engineering of great sophistication.

Werner Former Archive/Art Resource, N.Y.

as a whole. This was the work of Frumentius, a Syrian bishop of Aksum who served as secretary and treasurer to the king. Subsequently, under Alexandrian influence, the Ethiopian church embraced the Monophysite belief that Christ had only one, divine nature. Constantinople persecuted Monophysites within its empire, but religious disagreement did not hamper its trade with Aksum. In the fifth century C.E., the native Semitic language, Ge'ez, began to replace Greek in the liturgy, a major step toward the development of a distinctive Ethiopic or Abyssinian Christian Church.

ISOLATION OF CHRISTIAN ETHIOPIA

Aksumite trade continued to thrive through the sixth century, despite the decay of Rome. Strong enough at times to extend to the Yemen, Aksumite power was eclipsed in the end by the rise of Arab Islamic power. Aksum ceased to be a center of foreign trade and became increasingly isolated. Its center of gravity shifted south from the coast to the more rugged parts of the plateau. There, surrounded largely by Muslim peoples, a Monophysite Christian, Ge'ez-speaking culture emerged (modern Ethiopia) and survived in relative isolation until modern times.

Ethiopia's northern neighbors, the Christian states of Maqurra and Alwa, also survived for centuries in the former Meroitic lands of the Nilotic Sudan. However, incursions from Muslim Egypt in the 14th and 15th centuries and Arab migration from about 1300 led ultimately to the Islamization of the whole Nubian region. Ethiopia was left as the sole predominantly Christian state in Africa.

THE WESTERN AND CENTRAL SUDAN

AGRICULTURE, TRADE, AND THE RISE OF URBAN CENTERS

WHAT ROLE did trade play in the rise of large political entities in the western and central Sudan?

By the first or second century C.E., most of the inhabitants of the western Sudan had become settled farmers using iron tools, and their way of life was spreading into forest regions farther south. The savannah areas seem to have experienced a substantial population explosion, especially around major water sources: along the Senegal River, around the great northern bend in the Niger River, and in the Lake Chad basin. The largest political organizations remained villages or chiefdoms consisting of several villages. As time went on, their growth led to the development of larger towns and political units.

Trade promoted, or accompanied, the eventual rise of larger political entities in the western and central Sudan. Regional and interregional trade networks here date to ancient times. Extensive east-west trade connected the western Sahel to Egypt and the Nilotic Sudan. From the western Sahel, traders also found Saharan routes leading to the north (see Map 5–2).

By the latter half of the first millennium B.C.E., substantial urban settlements—such as Gao, Kumbi (or Kumbi Saleh), and Jenne—had emerged in the western Sahel. Excavations at Jenne, in the upper Niger (the so-called Inland Delta), date settlement there from 250 B.C.E. and indicate that its population reached more than 10,000 by the late first millennium C.E.[2]

The Western and Central Sudan: Probable Dates for Founding of Regional Kingdoms

ca. 400 C.E.	Takrur (Senegal River valley) or earlier
400–600 C.E.	Ghana (in Sahel between great northern bends of the Senegal and Niger Rivers)
ca. 700–800 C.E.	Gao (on the Niger River or before southeast of great bend)
ca. 700–900 C.E.	Kanem (northeast of Lake Chad)

[2]S. J. and R. J. McIntosh, pp. 41–59, 434–461; and R. Oliver, *The African Experience* (1991) pp. 90–101.

MAP 5–2
Africa: Early Trade Routes and Early States of the Western and Central Sudan.   This map shows some of the major routes of north–south trans-Saharan caravan trade and their links with Egypt and with Sudanic and forest regions of West Africa.

HOW DID Africa's geography help determine its trade routes?

These early urbanized areas were supported by a mix of farming, fishing, and hunting. All of them developed in oasis or river regions rich enough to sustain dense populations and trade. Over time, the relatively autonomous settlements formed loose confederations or widely dispersed imperial networks.

The introduction of the domesticated camel from the east around the beginning of the Christian era greatly increased the viability of trans-Saharan trade. By the early Christian centuries, the West African settled communities had developed trading centers of considerable importance on their northern

QUICK REVIEW

Trade
• Trade contributed to rise of larger political entities
• Regional and interregional trade networks date to ancient times
• Trade routes connected western and central Sudan with Egypt

A Camel Caravan Crossing the Sahara.
Use of the camel as a beast of burden from the first century C.E. onward greatly increased trans-Saharan trade.

© Michael S. Lewis/Corbis.

QUICK REVIEW

Ghana and Gold

- The people of Ghana depended on gold for Saharan trade
- Ghana was famous outside the region for control of gold
- Ruler of region inherited throne through matrilineal descent

---

WHY DID the coastal and inland regions of East Africa have different histories?

peripheries in the Sahel near the edge of the true desert. Salt and gold were the prime commodities exchanged.

Towns such as Awdaghast, Walata, Timbuktu, Gao, Tadmekka, and Agades were the most famous southern terminals for trade over the centuries. These centers allowed the largely Berber middlemen who plied the desert routes to cross the ever-dangerous Sahara via oasis stations en route to the North African coasts and Egypt. Because a typical crossing could take two to three months, this was not an easy route for transporting goods.

FORMATION OF SUDANIC KINGDOMS IN THE FIRST MILLENNIUM

The first millennium C.E. saw the growth of settled agricultural populations and the expansion of trans-Saharan and other internal trade. These developments coincided with the rise of sizable states in the western and central Sudan. The most important of these were located in Takrur on the Senegal River, from the fifth century or earlier; Ghana, between the northern bends of the Senegal and the Niger, from the fifth or sixth century; Gao, on the Niger southeast of the great bend, from before the eighth century; and Kanem, northeast of Lake Chad, from the eighth or ninth century. Each represents the first of a series of large political entities in its region. All continued to figure prominently in subsequent West African history (see Chapter 18).

The states developed by the Fulbe people of Takrur and the Soninke people of Ghana thrived by obtaining gold for the Saharan trade with Morocco from the savannah region west of the upper Senegal. Of all the sub-Saharan kingdoms of the late first millennium, Ghana was the most famous outside of the region, thanks to the major role it played in the gold trade. Its people built a large regional empire with its capital at Kumbi (or Kumbi Saleh). Its throne passed through matrilineal descent, and its king was regarded as semidivine. The king's subjects approached him through a hierarchy of government ministers. In contrast to the Soninke of Ghana, the Songhai rulers of Gao had no gold trade until the 14th century, and Gao, unlike its western neighbors, was oriented through its forest trade routes toward the lower, not the upper, Niger basin and in its Saharan ties toward eastern Algeria, not Morocco.

These states were supported by settled, farming populations. By contrast, the power of Kanem, on the northwestern side of Lake Chad, originated in the borderlands of the central Sudan and southern Sahara from a nomadic federation of black tribal peoples that persisted long enough for the separate tribes to merge as a single people, the Kanuri. Their kingdom controlled the southern terminus of perhaps the best trans-Saharan route—that running north via good watering stations to the oasis region of Fezzan in modern central Libya and thence to the Mediterranean (see Chapter 17).

CENTRAL, SOUTHERN, AND EAST AFRICA

The African subcontinent is the part of central, southern, and East Africa that lies south of a line from roughly the Niger delta and Cameroon across to southern

Somalia on the east coast. Paucity of sources makes it difficult to reconstruct in any detail the history of this region before 1,000 C.E. Some relatively certain facts and reasonable hypotheses have, however, emerged from linguistic, archaeological, and other research.

BANTU MIGRATIONS AND DIFFUSION

In the southern subcontinent, most people speak one of more than four hundred languages that belong to a single language group known as *Bantu*. These languages are as closely related as are the Germanic or Romance tongues of Europe. Although the place of origin and routes of diffusion of Bantu tongues have long been debated, there is increasing consensus that the location of the proto-Bantu language was the region south of the Benue River, in eastern Nigeria and modern Cameroon. During the later centuries B.C.E. and the first millennium C.E., migrations of Bantu-speaking peoples must have carried their languages in two basic directions: (1) south into the lower Zaïre (Kongo) basin and ultimately to the southern edge of the equatorial forest in present-day northern Katanga; and (2) east around the equatorial forests into the lakes of highland East Africa. How the Bantu peoples managed to impose their languages on the earlier cultures of these regions remains unexplained. In any case, Bantu cultures became fully interwoven with those of the peoples among whom they settled. For example, Bantu-Arab mixing on the eastern coasts produced the Swahili culture (see Chapter 18). We find Bantu-speaking peoples as slash-and-burn farmers in the Zaïre River savannah, as cattle herders in the East African high plains, as perennial floodplain cultivators on the Zambezi River, and as terracing and irrigating farmers among the highland Kikuyu and Chagga peoples.

EAST AFRICA

The history of East Africa along the coast before Islam differed from that of the inland highlands. Long-distance travel was easy and common along the seashore but less so inland. The coast had had maritime contact with India, Arabia, and the Mediterranean via the Indian Ocean and Red Sea trade routes from at least as early as the second century B.C.E. By contrast, we know little about the long-distance contacts of inland regions with the coastal areas until after 1000 C.E. Nonetheless, both regional inland and coastal trade must also be ancient. Both coastal and overseas trade remained important and interdependent over the centuries, because the Indian Ocean trade depended on the monsoon winds and could, therefore, use only the northernmost coastal trading harbors of East Africa for round-trip voyages in the same year. The monsoon winds blow from the northeast from December to March and thus can carry sailing ships south from Iran, Arabia, and India only during those months; the winds blow from the southwest from April to August, so ships can sail from Africa northeast during those months. Local coastal shipping had to haul cargoes from south of Zanzibar and then transfer them to other ships for the annual round-trip voyages to Arabia and beyond.

Long-distance trade came into its own in Islamic times—about the ninth century—as an Arab monopoly. However, long before the coming of

11.2
The Cities of the Sanj and the Indian Ocean Trade

Prehistoric San rock painting from southern Africa.

Christopher and Sally Gable© Dorling Kindersley.

Islam, trade was apparently largely in Arab hands. Many Arabs had settled in the East African coastal towns and in Iran and India to handle this international commerce. We have documentation of Greco-Roman contact with these East African centers of Red Sea and Indian Ocean trade from as early as the first century C.E.

Overseas trade was, however, evidently even more international than the earliest sources indicate. Today, Malagasy, the imported Malayo-Polynesian language of Madagascar, points to the antiquity of substantial contact with the East Indies via the coastal trading routes of Asia's ancient southern rim. Evidence of an Indonesian migration even before the beginning of our era is seen in the spread of bananas, coconut palms, and other food crops indigenous to Southeast Asia across the entire African continent as staple foods. Further, as a result of the early regular commercial ties to distant lands of Asia, extra-African ethnic and cultural mixing has long been the rule for the East African coast; even today, its linguistic and cultural traditions are rich and varied (see Chapter 18).

Other African imports included Persian Gulf pottery, Chinese porcelain, and cotton cloth. The major African export, around which the east coast trade revolved, was ivory. The slave trade was also important. Slaves were exported to the Arab and Persian world, as well as to India or China.

The history of inland East Africa south of Ethiopia is much more difficult to trace than that of the coast, again because of the absence of written sources and the immense difficulty of access until relatively recent times. We can, however, infer from linguistic clues and other evidence some key developments in the eastern highlands. These regions had seen an early diffusion of peoples from the north, and changing conditions of subsistence over the centuries continued to propel movements of small groups into new areas. Of the early migrants from the north, first came peoples speaking Kushitic languages of the Afro-Asiatic family, likely cattle herders and grain cultivators. Perhaps as early as 2000 B.C.E., they pushed from their homeland on the Ethiopian plateau south down the Rift Valley as far as the southern end of Lake Tanganyika.

Later, by about 1000 C.E., Nilotic-Saharan speakers moved from the southwestern side of the Ethiopian plateau west over the upper Nile valley. Then they pushed east and south, following older Kushite paths, to spread across the Rift Valley area (by the 15th century) and subsequently much of the East African highlands of modern-day Uganda, Kenya, and Tanzania. Here they all but completely supplanted their Kushite predecessors. Two of these Nilotic peoples were the Lwo and Maasai. The Lwo populated over a 900-mile-long swath of modern Uganda and parts of southern Sudan and western Kenya. They mixed readily with other peoples, absorbing new cultural elements and adapting to new situations wherever they went. The Maasai, on the other hand, were and still are cattle pastoralists fiercely proud of their separate language, way of life, and cultural traditions. These features have distinguished them sharply from the farming or hunting peoples whose settlements abutted their pasturages at the top of the southern Rift Valley in modern Kenya and Tanzania. Here, the Maasai have concentrated and remained.

These migrations from the north and those of the Bantu peoples, who also entered the eastern highlands over

Movement and Contact of Peoples in Central, Southern, and East Africa

ca. 1300–1000 B.C.E.	Kushitic-speaking peoples migrate from Ethiopian plateau south along Rift Valley
ca. 400 B.C.E.–1000 C.E.	Probable era of major Bantu migrations into central, East, and southeastern Africa
200–100 B.C.E.	East African coast becomes involved in Indian Ocean and Red Sea trade
ca. 100 B.C.E.	Probable time of first Indonesian immigration to East African coast
ca. 100–1500 C.E.	Nilotic-speaking peoples spread over upper Nile valley; Nilotic peoples spread over Rift Valley region

many centuries from the west, have made the highlands a melting pot for an immense diversity of languages and cultures. Here the radical diversity of peoples and cultures of the entire African continent is mirrored by a single region.

SUMMARY

Geography and History The human species, *homo sapiens* (*sapiens*) probably originated in Africa. Africa's geography and climate limited Africans' contact with peoples outside the continent and their development and preservation of historical records. Nonetheless, Africa does have a significant history. Archaeology produces evidence for extensive migrations of peoples across the continent from the earliest times diffusing cross-cultural influences throughout huge regions.

Contact with Other Cultures In three parts of Africa, there was considerable contact with non-African civilizations. In the Nile River valley, Egypt had extensive interaction with the Nubian peoples to its south. Nubian kingdoms—Kush, Napata, Meroe, and Axum (Ethiopia)—adopted many features of Egyptian civilization and sometimes dominated Egypt itself. Axum adopted Christianity in the fourth century C.E.

On the coast of East Africa, trade across the Red Sea and the Indian Ocean with Arabia and east Asia fostered a distinct and sophisticated culture. Extensive trade across the Sahara between North Africa and the western and central Sudan enabled products and ideas from the Mediterranean to reach the African interior in exchange for African products, such as gold, ivory, and salt.

IMAGE KEY
for pages 104–105

a. Great battle of Archers
b. Cave painting-prehistory; women gathering grain
c. Camel
d. Nigeria, Nok head
e. Homo habilis skull (reconstructed)
f. Cattle in a Saharan rock painting from Tassili n'Ajjer
g. Ruins of pyramids in ancient kingdom of Kush-Sudan
h. A carving from the ancient site of Great Zimbabwe
i. A giant stela at Aksum; perhaps a funerary monument
j. A Saharan camel train

REVIEW QUESTIONS

1. Were early African societies truly civilized? What unique conditions hamper current understanding of their histories?
2. How did the diffusion of peoples and languages affect early African history?
3. How did the political systems of the Meroitic Empire and Egypt compare?
4. How did Aksum become a Christian state?
5. What were the most important goods for African internal trade? Which products were traded abroad?
6. How did geography influence early African history?

KEY TERMS

Kalahari (p. 106)
Nilotic Africa (p. 107)

Sahara (p. 106)
Sahel (p. 106)

savannah (p. 106)

 For additional study resources for this chapter, go to:
www.prenhall.com/craig/chapter5

6 Republican and Imperial Rome

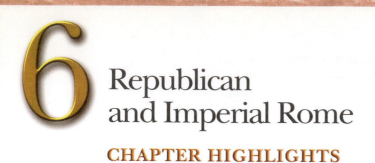

CHAPTER HIGHLIGHTS

Republican Rome Rome began as a small settlement ruled by kings; it became a republic in 509 B.C.E. The Roman constitution divided power between elected magistrates, an appointed Senate, and popular assemblies. During the third century B.C.E., the aristocratic patricians were forced to share power with the common people, the plebians.

Roman Expansion By the early fourth century, Rome had expanded to control all of Italy. Between 264 and 146 B.C.E., Rome fought three wars with Carthage for control of the western Mediterranean. These Punic Wars ended with the destruction of Carthage.

In the third century B.C.E., Rome turned to the east and defeated the Hellenistic monarchies that had succeeded Alexander's empire. This led to the rapid Hellenization of Roman culture. By the first century B.C.E., Rome controlled most of the Mediterranean world.

The Empire The Roman Republic was destroyed by social unrest and rivalry among ambitious generals and politicians, the most successful of whom was Julius Caesar. After Caesar's assassination in 44 B.C.E., his nephew Octavian emerged as the most powerful man in Rome. Under the title of Augustus, he set up a system that, while preserving the façade of republican institutions was in fact a monarchy.

Peace and stability prevailed throughout the Empire for two centuries. Christianity, which arose in the Roman province of Judaea in the first century C.E., spread throughout the empire despite occasional persecutions by the Roman state, which itself became Christian in the late fourth century.

Decline and Fall In the third century C.E., the Roman peace collapsed under the pressure of invasions by barbarians in the west and the Persians in the east. The emperors Diocletian and Constantine managed to arrest the decline, but in the fifth century C.E. Roman authority in the West collapsed. In the East, however, a Christian Roman Empire based in the city of Constantinople survived and evolved into the Byzantine Empire.

CHAPTER QUESTIONS

HOW DID the Etruscans influence early Rome?

WHY DID Rome and Carthage fight the Punic Wars?

HOW DID the Roman Republic come to an end?

WHAT ROLE did cities play in the Roman Empire?

HOW DID a Catholic Church emerge from early Christianity?

HOW DID the Roman Empire change under Diocletian and Constantine?

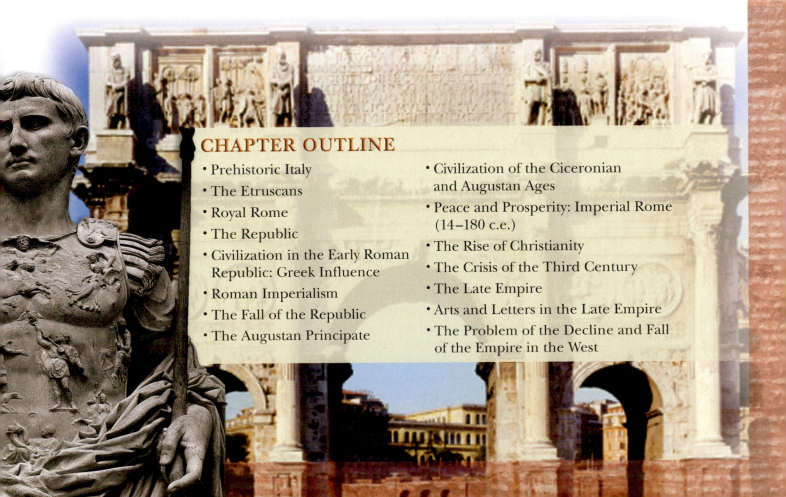

CHAPTER OUTLINE

- Prehistoric Italy
- The Etruscans
- Royal Rome
- The Republic
- Civilization in the Early Roman Republic: Greek Influence
- Roman Imperialism
- The Fall of the Republic
- The Augustan Principate

- Civilization of the Ciceronian and Augustan Ages
- Peace and Prosperity: Imperial Rome (14–180 c.e.)
- The Rise of Christianity
- The Crisis of the Third Century
- The Late Empire
- Arts and Letters in the Late Empire
- The Problem of the Decline and Fall of the Empire in the West

The ancient Romans were responsible for one of the most remarkable achievements in history. From their city in central Italy, they conquered most of the Near East and much of Europe. They brought peace, prosperity, and unity to this vast region for the only time in history.

Rome's legacy was not just military prowess and superb political organization. The Romans transformed the intellectual and cultural achievements of the Greeks, creating the Graeco-Roman tradition in literature, philosophy, and art. This tradition remains the heart of Western civilization.

PREHISTORIC ITALY

About 1000 B.C.E. bands of warlike people speaking related Italic dialects (belonging to the Indo-European family of languages) began to infiltrate Italy. They spread through the peninsula's Apennine mountains and then contested control of the western agricultural plains with earlier settlers. The Romans were the descendants of some of these hardy folk.

THE ETRUSCANS

Etruscan civilization, which was to have a powerful influence on the Romans, arose about 800 B.C.E. The **Etruscans** constituted a military ruling class, dominating the native people they had dispossessed. From their base in northern Italy (modern Tuscany), they took to the sea and established trade contacts with the Greeks and the Cartholginians of North Africa. Their influence spread south to the plains of Latium and Campania in the seventh and sixth centuries, but their power declined rapidly after 500 B.C.E.

ROYAL ROME

Rome, which was located on the northeastern rim of the plain of Latium, came under the control of Etruscan kings in the sixth century B.C.E. Geographical location made Rome a center for communication and trade. With Etruscan leadership, the Roman army conquered most of Latium.

GOVERNMENT

Roman kings had the awesome power of *imperium*, the right to issue commands and enforce them by fines, arrests, and physical punishment, including execution. Although the crown tended to remain in families, kingship was elective. The Roman Senate approved the candidate, and the Roman people, voting in assembly, formally granted him the *imperium*. This procedure—the granting of great power to executive officers contingent on the approval of the Senate and ultimately the people—remained a characteristic of Roman government.

The Senate, the second branch of the early Roman government, ostensibly had neither executive nor legislative power, but its authority was great. Senators, like kings, served for life. The Senate enrolled the most powerful men in the state. They provided continuity for government and experienced counsel.

The third branch of government, the curiate assembly, was made up of all citizens. The body of citizens was divided into 30 groups. Voting was by group; a majority within each group determined its single vote, and decisions were made by majority vote of the groups. Group voting remained the custom for future forms of Roman political assembly.

HOW DID the Etruscans influence early Rome?

Etruscans A people of central Italy who exerted the most powerful external influence on the early Romans.

imperium In ancient Rome, the right to issue commands and to enforce them by fines, arrests, and even corporal and capital punishment.

FAMILY

The center of Roman life was the family. At its head stood the father, whose power and authority resembled those of the king within the state. He held broad powers analogous to *imperium* over his children; he could sell them into slavery and might even kill them. Over his wife he had less power; he could not sell or kill her. In practice his power to dispose of his children was limited by other family members, by public opinion, and, most of all, by tradition. A wife could be divorced only for serious offenses. The Roman woman had a respected position and significant responsibility as the primary manager of her husband's household.

CLIENTAGE

Clientage was one of Rome's most important institutions. The client was said to be in the *fides*, or trust, of his patron, giving the relationship a moral dimension. The patron provided his client with physical and legal protection and economic support. In return, the client would fight for his patron, work his land, and support him politically. These mutual obligations were enforced by public opinion and tradition. Because the client-patron relationship was hereditary and was sanctioned by religion and custom, it was a major factor in the organization of Roman society and political life.

PATRICIANS AND PLEBEIANS

Roman society was divided into two classes based on birth. The wealthy **patrician** upper class held a monopoly of power and influence. Its members alone could conduct state religious ceremonies, sit in the Senate, or hold office. They formed a closed caste by forbidding marriage outside their own group.

   The **plebeian** lower class may have originally consisted of poor, dependent small farmers, laborers, and artisans, the clients of the nobility. As Rome grew, some of these nonpatrician plebeian families acquired wealth, and some patrician families fell into poverty from incompetence or bad luck. The line between the classes and the monopoly of privileges nevertheless remained firm.

patricians Hereditary upper class of early republican Rome.

plebeians Hereditary lower class of early republican Rome.

THE REPUBLIC

oman legend claimed that outrageous behavior by the last kings provoked the city's noble families to revolt in 509 B.C.E. They abolished monarchy and reorganized Rome as a republic.

WHY DID Rome and Carthage fight the Punic Wars?

CONSTITUTION

The Roman constitution was an unwritten accumulation of laws and customs that evolved over many generations.

Consuls The Romans granted consuls, their chief magistrates, the power of the *imperium* that kings had exercised. Like the kings, the consuls led the army, had religious duties, and served as judges. But the power of the consul was kept in check in two ways. Two men held consulships simultaneously, and each could overrule the other. Both were limited to a term of only one year. Their *imperium* was also limited. Although the consuls had full powers of life and death in the field with the army, within the city of Rome, citizens could appeal to the popular assembly any cases involving capital punishment. After their year in office, a consul also knew that he would spend the rest of his life as a member of the Senate, so only a reckless consul would ignore its advice. In serious crises, the consuls

A Roman warship. Rome became a naval power late in its history, in the course of the First Punic War. Roman sailors initially lacked the skill and experience in sea warfare of their Carthaginian opponents, who could maneuver their oared ships to ram the enemy. To compensate for this disadvantage, the Romans sought to make a sea battle more like an encounter on land by devising ways to grapple enemy ships and board them with armed troops. In time they also mastered the skillful use of the ram. This picture shows a Roman ship, propelled by oars, with both ram and soldiers, ready for either kind of fight.

Direzione Generale Musei Vaticani.

could, with the advice of the Senate, appoint a single *dictator*, who would hold *imperium* not subject to appeal both inside and outside the city for six months.

Financial officials called *quaestors* assisted consuls, and in 325 B.C.E., the Romans created the office of *proconsul,* which permitted a consul in the field to retain command for more than a year during a long campaign. Another new office, that of *praetor,* was primarily judicial. After the middle of the fifth century B.C.E., the job of identifying citizens and classifying them according to age and property was delegated to a **censor.** The Senate elected two censors every five years. They conducted a census and drew up the citizen rolls, and by the fourth century B.C.E. could exclude senators from the Senate on moral as well as financial grounds. The office was regarded as the ultimate prize of a political career.

Senate and Assembly   The end of the monarchy increased the power of the Senate. It was the only ongoing deliberative body in the Roman state and soon took control of finances and foreign policy.

The *centuriate assemble*, the early republic's most important popular assembly, was, in a sense, the Roman army acting in a political capacity. Its basic unit was the century, 100 fighting men who fought with the same kind of equipment. Because each man equipped himself, this divided the assembly into classes according to wealth—that is, according to the weapons a man could afford.

Struggle of the Orders   Patricians monopolized power in the early republic. Plebeians, however, made up much of the Roman army, and this gave them great political leverage. Their fight for political, legal, and social equality, the "struggle of the orders," lasted 200 years. They won the right to a plebeian tribal assembly led by elected officials called **tribunes.** A tribune could veto any action of a magistrate or any bill proposed in a Roman assembly or by the Senate. In 367 B.C.E., one of the consulships was opened to men of plebeian rank. In 287 B.C.E., the plebeians secured the passage of a law making the decisions of the plebeian assembly binding on all Romans without the approval of the Senate.

The victory of the plebeians in the "struggle of the orders" primarily benefited wealthy plebeian families by allowing them to share the political privileges of the patrician aristocracy. The *nobiles*—a small group of wealthy families, both patrician and plebeian—dominated the Senate and controlled the highest offices of the state.

CONQUEST OF ITALY

Initial Expansion and Gallic Invasion   By the beginning of the fourth century B.C.E., the Romans had become the chief power in central Italy. In 340 B.C.E., the city's Latin neighbors, the Latin League, sought to curtail Rome's expansion, but in 338 B.C.E., the Romans defeated the league and dissolved it.

censor   Official of the Roman republic charged with conducting the census and compiling the lists of citizens and members of the Senate.

tribunes   Roman officials who had to be plebeians and were elected by the plebeian assembly to protect plebeians from the arbitrary power of the magistrates.

Roman Policy Toward the Conquered   The Romans did not destroy any of the Latin cities. To some near Rome they granted full citizenship. To others farther away they granted municipal status, which included the right to local self-government and the right to trade and intermarry with Romans. Still other states became allies of Rome. The Romans established permanent colonies of veteran soldiers in conquered lands. The colonists remained Roman citizens and deterred rebellion. A network of durable roads—some still in use—connected the colonies to Rome.

Rome divided its enemies and extended its influence through military force and diplomatic skill. Rebels were punished harshly, but Rome was generous to those who submitted. Loyal allies could gain full Roman citizenship. This policy gave allies a stake in Rome's future and, as a result, most remained loyal.

ROME AND CARTHAGE

In the ninth century B.C.E., the Phoenician city of Tyre had planted a colony on the North African coast, calling it Carthage. In the sixth century B.C.E., Carthage became independent and expanded west and east. Carthage claimed an absolute monopoly on trade in the western Mediterranean.

First Punic War (264–241 B.C.E.)   Sicily was strategically important to both Carthage and Rome. It was there, in 264 B.C.E., that the two expanding powers first came to blows. Because the Romans called the Carthaginians *Poeni* or *Puni* (meaning "Phoenician"), the conflicts between them are called the **Punic Wars**.

Because Rome's strength was its army and Carthage's power was its navy, neither side could make much progress against the other in the First Punic War until the Romans built a fleet. Once they were able to blockade the Carthaginian ports in Sicily, the tide turned. Carthage capitulated in 241 B.C.E., giving up Sicily and agreeing to pay a war indemnity. Neither side was to attack the allies of the other.

Second Punic War (218–202 B.C.E.)   After 241 B.C.E., Carthage recovered strength by building a rich empire in Spain. In 221 B.C.E., Hannibal (247–182 B.C.E.) took command of Carthaginian forces in Spain. A few years earlier, Rome had received an offer of alliance from the Spanish town of Saguntum. The Romans accepted, and the Saguntines, confident of Rome's protection, began to stir up Spanish tribes allied with Hannibal. The Romans warned Hannibal to let Saguntum alone, but he ignored Rome's warning and captured it. Rome declared war in 218 B.C.E., but Hannibal struck first, marching overland from Spain to launch a swift and daring invasion of Italy. His army defeated the Romans in three battles, but his hopes for final victory were pinned on persuading Rome's allies to switch sides.

In 216 B.C.E., at Cannae, Hannibal destroyed a Roman army of 80,000 men. It was the worst defeat in Roman history, and many of Rome's allies went over to Hannibal. In 215 B.C.E., Philip V (r. 221–179 B.C.E.), king of Macedon, allied with Hannibal and launched a war to recover his influence on the Adriatic. For more than a decade Hannibal was free to roam Italy and do as he pleased, but victory was denied him so long as crucial

Punic Wars   Three wars between Rome and Carthage for dominance of the western Mediterranean that were fought from 264 B.C.E. to 146 B.C.E.

The Punic Wars

264–241 B.C.E.	First Punic War
238 B.C.E.	Rome seizes Sardinia and Corsica
221 B.C.E.	Hannibal takes command of Punic army in Spain
218–202 B.C.E.	Second Punic War
216 B.C.E.	Battle of Cannae
202 B.C.E.	Battle of Zama
149–146 B.C.E.	Third Punic War
146 B.C.E.	Destruction of Carthage

5.1
A Hero Under Fire: Livy Relates the Trials and Tribulations of Scipio Africanus

allies remained loyal to Rome. He had neither the numbers nor the supplies to besiege the city itself.

The turning point in the conflict came when the Romans appointed Publius Cornelius Scipio (237–183 B.C.E.), later called Scipio Africanus, to the command in Spain. He was almost as talented as Hannibal. Within a few years Scipio had conquered all Spain and deprived Hannibal of help from that region. In 204 B.C.E., Scipio invaded Africa and forced Hannibal to return to protect Carthage. In 202 B.C.E., Scipio defeated Hannibal at Zama. Carthage was stripped of its empire, and Rome emerged dominant at seas and over the Mediterranean coast from Italy westward.

The New Imperial System The old practice of extending citizenship in exchange for loyalty to Rome to defeated opponents stopped at the borders of Italy. The Romans made Sicily, Sardinia, and Corsica provinces. The governors of these provinces exercised an *imperium* free of the limits put on the power of officials in Rome. The natives of provinces became tribute-paying subjects of a Roman empire. Rome collected their taxes by "farming them out"; that is, by auctioning the right to collect taxes to the man who made the highest bid. The treasury got a guaranteed sum, and the tax collector made a profit by exploiting the provincials. Provincial government spread so much corruption that it strained the constitution and traditions of Rome and threatened to destabilize the republic.

MAP 6–1

The Western Mediterranean Area During the Rise of Rome. This map covers the theater of conflict between the growing Roman dominions and those of Carthage in the third century B.C.E. The Carthaginian Empire stretched westward from Carthage along the North African coast and into southern Spain.

WHY WAS conflict between Rome and Carthage inevitable?

HISTORY'S VOICES

SALLUST ON FACTIONS AND THE DECLINE OF THE REPUBLIC

S allust (86–35 B.C.E.) was a supporter of Julius Caesar and of the political faction called populares, translated here as "the democratic party," opponents of the optimates, translated here as "the nobility." In this selection from his monograph on the Jugurthine War, Sallust tries to explain Rome's troubles in the period after the destruction of Carthage in 146 B.C.E.

WHY DID Sallust think the destruction of Carthage marked the beginning of the decline of the Roman republic? Does his account of events seem fair and dispassionate? How would a member of "the nobility" have evaluated the same events? Is the existence of factions or "parties" inevitably harmful to a republic?

The division of the Roman state into warring factions, with all its attendant vices, had originated some years before, as a result of peace and of that material prosperity which men regard as the greatest blessing. Down to the destruction of Carthage, the people and Senate shared the government peaceably and with due restraint, and the citizens did not compete for glory or power; fear of its enemies preserved the good morals of the state. But when the people were relieved of this fear, the favourite vices of prosperity—licence and pride—appeared as a natural consequence. Thus, the peace and quiet which they had longed for in time of adversity proved, when they obtained it, to be even more grievous and bitter than the adversity. For the nobles started to use their position, and the people their liberty, to gratify their selfish passions, every man snatching and seizing what he could for himself. So the whole community was split into parties, and the Republic, which hitherto had been the common interest of all, was torn asunder. The nobility had the advantage of being a close-knit body, whereas the democratic party was weakened by its loose organization, its supporters being dispersed among a huge multitude. One small group of oligarchs had everything in its control alike in peace and war—the treasury, the provinces, public offices, all distinctions and triumphs. The people were burdened with military services and poverty, while the spoils of war were snatched by the generals and shared with a handful of friends. Meantime, the soldiers' parents or young children, if they happened to have a powerful neighbour, might well be driven from their homes. Thus, the possession of power gave unlimited scope to ruthless greed, which violated and plundered everything, respecting nothing and holding nothing sacred, till finally it brought about its own downfall. For the day came when noblemen rose to power who preferred true glory to unjust dominion: then the state was shaken to its foundations by civil strife, as by an earthquake.

Excerpt from Sallust, *The Jugurthine War: The Conspiracy of Catiline*, trans. by S. A. Hanford (London: Penguin Classics, 1963). Copyright © S. A. Hanford, 1963.

THE REPUBLIC'S CONQUEST OF THE HELLENISTIC WORLD

The East By the mid-third century B.C.E., the eastern Mediterranean had reached a stable balance of power. That equilibrium was threatened by two aggressive monarchs, Philip V of Macedon and the Seleucid emperor Antiochus III (223–187 B.C.E.). In 200 B.C.E., the Romans ordered Philip not to attack any Greek city and to pay reparations to the kingdom of Pergamum in Asia Minor. Philip refused. Two years later, the Romans demanded that Philip withdraw from Greece entirely. In 197 B.C.E., with Greek support, they defeated Philip in Thessaly. The Greek cities taken from Philip were made autonomous and declared free.

QUICK REVIEW

Rome Conquers Greece
- Romans forbid interference in Greek cities by Macedonia
- Rome saw Greek cities as a kind of protectorate
- Rome responded with force to sign of anti-Roman feeling in Greek cities

Soon after, Antiochus landed an army on the Greek mainland. The Romans drove him from Greece, and in 189 B.C.E. they crushed his army at Magnesia in Asia Minor. The Romans left Greek cities free, but they regarded Greece and Asia Minor as protectorates in which they could intervene as they chose.

In 179 B.C.E., Perseus (r. 179–168 B.C.E.) succeeded Philip V as king of Macedon. He tried to gain popularity in Greece by favoring the democratic and revolutionary forces in the cities. The Romans defeated him in 168 B.C.E. and divided Macedon into four separate republics. The new policy reflected a stern, businesslike policy promoted by the conservative censor Cato (234–149 B.C.E.). Leaders of anti-Roman factions in the Greek cities were punished severely, and in 146 B.C.E., the city of Corinth was destroyed. The Roman treasury benefited so much from these wars that Rome abolished direct property taxes on its citizens. Romans were learning that foreign campaigns could bring profit to the state, rewards to soldiers, and wealth, fame, and power to their generals.

The West   Although Carthage posed no threat, some Romans could not shake their hatred and fear of the enemy that had come so close to defeating them. In 146 B.C.E., Scipio Aemilianus took the city, and the Romans incorporated Carthage as the province of Africa (see "Sallust on Factions and the Decline of the Republic").

CIVILIZATION IN THE EARLY ROMAN REPUBLIC: GREEK INFLUENCE

*A*mong the most important effects of Rome's expansion overseas were changes in the Roman style of life and thought. Such Roman aristocrats as the Scipios surrounded themselves with Greek intellectuals. Even conservatives, such as Cato, learned Greek and absorbed Greek culture.

RELIGION

Almost from the beginning, the Romans identified their gods with Greek equivalents and incorporated Greek mythology into their own. However, in the third century B.C.E. important new cults were introduced from the east: the worship of Cybele, the Great Mother goddess from Asia Minor, and of Dionysus, or Bacchus. Interest in Babylonian astrology also grew.

EDUCATION

Education was entirely the responsibility of the Roman family. It is not clear whether girls received any education in early Rome, although they did later on. Boys' education aimed at making them moral, pious, patriotic, law-abiding, and respectful of tradition. Contact with the Greeks of southern Italy produced momentous changes in Roman curricula. Greek teachers introduced the study of language, literature, and philosophy, as well as the idea of a liberal education, or what the Romans called *humanitas*.

Schools were established in which the teacher

HOW DID Greek culture influence Roman civilization?

humanitas Roman name for a liberal arts education.

A Master Among His Students.
This carved relief from the second century C.E. shows a schoolmaster and his pupils. The student at the right is arriving late.
Rheinisches Landesmuseum, Triern, Germany/ Alinari/Art Resource, N.Y.

taught his students the Greek language and its literature, particularly the works of Homer. Thereafter, educated Romans were expected to be bilingual. Roman boys of the upper classes studied rhetoric, which was of great use in legal disputes and political life.

By the last century of the Roman republic, the new Hellenized education had become dominant. Latin literature formed part of the course of study, but much of it was modeled after Greek examples.

Girls of the upper classes were educated similarly to boys. They were probably taught by tutors at home, although they were usually married by the age when men were pursuing higher education. Still, some women became prose writers or poets.

A rich, socially ambitious Roman might support a Greek philosopher in his own home, so that his son could acquire through conversation the learning and polished thought necessary for the fully cultured gentleman. Some, like the great orator Cicero (106–43 B.C.E.), traveled to Greece to study with great teachers of rhetoric and philosophy. This style of education made the Romans part of the culture of the Hellenistic world, a world they ruled and, therefore, needed to understand.

ROMAN IMPERIALISM

Rome's expansion in Italy and overseas was accomplished without a grand general plan. But whether intended or not, it brought the Romans an empire, and with it, power, wealth, and responsibilities.

AFTERMATH OF CONQUEST

War and expansion changed the economic, social, and political life of Italy. The Second Punic War did terrible damage to the Italian farmland. Many veterans found it impossible or unprofitable to go back to their farms. Most became tenant farmers or hired hands. Often the land they abandoned was acquired by the wealthy who converted these farms, later called *latifundia*, into large plantations.

Land was inexpensive, and slaves conquered in war provided cheap labor. By fair means and foul, large landholders obtained sizable quantities of public land and forced small farmers off it. These changes separated the people of Rome and Italy more sharply into rich and poor, landed and landless, privileged and deprived. The result was conflict that threatened the republic.

THE GRACCHI

By the middle of the second century B.C.E., the problems caused by Rome's rapid expansion troubled perceptive Roman nobles. Tiberius Gracchus (168–133 B.C.E.) tried to solve these problems. He became tribune in 133 B.C.E. on a program of land reform. The program aroused great hostility. When Tiberius put it before the tribal assembly, another tribune vetoed it. Tiberius responded by persuading the assembly to remove from office the tribune who had blocked his popular legislation. Tiberius then proposed and passed a second bill, harsher than the first and even more appealing to the people. Because no tribune dared to oppose him, he got his way. But the cost was the destruction of the Roman constitution.

Tiberius understood the danger to himself and to prospects for implementing his reforms once his term as tribune came to an end, so he announced his candidacy for a second successive term. This violated the term limits posed by

WHY WAS there social unrest in Rome after the Second Punic war?

latifundia Large plantations for growing cash crops owned by wealthy Romans.

Roman Overseas Engagements

215–205 B.C.E.	First Macedonian War
200–197 B.C.E.	Second Macedonian War
196 B.C.E.	Proclamation of Greek Freedom
189 B.C.E.	Battle of Magnesia; Antiochus defeated in Asia Minor
172–168 B.C.E.	Third Macedonian War
168 B.C.E.	Battle of Pydna
154–133 B.C.E.	Roman wars in Spain
134 B.C.E.	Numantia taken

populares Roman politicians who sought to pursue a political career based on the support of the people rather than just the aristocracy.

equestrians Literally "cavalrymen" or "knights." In the earliest years of the Roman republic, those who could afford to serve as mounted warriors.

the Roman constitution. Having no legal recourse left, a mob of senators and their clients resorted to violence. They killed Tiberius and some 300 of his followers and threw their bodies into the Tiber River.

The tribunate of Tiberius Gracchus and the violent acts that ended it created a new situation. Tiberius had shown the Romans how to build a political career that was based not on aristocratic influence but on pressure from the people. In the last century of the republic, such politicians were called *populares*, whereas those who supported the traditional role of the Senate were called *optimates* ("the best men").

The tribunate of Gaius Gracchus (ca. 159–121 B.C.E.), brother of Tiberius, was much more dangerous to the Senate than that of Tiberius because all the tribunes were Gaius's supporters. There could be no veto, and tribunes could now be reelected (and, therefore, monopolize power). Gaius courted popularity by establishing colonies for landless veterans and passing a law stabilizing the price of grain in Rome. He also divided the wealthy, by winning the backing of the equestrian order in his struggles with the Senate. The **equestrians** were rich men who supplied goods and services to the Roman state and collected its taxes in the provinces. They had a special interest in Roman expansion and in the exploitation of the provinces. When Pergamum became the Roman province of Asia in 129 B.C.E., Gaius gave them the right to collect taxes there.

Gaius easily won reelection as tribune for 122 B.C.E., but then he made a misstep. He proposed giving citizenship to Italian allies, but the common people did not want to share the advantages of their Roman citizenship. The Senate seized on this to drive a wedge between Gaius and his supporters. After Gaius failed reelection in 121 B.C.E., a hostile consul provoked an incident that led to violence. Gaius was killed, and 3,000 of his followers were put to death without trial.

MARIUS AND SULLA

Before long the senatorial oligarchy faced a stronger opponent who got his start in a war with Jugurtha (d. 104 B.C.E.), king of Numidia. When the war dragged on, the people elected Gaius Marius (157–86 B.C.E.) to the consulship for 107 B.C.E. Marius was a *novus homo*, a political outsider, the first man from his family to win a consulship. He did so by promising the voters that popular military reforms would lead to speedy victory. He eliminated the traditional property qualification for military service and opened the ranks to volunteers, mostly dispossessed farmers and rural proletarians. They enlisted for long terms of service, looked on the army as a career, and expected land as a bonus when they retired. They became semiprofessional clients of their general and backed the politician who seemed most likely to be able to get them what they wanted. They looked to their commander rather than to the state for their rewards. Marius had to obtain grants from the Senate to maintain his power and reputation. But with a large, loyal army behind him, he could frighten the Senate into doing his bidding. Marius's innovation created both the opportunity and the necessity for military leaders to challenge the authority of civilian government.

Marius quickly routed Jugurtha, but a guerrilla war dragged on. Finally, Marius's subordinate, Lucius Cornelius Sulla (138–78 B.C.E.), captured Jugurtha and ended the war. Marius, however, took the credit, leaving Sulla to plot his revenge.

WAR AGAINST THE ITALIAN ALLIES (90–88 B.C.E.)

For a decade, Rome ignored the grievances of its Italian allies. In frustration, they took up arms. By 88 B.C.E., the revolt was put down, largely by giving the Italians what they wanted. They became Roman citizens, but their municipalities retained local self-government. The forging of Romans and Italians into a single people helped Italy to flourish.

SULLA'S DICTATORSHIP

Sulla was elected consul for 88 B.C.E. He backed the Senate in a war against Marius and his supporters, and following its victorious conclusion, he had himself appointed dictator. He used his power to restore the traditional Roman constitution and the power of the Senate. He could not, however, undo the effect of his example. Sulla had taken possession of Rome with its own army and led Romans in slaughtering Romans. Others were soon to do the same.

FALL OF THE REPUBLIC

HOW DID the Roman republic come to an end?

POMPEY, CRASSUS, AND CAESAR

Marcus Licinius Crassus (115–53 B.C.E.) and Cnaeus Pompey (106–48 B.C.E.) won election to the consulship for the year 70 B.C.E. and repealed most of Sulla's laws. In 67 B.C.E., a special law gave Pompey *imperium* for three years over the entire Mediterranean and 50 miles in from the coast to rid the area of pirates. When he returned to Rome in 62 B.C.E., he had more power, prestige, and popular support than any Roman in history.

Crassus had the most reason to fear Pompey's return. Although rich and influential, he did not have the confidence of the Senate, a firm political base of his own, or the kind of military support needed to rival Pompey. During the 60s B.C.E., therefore, he allied himself with a promising young soldier politician, Gaius Julius Caesar (100–44 B.C.E.).

FIRST TRIUMVIRATE

To general surprise, Pompey disbanded his army and returned to Italy as a private citizen. He needed a grant of land for his veterans from the Senate and was dismayed when the fearful Senate decided to try to turn his men against him by refusing his request. This drove Pompey into an alliance with Crassus and Caesar called the First Triumvirate.

DICTATORSHIP OF JULIUS CAESAR

Caesar was elected consul for 59 B.C.E. and enacted the Triumvirate's program. Caesar got an opportunity to raise a great army for the conquest of Gaul; Crassus got a similar military command in the Middle East; and Pompey got land for his veterans and confirmation of his treaties from the Senate. By the time Caesar had conquered Gaul and was ready to return to Rome, the Triumvirate had dissolved. Crassus's invasion of Parthia had ended with his death at Carrhae in 53 B.C.E., and Pompey had allied with the Senate against Caesar.

Fall of the Roman Republic

Date	Event
133 B.C.E.	Tribunate of Tiberius Gracchus
123–122 B.C.E.	Tribunate of Gaius Gracchus
111–105 B.C.E.	Jugurthine War
104–100 B.C.E.	Consecutive consulships of Marius
90–88 B.C.E.	War against the Italian allies
70 B.C.E.	Consulship of Crassus and Pompey
60 B.C.E.	Formation of First Triumvirate
58–50 B.C.E.	Caesar in Gaul
53 B.C.E.	Crassus killed in Battle of Carrhae
49 B.C.E.	Caesar crosses Rubicon; civil war begins
46–44 B.C.E.	Caesar's dictatorship
43 B.C.E.	Formation of Second Triumvirate
42 B.C.E.	Battle of Philippi
31 B.C.E.	Octavian defeats Antony at Actium

Early in January of 49 B.C.E., when Caesar's term as governor came to its end, the Senate ordered him to lay down his command. Instead, Caesar's legions crossed the Rubicon River, the boundary of his province. This began a civil war that ended in 45 B.C.E. with Caesar's victory over Pompey and the Senate.

Caesar made few changes in the government of Rome, but his monopoly of military power made a sham of the republic. His Senatorial enemies conspired against him, and on March 15, 44 B.C.E., they stabbed him to death at a meeting of the Senate. The assassins expected his death automatically to restore the republic, but 13 more years of civil war ensued and fatally undercut what was left of the republic.

SECOND TRIUMVIRATE AND THE EMERGENCE OF OCTAVIAN

Caesar's heir was his grandnephew, Octavian (63 B.C.E.–14 C.E.). Marcus Antonius (Mark Antony) (ca. 83–30 B.C.E.) and Lepidus (d. 13 B.C.E.), two of Caesar's officers, joined him in forming the Second Triumvirate, an alliance dedicated to punishing Caesar's assassins. The triumvirs defeated their enemy in 42 B.C.E., but soon quarreled among themselves. Octavian gained control of the western part of the empire. Antonius, together with Cleopatra (r. 51–30 B.C.E.), queen of Egypt, ruled the east. In 31 B.C.E., Octavian crushed the fleet and army of Antony and Cleopatra at Actium and ended the civil war. Octavian emerged in control of the Mediterranean world but faced a daunting challenge. He had to restore peace, prosperity, and confidence, without making the mistake that had cost Caesar his life. He had to excercise the power of a king without appearing to threaten the republican traditions to which his fellow Romans were passionately attached.

THE AUGUSTAN PRINCIPATE

Octavian's constitutional solution was to drape a monarchy in republican trappings by apparently sharing authority with the Senate. All real power, however, lay with the ruler, whether he was called by the unofficial title of "first citizen" (*princeps*) like Octavian, or "emperor" (*imperator*) like those who followed. The outline of his plan emerged in 27 B.C.E.: He was to rule the provinces of Spain, Gaul, and Syria with proconsular power for military command and retain a consulship in Rome. The Senate would govern the other provinces. Twenty of Rome's 26 legions just happened to be stationed in Octavian's provinces, giving him effective control of the empire. The Senate, however, was grateful to him for establishing peace after Rome's long civil war, and it voted him many honors, including the semireligious title "**Augustus**," which connoted veneration, majesty, and holiness. Historians refer to Octavian in his role as Rome's first emperor as Augustus and characterize his regime as the Principate, a government that tried to conceal the naked power on which it rested.

ADMINISTRATION

Augustus made important changes in the government of Rome, Italy, and the provinces to reduce inefficiency and corruption, to eliminate the threat to peace and order by ambitious individuals, and to reduce the distinction between Romans and Italians, senators and equestrians. Augustus controlled the elections and saw to it that promising young men, whatever their origin, served the state.

WHAT WERE the bases of Augustus's power?

imperator Under the Roman republic, the title given to a victorious general. Under Augustus and his successors, it became the title of the ruler of Rome, meaning "emperor."

Augustus Title given to Octavian in 27 B.C.E. and borne thereafter by all Roman emperors.

QUICK REVIEW

The Army Under Augustus
- Augustus professionalized army
- 20-year enlistment with good pay and pension
- 300,000 men formed frontier army

Equestrians and Italians who had no connection with the Roman aristocracy were admitted to the Senate, which Augustus treated with respect and honor.

The Augustan period was prosperous. Its economy was stimulated by wealth from newly conquered Egypt, by a general peace that stimulated commerce and industry, by a vast program of public works, and by a revival of small farming on the lands granted to Augustus's veterans.

THE ARMY AND DEFENSE

Under Augustus, Rome's soldiers became true professionals. Enlistment was for 20 years, but the pay was good, and there were bonuses and a pension on retirement. The citizen legions, together with auxiliary units staffed by provincials, stationed about 300,000 men on the empire's frontiers—barely enough to hold the line. The army in the provinces brought Roman culture to the natives. The soldiers spread their language and customs, often marrying local women and settling down there. They attracted merchants, who became the nuclei of new towns that became centers of Roman civilization. As time passed, the provincials on the frontiers became Roman citizens and helped strengthen Rome's defenses against the barbarians.

RELIGION AND MORALITY

A century of political strife and civil war had undermined Roman society. Augustus believed that restoration of traditional family and religious values would give the Romans the strength they needed to hold their empire. He curbed adultery and divorce, encouraged marriage and the procreation of legitimate children, and restored the dignity of formal Roman religion by building temples and reviving cults. Like Julius Caesar, he was deified after his death, and a state cult was dedicated to his worship.

CIVILIZATION OF THE CICERONIAN AND AUGUSTAN AGES

*R*oman civilization reached its peak in the late republican era and during the Principate of Augustus.

THE LATE REPUBLIC

Cicero (106–43 B.C.E.) Cicero is most famous for his orations delivered in the law courts and the Senate. Many of his letters also survive, giving us a fuller insight into his mind than we have of any other figure in antiquity. He also wrote treatises on rhetoric, ethics, and politics, and believed in a world governed by divine and natural law. He looked to law, custom, and tradition to produce both stability and liberty.

Emperor Augustus (r. 27 B.C.E.–14 C.E.). This statue, now in the Vatican, stood in the villa of Augustus's wife Livia. The figures on the elaborate breastplate are all of symbolic significance. At the top, for example, Dawn in her chariot brings in a new day under the protective mantle of the sky god; in the center, Tiberius, Augustus's successor, accepts the return of captured Roman army standards from a barbarian prince; and at the bottom, Mother Earth offers a horn of plenty.

Charitable Foundation, Gemeinnutzige Stiftung Leonard von Matt.

WHAT WERE the main achievements of Augustan civilization?

Law   The period from the Gracchi to the fall of the republic was important for the development of Roman law. The edicts of the magistrates who dealt with foreigners developed the idea of a comprehensive *jus gentium*, or "law of peoples," as opposed to a law based strictly on Roman custom. In the first century B.C.E., under the influence of the Greeks, the *jus gentium* was equated with the *jus naturale*, or "natural law," taught by the Stoics.

Poetry   Two of Rome's greatest poets, Lucretius and Catullus, were citizens of the late republic. The Hellenistic literary theorists believed that poetry should educate as well as entertain, a task Lucretius (ca. 99–ca. 55 B.C.E.) undertook in his epic poem *De Rerum Natura* (*On the Nature of Things*). It explained and advocated the scientific and philosophical theories of Epicurus and Democritus, which Lucretius believed would liberate people from superstition and the fear of death.

Catullus's (ca. 84–ca. 54 B.C.E.) poems were personal. He wrote of the joys and pains of love, and amused himself composing witty poetic exchanges. He illustrates the mindset of the proud, independent, pleasure-seeking, late republican nobility.

THE AGE OF AUGUSTUS

The literary works of the Augustan Age, the Golden Age of Roman literature, reflected the new conditions of society. As the old aristocratic order declined, poets lost their traditional patrons, the nobility. Henceforth, support for artists flowed from the *princeps*.

Virgil   Virgil (70–19 B.C.E.) was the most important of the Augustan poets. His greatest work is the *Aeneid*, a long epic that linked the history of Rome with the Homeric tradition of the Greeks. Its hero, the Trojan Aeneas, personifies the ideal Roman qualities of duty, responsibility, serious purpose, and patriotism. Virgil celebrated the peace and prosperity Augustus established for the empire and supported Augustus's program for the revival of traditional Roman virtues.

Horace   Horace's (65–8 B.C.E.) great skills as a lyric poet are best revealed in his *Odes*. Many of them glorify the new Augustan order, the imperial family, and the empire.

Ovid   Ovid (43 B.C.E.–18 C.E.) wrote entertaining love elegies that reveal the sophistication and the loose sexual conduct of the Roman aristocracy. His most popular work is *Metamorphoses*, a graceful, lively poem of epic length that retells Greek myths as charming stories.

History   The most important and influential prose writer of the time was Livy (59 B.C.E.–17 C.E.). His *History of Rome* traced the period from Rome's legendary origins until 9 B.C.E. Only one-fourth of his work survives. His great achievement was the creation of a continuous, impressive narrative encompassing the full sweep of Roman history. Its purpose was to promote traditional morality and patriotism. He glorified Rome's greatness and, like Augustus, grounded it in Rome's hardy virtues.

Architecture and Sculpture   Augustus embarked on a building program that beautified Rome, glorified his reign, contributed to the general prosperity, and enhanced his popularity. The greatest sculptural monument of the age is the Altar of Peace (*Ara Pacis*), dedicated in 9 B.C.E. Its walls show a procession in which

Imperial Procession from the Frieze of the Ara Pacis. The altar was dedicated in 9 B.C.E. It was part of a propaganda campaign—involving poetry, architecture, myth, and history—that Augustus undertook to promote himself as the savior of Rome and the restorer of peace.

Saturnia, Tellus, Goddess of Earth, Air and Water. Panel from the Ara Pacis. 13–9 B.C.E. Museum of the Ara Pacis, Rome. Nimatallah/Art Resource, N.Y.

Augustus and his family appear to move forward, followed by the magistrates, the Senate, and the people of Rome. There is no better symbol of the new order.

PEACE AND PROSPERITY: IMPERIAL ROME (14–180 C.E.)

Augustus tried to cloak the monarchical nature of his government, but his successors soon abandoned all pretense. They were called *imperator*—from which comes our word *emperor*—as well as *Caesar*. The latter title signified connection with the imperial house, and the former indicated the military power on which their authority was based. Augustus designated his heirs by giving them a share in the imperial power and responsibility (see Map 6–2).

WHAT ROLE did cities play in the Roman Empire?

MAP 6–2

Provinces of the Roman Empire to 117 C.E.   The growth of the empire to its greatest extent is shown in three states—at the death of Augustus in 14 B.C.E., at the death of Nerva in 98 C.E., and at the death of Trajan in 117 C.E. The division into provinces is also indicated. The inset outlines the main roads that tied together the far-flung empire.

WHY WAS the Mediterranean central to the Roman Empire?

Tiberius (emperor 14–37 C.E.), Gaius (Caligula, 37–41 C.E.), Claudius (41–54 C.E.), and Nero (54–68 C.E.) descended from Augustus's family. After their line died out in 68 C.E., various Roman armies marched on Italy and elevated four men in rapid succession to the throne.

Vespasian (69–79 C.E.) emerged victorious from the chaos, and his sons, Titus (79–81 C.E.) and Domitian (81–96 C.E.), carried forward his line, the Flavian dynasty. Vespasian was the first emperor who did not come from the old Roman nobility.

Following Domitian's assassination, the Senate appointed Nerva (96–98 C.E.) emperor. He was the first of the five "good emperors": Trajan (98–117 C.E.), Hadrian (117–138 C.E.), Antoninus Pius (138–161 C.E.), and Marcus Aurelius (161–180 C.E.). Until Marcus Aurelius, none of these men had sons, so they were each free to choose an able successor. The result was almost a century of excellent administration. This ended when Marcus Aurelius's incompetent son, Commodus (180–192 C.E.), succeed him. The "good emperors" had all enlisted the cooperation of the upper class by courteous and modest deportment.

ADMINISTRATION OF THE EMPIRE

The empire was a collection of cities and towns. Roman policy during the Principate was to raise urban centers to the status of Roman municipalities. The upper classes of the provinces were enlisted in the governments of their regions. This spread Roman culture and won the loyalty of influential people.

As the imperial bureaucracy grew and became more efficient, however, the scope of its functions grew. The importance and autonomy of the municipalities shrank as the central administration took a greater role in local affairs. Efficient centralized control was obtained at the cost of the vitality of the cities.

Augustus and his successors had not tried to expand the empire, but Trajan launched a sustained offensive into neighboring territory. Between 101 and 106 C.E., he established the new province of Dacia north of the Danube. His intent was probably to defend the empire by driving wedges into enemy territory. The same strategy led him to invade the Parthian Empire in the east (113–117 C.E.).

Hadrian retreated to a defensive posture, and gradually the military initiative passed to the barbarians. Marcus Aurelius spent most of his reign repulsing their attacks on the frontiers. This put enormous pressure on the empire's resources.

CULTURE OF THE EARLY EMPIRE

Literature   In Latin literature, the years between the death of Augustus and Marcus Aurelius are known as the Silver Age. Writers of the Silver Age were gloomy, negative, and pessimistic. They were prone to criticism and satire. Historians of the era wrote about remote periods to avoid the risk of offending an emperor's sensibilities. Scholarship was encouraged, but we hear little of poetry. Romances written in Greek became popular as an escape from contemporary realities.

Rulers of the Early Empire

27 B.C.E.–14 C.E.	Augustus
The Julio-Claudian Dynasty	
14–37 C.E.	Tiberius
37–41 C.E.	Gaius (Caligula)
41–54 C.E.	Claudius
54–68 C.E.	Nero
69 C.E.	Year of the four emperors
The Flavian Dynasty	
69–79 C.E.	Vespasian
79–81 C.E.	Titus
81–96 C.E.	Domitian
The "Good Emperors"	
96–98 C.E.	Nerva
98–117 C.E.	Trajan
117–138 C.E.	Hadrian
138–161 C.E.	Antoninus Pius
161–180 C.E.	Marcus Aurelius

Pompeiian Woman. The Roman provincial city of Pompeii, near the Bay of Naples, was buried by an eruption of Mount Vesuvius in 79 C.E. As a result, the town, together with its private houses and their contents, was remarkably well preserved until recovery in the 18th century. Among the discoveries were a number of works of art, including pictorial mosaics and paintings. This depiction of a young woman, on a round panel from a house in Pompeii, is part of a larger painting that includes her husband holding a volume of Plato's writings. The woman is holding a stylus and a booklet of wax tables and is evidently in the process of writing. Her gold earrings and hair net show that she is a fashionable person of some means. Late first century C.E. Diameter: 14 5/8 inches.

Sappho, idealized portrait of a girl poising as a poetess. Fresco from Pompeii, Insula occidentale. Museo Archeologico Nazionale, Naples, Italy, © Erich Lessing/Art Resource, N.Y.

Architecture   The prosperity and relative stability of the first two centuries of imperial Rome brought Roman architecture to full flower. Roman contributions to the building arts were largely advances in engineering that made huge structures feasible. To the basic post-and-lintel construction used by the Greeks, the Romans added the semicircular arch, borrowed from the Etruscans. When used internally in the form of vaults and domes, the arch permitted great buildings like the Roman baths. Romans also made good use of concrete, a building material first used by the Hellenistic Greeks. The arena in Rome called the Colosseum, which was built by the Flavian emperors, is an excellent example of Roman architecture. The only major Roman temple to survive intact is the Pantheon, a building roofed by a great dome. Roman engineers also spread impressive bridges, roads, and aqueducts throughout the empire.

Society   The first two centuries of the Roman Empire deserve their reputation as a Golden Age, but by the second century C.E., troubles had arisen—troubles that foreshadowed difficult times ahead. In the first century C.E., the upper classes had vied for election to municipal office, but by the second century, emperors were having to force the ruling classes to accept public office. The reluctance to serve was caused largely by the imperial practice of holding magistrates and councilmen personally and collectively responsible for the revenues that were due from their communities.

These difficulties reflected more basic problems. The prosperity created in Augustus's day by the end of the civil war and the influx of wealth from the east could not be sustained. Population also seems to have declined. The cost of government, however, kept rising, for emperors had to maintain an expensive standing army, keep the people in Rome quiet with "bread and circuses," pay for an increasingly large bureaucracy, and defend frontiers against dangerous and determined enemies. The ever-increasing need for money compelled the emperors to oppress their subjects and debase the coinage. The result was a series of crises that destroyed the empire.

LIFE IN IMPERIAL ROME: THE APARTMENT HOUSE

The civilization of the Roman Empire was the product of the vitality of its cities. The typical city had about 20,000 inhabitants; Rome probably had in excess of half a million.

Most of its residents were squeezed into tall apartment buildings, which the Romans called *insulae* ("islands"). The buildings, which were five or more stories tall, were uncomfortable and dangerous. Built cheaply, they were prone to collapse, and they were easily set on fire by the many torches, candles, oil lamps, and braziers their inhabitants used. They had no running water or other conveniences. Little wonder that Romans spent most of their time out of doors.

Roman Apartment House. This is a reconstruction of a typical Roman apartment house found at Ostia, Rome's port. The ground floor contained shops, and the stories above it held many apartments.

Gismondi (20th c.e.). Museo della Civilta Romana, Rome, Italy/ © Scala/Art Resource, N.Y.

RISE OF CHRISTIANITY

The story of how Christianity ultimately conquered the Roman Empire is one of the most remarkable in history. Christianity was opposed by the established religious institutions of its native Judaea and had to compete not only against the official cults of Rome and the sophisticated philosophies of the educated classes, but also against **"mystery" religions** such as the cults of Mithra, Isis, and Osiris. Christians were also at times officially persecuted by the state. But despite all this, Christianity became the official religion of the empire.

HOW DID a Catholic Church emerge from early Christianity?

JESUS OF NAZARETH

An attempt to understand the triumph of Christianity must begin with Jesus of Nazareth. The Gospel authors believed that Jesus was the son of God who came to redeem humanity and bring immortality to those who followed his way; to the Gospel writers, Jesus' resurrection was striking proof of his teachings.

Jesus was born in Judaea in the time of Augustus and was a most effective teacher in the tradition of the Jewish prophets. This tradition promised the coming of a Messiah (in Greek, *christos*—*Jesus Christ* means "Jesus the Messiah"), a redeemer who would make Israel triumph over its enemies and establish the kingdom of God on Earth. Jesus seems to have insisted that the Messiah would not establish an earthly kingdom but, at the Day of Judgment, God would reward the righteous and condemn the wicked. Until that day, which his followers believed would come soon, Jesus taught the faithful to abandon sin and worldly concerns; to follow the moral code described in the Sermon on the Mount, which preached love, charity, and humility; and to believe in him and his divine mission.

Jesus won a following, especially among the poor. This provoked the hostility of Jerusalem's religious leaders, and they convinced the Roman governor that Jesus and his followers might be dangerous revolutionaries. He was put to death in Jerusalem by the cruel and degrading method of crucifixion, probably in 30 C.E. His followers believed that he was resurrected on the third day after his death, and that belief became a critical element in their religion.

"mystery" religions Cults of Isis, Mithra, and Osiris, which promised salvation to those initiated into the secret or "mystery" of their rites.

Although faith in Jesus as the Christ spread to some Jewish communities in Syria and Asia Minor, without Saint Paul it might have remained a small, heretical cult within Judaism.

PAUL OF TARSUS

Paul (?5–67 C.E.), whose Hebrew name was Saul, was born in Tarsus in Asia Minor. He had an excellent Hellenistic education and held Roman citizenship. He was also a **Pharisee**, a strict adherent of the Jewish law. He persecuted the early Christians until his own sudden conversion while travelling to Damascus about 35 C.E. The great problem facing the early Christians, like Paul, was their relationship to Judaism. If the new faith was a version of Judaism, then it must adhere to the Jewish law and seek converts only among Jews. James, called the brother of Jesus, held that view, whereas Hellenist Jews tended to see Christianity as a new and universal religion.

Paul supported the position of the Hellenists and soon won many converts among the gentiles. He believed that the followers of Jesus were called to be evangelists ("messengers"), to spread the gospel ("good news") of God's gracious gift of salvation during the short time that remained before Jesus returned for the Day of Judgment. Faith in Jesus as the Christ was necessary for salvation, but salvation was a gift of God's grace, not something earned by good works.

ORGANIZATION

The new religion had its greatest success in the cities and among the poor and uneducated. The rites of the early Christians appear to have been simple and few. Baptism by water removed original sin and permitted participation in the community and its activities. The central ritual was a common meal called the *agape* ("love feast"), followed by the ceremony of the *Eucharist* ("thanksgiving"), a celebration of the Lord's Supper in which unleavened bread was eaten and unfermented wine drunk. There were also prayers, hymns, and readings from works that eventually became the Christian scriptures.

At first the churches had little formal organization, but by the second century C.E., most cities had leaders called bishops (*episkopoi* or "overseers"), who administered their Christian congregations. The doctrine of Apostolic Succession asserted that the message and authority Jesus had entrusted to his original disciples were passed on from bishop to bishop by the rite of ordination.

The bishops maintained discipline within their churches and dealt with the civil authorities. In time they began coming together in councils to settle difficult questions, define orthodox belief, and expel those who would not accept it. Christianity could probably not have survived without such strong internal organization and government.

PERSECUTION OF CHRISTIANS

The new faith soon incurred the distrust of the pagan world and of the imperial government. The Christians' refusal to demonstrate their patriotism by worshipping the emperor was considered treason. By the end of the first century, membership in the Christian community had become a crime.

EMERGENCE OF CATHOLICISM

Most Christians held to traditional, simple, conservative beliefs. This body of majority opinion and the church that enshrined it came to be called **Catholic**, which means "universal." Its doctrines were deemed **orthodox**; those holding contrary opinions were called **heretics**.

Pharisees Group that was most strict in its adherence to Jewish law.

agape Meaning "love feast." A common meal that was part of the central ritual of early Christian worship.

Eucharist Meaning "thanksgiving." Celebration of the Lord's Supper. Considered the central ritual of worship by most Christians. Also called Holy Communion.

Catholic Meaning "universal." The body of belief held by most Christians enshrined within the church.

orthodox Meaning "holding the right opinions." Applied to the doctrines of the Catholic Church.

heretics Persons whose religious beliefs differ from the official doctrines of their faith.

By the end of the second century, an orthodox scriptural canon had emerged that included the Old Testament, the Gospels, and the Epistles of Paul. The orthodox declared the church the guardian of authentic Christian belief and granted bishops power to define it. They drew up creeds, brief statements of faith to which true Christians should adhere. By the end of the second century, an orthodox Christian—that is, a member of the Catholic Church—had to accept its creed, its canon of holy writings, and the authority of the bishops.

ROME AS A CENTER OF THE EARLY CHURCH

The church in the city of Rome acquired special prominence. Rome benefited from the tradition that both Jesus' apostles Peter and Paul were martyred there. Peter was thought to be the first bishop of Rome, and the Gospel of Matthew (16:18) reported Jesus saying to Peter, "Thou art Peter [in Greek, *Petros*] and upon this rock [in Greek, *petra*] I will build my church." Subsequent bishops of Rome claimed supremacy over the Catholic Church as heirs to the role Jesus granted to Peter.

THE CRISIS OF THE THIRD CENTURY

*P*ressure on Rome's frontiers reached massive proportions in the third century C.E. In the east, a new Iranian dynasty, the Sasanids, reinvigorated Persia (see Chapter 10) and raided Roman territory. On the western and northern frontiers the threat came from German tribes.

BARBARIAN INVASIONS

Developments within the empire made it difficult for the Romans to meet the challenges to their empire. Septimius Severus (emperor 193–211 C.E.) and his successors changed the character of the Roman army. Septimius subordinated

WHAT PROBLEMS did Rome experience during the third century?

civil society to the support of a militarized monarchy and drew recruits for his army from peasants from the less civilized provinces. The result was a barbarization of Rome's military forces and a deline in their patriotism.

ECONOMIC DIFFICULTIES

Inflation had forced Commodus (r. 180–192 C.E.) to raise the soldiers' pay, but the Severan emperors had to double it to keep up with prices. This increased the imperial budget by as much as 25 percent. The emperors invented new taxes, debased the coinage, and even sold the palace furniture to raise money. Even then it was hard to recruit troops.

As external threats distracted the emperors, they were less able to preserve domestic peace. Piracy, brigandage, and the neglect of roads and harbors hampered trade. So, too, did inflation. As the money supply deteriorated, the government began to demand payment in food, supplies, and labor. The upper classes in the cities were ordered to serve as administrators without pay and to meet deficits in revenue out of their own pockets. Rebellions erupted in some provinces, and peasants and even town administrators fled to escape their burdens. The result was further diminishment of the Roman economy.

THE SOCIAL ORDER

The new conditions caused important changes in the social order. The state began to take on a military appearance. People's clothing became a kind of uniform that indicated their status. Titles were assigned to ranks in civilian society as to ranks in the army. The most important distinction was the one formally established by Septimius Severus between the *honestiores* (senators, equestrians, municipal aristocracy, and soldiers) and the lower classes, or *humiliores.* Septimius granted the *honestiores* legal privileges: lighter punishments, exemption from torture, and right of appeal to the emperor. It became more difficult to move from the lower order to the higher. Freedom and private initiative were suppressed as the state's needs forced it steadily to increase its control over its citizens.

CIVIL DISORDER

By the mid-third century, the empire seemed on the point of collapse, but a series of able military emperors gave it new life. Rome and other cities were given defensive walls to guard them from barbarian attack. The best troops were withdrawn from the frontiers to the emperor's command post. Rome relied on a newly organized heavy cavalry and a mobile army composed largely of German mercenaries whose loyalty was to the emperor, not the empire. Their officers became a new, if foreign, hereditary aristocracy. They increasingly filled the high administrative posts within the empire and some became emperors. In effect, the Roman people succumbed to an army of mercenaries they hired to protect them.

THE LATE EMPIRE

THE FOURTH CENTURY AND IMPERIAL REORGANIZATION

The reigns of Diocletian (r. 284–305 C.E.) and Constantine (r. 306–337 C.E.) marked an era of reconstruction and reorganization.

Diocletian   Diocletian rose to the throne through the army. He concluded that the job of defending and governing the entire empire was too great for one man. He, therefore, devised a new administrative system, a **tetrarchy,** a

HOW DID the Roman Empire change under Diocletian and Constantine?

tetrarchy Diocletian's (r. 306–337 C.E.) system for ruling the Roman Empire by four men with power divided territorially.

division of territorial responsibility for the empire among four men: two emperors and two assistants who were designated as their successors.

Constantine   In 305, Diocletian retired and compelled his co-emperor to do the same. But his plan for a smooth succession failed. By 310, five men were competing for the throne. In 324, Constantine emerged as sole emperor.

The emperor had now become almost unapproachable. Those admitted to his presence had to prostrate themselves before him and kiss the hem of his robe. He was addressed as *dominus* ("lord"), and he claimed a divine right to rule. Remoteness and ceremony helped to secure the emperor against assassination by making him an awe-inspiring figure.

Constantine moved the capital of the empire to a new city called Constantinople on the site of ancient Byzantium on the Bosphorus. Its strategic location was excellent. The city was surrounded on three sides by water and was easily defended, and it enabled the emperor to stay in close touch with the endangered eastern and Danubian frontiers.

Administration and Finance   The autocratic emperors governed through a civilian bureaucracy, which was kept separate from the army to divide power and reduce the temptation an official might have to challenge the emperor. The system was kept under surveillance by a network of spies and secret police, but they failed to eliminate corruption and inefficiency.

The cost of maintaining a 400,000-man army, a vast civilian bureaucracy, and an expensive imperial court, strained an already weak economy. Peasants unable to pay their taxes and officials unable to collect them fled their posts. Wealthy individuals moved from cities to their rural estates, and many peasants sought protection from the government's tax collectors by becoming tenant farmers on these estates. They were tied to the land, as were their descendants, as a caste system hardened.

Division of the Empire   The peace and unity established by Constantine did not last. The Germans in the west attacked along the Rhine, but even greater trouble was brewing along the Danube where the Visigoths had been driven from their home in the Ukraine by the Huns. The Emperor Valentinian (r. 364–375) saw that he could not defend the empire alone and appointed his brother Valens (r. 364–378) as co-ruler in the east. The empire was again divided in two, and the cultures of Latin west and Greek east grew increasingly distinct. In 376, the Goths began to plunder the Balkan provinces. In 378, Valens met them in battle at Adrianople in Thrace, and he was cut down with most of the eastern army. Theodosius (r. 379–395), an able and experienced general, unified the empire, but at his death in 395 it was divided between his sons and never reunited again.

The west became increasingly rural as barbarian invasions grew. The villa, a fortified country estate, became the basic unit of society. *Coloni* (tenant farmers) served local magnates in return for economic assistance and protection. Cities were depopulated and shrank to tiny walled fortresses ruled by military commanders and bishops. The upper classes left the cities and moved to the country to escape the imperial authorities. The inability of the central authority to maintain and police roads curtailed trade and communications, and living conditions became increasingly primitive. By the fifth century, the west was devolving into rural enclaves ruled by independent aristocrats and worked by a dependent

5.7
Sidonius Appolinaris: Rome's Decay and the Glimpse of the New Order

labor force. The only unifying institution was the Christian church. The pattern of life that was to prevail in the west during the early Middle Ages had been generally established.

While the west was being overrun by barbarians, the Roman Empire, in altered form, persisted in the east. Constantinople flourished as the "New Rome." Although its people continued to call themselves "Romans," their lifestyles were so different from those of ancient Rome that historians refer to them as subjects of medieval *Byzantine* empire. Constantinople's defensible location, the services of some skillful emperors, and the resources of its base in Asia Minor, enabled the eastern empire to deflect and repulse barbarian attacks. A strong Byzantine navy allowed commerce to flourish and cities to prosper. Emperors generally kept the upper hand in dealing with restive aristocratic elements. Byzantine civilization was a unique combination of classical culture, Christian religion, Roman law, and eastern artistic influences. When historians speak of the decline and fall of the Roman Empire in the fourth and fifth centuries, they reference only the west. A form of classical culture persisted in Byzantium for another thousand years.

TRIUMPH OF CHRISTIANITY

Religious Currents in the Empire   In the troubled fourth and fifth centuries people sought the help of powerful, personal deities. It was by no means unusual for people to worship new deities alongside traditional ones and to intertwine features of several gods to create new ones, a phenomenon called **syncretism**. Christianity bore some resemblance to other new faiths of the period, but none of them developed its universal appeal.

syncretism In religion, the equating or combining of deities.

The Triumph of Christianity

ca. 4 B.C.E.	Jesus of Nazareth born
ca. 30 C.E.	Crucifixion of Jesus
64 C.E.	Fire at Rome: persecution by Nero
ca. 70–100 C.E.	Gospels written
ca. 250–260 C.E.	Major persecutions by Decius and Valerian
303 C.E.	Persecution by Diocletian
311 C.E.	Galerius issues Edict of Toleration
312 C.E.	Battle of Milvian Bridge; conversion of Constantine to Christianity
325 C.E.	Council of Nicaea
ca. 330 C.E.	Georgia and Armenia become first Christian kingdoms
395 C.E.	Christianity becomes official religion of Roman Empire

Imperial Persecution   In 303, Diocletian had launched the most serious persecution inflicted on the Christians in the Roman Empire. It failed to stem the Christian tide. Ancient states could not carry out a program of terror with the thoroughness of modern totalitarian governments, and the witness of Christian martyrs may have strengthened the faith. In short order, Christians witnessed a miraculous reversal of fortune.

The conversion of Diocletian's ultimate successor, Constantine, and his ascent as sole ruler of the empire transformed Christianity's prospects. Constantine provided lavish patronage for the church and encouraged widespread conversion. In 394, the emperor Theodosius forbade the celebration of pagan cults, and by the time he died, Christianity had become the official religion of the Roman Empire.

Temptations of power and privilege constituted new threats to the moral standards and spiritual fervor of some Christians. State support for the faith threatened to subordinate the church to the state, as the pagan cults of empire had been. In the east, that was generally the church's fate, but in the west, the weakness of emperors permitted church leaders to exercise independence. In 390, when Ambrose (ca. 339–397), bishop of Milan, excommunicated

MAP 6–3

The Empire's Neighbors. In the fourth century the Roman Empire was nearly surrounded by more threatening neighbors. The map shows where these so-called barbarians lived and the invasion routes many of them took in fourth and fifth centuries.

HOW DID barbarian invasions transform the Roman world?

Emperor Theodosius, the emperor submitted to his authority and did penance. This set an important precedent for future assertions of the church's autonomy and authority.

Arianism and the Council of Nicea   The Christian emperors hoped to unify their increasingly decentralized realms by imposing Christianity as the only religion, but Christianity divided society in new ways. Safety from persecution allowed Christians the freedom to fight among themselves, and disputes over doctrine spread through the general population and caused serious disturbances as Christians sought to distinguish orthodox from heretical teachings. The most important controversy concerned **Arianism**, a debate begun by a priest named Arius of Alexandria (ca. 280–336). Arius's view that Jesus was not co-equal and co-eternal with God the Father was dismissed by his orthodox opponents, who argued that it undercut Jesus' power as savior. In 325, Constantine summoned a great church, **council of Nicaea**, to settle the issue. The **Nicene Creed** the council issued endorsed the doctrine of the Trinity: the belief that God is three persons (Father, Son, and Holy Spirit) who share one substance. Arianism, however, survived and spread and continued to create political difficulties for generations.

Arianism Belief formulated by Arius of Alexandria (ca. 280–336 C.E.) that Jesus was a created being, neither fully man nor fully God, but something in between.

Council of Nicea Council of Christian bishops at Nicaea in 325 C.E. that formulated the Nicene Creed, a statement of Christian belief that rejected Arianism in favor of the doctrine that Christ is both fully human and fully divine.

Nicene Creed A declaration of faith that the Council of Nicaea hoped would be endorsed by all Christians.

OVERVIEW THE FALL OF THE ROMAN EMPIRE IN THE WEST

For centuries scholars have proposed theories to explain why the ancient world collapsed, but the great English historian Edward Gibbon (1737–1794), the author of *The Decline and Fall of the Roman Empire*, said that we should really ask not why Rome fell but how so vast an empire managed to survive for so long. The following are some of the explanations scholars have proposed for the fall of Rome. They range from the plausible to the ridiculous.

Cause	Explanation
Climate change	A gradual drying and cooling climate destroyed the productivity of ancient agriculture on which the empire depended.
Soil exhaustion	Depleted soil around the Mediterranean no longer produced enough food to feed the population, which weakened and declined.
Lead poisoning	Use of lead pipes for drinking and cooking water led to widespread lead poisoning and sterility, especially among the upper classes who had most access to running water.
Racial pollution	Eastern immigrants to Rome—Syrians, Greeks, and Jews—sapped the vitality of the Romans and destroyed their ability to rule and defend themselves.
Slavery	The prevalence of slavery made the Romans lazy and undercut free labor.
Intellectual stagnation	Failure to make advances in science and technology—to achieve a scientific revolution— led the empire to an intellectual and economic dead end.
Social disorder	The destruction of the middle class through civil war, invasion, and over taxation wiped out the most productive and culturally aware part of the Roman population. Third-century emperors encouraged the rural poor to plunder the middle and upper classes.
Excessive government	Government exactions and regulations destroyed the operation of a market economy, which was the basis for prosperity.
Christianity	Adoption of Christianity as the official religion of the empire in the fourth century weakened the Roman state, diverted scarce resources to building and staffing churches and monasteries, and led large segments of the population to embrace pacifism.
Immorality	Gluttony, sloth, and sexual depravity replaced the old Roman virtues that had enabled Rome to conquer its empire.

HOW IS late antiquity a transition period from the Classical to the Medieval?

6.7
Paulus Orosius, History Against the Pagans

ARTS AND LETTERS IN THE LATE EMPIRE

*T*he art and literature of the late empire reflect both the confluence of pagan and Christian ideas and traditions and the conflict between them. Much of the literature is polemical, and much of the art is propaganda.

PRESERVATION OF CLASSICAL CULTURE

One of the major accomplishments of this period was the preservation of many of the great works of classical literature at a time when declining literacy and education threatened their loss. Books that were fundamental to the classical tradition were reproduced in many copies. Scholars saved some materials by condensing long works (e.g., Livy's *History of Rome*) into shorter versions, and they wrote learned commentaries and grammars that enabled later generations to comprehend their legacy from the ancient world.

MAP EXPLORATION

Interactive map: To explore this map further, go to **http://www.prenhall.com/craig/map6.4**

(A) 200

Christian Areas, 200

(B) 200 – 400

Christian Areas, 200
Expansion, 200 – 400

(C) 400 – 600

Christian Areas, 400
Expansion, 400 – 600

MAP 6–4

The Spread of Christianity. Christianity grew swiftly in the third, fourth, fifth, and sixth centuries—especially after the conversion of the emperors in the fourth century. By 600, on the eve of the birth of the new religion of Islam, Christianity was dominant throughout the Mediterranean world and most of Western Europe.

WHICH AREAS remained largely non-Christian at the end of the seventh century?

CHRISTIAN WRITERS

Christianity inspired scholars who did important original work. Jerome (348–420), a Christian who had superb classical education, used his linguistic skills to create the Vulgate, a revised version of the Bible in Latin. It became the official version of the Bible used by the medieval Catholic Church.

The most important Christian scholar in the east may have been Eusebius of Caesarea (ca. 260–ca. 340). His *Ecclesiastical History* attempted to develop a Christian theory of history as a working out of God's will. All of history, he claimed, had divine significance and direction. Constantine's victory and the subsequent unity of empire and church was its culmination.

The closeness and complexity of the relationship between classical pagan culture and the Christianity of the late empire are nowhere better displayed than in the career and writings of Augustine (354–430), bishop of Hippo in North Africa. His skill in pagan rhetoric and philosophy made him peerless among his contemporaries as a defender of Christianity and a theologian. His greatest works are his *Confessions*, an autobiography that describes his conversion, and *The City of God*. The latter was a response to Rome's sack by the Goths in 410. Augustine separated the fate of Christianity from that of the Roman Empire. He contrasted the secular world—the city of Man—with the spiritual—the City of God. The former was selfish, the latter unselfish; the former evil, the latter good. All states, even a Christian Rome, were part of the City of Man and therefore corrupt, mortal, and destined to pass away. Only the City of God was eternal and unaffected by earthly calamities.

SUMMARY

Republican Rome Rome began as a small settlement in Latium in central Italy ruled by Etruscan kings; Rome became a republic in 509 B.C.E. The Roman constitution divided power between elected magistrates, the chief of whom were two consuls: an appointed Senate, whose members served for life; and popular assemblies. During the third century B.C.E., the aristocratic patricians were forced to share power with the common people, the plebians. The institution of clientage by which clients pledged their loyalty to powerful patrons in return for legal and political protection was an important part of Roman political life.

Roman Expansion By the early fourth century, Rome had expanded to control all of Italy through a policy of conquest, alliances, colonies of Roman veterans, and generosity to foes who submitted. Between 264 and 146 B.C.E., Rome fought three wars with Carthage for control of the western Mediterranean. These Punic Wars ended with the destruction of Carthage, but led to resolve social and political disorder in Italy. Many small farmers lost their land, and efforts by the Gracchi brothers to resolve the problems ended in their murders.

In the third century B.C.E., Rome turned to the east and defeated the Hellenistic monarchies that had succeeded Alexander's empire. Macedon and Greece fell under Roman rule. This led to the adoption of Greek culture by the Roman aristocracy and the rapid Hellenization of Roman culture. By the first century B.C.E., Rome controlled most of the Mediterranean world.

The Empire The Roman republic was destroyed by social unrest and rivalry among ambitious generals and politicians, the most successful of whom was Julius Caesar. After a civil war that followed Caesar's assassination in 44 B.C.E., his nephew Octavian emerged as the most powerful man in Rome. Under the title of Augustus, he set up a system that, while preserving the façade of republican institutions, was in fact a monarchy.

The Roman Empire stretched from Scotland to Iraq. Rome fostered the growth of cities, developed the rule of law, built a vast network of roads and other public works, and established two centuries of peace and stability. Christianity, which arose in the Roman province of Judaea in the first century C.E., spread throughout the empire despite occasional persecutions by the Roman state, which itself became Christian in the late fourth century.

Decline and Fall In the third century C.E., the Roman peace collapsed under the pressure of invasions by barbarians in the west and the Persians in the east. Rival generals murdered emperors and usurped the throne. The economy declined. The state exacted more and more taxes and resources from its citizens. The emperors Diocletian and Constantine managed to arrest the decline, but in the fifth century C.E. Roman authority in the west collapsed. In the East, however, a Christian Roman Empire based in the city of Constantinople survived and evolved into the Byzantine Empire that did much to preserve the Greek and Roman heritage for 1,000 years.

REVIEW QUESTIONS

1. How did the institutions of family and clientage help to organize the early Roman republic?

2. What events and motives led Rome to bring Italy, Greece, and Asia Minor under its control?

3. How did Rome's victories over Carthage change Rome?

4. Why was the Roman republic plagued by civil war throughout the last century B.C.E.?

5. Why was the Roman population willing to accept Augustus's empire?

6. Why were Christians persecuted by Roman authorities? What explains Christianity's success?

IMAGE KEY

for pages 122–123

a. A Roman warship
b. Clay Plaque showing emblem of 20th Roman Legion - charging Boar
c. Pompeian, Boscoreale. "Lady playing the cithara"
d. Ancient bronze Roman flutes
e. Detailed scale model of the Roman Coliseum
f. Sarcophagus of an Etruscan couple, sixth century B.C.E.
g. A relief from Titus's Arch of Victory in the Roman Forum
h. Statue of Emperor Augustus of Prima Porta, Rome
i. Reconstruction of a large house and apartments at Ostia
j. Early Christian art showing the arrest of Christ
k. Arch of Constantine, Rome, Italy

KEY TERMS

agape (p. 142)
Arianism (p. 147)
Augustus (p. 134)
Catholic (p. 142)
censor (p. 126)
Council of Nicaea (p. 147)
equestrians (p. 132)
Etruscans (p. 124)
Eucharist (p. 142)

heretics (p. 142)
humanitas (p. 130)
imperator (p. 134)
imperium (p. 124)
latifundia (p. 131)
"mystery" religions (p. 141)
Nicene Creed (p. 147)
orthodox (p. 142)

patricians (p. 125)
Pharisee (p. 142)
plebeians (p. 125)
populares (p. 132)
Punic Wars (p. 127)
syncretism (p. 146)
tetrarchy (p. 144)
tribunes (p. 126)

 For additional study resources for this chapter, go to:
www.prenhall.com/craig/chapter6

7

China's First Empire
221 B.C.E. — 589 C.E.

CHAPTER HIGHLIGHTS

Unification of China China first became a unified state under the Qin dynasty (256–206 B.C.E.). The first Qin emperor built the Great Wall to contain the northern nomadic peoples. The Ch'in ruled through a strong bureaucracy, but their centralized administration collapsed after the death of the first emperor.

Han Dynasty Under the Han (256 B.C.E.–220 C.E.), China's centralized administration was revived. The bureaucracy grew, population expanded, and culture flourished. The Confucian classics became the standard for education. Buddhism arrived in China in the first century C.E. Under the Han it spread across China and adapted itself to Chinese culture. The Han eventually collapsed through a welter of court intrigue, rebellion, and military seizure of power.

CHAPTER QUESTIONS

HOW DID the Qin unify China?

WHAT WAS the dynastic cycle?

HOW DID the Han empire collapse?

TO WHAT extent did China become Buddhist under the Han dynasty?

CHAPTER OUTLINE

• Qin Unification of China

• Former Han Dynasty (206 B.C.E.–8 C.E.)

• Later Han (25–220 C.E.) and Its Aftermath

• Han Thought and Religion

154   **CHAPTER 7**   CHINA'S FIRST EMPIRE 221 B.C.E.–220 C.E.

One hallmark of Chinese history is its striking continuity of culture, language, and geography. The Shang and Zhou dynasties were centered in north China along the Yellow River or its tributary, the Wei. The capitals of China's first empire were in exactly the same areas, and north China has remained China's political center up to the present. If Western civilization had experienced similar continuity, it would have progressed from Thebes in the valley of the Nile to Athens on the Nile; Rome on the Nile; and then, in time, to Paris, London, and Berlin on the Nile; and each of these centers of civilization would have spoken Egyptian and written in Egyptian hieroglyphics.

The many continuities in its history did not mean, however, that China was unchanging. One key turning point came in the third century B.C.E., when the old, quasi-feudal, multistate Zhou system gave way to a centralized bureaucratic government. The new centralized state built an empire stretching from the steppe in the north to Vietnam in the south.

The history of the first empire is composed of three segments: the Qin dynasty, the Former Han dynasty, and the Later Han dynasty. The English word China *is derived from the name of the first dynasty. The Qin overthrew the previous Zhou dynasty in 256 B.C.E. and went on to unify China in 221 B.C.E. In reshaping China, the Qin developed such momentum that it overextended, and its realm collapsed only a generation after the unification. The succeeding Han dynasties each lasted about 200 years, the Early Han from 206 B.C.E. to 8 C.E., the Later Han (founded by a descendant of the Former Han rulers) from 25 to 220 C.E. Historians usually treat each of the Han dynasties as separate periods, although they were almost back to back and shared many institutions and cultural traits. So deep was the impression left by these two dynasties on the Chinese that even today they call themselves—in contrast to Mongols, Manchus, Tibetans, and other minorities—the "Han people," and their ideographs, "Han writing."*

QIN UNIFICATION OF CHINA

HOW DID the Qin unify China?

O f the territorial states of the Late Zhou era, none was more innovative and ruthless than Qin. Its location on the Wei River in northwest China—the same area from which the Zhou had launched their expansion a millennium earlier—gave it strategic advantages: It controlled the passes leading to the Yellow River plain, so it was easy to defend and was a secure base from which to attack other states. In the late fourth century B.C.E., the Qin conquered a part of Szechwan. This, with its home territory, gave the Qin control over two of the most fertile regions of ancient China. It welcomed Legalist administrators, who developed policies for enriching the country and strengthening its military. Despite the Qin's harsh laws, the order and stability of its society attracted farmers from other areas. Its armies had been forged by centuries of warfare against the nomadic raiders by whose lands it was half encircled. To counter their raid, Qin soldiers learned the skills of the nomads and developed cavalry in the fourth century. Other states saw the Qin as tough, crude, and brutal, but recognized its formidable strengths.

In 246 B.C.E., the man who would unify China succeeded to the Qin throne at the age of 13. Vigorous, ambitious, intelligent, and decisive, the First Qin Emperor is famous as a Legalist autocrat; but he was well liked by his ministers, whose advice he usually followed (see Chapter 2 for a description of Legalism). In 232 B.C.E., at the age of 27, he began the campaigns that destroyed the six remaining territorial states. In 221 B.C.E., he signified his victory and declared his superiority to the kings he conquered by adopting a glorious title. We translate it as "emperor," but it is a combination of ideographs hitherto used only for gods or mythic heroes. Then, aided by officials of great talent, this First Emperor implemented reforms throughout China that had been tried and found effective in his own realm. His accomplishments in the 11 years before his death, in 210 B.C.E., were stupendous.

Having conquered the civilized world of north China and the Yangtze River basin, the First Emperor sent his armies farther afield. They reached the northern edge of the Red River basin in what is now Vietnam. They occupied China's southeastern coast and the area about the present-day city of Canton (see Map 7–1). In the north and the northwest, the emperor's armies fought against the Hsiung Nu, Altaic-speaking Hunnish nomads. During the late Zhou, northern border states had built long walls to protect settled lands from incursions by nomadic horsemen. The Qin emperor joined into a single Great Wall that extended 1,400 miles from the Pacific Ocean into Central Asia. Construction of the Great Wall cost the lives of vast numbers of conscripted laborers—by some accounts, 100,000; by others, as many as 1 million.

The most significant Qin reform, carried out by the Legalist minister Li Si, extended the Qin system of bureaucratic government to the entire empire. Li Si divided China into 40 prefectures, which were further subdivided into counties. The county heads were responsible to prefects, who, in turn, were responsible to the central government. Officials were chosen by ability. Bureaucratic administration was impersonal, based on laws to which all were subject. No one, for example, escaped Qin taxation. This kind of bureaucratic centralism broke sharply with the old Zhou pattern of creating dependent principalities for members of a ruler's family. Furthermore, to ensure the smooth functioning of local government offices, former aristocrats of the territorial states were removed from their lands and resettled in the Qin capital, near present-day Xian. They were housed in mansions on one side of the river, from which they could gaze across at the enormous palace of the First Emperor.

Other policies contributed to the unity of the First Emperor's vast domain. Roads were built radiating out from the capital city. The emperor decreed a system of uniform weights and measures. He regulated the Chinese writing system, establishing standard ideographs to replace the great variety that had hitherto prevailed. He established uniform axle lengths for carts. Even thinkers were expected to conform to the government's standards. Following the precepts of Legalism, the emperor and his advisers launched a campaign for which they have been execrated throughout Chinese history. They collected and burned the books of the Confucian and other schools and were said to have buried alive several hundred scholars who rejected the Legalist philosophy. Only books considered useful—on agriculture, medicine, or Legalist teachings—were spared.

The Qin changed too much too quickly. To pay for the roads, canals, and the Great Wall, burdensome taxes were levied. Commoners hated conscription and labor service, and nobles resented their subordination to government authority. Merchants felt exploited, and scholars (except for Legalists) oppressed.

MAP 7–1
Unification of China by the Qin State.   Between 232 and 221 B.C.E., the Qin state expanded and unified China.

WHY DID Qin expansion fail to move westward?

The Great Wall of China. It was originally built during the Qin dynasty (256–206 B.C.E.), but what we see today is the wall as it was completely rebuilt during the Ming dynasty (1368–1644 C.E.).

Paolo Koch/Photo Researchers, Inc.

2.7
Sima Qian: The Historian's Historian writes about the builder of the Great Wall

A Chinese historian later wrote: "The condemned were an innumerable multitude; those who had been tortured and mutilated formed a long procession on the roads. From the princes and ministers down to the humblest people everyone was terrified and in fear of their lives."[1] After the First Emperor died, in 210 B.C.E., intrigues broke out at court, and rebellions arose in the land. At the end, the Qin was destroyed by the domino effect of its own legal codes. When the generals sent to quell a rebellion were defeated, they joined the rebellion rather than returning to the capital to suffer the severe punishment decreed for failure. The dynasty collapsed in 206 B.C.E.

In 1974, a farmer near Xian discovered the army of 8,000 life-size terracotta horses and soldiers that guarded the tomb of the First Emperor. The historical record tells us that in the tomb itself, under a mountain of earth, are a replica of his capital; a relief model of the Chinese world with quicksilver rivers; other warriors with chariots of bronze; and the remains of horses, noblemen, and criminals sacrificed to accompany in death the emperor whose dynasty was to have lasted for 10,000 generations.

FORMER HAN DYNASTY (206 B.C.E.–8 C.E.)

THE DYNASTIC CYCLE

WHAT WAS the dynastic cycle?

Confucian historians of China have seen a pattern in every dynasty of long duration. They call it the **dynastic cycle**. The stages of the cycle are explained as the "Mandate of Heaven." The cycle begins with internal wars that eventually lead to the military unification of China. Unification is proof that heaven has given the unifier the mandate to rule. Strong and vigorous, the first ruler consolidated his political power and restores peace and order to China. Economic growth follows, almost automatically. The peak of the cycle is marked by public works, more energetic reforms, and aggressive military expansion. During this phase, China

dynastic cycle Term used to describe the rise, decline, and fall of China's imperial dynasties.

[1]C. P. Fitzgerald, *China, A Short Cultural History* (New York: Praeger, 1935), p. 147.

OVERVIEW   THE DYNASTIC CYCLE

Confucian historians of China saw a pattern in the rise and fall of China's imperial dynasties that they called the "dynastic cycle." They saw it as a process under which a ruling family won and eventually lost "the Mandate of Heaven," the divine sanction to rule China. The dynastic cycle had the following stages:

Internal wars	China is wracked by disorder and divisions.
Unification	Eventually a strong ruler quells the disorder and reunifies China. His success is proof that he enjoys the Mandate of Heaven.
Strong government	His successors are wise and upright rulers under whom the economy flourishes, China expands, and public works and reforms are promoted. China appears invincible.
Decline	Government costs exceed revenues. The imperial court becomes overly luxurious and riven by intrigues. Emperors neglect their duties. Central controls weaken.
Collapse	Finally, public works decay, floods and plague occur, rebellions break out, and the dynasty collapses. Confucians consider the last emperors in the cycle morally culpable. They have lost the Mandate of Heaven.

appears invincible. But then the cycle turns downward. The costs of expansion, coupled with increasing opulence at court, place a heavy burden on tax revenues just as they are beginning to decline. The vigor of the monarchs wanes. Intrigues develop at court. Central controls loosen, and provincial governors and military commanders gain autonomy. Finally, public works fall into disrepair, floods and pestilence occur, rebellions break out, and the dynasty collapses. For Confucian historians, the last emperors in a cycle are not only politically weak but morally culpable.

EARLY YEARS OF THE FORMER HAN DYNASTY

The first 60 years of the Han may be thought of as the early phase of its dynastic cycle. After the collapse of the Qin, one rebel general gained control of the Wei basin and went on to unify China. He became the first emperor of the Han dynasty and is known by his posthumous title of Gaozu (r. 206–195 B.C.E.). He rose from plebeian origins to become emperor, which only happened one other time in Chinese history. Gaozu built his capital at Chang'an, not far from the former capitals of the Western Zhou and the Qin. It took Gaozu and his immediate successors many years to consolidate their power, for they wanted to avoid the appearance of reinstituting the hated Qin despotism. They made punishments less severe and reduced taxes. Good government prevailed, the economy rebounded, granaries were filled, and the government accumulated vast cash reserves. Later historians often singled out the early Han rulers as model sage-emperors.

HAN WUDI

The second phase of the dynastic cycle began with the rule of Wudi (the "martial emperor"), who came to the throne in 141 B.C.E. at the age of 16 and ruled for 54 years (141–87 B.C.E.). Wudi was daring, vigorous, and intelligent, but also superstitious, suspicious, and vengeful. He wielded tremendous personal authority.

    Building on the prosperity achieved by his predecessors, Wudi initiated new economic policies. A canal was built from the Yellow River to the capital in

A soldier. From the army of life-size terracotta soldiers, this was found in the tomb of the first emperor of the Qin dynasty (256–206 B.C.E.).

Adam Crowley/Getty Images, Inc./PhotoDisc, Inc.

northwest China, linking the two major economic regions of north China. "Ever-level granaries" were established throughout the country so that the surplus from bumper crops could be bought and then resold in time of scarcity. To increase revenues, taxes were levied on merchants, the currency was debased, and some offices were sold. Wudi also moved against merchants who had built fortunes in untaxed commodities by reestablishing government monopolies—a practice of the Qin—on copper coins, salt, iron, and liquor. For fear of Wudi, no one spoke out against the monopolies, but a few years after his death, a famous debate took place at court.

Known as the "Salt and Iron Debate," from the title of the chronicle that records it, the discussion was frequently cited thereafter in China, Japan, and Korea. Quasi-Legalist officials argued that the state should enjoy the profits from the sale of salt and iron. They were opposed by Confucians, who argued that these resources should be left in private hands, for the moral purity of officials would be sullied if they had to deal with merchants. The Confucian scholars who compiled the chronicle made themselves the winners in the debate; but state monopolies became a regular part of Chinese government finance.

Wudi also aggressively expanded Chinese territory—a policy that would characterize every strong dynasty. His armies swept south into what is today northern Vietnam and northeast across Manchuria to establish a military out-post in northern Korea that survived until 313 C.E.

THE XIONGNU

The principal threat to the Han was from the Xiongnu Empire to the north. Their mounted archers could raid China and flee before an army could be mobilized to send against them. Wudi responded by developing policies that became standard thereafter. When possible, he "used the barbarian to control the barbarian," making allies of border nomads against more distant nomads. These allies were allowed to trade with Chinese merchants; they were awarded titles and honors; and their kings were sent Chinese princesses as brides. When this method did not work, Wudi used force. Between 129 and 119 B.C.E. he sent several armies of more than 100,000 troops into the steppe, destroying Xiongnu power south of the Gobi Desert in southern Mongolia. To establish a strategic line of defense aimed at the heart of the Xiongnu Empire farther to the west, Wudi then sent 700,000 Chinese colonists to the arid Kansu panhandle and extended the Great Wall to the Jade Gate outpost at the eastern end of the Tarim basin. From this outpost, Chinese influence was extended over the rim oases of Central Asia, establishing the **Silk Road** that linked Ch'ang-an with Rome (see Map 7–2).

GOVERNMENT DURING THE FORMER HAN

To demonstrate their difference from the Qin emperor, the early Han emperors set up some Zhou-like principalities: small, semiautonomous states with independent lords. This, however, was a token gesture. The principalities were closely superintended and then curtailed after several generations. Basically, despite its repudiation of the Qin and all its works, the Han continued the Qin form of centralized bureaucratic administration. Officials were organized by grades and were paid salaries in grain, plus cash or silk. They were recruited by sponsorship or recommendation. Provincial officials had the duty of recommending promising candidates, and a school that trained them at Chang'an was said to have 30,000 students by the Later Han. The bureaucracy grew until, by the first century B.C.E., there were

Silk Road Trade route from China to the West that stretched across Central Asia.

MAP EXPLORATION

Interactive map: To explore this map further, go to **http://www.prenhall.com/craig/map7.2**

MAP 7–2

The Han Empire 206 B.C.E.–220 C.E.   At the peak of Han expansion, Han armies advanced far out into the steppe north of the Great Wall and west into Central Asia. The Silk Road to Rome passed through the Tarim basin to the Kushan Empire, and on to western Asia and the Middle East.

WHY DID the Han seek to expand their empire to the west and south?

more than 130,000 officials. This, however, may not have been too many for a population that, by then, numbered 60 million.

During the Han dynasty, this Legalist governmental system was slowly and partially Confucianized. The first Han emperor despised Confucians as bookish pedants—he once urinated in the hat of a scholar! But Confucian ideas proved useful. The Mandate of Heaven provided an ethical justification for dynastic rule. The vast bookkeeping the empire entailed engendered respect for old records and the written word. The Confucian classics gradually were accepted as the standard texts for educating government officials. Confucius taught that ethical cultivation could transformation the self, and he envisioned a benevolent government by virtuous, talented men who needed no external constraint

This painted banner is from the tomb of an aristocratic lady, Hunan Province, China, Han dynasty, ca. 160 B.C.E.

to keep them honest. No one attempted to replace laws with a code of etiquette, but increasingly laws were interpreted and applied by men with a Confucian education.

The court during the Han dynasty exhibited features that would appear in later dynasties as well. Everything centered on the emperor, the all-powerful "son of heaven." The will of a strong adult emperor was paramount. If he was weak, however, or ascended the throne when still a child, others competed to rule in his name. Four types of contenders for this surrogate role appeared and reappeared throughout Chinese history: court officials, the empress dowager, court eunuchs, and military commanders.

Court officials were selected for their ability. They staffed the apparatus of government and directly advised the emperor on matters of policy. Apart from the emperor himself, they were usually the most powerful men in China. Their position, however, was often precarious. Few officials escaped being removed from office or banished at least once or twice during their careers. Of the seven prime ministers who served Wudi, five were executed by his order.

Of the emperor's many wives, the empress dowager was the one whose child was designated heir to the throne. Her influence sometimes continued even after her son became an adult, but she was most powerful as a regent for an emperor during his minority. On Gaozu's death in 195 B.C.E., for example, the Empress Lu became the regent for her child, the new emperor. Aided by her relatives, she seized control of the court and murdered a rival. When her son was about to come of age, she killed him and made a younger son the heir so that she could continue to rule as regent. When she died in 180 B.C.E., loyal adherents of the imperial family who had opposed her rule massacred her relatives.

Court eunuchs came mostly from families of low social status. They were brought to court as boys, castrated, and assigned to work as servants in the emperor's harem. They were thus in contact with the future emperor from the day he was born. They became his childhood confidants, and they often continued to advise him after he had gained the throne. Emperors found eunuchs, who had no family ties, useful as counterweights to officials. But the scholars who wrote China's history characterized the eunuchs as greedy half men, given to evil intrigues.

Military leaders, whether generals or rebels, were the usual founders of dynasties. In the later phase of most dynasties, regional military commanders often became semi-independent rulers. A few even usurped the throne. Yet they were less powerful at the Chinese court than they were, for example, in imperial Rome, partly because military men were regarded as inferior in prestige to the better-educated civil officials. The court also took great pains to prevent its generals from establishing bases of personal power. An appointment to command a Han army was given only for a specific campaign, and commanders were appointed in pairs so that each would check the other.

Another characteristic of government during the Han and subsequent dynasties was that its functions were limited. It collected taxes, maintained military forces, administered laws, supported the imperial household, and carried out public works that were beyond the powers of local jurisdictions. But government in a district that remained orderly and paid its taxes was left largely in the hands of local notables and large landowners. This pattern was not, to be sure, unique to China. Most premodern governments, even those that were bureaucratic, were not able to reach down and interfere in the everyday lives of their subjects.

THE SILK ROAD

Romans loved Chinese silks, and the Chinese coveted Roman glass and gold. No single caravan conveyed these goods from one empire to the other, but they were passed through many hands, like batons in a relay race. During the Han and later dynasties, a route began to evolve that ran from the Chinese capital to Kashgar and then north through Tashkent and Samarkand or south through Teheran and Bagdad to Mediterranean ports such as Tyre, Antioch, and Byzantium. Only a small portion of the original shipments made it to the end of the line, a journey of thousands of miles that took more than half a year. Only the most valuable goods were worth the effort of moving them so far.

The Chinese and Romans had no direct contact. Each was unsure of the other's location and knew little about the civilization of the land with which it traded. Ideas and technologies, however, moved along the silk road and were more important than exotic luxury goods. China borrowed the chariot, compound bow, wheat, the domesticated horse, the stirrup, and maybe even the technology for bronze casting from western Asia. Papermaking, iron casting, water-powered mills, shoulder collars for draft animals, compasses, and gunpowder spread from China to the West. Plants and animals were exchanged. Religions migrated, and horrific plagues swept from one region to the other.

DECLINE AND USURPATION

During the last decade of Wudi's rule in the early first century B.C.E., military expenses began to run ahead of revenues. His successor cut back on military costs, eased economic controls, and reduced taxes. But over the next several generations, large landowners used their growing influence in provincial politics to avoid paying taxes. State revenues declined. The tax burden on smaller landowners and free peasants grew heavier. In 22 B.C.E., rebellions broke out in several parts of the empire. At the court, too, decline set in through a series of weak emperors, intrigues, nepotism, and factional struggles. Officials worried that Heaven had withdrawn its mandate and that the dynastic cycle approached its end.

Galloping Horse. China traded with steppe merchants to obtain the horses needed to equip its armies against steppe warriors. Especially desired by the Chinese were the fabled "blood sweating" horses of far-off Ferghana (present-day Tajikistan).

The New York Public Library for the Performing Arts/Art Resource.

Many courtiers urged Wang Mang, the regent for the infant emperor and the nephew of an empress, to take the throne and found a new dynasty. Wang Mang refused several times—to demonstrate his lack of eagerness—and then, in 8 C.E., accepted. He drew up a program of sweeping reforms based on ancient texts. He was a Confucian, but he relied on new institutional arrangements rather than moral reform to improve society. He revived ancient titles, expanded state monopolies, abolished private slavery (affecting about 1 percent of the population), made loans to poor peasants, and confiscated large private estates.

These reforms alienated many. Merchants disliked the monopolies. Large landowners resisted the expropriation of their lands. Even nature seemed to turn against Wang Mang. The Yellow River overflowed its banks, changed its course, and destroyed the northern Chinese irrigation system. Several years of poor harvests resulted in famines. The Xiongnu overran China's northern borders. In 18 C.E., a peasant secret society rose in rebellion, and in 23 C.E., rebels attacked Chang'an. Wang Mang was killed and eaten by rebel troops. He had tried to found a new

The Dynastic History of China's First Empire

256–206 B.C.E.	Qin dynasty
206 B.C.E.–8 C.E.	Former Han dynasty
25–220 C.E.	Later Han dynasty

HOW DID the Han empire collapse?

dynasty from within a decrepit court, but without a base of military support, the attempt was futile. Internal wars continued in China for two more years until a large landowner, the leader of a rebel army, emerged triumphant (25 C.E.). He was from a branch line of the imperial family, and his new dynasty was seen as a restoration of the Han.

LATER HAN (25–220 C.E.) AND ITS AFTERMATH

FIRST CENTURY

The founder of the Later Han moved his capital east to Loyang. Under the first emperor and his two successors there was a return to strong central government and a laissez-faire economy. Agriculture and population recovered. By the end of the first century C.E., China was as prosperous as it had been during the good years of the Former Han. And as in the case of the Former Han, military expansion followed pacification and recuperation. This time the transition came much earlier. South China and Vietnam were retaken during the reign of the first emperor. Dissension among the Xiongnu enabled the Chinese to secure an alliance with some of the southern tribes in 50 C.E., and in 89 C.E. Chinese armies crossed the Gobi Desert and defeated the northern Xiongnu. This defeat sparked the migrations that some historians believe sent the Xiongnu across the southern Russian steppes and then, in the fifth century C.E., to Europe, where they were known as the Huns. In 97 C.E., a Chinese general led an army to the shores of the Caspian Sea. The Chinese expansion in inner Asia, coupled with more lenient government policies toward merchants, facilitated the camel caravans that carried Chinese silk across the Tarim basin to Iran, Palestine, and Rome.

DECLINE DURING THE SECOND CENTURY

Until 88 C.E. the emperors of the Later Han were vigorous, but their successors were ineffective and short-lived. Empresses plotted to advance the fortunes of their families. Emperors turned for help to palace eunuchs, whose power at times surpassed that of officials. In 159 C.E., a group of eunuchs in the service of an emperor slaughtered the family of a scheming empress dowager and took over the court. When officials and students protested against the eunuch dictatorship, more than 100 were killed and 1,000 were tortured or imprisoned. In another incident in 190 C.E., a general deposed one emperor, installed another, killed the empress dowager, and massacred most of the eunuchs at the court.

In the countryside, large landowners who had been powerful from the start of the dynasty grew more so. They harbored private armies. Farmers on their estates were reduced to serfs, and they used their influence to avoid taxes. Great numbers of free farmers escaped their taxes by fleeing south, leaving the remaining freeholders obligated for ever-increasing taxes and labor services. Many peasants turned to neo-Daoist religious movements that provided the justification and organization they needed to turn their discontent into action. In 184 C.E., rebellions organized by members of the religious movements broke out against the government. Han generals suppressed the rebellions but then took personal control of the provinces they had pacified. In 220 C.E., they deposed the last Han emperor.

AFTERMATH OF EMPIRE

For more than three and a half centuries after the fall of the Han, China was fragmented. For several generations it was divided into three kingdoms, whose heroic warriors and scheming statesmen were made famous by wandering storytellers. These characters are included in the *Tale of the Three Kingdoms*, a Chinese romantic epic.

Chinese history during the post-Han centuries had two characteristics. The first was the dominant role played by the great aristocratic landowning families. With vast estates, huge numbers of serfs, fortified manor houses, and private armies, no king could control them. Because they took over many of the functions of local government, some historians see post-Han China as reverting to the quasi-feudalism of the Zhou. The second feature of this period was divergence in the ways that northern and southern China were developing.

In the south, a succession of ever weaker dynasties centered on Nanjing. Although the period of Chinese history from 220 C.E. to 589 C.E. is called the Six Dynasties era, these six southern states were in fact short-lived kingdoms, plagued by intrigues, usurpations, and coups d'état. They were frequently at war with northern states and in constant fear of their own generals. The main developments in the south were: (1) continuing economic growth and the emergence of Nanking as a thriving center of commerce, (2) the ongoing absorption of tribal peoples into Chinese society and culture, (3) large-scale immigrations of Chinese fleeing the north, and (4) the penetration of Buddhism to the heart of Chinese culture.

In the north, state formation depended on interaction between nomads and the Chinese. During the Han dynasty, Chinese invasions of the steppe had led to the establishment of semi-Sinicized Xiongnu as the northernmost tier of the Chinese defense system—just as Germanic tribes protected the late Roman Empire. But as the Chinese state weakened, the highly mobile nomads broke loose, joined with other tribes, and began to invade China. The short-lived states that they formed are usually referred to as the "Sixteen Kingdoms." One was founded by invaders of Tibetan stock. Most spoke Altaic languages: the Xianbii (proto-Mongols), the Tuoba (proto-Turks), and the Ruan Ruan (who would later appear in eastern Europe as the Avars). But differences were less important than these tribes' similarities:

1. All began as steppe nomads with a way of life different from that of agricultural China.

2. After forming states, all became at least partially Sinicized. Chinese from great families, which had preserved Han traditions, served as their tutors and administrators.

3. All were involved in wars—among themselves, against southern dynasties, or against conservative steppe tribes that resisted Sinicization.

4. Buddhism was as powerful in the north as in the south. As a universal religion, it acted as a bridge between "barbarians" and Chinese—just as Christianity was a unifying force in post-Roman Europe. The barbarian rulers of the north were especially attracted to its magical side and usually made Buddhism their state religion. Of the northern states, the most durable was the Northern Wei (386–534 C.E.), famed for its Buddhist sculpture.

TO WHAT extent did China become Buddhist under the Han dynasty?

HAN THOUGHT AND RELIGION

Poems describe the splendor of Chang'an and Luoyang: broad boulevards, tiled gateways, open courtyards, watchtowers, and imposing walls. Most splendid of all were the palaces of emperors, with their audience halls, vast chambers, harem quarters, and parks containing artificial lakes and rare animals and birds. Today, however, little remains of the grandeur of the Han. Whereas Roman ruins abound in Italy and circle the Mediterranean, in China nothing remains above ground. Only from pottery, bronzes, musical instruments, gold and silver jewelry, lacquerware, and clay figurines that were buried in tombs can we get a feeling for the rich material culture of the Han period. And only from paintings on the walls of tombs do we know of its art. But a wealth of written records survives to document the intellectual achievements of Han culture, particularly in the fields of philosophy and history.

HAN CONFUCIANISM

A major accomplishment of the early Han was the recovery of texts lost during the Qin persecution of scholars. Some were retrieved from the walls of houses where they had been hidden; others were reproduced from memory by scholars. (The degree of authenticity of the texts was debated then as now.) In 51 B.C.E. and again in 79 C.E., councils were held to determine the true meaning of the Confucian classics. In 175 C.E., an approved, official version of the texts was inscribed on stone tablets. Han scholars also began writing commentaries on the classics, a major scholarly activity throughout Chinese history. Scholars learned the classics by heart and used classical allusions in their writing.

The first dictionary was compiled about 100 C.E. Containing about 9,000 characters, it helped promote a uniform system of writing. In Han times, as today, Chinese from the north could not converse with Chinese from the southeastern coast. But a common written language bridged differences of pronunciation and fostered Chinese unity.

Han philosophers augmented Zhou Confucianism with ideas characterized as cosmological naturalism. Zhou Confucianists had assumed that the moral force of a virtuous emperor would both order society and harmonize nature. Han Confucianists explained why. Dong Zhongshu (ca. 179–104 B.C.E.), for example, held that all nature was a single, interrelated system. Just as summer always follows spring, so does one color, one virtue, one planet, one element, one number, and one officer of the court always take precedence over another. All

Han Dynasty Tomb Painting. Court figures painted on ceramic tile in a Han dynasty tomb (Gray earthenware; hollow tiles painted in ink and colors on a whitewashed wound 73.8 × 204.7 cm).

"Lintel & Pediment of a Tomb." China, Western Han dynasty, first century B.C. Gray earthenware; hollow tiles painted in ink & colors on a whitewashed ground. 73.8 × 204.7 cm. Denman Waldo Ross Collection, & Gift of C.T. Loo. Courtesy Museum of Fine Arts, Boston.

reflect the systematic workings of yang and yin and the five elements. And just as one dresses appropriately for each season, so was it important for the emperor to choose policies appropriate to the sequences inherent in nature. If he was moral, if he acted in accord with heaven's natural system, then all would go well. But if he acted inappropriately, then heaven would send a portent as a warning—a blue dog, a rat holding its tail in its mouth, an eclipse, or a comet. If the portent was not heeded, wonders and then misfortunes would follow. It was the Confucian scholars themselves, of course, who claimed to understand these omens, a skill that made them essential advisers to emperors.

It is easy to criticize Han philosophy as a pseudo-scientific or mechanistic view of nature. But it represented a new effort by the Chinese to comprehend the interrelationships of the natural world. This effort led to inventions like the seismograph and to advances in astronomy, music, and medicine. It was also during the Han that the Chinese invented paper, the wheelbarrow, the stern-post rudder, and the compass (known as the "south-pointing chariot").

HISTORY

The Chinese were the greatest historians of the premodern world. They wrote more history than anyone else, and what they wrote was usually more accurate than other accounts. Apart from the *Spring and Autumn Annals* and the scholarship of Confucius himself, history writing in China began during the Han dynasty. Various explanations are proposed for why the Chinese were so history-minded. It may be because Chinese tradition is this-worldly or because veneration of the Confucian classics created respect for the written word. It could be because history was seen as a lesson book (the Chinese called it a mirror) for statesmen, and thus knowledge of it was a necessity for the literate men who ran the Chinese state.

The practice of using actual documents and firsthand accounts of events began with Sima Qian (d. 85 B.C.E.), who attempted to write a history of the known world from the most ancient times down to the age of the emperor Wudi. His *Historical Records* consisted of 130 substantial chapters. It was divided into "Basic Annals"; "Chronological Tables"; "Treatises" (on rites, music, astronomy, the calendar, and so on); "Hereditary Houses"; and "Biographies" (70 chapters including descriptions of foreign people). A second great work, *The Book of the Han*, was written by Ban Gu (d. 92 C.E.). It applied the analytical schema of Sima Qian to a single dynasty, the Former Han, and established the pattern by which each dynasty wrote the history of its predecessor.

NEO-DAOISM

As the Han dynasty waned, the effort to realize the Confucian ethic in the sociopolitical order became increasingly difficult. Some scholars abandoned Confucianism altogether in favor of **Neo-Daoism**, or "mysterious learning," as it was called. A few wrote commentaries on the classical Daoist texts that had been handed down from the Zhou. The *Zhuangzi* was especially popular. Other scholars, defining the natural as the pleasurable, withdrew from society to engage in witty "pure conversations." They discussed poetry and philosophy, played the lute, and drank wine. The most famous were the Seven Sages of the Bamboo Grove of the third century C.E. One sage was always accompanied by a servant carrying a jug of wine and a spade—the one for his pleasure, the other to dig his grave should he die. Another wore no clothes at home. When criticized, he replied that the cosmos was his home, and his house his clothes. "Why are you in my pants?" he asked a discomfited visitor. Still another took a boat to visit a friend on a snowy night, but on

Neo-Daoism A revival of Daoist "mysterious learning" that flourished as a reaction against Confucianism during the Han dynasty.

arriving at his friend's door, turned around and went home. When pressed for an explanation, he said that it had been his pleasure to go, and that when the impulse died, it was his pleasure to return. This story reveals a scorn for convention coupled with an admiration for an inner spontaneity, however eccentric (see "The Peach Blossom Spring").

Another concern of Neo-Daoism was the achievement of immortality. Some people sought it in dietary restrictions and Yogalike meditation, some in sexual abstinence or orgies. Others, trying to discover elixirs to prolong life, dabbled in alchemy, and although no magical formula was ever found, the schools of alchemy to which the search gave rise are credited with the discovery of medicines, dyes, glazes, and gunpowder. Popular religious cults arose among the common people that, because they included the Daoist classics among their sacred texts, are considered Neo-Daoist. Like most folk religions, they were an amalgam of beliefs, practices, and superstitions. They had a pantheon of gods and immortals and taught that the good or evil done in this life would be rewarded or punished in the innumerable heavens or hells of an afterlife. These cults had priests, shamans who practiced faith healing, seers, and sorceresses. For a time, they also had hierarchical religious organizations, but these were smashed at the end of the second century C.E. Local Daoist temples and monasteries, however, survived until modern times. With many Buddhist accretions, they furnished the religious beliefs of the bulk of the Chinese population. Today, these sects continue in Taiwan and in Chinese communities in Southeast Asia. They were suppressed in China during the Maoist era but revived during the 1990s.

BUDDHISM

Central Asian missionaries, following the trade routes east, brought Buddhism to China in the first century C.E. It was at first viewed as a new Daoist sect, which is not surprising because early translators used Daoist terms to render Buddhist concepts. *Nirvana*, for example, was translated as "not doing" (*wuwei*). In the second century C.E., confusion about the two religions led to the very Chinese view that Laozi had gone to India, where the Buddha had become his disciple, and that Buddhism was the Indian form of Daoism.

Then, as the Han sociopolitical order collapsed in the third century C.E., Buddhism spread rapidly. We are reminded of the spread of Christianity at the end of the Roman Empire. Although an alien religion in China, Buddhism had some advantages over Daoism:

1. It was a doctrine of personal salvation, offering several routes to that goal.

2. It upheld high standards of personal ethics.

3. It had systematic philosophies, and during its early centuries in China, it continued to receive inspiration from India.

4. It drew on the Indian tradition of meditative practices and psychologies, which were the most sophisticated in the world.

By the fifth century C.E. Buddhism had spread over all of China (see Map 7–3 on page 166). Occasionally it was persecuted by Daoist emperors—in the north between 446 and 452 C.E., and again between 574 and 578 C.E. But most courts supported Buddhism. The "Bodhisattva Emperor" Wu of the southern Liang dynasty three times dedicated himself to a monastery and had to be ransomed back by his disgusted courtiers. Temples and monasteries abounded in both the north and the south. There were communities of women as well as of men. Chinese produced Buddhist painting and sculpture of surpassing beauty, and

nirvana In Buddhism the attainment of release from the wheel of *karma*.

HISTORY'S VOICES

THE PEACH BLOSSOM SPRING

he poet Dao Qian wrote in 380 C.E. of a lost village without taxes and untouched by the barbarian invasions and wars of the post-Han era. The simplicity and naturalness of his utopian vision were in accord, perhaps, with certain strains of Neo-Daoist thought. It struck a chord in the hearts of Chinese, and then Koreans and Japanese, inspiring a spate of paintings, poetry, and essays.

UTOPIAS ARE often based on religion, but this one is not. What does this suggest regarding the Chinese view of human nature?

During the T'ai-yuan period of the Ch'in [Qin] dynasty a fisherman of Wuling once rowed upstream, unmindful of the distance he had gone, when he suddenly came to a grove of peach trees in bloom. For several hundred paces on both banks of the stream there was no other kind of tree. The wild flowers growing under them were fresh and lovely, and fallen petals covered the ground—it made a great impression on the fisherman. He went on for a way with the idea of finding out how far the grove extended. It came to an end at the foot of a mountain whence issued the spring that supplied the stream. There was a small opening in the mountain and it seemed as though light was coming through it. The fisherman left his boat and entered the cave, which at first was extremely narrow, barely admitting his body; after a few dozen steps it suddenly opened out onto a broad and level plain where well-built houses were surrounded by rich fields and pretty ponds. Mulberry, bamboo and other trees and plants grew there, and criss-cross paths skirted the fields. The sounds of

cocks crowing and dogs barking could be heard from one courtyard to the next. Men and women were coming and going about their work in the fields. The clothes they wore were like those of ordinary people. Old men and boys were carefree and happy.

When they caught sight of the fisherman, they asked in surprise how he had got there. The fisherman told the whole story, and was invited to go to their house, where he was served wine while they killed a chicken for a feast. When the other villagers heard about the fisherman's arrival they all came to pay him a visit. They told him that their ancestors had fled the disorders of Ch'in [Qin] times and, having taken refuge here with wives and children and neighbors, had never ventured out again; consequently they had lost all contact with the outside world. They asked what the present ruling dynasty was, for they had never heard of the Han, let alone the Wei and the Ch'in [Qin]. They sighed unhappily as the fisherman enumerated the dynasties one by one and recounted the vicissitudes of each. The visitors all asked him to come to their houses in turn, and at every house he had wine and food. He stayed several days. As he was about to go away, the people said, "There's no need to mention our existence to outsiders." After the fisherman had gone out and recovered his boat, he carefully marked the route. On reaching the city, he reported what he had found to the magistrate, who at once sent a man to follow him back to the place. They proceeded according to the marks he had made, but went astray and were unable to find the cave again.

Source: *The Poetry of Ta'o Ch'ien* by J. R. Hightower. Copyright © 1970 Clarendon Press. pp. 254–255. Reprinted by permission of Oxford University Press.

thousands of monk-scholars labored to translate sutras and philosophical treaties. Chinese monks went on pilgrimages to India. The record left by Fa Xian, who traveled to India overland and back by sea between 399 and 413 C.E., became a prime source of Indian history. The Tang monk Xuanzang went to India from 629 until 645. Several centuries later, a novelized version of his pilgrimage (combining faith, magic, and adventure) appeared under the title *Journey to the West.*

MAP 7–3

The Spread of Buddhism and Chinese States in 500 C.E. Buddhism originated in a Himalayan state in northwest India and spread in one wave south to India and on to Southeast Asia as far as Java. But Buddhism also spread into northwest India, Afghanistan, Central Asia, and then to China, Korea, and Japan.

WHAT IS the relationship between the spread of Buddhism and trade?

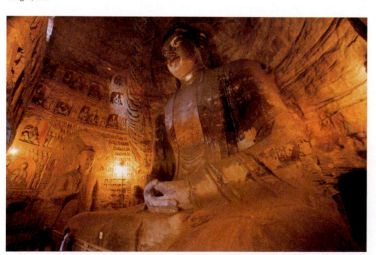

Buddha. A giant statue of the Buddha dwarfs visitors to the Yungang Grotto in Datong, China. Note the little Buddhas in the walls of the grotto.

China Tourism Press/Chan, Yat Nin/Getty Images, Inc.

A comparison of Indian and Chinese Buddhism highlights some distinctive features of its spread. Buddhism in India had begun as a reform movement. The Buddha had advised people to forget speculative philosophies and elaborate metaphysics and concentrate on simple truths: Life is suffering; the cause of suffering is desire; death does not stop the endless cycle of birth and rebirth; only the attainment of *nirvana* releases one from the "wheel of *karma*." In this most otherworldly of world religions, the cosmic drama of salvation was compressed into single figure— the Buddha meditating under the Bodhi tree. Over the centuries, however, Indian Buddhism developed contending philosophies and conflicting sects. It became virtually indistinguishable from Hinduism and was reabsorbed after 1000 C.E.

In China, there were a number of sects with different doctrinal positions. But the Chinese genius was more syncretic. It adopted the sutras and meditative practices of early Buddhism. It took in the Mahayana philosophies that depicted a succession of Buddhas, cosmic and historical, past and future, all embodying a single ultimate reality. It also honored the sutras and practices of Buddhist devotional sects. Finally, in the Tiantai sect, the Chinese joined together these various elements, explaining them as different levels of a single truth. Thus, the monastic routine of a Tiantai monk would include reading sutras, meditating, and practicing devotional exercises.

Socially, too, Buddhism adapted to China. Ancestor worship demanded heirs to perform the sacrifices. Without progeny, ancestors might become "hungry ghosts." Hence, the first son would be expected to marry and have children, whereas the second son, if he were so inclined, might become a monk. The practice also arose of holding Buddhist masses for dead ancestors. Still another difference between China and India was the more extensive regulation of Buddhism by the state in China. Just as Buddhism was not to threaten the integrity of the family, so Buddhism was not to reduce the taxes paid on land. As a result, limits were placed on the number of monasteries, nunneries, and monastic lands, and men and women had to get permission from the state before they could abandon the world to enter a religious establishment. This regulation, to be sure, was not always enforced.

SUMMARY

Unification of China China first became a unified state under the Qin dynasty (256–206 B.C.E.). In the north, the first Qin emperor built the Great Wall to contain the northern nomadic peoples. The Qin ruled through a strong bureaucracy, but their centralized administration collapsed after the death of the first emperor.

Han Dynasty Under the Han (256 B.C.E.–220 C.E.), China's centralized administration was revived. The Han made such a profound impression on Chinese history that the Chinese still speak of themselves as the "Han people." The Confucian classics became the standard for education and Buddhism arrived in China in the first century C.E.. The Han eventually collapsed through a welter of court intrigue, rebellion, and military seizure of power.

REVIEW QUESTIONS

1. What were the main features of Qin administration? Why did the Qin collapse?

2. What was the "Mandate of Heaven?" What was the "dynastic cycle?"

3. Who were the players who sought power at the Han court? Did the means they used reflect differences in their positions?

4. Did Buddhism "triumph" in China in the same sense in which Christianity triumphed in the Roman world? What problems did both China and the Roman Empire face and how did they try to resolve them?

KEY TERMS

dynastic cycle (p. 156)
Neo-Daoism (p. 165)

nirvana (p. 166)
Silk Road (p. 158)

IMAGE KEY

for pages 152–153

a. Bronze horse bit from Han Dynasty
b. Great Wall near Peking, China
c. "Prince Charming"—stem with flowers
d. Ancient Chinese armored terra cotta soldier
e. China, Xian, The army of terracotta warriors, close-up
f. Han sculpture of Chinese galloping horse
g. Bronze mirror, Han Dynasty
h. The lintel of an ancient tomb from the Western Han dynasty
i. Scabbard from the Dian Kingdom
j. A Chinese seismograph
k. A pottery model of a Later Han dynasty watch tower
l. A tomb figure; Former Han dynasty

 For additional study resources for this chapter, go to:
www.prenhall.com/craig/chapter7

Visualizing The Past

Visualizing the Past: The Silk Road in Late Antiquity

WHAT IS the relationship between trade and cultural exchange?
Why is the Silk Road a uniquely Eurasian phenomenon?

In late antiquity Eurasia was connected by a series of political, economic, and cultural networks that extended from China to Rome. The Silk Road (see page 161) was the most important link in this nexus of trade and cultural exchange. Along this great route ideas, religions, and artistic styles were transmitted across Eurasia.

◄ **The Story of the Silk Princess.** This sixth-century C.E. wooden panel comes from a Buddhist sanctuary in Khotan, a Central Asian kingdom that flourished along the Silk Road in late antiquity. This scene illustrates the introduction of silk moths to Khotan from China, which first domesticated the insect around 5000 B.C.E and strenuously tried to prevent the spread of silk cultivation. A Chinese princess (second from left) defied the emperor's embargo by hiding mulberry seeds and eggs of the silk moth in her crown and smuggled them past a border-post. An attendant draws the viewer's attention to this by pointing to her head-dress. The basket of cocoons between them signifies the mission's success. On the far right, a figure holding a comb stands in front of a loom with a reel of thread behind. The four-armed deity is the patron of weaving.
© Copyright The British Museum.

Standing Buddha. In the early centuries of the first millennium C.E. the Kushan empire straddled the trade routes that intersected the steppes of Central Asia to become an influential power facilitating the spread of culture and ideas. One of the legacies of Kushan is the Gandharan school of art which fused Greek (Hellenistic) and Indian influences into its own unique style (see chapter 4), as exemplified by this standing Buddha.
National Museum of New Delhi.

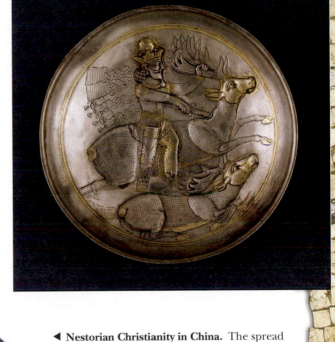

Shapur II. Located on the western end of the Silk Road, the Sasanian ▶ Empire (224–651 C.E.), the last Persian dynasty before the advent of Islam, extended its cultural reach far beyond its borders. Sasanian ideals of kingship would later influence Arab notions of imperial splendor as well as the pretensions of regional powers, such as Armenia and Georgia. This silver plate depicts the great fourth-century Sasanian emperor Shapur II (r. 531–579) slaying a deer. The ideal of the king as a mighty hunter is a common motif in late antiquity.
4th century C.E. British Library/London/Great Britain. Hunting Scene. Plate. Sasanian (224–649 C.E.). Shapur II (310–379). Silver. HIP/Art Resource, N.Y.

◀ **Nestorian Christianity in China.** The spread of Christianity along the Silk Road perfectly illustrates the close connection between missionary activity and trading routes in late antiquity. The Nestorians (named after Nestorius, a fifth-century Greek theologian) were an early Christian sect that flourished initially in what is present-day Iraq and Iran. They stressed the human as opposed to the divine aspect of Jesus Christ. Although the Nestorians had little impact on Christian communities in the Mediterranean and Europe, their faith extended east along the Silk Road. The **stele** depicted here, built in 781 C.E., commemorates the introduction of Nestorian Christianity in China.
Musée des Arts Asiatiques–Guimet, Paris, France. Réunion des Musée Nationaux/Art Resource, N.Y.

PART THREE   Consolidation and Interaction of World Civilizations

EUROPE

511	Death of Clovis, Frankish ruler of Gaul
529	Benedict of Nursia founds Benedictine Order
590–604	Pontificate of Gregory I, "the Great"
768–814	Charles the Great (Charlemagne)

◀ *Crown of the Holy Roman Emperor*
Kunsthistorisches Museum, Vienna.

▲ *Charlemagne*

ca. 800–1000	Invasions of England and the Carolingian Empire (Vikings, Magyars, and Muslims)
843	Treaty of Verdun divides Carolingian Empire
910	Cluny Monastery founded
1019–1054	Yaroslav the Wise reigns; peak of Kievan Russia
1054	Schism between Latin and Greek churches
1066	Norman Conquest of England
1073–1085	Investiture controversy
1096–1270	The Crusades

▲ *Battle of Hastings*

NEAR EAST / INDIA

527–565	Justinian's reign
531–579	Reign of Chosroes Anosharvian in Iran
ca. 570–632	Muhammad
622	The Hijra
616–657	Reign of Harsha; neo-Gupta revival in India
651	Death of last Sasanid ruler
661–750	Umayyad dynasty
680	Death of Al-Husayn at Karbala; second civil war begins
ca. 710	First Muslim invasion of India
750–1258	Abbasid dynasty
786–809	Caliph Harun Al-Rashid reigns

800–1200	Period of feudal" overlordship in India
900–1100	Golden age of Muslim learning
909–1171	Fatimids in North Africa and Egypt
945–1055	Buyid rule in Baghdad
994–1186	Ghaznavid rule in northwestern India, Afghanistan, and Iran
1055–1194	Seljuk rule in Baghdad
1071	Seljuk Turks capture Jerusalem
1081–1118	Byzantine emperor Alexius Comnenus reigns
ca. 1000–1300	Turko-Afghan raids into India

Manichaean priests ▶

EAST ASIA

589–618	Sui dynasty reunifies China
607	Japan begins embassies to China
618–907	Tang dynasty in China
701–762	Li Bo, Tang poet
710–784	Nara court, Japan's first permanent capital
712	*Records of Ancient Matters,* in Japan
713–756	Emperor Hsuan Tsung reigns in China
755	An Lushan rebellion in China
794–1185	Heian (Kyoto) court in Japan

◀ *Song dynasty wine pot*

856–1086	Fujiwara dominate Heian court
960–1279	Song dynasty in China
ca. 1000	*Pillow Book* by Sei Shōnagon and *Tale of Genji* by Murasaki Shikibu
1037–1101	Su Dungpo, Song poet

AFRICA

ca. 500	States of Takrur and Ghana founded
ca. 500–700	Political and commercial ascendancy of Aksum (Ethiopia)
ca. 600–1500	Extensive slave trade from sub-Saharan Africa to Mediterranean
ca. 700–800	Ghanians begin to supply gold to Mediterranean
ca. 700–900	States of Gao and Kanem
ca. 800	Appearance of the Kanuri people around Lake Chad

ca. 800–900	Decline of Aksum
ca. 900–1100	Kingdom of Ghana; capital city, Kumbi Saleh
ca. 1000–1100	Islam penetrates sub-Saharan Africa
1000–1500	"Great Zimbabwe" center of Bantu Kingdom in southeastern Africa

◀ *Stela at Aksum*

THE AMERICAS

ca. 150–900	Classic period. Dominance of Teotihuacán in central Mexico, Tikal in southern Yucatán

ca. 600–1000	Middle (Huari/Tiwanaku) Horizon in Andean South America

Ruins of Tikal ▶

1154–1158	Frederick Barbarosa invades Italy
1182–1226	St. Francis of Assisi
1198–1216	Pontificate of Innocent III
ca. 1100–1300	Growth of trade and towns
1215	Magna Carta granted
ca. 1225–1274	St. Thomas Aquinas
1265–1321	Dante Alighieri

1337	Hundred Years' War begins
ca. 1340–1400	Geoffrey Chaucer
1347–1349	The Black Death
1375–1527	The Italian Renaissance
1485	Battle of Bosworth Field; accession of Henry Tudor to the throne of England
1492	Columbus's first voyage to the New World

Book of Hours ▶
(15th century)

1174–1193	Saladin reigns
1192	Muslim conquerors end Buddhism in India
1206–1526	Delhi Sultanate in India; Indian culture divided into Hindu and Muslim
ca. 1220	Mongol invasions of Iran, Iraq, Georgia, Armenia, Syria, India
1258	Hulagu Khan, Mongol leader, conquers Baghdad
1260–1335	Il-Khans rule Iran

1250–1517	Mamluk rule in Egypt
1366–1405	Timur (Tameriane) reigns
1405–1494	Timurids rule in Transoxiana and Iran
1453	Byzantine Empire falls to the Ottoman Turks, with capture of Constantinople

◄ *Bronze Shiva*

1130–1200	Zhu Xi, Song philosopher
1167–1227	Genghis Khan, founder of Mongol Empire
1185–1333	Kamakura shogunate in Japan
1274–1281	Mongol invasions of Japan
1279–1368	Mongol (Yuan) dynasty in China

1336–1467	Ashikaga shogunate in Kyoto
1368–1644	Ming dynasty in China
1405–1433	Voyages of Cheng Ho to India and Africa
1467–1568	Warring States era in Japan
1472–1529	Wang Yang-ming, Ming philosopher

◄ *Genghis Khan*

▲ *Sesshū painting of a market day in Japan*

ca. 1100–1897	Kingdom of Benin in tropical rain forest region
1194–1221	Kanem Empire achieves greatest expansion
1203	Kingdom of Ghana falls to Sosso people
1230–1255	King Sundiata, first ruler of Mali Empire; Walata and Timbuktu become centers of trade and culture
ca. 1230–1450	Kingdom of Mali Empire

1307–1332	Mansa Musa, greatest king of Mali
1490s	Europeans establish trading posts on western African coast
mid–1400s	Decline of Mali Empire; creation of Songhai Empire
1468	Sonni Ali captures Timbuktu
1476–1507	Reign of King Mai Ali of Bornu in central Sudan
1493–1528	Songhai ruler Askia Muhammed reigns; consolidates Songhai Empire

▲ *Fatimid ceramic bowl*

| ca. 800–1400 | Chimu Empire on north coast of Peru |

1325	Founding of Aztec capital of Tenochtitlán
1428–1519	Period of Aztec expansion
1492	European encounter with America
1519	Cortes conquers Aztec Empire
ca. 1350–1533	Inca Empire in Peru
1533	Pizarro executes Inca ruler Atahualpa

Pre-Columbian ▶
Aztec sun stone

8 Imperial China
589 B.C.E. – 1368 C.E.

CHAPTER HIGHLIGHTS

Sui and Tang Dynasties The Sui and Tang dynasties (589–907) reunited China's empire. Under the Tang, China expanded into Central Asia, taking control of much of the lucrative Silk Road along which trade moved to the West. Chang'an, the Tang capital, became the largest city in the world. Tang culture was rich and cosmopolitan, much influenced by its contacts with other cultures. The Tang dynasty was also the golden age of Buddhism in China.

Song Dynasty Under the Song dynasty (960–1279), China experienced an agricultural revolution in which large aristocratic estates worked by serfs gave way to small land holdings owned by free farmers. Advances in technology led to the invention of printing and the development of a coal and iron-smelting industry. The growth of a money economy encouraged the expansion of trade. Song culture was particularly rich in philosophy, poetry, and painting.

The Mongols After their unification by Genghis Khan (1167–1227), the Mongols created the greatest empire in history. The highly mobile Mongol cavalry overwhelmed Chinese armies. By 1279 the Mongols ruled all of China. But Mongol rule in China was short lived and enjoyed only shallow Chinese support. Mongol rule in China ended in 1368.

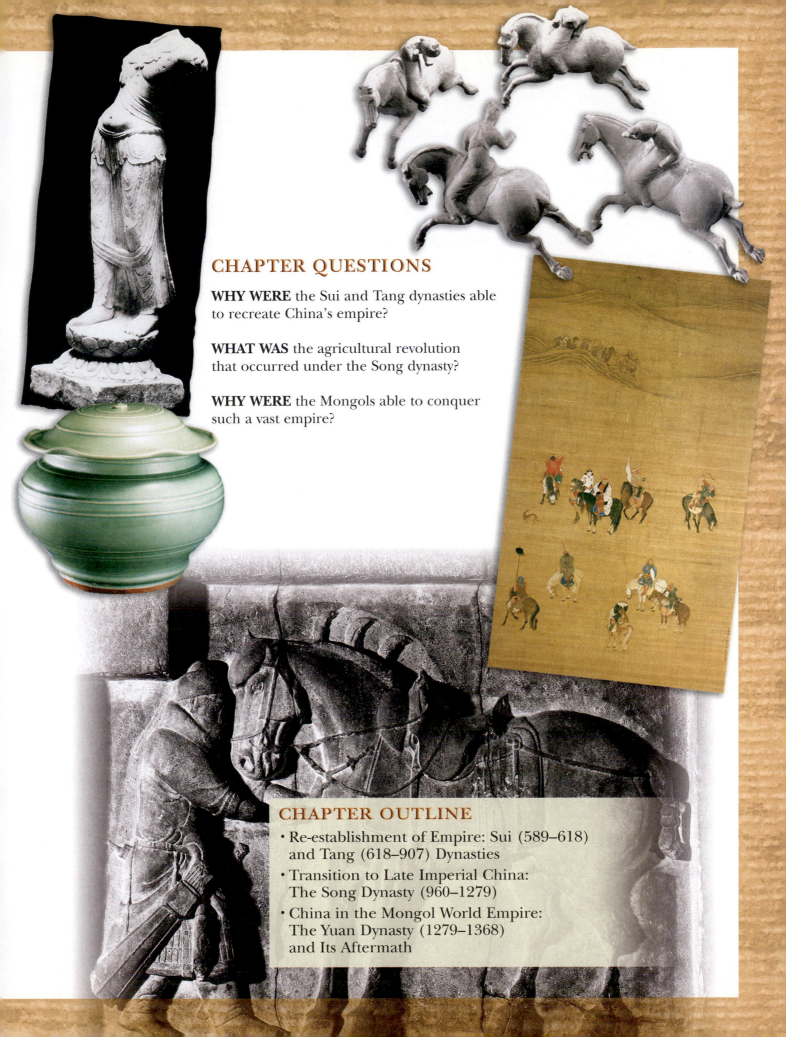

CHAPTER QUESTIONS

WHY WERE the Sui and Tang dynasties able to recreate China's empire?

WHAT WAS the agricultural revolution that occurred under the Song dynasty?

WHY WERE the Mongols able to conquer such a vast empire?

CHAPTER OUTLINE

- Re-establishment of Empire: Sui (589–618) and Tang (618–907) Dynasties
- Transition to Late Imperial China: The Song Dynasty (960–1279)
- China in the Mongol World Empire: The Yuan Dynasty (1279–1368) and Its Aftermath

If Chinese dynasties from the late sixth to the mid-14th centuries were given numbers like those of ancient Egypt, the Sui and Tang dynasties would be called the Second Empire; the Song, the Third; and the Yuan, the Fourth. Numbers, however, would not convey the distinct personalities of these dynasties. The Tang (618–907) is everyone's favorite dynasty: open, cosmopolitan, expansionist, exuberant, and creative. It was the example of Tang China that decisively influenced the formation of states and high cultures in Japan, Korea, and Vietnam. Poetry during the Tang attained a peak that has not been equaled since. The Song (960–1279) rivaled the Tang in the arts; it was China's great age of painting and the most significant period for philosophy since the Zhou, when Chinese philosophy began. Although not militarily strong, the Song dynasty also witnessed an important commercial revolution. The Yuan (1279–1368) was a short-lived dynasty of Mongol rulers during which China became the most important unit in the largest empire the world has yet seen.

WHY WERE the Sui and Tang dynasties able to recreate China's emperor?

Reestablishment of Empire: Sui (589–618) and Tang (618–907) Dynasties

*I*n the period corresponding to the European early Middle Ages, the most notable feature of Chinese history was the reunification of China, the recreation of a centralized bureaucratic empire consciously modeled on the earlier Han dynasty (206 B.C.E.–220 C.E.). Reunification, as usual, began in the north. The first steps were taken by the Northern Wei (386–534), the most enduring of the northern Sino-Turkic states. It moved its court south to Luoyang, made Chinese the language of the court, and adopted Chinese dress and surnames. It also used the leverage of its nomadic cavalry to impose a new land tax, mobilizing resources for state use. The Northern Wei was followed by several short-lived kingdoms. Because the emperors, officials, and military commanders of these kingdoms came from the same aristocratic stratum, none had an advantage over the others, and the throne was often in contention among them.

The Sui Dynasty

A general of mixed Chinese-Turkic ancestry, Sui Wen-ti (d. 605), who came to power in 581 and began the Sui dynasty (589–618), was no exception to this rule. He was, however, talented and succeeded in unifying the north, restoring the tax base, and reestablishing a centralized bureaucratic government. He went on to conquer and unify southern China. Huge palaces arose in his Wei valley capital. The Great Wall was rebuilt. The Grand Canal was constructed, linking the Yellow and Yangtze Rivers. This canal enabled the northern conquerors to tap the wealth of central and southern China. Peace was maintained with the Turkic tribes along China's northern borders. Eastern Turkic khans (chiefs) were honored with Chinese princesses as brides.

The early years of the Second Sui emperor were also constructive, but then meddling in the politcs of the steppe peoples stirred up wars. The hardships and casualties created by campaigns against Korea and along China's northern border spawned discontent. Natural disasters occurred. The court became bankrupt and demoralized. Rebellions broke out, and a free-for-all again broke out among the armies of aristocratic military commanders. The winner, and the founder of the Tang dynasty, was a relative of the Sui empress and a Sinobarbarian aristocrat of the same social background as those who had ruled before him.

Chinese historians often compare the short-lived Sui dynasty with that of the Qin (256–206 B.C.E.). Each unified China after centuries of fragmentation.

QUICK REVIEW

Sui Wen-ti (d. 605)

- Founder of the Sui dynasty (589–618)
- Talented ruler who unified China
- Grand Canal constructed and Great Wall rebuilt during his reign

Each achieved a great deal and then fell to be replaced by a long-lasting dynasty. The Tang built on the foundations that had been laid by the Sui, just as the Han had built on those of the Qin.

THE TANG DYNASTY

The first Tang emperor took over the Sui capital, renamed it Chang'an, and made it his own. Within a decade the Tang had extended its authority over all of China. It collected adequate tax revenues to govern effectively, and it inaugurated military campaigns that brought more territory than ever before under Chinese control (see Map 8–1). Confucian scholars served the court. Buddhist temples and monasteries flourished, and good order prevailed throughout the land, particularly from 624 to 755.

Government   The first Tang emperor had been a provincial governor before he became a rebel general. Many of those whom he appointed to posts in the new Tang administration were former Sui officials who had served with him. In building the new administration, he and his successors had to reconcile two conflicting sets of interests. On the one hand, the emperor wanted a bureaucratic

9.1
The T'ang Dynasty (618–907): The Art of Government

 MAP EXPLORATION
Interactive map: To explore this map further, go to **http://www.prenhall.com/craig/map8.1**

MAP 8–1
The Tang Empire at its Peak During the Eighth Century.   The Tang expansion into Central Asia reopened trade routes to the Middle East and Europe. Students from Bohai, Silla (Korea), and Japan studied in the Tang capital of Chang'an, and then returned, carrying with them Tang books and technology.

WHY DID the Chinese Empire continually seek to expand into Central Asia?

government in which authority was centralized in his own person. On the other hand, he had to make concessions to the aristocrats whose dominance of Chinese society during the late Han continued during the early Tang.

The degree to which political authority was centralized was apparent in the formal organization of the bureaucracy. At the highest level were three organs: Military Affairs, the **Censorate**, and the Council of State. Military Affairs supervised the Tang armies, of which the emperor was commander-in-chief. The Censorate had watchdog functions; it reported instances of misgovernment directly to the emperor and could also remonstrate with the emperor when it considered his behavior improper. The Council of State, which was made up of the heads of the Secretariat, was the most important body. It met daily with the emperor. The Secretariat drafted policies. The Chancellery reviewed them, and State Affairs carried them out. Beneath State Affairs were the Six Ministries, which remained the core of the central government down to the 20th century. Beneath them were several levels of local administration.

The tax system made concessions to the aristocratic families. All land was declared to be the property of the emperor. He distributed it to able-bodied cultivators, who owed him taxes in labor and grain for its use. Because all able-bodied adult males received an equal allotment of land (women got less), the land-tax system was called the "equal field system." Aristocrats, however, were given exemptions and grants of "rank" and "office" lands that, in effect, allowed them to preserve their estates.

Aristocrats were also favored in the recruiting of officials. Most officials either were recommended for posts or received posts because their fathers had been officials. They were drawn almost exclusively from the aristocracy. A tiny percentage were recruited by the Confucian system of examinations. Those who passed the examinations had the highest prestige and were more likely to have brilliant careers. But as only well-to-do families could afford the years of study needed to pass the rigorous examinations, even the examination bureaucrats were usually noble. Entrance to government schools at Chang'an and the secondary capital at Luoyang was restricted to the sons of nobles and officials.

The Empress Wu   Women of the inner court continued to play a role in government. Wu Zhao (626–ca. 706), a young concubine of the strong second emperor, so entranced his weak heir that when he succeeded to the throne, he recalled her from the nunnery to which all the former wives of deceased emperors were routinely consigned and installed her at the court. She poisoned or otherwise removed her rivals and became his empress. She also murdered or exiled the statesmen who opposed her. When the emperor suffered a stroke in 660, she completely dominated the court. After his death in 683 she ruled for seven years as regent and then, deposing her son, became emperor herself, the only woman in Chinese history to hold the title. Empress Wu moved the court to Luoyang in her native area and proclaimed a new dynasty. A fervent Buddhist with an interest in magic, she saw herself as the incarnation of the messianic Buddha Maitreya and built temples throughout the land. She patronized the White Horse Monastery, appointing one of her favorites as its abbot. Her sexual appetites were said to have been prodigious. She ruled China until 705, when at the age of 80 she was deposed.

After Empress Wu, no woman would ever become emperor again; yet her machinations did not seriously weaken the court. So highly centralized was power during these early years of the dynasty that the ill effects of her intrigues could be absorbed without provinces breaking away or military commanders becoming

Censorate Branch of the imperial Chinese government that acted as a watchdog, reporting instances of misgovernment directly to the emperor and remonstrating when it considered the emperor's behavior improper.

autonomous. In fact, her struggle for power may have strengthened the central government, for she sought help in controling the old northwestern Chinese aristocrats, not from her family, but from men who passed through the examination system, the Scholars of the North Gate. This broadened her government's base by bringing in aristocrats from other regions of China. The dynamism of a young dynasty may also explain why her rule coincided with the maximal geographical expansion of Tang military power.

The Chang'an of Emperor Xuan Zong   Only a few years after Empress Wu was deposed—years filled with tawdry intrigues—Xuan Zong (r. 713–756) came to the throne. In reaction to Empress Wu, he shifted favor from examination bureaucrats and established government commissions headed by distinguished aristocrats to reform government finances. The Grand Canal was repaired and extended. A new census added to the tax rolls, and wealth and prosperity inspired a cultural flowering. Years later, the great poet Li Bo (701–762) recalled the exhilaration of his youth and the glory of the capital of Xuan Zong:

> Long ago, among the flowers and willows,
>
> We sat drinking together at Chang'an.
>
> The Five Barons and Seven Grandees were of our company,
>
> But when some wild stroke was afoot
>
> It was we who led it, yet boisterous though we were
>
> In the arts and graces of life we could hold our own
>
> With any dandy in the town—
>
> In the days when there was youth in your cheeks
>
> And I was still not old.
>
> We galloped to the brothels, cracking our gilded whips,
>
> We sent in our writings to the palace of the Unicorn,
>
> Girls sang to us and danced hour by hour on tortoise-shell mats.
>
> We thought, you and I, that it would be always like this.
>
> How should we know the grasses would stir and dust rise on the wind?
>
> Suddenly foreign horsemen were at the Hsien-ku Pass
>
> Just when the blossom at the palace of Ch'in was opening on the sunny boughs.[1]

Chang'an was an imperial city, an administrative center that lived on taxes. It was designed to exhibit the power of the emperor and the majesty of his court. At

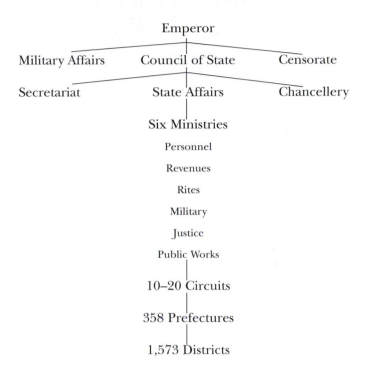

Tang Government Organization

Emperor

Military Affairs   Council of State   Censorate

Secretariat   State Affairs   Chancellery

Six Ministries

Personnel

Revenues

Rites

Military

Justice

Public Works

10–20 Circuits

358 Prefectures

1,573 Districts

QUICK REVIEW

Chang'an

- Chang'an was an administrative center that lived on taxes
- Designed to show power and majesty of emperor and his court
- City was laid out on a grid

---

[1]Arthur Waley, *The Poetry and Career of Li Po* © 1950, George Allen & Unwin Ltd, an imprint of HarperCollins Publishers, Ltd.

MAP 8–2

Chang'an. The great city of Chang'an had been a Chinese capital since the Han period. By the eighth century there were around a million people within the city walls with the same number close by outside, making it the largest city in the world at the time. The rigorous grid structure accommodates a variety of districts, each with its own function.

HOW DOES the layout of Chang'an exhibit the power of the emperor?

the far north of the city, the palace faced south. The placement was traditional: Confucius, speaking of Shun, said he had only "to hold himself in a respectful posture and to face due south." In front of the palace was a complex of government offices from which an imposing 500-foot-wide avenue led to the main southern gate. The city was laid out on a north-south, east-west grid, which one Tang poet compared to a chessboard. Each block of the city was administered as a ward with interior streets and gates that were locked at night. Enclosed by great walls, the city covered 30 square miles. It was the largest city in the world, having a population of more than one million (half within the walls; the other half in suburbs). The population of China in the year 750 was about 50 million—about 4 percent of the country's present-day population. Chang'an was also a trade center from which caravans set out across Central Asia. Merchants from India, Iran, Syria, and Arabia hawked the wares of the Middle East and all of Asia in its two government-controlled markets.

The Tang Empire　A Chinese dynasty is like an accordion, first expanding into the territories of its barbarian neighbors and then contracting back toward its original, densely populated core. The principal threats to the Tang state were from Tibetans in the west, Turks in the northwest and north, and Khitan Mongols in Manchuria.

OVERVIEW　CHINESE POLICY TOWARD BARBARIANS

Nomadic peoples from the west and north, whom the Chinese considered to be barbarians, posed a recurrent threat to the Chinese Empire for much of its history. The imperial Chinese government adopted a variety of strategies for dealing with this threat.

Armies	When nothing else worked, the Chinese went on the offensive and sent armies against the nomads. But armies were expensive, and victories over nomads were transitory. Within a few years the tribes would regroup and menace China anew.
Nomads against nomads	The Chinese were adept at inducing their nomadic neighbors to fight among themselves. This distracted the nomads and diverted their energy and attention away from China.
Defense	The Chinese fortified their northern borders, most conspicuously with the Great Wall. At times China also put its frontier provinces under military rule.
Diplomacy	China sought to neutralize its neighbors by loosely attaching them to its empire. Nomadic tribes, Central Asian states, and Korea became "tributaries" of the emperor. Their rulers sent embassies bearing gifts ("tribute") to the imperial court, which fed and housed them, and sent them home with even costlier gifts and reports of China's power, wealth, splendor, and cultural achievements. The Chinese hoped that these "barbarians" would be too overawed to pose a threat.

To protect their border, the Tang employed a four-tier policy. When nothing else would work, the Tang dispatched an army. But armies were expensive, and using them against nomads was like sweeping back the waves with a broom. A victory might dissolve a tribal confederation, but a decade or two later the federation would reorganize under a new leader. For example, in 630 Tang armies defeated the eastern Turks; in 648, they took the Tarim basin and kept trade routes to western Asia open for almost a century. In 657, they defeated the western Turks and extended Chinese influence across the Pamir Mountains to petty states near Samarkand. By 698, however, the Turks were again invading northeastern China, and from 711 to 736 they controlled the steppe from the Oxus River to China's northern frontier.

China's experience with Tibet was much the same. From 670 Tibet expanded and threatened China. In 679, it was defeated, but in 714 it rose again. More wars were fought from 727 to 729. A settlement was reached in 730, but wars then broke out again. In 752, Tibet allied with the state of Nan Chao in Yunnan. In 763, Tibetan forces captured and looted Chang'an. They were driven out, but even at the height of Tang power, no final victory was possible.

The second defensive strategy the Chinese employed was to use nomads against nomads. The critical development for the Tang was the rise to power of the Uighur Turks. From 744 to 840, the Uighurs controlled Central Asia and were staunch allies of the Tang. Without their support, the Tang dynasty would never have lasted as long as it did.

The third option was to station military along China's borders, including the Great Wall. At mid-dynasty, whole frontier provinces in the north and the northwest were assigned to military commanders, who in time came to control civil as well as military affairs. The bulk of the Tang military was stationed in frontier commands. At times the autonomy and rebel potential of these forces were as much a threat to the Tang court as to the nomadic enemy.

Diplomacy is always cheaper than war, and the fourth line of defense was to bring potential enemies into the empire as tributaries. The Tang defined "tributary" broadly. It included principalities that were truly dependent on China, Central Asian states conquered by China, enemy states (such as Tibet or the Thai state of Nan Chao in Yunnan) when they were not actually at war with China, the Korean state of Silla (which had unified the peninsula with Tang aid but then blocked Tang armies that tried to impose Chinese hegemony), and wholly independent states, such as Japan. All sent embassies and gifts to the Tang court, which hosted them and sent them home with costly presents.

For some countries these embassies had a special significance. As the only "developed nation" in eastern Asia, China was a model for countries still in the throes of state formation. Foreign embassies to the Chinese court were exposed to Tang culture and technology: its philosophy and literature; its administrative and land systems; its Buddhism; and its arts, architecture, and medicine. In 640, there were 8,000 Koreans, mostly students, in Chang'an. Never again would China exert such an influence, for never again would its neighbors be at such a formative and receptive stage of development.

Rebellion and Decline   In the mid–eighth century, signs of decline began to appear. China's frontiers started to contract. Tribes in Manchuria became unruly. Tibetans threatened China's western border. In 751, an overextended Tang army led by a Korean general was defeated

Imperial China

589–618	Sui dynasty
618–907	Tang dynasty
960–1279	Song dynasty
1279–1368	Yuan (Mongol) dynasty

by Arabs near Samarkand in western Asia, shutting down China's caravan trade with the West for more than five centuries. Furthermore, in 755 a Sogdian general, An Lu-shan, who commanded three Chinese provinces on the northeastern frontier, led his 160,000 troops in a rebellion that swept across northern China, capturing Luoyang and then Chang'an. The emperor fled to Sichuan.

The event contained an element of romance. Ten years earlier the emperor Xuan Zong had taken a young woman, Yang Guifei, from the harem of his son. (He gave his son another beauty in exchange.) So infatuated was he that he neglected not only the other "3,000 beauties of his inner chambers" but the business of government as well. For a while this did not matter because he had an able chief minister. But when the minister died and Xuan Zong appointed his concubine's second cousin to the post, he set a train of events in motion that led to a rebellion. En route to Sichuan, his soldiers, blaming Yang Guifei for their plight, strangled her. The event was later immortalized in a poem that described her "snow-white skin," "flowery face," and "moth eyebrows," as well as the 72-year-old emperor's "eternal sorrow." After a decade of wars and much devastation, a new emperor restored the dynasty with the help of the Uighur Turks, who rewarded themselves by looting Chang'an. The recovery and the century of relative peace and prosperity that followed testify to the resilience of Tang institutions. China was smaller, but military governors secured its diminished frontiers. Provincial governors were more autonomous, but they still sent taxes to the capital. Occasional rebellions were suppressed by imperial armies, sometimes led by eunuchs. Most of the emperors were weak, but three were strong and able to implement reforms. Edwin O. Reischauer, who translated the diary of a Japanese monk who studied in China during the early ninth century, commented that the "picture of government in operation" that the diarist painted "is amazing for the ninth century, even in China:"

> The remarkable degree of centralized control still existing, the meticulous attention to written instructions from higher authorities, and the tremendous amount of paper work involved in even the smallest matters of administration are all the more striking just because this was a period of dynastic decline.[2]

Of the reforms of this era, none was more important than the reorganization of the land system. The official census, on which land allotments and taxes were based, showed a drop in population from 53 million before the An Lushan rebellion to 17 million afterward. Unable to find enough people to fill the registers, the government's revenue from land fell below what it received from salt and iron. It, therefore, replaced the equal field system with a fixed quota of taxes levied on each province and paid twice a year. The new system began in 780 and continued into the 16th century.

During the second half of the ninth century the government weakened further. Most provinces were autonomous and ruled by military commanders who resisted efforts to enforce centralized control. Wars were fought with the state of Nan Chao in the southwest. Bandits appeared. Droughts sparked peasant uprisings. By the 880s, warlords had divided China into independent kingdoms, and in 907 the Tang dynasty fell.

Within half a century, however, a new dynasty arose. The fall of the Tang did not lead to centuries of division as had the collapse of the Han. Something had changed within China.

Tang Figurine. During the Tang dynasty (618–907), well-to-do families placed glazed pottery figurines in the tombs of their dead. Perhaps they were intended to accompany and amuse the dead in the afterlife. Note the fancy chignon hairstyle of this female flutist, one figure in a musical ensemble. Today these figurines are sought by collectors around the world.

Werner Forman/Art Resource, N.Y.

[2]E. O. Reischauer, *Ennin's Travels in Tang China* (New York: Ronald Press, 1955), p. 7.

Relief of Tang Emperor's Horse. A bearded "barbarian" groom tends the charger of the second Tang emperor (r. 626–649). This stone relief was found on the emperor's tomb. Note the stirrup, a Chinese invention of the fourth century C.E.

A Relief of Emperor T'ai T'song's Horse, "Autumn Dew." University of Pennsylvania Museum, Philadelphia (NEG.# S8-62840).

Tang Culture   The creativity of the Tang period arose from the juxtaposition and interaction of cosmopolitan, medieval Buddhist, and secular elements—a development rooted in the wealth and the social order of the recreated empire. Tang culture was cosmopolitan not just because of its broad contacts with other cultures and peoples but also because of its openness to them. Buddhist pilgrims journeyed to India, and Indian art and thought returned to China. The influence of voluptuous Indian painting and sculpture can be seen, for instance, in the Tang representation of the *bodhisattva*. Commercial contacts were also widespread, and foreign goods were sold in Chang'an marketplaces. Communities of central and western Asians were established in the capital, and Arab and Iranian quarters grew in the seaports of southeastern China. Merchants imported religions as well as goods: Nestorian Christianity, Zoroastrianism, Manichaeism, Judaism, and Islam. Most of these were suppressed by persecution during the ninth century, but Islam and small pockets of Judaism survived until the 20th century. Central Asian music and musical instruments became so popular as almost to displace the native traditions. Tang ladies adopted foreign hairstyles. Foreign dramas and acrobatic performances by western Asians could be seen in the streets of the capital. Even among the pottery figurines customarily placed in tombs were representations of western Asian traders and Central Asian grooms, along with those of horses, camels, and court ladies that today may be seen in museums around the world. In Tang poetry, too, what was foreign was not shunned but judged on its own merits or presented as exotically attractive.

The Tang dynasty was slightly less an age of faith than the preceding Six Dynasties, but it was, nonetheless, the golden age of Buddhism in China. Patronized by emperors and aristocrats, the Buddhist establishment acquired vast landholdings and great wealth. Temples and monasteries were constructed

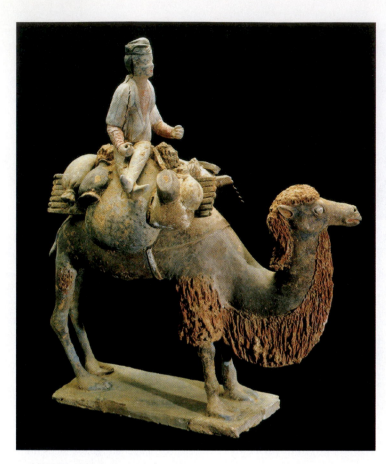

Caravaneer on a Camel. The animal's shaggy mane indicates that it is a Bactrian camel from Central Asia.

Réunion des Musées/Art Resource, N.Y.

Amitabha Buddha Buddhist Lord of the Western Paradise, or Pure Land.

Zen A form of Buddhism, which taught that Buddha was only a man and exhorted each person to attain enlightenment by his or her own efforts.

throughout China. To gain even an inkling of the beauty and sophistication of the temple architecture, the wooden sculpture, or the paintings on the temple walls, one must see Hryji or the ancient temples of Nara in Japan, for little of note has survived in China. The single exception is the Caves of the Thousand Buddhas at Dunhuang in China's far northwest, which were sealed during the 11th century for protection from Tibetan raiders and not rediscovered until the 20th century. They contained stone sculptures, Buddhist frescoes, and thousands of manuscripts in Chinese and Central Asian languages.

Only during the Tang did China have a religious institution that was at all comparable to medieval Europe's church, but even then it was subservient to the far stronger Tang state. Buddhist wealth and learning entailed secular obligations. Tang temples served as schools, inns, and even bathhouses. The temples lent money. Priests performed funerals and dispensed medicines. Occasionally the state recaptured revenues gifted to temples. The fortunes of Chinese Buddhism began to decline when, between 841 and 845, an ardent Daoist emperor confiscated millions of acres of tax-exempt lands, put 260,000 monks and nuns back on the tax registers, and destroyed 4,600 monasteries and 40,000 shrines.

During the early Tang, the principal Buddhist sect was the Tiantai, but after the mid-ninth-century suppression of Buddhist temples, other sects came to the fore:

1. One devotional sect focused on Maitreya, a Buddha of the future, who would create a paradise on earth. Maitreya was a cosmic messiah, not a human figure. The messianic teachings of the sect often furnished the ideology for popular uprisings and rebellions like the White Lotus, which claimed that it was renewing the world in anticipation of Maitreya's coming.

2. Another devotional sect worshiped the **Amitabha Buddha**, the Lord of the Western Paradise or Pure Land. This sect taught that in the early centuries after the death of the historical Buddha, his teachings had been accurately transmitted and people could obtain enlightenment by their own efforts, but that at present the Buddha's teachings had become so distorted that only by reliance on Amitabha could humans obtain salvation. All who called on Amitabha with a pure heart and perfect faith would be saved. Developing a congregational form of worship, this sect became the largest in China and deeply influenced Chinese popular religion.

3. A third sect, and the most influential among the Chinese elites, was known in China, where it began, as Chan and is better known in the West by its Japanese name, **Zen**. Zen had no cosmic Buddhas. It taught that the historical Buddha was only a man and exhorted each person to attain

enlightenment by his or her own efforts. Although its monks were often the most learned in China, Zen was anti-intellectual in its emphasis on direct intuition into one's own Buddha-nature. Enlightenment was to be obtained by a regimen of physical labor and meditation. To jolt the monk into enlightenment—after preparation by long hours of meditation— some Zen sects used little problems not answerable by normal ratiocination: "What was your face before you were conceived?" "If all things return to the One, what does the One return to?" "From the top of a hundred-foot pole, how do you step forward?" The psychological state induced by attempting to deal with these problems is compared to that of "a rat pursued into a blocked pipe" or "a mosquito biting an iron ball." The discipline of meditation, combined with a Zen view of nature, profoundly influenced the arts in China and subsequently in Korea and Japan as well.

Another characteristic of Tang culture was the reappearance of secular scholarship and letters. The reestablishment of a centralized bureaucratic government stimulated the tradition of learning that had been partially interrupted by the fall of the Han dynasty in the third century C.E. Most men of letters were officials, and most high-ranking officials were also painters or poets. An anthology of Tang poetry compiled during the Ming period (1368–1644) contained 48,900 poems by almost 2,300 authors. This secular stream of Tang culture was not ideologically anti-Buddhist. Officials were often privately sympathetic to Buddhism. But as men of affairs active in government, their values became increasingly this-worldly.

Court historians of the Tang revived the Han practice of writing official histories of preceeding dynasties. For the first time scholars wrote comprehensive institutional histories and regional and local gazetteers. They compiled dictionaries and wrote commentaries on the Confucian classics. Other scholars wrote ghost stories or tales of adventure, using the literary language. Buddhist sermons were often written in the vernacular, and more paintings were Buddhist than secular. Chinese landscape painting originated during the Tang. Nowhere, however, was the growth of a secular culture more evident than in poetry, the greatest achievement of Tang letters.

Li Bo (701–762) was exceptional among Tang poets in never having sat for the civil service examinations. Whether he can be called wholly secular is questionable. Li Bo might better be called Daoist. But he clearly was not Buddhist. Born in Sichuan, his poetic reputation won him an official post at Chang'an, which he held for a short time. Large and muscular, he was a swordsman and a carouser. Of the 20,000 poems he is said to have composed, 1,800 have survived, and a fair number have titles like "Bring on the Wine" or "Drinking Alone in the Moonlight." According to legend, he drowned while drunkenly attempting to embrace the reflection of the moon in a lake. His poetry is clear, powerful, passionate, and always sensitive to beauty (see "A Poem by Li Bo").

Du Fu (712–770), an equally famous Tang poet, was from a literary family. He failed the metropolitan examination at the age of 23 and spent years in wandering and poverty. At 39, he received an official appointment after presenting his poetry to the court. Four years later he was given a military post. He fell into rebel

Great Wild Goose Pagoda at Ci'en Temple, Xi'an, China, Tang Dynasty, 645. During the Tang dynasty, Buddhism reached its greatest development, although under the patronage of the later Tang emperors a conservative reaction reasserted Confucian influence at the expense of Buddhism.

HISTORY'S VOICES

A Poem by Li Bo

IT HAS been said that concreteness of imagery is the genius of Chinese poetry. How does this poem support that contention?

THE RIVER MERCHANT'S WIFE: A LETTER

While my hair was still cut straight across my
    forehead
I played about the front gate, pulling flowers.
You came by on bamboo stilts, playing horse,
You walked about my seat, playing with blue plums.
And we went on living in the village of Chokan:
Two small people, without dislike or suspicion.
At fourteen I married My Lord you.
I never laughed, being bashful.
Lowering my head, I looked at the wall.
Called to, a thousand times, I never looked back.
At fifteen I stopped scowling,
I desired my dust to be mingled with yours
Forever and forever and forever.
Why should I climb the look out?

At sixteen you departed,
You went into far Ku-to-yen, by the river of swirling
    eddies,
And you have been gone five months.
The monkeys make sorrowful noise overhead.
You dragged your feet when you went out.
By the gate now, the moss is grown, the different
    mosses,
Too deep to clear them away!
The leaves fall early this autumn, in wind.
The paired butterflies are already yellow with August
Over the grass in the West garden;
They hurt me. I grow older.
If you are coming down through the narrows of the
    river Kiang,
Please let me know beforehand,
And I will come out to meet you,
As far as Cho-fu-Sa.

Source: "The River Merchant's Wife: A Letter" by Ezra Pound, from *Personae.* Copyright © 1926 by Ezra Pound. Reprinted by permission of New Directions Publishing Corp.

hands during the An Lushan rebellion but escaped. He was reappointed to a civil post, but was ultimately dismissed and condemned to further hardships. His poetry is less lyrical and more allusive than Li Bo's. It also reflects more compassion for human suffering. For example, he writes about the mother whose sons have been conscripted and sent to war; the brothers scattered by war; his own family, to whom he returned after having been given up for dead. Like Li Bo, he felt that humans are short-lived and that only nature endures. Visiting the ruins of the palace of the second Tang emperor, he saw "grey rats scuttling over ancient tiles" and "in its shadowed chambers ghost fires green." In describing the ruins, he writes, "Its lovely ladies are the brown soil" and only "tomb horses of stone remain." His response to this sad scene was somewhat Stoic and un-Buddhist:

Sing wildly, let the tears cover your open hands.

Then go ever onward and on the road of your travels,

Meet none who prolong their fated years.[3]

[3]S. Owen, *The Great Age of Chinese Poetry: The High Tang.* © 1980, New Haven, CT: Yale University Press, pp. 223–224. Reprinted by permission.

Transition to Late Imperial China: The Song Dynasty (960–1279)

WHAT WAS the agricultural revolution that occurred under the Song dynasty?

Most traditional Chinese history was written to illustrate what Chinese scholars assumed to be an inevitable dynastic cycle—a pattern of rise and fall, of expansion and contraction, that was the fate of every dynasty. Certainly the Song fit this model. It reunified China in 960 and established its capital at Kaifeng on the Yellow River (see Map 8–3). It provided effective government for 170 years, a period called the Northern Song. In 1127, the Song lost control over the north, but for another 150 years it continued to rule the south from a new capital at Hangzhou in east-central China. The Southern Song fell before the Mongol onslaught in 1279.

But there is more to Chinese history than a repetitive dynastic cycle. Important longer-term changes cut across dynasties. One such set of changes began during the late Tang and continued into the Song period. Its affects on economy, society, state, and culture help to explain why China after the Tang did not relapse into centuries of disunity as it had after the Han—and why China never again experienced more than brief intervals of disunity. Fundamental transformations contributed more to these changes than emperors, empresses, eunuchs, and generals.

AGRICULTURAL REVOLUTION OF THE SONG: FROM SERFS TO FREE FARMERS

Landed aristocrats had dominated local society in China during the Sui and Tang periods. The tillers of their estates were little more than serfs. Labor service was the heaviest tax, and whether performed on the lands aristocrats held by office or rank, or on other government lands, it created a system of social subordination.

The aristocracy declined under the Tang and after the Tang's fall. Estates shrank as they were divided among all a man's male children after his death. Artistocracts, whose local property diminished, were attracted to the capital where they became a metropolitan elite. After the fall of the Tang, the aristocratic estates were often seized by warlords. The fading power of the aristocracy and changes in the land and tax systems worked in favor of those who tilled the soil. The end of the equal field system freed farmers to buy and sell land, and ownership of land as private property gave cultivators greater independence. They could now move about as they pleased. Taxes paid in grain gave way during the Song to taxes in money. The commutation of the labor tax to a money tax gave farmers more control over their time. Conscription, the cruelest and heaviest labor tax of all, disappeared as the conscript armies of the early and middle Tang were replaced by professional soldiers.

Changes in technology also benefited the cultivator. New strains of an early-ripening rice permitted double cropping. In the Yangzi region, extensive water-control projects were carried out, and more fertilizers were used. New commercial crops were developed. Tea, which had been introduced during the Six Dynasties as a medicine and had been drunk by monks during the Tang, became widely cultivated. Cotton also became a common crop. Because taxes paid in money tended to become fixed, much of the profit generated by increased productivity accrued to the cultivator. Of course, not all benefited equally. Landlords and landless tenants as well as independent small farmers still existed.

MAP 8–3

The Northern Song and Liao Empires (Top) and the Southern Song and Jin Empires (Bottom).   During the Northern Song, the Mongol Liao dynasty ruled only the extreme northern edge of China. During the Southern Song, in contrast, the Manchurian Jin dynasty ruled half of China.

WHY DID the authority of the Song dynasty not extend beyond southern China after 1279?

The disappearance of the aristocrats also increased the authority of district magistrates, who no longer had to contend with their interference in local affairs. The Song magistrate became the sole representative of imperial authority in each locality, but there were too many villages in his district for him to be involved regularly in their internal governance. As long as taxes were paid and order maintained, affairs were left in the hands of the village elites. The Song farmer, therefore, enjoyed rising income, greater freedom, and substantial self-government.

One other development that began during the Song—and became vastly more important later—was the appearance of a scholar-gentry class. The typical gentry family lived in the district seats or market towns and had at least one member who had passed the provincial civil service examination. Socially and culturally, these gentry were closer to magistrates than villagers, but they usually owned land in the villages and thus shared some interests with the local landholders. Although much less powerful than the former aristocrats, the gentry took a hand in local affairs and at times functioned as a buffer between the village and the magistrate's office.

COMMERCIAL REVOLUTION OF THE SONG

Changes in the countryside contributed to, and were stimulated by, several factors: demographic shifts, innovative technologies, growth of cities, spread of money, and rising trade. The effects of these developments varied by region, but overall the Song economy reached new heights of prosperity.

Emergence of the Yangzi Basin   Until late in the Tang, the north had been China's most populous and productive region. But from the late ninth-century the center of gravity of China's population, agricultural production, and culture shifted to the lower and eastern Yangzi region. Between 800 and 1100, the population of the region tripled as China's total population increased to about 100 million. The Yangzi's rice paddies yielded more per acre than the wheat or millet fields of the north, making rice the tax base of the empire. The area's wealth led to the establishment of so many schools that the government set quotas for the examination system to prevent the Yangzi region from dominating China. The Northern Song capital itself was kept in the north for strategic reasons, but it was situated at Kaifeng, further east than Luoyang, at the point where the Grand Canal, which carried tax rice from the south, joined the Yellow River.

New Technology   During the Northern Song a coal and iron-smelting industry developed in north China, providing the Chinese with better tools and weapons. Using coke and bellows to heat furnaces to temperatures required for carbonized steel, Song technology was the most advanced in the world.

Printing began in China with the use of carved seals. The earliest woodblock texts, mostly on Buddhist subjects, appeared in the seventh century. By the 10th century, a complete edition of the classics had been published, and by the mid-Song books printed with movable type were fairly common. Other advances during the Song were the abacus, the use of gunpowder in grenades and projectiles, and improvements in textiles and porcelains.

Rise of a Money Economy   Exchange during the Tang had been based on silk. Coins had been issued, but their circulation was limited. During the Northern Song large amounts of copper cash were coined, but the demand rose more rapidly than the supply. Coins were made with holes in the center so that they could be strung together (a string of 1,000 was the usual unit for large transactions). In the Southern Song, silver began to be minted to complement copper cash (10 times as much silver in the late 12th century as in the early 11th century). Letters of credit were used by merchants, and various kinds of paper money were issued. The penetration of money into the village economy was such that by 1065 tax receipts paid in money had risen to 38 million strings of cash—compared with a mere two million in mid-Tang.

Irrigation Methods on a Farm in the Yangzi Valley. A farmer and his wife use their legs and feet to work the square-pallet chain pump, a boy drives a water buffalo to turn a water-pumping device, and another boy fishes.

© Photograph by Wan-go Weng/Collection of H. C. Weng.

Trade   The growth of trade spurred the demand for money. During the Tang most cities had been administrative centers supported by taxes from the countryside. The salaries and government expenditures made possible by these taxes created a demand for services and commercial products that turned these cities into islands of commerce in a noncommercial hinterland. In most of China's seven or eight economic regions, this pattern continued during the Song, but in the capital and the economically advanced regions along the Yangzi, cities became the hubs of regional commercial networks, with district seats or market towns serving as secondary centers for the local markets beneath them.

As this transition occurred, cities with more than 100,000 households almost quadrupled in number. The Northern Song capital at Kaifeng had 260,000 households—probably more than one million inhabitants—and the Southern Song capital at Hangzhou had 391,000 households. Compare these capitals to those of backward Europe: London during the Northern Song had a population of about 18,000; Rome during the Southern Song had 35,000; and Paris even a century later had fewer than 60,000.

Furthermore, these Song capitals, unlike Chang'an with its walled wards that closed at night, were open within and spread beyond their outer walls. As in present-day Chinese cities, their main avenues were lined with shops. Merchant guilds replaced government officials as the managers of marketplaces. Growing

Chinese Ladies Preparing Silk. The manufacture of silk was an important part of the Song economy and was exported abroad.

Emporer Hui Tsung, Chinese, 1082–1135. Ladies Preparing Newly Made Silk, Part 11. Chinese scroll painting, Song Dynasty. Courtesy, Museum of Fine Arts, Boston. Reproduced with permission. © 2006 Museum of Fine Arts, Boston. All Rights Reserved.

wealth also led to a taste for luxury and an increasingly secular lifestyle. Restaurants, theaters, wine shops, and brothels abounded. Entertainment quarters with fortunetellers, jugglers, chess masters, acrobats, and puppeteers sprang up. Such amusements had previously been available in Chang'an, but now their numbers increased, and they catered to traders and rich merchants as well as to officials.

Trade between regions during the Song was limited mainly to luxury goods like silk, lacquerware, medicinal herbs, and porcelains. Only where transport was cheap—along rivers, canals, or the coast—was interregional trade in bulk commodities economical, and even there it usually thrived only temporarily to make up for specific shortages.

Foreign trade also reached new heights during the Song. In the north, Chinese traders bought horses from Tibetan, Turkic, and Mongol border states, and sold silks and tea. Along the coast, Chinese merchants took over the port trade that during the Tang had been in the hands of Korean, Arab, and Persian merchants. The new hegemony of Chinese merchants was based on improved ships using both sail and oars and equipped with watertight compartments and better rudders. Chinese captains, navigating with the aid of the compass, came to dominate the sea routes from Japan in the north to Sumatra in the south. The products traded overseas reflected China's advanced economy. China imported raw materials and exported finished goods. Porcelains were sent to Southeast Asia and then were carried by Arab ships to medieval trading centers on the Persian Gulf and down the coast of East Africa as far south as Zanzibar.

GOVERNMENT: FROM ARISTOCRACY TO AUTOCRACY

The millennium of late imperial China after the Tang is often spoken of as the age of autocracy or as China's era of absolute monarchy. Earlier emperors were often personally powerful, but beginning with the Song, changes occurred that made it easier for emperors to be autocrats.

Song emperors had the advantage of direct personal control over more offices than their Tang predecessors. Also, the Board of Academicians, an advisory office, presented the emperor with policy options separate from those presented by the Secretariat-Chancellery. The emperor could thus use the one against the other and prevent bureaucrats in the Secretariat-Chancellery from dominating his government.

The central government of the Song was better funded than previous administrations. Revenues in 1100 were three times the peak revenues of the Tang. Income was derived from increasing population and agricultural wealth, government monopolies (on salt, wine, and tea), and various duties, fees, and taxes levied on domestic and foreign trade. During the Northern Song these commercial revenues rivaled the land tax; during the Southern Song they surpassed it. Confucian officials continued to stress the primacy of land, but throughout late imperial China, commerce was a vital source of revenues.

Another change that strengthened the emperors was the disappearance of the aristocracy. During the Tang the emperor had come from the same Sino-Turkic nobility of northwestern China as most of his principal ministers, and he was essentially the organ of a state that ruled on behalf of this aristocracy. Aristocrats monopolized the high posts of government. They married among themselves and with the imperial family. They called the emperor the Son of Heaven, but they knew he was one of them. During the Song, however, government officials were commoners and mostly products of the examination system. They were separated from the emperor by an enormous social gulf and saw him as a person apart.

The Song examination system was larger than that of the Tang, but smaller than under later dynasties. Whereas only 10 percent of officials had been recruited by examination during the Tang, the Song figure rose to more than 50 percent and included the most important officials. The first examination was given at regional centers. The applicant took the examination in a walled cubicle under close supervision. To ensure impartiality, his answers were recopied by clerks and his name was replaced by a number before his examination was sent to the officials who graded it. Of those who sat for the examination, only a tiny percentage passed. The second hurdle was the metropolitan examination at the national capital, where the precautions were equally elaborate. Only one in five, or about 200 a year, passed. The average successful applicant was in his mid-30s. The final hurdle was the palace examination, which weeded out a few more and assigned rankings to the rest.

To pass the examinations, the candidate had to memorize the Confucian classics, interpret selected passages, write in the literary style, compose poems on themes given by the examiners, and propose solutions to contemporary problems in terms of Confucian philosophy. The quality of the officials produced by the Song system was impressive. A parallel might be drawn with 19th-century Britain, where students in the classics at Oxford and Cambridge went on to become generalist bureaucrats. The Chinese examination system that flourished during the Song continued, with some interruptions, into the 12th century. The continuity of Chinese government during this millennium depended on the common culture and values of the examination elite.

The examination meritocracy was sustained by land, education, and office. Landed wealth paid the costs of education. A poor peasant or city dweller could not afford the years of study needed to pass the examinations, and without passing the examinations, an official position was unobtainable. Family wealth, however, could not be preserved unless one held an office. The Chinese pattern of inheritance, as noted earlier, divided property at each change of generation. China's extended-family or clan system, however, meant that bright children were often educated by a wealthy relative who held an office. Some families passed the civil service examinations for several generations running. More often, the sons of well-to-do officials did not study as hard as those with scant means. The adage "shirt sleeves to shirt sleeves in three generations" describes a common fate during the Song and later dynasties.

How the merchants related to this system is unclear. They had wealth but were despised by scholar-officials as grubby profit seekers and were barred from taking the examinations. Some merchants avoided the system altogether, for an education in the Confucian classics did little to fit a merchant's son for a career in commerce. Others bought land for status and security, and their sons or grandsons became eligible to take the exams. Similarly, a small peasant might build up his holdings, become a landlord, and educate a son or grandson. The system was steeply hierarchical, but it was not closed and did not produce a new, self-perpetuating aristocracy.

SONG CULTURE

As society and government changed during the Tang-Song transition, so too did culture. Song culture retained some of the energy of the Tang while becoming more intensely and perhaps more narrowly Chinese. The rich Song culture was

9.2
Song China: Imperial Examination System

encouraged by a rising economy, an increase in the number of schools, higher literacy rates, and the spread of printing. Song culture was less aristocratic, less cosmopolitan, and more closely associated with the officials and the scholar-gentry, who were both its practitioners and its patrons. It also was less Buddhist than the Tang had been. Only the Buddhist Zen (Chan) sect remained vital, and many Confucians were outspokenly anti-Buddhist and anti-Daoist. The secular culture of officials that originated during the Tang broadened to become the mainstream during the Song.

Chinese believe that the Song dynasty marked the peak of their traditional culture. It was, for example, China's greatest age of pottery and porcelains. High-firing techniques were developed, and kilns were established in every area. There was a rich variety of beautiful glazes. Shapes were restrained and harmonious. Song pottery, like nothing produced in the world before it, made ceramics a major art form in East Asia. This was also an age of great historians. Sima Guang (1019–1086) wrote *A Comprehensive Mirror for Aid in Government*, which treated not a single dynasty but all Chinese history. His work was more sophisticated than previous histories in that it included a discussion of documentary sources and an explanation of why he chose to rely on one source rather than another. The greatest achievements of the Song, however, were in philosophy, poetry, and painting.

Philosophy The Song was second only to the Zhou as a creative age in philosophy. A series of original thinkers culminated in the towering figure of Zhu Xi (1130–1200). Zhu Xi studied Daoism and Buddhism in his youth, along with Confucianism. A brilliant student, he passed the metropolitan examination at the age of 18. During his 30s, he focused his attention on Confucianism, deepening and making more systematic its social and political ethics by drawing on Buddhist and native metaphysical elements. He pioneered a new Confucianism as a viable alternative to Buddhism for Chinese intellectuals. Zhu Xi became famous as a teacher at the White Deer Grotto Academy, and his writings were widely distributed. Before the end of the Song, his version of Confucianism had become the standard interpretation used in the civil service examinations, and it remained so until the 20th century.

Comparable figures in other traditions include Saint Thomas Aquinas (1224–1274) of medieval Europe and the Islamic theologian al-Ghazali (1058–1111), both of whom produced a new synthesis or worldview that lasted for centuries. Aquinas combined Aristotle and Latin theology just as Zhu Xi combined Confucian philosophy and metaphysical notions from other sources. Because Zhu Xi used terms such as the "great ultimate" and because he emphasized a Zen-like meditation called "quiet sitting," some contemporary critics claimed that his Neo-Confucian philosophy was a Buddhist wolf in the clothing of a Confucian sheep. This was unfair. Whereas Aquinas would make philosophy serve religion, Zhu Xi made religion or metaphysics serve philosophy. In his hands, the "great ultimate" or *li* ("principle") lost its otherworldly character and became a constituent of all things in the universe. Perhaps Zhu Xi's philosophy should be characterized as innerworldly.

Later critics often argued that Zhu Xi's teachings encouraged metaphysical speculation at the expense of practical ethics. Zhu Xi's followers

An Elegant Song Dynasty Wine Pot. This pot has green celadon glaze (24.8 cm high).

Ewer with carved flower sprays. Porcelain with molded and carved low-relief decoration in grayish-green glaze approx. 1000–12000. Northern Song Dynasty (960–1127) H. 9 5/8 in × W. 5 1/4 in × D. 7 3/4 in, H. 24.5 cm × W. 13.4 cm × D. 19.7 cm. China; Shaanxi province. © Gift of The Asian Art Museum Foundation.

replied that, on the contrary, his teachings gave practical ethics a systematic underpinning and positively contributed to individual moral responsibility. What was discovered within by Neo-Confucian quiet sitting was just those positive ethical truths enunciated by Confucius more than 1,000 years earlier. The new metaphysics did not change the Confucian social philosophy.

Zhu Xi urged that scholar-officials be chosen by schools rather than by examinations, and it is ironic that his teachings became a new orthodoxy that was maintained by the channelizing effect of the civil service examinations. However, Zhu Xi's teachings may have contributed to the stability of late imperial China, for like the examination system, the imperial institution, the scholar-gentry class, and the land system, his interpretation of Confucianism maintained continuity and impeded change. Some historians fault the Zhu Xi orthodoxy for stifling intellectual creativity during later dynasties, but this probably overstates its power. There were always contending schools.

Poetry   Song poets were in awe of those of the Tang, yet Song poets were also among China's best. A Japanese authority on Chinese literature wrote:

> Tang poetry could be likened to wine, and Song poetry to tea. Wine has great power to stimulate, but one cannot drink it constantly. Tea is less stimulating, bringing to the drinker a quieter pleasure, but one which can be enjoyed more continuously.[4]

The most famous poet of the Northern Song was Su Dungpo (1037–1101), a man skilled in all the cultural activities of his era. He was a painter and a calligrapher who was particularly knowledgeable about inks. He practiced Zen and wrote commentaries on the Confucian classics. Su superintended engineering projects, and he was a connoisseur of cooking and wine. His life was shaped by politics. He was a conservative, who believed in a limited role for government and in relying on morality to maintain social control. Opponents in the Song bureaucracy, the reformers, stressed law and an expanded role for government.

Passing the metropolitan examination, Su rose through a succession of posts to become the governor of a province—a position of immense power. One of his poems reflected on his duty to authorize death sentences, which could not be carried over into a new year:

> New Year's Eve—you'd think I could go home early
>
> But official business keeps me.
>
> I hold the brush and face them with tears:
>
> Pitiful convicts in chains,
>
> Little men who tried to fill their bellies,
>
> Fell into the law's net, don't understand disgrace.
>
> And I? In love with a meager stipend

Song Dynasty Philosopher Zhu Xi (1130–1200). His Neo-Confucian ideas remained central up to the 20th century.

Collection of the National Palace Museum, Taiwan, R.O.C.

[4]Kojiro Yoshikawa, *An Introduction to Song Poetry*, trans. by Burton Watson (Cambridge: Harvard University Press, Harvard-Yenching Institute Monograph Series, 1967), p. 37.

I hold on to my job and miss the chance to retire.

Do not ask who is foolish or wise;

All of us alike scheme for a meal.

The ancients would have freed them a while at New Year's—Would

I dare do likewise? I am silent with shame.[5]

Eight years later, when the reformers came to power, Su himself was arrested and spent 100 days in prison, awaiting execution on a charge of slandering the emperor. Instead, he was released and exiled. He wrote:

"Out the gate, I do a dance, wind blows in my face; our galloping horses race along as magpies cheer."[6]

Arriving at his place of exile, he reflected:

Between heaven and earth I live,

One ant on a giant grindstone,

Trying in my petty way to walk to the right

While the turning of the mill wheel takes me endlessly left.

Though I go the way of benevolence and duty,

I can't escape from hunger and cold.[7]

Su turned his place of exile into a work of art. He farmed a plot of land at the "eastern slope" from which he took his literary name, Dungpo. Of his work there, he wrote:

A good farmer hates to wear out the land;

I'm lucky this plot was ten years fallow.

It's too soon to count on mulberries;

My best bet is a crop of wheat.

I planted seed and within the month

Dirt on the rows was showing green.

An old farmer warned me,

Don't let seedlings shoot up too fast!

If you want plenty of dumpling flour

Turn a cow or sheep in here to graze.

Good advice—I bowed my thanks;

I won't forget you when my belly's full.[8]

The conservatives regained control of the government in 1086, and Su resumed his official career. In 1094 power shifted once more, and Su was again exiled to the distant southern island of Hainan. Su was on his way back to the capital after another change of government when he died in 1101.

Painting　In the West, penmanship and painting are quite separate, one merely a skill and the other esteemed as an art. In China, calligraphy and painting were

[5]Yoshikawa, p. 119
[6]Yoshikawa, p. 117
[7]Yoshikawa, p. 105
[8]Yoshikawa, p. 119–120

equally appreciated and were seen as related. A scholar spent his life with brush in hand. The same qualities of line, balance, and strength needed for calligraphy carried over to painting. Chinese calligraphy is immensely pleasing even to the untutored Western eye, and it is not difficult to distinguish between the elegant strokes of Huineng, the last emperor of the Northern Song, and the powerful brushwork of the Zen monk Zhang Jizhi.

Song painters chose a wide variety of subjects—birds, flowers, fish, insects, horses, monkeys, water buffalo, scholars, emperors, Buddhas, and Daoist immortals. But its crowning achievement was landscape. Song landscapes are different from those of the West. Each stroke of the brush on silk or paper was final, for a mistake could not be covered up. Each element within a painting was represented in its most pleasing aspect; the painting as a whole was not constrained by single-point perspective. It had no single source of illumination, but an overall diffusion of light. Space was an integral part of its composition. A typical painting might have craggy rocks or twisted pine trees in the foreground, then mist or clouds or rain to create distance, and in the background the outlines of mountains or cliffs. If the painting contained human figures at all, they were tiny elements set in a world of nature that was very large. Chinese painting thus reflected the same worldview as Chinese philosophy and poetry. The painter sought to grasp the inner reality of a scene and not to be preoccupied by surface details.

In paintings by monks or masters of the Zen school, the presentation of an intuitive vision of an inner reality became even more pronounced. A Zen "broken ink" landscape might feature rocks, water, mountains, and clouds, each represented by a few explosive strokes of the brush. Paintings of Bodhidharma, the legendary founder of the Zen sect, are often dominated by a single powerful downstroke of the brush, defining the edge of his robe. Paintings of patriarchs tearing up sutras or sweeping dust from the mirror of the mind with a broom are almost calligraphic.

CHINA IN THE MONGOL WORLD EMPIRE: THE YUAN DYNASTY (1279–1368)

*T*he Mongols created the greatest empire in the history of the world. Their domain extended from the Caspian Sea to the Pacific Ocean; from Russia, Siberia, and Korea in the north to Persia and Burma in the south. Invasion fleets were even sent to Java and Japan, although without success. Mongol rule in China is one chapter of this larger story.

RISE OF THE MONGOL EMPIRE

The Mongols were a nomadic people who lived to the north of China on grasslands where they raised horses and herded sheep. They lived in felt tents (yurts) and sometimes called themselves "the people of the felt tents." Women performed much of the work and were freer and more easygoing than women in China. Families belonged to clans, and related clans to tribes. Tribes would gather during the annual migration from the summer plains to winter pasturage. Chiefs were elected, most often from noble lineages, and chosen for their courage, military prowess, judgment, and leadership. Like Manchu or Turkic, the Mongol tongue was Altaic. The Mongols worshipped nature deities and a supreme sky god. (Sky blue was their sacred color.) They communicated with

WHY WERE the Mongols able to conquer such a vast empire?

their gods through religious specialists called *shamans*. Politically divided, they traded and warred among themselves and with settled peoples on the borders of their vast grassland domains.

The founder of the Mongol Empire, Temujin, was born in 1167, the son of a tribal chief. While Temujin was still a child, his father was poisoned. He fled and after wandering for some years, returned to the tribe, avenged his father, and in time became chief himself. By the time he was forty, Temujin's shrewd alliances and remarkable skill as a survivor had enabled him to unite the Mongol tribes and become their great khan or ruler. It is by the title *Genghis* (also spelled *Jenghiz* or *Chinggis*) *Khan* that he is known to history. Genghis possessed an extraordinary charisma, and his sons and grandsons were wise and talented leaders. Why the Mongol tribes, almost untouched by the higher civilizations of the world, should have produced such leaders at this point in history is difficult to explain.

A second conundrum is how the Mongols, who numbered only about 1.5 million, created the army that conquered vastly denser populations. Part of the answer is institutional. Genghis organized his armies into "myriads" of 10,000 troops, with decimal subdivisions of 1,000, 100, and 10. Elaborate signals were devised so that in battle, even large units could be manipulated like the fingers of a hand. Mongol tactics were superb: Units would retreat, turn, flank, and destroy their enemies. The historical record makes amply clear that Genghis's nomadic cavalry had a paralytic effect on its opponents. The most dreaded weapon of the peerless Mongol horseman was the compound bow. It was short enough to be shot from the saddle yet more powerful than the English longbow.

The Mongol cavalry was astonishingly mobile. Men carried their own supplies, and, trailing remounts, they covered vast distances quickly. By 1241, a Mongol army had reached Hungary, Poland, and the shore of the Adriatic. It was poised to continue its advance into western Europe when word of the death of the great khan caused it to hasten back to Mongolia to help choose his successor.

Conquered enemies taught the Mongols how to use siege weapons to take walled cities. Chinese engineers were employed in campaigns in Persia. The Mongols also used terror as a weapon. Inhabitants of cities that refused to surrender were put to the sword. Large areas in north China and Sichuan were devastated and depopulated. Descriptions of the Mongols by those whom they conquered dwell on their physical toughness and pitiless cruelty.

But Mongol strength was more than military. Genghis opened his armies to recruits from the Uighur Turks, the Manchus, and other nomadic peoples. As long as they complied with the military discipline demanded of his forces, they could share his triumphs. In 1206, Genghis promulgated laws designed to prevent the traditional wrangling and warring between tribes that might otherwise have undermined his empire. Genghis also obtained pledges of personal loyalty from thousands of his followers, and he used these "vassals"

Kublai Khan. Wearing an ermine coat, the Mongol emperor sits on a horse among Mongol warriors at the hunt.

National Palace Museum, Taiwan, R.O.C.

to command his armies and staff his government. This gave his forces an inner coherence that countered the divisive effect of tribal loyalties.

Mongol conquests were all the more impressive in that, unlike the earlier Arab expansion, the Mongols lacked the unifying force of religious zeal. To be sure, at an assembly of chiefs in 1206, an influential shaman revealed that it was the sky god's will that Genghis conquer the world. Yet other unabashedly frank words attributed to Genghis may reveal a truer image of what lay behind the Mongol drive to conquest: "Man's highest joy is in victory: to conquer one's enemies, to pursue them, to deprive them of their possessions, to make their beloved weep, to ride on their horses, and to embrace their wives and daughters."[9]

Genghis divided his far-flung empire among his four sons. Trade and communications were maintained between the parts, but over several generations, each of the four khanates became independent. The khanate of Chagatai was in Central Asia and remained purely nomadic. A second khanate of the Golden Horde ruled Russia from the lower Volga. The third was in Persia, and the fourth, led by those who succeeded Genghis as great khans, centered first in Mongolia and then in China (see Map 8–4).

MONGOL RULE IN CHINA

The standard theory used to organize Chinese history is the dynastic cycle, but a second theory explains Chinese history in terms of the interaction between the settled peoples of China and the nomads of the steppe. When strong states emerged in China, their wealth and population enabled them to expand militarily onto the steppe. But when China was weak, as was more often the case, the steppe peoples overran China. To review briefly:

1. During the Han dynasty (206 B.C.E.–220 C.E.), the most pressing problem in foreign relations was the Hsiung Nu Empire to the north.

2. During the centuries that followed the Han, various nomadic peoples invaded and ruled northern China.

3. The energy and institutions of these Sino-Turkic rulers of the northern dynasties shaped China's reunification during the Sui (589–618) and Tang (618–907) dynasties. The Uighur Turks also played a major role in Tang defense policy.

4. Northern border states became even more important during the Song. The Northern Song (960–1126) bought peace with payments of gold and silver to the Liao. The Southern Song (1126–1279), for all its cultural brilliance, was little more than a tributary state of the Chin dynasty, which had expanded into northern China.

From the start of the Mongol pursuit of world hegemony, the riches of China were a target. But Genghis proceeded cautiously, determined to leave no enemy at his back. He first disposed of the Tibetan state to the northwest of China and then the Manchu state of Chin that ruled north China. Mongol forces took Beijing in 1227, the year Genghis died. They went on to take Luoyang and the southern reaches of the Yellow River in 1234, and all of north China by 1241. During this time, the Mongols were interested mainly in loot. Only later did Chinese advisers persuade them that more wealth could be obtained by taxation.

---

[9]J. K. Fairbank, E. O. Reischauer, and A. M. Craig, *East Asia, Tradition and Transformation* (Boston: Houghton Mifflin, 1973), p. 164.

MAP 8–4

The Mongol Empire in the Late 13th Century. Note the four khanates: the Golden Horde in Russia, the Ilkhanate in Persia, Chagatai in Central Asia, and the Great Khanate extending from Mongolia to southern China.

HOW DID the size of the Mongol Empire facilitate trade and communication?

Kublai, a grandson of Genghis, was chosen as the great khan in 1260. In 1264, he moved his capital from Karakorum in Mongolia to Beijing. It was only in 1271 that he adopted a Chinese dynastic name, the Yuan, and, as a Chinese ruler, went to war with the Southern Song. The Mongols swept across southern China, and the last Song stronghold fell in 1279.

Kublai Khan's rule in Beijing reflected the mixture of cultural elements in Mongol China. From Beijing, Kublai could rule as a Chinese emperor, which would not have been possible in Karakorum. He adopted the Chinese custom of hereditary succession. He rebuilt Beijing as a walled city. It was known to the West as Cambulac, "the city (baliq) of the khan." Beijing was far to the north of any previous Chinese capital, away from centers of wealth and population, and the Grand Canal had to be extended to provision it. But from Beijing, Kublai could watch over Manchuria and Mongolia and maintain ties with the other khanates. Residence in the city proper was limited to Mongols. Chinese were segregated in an adjoining walled city. The palace of the khan was designed in a Central Asian style by an Arab architect. Kublai also maintained a summer palace at Shangdu (the "Xanadu" of Samuel Taylor Coleridge's poem) in Inner Mongolia, where he could hawk and ride and hunt in Mongol style.

Early Mongol rule in northern China was rapacious and exploitative, but it later came to employ Chinese forms of government and taxation, especially in the south and at the local level. As a foreign military occupation, its civil administration was highly centralized. Under the emperor was a Central Secretariat, and beneath it were 10 "Moving Secretariats," which became provinces under later dynasties. These highly centralized institutions and the arbitrary style of Mongol decision making accelerated the trend toward absolutism that had started during the previous dynasty.

About 400,000 Mongols lived in China during the Yuan period. For such a tiny minority to control the Chinese majority, it had to maintain itself as a separate and distinct people. One technique was to limit military service to Mongols and their nomadic allies and to station garrisons throughout China, while maintaining a strategic reserve on the steppe. Military officers were always regarded as more important than civil officials. A second technique for assuring Mongol superiority was to use ethnic classifications when appointing civil officials. Mongols held the top civil and military posts. The second rank category of high civilian offices was open to Persians, Turks, and other non-Chinese. The third rank admitted the northern Chinese, including Manchus and other border peoples, and the fourth employed the southern Chinese. Even when the examination system was sporadically revived after 1315, the Mongols and their allies were favored by easier examinations. Their quota was as large as that for the much more numerous Chinese, and they were appointed to higher offices.

The net result was an uneasy symbiosis. Chinese officials at the lower levels directly governed the Chinese populace, collecting taxes, settling disputes, and maintaining local order. Few of them learned to speak Mongolian, but without their cooperation, Mongol rule in China would have been impossible. The Mongols, concentrated in Beijing, large cities, and in garrisons, spoke Mongolian among themselves and usually did not bother to learn Chinese. A few exceptional Mongols learned to write poetry in Chinese and to paint in the Chinese style, but most were content to communicate through interpreters. When a Chinese district magistrate sent a query to the court, the response was written in Mongolian with a word-for-word Chinese translation.

(The Mongols borrowed the alphabet of the Uighurs to transcribe their tongue.) As the two languages are syntactically very different, the resulting Chinese was grotesque.

FOREIGN CONTACTS AND CHINESE CULTURE

11.5
William of Rubruck:
*Impressions of the
Medieval Mongols*

Diplomacy and trade within the greater Mongol Empire brought China into contact with other higher civilizations for the first time since the Tang period. Persia and the Arab world were especially important. Merchants, missionaries, and diplomats voyaged from the Persian Gulf and across the Indian Ocean to seaports in southeastern China. The Arab communities in Canton and other ports were larger than they had been during the Song. Camel caravans carrying silks and ceramics left Beijing to pass through the Central Asian oases and on to Baghdad. Although the Mongols did not favor Chinese merchants and most trade was in other hands, Chinese trade expanded. Chinese communities were established in Tabriz, the center of trading in western Asia, and in Moscow and Novgorod. During this period knowledge of printing, gunpowder, and Chinese medicine spread to western Asia. Chinese ceramics influenced those of Persia, and Chinese painting influenced Persian miniatures.

11.6
The Book of Ser
Marco Polo

In Europe, knowledge of China was transmitted by the Venetian trader Marco Polo, who said he had served Kublai as an official between 1275 and 1292. His book, *A Description of the World*, was translated into most European languages. Many readers doubted that a land of such wealth and culture could exist so far from Europe, but the book excited an interest in geography. When Christopher Columbus set sail in 1492, his goal was to reach Polo's Zipangu (Japan). A great Muslim explorer, Ibn Battuta (1304–c. 1370) of Morocco, also toured much of the Mongol world and left us a description of customs of the peoples he encountered. He characterized the Chinese as wealthy, but disinclined to flaunt their riches.

Other cultural contacts were fostered by the Mongol toleration or encouragement of religion. Nestorian Christianity spread from Persia to Central Asia and reentered China during the Mongol era. Churches were built in main cities. The mother of Kublai Khan was a Nestorian Christian. Several papal missions were sent from Rome to the Mongol court. An archbishopric was established in Beijing, where a church was built, sermons preached in Turkish and Mongolian, and choirboys sang hymns. Kublai gave Marco Polo's father and uncle a letter for the pope asking him to send 100 educated men to Kublai's court.

Tibetan Buddhism, with its magical doctrines and elaborate rites, was the religion most favored by the Mongols, but Chinese Buddhism also flourished. Priests and monks of all religions were given tax exemptions. Half a million Chinese became Buddhist monks during the Mongol century. The foreign religion that

The Journey of Marco Polo. Marco Polo and compagnions en route to China on the Silk Road.

Getty Images, Inc/Hulton Archive Photos.

made the greatest gains was Islam. It took permanent root in Central Asia and western China. Mosques were built in these areas, in Beijing, and in southeastern port cities. Confucianism was regarded as a religion by the Mongols. Its teachers were exempted from taxes, but as the scholar-gentry rarely obtained important offices, they saw the Mongol era as a time of hardship.

Despite these wide contacts with other peoples and religions, the high culture of China appears to have changed little if at all—partly because China had little to learn from other areas, and partly because the centers of Chinese culture were in the south, the last area to be conquered and the area least affected by Mongol rule. In reaction to the Mongol conquest, Chinese culture became conservative and turned in on itself. Scholars wrote poetry in the style of the Song. New schools of painting appeared, but they evolved within the Chinese tradition. The greatest Yuan paintings continued the style of the Song. The head of the court bureau of historiography was a Mongol, but the histories produced by his Chinese staff were in the traditional mold. As the dynasty waned, unemployed scholars wrote essays professing loyalty to the Song and satirizing the Mongols. Their works were not censored, for the Mongols either could not read them or did not care.

The major contribution to Chinese arts during the Yuan was by dramatists. They combined poetic arias with vaudeville theater to produce a new operatic drama. Performed by traveling troupes, the operas used few stage props and relied for effect on makeup, costumes, pantomime, and stylized gestures. Female roles were usually played by men. Except for the arias—the highlights of the performance—the dramas used vernacular Chinese to appeal to a popular audience. The unemployed scholars who wrote the scripts drew on the entire repertoire of the Song storyteller. Among the stock figures of the operas were a Robin Hood-like bandit, a famous detective-judge, a Tang monk who traveled to India, warriors and statesmen of the Three Kingdoms, and an assortment of romantic heroes, villains, and ghosts. Justice always triumphed, and the dramas usually ended happily. In several famous plays the hero got the girl, despite objections by her parents and seemingly insurmountable obstacles, by passing the civil service examinations in first place. As the examinations were not employed during most of the Yuan, this resolution of the hero's predicament harked back to the Song traditions of government. Yuan drama continued almost unchanged in later dynasties, and during the 19th century it merged with a form of southern Chinese theater to become today's Beijing Opera.

LAST YEARS OF THE YUAN

Despite the Mongol military domination of China and the highly centralized institutions of the Mongol court, the Yuan was the shortest of China's major dynasties. Little more than a century elapsed between Kublai's move to Beijing in 1264 and the dynasty's collapse in 1368. The rule of Kublai and his successor had been effective, but thereafter decline set in. By then, the Mongol Empire as a whole no longer lent strength to its parts. The khanates became separated by religion and culture as well as distance. Tribesmen in Mongolia rebelled now and then against the great khans in Beijing, who, in their eyes, had become too Chinese. The court at Beijing had never gained legitimacy. Some Chinese officials served it loyally to the end, but most Chinese viewed it as a government of carpetbaggers and Mongol rule as a military occupation. When succession disputes, bureaucratic factionalism, and pitched battles between

Mongol generals broke out, the Chinese showed little inclination to rally to the support of the dynasty.

Problems also arose in the countryside. Taxes were heavy, and some local officials were corrupt. The government issued excessive paper money and then refused to accept it in payment for taxes. The Yellow River changed its course, flooding the canals that carried grain to the capital. At great cost and suffering, a labor force of 150,000 workers and 20,000 soldiers rerouted the river to the south of the Shandung Peninsula. Further natural disasters during the 1350s led to popular uprisings. The White Lotus sect preached the coming of Maitreya. Regional military commanders, who combated the rebellions, broke free from central control, and became independent warlords. Important economic regions were devastated and partially depopulated. At the end, a rebel army threatened Beijing, and the last Mongol emperor and his court fled on horses to Shangdu. When it fell, they fled deeper into Mongolia.

IMAGE KEY
for pages 174–175

a. Song dynasty philosopher Chu Hsi (1130–1200)
b. A painting of irrigation methods on a farm south of the Yangtze
c. Animal-shaped vessel from China
d. Longquanware celadon jar with lotus petal lid
e. Song dynasty wine pot
f. Chinese, Song Dynasty incense burner (possibly Lao-Tzu on a Water buffalo)
g. A Mongol warrior's boots
h. Tang poet Li Po, as imagined by Song artist Liang Kai
i. Stone sculpture of bodhisattva
j. Pottery figures of court ladies playing polo, seventh century, Tang dynasty
k. Kublai Khan with Mongol warriors at the hunt
l. A "Barbarian" groom tends his steed

SUMMARY

Sui and Tang Dynasties The Sui and Tang dynasties (589–907) reunited China's empire. Under the Tang, China expanded into Central Asia, taking control of much of the lucrative Silk Road along which trade moved to the West. Chang'an, the Tang capital, became the largest city in the world. Tang culture was rich and cosmopolitan, much influenced by its contacts with other cultures. The Tang dynasty was also the golden age of Buddhism in China, and a variety of Buddhist sects flourished.

Song Dynasty Under the Song dynasty (960–1279), China experienced an agricultural revolution in which large aristocratic estates worked by serfs gave way to small land holdings owned by free farmers. Advances in technology led to the invention of printing and the development of a coal and iron-smelting industry. The growth of a money economy encouraged the expansion of trade, both within China and with foreign countries. Song culture was particularly rich in philosophy, poetry, and painting.

The Mongols After their unification by Genghis Khan (1167–1227), the Mongols created the greatest empire in history. The highly mobile Mongol cavalry overwhelmed Chinese armies. By 1279, the Mongols controlled all of China. Mongol rulers, however, enjoyed only shallow Chinese support, and their reign came to an end in 1368.

REVIEW QUESTIONS

1. Why was China able to reestablish its empire just 400 years after the fall of the Han, when Rome could not?

2. How did the Chinese economy and government change from the Tang to the Northern Song to the Southern Song?

3. What position did poets occupy in Chinese society?

4. How were the Mongols able to conquer most of the known world? What was the Chinese response to Mongol rule?

KEY TERMS

Amitabha Buddha (p. 184)   **Censorate** (p. 178)   **Zen** (p. 184)

 For additional study resources for this chapter, go to:
www.prenhall.com/craig/chapter8

9 Japan
Early History to 1467

CHAPTER HIGHLIGHTS

Yamato Japan Early Japanese history has two main turning points. The first occurred in the third century B.C.E. when an Old Stone Age Japan became an agricultural, metal-working society. The new technologies came to Japan from Korea. By the fifth century C.E., the Yamato court ruled most of Japan. It was heavily influenced by Korea until the seventh century when, in the second main turning point of their history, the Japanese began to adopt and adapt many features of Chinese culture, including Buddhism and Chinese writing, literature, and political institutions.

Nara and Heian Japan In this period, Japan was ruled by a civil aristocracy under the emperor. An enormous gulf existed between aristocrats and commoners. Japanese government was heavily influenced by the Chinese imperial system. Japanese culture, however, was increasingly self-confident and was aristocratic in its tastes and forms of expression. Noblewomen wrote many of the great works of Japanese literature during this age. Buddhism, heavily influenced by Shintoism, became increasingly assimilated in Japan.

The Early Feudal Age In the eighth century, mounted warriors called *samurai* began to dominate local government. By the late 1100s, power passed from the civil bureaucracy to military aristocrats. A series of *shōguns*, military officials, ruled in the emperor's name. The *shōguns'* power was based on their ability to command the loyalty of military vassals. Minamoto Yoritomo's seizure of power in 1185 marked the beginning of Japan's feudal age. He established *bakufu*, or "tent government." It would endure in Japan until the mid-nineteenth century. In 1274 and 1281, the Japanese, with the help of storms that destroyed the Mongol fleet, managed to defeat Mongol invaders sent by Kublai Khan.

CHAPTER QUESTIONS

HOW DID contact with Korea influence the Yamato Court?

WHAT FEATURES of Chinese civilization did Japan adopt during the Nara and Heian periods?

WHAT ROLE did women play in aristocratic Japanese culture?

HOW DID a military aristocracy come to dominate medieval Japan?

WHAT VARIETIES of Buddhism emerged in medieval Japan?

CHAPTER OUTLINE

• Japanese Origins and the Yayoi Revolution
• Nara and Heian Japan
• Aristocratic Culture and Buddhism
• Japan's Early Feudal Age
• Buddhism and Medieval Culture

Japanese history has three main turning points, each marked by a major influx of an outside culture and each followed by a massive restructuring of Japanese institutions. The first was in the third century B.C.E., when an Old Stone Age Japan became an agricultural, metal-working society. The second turning point came during the seventh century, when whole complexes of Chinese culture entered Japan directly, and Japan made the leap to a higher historical civilization, associated with the writing system, technologies, and philosophies of China, and with Chinese forms of Buddhism. Japan remained within this cultural sphere until the third turning point, in the 19th century, when it encountered the West.

HOW DID contact with Korea influence the Yamato Court?

Jōmon Figurine. Along with the cord-patterned pots, the hunting and gathering Jōmon people produced mysterious figurines. Is this a female deity? Why are the eyes slitted like snow goggles? Earthenware with traces of pigment (Kamegoaka type); 24.8 cm high.

Asia Society, N.Y.: Mr. and Mrs. John D. Rockefeller 3rd Collection.

JAPANESE ORIGINS AND THE YAYOI REVOLUTION

The earliest evidence of human habitation in Japan dates from about 30,000 B.C.E. Pottery, the oldest in the world, appeared about 10,000 B.C.E., and from about 8000 B.C.E. the Jōmon or "cord-pattern" pottery style developed. Archaeologists are baffled by its appearance in an Old Stone Age society, for in all other early societies pottery does not predate New Stone Age cultures.

After 8,000 years of Jōmon culture, the second phase of Japanese prehistory began about 300 B.C.E. It is called the Yayoi culture, after a place in Tokyo where its distinctive hard, pale orange pottery was first unearthed. There is no greater break in the cultural history of Japan than that between the Jōmon and the Yayoi. For at the beginning of the third century B.C.E., the agricultural revolution, the bronze revolution, and the iron revolution simultaneously burst on Japan. The new technologies were brought to Japan from Korea and rapidly replaced Jōmon culture as far east in Japan as the modern city of Nagoya. After that, the Yayoi culture diffused more slowly overland into eastern Japan, where conditions were less favorable for agriculture and a mixed agricultural-hunting economy lingered.

By the first century C.E., the Yayoi population had so expanded that wars were fought for the best land. From these wars emerged a more peaceful order of regional states ruled by a class of aristocratic warriors. During the third century C.E., a temporary hegemony was established over a number of these states.

TOMB CULTURE, THE YAMATO STATE, AND KOREA

A period (300–600 C.E.) emerged directly from the Yayoi culture that was characterized by giant tomb mounds. (They still dot the landscape of the Nara-Osaka region.) The early tombs imitated Korean models: circular mounds of earth built atop megalithic burial chambers. Like the Yayoi graves that preceded them, the tombs contained mirrors, jewels, and other ceremonial objects. From the fifth century C.E., these objects were replaced by armor, swords, spears, and military trappings. The change reflected a new wave of continental influences from the Korean peninsula—a flow of people and culture into Japan that began with Yayoi was continuous into historical times.

Japan appeared in Chinese chronicles in the fifth century C.E., a period also covered in the earliest Japanese accounts of their own history, the *Records of Ancient Matters* (*Kojiki*), compiled in 712, and the *Records of Japan* (*Nihongi*), dating from 720. A picture emerges of regional aristocracies under the loose hegemony of the Yamato "great kings" whose courts were located on the Yamato plain, near present-day Osaka, ancient Japan's richest agricultural region. The Yamato rulers held lands and granaries throughout Japan. The tomb of the great king Nintoku, which is 486 meters long and 36 meters high, has twice the volume of material found in the Great Pyramid of Egypt. By the fifth century C.E., the great kings must have had great authority to be able to commandeer laborers for a project on such a scale.

The great kings awarded Korean-type titles to court and regional aristocrats, titles that implied a national hierarchy centering on the Yamato court. Regional rulers used a similar system to govern their populations.

The basic social unit of Yamato aristocratic society was the extended family (*uji*). Groups of specialist workers and peasants called *be* were attached to these families. Yamato society had a small class of slaves, but many peasants were neither slaves nor members of aristocratic clans or specialized workers' groups.

The court was the scene of incessant struggles for power between aristocratic families and an ongoing campaign to control outlying regions. Rebellions were frequent, and there were constant wars with "barbarian tribes" in southern Kyushu and eastern Honshu on the frontiers of "civilized" Japan. Under the Yamato court, a three-cornered military balance emerged on the Korean peninsula between the states of Paekche, Silla, and Koguryo (see Map 9–1). Japan was an ally of Paekche, and the Paekche connection enabled the Yamato court to expand its power within Japan. Imports of iron weapons and tools increased its military strength. The migration to Japan of Korean artisans expanded its wealth and influence, and many immigrants founded noble families. Paekche also served as a conduit for elements of Chinese culture to reach Japan. Chinese writing was adopted for the transcription of Japanese names during the fifth or sixth century. Confucianism entered in 513 and Buddhism in 538.

In 532, Paekche turned against Japan, but by this time Japan had established direct relations with China.

RELIGION IN EARLY JAPAN

The indigenous religion of Yamato Japan was an animistic worship of the forces of nature, later given the name of *Shintō*, or "the way of the gods," to distinguish it from Buddhism. Shintō, which probably appeared in Japan as part of Yayoi culture, saw the underlying forces of nature embodied in a waterfall, a twisted tree, a strangely shaped boulder, a mountain, or in a great leader who would be worshipped as a deity after his death. Mount Fuji was regarded as holy not because it was thought to be the abode of a god, but because the mountain itself was an upwelling of a vital force of nature. Even today in Japan, a gnarled tree trunk may be girdled with a straw rope to mark it as an object of veneration. The sensitivity to nature and natural beauty that pervades Japanese art and poetry owes much to Shintō.

Early Japanese History

8000–300 B.C.E.	Jōmon culture
Early Continental Influences	
300 B.C.E.–300 C.E.	Yayoi culture
300–680 C.E.	Tomb culture and the Yamato state
680–850 C.E.	Chinese Tang pattern in Nara and Early Heian Japan

Shintō "The way of the gods." The animistic worship of the forces of nature that is the indigenous religion of Japan.

Terra-cotta Tomb Figurine. A clay statue of a Japanese warrior in armor from an ancient tomb.

Tokyo National Museum.

MAP 9–1
Yamato Japan and Korea (ca. 500 C.E.).   Paekche was Japan's ally on the Korean peninsula. Silla, Japan's enemy, was the state that would eventually unify Korea. (Note: Nara was founded in 710; Heian in 794.)

HOW DID Japan's proximity to Korea and China influence its cultural development?

A second aspect of early Shintō was its connection with the state and the aristocracy. The more potent forces of nature such as the sea, the sun, the moon, the wind, and thunder and lightning became personified as deities. Each clan, or extended family, had its own myth centering on a nature deity (*kami*) that it claimed as its original ancestor. Aristocratic families developed genealogies to trace their descent from such a deity, and the head of a clan was the chief priest who led its worship. When Japan was unified by the Yamato court, the myths of several clans apparently were joined into a composite national myth. The deity of the Yamato great kings was the sun goddess, so she became the chief deity.

The *Records of Ancient Matters* and *Records of Japan* narrate myths of Japan's origin and the deeds and misdeeds of gods, but in mid-volume the stories of the gods give way to stories about early emperors and events in Japanese history. The Japanese emperors, today the oldest royal family in the world, were viewed

JAPAN CHAPTER 9 209

as the lineal descendants of the sun goddess and as "living gods." The Great Shrine of the sun goddess at Ise has always been Japan's most important.

NARA AND HEIAN JAPAN

The second major turning point in Japanese history was its adoption of the higher civilization of China. This is a prime example of the worldwide process (described in Chapter 2) by which the heartland civilizations spread into outlying areas. In Japan, this happened between the seventh and 12th centuries and can best be understood as occurring in three stages. First, the Japanese studied China. Then, during the eighth and ninth centuries, they imported Chinese institutions, and finally they adapted these institutions to fit conditions in Japan. By the 11th century, the creative reworking of Chinese elements had created a Japanese culture distinct from China's and that of the Yamato court.

COURT GOVERNMENT

Japan began to send official embassies—traders, students, and Buddhist monks—to China in 607 C.E. Like Third World students who study abroad today, Japanese who studied in China returned home with technology, art, Buddhism, and a knowledge of Tang legal and governmental systems. Large-scale institutional changes inspired by the Tang model began in the 680s with the Emperor Temmu and his successor, the Empress Jito (r. 686–697).

Temmu usurped the throne from his nephew and then used Chinese systems to consolidate his power. A Chinese-type law code greatly augmented his authority. He styled himself "heavenly emperor" (**tennō**), which thereafter replaced the title of "great king." He rewarded his supporters with court ranks and positions in government patterned after the Tang example. He extended the authority of the court and increased its revenues by a survey of agricultural lands and a census. In short, although admiration for Chinese things must have been enormous, much of the borrowing was dictated by Japanese concerns.

Until the eighth century, the capital was usually moved each time an emperor died. Then, in 710 a new capital was laid out at Nara on a checkerboard grid pattern (similar to the Chinese capital at Chang'an). The capital was intended to be permanent, but it was moved again in 794 to Heian (later Kyoto) on the plain north of Nara. The imperial capital remained there until its relocation to Tokyo in 1869.

The superimposition of a Chinese-type capital on a still backward Japan produced a stark contrast. In the villages, peasants lived in pit dwellings and either planted in crude paddy fields or used slash-and-burn techniques of dry-land farming. In the capital, the emperor and nobles, believed to be descendants of the gods, dwelt in pillared palaces, drank wine, wore silk,

WHAT FEATURES of Chinese civilization did Japan adopt during the Nara and Heian periods?

tennō "Heavenly emperor." The official title of the emperor of Japan.

Prince Shōtoku (574–622). Shown here with two of his sons, he was a Buddhist and a reformer who began sending regular embassies to China in 607.

Corbis/Bettmann.

9.4
Prince Shotoku's
Seventeen Article
Constitution

9.5
Pilgrimage to
China (840) Ennin

and enjoyed the paintings, perfumes, and pottery of the Tang. Clustered about the capital were Buddhist temples with soaring pagodas and tile roofs.

Emperors at the Heian court were seen both as Confucian rulers with the majesty accorded by Chinese law and as Shintō rulers descended from the sun goddess. Their lineage was never usurped. Japanese history constitutes a single dynasty, although a few emperors were killed and replaced by other family members.

Beneath the emperor, the same modified Chinese pattern prevailed. A Council of State representing leading clans manipulated the authority of an emperor who usually reigned but did not rule. Beneath this council were eight ministries, including the Imperial Household Ministry. Size affected function: Where China had a population of 60 million, Japan had only four or five million. There were no significant external enemies, and local rule, in the Yamato tradition, was mostly in the hands of local clans. Consequently, much of the business of court government concerned the court itself. Of the 6,000 persons in the central ministries, more than 4,000 were concerned with the care of the imperial house.

Under the central court government were about 60 provinces, subdivided into districts and villages. Provincial governors were sent out from the capital. This change reduced the regional aristocrats to district magistrates and increased the power of the central aristocracy.

Japanese court government was, in other regards, unlike China's. There were no eunuchs. There was little tension between the emperor and the bureaucracy. (The main struggles were between clans.) The Tang shift from aristocracy

---

OVERVIEW   DEVELOPMENT OF JAPANESE WRITING

No two languages could be more different than Chinese and Japanese. Chinese is nonsyllabic, uninflected, and tonal. Japanese is polysyllabic, highly inflected, and atonal. To adopt Chinese writing for use in Japanese was thus no easy task. What the Japanese did at first—when they were not simply learning to write in Chinese—was to use certain Chinese ideographs as a phonetic script. For example, in the *Man'yōshū*, the eighth-century poetic anthology, *shira-nami* (white wave) was written with 之 for *shi*, 良 for *ra*, 奈 for *na*, and 美 for *mi*. Over several centuries, these phonetic ideographs evolved into a unique Japanese phonetic script:

Original Chinese Ideograph	Simplified Ideograph	Phonetic Script (kana)
之	乃	し
良	戻	ら
奈	亦	な
美	歺	み

It is apparent in the above examples how the original ideograph was first simplified according to the rules of calligraphy and was then further simplified into a phonetic script known as *kana*. In modern Japanese, Chinese ideographs are used for nouns, verb stems, and adjectives, and the phonetic script is used for inflections and particles.

学生 は 図書館 へ 行きました Students/as for/library/to/went. (The students went to the library.)

In the above sentence, the Chinese ideographs are the forms with many strokes, and the phonetic script is shown in the simpler, cursive form.

toward meritocracy did not take place, and only aristocrats were appointed to important official posts. A feeble attempt to establish an examination meritocracy on the Chinese model failed completely. Japan simply did not need the elaborate structures of Chinese imperial government. In the early Heian period, three new departments outside the Chinese system handled most of the functions of government: an office of auditors handled taxation, a bureau of archivists exercised executive power through the drafting of decrees, and police commissioners enforced laws and maintained order in the capital. Power shifted during the Heian period, but always revolved around the emperor. Until the mid-ninth century, some emperors ruled directly. In 856, the northern branch of the Fujiwara clan began to establish a stranglehold on power which was not broken until the last half of the 11th century. In 1072, the Emperor Shirakawa regained control of the government and strengthened the imperial family, but by then the capital was increasingly isolated and threatening developments were taking place in the countryside.

LAND AND TAXES

The last Japanese embassy to China was in 839. By then, the Japanese were sufficiently self-confident to use Chinese ideas in innovative ways. The 350 years that followed until the end of the 12th century were a time of assimilation and evolutionary change. Nowhere was this more evident than in the system of taxation.

The land system of early Heian Japan was patterned after China's equal field system. All land belonged to the emperor. It was redistributed to all able-bodied persons every six years, and taxes were levied on them, not on the land. The system was complex, requiring land surveys, the redrawing of boundaries, and elaborate land and population registers. Even China, with its sophisticated bureaucracy, could not prevent the system from breaking down. The attempt to implement the system demonstrates the energy and ability of the early Japanese.

The evolution of taxation in late Heian Japan was a messy affair driven by haphazard local developments. Court officials were not able to maintain the elaborate records needed to administer the equal field system, so they simply assigned each governor a fixed sum to be collected from his province. The governor assigned quotas to district magistrates, who collected as much as they could and pocketed the surplus. This began the evolution of a new local ruling class.

Nobles and powerful temples in Kyoto used their influence at court to obtain exemptions from taxation for their lands. From the ninth century, many cultivators of small holdings began to commend their land to such nobles, judging that they would be better off as serfs on tax-free estates than as free farmers subject to taxation. The estates were managed by stewards, appointed from among local notables. They took a share of the harvests for themselves and thus had a vital interest in upholding local order.

RISE OF THE SAMURAI

During the Nara period, Japan followed China's example and experimented with conscripted armies. These, however, proved inefficient, and in 792, the court ended conscription and established a system of mounted warriors whose taxes were remitted in exchange for military service. They were stationed in the capital and in the provinces. The Japanese verb "to serve" is *samurau*, so those who served became known as **samurai**. Nonofficial private bands of local warriors

samurai Professional Japanese warriors.

Japanese Sword. From medieval times, Japanese artisans made the world's finest swords. They became a staple export to China. Worn only by samurai, they were also an emblem of class status, distinguishing them from commoners.

Philip Gatward © Dorling Kindersley.

sprang up to replace the official appointees, and they constituted Japan's military until the 15th and 16th centuries, when a new emphasis was placed on foot soldiers.

Being a samurai was expensive. Horses, armor, and weapons were costly, and their use required long training. The primary weapon was the bow and arrow, used from the saddle. Most samurai were from well-to-do local families. Their initial function was to preserve local order and, possibly, to help with tax collection. But at times they contributed to disorder. District magistrates sometimes led local forces against provincial governors to protest taxation.

Regional military coalitions or confederations formed and first made history in 935–940, when a descendant of an emperor, who headed such a group, became involved in a tax dispute. He captured several provinces and declared himself emperor. The Kyoto court recruited another military band as its champion, and quelled the rebellion. It, however, was only the first of a number of conflicts between regional military bands. By the mid-12th century, local and regional military bands existed in every part of Japan. In 1156, a power struggle at court enabled a band led by Taira Kiyomori to seize control of Kyoto and the emperor. But, like the earlier Fujiwara family, he did not change the system. He only imposed a new stratum atop the many power centers already established at court.

ARISTOCRATIC CULTURE AND BUDDHISM

*I*f the features of a culture could be weighed, the culture of Nara and early Heian Japan would appear to have been consisted largely of Shintō religious practices and village folkways—an extension of the culture of the late Yamato period. The aristocracy was small and encapsulated at court, just as Buddhist monks were contained within their monastic environment. The early Heian aristocracy comprised one-tenth of 1 percent of Japan's population, and most of its court culture had only recently been imported from China. There had not been time for commoners to ape their betters or for the powerful force of the indigenous culture to reshape that of the elite.

The resulting cultural gap helps explain why the aristocrats believed that commoners were hardly human. The writings of courtiers reflect little sympathy for the people. Heian high culture resembled a hothouse plant. It was protected by the political influence of the court and nourished by the flow of tax revenues and income from estates. Its indulged aristocrats developed a unique way of life guided by canons of elegance and taste that are striking even today.

CHINESE TRADITION IN JAPAN

Education at the Nara and Heian courts was largely a matter of reading Chinese books and acquiring the skills to compose poetry and prose in Chinese. These were daunting tasks, but the challenge was met. From the Nara period until the 19th century, most philosophical and legal writings, as well as most of the histories, essays, and religious texts in Japan, were written in Chinese.

Not only were Japanese writings in Chinese a vital part of the Japanese cultural tradition, but the original Chinese works themselves also became a part of the same tradition. Chinese history was read, and its stock figures provided the types of heroes and villains through whom the Japanese

---

QUICK REVIEW

Samurai

- Word comes from Japanese verb "to serve"
- Constituided Japan's military until 15th century
- Samurai were responsible for their own equipment and training

---

WHAT ROLE did women play in aristocratic Japanese culture?

QUICK REVIEW

The Place of China in Japanese Education and Literature

- Court education was almost synonymous with Chinese literature
- Chinese history was widely read
- Buddhisist stories and works of Confucianism part of Japanese culture

---

Who Was in Charge at the Nara and Heian Courts?

710–856	Emperors or combinations of nobles
856–1086	Fujiwara nobles
1086–1160	Retired emperors
1160–1180	Military house of Taira

viewed their own history. Chinese history became the mirror in which Japan saw itself, despite the differences between the two societies. Buddhist stories and the books of Confucianism also became Japanese classics. A Western parallel might be the role that "foreign books," such as the Bible and works of Plato and Aristotle, played in medieval and Renaissance England.

Birth of Japanese Literature

Stimulated by Chinese models, the Japanese began to compose poetry in their native tongue. The first major anthology, the *Collection of Ten Thousand Leaves* (*Man'yōshū*), dates from about 760 and contains 4,516 poems. Sentiments in the poems reveal a deep sensitivity to nature and strong human relationships between husband and wife, parents and children. They also display a love for the land of Japan and links to a Shintō past.

An early obstacle to the development of a Japanese poetic tradition was the difficulty of transcribing Japanese sounds. In the *Ten Thousand Leaves*, Chinese characters were used as phonetic symbols. But because there was no standardization for transcription, it soon became unintelligible. In 951, a committee of poets deciphered the work and put it into *kana*, a new syllabic script or alphabet that had developed during the ninth century.

An Album Leaf. This album leaf from the Ishiyama-gire is part of a collection from the works of 36 poets compiled in the early 12th century. The poem is by Ki no Tsurayuki (868?–945?), who in the preface to another anthology wrote: "The poetry of Japan has its roots in the human heart and flourishes in the countless leaves of words . . . Hearing the warbler sing among the blossoms and the frog in his fresh waters—is there any living being not given to song? It is poetry which, without exertion, moves heaven and earth, stirs the feelings of gods and spirits invisible to the eye, softens the relations between men and women, calms the hearts of fierce warriors." The calligraphy is by Fujiwara no Sadanobu (1088–1154). The poem is written on layered rice paper with gold and silver and foliage designs. Even to the untutored eye, the effect is elegant.

Freer Gallery of Art, Smithsonian Institution, Washington, D.C.

The invention of *kana* opened the gate to the most brilliant developments of the Heian period. Most of the new works and certainly the greatest were by women—particularly Sei Shōnagon and Murasaki Shikibu. Both were daughters of provincial officials serving at the Heian court. The *Pillow Book of Sei Shōnagon* contains sharp, satirical, amusing essays and literary jottings that illustrated the demanding aristocratic taste of the early 11th-century Heian court.

The *Tale of Genji*, written by Murasaki Shikibu (about 1010), is the world's first novel. *Genji* is a work of sensitivity, originality, and acute psychological delineation of character. It had no Chinese model. It tells of the life, loves, and sorrows of Prince Genji, son of an imperial concubine, and, after his death, of his son Kaoru. The novel spans three-quarters of a century and may be seen as having had a "definite and serious purpose." In one passage Genji twits a court lady whom he finds reading an extravagant romance. But then Genji says:

> I think far better of this art than I have led you to suppose. Even its practical value is immense. Without it what should we know of how people lived in the past, from the Age of the Gods down to the present day? For history books such as the *Chronicles of Japan* show us only one small corner of life; whereas these diaries and romances, which I see piled around you contain, I am sure, the most minute information about all sorts of people's private affairs.[1]

[1] R. Tsunoda, W. T. deBary, and D. Keene, eds., *Sources of the Japanese Traditon* (New York: Columbia University Press, 1958), p. 181.

NARA AND HEIAN BUDDHISM

The Six Sects of the Nara period each represented a separate philosophical doctrine within Mahayana Buddhism. Their monks, trained in monastic communities set apart from the larger society, studied, read sutras, copied texts, meditated, and joined in rituals. As in China, monasteries and temples were tied closely to the state. Tax revenues supported them, and monks prayed for the health of the emperor and for rain in time of drought.

Japan in the seventh and eighth centuries was much less culturally developed than China. The Japanese came to Buddhism not from the philosophical perspectives of Confucianism or Daoism but from the magic and mystery of Shintō. What appealed to the early Japanese in Buddhism was, consequently, its colorful and elaborate rituals; the gods, demons, and angels of the Mahayana pantheon; and, above all, the beauty of Buddhist art. The philosophy took longer to establish itself.

Japan's cultural identity was also different. In China, Buddhism was always viewed as Indian and alien—a factor leading to the Chinese persecution of Buddhists during the ninth century. In contrast, Japan's cultural identity or cultural self-consciousness took shape only during the Nara and early Heian periods. One element in that identity was the imperial cult derived from Shintō, but Shintō was no match for Buddhism as a religion. Buddhism was no more foreign to Japan than Confucianism and the rest of the Chinese culture that had helped reshape the Japanese identity, so there was no bias against it. Consequently,

The Hōryūji Temple. Built by Prince Shōtoku in 607, it contains the oldest wooden buildings in the world. They are the best surviving examples of Chinese Buddhist architecture. Note the groups of visiting students in the foreground.

Susumu Takahashi/Reuters/Corbis-Bettmann.

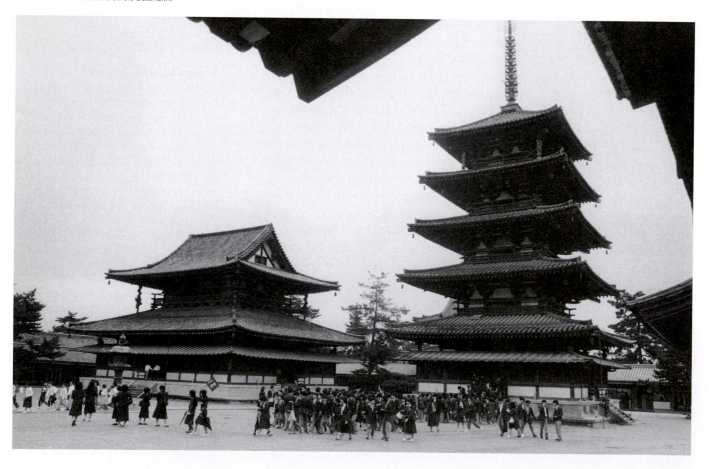

Buddhism entered deeply into Japanese culture and retained its vitality longer than in China. Not until the 17th or 18th centuries did Japanese elites became so Confucian as to be anti-Buddhist. In 794, when the court moved to Heian (Kyoto), the two great new Buddhist sects were Tendai and Shingon.

Tendai's champion was a monk named Saichō (767–822) who, in 785, founded a temple on Mount Hiei to the northwest of Kyoto. He went to China to study in 804 and returned the following year imbued with the teachings of the Tendai sect. He taught that salvation could be attained by all who led a life of contemplation and moral purity. He instituted strict monastic rules and a 12-year training curriculum for novices who sought admission to his monastery. The sect grew until thousands of temples had been built on Mount Hiei. Many later Japanese sects emerged from the Tendai fold.

The Shingon sect was begun by Kūkai (774–835), who became a monk at the age of 18. In 804, he went to China with Saichō. He returned two years later bearing the Shingon doctrines and founded a monastery on Mount Kōya. Kūkai was a bridge builder, a poet, an artist, and one of the three great calligraphers of his age. He is sometimes credited with inventing the *kana* syllabary and with introducing the Japanese to tea. Shingon doctrines center on an eternal and cosmic Buddha, of whom all other Buddhas are manifestations. *Shingon* means "true word" or "mantra," a verbal formula with mystical powers. It is sometimes called *esoteric Buddhism* in that it had secret teachings that were passed from master to disciple. In China, Shingon died out as a sect in the persecutions of the mid-ninth century, but in Japan its doctrines even influenced the Tendai center on Mount Hiei.

During the later Heian period, Buddhism began to be more widely assimilated. At the village level, the folk religion of Shintō took in many Buddhist elements. In the high culture of the capital, Shintō was almost absorbed by Buddhism. Shintō deities came to be seen as the local manifestations of universal Buddhas. The cosmic or "Great Sun Buddha" of the Shingon sect, for example, was easily identified with the sun goddess. Often, great Buddhist temples had smaller Shintō shrines on their grounds. Not until the mid-19th century was Shintō disentangled from Buddhism, and then the motive was political, not religious.

JAPAN'S EARLY FEUDAL AGE

The year 1185, or 1160, if we include Taira rule in Kyoto, marked the shift from centuries of rule by a civil aristocracy to centuries of rule by military nobles. It saw the formation of the *bakufu* (tent government), a completely non-Chinese type of government. During this time the *shōgun* emerged as the de facto ruler of Japan, although in theory he was a military official of the emperor. The year marked the beginning of new cultural forms and initiated changes in family and social organization.

THE KAMAKURA ERA

Taira Kiyomori's seizure of Kyoto in 1160 fell short of establishing a national military hegemony, for other bands flourished elsewhere in Japan beyond his control. After Kiyomori's victory, the Taira embraced the elegant lifestyle of the Kyoto court. They expected their tutelage over the court to be as enduring as that of the Fujiwara. But in 1180, Minamoto Yoritomo (1147–1199) responded to a call to

HOW DID a military aristocracy come to dominate medieval Japan?

bakufu "Tent government." Military regime that governed Japan under the shguns.

shōgun Military official who was the actual ruler of Japan in the emperor's name from the late 1100s until the mid-19th century.

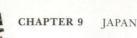

arms by a disaffected prince, seized control of eastern Japan (the rich Kanto plain), and began the war that ended in 1185 with the downfall of the Taira.

Yoritomo's authority was national, for his armies had ranged over most of Japan. After his victory in 1185, warriors from every area became his vassals. Wary of Kyoto, Yoritomo set up his headquarters at Kamakura, 30 miles south of present-day Tokyo, at the edge of his base of power in eastern Japan. He called his government the bakufu in contrast to the civil government in Kyoto. The offices he established were few and practical: one to deal with his samurai retainers, one to administer and execute his policies, and one to hear legal suits. Each office was staffed by vassals. Yoritomo also appointed military governors in each province and military stewards on the former estates of the Taira and of others who had fought against him. These appointments carried the right to some income from the land, but the rest of the income went to Kyoto as taxes or as revenues for the noble owners of these estates.

When Yoritomo died in 1199, his widow and her Hōjō kinsmen moved to usurp the power of the Minamoto house. The widow, having taken holy orders after her husband's death, was known as the Nun Shōgun. One of her sons was pushed aside. The other became Shōgun but was murdered in 1219. After that, the Hōjō ruled as regents for a puppet Shōgun. The Kyoto court led an armed uprising against Kamakura in 1221, but it was suppressed. Any society based on personal bonds faces the problem of how to transfer loyalty from one generation to another. That the Kamakura vassals fought for the Hōjō in 1221 suggests that they were loyal to the bakufu, which guaranteed their income from land. Their personal loyalty to the Minamoto had ended with the death of Yoritomo.

The Mongols In 1266, Kublai Khan (see Chapter 8) sent envoys demanding that Japan submit to his rule. He had subjugated Korea in 1258. The Hōjō at Kamakura refused. The first Mongol invasion fleet arrived with 30,000 troops in 1274, but withdrew after initial victories. A second invasion force arrived in 1281. Carrying 140,000 troops, the scale of this amphibious operation was unprecedented in world history. With gunpowder bombs and phalanxes of

Minamoto Yoritomo. Founder of the Kamakura Shogunate. He is depicted here in court robes as a statesman and official, though he was, above all, a warrior-general.

Seka Bunka Photo.

Japanese Scroll Painting. Mongol invaders battling with an intrepid samurai horseman. Note the bomb bursting in the air at the upper right of this late 13th-century Japanese scroll painting.

© Museum of Imperial Collections–Sannomaru Shozo Kan. Courtesy of the International Society for Educational Information, Inc.

archers protected by a forward wall of soldiers carrying overlapping shields, the Mongol forces were formidable.

Although the Japanese strategy of fierce individual combat was not very effective against the Mongols' tactics, the Japanese held out for two months until *kamikaze* ("divine winds") sank a portion of the Mongols' fleet and forced the rest to retreat. Preparations for a third invasion ended with Kublai's death in 1294. The defensive campaign yielded no new lands or booty to be distributed among the soldiers, and this caused considerable complaint.

THE QUESTION OF FEUDALISM

Scholars often contend that Yoritomo's rule marks the start of feudalism in Japan. Feudalism may be defined in terms of three criteria: lord-vassal relationships, fiefs given in return for military service, and a warrior ethic. It can be asked, however, whether these criteria truly apply to Kamakura Japan.

Certainly, the mounted warriors who made up the armies of Yoritomo were predominantly his vassals, not his kin. As for fiefs, the situation is ambiguous. Kamakura vassals received rights to income from land in exchange for military service, but fiefs, as such, did not appear until the late 15th century. The warrior ethic, however, is beyond doubt. It had been developing among regional military bands for several centuries before 1185. The samurai prized bravery, cunning, physical strength, and endurance. They gave their swords names. Their sports were hunting, hawking, and archery. Warriors thought of themselves as a military aristocracy that practiced "the way of the bow and arrow," "the way of the bow and horse," "the way of the warriors," and so on.

The common definition of feudalism describes the Kamakura military band, but warrior bands were only one part of society. Kamakura Japan had two political centers. The bakufu had military authority, but the Kyoto court continued the late Heian pattern of civil rule by appointing civil governors, collecting tax revenues, and controlling the region about Kyoto. Noble families, retired emperors, and the great Buddhist temples also contributed to Kyoto's influence. It also remained the fount of rank and honors. After his victory in 1185, Yoritomo asked the emperor for the title of "barbarian-quelling generalissimo" (*Sei i tai shōgun*, shortened to *shōgun*). He was refused, but in 1192 he finally got the title. Even then, the award had to be justified by the argument that Yoritomo was a Minamoto offshoot of the imperial line.

The small size of Yoritomo's vassal band is an even more telling argument against viewing Kamakura Japan as fully feudal. Numbering about 2,000 before 1221 and 3,000 thereafter, most of the band were concentrated in eastern Japan. But even if as many as half were distributed about the rest of the country as military governors and stewards, there would have been only 100 in a region the size of Massachusetts. (Japan in 1180 was about 15 times larger than that state.) How could so few control such a large area? The answer is that they did not have to.

The local social order of the late Heian era continued into the Kamakura period. The Kyoto court, governors, district magistrates, and local notables functioned more or

Mongol Invasion
- 1266: Kublai Khan demands Japan submit to his rule
- 1274: Invasion fleet withdraws after initial victories
- 1281: Huge invasion force destroyed by *kamikaze*, or "divine winds"

kamikaze "Divine winds" that sank a portion of the invading Mongol fleet in Japan in 1281.

Government by Military Houses

1160–1180	Taira rule in Kyoto
1185–1333	Kamakura bakufu
1185	Founded by Minamoto Yoritomo
1219	Usurped by Hōjō
1221	Armed uprising by Kyoto court
1232	Formation of Jōei Code
1274 and 1281	Invasion by Mongols
1336–1467	Ashikaga bakufu
1336	Begun by Ashikaga Takauji
1392	End of Southern Court
1467	Start of warring states period

less as they had earlier. To influence the local scene, the newly appointed Kamakura vassals had to win the cooperation of the existing local power-holders. In short, even if the Kamakura vassals themselves could be called feudal, they were only a thin skin on the surface of a society still constructed on older principles.

THE ASHIKAGA ERA

By 1331, various tensions had developed within Kamakura society. Because the patrimony of a warrior was divided among his children, vassals became poorer over time and often fell into debt. High-ranking vassals of Kamakura were also dissatisfied with the Hōjō monopolization of key bakufu posts. While the ties of vassals to Kamakura weakened, the ties to other warriors within their region grew stronger until new regional bands were ready to emerge. The precipitating event was a revolt in 1331 by an emperor who thought emperors should actually rule. Kamakura sent Ashikaga Takauji (1305–1358), the head of a branch family of the Minamoto line, to put down the revolt; instead he joined it. Other regional lords then rose up and destroyed the Hōjō bakufu in Kamakura.

What emerged from the turmoil of the years from 1331 to 1336 was a regional multistate system centering on Kyoto. Each region was based on a warrior band. In the central Kyoto region, Ashikaga Takauji established his bakufu. Its offices were simple and functional: a samurai office for police and military matters, an administrative office for financial matters, a documents office for land records, and a judicial board to settle disputes. The offices were staffed by Takauji's vassals. They became lords (called *daimyo*) in their own right and usually held appointments as military governors in the provinces surrounding Kyoto. The bakufu also appointed vassals to watch over its interests in the far north, in eastern Japan, and in Kyushu.

Government in the outlying regions was more diverse. Some lords held several provinces, some only one. Some had integrated most of the warriors in their areas into their bands. Others had several unassimilated military bands in their territories, forcing them to rely more on the authority of Kyoto. Formally, all regional lords or daimyo were the vassals of the shōgun, but the relationship was often nominal. Sometimes the regional lords lived on their lands; sometimes they lived in Kyoto.

The relationship between the Kyoto bakufu and the regional lords fluctuated from 1336 to 1467. At times, able lords turned their regions into virtually independent states. At other times, the power of the Kyoto bakufu grew. In 1394, the third shōgun strengthened its power by relinquishing his military post as shōgun to his son and taking the highest civil post, grand minister of state. He improved relations with the great Buddhist temples and Shintō shrines and established ties with Ming China. His military campaigns dented the autonomy of regional lords outside of the inner Kyoto circle.

Even the third shōgun, however, depended heavily on his vassals. He gave them the authority to levy taxes; to pull into their own hands all judicial, administrative, and military authority in their regions; and to take on unaffiliated warriors as their own vassals. This created problems for his successors. As ties of personal loyalty wore thin, new local warrior bands formed.

WOMEN IN WARRIOR SOCIETY

The Nun Shōgun was one of a long line of important women in Japan. The central figure of Japanese mythology was the sun goddess, who ruled the Plain of High Heaven. The empresses of the Yamato and Nara courts were followed by the great women writers of the Heian period. Under the Kamakura bakufu, daughters of warrior families often trained in archery and other military arts. Women also occasionally inherited the position of military steward. But as fighting became more common in the 14th century, their position declined, and as warfare became endemic in the 15th, their status plummeted. To protect the integrity of the military fief—the warrior's reward for serving his lord in battle and the lord's guarantee that his warriors would continue their service—multigeniture, the custom by which daughters as well as sons inherited property, gave way to inheritance of an undivided patrimony by a man's most able son.

AGRICULTURE, COMMERCE, AND MEDIEVAL GUILDS

Population figures for medieval Japan were about 6 million for the year 1200 and 12 million for 1600. The increase was brought about by land reclamation and improvements in agricultural technology. Iron-edged tools became available to all. New strains of rice were developed. Irrigation and diking improved. Vegetables were planted during the fall and winter in dry fields, which were flooded and planted with rice during the spring and summer.

In the Nara and early Heian periods, the economy was almost exclusively agricultural. The government had established a mint, but little money actually circulated. Taxes were paid in grain and labor. Commercial transactions were largely barter, with silk or grain as the medium of exchange. Artisans produced for the noble households or temples to which they were attached. Peasants were self-sufficient.

From the late Heian period, more of the growing agricultural surplus stayed in local hands. During the Kamakura and Ashikaga periods, income was transfered from the court aristocrats to the warrior class. As this took place, artisans began to produce for new consumers. Military equipment was an early staple of commerce, but gradually *sake*, lumber, paper, vegetable oils, salt, and products of the sea were also commercialized. A demand for copper coins developed, and they were imported in huge quantities from China.

During the Kamakura period, a class of merchants emerged to market the products of artisans. Trade networks spread throughout Japan. Artisan and merchant guilds, not unlike those of medieval Europe, paid a fee in exchange for monopoly rights in a given area. From the Kamakura period onward, markets were held periodically in many parts of Japan. During the 14th and 15th centuries, markets were held with increasing frequency until they evolved into permanent towns.

BUDDHISM AND MEDIEVAL CULTURE

WHAT VARIETIES of Buddhism emerged in medieval Japan?

The Nara and Heian periods are often referred to as Japan's Classical Age, and the period that followed (approximately 1200 to 1600) is characterized as its Middle Ages. It was medieval in the root sense of the word in that it lay between two major spans of premodern Japanese history. It was also medieval in that it shared some of the characteristics of societies that are labeled medieval in Europe and China. However, there was an important difference. Medieval Japan transitioned from its classical era without interruption. The two periods even overlapped during the early Kamakura, whereas in Europe, a millennium of recovery from barbarian incursions separated classical

Rome from the high medieval era. Similarly, China endured 400 years of political disunity and barbarian invasions.

The continuity of Japanese culture is visible throughout its history. The earlier poetic tradition continued with vigor. The style of painting that had reached a peak in the *Genji Scrolls* continued into the medieval era with scrolls dealing with historical and religious themes or fairy-tale adventures. Artisanal production was never interrupted. In short, Heian culture bridged smoothly into medieval Japanese culture. The latter, however, added some new characteristics. First, as the leadership of society shifted from court aristocrats to military aristocrats, new forms of literature appeared. The medieval military tales were as different from the *Tale of Genji* as the elaborate armor of the mounted warrior was from the colorful silken robes of the court nobility. Second, a new wave of culture influence entered from Sung China. Third, and most important, the medieval centuries were Japan's age of Buddhist faith. A religious revolution took place and deeply influenced the arts of Japan.

JAPANESE PIETISM: PURE LAND AND NICHIREN BUDDHISM

Among the doctrines of the Heian Tendai sect was the belief that the true teachings of the historical Buddha had been lost and that salvation could be had only by calling on the name of Amida, the Buddha who ruled over the Western Paradise (or **Pure Land**). During the 10th and 11th centuries, itinerant preachers began to spread Pure Land doctrines and practices beyond Kyoto and into remote provinces. The doctrine that the world had fallen on evil times and that only faith would suffice was given credence by earthquakes, epidemics, fires, banditry, and wars.

Two early Kamakura religious geniuses were behind the surge of interest in Buddhism. Hōnen (1133–1212) was perhaps the first to say that the invocation of the name of Amida alone was enough for salvation and that only faith counted. These claims brought Hōnen into conflict with the older Buddhist establishment and marked the emergence of Pure Land as a separate sect. Shinran (1173–1262) taught that even a single invocation in praise of Amida, if done with perfect faith, was sufficient for salvation. But perfect faith was a gift from Amida. Shinran taught that pride was an obstacle to purity of heart. He famously said: "If even a good man can be reborn in the Pure Land, how much more so a wicked man." In other words, the evil man is less inclined to assume that he is the source of his own salvation and is, therefore, more inclined to trust in Amida.

Shinran's emphasis on faith alone led him to break many of the monastic rules of earlier Buddhism: He ate meat and married a nun, thus authorizing a married clergy for the Pure Land sect. He taught that all occupations were equally "heavenly" if performed with a pure heart, and he traveled about Japan establishing "True Pure Land" congregations. These often developed political and military power. The sect believed that a strong "church" was needed to protect the saved while they were still in this world. During the 15th century, some Pure Land village congregations established self-defense forces. At times they rebelled against feudal lords. Although their power was destroyed in the late 16th century and their sect was depoliticized, a line of distinguished teachers kept them true to their original doctrinal simplicity and reliance on piety. Pure Land Buddhism remains the dominant form of Buddhism in Japan today.

Kūja Invoking Buddha. The mid-Heian monk Kūja (903–972) preached Pure Land doctrines in Kyoto and throughout Japan. Little Buddhas emerge from his mouth.

PPS/Pacific Press Service.

Pure Land Buddhism Variety of Japanese Buddhism that maintained that only faith was necessary for salvation.

HISTORY'S VOICES

HAKUIN'S ENLIGHTENMENT

akuin (1686–1769) was a poet, painter, and Zen master. He wrote in colloquial Japanese as well as in Chinese. He illustrated the continuing power of the Zen tradition in postmedieval times. The following passages are from an autobiographical account of his spiritual quest. The first follows a recounting of his disappointments and failures and tells of his initial enlightenment. His teacher did not accept this as adequate, however. The second passage tells of his experience eight years later.

1

In the spring of my twenty-fourth year, I was painfully struggling at the Eiganji in the province of Echigo. I slept neither day nor night, forgetting either to eat or sleep. A great doubt suddenly possessed me, and I felt as if frozen to death in the midst of an icy field extending thousands of *li*. A sense of an extraordinary purity permeated my bosom. I could not move. I was virtually senseless. What remained was only "*Mu*." Although I heard the master's lectures in the Lecture Hall, it was as though I were listening to his disclosure from some sixty or seventy steps outside the Hall, or as if I were floating in the air. This condition lasted for several days until one night I heard the striking of a temple bell. All at once a transformation came over me, as though a layer of ice were smashed or a tower of jade pulled down. Instantly I came to my senses. Former doubts were completely dissolved, like ice which had melted away. "How marvelous! How marvelous!" I cried out aloud. There was no cycle of birth and death from which I had to escape, no enlightenment for which I had to seek.

2

At the age of thirty-two I settled in this dilapidated temple [Shoinji]. In a dream one night my mother handed me a purple silk robe. When I lifted it I felt great weights in both sleeves. Examining it, I found in each sleeve an old mirror about five or six inches in diameter. The reflection of the right-hand mirror penetrated deep into my heart. My own mind, as well as mountains and rivers, the entire earth, became serene and bottomless. The left-hand mirror had no luster on its entire surface. Its face was like that of a new iron pan not yet touched by fire. Suddenly I became aware that the luster on the left-hand mirror surpassed that of the right by a million times. After this incident, the vision of all things was like looking at my own face. For the first time I realized the meaning of the words, "The eyes of the Tatha-gata behold the Buddha-nature."

Source: *The Buddhist Tradition in India, China, and Japan* by William Theodore de Bary. Copyright © 1969 by William Theodore de Bary. Reprinted by permission of Modern Library, a division of Random House Inc.

A second devotional sect was founded by Nichiren (1222–1282), who believed that the Lotus Sutra perfectly embodied the teachings of the Buddha. He instructed his adherents repeatedly to chant, "Praise to the Lotus Sutra of the Wondrous Law," usually to the accompaniment of rapid drumbeats. The chanting optimally induced a state of religious rapture. Nichiren was remarkable for a Buddhist in being both intolerant and nationalistic. He blamed the ills of his age on rival sects and asserted that only his sect could protect Japan. Even his adopted Buddhist name, the Sun Lotus, combined the term for the rising sun of Japan with that of the flower that had become the symbol of Buddhism.

ZEN BUDDHISM

Meditation had long been a part of Japanese monastic practice. Zen meditation and doctrines were introduced by monks returning from study in Sung China. Zen in Japan was a religion of paradox. Its monks were learned, yet it stressed a return to the uncluttered "original mind," a state attained in a flash of intuitive understanding (see "Hakuin's Enlightenment"). Zen was punctiliously traditional and the most Chinese of Japan's medieval sects. The authority of the Zen master over his pupil-monks was absolute. Yet Zen was also iconoclastic. Its sages were depicted tearing up sutras to make the point that it is religious experience and not words that count. Within a rigidly structured monastic regimen, monks tested their understanding, gained through long hours of meditation, in encounters with their master. Buddhism stressed compassion for all sentient beings, yet in Japan the Zen sect included many samurai whose duty it was to fight and kill. A few military leaders encouraged the practice of Zen among their retainers in the hope of instilling a single-minded attention to duty.

The most remarkable aspect of Zen was its influence on the arts of medieval Japan. The most beautiful gardens, for example, were in Zen temples. Zen monks, such as Josetsu, Shūbun (ca. 1415), and Sesshū (1420–1506) are among the masters of ink painting in East Asia. Because the artist's creativity itself was seen as grounded in his experience of meditation, a painting of a waterfall or of a crow on a leafless branch in late fall was viewed as no less religious than a painting of the mythic Zen founder Bodhidharma.

Nō Plays

Another fascinating product of medieval culture was the Nō play, a kind of mystery drama without parallels in East Asia. The play was performed on an almost square, bare wooden stage (often outdoors) by male actors wearing robes of great beauty and carved, painted masks with enigmatic expressions. Many such masks and robes are regarded as Japan's national treasures. The chorus was chanted to the accompaniment of flute and drums. The language was poetic. The action was slow and highly stylized. At a critical juncture in most plays, the protagonist was possessed by the spirit of another and performed a dance. Spirit possession was common in Japanese folk religion and also occurred in the *Tale of Genji*.

Summary

Yamato Japan Early Japanese history has two main turning points. The first occurred in the third century B.C.E. when an Old Stone Age Japan became an agricultural, metal-working society. The new technologies came to Japan from Korea. By the fifth century C.E., the Yamato court ruled most of Japan. It was heavily influenced by Korea until the seventh century when, in the second main turning point of their history, the Japanese began to adopt and adapt many features of Chinese culture, including Buddhism and Chinese writing, literature, and political institutions.

Nara and Heian Japan In this period, Japan was ruled by a civil aristocracy under an emperor. An enormous gap existed between aristocrats and commoners. Japanese government was heavily influenced by the Chinese imperial system. Japanese culture, however, grew increasingly self-confident and aristocratic in its tastes and forms of expression. Noblewomen wrote many of the great works of Japanese literature during this age. Buddhism, heavily influenced by Shintōism, was increasingly assimilated.

IMAGE KEY

for pages 204–205

a. Ishiyama-Gire (Fragment)
b. Naran tomb paining in Japan
c. Antique Japanese No mask
d. Horyuji temple
e. A clay statue of a warrior in armor from an ancient tomb
f. The Prince Shotoku (574–622)
g. Fan-shaped sutra, Heian period
h. Scroll with depictions of the13th century attack on the Sanjo Palace
i. Mid-Heian monk

The Early Feudal Age In the eighth century, mounted warriors called *samurai* began to dominate local government. By the late 1100s, power passed from the civil bureaucracy to military aristocrats, and a series of shōguns, military officials, ruled in the emperor's name. The shōguns' power was based on their ability to command the loyalty of military vassals. Minamoto Yoritomo's seizure of power in 1185 marked the beginning of Japan's feudal age. He established bakufu, or "tent government," which endured in Japan until the mid-19th century. In 1274 and 1281, the Japanese, with the help of storms that destroyed the Mongol fleet, managed to defeat Mongol invaders sent by Kublai Khan.

REVIEW QUESTIONS

1. How did Chinese culture influence Japan's government and religion? How did the Japanese change what they borrowed?

2. How did the Buddhism of the Nara and Heian periods differ from that of the early medieval era?

3. How did Japan become a society dominated by military lords and their vassals?

4. How and why did the role of women change from the Heian to the Ashikaga eras?

KEY TERMS

bakufu (p. 215)   **samurai** (p. 211)   **Shōgun** (p. 215)
kamikaze (p. 217)   **Shintō** (p. 207)   **tennō** (p. 209)
Pure Land Buddhism (p. 220)

 For additional study resources for this chapter, go to:
www.prenhall.com/craig/chapter9

BUDDHISM

Hinduism, Buddhism. and Jainism all arose out of the spiritual ferment of Vedic India after 700 B.C.E. Buddhism shares a kinship with these other religions much as Judaism, Christianity, and Islam have a relationship.

The founder of Buddhism, Siddhartha Gautama, was born about 563 B.C.E. A prince in a petty kingdom near what is now the border of India and Nepal, Gautama was reared amid luxury and comforts, married at 16, and had a child. According to legend, at age 29 he saw a decrepit old man, sick and suffering, and a corpse. He suddenly realized that all humans would suffer the same fate. Gautama renounced his wealth and family and entered the life of a wandering ascetic. He visited famous teachers, for almost six years practiced extremes of ascetic self-deprivation, and finally discovered the Middle Path between self-indulgence and self-mortification. At the age of 35 he attained *nirvana*, becoming the *Buddha*, or the Enlightened One. The Buddha spent the rest of his 80 years teaching others the truths he had learned.

Basic to the Buddha's understanding of the human condition were the "Four Noble Truths:"

1. All life is suffering—an endless chain of births and rebirths (karma).

2. The cause of the suffering is desire. It is desire that binds humans to the wheel of karma.

3. Escape from suffering and endless rebirths can come only by the cessation of desire and the attainment of nirvana.

4. The path to nirvana is eightfold, requiring right views, thought, speech, actions, living, efforts, mindfulness, and meditation. Buddhists say that nirvana cannot be described: It is the ground of all existence, ineffable, and beyond time and space—an ultimate reality that may be experienced, but not grasped intellectually.

The Buddha was a religious teacher, not a social reformer, yet his religious understanding led to ethical conclusions. He condemned the caste system that flourished in the India of his day. He denounced war, slavery, and the taking of life. He opposed appeals to miracles. He did not demand a blind faith in his doctrines: He told his followers to accept his teachings only after they had tested them against their own experience. He taught that poverty was a cause of immorality, and that it was futile to attempt to suppress crime with punishments. He identified with all humanity, saying, "He who attends on the sick attends on me." Because the goal of Buddhism is for all humans to become Buddhas, some have called Buddhism the most contemplative and otherworldly of the great world religions. For the spiritually unprepared, and even for the historical Buddha, the way was not easy, and one lifetime was not enough.

Monks and nuns might practice the Eightfold Path, meditate for months and years, and experience an inner spiritual awakening, but only a few would gain enlightenment,

Two seated Buddhas. This fifth- to sixth-century painting adorns a wall of a cave in Ajanta, India.
Borromeo/Art Resource, N.Y.

Tibetan Buddhist nuns. They belong to a Tibetan sect of the Mahayana (Greater Vehicle) Buddhism that swept north to Central Asia and Tibet, and then East to China, Korea and Japan. Behind them, prayer flags blow in the wind.
Patrick Feld/Eye Ubiquitous/Corbis.

the release from karmic causation. Most could only hope for a rebirth in a higher spiritual state—to begin again closer, to the goal. For laypeople the emphasis of Buddhism was on ethical living in human society as a preparation for a more dedicated religious quest in a future life.

Buddhism spread rapidly along the Ganges River and through northern India. In the time of King Ashoka (272–232 B.C.E.) of the Mauryas, it spread to southern India, Ceylon, and beyond. This was its great missionary age. As it spread throughout India its influence on religious practice at the village level was enormous, and its meditative techniques helped reshape Hindu yogic exercises. Eventually, however, Buddhism in India was re-Hinduized. It developed competing schools of metaphysics, a pantheon of gods and cosmic Buddhas, and devotional sects focusing on one or another of these cosmic figures. Its original character as a reform movement of Hinduism was lost, and between 500 and 1500 C.E. it was largely reabsorbed into Hinduism.

Beyond India, two major currents of Buddhism spread over Asia. One, known as the "Way of the Elders" (*Theravada*), swept through continental Southeast Asia and the islands that are today Indonesia. The Theravada teaching was close to early Indian Buddhism and, as it spread, it carried with it other strands of Indian culture as well.

Buddhism remains the predominant religion of Burma, Thailand, Cambodia, and Laos, although it must contend with more recent secular ideologies. In Thailand, it remains the state religion: Thai kings rule as Buddhist monarchs; Thai boys spend short periods as Buddhist monks; and Thai temples (*wats*) continue as one center of village life. Before the spread of Islam, Buddhism also once flourished in Malaya, Sumatra, and Java.

The second major current, known as the "Greater Vehicle" (*Mahayana*), spread through northwest India to Afghanistan and Central Asia, and then to China, Tibet and Mongolia, Vietnam, Korea, and Japan. In each region the pattern that unfolded was different. In what is today Pakistan, Afghanistan, and Central Asia, Buddhism was overtaken and replaced by Islam. Mahayana doctrines entered Tibet during the sixth century C.E. and became firmly established several centuries later.

Today Tibetan Buddhism is the predominant religion of Tibet, Nepal, Sikkim, Bhutan, and Mongolia (although there it is severely curtailed by Chinese authorities). In China, and then spreading from China to Korea, Vietnam, and Japan, Mahayana Buddhism saw its fullest development. One key doctrine in this current was the ideal of the *bodhisattva*, a being who had gone all the way to nirvana, but held back to help others attain salvation.

Another Mahayana doctrine, that of the Chan (in China) or Zen (in Japan) sect, stressed meditation and perhaps was closer to the teachings of the historical Buddha.

In China, the Tang dynasty (618–907) was the great Buddhist age, a time of unparalleled creativity in religious art, sculpture, and music. After that, although Buddhism continued to flourish at the village level, the governing scholar-gentry class shifted to the more worldly doctrines of Neo-Confucianism. In Vietnam, Korea, and Japan, the overall process replicated that of China, but the shift occurred later and with many local variations.

During modern times Buddhism—like all structures of faith—has struggled, with the secular doctrines of the scientific, and industrial, and communist revolutions exerting a powerful influence in the 19th and 20th centuries. The future is unclear, but undoubtedly Buddhism will be powerfully affected by the ongoing transformations of Asian societies.

- In what way is Buddhism's relation to Hinduism parallel to Christianity's relation to Judaism?
- How can the teachings of a religion be tested against an individual's experience? If you were a Buddhist, how would you define a fair test?

10 Iran and India Before Islam

CHAPTER HIGHLIGHTS

Iran Under the Parthians (247 B.C.E.–223 C.E.) and the Sasanids (224–651 C.E.), Iran was a rival to Roman and Byzantine power in the Near East. The Sasanids, in particular, sought to restore the glory of the ancient Achaemenid Empire and promoted native Persian culture. They also based their rule on orthodox Zoroastrianism and suppressed the Manichaeans as heretics. Although foreign trade flourished, the Parthian and Sasanid rulers favored the landed aristocracy at the expense of the peasantry, who were heavily taxed. The long wars with Rome and Byzantium ultimately sapped Sasanid strength and left the empire vulnerable to Islamic Arab invasion in the seventh century.

India The Gupta period (320–467 C.E.) is considered one of the high points of Indian civilization. Art, especially architecture and sculpture, flourished, and Indian civilization took on its enduring "Hindu" social, religious, and cultural shape. In society the fundamentally hierarchic nature of the caste system solidified. Hindu piety emphasized devotional cults to deities, especially Vishnu and Shiva. Indian Buddhism developed two main schools, the Mahayana and the Theravada, and spread to other parts of Asia.

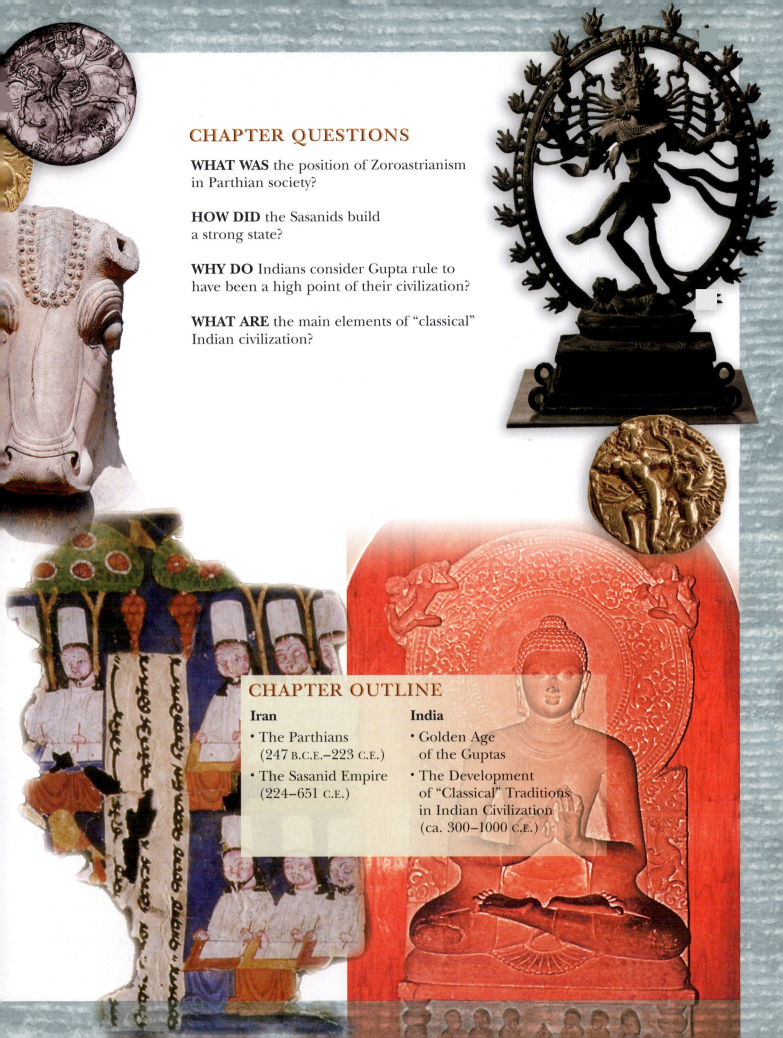

CHAPTER QUESTIONS

WHAT WAS the position of Zoroastrianism in Parthian society?

HOW DID the Sasanids build a strong state?

WHY DO Indians consider Gupta rule to have been a high point of their civilization?

WHAT ARE the main elements of "classical" Indian civilization?

CHAPTER OUTLINE

Iran
- The Parthians (247 B.C.E.–223 C.E.)
- The Sasanid Empire (224–651 C.E.)

India
- Golden Age of the Guptas
- The Development of "Classical" Traditions in Indian Civilization (ca. 300–1000 C.E.)

In this chapter we look at Southwest and South Asia before the spread of Islam. In Iran the Sasanids, a dynasty of Persian imperial rulers, reigned from the breakdown of Parthian rule in the early third century C.E. to the coming of Islam in the seventh. Although Zoroastrian traditions regained their vitality, a small ruling nobility dominated the social and political system, and there was constant competition with the Byzantine Empire. This competition finally exhausted both Sasanid and Byzantine resources. Both empires were defeated by the Arabs under the banner of Islam in the mid-seventh century.

In India the imperial Gupta kings presided also over a cultural flowering of unprecedented magnificence until new incursions of steppe peoples from about 500 C.E. led to political fragmentation. Nevertheless, regional empires lasted until the 13th century, when Islamic power under the Delhi sultans began to forge new patterns of power and culture north and south.

The coming of Islamic civilization—with Muslim conquerors or, more often, with Muslim traders and religious brotherhoods—took place at different times and with differing consequences in Iran and India.

In Iran, Islam was prominent in government and public life from the early years of the Arab conquests in the mid-seventh century, although the populace in the regions of the traditional Iranian cultural sphere did not convert until much later.

In India, Arab armies penetrated the Indus region as early as 711, and Muslim rulers of Central Asian extraction controlled the Panjab from around 1000. The establishment of the so-called Delhi Sultanate in 1205 marked the entrenchment of Muslim ruling dynasties in the Indian heartlands. Similarly, Sufi brotherhoods made significant converts in India from about the 13th century onward. Even earlier, in trading communities on the coasts of Gujarat and South India, Muslim settlers and converts had already provided the nuclei of smaller, often scattered Muslim communities that grew up within the larger Hindu society.

IRAN

THE PARTHIANS

WHAT WAS the position of Zoroastrianism in Parthian society?

Parthian Arsacid rule (ca. 247 B.C.E.–223 C.E.) began in the eastern Iranian province of Parthia in Seleucid times and eventually dominated the Iranian heartlands of the Achaemenids (see Chapter 4). The Parthians even managed by 129 B.C.E. to extinguish Seleucid power east of the Euphrates. They also continued the Iranian imperial and cultural traditions of the Achaemenids. The relative Parthian tolerance of religious diversity was paralleled by the growth of regionalism in political and cultural affairs. A growing nobility built strong local power bases and became the backbone of Parthian military power. Aramaic, the common language of the empire, gradually lost ground to regional Iranian tongues after the second century B.C.E., although Greek was widely spoken.

Despite their general religious tolerance, the Parthians upheld such Zoroastrian traditions as maintenance of a royal sacred fire at a shrine in their Parthian homeland and included priestly advisers on the emperor's council. The last century of their rule saw increased emphasis on Iranian as opposed to foreign traditions in religious and cultural affairs, perhaps in reaction to the almost constant warfare with the Romans on their west flank and the Graeco-Bactrian Kushan threat to the east. By this time Christianity and Buddhism were making sufficient converts in border areas to threaten Zoroastrian tradition. These threats may have stimulated Parthian attempts to collect the largely oral

Zoroastrian textual heritage. In such ways, Parthian rule laid the groundwork for the nationalistic emphases of subsequent centuries.

THE SASANID EMPIRE (224–651 C.E.)

HOW DID the Sasanids build a strong state?

The Sasanids were a Persian dynasty and claimed to be the rightful Achaemenid heirs. They championed Iranian legitimacy and tried to brand the Parthians as outside invaders from the northeast who followed Greek and other foreign ways. The first Sasanid king, Ardashir (r. 224–ca. 239 C.E.), was a Persian warrior noble from a priestly family. The Sasanid name came from his grandfather, Sasan. Ardashir and his son, Shapur I (r. ca. 239–272), built a strong internal administration in Persia (Fars), extended their sway to Ctesiphon, and took Bactria from the Kushans. Under Shapur's long rule, the empire grew in the east, beyond the Caucasus, and into Syria, Armenia, and parts of Anatolia. Shapur defeated three Roman emperors, even capturing one of them, Valerian (r. 253–260). Thus he could justifiably claim to be a restorer of Iranian glory and a "king of kings," or *shahanshah*. He also centralized and rationalized taxation, the civil ministries, and the military, although neither he nor his successors could fully contain the growing power of the nobility.

With the shift of the Roman Empire east to Byzantium in the early fourth century C.E., the stage of imperial conflict was set for the next 350 years. Byzantium (Constantinople) on the Bosphorus and Ctesiphon on the Tigris were home to the two mightiest thrones of Eurasia until the coming of the Arabs. Each won victories over the other and championed a different religious orthodoxy, but neither could ever completely conquer the other. In the sixth century, each produced its greatest emperor: the Byzantine Justinian (r. 527–565) and the Sasanid Chosroes Anosharvan ("Chosroes of the Immortal Soul," r. 531–579). Yet, less than a century after their deaths, the new Arab power reduced one empire dramatically and destroyed the other. Byzantium survived with the loss of most of its territory for another 800 years, but the Sasanid imperial order was swept away in 651. Memory of the Sasanids did not, however, entirely die. Chosroes, for example, became a legendary model of greatness for Persians and a symbol of imperial splendor among the Arabs. The Pahlavi monarchy in 20th-century Iran also utilized the historical memory of the Sasanid to legitimize their own rule and persuade modern-day Iranians of their cultural distinctiveness.

SOCIETY AND ECONOMY

Sasanid society was largely like that of earlier times. The extended family was the basic social unit. Zoroastrian orthodoxy recognized four classes: priests, warriors, scribes, and peasants. However, a great divide separated the royal house, the priesthood, and the warrior nobility from the common people (artisans, traders, and the rural peasantry).

The basis of the economy remained agriculture, but land became increasingly concentrated in the hands of an ever-richer minority of the royalty, nobility, and priesthood. As in Roman domains, the growth of great estates was responsible for a growing imbalance between the rich few and the impoverished many. Many small farmers were reduced to serfdom. The burden of land taxation, like

Shapur I. A cameo depicts the capture of the Emperor Valerian by Shapur I, following the great Persian victory against the Romans near Edessa in 259 C.E.
Bibliotheque Nationale. Paris, France.

that of conscript labor work and army duty, hit hardest those least able to afford it. This produced a popular reaction, as the Mazdakite movement, discussed below, shows.

The Sasanids also closely oversaw and heavily taxed the lucrative caravan and sea trade in their territory. Silk and glass production increased under government monopoly, and the state also controlled mining. The empire's many urban centers and its foreign trade relied on a money system. It was from Jewish bankers in Babylonia and their Persian counterparts that Europe and the rest of the world got the use of bills of exchange (the term *check* comes from a Pahlavi word).[1]

Sasanid aristocratic culture drew on diverse traditions, from Roman, Hellenistic, and Bactrian-Indian to Achaemenid and other native Iranian ones. Its heyday was the reign of Chosroes. Indian influences—not only religious ones, as in the case of Buddhist ideas, but also artistic and scientific ones—were especially strong. Indian medicine and mathematics were notably in demand. Hellenistic culture was also revived in the academy at Jundishapur in Khuzistan, where refugee scholars from Byzantium came to teach medicine and philosophy after Justinian closed the Greek academies in the West.

RELIGION

Zoroastrian Revival The Sasanids institutionalized Zoroastrian ritual and theology as state orthodoxy. Although they were continuing the Arsacid patronage of Zoroastrian worship, the Sasanids claimed to be restoring the true faith after centuries of neglect. The initial architect of this propaganda and the Zoroastrian revival was the first chief priest (Mobad) of the empire, Tosar (or Tansar). Under Ardashir, Tosar instituted a state church and began to compile an authoritative, written canon of the Avesta, the scriptural texts that include the hymns of Zarathushtra (see Chapter 4). He may also have instituted a calendar reform and replaced all images in the temples with the sacred altar fires of Zoroastrian tradition.

The most influential figure in Sasanid religious history was Tosar's successor, Kartir (or Kirdir), who served as chief priest to Shapur I and three successors (ca. 239–293). Although his zealotry was initially restrained by the religiously tolerant Shapur, Kirdir gained greater power and influence after Shapur's death. He seems to have tried to convert not only pagans, but also Christians, Buddhists, and others. His chief opponents were the Manichaeans, whom he considered Zoroastrian heretics, much as Christian groups saw them as Christian heretics.

Manichaeism Mani (216–277 C.E.) was born of a noble Parthian family but raised in Babylonia. A cosmopolitan who spoke Aramaic, Persian, and Greek and traveled to India, Mani preached a message both similar to and sharply divergent from its Zoroastrian, Judaic, and Christian forerunners. **Manichaeism**

Manichaeism A dualistic and moralistic view of reality in which good and evil, spirit and matter warred with each other.

Manichaean Priests. This leaf from a Manichaean book (ca. eighth–ninth century C.E.) shows priests in white robes and tall hats kneeling in front of low desks. Each has a sheet of white paper and some hold pens. Works such as this are an important source for our knowledge of Manichaean communities.

A leaf from a Manchurian book, Roko, Templek (MIK III 6368), 8th-9th century, a manuscript painting 17.2 × 11.2 cm. Museum fur Indische Kunst, Staatliche Museen Preussischer Kulturbesitz, Berlin.

---

[1] R. Girshman, *Iran* (Harmondsworth, U.K.: Penguin Books, 1954), pp. 341–346. "Pahlavi" is the name of the Middle Persian language.

centered on a radically dualistic and moralistic view of reality in which good and evil, spirit and matter, were constantly at war with one another. Mani sought to convert others to his views which he presented as the culmination and restoration of the original unity of Zoroastrian, Christian, and Buddhist teachings. He may have been the first person in history whose conscious intent was to "found" a new religious tradition or to seek to create a "scripture" for his followers. He called his new system "Justice," although outsiders called it *Manichaeism*. The popularity of Mani's movement probably contributed to Kirdir's and later attempts to establish a Zoroastrian "orthodoxy" and scriptural canon.[2]

Kirdir eventually had Mani executed as a heretic in 277, but Mani's movement had great consequences. It spread westward to challenge the Christian church (Saint Augustine was once a Manichaean) and eastward along the Silk Route to Central Asia. The movement's ideas figured even centuries later in both Christian and Islamic heresies. Its adherents probably carried the Western planetary calendar to China, where in some areas it was used for centuries.

Zoroastrian Orthodoxy   Kartir had firmly grounded Zoroastrian orthodoxy despite the persistence of challenges to it, such as Mani's. This orthodoxy became the backbone of Sasanid culture. When the Sasanids' Persian dialect, *Pahlavi*, became the official imperial language, the Zoroastrian sacred texts were written in Pahlavi. Throughout Sasanid times, the priesthood increased its power. Priests served as the empire's jurists and legal interpreters as well as its liturgists and scholars. With increasing endowments for new fire temples, the church establishment also came to control much of Iran's wealth.

LATER SASANID DEVELOPMENTS

Despite the Zoroastrian moral idealism of many of their rulers, the Sasanid concept of justice did not include equal distribution of the empire's bounty. The radical inequality of wealth between the aristocracy and the masses sparked a conflict with what is called the Mazdakite movement at the end of the fifth century. The movement's leader, Mazdak, preached asceticism, pessimism about the evil state of the material world, the virtues of vegetarianism, tolerance, and brotherly love—all ideas apparently drawn ultimately from Manichaeism—and the need for a more equal distribution of society's goods. This appealed to the oppressed classes, although even one Sasanid ruler, Kavad I (r. 488–531), was sympathetic for a time to Mazdak's ideas of social justice. However, in 528 Kavad's third son, the later Chosroes Anosharvan, massacred Mazdak and his most important followers. Although this finished the Mazdakites, their name was used later, in Islamic times, for various Iranian popular revolts.

Sasanid Iran

223–224 C.E.	Ardashir (r. 224–ca. 239) defeats the last Arsacid ruler, becomes *shahanshah* of Iran
ca. 225–ca. 239	Tosar chief priest (Mobad) of realm
239–272	Reign of Shapur I; expansion of the empire east and west
ca. 239–293	Kirdir chief priest (Mobad) of the realm
216–277	Mani
ca. 307–379	Reign of Shapur II
488–531	Reign of Kavad I; height of Mazdakite movement
528	Mazdak and many of his followers massacred
531–579	Reign of Chosroes Anosharvan at Ctesiphon
651	Death of last Sasanid; Arabs conquer Persian Empire

[2]W. C. Smith, *The Meaning and End of Religion* (New York: Harper & Row, 1962), pp. 92–98.

INDIA

GOLDEN AGE OF THE GUPTAS

Indians have always considered the Gupta era a high point of their civilization. Historians have seen in it the source of "classical" norms for Hindu religion and Indian culture—the symbolic equivalent of Periclean Athens, Augustan Rome, or Han China. The Guptas ruled when the various facets of Indian life came together to create the recognizable patterns of a single civilization that extended over the whole subcontinent. A major factor in this development was the relative peace and stability that marked most of the Guptas' reign.

GUPTA RULE

The first Gupta king was Chandragupta (r. 320–ca. 330 C.E.). He ruled first in Magadha and then became prominent in the whole Ganges basin after he married Princess Kumaradevi, daughter of a powerful tribal leader north of the Ganges. Although their reign inaugurated Gupta power, it was their son, Samudragupta (r. ca. 330–375), and especially their grandson, Chandragupta II (r. ca. 375–415), who turned kingdom into empire and presided over the Gupta "golden age."

The Gupta realm extended from the Panjab and Kashmir south to the Narbada River in the western Deccan and east to modern Assam (see Map 10–1), and their sphere of influence included some of the Kushan and Saka kingdoms of the northwest and much of the eastern coast of India and possibly Ceylon (Sri Lanka). Unlike the Mauryans, the Guptas usually made a defeated ruler into a vassal prince rather than attempting to take direct control of his kingdom. Seated at the old Mauryan capital, Pataliputra, Gupta splendor and power had no rival. Under Chandragupta II, India was arguably the most civilized and peaceful country in the world (see "A Chinese Traveler's Report on the Gupta Realm").

Two further Gupta kings sustained this prosperity for another half century, despite invasions by a new wave of steppe nomads, the Huns, after about 440. By about 500 the Huns had overrun western India, and the Gupta Empire collapsed about 550. Harsha, a descendant of the Guptas through his grandmother, did revive a semblance of former Gupta splendor between 616 and 657. His loosely held dominions again spanned North India, but when he died without heirs, the empire broke up again.

The succeeding centuries before the arrival of Muslim invaders about 1000 C.E. saw several dynasties in North India share power, but no unified rule of any duration. Outside the north, several long-lived dynasties built regional empires in the western Deccan and Tamilnad (the extreme south) after Gupta times, and the main centers of Indian civilization shifted to those areas.

GUPTA CULTURE

With the decline of Rome in the West, Indian culture experienced little new outside influence from the Gupta

3.8
Fa-Hsien: A Chinese perspective on Gupta India

India from the Gupta Age to ca. 1000 C.E.

320 C.E.–ca. 467	Gupta period
320–330	Reign of Chandragupta, first Gupta king
375–454	Reigns of Chandragupta II and Kumaragupta: Kalidasa flourishes; heyday of Gupta culture
399–414	Chinese Buddhist monk, Fa-Hsien, travels in India
ca. 440	Beginning of Hun invasions from Central Asia
616–657	Reign of Harsha; revival of Gupta splendor and power
820	Death of Vedantin philosopher-theologian, Shankara
550–ca. 1000	Regional Indian kingdoms in north and south; major Puranas composed; age of first great Vaishnava and Shaivite devotional poets in southern India

MAP EXPLORATION

Interactive map: To explore this map further, go to **http://www.prenhall.com/craig/map10.1**

MAP 10–1

International Trade Routes in Gupta and Sasanid Times. This map shows the Gupta and Sasanid Empires and the trade routes that linked them to each other and to other areas of the world.

HOW DID the Indian Ocean facilitate trade between different regions?

era until Muslim times. India's chief contacts were now with Southeast Asia and China, and most of the cultural transmission was from India eastward, not vice versa.

The claim of the Gupta era to being India's golden age of culture could be sustained solely by its magnificent architecture and sculpture, the wall paintings of the Ajanta caves, and Kalidasa's matchless drama and verse. Kalidasa, the "Shakespeare" of Sanskrit letters, flourished in the time of Chandragupta II and his successor.

The depth of Gupta culture is indicated by the era's strong emphasis on education, whether in Jain and Buddhist monasteries or in Brahmanical schools. In addition to religious texts, typical subjects included rhetoric, prose and poetic composition, grammar, logic, medicine, and metaphysics. Using an older Indian

HISTORY'S VOICES

A CHINESE TRAVELER'S REPORT ON THE GUPTA REALM

a-Hsien, a Chinese Buddhist monk, was the first of several Chinese known for traveling to India to study and bring back Buddhist scriptures from the intellectual centers of Buddhist thought there. He wrote an account of his travels, first through Central Asia, then all over India, and finally through Ceylon and Indonesia again to China (399–414 C.E.).

WHAT THINGS about India seem most to surprise Fa-Hsien? Is his image of Indian rule a positive one? What do his remarks say about the prestige of the Buddhist tradition and its monks in the Indian state? What does he tell us about Indian society?

On the sides of the river, both right and left, are twenty san ghârâmas [monasteries], with perhaps 3,000 priests. The law of the Buddha is progressing and flourishing. Beyond the deserts are the countries of Western India. The kings of these countries are all firm believers in the law of Buddha. They remove their caps of state when they make offerings to the priests. The members of the royal household and the chief ministers personally direct the food-giving; when the distribution of food is over, they spread a carpet on the ground opposite the chief seat (the president's seat) and sit down before it. They dare not sit on couches in the presence of the priests. The rules relating to the almsgiving of kings have been handed down from the time of Buddha till now. Southward from this is the so-called middle-country (Mâdhyade´sa). The climate of this country is warm and equable, without frost or snow. The people are very well off, without poll tax or official restrictions. Only those who till the royal lands return a portion of profit of the land. If they desire to go, they go; if they like to stop, they

stop. The kings govern without corporal punishment; criminals are fined, according to circumstances, lightly or heavily. Even in cases of repeated rebellion they only cut off the right hand. The king's personal attendants, who guard him on the right and left, have fixed salaries. Throughout the country the people kill no living thing nor drink wine, nor do they eat garlic or onions, with the exception of Chandâlas [outcasts] only. The Chandâlas are named "evil men" and dwell apart from others; if they enter a town or market, they sound a piece of wood in order to separate themselves; then men, knowing who they are, avoid coming in contact with them. In this country they do not keep swine nor fowls, and do not deal in cattle; they have no shambles or wine-shops in their market places. In selling they use cowrie shells. The Chandâlas only hunt and sell flesh. Down from the time of Buddha's Nirvâna, the kings of these countries, the chief men and householders, have raised vihâras [monasteries] for the priests, and provided for their support by bestowing on them fields, houses, and gardens, with men and oxen. Engraved title-deeds were prepared and handed down from one reign to another; no one has ventured to withdraw them, so that till now there has been no interruption. All the resident priests having chambers (in these vihâras) have their beds, mats, food, drink, and clothes provided without stint; in all places this is the case. The priests ever engage themselves in doing meritorious works for the purpose of religious advancement (karma—building up their religious character), or in reciting the scriptures, or in meditation.

Source: "Buddhist Country Records," in Si-Yu-Ki, *Buddhist Records of the Western World,* trans. by Samuel Beal (London, 1884; reprint, Delhi: Oriental Books Reprint Corporation, 1969), pp. xxxvii–xxxviii. Reprinted by permission of Motilal Banarsidass Publishers Pvt. Ltd., Delhi, India.

number system that the Arabs transmitted to the West as "Arabic numerals," Gupta scholars were especially adept at mathematics.

In sculpture, the monastic complex at Sarnath was a great center of activity. The superb technique and expressive serenity of Gupta style grew out of native Mathura and Greco-Roman schools. Hindu, Jain, and Buddhist works all shared the same style and conventions. Even in handwork and luxury crafts (silks, muslin, linen, ivory and other carvings, bronze metalwork, gold and silver work, and cut stones), Gupta products achieved new levels of quality and were in great demand abroad. In architecture, Gupta splendor is less evident, except in the culmination of cave-shrine (Chaitya-hall) development at Ajanta and in the erection of the earliest surviving free-standing temples in India. The Hindu temple, however, underwent its most important development in post-Gupta times, beginning in the eighth century.

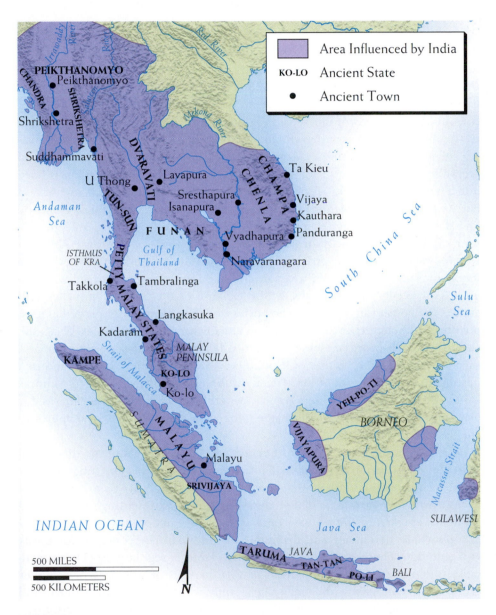

MAP 10–2

Indian influence in Southeast Asia, ca. 650 C.E.   By the middle of the seventh century C.E., Indian traditions, art, and music had a pervasive influence throughout Southeast Asia, even though the number of Indians who traded and migrated there was not great.

HOW DOES the influence of India on Southeast Asian civilization demonstrate the role of trade in spreading ideas and customs?

jatis The many subgroups that make up the Hindu caste system.

varnas The four main classes that form the basis for Hindu caste relations.

Gupta Sculpture. Fifth-century C.E. statue of Lokanatha from Sarnath, which despite damage, shows the fine sculptural work of the important school of Gupta artists at Sarnath and the influence on them of both Graeco-Roman antecedents and native Indian traditions and conventions.

Scala/Art Resource, N.Y.

THE DEVELOPMENT OF "CLASSICAL" TRADITIONS IN INDIAN CIVILIZATION (CA. 300–1000 C.E.)

*T*he Guptas' support of Brahmanic traditions and Vaishnava[3] devotionalism reflected the waning of Buddhist traditions in the mainstream of Indian religious life. In Gupta times and subsequently, down to the advent of Muslim rule, Indian civilization assumed its classical shape, its enduring "Hindu" forms of social, religious, and cultural life.

SOCIETY

In these centuries, the fundamentally hierarchical character of Hindu/Indian society solidified. The oldest manual of legal and ethical theory, the *Dharmashastra* of Manu, dates from about 200 C.E. Based on Vedic tradition, it treats the *dharma* (duties) appropriate to one's class and stage of life, rules for rites and for the study of the Veda, pollution and purification measures, dietary restrictions, royal duties and prerogatives, and other legal and moral questions.

The manual presents a classic statement of the four-class theory of social hierarchy. This ideal construct rests on the principle that every person is born into a particular station in life as a result of *karma* from earlier lives. Every station has its particular *dharma*, or appropriate duties and responsibilities, from the lowest servant to the highest prince or Brahman. The Brahmans' ancient division of Aryans into the four *varnas* or classes—*Brahman* (priest), *Kshatriya* (noble/warrior), *Vaishya* (tradesperson), and *Shudra* (servant)—provided a schematic structure designed to assure the status and power of the upper three groups, especially the Brahmans, at the expense of the Shudras and the "fifth estate," the non-Aryan "outcasts" who performed the jobs society regarded as most polluting. Although class distinctions had already hardened before 500 B.C.E., the classes were, in practice, somewhat fluid. If the traditional occupation of a varna was unavailable to one of its members, he could often take up another, despite theory to the contrary. When Brahmans, Vaishyas, or even Shudras gained political power as rulers (as was evidently the case with the Mauryas, for example), their family gradually came to be viewed as *Kshatriyas*, the appropriate class for princes.

Although the four classes, or *varnas* (see "Overview"), are the theoretical basis for *caste* relations, much smaller and far more numerous subgroups, or *jatis*, are the units closest to what "caste" means in English. (*Caste* comes from *casta*, Portuguese for *jati*.) These divisions (most representing occupational groups) were already the primary units of social distinction in Gupta times. *Jati* groupings are hereditary and distinguished essentially by concerns for purity and pollution. These are determined by three kinds of regulations: (1) commensality (one may take food only from or with persons of the same or a higher group); (2) endogamy (one may marry only within one's own group); and (3) trade or craft limitation (one must practice only the trade of one's group).[4]

The caste system has been the basis of Indian social organization for at least two millennia. It enabled Hindus to accommodate foreign cultural, racial, and religious communities within Indian society by treating them as new caste

---

[3]*Vaishnava* or *Vaishnavite* means "related to Vishnu"; similarly, *Shaiva* or *Shaivite* refers to Shiva worship.
[4]A. L. Basham, *The Wonder that was India* (New York: 1963), pp. 148–149.

groups. The caste system promoted social stability and individual security by permitting everyone to tell by dress and other marks how to relate to others. It was also the logical extension of the religious doctrine of karma into society—whether as justification, result, or partial cause of the system itself (see Chapter 2).

RELIGION

Hindu Religious Life   Gupta and later times saw the growth of devotional cults of deities, preeminently Vishnu and Shiva, who were unknown or unimportant in Vedic religion. The temple worship of a particular deity has ever since been a basic form of Hindu piety. After Vishnu (especially in his form as the hero-savior Krishna) and Shiva (originally a fertility god), the chief focus of devotion came to be the Goddess in one of her many forms, such as Parvati, Shakti, Durga, or Kali. Vishnu and Shiva, like Parvati, have many forms and names and have always been easily identified with other deities, who are then worshipped as one form of the Supreme Lord or Goddess. Animal or nature deities were presumably part of popular piety from Indus Valley days forward. Indian reverence for all forms of life and stress on *ahimsa,* or "noninjury" to living beings (see Chapter 2), are most vivid in the sacredness of the cow, which has always been a mainstay of life in India.

In the development of Hindu piety and practice, a major strand was the tradition of ardent theism known as *bhakti,* or "loving devotion." *Bhakti* was already evident, at the latest by 200 C.E., in the Bhagavad Gita's treatment of Krishna. Gupta and later times saw the rise, especially in the Tamil-speaking south, of schools of bhakti poetry and worship. The central bhakti strand in Hindu life

The Bodhisattva Avalokiteshvara. Detail of a Buddhist wall painting from the cave shrines at Ajanta (Maharashtra, India), Gupta period, ca. 475 C.E. Avalokiteshvara (known in China as Kwan-yin and in Japan as Kannon) is the supreme figure of infinite mercy.

Art Resource, N.Y.

OVERVIEW   THE FOUR MAIN HINDU CASTES

Traditional Hindu/Indian society is fundamentally hierarchic in character. There are four main classes (*varnas*) into which a person is born according to how he or she lived in a previous life. Every class has its appropriate duties and responsibilities. In addition, there are numerous subgroups (*jatis*) based on a person's occupation. The English word "caste" is used to refer to all of these groups.

Brahman	Priest. This is the highest caste.
Kshatriya	Warrior or aristocrat. This is considered the appropriate caste for rulers.
Vaishya	Tradespeople and merchants.
Shudra	Servant. This caste includes peasants and manual laborers as well as domestic servants.

In addition, there is a fifth group of "outcastes" who performed the necessary but most polluting tasks in society, such as removing human waste. Persons in this category were considered "untouchable," and contact with them was considered morally and spiritually unclean.

Vishnu. A bronze statue of Hindu deity Vishnu from Thailand reflects the impact of Indian civilization on Southeast Asia.

Luca I. Tettoni/Corbis N.Y.

QUICK REVIEW

Bhakti

- *Bhakti*, or loving devotion, evident in the Bhagavad Gita's treatment or Krishna
- Derives in part from Tamil and other vernacular poets
- Through bhakti, pre-Aryan religious sensibilities reasserted themselves

Mahayana The "Great Vehicle" for salvation in Buddhism. It emphasized the Buddha's infinite compassion for all beings.

Theravada The "Way of the Elders." A school of Buddhism that emphasized the monastic ideal.

bodhisattva A "Buddha to be" who postpones his own nirvana until he has helped all other beings become enlightened.

derives in good part from Tamil and other vernacular poets who first sang the praises of Shiva or Vishnu as Supreme Lord. Here, pre-Aryan religious sensibilities apparently reasserted themselves through the non-Aryan Dravidian peoples of the south. The great theologian of devotional Hinduism, Ramanuja (d. ca. 1137), would later come from this same Dravidian tradition. Of major importance also to devotional piety was the development in this era of the Puranas—epic, mythological, and devotional texts. They are still today the functional sacred scriptures of grassroots Hindu religious life (the Vedic texts remaining the special preserve of the Brahmans).

Whatever god or goddess a Hindu worships, it is usual to pay homage on proper occasions also to other appropriate deities. Most Hindus view one deity as Supreme Lord but see others as manifestations of the Ultimate at lower levels. Hindu polytheism is not "idolatry" but a vivid affirmation of the infinite forms that transcendence takes in this world. The sense of the presence of the Divine everywhere is evident in the importance attached to sacred places. India is the land of religious pilgrimage *par excellence.* Sacred mountains, rivers, trees, and groves are all *tirthas*, or "river fords" to the Divine.

The intellectual articulation of Hindu polytheism and relativism found its finest expression in post-Gupta formulations of Vedanta ("the end of the Veda"). The major Vedantin thinker, Shankara (d. 820), stressed a strict "non-duality" of the Ultimate, teaching that Brahman was the only Reality behind the "illusion" (*maya*) of the world of sense experience. Yet he accepted the worship of a lesser deity as appropriate for those who could not follow his extraordinary norm—the intellectual realization of the formless Absolute beyond all "name and form."

Buddhist Religious Life The major developments of these centuries were: (1) the solidification of the two main strands of Buddhist tradition, the **Mahayana** and the **Theravada**, and (2) the spread of Buddhism abroad from its Indian homeland. The Mahayana ("Great Vehicle [of salvation]") arose in the first century B.C.E, Its proponents differentiated it sharply from the older, more conservative traditions of monk-oriented piety and thought, which they labeled the Hinayana ("Little Vehicle"). In Mahayana speculation Buddhas were seen as manifestations of a single principle of "Ultimate" Reality, and Siddhartha Gautama was held to be only one Buddha among many. The Mahayana stressed the example of the Buddha's infinite compassion for all beings. The highest goal was not a *nirvana* of "selfish" extinction but the status of a **bodhisattva**, or "Buddha-to-be," the one who postpones his own nirvana to help all other beings become enlightened.

The *bodhisattva* can offer this aid because his long career of self-sacrifice has gained him infinite merit. Salvation becomes possible not only through individual effort, but also through devotion to the Buddhas and *bodhisattvas*. At the popular level, this idea translated into devotional cults focusing on transcendent Buddhas and *bodhisattvas* conceived of as cosmic beings. One of the most important was that of the Buddha Amitabha, the personification of infinite compassion. Amitabha presides over a Western Paradise, or Pure Land, to which (through his infinite compassion) all who have faith in him have access (see Chapter 9 for a discussion of Pure Land Buddhism in Japan).

The older, more conservative "Way of the Elders" (Theravada) always focused on the monastic community, but taught that service and gifts to the

‍‌

monks were a major source of merit for the laity. It emphasized gaining merit for a better rebirth through high standards of conduct, lay devotion to the Buddha, and pilgrimage to his relics at various **stupas**. The Mahayana also held monastic life as the ideal, but some of its greatest attractions were its strong devotionalism and virtually polytheistic delight in divine Buddhas and *bodhisattvas* to whom one could pray for mercy, help, and rebirth in paradise. The basis of Theravada piety and practice was the scriptural collection of the traditional teachings ascribed to the Buddha, as reported by his disciples. Theravadins rejected the Mahayana claim that later texts (e.g., the Lotus Sutra) contained the highest teachings of the Buddha.

stupa   A Buddhist shrine.

MAP 10–3

Spread of Buddhism throughout Southeast Asia.   By the 12th century C.E., Buddhism had taken root in many parts of Southeast Asia, often blending with local customs, as well as Hindu traditions that had been introduced earlier.

HOW DID the spread of Buddhism in Southeast Asia replicate the spread of Hindu traditions earlier?

India gave Theravada Buddhism to Ceylon, Burma, and parts of Southeast Asia. Mahayana Buddhism predominated in Central Asia and China, from which it spread in the fifth to eighth centuries to Korea and Japan. Tantric Buddhism, an esoteric Mahayana tradition heavily influenced by Hinduism, entered Tibet from North India in the seventh century and became the dominant tradition there.

SUMMARY

IMAGE KEY

for pages 226–227

a. Four-armed Ganesa
b. Relief carving of the Hindu deity Vishnu reclining on the serpent Sesa at the Temple of Vishnu in Rajasthan, India.
c. Gupta coin with horse on it
d. Gupta coin with horseman on it
e. Statue of Lokanatha from Sarnath
f. The ruins of the Great Hall in the Palace of the Parthian Kings
g. Bottom of a silver bowl with Sassanid relief work
h. Seated Buddha
i. Shiva Nataraja
j. Bull from Persian ruin
k. Manichaean book leaf showing priests in white robes

Iran Under the Parthians (247 B.C.E.–223 C.E.) and the Sasanids (224–651 C.E.), Iran was a rival to Roman and Byzantine power in the Middle East. The Sasanids, in particular, sought to restore the glory of the ancient Achaemenid Persian Empire and promoted native Persian culture. They also based their rule on orthodox Zoroastrianism and suppressed the Manichaeans as heretics. The Parthian and Sasanid rulers favored the landed aristocracy at the expense of the peasantry, who were heavily taxed. The long wars with Rome and Byzantium ultimately sapped Sasanid strength and left the empire vulnerable to Islamic Arab invasion in the seventh century.

India The Gupta period (320–467 C.E.) is considered one of the highlights of Indian civilization. Art, especially architecture and sculpture, flourished, and Indian civilization took on its enduring "Hindu" social, religious, and cultural shape. In society the fundamentally hierarchic nature of the caste system solidified. Hindu piety emphasized devotional cults to deities, especially Vishnu and Shiva. Indian Buddhism developed two main schools, the Mahayana and the Theravada, and spread to other parts of Asia.

REVIEW QUESTIONS

1. How did the Sasanid Empire develop after the fall of the Parthians?

2. What were the major religious issues in the Sasanid empire?

3. Why is the high Gupta period (ca. 320–450) considered a "golden age"?

4. What are some similarities and differences between the classical Buddhist and Hindu traditions that crystallized in the first half of the first millennium?

5. What might have contributed to the fact that Persia and India fell to Arab invaders?

KEY TERMS

bodhisattva (p. 238)   *Manichaeism* (p. 230)   **Theravada** (p. 238)
jatis (p. 236)   **stupa** (p. 239)   *varnas* (p. 236)
Mahayana (p. 238)

  For additional study resources for this chapter, go to:
www.prenhall.com/craig/chapter10

HINDUISM

The term *Hinduism* is our modern word for the whole of the diverse religious traditions of India. Until the word was coined in the 19th century, Hinduism (like *Buddhism*) was not even a concept in the West, let alone in India. In contemporary usage, it has become a catchall term for all the Indian religious communities that look upon the texts of the Vedas (see Chapter 1) as eternal, perfect truth.

The historical beginnings of the varied Hindu traditions can be traced to the ancient Aryan migrations into southern Asia in the second millennium B.C.E. During this era the Vedic hymns were composed. They describe a pantheon of gods not unlike that among the Greeks, the Romans, and other Indo-European peoples. Centered on a sacrificial cult of these gods, Vedic religion increasingly became the preserve of the Brahman priestly class of early Indian society. The Brahmans gradually elaborated a cult characterized by sacrificial rituals, purificatory rules, and fixed distinctions of birth on which India's later caste system was based.

These developments are mirrored in the later Vedic, or Brahmanical, texts (ca. 1000–500 B.C.E.) that provide commentary on and instructions for ritual use of the Vedic hymns.

After about 700 B.C.E. new developments emerged. North India produced a series of religious reformers, some of whom broke with Vedic tradition and championed knowledge and ascetic discipline over purity and ritual action. Of these, the most famous were Siddhartha Gautama (the Buddha, b. ca. 563 B.C.E.) and Mahavira Vardhamana (founder of the Jain tradition, b. ca. 550 B.C.E.). Other religious leaders reinterpreted the older sacrifice as an inner activity and deepened its spiritual dimensions. Their thinking is represented especially in the Upanishads, which many Hindus consider the most sublime philosophical texts in the Indian tradition.

Developed so long ago, such notions have been part of the complex vision of existence that lies behind the myriad forms of religious life known to us as Hinduism. In this vision the immortal part of each human being, the *atman*, is enmeshed in existence, but not ultimately of it. The nature of existence is *samsara*, a ceaseless round of cause and effect determined by the inescapable consequences of *karma*, or "action." The doctrine of *karma* is a moral as well as physical economy in which every act has unavoidable results; so long as mental or physical action occurs, life and change go on repeatedly. Birth determines one's place and duties in the traditional Indian caste system. Caste is the most visible and concrete reminder of the pervasiveness of the Hindu concept of absolute causality. The final goal is to transcend this cycle, or *samsara*, in which we are all caught. The only way out of this otherwise endless becoming and rebirth is *moksha*, which may be gained through knowledge, action, or devotion.

On the popular level, the period after about 500 B.C.E. is most notable in Indian religious life for two developments. Both took place alongside the ever deeper entrenchment in society of caste distinctions and a supporting ethic of obligations and privileges. The first was

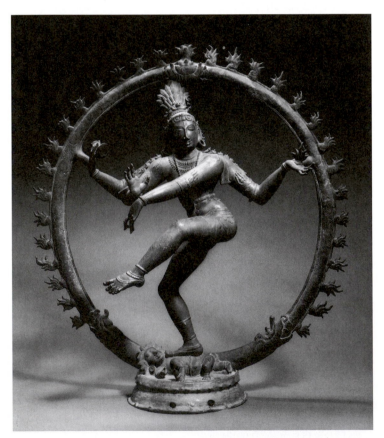

Shiva. This exquisitely crafted bronze figure of Shiva dating from the 11th century C.E. depicts him as Lord of the Dance. He is surrounded by a circle of fire, which symbolizes both death and rebirth.
The Cleveland Museum of Art, 2002, Purchase from the J.H. Wade Fund 1930.331.

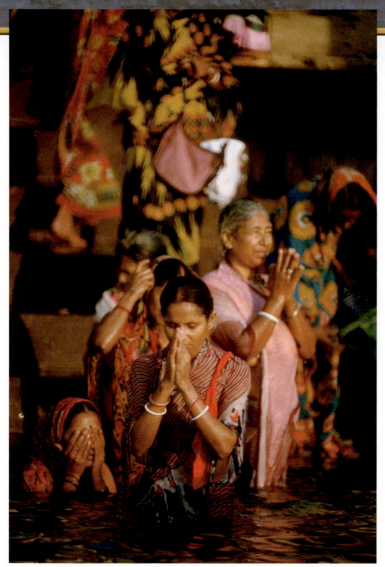

Purification rituals in the waters of the holy Ganges. Purification rituals are part of the obligatory daily rituals of all "twice-born" Hindus. The morning rituals performed by the women here in the Ganges include greeting the sun with recitation and prayer and purification by bathing.

Ian Berry/Magnum Photos, Inc.

worship one deity, but they do so in the awareness that faith in other deities can also lead one to the Ultimate.

The period between about 500 B.C.E. and 1000 C.E. saw the rise to special prominence of two gods, Vishnu and Shiva, as the primary forms in which the Supreme Lord was worshipped. Along with the mother-goddess figure, who takes various names and forms (Kali and Durga, for example), Vishnu and Shiva have remained the most important manifestations of the Divine in India. Their followers are known as Vaishnavas and Shaivas, respectively. A few recurring phenomena and ideas can suggest something of Indian religiousness in practice.

Hindu practice is characterized especially by temple worship (*puja*), in which *worshippers bring* offerings of flowers, food, and the like. They especially seek out temple images for the blessing that the sight of these images brings. Another important part of Hindu devotionalism is the recitation of sacred texts, many of which are vernacular hymns of praise to a particular deity. *Mantras*, or special recitative texts from the Vedas, are thought to have extraordinary power and are used by many Hindus in their original Sanskrit form. Pilgrimage to sacred sites, especially rivers, mountains, and famous shrines, is a prominent part of Hindu religious life. India's landscape is filled with sacred sites and sacred pilgrim routes, both local and national in reputation. A prominent feature of Hindu life is preoccupation with purity and pollution, most evident in the food taboos associated with caste groupings.

The ascetic tendency in India is also highly developed. Although only a tiny minority of Indians take up a life of full renunciation, they are influential. Ascetic worshippers do not settle in one place, acquire possessions, or perform regular worship. Rather, they wander about in search of teachers and devote themselves to meditation and self-realization. Even though most Hindus have families and work at their salvation through *puja* and moral living, the ascetic ideal has an important place in the overall Indian worldview. It stands as a constant reminder of the deeper reality beyond the everyday world and any individual, life.

the elaboration of ascetic traditions of inner quest and self-realization, such as that of yoga. The second was the rise of devotional worship of specific gods and goddesses who were seen by their worshippers as identical with the Ultimate—in other words, as supreme deities for those who served them. The latter development was of particular importance for popular religion in India. Evident in the famous and beloved Hindu devotional text, the Bhagavad Gita, it reached its highest level after 500 B.C.E. in the myriad movements of fervent, loving devotionalism, or *bhakti*, many of which remain important today. A striking aspect of Hindu piety has been its willingness to accommodate the focus on one "chosen deity" who is worshipped as supreme to a worldview that holds that the Divine can and does take many forms. Thus most Hindus

- Compared to other faiths that have expanded globally, such as Christianity and Islam, why has Hinduism been largely confined to India?

- How has Hinduism accomodated and absorbed different beliefs and value systems?

11

The Formation of Islamic Civilization 622–945

CHAPTER HIGHLIGHTS

Muhammad The Prophet Muhammad (570-632) was the founder of Islam. At about age 40, he had a religious experience during which, Muslims believe, the angel Gabriel repeatedly recited *(qur'an)* God's word to him. The message of the Qur'an was that social justice and worship of the one true God are required of every person. The proper response to God is submission *(islam)* to his will by becoming a Muslim (one who submits).

Islamic Conquest By the time of Muhammad's death, his followers had conquered all of Arabia. Under his successors, the caliphs, Muslim Arab armies conquered most of the Middle East, North Africa, Spain, Iran, and northwest India. Many of the peoples of these territories welcomed Islamic rule and eventually converted to Islam and became part of the *(umma)*, the community of Islamic believers.

The High Caliphate Under the Abbasid caliphs, Islamic culture enjoyed its "classical" phase. Arabic translations of Greek and Sanskrit works stimulated progress in astronomy and medicine. Arabic literature and poetry flourished and Arabic language spread throughout the Islamic world. Arabic artists and architects built on earlier traditions to develop a distinctive Islamic style in decoration, painting, and architecture. The *ulama*, Islamic religious and legal scholars, played a prominent part in Islamic society as interpreters of Islamic tradition and law.

Decline of the Caliphate The Islamic empire began to splinter early. Disputes over the succession to the Prophet divided Muslims. Large parts of the Empire–Spain, North Africa, Iran– seceded. Military commanders reduced the caliphs to mere figureheads. The last Abbasid caliph was killed by the Mongols when they sacked Baghdad in 1258.

CHAPTER QUESTIONS

WHAT WAS the Qur'anic message as expressed to Muhammad?

WHY DID Islam expand so rapidly in the seventh century?

WHAT ROLES did the caliphate and the ulama play in Islamic states?

WHY DID the caliphal empire decline?

WHAT WERE the main achievements of "classical" Islamic culture?

CHAPTER OUTLINE

- Origins and Early Development
- Women in Early Islamic Society
- Early Islamic Conquests
- The New Islamic Order
- The High Caliphate
- "Classical" Islamic Culture

Islamic civilization has been the last great world civilization to appear to date, if one excepts the post-Enlightenment modern West. The basic ideas and ideals of the Islamic worldview derived from a single, prophetic-revelatory event, Muhammad's proclamation of the Qur'an. This event galvanized the Arabs into a new kind of unity—that of the community of Muslims, or "submitters" to God. This community subsequently spread far beyond Arabia, and Persians, Indians, and others raised it to new heights. Their acceptance of a new vision of society (and also of reality) as more compelling than any older vision— Jewish, Greek, Iranian, Christian, Buddhist—brought an Islamic civilization into being.

ORIGINS AND EARLY DEVELOPMENT

THE SETTING

WHAT WAS the Qur'anic message as expressed to Muhammad?

By 600 C.E., the dominant Eurasian political powers, Christian Byzantium and Sasanid Iran, had confronted one another for centuries. This rivalry did not, however, continue much longer. In the wake of one final, mutually exhausting conflict (608–627), a new Arab power humbled one and destroyed the other.

Pre-Islamic Arabia was not just a land of desert nomads. In the Fertile Crescent, Byzantium and Iran had kept the nomads of the Syrian and northern Arabian steppe at bay by enlisting small Arab client kingdoms on the edge of the desert as buffer states. One of the biggest of these was Christian. There had long been settled Arab kingdoms in the highlands of southern Arabia, which had direct access to the international trade that moved along the peninsula's coasts (see Chapter 4). Some of these kingdoms, including a Jewish one, had been independent; others had been under Persian or Abyssinian control. In the western Arabian highland of the Hijaz, the town of Mecca was a center of the caravan trade. It was also a pilgrimage center because of its famous sanctuary, the **Ka'ba** (or Kaaba), where many pagan Arab tribes had gods enshrined. Mecca was a merchant republic in which older tribal values were breaking down under the strains of urban and commercial life. But neither the Meccans nor other settled Arabs were wholly cut off from the nomads. The Arabic language defined and linked the Arab peoples, however divided they were by religion, blood feuds, rivalry, and conflict.

QUICK REVIEW

Mecca
• Center of caravan trade
• Pilgrimage center because of presence of Ka'ba
• A merchant republic

The popular notion of Islam as a "religion of the desert" is largely untrue. Islam began in a commercial center and first flourished in an agricultural oasis. Its first converts were settled Meccan townsfolk and date farmers of Yathrib (Medina). Before becoming Muslims, most of these Arabs were pagans, but some were Jews or Christians, or influenced by them. Caravans passed north and south through Mecca, and no merchant involved in this traffic, as Muhammad himself was, could have been ignorant of diverse cultures. Early Muslim leaders used the Arabs as warriors and looked to Arab culture for roots long after the locus of Islamic power had left Arabia. But the empire and civilization they built were centered in the heartlands of Eurasian urban culture and based on settled communal life rather than desert tribal anarchy.

MUHAMMAD AND THE QUR'AN

8.1
Koran

Muhammad (ca. 570–632) was raised an orphan in one of the commercial families of the old Meccan tribe of Quraysh. Later, in the midst of a successful business career made possible by his marriage to Khadija (d. ca. 619), a wealthy Meccan widow and entrepreneur, he grew troubled by the idolatry, worldliness, and lack of social conscience around him. These traits would have offended Jewish or Christian morality, about which he knew something. But for most

Ka'ba A black meteorite in the city of Mecca that became Islam's holiest shrine.

Arabs, these religious traditions were foreign, even though some Arab tribes were Jewish or Christian.

Muhammad's discontent paved the way for a religious experience that changed his life when he was about 40 years old. He felt himself called by the one true God to "rise and warn" his fellow Arabs about their disregard for morality and neglect of the worship of their creator. On repeated occasions, revelation came to him through God's messenger angel, Gabriel. It took the form of a "reciting" (*qur'an*) of God's word—now rendered in "clear Arabic" for the Arabs, just as it had been given in other languages to previous prophets for their people.

The message of the Qur'an was clear: The Prophet is to warn his people against false gods and immorality, especially injustice to the poor, orphans, widows, and women in general. At the end of time, on judgment day, every person will be bodily resurrected to face eternal punishment in hellfire or joy in paradise, according to how he or she lived. The way to paradise lies in gratitude to God for the bounties of creation, His prophetic and revelatory guidance, and His readiness to forgive. Social justice and worship of the one Lord are required of every person. Each is to recognize his or her creatureliness and God's transcendence. The proper response is "submission" (*islam*) to God's will, becoming *muslim* ("submissive" or "surrendering") in one's worship and morality. All of creation praises and serves God by nature except humans, who can choose to obey or to reject him (see "The Qur'an, or 'Recitation,' of God's Word").

In this Qur'anic message, the ethical monotheism of Judaic and Christian tradition (probably reinforced by Zoroastrian and Manichaean ideas) reached its logical conclusion—it demanded absolute obedience to the one Lord of the universe. The Qur'anic revelations state that Muhammad is the last in a line of prophets chosen to bring God's word. Noah, Abraham, Moses, Jesus, and non-biblical Arabian figures such as Salih had been sent on similar missions. But because the followers of these earlier prophets had strayed from their teachings or altered them, Muhammad was given one final iteration of God's message. Jews and Christians, like pagans, were summoned to respond to the moral imperatives of the Qur'an.

The Prophet's preaching fell largely on deaf ears in the first years after his calling. A few followed the lead of his wife, Khadija, in recognizing him as a divinely chosen reformer, but the merchant aristocracy as a whole resisted. His preaching against their traditional gods and goddesses threatened both their ancestral ways and also the Meccan pilgrimage shrine and the lucrative trade it attracted. The Meccans began to persecute Muhammad's followers. After the deaths of Khadija and Muhammad's uncle and protector, Abu Talib, the situation worsened. Then, as a result of his growing reputation as a moral and holy man, Muhammad was called to Yathrib (an agricultural oasis about 240 miles north of Mecca) as a neutral arbitrator among its five quarrelsome tribes, three of which were Jewish. Having sent his Meccan followers ahead, Muhammad fled Mecca in July 622 for Yathrib, afterward to be known as Medina (al-Madina, "the City [of the Prophet]"). Some dozen years later, this "emigration," or **Hegira**, became the starting point for the Islamic calendar, the event marking the creation of a distinctive Islamic community, or *Umma*.[1]

Qur'an "A reciting." Islamic bible, which Muslims believe God revealed to the prophet Muhammad.

Islam "Submission." Religion founded by the prophet Muhammad.

Hegira Flight of Muhammad and his followers from Mecca to Medina in 622 C.E. It marks the beginning of the Islamic calendar.

Umma Islamic community.

---

[1] The 12-month Muslim lunar year is shorter than the Christian solar year by about 11 days, giving a difference of about three years per century. Muslim dates are reckoned from the month in 622 in which Muhammad began his Hegira (Arabic: *Hijra*). Thus Muslims celebrated the start of their lunar year 1401 in November 1980 (1979–1980 C.E. = A.H. [Anno Hegirae] 1400), whereas it was only 1,358 solar years from 622 to 1980.

HISTORY'S VOICES

THE QUR'AN, OR "RECITATION," OF GOD'S WORD

The Qur'an has many themes, from moral admonition, social justice, eternal punishment for the ungodly, and exemplary stories of past peoples and their prophets, to God's majesty and uniqueness, his bountiful natural world and compassion for humankind, and the joys of paradise.

CAN YOU identify at least four major Qur'anic themes in the selections that follow? To what end are the bounties of creation cited? What is the image of God conveyed in these selections? What can you infer about the Qur'anic conception of prophethood? Of the Judgment Day?

The revelation of the Book is from God who is mighty and wise. There are signs for men of faith, in the heavens and in the earth, in your being created and in God's scattered throng of creatures—signs for people with a grasp of truth.

There are signs, too—for those with a mind to understand—in the alternation of night and day, and in the gracious rain God sends from heaven to renew the face of the parched earth, and in the veering of the winds.

These are the signs of God which truly We recite to you. Having God and His signs, in what else after that will you believe as a message?

—*Sura 45:1–6*

Were you set to count up the mercies of God you would not be able to number them. God is truly forgiving and merciful.

—*Sura 16:18*

Such is God your Lord. There is no god but He, creator of all things. Then worship Him who is guardian over all there is. No human perception comprehends Him, while He comprehends all perception. He is beyond all conceiving, the One who is infinitely aware.

—*Sura 6:102–103*

To God belong the east and the west, and wheresoever you turn there is the face of God. Truly God is all-pervading, all-knowing.

—*Sura 2:115*

You people of the Book, why are you so argumentative about Abraham, seeing that the Torah and the Gospel were only sent down after his time? Will you not use your reason? You are people much given to disputing about things within your comprehension: why insist on disputing about things of which you have no knowledge? Knowledge belongs to God and you lack it!

Abraham was not a Jew, nor was he a Christian. He was a man of pure worship (a hanif) and a Muslim: he was not one of those pagan idolaters . . . .

—*Sura 3:65–67*

Yet you [people] deny the reality of the judgement. There are guardians keeping watch over you, noble beings keeping record, who know your every deed. The righteous will dwell in bliss. The evil-doers will be in *Jahim*, in the burning on Judgement Day, and there will be no absconding for them.

What can make you realize the Day of judgement as it is? . . . the Day when there is no soul that can avail another soul. For the authority on that Day is God's alone.

—*Sura 82.1–5, 9, 19*

Excerpt from *Readings in the Qur'an* by Kenneth Cragg. Copyright © 1988 by Kenneth Cragg. Reprinted by permission of HarperCollins, Inc.

8.3
Orations: The Words of the Prophet Through His Speeches

Muhammad quickly cemented ties between the Meccan emigrants and the Medinans, many of whom became converts. Raids on his Meccan enemies' caravans established his leadership. The Arab Jews of Medina largely rejected his religious message. And when they made contact with his Meccan enemies, he turned on them and took their lands. Many of the revelations of the Qur'an from this period pertain to communal order and to the Jews and Christians who rejected Islam.

The basic Muslim norms took shape in Medina: allegiance to the *Umma;* honesty; modesty; abstention from alcohol and pork; fair division of inheritances; improved treatment of women, especially as to property and other rights in marriage; regulation of marriage and divorce; ritual ablution before worship (Qur'an reciting or prayer); three—later five—daily prayers facing the Meccan shrine of the Ka'ba; payment to support less fortunate Muslims; daytime fasting for one month each year; and, eventually, pilgrimage to Mecca at least once in a lifetime, if one can. These constitute the five pillars of Islam: (1) *Shahada*, the creed, "There is no god but God and Muhammad is God's prophet"; (2) *Salat*, prayer; (3) *Sawm*, fasting during the month of Ramadan; (4) *Zakat*, alms; and (5) *Hajj*, pilgrimage.

Groups that accepted the political authority of Islam were granted religious tolerance. A Jewish oasis that yielded to Muhammad was allowed, unlike the resistant Medinan Jews, to keep its lands, practice its faith, and receive protection in return for the payment of a head tax. This set a precedent that was followed ever after by Jews, Christians, and other "people of Scripture" who accepted Islamic rule. After long conflict, the Meccans surrendered to Muhammad, and his generosity in receiving them into the *Umma* set the pattern for the later Islamic conquests. Muhammad cemented many of his alliances with marriages. In the last years of the Prophet's life, his once tiny band of Muslims became the heart of a pan-Arabian tribal confederation, bound together by personal allegiance to Muhammad, submission (*islam*) to God, and membership in the *Umma* of "submitters."

The Ka'ba in Mecca. The Ka'ba is viewed in Muslim tradition as the site of the first "house of God" built by Abraham and his son Ishmael at God's command. It is held to have fallen later into idolatrous use until Muhammad's victory over the Meccans and his cleansing of the holy cubical structure (*Ka'ba* means "cube"). The Ka'ba is the geographical point toward which all Muslims face when performing ritual prayer. It and the plain of Arafat outside Mecca are the two foci of the pilgrimage of Hajj that each Muslim aspires to make at least once in a lifetime.

Mehmet Biber/Photo Researchers, Inc.

Hajj Pilgrimage to Mecca that all Muslims are enjoined to perform at least once in their lifetime.

WOMEN IN EARLY ISLAMIC SOCIETY

HOW DID the status of women improve under Islam?

*T*he Qur'an introduced the Arabs to ideas that drastically improved the status of women. It prohibited the common practice of female infanticide, and guaranteed a woman the right to inherit, own, and manage property. The Qur'an recognized a woman's right to contract her own marriage, and stipulated that she, not a male relative, receive the dowry provided by her husband. In effect, it declared that a bride was not an object to be sold by one man to another, but a party to a negotiated contract.

The Qur'an, however, did not envision the kind of gender equality that is expected by many in the modern world. Islamic law stipulates that a senior male control and guide the family unit. He is to receive a larger share in an inheritance. He is freer to initiate divorce, and in court his eye-witness testimony is weighted more heavily than that of a woman.

Veiled Women. Women mourning the death of martyrs in combat. Safavid fresco, 17th century.

Art Resource, N.Y.

The Qur'an presupposes and legitimizes patriarchal authority and it does not outlaw customs that have prevented women from reaching full equality. It tolerates, but seeks to control, polygamy. The Qur'an permits a man to have as many as four wives on condition that he treat each equally and fairly. (Some Muslims claim that this is a prohibition of polygamy, for absolutely equal treatment is impossible.) The veiling of women is associated with Islam, but Muslims did not invent the custom. It was a common practice among upperclass women in the Byzantine and Sasanid Empires. The Qur'an, however, does stipulate that both men and women conduct themselves with modesty and that women "should draw their veils over their bosom and display their beauty only to their husbands and their fathers." (Q. 24:31). Rigid implementation of this rule has led, at some times and in some places, to practices of extreme veiling, seclusion of women in their homes, and their exclusion from all roles in public life. Some modern Muslim women have, however, interpreted these verses in ways that bring them more in line with modern ideas of gender equality. They can point to history for support, for many women—among them some of Muhammad's wives—played influential roles in the development of Islam.

EARLY ISLAMIC CONQUESTS

WHY DID Islam expand so rapidly in the seventh century?

*I*n 632, Muhammad died. Because he left no son and did not designate a successor, the new *Umma* faced its first major crisis. A political struggle erupted between Meccan and Medinan factions, which ended in a pledge of allegiance to Abu Bakr, the most senior of the early Meccan converts. Many tribes assumed that their allegiance had been to the Prophet and ended at his death. But Abu Bakr's rule (632–634) as Muhammad's successor, or "caliph" (Arabic: *khalifa*), reestablished at least nominal religious unity among the Arabs. They were forced to recognize in the *Umma* a new kind of supra-tribal community that demanded more than fidelity to a particular leader.

COURSE OF CONQUEST

Under the next two caliphs, Umar (634–644) and Uthman (644–656), Arab armies burst out of the peninsula. By 643, they had conquered the Byzantine and Sasanid territories of the Fertile Crescent, Egypt, and most of Iran. For the first time in centuries, the lands from Egypt to Iran came under one rule. Finally, Arab armies swept west over the Byzantine-controlled Libyan coast, and in the east in 651, they defeated the last Sasanid ruler.

An interlude of civil war followed during the disputed caliphate of Ali (656–661). Then expansion resumed under the fifth caliph, Mu'awiya (661–680). An Islamic fleet conquered Cyprus, plundered Sicily and Rhodes, and crippled Byzantine sea power. By 680, control of greater Iran was solidified by permanent Arab garrisoning of Khorasan, much of Anatolia was raided, Constantinople was besieged (but not taken), and Armenia was under Islamic rule.

Succeeding decades saw the eastern Berbers of Libyan North Africa defeated and converted to Islam. With their help, "the West" (al-Maghrib, modern Morocco and Algeria) was quickly overrun. By 716, the disunited Spanish Visigoth kingdoms had fallen, and much of Iberia had come under Islamic control. Pushing north into France, the Arabs were finally checked by the Frankish leader, Charles Martel, south of Tours (732). In 710, when Arab armies reached the Indus region, Islamic power stretched from the Atlantic to central Asia (see Map 11–1).

FACTORS OF SUCCESS

A combination of factors underlay this rapid expansion. The basic one was the weakened military and economic condition of the Byzantines and Sasanids—the result of their chronic warfare with one another. Also important was the power of

OVERVIEW   THE BASIC TENETS OF ISLAM

Islam, meaning "submission to God's will," is a monotheistic religion without an ordained clergy or elaborate ritual. From its earliest days, Islam has required or enjoined all Muslims (those who submit or surrender themselves to God) to adhere to a few relatively simple norms.

Allegiance to the *Umma*, the community of Islamic believers

Honesty

Modesty in dress and demeanor

Abstention from alcohol or pork

Benevolence and fair treatment to women, especially in regard to property and marriage rights

Ritual washing before worship

Prayer five times a day facing Mecca

Giving alms

Daytime fasting once a year during the month of Ramadan

Pilgrimage to Mecca at least once in a person's lifetime if possible

MAP EXPLORATION

Interactive map: To explore this map further, go to **http://www.prenhall.com/craig/map11.1**

MAP 11–1

Muslim Conquests and Domination of the Mediterranean to about 750 C.E.   The rapid spread of Islam (both religion and political-military power) is shown here. Within 125 years of Muhammad's rise, Muslims came to dominate Spain and all areas south and east of the Mediterranean.

WHY DID so many subject peoples welcome Islamic rule?

jihad "Struggle in the path of God." Although not necessarily implying violence, it is often interpreted to mean holy war in the name of Islam.

the new Islamic vision of society and life to unite the Arabs and attract converts from other peoples. An implication of the vision was a duty to support campaigns to extend "the abode of submission" (*Dar al-Islam*) abroad. Paradise was assured for those who engaged in *jihad*, or "struggle (in the path of God)," but it is less likely to have motivated the average Arab tribesman than booty. The marginal life in the peninsula was such that the hope of greater prosperity must have been compelling. Still, religious zeal cannot be discounted.

Another major factor was the excellent leadership of the first caliphs and generals, which, combined with Byzantine and Iranian exhaustion, gave Arab armies an advantage. Also important was the readiness of many subject populations to welcome Islamic rule as a relief from Byzantine or Persian oppression. Crucial here was the Muslim willingness to allow Christian, Jewish, and even Zoroastrian groups to continue as minorities (with their own legal systems and no military obligations) under the protection of Islamic governments. These religious communities had to recognize Islamic political authority, pay a non-Muslim head tax (*jizya*), and refrain from proselytizing or interfering with Muslim religious practice. As time went on, the head tax and other strictures on non-Muslims encouraged Christians and Jews to convert.

Finally, the astute policies of the early leaders led to the permanence of the conquests: relatively little bloodshed, destruction, or disruption in conquest; adoption of existing administrative systems (and personnel) with minimal changes; adjustment of unequal taxation; appointment of capable governors; and strategic siting of new garrison towns such as Basra, Kufa, and Fustat (later Cairo).

THE NEW ISLAMIC ORDER

Although they were quick to adopt and adapt existing traditions, the Muslims brought with them a new worldview that demanded a new political, social, and cultural reality. Beyond military and administrative problems loomed the question of the nature of Islamic society. Under the Prophet, the new community of the *Umma* had replaced, at least in theory, the tribal, blood-based sociopolitical order in Arabia. Yet once the Arabs (most of whom became Muslims) had to rule non-Arabs and non-Muslims, new problems tested the ideal of an Islamic polity. Chief among these were leadership and membership qualifications, social order, and religious and cultural identity.

THE CALIPHATE

Allegiance to Muhammad had rested on his authority as a divine spokesperson and gifted leader. His first successors were chosen much as were Arab *shaykhs* ("sheiks"), or tribal chieftains. Leaders, or elders, of the new religious "tribe" of

WHAT ROLES did the caliphate and the ulama play in Islamic states?

The Dome of the Rock, Jerusalem. An early example of Islamic architecture, it dates from the seventh century and the first wave of Arab expansion. It is built on the rock from which Muslims believe Muhammad ascended into heaven and on which Jews believe Abraham prepared to sacrifice Isaac. The Dome of the Rock has special symbolic significance for Muslims because the site is associated with the life and story of the Prophet. For a few years of Muhammad's time in Medina, Muslims faced Jerusalem when they prayed, before a new Qur'anic revelation changed the direction to Mecca.

Scala/Art Resource, N.Y.

Muslims came to agreement on the choice of an individual on the basis of his superior personal qualities. In addition to these attributes, precedence in the faith deriving from a reputation for piety and a history of association with the Prophet were also important. The men chosen bore several titles: "successor" (*khalifa*, or caliph), "leader" (*imam*—literally, the one who stands in front to lead the ritual prayer), and "commander (*amir*) of the faithful." These terms underscored the caliph's function as the guardian of the *Umma*. Most Muslims agreed that the necessary qualities were to be found in the caliphs Abu Bakr and Umar, and potentially in Uthman and Ali. But by the time of Uthman and Ali, dissension arose and led to civil war. The first four caliphs had all been close to Muhammad, and this closeness gave their reigns a nostalgic aura of pristine purity, especially as the later **caliphate** institution was based largely on sheer power legitimized by hereditary succession.

The nature of Islamic leadership became an issue with the first civil war (656–661) and the recognition of Mu'awiya, a kinsman of Uthman, as caliph. He founded the first dynastic caliphate, that of his Meccan clan of Umayya (661–750). Umayyad descendants held power until they were ousted in 750 by the Abbasid clan, which based its legitimacy on descent from Abbas, an uncle of the Prophet. The Umayyads had the prestige of an office held by the first four, "rightly guided" caliphs. Many, however, considered them to be worldly kings in comparison to the first four, who were seen as true Muslim successors to Muhammad.

The Abbasids launched a rebellion in 750 that won them the caliphate. Their followers were inspired by pious dissatisfaction with Umayyad worldliness, non-Arab Muslim resentment (primarily in Iran) of preferential treatment given Arabs, and ongoing dissension among Arab tribal factions in the garrison towns. The Abbasids, however, proved to be scarcely less worldly than the Umayyads and continued the custom of hereditary succession to the caliphate begun by the Umayyads. They retained control of most of the Islamic territories until 945. Thereafter, although their line continued until 1258, the caliphate was primarily a titular office representing an Islamic unity that existed, in the political realm, in name only.

THE ULAMA

The caliph was never "emperor and pope combined." Religious leadership in the *Umma* devolved on another group, those Muslims whose reputations for piety and learning led them to be regarded as authorities. Initially, they were the "Companions" (male and female) of Muhammad. This generation was succeeded by younger believers who were concerned with preserving, interpreting, and applying the Qur'an, and maintaining the norms of the Prophet's original *Umma*. Because the Qur'an contained few actual legal prescriptions, they had to draw on precedents from Meccan and Medinan practice, as well as on oral traditions from and about the Prophet and his Companions. They also had to develop and standardize grammatical rules for a common Arabic language based on the Qur'an and pre-Islamic poetry. Furthermore, they had to improve the phonetic, cursive Arabic script, a task done so well that the script gradually became the standard written medium for languages wherever Islamic religion and culture was dominant: among Iranians, Turks, Indians, Indonesians, Malays, East Africans, and others. They also developed an enduring pattern of education based on study under persons who could claim high rank in an unbroken succession of trustworthy Muslims stretching back to the earliest *Umma*.

imam Islamic prayer leader.

amir/emir Islamic military commander.

caliphate Spiritual and temporal rule of the Muslim community.

These scholars came to be known as **ulama** ("persons of right knowledge"). Their legal opinions and collective discussions of issues, from theological doctrine to criminal punishments, established a basis for religious and social order. By the ninth century, they had largely defined the understanding of the divine law, or *Shari'a*, that Muslims ever after have held to be the definitive guide for legal, social, commercial, political, ritual, and moral concerns. This understanding and the methods by which it was derived together form the Muslim science of jurisprudence, the core discipline of Islamic learning.

In Umayyad time, the *ulama* became a new elite. Caliphs and their governors regularly sought their advice, but often only for moral or legal (the two are, in Muslim view, the same) sanction of a contemplated (or accomplished) action. Some *ulama* compromised themselves. Yet, incorruptible *ulama* were seldom persecuted for their opinions, mostly because of the respect they enjoyed in the Muslim community.

Thus, without building a formal clergy, Muslims developed a workable moral-legal system based on a formally trained scholarly elite and a tradition of concern with religious ideals in public affairs and social order. Because the caliphs and their deputies had at least to act with circumspection and support for pious standards in public, the *ulama* enjoyed de facto leadership in Muslim societies with the rulers—a pattern that has endured in Islamic states.

THE UMMA

A strength of the Qur'anic message was its universalism, the acceptance into the *Umma* of anyone who would submit to God and follow Muslim precepts. Non-Arab converts had to be accepted, even if it meant loss of tax revenue. The social and political status of new converts was, however, clearly second to that of Arabs. Umar had organized the army register, or *diwan*, according to tribal precedence in converting to Islam. Because the diwan served as the basis for distribution and taxation of the new wealth, this perpetuated Arab precedence. The garrisons the Arabs planted in conquered lands became centers of Islamic culture, and they kept the Arabs sufficiently separate from native populations that they were not simply absorbed into the cultures of their new subjects. The dominance of the Arabic language was ensured by the centrality of the Qur'an in Muslim life and the notion of its perfect Arabic form, together with the increasing administrative use of Arabic to replace Aramaic, Greek, Middle Persian, or Coptic languages.

Non-Arab converts routinely attached themselves to Arab tribes as "clients," which assured a place in the diwan. This attachment, however, still meant second-class citizenship alongside the Arabs. Dissatisfaction among client Muslims was widespread and led to uprisings. Persian-Arab tensions were strong in Umayyad and early Abbasid times. Nevertheless, a Persian cultural renaissance raised the Islamicized modern Persian language to high status in Islamic culture. Consequently, it affected religion, art, and literature in much of the Islamic world.

Caliphal administration joined with the evolution of legal theory and practice and the consolidation of religious norms to give stability to the emerging Islamic society. So powerful was the Muslim vision of society that, upon the demise of a caliph, or even a dynasty such as the Umayyads, the *Umma* and the caliphal office continued. There were, however, conflicting notions of that vision. In the first three Islamic centuries, two major interpretations crystallized that reflected idealistic interpretations of the *Umma*—its

ulama "Persons with correct knowledge." Islamic scholarly elite who served a social function similar to the Christian clergy.

The Ritual Worship, or Prayer. These illustrations show the sequence of movement prescribed for the ritual prayers that each Muslim should perform five times a day. Various words of praise, prayer, and recitation from the Qur'an accompany each position and movement. The ritual symbolizes the Muslim's complete obedience to God and recognition of God as the one, eternal, omnipotent Lord of the universe.

Library of Congress.

leadership and membership. When neither proved viable in the practical world, they failed to win broad-based support. A third, "centrist," vision found favor with the majority because it accommodated inevitable compromises in the higher cause of Islamic unity.

The Kharijites   The most radical idealists traced their political origin to the first civil war (656–661). They were the Kharijites, or "seceders" — those who left Ali's camp because, in their view, he compromised with his enemies. The Kharijites' position was that the Muslim polity must be based on strict Qur'anic principles. They espoused total equality of the faithful and held that the leader of the *Umma* should be the best Muslim, whoever that might be. They took a moralistic view of membership in the *Umma:* Anyone who committed a major sin was no longer a Muslim. Extreme Kharijites were rallying points for opposition to the Umayyads and the Abbasids. Although the movement declined, Kharijite groups survive today in Oman and North Africa.

The Shi'a   A second position was defined largely in terms of a dispute over qualifications for leadership of the *Umma.* Muhammad had no surviving sons, and his son-in-law and cousin Ali claimed the caliphate in 656, partly on the basis of his blood tie to the Prophet. His claim was contested by Mu'awiya in the first Islamic civil war. After a Kharijite murdered Ali in 661, Mu'awiya took over. The "partisans of Ali" (*Shi'at Ali,* or simply the **Shi'a**, or *Shi'ites*) originated with Ali's murder and the death of his son Husayn at Karbala, in Iraq, at the hands of Umayyad troops (680).

Whereas all Muslims esteem Ali for his closeness to Muhammad, Shi'ites believe him to be the Prophet's appointed successor. Ali's blood tie with Muhammad was augmented in Shi'ite thinking by belief in the Prophet's designation of him as the true imam, or Muslim leader, after him. Numerous rebellions in Umayyad times rallied around persons claiming to be such a true successor, whether as an Alid or merely a member of Muhammad's clan, the Hashim. Even the Abbasids based their right to the caliphate on their Hashimite ancestry. The major Shi'ite pretenders who emerged in the 9th and 10th centuries based their claims on both the Prophet's designation and their descent from Ali and Fatima, Muhammad's daughter. They also stressed the idea of a

Shi'a Muslims who trace their beliefs to the caliph Ali, who was assassinated in 661 C.E.

divinely inspired knowledge passed on by Muhammad to his designated heirs. Thus, the true Muslim was the faithful follower of the imams, who carried Muhammad's blood and spiritual authority.

Shi'ites saw Ali's assassination by a Kharijite and the massacre of Husayn and his family as proofs of the evil nature of this world's rulers, and as rallying points for true Muslims. True Muslims, like their imams, must suffer. But they would ultimately be vindicated by a *mahdi*, or "guided one," who would usher in a messianic age and a judgment day when the faithful would be rewarded.

On several occasions, Shi'ite rulers headed Islamic states. But only after 1500, in Iran, did Shi'ism prevail as the majority faith in a major Muslim state. The Shi'ite vision of the true *Umma* has not been able to dominate the larger Islamic world.

The Centrists It was a third, less sharply defined position on the nature of leadership and membership in the *Umma* that most Muslims accepted. It proved acceptable not only to lukewarm Muslims or pragmatists but also to persons of piety as intense as that of any Kharijite or Shi'ite. We may term the proponents of this position *centrists*. They called themselves *Sunnis*—followers of the tradition (*sunna*) established by the Prophet and the Qur'an. Neither they, nor the Shi'ites, nor the Kharijites, have ever been a single sect, but have always encompassed a wide range of ideas and groups. They have made up the broad middle spectrum of Muslims who tend to put communal solidarity and maintenance of the Islamic polity above purist adherence to particular theological tenets. They have been inclusivist rather than exclusivist, a trait that has typified the Islamic (unlike the Jewish or Christian) community.

The centrist position was the most workable framework for the new Islamic state. Its basic ideas were:

1. The *Umma* is a theocratic entity, a state under the authority of God's law, the Shari'a. The sources of guidance are, first, the Qur'an; second, Muhammad's precedent; and, third and fourth, the interpretive efforts and consensus of the Muslims (that is, of the *ulama*).

2. The caliph is the absolute temporal ruler, charged with administering and defending the Abode of Islam and protecting Muslim norms and practice; he possesses no greater authority than other Muslims in matters of faith.

3. A person who professes to be Muslim by witnessing that "There is no god but God, and Muhammad is His Messenger" should be considered a Muslim (because "only God knows what is in the heart"), and not even a mortal sin excludes such a person from the *Umma*.

These and other basic premises of Muslim community came to be the theological underpinnings of both the caliphal state and the international Islamic social order.

Origins and Early Development of Islam

ca. 570	Birth of Muhammad
622	The Hegira ("emigration") of Muslims to Yathrib (henceforward *al-Madina*, "The City [of the Prophet]"); beginning of Muslim calendar
632	Death of Muhammad; Abu Bakr becomes first "successor" (*khalifa*, caliph) to leadership, reigns 632–634
634–644	Caliphate of Umar; rapid conquests in Egypt and Iran
644–656	Caliphate of Uthman (member of Umayyad clan); more conquests; Qur'an text established; growth of sea power
656–661	Contested Caliphate of Ali; first civil war
661–680	Caliphate of Mu'awiya; founding of Umayyad dynasty (661–750); capital moved to Damascus; more expansion
680	Second civil war (680–692) begins with death of al-Husayn at Karbala

Sunna "Tradition." Dominant Islamic group.

WHY DID the caliphal empire decline?

THE HIGH CALIPHATE

*T*he consolidation of the caliphal institution began with the victory of the Umayyad caliph Abd al-Malik in 692, in the second civil war. The ensuing century and a half mark the era of the "high caliphate" that flourished first under the Umayyads in Damascus and then in the Abbasid capital of Baghdad. The height of caliphal power and splendor came in the first century of Abbasid rule, notably during the caliphates of the fabled Harun al-Rashid (786–809) and his third son, al-Ma'mun (813–833; see Map 11–2).

THE ABBASID STATE

The Abbasids' victory effectively ended Arab dominance as well as Umayyad ascendancy (except in Spain). The shift of the imperial capital from Damascus to Baghdad on the Tigris (762–766) was indicative of the influence the eastern cultures had on the new regime as more and more Persians entered its bureaucracy. Although the Abbasids stressed their descent from al-Abbas (ca. 565–653), uncle of both Muhammad and Ali, their religious policy was to disavowal support for Shi'ite hopes for a divinely inspired imamate. This made their rule attractive to a broad spectrum of Muslims.

Whereas the Umayyads had relied on Syrian Arab forces, the Abbasids used Khorasanian Arabs and Iranians. Beginning in the ninth century, however, they began to enlist slave soldiers (*mamluks*), mostly Turks from the northern steppes, as their personal troops. The officers of these forces, who were also mamluks,

MAP 11–2

The Abbasid Empire, ca. 900 C.E. A great diversity of peoples and nations were united by the Abbasids. Their capital at Baghdad became the center of a trading network that linked India, Africa, and China.

WHICH MUSLIM regions were not part of the Abbasid Empire?

soon seized the positions of power in the bureau-cracies and the army and dominated the caliphs. This increasingly alienated the Muslim populace from their own rulers.

SOCIETY

A deep division between rulers and populace became typical of Islamic societies. However, even while Abbasid central power declined (after the mid-ninth century) as more provincial rulers asserted indepdencence, these rulers generally chose to recognize nominal caliphal authority. This underscored their role as guardians of the Islamic order, which found its real cohesiveness in the Muslim ideals propagated by the *ulama*.

Conversion of the diverse populace of the Islamic Empire lagged behind centralization of political power and development of Islamic institu-tions. Prior to the mid-12th century, Iraq and Iran (especially Khorasan, which had substantial early Arab Muslim immigration) experienced the most complete Islamization of local elites. They were fol-lowed by Spain, North Africa, and Syria. As conversion and Islamization pro-gressed, a more self-confident Muslim community appeared that had less need for centralized caliphal power.[2]

The Great Mosque of Samarra. Built in the middle of the ninth century by the Abbasid caliph al Mutaanakkil, this Friday, or congregational Mosque has a prayer space larger than nine football fields, making it the largest enclosed such space in the Islamic world. The style of the Minaret recalls the ziggu-rats of ancient Babylon.

Aerofilms.

DECLINE

The eclipse of the caliphal empire was foreshadowed at the outset of Abbasid rule, when one of the last Umayyads founded the Islamic state (756–1030) on the Iberian peninsula that produced the spectacular Moorish culture of Spain. In 929, the Spanish Umayyads claimed the title of caliph. In all the Abbasid provinces, regional governments always had the potential to become independent states. Harun al-Rashid's governor of what is today Tunisia set up a separate state in North Africa in 801. A later North African dynasty, the Fatimids, conquered Egypt in 969 and established a Shi'ite dynasty that claimed to be the only true caliphate.

In the East, Baghdad had a difficult time control-ling Iran. For two centuries, beginning in 821 in Khorasan, Abbasid governors or rebel groups founded independent dynasties, and the caliph usually had to rec-ognize their rule. The Samanids of Khorasan and Transoxiana ruled at Bukhara as nominal Abbasid vassals from 875 until 999. They gave northeastern Iran a long period of economic and political security from Turkish steppe invaders. Under their aegis, Persian poetry and Arabic scientific studies began a Persian Islamic cultural renaissance and influential scientific tradition.

Early Period of the High Caliphate

680–692	Second civil war
685–705	Caliphate of Abd al-Malik; consolidation, Arabization of administration
705–715	Caliphate of al-Walid; Morocco conquered, Spain invaded; Arab armies reach the Indus
ca. 750	Introduction of paper manufacture from China through Samarqand to Islamic world
750	Abbasids seize caliphate from Umayyads, begin new dynasty (750–1258)
756	Some Umayyads escape to Spain, found new dynasty (756–1030)
762–766	New Abbasid capital built at Baghdad

[2]Richard W. Bulliet, *Conversion to Islam in the Medieval Period* (Cambridge: Harvard University Press, 1979), especially pp. 7–15, 128–138.

Of greatest consequence for the Abbasid caliphate, however, was the rise of a Shi'ite clan, the Buyids. In 945, they brought the Abbasid caliphs under their control, and henceforth the caliph was a puppet in the hands of Buyid "commanders" (*amirs* or *emirs*; later, *sultans*). In 1055, the Buyids were replaced by the more famous Seljuk *sultans*. Abbasid caliphs continued as figureheads of Muslim unity until Mongol invaders killed the last of them in 1258.

WHAT WERE the main achievements of "classical" Islamic culture?

8.7
Islamic Science and Mathematics

An illustration from The Maqamat of al Hariri (d.1122), one of the great masterpieces of Arabic literature of the later Middle Ages. It is a narrative written in rhymed prose for the purposes of entertainment.

Maquamat of al Hariri, Library in a mosque, Arab manuscript, 13th century (1237). Paris, France Bibliotheque Nationale (National Library), Photos 12.com-ARS.

"CLASSICAL" ISLAMIC CULTURE

The splendor of the Abbasid court became the stuff of Islamic legends, such as those in *The Thousand and One Nights*. Its rich cultural legacy outlived the Abbasids themselves. Their achievements had been made possible by a strong army and central government and vigorous internal and external trade. The latter may have been stimulated by the Tang Empire of China, with which the Islamic world had overland and sea contact. Material factors, such as the introduction of paper manufacture (from China about 750) or the flight of Byzantine scholars east to new Abbasid centers of learning, also contributed to making the early Abbasid Era special.

INTELLECTUAL TRADITIONS

The Abbasid heyday was marked by sophisticated tastes and an insatiable thirst for knowledge—*any* knowledge. Contacts (primarily among intellectuals) between Muslims and Christian, Jewish, Zoroastrian, and other "protected" religious communities contributed to the cosmopolitanism of the age. Some older intellectual traditions experienced a revival in early Abbasid times, as with Hellenistic learning. Philosophy, astronomy, mathematics, medicine, and other natural sciences enjoyed patronage. Islamic culture took over the tradition of rational inquiry from the Hellenistic world and developed and preserved it at a time when Europe was by comparison a cultural wasteland.

Arabic translations of Greek and Sanskrit works stimulated progress in astronomy and medicine. Translation reached its peak in al-Ma'mun's new academy headed by a Nestorian Christian, Hunayn ibn Ishaq (d. 873), noted for his medical and Greek learning. There were Arabic translations of everything from the Greek authors Galen, Ptolemy, Euclid, Aristotle, Plato, and the Neo-Platonists to the Indian fables that had been rendered into Middle Persian under the Sasanids. Such translations stimulated not only Arabic learning, but that of the less advanced European world, especially in the 12th and 13th centuries.

LANGUAGE AND LITERATURE

Arabic language and literature developed greatly in the expanded cultural sphere of the new empire. In *belles lettres* there arose a significant genre of Arabic writing known as *adab*, or "manners" literature. It included essays and didactic literature influenced by earlier Persian examples. While translations of different literary genres increased the range of the Arabs' original bedouin idiom, poetry flourished by building on the sophisticated tradition of the Arabic ode, or *qasida*. Grammar was central to the interpretation of the Qur'an that occupied the *ulama*, and this linguistic concern undergirded an emerging curriculum of Muslim learning. Historical and biographical writings became major genres of Arabic writing. They arose primarily to record first the lives and times of the Prophet and his earliest companions, then those of subsequent generations of Muslims. This information was crucial to judging the reliability of the "chains" of transmitters attached to each traditional report, or **hadith**. A *hadith* consisted of words or actions ascribed to Muhammad and the Companions; it became the chief source of Muslim legal and religious norms alongside the Qur'an, as well as the basic unit of most prose genres, from history to Qur'an exegesis. Collections of the *hadith* also formed a separate genre that was mined by preachers and by the developing schools of legal interpretation, whose crowning glory was al-Shafi'i's (d. 820) work on legal reasoning.

ART AND ARCHITECTURE

In art and architecture the Abbasid Era saw the crystallization of a "classical" Islamic style by about 1000 C.E. Except for ceramics and Arabic calligraphy, most of the discrete elements of Islamic art and architecture had antecedents in Greco-Roman, Byzantine, or Iranian art. What was new was the use of older forms and motifs for new purposes and combinations, and also the spread of such elements to new locales, generally from east (especially the Fertile Crescent) to west (Syria, Egypt, North Africa, and Spain). The combination and elaboration of discrete forms, as in the case of the colonnade (or hypostyle) mosque or complex arabesque designs, were also introduced.

The Muslims had good reason for confidence in their faith and culture and to want to distinguish themselves from others. Particular formal items, such as calligraphic motifs and inscriptions on buildings, characterize Islamic architecture and define its functions. Most striking was the avoidance of pictures or icons in public art. This was, of course, in line with the Muslim aversion to idolatry and to Byzantine Christian art. Although this iconoclasm later diminished, it was a telling proclamation of the general thrust of Muslim faith.

Decorated Ceramic Bowl. A glazed ceramic bowl decorated with a gazelle or antelope, a symbolic figure of beauty and grace. From North Africa, Tunisian area, Fatimid (10th–12th centuries).

Werner Forman/Art Resource, N.Y.

hadith   Saying or action ascribed to Muhammad.

"Classical" Period of the High Caliphate

786–809	Caliphate of Harun al-Rashid; apogee of caliphal power
813–833	Caliphate of al-Ma'mun; strong patronage of translations of Greek, Sanskrit, and other works into Arabic; first heavy reliance on slave soldiers (*mamluks*)
875	Rise of Sasanid power at Bukhara; patronage of Persian poetry paves way for Persian literary renaissance
945–1055	Buyid amirs rule the eastern empire at Baghdad; the Abbasid caliphs continue largely as figureheads
969	Rise of Shi'ite Fatimid dynasty in North Africa
1055	Buyid amirs replaced by Seljuk sultans as effective rulers at Baghdad and custodians of the caliphate

A

B

The Congregational Mosque. Two examples of the finest great mosques of the classical Islamic world. Such buildings were designed not only for worship; their large courtyards and pillared halls were also intended to hold the population of a given city and could be used for governmental purposes or for mustering troops in time of war. Their splendor also announced the power and wealth of Islamic rule. Figure A is the Great Mosque at Qayrawan in modern Tunisia, built between the 8th and 9th centuries. Figure B shows the Spanish Umayyad mosque in Cordoba, built and added to from the 8th to the 10th centuries, in a series of roofed extensions—unlike that in Qayrawan, which has only covered colonnades and one great hall (behind the photographer in this picture).

SUMMARY

Muhammad The Prophet Muhammad (570–632) was the founder of Islam. Born in the Arabian commercial city of Mecca, he was influenced by contact with Arab Christians and with Jews. At about age 40, he had a religious experience during which, Muslims believe, God's messenger angel Gabriel repeatedly recited (*qur'an*) God's word to him. The message of the Qur'an was that social justice and worship of the one true God are required of every person. At the end of time, people will be resurrected and judged by God to be rewarded or punished according to how they lived. The proper response to God is submission (*islam*) to His will by becoming a Muslim (one who submits).

Islamic Conquest By the time of Muhammad's death, his followers had conqured all of Arabia. Under his successors, the caliphs, Muslim Arab armies conquered most of the Middle East, North Africa, Spain, Iran, and northwest India. Many of the peoples of these territories converted to Islam.

The High Caliphate Under the Abbasid caliphs who ruled from the city of Baghdad, Islamic culture enjoyed its "classical" phase. As the sacred medium of God's final revelation, the Arabic language spread throughout the Islamic world. Arabic artists and architects developed a distinctive Islamic style. The *ulama*, Islamic religious and legal scholars, played a prominent part in Islamic society as interpreters of Islamic tradition and law.

Decline of the Caliphate The Islamic empire began to splinter early. Disputes over the succession to the Prophet divided Muslims. Large parts of the Empire seceded. Military commanders (*amirs*) reduced the caliphs to figureheads. The last Abbasid caliph was when the Mongols sacked Baghdad in 1258.

IMAGE KEY

for pages 244–245

a. Mohammed, Abu Bakr and Ali travel to the Ukaz Fair, from Siyar-i-Nabi (Life of the Prophet) IV. 2, f. 132v. Ink, color, gold on paper, 1594–95. Spencer Collection, Astor, Lenox and Tilden Foundations.

b. Tenth century, earthenware bowl

c. The Ka'ba in Mecca

d. Recitation of the Muslim religion, written in black Sanskrit

e. Page from a Koran, 8th–9th century Kufic script.

f. The Great Mosque at Kairouan

g. Ritual worship, or prayer

h. Dome of the Rock

i. Spanish Umayyad mosque in Cordoba

REVIEW QUESTIONS

1. What was Arabian society like before the coming of Islam?

2. How do Islamic ideas about history, salvation, law, social justice, and other key issues compare with those of Christianity and Judaism?

3. To what extent were political and religious leadership separated in early Islam?

4. What explains the initial rapid conquests of the Arab armies?

5. What role did foreign traditions play during the high caliphate?

KEY TERMS

caliphate (p. 254)

emir (p. 254)

hadith (p. 261)

Hajj (p. 249)

Hegira (p. 247)

imam (p. 254)

islam (p. 247)

jihad (p. 252)

Ka'ba (p. 246)

Qur'an (p. 247)

Shi'a (p. 256)

Sunna (p. 257)

ulama (p. 255)

Umma (p. 247)

For additional study resources for this chapter, go to:
www.prenhall.com/craig/chapter11

12 The Byzantine Empire and Western Europe to 1000

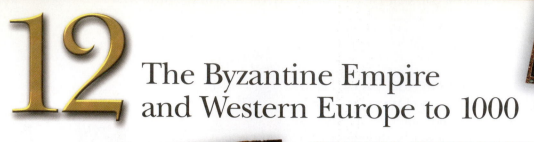

CHAPTER HIGHLIGHTS

The Byzantine Empire In the fifth century, Roman authority in the west collapsed under the impact of Germanic invasions. However, imperial power shifted to the eastern part of the Roman Empire, known as the Byzantine Empire. The Byzantine Empire would endure until 1453. The Byzantine Empire provided a model of civilized society to medieval Europe, helped protect it from Muslim invaders, and preserved much of classical learning.

The Islamic world also acted as a conduit for classical learning to the West, particularly in medicine, astronomy, and mathematics.

The Roman Church The church was the strongest and most prestigious institution in early medieval Europe where it filled the vacuum created by the collapse of Roman authority. Monasteries were an economic, political, and spiritual force throughout the West.

With the collapse of imperial authority in the West, the bishops of Rome, the popes, developed the doctrine of papal primacy by which they claimed supreme authority over church doctrine and the clergy. These claims were unacceptable in the East, where a separate Greek Orthodox Church developed under the control of the Byzantine emperors.

Charlemagne's Empire The Frankish ruler Charlemagne (r. 768–814) sought to re-create a universal Western empire and was crowned emperor by the pope in 800. Charlemagne formed a close alliance with the church and relied on churchmen as royal agents and administrators. His palace school at Aachen was the center of a modest renaissance of classical learning. After Charlemagne's death, his empire dissolved amid quarrels among his heirs, the revolts of powerful nobles, and invasions by Vikings, Magyars, and Muslims.

Feudal Society The Middle Ages were characterized by a chronic absence of central government and the constant threat of famine, disease, and invasion. Feudal society was one in which local lords offered security in return for allegiance from his dependents or vassals.

The feudal economy was organized and controlled through agrarian villages known as manors, worked by free peasants or by serfs.

CHAPTER QUESTIONS

HOW DID the Western Roman Empire end?

WHAT ROLE did the Byzantine Empire play in the history of Western Europe?

HOW DID the Islamic world influence medieval Western civilization?

WHAT WAS the doctrine of papal supremacy?

WHY DID Charlemagne's empire break up after his death?

WHAT IS a feudal society?

CHAPTER OUTLINE

THE BIRTH OF EUROPE
- The End of the Western Roman Empire
- The Byzantine Empire
- The Impact of Islam on East and West
- The Developing Roman Church
- The Kingdom of the Franks
- Feudal Society

The early Middle Ages marks the birth of Europe. Within what had been the northern and western provinces of the Roman Empire, Greco-Roman culture combined with Germanic culture and Christianity to create distinctive political and cultural forms. In government, religion, and language, as well as geography, these regions grew separate from the eastern Byzantine world and the Islamic Arab world that extended across North Africa from Spain to the eastern Mediterranean.

Surrounded and assailed from north, east, and south, western Europe became insular and stagnant, its people losing touch with classical, especially Greek, learning and science. They worked hard to develop their native resources, and the reign of Charlemagne saw a modest renaissance of antiquity. The social and political forms that emerged during this period—manorialism and feudalism—proved to be fertile seedbeds for the growth of distinctively Western institutions.

THE END OF THE WESTERN ROMAN EMPIRE

HOW DID the Western Roman Empire end?

*I*n the early fifth century, Italy and Rome suffered devastating blows. In 410, the Visigoths sacked the city of Rome. In 452, the Huns, led by Attila, invaded Italy. In 455, Rome was overrun by the Vandals.

By the mid-fifth century, power in western Europe had passed to barbarian chieftains. In 476, the barbarian Odovacer (ca. 434–493) deposed the last western emperor Romulus Augustulus. The eastern emperor Zeno (r. 474–491) recognized Odovacer as his western viceroy. But Zeno had little power to command in what had been the western empire, which by the end of the fifth century, was completely overrun by German barbarians (see Map 12-1).

The barbarians admired Roman culture and had no desire to destroy it. Except in Britain and northern Gaul, Roman law and government and Latin coexisted with the new Germanic institutions. Only the Vandals and the Anglo-Saxons refused to profess titular obedience to the emperor in Constantinople.

The Visigoths, the Ostrogoths, and the Vandals were followers of the Arian creed, which had been condemned at the Council of Nicea in 325 and was considered heretical in the west (see Chapter 6). Later, around 500, the Franks, who had settled in Gaul, would convert to the orthodox, or "Catholic," form of Christianity supported by the bishops of Rome. The Franks ultimately helped convert the other barbarians to Roman Christianity.

A gradual interpenetration of two strong cultures marked the period of the Germanic migrations. Despite western military defeat, the Goths and the Franks became far more romanized than the Romans were germanized. Latin, Nicene Christianity, and Roman law and government were to triumph in the west during the Middle Ages.

THE BYZANTINE EMPIRE

WHAT ROLE did the Byzantine Empire play in the history of Western Europe?

*A*s barbarian invaders overran the western half of the Roman Empire, its eastern half thrived under the rule of emperors who ruled from the city of Byzantium (modern Istanbul). Between 324 and 330, the emperor Constantine the Great rebuilt the city and renamed it Constantinople. It was regarded as the capital of the old Roman Empire, but its future was as the capital of a new Byzantine Empire. The term Byzantine indicates the Greek, Hellenistic Roman, and Judaic monotheistic elements that came, during the Middle Ages, to distinguish the culture of the East from the Latin West.

MAP EXPLORATION
Interactive map: To explore this map further, go to **http://www.prenhall.com/craig/map12.1**

MAP 12–1
Barbarian Migrations into the West in the Fourth and Fifth Centuries. The forceful intrusion of Germanic and non-Germanic tribes into the Empire from the last quarter of the fourth century through the fifth century made for a constantly changing pattern of movement and relations. The map shows the major routes taken by the usually unwelcome newcomers and the areas most deeply affected by the main groups.

WHICH PART of the Roman Empire was least affected by barbarian migrations?

The history of the Byzantine Empire divides into three periods:

1. From the founding of Constantinople in 324 to the spread of Islam in 632;

2. From 632 to the loss of Asia Minor to the Seljuk Turks in 1071 and the sack of Constantinople by Latin Cusaders in 1204; and

3. to the conquest of Constantinople and the Byzantine Empire by the Ottoman Turks in 1453.

THE REIGN OF JUSTINIAN

The first period of Byzantine history (324–632) was by far its greatest, and its pinnacle was the reign of the emperor Justinian (r. 527–565). He ruled with the assistance of his remarkable wife, Theodora. Born a commoner, Theodora had allegedly been a circus entertainer and a prostitute before attracting the emperor's eye. She equaled her husband in intelligence and may have exceeded him in toughness. In 532, when a riot threatened to overthrow their administration, she dissuaded him from flight and urged him to put down the rebellion by ordering the slaughter of tens of thousands of protesters.

QUICK REVIEW

Justinian Government
- *Corpus Juris Civilis* collated and revised Roman law
- Close ties between rulers and church
- Empire had many large cities and was the crossroads of Asian and European civilizations

Hagia Sophia. One of the greatest achievements of Byzantine civilization, Hagia Sophia (the church of Holy wisdom) was completed in 537 by Anthemius of Tralles and Isidone of Miletus. Circled with numerous windows, the great dome floods the hall with light and, together with the church's many other windows, mosaics, and open spaces, gives the interior a remarkable airiness and luminosity. With the Turkish conquest of Constantinople in 1453, Hagia Sophia was transformed into a mosque.

Hagia Sophia, Istanbul. Erich Lessing/Art Resource. N.Y.

Cities The strength of Justinian's empire was its more than 1,500 cities. The largest, Constantinople, was the crossroad of Asian and European cultures. It had about 350,000 inhabitants, and the larger provincial cities of its empire numbered approximately 50,000. These towns were administered at first by councils of wealthy local landowners, the *Decurions*. But being heavily taxed, they were prone to rebellion. Consequently, by the sixth century the emperor had replaced them with governors chosen for their loyalty to his person. Tighter central control was encouraged by the need to resist barbarian pressures on the empire from the north and east (see Map 12-2).

Law Justinian's policy—"one God, one empire, one religion"—was to centralize government by imposing legal and doctrinal conformity throughout his domain. To this end he ordered a codification of the mass of legal materials he had inherited from his predecessors. The result was the *Corpus Juris Civilis*, or "Body of Civil Law." It was organized in four parts. The *Code* revised imperial edicts issued by emperors since the reign of Hadrian (r. 117–138). The *Novellae*, or "New Things," dealt with decrees issued by emperors since 534, including Justinian. The *Digest* organized opinions penned by famous jurists, and the *Institutes* was a kind of text-book for young scholars. Because Roman law emphasized the authority of a single sovereign, rulers who struggled to centralize governments found Justinian's collection useful. Between the Renaissance and the 19th century, his code powerfully influenced the development of governments throughout Europe.

Avars, Slavs, and Bulgars   Justinian attempted to regain control of the western Roman Empire, but his success was partial and temporary. He reoccupied Italy, North Africa, and parts of Spain, but at a cost that his beleaguered empire could ill afford.

Avars, Slavs, and Bulgars, nomadic barbarian tribes, invaded the lands north and west of Constantinople in the sixth and seventh centuries. The Slavs were converted to Eastern Orthodoxy (Byzantine Christianity) by two learned missionaries sent from Constantinople: the future Saints Cyril and Methodius. They created a Greek-based alphabet adapted to writing the Slavic language.

MAP 12–2
The Byzantine Empire at the Death of Justinian.   The inset shows the Empire in 1025, before its losses to the Seljuq Turks.

WHY DID the Byzantine Empire suffer major territorial losses between the death of Justinian and the 11th century?

Emperor Justinian and His Attendants.
Mosaic in the Church of San VItale,
Ravenna, Italy, ca 547.

Scala/Art Resource, N.Y.

When the Bulgars conquered and absorbed the Slavs, this script was revised and is now known as Cyrillic or Old Church Slavonic. It facilitated the spread of Byzantine Christianity and culture in eastern Europe and Russia.

Persians and Muslims During the reign of the emperor Heraclius (r 610–641), Constantinople decidedly oriented itself toward the East. Heraclius spoke Greek, not Latin, and spent his reign combating Persian and Islamic invaders. The Persians were repulsed, but Heraclius suffered a defeat by the Muslims in 632 that cleared the way for them to overrun much of his empire. Not until the reign of Leo III (r. 717–740), founder of the Isaurian dynasty, did the Byzantines drive the Arab armies back and regain most of Asia Minor. Their larger Mediterranean empire, however, was gone forever.

The loss of territory required a restructuring of Constantinople's empire. The older hierarchical administration gave way to locally governed and garrisoned provincial strongholds headed by generals appointed by the emperor. This created a stronger, more flexible military defense for the remaining Byzantine lands.

In the 11th century, Constantinople again suffered major losses. The Muslim Seljuk Turks destroyed the imperial army at the battle of Manzikert in 1071 and then overran Asia Minor, the heartland from which Constantinople recruited its soldiers. This foreshadowed the inevitable fall of Constantinople, but in the interim the Byzantines and Muslims were distracted by the intervention in their affairs of Latin crusaders.

The Religious Diversity of Christendom Religious belief encouraged the unity of the Byzantine Empire, and religious controversy undermined it. Christianity was declared the empire's official faith in 391 and all other religions dismissed as "demented and insane." Emperors were crowned by the patriarch of Constantinople. Lavish endowments were provided for the church. It acted as the state's welfare agency, and its clergy were tightly bound to state service.

Although Christianity in one form or another was the dominant faith, large numbers of Jews lived within the Byzantine Empire. Roman law had protected them, so long as they did not proselytize Christians, but some Byzantine emperors tried to induce or to compel their conversion to Christianity. Neither approach was successful.

Despite the fact that the state religion was Orthodox Christianity, some Christian heresies attracted large followings and occasionally received imperial support. Justinian, for instance, was passionately orthodox, but his wife, the empress Theodora, was a Monophysite, a popular eastern variant of the faith, which the West regarded as a heresy. The Monophysites taught that Christ had a single, immortal nature and was not a union of eternal God and mortal man. The modern Coptic, Syrian, and Armenian churches endorse this belief.

The theological debates that thrived in the East were regarded with suspicion in the West. The West, for instance, rejected the Monophysites' view of Christ as incompatible with its understanding of the doctrine of the Trinity. It also disagreed with the east on interpretations of the Holy Spirit. To oppose Arian Christianity, which had spread among some German tribes, the western church insisted that the Holy Spirit proceeded from both the Father and the Son. This made it clear that the Son was not, as the Arians claimed, subordinate to the Father.

A dispute over the use of sacred images (icons) in worship, which erupted in the eighth century, further divided the east and west. In 726, Emperor Leo III (r. 717–741) forbade the use of images and icons by all Christians. His intention may have been to weaken the monastic owners of popular icons and to court populations influenced by Muslim and Jewish contempt for image worshipers. At any rate, his attack on traditional practices shocked the West and helped drive the Roman popes into an alliance with Europe's strongest emerging rulers, the Frankish kings. Constantinople underwent a spate of iconoclasm (destruction of icons) but reversed itself in the mid-ninth century and restored respect for sacred images.

If the Western church rejected eastern ideas, the Eastern church also dismissed beliefs that were winning popular support in the West. It denied the existence of Purgatory. It permitted the laity to divorce and to remarry. It allowed its priests, but not its bishops, to marry. It endorsed liturgies in vernacular languages. It also embraced Caesaropapism—an elevation of the emperor to sovereignty over the church as well as the state.

In 1054, these accumulating differences finally precipitated the formal separation of the western Catholic and the eastern Orthodox churches. The pope's

OVERVIEW   BARBARIAN INVASIONS OF THE WESTERN ROMAN EMPIRE

The Germanic tribes—the barbarians—who overran the Western Roman Empire had coexisted with the Romans for centuries in a relationship marked more by the commingling of cultures and by trade than by warfare. The arrival of the Huns from the east in the late fourth century, however, caused many of the tribes, beginning with the Visigoths in 376, to flee westward and seek refuge within the empire. They found the western half of the empire weakened by famine, disease, overtaxation, and an enfeebled military. The Romans lost control of their frontiers, and in the fifth century, the tribes overran the West and set up their own domains. The following is a list of the most important tribes and the areas they controlled by the year 500.

Tribes	Area of Control
Anglo-Saxons	most of England
Franks	northeast France
Burgundians	eastern-central France
Alemani	Switzerland
Visigoths	most of Spain and southern France
Suevi	northwest Spain
Vandals	North Africa
Ostrogoths	Italy, Austria, Croatia, Slovenia

HOW DID the Islamic world influence medieval Western civilization?

Religious Diversity. A Muslim and a Christian play the *ud* or lute together, from a 13th-century *Book of Chants* in the Escorial Monastery of Madrid. Medieval Europe was deeply influenced by Arab-Islamic culture, transmitted particularly through Spain. In music some of the many works in Arabic on musical theory were translated into Latin and Hebrew, but the main influence came from the actual arts of singing and playing spread by minstrels.

A Moor and a Christian playing the lute, miniature in a book of music from the 'Cantigas' of Alfonso X 'the Wise' (1221–84). Thirteenth century (manuscript). Monastero de El Escorial, El Escorial, Spain/Index/Bridgeman Art Library.

envoy, Cardinal Humbertus, who was sent to Constantinople to try to resolve some of the points in contention, excommunicated his Eastern colleagues, and they in turn condemned the West. The result was a breach that remained until 1965, when a Roman pope met with the patriarch of Constantinople to revoke the mutual medieval condemnations.

THE IMPACT OF ISLAM ON EAST AND WEST

A new drama began to unfold for the West in the seventh century with the rise of Islam (see Chapter 11). By the middle of the eighth century, Arabs had conquered the southern and eastern Mediterranean coastline and occupied parts of Spain. Assaulted from east and west, Christian Europe developed a lasting fear of the Muslims. In 718, the Byzantine Emperor Leo III halted the Muslim advance on Constantinople and began a counteroffensive that, during the next several centuries, pushed the Arabs back. In 732, the Franks defeated the Arabs near Tours (in central France), but Muslims preserved their hold on Andalusia, which they had taken from the Visigoths in 711, for another 700 years. Although the momentum of the Muslim advance was broken, the Mediterranean had become (and until the mid-11th century remained) something of a Muslim lake. The center of evolving European civilization shifted north away from the sea, but positive contacts between Muslims and Christians did not end. Western trade with the East continued to be important.

THE WESTERN DEBT TO ISLAM

The Arab invasions during the early Middle Ages helped western Europe develop a unique civilization of its own. Arab belligerence forced western Europeans to fall back on and exploit the cultural potential of their own resources: their Germanic tribal, Judeo-Christian, and Greco-Roman heritages. By diverting the energies of the Byzantine Empire, the Arabs also prevented Constantinople from expanding into western Europe. This gave the Frankish and the Lombard kingdoms an opportunity to establish themselves.

Despite hostilities, a creative interchange developed between the Christian West and the Muslim world. The backward West stood to gain most from this, for Arab civilization was enjoying its golden age. Moorish Cordoba was a model multicultural city and a conduit through which Arab products and ideas reached Europe. The Arabs taught Western farmers how to irrigate fields and Western artisans how to tan leather and refine silk. Arabic scholars passed on knowledge of ancient Greek works on astronomy, mathematics, and medicine. Jewish scholars also thrived. The era produced numerous major researchers, thinkers, and poets whose influence was far-reaching.

THE DEVELOPING ROMAN CHURCH

Throughout this period in which most of the institutions of the old Roman Empire decline, one gained in strength: the Christian church. As the Western empire crumbled, local bishops and cathedral chapters (ruling bodies of clergy) filled the resulting vacuum of leadership. The local cathedral became the center of urban life and the local bishop the highest authority for those who remained in Europe's shrinking cities. German leaders, who struggled to found new kingdoms amid the ruins of the empire, discovered that the Christian church was a valuable repository of Roman administrative skills and classical culture. The church also had a religious message of providential purpose and individual worth that could give solace and meaning to life at a time when encouragement was desperately needed. The church's ritual of baptism and creed united people across traditional barriers of class, education, and gender. And alone in the West, the church retained an effective, if somewhat scattered, hierarchical administration. It was staffed by the best-educated minds in Europe, and it centered on Rome, whose bishop had stepped into the vacancy created by the departure of emperors.

MONASTIC CULTURE

Monasticism provided a major support for Europe's Christian faith throughout the early medieval period. The first monks were hermits, such as Anthony of Egypt (ca. 251–356), who felt compelled to withdraw from society and give up all worldly attachments to pursue a purely spiritual life. So many people were attracted to the movement the hermits began that communal organizations had to be devised to serve them. Pachomius (ca. 286–436), another Egyptian, founded some of the earliest of these. The monastic life, which was guided by the biblical "counsels of perfection" (chastity, poverty, and obedience), came to be regarded as the purest form of religious practice.

The extreme asceticism of the early hermits was soon tempered by men who had a different vision of what was required to live a life in imitation of Christ. Basil the Great (329–379), whose rule (regulations to govern a monastery) spread widely throughout the East, urged monks to leave their protected enclaves and serve the needs of others by caring for orphans, widows, and the infirm.

Benedict of Nursia (ca. 480–547) devised the rule that became popular in western Europe. In 529, he established a monastery at Monte Cassino, in Italy. It became the mother-house of the Benedictine order of monks. His *Rule for Monasteries* defined a regimented but humane way of life for monks. Benedictine monasteries were hierarchically organized under an abbot. His command was beyond question, but he was to care for his subordinates—discouraging extreme asceticism and making sure that they had adequate, if simple, food and clothing. The Benedictine Rule also deceed that monks should do manual labor to support themselves and set aside time for study. The pattern of life in Benedictine houses followed a cycle of periods for prayer, study, and labor. Monasteries were organized for self-sufficiency. Therefore, they did a better job than most late Roman institutions of surviving the decline of the empire. In the wake of the barbarian invasions, Benedictine missionaries were equipped to begin the process of Christianizing England and Germany. Their disciplined organization and devotion to hard work made the Benedictines an economic and political power as well as a spiritual force. The

6.8 St. Benedict

Major Political and Religious Developments of the Early Middle Ages

313	Emperor Constantine issues the Edict of Milan
325	Council of Nicea defines Christian doctrine
410	Rome invaded by Visigoths under Alaric
413–426	St. Augustine writes *The City of God*
451–453	Europe invaded by the Huns under Attila
476	Barbarian Odovacer deposes western emperor and rules as king of the Romans
488	Theodoric establishes kingdom of Ostrogoths in Italy
529	St. Benedict founds monastery at Monte Cassino
533	Justinian codifies Roman law
732	Charles Martel defeats Arabs at Tours
754	Pope Stephen II and Pepin III ally

apostolic primacy Doctrine that the popes are the direct successors to the Apostle Peter and as such heads of the church.

plenitude of power Teaching that the popes have power over all other bishops of the church.

schools and libraries that survived within the shelter of their walls played a major role in the rescue and revival of medieval Europe's literary culture.

THE DOCTRINE OF PAPAL PRIMACY

The Eastern emperors treated the Byzantine church like a department of the state, but their power did not reach to Rome, whose bishops resisted royal intervention. Their doctrine of "papal primacy," which declared the Roman pontiff supreme within the church, gave him the power to define doctrine and command the clergy. This doctrine also enabled the pope to make important secular claims, leading to repeated conflicts between church and state, pope and emperor, throughout the Middle Ages.

Pope Damasus I (366–384) laid the foundation for papal claims to absolute authority by asserting Rome's **apostolic primacy**. He pointed to Jesus' words to Peter in the Gospel of Matthew (16:18): "Thou art Peter, and upon this rock I will build my church." Because tradition maintained that Peter was the first bishop of Rome and that he died there, Damasus insisted that Rome's popes, Peter's successors, were heirs to the role Jesus had decreed for Peter. Pope Leo I (440–461) assumed the title *pontifex maximus*—"supreme priest" and laid claim to a "**plenitude of power**," supremacy over all other bishops in the church. Pope Gelasius I (492–496) stated that the authority of the clergy was "more weighty" than the power of kings, for priests were given charge over divine affairs.

DIVISION OF CHRISTENDOM

The division of Christendom into Eastern (Byzantine) and Western (Roman Catholic) churches arose in the early Middle Ages in response in part to linguistic and cultural differences between the Greek East and the Roman West. In both regions, church organization closely followed the structure of the secular state. A "patriarch" ruled over "metropolitans" and "archbishops" in the cities and provinces, and they in turn ruled over bishops, who ruled the local clergy. A novel combination of Greek, Roman, and Asian elements, however, shaped Byzantine culture, giving Eastern Christianity more of a mystical orientation and a greater preoccupation with the hereafter than Western Christianity. This difference in outlook may have predisposed Eastern patriarchs to submit more readily to royal intervention in their affairs than Western popes ever would.

Three major factors lay behind the religious break that separated the Eastern and Western churches in 1054. The first revolved around questions of doctrinal authority. The Eastern church put more stress on the authority of the Bible and ecumenical councils of the church to define Christian doctrine than on the decrees of the bishop of Rome. The claims of Roman popes were unacceptable to the East. A second factor was the western addition of the *filioque* clause to the Nicene Creed. According to this anti-Arian clause, the Holy Spirit proceeds "also from the Son" (*filioque*) as well as from the Father, making clear the western belief that Christ was fully one essence with God the Father and not a lesser being. The third factor dividing the Eastern and Western churches was the iconoclastic controversy of the eighth century. As noted earlier, when the Byzantine Emperor Leo III (r. 717–741) ordered western popes to abolish the use of images in their churches, he met fierce resistance. In 754, Pope Stephen II (752–757) solved two problems at one time. He enlisted the aid of the Franks and their ruler, Pepin III, against his Italian enemies, the Lombards, and used this alliance with the Franks as a counterweight to the influence of the Eastern emperor. Cooperation between Roman pope and Frankish king chartered a new course for Western history.

THE KINGDOM OF THE FRANKS

MEROVINGIANS AND CAROLINGIANS: FROM CLOVIS TO CHARLEMAGNE

Clovis (ca. 466–511), a chieftain who converted to orthodox Christianity around 496, founded the first Frankish dynasty, the Merovingians. Clovis and his successors gave the Franks a major role in the recovery of western Europe. The territory under their control included modern France, Belgium, the Netherlands, and western Germany. In attempting to govern this extensive kingdom, the Merovingians encountered the most persistent problem of medieval political history—the competing claims of the "one" and the "many," the struggle of a lone king to impose centralized government on local magnates.

The Merovingian kings addressed this problem by making pacts with the landed nobility and creating officials called *counts*. The men they appointed as counts had no personal powerbases in the regions they governed and were, therefore, presumed to be dependent on and loyal to the king. But like local landed aristocrats, the Merovingian counts soon laid claim to authority in their own names, and the Frankish kingdom fragmented into independent, tiny principalities. This tendency was aggravated by the Frankish custom of dividing the kingdom among the king's legitimate male heirs.

By the seventh century, the Frankish king had no effective authority left. Real power was concentrated in the office of the mayor of the palace, who was the spokesman at the king's court for the great landowners. The Carolingian dynasty used this office to rise to power and unseat the Merovingians.

The Carolingians (named for the dynasty's greatest ruler, Carolus, later known as Charlemagne, or Charles the Great) controlled the office of the mayor of the palace from the ascent to that post of Pepin I (d. 639) until 751, when, with the connivance of the pope, they expropriated the Frankish crown. Pepin II (d. 714) was king in fact if not in title over the Frankish realm. His son, Charles Martel ("the Hammer," d. 741), created a great cavalry by bestowing lands (*benefices* or *fiefs*) on nobles in exchange for their military service. The army he created checked the Arabs at Tours in 732.

The fiefs bestowed by Charles Martel came in large part from land usurped from the church. The Carolingians chose their counts almost entirely from the

Scribes at work. During the Carolingian Renaissance, scholars made editions of the works of Gregory the Great, shown here in a monastic scriptorium (an area devoted to copying and preserving books) receiving the divine word from a dove perched on his shoulder. Below St. Gregory three monks are shown writing. Note the inkwell held by the middle monk. Before the invention of the printing press in about 1450, manuscripts could only be duplicated by laborious hand copying. Much of this painstaking work was done by monks.
Kunsthistorisches Museum, Vienna.

WHY DID Charlemagne's Empire break up after his death?

fief Land granted to a vassal in exchange for services, usually military.

ranks of the landed nobility. The Merovingians had tried to compete with these great aristocrats by raising landless men to power, but this strategy had failed. By playing to strength rather than challenging it, the Carolingians empowered themselves, at least for the short term. The church had little choice but to tolerate the seizure of its lands to support the army that defended Christian Europe from Muslim attack.

Frankish Church   The church, particularly its monasteries, played a large role in the Frankish government. Many monasteries had rich landed estates, and their abbots were wealthy, powerful magnates. The higher clergy were employed as royal agents, and the Carolingians used the missionary clergy to pacify the tribes whose lands they conquered. Christian bishops became lords, appointed by and subject to the king.

In 751 Pope Zacharias (741–752) sanctioned the deposition of the last of the Merovingians, and Pepin III was proclaimed king by the nobility in council Zacharias's successor, When Pope Stephen II (752–757) was driven from Rome in 753 by the Lombards, he appealed to Pepin to cast out the invaders and guarantee papal claims to rule central Italy, a region then under the jurisdiction of the eastern emperor. In 754, the Franks and the church allied against the Lombards and the eastern emperor. Carolingian kings officially became the protectors of the Catholic Church. Pepin was proclaimed *patricius Romanorum*, "father-protector of the Romans," a title heretofore borne by the representative of the Eastern emperor. In 755, the Franks defeated the Lombards and gave the pope the lands surrounding Rome. This created a political entity called the **Papal States**. During this time the papacy began to circulate a fraudulent document, *Donation of Constantine*, which was intended to prove to the Franks that the church was the heir to the legacy of Rome's empire. It was exposed as a forgery in the 15th century.

The papacy had looked to the Franks to protect it from the Eastern emperors. But the Carolingian dynasty drew almost as slight a boundary between state and church as did Eastern emperors. Although preferable to Eastern domination, Carolingian patronage of the church proved to be no less constraining.

REIGN OF CHARLEMAGNE (768–814)

Charlemagne, son of Pepin the Short, continued his father's policies. He served as papal protector in Italy and pursued the conquest of additional territory in the north. In 774 Charlemagne defeated the Lombards of northern Italy and assumed their crown The subjugation of neighboring pagan tribes, especially the Saxons whom the Franks Christianized and dispersed, brought more of Europe under his control. The Danubian plains were drawn into the Frankish orbit by a war that routed the Avars. The Arabs were chased beyond the Pyrenees. By the time of his death on January 28, 814, Charlemagne's kingdom embraced modern France, Belgium, Holland, Switzerland, almost all of Germany, much of Italy, and part of Spain (see Map 12–3).

The New Empire   Charlemagne aspired to recognition as emperor. To support his case, he constructed a palace city, Aachen, in imitation of the courts of the ancient Roman and the Eastern emperors. He treated the church with a paternalism almost as great as that of any Eastern emperor and used it to help build his empire. Frankish Christians professed the Nicene Creed (with the

Papal States   Territory in central Italy ruled by the pope until 1870.

MAP 12–3

The Empire of Charlemagne to 814. Building on the successes of his predecessors, Charlemagne greatly increased the Frankish domains. Such traditional enemies as the Saxons and the Lombards fell under his sway.

HOW DOES the extent of Charlemagne's Empire compare with that of the Roman Empire in the west?

filioque clause the emperor endorsed) and were taught by their clergy to revere Charlemagne.

On Christmas Day 800, Pope Leo III (795–816) crowned Charlemagne emperor. This event created what would later be called the Holy Roman Empire, a revival (confined after 870 largely to Germany) of the old Roman Empire in the West. The coronation benefited both the church and Charlemagne. Before his coronation, Charlemagne had been a minor Western potentate in the eyes of

Charlemagne. An equestrian figure of Charlemagne (or possibly one of his sons) from the early ninth century.

Bronze equestrian statuette of Charlemagne, from Metz Cathedral, 9th–10th century 3/4 view. Louvre, Paris, France. Copyright Bridgeman-Giraudon/Art Resource, N.Y.

7.5
The Missi Domenici

Eastern emperors. After the coronation, Eastern emperors reluctantly recognized his new imperial dignity.

The New Emperor   Charlemagne was a physically daunting man. An examination of his remains conducted in 1861 verified that he was six feet, three and one half inches tall. Contemporary witnesses describe him as athletic, energetic, restless, and ever ready for a hunt or a swim in Aachen's hot springs. Informal and gregarious, he was known for his humor and hospitality. Aachen was a festive palace city to which people and gifts came from all over the world. Baghdad's famous caliph, Harun-al-Rashid once honored him with a truly imperial present—a white elephant.

Charlemagne had a series of five official wives by whom he sired numerous children. This created problems. His oldest son, Pepin grew jealous of the attention he gave to the sons of his second wife and joined in a conspiracy against him. The plot was exposed, and Pepin was confined to a monastery for the rest of his life.

Problems of Government   Charlemagne governed his kingdom through counts, strategically located within the administrative districts into which the kingdom was divided. Carolingian counts tended to be local magnates who already had armed followings and the self-interest to enforce the will of the king. Their three main duties were to maintain a local army loyal to the king, to collect tribute and dues, and to administer justice. They discharged this last responsibility through a district law court known as the *mallus.* The court heard testimony, passed judgment, and assessed a monetary compensation to be paid to injured parties.

Many counts used their official position and judicial powers to their own advantage. They set themselves up as local despots and claimed the land grants with which they were paid as hereditary possessions, not loans that the emperor could cancel. Charlemagne tried to supervise his officials by dispatching royal envoys, the *missi dominici,* to visit their counties and report on how they were discharging their duties. But this policy had minimal effect. The king appointed various kinds of provincial governors with titles like prefect, duke, or margrave, but none of them was incorruptible.

Charlemagne never solved the problem of creating a loyal bureaucracy. His ecclesiastical agents had the same responsibilities, secular lifestyles, and aspirations as his counts. Except for duties involving liturgy and prayers, they were indistinguishable from the lay nobility. Capitularies, or royal decrees, discouraged the more outrageous behavior of the clergy. But Charlemagne also sensed that reform-minded ecclesiastical landowners could, for different reasons, undercut royal authority. Charlemagne treated his bishops as vassals who served at his pleasure.

Alcuin and the Carolingian Renaissance   Charlemagne used some of his wealth to encourage a revival of literacy and learning. His generous patronage brought notable scholars, such as his biographer Einhard (ca. 770–840) and

Alcuin of York (735–804), director of his palace school, to Aachen. There, they set about developing a court culture and a new educational program. Their labors were richly rewarded. Alcuin's classical and Christian learning earned him the income from several wealthy monasteries.

Although Charlemagne appreciated learning for its own sake, his palace school was intended to upgrade the administrative skills of his officials by providing training in the basic tools of bureaucrats: reading, writing, speaking, logic, and counting. To this end Charlemagne's scholars created a new, clear, standardized style of handwriting—Carolingian minuscule—and fostered the use of accurate Latin in official documents. These developments helped increase lay literacy. Alcuin created a genuine community of scholars and clerics at court and infused the highest administrative levels with a sense of comradeship and common purpose.

The result was a modest renaissance, or rebirth, of interest in antiquity at the palace school. Its scholars collected and preserved ancient manuscripts and attempted to immitate the styles and forms employed by classic authors. These scholarly activities served official efforts to bring uniformity to church law and liturgy, educate the clergy, and elevate spiritual life.

The Manor and Serfdom   The agrarian economy of the Middle Ages was organized and controlled through village farms known as **manors**. Here peasants labored as farmers in subordination to a lord, that is, a more powerful landowner who gave them land and a dwelling in exchange for their services and a portion of their crops. The land farmed by the peasants for the lord was the **demesne**, about one-quarter to one-third of the arable land. All crops grown there belonged to the lord.

manors   Village farms owned by a lord.

demesne   Part of a manor that was cultivated directly for the lord of the manor.

Moldboard plow.   The invention of the moldboard plow greatly improved farming. The heavy plow cut deeply into the ground and furrowed it. This illustration from the Luttrell Psalter (ca. 1340) also shows that the traction harness, which lessened the strangulation effect of the yoke on the animals, had not yet been adopted. Indeed, one of the oxen seems to be on the verge of choking.

The British Library/The Art Archive.

Peasants were treated according to their social status and the size of their land holdings. A freeman—that is, a peasant with his own modest property—became a **serf** by surrendering his property to a lord in exchange for protection and assistance. The freeman received his land back from the lord with a clear definition of his economic and legal rights. Although the land was no longer his property, he had full possession and use of it and could not be separated from it. The services and goods he was to supply to the lord were also spelled out. Peasants who had little real property to bargain with ended up as unfree serfs and were more vulnerable to the lord's demands. Impoverished peasants were the most vulnerable to abuse.

Serfs were subject to dues in kind. They owed firewood for cutting wood in the lord's forests, sheep for grazing their sheep on the lord's land, and the like. The lord, who furnished shacks and small plots of land from his vast domain, had an army of servants who provided him with everything from eggs to boots. Many serfs were discontented and fled their lords hoping to find better deals under new masters.

By the time of Charlemagne, the moldboard plow, which was needed in northern Europe where the soil was heavy, and the **three-field system** were coming into use. These developments improved agricultural productivity. The moldboard cut deep into the soil and turned it to form a ridge, providing a natural drainage system as well as permitting deep planting. Unlike the earlier two-field system, which alternated fallow with planted fields each year, the three-field system increased the amount of cultivated land by leaving only one-third fallow.

Religion and the Clergy   As owners of the churches on their lands, the lords had the right to chose serfs to serve as priests for the parishes on their estates. Church law directed the lord to set a serf free before he entered the clergy, but lords preferred a "serf priest," one who not only said Mass but continued to serve his lord. Frankish lords cultivated a docile parish clergy.

Ordinary people baptized themselves and their children, confessed the Creed at mass, tried to learn the Lord's Prayer, and hoped to receive last rites from the priest at death. Local priests were no better educated than their congregations, and instruction in Christian doctrine remained at a minimum.

BREAKUP OF THE CAROLINGIAN KINGDOM

In his last years, Charlemagne knew that his empire was becoming ungovernable. The seeds of dissolution lay in the determination of each locality to protect its self-interests. In medieval society, a direct relationship existed between physical proximity to authority and loyalty. Local people obeyed local lords more than a distant king, and Charlemagne had courted the support of regional magnates by enhancing their power.

Louis the Pious   Charlemagne's successor, Louis the Pious (r. 814–840), had three sons by his first wife; according to Salic or Germanic law, a ruler partitioned his kingdom equally among his surviving sons. Louis tried to break this tradition by making his eldest son, Lothar (d. 855), coregent and sole imperial heir in 817. To Lothar's brothers he gave lesser appanages, or hereditary lands.

serfs   Peasants tied to the land they tilled.

three-field system   Medieval innovation that increased the amount of land under cultivation by leaving only one-third fallow in a given year.

Pepin (d. 838) became king of Aquitaine, and Louis "the German" (d. 876) became king of Bavaria over the eastern Franks.

In 823, Louis's second wife, Judith of Bavaria, bore him a fourth son, Charles (d. 877). Determined that her son should receive more than just a nominal inheritance, the queen incited Pepin and Louis to war against Lothar, and persuaded Louis to divide the kingdom equally among his four living sons. The pope had an important stake in the preservation of the revived Western empire and the imperial title, which Louis's partition of his kingdom threatened to undo. The pope, therefore, restored Lothar to his inheritance, but he could not prevent Lothar's brothers from renewing war against him.

The Treaty of Verdun and Its Aftermath In 843, with the Treaty of Verdun, the Carolingian Empire was partitioned into three equal parts. Lothar received a middle section, which embraced modern Holland, Belgium, Switzerland, Alsace-Lorraine, and Italy; Charles the Bald received roughly modern France; and Louis the German got territory approximating modern Germany (see Map 12–4). This terminated the universal empire to which Charlemagne and Louis the Pious aspired.

MAP 12–4
The Treaty of Verdun (843) and the Treaty of Mersen (870). The Treaty of Verdun divided the kingdom of Louis the Pious among his three feuding children: Charles the Bald, Lothar, and Louis the German. After Lothar's death in 855, the middle kingdom was so weakened by division among his three sons that Charles the Bald and Louis the German divided it between themselves in the Treaty of Mersen.

HOW DID the division of the Carolingian Empire lay the basis for modern nation states?

The Treaty of Verdun proved to be only the beginning of Carolingian fragmentation. When Lothar died in 855, his kingdom was divided among his three surviving sons. Henceforth, Western Europe would be split between eastern and western Frankish kingdoms—roughly Germany and France—perpetually at war to claim portions of the fractionalized middle kingdom. The contest continued into modern times.

Vikings, Magyars, and Muslims   The political breakdown of the Carolingian Empire coincided with new external threats. In the late 9th and 10th centuries, waves of Normans (North men), better known as Vikings, swept into Europe from Scandinavia. *Vikings* was a catchall term for Scandinavians who visited Europe to trade and raid. Their rugged ocean-going longboats enabled them to threaten the coastal and river towns of the continent and British Isles. Danes penetrated as far as Paris in the ninth century. Other Vikings established themselves in northern England and Ireland. They colonized Greenland and appear to have explored the shores of New England 500 years before Columbus sailed. Their foreign adventures continued into the 11th century.

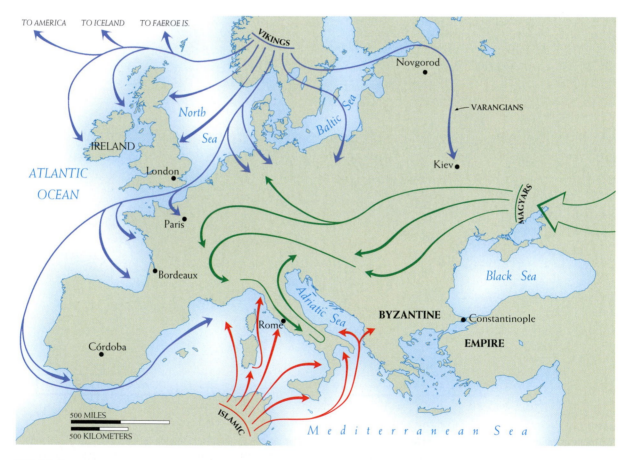

MAP 12–5

Viking, Muslim, and Magyar Invasions to the 11th Century.   Western Europe was sorely beset by new waves of outsiders from the 9th to the 11th century. From north, east, and south, a stream of invading Vikings, Magyars, and Muslims brought the West at times to near collapse and of course gravely affected institutions within Europe.

HOW DID early medieval Europe respond to invasions?

Magyars, or Hungarians, likewise swept in from the eastern plains, while Muslims made incursions from North Africa (see Map 12–5). The Franks built fortified towns and castles as refuges or bought off the invaders with land and silver. In this turmoil, local populations became more dependent on local strongmen, creating the precondition for feudal society.

FEUDAL SOCIETY

The Middle Ages were characterized by a chronic absence of effective central government and the constant threat of famine, disease, and invasion. The true lords were those who could guarantee protection from rapine and starvation. *Feudal society* refers to the social, political, military, and economic system that emerged in these circumstances. It is a social order in which a regional prince or a local lord is dominant, and society is held together by trust in pledges of fidelity. In a feudal society, people require the assurance that others can be depended on in time of need. It is a system of mutually recognized rights and responsibilities.

During the early Middle Ages, the landed nobility ruled over their domains as miniature kingdoms. They maintained their own armies and courts, regulated local tolls, and even minted their own coins. Large groups of warrior **vassals** were created by bestowals of land, and these constituted a professional military class with its own code of conduct. In feudal society, serfs worked the land, the clergy prayed and gave counsel, and lords and knights maintained law and order.

ORIGINS

The origins of feudal government can be found in the divisions and conflicts of Merovingian society when freemen began placing themselves under the protection of more powerful men. The latter became local magnates, and the former solved the problem of survival. Freeman who so entrusted themselves to others or gave themselves to the king came to be described as *vassi* ("those who serve"), from which evolved the term *vassalage*, meaning to pledge oneself to the personal service of someone who promises protection.

Landed nobles, like kings, tried to acquire as many vassals as they could, because military strength lay in numbers. To maintain these growing armies, they were granted land, which came to be known as a *benefice*, or a *fief*. Vassals were expected to dwell on it and maintain their accouterments of war in good order.

VASSALAGE AND THE FIEF

Vassalage involved **fealty** to the lord. To swear fealty was to promise not to act against the lord's well-being and to perform personal services for him whenever requested. Chief among the expected services was military duty as a mounted knight. Continuous bargaining and bickering occurred over the terms of service.

Limitations were placed on the number of days a lord could require services from a vassal. In France in the 11th century, about 40 days of service per year were considered sufficient. Vassals could also buy their way out of military service by a monetary payment known as *scutage*. The lord, in turn, used this payment to hire mercenaries. The vassal was also expected to give the lord advice and to sit as a member of his court.

Magyars Majority ethnic group in Hungary.

WHAT IS a feudal society?

feudal society Social, political, military, and economic system that prevailed in the Middle Ages and beyond in some parts of Europe.

vassal Person granted an estate or cash payments in return for accepting the obligation to render services to a lord.

fealty Oath of loyalty by a vassal to a lord, promising to perform specified services.

The lord's obligations to his vassals were specific. He was obligated to protect the vassal from physical harm and to stand as his advocate. After fealty was sworn and homage paid, the lord bestowed a benefice, or fief. The fief was the physical or material wherewithal to meet the vassal's obligations. It could take the form of liquid wealth. Money fiefs empowered a vassal to receive regular payments from the lord's treasury. Normally, however, the fief consisted of a landed estate or a castle.

In Carolingian times, a benefice varied in size from one or more small villas to several *mansi* of 25 to 48 acres. The king's vassals received benefices of at least 30 and as many as 200 such mansi. Royal vassalage with a benefice was widely sought by the highest classes of Carolingian society; however, it proved deadly to the king. Although Carolingian kings guarded their rights over property granted in benefice to vassals, vassals were still free to dispose of their benefices as they pleased. Vassals of the king, in turn, created their own vassals. These vassals created still further vassals of their own—vassals of vassals of vassals—in a reverse pyramiding effect that by the late ninth century fragmented both land and authority from the highest to the lowest levels.

Beginning with the reign of Louis the Pious (r. 814–840), bishops and abbots swore fealty and received their offices from the king as a benefice. The king invested these clerics with a ring and a staff, the symbols of high spiritual office. Lay investiture would eventually provoke a great confrontation between church and state (see "Bishop Fulbert Describes Obligations of Vassals and Lords").

Carolingian Dynasty (751–987)

751	Pepin III "the Short" becomes king of the Franks
755	Franks drive Lombards out of central Italy; creation of Papal States
768–814	Charlemagne rules as king of the Franks
774	Charlemagne defeats Lombards in northern Italy
750–800	Fraudulent *Donation of Constantine* created in an effort to counter Frankish domination of church
800	Pope Leo III crowns Charlemagne
814–840	Louis the Pious succeeds Charlemagne as "Emperor"
843	Treaty of Verdun partitions the Carolingian Empire
870	Treaty of Mersen further divides Carolingian Empire
875–950	Invasions by Vikings, Muslims, and Magyars
962	Ottonian dynasty succeeds Carolingian in Germany
987	Capetian dynasty succeeds Carolingian in France

FRAGMENTATION AND DIVIDED LOYALTY

Occupation of the land led to claims of hereditary possession. Hereditary possession became legally recognized in the ninth century and laid the basis for claims to real ownership. Further, to accumulate as much land as possible, one man could become a vassal to several different lords. This led in the ninth century to the concept of a "liege lord"—one master whom the vassal must obey even to the harm of the others, should a direct conflict among them arise.

The problem of loyalty was reflected in the ceremonial development of the act by which a freeman became a vassal. In the mid-eighth century, an "oath of fealty" highlighted the ceremony. A vassal reinforced his promise of fidelity to the lord by swearing a special oath with his hand on a sacred relic or the Bible. In the 10th and 11th centuries, paying homage also involved placing the vassal's hands between the lord's and sealing the ceremony with a kiss.

Despite their limitations and risks, feudal arrangements provided stability in the early Middle Ages and aided the process of political centralization during the High Middle Ages. Feudal government was adaptable. The foundations of the modern nation-state would emerge in France and England from fine-tuning feudal arrangements as kings sought to adapt their goal of centralized government to local power and control.

HISTORY'S VOICES

BISHOP FULBERT DESCRIBES OBLIGATIONS OF VASSALS AND LORDS

Trust held the lord and vassal together. Their duties in this regard were carefully defined. Here are six general rules for vassal and lord, laid down by Bishop Fulbert of Chartres in a letter to William, Duke of Aquitaine, in 1020.

WHAT ARE the respective obligations of vassal and lord? Do they seem fair for each side? Why might a vassal have more responsibilities and a lord fewer?

He who swears fealty to his lord ought always to have these six things in memory: what is harmless, safe, honorable, useful, easy, practicable. Harmless, that is to say, that he should not injure his lord in his body; safe, that he should not injure him by betraying his secrets or the defenses upon which he relies for his safety; honorable, that he should not injure him in his possessions; easy and practicable, that that good which his lord is able to do easily he make not difficult, nor that which is practicable he make not impossible to him.

That the faithful vassal should avoid these injuries is certainly proper, but not for this alone does he deserve his holding; for it is not sufficient to abstain from evil, unless what is good is done also. It remains, therefore, that in the same six things mentioned above he should faithfully counsel and aid his lord, if he wishes to be looked upon as worthy of this benefice and to be safe concerning the fealty which he has sworn.

The lord also ought to act toward his faithful vassal reciprocally in all these things. And if he does not do this, he will be justly considered guilty of bad faith, just as the former, if he should be detected in avoiding or consenting to the avoidance of his duties, would be perfidious and perjured.

Source: James Harvey Robinson, ed., *Readings in European History*, Vol. 1 (Boston: Athenaeum, 1904), p. 184.

SUMMARY

The Byzantine Empire   In the fifth century, Roman authority in the west collapsed under the impact of Germanic invasions. However, imperial power shifted to the eastern part of the Roman Empire—known as the Byzantine Empire—with its capital at Constantinople. The Byzantine Empire would endure until the Ottoman Turks captured Constantinople in 1453. The peak of Byzantine power occurred during the reign of Justinian (527–565), one of whose major achievements was the *Corpus Juris Civilis*, a codification of Roman law on which most European law was based until the 19th century. The Byzantine Empire provided a model of civilized society to medieval Europe, helped protect it from Muslim invaders, and preserved much of classical learning.

The Islamic world also acted as a conduit for classical learning to West, particularly in medicine, astronomy, and mathematics.

The Roman Church   The church was the strongest and most prestigious institution in early medieval Europe where it filled the vacuum created by the collapse of Roman authority. Monastic culture was especially strong. The greatest organizer of Western monasticism was St. Benedict of Nursia (480–547). Benedictine monasteries were an economic, political, and spiritual force throughout the West.

IMAGE KEY

for pages 264–265

a. An illustration from the Luttrell Psalter (ca.1340)

b. A vassal

c. Book of Kells: St. Matthew, Chi Rho initial.

d. Reliquary of the True Cross, Constantinople, c.960

e. Byzantine empress Theodora with ladies of the court

f. Non-Ptolemaic model for the motions of sun, moon and planets

g. The coronation of Charlemagne by Pope Leo III in Rome

h. Bronze equestrian statuette of Charlemagne

i. The Hagia Sophia, exterior

j. The Hagia Sophia, interior

k. Relief of a monastic scriptorium

With the collapse of imperial authority in the West, the bishops of Rome, the popes, developed the doctrine of papal primacy by which they claimed supreme authority over church doctrine and the clergy. These claims were unacceptable in the East, where a separate Greek Orthodox Church developed under the control of the Byzantine emperors.

Charlemagne's Empire The Frankish ruler Charlemagne (r. 768–814) sought to recreate a universal Western empire and was crowned emperor by the pope in 800. Charlemagne's realm embraced modern France, Belgium, Holland, and Switzerland, most of Germany, and parts of Italy and Spain. He formed a close alliance with the church and relied on churchmen as royal agents and administrators. His palace school at Aachen was the center of a modest renaissance of classical learning under scholars such as Alcuin of York (735–804).

Yet, despite his efforts at administrative control, Charlemagne's empire proved to be ungovernable. Charlemagne had increased the power of local lords whose support he needed to rule, but their power and wealth became so great that they were able to put their self-interests above royal authority. After Charlemagne's death, his empire dissolved amid quarrels among his heirs, revolts of powerful nobles, and invasions by Vikings, Magyars, and Muslims.

Feudal Society The Middle Ages were characterized by a chronic absence of central government and the constant threat of famine, disease, and invasion. Lords were those who could guarantee protection under these conditions. Feudal society was one in which a local lord is dominant and offers security in return for allegiance from his dependents or vassals. It was a system of mutual rights and responsibilities. Medieval vassals pledged fealty to their lord in return for a fief, or grant of land. They promised to support their "liege lord" with troops or money when he called upon them for aid.

The feudal economy was organized and controlled through agrarian villages known as manors, worked by free peasants, who had their own modest property and economic and legal rights, or by serfs, impoverished peasants who were bound to the land and obliged to provide their lords with an array of services, dues in kind, and products.

REVIEW QUESTIONS

1. How did the situation that faced the church in the western Roman Empire differ from that it confronted in the east at the start of the Middle Ages?

2. How did the Franks become the dominant force in western Europe? Why did Charlemagne's empire break apart?

3. How and why was the history of the eastern or Byzantine half of the Roman Empire so different from the western half?

4. What were the defining features of feudalism? Is a feudal society a "backward" society?

KEY TERMS

apostolic primacy (p. 274)
demesne (p. 279)
fealty (p. 283)
feudal society (p. 283)

fief (p. 275)
Magyars (p. 283)
manor (p. 279)
Papal States (p. 276)

plenitude of power (p. 274)
serf (p. 280)
three-field system (p. 280)
vassal (p. 283)

 For additional study resources for this chapter, go to:
www.prenhall.com/craig/chapter12

13 Islam in the Heartlands and Beyond, ca. 1000–1600

CHAPTER HIGHLIGHTS

Religion Between 1000 and 1500, Sunnism was the dominant tradition across the Islamic world, but in both main branches of Islam, the *ulama* joined the religious, social, and political elites and discouraged religious innovation. Shiism flourished in Iran under the Savafid rulers. Sufi fraternal orders, whether Sunni or Shi'ite, became the chief instruments for the spread of Muslim faith in most Islamic societies.

Regional Developments Muslims were gradually pushed out of Spain by the Spanish Christian states between 1000 and 1492. In Egypt, the Shi'ite Fatamids established a separate caliphate from 969 to 1171. The Mamluks, whose rule in Egypt lasted from 1260 to 1517, were the only Muslim dynasty to withstand the Mongol invasions. The Seljuks were the first major Turkish dynasty of Islam.

Mongol Invasions In 1255, the Mongols invaded the Muslim world and swept all before them, conquering Transoxiana, Iran, and Iraq, before being defeated by the Mamluks in Syria in 1260. Thereafter, the Mongols established the Ilkhanid dynasty in Iran and converted to Islam. Another wave of Turko-Mongol conquest under Timur-I Lang further devastated much of the Middle East between 1379 and 1405.

India Muslim invaders and rulers spread Islam in India, where it became an enduring and influential part of Indian civilization. There was reciprocal influence between Muslims and Hindus, and Hindu religion and culture flourished, even under Muslim control.

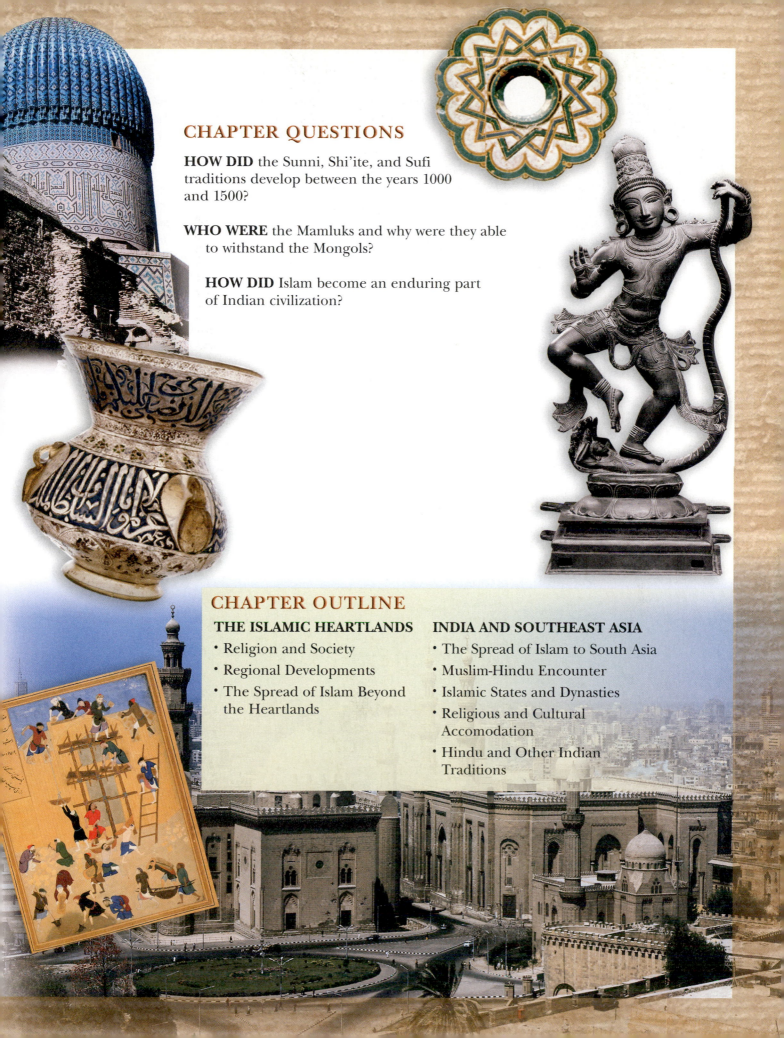

CHAPTER QUESTIONS

HOW DID the Sunni, Shi'ite, and Sufi traditions develop between the years 1000 and 1500?

WHO WERE the Mamluks and why were they able to withstand the Mongols?

HOW DID Islam become an enduring part of Indian civilization?

CHAPTER OUTLINE

THE ISLAMIC HEARTLANDS
- Religion and Society
- Regional Developments
- The Spread of Islam Beyond the Heartlands

INDIA AND SOUTHEAST ASIA
- The Spread of Islam to South Asia
- Muslim-Hindu Encounter
- Islamic States and Dynasties
- Religious and Cultural Accomodation
- Hindu and Other Indian Traditions

The centralized power of the caliphate in the Islamic world had broken down by the mid-10th century. Regional Islamic states with distinctive political and cultural identities took its place—a pattern that endured into modern times (see Map 13–1). Yet the diverse Islamic lands remained part of a larger civilization.

Socially and religiously, the next 500 years saw the growth of a truly international Islamic community, united by shared norms of communal order represented and maintained by the Muslim religious scholars (the ulama). Sufism, a strand of Islam stressing piety and allegiance to a spiritual master, gained widespread popularity, especially after 1200, through the growth of Sufi affiliations or brotherhoods. Shi'ite ideas also offered an alternative vision of society for many. Movements loyal to Ali and his heirs challenged but failed to reverse centrist, Sunni predominance, even though Shi'ite dynasties ruled much of the Islamic heartlands in the 10th and 11th centuries.

Culturally, the rise of the New Persian language in the 10th century resulted in a rich new Islamic literature. A cultural renaissance fueled the spread of Persian as the major language of Islam alongside Arabic. The Persian-dominated Iranian and Indian Islamic world became increasingly distinct from the western Islamic lands.

MAP 13–1

The Islamic World, 1000 ca. 1500. Compare this with Map 11–1 on page 252. Though the Muslim world had expanded deep into Africa, India, and Central Asia, it had also lost Spain to Christian reconquest.

GIVEN THE many Muslim states shown on this map, to what extent is it correct to speak of a single Islamic civilization?

Two Asian steppe peoples, the Mongols and the Turks, came to rule much of the Islamic world in these centuries, while Islam impinged more and more on the Indian subcontinent, Southeast Asia, and sub-Saharan Africa. Although Muslims remained a minority in these regions, Islam became the major new influence in all of them.

THE ISLAMIC HEARTLANDS

RELIGION AND SOCIETY

uring this period Islamic society was shaped by consolidation of Sunni orthodoxy, Sufi piety and organization, and Shi'ite traditions.

CONSOLIDATION OF SUNNI ORTHODOXY

The *ulama* (both Sunni and Shi'ite) gradually became entrenched religious, social, and political elites throughout the Islamic world, especially after the breakdown of the caliphate's centralized power in the 10th century. Their integration into local merchant, landowning, and bureaucratic classes led to stronger identification of these economic and political groups with Islam.

From the 11th century onward, the *ulama's* power and continuity as a class were expressed in the institution of the ***madrasa***, or college of higher learning. In contrast to the university, with its corporate organization and institutional degrees, the *madrasa* was a support institution for individual teachers, who personally certified students' mastery of particular subjects. It gave an institutional base (often providing not only teaching space but stipends and student living quarters) to Islam's long-developed system of students seeking out the best

HOW DID the Sunni, Shi'ite, and Sufi traditions develop between the years 1000 and 1500?

 12.1
Sunni versus Shi'ite: "We Exhort You to Embrace the True Faith!"

madrasa Islamic college of higher learning.

The Sultan Hasan Madrasa and Tomb-Mosque. This imposing Mamluk building (1356–1363) was built to house teachers and students studying all four of the major traditions or "schools" of Islamic law. Living and teaching spaces are combined here in a building with a mosque and the Sultan's tomb enclosure.

SuperStock, Inc.

جون روا وار که بسک ان او در آتش بسوز ند حضرت رسالت صلی الله علیه وآله وسلم

Dancing Dervishes. This image from a 1552 Persian manuscript depicts a Sufi master dancing with his disciples. Sufis often use music and bodily movement to induce a feeling of ecstacy which they feel brings them closer to God.

Bodleian Library, University of Oxford.

Ramadan Month when Muslims must fast during daylight hours.

orthopraxy Correct practice of a religion.

Sufi Movement within Islam that emphasizes the spiritual and mystical.

teachers and studying texts with them until they received the teachers' formal certification, or "permission" to transmit and teach those same texts themselves.

Popular "unofficial" piety flourished in pilgrimages to saints' tombs, in folk celebrations of Muhammad's birthday, in veneration of him in poetry, and in ecstatic chant and dance among Sufi groups. But the shared traditions that directed family and civil law, the daily worship rituals, fasting in the month of **Ramadan**, and the yearly Meccan pilgrimage remained the public bond uniting almost all Muslims. The tendency among Muslims, despite their theological disputes, was to define Islam in terms of what Muslims do—namely by **orthopraxy** (practice) rather than by ortho*doxy* (beliefs). The chief arbiters of "normative" Sunni and Shi'i Islam among the ulama were the legal scholars, not the theologians.

A basic Sunni orthopraxy, discouraging religious or social innovation, was well established by the year 1000 as the dominant tradition. Further, a growing social conservatism among the ulama reflected their integration in regional social aristocracies. The ulama were often committed to the status quo, as were the rulers.

SUFI PIETY AND ORGANIZATION

Sufi piety stresses the spiritual and mystical dimensions of Islam. The term *Sufi* apparently came from the Arabic *suf* ("wool"), recalling an old ascetic practice of wearing only a coarse woolen garment. Sufi simplicity and humility developed as a distinctive tendency when, after about 700 C.E., male and female pietists emphasized a godly life over and above mere observance of Muslim duties. Some stressed ascetic avoidance of temptations, others loving devotion to God. Sufi piety mystically bridged the abyss between the human and the divine that is implied in the exalted Muslim concept of the omnipotent God of creation. Sufi piety merged with folk piety in saint veneration, shrine pilgrimage, ecstatic worship, and seasonal festivals. Sufi writers composed some of the world's finest mystical poetry.

Some Sufis were revered as spiritual masters and saints. Their disciples formed brotherhoods that, from about the 11th century on, became both regional and international organizations. Each had its distinctive mystical teaching, Qur'anic interpretation, and devotional practice. These fraternal orders became the chief instruments for spreading Muslim faith in almost all Islamic societies. Indeed, Sufi orders became in this age one of the typical social institutions of everyday Muslim life. Whether Sunni or Shi'ite, casually or seriously pious, many Muslims have ever since identified in some degree with one or another Sufi order.

CONSOLIDATION OF SHI'ITE TRADITIONS

Shi'ite traditions crystallized between the 10th and 12th centuries. Numerous states came under Shi'ite rulers despite the fact that substantial Shi'ite populations developed only in Iran, Iraq, and the lower Indus (Sind).

Two Shi'ite groups emerged as the most influential. The first were the "Seveners," or "Isma'ilis," who recognized Isma'il (d. ca. 760), first son of the sixth Alid *imam*, as the seventh *imam*. Isma'ili groups were often revolutionary, and one Isma'ili group, the Qarmatians of eastern Arabia, ruled or agitated in Iraq, Syria, and Arabia through much of the 10th century.

By the 11th century, however, most Shi'ites accepted a line of 12 *imams* descended through another son of the sixth *imam*. The last of these is said to have disappeared in Samarra (Iraq) in 873 and to have been cosmically concealed until the time comes for him to emerge as the Mahdi, or "Guided One." His return is to usher in the messianic age and final judgment. The "Twelvers," the Shi'ite majority, focus their faith on the martyrdom of the 12 *imams* and look for their intercession on the Day of Judgment. The "Twelvers" have flourished best in Iran, where most Shi'ite doctrines have originated, no matter the sect. The Safavids of Iran made Twelver theology the "state religion" in the 16th century (see Chapter 23).

REGIONAL DEVELOPMENTS

Beginning in the 10th century, the western half of the Islamic world evolved two regional foci: (1) Spain, Moroccan North Africa, and to a lesser extent, West Africa; and (2) Egypt, Syria-Palestine, Anatolia, along with Arabia and Libyan North Africa. The eastern half of the Islamic world, in the period between 1000 and 1500, was profoundly affected by the incursion of the Mongols in the 13th century.

THE ISLAMIC WEST: SPAIN AND NORTH AFRICA

The grandeur of Spanish Islamic ("Moorish") culture can still be seen in Córdoba's great mosque and the remnants of the legendary Alhambra castle. Abd al-Rahman I (r. 756–788) established the Umayyad dynasty at Córdoba, the cultural center of the western world for the next two centuries. Renowned for its intellectual life, commercial activity, public baths and gardens, and elegance, Córdoba reached its zenith under Abd al-Rahman III (r. 912–961). He took the title of caliph in 929, and as an absolute but benevolent ruler, he presided over a largely unified, peaceful Islamic Spain. The mosque-university of Córdoba that he founded was the earliest of its kind. It attracted students from Europe as well as the Islamic world. A sad irony of this cosmopolitan culture was recurring religious exclusivism in both the Muslim and Christian camps, which sparked conflict between them.

QUICK REVIEW

Islamic Higher Education
- *Madrasa*: College of higher learning
- *Madrasa* were support institutions for individual teachers
- Operated within Islamic tradition of students seeking best teachers

WHO WERE the Mamluks and why were they able to withstand the Mongols?

Western Islamic Lands

756–1021	Spanish Umayyad dynasty
912–961	Rule of Abd al-Rahman III; height of Umayyad power and civilization
969–1171	Fatimid Shi'ite dynasty in Egypt
ca. 1020	Origin of Druze community (Egypt/Syria)
1171	Fatimids fall to Salah al-Din (Saladin), Ayyubid lieutenant of the ruler of Aleppo
1056–1275	Almoravid and Almohad dynasties in North Africa, West Africa, and Spain
1096–1291	Major European Christian crusades into Islamic lands; some European presence in Syria-Palestine
1198	Death of Ibn Rushd (Averroës), philosopher
1204	Death of Ibn Maymun (Maimonides), philosopher and Jewish savant
1240	Death of Ibn al-Arabi, theosophical mystic
1250–1517	Mamluk sultanate in Egypt and (from late 1200s) Syria; claim laid to Abbasid caliphate
1260	Mamluk victory at Ain Jalut halts Mongol advance into Syria
1406	Death of Ibn Khaldun, historian and social philosopher
ca. 1300	Rise of Ottoman state in western Anatolia

Eastern Islamic Lands

875–999	Samanid dynasty, centered at Bukhara
945–1055	Buyid Shi'ite dynasty in Baghdad, controls caliphs
994–1186	Ghaznavid dynasty in Ghazna (modern Afghanistan) and Lahore (modern Pakistan), founded by Subuktigin (r. 976–997) and his son, Mahmud of Ghazna (r. 998–1030)
ca. 1020	Death of Firdawsi, compiler of *Shahnama*
ca. 1048	Death of al-Biruni, scientist and polyglot
1055–1194	Seljuk rule in Baghdad
1063–1092	Viziership of Nizam al-Mulk
1111	Death of al-Ghazzali, theologian and scholar
1219–1222	Genghis Khan plunders eastern Iran to Indus region
1258	Hulagu Khan conquers Baghdad
1261	Mamluk-Mongol treaty halts westward Mongol movement
1260–1335	Hulagu and his Il-Khanid successors rule Iran
1379–1405	Campaigns of Timur-i Lang (Tamerlane) devastate entire Islamic East
1405–1494	Timurids, successors of Tamerlane, rule in Transoxiana and Iran
1405–1447	Shahrukh, Timurid ruler at Herat; great patronage of the arts and philosophy

Reconquista Christian reconquest of Spain from the Muslims from 1000 to 1492.

Abd al-Rahman III checked both the new Fatimid power in North Africa and the Christian kingdoms in northern Spain, making possible a golden era of Moorish power and culture. But after his death, his realm broke up into warring Muslim principalities. This made them vulnerable to attack by Spain's Christian states. Between 1000 and 1085, when Christians took the key city of Toledo, these states won control of the northern half of the Iberian peninsula.

Brief Islamic revivals in Spain and North Africa were sparked by religious reform movements led by the Almoravids and Almohads. The Almoravids originated as a religious-warrior brotherhood among Berber nomads in West Africa. In 1086, they carried their zealotry into Spain and reunited its Islamic kingdoms. Under their rule, arabized Christians (Mozarabs) were persecuted, as were some Moorish Jews. The subsequent wars began the last major phase of the Spanish "Reconquest" (**Reconquista**) in which Christian rulers sought to regain and Christianize the peninsula.

The Almohads ended Almoravid rule in Morocco in 1147 and then conquered much of southern Spain. Before their demise (1225 in Spain; 1275 in Africa), they stimulated a brilliant revival of Moorish culture. During this era, paper manufacture reached Spain and then the rest of western Europe. Fables originating in India also completed a long westward journey at this time and were circulated in Spanish and Latin translations. The greatest of Spain's Islamic intellectuals were the philosopher and physician, Ibn Rushd (Averroës, d. 1198); the Muslim mystical thinker, Ibn al-Arabi (d. 1240); and the Arab-Jewish philosopher, Ibn Maymun, or Maimonides (d. 1204).

THE ISLAMIC WEST: EGYPT AND THE EASTERN MEDITERRANEAN WORLD

The Fatimids The Shi'ite Fatimids were the strongest Islamic power in the Mediterranean region from the 10th to the 12th century. Their name advertized their claim to descent from Muhammad's daughter, Fatima. They began as a Tunisian dynasty, then conquered Morocco, Sicily, and Egypt (969). They founded a new city in Egypt to serve as their capital, Cairo (*al-Qahira*, "the Victorious"). It was located near the first garrison town that the early Muslims had established when they occupied Egypt. Because the Fatimids assumed the title of caliph, for a time there were three "caliphates"—headquartered in Baghdad, Córdoba, and Cairo. The Fatimids were Isma'ilis (see above). They won the allegiance of a Yemeni Shi'ite state and were able, for a time, to take western Arabia and most of Syria.

Fatimid rule spawned two splinter groups. The Druze of modern Lebanon and Syria originated around 1020. They were founded by members of the Fatimid court who professed belief in the divinity of one of the Fatimid caliphs. Their beliefs range too far from Islam for them to be considered a

Muslim sect. The Isma'ili Assassins, on the other hand, were a radical Muslim movement founded in Iran by a Fatimid defector around 1100. The name "Assassins" comes not from the political assassinations that made them infamous but from the Arabic *Hashishiyyin* ("users of hashish"). It was possibly connected with the story that drugs were used to induce their assassins to undertake suicidal missions. The Assassins were destroyed by the Mongols in the 13th century.

Fatimid rulers treated Egypt's Coptic Christians and Jews generally as well as they did their Sunni majority. Many Copts held high offices. After 1100 the Fatimids weakened, falling in 1171 to Salah al-Din (Saladin, 1137–1193), a general serving the Turkish ruler of Syria, Nur al-Din (1118–1174). After Nur al-Din's death, Saladin, a Sunni Kurd, struck out on his own. He added Syria-Palestine and Mesopotamia to his Egyptian dominions and founded the Ayyubid dynasty. It controlled these areas until 1250, when Egypt fell to the Mamluks, and 1260, when the Mongols overran most of Syria and Mesopotamia.

Like Nur al-Din, and on the model of the Seljuks (see Chapter 11), Saladin founded madrasas to teach and promote Sunni law. A self-conscious Sunnism entrenched itself in Egypt under his dynasty, and Shi'ite Islam disappeared.

The Mamluks The heirs of the Fatimids and Saladin in the eastern Mediterranean were the redoubtable sultans of the Mamluk dynasty. The Mamluks were the only Islamic dynasty to withstand the Mongol invasions. Their victory at Ain Jalut in Palestine in 1260 halted the Mongols' westward movement. The first Mamluk **sultan**, Aybak (r. 1250–1257), and his successors were elite Turkish and Mongol slave officers. Whereas the early Mamluk sultans passed down their office within their families, after the 1390s succession was vigorously contested. No sultan reigned more than a few years. The Mamluk state consisted of military fiefs and was totally controlled by its slave-officer elite.

The Mamluk sultan Baybars (r. 1260–1277), who took the last Crusader fortresses, is a larger-than-life figure in Arab legend. To legitimize his rule, he installed an uncle of Baghdad's last Abbasid caliph as caliph at Cairo. This, nominally at least, revived the Abbasid caliphate after its extinction by the Mongols who sacked Baghdad in 1258 (discussed later). He extended Mamluk rule south to Nubia and west among the Berbers.

As trade relations with the Mongol domains improved after 1300, the Mamluks enjoyed prosperity. At their zenith, they commanded an empire worthy of the early Abbasids or the later Ottomans. The prosperity and peace of the reign of Ibn Qala'un (1310–1340) marked the heyday of Mamluk rule. The Black Death epidemic of 1347–1348 in the Arab Middle East hurt the Mamluk and other regional states. However, the Mamluks survived this and even the Ottoman conquest of Egypt in 1517. Mamluks continued to rule Egypt as Ottoman governors into the 19th century.

Architecture, especially from the reigns of Baybars and al-Nasir (r. 1293–1340), much of which still graces Cairo, is the most magnificent Mamluk bequest to posterity. Mosaics, calligraphy, and metalwork from their era

Military Banner. Made in southern Spain in the early 13th century, the banner of Las Navas de Tolosa, of silk tapestry with gold parchment (3.3 × 2.2 m), reflects the emphasis on architectural designs that emerged at this time among Spanish weavers. The central section of the banner, bordered with Qur'anic inscriptions, resembles a Spanish courtyard garden. The banner was captured in battle by Christians not long after it was made.

Banner of Las Navas de Tolosa, from southern Spain. First half of 13th century. Silk tapestry-weave w/gilt parchment, 10'9 7/8" × 7'2 5/8" (3.3 × 2.2 m) Museo de Telas Medievales, Monasterio de Santa Maria la Real de Las Huelgas, Burgos, Spain. Patrimonio Nacional. Arxiu Mas.

sultan Muslim royal title that means "authority."

Mamluk Trade. Trade in spices and other precious commodities between the Mamuluks and western Europe was of great importance. In this painting from about 1500 we see Venetian ambassadors being received by the governor of Damascus, who sits on a low platform and wears a distinctively-shaped turban.

Erich Lessing/Art Resource, N.Y.

are also worthy of note. The Mamluks were great patrons of scholars as well as artists. The most important of these was Ibn Khaldun (d. 1406), a great social historian and philosopher (see "Ibn Khaldun 'The Muqaddimah'").

THE ISLAMIC EAST: BEFORE THE MONGOL CONQUESTS

The Iranian dynasties of the Samanids at Bukhara (875–999) and the Buyids at Baghdad (945–1055) were the major usurpers of the eastern Abbasid dominions. Their successes epitomized the rise of regional states that had begun to undermine the caliphate by the ninth century. Their demises reflected a second pattern: the ascendancy of Turkish slave-rulers (like the Mamluks in the west) and of Oghuz Turkish peoples (called Turkomans). With the Seljuks (successors of the Buyids), the process begun by the use of Turkish slave troops in ninth-century Baghdad ended with the establishment in the Islamic world of Turkish ruling dynasties. As is typical of late converts, they became the most zealous of Sunni Muslims.

The Ghaznavids   The rule of the Samanids in Transoxiana was ended by a Turkoman group in 999. Previously, by 994, the Samanids had lost all of eastern Iran south of the Oxus to one of their slave governors, Subuktigin (r. 976–997). He set up his own state in modern Afghanistan, at Ghazna, whence he and his son and successor, Mahmud of Ghazna (r. 998–1030), launched campaigns against his former masters. The Ghaznavids are notable for their patronage of Persian culture and for their conquests in northwestern India, which established a lasting Muslim presence in India. Mahmud was their greatest ruler. His empire stretched from western Iran to the Oxus and the Indus.

HISTORY'S VOICES

IBN KHALDUN "THE MUQADDIMAH"

bd al-Rahman Ibn Khaldun (1336–1406) of Tunisia was a brilliant thinker who has sometimes been called the first modern social scientist. He studied and held important positions in Granada, Cairo, and Fez. His most famous work, the Muqaddima, *or Introduction to Universal History, was a major intellectual contribution. In this text, a portion of which follows, he presented his philosophy of history. Like many Roman and Greek historians before him, he considered history to be cyclical. He considered culture, geography, climate, and economic trends to be the major forces behind historical changes. In the following chapter, Ibn Khaldun examines how dynasties rise and fall.*

WHAT MAKES Ibn Khaldun a "modern" thinker? Does this description seem applicable today?

We have stated that the life of a dynasty does not as a rule extend beyond three generations. The first generation retains the desert qualities, desert toughness, and desert savagery. (Its members are used to) privation and to sharing their glory (with each other); they are brave and rapacious. Therefore, the strength of group feeling continues to be preserved among them. They are sharp and greatly feared. People submit to them.

Under the influence of royal authority and a life of ease, the second generation changes from the desert attitude to sedentary culture, from privation to luxury and plenty, from a state in which everybody shared in the glory to one in which one man claims all the glory for himself while the others are too lazy to strive for glory, and from proud superiority to humble subservience. Thus, the vigour of group feeling is broken to some extent. People become used to lowliness and obedience. But many of the old virtues remain in them, because they had had direct personal contact with the first generation and its conditions, and had observed with their own eyes its prowess and striving for glory and

its intention to protect and defend (itself). They cannot give all of it up at once, although a good deal of it may go. They live in hope that the conditions that existed in the first generation may come back, or they live under the illusion that those conditions still exist.

The third generation, then, has (completely) forgotten the period of desert life and toughness, as if it had never existed. They have lost (the taste for) the sweetness of fame and for group feeling, because they are dominated by force. Luxury reaches its peak among them, because they are so much given to a life of prosperity and ease. They become dependent on the dynasty and are like women and children who need to be defended. Group feeling disappears completely. People forget to protect and defend themselves and to press their claims. With their emblems, apparel, horseback-riding, and (fighting) skill, they deceive people and give them the wrong impression. For the most part, they are more cowardly than women upon their backs. When someone comes and demands something from them, they cannot repel him. The ruler, then, has need of other, brave people to support him. He takes many clients and followers. They help the dynasty to some degree, until God permits it to be destroyed, and it goes with everything it stands for.

As one can see, we have there three generations. In the course of these three generations, the dynasty grows senile and is worn out. Therefore, it is in the fourth generation that (ancestral) prestige is destroyed. . . .

In this way, the life span of a dynasty corresponds to the life span of an individual; it grows up and passes into an age of stagnation and thence into retrogression. Therefore, people commonly say that the life span of a dynasty is one hundred years. . . .

Source: Ibn Khaldun, *The Muqaddimah: An Introduction to History,* ed. N.J. Dawood, trans. Franz Rosenthal (Princeton NJ: Princeton University Press, 1967) pp. 137–138.

11.5
William of Rubrick:
Impressions of the
Medieval Mongols

Mamluk Bottle This elegant glass bottle was made in Mamluk workshops in Syria in the mid–14th century for the rulers of the Yemen in southern Arabia.

John Tsantes/Courtesy of the Freer Gallery of Art, Smithsonian Institution, Washington, D.C.

Mahmud attracted to Ghazna numerous scholars and artists, notably the great scientist and mathematician al-Biruni (d. 1048) and the epic poet Firdawsi (d. ca. 1020). Firdawsi's *Shahnama* ("The Book of Kings") is the chief masterpiece of Persian literature, an epic of 60,000 verses that helped fix the New Persian language and revive the pre-Islamic Iranian cultural tradition. After Mahmud the empire began to break up, although Ghaznavids ruled at Lahore until 1186.

The Seljuks   The Seljuks, a steppe clan who became avid Sunnis, were the first major Turkish dynasty of Islam. In 1055 they took Baghdad. As the new guardian of the caliphate and master of an Islamic empire, the Seljuk leader Tughril Beg (r. 1037–1063) took the title of *sultan* ("authority") to signify his power. He was invested by the caliph as "king of east and west."

As new Turkish tribes joined their ranks, the Seljuks extended Islamic rule into the central Anatolian plateau at Byzantine expense, even capturing the Byzantine emperor in 1071. They also conquered much of Syria and wrested Mecca and Medina from the Shi'ite Fatimids. Turkish rule in Anatolia dates from 1077, when the Seljuk governor there formed a sultanate. Known as the Seljuks of Rum ("Rome," i.e., Byzantium), these Seljuks were displaced after 1300 by the Ottomans (see Chapter 21).

The most notable figure of Seljuk rule was the vizier Nizam al-Mulk from 1063 to 1092. In his time, new roads and inns (caravanserais) for trade and pilgrimage were built, canals were dug, mosques and other public buildings were founded, and science and culture were patronized. He appointed as professor in his Baghdad madrasa Muhammad al-Ghazzali (d. 1111), probably the greatest of Muslim religious thinkers. He also patronized the mathematician and astronomer Umar Khayyam (d. 1123), whose Western fame rests on the poetry of his "Quatrains," or *Ruba'iyat.*

By 1194, Iranian Seljuk rule was erased by another Turkish slave dynasty from Khwarizm in the lower Oxus basin. By 1200, these Khwarizm Shahs had built a large but shaky empire covering Iran and Transoxiana. In the same era, the Abbasid caliph at Baghdad, al-Nasir (r. 1180–1225), established an independent caliphal state in Iraq. But neither his heirs nor the Khwarizm Shahs survived for long.

THE ISLAMIC EAST: THE MONGOL AGE

Mongols and Ilkhanids   The building of a vast Mongol empire (see Chapter 8) proved momentous for Islamic Eurasia and India. The Great Khan, Genghis (ca. 1162–1227) plundered mercilessly (1219–1222) from Transoxiana and Khorasan to the Indus, razing entire cities. After his death, a division of his empire into four khanates under his four sons gave the Islamic world a respite. Then in 1255 Hulagu Khan (r. 1256–1265), a grandson of Genghis, again led a massive army across the Oxus. He went from victory to victory, destroying every Iranian state. In 1258, Hulagu's troops smashed Baghdad's defenses and plundered the city, killing at least 80,000 inhabitants, including the caliph and his sons.

At the urging of his wife and of Nestorian Christians and Buddhists in his inner circle, Hulagu spared the Christians of Baghdad and followed this policy in his other conquests. When Damascus surrendered, Western Christians hoped (in vain, as it turned out) that Mamluk Cairo and Islamic power would collapse. But Hulagu's drive west was slowed by

MAP 13–2

The Seljuk Empire, ca. 1095. By the end of the 11th century, the Seljuks had conquered Persia, Mesopotamia, and Syria, and had inflicted a devasting blow against the Byzantine Empire at the battle of Manzikert in 1071, altering the balance of power in the eastern Mediterranean and the Near East.

HOW DO the Seljuk conquests reveal the power of steppe peoples to overturn settled societies?

rivalry with his kinsman Berke. A Muslim convert, Berke ruled the khanate of the Golden Horde, the Mongol state centered in southern Russia. He was in contact with the Mamluks, and some of his Mongol troops even fought with them when they won a victory over Hulagu in Palestine (1260), which prevented his advance into Egypt. A treaty in 1261 between the Mamluk sultan and Berke established a formal alliance that confirmed the breakup of Mongol unity and the autonomy of the four khanates: in China (the Yuan dynasty), in Iran (the Ilkhans), in Russia (the Golden Horde), and in Transoxiana (the Chagatays).

Hulagu pledged allegiance to the new Great Khan of China, and he and his heirs ruled the old Persian Empire from Azerbaijan for some 75 years as the Great Khan's viceroys (or *Il-Khans*; the title from which Hulagu's line takes its name *Ilkhanid*). Here, as elsewhere, the Mongols did not eradicate the society they inherited. Instead, both their native paganism and their Buddhist and Christian leanings yielded to Muslim faith and practice. Religious tolerance, however, remained the norm under their rule. After 1335, Ilkhanid rule fell prey to the familiar pattern of a gradual breaking away of provinces, and for 50 years, Iran was again fragmented.

Genghis Khan.
The Granger Collection, N.Y.

HOW DID Islam become an enduring part of Indian civilization?

Tamerlane's Army. A miniature painting of the Army of Tamerlane storming the walls of the Rajput city of Bhatnair in 1398. Bhatnair was one of the many North Indian cities and fortresses that fell to the relentless onslaught of Tamerlane's armies.

Art Resource/Bildarchiv Preussischer Kulturbesitz.

Timurids and Turkomans This situation prepared the way for a new Turko-Mongol conquest from Transoxiana, under Timur-i Lang ("Timur the Lame," or "Tamerlane," 1336–1405). Timur's savage campaigns, between 1379 and his death in 1405, were aimed at sheer conquest. Timur was a Muslim convert who evidently possessed a strong sense of a calling to be the protector of commerce and punisher of the injustices of regional petty tyrants and extremist groups. His means were brutal. His campaign spread a wave of devastation through eastern Iran (1379–1385); western Iran, Armenia, the Caucasus, and upper Mesopotamia (1385–1387); southwestern Iran, Mesopotamia, and Syria (1391–1393); Central Asia from Transoxiana to the Volga and as far as Moscow (1391–1395); North India (1398); and northern Syria and Anatolia (1400–1402). In his wake he left ruins, death, disease, and political chaos across the entire eastern Islamic world. His was, however, the last great steppe invasion, for firearms soon ended the advantage that the steppe's horsemen had long enjoyed.

Timur's sons, the Timurids, ruled after him with varying results in Transoxiana and Iran (1405–1494). The most successful of them was Shahrukh (r. 1405–1447), who ruled a united Iran for a time. His capital, Herat, became an important center of Persian Islamic culture and Sunni piety. He provided patronage for the famous Herat school of miniature painting as well as for Persian authors and philosophers. The Timurids had to share Iran itself with Turkoman dynasties in western Iran, once even losing Herat to one of them. They and the Turkomans were the last Sunnis to rule Iran. Both were eclipsed at the end of the 15th century by the militant Shi'ite dynasty of the Safavids, who ushered in a new, Shi'ite era in the Iranian world (see Chapter 21).

THE SPREAD OF ISLAM BEYOND THE HEARTLANDS

The period from roughly 1000 to 1500 saw the spread of Islam as a lasting religious, cultural, and political force into new areas. India, Malaysia, and Indonesia became major spheres of Islamic political or commercial power even though large numbers, often the majority, of their inhabitants continued the practice of their traditional religions.

Islamic civilization in India was formed by creative interaction between invading foreigners and indigenous peoples. The early Arab and Turkish invaders were a foreign Muslim minority, but their heirs became truly "Indian" as well as Muslim. From then on, Indian civilization both included and enriched Islamic traditions.

INDIA AND SOUTHEAST ASIA

The port cities of Gujarat and southern India attracted Muslim merchants who hoped to profit from internal Indian trade as well as from trade with the Indies and China (see Map 13–2). Wherever Muslim traders went, converts to Islam followed. Sufi orders also drew converts.

India	
ca. 900–1300	Chola dynasty in southern India
1137	Death of Ramanuja
1206–1290	Slave Sultans of Delhi
1290–1320	Khalji sultans of Delhi
1320–1413	Tughluqid sultans of Delhi
1414–1526	Sayyid sultans of Delhi
1336–1565	Hindu dynasty of Vijayanagar
1347–1527	Muslim Bahmanid dynasty in the Deccan
1398	Timur's sack of Delhi

MUSLIM-HINDU ENCOUNTER

From the outset, Muslim leaders faced the problem of ruling a country dominated by utterly different cultural and religious traditions. The first Arab conquerors in Sind (711) had treated Hindus as "protected peoples" under Muslim sovereignty. These precedents gave later Indian Muslim rulers a legal basis for coexistence with their Hindu subjects, but they did not eliminate Hindu resistance to Muslim rule.

The chief obstacle to Islamic expansion in India was the military prowess of the Hindu warrior class, known from about the mid-seventh century as *Rajputs*. The Rajputs were a large group of clans bound together by a fierce warrior ethic and strong Hindu cultural and religious traditionalism. They fought the Muslims with tenacity, but their inability to form a common front against their enemy resulted, in the 16th century, in their dominance by the Muslims (see Chapter 21).

The Qutub Minar (Victory Tower) in Delhi in India is an example of classic Indo-Muslim art and architecture. Constructed in the 12th century, this soaring tower made from red sandstone commemorated a decisive Muslim military victory.

Getty Images, Inc.-Taxi.

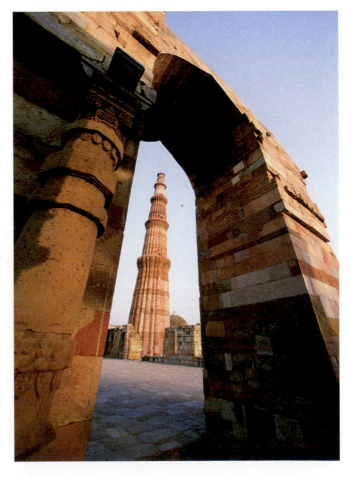

ISLAMIC STATES AND DYNASTIES

After the Ghaznavids and a brief period of Afghan rule, Turkish-Afghan rulers (the "Slave Sultans of Delhi") extended Islamic power over North India (1206–1290). Four later Muslim dynasties—the Khaljis, Tughluqs, Sayyids, and Lodis—continued the Delhi sultanate through the 15th century. Their reigns were interrupted by several years of chaos following the Mongol-Turkish invasion and Timur's sack of Delhi in 1398, from which the city took decades to recover. Throughout its history the Delhi sultanate's authority over its provincial governors fluctuated, even in the heart of North India. Before the advent of the Mughals in the mid-16th century, many regions split off from the sultanate and became independent. Regional rule predominated across the subcontinent.

MAP EXPLORATION

Interactive map: To explore this map further, go to **http://www.prenhall.com/craig/map13.3**

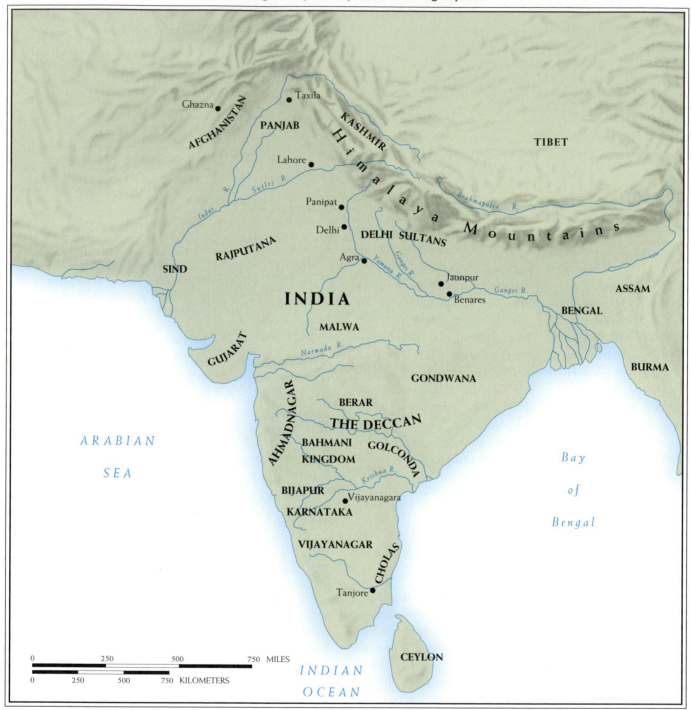

MAP 13–3

The Indian Subcontinent, 1000–1500. Shown are major kingdoms and regions.

WHERE IN India were the principle Islamic states located during this period?

The years between 1000 and 1500 were marked by political fragmentation in the Islamic world. While the Muslims eventually defeated the Crusader states in Palestine and Syria, in Spain the Christians gradually conquered every Islamic state. The Mongol invasions of the mid-13th century and the campaigns of Timur-i Lang in the 14th century devastated much of the eastern Islamic world. Yet, despite these reverses and the rise and fall of dynasties, Islamic civilization endured, and the Muslim faith spread to new areas in Africa, India, and East Asia.

Dynasty	Location
Umayyads	Spain
Almoravids	West Africa, North Africa, Spain
Almohads	Morocco, Spain
Fatimids	Tunisia, Egypt
Ayyubids	Egypt, Syria
Mamluks	Egypt, Syria
Samanids	Transoxiana
Buyids	Iraq
Seljuks	Anatolia, Iraq
Abbasids	Iraq
Ghaznavids	Transoxiana, Pakistan
Khwarzims	Iran
Ilkhanids	Iran
Timurids	Transoxiana, Iran
Delhi Sultans	Northern India
Bahmanids	Deccan

SOUTHEAST ASIA

The most important independent Islamic state was that of the Bahmanids in the Deccan (1347–1527). Bahmanid rulers were famous for their architecture and the intellectual life of their court, as well as for their role in containing the powerful South Indian Hindu state of Vijayanagar (1336–1565). Most regional capitals boasted rich cultures. After Timur's sack of Delhi in 1398, its artists and intellectuals found refuge in Jaunpur, which developed an impressive tradition of Islamic architecture. Many Indian texts were translated into Persian in the Kashmir, which, from 1346 to 1589, was an independent sultanate.

Geographically, the islands in Southeast Asia linked India and China, and by the 15th century they had developed as an important trade route. Islam's

HOW DID local traditions influence the spread of Islam in Southeast Asia?

Spread of Islam
- 13th – 14th Centuries
- 15th Century
- 16th Century
- 17th – 18th Centuries
- 19th – 20th Centuries
- → Spread of Islam

MAP 13–4
The Spread of Islam in Southeast Asia.

WHAT WERE the main reasons for the spread of Islam in Southeast Asia?

spread in the region was, however, not steady and progressive, but idiosyncratic. The result was the emergence of a number of distinct Islamic traditions clustering in five areas: Java, Samudra, Melaka, Acheh, and Moluccas (see Map 13–3). In some places Islam coexisted with worship of ancestors, sorcery, and magic. Some significant Islamic rites (the *hajj*, for example) were viewed as Arab customs and, therefore, not regarded as integral to the true practice of the faith for all Muslims. Islam's support for centralization and consolidation of power, however, encouraged many political leaders to adopt a more stringent version of Islam.

Major tensions in the region derived not from religion but from a struggle between the coastal districts and the interior. Urban (mostly port) rulers, who profited most from the era's growing trade, tried to assert their authority over hereditary chiefs of rural areas. They invoked Islam's vision of a perfect society to justify this, but local traditions proved durable. Muslims in Southeast Asia adapted Islam to their needs and customs rather than substituting it for their indigenous practices.

RELIGIOUS AND CULTURAL ACCOMMODATION

HOW DID India accomodate Hinduism and Islam?

Despite the enduring division of the subcontinent into multiple and diverse units, the five centuries after Mahmud of Ghazna's (r. 998–1030) planting of Islam in India saw the faith become an enduring, influential, and transregional, if still minority, element in Indian culture. Its greatest strength was in the north and in the Deccan. The Delhi sultans provided a basic political and social framework within which Islam could take root. Although the ruling class remained a Muslim minority of Persianized Turks and Afghans governing a Hindu majority, converts were to be found at various levels of society.

Ghazis ("warriors") spread Islam by force of arms to pagan groups in eastern Bengal and Assam. More significantly, Sufi orders converted numerous Hindus among the lower classes across the North. The Muslim aristocracy was usually treated in Indian society as a separate caste group or groups. When lower class or other Hindus converted, they were assimilated into lower "Muslim castes," often identified by occupation.

Sanskrit had long been the Indian scholarly language and lingua franca, but in this period regional languages, such as Tamil in the south, gained status, and Persian became the language of intellectual and cultural life for the ruling elites of North India. However, a new language with both Perso-Arabic and indigenous Indian elements, **Urdu-Hindi**, grew in popularity until it gained wide

ghazis Warriors who carried Islam by force of arms to pagan groups.

Urdu-Hindi Language that combines Persian-Arabic and native Indian elements. Urdu is the Muslim version of the language; Hindi is the Hindu version.

use in the subcontinent by modern times. It began to take shape not long after the initial Muslim influx in the 11th century and developed in response to the increasing need of Hindus and Muslims for a shared medium of communication. The name *Urdu* designated the Muslim version that continued to draw on its Perso-Arabic heritage, whereas Hindi ("Indian") was used for the version associated with Hindu culture and Sanskritic heritage. Each would later become an official national language: Urdu for modern Pakistan and Hindi for modern India.

Indian Muslims were always susceptible to Hindu influence (in language, marriage customs, and caste consciousness), but they were never completely absorbed into Hindu culture. Consciousness of their uniqueness in the Hindu world made them proud of their distinctness. Nevertheless, Muslims and Hindus inevitably influenced one another, especially in popular piety. Sufi devotion had an appeal similar to that of Hindu devotional, or *bhakti*, movements (see Chapter 10), and each influenced the other. Various theistic mystics preached devotion to a God who saves His worshipers without regard either to Hindu caste obligations or to the legalistic observance of Muslim orthopraxy. The poet-saints Ramananda (d. after 1400) and Kabir (d. ca. 1518) were the two most famous such reformers.

bhakti Hindu devotional movements.

HINDU AND OTHER INDIAN TRADITIONS

The Jain tradition continued to flourish, but in the north by the 11th century the Muslim conquests had effectively ended India's Buddhist monastic and lay traditions. Buddhism was already waning long before Islam came to India, and the coming of Islam either dealt it a death blow or coincided with its reduction to small-minority status.

Hindu religion and culture continued to flourish, even under Muslim control. *Bhakti* was especially creative. The great Hindu Vaishnava Brahman, Ramanuja (d. 1137), provided a theological basis for bhakti, reconciling its ideas with the classical Upanishadic Hindu worldview in the Vedantin tradition. Important examples of bhakti movements are the Shaivite and Vaishnavite traditions. Bhakti piety underlies the masterpiece of Hindu mystical love poetry, Jayadeva's *Gita Govinda* (12th century), which is devoted to Krishna, the most important of Vishnu's incarnations.

The south continued to be the center of Hindu cultural, political, and religious activity. Of several important dynastic states in the south during this age, the foremost was that of the Cholas, which flourished from about 900–1300. Their mightiest successor, the kingdom of Vijayanagar (1336–1565), subjugated the entire south in the 14th century and resisted its Muslim foes longer than any other kingdom. Vijayanagar itself was one of India's most lavishly developed cities and a center of the cult of Shiva.

SUMMARY

Religion Between 1000 and 1500, the most important developments for shaping of Islamic society were of Sunni and Shi'ite legal and religious norms and of Sufi traditions and personal piety. Sunnism was the dominant tradition across the Islamic world, but in both main branches of Islam, the ulama joined the religious, social, and political elites and discouraged religious innovation.

IMAGE KEY

for pages 288–289

a. Folio from a manuscript of "Khusraw and Shirin" by Nizami.

b. Bowl. Iran, late 12th century

c. Mosaic from the Alhambra Palace, Granada, Spain

d. The Sultan Hasan Madrasa and tomb-mosque

e. A mamluk lamp covered in arabic

f. The Gur-i-mir, the tomb of Timur in Samarkand

g. A picture from a Hebrew Haggada, Spain, fourteenth century

h. South Indian bronze figure of Krishna

Shiism flourished in Iran under the Savafid rulers. Sufi piety stresses the spiritual and mystical dimensions of Islam. Sufi fraternal orders, whether Sunni or Shi'ite, became the chief instruments for the spread of Muslim faith in most Islamic societies.

Regional Developments Despite general religious tolerance and high cultural achievements, the Muslims were gradually pushed out of Spain by the Spanish Christian states between 1000 and 1492. In Egypt, the Shi'ite Fatamids established a separate caliphate from 969 to 1171. The Mamluks, whose rule in Egypt lasted from 1260 to 1517, were the only Muslim dynasty to withstand the Mongol invasions. The Seljuks, based in Anatolia and Iraq, were the first major Turkish dynasty of Islam. Other notable Islamic dynasties were the Ghaznavids in Transoxiana and the Khwarizam shahs in Iran.

Mongol Invasions In 1255, the Mongols invaded the Muslim world and swept all before them, conquering Transoxiana, Iran, and Iraq, where they captured Baghdad and killed the last Abbasid caliph in 1258, before being defeated by the Mamluks in Syria in 1260. Thereafter, the Mongols established the Ilkhanid dynasty in Iran and converted to Islam. Another wave of Turko-Mongol conquest under Timur-I Lang further devastated much of the Middle East between 1379 and 1405.

India Muslim invaders and rulers spread Islam in India, where it became an enduring and influential part of Indian civilization. There was reciprocal influence between Muslims and Hindus, and a new language, Urdu-Hindi, combined Persian-Arabic and indigenous Indian elements. Buddhism all but disappeared from India during these years, but Hindu religion and culture flourished, even under Muslim control. Hindu devotional, or Bhakti, movements were especially creative.

REVIEW QUESTIONS

1. In the period 1000–1500, why did no Muslim leader build a large-scale Islamic empire of the extent of the early Abbasids?

2. Who were the ulama? What was their relationship to political leadership? What social roles did they play?

3. How did Córdoba become a model of civilized culture?

4. Why was Islam able to survive the invasions by steppe peoples from 945 on? What were the lasting results of these "invasions" for the Islamic world?

5. How did Islam affect India? What happened to Islam as it spread through Southeast Asia?

KEY TERMS

bhakti (p. 305)   orthopraxy (p. 292)   Sufi (p. 292)
ghazis (p. 304)   Ramadan (p. 292)   sultan (p. 295)
madrasa (p. 291)   *Reconquista* (p. 294)   Urdu-Hindi (p. 304)

   For additional study resources for this chapter, go to:
www.prenhall.com/craig/chapter13

Visualizing The Past

The Divine in the Middle Ages

HOW DID artists of different religions depict the divine? How did their differing conceptions of the divine, and rules within religions about how and whether, the divine should be depicted, shape religious art?

The Middle Ages (500 C.E.–1300 C.E.) witnessed the creation of a new world religion, Islam, and the expansion and consolidation of others, including Christianity, Buddhism, and Hinduism. Each of these religions fostered forms of religious art suited to its conception of the divine. Religious and secular leaders alike commissioned the art as objects or focuses of worship, teaching tools, and decorations. Secular leaders enhanced their status by associating themselves with the divine through patronage of religious art.

Hinduism. "Standing Parvati," India, Chola Period (880–1279), circa first quarter of the 10th century. This statue of the Hindu goddess Parvati hails from the Chola-ruled region of South India. Chola art, known for its exceptional grace and beauty, influenced Hindu art throughout south Asia. Hinduism is the only major polytheistic world religion of the medieval period and it also was the only one to retain female as well as male gods.

Indian, Tamil Nadu, Standing Parvati, Chola period (ca. 860–1279), ca. first quarter of 10th century, Copper alloy. H. 27 3/8 in. (69.5 cm). "The Metropolitan Museum of Art, Bequest of Cora Timken Burnett, 1956. (57.5.3). Photograph by Bruce White. © 1994 The Metropolitan Museum of Art."

▼

Islam. This is a page from a vellum medieval Koran with a rosette in the margin, by the medieval Islamic School. Islam follows the Jewish tradition in prohibiting images of God (Allah). Because Islam also prohibits depicting the human form (although some Islamic artists did produce images of people and animals), as this picture shows, Islamic art tended to be highly abstract, and Islamic writing itself became an art form of great beauty and refinement.

Page from the Koran with a rosette in the margin by Islamic School Musee Conde, Chantilly, France, France/Bridgeman Art Library.

◀**Christianity.** This cloisonné and gold medallion crafted by Georgian artisans for a Byzantine icon frame, circa 1100 C.E., shows Jesus Christ, his divinity communicated by his halo, and his wisdom as a human teacher by the book he carries. By the Middle Ages, the Byzantine world had produced many icons, and the defeat of the iconoclasts, who opposed the creation of religious images for fear that ordinary people would worship them, in the ninth century ensured that religious art replete with images of God, Jesus, and the saints would dominate medieval Christian art throughout Europe.
Giraudon/Art Resource, N.Y.

Buddhism. This seated porcelain *bodhisattva* from the Chinese ▶ Yuan dynasty (1279–1368) symbolizes the spirituality of medieval Mahayana Buddhism. Siddhartha Gautama (563–483 B.C.E.) was a wealthy nobleman from India whose search for enlightenment led him to found a new religion, the goal of which was not salvation but, rather, attainment of *nirvana*. By the medieval period, however, some Buddhist theologians had begun to worship the Buddha as divine, and also had developed the concept of bodhisattvas, enlightened individuals who, like Christian saints, spent the afterlife assisting humans to reach nirvana, and also served as role models of spiritual excellence for the living.
Thierry Ollivier/Art Resource, N.Y.

14 Ancient Civilizations of the Americas

CHAPTER HIGHLIGHTS

Mesoamerica Although there was no single Mesoamerican civilization, the civilizations of the Olmecs, the people of Monte Alban and Teotihuacan, the Maya, the Toltecs, and the Aztecs shared many features: urban centers with monumental buildings arranged around large plazas, writing, a sophisticated calendrical system, religions that included human sacrifice, and the cultivation of certain crops, especially maize and beans.

The Aztecs established the largest Mesoamerican state before the coming of the Spanish in the sixteenth century. The Aztec Empire depended on tribute from conquered peoples. It was a society organized for war. Women could own property and participate in trade, but were subordinate to men and excluded from high authority.

Andean South America Monumental architecture and public buildings in Peru date from the third millenium B.C.E. Over the next 3,000 years, the Andean peoples developed pottery, urban centers, intricate cotton weaving, and sophisticated agriculture.

The Incas built the most extensive Andean empire. It spanned 2,600 miles from Ecuador to Chile between the Pacific and the Amazon basin, with over 14,000 miles of roads and numerous rope bridges. Although the Inca lacked writing, they kept detailed accounts using a system of knotted strings.

CHAPTER QUESTIONS

WHAT PROBLEMS do scholars face in reconstructing the history of native American civilization?

WHAT GROUPS dominated Olmec society?

WHAT WERE some of the main achievements of the Classic period civilizations in Mesoamerica?

WHAT ROLE did human sacrifice play in the Aztec Empire?

WHEN DID Andean people first become dependent on agriculture?

HOW DID the Inca enlarge and organize their empire?

CHAPTER OUTLINE

- Problems in Reconstructing the History of Native American Civilization
- Mesoamerica
- The Formative Period and the Emergence of Mesoamerican Civilization
- The Classic Period in Mesoamerica
- The Post-Classic Period
- Andean South America

- The Preceramic and the Initial Period
- Chavín de Huantar and the Early Horizon
- The Early Intermediate Period
- The Middle Horizon Through the Late Intermediate Period
- The Inca Empire

Humans first settled the American continents between 12,000 and 40,000 years ago. At that time, glaciers locked up much of the world's water, lowering the sea level and opening a bridge of dry land between Siberia and Alaska. When the glaciers receded, the oceans rose, severing Asia from America. The inhabitants of the Americas were isolated from the inhabitants of Africa and Eurasia and remained so until 1492.

Although separated from one another, the peoples of the Americas, Africa, and Eurasia experienced similar cultural changes at the end of the Paleolithic period. People in some regions shifted from hunting and gathering to a settled, agricultural way of life. And in some places civilization emerged.

Mesoamerica (modern Mexico and Central America) and the Andean region of South America have histories of civilization reaching back thousands of years. At the time of the European conquest of the Americas in the 16th century, both regions were dominated by powerful empires—the Aztecs, or Mexica, in Mesoamerica and the Inca in the Andes. Spanish conquerors obliterated both empires. But Native American traditions have endured, overlaid, and combined with Hispanic culture to provide clues to the pre-Hispanic past.

RECONSTRUCTING THE HISTORY OF NATIVE AMERICAN CIVILIZATION

WHAT PROBLEMS do scholars face in reconstructing the history of Native American civilization?

Andean civilizations never developed writing, and in Mesoamerica much of the written record was destroyed by time and conquest. Archaeologists have been able to create a picture of the economic and social organization of ancient American civilizations, but archaeology alone cannot produce the kind of narrative history that thousands of years of written records have made possible for Eurasian civilizations. From one ancient Mesoamerican people, however—the Maya—specimens of writing survive, and scholars have deciphered their script and attached names, dates, and events to silent ruins.

We also have information about the history and culture of the Aztecs and Inca that was told to the Spanish in the wake of their conquests of these peoples. But these accounts are colored by the interests and prejudices of the conquerors. Scholars seeking to understand Native American civilization have had to rely on the language and categories of European thought to investigate peoples and culturals that had nothing to do with Europe. Cultural blinders and arrogance exacerbate this situation.

MESOAMERICA

Mesoamerica, which means "middle America," extends from central Mexico into Central America. It also designates a distinctive and enduring cultural tradition that emerged between 1000 and 2000 B.C.E. and manifested itself in a succession of impressive states that flourished prior to the arrival of European conquerors in the 16th century. The peoples of Mesoamerica were and are ethnically and linguistically diverse. There was no single Mesoamerican civilization or linear development of civilization in the region. Nonetheless, Mesoamerican civilizations shared many traits, including writing, a sophisticated calendrical system, religious ideas, a ritual ball game, and urban centers with buildings arranged around large plazas.

Throughout their history, the peoples of the region were linked by trade. Metallurgy came late to Mesoamerica and was used primarily for ceremonial

OVERVIEW   PERIODS OF MESOAMERICAN AND ANDEAN CIVILIZATIONS

Scholars divide the history of the Mesoamerican and Andean peoples into several distict periods.

MESOAMERICA

Period	Civilization
Archaic, 8000–2000 B.C.E.	agricultural villages; maize cultivation
Formative, 2000 B.C.E.–150 C.E.	Olmecs, Monte Alban; urban centers, writing, calendar
Classic, 150–900 C.E.	Maya, Teotihuacán; sophisticated mathematics, astronomy, and calendar
Post-Classic, 900–1521 C.E.	Toltecs, Aztecs

ANDES

Period	Civilization
Preceramic and Initial, ca. 3000–800 B.C.E.	coastal peoples; monumental architecture, pottery
Early Horizon, ca. 800–200 B.C.E.	Chavin; innovations in ceramics, weaving, and metallurgy
Early Intermediate, ca. 200 B.C.E.–600 C.E.	Nazca, Moche; political centralization, monumental earthworks, advanced pottery and metallurgy
Middle Horizon and Late Interemediate, ca. 600 C.E.–1475	Tiwanaku, Huari, Chimu; expansionist empires, sophisticated agriculture
Inca Empire, ca. 1475–1532	extensive network of roads and bridges, sophisticated record keeping, advanced architecture

objects. In place of metal, Mesoamericans made weapons and tools from **obsidian**, a volcanic glass highly valued for its ability to hold a razor-sharp edge.

Mesoamerican history before the Spanish conquest is conventionally divided into four major periods: the Archaic, Formative (Olmecs), Classic (Maya), and Post-Classic (Toltecs and Aztecs). The term "Classic" reflects the view of many early Mesoamericanists that the era during which the Maya civilizations of the southern Yucatán erected dated stone monuments was the high point of Mesoamerican civilization. Although that view is no longer so prevalent, the terminology has endured, and the four periods still provide a useful framework for understanding Mesoamerican history.

During the Archaic period some people in Mesoamerica made the transition from hunting and gathering to settled village life. The key to this development was the domestication of maize (corn) and other staple crops, including beans, squash, tomatoes, chili peppers, and avocado. Maize and beans together provide a superior source of protein to the grains that were the basis of the Neolithic revolution in the Ancient Middle East and China. Eurasians relied to some extent on domesticated animals for protein, but Mesoamerica had few domesticated species—among them dogs and turkeys—and no large herd animals like the cattle, sheep, and goats of the Old World.

Probably because they had no large draft animals, the people of the Americas, including Mesoamerica, utilized the wheel only for toys. In Mesoamerica, humans did the carrying, and armies were composed of foot soldiers.

QUICK REVIEW

Transition to Settled Village Life

- Occurred during Archaic period
- Cornerstone of process was domestication of maize
- Mesoamerica had few domesticated animals

obsidian Hard volcanic glass that was widely used in Mesoamerica.

WHAT GROUPS dominated Olmec society?

THE FORMATIVE PERIOD AND THE EMERGENCE OF MESOAMERICAN CIVILIZATION

By about 1500 B.C.E., Mesoamerica's agricultural villages were beginning to coalesce into more complicated societies, with towns and monumental architecture, social classes, trade among regions, and sophisticated artistic traditions.

THE OLMEC

The most prominent of the early Formative period cultures is that of the Olmec, centered on the lowlands of Mexico's Gulf Coast. Most of what is known about the Olmecs comes from the archaeological sites of San Lorenzo and La Venta (see Map 14–1). San Lorenzo had developed into a prominent center by about 1200 B.C.E. It included public buildings, a drainage system linked to artificial ponds, and what was probably the earliest court for the unique Mesoamerican ball game. The settlement flourished until about 900 B.C.E., then went into decline and was abandoned by about 400 B.C.E. La Venta thrived during the era in which San Lorenzo faded. Its most conspicuous feature is a 110-foot scalloped pyramid, known as the Great Pyramid, which stands at one end of a group of platforms and plazas aligned along a north–south axis.

Olmec Monument. A large carved monument from the Olmec site of La Venta with a naturalistically rendered human figure.

Robert and Linda Mitchell Photography.

MAP 14–1
Mesoamerica in the Formative Periods.

WHAT ROLE did trade play in the formation of Mesoamerican civilizations?

San Lorenzo and La Venta probably had fewer than 1,000 inhabitants. They were, in all likelihood, a powerful elite who were supported by farmers in outlying villages. The monumental architecture and sculpture at these sites suggests that Olmec society was dominated by a class of ruler-priests who could mobilize large gangs of laborers.

The raw material for many Olmec artifacts, such as jade and obsidian, comes from other regions of Mesoamerica. Likewise, Olmec goods and iconography are found in other regions. This suggests that from an early time, the parts of Mesoamerica were linked in a web of trade. Trade contacts would have contributed to the formation of common Mesoamerican traditions.

THE VALLEY OF OAXACA AND THE RISE OF MONTE ALBAN

Olmec civilization had disappeared by about 200 B.C.E., but by then important developments were taking place elsewhere. Some of the most significant settlements in the Late Formative period were in the Valley of Oaxaca. Around 500 B.C.E., Monte Alban was built on a hill where three branches of the valley meet. Its population grew to about 5,000, and it emerged as the capital of a state that dominated the Oaxaca region. Carved images of bound prisoners imply that warfare played a role in establishing its authority. These images also suggest an early origin for the ritual human sacrifice that characterized most Mesoamerican cultures. Monte Alban maintained its independence against the growing power of the greatest Classic period city, Teotihuacán.

Major Periods in Ancient Mesoamerican Civilization

Archaic	8000–2000 B.C.E.
Formative (or Pre-Classic)	2000 B.C.E.–150 C.E.
Classic	150–900 C.E.
Post-Classic	900–1521 C.E.

WHAT WERE some of the main achievements of the Classic period civilizations in Mesoamerica?

THE EMERGENCE OF WRITING AND THE MESOAMERICAN CALENDAR

The earliest evidence of writing and the Mesoamerican calendar has been found in the Valley of Oaxaca. The Mesoamerican calendar is based on two interlocking cycles. One cycle, tied to the solar year, was of 365 days; the other was of 260 days. Combining the two cycles produced a "century" of 52 years, the amount of time required before a combination of days in each cycle would repeat itself. At the time of the Spanish conquest, all the peoples of Mesoamerica used this 52-year calendrical system. Only the Maya developed a calendar based on a longer time period, anchored—like the Jewish, Christian, or Muslim calendars—to a fixed starting point in the past.

THE CLASSIC PERIOD IN MESOAMERICA

*T*he Classic period was a time of cultural florescence. The Maya, who built densely populated cities in the rain forests of the southern Yucatán, developed a sophisticated system of mathematics and Mesoamerica's most advanced hieroglyphic writing. Indeed, Classic period urban life in Mesoamerica was richer and on a larger scale than in Europe north of the Alps at the same time.

Classic period cities were religious and administrative centers whose rulers combined secular and religious authority. Warfare was common and rulers used force to expand and maintain their power. The ritual sacrifice of captive enemies was a feature of Classic period societies.

TEOTIHUACÁN

In the late Formative period, two centers competed for dominance over the growing population of the Valley of Mexico. One of these, Cuicuilco, was at the southern end of the valley. The other, Teotihuacán, was about 30 miles northeast of Mexico City. When a volcano destroyed Cuicuilco in the first century C.E., Teotihuacán grew into a great city, perhaps Mesoamerica's first true city-state. It dominated central Mexico for centuries and influenced the rest of Mesoamerica.

Natural advantages contributed to Teotihuacán's rise. A network of caves recently discovered under its most prominent monument, the Pyramid of the Sun (the name by which the Aztecs knew it), may have been considered an entrance to the underworld. Stone quarried from the caves was used to construct the city, creating a symbolic link between the city's buildings and its sacred origins. Teotihuacán is also near a source of obsidian, and it straddled a trade route to the Gulf Coast and southern Mesoamerica. The quarrying of obsidian and the manufacture and trade of obsidian goods were apparently major sources of the city's wealth and influence, but it was also surrounded by fertile farmland.

At its height in about 500 C.E., Teotihuacán extended over almost 9 square miles and had a population of more than 150,000, making it, at that time, one of the largest cities in the world. Its size and organization suggest that it was ruled by a powerful, centralized authority. Teotihuacán is laid out on a rigid grid plan dominated by a broad, 3-mile-long thoroughfare known as the Avenue of the Dead. Religious and administrative structures and a market occupy the center of the city. At one end of the Avenue of the Dead is the 210-foot-high Pyramid of the Sun. More than 2,000 residences surround the city center. The lavish homes of the city's elite lie nearest its center. Most residents lived in walled apartment compounds located farther out. In addition to being residences,

The Pyramid of the Sun. This monumental structure stands near the southern end of Teotihuacán's great central thoroughfare, the Avenue of the Dead.

Kal Muller/Woodfin Camp & Associates.

these compounds housed craft manufacture. Neighborhoods specialized in different products, such as pottery or obsidian work. Parts of the city were reserved for foreign traders. Murals adorned the interiors of many buildings. The humble dwellings of poor farmers occupied the city's periphery. As the city grew, local farmers were forced to move to Teotihuacán, which is another indication of the power of its rulers.

Teotihuacán's influence extended throughout Mesoamerica. In the central highlands, dispersed settlements were consolidated into larger centers laid out similarly to Teotihuacán, suggesting conquest and direct control—a Teotihuacán empire. The city's influence in more distant regions may reflect close trading ties rather than conquest. The city's obsidian and pottery were exchanged widely for items like the green feathers of the quetzal bird and jaguar skins, materials used to make ritual garments.

Many of the buildings in Teotihuacán were decorated with sculptures and murals depicting the city's gods and ritual practices. Among the deities of Teotihuacán are a storm god and his goddess counterpart, who may be linked to the Aztecs' rain god and his consort. The people of Teotihuacán also worshipped a feathered serpent who is recognizable as the antecedent of the deity the Aztecs worshipped as Quetzalcoatl and the Maya as Kukulcan. Murals also suggest that the Teotihuacán elite, like the Maya and later Mesoamerican peoples, drew their own blood as a form of sacrifice to the gods. They also practiced human sacrifice.

After 500 C.E., Teotihuacán's influence began to decline, and in the eighth century its authority collapsed. The ritual center and the residences of the elite were destroyed by fire, perhaps as a consequence of a popular uprising. The city never regained its former status, but it retained its hold on the imaginations of succeeding generations of Mesoamericans—much like the appeal the ruins of ancient Greece and Rome had for Europeans. Teotihuacán is an Aztec word meaning "City of the Gods," and it was still a revered pilgrimage site at the time of the Spanish conquest.

THE MAYA

Maya civilization arose in southern Mesoamerica. During the Classic period, it experienced a remarkable florescence in the lowland jungles of the southern Yucatán.

All the pre-Spanish societies of Mesoamerica were literate. They recorded historical and religious information on scrolled or screenfold books made with deerhide or bark paper, but only a handful of these documents have survived. The Maya of the Classic period developed Mesoamerica's most advanced writing system, and they were unique in the extent to which they inscribed words and calendrical symbols on stone, pottery, and other imperishable materials.

The largest Maya city, Tikal, probably had a population of between 50,000 and 70,000 at its height. Powerful ruling families and their elite retainers dominated Maya cities, supported by a large class of farmer-commoners. Maya inscriptions are almost entirely devoted to recounting important events in the lives of these rulers. Warfare between cities was chronic, and as murals and sculptures document, captured prisoners were sacrificed to appease the gods and glorify victorious leaders.

Religion profoundly influenced the social and political lives of the Maya, for they recognized no clear distinction between a natural and a supernatural

Mayan Mural. This reproduction of one of the remarkable murals found at the Maya site of Bonampak shows the presentation of captives to the city's ruler, Chan Muan.

Copyright © President and Fellows of Harvard College 1998. All rights reserved Peabody Museum, Harvard University. Photograph by Hillel Burger.

world. As had probably been true in Teotihuacán, rulers and an elite exercised a combination of religious and political authority. Rulers claimed association with the gods and mediated between humans and gods by means of elaborate rituals. They wore special regalia to symbolize their power, and the ceremonies over which they presided were believed to be essential to sustaining the gods and the cosmic order. Religious rituals included bloodletting ceremonies, the sacrifice of captives, and ball games.

Maya believed that the world had gone through several cycles of creation, and a creation myth explains why all Maya cities had courts on which a unique sacrificial ball game was played. The myth tells how the Hero Twins defeated the gods of the underworld in the ball game and returned to life after being sacrificed. One became the sun and the other Venus. The regular rising and setting of these heavenly bodies represented the Twins' descent into the underworld and their subsequent rebirth. The games were ritual reinactments of the confrontation between the Hero Twins and the lords of the underworld. The losing team was sometimes sacrificed.[1]

During the Classic period, Maya developed a sophisticated mathematics and were among the first peoples in the world to invent the concept of zero. In addition to the 52-year calendar based on interlocking 260- and 365-day cycles they shared with other Mesoamerican societies, the Maya developed an absolute calendar. It was known as the **Long Count**, for it was reckoned from a fixed point in the past. The calendar had great religious as well as practical significance for the Maya, because it was determined by the movements of certain celestial bodies that were worshipped as deities. Great skill in astronomical observation was required to achieve the complexity and accuracy of the Maya calendar. The lunar calendar was adjusted to remain in sync with the actual length of the lunar cycle (29.53 days), and it may have had provisions like our leap years to coordinate with the solar year. Maya also made accurate observations of Venus and recognized before other peoples that it is both the morning and the evening star. The importance of the calendar, its association with divine forces, and the esoteric knowledge required to maintain it go a long way toward explaining the prestige and power of the elite who were its guardians.

During the Classic period, no single center dominated the Maya region. Many independent units, consisting of a capital city and smaller subject towns and villages, rose and fell in prominence. Tikal, which emerged as an important center in the Late Formative period, is a good example. At its height, it was the largest Classic Maya city, having a residential center covering more than 14 square miles and containing about 3,000 structures. The city follows the uneven terrain of the rain forest. It is not, like Teotihuacán, laid out on a grid, but monumental causeways link its major structures. Tikal benefited from its strategic location near a source of flint, a valued raw material for stone tools. Nearby swamps, with modification, might have been agriculturally productive. River systems connect the city to the coasts.

A single dynasty of 39 rulers reigned in Tikal from the Early Classic period until the eighth century. Early rulers in this Jaguar Paw line were buried in a structure known as the North Acropolis. Inscriptions associated with their tombs provide details about them, including in many cases their names and the dates of their reigns and military victories.

Long Count Mayan calendar that dated from a fixed point in the past.

---

[1]Robert J. Sharer, *The Ancient Maya*, 5th ed. (Stanford, CA: Stanford University Press, 1994), p. 522.

For about 100 years beginning in the mid-sixth century, Tikal and most other lowland Maya sites undertook little new construction. Tikal may have suffered a serious defeat at the hands of the city of Caracol, but in 682, the ruler Ah Cacau (r. 682–723?) initiated a new period of vigor and prosperity for Tikal. He extended its influence through conquests and strategic marriage alliances, and he and his two immediate successors began an ambitious building program. They created most of Tikal's surviving monumental structures, including the dramatic, soaring temples that dominate the site. After the death of Chitam (r. 769–?), the last ruler in the Jaguar Paw dynasty, Tikal declined and never recovered.

Similar dynastic histories are being recovered at other Classic Maya sites. Inscriptions above the tomb of Lord Pacal (r. 615–683), the greatest ruler of the city of Palenque, located in the western Mayan region, trace the city's entire dynastic history back to mythic ancestors. Two of its rulers were women, one of them Pacal's mother, Lady Zac Kuk (r. 612–640), and another predecessor, Lady Kanal Ikal (r. 583–604).

Between 800 and 900 C.E., Classic period civilization collapsed in the southern lowlands. The ruling dynasties came to an end, and the great cities were virtually abandoned. The cause of the collapse is not known with certainty, but it is clear that the Maya exceeded their resources. Intensifying warfare, population growth and concentration, and attempts to increase agricultural production that ultimately backfired may all have worked to bring down the civilization. As the urban areas around the ceremonial centers grew, so did the demand for food. But because ambitious building projects continued right up to the collapse, a growing proportion of the population must have been employed on these projects, leaving fewer to produce food. Overfarming may then have led to soil exhaustion, and a major drought may also have occurred.

The focus of Maya civilization next shifted to the northern Yucatán. There the site of Chichén Itzá, located next to a sacred well, flourished from the 9th to the 13th centuries. Stylistic resemblances between Chichén Itzá and Tula, the capital of the Post-Classic Toltec Empire in central Mexico (see the next section), suggest ties between the two cities. After Chichén Itzá fell, Mayapan became the main Maya center. But by the time of the Spanish conquest, only small, competing Maya settlements remained.

THE POST-CLASSIC PERIOD

After Teotihuacán's collapse in the eighth century, smaller, militaristic states emerged. Many centered on fortified hilltop cities. Interregional trade and market systems became increasingly important, and secular and religious authorities began to diverge.

WHAT ROLE did human sacrifice play in the Aztec Empire?

THE TOLTECS

About 900 C.E., a people known as the Toltecs rose to prominence. Their capital, Tula, is near the northern periphery of Mesoamerica. Like Teotihuacán, it lay close to an important source of obsidian. The Toltecs themselves were apparently descendants of one of many "barbarian" northern peoples (like the later Aztecs) who began migrating into Mesoamerica during the Late Classic.

Aztec mythology glorified the Toltecs as the fount of civilization, attributing to them a vast empire to which the Aztecs were the heirs. Other Mesoamerican peoples also attributed legendary status to the Toltecs. However, Tula, although a substantial city with a population of between 35,000 and 60,000 people, was never as large or as organized as Teotihuacán. Toltec influence reached many regions of Mesoamerica, but archaeologists are uncertain whether that influence translated into political control.

Toltec iconography, which stresses human sacrifice, death, blood, and military symbolism, supports their warlike reputation. But Toltec power was short-lived. By about 1100, Tula was in decline and its influence gone.

THE AZTECS

The people commonly known as the Aztecs referred to themselves as the **Mexica**. When the Spanish arrived in 1519, the Aztecs dominated much of Mesoamerica. Their capital city, Tenochtitlán, was the most populous in Mesoamerica up to that time. Built on islands in the southern part of Lake Texcoco in the Valley of Mexico, it was home to between 200,000 and 300,000 people. Tenochtitlán had great temples and palaces. Traders brought goods from distant regions, and vast wealth flowed to the city from subject territories. Yet the Aztecs were relative newcomers, having begun their rise to power only about 200 years before the Spaniards arrived.

According to their legends, the Aztecs were originally a nomadic people from somewhere to the northwest of the Valley of Mexico. At the urging of their patron god Huitzilopochtli, they began to migrate, arriving in the Valley of Mexico early in the 13th century. Scorned by the people already living there, they settled in 1325 on the island that became Tenochtitlán. The site was indicated to them by an omen from Huitzilopochtli: an eagle perched on a prickly pear cactus.

At first the Aztecs paid tribute to and served as mercenaries for Azcazpotzalco, the most powerful state in the valley. Soon, however, they became independent allies with their own tribute-paying territories. They consolidated their position by marriage alliances with ruling families of other cities. These marriages gave their rulers claim to descent from the Toltecs. In 1428, under their fourth ruler, Itzcoatl (r. 1427–1440), the Aztecs formed a triple alliance with Texcoco and Tlacopan and became the dominant power in the Valley of Mexico. Less than 100 years before the arrival of Cortés, the Aztecs, at the head of this Triple Alliance, began the aggressive expansion that brought them their vast tribute-paying empire (see Map 14–2).

Itzcoatl inaugurated the official Aztec imperial ideology by burning all the ancient books in the valley, expunging any histories that conflicted with Aztec pretensions, and restructuring Aztec religion to support Aztec preeminence. The Aztecs wished to present themselves as the divinely ordained successors to the Toltecs.

Aztec conquests ultimately included almost all of central Mexico. To the west,

Mexica Aztecs' name for themselves.

Human Sacrifice. Illustration from a colonial era manuscript volume, known as the Codex Magliabecchiano, presenting Aztec ritual sacrifice on a temple altar.

Scala/Art Resource.

MAP 14–2

The Aztec and Inca Empires on the Eve of the Spanish Conquest.

WHAT WERE the chief differences between the Aztec and Inca Empires?

however, they were unable to conquer the rival Tarascan Empire. And within their realm, several pockets of resistance (notably, Tlaxcala) remained at war with the Aztecs.

The Aztec Extractive Empire   The Aztec Empire was extractive; meaning that after a conquest, the Aztecs usually left the local elite in power but extracted heavy tribute in goods and labor from their people. Tribute included agricultural products, fine craft goods, gold and jade, textiles, and feathers. The volume was considerable. For instance, up to 7,000 tons of maize and two million cotton cloaks flowed into Tenochtitlán's coffers annually. This wealth underwrote the grandeur of Tenochtitlán (see "A Spaniard Describes the Glory of the Aztec Capital").

Aztec Religion and Human Sacrifice   Aztec imperial exploitation did not end with valued craft goods. Human sacrifice on a prodigious scale was central to Aztec ideology. The Aztecs believed that Huitzilopochtli, the sun god, required human blood to rise again each day, and that it was their responsibility to provide the victims. The prime candidates for sacrifice were war captives, and the Aztecs often engaged in "flowery wars" with traditional enemies like Tlaxcala just to obtain captives. On major festivals, thousands of victims might perish. Led up the steps of the temple of Huitzilopochtli, a victim was thrown backward over a stone, his arms and legs pinned, while a priest cut out his heart. He would then be rolled down the steps of the temple, his head placed on a skull rack, and his limbs butchered and distributed to be eaten. Small children were sacrificed to the rain god Tlaloc, who, it was believed, was pleased by their tears.

Victims were also selected as stand-ins for particular gods and were sacrificed after a series of rituals. In ceremonies honoring the powerful god Tezcatlipoca, a beautiful male youth was chosen to represent the god for a year, during which he was treated with reverence. He wandered through the city dressed as the god and playing the flute. A month before the end of his reign he was given four wives. Twenty days before his death he was dressed as a warrior, and for a few days he was virtual ruler of the city. Then he was sacrificed.

No other Mesoamerican people practiced human sacrifice on the scale of the Aztecs. The slaughter doubtless served a variety of spiritual functions, but on a practical level it intimidated subject peoples and, by reducing their population of fighting-age men, headed off rebellions. But human sacrifice and the heavy burden of tribute also fed resentment and fear that may explain why so many subject peoples were willing to support Cortés when he challenged the Aztecs.

Tenochtitlán   Three great causeways linked Tenochtitlán to the mainland. They met at the ceremonial core of the city, which was dominated by the temple to Huitzilopochtli and Tlaloc where most of the Aztecs' sacrificial victims met their fates. The palaces of the ruler and high nobles lay just outside the central precinct. The ruler's palace was the empire's administrative center, with government officials, artisans and laborers, gardens, and a zoo. The rest of the city was divided into wards (**calpulli**). Some *calpulli* were reserved for merchants (*pochteca*) or artisans. The city was laid out on a grid formed of streets and canals. Agricultural plots of great fertility bordered the canals and the lake. Aqueducts

calpulli Wards into which the Aztec capital, Tenochtitlan, was divided.

HISTORY'S VOICES

A SPANIARD DESCRIBES THE GLORY OF THE AZTEC CAPITAL

On November 8, 1519, a group of approximately 400 Spaniards under the command of Hernán Cortés entered the Aztec capital of Tenochtitlán. One of them was Bernal Díaz del Castillo (b. 1492) who later wrote The Conquest of New Spain, a chronicle of his experience. This gives some sense of the magnificence of the Aztec capital.

WHICH ELEMENTS of Aztec life especially astonished Díaz? What can one conclude about the social and political life of the Aztec elite from the manner in which Montezuma was attended? Which forms of wealth were most apparent?

Early next day we left Iztapalapa [where Cortés forces had been camped] with a large escort of these great Caciques [Aztec nobles], and followed the causeway, which is eight yards wide and goes so straight to the city of Mexico [Tenochtitlán] that I do not think it curves at all. Wide though it was, it was so crowded with people that there was hardly room for them all. Some were going to Mexico and others coming away, besides those who had come out to see us, and we could hardly get through the crowds that were there. For the towers and the cues [temples] were full, and they came in canoes from all parts of the lake. No wonder, since they had never seen horses or men like us before.

With such wonderful sights to gaze on we did not know what to say, or if this was real that we saw before our eyes. On the land side there were great cities, and on the lake many more. The lake was crowded with canoes. At intervals along the causeway there were many bridges, and before us was the great city of Mexico . . . .

We marched along our causeway to a point where another small causeway branches off to another city . . . and there, beside some towerlike buildings, which were their shrines, we were met by many more Caciques and dignitaries in very rich cloaks. The different chieftains wore different brilliant liveries, and the causeways were full of them. . . .

. . . When we came near to Mexico, at the place where there were some other small towers, the great Montezuma descended from his litter, and these other great Caciques supported him beneath a marvelously rich canopy of green feathers, decorated with gold work, silver, pearls . . . which hung from a sort of border. It was a marvelous sight. The great Montezuma was magnificently clad, in their fashion and wore sandals . . . the soles of which are of gold and the upper parts ornamented with precious stones. And the four lords who supported him were richly clad also in garments that seem to have been kept ready for them on the road so they could accompany their master . . . and many more lords . . . walked before the great Montezuma, sweeping the ground on which he was to tread, and laying down cloaks so that his feet should not touch the earth. Not one of these chieftains dared to look him in the face. All kept their eyes lowered most reverently except those four lords, his nephews, who were supporting him.

. . . Who could now count the multitude of men, women, and boys in the streets, on the roof-tops and in canoes on the waterways, who had come out to see us? . . .

They led us to our quarters, which were in some large houses capable of accommodating us all and had formerly belonged to the great Montezuma's father . . . . Here Montezuma now kept the great shrines of his gods, and a secret chamber containing gold bars and jewels. This was the treasure he had inherited from his father, which he never touched.

Source: *The Conquest of New Spain*, by Bernal Díaz, trans. by J. M. Cohen (New York: Penguin Books, 1963), copyright © J. M. Cohen, 1963, pp. 216–218.

carried water into the city. A dike kept the briny water of the northern part of Lake Texcoco from contaminating the waters around Tenochtitlán.

Society Aztec society was hierarchical, authoritarian, and militaristic. It was divided into two broad classes, noble and commoner, with merchants and certain artisans forming an intermediate category. The nobility enjoyed wealth and luxury. Laws and regulations relating to dress reinforced social divisions. Elaborate and brilliantly colored regalia distinguished nobles from commoners, who were required to wear rough, simple garments.

The Aztecs were morally austere. They valued obedience, respectfulness, discipline, and moderation. Laws were strict and punishment severe. Standards for the nobility were higher than for commoners and punishments for sexual and social offenses were more strictly enforced for them. Drunkenness was harshly punished among the elite.

The most exalted rank in the nobility was that of *tlatoani* (plural *tlatoque*), or ruler of a major political unit. Of these, the chiefs were the rulers of the three cities of the Triple Alliance, and of them, the highest was the *tlatoani* of Tenochtitlán. Below these rulers were the *tetcutin*, the lords of subordinate units, and below them were the *pipiltin*, the bureaucrats and priests.

The bulk of the population, the commoners, farmed, harvested fish from the lake, and provided labor for public projects. All commoners belonged to a *calpulli*, each of which had its own temple. Children received training in the song houses attached to these temples. *Calpulli* officials assured that the *calpulli* fulfilled its tribute obligations. Commoners who could not pay their debts or the tribute they owed could be enslaved. Slavery was also the punishment for some criminal offenses. Serfs worked the estates of noblemen.

Traders and merchants (*pochteca*) were important figures in Aztec society. Together with the Aztec armies, they helped spread Aztec influence, and their far-reaching expeditions obtained luxury goods for the lords of Tenochtitlán. The pochteca organized guilds and established laws and customs for doing business. Their wealth gave them a somewhat ambiguous position in Aztec society, and they usually avoided ostentatious display so as not to attract unwanted attention. Artisans who made luxury goods, like the merchants who sold them, also enjoyed special status.

Markets were central to Aztec economic life. More than 60,000 people bought and sold in the great market at Tlatelolco each day. Market administrators, some of whom were women, regulated transactions. Cacao beans and cotton cloaks served as mediums of exchange.

Above all, Aztec society was structured and constantly mobilized for war. All young men received military training. Battles were fought to capture new territory, punish rebellious tributaries, protect trading expeditions, secure natural resources, and replenish the supply of sacrificial victims. Battles were not coordinated confrontations of massed infantry units, but fields on which a myriad of simultaneous individual combats took place. A warrior's goal was to subdue and capture prisoners for sacrifice. Prowess in battle was key to social advancement and to rewards for both commoners and nobles. On the other hand, failure in battle entailed social disgrace.

Women in Aztec society could inherit and own property. They traded in the marketplace and served as market officials. Their craft work provided their

14.6
Bernal Díaz del Castillo

tlatoani An Aztec ruler.

tetcutin Subordinate Aztec lords.

pipiltin Aztec bureaucrats and priests.

pochteca Aztec merchants.

families with income. Girls and boys alike were educated in the song houses, and women had access to priestly roles, although they were barred from the higher religious positions. In general, however, Aztec society's fixation on war relegated women to subordinate status and excluded them from major leadership roles. A man's function was to wage war, and a woman's purpose was to bear children. Childbirth was compared to battle, and death in childbirth, like death in battle, guaranteed rewards in the afterlife.

ANDEAN SOUTH AMERICA

HOW HAVE the Andes affected the development of civilization in South America?

*T*he Andean region of South America—primarily modern Peru and Bolivia—had, like Mesoamerica, a long history of civilization before the Spanish conquerors arrived in the 16th century. Andean civilization is conventionally divided into seven periods: Preceramic, Initial, Early Horizon, Early Intermediate, Middle Horizon, Late Intermediate, and Late Horizon (Inca Empire). During the Early, Middle, and Late Horizon periods, a homogeneous art style spread over a wide area. The intermediate periods are characterized by regional stylistic diversity.

THE PRECERAMIC AND THE INITIAL PERIOD

WHEN DID Andean people first become dependent on agriculture?

*T*he earliest monumental architecture in Peru dates to the early third millennium B.C.E., roughly contemporary with the Great Pyramids of Egypt. Located on the coast mostly near the shore, these earliest centers, which predate the introduction of pottery to Peru, feature ceremonial mounds and plazas. Coastal people at this time subsisted primarily on the bounties of the sea, supplemented by squash, beans, and chili peppers. They also cultivated cotton. Their cotton fishing nets and textiles mark the start of a sophisticated Andean textile tradition.

The earliest public buildings in the highlands date to before 2500 B.C.E. Highland people were more dependent on agriculture than coastal people during the late Preceramic, cultivating maize as well as potatoes and other tubers. Llamas and alpacas were fully domesticated by about 2500 B.C.E.

There is little evidence of social stratification for the late Preceramic. Public structures of both the coast and the highlands appear to have been centers of community ritual for relatively egalitarian societies.

The introduction of pottery to Peru around 2000 B.C.E. marks the beginning of the Initial period and corresponds to a major shift in settlement and subsistence patterns on the coast. People became dependent on agriculture as well as on maritime resources. They moved their settlements inland, constructed irrigation systems, began cultivating maize, and built large ceremonial centers adorned with sculpture and brightly painted façades. Population grew, society became stratified, and incised carvings of bodies with severed heads suggest

MAP 14–3
Pre-Inca Sites.

WHAT WERE the differences between highland and coastal cultures in early South American history?

that conflicts were increasing. Centers appear, however, to have maintained their independence of any overarching political authority.

CHAVÍN DE HUANTAR AND THE EARLY HORIZON

The large coastal centers of the Initial period declined early in the first millennium B.C.E. At about the same time, beginning around 800 B.C.E., a site in the highlands, Chavín de Huantar, was growing in influence. Located on a trade route between the coast and the lowland tropical rain forest and boasting a powerful religious cult, Chavín had a population of perhaps 3,000 at its height. Between about 400 and 200 B.C.E., Chavín influence spread widely throughout Peru, due probably to the prestige of its cult and not to political or military expansion.

The flowering of the Chavín culture was marked by innovations in ceramics, weaving, and metallurgy. Excavations also point to increasing social stratification. Skeletal remains at Chavín, for example, suggest that people who lived closer to the ceremonial center ate better than people living on the margins of the site.

The Periods of Andean Civilization	
Preceramic	ca. 3000–ca. 2000 B.C.E.
Initial Period	ca. 2000–ca. 800 B.C.E.
Early Horizon	ca. 800–ca. 200 B.C.E.
Early Intermediate Period	ca. 200 B.C.E.–ca. 600 C.E.
Middle Horizon	ca. 600 C.E.–ca. 800/1000 C.E.
Late Intermediate Period	ca. 800/1000–ca. 1475
Late Horizon (Inca Empire)	ca. 1475–1532

THE EARLY INTERMEDIATE PERIOD

Signs of increasing warfare accompany the collapse of the Chavín culture and the ideological unity it had brought to the Andes. During the Early Intermediate period that followed, both regional diversity and political centralization developed as the first territorial states appeared in the Andes.

WHICH CULTURES followed in the wake of Chavín?

NAZCA

The Nazca culture, which flourished from about 100 B.C.E. to about 700 C.E., was centered in the Ica and Nazca valleys. The people of the Nazca valley built underground aqueducts to divert ground water from the middle of the valley to supply their irrigation canals. Cahuachi, the largest Nazca site, may have been the capital of a Nazca confederation. It was, however, empty most of the year and filled only when pilgrims arrived to celebrate religious festivals.

The Nazca are renowned for their textiles and fine pottery, decorated with images of Andean plants and animals. They are most famous, however, for their colossal earthworks, or geoglyphs, the so-called Nazca lines. These massive designs were created by brushing away the dark gravel of the desert to reveal the lighter-colored subsurface. Some geoglyphs are located on hillsides and visible from ground level, but others can be seen only from the air.

MOCHE

The Moche culture, named for the Moche valley on the north coast of Peru, flourished from about 200 to 700 C.E. Two huge structures, the Pyramid of the Sun and the Pyramid of the Moon, overlook this site. The cross-shaped Pyramid

The Nazca Geoglyph. Located in the Peruvian desert, the geoglyph depicts a vast hummingbird. The lines were constructed by the Nazca people probably sometime between 250 C.E. and 600 C.E. They appear to have been sacred paths walked by Nazca people perhaps somewhat as medieval Europeans walked a labyrinth. At the summer solstice the final parallel line points to the sun. Features of this and other geoglyphs can only be discerned from the air, and their exact purpose remains a matter of speculation.

Marilyn Bridges/Corbis Bettman.

HOW DO Tiwanaku and Huari foreshadow the achievements of the Inca?

of the Sun is the largest adobe structure in the Americas. It was some 1,200 feet long by 500 feet wide and rose in steps to a height of 60 feet. Its construction required more than 143 million adobe bricks.

The Moche were skilled potters. They sculpted realistic portrait vessels that may depict actual people. Ceremonial scenes feature elaborately dressed figures drinking the blood of sacrificed prisoners. The Moche were also the most sophisticated smiths in the Andes. They developed innovative alloys, cast weapons and agricultural tools, and used the lost-wax process to create small, intricate works.

THE MIDDLE HORIZON THROUGH THE LATE INTERMEDIATE PERIOD

TIWANAKU AND HUARI

In the fifth century C.E., as the Roman Empire was crumbling under the pressure of Germanic invasions and as Teotihuacán was reaching its height in Mesoamerica, the first expansionist empires were emerging in the Andean highlands. One of these was centered at Tiwanaku in Bolivia and the other at Huari in Peru. Both are associated with new agricultural technologies and show signs of statecraft that foreshadow the administrative practices of the later Inca

Empire. The artistic symbols used by both peoples also suggest that they shared a religious ideology.

Tiwanaku lies more than 12,600 feet above sea level, making it the highest capital in the ancient world. Construction apparently began at the site about 200 C.E., and it experienced its greatest growth from about 500 to 600 C.E. It collapsed some 500 years later. The city occupied one to two square miles, and may have had a population of 20,000 to 40,000 people at its height. Laid out on a grid, Tiwanaku is dominated by large public structures and ceremonial gateways. The effort expended to transport the stone for these monuments was enormous, and their existence is evidence of the power of Tiwanaku's rulers.

An economy based on raised-field agriculture on the shores of Lake Titicaca sustained Tiwanaku. This system involved farming on artificial platforms capped with rich topsoil and separated by basins of water. Experimental reconstructions have shown it to be extremely productive.

Tiwanaku dominated the Titicaca basin and neighboring regions. It probably owed its influence to its religious prestige and to a policy of establishing colonies and religious-administrative structures in distant territories.

The Huari Empire, which flourished from about 600 to 800 C.E., dominated the highlands from near Cuzco in the south to Cajamarca in the north. Its capital city, Huari, covers about 1.5 square miles and had a population of 20,000 to 30,000 people.

Huari is located in a valley, and its origin is associated with development of techniques for terracing and irrigating hillsides to increase productivity. Huari administrative centers were undefended and built in accessible places. Many archaeologists think they may have functioned like later Inca administrative centers; that is, they housed a small Huari elite that organized local labor for state projects. Also like the Inca, Huari administrators used *quipu*, record-keeping devices made of string.

THE CHIMU EMPIRE

After the demise of the Moche, two new states emerged on the north coast. One is named for the site of Sican and was centered in the Lambayeque Valley. The other, known as Chimu, was centered in the Moche valley. In two waves of expansion, the Chimu built an empire that took over the Lambayeque valley and stretched for 800 miles along the coast. Its administrative capital, Chan Chan, was a vast walled city covering 8 square miles. The city's focal points are some 10 immense adobe-walled enclosures that probably housed the empire's ruling elite. Smaller compounds probably belonged to lesser nobility. Surrounding these were the homes and workshops of the artisans and

quipu Knotted string used by Andean peoples for recordkeeping.

The Inca *Quipumayoc*. The Inca Guipumayoc grand treasurer, is shown holding a *quipu*, a device made of knotted strings, used to record administrative matters and sacred histories. Information was encoded in the colors of the strings and the style of the knots.
The Granger Collection.

workers who served the upperclasses. Two areas were apparently transport centers, where llama caravans brought raw materials to the capital from the empire's territories. The total population of the city was between 30,000 and 40,000. All of this was swept away about 1470 by the rising Inca Empire.

THE INCA EMPIRE

*I*n 1532, when Francisco Pizarro and his companions happened on it, the Inca Empire was one of the largest states in the world. It spanned the region between the Pacific Coast and the Amazon basin and stretched some 2,600 miles from Ecuador to northern Chile (see Map 14–2). Its population numbered in the millions.

The Inca called their domain the Land of the Four Quarters. Their capital, Cuzco, lay at the intersection of these divisions. Home to the ruler (Inca) and the ruling elite, the city enjoyed great splendor. Its principal temples, dedicated to the sun and moon, gleamed with gold and silver.

The origins of the Inca are obscure. According to their own traditions, Inca expansion began only in the 15th century in the wake of a revolt by the Chanca people that nearly destroyed Cuzco. Inca Yupanqui, son of the city's aging ruler, crushed the revolt, and he and his successors expanded their domains, spreading civilization through the Andean region. There is an element of imperial propaganda in this legend, for archaeological evidence suggests that the Inca had been expanding for decades—perhaps centuries—before the Chanca revolt.

The Inca enlarged their empire through alliance, intimidation, and conquest. They ruled their realm through a hierarchical administrative system and imposed their language, **Quechua**, as the official tongue. Quechua is still widely spoken in the Peruvian Andes.

The Inca relied on various forms of labor taxation. They divided agricultural lands into categories, allowing local populations to retain some for their own support and reserving the rest for the state and the gods. In a system known as the *mita*, local people worked for the state on a regular basis, receiving in return gifts and ritual entertainments. Men also owed military service and labor on public works projects. The Inca designated entire communities as *Mitimaqs* and relocated them at will to exploit various resources of their empire. They sometime pacified territories by settling loyal people in hostile regions and moving hostile people to loyal regions.

Several groups of people were employed in full-time state service. The *mamakuna*, the so-called Virgins of the Sun, formed one of these groups. These women lived privileged but celibate, regulated lives in cities and towns scattered throughout the empire. They could be given in marriage by Inca rulers to cement alliances, and they had important economic as well as religious roles. They wove cloth and brewed the maize beer known as *chicha*, which was consumed at state religious festivals. Another group of full-time state workers were men whose duties included tending the royal llama herds.

Cloth and clothing were means of communication. Inca warehouses were filled with textiles as well as with food and other craft goods. Complex textile patterns indicated a person's rank and ethnic affiliation. The Incas controlled their empire through regional administrative centers and warehouses linked

---

Quechua   Inca language.

mita   Inca system of forced labor in return for gifts and ritual entertainments.

Mitimaqs   Communities whom the Incas forced to settle in designated regions for strategic purposes.

mamakuna   Inca women who lived privileged but celibate lives and had important economic and cultural roles.

chicha   Maize beer brewed by the mamakuna for the Inca elite.

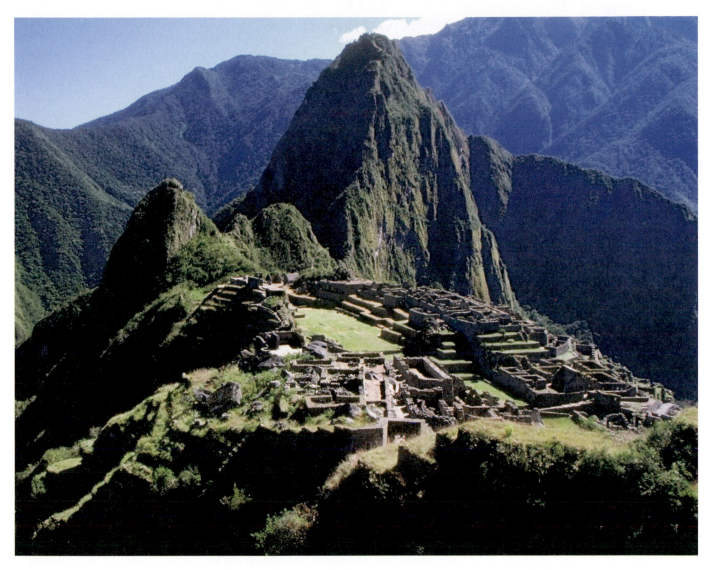

Machu Picchu. The Inca city of Machu Picchu perches on a saddle between two peaks on the eastern slopes of the Andes.

Robert Frerk/Odyssey Productions.

by roads. These facilities organized, housed, and fed people engaged in mita labor service and staged feasts and rituals to impress them with the power and beneficence of the state. The wealth of the empire, collected in storehouses, sustained the mita laborers, fed and clothed the army, and enriched the Inca elite. Although the Inca lacked writing, they kept detailed administrative records on quipu, accounting devices made from knotted strings. The Inca also built more than 14,000 miles of road, ranging from narrow paths to wide thoroughfares. Rope bridges crossed gorges and rivers, and stairways made ascent of steep slopes easier. A system of relay runners sped messages to Cuzco from the far reaches of the empire.

Over their long history, the people of the Andes developed an adaptation to their challenging environment that allowed them to prosper and grow. They brought more land under cultivation than is farmed in that part of the world today, and they engineered an economy that brought them a measure of well-being superior to that which followed the destruction of the Inca Empire by the Spanish invaders.

IMAGE KEY

for pages 310–311

a. Mayan numbers on terra-cotta, 100 C.E.
b. Corn seeds
c. Separated head, limbs, and torso of the Aztec goddess Coyolxauhqui
d. Sipan earspool
e. Aztec sun stone
f. A ball game player, Mayan funerary gift
g. Chichen Itza, Mexico, El Castillo/ Pyramid of Kukulcan
h. Tula statuary
i. El Castillo, Mayan castle at Tulum, on the Yucatan peninsula, Mexico
j. Olmec Monument
k. Machu Picchu

SUMMARY

Mesoamerica Mesoamerica means "middle America." It extends from central Mexico through Central America. Although there was no single Mesoamerican civilization, the civilizations of the Olmecs, the peoples of Monte Alban and Teotihunacán, the Maya, the Toltecs, and the Aztecs shared many features: urban centers with monumental buildings arranged on large plazas, writing, a sophisticated calendrical system, religions that included human sacrifice, and the cultivation of certain crops, especially maize and beans. Throughout its history, the cities of Mesoamerica also were linked by trade.

The Aztecs established the largest Mesoamerican state before the coming of the Spanish in the 16th century. The Aztec Empire depended on tribute from conquered peoples. Aztec society was organized for war and was divided into nobles and commoners, with merchants and certain artisans forming intermediate categories. The Aztecs practiced widescale human sacrifice. Most of the victims were captured warriors. Women could own property and participate in trade, but were subordinate to men and excluded from high authority.

Andean South America Monumental architecture and public buildings in Peru date from the third millennium B.C.E. Over the next 3,000 years, the Andean peoples developed pottery, urban centers, intricate cotton weaving, and sophisticated agriculture. The first expansionist empires emerged in the Andean highlands in the fifth century C.E..

The Incas built the most extensive Andean empire. It spanned 2,600 miles from Ecuador to Chile between the Pacific and the Amazon basin. Inca rule relied on conquest, intimidation, and alliances with other peoples. The Inca exacted taxation in terms of forced labor and constructed more than 14,000 miles of roads and numerous rope bridges. Although the Inca lacked writing, they kept detailed accounts using knotted strings.

REVIEW QUESTIONS

1. What did the rise of civilization in Mesoamerica and Andean South America have in common with the rise of civilization in Africa and Eurasia? How did these regions differ?
2. What were the distinguishing characteristics of the Classic period civilizations of Mesoamerica?
3. How was the Aztec Empire organized? The Inca Empire?
4. Both the Aztec and Inca Empires fell in the early 16th century when confronted with Spanish forces of a few hundred men. What might explain this?

KEY TERMS

calpulli (p. 323)

chicha (p. 330)

Long Count (p. 319)

Mexica (p. 321)

mita (p. 330)

Mitimaqs (p. 330)

manakuna (p. 330)

obsidian (p. 313)

pipiltin (p. 325)

pochteca (p. 325)

quipu (p. 329)

Quechua (p. 330)

tlatoani (p. 325)

tetcutin (p. 325)

  For additional study resources for this chapter, go to:
www.prenhall.com/craig/chapter14

Visualizing The Past
Mapping the World before 1500

HOW DO world maps convey a culture's understanding of its place in the cosmos? Is it possible for any map of the world to be objective?

Long before explorers knitted the globe into a single planet, humans mapped their world. Environmental factors and cultural values influenced the way mapmakers executed their craft. Despite these differences, the maps below share a technical proficiency matched only by their intrinsic beauty.

Arabia. The Arab scholar al-Idrisi created this world map in 1154. In keeping with Arab cartographic traditions, the map is oriented with south on top. Europe appears as a fairly insignificant appendage of Asia while Africa is depicted as a huge landmass turning all the way east towards China. The entire world is surrounded by an "All-Encompassing Ocean."

Map of World by Islamic scholar, Al Idrisi, copy made in 1553 (960 AH or Anno Hegirae) of original of 1154, Arabic. Pococke 375 folio 3v-4r. Bodleian Library Oxford.

Africa. This is a late 15th-century map of ▶ the world based on a description by the second century CE scholar Claudius Ptolemaeus of Alexandria, more commonly known as Ptolemy. The Ptolemaic view of the world held sway in western Europe until the great age of discovery. Note how, in contrast to the map of al-Idrisi, Africa curves eastward to connect with China on the far right, making the Indian Ocean an enclosed sea—which for Europeans it practically was until Vasco da Gama sailed to the Indian Ocean in 1497–1499.

Courtesy of the Library of Congress.

◀ **The New World.** More a cosmic diagram than a map, this startling image, painted on animal hide sometime between 1400 and 1500 by either the Mixtec or Aztec peoples of present-day Mexico, illuminates a native American worldview before the arrival of Europeans. At the center is the fire god Xiuhtecutli. Radiating out from him are the four directions—each represented by a specific color, deity, and tree with a bird in its branches. In each corner, to the right of a U-shape, is one of the attributes of Tezcatlipoca, the Smoking Mirror, a primal god who could see humankind's thoughts and deeds. Intense symbolism, such as the kind depicted here, played a central role in the cultures of pre-Colombian America.

Liverpool Museum, Liverpool, Great Britain.

Polynesia. Polynesians were among the world's greatest explorers ▶ in the pre-modern era. Starting out from their ancestral homeland in New Guinea, by 1000 CE they had discovered almost every island in the Pacific. Expert navigators, they sailed in twin-hulled canoes and used the sun, stars, and the direction of prevailing winds and ocean currents to cross vast stretches of ocean. Stick charts, like the one depicted here, were used to record patterns of ocean swells. The shells indicate islands.

Courtesy of the Library of Congress.

15 Europe to the Early 1500s
Revival, Decline, and Renaissance

CHAPTER HIGHLIGHTS

Medieval Society Medieval society was divided, in theory, into three main groups: clergy, nobility, and laborers. The rise of merchants, self-governing towns, and universities helped break down this division. By supporting rulers against the nobility, towns gave kings the resources to build national governments. Much of medieval history involves the struggle by rulers to assert their authority over powerful local lords and the church.

Church and State The medieval papacy sought to extend its power over both church and state. In the tenth century, the Cluny reform movement increased popular respect for the church and strengthened the papacy. In the Investiture Struggle, the papacy secured the independence of the clergy, in the process weakening imperial power in Germany. The First Crusade further strengthened papal prestige. But, by the end of the thirteenth century, kings had become more powerful than popes. In the fourteenth century, the Great Schism further weakened papal prestige.

Nation Building By the fifteenth century, England, France, and Spain had developed into strong national monarchies with centralized bureaucracies and professional armies. The Great Schism, the Hundred Years' War, and the Black Death had weakened the church and the nobility, while townspeople supported kings. A similar process began in Russia where rulers of Moscow extended their authority after throwing off Mongol rule.

The Renaissance The Renaissance, which began in the Italian city-states in the late fourteenth century, marked the transition from the medieval to the modern world. Humanism promoted a rebirth of ancient norms and values and the classical ideal of an educated, well-rounded person. The growth of secular values led to a great burst of artistic activity. The political weakness of the Italian states invited foreign intervention by France, Spain, and the Habsburgs. The sack of Rome by imperial forces in 1527 marked the end of the Renaissance.

CHAPTER QUESTIONS

HOW DID the Investiture Controversy weaken the Holy Roman Empire?

WHAT WERE the three basic social groups in the medieval society?

HOW DID England and France develop strong royal governments by the thirteenth century?

WHAT WERE the causes of the political and social breakdown that occurred during the fourteenth century?

WHY WAS the Renaissance a transition from the medieval to the modern world?

WHAT WERE the bases for the rise of the modern sovereign state in the fifteenth century?

CHAPTER OUTLINE

- Revival of Empire, Church, and Towns
- Society
- Growth of National Monarchies
- Political and Social Breakdown and Revival: The Late Medieval Church
- The Renaissance in Italy (1375–1527)
- Revival of Monarchy: Nation Building in the Fifteenth Century

The High Middle Ages (from the eleventh through the thirteenth centuries) were a period of both political expansion and consolidation and intellectual flowering and synthesis. The Latin, or Western, church established itself as a spiritual authority independent of secular monarchies, which themselves became more powerful and self-aggrandizing. The parliaments and popular assemblies that accompanied the rise of these monarchies pioneered modern representative institutions.

The High Middle Ages saw a revolution in agriculture that increased food supplies and populations. Trade and commerce revived, towns expanded, protomodern forms of banking and credit developed, and a "new rich" merchant class rose to power in Europe's cities. Universities were established, and contact with the Arab world led to the beginning of the recovery of the works of the ancient Greek philosophers. This helped to stimulate the great expansion of Western education and culture that was achieved during the late Middle Ages and the Renaissance.

The late Middle Ages and the Renaissance (the fourteenth, fifteenth, and early sixteenth centuries) were a time of unprecedented calamity and of bold new beginnings in Europe. France and England grappled with each other in a bitter conflict, the Hundred Years' War (1337–1453). Between 1348 and 1350, Bubonic plague, which contemporaries called the Black Death, reduced the population in many regions by approximately one-third. A schism divided the papacy and the church (1378–1417), and in 1453 the Turks captured Constantinople and expanded into Europe. From this perspective, Western civilization seemed to be collapsing.

But the late Middle Ages also witnessed an intellectual and artistitic renaissance that continued into the seventeenth century. Scholars criticized medieval assumptions about the nature of God, humankind, and society. Italian and northern humanists made a full recovery of classical learning and languages and conceived of ideas that would spread and transform life in Europe. The "divine art" of printing was invented. The vernaculars, the languages of ordinary people, began to take their place alongside Latin as vehicles for art and serious discourse, and patriotism and incipient nationalism became important factors in the politics of Europe's independent nation-states.

REVIVAL OF EMPIRE, CHURCH, AND TOWNS

OTTO I AND THE REVIVAL OF THE EMPIRE

HOW DID the Investiture Controversy weaken the Holy Roman Empire?

The fortunes of both the old empire and the papacy began to revive in 918, when the Saxon Henry I ("the Fowler"; d. 936) became the first non-Frankish king of Germany. Henry rebuilt royal power and left his son and successor Otto I (r. 936–973) in a strong territorial position. Otto maneuvered his own kin to dominate Bavaria, Swabia, and Franconia. Then, in 951, he invaded Italy and proclaimed himself its king. In 955, he defeated the Hungarians at Lechfeld, which secured German borders against barbarian attacks. All this earned Otto the title "the Great."

Otto enlisted the help of the church in rebuilding his realm. As agents to administer his lands, he preferred to appoint bishops and abbots. These men possessed a sense of universal empire but they could not marry and found families to compete with his own. In 961, Otto responded to a call for help from Pope John XII (955–964), and on February 2, 962, Otto received from the pope in return the imperial coronation he had long desired. The church was brought ever more under royal control, but it was increasingly determined to assert its independence.

THE REVIVING CATHOLIC CHURCH

Otto's successors became so preoccupied with Italy that they allowed their German base to disintegrate. As the revived empire began to crumble in the 11th century, the church, long unhappy with imperial domination, declared its independence by embracing a reform movement pioneered by a monastic order.

Cluny Reform Movement   In 910, a monastery was founded at Cluny in east-central France, and the Cluniac monks launched a campaign to free the church from lay control. Their cause was aided by the popular respect the church commanded. The church was medieval society's most democratic institution. Theoretically, any man could become pope, for the pope was usually elected by the people and the clergy of Rome. The grace and salvation the church dispensed were available to everyone, and the church promised a better life to come to the great mass of ordinary people, who found their earthly circumstances brutish and hopeless.

The Cluny reformers maintained that clergy should not be subservient to kings, and that all clergy should come directly under the authority of the pope. They denounced "secular" parish clergy, who by living with concubines in a relationship akin to marriage, fell short of Cluny's ascetic ideals. Distinctive features of Western religion—separation of church and state and the celibacy of the Catholic clergy—had their definitive origins in the Cluny reform movement. From Cluny, reformers were dispatched throughout France and Italy, and in the late 11th century the papacy embraced their reforms.

Otto I and the Church.   Otto I presents the Magdeburg Cathedral to Christ, as the pope (holding the keys to the kingdom of heaven) watches, a testimony to Otto's guardianship of the Church.

"Christ Enthroned with Saints and Emperor Otto I" (r. 962–973). One from a series of 19 known as the Magdeburg Ivories. Ivory H 5" × W 41/2" (12.7 × 11.4 cm).

Investiture Struggle: Gregory VII and Henry IV   In 1075, Pope Gregory VII (r. 1073–1085), a fierce advocate of church reform, condemned under penalty of excommunication the well-established custom of king's appointing bishops to administer their estates and "investing" them with the ring and staff that symbolized their ecclesiastical office. The emperor Henry IV of Germany considered Gregory's action a direct challenge to his authority. Germany's territorial princes, on the other hand, were inclined to support the pope, for they believed that anything that weakened the emperor strengthened them.

The lines of battle were quickly drawn. Henry assembled his loyal German bishops at Worms in January 1076 and had them declare their independence from Gregory. Gregory promptly excommunicated Henry and absolved all Henry's subjects from loyalty to him. The German princes were delighted. Henry, facing a general revolt, had to come to terms with Gregory. In a famous scene, he prostrated himself outside Gregory's castle retreat at Canossa in northern Italy. Reportedly he stood barefoot in the snow off and on for three days before the pope absolved him. Papal power seemed to triumph, but the struggle was not yet over.

The investiture controversy was not settled until 1122. In the Concordat of Worms, Emperor Henry V (r. 1106–1125) agreed not to invest bishops with the ring and staff that signified their spiritual authority, and Pope Calixtus II (r. 1119–1124) recognized the emperor's right to be present at episcopal consercrations and to grant bishops their secular fiefs before or after their investment

QUICK REVIEW

Church and State

- Investiture crisis centered on authority to appoint and control clergy
- Pope Gregory excommunicated Henry IV when he proclaimed his independence from papacy
- Crisis settled in 1122 with Concordat of Worms

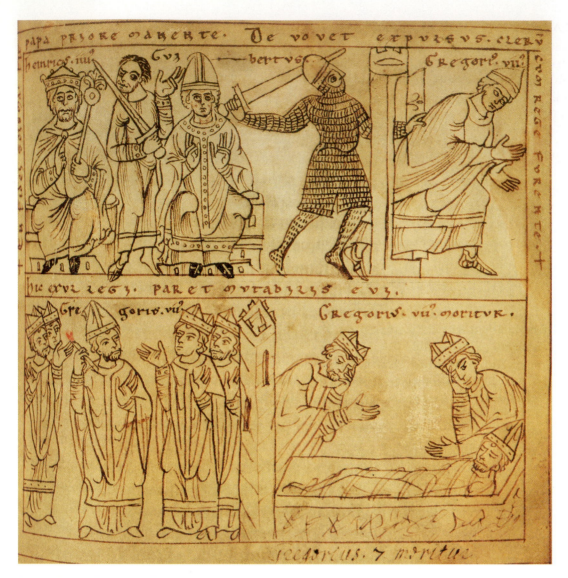

Struggle Between Emperor and Pope. A 12th-century German manuscript portrays the struggle between Emperor Henry IV and Pope Gregory VII. In the top panel, Henry installs the puppet pope Clement III and drives Gregory from Rome. Below, Gregory dies in exile. The artist was a monk, whose sympathies were with Gregory, not Henry.

Thuringer Universities and Landesbibliothek, Jena: Bos. q. 6, Blatt 79r.

Crusades Religious wars directed by the church against infidels and heretics.

with the spiritual symbols by the church. The emperor effectively retained the right to nominate or veto a candidate. The settlement had the effect of separating spheres of ecclesiastical and secular authority and setting the stage for future and greater conflicts between church and state.

THE CRUSADES

If evidence of a surge of popular piety and support for the pope in the High Middle Ages is needed, the **Crusades** provide it. What the Cluniac reform was to the clergy, the First Crusade to the Holy Land was to the laity: an outlet for heightened religious zeal.

Late in the 11th century, the Byzantine Empire was under severe pressure from the Seljuk Turks, and Emperor Alexius I Comnenus (r. 1081–1118) appealed for Western aid. At the Council of Clermont in 1095, Pope Urban II (r. 1088–1099) responded by launching the First Crusade. Scholars debate the motives of the Crusaders. Genuine religious piety played a major part. The papacy promised crusaders forgiveness for all their sins should they die in battle, and a crusade to the Holy Land was the ultimate religious pilgrimage. But the pope and others may also have hoped to stabilize the West by sending large numbers of restless, feuding young nobles off to foreign lands. (About 100,000 took part in the First Crusade.) Younger sons of nobleman, for whom there were no estates at home, may have hoped that the crusade would make their fortunes. Urban also saw the crusade as an opportunity to reconcile Eastern and Western Christianity.

The First Victory   Drawn by the dream of liberating the holy city of Jerusalem, which the Seljuk Turks had held since the seventh century, three great armies gathered in France, Germany, and Italy. As the crusaders marched by different overland routes toward Constantinople, they seized the opportunity to rid Europe of Jews as well as Muslims. Jewish communities, especially in the Rhineland, suffered bloody pogroms (see Map 15-1).

The eastern emperor was suspicious of the uncouth, spirited soldiers who gathered at his capital, and his subjects, whose villages the Europeans plundered, were openly hostile. Nevertheless, the Crusaders succeeded in doing what Byzantine armies had failed to do. They routed the Seljuks and on July 15, 1099,

7.6
Launching the Crusades (1095): "It Is the Will of God!"

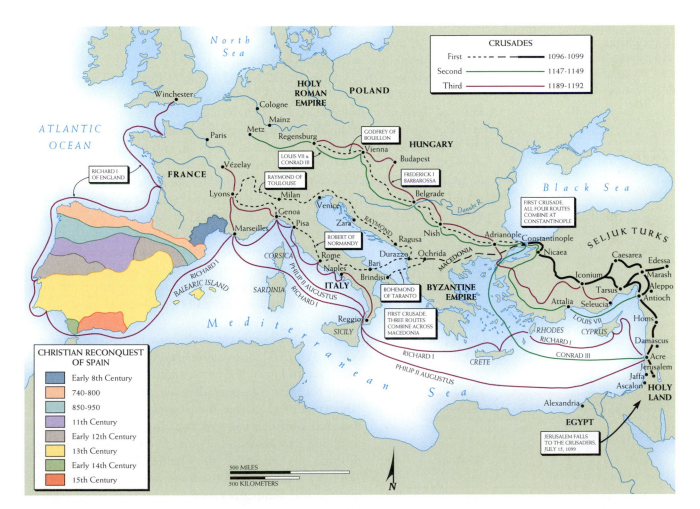

MAP 15–1
The Early Crusades.   Routes and several leaders of the Crusades during the first century of the movement are shown. The names on this map do not exhaust the list of great nobles who went on the First Crusade. The even showier array of monarchs of the Second and Third Crusades still left the Crusades, on balance, ineffective in achieving their goals.

WHAT obstacles did the Crusaders encounter?

Seige of Jerusalem. Godfrey of Bouillon leads the attack on Jerusalem in 1099. The capture of the city was hailed as a miracle, followed by the massacre of its inhabitants.

Bibliotheque Nationale, Paris, France.

took the city of Jerusalem. They owed their success to their superior military discipline and weaponry and to the fact that the Muslims failed to unite to oppose them.

The Crusaders set up a "kingdom of Jerusalem" composed of a number of tiny feudal states. These were tenuously held islands in a sea of Muslims intent on their destruction. As the crusaders built castles for the defense of their new territories, their focus shifted from conquest to economic development. Some, like the military-religious order of the Knights Templar, acquired vast fortunes.

The Second and Third Crusades Europeans held their own for about 40 years, and then the crusader states began to fall. The first to go was Edessa. Its loss in 1144 sparked a drive for a Second Crusade (1147–1149), which was effectively preached by Bernard of Clairvaux (1091–1153), a Cistercian monk and one of Europe's most eminent religious leaders. The venture was a dismal failure.

In October 1187, Saladin (r. 1138–1193), king of Egypt and Syria, retook Jerusalem. Its loss inspired the Third Crusade (1189–1192), a joint effort by three of Europe's greatest kings: Richard the Lion-Hearted of England, Frederick Barbarossa of the Holy Roman Empire, and Philip Augustus of France. Barbarossa died in an accident en route to the front, and Philip Augustus soon returned to France to prey on Richard's lands. Left alone, Richard could do little. When he finally acknowledged that fact and headed home, he was captured by Emperor Henry VI. England paid a huge ransom to win his release. Popular resentment at the failed, costly venture contributed to the events that produced the Magna Carta in 1215, an effort to curb the power of England's kings.

The Crusades did not change the international political situation. The Holy Land reverted as firmly as ever to Muslim control. But the Crusades did transform international commerce by creating new trade routes and reopening old ones. Italy's great port cities—particularly Venice, Pisa, and Genoa—profited greatly.

The Fourth Crusade Venetian commercial ambitions helped to make the Fourth Crusade a travesty. In 1202, 30,000 crusaders gathered at Venice, intending to sail to Egypt. When they could not raise the money to pay for their transport, they negotiated a deal with the Venetians. In exchange for passage, they agreed to take the rival Christian port of Zara for Venice. Europe was stunned, but worse was to come. The Crusaders were next diverted to Constantinople, which fell to their assault in 1204. A Latin ascended the Byzantine throne, and Venice became the dominant commercial power in the eastern Mediterranean.

Pope Innocent III was chagrined by the misdirection of a crusade he had authorized, but once Constantinople was in Latin hands, he changed his mind. The opportunity to bring Greek Christians under the control of the Latin church was too tempting. The Greeks, however, could not

The Crusades

1095	Pope Urban II launches the First Crusade
1099	The Crusaders take Jerusalem
1147–1149	The Second Crusade
1187	Jerusalem retaken by the Muslims
1189–1192	Third Crusade
1202–1204	Fourth Crusade

be reconciled to Latin rule, and in 1261 the man they recognized as their legitimate emperor, Michael Paleologus, recaptured the city. He had help from Venice's rival, Genoa. The Fourth Crusade did nothing to heal the political and religious divisions that separated East and West.

TOWNS AND TOWNSPEOPLE

In the 11th and 12th centuries, most towns were small. Only about 5 percent of western Europe's population lived in an urban context, but they were some of the most creative members of medieval society.

The Chartering of Towns   Towns were originally dominated by the feudal lords who issued charters spelling out terms for their organization. The lords' purpose was to court skilled laborers who could manufacture the finished goods the feudal nobility desired. A charter guaranteed a town's safety and gave its residents a degree of independence unknown to a rural peasant.

As towns grew and their privileges beckoned, many serfs migrated to the new urban centers. There they found the freedom and opportunity to earn the wealth that elevated an industrious craftsperson's social standing. As movement of serfs to towns accelerated, the lords in the countryside were forced to offer serfs more favorable terms of tenure to keep them on the land. The growth of towns thus improved the lot of serfs in several ways.

The Rise of Merchants   Rural society not only provided craftspeople and day laborers for towns, but the first merchants may have been enterprising serfs. Certainly, some of the long-distance traders were people who had nothing to lose and everything to gain from the enormous risks of foreign trade. They traveled together in armed caravans and convoys, buying goods and products as cheaply as possible at the source, and selling them for all they could get.

At first the merchants were disliked because they were outside the traditional social groups of nobility, clergy, and peasantry. Over time, however, the powerful came to respect the merchants and the weak to imitate them. Merchants brought prosperity and a higher standard of living.

As traders established themselves in towns and grew in wealth and numbers, they formed their own protective associations. These soon challenged seigneurial authority over their communities. Merchants especially wanted to end the arbitrary tolls and tariffs that regional magnates imposed on the goods merchants moved through the countryside.

Townspeople needed simple, uniform laws and a government sympathetic to their new forms of business activity. Commerce was incompatible with the defensive, fortress mentality of the lords of the countryside. The result was often a struggle with the old nobility within and outside the towns. This conflict led townspeople in the High and late Middle Ages to form independent communes and to ally themselves with kings against the rural nobility, a development that rearranged the centers of power in medieval Europe and ended classic feudal government.

Foundry in Florence. Skilled workers were an integral component of the commerce of medieval towns. This scene shows the manufacture of cannons in a foundry in Florence.
Scala/Art Resource, N.Y.

MAP EXPLORATION

Interactive map: To explore this map further, go to **http://www.prenhall.com/craig/map15.2**

MAP 15–2

Medieval Trade Routes and Regional Products.   Trade in Europe varied in intensity and geographical extent in different periods during the Middle Ages. The map shows some of the channels that came to be used in interregional commerce. Labels tell part of what was carried in that commerce.

HOW STRONG were the connections among Europe, the Middle East, and Africa at this time?

Because the merchants were the engine of the urban economy, small shopkeepers and artisans identified far more with them than with the aloof lords and bishops who were medieval society's traditional masters. The lesser nobility (small knights) also recognized the new mercantile economy as the wave of the future. During the 11th and 12th centuries, the burgher upper classes increased their economic strength and successfully challenged the old noble urban lords for control of towns.

New Models of Government   With urban autonomy came new models of self-government. Around 1100 the old urban nobility and the new burgher upper class merged to form an urban patriciate. It was a marriage between those wealthy by birth (inherited property) and those who made their fortunes in long-distance trade. From this new ruling class was born the aristocratic town council, which henceforth governed towns.

Enriching and complicating the situation, small artisans and craftspeople also slowly developed their own protective associations or **guilds** and began to gain a voice in government. The opportunities towns created for the "little people" established a new principle: "Town air brings freedom." Within town walls people thought of themselves as citizens with basic rights, not subjects liable to a master's whim.

Towns and Kings   By providing kings with the resources they needed to curb factious noblemen, towns became a major force in the transition from feudal societies to national governments. Towns were a ready source of educated bureaucrats and lawyers who knew Roman law, an effective tool for building royal government. The money that towns could provide for kings also enabled kings to hire their own armies and free themselves from dependence on the nobility. In turn, towns won political recognition and had their privileges guaranteed by national governments. In France, towns were integrated early into the royal administration. In Germany, they came under ever-tighter control by princes. In Italy, uniquely, they grew into genuine city-states that reached the peak of their power and influence during the Italian Renaissance.

Jews in Christian Society   Towns also attracted Jews who plied trades in small businesses. Many became wealthy as moneylenders to kings, popes, and business-people. Jewish intellectual and religious culture both dazzled and threatened Christians. These various factors encouraged suspicion and distrust among Christians, and led to a surge in anti-Jewish sentiment in the late 12th and early 13th centuries.

Schools and Universities   In the 12th century, translations and commentaries by Byzantine and Spanish Islamic scholars introduced western Europeans to the philosophical works of Aristotle, the writings of Euclid and Ptolemy, the texts of Greek physicians and Arab mathematicians, and the corpus of Roman law. The intellectual ferment created by this explosion of information began the development of the modern universities. The first important Western university was established in 1158 in Bologna. It specialized in the study of Roman law and became the model for the universities of Spain, Italy, and southern France. Paris provided a different model for northern European universities, and it was leading school for theologians

At the start of the High Middle Ages, learning involved mastering what was already known. People assumed that all truth had been discovered and only needed to be properly organized, elucidated, and defended. Students wrote commentaries on authoritative texts, especially those of Aristotle and the church fathers. Teachers did not encourage students to strive independently for undiscovered truth. They taught them to organize and harmonize the accepted truths of tradition and drilled these into them.

Under this method of study, called **Scholasticism**, students summarized the opinions of the received authorities in their field, debated their arguments pro

guild Association of merchants or craftsmen that offered protection to its members and set rules for their work and products.

Scholasticism Method of study based on logic and dialectic that dominated the medieval schools. It assumed that truth already existed; students had only to organize, elucidate, and defend knowledge learned from authoritative texts, especially those of Aristotle and the Church Fathers.

Dominicans (left) and Franciscans (right). Unlike the other religious orders, the Dominicans and Franciscans did not live in cloisters but wandered about preaching and combating heresy. They depended for support on their own labor and the kindness of the laity.

Cliché Bibliothèque Nationale de France, Paris.

and con, and then drew logical conclusions. The arrival of Aristotle's works in the West honed the tools of logic and dialectic they used to discipline their thinking. Dialectic is the art of testing a truth by examining arguments against it. The assumption that truth could be discovered by debating authoritative texts was accepted even in fields such as medicine—to the detriment of practical experience and empirical research.

Abelard   Peter Abelard (1079–1142) was the boldest and most controversial of the advocates for the new Aristotelian learning. As the leading philosopher and theologian of his day, he was the first European scholar to attract a large student following. His audacious logical critique of religious doctrine, however, earned him powerful enemies. His thinking was unique in its appreciation of subjectivity. He claimed, for instance, that the motives of an act's agent determined whether that act was good or evil, not the act itself. He also said that an individual's feeling of repentance was a more important factor in receiving God's forgiveness than the church's sacrament of penance.

Abelard, as he laments in his autobiography, played into the hands of his enemies by seducing Heloise, a young woman he was hired to tutor. She was the niece of a powerful canon of Paris's cathedral of Notre Dame. After she became pregnant, Abelard wed her—but kept the marriage secret, for university teachers, like clergy, were required to be celibate. Her chagrined uncle hired men to break into Abelard's rooms and castrate him.

Abelard sought refuge in the monastic life and induced Heloise to enter a convent. They exchanged letters in which he denigrated his love for her as wretched desire. Repentance failed, however, to ingratiate him with the church authorities. In 1121, his works were burned, and in 1140, 19 propositions that he had taught were condemned as heresies. Heloise outlived him by 20 years and won renown for her efforts to improve conditions for cloistered women.

SOCIETY

WHAT WERE the three basic social groups in the medieval society?

THE ORDER OF LIFE

Medieval commentators described society as consisting of only three categories of people: those who fought as mounted knights (the landed nobility), those who prayed (the clergy), and those who labored in fields and shops (the peasantry and village artisans). After the revival of towns in the 11th century, a fourth social group emerged: the long-distance traders and merchants.

Nobles By the late Middle Ages, separate classes of higher and lower nobility had evolved. The higher were the great landowners and territorial magnates, long the dominant powers in their regions; the lower were petty landlords, the descendants of minor knights, newly rich merchants, or wealthy farmers.

Arms were the nobleman's profession and waging war his sole occupation. In the eighth century, the adoption of stirrups made mounted warriors Europe's most valued military assets. The chief virtues of these knights were physical strength, courage, and beligerancy. For them, warfare was an opportunity to win wealth, honor, and glory. Peace, on the other hand, meant economic stagnation and boredom.

No medieval social group was absolutely uniform. Noblemen formed a broad spectrum—from minor vassals without subordinate vassals to mighty barons, the principal vassals of a king or prince, who had many vassals of their own. Dignity and status within the nobility were directly proportional to how much authority one exercised over others; a chief with many vassals far excelled the small country nobleman who was lord over none but himself.

By the late Middle Ages, several developments were forcing the landed nobility into a steep economic and political decline from which it never recovered. Climatic changes and agricultural failures created large famines, while the great plague (discussed later in this chapter) brought about unprecedented population losses. Changing military tactics and the appearance of heavy artillery during the Hundred Years' War empowered infantry and made the noble cavalry nearly obsolete. The support wealthy towns gave to kings enabled strong royal governments to reduce the power nobles once had over their private domains. After the 14th century, land and wealth counted for far more than noble lineage as qualifications for entrance into the highest social class.

Clergy Unlike a noble or a peasant, one was not born into the clerical estate. It was acquired by religious training and ordination and was, in theory at least, open to anyone. There were two fundamental categories of clergy. The **regular clergy** were the monks who lived according to a special ascetic rule (*regula*) in cloisters apart from the world. In the 13th century, the papacy authorized a different kind of monastic order. The friars—the Franciscans and the Dominicans—stayed in the world to preach, combat heresy, and provide social services. The **secular clergy** lived and worked among the laity in the world (*saeculum*). They staffed a vast hierarchy. At the top were the wealthy cardinals, archbishops, and bishops who were drawn almost exclusively from the nobility. Below them were the urban priests, cathedral canons, and court clerks. Finally, there was the great mass of poor parish priests, who were neither financially nor intellectually much above the common people they served.

During most of the Middle Ages, the clergy were honored as the first estate, and theology was the queen of the sciences. There was great popular respect and reverence for the clergy's function as mediators between God and humanity. The priest brought the Son of God down to earth when he celebrated the sacrament of the Eucharist, and his absolution released penitents from punishment for sin. Mere laypeople were not to presume to sit in judgment on such a priest.

Peasants The largest and lowest social group in medieval society was the one on whose labor the welfare of all the others depended: the agrarian peasantry. Many peasants lived and worked on the manors of the nobility, the vital cells of rural social life. The lord of a manor was owed a fixed amount of produce (grain,

regular clergy Monks and nuns who belong to religious orders.

secular clergy Parish clergy who did not belong to a religious order.

OVERVIEW   MEDIEVAL UNIVERSITIES

In the 12th century, Latin translations of of ancient texts in law, astronomy, philosophy, and mathematics, and of learned commentaries on them by Islamic and Byzantine scholars, reached the West. The resulting intellectual ferment gave rise to the medieval universities. The first university was established at Bologna in Italy in 1158. By 1500, there were almost 50 universities across Europe from Scotland to Poland. Universities helped bring wealth and prestige to towns; graduated professionals, such as lawyers, physicians, and theologians; and provided rulers with trained bureaucrats for their increasingly complex administrations. The following is a list of the medieval universities and the dates of their founding:

University	Country	Date of Founding	University	Country	Date of Founding
Bologna	Italy	1158	Erfurt	Germany	1379
Paris	France	ca. 1150–1160	Heidelberg	Germany	1385
Oxford	England	1167	Ferrara	Italy	1391
Vicenza	Italy	1204	Wurzburg	Germany	1402
Cambridge	England	1209	Leipzig	Germany	1409
Salamanca	Spain	1218	St. Andrews	Scotland	1411
Padua	Italy	1222	Turin	Italy	1412
Naples	Italy	1224	Louvain	Belgium	1426
Toulouse	France	1229	Poitiers	France	1431
Rome	Italy	1244	Caen	France	1437
Siena	Italy	1247	Bourdeaux	France	1441
Piacenza	Italy	1248	Barcelona	Spain	1450
Montpellier	France	1289	Trier	Germany	1450
Lisbon	Portugal	1290	Glasgow	Scotland	1451
Avignon	France	1303	Freiburg	Germany	1455
Orleans	France	1305	Ingolstadt	Germany	1459
Perugia	Italy	1308	Basel	Switzerland	1460
Coimbra	Portugal	1308	Nantes	France	1463
Grenoble	France	1339	Bourges	France	1465
Pisa	Italy	1343	Ofen	Germany	1475
Valladolid	Spain	1346	Tubingen	Germany	1477
Prague	Bohemia	1348	Uppsala	Sweden	1477
Pavia	Italy	1361	Copenhagen	Denmark	1479
Vienna	Austria	1364	Aberdeen	Scotland	1494
Cracow	Poland	1364			

eggs, and the like) and services from its peasant families, and he held judicial and police authority over them. He owned and operated the machines that processed their crops into food and drink, and he had the right to subject his tenants to exactions called *banalities*. He could, for example, force them to breed their cows with his bull, to grind their bread grains in his mill, to bake their bread in his oven, and to make their wine in his wine press—all for a fee. He might also compel them to buy their beer from his brewery and even give him the choice parts of all animals slaughtered on his lands. He collected as an inheritance tax a serf's best animal. Without the lord's permission, a serf could neither travel nor marry outside the manor to which he was attached.

However, the serfs' status was not chattel slavery. It was to a lord's advantage to keep his serfs healthy and happy, for his welfare, like theirs, depended on the quality of their work. Serfs had their own dwellings and strips of land that produced their incomes. They organized their own labor and could market for their own profit any surpluses that remained after they met their obligations. Serfs could pass their property (their dwellings, fields, and personal possessions) on to their children.

Two basic changes transformed conditions of life for the peasantry during the course of the Middle Ages. The first was increasing importance of single-family holdings. As families acquired and retained property from generation to generation, family farms replaced manorial units. The second was the conversion of the serf's dues into money payments, a change made possible by the revival of trade, the rise of town markets, and the return of a monetary economy. By the 13th century, many peasants held their land as rent-paying tenants and no longer had servile status.

In the mid-14th century, when the great plague and the Hundred Years' War created a labor shortage, nobles in England and France tried to turn back the clock by increasing taxes on the peasantry and restricting their migration to the cities. Their efforts triggered rebellions. The revolts of the agrarian peasantry, like those of the urban proletariat, were brutally crushed, but they were only one of the stresses that were threatening to destabilize European society at the end of the Middle Ages.

MEDIEVAL WOMEN

The image of women and the reality of their lives were quite different in the Middle Ages. The image was sketched by celibate male clergy who viewed virginity as morally superior to marriage. Drawing on ancient pagan as well as biblical sources, they claimed that women were physically, mentally, and morally inferior to men. They defined only two respectable roles for them: subjugated housewife, or confined nun. Many medieval women were neither.

Image and Status   The clerical view of women was contradicted both within the church itself and in secular society. During the 12th and 13th centuries, the burgeoning popularity of the cult of the Virgin Mary, of chivalric romances, and of courtly love literature celebrated women as natural moral superiors of men. The church also condemned extreme misogyny.

Virgin and Child, surrounded by angels, by Giovanni Cimabue (1240–1302).
SuperStock, Inc.

Medieval Marketplace. A 15th-century rendering of an 11th- or 12th-century marketplace. Medieval women were active in all trades, but especially in the food and clothing industries.

Scala/Art Resource, N.Y.

10.3
The Goodman of Paris

vernacular Everyday language spoken by the people as opposed to Latin.

HOW DID England and France develop strong royal governments by the 13th century?

Peter Lombard (1100–1169), an influential theologian, taught that God created Eve from Adam's rib because God intended woman neither to rule nor be ruled, but to be at man's side as his partner in a mutual relationship.

Germanic customary law also treated women better than Roman law. German women married men of their own age, and a German bride was entitled to a gift of property from her husband that she retained in case of his death. German law gave women the right to inherit, administer, dispose of, and confer property, and it allowed women to take men to court and sue for bodily injury and rape.

Life Choices The nunnery was an option only for women from the propertied classes, for admission to a cloister was contingent on payment of a substantial dowry. The number of nuns was never very large in the Middle Ages, but the cloister was an appealing refuge for some. Within a nunnery a woman could rise to a position of leadership and exercise a kind of authority often denied her sisters in the outside world. Even cloistered women, however, had to submit to supervision by male clergy.

In the ninth century, the Carolingian monarchs obeyed the church and began to enforce monogamy. This was both a gain and a loss for women. Wives were accorded greater dignity and legal security, but their burdens as household managers and bearers of children multiplied. The mortality rates of Frankish women increased and their longevity decreased in the ninth century.

Working women The vast majority of medieval women were neither housewives nor nuns, but working women. Evidence suggests that they were respected and loved by their husbands, perhaps because they worked shoulder to shoulder with them. Between the ages of 10 and 15, girls were apprenticed to learn productive trades, much like boys. If they married, they might operate businesses of their own or go to work in their husband's shops. Women appeared in virtually every "blue-collar" trade, but were especially prominent in the food and clothing industries. They belonged to guilds, and they could become craftmasters, but working women were paid less than men who did the same jobs. In the late Middle Ages, townswomen had opportunities to get some schooling and acquire **vernacular** literacy, but they were excluded from the learned professions.

GROWTH OF NATIONAL MONARCHIES

ENGLAND AND FRANCE: HASTINGS (1066) TO BOUVINES (1214)

William the Conqueror Medieval England's political destiny was determined by the response to the death of the childless Anglo-Saxon ruler Edward the Confessor (r. 1042–1066). Through a connection with Edward's mother, a Norman princess, Duke William of Normandy (d. 1087) laid claim to the vacant English throne. The Anglo-Saxon assembly preferred a native nobleman, Harold Godwinsson (ca. 1022–1066). William reacted by invading England and defeating Harold's army at Hastings on October 14, 1066. William I "the Conqueror" was crowned king of England in Westminster Abbey within weeks of the invasion.

Battle of Hastings. William the Conqueror on horseback urging his troops into combat with the English at the Battle of Hastings (October 14, 1066). From the Bayeux Tapestry, about 1073–1083.

Giraudon/Art Resource, N.Y.

As England's conqueror, William was free to establish a strong monarchy. He kept the Anglo-Saxon tax system and practice of issuing court writs (legal warnings). He continued the Anglo-Saxon quasi-democratic tradition of frequent *parleying*; that is, conferring with the lesser powers who had vested interests in royal decisions. This led eventually to the balance between monarchical and parliamentary elements that remains a characteristic of England's government.

Popular Rebellion and Magna Carta   The Duke of Normandy, who after 1066 was master of England, was also a vassal of the French king in Paris. France's Capetian kings understandably watched with alarm as the power of their Norman vassal grew alarmingly during the reign of William's grandson, Henry II (r. 1154–1189). From his mother Henry inherited Normandy. His father left him Maine, Touraine, and Anjou. Marriage to Eleanor of Aquitaine (1122–1204) brought him her huge duchy in southern France and completed the so-called Angevin or English-French empire. Henry used his resources to promote royal power, but this was met by strong resistance from both the nobility and the clergy.

Under Henry's successors, the brothers Richard the Lion-Hearted (r. 1189–1199) and John (r. 1199–1216), burdensome taxes levied to support Crusades and a failing war with France turned resistance into rebellion. With the full support in 1215 of the clergy and the townspeople, England's barons forced King John grudgingly to agree to terms spelled out in the **Magna Carta** ("Great Charter") in 1215. This famous cornerstone of modern English law limited royal power and secured the right of the privileged classes to representation when the government considered important matters like taxation. The Great Charter charted a path between dissolution of the monarchy by the nobility and the abridgment of the rights of the nobility by the monarchy.

Philip II Augustus   Powerful feudal princes dominated France from the beginning of the Capetian dynasty (987) until the reign of Philip II Augustus (1180–1223). During this period the Capetian kings wisely concentrated their limited resources on securing the territory surrounding Paris, the Île-de-France. By the time of Philip II, Paris had become the center of French government and culture, and the Capetian dynasty had acquired a secure hereditary right to the throne. Thereafter, the kings of France steadily enhanced their power over the French nobles.

Philip Augustus waged both internal and international campaigns, and he succeeded at both. His armies reclaimed all of England's continental fiefdoms,

Magna Carta   The "Great Charter" limiting royal power, which the English nobility forced King John to sign in 1215.

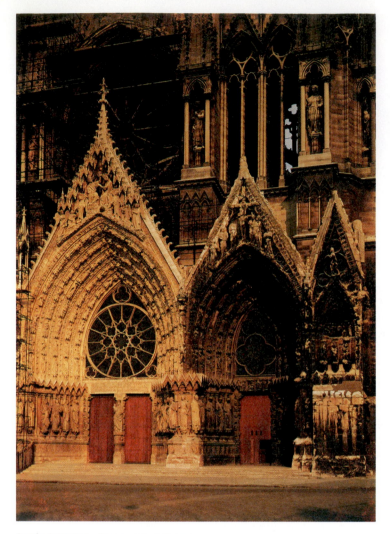

Gothic Cathedral. The portal of Reims Cathedral, where the kings of France were crowned. The cathedral was built in the Gothic style—emblematic of the High and late Middle Ages—that originated in France in the mid–12th century. The earlier Romanesque (Roman-like) style from which it evolved is characterized by fortresslike buildings with thick stone walls, rounded arches and vaults, and few windows. The Gothic style, in contrast, is characterized by soaring structures, their interiors flooded with colored light from vast expanses of stained glass.

Scala/Art Resource, N.Y.

except for Aquitaine. At Bouvines on July 27, 1214, the French won a decisive victory over the English and their German allies. Philip solidly united France behind its king and laid the foundation for French ascendancy in the late Middle Ages.

FRANCE IN THE 13TH CENTURY: REIGN OF LOUIS IX

Louis IX (r. 1226–1270), the grandson of Philip Augustus, embodied the medieval ideal of kingly authority. Louis's greatest achievements were on the domestic front. Under him, the efficient French bureaucracy established order and fair play in local government. He dispatched commissioners to monitor the conduct of the royal officials who were responsible for local administration and enforcing justice. These royal ambassadors were perceived as genuine champions of the people. Louis abolished private wars among nobles and serfdom within the royal domain, gave his subjects the right of appeal from local to higher courts, and made the tax system more equitable. The French people came to associate their king with justice, and their awareness of themselves as possessors of a unifying national identity grew strong during his reign.

French society and culture, during Louis's lifetime, set a standard for all of Europe, a pattern that continued into the modern period. Northern France became the showcase of monastic reform, chivalry, and Gothic art and architecture. Louis's reign also coincided with the golden age of Scholasticism, in which Europe's greatest thinkers converged on Paris, among them the famous Thomas Aquinas.

THE HOHENSTAUFEN EMPIRE (1152–1272)

Frederick I Barbarossa While different, but stable, monarchies developed in France and England, the Holy Roman Empire fragmented (see Map 15-3). Frederick I Barbarossa (1152–1190), founder of the Hohenstaufen dynasty, reestablished imperial authority but also initiated a new phase in the contest between popes and emperors. Frederick attempted to consolidate an empire uniting Germany and Italy by stressing feudal bonds, but his reign ended with stalemate in Germany and rising tensions in Italy. In 1186 his son—the future Henry VI (r. 1190–1197)—married Constance, heiress to the kingdom of Sicily. This union of the empire with Sicily threatened the papacy by encircling the Papal States, and turned the popes into determined opponents of the German emperor.

When Henry VI died in September 1197, chaos followed. Civil war erupted in Germany. Henry VI's four-year-old son, Frederick, the heir to the imperial crown, had for his own safety been made—fatefully, it would prove—a ward of Pope Innocent III (r. 1198–1215). Innocent had both the will, the means, and the opportunity to challenge the power of the Hohenstaufens.

North Sea

Baltic Sea

Danzig

Lübeck

POMERANIA

BRANDENBURG

FRIESLAND

SAXONY

Weser R.

POLAND

Rhine R.

Meuse R.

Cologne

GERMAN

SILESIA

THURINGIA

Elbe R.

LOWER
LORRAINE

Aachen

Prague

Mainz

Main R.

BOHEMIA

STATES

Trier

PALATINATE

MORAVIA

UPPER
LORRAINE

FRANCONIA

Danube R.

AUSTRIA

FRANCE

Strasbourg

Augsburg

Vienna

SWABIA

BAVARIA

Constance

STYRIA

Rhone R.

HUNGARY

BURGUNDY

TYROL

Milan

Venice

LOMBARDY

Pavia

Po R.

Canossa

Ferrara

Genoa

Bologna

Ravenna

Zara

Avignon

Pisa

Florence

Adriatic Sea

TUSCANY

Siena

ITALY

Assisi

CORSICA
(PISA)

Rome

PAPAL
STATES

Anagni

SARDINIA
(PISA & GENOA)

Naples

APULIA

KINGDOM OF
THE TWO SICILIES

CALABRIA

Palermo

SICILY

AFRICA

400 MILES

400 KILOMETERS

MAP 15–3

Germany and Italy in the Middle Ages. Medieval Germany and Italy were divided lands. The Holy Roman Empire (Germany) embraced hundreds of independent territories that the emperor ruled only in name. The papacy controlled the Rome area and tried to enforce its will in the Romagna. Under the Hohenstaufens (mid–12th to mid–13th centuries), internal German divisions and papal conflict reached new heights; German rulers sought to extend their power to southern Italy and Sicily.

WHY WERE the emperors unable to unite Germany and Italy in the Middle Ages?

Frederick II In December 1212, shifting alliances in the German war induced the pope to support his ward's coronation as Emperor Frederick II. But Frederick soon disappointed his papal sponsor. He was a Sicilian by upbringing, and he was to spend only 9 of the 38 years of his reign in Germany. To secure the imperial title for himself and his sons, he gave the German princes what they wanted—undisputed authority over their territories. Germany was fragmenting into a gaggle of petty kingdoms.

Frederick had a disastrous relationship with the papacy. Popes excommunicated him four times and roused the German princes against him, launching the church into European politics on a massive scale. Efforts by the papacy to become a formidable political and military power made the church highly vulnerable to criticism from religious reformers and royal apologists.

When Frederick died in 1250, the German monarchy died with him. The princes established an electoral college in 1257 to pick the emperor, and the "king of the Romans" became their puppet. The Hohenstaufen dynasty effectively ended with Frederick.

POLITICAL AND SOCIAL BREAKDOWN

HUNDRED YEARS' WAR

WHAT WERE the causes of the political and social breakdown that occurred during the 14th century?

The Causes of the War The Hundred Years' War, which began in May 1337 and lasted until October 1453, started when the English king Edward III (r. 1327–1377), the grandson of Philip the Fair of France (r. 1285–1314), claimed the French throne. But the war was more than a dynastic quarrel. England and France were territorial and economic rivals with a long history of mutual prejudice and animosity This made the Hundred Years' War a struggle for national identity.

Although France had three times the population of England, was far wealthier, and fought on its own soil, most of the major battles were stunning English victories. The primary reason for France's failure was internal disunity caused by endemic social conflict. France lagged behind England in making the transition from a fragmented feudal society to a centralized modern state.

France's defeats also owed much to incompetent leadership and English military superiority. The English infantry was more disciplined than the French feudal cavalry, and English archers could fire six arrows a minute with enough force to pierce an inch of wood or the armor of a knight at 200 yards. Eventually, thanks in part to the inspiring leadership of Joan of Arc (1412–1431), and a sense of national identity and self-confidence, the French were able to expel the English from France. By 1453, all that remained to the English was a coastal enclave at Calais.

Joan was poorly repaid by the king she helped to the throne. When the Burgundians captured her in May 1430, Charles could have secured her release but did not. The Burgundians and the English wanted her publicly discredited, believing this would demoralize French resistance. She was turned over to the Inquisition in English-held Rouen, where, after 10 weeks of interrogation, she was executed on May 30, 1431.

The Hundred Years' War had lasting political and social consequences. It devastated France, but it also awakened French nationalism and hastened the country's transition from a feudal monarchy to a centralized state. In both France and England the burden of the war fell most heavily on the peasantry, who were forced to support it with taxes and services.

THE BLACK DEATH

Preconditions and Causes   In the late Middle Ages, improvements in agriculture increased the food supply, spurring a growth in population. It is estimated that Europe's population doubled between the years 1000 and 1300, and then began to outstrip food production. Finally, there were more people than food to feed them or jobs to employ them. The average European

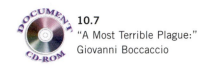

10.7
"A Most Terrible Plague:"
Giovanni Boccaccio

MAP 15–4

Spread of the Black Death.   Apparently introduced by sea-borne rats from areas around the Black Sea where plague-infested rodents have long been known, the Black Death had great human, social, and economic consequences. According to one of the lower estimates, it killed 25 million in Europe. The map charts the spread of the plague in the mid–14th century. Generally following trade routes, it reached Scandinavia by 1350, and some believe it then went on to Iceland and even Greenland. Areas off the main trade routes were largely spared.

WHAT WERE the social and economic consequences of the plague?

faced the probability of famine at least once during his or her average 35-year life-span.

Between 1315 and 1317, crop failures produced the greatest famine of the Middle Ages. Decades of overpopulation, economic depression, famine, and bad health made Europeans vulnerable to a virulent plague that struck with full force in 1348.

This **Black Death**, so called because it discolored the body, travelled the trade routes from Asia into Europe. Appearing in Sicily in late 1347, it entered Europe through Venice, Genoa, and Pisa in 1348, and from there it swept rapidly through Spain and southern France and into northern Europe. Areas outside the major trade routes, like Bohemia, appear to have remained virtually unaffected. The plague made numerous reappearances after its first onslaught, and it is estimated that the population of Europe had been reduced by two-fifths by the early 15th century.

Popular Remedies   The plague was transmitted by fleas and rats, but it also sometimes entered the lungs and was spread by sneezes. Contemporary physicians had little understanding of how diseases worked and no idea how to help people fend off or recover from infection. Popular wisdom held that bad air caused the disease. Some thought that earthquakes had released poisonous fumes. Psychological reactions sometimes went to extremes. Some hoped that moderation and temperance would save them; some wildly indulged their bodily appetites; some fled in panic, and some developed a morbid religiosity. Parades of flagellants whipped themselves, hoping to induce God to show mercy and intervene. Jews were baselessly accused of spreading the disease, and pogroms flared again. The church tried to maintain order, but across Western Europe people developed an obsession with death and dying and a deep pessimism that endured for decades.

Social and Economic Consequences   Whole villages vanished in the wake of the plague. With them went much of the labor force that made the estates of the nobility profitable. Demand for farm laborers and skilled artisans drove wages up. Many serfs negotiated substitution of money payment for their traditional servile

Black Death Bubonic plague that killed millions of Europeans in the 14th century.

Black Death. Men and women carrying plague victims in coffins to the burial ground in Tournai, Belgium, 1349.

The Granger Collection, N. Y.

obligations, or they abandoned the farm altogether and sought jobs in cities. Agricultural prices fell because of lowered demand from a shrunken market, but the price of luxury and manufactured goods—the scarce work of skilled artisans—rose. The standard of living of the nobility was seriously threatened by these developments. Landed aristocrats had to pay more for finished products and for farm labor, but received less for their agricultural produce. Their rents also declined.

Peasants Revolt   To recoup their losses, some landowners converted arable land to sheep pasture. Wool production was less labor-intensive than grain farming. The propertied classes also used their political influence to pass repressive legislation that forced peasants to stay on their farms and froze wages at low levels. The result was the eruption of peasant rebellions in France and England.

Cities Rebound   Although the plague hit urban populations especially hard, the cities and their skilled industries ultimately prospered from its effects. Cities had always protected their interests by regulating competition and immigration from rural areas. After the plague the reach of such laws was extended beyond the cities to include the lands of nobles and landlords, many of whom were now integrated into urban life.

The omnipresence of death whetted the appetite for goods that only skilled urban industries could produce. Expensive cloths, jewelry, furs, and silks were in great demand. Faced with life at its worst, people insisted on having the best. Initially this new demand could not be met, for the first wave of plague transformed an already limited supply of skilled artisans into a shortage almost overnight. As a result, the prices of manufactured and luxury items soared to new heights. This, however, encouraged workers to migrate to the city to become artisans. Urban dwellers enjoyed every advantage. Their products sold at premium prices, but the depressed market for agricultural goods reduced the cost of the things they bought from the countryside.

There was gain and loss for the church as well. As a great landhold, its income and therefore its political influence declined. But it received new revenues from the vastly increased demand for religious services for the dead and the dying and from the multiplication of gifts and bequests.

New Conflicts and Opportunities   The plague contributed to social conflicts within cities. The merchant and patrician classes had long dominated urban government, but they lost ground to the growing economic and political power of artisan and trade guilds. Guilds used their political influence to pass restrictive legislation that protected their markets. Master artisans wanted to keep their numbers low to limit competition, but the journeymen they employed wanted access to the guild so that they could set up shops of their own. To the old conflict between the urban patriciate and the guilds was now added a struggle within the guilds themselves.

In the years following the plague, two groups that had helped to contain the growth of royal power, the landed nobles and the church, were thrust onto the defensive, and kings seized the opportunity to exploit growing national sentiment and work toward the centralization of governments and economies. The nobles lost clout as the new infantry forces that appeared during the Hundred Years' War diminished the importance of the feudal cavalry. The church suffered a reduction in the numbers of clergy—up to one-third in places. To make things worse, the leadership of the church blundered badly.

WHAT ISSUES led to the papal crisis of the late Medieval ages?

ECCLESIASTICAL BREAKDOWN AND REVIVAL: THE LATE MEDIEVAL CHURCH

BONIFACE VIII AND PHILIP THE FAIR

By the 14th century, popes faced rulers far more powerful than the they were. When Pope Boniface VIII (r. 1294–1303) issued the bull, *Clericis Laicos*, which forbade lay taxation of the clergy without prior papal approval, King Philip the Fair of France (r. 1285–1314) unleashed a ruthless antipapal campaign. On November 18, 1302, Boniface made a last-ditch stand against attempts by states to assert their authority over the churches within their borders. He issued the bull *Unam Sanctam,* which declared that temporal authority was "subject" to the spiritual power of the church. The French, however, responded with force. Philip sent troops into Italy who captured the pope, beat him badly, and might have executed him had not an aroused populace rescued him. No pope ever again seriously tried to threaten a king or emperor. Relations between church and state henceforth were characterized by increasing state control of religion.

THE GREAT SCHISM (1378–1417) AND THE CONCILIAR MOVEMENT TO 1449

After Boniface VIII's death, his successor, Clement V (r. 1305–1314), moved the papal court to Avignon on the southeastern border with France, where it remained until Pope Gregory XI (r. 1370–1378) returned the papacy to Rome in January 1377. His successor, Pope Urban VI (r. 1378–1389), proclaimed his intention to reform the **Curia**. This announcement alarmed the cardinals, most of whom were French. Not wanting to surrender the benefits of a papacy under French influence, the French king, Charles V (r. 1364–1380), supported a schism in the church, and on September 20, 1378, 13 cardinals, all but one of whom was French, elected a cousin of the French king as Pope Clement VII (r. 1378–1397). Clement's papacy was seated in Avignon. This **Great Schism** created two papal courts, and support for them divided along political lines: England and its allies (the **Holy Roman Empire**, Hungary, Bohemia, and Poland) acknowledged Urban VI, whereas France and its allies (Naples, Scotland, Castile, and Aragon) backed Clement VII. Today, only the Roman line of popes is recognized as legitimate by the church.

In 1409, a council at Pisa deposed both the Roman and the Avignon popes and elected its own new pope. But neither Rome nor Avignon accepted its action, so after 1409 there were three contending popes. This intolerable situation ended when Emperor Sigismund (r. 1410–1437) prevailed on the Pisan pope to summon a council of the church in Constance in 1414. The Roman pope Gregory XII (r. 1406–1415) also eventually recognized its legitimacy. After the three contending popes had either resigned or been deposed, the council elected a new pope, Martin V (r. 1417–1431), in November 1417. After nearly 30 years of schism, the church was again reunited

Under Pope Eugenius IV (r. 1431–1447), the papacy regained much of its prestige and authority, and in 1460 the papal bull *Execrabilis* condemned all appeals to councils as "completely null and void." But the conciliar movement had planted deep within the conscience of all western peoples the conviction that the leader of an institution must be responsive to its members and not act against their best interests.

Curia Papal government.

Great Schism Appearance of two and at times three rival popes between 1378 and 1415.

Holy Roman Empire Revival of the old Roman Empire, based mainly in Germany and northern Italy, that endured from 870 to 1806.

The Renaissance in Italy (1375–1527)

Most scholars agree that the **Renaissance** was a transition from the medieval to the modern world. Medieval Europe, especially before the 12th century, had been a fragmented feudal society with an agricultural economy, its thought and culture dominated by the church. Renaissance Europe, especially after the 14th century, was characterized by growing national consciousness and political centralization, an urban economy based on organized commerce and capitalism, and ever greater lay and secular control of thought and culture.

The distinctive features and achievements of the Renaissance are most strikingly revealed in Italy from roughly 1375 to 1527, the year Rome was sacked by imperial soldiers. What was achieved in Italy during these centuries also deeply influenced northern Europe.

THE ITALIAN CITY-STATE: SOCIAL CONFLICT AND DESPOTISM

The Renaissance began in the cities of late medieval Italy. Italy was the natural gateway between East and West. Its vibrant urban societies, such as Venice, Genoa, and Pisa, traded uninterruptedly with the Middle East throughout the Middle Ages. During the 13th and 14th centuries, the trade-rich Italian cities became powerful city-states, dominating the political and economic life of their surrounding countrysides. By the 15th century, the great Italian cities had become the bankers for much of Europe. There were five major and competing states in Italy: the duchy of Milan, the republics of Florence and Venice, the Papal States, and the kingdom of Naples.

Social strife and competition for political power were so intense within the cities that to maintain order and survive, most had, by the 15th century, found it necessary to submit to the control of a despot. Venice, ruled by a successful merchant oligarchy, was the notable exception. Elsewhere, the new social classes and divisions within society produced by rapid urban growth fueled chronic, near-anarchic conflict.

In Florence, divisions created turmoil at every level of society. True stability was not established until the ascent to power in 1434 of Cosimo de' Medici (1389–1464), the wealthiest man in Florence and a most astute statesman. Cosimo controlled the city internally from behind the scenes, skillfully manipulating its constitution and influencing elections. His grandson Lorenzo the Magnificent (1449–1492, r. 1478–1492) exercised near totalitarian authority.

Despotism was less subtle elsewhere in Italy. To prevent internal social conflict and foreign intrigue from paralyzing their cities, the dominant groups in many cities cooperated to install a hired strongman,

WHY WAS the Renaissance a transition from the medieval to the modern world?

Renaissance   Revival of ancient learning and the supplanting of traditional religious beliefs by new secular and scientific values that began in Italy in the 14th and 15th centuries.

Cosimo de' Medici (1389–1464). Florentine banker and statesman, in his lifetime the city's wealthiest man and most successful politician. This portrait is by Jacopo da Pontormo (1494–1556).

Jacopo Pontormo (1494–1556), "Cosimo de' Medici the Elder, Pater Patriae," (1389–1464). Oil on wood, 87 × 65 cm. Inv. 3574. Uffize, Florence. Photograph © Erich Lessing/Art Resource, N.Y.

Church and Empire

humanism Study of the Latin and Greek classics and of the Church Fathers both for their own sake and to promote a rebirth of ancient norms and values.

studia humanitatis During the Renaissance, a liberal arts program of study that embraced grammar, rhetoric, poetry, history, philosophy, and politics.

a *podesta*, to maintain law and order. Because these despots could not depend on the cooperation of a divided populace, they relied on mercenary armies to maintain order.

Political turbulence and warfare motivated the development of diplomacy. Most city-states established resident embassies during the 15th century, and their ambassadors were their watchful eyes and ears at rival courts. They stayed abreast of foreign military developments and, if shrewd enough, gained power and advantage without actually going to war.

HUMANISM

Humanism was the scholarly study of the Latin and Greek classics and the ancient Church Fathers both for their own sake and to promote a rebirth of ancient norms and values. Humanists advocated the *studia humanitatis*, a liberal arts program consisting of rhetoric, poetry, history, politics, and moral philosophy.

The first humanists were orators and poets. They wrote in both the classical and the vernacular languages and drew their inspiration from newly discovered works of the ancients. They taught rhetoric within the universities, and they were sought as secretaries, speech writers, and diplomats in princely and papal courts.

Classical and Christian antiquity had been studied before the Italian Renaissance. However, the Italian Renaissance of the late Middle Ages was more secular and lay dominated, had broader interests, recovered more manuscripts, and possessed far superior technical skills than the earlier medieval rebirths of interest in antiquity.

Unlike their Scholastic rivals, humanists were not content only to summarize and compare the views of recognized authorities on a question, but instead went directly to original sources and drew their own conclusions. Avidly searching out manuscript collections, Italian humanists made the full corpus of Greek and Latin antiquity available to scholars during the 14th and 15th centuries. Mastery of Latin and Greek was their primary instrument. There is a kernel of truth—but only a kernel—in the arrogant boast of the humanists that the period between themselves and classical civilization was a "dark middle age."

Petrarch, Dante, and Boccaccio Francesco Petrarch (1304–1374), the father of humanism, left the legal profession to pursue his love of letters and poetry. Petrarch celebrated ancient Rome in his writings and tirelessly collected ancient manuscripts; among his finds were letters by Cicero. His critical textual studies, elitism, and contempt for the allegedly useless learning of the Scholastics were shared by many later humanists.

Petrarch had a far more secular orientation than Dante Alighieri (1265–1321), whose *Vita Nuova* and *Divine Comedy* form, with Petrarch's sonnets, the cornerstones of Italian vernacular literature. Petrarch's student and friend Giovanni Boccaccio (1313–1375), author of the *Decameron*, 100 bawdy tales told by three men and seven women in a country retreat from the plague that ravaged Florence in 1348, also pioneered humanist studies. An avid

HISTORY'S VOICES

PICO DELLA MIRANDOLA STATES THE RENAISSANCE IMAGE OF MAN

O ne of the most eloquent Renaissance descriptions of the abilities of humankind comes from the Italian humanist Pico della Mirandola (1463–1494). In his famed *Oration on the Dignity of Man* (ca. 1486), Pico described humans as free to become whatever they choose.

IN WHAT does the dignity of humankind consist? Does Pico reject the biblical description of Adam and Eve's fall? Does he exaggerate a person's ability to choose freely to be whatever he or she wishes? What inspired such seeming hubris during the Renaissance?

The best of artisans [God] ordained that that creature (man) to whom He [God] had been able to give nothing proper to himself should have joint possession of whatever had been peculiar to each of the different kinds of being. He therefore took man as a creature of indeterminate nature and, assigning him a place in the middle of the world, addressed him thus: "Neither a fixed abode nor a form that is thine alone or any function peculiar to thyself have we given thee, Adam, to the end that according to thy longing and according to thy judgment thou mayest have and possess what abode, what form, and what functions thou thyself shalt desire. The nature of all other beings is limited and constrained within the bounds of laws prescribed by Us. Thou, constrained by no limits, in accordance with thine own free will, in whose hand We have placed thee, shalt ordain for thyself the limits of thy nature. We have set thee at the world's center that thou mayest from thence more easily observe whatever is in the world. We have made thee neither of heaven nor of earth, neither mortal nor immortal, so that with freedom of choice and with honor, as though the maker and molder of thyself, thou mayest fashion thyself in whatever shape thou shalt prefer. Thou shalt have the power to degenerate into the lower forms of life, which are brutish. Thou shalt have the power, out of thy soul's judgment, to be reborn into the higher forms, which are divine." O supreme generosity of God the Father, O highest and most marvelous felicity of man! To him it is granted to have whatever he chooses, to be whatever he wills.

Source: Giovanni Pico della Mirandola, *Oration on the Dignity of Man*, in *The Renaissance Philosophy of Man*, ed. by E. Cassirer et al. Phoenix Books, 1961, pp. 224–225. Reprinted by permission of The University of Chicago Press.

collector of manuscripts, Boccaccio assembled an encyclopedia of Greek and Roman mythology.

Educational Reforms and Goals   The classical ideal of a useful education that produces well-rounded people inspired far-reaching reforms in traditional education. The most influential Italian Renaissance tract on education, Pietro Paolo Vergerio's (1349–1420) *On the Morals That Befit a Free Man*, was derived directly from classical models. Vittorino da Feltre (d. 1446) guided his students through a highly disciplined curriculum that combined the reading of ancient authors with vigorous physical exercise (see "Pico della Mirandola States the Renaissance Image of Man").

Educated and cultured noblewomen also had a prominent place at Renaissance courts, among them Christine de Pisan (1363?–1434). She was an expert in classical, French, and Italian languages and literature and became a well-known woman of letters in the courts of Europe. Her most famous work, *The City of Ladies*, describes the accomplishments of the great women of history.

RENAISSANCE ART

In Renaissance Italy, as later in Reformation Europe, the values and interests of the laity were less subordinated to those of the clergy. In education, culture, and religion, medieval Christian values were adjusting to a more this-worldly spirit. Men and women began again to appreciate and even to glorify the secular world, secular learning, and purely human pursuits as ends in themselves.

This perspective on life is especially prominent in the painting and sculpture of the High Renaissance (late 15th and early 16th centuries), when Renaissance art reached its full maturity. In imitation of Greek and Roman art, painters and sculptors attempted to create harmonious, symmetrical, and properly proportioned figures, portraying the human form with a glorified realism. Whereas Byzantine and Gothic art had been religious and idealized in the extreme, Renaissance art, especially in the 15th century, realistically reproduced nature and human beings as a part of nature.

Renaissance artists took advantage of new technical skills and materials developed during the 15th century: the use of slow-drying oil paints, of contrast of light and shade to enhance realism (**chiaroscuro**), and of linear perspective to give the viewer the illusion of three-dimensional space. Compared with their flat Byzantine and Gothic counterparts, Renaissance paintings seem filled with energy and life. The great masters of the High Renaissance include Leonardo da Vinci (1452–1519), Raphael (1483–1520), and Michelangelo Buonarroti (1475–1564).

chiaroscuro Use of shading to enhance naturalness in painting and drawing.

Aviation Drawings by Leonardo da Vinci (1452–1519). He imagined a possible flying machine with a retractable ladder for boarding.

David Forbert/SuperStock, Inc.

Leonardo da Vinci Leonardo personified the Renaissance ideal of the universal person, one who is not only a jack-of-all-trades but also a master of many. A military engineer and advocate of scientific experimentation, he dissected corpses to learn anatomy and was a self-taught botanist. He sketched designs for such modern machines as airplanes and submarines. The variety of his interests tended, however, to shorten his attention span, so that he constantly moved from one activity to another. As a painter, his great skill lay in conveying inner moods through complex facial features. This is the intriguing characteristic of his most famous painting, the *Mona Lisa*.

Raphael Raphael, who died young (37), is reknowned for his tender depictions of the Virgin Mary and the infant Jesus. Art historians also consider his fresco *The School of Athens*, which depicts Plato and Aristotle surrounded by philosophy and science, one of the best examples of Renaissance artistic theory and technique.

Michelangelo This melancholy genius also excelled in a variety of arts and crafts. His 18-foot statue *David* is a perfect example of the Renaissance artist's devotion to harmony, symmetry, and proportion, and to the extreme glorification of the human form. Four different popes commissioned works by Michelangelo, the best known of which are the frescoes for the Sistine Chapel, which he painted for Pope Julius II (r. 1503–1513).

His later works mark the passing of High Renaissance painting and the advent of a new, experimental style called *mannerism,* which flourished in the late 16th and early 17th centuries. Mannerism derived its name from the "mannered" or "affected" way in which artists expressed their individual perceptions and feelings. Tintoretto (d. 1594) and especially El Greco (d. 1614) are its supreme representatives.

ITALY'S POLITICAL DECLINE: THE FRENCH INVASIONS (1494–1527)

Italy's autonomous city-states had always worked together to oppose foreign invaders. But in 1494, when Naples, backed by Florence and the Borgia pope Alexander VI (1492–1503), prepared to attack Milan, the Milanese despot Ludovico il Moro (r. 1476–1499) invited the French to invade to assert a dynastic claim France had to Naples. France, however, also laid claim to Milan, and the French appetite for territory became insatiable once French armies had crossed the Alps and reestablished themselves in Italy.

The French king Charles VIII (r. 1483–1498) quickly responded to Ludovico's call. Within five months, he had crossed the Alps (August 1495) and raced as conqueror through Florence and the Papal States into Naples. Charles's lightning march through Italy alarmed Ferdinand (r. 1479–1516), king of Aragon and Sicily. He organized a counteralliance (the League of Venice) that forced Charles to retreat.

The French returned to Italy under Charles's successor, Louis XII (r. 1498–1515), this time assisted by the Borgia pope Alexander VI (1492–1503). Alexander, probably the most corrupt pope in history, wanted to carve out a duchy for his son Cesare, in Romagna, officially part of the Papal States. Hoping that a French alliance would allow him to regain control of the region, Alexander abandoned the League of Venice. This made the league too weak to defend Milan, which Louis successfully invaded in August 1499. In 1500, he and Ferdinand of Aragon divided Naples, while the pope and Cesare Borgia conquered the Romagna without opposition.

In 1503, Cardinal Giuliano della Rovere became Pope Julius II (1503–1513). He suppressed the Borgias and placed their newly conquered lands in Romagna under papal jurisdiction. After securing the Papal States with French aid, Julius changed sides and sought to rid Italy of his former allies. Julius, Ferdinand of Aragon, and Venice formed the Holy League in October 1511, which was soon joined by Emperor Maximilian I (r. 1493–1519) and the Swiss. By 1512 the French were in full retreat.

The French invaded Italy again under Louis's successor, Francis I (r. 1515–1547). French armies massacred the Holy League's Swiss army at Marignano in September 1515, and forced the Medici pope Leo X (r. 1513–1521) to agree to the Concordat of Bologna (August 1516). The agreement gave the French king control over the French clergy and the right to collect

mannerism A style of art in the mid to late 16th century that permitted artists to express their own "manner" or feelings in contrast to the symmetry and simplicity of the art of the High Renaissance.

Major Political Events of the Italian Renaissance (1375–1527)

1378–1382	Ciompi revolt in Florence
1434	Medici rule in Florence established by Cosimo de' Medici
1454–1455	Treaty of Lodi allies Milan, Naples, and Florence (in effect until 1494)
1494	Charles VIII of France invades Italy
1495	League of Venice unites Venice, Milan, the Papal States, the Holy Roman Empire, and Spain against France
1499	Louis XII invades Milan (the second French invasion of Italy)
1500	The Borgias conquer Romagna
1512–1513	The Holy League (Pope Julius II, Ferdinand of Aragon, Emperor Maximilian I, and Venice) defeat the French
1513	Machiavelli writes *The Prince*
1515	Francis I leads the third French invasion of Italy
1516	Concordat of Bologna between France and the papacy
1527	Sack of Rome by imperial soldiers

Niccolò Machiavelli. Santi di Tito's portrait of Machiavelli, perhaps the most famous Italian political theorist, who advised Renaissance princes to practice artful deception and inspire fear in their subjects if they wished to succeed.

Scala/Art Resource, N.Y.

taxes from them in exchange for France's recognition of the pope's superiority to church councils. The terms helped keep France Catholic after the outbreak of the Protestant Reformation. But France's thrust into Italy began the first of four major wars with Spain, the Habsburg-Valois wars. These wars stretched over the first half of the 16th century, and France won none of them.

NICCOLÒ MACHIAVELLI

Invasions and wars made a shambles of Italy, and Niccolò Machiavelli (1469–1527) watched as French, Spanish, and German armies wreaked havoc on his country. The more he saw, the more convinced he became that the creation of a unified, independent Italy was an end that justified any means needed to achieve it. Machiavelli admired the heroic acts of ancient Roman rulers, what Renaissance people called their *Virtu*. Romanticizing the old Roman citizenry, he lamented the absence of comparable heroism among his compatriots. His perspective led him to pen distorted interpretations of both ancient and contemporary history.

Machiavelli's comparison of the noble achievements of idealized ancient Romans with the failures of his "Roman" contemporaries led him to conclusions that have made *Machiavellian* synonymous with cynicism. Only an unscrupulous strongman, he argued, using duplicity and terror, could impose order on so divided and selfish a people as his countrymen. Machiavelli was probably in earnest when he advised rulers to consider the advantages of fraud and brutality. He apparently hoped to see a strong ruler emerge from the Medici family. The Medicis, however, were not destined to be Italy's deliverers. The second Medici pope, Clement VII (r. 1523–1534), watched helplessly as Rome was sacked by the army of Emperor Charles V (r. 1519–1556) in 1527, the year of Machiavelli's death.

WHAT WERE the bases for the rise of the modern sovereign state in the 15th century?

REVIVAL OF MONARCHY: NATION BUILDING IN THE 15TH CENTURY

After 1450, unified national monarchies progressively replaced fragmented and divisive feudal governance. The dynastic and chivalric ideals of feudalism did not, however, disappear. Minor territorial princes survived, and representative assemblies even gained influence in some regions. But by the late 15th and early 16th centuries, the old problem of the one and the many was being decided clearly in favor of monarchy.

The feudal monarchies of the High Middle Ages split the basic powers of government between a king and his semiautonomous vassals. The nobility and the towns worked with varying degrees of unity and success through evolving representative bodies, such as the English Parliament, the French Estates General, and the Spanish Cortes, to thwart the centralization of royal power. However, the Hundred Years' War and the schism in the church undercut the power of the landed nobility and the clergy respectively in the late Middle Ages, and the increasingly important towns sided with the kings. Loyal, businesswise townspeople, not the nobles and the clergy, staffed offices in royal governments, becoming the king's lawyers, bookkeepers, military tacticians, and diplomats. This alliance between king and town slowly broke the bonds of feudal society and promoted the rise of the modern sovereign state.

In a sovereign state, the powers of taxation, war making, and law enforcement are no longer the right of local semiautonomous vassals but are concentrated at the center in the monarch and exercised by his chosen agents. Taxes, wars, and laws become national rather than merely regional matters. Only as monarchs won free of the nobility and representative assemblies could they overcome the decentralization that was the chief obstacle to nation building.

Monarchies also began to create standing national armies in the 15th century. As the aristocratic cavalry receded in importance and the infantry and the artillery emerged as the primary forces, many kings employed mercenary soldiers recruited from Switzerland and Germany. The growing cost of warfare increased a king's need to develop new sources of income, but expansion of royal revenues was hampered by the upper classes' stubborn belief that they were immune from taxation. The nobility guarded their properties and traditional rights and despised taxation as an insult and a humiliation. Royal revenues accordingly grew at the expense of those least able to resist and least able to pay. Monarchs had several options. As feudal lords they collected rents from their personal domains. They might also levy national taxes on basic food and clothing, such as the *gabelle* or salt tax in France and the *alcabala* or 10 percent sales tax on commercial transactions in Spain. Kings could also levy direct taxes on the peasantry (such as the French *taille*) and on commercial transactions in towns that were under royal protection. They did this with the cooperation of assemblies that represented the privileged classes but not the peasants who paid the taxes. In the 15th century innovative fund-raising devices, such as sale of public offices and issuance of high-interest government bonds, appeared. But kings still did not levy taxes on the powerful aristocrats. Instead, they turned to rich nobles, as they did to the great bankers of Italy and Germany, for loans, bargaining with the privileged classes, who were often as much the kings' creditors and competitors as their subjects.

MEDIEVAL RUSSIA

In the late 10th century, Prince Vladimir of Kiev (r. 972–1015), then Russia's chief city, converted to Greek Orthodoxy. It became the religion of Russia and added a new cultural bond to the long-standing commercial ties the Russians had with the Byzantine Empire.

Vladimir's successor, Yaroslav the Wise (r. 1016–1054), turned Kiev into a magnificent political and cultural center, but after his death, rivalry among princes challenged Kiev's dominance, and it became just one of several national centers.

Mongol Rule (1243–1480)   Mongol (or Tatar) armies (see Chapters 8 and 13) invaded Russia in 1223, and Kiev fell to them in 1240. Russia's cities became tribute-paying principalities of the portion of the Mongol Empire called the **Golden Horde**. It had its capital at Sarai, on the lower Volga. Mongol rule drew Russia away from the West but left Russia's traditional political institutions and religion largely intact. Mongolian power and trade contacts also enhanced the peace and prosperity of Russia.

taille   Direct tax on the French peasantry.

Golden Horde   Name given to the Mongol rulers of Russia from 1240 to 1480.

Exterior of a Russian Orthodox Church in Novgorod, Russia.

UNESCO, Ann Ronan/ The Image Works.

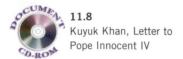

11.8
Kuyuk Khan, Letter to
Pope Innocent IV

Russian Liberation   The princes of Moscow cooperated with the Mongols, grew wealthy, and gradually expanded their principality through land purchases, colonization, and conquest. In 1380, Grand Duke Dimitri of Moscow (1350–1389) defeated Tatar forces at Kulikov Meadow in a victory that marked the beginning of the decline of Mongolian hegemony. Another century passed before Ivan III, called Ivan the Great (d. 1505), brought all of northern Russia under Moscow's control and ended Mongol rule (1480). By the last quarter of the 15th century, Moscow had replaced Kiev as the political and religious center of Russia. After the fall of Constantinople to the Turks in 1453, Russians laid claim to the legacy of the Byzantine Empire and proclaimed Moscow the "third Rome."

FRANCE

There were two cornerstones of French nation building in the 15th century. The first was England's retreat from the continent following its loss of the Hundred Years' War. The second was the defeat of Charles the Bold (r. 1467–1477) and his duchy of Burgundy. The dukes of Burgundy were probably Europe's strongest rulers in the mid-15th century, and they hoped to build a dominant middle kingdom between France and the Holy Roman Empire. They might have succeeded had not the Continental powers joined forces to oppose them. The dream of Burgundian empire died in 1477, when Charles the Bold was killed in battle at Nancy.

The dissolution of Burgundy removed a serious threat to France and cleared the way for its King Louis XI (r. 1461–1483) to build a powerful monarchy. By annexing and adding Burgundian lands to his own Angevin inheritance, Louis doubled the size of his kingdom. He harnessed the nobility and expanded trade and industry.

Strength does not necessarily ensure a healthy future for a nation. It was because Louis left his successors such a secure and efficient government that they were able to pursue Italian conquests in the 1490s and to fight a long series of losing wars with the Habsburgs in the first half of the 16th century. By the mid-16th century, France was again a defeated nation and almost as divided internally as it had been during the Hundred Years' War.

SPAIN

Spain, too, became a strong country in the late 15th century. Both Castile and Aragon had been poorly ruled, divided kingdoms in the mid-15th century, but the marriage in 1469 of Isabella of Castile (r. 1474–1504) and Ferdinand of Aragon (r. 1479–1516) changed that trend. Their union was strongly protested by their neighbors, Portugal and France, who foresaw the formidable European power it would create. Castile was by far the richer and more populous of the two kingdoms, having an estimated five million inhabitants to Aragon's less than one million. Castile also had a lucrative sheep-farming industry. An example of the growing trend toward centralized economic planning, it was run by a government-backed organization called the *Mesta*. Although the two kingdoms were dynastically united by the marriage of Ferdinand and Isabella in 1469, each retained its own laws, armies, coinage, tax systems, and cultural traditions.

Ferdinand and Isabella could do together what neither could accomplish alone: subdue their realms, secure their borders, and conduct foreign military ventures. Townspeople allied themselves with the crown and progressively replaced nobles within the royal administration. The crown further circumscribed the power of the nobility by extending its authority over the wealthy chivalric orders.

Spain had long been remarkable as a place where three religions—Islam, Judaism, and Christianity—coexisted with a certain degree of toleration. This changed dramatically as Ferdinand and Isabella exerted state control over religion. They totally dominated the Spanish church and made religion serve the cause of national unity. They appointed the higher clergy and the officers of the Inquisition. The Inquisition was a key national agency established in 1479 to monitor the activity of Spain's converted Jews (*conversos*) and Muslims (*Moriscos*). It was run by Isabella's confessor, Tomás de Torquemada (d. 1498). In 1492, Ferdinand and Isabella exiled all Jews from Spain and confiscated their properties. In 1502, nonconverting Moors in Granada were driven into exile. The state imposed regimented, uniform spiritual practices on its subjects. Spain remained a loyal Catholic country through the era of the Reformation and provided a base of operation for the Counter-Reformation resurgence of the Catholic Church.

Ferdinand and Isabella had wide horizons. The anti-French marriage alliances they arranged for their children determined much of European history in the 16th century. In 1496, their eldest daughter, Joanna, later known as "the Mad" (1479–1555), married Archduke Philip (1478–1506), the son of Emperor Maximilian I (r. 1493–1519). Their son, Charles I, the first king of a united Spain, acquired by inheritance and his election as Emperor Charles V in 1519 a European realm almost equal in size to Charlemagne's. A second daughter, Catherine of Aragon (1485–1536), married King Henry VIII of England. The failure of this marriage led to the English Reformation.

Ferdinand and Isabella's vision for Spain's future was also revealed by their sponsorship of overseas exploration. They sent the Genoese adventurer Christopher Columbus (1451–1506) west in search of a shorter route to the spice markets of the Far East. The islands he discovered in the Caribbean began the creation of the Spanish Empire in Mexico and Peru. Gold and silver from their mines helped to make Spain Europe's dominant power in the 16th century.

ENGLAND

The last half of the 15th century was a difficult period for England. Following its loss of the Hundred Years' War, civil war broke out in England between two rival branches of the royal family, the House of York and the House of Lancaster. This conflict, named the Wars of the Roses (York's symbol, according to legend, was a white rose, and Lancaster's a red rose), kept England in turmoil from 1455 to 1485.

The Lancastrian, King Henry VI (r. 1422–1461), was challenged by the Duke of York and his supporters in the prosperous southern towns. In 1461 the Duke of York's son seized power and became King Edward IV (r. 1461–1483). Assisted by loyal and able ministers, he bent Parliament to his will. His brother and successor, Richard III (r. 1483–1485), was confronted by growing support for the exiled Lancastrian leader Henry Tudor. Henry defeated Richard on Bosworth Field in August 1485 to become King Henry VII (r. 1485–1509), founder of a Tudor dynasty that endured until 1603.

To bring the rival royal families together and give his offspring an incontestable hereditary claim to the throne, Henry married Edward IV's daughter, Elizabeth of York. With the aid of a much-feared instrument of royal power, the Court of Star Chamber, he imposed discipline on the English nobility. He shrewdly construed legal precedents to the advantage of the crown and used English law to further his own ends. He confiscated so much noble land and so many fortunes that he was able to govern without depending on Parliament for grants. Henry constructed a powerful monarchy that became one of early modern Europe's most exemplary governments during the reign of his granddaughter, Elizabeth I (r. 1558–1603).

IMAGE KEY

for pages 336–337

a. Two-handed sword, circa 1600

b. Raphael's portrait (ca.1515) of Baldassare Castiglione (1478–1529)

c. Students attending a lecture, detail of the Tomb of Giovanni da Legnano

d. From the Bayeux Tapestry (ca. 1073–1083), William the Conqueror on horseback

e. An eleventh- or twelfth-century marketplace in a fifteenth-century rendering

f. Pope Innocent III

g. Michelangelo's *Pietà* (ca. 1498–1500)

h. Statue of Pope Boniface VIII

i. Cosimo de' Medici

j. Joan of Arc

SUMMARY

Medieval Society   Medieval society was divided in theory into three main groups: clergy (those who prayed), nobility (those who fought as mounted warriors), and laborers (peasants and artisans). The rise of merchants, self-governing towns, and universities helped break down this division. By supporting rulers against the nobility, towns gave kings the resources—money and university-trained bureaucrats and lawyers—to build national governments. Much of medieval history involves the struggle by rulers to assert their authority over powerful local lords and the church.

Church and State   The medieval papacy sought to extend its power over both church and state. In the 10th century, the Cluny reform movement increased popular respect for the church and strengthened the papacy. In the Investiture Struggle, the papacy secured the independence of the clergy by enlisting the support of the German princes against the Holy Roman Emperors, thus weakening imperial power in Germany. The First Crusade further strengthened papal prestige. But, by the end of the 13th century, kings had become more powerful than popes, and the French king, Philip the Fair, was able to defy the papacy. In the 14th century, the Great Schism further weakened papal prestige. Although the papacy was able to fend off a movement to make church councils superior to popes, it never recovered its authority over national rulers.

Nation Building   By the 15th century, England, France, and Spain had developed into strong national monarchies with centralized bureaucracies and professional armies. Although medieval institutions, such as the English Parliament, in theory limited royal power, in practice monarchs in these countries held unchallenged authority. The Great Schism, the Hundred Years' War, and the Black Death had weakened the church and the nobility, while townspeople supported kings. A similar process was beginning in Russia where the rulers of Moscow were extending their authority after throwing off Mongol rule. In the empire, however, regional lords had defeated the emperors' attempts to build a strong central state.

The Renaissance   The Renaissance, which began in the Italian city-states in the late 14th century, marks the transition from the medieval to the modern world. Humanism, the scholarly study of the Greek and Latin classics and the ancient Church fathers, promoted a rebirth of ancient norms and values and the classical ideal of an educated, well-rounded person. The growth of secular values led to a great burst of artistic activity by artists such as da Vinci, Raphael, and Michelangelo. The political weakness of the Italian states invited foreign intervention by France, Spain, and the Habsburgs. The sack of Rome by imperial forces in 1527 marks the end of the Renaissance.

REVIEW QUESTIONS

1. What were the objectives of the Cluny reform movement? Why did it succeed?

2. Was the investiture controversy a political or a religious conflict?

3. Why did Germany remain divided while France and England were able to begin forming strong, unified states during the High Middle Ages?

4. How did the Hundred Years' War, the Black Death, and the Great Schism in the church affect the course of history?

5. What gave rise to towns? How did they change medieval society?

6. What was "reborn" in the Renaissance?

KEY TERMS

Black Death (p. 356)

chiaroscuro (p. 362)

Crusades (p. 340)

Curia (p. 358)

Golden Horde (p. 365)

Great Schism (p. 358)

guild (p. 345)

Holy Roman Empire (p. 358)

humanism (p. 360)

Magna Carta (p. 351)

mannerism (p. 363)

regular clergy (p. 347)

Renaissance (p. 359)

Scholasticism (p. 345)

secular clergy (p. 347)

studia humanitatis (p. 360)

taille (p. 365)

vernacular (p. 350)

 For additional study resources for this chapter, go to:
www.prenhall.com/craig/chapter15

PART FOUR · THE WORLD IN TRANSITION

EUROPE

1517–1555	Protestant Reformation
1533–1584	Ivan the Terrible of Russia reigns
1540	Jesuit Order founded by Ignatius Loyola
1543–1727	Scientific Revolution
1556–1598	Philip II of Spain reigns
1558–1603	Elizabeth I of England reigns
1562–1598	French Wars of Religion
1581	The Netherlands declares its independence from the Spanish Habsburgs
1588	Defeat of the Spanish Armada
1589–1610	Henry IV, Navarre, founds Bourbon dynasty of France

▲ *Queen Elizabeth I*

NEAR EAST / INDIA

1500–1722	Safavid Shi'ite rule in Iran
1512–1520	Ottoman ruler Selim I
1520–1566	Ottoman ruler Suleiman the Magnificent
1525–1527	Babur founds Mughal dynasty in India
1540	Hungary under Ottoman rule
1556–1605	Akbar the Great of India reigns
1571	Battle of Lepanto; Ottomans defeated
ca. 1571–1640	Safavid philosopher-writer Mullah Sadra
1588–1629	Shah Abbas I of Iran reigns

Leaf from "Divan" ▶
by the poet, Hafiz

EAST ASIA

1500–1800	Commercial revolution in Ming-Ch'ing China; trade with Europe; flourishing of the novel
1543	Portuguese arrive in Japan
1568–1600	Era of unification follows end of Warring States Era in Japan
1587	Spanish arrive in Japan
1588	Hideyoshi's sword hunt in Japan
1592–1598	Ming troops battle Hideyoshi's army in Korea

AFRICA

Feluccas ▶
on the Nile

1506	East coast of Africa under Portuguese domination
1507	Mozambique founded by Portuguese
1517	Spanish crown authorizes slave trade to its South American colonies; rapid increase in importation of slaves to the New World
1554–1659	Sa'did Sultanate in Morocco
1575	Union of Bornu and Kanem by Idris Alawma (r. 1575–1610); Kanem-Bornu state the most fully Islamic in West Africa
1591	Moroccan army defeats Songhai army; Songhai Empire collapses

THE AMERICAS

1519	Conquest of the Aztecs by Cortes; Aztec ruler, Montezuma (r. 1502–1519) killed; Tenochtitlán destroyed
1529	Mexico City becomes capital of the viceroyalty of New Spain
1533	Pizarro begins his conquest of the Incas
1536	Spanish under Mendoza arrive in Argentina
1544	Lima becomes capital of the viceroyalty of Peru
1584	Sir Walter Raleigh sends expedition to Roanoke Island (North Carolina)

◀ *Aztec drawing of Spanish conquest of Mexico*

▲ *Algonquin village of Secotton*

1618–1648	Thirty Years' War
1640–1688	Frederick William, the Great Elector, reigns in Brandenburg-Prussia
1642–1646	Puritan Revolution in England
1643–1715	Louis XIV of France reigns
1682–1725	Peter the Great of Russia reigns
1688	Glorious Revolution in England
1690	"Second Treatise of Civil Government," by John Locke

◄ *Louis XIV of France*

1701	Act of Settlement provides for Protestant succession to English throne
1702–1713	War of Spanish Succession
1740–1748	War of Austrian Succession
1756–1763	Seven Years' War
ca. 1750	Industrial Revolution begins in England
1772	First partition of Poland
1789	First French Revolution
1793 and 1795	Last two partitions of Poland

▲ *"Evening" by Francis Wheatley*

1628–1657	Shah Jahan reigns; builds Taj Mahal as mausoleum for his beloved wife
1646	Founding of Maratha Empire
1648	Delhi becomes the capital of Mughal Empire
1658–1707	Shah Aurangzeb, the "World Conqueror," reigns in India; end of religious toleration toward Hindus; beginning Mughal decline
1669–1683	Last military expansion by Ottomans: 1669, seize Crete; 1670s, the Ukraine; 1683, Vienna

▲ *The Taj Mahal*

1700	Sikhs and Marathas bring down Mughal Imperial Power
1708	British East India Company and New East India Company merge
1722	Last Safavid ruler forced to abdicate
1724	Rise in the Deccan of the Islamic state of Hyderabad
1725	Nadir Shah of Afganhistan becomes ruler of Persia
1739	Persian invasion of northern India, by Nadir Shah
1748–1761	Ahmad Shah Durrani of Afghanistan invades India
1757	British victory at Plassey, in Bengal

1600	Tokugawa Ieyasu wins battle of Sekigahara, completes unification of Japan
1600–1868	Tokugawa shogunate in Edo
1630s	Seclusion adopted as national policy in Japan
1644–1694	Bashō, Japanese poet
1644–1911	Ch'ing (Manchu) dynasty in China
1661-1722	K'ang Hsi reign in China
1673–1681	Revolt of southern generals in China
1699	British East India Company arrives in China

◄ *"White Heron" castle in Jimeji*

1701	Forty-seven ro-nin incident in Japan
1716–1733	Reforms of Tokugawa Yoshimune in Japan
1737–1795	Reign of Qianlong in China
1742	Christianity banned in China
1784	American traders arrive in China
1787–1793	Matsudaira Sadanobu's reforms in Japan
1798	White Lotus Rebellion in China

Manchu emperor ► *Ch'ien Lung*

1600s	English, Dutch, and French enter the slave trade; slaves imported to sugar plantations in the Caribbean
1619	First African slaves in North America land in Virginia
1652	First Cape Colony settlement of Dutch East India Company
1660–1856	Omani domination of East Africa; Omani state centered in Zanzibar; 1698, takes Mozambique from Portuguese

1702	Asiento Guinea Trade Company founded for slave trade between Africa and the Americas
1700s	Transatlantic slave trade at its height
1741–1856	United Sultanate of Oman and Zanzibar
1754–1817	Usman Dan Fodio, founder of sultanate in northern and central Nigeria; the Fulani become the ruling class in the region
1762	End of Funj Sultanate in eastern Sudanic region

◄ *The Friday Mosque at Shela*

◄ *Slave labor on sugar plantation in Brazil*

1607	The London Company establishes Jamestown Colony (Virginia)
1608	Champlain founds Quebec
1619	Slave labor introduced at Jamestown (Virginia)

1733	Georgia founded as last English colony in North America
1739–1763	Era of trade wars in Americas between Great Britain and the French and Spanish
1763	Peace of Paris establishes British government in Canada
1776–1781	American Revolution
1783–1830	Simón Bolívar, Latin American soldier, statesman
1789	U.S. Constitution
1791	Negro slave revolt in French Santo Domingo
1791	Canada Constitution Act divides the country into Upper and Lower Canada

16 Europe 1500–1650: Expansion, Reformation and Religious Wars

CHAPTER HIGHLIGHTS

Voyages of Discovery In the late fifteenth century, Europe began to expand around the globe. The Portuguese pioneered a sea route around Africa to India and the Far East, and the Spanish discovered the Americas. The consequences were immense for Europeans, native Americans, Africans, and Asians. In time, a truly global society would emerge.

The Reformation The Reformation began in Germany with Martin Luther's attack on indulgences in 1517. Despite the opposition to the Reformation of Emperor Charles V, Luther had the support of many German princes. The Reformation shattered the religious unity of Europe. In Switzerland, Zwingli and Calvin launched their own versions of Protestantism. In England, Henry VIII repudiated papal authority when the pope refused to grant him a divorce. The Reformation also led to far-reaching changes in religious practices and social attitudes, including steps toward the advancement of women.

The Roman Catholic Church also acted to reform itself. The Council of Trent tightened church discipline and reaffirmed traditional doctrine. The Jesuits converted many Protestants back to Catholicism.

The Wars of Religion The religious divisions of Europe led to more than a century of warfare from the 1520s to 1648. When the Thirty Years' War ended in 1648, Europe was permanently divided into Catholic and Protestant areas.

Superstition and Enlightenment The Reformation led to both dark and constructive views of human nature. Perhaps the darkest view was the witch crazes that erupted across Europe. Thousands of innocent people, mostly women, were persecuted and executed as witches between 1400 and 1700.

In literature and philosophy, however, these years witnessed an outpouring of creative thinking. Among the greatest writers of the age were Cervantes, Shakespeare, Pascal, Spinoza, Hobbes, and Locke.

CHAPTER QUESTIONS

WHAT WERE the motives for the European voyages of discovery in the late fifteenth and sixteenth centuries?

WHY DID Martin Luther break with the Roman Catholic Church?

HOW DID the Reformation change religious and social life?

WHAT WAS the final result of the wars of religion in France, the Netherlands, and Germany?

WHY DID witch hunts and panics erupt across Western Europe between 1400 and 1700?

CHAPTER OUTLINE

- The Discovery of a New World
- The Reformation
- The Reformation's Achievements
- The Wars of Religion
- Superstition and Enlightenment: The Battle Within

In the second decade of the 16th century, a powerful religious movement began in Saxony in Germany and rapidly spread throughout northern Europe, deeply affecting society and politics as well as spiritual life. Attacking what they believed to be burdensome superstitions that robbed people of their money and their peace of mind, Protestant reformers led a revolt against the medieval church. In a short time, hundreds of thousands of people from all social classes set aside the beliefs of centuries and adopted a more simplified religious practice.

The Protestant Reformation challenged aspects of the Renaissance, especially its loyalty to traditional religions and humanism's tendency to follow classical sources in glorifying human nature. Protestants were more convinced of the human potential for evil than by any human inclination to do good. This led them to urge parents, teachers, and magistrates to be firm disciplinarians. On the other hand, Protestants also embraced many Renaissance ideas, especially educational reform and the study of ancient languages. These provided the tools they used to interpret Scripture and challenge the papacy.

Protestantism was not the only reform movement to grow out of the religious grievances of the late Middle Ages. Within the Catholic Church itself a reform was emerging that would give birth to new religious orders, rebut Protestantism, and win back a great many of its converts.

As different groups identified their political and social goals with either Protestantism or Catholicism, a hundred years of bloody war between Protestants and Catholics darkened the second half of the 16th century and the first half of the 17th. In the second half of the 16th century, the political conflict that had previously been confined to central Europe and a struggle for Lutheran rights and freedoms shifted to Western Europe—to France, the Netherlands, England, and Scotland—where it became a struggle for Calvinist recognition. In France, Calvinists fought Catholic rulers for the right to form their own communities, to practice their chosen religion openly, and to exclude from their lands those they deemed heretical. During the Thirty Years' War (1618–1648), international armies of varying religious persuasions clashed in central and northern Europe. By 1649 English Puritans had overthrown the Stuart monarchy and the Anglican Church.

For Europe the late 15th and the 16th centuries were also a period of unprecedented territorial expansion. Permanent colonies were established within the Americas, and the exploitation of the New World's human and mineral resources began. Imported American gold and silver spurred scientific invention and a new weapons industry. The new bullion helped fund an international traffic in African slaves as rival tribes sold their captives to the Portuguese. These slaves were brought in ever-increasing numbers to work the mines and the plantations of the New World as replacements for faltering American natives.

WHAT WERE the motives for the European voyages of discovery in the late 15th and 16th centuries?

THE DISCOVERY OF A NEW WORLD

The discovery of the Americas dramatically expanded the geographical and intellectual horizons of Europeans. Knowledge of the New World's inhabitants and exploitation of its vast wealth set new cultural and economic forces in motion throughout Western Europe. Beginning with the successful voyages of Christopher Columbus (1451–1506) in the late 15th century, commercial supremacy started to shift from the Mediterranean and the Baltic to the Atlantic seaboard, and western Europe's global expansion began in earnest (see Map 16–1).

The Portuguese Chart the Course   Seventy-seven years before Columbus sailed for Spain, Portugal's Prince Henry the Navigator (1394–1460) began exploration of Africa's Atlantic coast. The Portuguese first sought gold and slaves. During the second half of the 15th century, the Portuguese delivered

MAP 16–1
European Voyages of Discovery and the Colonial Claims of Spain and Portugal in the 15th and 16th Centuries. The map dramatizes Europe's global expansion in the 15th and 16th centuries.

WHY DID the Europeans want to find a sea route to Asia?

150,000 slaves to Europe. By the end of that century, however, they were hoping to find a sea route around Africa to Asia's spice markets. Spices, especially pepper and cloves, were in great demand both as preservatives and taste enhancements to food. Overland routes to India and China had long existed, but they were difficult and expensive and monopolized by the Venetians and Turks. The first exploratory voyages were slow and tentative, but the experience they provided taught sailors the skills needed to cross the oceans to the Americas and and Orient.

In 1455, a pope gave the Portuguese rights to all the lands, goods, and slaves they might discover from the coast of Guinea to the Indies. The church hoped that conquests would be followed by mass conversions and the development of allies against the Muslims. Bartholomew Dias (d. 1500) opened the Portuguese Empire in the East when he rounded the Cape of Good Hope at the tip of Africa in 1487. A decade later, in 1498, Vasco da Gama (d. 1524) stood on the shores of India. When he returned to Portugal, his cargo was worth 60 times the cost of the voyage. Later, the Portuguese established colonies in Goa and Calcutta and successfully challenged the Arabs and the Venetians for control of the European spice trade.

While the Portuguese concentrated on the Indian Ocean, the Spanish set sail across the Atlantic, hoping to establish a shorter route to the rich spice markets of

14.5
Christopher Columbus

the East Indies. Rather than beat the Portuguese at their own game, however, Columbus discovered the Americas—although he did not at first realize that.

The Spanish Voyages of Christopher Columbus   On October 12, 1492, after a 33-day voyage from the Canary Islands, Columbus landed in San Salvador (Watlings Island) in the eastern Bahamas. He thought San Salvador was an outer island of Japan, for his knowledge of geography was based on Marco Polo's account of his years in China during the 13th century and a global map by Martin Behaim, a Nuremberg map-maker, which showed only ocean between the west coast of Europe and the east coast of Asia.

The friendly naked natives, who greeted Columbus and his crew on the beaches of the New World, were Taino Indians. They spoke a variant of a language known as Arawak. Mistaking the island for the East Indies, Columbus called the people Indians, and the name stuck even after it became known that he had discovered a new continent. The natives' generosity amazed Columbus. They freely gave his men all the corn and yams—and sexual favors—they desired. "They never say no," Columbus marveled and predicted that they could easily be enslaved.

On the heels of Columbus, Amerigo Vespucci (1451–1512), after whom America is named, and Ferdinand Magellan (1480–1521) carefully explored the coastline of South America. Their travels proved that the lands discovered by Columbus were not the outermost territory of the Far East, but a new continent that opened on the still greater Pacific Ocean. Magellan, in search of a westward route to the East Indies, sailed to the Philippines, where he died.

Impact on Europe and America   Columbus's voyage of 1492 marked, unknowingly to those who undertook and financed it, the beginning of more than three centuries of Spanish conquest, exploitation, and administration of a vast American empire. What had begun as voyages of discovery soon became expeditions of conquest. The wars Christian Aragon and Castile waged against the Islamic Moors had just ended in 1492, and they imbued the early Spanish explorers with a zeal for conquering and converting non-Christian peoples.

The voyages to the New World had important consequences for both Europe and America. For Spain, the venture created Europe's largest and longest-surviving trading bloc and yielded the wealth that financed Spain's commanding role in the era's religious and political conflicts. It also fueled European-wide economic expansion, and spurred other European countries to undertake their own colonial ventures.

European expansion had major consequences for ecosystems. Numerous species of fruits, vegetables, and animals were introduced to Europe from America and vice versa. European diseases also devasted America's natives. The imprint that Spain left on the new territories—Roman Catholicism, economic dependence, and a hierarchical society—is visible today.

QUICK REVIEW

Impact on Europe and America

• Spurred other European nations to colonial expansion

• Financed Spain's role in the age's political and religious conflicts

• For native peoples of the Americas, contact brought disease, war, and destruction

THE REFORMATION

*T*he **Reformation** was a religious reform movement that began in Germany in the sixteenth Century and led to the establishment of Protestant Christianity.

WHY DID Martin Luther break with the Roman Catholic Church?

Reformation Sixteenth-century religious movement that sought to reform the Roman Catholic Church and led to the establishment of Protestantism.

Religion and Society   The Reformation broke out first in the free imperial cities of Germany and Switzerland. There were about 65 of these, and each was a little kingdom unto itself. Most developed Protestant movements, but with mixed success and duration. Some quickly turned Protestant and remained so. Some were Protestant for only a short time. Others developed mixed confessions and let Catholics and Protestants coexist.

The cities not only struggled with higher princely or royal authority, they also suffered deep internal social and political divisions. Certain groups favored the Reformation more than others. In many places, guilds like that of the printers, whose members were prospering both socially and economically and who had a history of conflict with local authority, were in the forefront of the Reformation. Evidence suggests that people who felt pushed around and bullied by either local or distant authority—a guild by an autocratic local government; a city or region by a prince or king—initially perceived an ally in the Protestant movement.

Social and political experience thus coalesced with the larger religious issues in both town and countryside. When Martin Luther and his comrades wrote, preached, and sang about a priesthood of all believers, scorned the authority of ecclesiastical landlords, and ridiculed papal laws as arbitrary human inventions, they touched political as well as religious nerves in German and Swiss cities. This was also true in villages, for the peasants also heard in the Protestant sermon and pamphlet a promise of political liberation and even a degree of social betterment.

Popular Movements and Criticism of the Church   The Protestant Reformation could not have occurred without the monumental crises of the late medieval church and the Renaissance papacy. For many people, the church had ceased to provide a viable vehicle for the expression of their piety. Laity and clerics alike began to seek more heartfelt, idealistic, and often—in the eyes of the pope—increasingly heretical religious outlets. The late Middle Ages were marked by independent lay and clerical efforts to reform local religious practice and by widespread experimentation with new religious forms that shared a common goal: the recovery of religious simplicity in imitation of Christ.

A variety of factors contributed to the growth of lay criticism of the church. The laity in the cities were becoming increasingly knowledgeable about the world and those who controlled their lives. They traveled widely—as soldiers, pilgrims, explorers, and traders. New postal systems and the printing press increased the information at their disposal. The new age of books and libraries raised literacy and heightened curiosity. Laypersons were increasingly able to take the initiative in shaping the cultural life of their communities.

Secular Control over Religious Life   On the eve of the Reformation, Rome's international network of church offices began to be pulled apart by a growing awareness of regional identity (incipient nationalism) and the increasing competence of local secular administrations. The late medieval church had permitted important ecclesiastical posts ("benefices") to be sold to the highest bidders and had not enforced residency requirements in parishes. Rare was the late medieval German town that did not have complaints about the maladministration, concubinage, or fiscal conduct of its clergy, especially the higher clergy (bishops, abbots, and prelates).

City governments also sought to restrict the growth of ecclesiastical properties and clerical privileges and to improve local religious life by bringing the clergy under the local tax code and by endowing new clerical positions for well-trained and conscientious preachers.

Gutenberg Bible. The printing press made possible the diffusion of Renaissance learning. But no book stimulated thought more at this time than did the Bible. With Gutenberg's publication of a printed Bible in 1454, scholars gained access to a dependable, standardized text, so that Scripture could be discussed and debated as never before.

Huntigton Library.

QUICK REVIEW

Criticism of the Church
- Many people did not see church as a foundation for religious piety
- Laity and clerics interested in alternatives and reform
- Layperson increasingly willing to take the initiative

THE NORTHERN RENAISSANCE

The scholarly works of northern humanists created a climate favorable to religious and educational reforms. Northern humanism was initially stimulated by the importation of Italian learning through such varied intermediaries as students who had studied in Italy, merchants, and a religious organization called the Brothers of the Common Life. The northern humanists tended to come from more diverse social backgrounds and to be more devoted to religious reforms than were their Italian counterparts. They were also more willing to write for lay audiences.

The growth of schools and lay education combined with the invention of cheap paper to create a mass audience for printed books. It was well served when, around 1450, Johann Gutenberg (d. 1468) invented printing with movable type in the German city of Mainz. Thereafter, books were rapidly and handsomely produced on topics both profound and practical. By 1500, printing presses operated in at least 60 German cities and in more than 200 throughout Europe. The provided politicians, humanists, and reformers with a new medium through which to promote their causes.

The most famous of the northern humanists was Desiderius Erasmus (1466–1536), the "prince of the humanists." Idealistic and pacifistic, Erasmus gained fame as both an educational and a religious reformer. He aspired to unite the classical ideals of humanity and civic virtue with the Christian ideals of love and piety. He believed that disciplined study of the classics and the Bible, if begun early enough, was the best way to reform both individuals and society. He summarized his own beliefs with the phrase *philosophia Christi*, a simple, ethical piety in imitation of Christ. He set this ideal against what he believed to be the dogmatic, ceremonial, and factious religious practice of the late Middle Ages. To promote his own religious beliefs, Erasmus edited the works of the Church Fathers and made a Greek edition of the New Testament (1516), which became the basis for a new, more accurate Latin translation (1519). Martin Luther later used both these works as the basis for his famous German translation.

The best known of early English humanists was Sir Thomas More (1478–1535), a close friend of Erasmus. While visiting More, Erasmus wrote his most famous work, *The Praise of Folly* (1511), an amusing and profound exposé of human self-deception. It was quickly translated from the original Latin into many vernacular languages. More's *Utopia* (1516), a criticism of contemporary society, depicts an imaginary society based on reason and tolerance that requires everyone to work and has rid itself of all social and political injustice. Although More remained a staunch Catholic, humanism in England, as in Germany, paved the way for the Reformation. A circle of English humanists, under the direction of Henry VIII's minister Thomas Cromwell, translated and disseminated late medieval criticisms of the papacy and many of Erasmus's satirical writings as well.

Whereas humanism helped the Protestants in Germany, England, and France, in Spain it entered the service of the Catholic Church. Here the key figure was Francisco Jiménez de Cisneros (1437–1517), a confessor to Queen Isabella, and after 1508 Grand Inquisitor—a position from which he was able to enforce the strictest religious orthodoxy. Jiménez was a conduit for humanist scholarship and learning. He founded the University of Alcalá near Madrid in 1509, printed a Greek edition of the New Testament, and translated many religious tracts that aided clerical reform and control of lay religious life. His greatest achievement, taking 15 years to complete, was the Complutensian Polyglot Bible. It is a six-volume work that prints, side by side, Hebrew, Greek, and Latin

QUICK REVIEW

Desiderius Erasmus (1466–1536)

- Prince of the humanists
- Saw study of Bible and classics as best path to reform
- Edited the works of the Church Fathers and made a Greek edition of the New Testament

versions of the Bible. Such scholarly projects and internal church reforms joined with the repressive measures of Ferdinand and Isabella to keep Spain strictly Catholic.

MARTIN LUTHER AND THE GERMAN REFORMATION TO 1525

13.4
Martin Luther

Late medieval Germany lacked the political unity to enforce "national" religious reforms during the late Middle Ages. What happened on a unified national level in England and France occurred only locally and piecemeal in Germany. As popular resentment of clerical immunities and ecclesiastical abuses spread among German cities and towns—especially regarding the selling of indulgences—an unorganized "national" opposition to Rome formed. German humanists had long voiced such criticism, and by 1517 it provided a solid foundation for Martin Luther's reform.

Luther (1483–1546), the son of a successful Thuringian miner, was educated by teachers who had been influenced by the Northern Renaissance. He received his master of arts degree from the University of Erfurt in 1505 and registered with the law faculty. He never began that course of study, for to the shock and disappointment of his parents, he joined the Order of the Hermits of Saint Augustine in Erfurt on July 17, 1505. This decision had apparently been forming in his mind for some time and was precipitated by a terrifying storm that caused him to promise the saint to whom he prayed that he would enter a monastery if he escaped death.

Luther was ordained in 1507 and was sent to Rome in 1510 on business for his order. There he witnessed the abuses for which the papacy was being criticized. In 1511, he was transferred to the Augustinian monastery in Wittenberg, where he earned his doctorate in theology (1512)—thereafter to become a leader within the monastery, the new university, and the spiritual life of the city.

John Tetzel. A contemporary caricature depicts John Tetzel, the famous indulgence preacher. The last lines of the jingle read: "As soon as gold in the basin rings, right then the soul to heaven springs." It was Tetzel's preaching that spurred Luther to publish his 95 theses.

Courtesy Stiftung Luthergedenkstaten in Sachsen-Anhalt/Lutherhalle, Wittenberg.

Justification by Faith Alone Reformation theology grew out of a problem common to many clergy and laity at this time: the failure of traditional medieval religion to provide full personal or intellectual satisfaction. Luther was especially plagued by the disproportion between his own sense of sinfulness and the perfect righteousness that medieval theology taught that God required for salvation. Traditional church teaching and the sacraments were no consolation. Luther wrote that he came to despise the phrase "righteousness of God," for it seemed to demand of him a perfection he knew neither he nor any other human being could ever achieve. His insight into the meaning of "justification by faith alone" was a gradual process that extended over several years, between 1513 and 1518. The righteousness God demands, he concluded, does not come from religious works but is present in full measure in those who believe and trust in the redemptive life and death of Christ, who alone exhibits the righteousness satisfying to God. To believe in Christ is to stand before God clothed in Christ's righteousness.

The Attack on Indulgences An **indulgence** was a remission of the temporal penalty imposed by the priest on penitents as a "work of satisfaction" for their sins. According to medieval theology, after the priest had absolved penitents of guilt for their sins, God still imposed on them a temporal penalty, a manageable "work of satisfaction" that the penitent could perform here and now (for example, through prayers, fasting, almsgiving, retreats, and pilgrimages). Penitents who defaulted on such prescribed works of satisfaction could expect to suffer for their sins in purgatory.

Originally, indulgences had been given only for the true self-sacrifice of going on a crusade to the Holy Land. But they came over time to be more commonly issued as a comfort to laity who were genuinely anxious that forgotten or unrepented sins would condemn them to suffering in purgatory. In 1343, Pope Clement VI (r. 1342–1352) proclaimed the existence of a "treasury of merit," on which popes could draw to issue "letters of indulgence" that canceled the works of satisfaction owed by penitents. By Luther's time, they were regularly dispensed for small cash payments (modest sums that were regarded as almsgiving) and were said to remit not only future punishment of the living, but also those of the dead in purgatory for whom they were purchased.

In 1517, a Jubilee indulgence, proclaimed under Pope Julius II (r. 1503–1513) to raise funds for the rebuilding of Saint Peter's in Rome, was revived and preached on the borders of Saxony in the territories of Archbishop Albrecht of Mainz, who had large debts. The selling of the indulgence was a joint venture by Albrecht, the Augsburg banking house of Fugger, and Pope Leo X (r. 1513–1521), half the proceeds going to the pope and half to Albrecht and his creditors. The famous indulgence preacher John Tetzel (d. 1519) exhorted the crowds:

> Don't you hear the voices of your dead parents and other relatives crying out, "Have mercy on us, for we suffer great punishment and pain. From this you could release us with a few alms.... We have created you, fed you, cared for you, and left you our temporal goods. Why do you treat us so cruelly and leave us to suffer in the flames, when it takes only a little to save us?"[1]

When on October 31, 1517, Luther posted his **ninety-five theses** against indulgences on the door of Castle Church in Wittenberg, he especially protested the impression Tetzel gave his customers that indulgences actually remitted sins and released the dead from purgatory. Luther thought that this was excessive and created the impression that salvation could be bought.

Election of Charles V Luther's theses made him famous overnight. Humanists endorsed them, but the church began official proceedings to discipline him. As sanctions were being prepared against Luther, Emperor Maximilian I died (January 12, 1519), diverting attention from heresy in Saxony to the contest for a new emperor. The pope backed the French king, Francis I. However, Charles I of Spain, then 19, succeeded his grandfather and became Emperor Charles V (r. 1519–1556). Charles was assisted by a long tradition of Habsburg imperial rule and massive Fugger loans, which secured the votes of the seven electors. The electors also won political concessions from Charles that prevented him from taking unilateral action against Germans, something for which Luther eventually had cause to be grateful.

indulgences Remission of the temporal penalty of punishment in purgatory that remained after sins had been forgiven.

ninety-five theses Document posted on the door of Castle Church in Wittenberg, Germany on October 31, 1517 by Martin Luther protesting, among other things, the selling of indulgences.

[1]*Die Reformation in Augenzeugen Berichten*, ed. by Helmar Junghans (Dusseldorf: Karl Rauch Verlag, 1967), p. 44.

A Catholic portrayal of Martin Luther tempting Jesus (1547). Reformation propaganda often portrayed the pope as the Antichrist or the devil. Here Catholic propaganda turns the tables on the Protestant reformers by portraying a figure of Martin Luther as the devil (note the monstrous feet and tail under his academic robes).

Versuchung Christi, 1547, Gemälde, Bonn, Rheinisches Landesmuseum, Inv. Nr. 58.3.

MAP 16–2

The Empire of Charles V. Dynastic marriages and good luck concentrated into Charles's hands rule over the lands shown here, plus Spain's overseas possessions. Crowns and titles rained down on him; election in 1519 as emperor gave him new burdens and responsibilities.

WHAT WERE the geographical advantages and disadvantages of the empire of Charles V?

Luther's Excommunication and the Diet of Worms In the same month in which Charles was elected emperor, Luther debated the Ingolstadt professor John Eck (1486–1543) in Leipzig (June 27, 1519). Luther challenged the infallibility of the pope and the inerrancy of church councils, and argued for the first time for Scripture as the sole and sovereign authority over faith. He burned all his bridges to the old church when he defended John Huss, a condemned heretic.

In 1520, Luther made his position clear by issuing three famous pamphlets. The *Address to the Christian Nobility of the German Nation* urged the German princes to force reforms on the Roman Church and especially to curtail its political and economic power in Germany. The *Babylonian Captivity of the Church* attacked the traditional seven sacraments and claimed that only two were legitimate. It also exalted the authority of Scripture and the decisions of church councils and secular princes over the judgments of popes. The last pamphlet, *Freedom of a Christian*, eloquently summarized his new teaching: that salvation came by faith alone—that it was the consequence of a "happy union" between the soul and Christ.

In April 1521, Luther presented his views before the imperial **Diet of Worms**, over which Charles V presided. Ordered to recant, Luther refused. On

Diet of Worms Meeting of the representatives (diet) of the Holy Roman Empire, presided over by the Emperor Charles V at the German city of Worms in 1521, at which Martin Luther was ordered to recant his ninety-five theses. Luther refused and was declared an outlaw although he was protected by the Elector of Saxony and other German princes.

May 26, 1521, he was placed under the imperial ban and became an "outlaw" within the empire. Friends hid him in Wartburg Castle. There he spent almost a year in seclusion (April 1521 to March 1522), translating Erasmus's new Greek text of the New Testament into German. He also attempted by correspondence to oversee the first stages of the Reformation in Wittenberg.

Imperial Distractions: France and the Turks   The Reformation was greatly assisted at its start by the fact that the emperor was forced to focus his attention on a war with France and the advance of the Ottoman Turks into eastern Europe. Against both adversaries, Charles V, who was also Spain's king and had dynastic responsibilities outside the empire, needed German troops. Consequently, he pursued friendly relations with the German princes. Between 1521 and 1559, Spain (the Habsburg dynasty) and France (the Valois dynasty) fought four major wars. In 1526, the Turks overran Hungary at the Battle of Mohacs, while in western Europe the French-led League of Cognac pushed Charles toward a second Habsburg-Valois war. Thus preoccupied, the emperor agreed at the German Diet of Speyer in 1526 that each German territory could be free to enforce the Edict of Worms (1521) against Luther "so as to be able to answer in good conscience to God and the emperor." That concession, in effect, gave the German princes territorial sovereignty in religious matters while giving the Reformation time to put down deep roots. In 1555, the Peace of Augsburg enshrined this princely privilege as imperial law.

How the Reformation Spread   The Reformation soon passed from the hands of theologians and pamphleteers into those of magistrates and princes. In many cities, Protestant preachers built sizable congregations that pressured urban governments to adopt religious reforms. Many magistrates had long pushed for reform and welcomed the preachers as allies. Reform slogans thus became laws binding on all townspeople.

Religious reform became a territorial political movement as well. It was led by the elector of Saxony and the prince of Hesse. Like the urban magistrates, the princes recognized political and economic opportunities for themselves in the demise of the Roman Catholic Church, and they urged the reform on their neighbors. By the 1530s, there was a powerful Protestant alliance prepared for war with the Catholic emperor.

The Peasants' Revolt   In its first decade, the Protestant movement suffered more from internal division than from imperial interference. By 1525, Luther had become as much an object of protest within Germany as was the pope. Original allies and sympathizers declared their independence from him.

The German peasants had at first believed Luther to be an ally. Since the late 15th century, they had organized to resist efforts by princes to jettison traditional customs and impose new regulations and taxes on them. Peasant leaders saw in Luther's teaching of religious freedom and his criticism of monastic landowners a point of view close to their own. They openly solicited his support of their political and economic rights, including their revolutionary request for release from serfdom.

Luther and his followers sympathized with the peasants, but the Lutherans were no social revolutionaries. Luther believed that Christian freedom was an inner release from guilt and anxiety, not the right to an egalitarian society. When the peasants revolted in 1524–1525, Luther condemned them in the strongest

Execution of a Peasant Leader. The punishment of a peasant leader in a village near Heilbronn. After the defeat of rebellious peasants in and around the city of Heilbronn, Jacob Rorbach, a well-to-do peasant leader from a nearby village, was tied to a stake and slowly roasted to death.

© Badische Landesbibliothek.

possible terms as "unchristian" and urged the princes to crush their revolt without mercy. Tens of thousands of peasants (estimates run between 70,000 and 100,000) had died by the time the revolt was put down.

For Luther, the freedom of the Christian was an inner release from guilt and anxiety, not a right to restructure society by violent revolution. Had Luther supported the Peasants' Revolt, he would have also ended any chance of his reform surviving beyond the 1520s.

Luther and the Jews   Luther's stand toward the Jews has also been controversial. In 1523 he published a pamphlet, "Jesus Christ was Born a Jew," in which he urged Christians to be kind to Germany's Jews in the hope that they might convert to reformed Christianity. But Luther came to regret his pamphlet and decided that the Jews were just another in a long history of foreign predators who threatened German Christians. He expressed these views in a series of pamphlets in the late 1530s and early 1540 in which he urged German princes to forcibly expel Jews who refused to convert. Fortunately, the Jews found a protector in Emperor Charles V, and Luther's colleagues were not inclined to abandon the hope that the Jews would eventually convert. However, in Hesse and Saxony rulers tightened restrictions on Jews, and Luther did not, as he might have, use his influence on their behalf.

ZWINGLI AND THE SWISS REFORMATION

Although Luther's was the first, reform movments occurred in Switzerland and France almost simultaneously with the German Reformation. Switzerland was a loose confederacy of 13 autonomous cantons or states and allied areas. Some became Protestant, some remained Catholic, and a few managed to effect a compromise. The two preconditions of the Swiss Reformation were the growth of national sentiment and a desire for church reform.

The Reformation in Zurich   Ulrich Zwingli (1484–1531), the leader of the Swiss Reformation, was widely known for opposition to the sale of indulgences and religious superstition. As a priest in Zurich, he made the city his base for reform. Zwingli's reform guideline was simple and effective: whatever lacked literal support in Scripture was to be neither believed nor practiced. After a public disputation in January 1523, based on his Scripture test, Zurich became, to all intents and purposes, a Protestant city and the center of the Swiss Reformation. Its rigorous enforcement of its religious ideals made it one of the first examples of a "puritanical" Protestant city.

The Marburg Colloquy   Landgrave Philip of Hesse (1504–1567) sought to unite Swiss and German Protestants in a mutual defense pact, a potentially significant political alliance. His efforts were spoiled, however, by theological disagreements between Luther and Zwingli over the nature of Christ's presence in the Eucharist. Zwingli maintained a symbolic interpretation of Christ's words, "This is my body"; Christ, he argued, was only spiritually, not bodily, present in the bread and wine of the Eucharist. Luther, to the contrary, insisted that Christ's human nature could share the properties of his divine nature. Hence, where Christ was spiritually present, he could also be bodily present, for his was a special nature (*transubstantiation*).

Philip of Hesse brought the two Protestant leaders together in his castle in Marburg in early October 1529, but they were unable to work out their differences

transubstantiation Doctrine that the entire substances of the bread and wine are changed in the Eucharist into the body and blood of Christ.

on this issue. Luther left thinking Zwingli a dangerous fanatic. The disagreement splintered the Protestant movement theologically and politically.

ANABAPTISTS AND RADICAL PROTESTANTS

The moderate pace and seemingly small ethical results of the Lutheran and Zwinglian reformations discontented many people, among them some of the original coworkers of Luther and Zwingli. Many desired a more rapid and thorough implementation of primitive Christianity and accused the major reformers of going only halfway. The most important of these radical groups were the Anabaptists, the 16th-century ancestors of the modern Mennonites and Amish. The Anabaptists take their name from their rejection of infant baptism and their insistence that only baptism as a consenting adult conformed to Scripture and was respectful of human freedom. (*Anabaptism* derives from the Greek word meaning "to rebaptize.")

Anabaptists withdrew from society to form more perfect communities modeled on what they believed to be the example of the first Christians. Due to the close connection between religious and civic life in this period, however, political authorities believed that their separatism was a threat to basic social bonds.

At first, Anabaptism drew adherents from all social classes. But as Lutherans and Zwinglians joined with Catholics in opposing it, a more rural, agrarian class came to make up the great majority of Anabaptists. In 1529, rebaptism became a capital offense throughout the Holy Roman Empire. It has been estimated that between 1525 and 1618 at least 1,000 and perhaps as many as 5,000 men and women were executed for rebaptizing themselves as adults.

JOHN CALVIN AND THE GENEVAN REFORMATION

Calvinism was the religious ideology that inspired or accompanied massive political resistance in France, the Netherlands, and Scotland. Believing in both divine predestination and the individual's responsibility to create a godly society, Calvinists were zealous reformers. In a famous and controversial study, *The Protestant Ethic and the Spirit of Capitalism* (1904), the German sociologist Max Weber argued that this peculiar combination of religious confidence and self-disciplined activism produced an ethic congenial to emergent capitalism.

Political Revolt and Religious Reform in Geneva

Whereas in Saxony religious reform paved the way for a political revolution against the emperor, in Geneva a political revolution against the local prince-bishop laid the foundation for religious change. In late 1533, the Protestant city of Bern sent Protestant reformers to Geneva and by the summer of 1535, after much internal turmoil, the Protestants triumphed. On May 21, 1536, the city voted officially to adopt the Reformation: "to live according to the Gospel and the Word of God ... without ... any more masses, statues, idols, or other papal abuses."

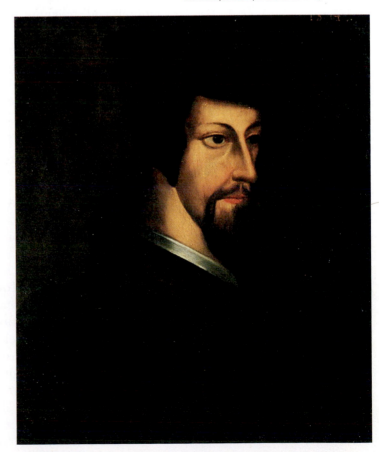

A portrait of the young John Calvin.
Bibliotheque Publique et Universitaire, Geneva.

John Calvin (1509–1564), a reform-minded humanist and lawyer, arrived in Geneva after these events, in July 1536. The local Protestant reformer persuaded him to stay and assist the Reformation. Before a year had passed, Calvin had drawn up articles for the governance of the new church, as well as a catechism to guide and discipline the people. As a result of the strong measures proposed to govern Geneva's moral life, the reformers were accused of trying to create a "new papacy," and in February 1538 they were exiled from the city.

Calvin went to Strasbourg, a model Protestant city, where he became pastor to a group of French exiles. During his two years in Strasbourg, he wrote biblical commentaries and a second edition of his masterful *Institutes of the Christian Religion*, which many consider the definitive theological statement of the Protestant faith. He also married and participated in the ecumenical discussions urged on Protestants and Catholics by Charles V. Most important, he learned from the Strasbourg reformer Martin Bucer (1491–1551) how to implement the Protestant Reformation successfully.

Calvin's Geneva   In 1540, Geneva elected officials favorable to Calvin, and he was invited to return. Within months of his arrival, new ecclesiastical ordinances were implemented that allowed the magistrates and the clergy to cooperate in matters of internal discipline.

Calvin and his followers were motivated above all by a desire to make society godly. The "elect," Calvin taught, should live a manifestly God-pleasing life, if they were truly God's elect. The majesty of God demanded nothing less. The *consistory*, a judicial body composed of clergy and laity, was established to enforce the strictest moral discipline. It meted out punishments for a broad range of moral and religious transgressions and became unpopular among many Genevans.

After 1555 the city's magistrates were all devout Calvinists, and Geneva became a refuge for thousands of exiled Protestants driven out of France, England, and Scotland. Refugees (more than 5,000), most of them utterly loyal to Calvin, constituted over one-third of the population of Geneva. From this time until his death in 1564, Calvin's position in the city was greatly strengthened and the magistrates were very cooperative.

POLITICAL CONSOLIDATION OF THE LUTHERAN REFORMATION

By 1530 the Reformation was irreversible, but it would take several decades and major attempts to eradicate it before this was accepted. The political success of Lutheranism in the empire, by the 1550s, gave Protestant movements elsewhere a new lease on life.

Expansion of the Reformation   In the 1530s, German Lutherans formed regional consistories, which oversaw and administered the new Protestant churches. These consistories replaced the old Catholic episcopates. Under the leadership of Philip Melanchthon (1497–1560), Luther's most admired colleague, educational reforms were enacted that provided for compulsory primary education, schools for girls, a humanist revision of the traditional curriculum, and catechetical instruction of the laity in the new religion.

The Reformation also dug in elsewhere. Introduced into Denmark by Christian II (r. 1513–1523), Lutheranism became the state religion under Christian III (r. 1536–1559). In Sweden, Gustavus Vasa (r. 1523–1560), supported by a nobility greedy for church lands, confiscated church property and subjected the clergy to royal authority at the Diet of Vesteras (1527). In politically splintered Poland, Lutherans, Calvinists, and others found room to practice their beliefs. The absence of a central political authority made Poland a model of religious pluralism and toleration in the second half of the 16th century.

Reaction Against Protestants: The "Interim"   Charles V made abortive efforts in 1540–1541 to enforce a compromise agreement between Protestants and Catholics. When these and other conciliar efforts failed, he sought a military solution. In 1547 imperial armies crushed a Protestant alliance called the Schmalkaldic League.

The emperor established puppet rulers in Saxony and Hesse and issued as imperial law the Augsburg Interim. It ordered Protestants everywhere to readopt Catholic beliefs and practices. The Reformation was, however, too entrenched by 1547 to be ended even by brute force. Confronted by fierce Protestant resistance and weary from three decades of war, the emperor was forced to relent.

The Peace of Augsburg in September 1555 made the division of Christendom permanent. This agreement recognized in law what had already been well established in practice: *cuius regio, eius religio*, meaning that the ruler of a land would determine the religion of the land. Lutherans were permitted to retain all church lands forcibly seized before 1552. Those discontented with the religion of their region were permitted to migrate to another.

Calvinism was not recognized as a legal form of Christian belief and practice by the Peace of Augsburg. Calvinists remained determined not only to secure the right to worship publicly as they pleased, but also to shape society according to their own religious convictions. They organized to lead national revolutions throughout northern Europe.

Progress of Protestant Reformation on the Continent

1517	Luther posts 95 theses against indulgences
1519	Charles I of Spain elected Holy Roman emperor (as Charles V)
1519	Luther challenges infallibility of pope and inerrancy of church councils at Leipzig Debate
1521	Papal bull excommunicates Luther for heresy
1521	Diet of Worms condemns Luther
1521–1522	Luther translates the New Testament into German
1524–1525	Peasants' Revolt in Germany
1529	Marburg Colloquy between Luther and Zwingli
1530	Diet of Augsburg fails to settle religious differences
1531	Formation of Protestant Schmalkaldic League
1536	Calvin arrives in Geneva
1540	Jesuits, founded by Ignatius of Loyola, recognized as order by pope
1546	Luther dies
1547	Armies of Charles V crush Schmalkaldic League
1555	Peace of Augsburg recognizes rights of Lutherans to worship as they please
1545–1563	Council of Trent institutes reforms and responds to the Reformation

THE ENGLISH REFORMATION TO 1553

Late medieval England had a well-earned reputation for defending the rights of the crown against the pope. It was, however, the unhappy marriage of King Henry VIII (r. 1509–1547) that precipitated England's break with the papacy.

The King's Affair   Henry had married Catherine of Aragon (d. 1536), a daughter of Ferdinand and Isabella of Spain, and the aunt of Emperor Charles V. By 1527, the union had produced only one surviving child, a daughter, Mary Tudor. Henry was justifiably concerned about the political consequences of leaving only a female heir. People in this period believed it unnatural for women to rule over men. At best, a woman ruler meant a contested reign; at worst, turmoil, revolution, and possible foreign invasion. After Henry's queen Catherine had numerous miscarriages and stillbirths, the king concluded

Main Events of the English Reformation

1529	Reformation Parliament convenes
1532	Parliament passes the Submission of the Clergy, an act placing canon law and the English clergy under royal jurisdiction
1533	Henry VIII weds Anne Boleyn
1534	Act of Succession makes Anne Boleyn's children legitimate heirs to the English throne
1534	Act of Supremacy declares Henry VIII the only supreme head of the Church of England
1535	Thomas More executed for opposition to Acts of Succession and Supremacy
1535	Publication of Coverdale Bible
1539	Henry VIII imposes the Six Articles, condemning Protestantism and reasserting traditional doctrine
1547	Edward VI succeeds to the throne
1549	First Act of Uniformity imposes Book of Common Prayer on English churches
1553–1558	Mary Tudor restores Catholic doctrine
1558–1603	Elizabeth I fashions an Anglican religious settlement

that their union had been cursed by God. Catherine had briefly been the wife of his late brother, Arthur.

By 1527, Henry was thoroughly enamored of Anne Boleyn (ca. 1504–1536), one of Catherine's young ladies in waiting. He decided to put Catherine aside and marry Anne, but this required papal annulment of the marriage—and therein lay a problem. In 1527, the reigning pope, Clement VII (r. 1523–1534), was a prisoner of Charles V, Catherine's nephew. Even if this had not been the case, it would have been virtually impossible for the pope to grant Henry an annulment. Not only had his marriage lasted for 18 years, but it had been made possible in the first place by a special papal dispensation. This had been required because of Catherine's previous marriage to Henry's deceased brother, Arthur.

After Cardinal Wolsey (1475–1530), Lord Chancellor of England since 1515, failed to secure the annulment the king wanted, Henry chose as advisers Thomas Cranmer (1489–1556) and Thomas Cromwell (1485–1540), both of whom harbored Lutheran sympathies. They urged the king to take a different course: Why not simply declare himself supreme in English spiritual affairs as he was in English temporal affairs? The king could then rule on the status of his own marriage.

Reformation Parliament   In 1529 Parliament convened for the seven-year session that earned it the title "Reformation Parliament." It passed a flood of legislation that subjected the clergy to royal authority. In January 1531, the clergy publicly recognized Henry as head of the church in England "as far as the law of Christ allows." In 1532, Parliament passed the Submission of the Clergy, effectively placing canon law under royal control and the clergy under royal jurisdiction.

In January 1533 Henry wed the pregnant Anne Boleyn, with Thomas Cranmer, his newly appointed archbishop of Canterbury, officiating. In 1534, Parliament ended all payments by the English clergy and laity to Rome and gave Henry sole jurisdiction over high ecclesiastical appointments. The Act of Succession in the same year made Anne Boleyn's children legitimate heirs to the throne, and the Act of Supremacy declared Henry "the only supreme head in earth of the church of England."

The Protestant Reformation Under Edward VI   Despite his political break with Rome, Henry remained decidedly conservative in his religious beliefs and continued to endorse Catholic doctrine and practices, despite agitation for Protestant reforms by some of his subjects. Henry forbade the English clergy to marry and threatened to execute clergy caught twice in concubinage. The Six Articles of 1539 reaffirmed belief in transubstantiation, denied the Eucharistic cup to the laity, declared that vows of celibacy could not be voided, provided for private Masses, and ordered the continuation of oral confession to a priest.

Edward VI (r. 1547–1553), Henry's son by his third wife, Jane Seymour, became king at age 10. Under his regents, England enacted much of the

Protestant Reformation. Henry's Six Articles and laws against heresy were repealed, and clerical marriage and Communion with the cup were sanctioned. An Act of Uniformity imposed Thomas Cranmer's Book of Common Prayer on all English churches, which were stripped of their images and altars. His 42-article confession of faith set forth a moderate Protestant doctrine.

These changes were short-lived because in 1553 young Edward died, and his half-sister, Catherine of Aragon's daughter, Mary Tudor (d. 1558), succeeded to the throne. She restored Catholic doctrine and practice with a single-mindedness that rivaled that of her father. It was not until the reign of Anne Boleyn's daughter, Elizabeth I (r. 1558–1603), that a lasting religious settlement was worked out in England.

CATHOLIC REFORM AND COUNTER-REFORMATION

The Protestant Reformation did not take the medieval church completely by surprise. There had been much criticism and many calls for reform before the **Counter-Reformation** began in response to Protestant successes.

Sources of Catholic Reform Before the Reformation began, ambitious proposals had been made for church reform. But 16th-century popes were mindful of how the Councils of Constance and Basel had tried to strip the pope of his traditional powers, and they squelched efforts to bring about basic changes in the laws and institutions of the church. Despite papal foot-dragging, the church was not without reformers. Many new religious orders sprang up in the 16th century to champion renewal within the church.

Ignatius of Loyola and the Society of Jesus Of the various reform groups, none was more instrumental in the success of the Counter-Reformation than the Society of Jesus, the new order of Jesuits. Organized by Ignatius of Loyola in the 1530s, it was officially recognized by the papacy in 1540. Within a century, the society had more than 15,000 members scattered throughout the world and had established thriving missions in India, Japan, and the Americas.

Ignatius of Loyola (1491–1556) was a heroic figure. A dashing courtier and caballero in his youth, he began his spiritual pilgrimage in 1521 while recuperating from a serious battle wound. During a lengthy and painful convalescence, he read Christian classics. So impressed was he with the heroic self-sacrifice of the church's saints and their methods of overcoming mental anguish and pain that he underwent a profound religious conversion. Henceforth, he too would serve the church as a soldier of Christ.

Counter-Reformation
Sixteenth-century reform movement in the Roman Catholic Church in reaction to the Protestant Reformation.

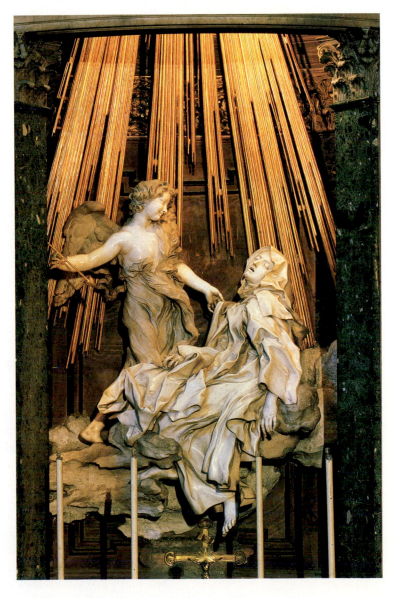

The Ecstasy of Saint Teresa of Avila, by Gianlorenzo Bernini (1598–1680). Catholic mystics like Saint Teresa and Saint John of the Cross helped revive the traditional piety of medieval monasticism.
© Scala/Art Resource, N.Y.

HISTORY'S VOICES

IGNATIUS OF LOYOLA'S "RULES FOR THINKING WITH THE CHURCH"

A s leaders of the Counter-Reformation, the Jesuits attempted to live by and instill in others the strictest obedience to church authority. The following are some of the 18 rules included by Ignatius in his Spiritual Exercises to give Catholics positive direction. These rules also indicate the Catholic reformers' refusal to compromise with Protestants.

WOULD PROTESTANTS find any of Ignatius's "rules" acceptable? Might any of them be controversial among Catholic laity as well as among Protestant laity?

In order to have the proper attitude of mind in the Church Militant we should observe the following rules:

1. Putting aside all private judgment, we should keep our minds prepared and ready to obey promptly and in all things the true spouse of Christ our Lord, our Holy Mother, the hierarchical Church.

2. To praise sacramental confession and the reception of the Most Holy Sacrament once a year, and much better once a month, and better still every week. . . .

3. To praise the frequent hearing of Mass. . . .

4. To praise highly the religious life, virginity, and continence; and also matrimony, but not as highly. . . .

5. To praise the vows of religion, obedience, poverty, chastity, and other works of perfection and supererogation. . . .

6. To praise the relics of the saints . . . [and] the stations, pilgrimages, indulgences, jubilees, Crusade indulgences, and the lighting of candles in the churches.

7. To praise the precepts concerning fasts and abstinences . . . and acts of penance. . . .

8. To praise the adornments and buildings of churches as well as sacred images. . . .

9. To praise all the precepts of the church. . . .

10. To approve and praise the directions and recommendations of our superiors as well as their personal behaviour. . . .

11. To praise both the positive and scholastic theology. . . .

12. We must be on our guard against making comparisons between the living and those who have already gone to their reward, for it is no small error to say, for example: "This man knows more than St. Augustine"; "He is another Saint Francis, or even greater." . . .

13. If we wish to be sure that we are right in all things, we should always be ready to accept this principle: I will believe that the white that I see is black, if the hierarchical Church so defines it. For I believe that between . . . Christ our Lord and . . . His Church, there is but one spirit, which governs and directs us for the salvation of our souls.

Source: *The Spiritual Exercises of St. Ignatius*, trans. by Anthony Mottola. Copyright © 1964 by Doubleday, a division of Bantam, Doubleday, Dell Publishing Group, Inc., pp. 139–141. Used by permission of Doubleday, a division of Random House, Inc.

Ignatius devised a program of religious and moral self-discipline called the *Spiritual Exercises*, which outlined a path to absolute spiritual self-mastery. Ignatius believed that a person could shape his or her own behavior, even create a new religious self, through disciplined study and regular practice (see Ignatius of Loyola's "Rules for Thinking with the Church").

Whereas in Jesuit eyes Protestants had distinguished themselves by disobedience to church authority and by religious innovation, Ignatius's exercises were intended to teach good Catholics to submit without question to higher church authority and spiritual direction. Perfect discipline and self-control were essential for achieving such obedience, as were a passion for traditional spirituality and mystical experience. This potent combination helped counter the Reformation and win many Protestants back to the Catholic fold, especially in Austria and Germany.

The Council of Trent (1545–1563)   The broad success of the Reformation and the insistence of the emperor Charles V forced Pope Paul III (r. 1534–1549) to call a general council of the church to reassert church doctrine. The pope also appointed a reform commission, whose report, presented in February 1537, bluntly criticized the fiscality and simony[2] of the papal Curia (court) as the primary source of the church's loss of esteem. The report was so critical that Pope Paul III attempted unsuccessfully to suppress its publication, and Protestants reprinted and circulated it to justify their criticism.

The long-delayed council met in 1545 in the imperial city of Trent in northern Italy. There were three sessions spread over 18 years with long interruptions due to war, plague, and politics. Unlike the general councils of the 15th century, Trent was strictly under the pope's control, with high Italian prelates prominent in the proceedings.

The council's most important reforms concerned internal church discipline. The selling of church offices and other religious goods was forbidden. Trent strengthened the authority of local bishops so they could effectively discipline popular religious practice. Bishops who resided in Rome were forced to move to their appointed seats of authority. They had to preach regularly and conduct annual visitations. Parish priests were required to be neatly dressed, better educated, strictly celibate, and active among their parishioners. To train better priests, Trent also called for the establishment of a seminary in every diocese.

The Council did not make a single doctrinal concession to the Protestants, however. In the face of Protestant criticism, the Council of Trent reaffirmed the traditional scholastic education of the clergy; the role of good works in salvation; the authority of tradition; the seven sacraments; transubstantiation; the withholding of the Eucharistic cup from the laity; clerical celibacy; the reality of purgatory; the veneration of saints, relics, and sacred images; and the granting of letters of indulgence.

Rulers initially resisted Trent's reform decrees, fearing a revival of papal political power within their lands. But in time the new legislation took hold, and parish life revived under the guidance of a devout and better-trained clergy.

THE REFORMATION'S ACHIEVEMENTS

Although politically conservative, the Reformation changed traditional religious practices and institutions in many lands. By the end of the 16th century, what had disappeared or was radically altered was often dramatic.

HOW DID the Reformation change religious and social life?

Religion in 15th-Century Life   Prior to the Reformation, the streets of the great cities of central Europe that later turned Protestant (for example, Zurich, Strasbourg, Nuremberg, or Geneva) were filled with people who had clerical vocations. They made up 6 to 8 percent of the total urban population, and they exercised considerable political as well as spiritual power. They legislated and taxed; they tried cases in special church courts; and they enforced their laws with threats of excommunication.

The church calendar regulated daily life. About one-third of the year was devoted to some kind of religious observance or celebration. There were frequent

---

[2]The sin of selling sacred or spiritual things, such as church offices.

periods of fasting. On almost a hundred days out of the year, a pious Christian could not, without special dispensation, eat eggs, butter, fat, or meat.

Monasteries and especially nunneries were prominent, influential institutions. Sons of society's most powerful citizens resided there. Local aristocrats were closely identified with particular churches and chapels, whose walls recorded their lineage and proclaimed their generosity. Friars from near and far worked the streets begging alms. The Mass and liturgy were read entirely in Latin. Images of saints were regularly displayed, and on certain holy days their relics were paraded about and venerated. Pilgrims gathered by the hundreds and thousands at religious shrines, many sick and dying in search of a cure or a miracle, but also "tourists" seeking diversion and entertainment. Several times during the year, special preachers appeared with letters of indulgence to sell. Many clergy lived openly with concubines and had children, although they were sworn to celibacy and forbidden marriage. The church tolerated such relationships if penitential fines were paid.

People everywhere could be heard complaining about the clergy's exemption from taxation and, in many instances, also from the civil criminal code. People also grumbled about having to support local church officials who actually lived and worked elsewhere. Townspeople expressed concern that the church had too much influence over education and culture.

Religion in 16th-Century Life   After the Reformation, few changes in politics and society were evident in these cities. The same aristocratic families governed, and the rich generally got richer and the poor poorer. But overall numbers of clergy fell by two-thirds and religious holidays shrank by one-third. Monasteries and nunneries were almost all gone. Many were turned into hospices for the sick and poor or into educational institutions, their endowments to these new purposes. A few cloisters remained for very devout old monks and nuns, who could not be pensioned off or who lacked families and friends to care for them. But these remaining cloisters died out with their inhabitants.

The number of churchgoers had been reduced by at least a third, and worship was conducted almost completely in the vernacular. In some, particularly those in Zwinglian cities, the walls were stripped bare and white-washed to make sure their congregations meditated only on God's Word. The laity observed no obligatory fasts. Indulgence preachers no longer appeared. Local shrines were closed down, and anyone found openly venerating saints, relics, and images was subject to fine and punishment.

Copies of Luther's translation of the New Testament, or more often excerpts from it, could be found in private homes, and meditation on them was encouraged by the new clergy. The clergy could marry, and most did. They paid taxes and were punished for their crimes in civil courts. Domestic moral life was regulated by committees composed of roughly equal numbers of laity and clergy, over whose decisions secular magistrates had the last word.

Not all Protestant clergy were enthusiastic about the new authority the laity enjoyed in religious affairs, and the laity themselves were ambivalent about some aspects of the Reformation. More than half of the original converts returned to the Catholic fold before the end of the 16th century. Half of Europe could be counted in the Protestant camp in the mid-16th century, but only a fifth were still there by the mid-17th century.[3]

[3]Geoffrey Parker, *Europe in Crisis, 1598–1648* (Ithaca, NY: Cornell University Press, 1979), p. 50.

FAMILY LIFE IN EARLY MODERN EUROPE

Changes in the timing and duration of marriage, family size, and child care suggest that social and economic pressures were altering family life in the 16th and 17th centuries. The Reformation was only one factor—and not the chief—of these changes.

Later Marriages Between 1500 and 1800 men and women married later than in previous centuries: men in their mid-to late 20s and women in their early to mid-20s. The medieval church had recognized marriages made by a private exchange of vows between competent adults, but after the Reformation both Catholics and Protestants required parental consent and public vows for a licit union.

Late marriages reflected the difficulties couples had in accumulating the capital needed to set up independent households. There was a large population of single women: one in five never married, and 15 percent were widowed. Late marriages meant shorter unions, older first-time mothers, and higher mortality in childbirth. That led to more frequent remarriages for men. Delayed marriage also increased incidences of premarital sex and the numbers of children born out of wedlock.

Arranged Marriages By the 15th century, it was usual for a future bride and groom to have known each other and to have had a prior relationship. Parents did not force strangers to wed, and the law protected children from coercion. Forced marriages where by definition invalid. But marriages were "arranged" in the sense that parents met and discussed terms before the prospective bride and groom began preparations.

Family Size Nuclear families were the rule in Western Europe: a father, a mother, and their children. They might live in larger households with in-laws, servants, and boarders. Children were conceived on the average of every two years. About one-third died by age five, and one-half by their teens.

Birth Control Artificial birth control methods had been known since antiquity. They were, however, not very effective, and the church opposed anything that might be done to prevent conception. St. Thomas Aquinas had argued that acts were moral only when they served nature's ends, and the production of children was the natural purpose of sex.

Wet Nursing The church and physicians both encouraged women to suckle their own newborns rather than hand them off to wet nurses (lactating women who sold their services). Wet nursing increased the risk of infant mortality, for the women who provided this service were not always as healthy, clean, or caring as the well-off women who employed them. Upper-class women, however, tended for reasons of vanity and convenience to employ wet nurses. Because nursing has a contraceptive effect, some women nursed to space out their pregnancies, and those who wanted many children used wet nurses.

A Young Couple in Love (ca. 1480)
by an anonymous artist.

Bildarchiv Preussischer Kulturbesitz.

Loving Families   Some features of family life in this period may seem cold to modern people. Between the ages of 8 and 13, children were usually sent away from home to school or to begin apprenticeships and take up employment. The widowed often remarried within a few months of their bereavement. Marriages between spouses of vastly different ages were common.

In context, these practices made sense. Parents showed love and affection for their children by ensuring that they acquired the skills needed to be self-supporting. The labor involved in maintaining a household pushed people to remarry rapidly, but extreme disparity in age did invite criticism and ridicule.

WHAT WAS the final result of the Wars of Religion in France, the Netherlands, and Germany?

THE WARS OF RELIGION

After the Council of Trent adjourned in 1563, Protestants were met by a Jesuit-led Catholic counteroffensive. At the time of John Calvin's death in 1564, Geneva had become both a refuge for Europe's persecuted Protestants and an international school training Protestant resisters—leaders fully equal to the new Catholic challenge.

Genevan Calvinism and the reformed Catholicism of the Council of Trent were equally dogmatic, aggressive, and unwilling to compromise. Calvinists may have looked like "new papists" to their critics in the cities they dominated, but when they were a minority fighting for civil and religious rights, they could become firebrands and revolutionaries.

Calvinists favored a presbyterian form of church government. Congregations elected boards of *presbyters* (elders) to govern them and represent them at synods and meetings that shaped the policy of the church at large. Calvinism, therefore, encouraged local and regional religious authority. By contrast, the Counter-Reformation affirmed Catholicism's dedication to a centralized episcopal system, a church governed by a clerical hierarchy and owing absolute obedience to the pope. The higher clergy—the pope and bishops—not synods of local churches, ruled supreme. Calvinism attracted proponents of political decentralization who opposed totalitarian rulers, whereas Catholicism was congenial to proponents of absolute monarchy who believed that order required "one king, one church, one law."

The wars of religion that erupted between these camps were both internal national conflicts and international wars. Catholic and Protestant struggled for control of France, the Netherlands, and England. The Catholic governments of France and Spain fought the Protestant regimes in England and the Netherlands. The Thirty Years' War, which began in 1618, illustrated the international nature of religious conflict. Before it ended, it drew in every major European nation.

FRENCH WARS OF RELIGION (1562–1598)

When Henry II (r. 1547–1559) died accidentally during a tournament in 1559, his sickly 15-year-old son, Francis II (d. 1560), came to the throne under the regency of the queen mother, Catherine de Médicis (1519–1589). With the monarchy so weakened, three powerful families competed to control France: the Bourbons based in the south and west, the Montmorency-Châtillons from the center, and the Guises from eastern France. The Guises were by far the strongest, and the name *Guise* was synonymous with militant, ultra-Catholicism. The Bourbon and Montmorency-Châtillon families, by contrast, had strong **Huguenot** sympathies,

Huguenots   French Calvinists.

primarily for political reasons. (French Protestants were called Huguenots after Besançon Hughes, the leader of a Genevan political revolt in the late 1520s.) The Bourbon Louis I, prince of Condé (d. 1569), and the Montmorency-Châtillon admiral Gaspard de Coligny (1519–1572) were the leaders of the French Protestant cause.

Ambitious aristocrats and discontented townspeople often joined Calvinist churches to oppose the Guise-dominated French monarchy. By 1561, there were more than 2,000 Huguenot congregations in France. Huguenots made up only about a 1/15 of the population, but they held important geographic areas and were well represented among the leaders of French society. More than 2/5 of the French aristocracy became Huguenots. Many apparently hoped to establish in France a principle of territorial sovereignty akin to the arrangement that the German princes won from the emperor in the Peace of Augsburg (1555). In this sense, Calvinism served the forces of political decentralization.

Catherine de Médicis and the Guises After Francis II's death in 1560, Catherine de Médicis continued as regent for her second son, Charles IX (r. 1560–1574). Fearing the Guises, Catherine, whose first concern was to

The St. Bartholemew's Day Massacre. In this notorious event, here depicted by the contemporary Protestant painter François Dubois, 3,000 Protestants were slaughtered in Paris and an estimated 20,000 others died throughout France. The massacre transformed the religious struggle in France from a contest for political power into an all-out war between Protestants and Catholics.

Le Massacre de la St–Barthelemy, entre 1572 et 1584. Oil on wood, 94 × 154 cm. Musée Cantonal des Beaux Arts, Lausanne. Photo: J.–C. Ducret Musée Cantonal des Beaux–Arts, Lausanne.

preserve the monarchy, sought allies among the Protestants. Early in 1562, she granted Protestants freedom to worship publicly outside towns—although only privately within them—and to hold synods, or church assemblies. In March 1562, the Duke of Guise surprised and massacred a Protestant congregation worshiping illegally at Vassy. This began the French Wars of Religion. Perpetually caught between fanatical Huguenot and Guise extremes, Queen Catherine tried to play one side against the other. She wanted a Catholic France but not under Guise domination.

On August 22, 1572, four days after the Huguenot Henry of Navarre had married Charles IX's sister—a royal alliance based on the queen mother's belief that Protestant power was growing—the Huguenot leader Coligny, who had influence over the king, was wounded by an assassin's bullet. Catherine may have been privy to this Guise plot to eliminate Coligny. After its failure, she feared both the king's response to her complicity and the Huguenots reaction to the attack on their leader. Catherine convinced Charles that a Huguenot coup was afoot and that only the swift execution of Protestant leaders could save the crown from a Protestant attack on Paris. On the eve of Saint Bartholomew's Day, August 24, 1572, Coligny and 3,000 fellow Huguenots were butchered in Paris. Within three days an estimated 20,000 Huguenots were killed in coordinated attacks throughout France.

This event changed the nature of the struggle between Protestants and Catholics throughout Europe. In France, it was no longer an internal political contest between Guise and Bourbon factions, nor was it simply a Huguenot campaign to win basic religious freedoms. Henceforth, Protestants viewed it as an international struggle to the death for survival against an adversary whose cruelty justified any means of resistance.

The Rise to Power of Henry of Navarre   Henry III (r. 1574–1589), who was Catherine's third son and the last Valois king, was caught between a radical Catholic League, formed in 1576 by Henry of Guise, and vengeful Huguenots. Like his mother, he tried to steer a middle course, which won him support from a growing body of neutral Catholics and Huguenots, who put the political survival of France above its religious unity. Such *politiques*, as they were called, were prepared to compromise religious creeds to save the nation.

In the mid-1580s the Catholic League, with Spanish help, totally dominated Paris. Henry III tried to rout the league with a surprise attack in 1588, but he failed and had to flee Paris. Resorting to guerrilla tactics, the king had both the Duke and the Cardinal of Guise assassinated. The Catholic League reacted with a fury that matched the earlier Huguenot response to the Massacre of Saint Bartholomew's Day. In April 1589, the king was forced into an alliance with his Protestant cousin and heir, Henry of Navarre.

However, as the two Henrys prepared to attack Paris, a fanatical Dominican friar murdered Henry III, clearing the way for the Bourbon Huguenot Henry of Navarre to become Henry IV of France (r. 1589–1610).

Henry IV was a *politique*, who valued peace more than religious unity. He believed that a policy of tolerant Catholicism would best achieve his objectives. On July 25, 1593, he abjured the Protestant faith and embraced the majority religion of his subjects. He is reported to have said: "Paris is worth a Mass."

The Edict of Nantes   Five years later, on April 13, 1598, Henry IV issued the Edict of Nantes, a formal religious settlement. In 1591, he had assured the

Huguenots of at least qualified religious freedoms, and the edict fulfilled his promise by sanctioning minority religious rights within what was to remain an officially Catholic country. This religious truce—and it was never more than that—granted the Huguenots, who by this time numbered well over a million, freedom of public worship, the right of assembly, admission to public offices and universities, and permission to maintain fortified towns. Most of these freedoms, however, were confined to specific Huguenot localities. Concession of the right to fortify towns reveals the continuing distrust between French Protestants and Catholics. The edict only transformed a long hot war between enemies into a long cold war. Critics believed the edict created a state within a state.

The Milch Cow. A 16th-century satirical painting depicting the Netherlands as a land all the great powers of Europe wish to exploit. Elizabeth of England is feeding her (England had long-standing commercial ties with Flanders); Philip II of Spain is attempting to ride her (Spain was trying to reassert its control over the entire region); William of Orange is trying to milk her (he was the leader of the anti-Spanish rebellion); and the king of France holds her by the tail (France hoped to profit from the rebellion at Spain's expense).

Rijksmuseum, Amsterdam.

A Catholic fanatic assassinated Henry IV in May 1610. Although Henry is best remembered for the Edict of Nantes, his political and economic policies were equally important. They laid the foundations for the transformation of France into the absolutist state it became in the 17th century. His grandson Louis XIV (r. 1643–1715), renewing the slogan "one king, one church, one law," revoked the Edict of Nantes in 1685 (see Chapter 20). Religion again violently disrupted French society. Rare is the politician who learns from the lessons of history.

IMPERIAL SPAIN AND THE REIGN OF PHILIP II (1556–1598)

Until the English defeated his mighty Armada in 1588, no ruler was greater in the second half of the sixteenth century than Philip II of Spain. During the first half of his reign, Philip II focused attention on the Mediterranean and Turkish expansion. On October 7, 1571, a Holy League of Spain, Venice, and the pope defeated the Turks at Lepanto in the largest naval battle of the 16th century. About 30,000 Turks were killed and more than one-third of the Turkish fleet was sunk or captured.

Revolt in the Netherlands   The spectacular Spanish military success in southern Europe was not repeated in northern Europe, where Philip tried to impose his will within the Netherlands and on England and France. The resistance of the Netherlands was key to undoing Spanish dreams of world empire.

The Netherlands were the richest area in Europe. The merchant towns of the region were, however, Europe's most independent. Many, like the great port of Antwerp, were Calvinist strongholds. Opposition to the Spanish overlords found a leader in a native nobleman, William of Nassau, the Prince of Orange (r. 1533–1584). Like other successful rulers in this period, William of Orange was a politique who valued the Netherlands' political autonomy above religious creeds. He was at various times Catholic, Lutheran, and Calvinist.

In 1564, political and religious opponents to Spain's rule united for the first time under Philip II's unwise insistence that the decrees of the Council of Trent be enforced throughout the Netherlands. They formed a national covenant called the Compromise, a solemn pledge to resist the decrees of Trent and the Inquisition.

Philip ordered the Duke of Alba (1508–1582) to lead an army of 10,000 men into the Netherlands from Milan in 1567, a show of combined Spanish and papal might. Alba put down the revolt and established a tribunal—known to the Spanish as the Council of Troubles and to the Netherlanders as the Council of Blood—to govern the land. Several thousand suspected heretics were publicly executed before Alba's reign of terror ended.

William of Orange, who was an exile in Germany during these turbulent years, emerged as the leader of a broad movement for the Netherlands' independence. In 1576, after a decade of persecution and warfare, the 10 predominantly Catholic southern provinces (roughly modern Belgium) joined the 7 largely Protestant northern provinces (roughly the modern Netherlands) in opposition to Spain. Their union, the Pacification of Ghent, granted each region of the country sovereignty in matters of religion—a Netherlands version of the Peace of Augsburg.

In January 1579, the southern provinces formed the Union of Arras and made peace with Spain. The northern provinces formed the Union of Utrecht and continued the struggle. Spanish preoccupation with France and England in the 1580s gave the northern provinces their chance to evict Spain's armies (1593), and in 1596, France and England formally recognized their independence. However, the northern provinces did not formally conclude peace with Spain until 1609, and Spain did not fully recognize their independence until the Peace of Westphalia in 1648.

ENGLAND AND SPAIN (1558–1603)

Elizabeth I   Elizabeth I (r. 1558–1603), daughter of Henry VIII and Anne Boleyn, was perhaps the most astute politician of the 16th century in both domestic and foreign policy. She repealed the anti-Protestant legislation of her predecessor Mary Tudor and guided a religious settlement through Parliament that prevented England from being torn asunder by religious differences in the 16th century, as the Continent was.

Catholic extremists hoped to replace Elizabeth with the Catholic Mary Stuart, Queen of Scots. But Elizabeth fended off Catholic assassination plots and rarely let emotion override her political instincts.

Elizabeth also dealt cautiously with England's Puritans, Protestants who wanted to "purify" the national church of every vestige of "popery" and make its theology purely Protestant. The Puritans had two special grievances: (1) the retention of Catholic ceremony and vestments by the Church of England, and (2) the continuation of the episcopal system of church governance. Sixteenth-century Puritans were not separatists, however. They worked through Parliament to create an alternative national church of semi-autonomous congregations governed by representative presbyteries, following the model of Calvin and Geneva. These were the Presbyterians. The more extreme Puritans, who wanted every congregation to be autonomous and a law unto itself, were called Congregationalists. Elizabeth considered their views subversive.

Deterioration of Relations with Spain   A series of events led inexorably to war between England and Spain, despite the sincere desires of both Philip II and Elizabeth to avoid it. Following Spain's victory at Lepanto in 1571, England signed a mutual defense pact with France. Also in the 1570s, Elizabeth's famous seamen, John Hawkins (1532–1595) and Sir Francis Drake (?1545–1596), began to prey on Spanish shipping in the Americas. Drake's circumnavigation of the globe (1577–1580) was one in a series of dramatic demonstrations of England's growing sea power. In 1585, Elizabeth signed a treaty that committed English soldiers to aid the Netherlands. These events pushed England and Spain toward a showdown, and the breakpoint was Elizabeth's reluctant decision to execute Mary, Queen of Scots (1542–1587) for complicity in a plot to assassinate her.

Philip assembled a great armada for an invasion of England, and on May 30, 1588, his fleet of 130 ships bearing 25,000 sailors and soldiers under the command of the Duke of Medina-Sidonia set sail for England. The English, however, ably countered his attack. The barges sent to transport Spanish soldiers from the galleons onto English shores were prevented from leaving Calais and Dunkirk. The swifter English and Netherlands ships, assisted by an "English wind (a storm)", dispersed the Spanish fleet, over a third of which never returned to Spain. The Armada's defeat gave heart to Protestant resistance everywhere, and Spain never fully recovered. By the time of Philip's death on September 13, 1598, his forces had been rebuffed by the French and the Dutch. His 17th-century successors were all inferior leaders, and Spain never again had an era of imperial grandeur comparable to Philip's reign. The French seized the opportunity to dominate the Continent, while the Dutch and the English whittled away at Spain's overseas empire.

Elizabeth died on March 23, 1603, leaving behind her a strong nation poised to expand into a global empire (see Map 16–3).

THE THIRTY YEARS' WAR (1618–1648)

The Thirty Years' War in the Holy Roman Empire was the last and most destructive of the Wars of Religion. Religious and political differences had long set Catholics against Protestants and Calvinists against Lutherans. What made the Thirty Years' War so devastating was the entrenched hatred of the various sides and their seeming determination to sacrifice everything for territorial sovereignty and religion. As conflicts multiplied, virtually every major European land became involved either directly or indirectly. When the hostilities ended in 1648, the peace terms redrew much of the map of northern Europe to conform to the pattern we know today.

Fragmented Germany   During the second half of the 16th century, Germany was an almost ungovernable land of 360 autonomous political entities. The Peace of Augsburg (1555) had given each a significant degree of sovereignty within its own borders. Each levied its own tolls and tariffs and coined its own money, practices that made land travel and trade between the various regions difficult, if not impossible. Many of these little "states" had political ambitions. Unlike France, Spain, and England at the start of the 17th century, Germany was radically decentralized and fragmented (see Map 16–3).

Religious Division   Religious conflict accentuated international and internal political divisions. The Holy Roman Empire was about equally divided between Catholics and Protestants, the latter having perhaps a slight numerical

⟡ MAP EXPLORATION

Interactive map: To explore this map further, go to **http://www.prenhall.com/craig/map16.3**

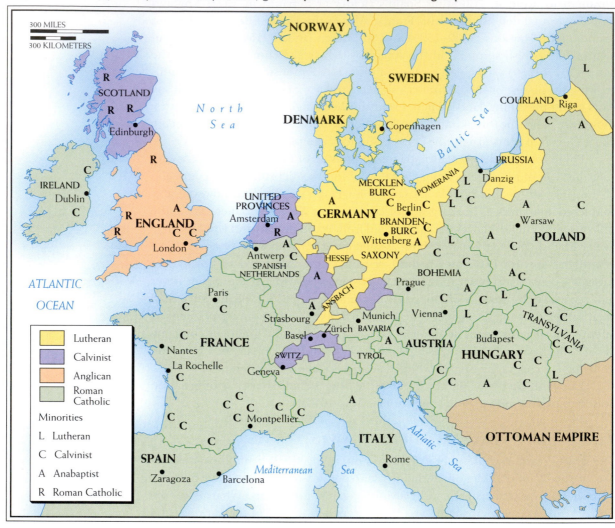

Legend:
- Lutheran
- Calvinist
- Anglican
- Roman Catholic

Minorities
- L   Lutheran
- C   Calvinist
- A   Anabaptist
- R   Roman Catholic

MAP 16–3

Religious Division ca. 1600.   By 1600 few could expect Christians to return to a uniform religious allegiance. In Spain and southern Italy, Catholicism remained relatively unchallenged, but note the existence elsewhere of large religious minorities, both Catholic and Protestant.

WHY DID the Wars of Religion fail to reestablish religious uniformity in the Holy Roman Empire?

edge by 1600. The terms of the Peace of Augsburg (1555) had attempted to freeze the amount of territory held by Lutherans and the Catholics. In the intervening years, however, the Lutherans had gained political control in many Catholic areas, and Catholics had taken over a few previously Lutheran areas. There was also religious strife between liberal and conservative Lutherans and between Lutherans and the growing numbers of Calvinists.

As elsewhere in Europe, Calvinism operated as political and religious leaven within the Holy Roman Empire. Calvinism was not recognized as a legal religion by the Peace of Augsburg, but in 1559 it established a strong foothold within the empire when Elector Frederick III (r. 1559–1576) of the Palatinate, a devout convert to Calvinism, made it his domain's official religion. By 1609,

EURO

PE 1500-1650

MAP 16–4

The Holy Roman Empire ca. 1618. On the eve of the Thirty Years' War, the empire was politically and religiously fragmented, as this somewhat simplified map reveals. Lutherans dominated the north and Catholics the south, while Calvinists controlled the United Provinces and the Palatinate and also had an important presence in Switzerland and Brandenburg.

DID THE Holy Roman Empire emerge from the Wars of Religion stronger or weaker?

Palatine Calvinists had organized a Protestant defensive alliance supported by Spain's enemies: England, France, and the Netherlands.

If the Calvinists were active within the Holy Roman Empire, so were their Catholic counterparts, the Jesuits. Staunchly Catholic Bavaria, with Spanish backing, was militarily and ideologically for Counter-Reformation Catholicism what the Palatinate was for Protestantism. From Bavaria, the Jesuits launched successful missions throughout the empire. In 1609, Maximilian, Duke of Bavaria (1573–1651), organized a Catholic League to counter a new Protestant

OVERVIEW THE RELIGIOUS DIVISIONS OF EUROPE

The Reformation permanently shattered the religious unity of Western Europe that had existed since the fifth century C.E. It also gave rise to more than a century of warfare, in which Catholics fought Protestants, and Protestants fought each other all in the name of faith. By 1648, when the Treaty of Westphalia ended the Thirty Years' War, Europe remained divided into mostly Catholic regions, mostly Protestant regions, and those areas with large religious minorities. Most of these divisions have persisted to the present day.

Country	Religion
Austria	Catholic
Belgium	Catholic
Bohemia (modern Czech Republic)	Catholic
Croatia	Catholic
England	Protestant (Anglicans, Calvinists, and Anabaptists); a declining Catholic minority
Estonia	Lutheran
France	Catholic, but with substantial numbers of Calvinists
Germany	North was predominately Protestant (Lutheran, Calvinist, Anabaptist); south and the Rhineland were mostly Catholic; but each area had religious minorities
Hungary	Mostly Catholic, but with a large Calvinist minority
Ireland	Mostly Catholic, but with a Protestant minority (Anglicans and Calvinists) mainly in the north
Italy	Catholic
Latvia	Lutheran
Lithuania	Catholic
Netherlands	Calvinist majority, but with a large Catholic minority
Poland	Catholic
Portugal	Catholic
Scandinavia	Lutheran
Scotland	Calvinist
Slovakia	Catholic
Slovenia	Catholic
Spain	Catholic
Switzerland	Almost evenly divided between Catholics and Protestants (both Calvinists and Lutherans)

alliance that had been formed by the Calvinist Elector Palatine, Frederick IV (r. 1583–1610). When the league fielded a great army under the command of Jean't Senclaes, Count of Tilly (1559–1632), the stage was set for the Thirty Years' War, the worst European catastrophe since the Black Death of the 14th century.

The Treaty of Westphalia   In 1648, all hostilities within the Holy Roman Empire were ended by the Treaty of Westphalia. The treaty reasserted the major feature of the religious settlement of the Peace of Augsburg (1555). Rulers were again permitted to determine the religion of their lands. Calvinists were given the legal recognition they had long-sought, but they were denied such status to various sectarians. The independence of the Swiss Confederacy and of the United Provinces of Holland was officially recognized.

By confirming the territorial sovereignty of Germany's many political entities, the Treaty of Westphalia prolonged Germany's division and political weakness into the modern era. However, two German states attained international significance during the 17th century: Austria and Brandenburg-Prussia. The petty regionalism within the empire reflected on a small scale the drift of larger European politics. During the 17th century Europe's distinctive nation-states, each with its own political, cultural, and religious identity, reached maturity and firmly established the competitive nationalism of the modern world.

SUPERSTITION AND ENLIGHTENMENT: THE BATTLE WITHIN

WHY DID witch hunts and panics erupt across Western Europe between 1400 and 1700?

Religious reform and warfare permanently changed religious institutions in major European countries. They also motivated rethinking traditional assumptions about human nature and society. On the one hand, this had dark consequence, for the peak years of religious warfare were also those of the great European witch hunts. On the other hand, however, the era spawned a constructive skepticism that inaugurated a period of significant scientific progress.

WITCH HUNTS AND PANIC

Nowhere is the dark side of the period better seen than in the witch hunts and panics that erupted in almost every western land. Between 1400 and 1700, courts sentenced an estimated 70,000 to 100,000 people to death for harmful magic (*maleficium*) and diabolical witchcraft. In addition to threatening their neighbors, witches were said to attend mass meetings known as *sabbats,* to which they were believed to fly. They were accused of indulging in sexual orgies with the devil, who appeared in animal form, most often as a he-goat. They were said to practice cannibalism (having a taste for Christian children) and a variety of ritual acts and practices that denied or perverted Christian beliefs.

Many factors may have contributed to the great witch panics of the second half of the 16th and the early 17th centuries. Religious division and warfare were major influences. The Reformation's rejection of the defenses against the devil and demons that the chuch had traditionally provided forced people to find alternative ways to handle their anxieties. The growing strength of governments intent on weeding out nonconformists also played a part.

Village Origins In village societies, "cunning folk," those who were both revered and feared by their neighbors, played a positive role in helping people cope with calamity. Neighbors turned to them for help in the face of natural disasters or physical disabilities, for they provided consolation and hope that, through magic, something might be done to avert or overcome difficulties.

Possession of magical powers, for good or ill, gave one status in village society. Not surprisingly, therefore, claims to such powers most often were made by the people most in need of security and influence—the old and the impoverished, especially single or widowed women. For villagers, witch beliefs may also have been a way of resisting pressure from urban Christian societies that wanted to impose their laws and institutions on the rural populace. From the perspective of church authorities, entrenched local fertility cults (semipagan practices intended to ensure good harvests) may have looked like diabolical witchcraft.

Influence of the Clergy Had ordinary people not believed that "gifted persons" could help or harm them by magical means and had they not been willing to make accusations against them, witch hunts would not have occurred. But the highly educated also contributed to the witch craze. The Christian clergy believed in and practiced magic—the holy sacraments and exorcism of demons. In the late 13th century the church declared its magic to be the only legitimate magic. Given that magical powers were not human, theologians reasoned that they had to come either from God or the devil. Anyone who practiced magic outside the church obviously derived their power from the devil. From such reasoning grew accusations of "pacts" between non-Christian magicians and Satan.

Attacking witches was one way in which the church brought regions into conformity with its doctrines and established its spiritual hegemony. The clergy viewed the cunning folk as competitors and obstacles. A campaign to root them out was a way to establish moral and policial authority over a village or territory.

Why Women? Roughly 80 percent of the victims of witch hunts were women, most of whom were single and between 45 and 60 years of age, suggesting to some that misogyny fueled the witch hunts. At a time when women threatened to break out from under male control, witch hunts, it has been argued, were simply a conspiracy of males against females.

Combating Witchcraft. Three women are burned to death as witches in Baden, Germany. Their alleged crimes are depicted on the right, where they are seen feasting with demons.

"Three witches burned alive from a German Broadside," circa 1555. Courtesy of Stock Montage, Inc.

Older single women may, however, have been vulnerable for more basic social reasons. They were a largely dependent social group in need of public assistance and natural targets for the "social engineering" of the witch hunts. For economic reasons, such women sometimes sought to protect and empower themselves by claiming supernatural powers. They thus found themselves on the front lines in disproportionate numbers when the church declared war against all who practiced magic without its blessing. Also, the practice by many of these women of midwifery associated them with the deaths of beloved wives and infants and made them targets of local resentment and accusations. Both the church and their neighbors were prepared to think and say the worst about these women. It was a deadly combination.

End of the Witch Hunts   Many factors helped end the witch hunts. The emergence of a new, more scientific worldview made it difficult to believe in the powers of witches. When, in the 17th century, mind and matter came to be viewed as independent realities, the belief faded that a witch's curse, mere words, could affect things. Advances in medicine and the beginning of insurance companies improved people's ability to cope with calamities and physical affliction and dissuaded them from thoughts of the supernatural. Witch hunts also tended to get out of hand. Accused witches sometimes alleged that important townspeople had attended their sabbats, sometimes even their judges. At this point the trials ceased to serve the purposes of those who were conducting them. They not only became dysfunctional but threatened anarchy as well.

WRITERS AND PHILOSOPHERS

By the end of the 16th century, many could no longer accept either old Catholic or new Protestant absolutes. Intellectually as well as politically, the 17th century was a period of transition for which the humanists and scientists of the Renaissance and post-Renaissance (see Chapter 22) had prepared the way. Writers and philosophers of the era were aware that they lived in a time of change. Some embraced emerging science attitudes wholeheartedly (Hobbes and Locke), some tried to straddle the two ages (Cervantes and Shakespeare), and still others ignored or opposed developments that seemed to threaten traditional values (Pascal).

Miguel de Cervantes Saavedra   Spanish literature of the 16th and 17th centuries was influenced by Spain's peculiar religious and political situation. Spain was dominated by a Catholic Church that enjoyed vigorous state support. The intertwining of Catholic piety and Spanish political power created a preoccupation with medieval chivalric virtues—in particular, honor and loyalty.

Generally acknowledged to be the greatest Spanish writer of all time, Cervantes (1547–1616) explored the strengths and weaknesses of religious idealism. The son of a nomadic physician, he received only a smattering of formal education. Cervantes educated himself by insatiable reading in vernacular literature and immersion in the school of life. As a young man, he worked in Rome for a Spanish cardinal. In 1570, he became a soldier and was decorated for gallantry at Lepanto (1571). He began to write his most famous work, *Don Quixote*, in 1603, while languishing in prison after conviction for theft.

The first part of *Don Quixote* appeared in 1605, and a second part in 1615. If, as many argue, the intent of this work was to satirize the chivalric romances so popular in Spain, Cervantes failed to conceal his deep affection for the character he created as an object of ridicule, Don Quixote. Don Quixote, a none-too-stable middle-aged man, is driven mad by reading too many romances. He comes to believe that he is an aspirant to knighthood and must prove his worthiness. To this end, he acquires a rusty suit of armor, mounts an aged horse, and chooses for his inspiration a quite unworthy peasant girl whom he imagines to be a noble lady to whom he can, with honor, dedicate his life.

Don Quixote's foil in the story—his squire, Sancho Panza, a clever, worldly wise peasant—watches with bemused skepticism and genuine sympathy, as his lord does battle with a windmill (which he mistakes for a dragon) and repeatedly makes a fool of himself. The story ends tragically with Don Quixote's humiliating defeat by a well-meaning friend, who, disguised as a knight, bests Don Quixote in combat and forces him to renounce his quest for knighthood. The humiliated Don Quixote does not, however, come to his senses as a result. He returns sadly to his village to die a shamed and broken-hearted old man.

Throughout *Don Quixote*, Cervantes juxtaposed the down-to-earth realism of Sancho Panza with the old-fashioned religious idealism of Don Quixote. Cervantes admired the one as much as the other. He wanted his readers to realize that to be truly happy, men and women need dreams just as much as a sense of reality.

William Shakespeare   There is much less factual knowledge about William Shakespeare (1564–1616), the greatest playwright in the English language, than one would expect of such an important figure. Shakespeare may have worked as a schoolteacher for a time and in this capacity acquired his broad knowledge of Renaissance learning and literature. His work shows none of the Puritan distress over worldliness. He took the new commercialism and the bawdy pleasures of the Elizabethan Age in stride and with amusement. In politics and religion, he was a man of his time and not inclined to offend his queen.

That Shakespeare was interested in politics is apparent from his historical plays and the references to contemporary political events that fill all his works. He seems to have viewed government simply as a function of the character of a ruler, whether a Richard III or an Elizabeth Tudor, not as the realization of a social ideal. By modern standards he was a political conservative, accepting the social rankings and the power structure of his day and demonstrating unquestioned patriotism.

Shakespeare knew the theater as an insider. A member and principal dramatist of a famous company of actors, the King's Men, he was a playwright, actor, and part owner of a theater. He synthesized the best of the past and current achievements in the dramatic arts. He was particularly skilled at exploring human motivation and passion and had a unique talent for psychological penetration.

Shakespeare wrote histories, comedies, and tragedies. The tragedies are his greatest achievements. Four were written within a three-year period: *Hamlet* (1603), *Othello* (1604), *King Lear* (1605), and *Macbeth* (1606). The most original of the tragedies, *Romeo and Juliet* (1597), transformed an old popular story into a moving drama of "star-cross'd lovers."

In his lifetime and ever since, Shakespeare has been immensely popular with both audiences and readers. As Ben Jonson (1572–1637), a contemporary classical dramatist who created his own school of poets, put it in a tribute affixed to the *First Folio* edition of Shakespeare's plays (1623): "He was not of an age, but for all time."

Blaise Pascal   Blaise Pascal (1623–1662) was a French mathematician and a physical scientist widely acclaimed by his contemporaries. Torn between the continuing dogmatism and the new skepticism of the 17th century, Pascal aspired to write a work that would refute both the Jesuits, whose *casuistry* (confessional

Pascal's calculator. Pascal invented this adding machine, the ancestor of mechanical calculators, around 1644. It has eight wheels with ten cogs each, corresponding to the numbers 0 through 9. The wheels move forward for addition, backward for subtraction.

Bildarchiv Preussischer Kulturbesitz

tactics designed to minimize or excuse sinful acts) he considered a distortion of Christian teaching, and the skeptics, who either denied religion altogether (atheists) or accepted it only as it conformed to reason (deists). Pascal failed to complete such a definitive work, and his views on these matters exist only in piecemeal form. He opposed the Jesuits in his *Provincial Letters* (1656–1657), and he left behind a provocative collection of reflections on humankind and religion that was published posthumously under the title *Pensées*.

Pascal was early influenced by the Jansenists, 17th-century Catholic opponents of the Jesuits. Although good Catholics, the Jansenists shared with the Calvinists St. Augustine's belief in the total sinfulness of human beings, their eternal predestination by God, and their complete dependence on faith and grace for knowledge of God and salvation.

Pascal believed that reason and science, although attesting to human dignity, remained of no avail in religion. Only the reasons of the heart and a "leap of faith" could found belief. Pascal saw two essential truths in the Christian religion: that a loving God, worthy of human devotion, exists; and that human beings, because they are corrupted in nature, are utterly unworthy of God. Pascal believed that the atheists and deists of the age had spurned the lesson of reason. For him, rational analysis of the human condition attested to humankind's utter mortality and corruption and exposed the inability of reason to resolve the problems of human nature and destiny. Those who truly heed reason should be driven by it to faith and dependence on divine grace.

Pascal made a famous wager with skeptics. It is a better bet, he argued, to believe that God exists and to stake everything on His promised mercy than not to do so; if God does exist, everything will be gained by the believer, whereas the loss incurred by having believed in God should He prove not to exist is, by comparison, slight.

Pascal was convinced that belief in God measurably improved earthly life psychologically and disciplined it morally, regardless of whether God proved in the end to exist. He thought that great danger lay in the surrender of traditional religious values. He urged his contemporaries to seek self-understanding through "learned ignorance" and to discover humankind's greatness by recognizing its misery. This, he hoped, would counter what he believed to be the false optimism of the new rationalism and science.

Baruch Spinoza   The most controversial thinker of the 17th century was Baruch Spinoza (1632–1677), the son of a Jewish merchant of Amsterdam. Spinoza's philosophy caused his excommunication by his own synagogue in 1656. In 1670, he published his *Treatise on Religious and Political Philosophy*, a work that criticized the dogmatism of Dutch Calvinists and championed freedom of thought. During his lifetime, both Jews and Protestants attacked him as an atheist.

Spinoza's most influential writing, *Ethics*, appeared after his death in 1677. Religious leaders universally condemned it for its apparent espousal of pantheism. God and nature were so closely identified by Spinoza that little room seemed left either for divine revelation in Scripture or for the personal immortality of the soul, denials equally repugnant to Jews and to Christians.

The most controversial part of *Ethics* deals with the nature of substance and of God. According to Spinoza there is only one substance, which is self-caused, free, and infinite, and God is that substance. From this definition, it follows that everything that exists is in God and cannot even be conceived of apart from him.

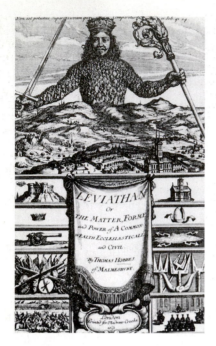

Leviathan. The famous title page from Hobbes's book depicts the ruler as absolute lord of his lands, but note that he incorporates the mass of individuals whose self interests are best served by their willing consent to accept him and cooperate with his rule.

Such a doctrine is not precisely pantheistic, because God is still seen to be more than the created world that he, as primal substance, embraces. Nonetheless, in Spinoza's view, statements about the natural world are also statements about divine nature. Mind and matter are seen to be extensions of the infinite substance of God; what transpires in the world of humankind and nature is a necessary outpouring of the Divine.

Such teaching clearly ran the danger of portraying the world as eternal and human actions as unfree and inevitable, the expression of a divine fatalism. Such points of view had been considered heresies by Jews and Christians because these views deny the creation of the world by God and destroy any voluntary basis for personal reward and punishment.

Thomas Hobbes Thomas Hobbes (1588–1679) was the most original political philosopher of the 17th century. Although he never broke with the Church of England, he came to share basic Calvinist beliefs, especially the low view of human nature and the ideal of a commonwealth based on a covenant, both of which find eloquent expression in his political philosophy.

Hobbes, an urbane and much-traveled man, was one of the most enthusiastic supporters of the new scientific movement. During the 1630s he visited Paris, where he came to know Descartes. After the outbreak of the Puritan Revolution (see Chapter 20) in 1640, he lived as an exile in Paris until 1651. Hobbes also spent time with Galileo (see Chapter 22) in Italy. He took a special interest in the works of William Harvey, a physiologist famed for the discovery of how blood circulated through the body; Harvey's scientific writings influenced Hobbes's own tracts on bodily motions.

Hobbes was driven to the vocation of political philosophy by the English Civil War (see Chapter 20). In 1651, his *Leviathan* appeared in which he examined the political consequences of human passions. This work's originality lay in (1) its making natural law, rather than common law (i.e., custom or precedent), the basis of all positive law; and (2) its defense of a representative theory of absolute authority against the theory of the divine right of kings. Hobbes maintained that statute law found its justification only as an expression of the law of nature and that rulers derived their authority from the consent of the people.

Hobbes viewed humankind and society in a thoroughly materialistic and mechanical way. Human beings are defined as a collection of material particles in motion. All their psychological processes begin with and are derived from bare sensation, and all their motivations are egotistical, intended to increase pleasure and minimize pain. Despite this seemingly low estimate of human beings, Hobbes believed much could be accomplished by the reasoned use of science. All was contingent, however, on the correct use of that greatest of all human powers, a commonwealth that unites people by their consent as one all-powerful person.

The key to Hobbes's political philosophy is a brilliant myth of the original state of humankind. According to this myth, human beings in the natural state are generally inclined to a "perpetual and restless desire of power after power that ceases only in death."[4] As all people desire—and in the state of nature have a natural right to—everything, their equality breeds enmity, competition, and

---

[4] *Leviathan*, Parts I and II, ed. By H. W. Schneider (Indianapolis, IN: Bobbs-Merrill, 1958), p. 86.

diffidence, and the desire for glory begets perpetual quarreling—"a war of every man against every man."[5]

Whereas earlier and later philosophers saw the original human state as a paradise from which humankind had fallen, Hobbes saw it as a corruption from which social life had delivered people. Contrary to the views of Aristotle and of Christian thinkers like St. Thomas Aquinas, Hobbes saw human beings not as sociable, political animals, but as self-centered beasts, laws unto themselves, utterly without a master unless one is imposed by force.

According to Hobbes, people escape the impossible state of nature only by entering a social contract that creates a commonwealth tightly ruled by law and order. The social contract obliges every person, for the sake of peace and self-defense, to agree to set aside personal rights to all things. We should impose restrictions on the liberty of others only to the degree that we would allow others to restrict our own.

Because words and promises are insufficient to guarantee this state, the social contract also establishes the coercive force necessary to compel compliance with the covenant. Hobbes believed that the dangers of anarchy were far greater than those of tyranny, and he conceived of the ruler's power as absolute and unlimited. There is no room in Hobbes's political philosophy for political protest in the name of individual conscience, nor for resistance to legitimate authority by private individuals—features of *Leviathan* criticized by his contemporaries, Catholics and Puritans alike.

John Locke   John Locke (1632–1704) has proved to be the most influential political thinker of the 17th century.[6] His political philosophy came to be embodied in the so-called Glorious Revolution of 1688–1689 (Chapter 20). Although he was not as original as Hobbes, his political writings were a major source of the later Enlightenment Era's criticism of absolutism, and they inspired both the American and French Revolutions.

Locke's two most famous works are the *Essay Concerning Human Understanding* (1690) (discussed in Chapter 22) and *Two Treatises of Government* (1690). He wrote the latter to refute the argument that rulers had absolute power. Rulers, Locke argued, are bound to the law of nature, which is the voice of reason that teaches that "all mankind [are] equal and independent, [and] no one ought to harm another in his life, health, liberty, or possessions,"[7] inasmuch as all human beings are the images and property of God. According to Locke, people enter social contracts, empowering legislatures and monarchs to "umpire" their disputes, precisely to preserve their natural rights and not to surrender them to an absolute authority.

"Whenever that end [namely, the preservation of life, liberty, and property for which power is given to rulers by a commonwealth] is manifestly neglected or opposed, the trust must necessarily be forfeited and the power devolved into the hands of those that gave it, who may place it anew where they think best for their safety and security."[8] From Locke's point of view, absolute monarchy was "inconsistent" with civil society and could be "no form of civil government at all."[9]

18.1
The Mortal God:
Leviathan (1651)

QUICK REVIEW

Important European writers and philosophers, 1600–1700
- Cervantes (1547–1616), Spain
- Shakespeare (1564–1616), England
- Pascal (1623–1662), France
- Spinoza (1632–1677), Netherlands
- Hobbes (1588–1679), England
- Locke (1632–1704), England

[5]Ibid., p. 106.
[6]Locke's scientific writings are discussed in Chapter 24.
[7]*The Second Treatise of Government*, ed. By P. T. Peardon (Indianapolis, IN: Bobbs-Merrill, 1952), chap. 2, sects. 4–6, pp. 4–6.
[8]Ibid., chap. 13, sect. 149, p. 84.
[9]Ibid.

IMAGE KEY
for pages 370–371

a. Fifteenth century Italian silver cross
b. Martin Luther tempting Jesus
c. *The Milch Cow* a sixteenth-century satirical painting
d. Gutenberg's Bible
e. Miguel de Cervantes Saavedra (1547–1616)
f. *The Ecstacy of Saint Teresa of Avila*, by Bernini
g. *Le Massacre de la St-Barthelemy, entre 1572 et 1584*
h. John Calvin
i. Elizabeth I

SUMMARY

Voyages of Discovery In the late 15th century, Europe began to expand around the globe. Driven by both mercenary and religious motives, the Portuguese pioneered a sea route around Africa to India and the Far East, and the Spanish discovered the Americas. The consequences were immense for Europeans, Native Americans, Africans, and Asians. In time, a truly global society would emerge.

The Reformation The Reformation began in Germany with Martin Luther's attack on indulgences in 1517. Despite the opposition to the Reformation of Emperor Charles V, Luther had the support of many German princes. The Reformation shattered the religious unity of Europe. In Switzerland, Zwingli and Calvin launched their own versions of Protestantism. In England, Henry VIII repudiated papal authority when the pope refused to grant him a divorce. The different Protestant sects were often as hostile to each other as they were to Catholicism. The Reformation also led to far-reaching changes in religious practices and social attitudes, including steps toward the advancement of women.

The Roman Catholic Church also acted to reform itself. The Council of Trent tightened church discipline and reaffirmed traditional doctrine. The Jesuits converted many Protestants back to Catholicism.

The Wars of Religion The religious divisions of Europe led to more than a century of warfare from the 1520s to 1648. The chief battlegrounds were in France, the Netherlands, and Germany. When the Thirty Years' War ended in 1648, Europe was permanently divided into Catholic and Protestant areas.

Superstition and Enlightenment The Reformation led to both dark and constructive views of human nature. Perhaps the darkest view was the witch crazes that erupted across Europe. Thousands of innocent people, mostly women, were persecuted and executed as witches between 1400 and 1700 by both Catholic and Protestant authorities.

In literature and philosophy, however, these years witnessed an outpouring of creative thinking. Among the greatest writers of the age were Cervantes, Shakespeare, Pascal, Spinoza, Hobbes, and Locke.

REVIEW QUESTIONS

1. What were the main problems of the church that contributed to the Protestant Reformation? Why was the church unable to suppress dissent as it had earlier?

2. Why did the Reformation begin in Germany?

3. What was the Catholic Reformation?

4. Why did Henry VIII break with the Catholic Church? Was the "new" religion he established really Protestant?

5. Were the Wars of Religion really over religion?

KEY TERMS

Counter-Reformation (p. 389)   **indulgences** (p. 380)   **Reformation** (p. 376)
Diet of Worms (p. 382)   **ninety-five theses** (p. 380) **transubstantiation** (p. 384)
Huguenot (p. 394)

 For additional study resources for this chapter, go to:
www.prenhall.com/craig/chapter16

CHRISTIANITY

Christianity is based on the teaching of Jesus of Nazareth, a Jew who lived in Palestine during the Roman occupation. His simple message of faith in God and self-sacrificial love of one's neighbor attracted many people. Roman authorities, perceiving his large following as a threat, crucifed him. After Jesus' crucifixion, his followers proclaimed that he had been resurrected from the dead and that he would return in glory, to defeat sin, death, and the devil, and take all true believers with him to heaven—a radical vision of judgment and immortality that has driven Christianity's appeal since its inception. In the teachings of the early church, Jesus became the Christ, the son of God, the long-awaited Messiah of Jewish prophecy. His followers called themselves Christians.

Christianity proclaimed the very incarnation of God in a man, the visible presence of eternity in time. According to early Christian teaching, the power of God's incarnation in Jesus lived on in the preaching and sacraments of the church under the guidance of the Holy Spirit. According to the Christian message, in Jesus, eternity has made itself accessible to every person here and now and forevermore.

The new religion attracted both the poor and powerless and the socially rising and well-to-do. For some, the gospel of Jesus promised a better material life. For others, it imparted a sense of spiritual self-worth regardless of one's place or prospects in society.

In the late second century, the Romans began persecuting Christians as "heretics" (because of their rejection of the traditional Roman gods) and as social revolutionaries (for their loyalty to a lord higher than the emperor of Rome). At the same time, dissenting Christians, particularly sects claiming direct spiritual knowledge of God apart from Scripture, internally divided the young church. To meet these challenges the church established effective weapons against state terrorism and Christian heresy: an ordained clergy, a hierarchical church organization, orthodox creeds, and a biblical canon (the New Testament). Christianity not only gained legal status within the Roman Empire, but also, by the fourth century, most favored religious status thanks to Emperor Constantine's embrace of it.

After the fall of the Western Roman Empire in the fifth century C.E., Christianity became one of history's great success stories. Aided by the enterprise of its popes and the example of its monks, the church cultivated an appealing lay piety centered around the Lord's Prayer, the Apostles' Creed, veneration of the Virgin, and the sacrament of the Eucharist. Clergy became both royal teachers and bureaucrats within the kingdom of the Franks. Despite a growing schism between the Eastern (Byzantine) and Western churches, and a final split in 1054, by 1000 the church held real economic and political power. In the 11th century reform-minded prelates put an end to presumptuous secular interference in its most intimate spiritual affairs by ending the lay investiture of clergy in their spiritual offices. For several centuries thereafter the church remained a formidable international force, able to challenge kings and emperors and inspire crusades to the Holy Land.

Pentecost. This exquisite enamel plaque, from the Mosan school that flourished in France in the 11th and 12th centuries, shows the descent of the Holy Spirit upon the apostles, 50 days after the resurrection of Jesus on the ancient Jewish festival called the "feast of weeks," or Pentecost.
Courtesy Metropolitan Museum of Art.

Female Bishop. Women are entering the ministry and priesthood of many Christian denominations. The first woman bishop of the Episcopal Church of North America is here shown consecrating the Eucharist. The Church of England has also voted to admit women to the priesthood.
Ira Wyman/Corbis/Sygma.

By the 15th century the new states of Europe had stripped the church of much of its political power. It was thereafter progressively confined to spiritual and moral authority. Christianity's greatest struggles ever since have been not with kings and emperors over political power, but with materialistic philosophies and worldly ideologies, matters of spiritual and moral hegemony within an increasingly pluralistic and secular world. Since the 16th century a succession of humanists, skeptics, Deists, Rationalists, Marxists, Freudians, Darwinians, and atheists have attempted to explain away some of traditional Christianity's most basic teachings. In addition, the church has endured major internal upheavals. After the Protestant Reformation (1517–1555) made the Bible widely available to the laity, the possibilities for internal criticism of Christianity multiplied exponentially. Beginning with the split between Lutherans and Zwinglians in the 1520s, Protestant Christianity has fragmented into hundreds of sects each claiming to have the true interpretation of Scripture. The Roman Catholic Church, by contrast, has maintained its unity and ministry throughout perilous times, although present-day discontent with papal authority threatens the modern Catholic Church almost as seriously as the Protestant Reformation once did.

Christianity has remained remarkably resilient. It possesses a simple, almost magically appealing gospel of faith and love in and through Jesus. In the present-day world where religious needs and passions still run deep, evangelical Christianity has experienced a remarkable revival. The Roman Catholic Church, still troubled by challenges to papal authority, has become more pluralistic than in earlier periods. The pope has become a world figure, traveling to all continents to represent the church and advance its position on issues of public and private morality. A major ecumenical movement emerging in the 1960s has promoted unprecedented cooperation among evangelical Christian denominations. Everywhere Christians of all sects are politically active, spreading their divine, moral, and social messages. Meanwhile, old hot-button issues, such as the ordination of women, are being overtaken by new ones, particularly the marriage of gay men and women and the removal of clergy who do not maintain the moral discipline of their holy orders.

- Over the century what have been some of the chief factors attracting people to Christianity?

- What forces have led to disunity among Christians in the past? What factors cause tensions among modern Christians?

413

17 Africa
ca. 1000–1800

CHAPTER HIGHLIGHTS

North Africa Developments in African history from 1000 to 1800 varied from region to region. In North Africa, the key new factor was the imperial expansion of the Ottoman Empire as far west as Morocco. But regionalism soon rendered Ottoman authority in North Africa purely nominal.

Empires of the Sudan Several substantial states arose south of the Sahara: Ghana, Mali, Songhai, and Kanem. The ruling elites of these states converted to or were heavily influenced by Islam, although most of their populations clung to their older traditions. Much of the wealth of these states was tied to their control of the trans-Saharan trade routes. Farther south, in Central Africa, another substantial kingdom arose in Benin, famous for its brass sculptures.

East Africa On the east coast, Islam influenced the development of the distinctive Swahili culture and language, and Islamic traders linked the region to India and East Asia.

The Coming of the Europeans The key development of the fifteenth century was the arrival of European traders, missionaries, and warships. The Portuguese and later Europeans came in search of commerce, converts to Christianity, and spheres of influence. Their arrival disrupted indigenous African culture and political relations and presaged Africa's involvement in a new, expanding global trading system dominated by Europeans.

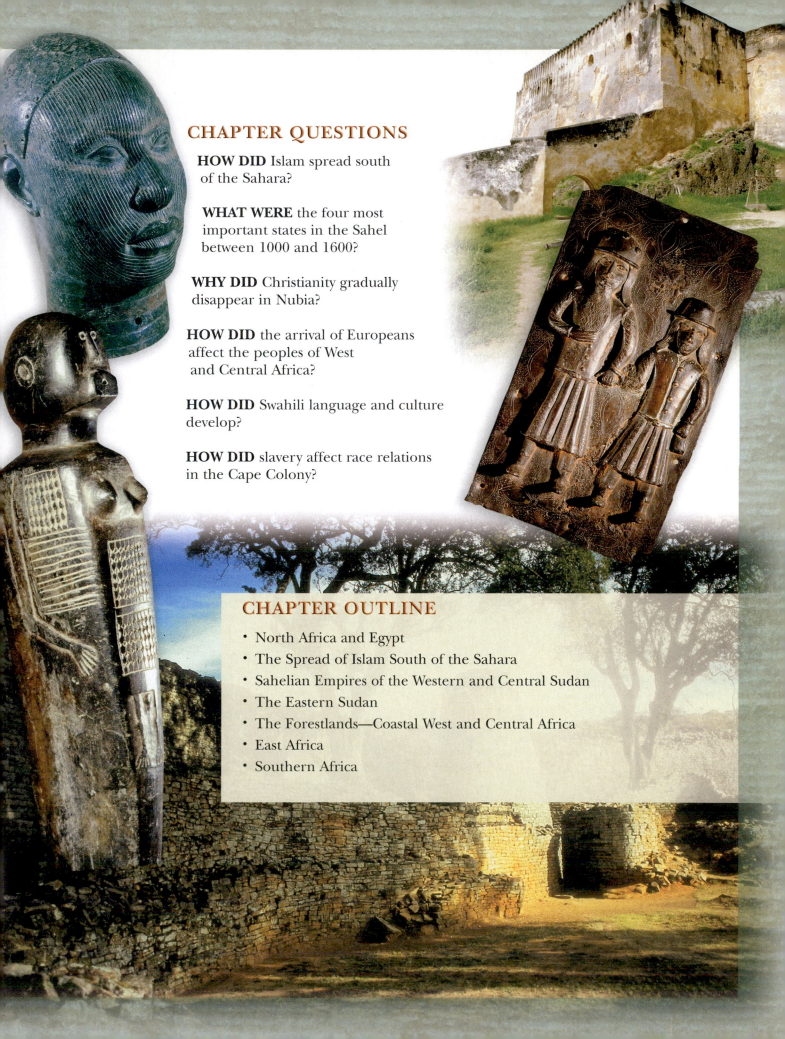

CHAPTER QUESTIONS

HOW DID Islam spread south of the Sahara?

WHAT WERE the four most important states in the Sahel between 1000 and 1600?

WHY DID Christianity gradually disappear in Nubia?

HOW DID the arrival of Europeans affect the peoples of West and Central Africa?

HOW DID Swahili language and culture develop?

HOW DID slavery affect race relations in the Cape Colony?

CHAPTER OUTLINE

- North Africa and Egypt
- The Spread of Islam South of the Sahara
- Sahelian Empires of the Western and Central Sudan
- The Eastern Sudan
- The Forestlands—Coastal West and Central Africa
- East Africa
- Southern Africa

In this chapter we explore, region by region, some salient developments in Africa from 1000 to 1800. While the Atlantic slave trade is treated in Chapter 18, its importance must be kept in mind as we review the period's other developments. We begin with Africa above the equator, where the influence of Islam increased and where substantial empires and kingdoms developed and flourished. Then we discuss west, east, central, and southern Africa and the effects of first Arab-Islamic and then European influence in both regions.

North Africa and Egypt

WHY WAS no single power able to control North Africa for long?

In politics, this period witnessed the influential dynasties of the Fatimids (909–969 in Tunisia; 969–1171 in Egypt), the Almoravids (1056–1147 in Senegal and the western Sudan; 1062–1118 in Marrakesh and western North Africa; 1086–1147 in Spain), the Almohads (1130–1269 in western North Africa; 1145–1212 in Spain), the Ayyubids (1169–1250 in Egypt), the Mamluks (1250–1517 in Egypt and the eastern Mediterranean); and the Ottomans (from the 14th century) across most of Mediterranean Africa. In general, a feisty regionalism characterized states, city-states, and tribal groups north of the Sahara and along the lower Nile, especially vis-à-vis external power centers, such as Baghdad and Spain. No single power controlled them for long. Regionalism persisted even after 1500, when most of North Africa came under the influence—and often direct control—of the Ottoman Empire.

By 1800, the nominally Ottoman domains from Egypt to Algeria were effectively independent principalities. In Egypt, the Ottomans had established direct rule after their defeat of the Mamluks in 1517, but by the 17th and 18th centuries, power had already passed to Egyptian governors descended from the former ruling Mamluks. The Mediterranean coastlands between Egypt and Morocco were officially Ottoman provinces, or regencies, whether under local governors or Ottoman deputies. By the 18th century, however, Algiers, Tripoli (in modern Libya), and Tunisia were virtually independent of the Ottomans. Morocco was the only North African sultanate to remain fully independent after 1700. Its most important dynasty was that of the Sa'dis (1554–1659).

The Spread of Islam South of the Sahara

HOW DID Islam spread south of the Sahara?

By 1800, Islamic influence in sub-Saharan Africa affected most of the Sudanic belt and the coast of East Africa as far south as modern Zimbabwe. Typically, Islam did not penetrate beyond the ruling or commercial classes of a region and tended to coexist or blend with indigenous ideas. Nevertheless, Islam and its carriers brought commercial and political changes as well as the Qur'an, new religious practices, and literate culture.

In East Africa, Islamic city-states along the coast from Mogadishu to Kilwa became a major factor. By contrast, in the western and central parts of the continent, Islam penetrated south of the Sahara into the Sudan by overland routes, primarily from North Africa and the Nile valley. Its agents were sometimes traders, but primarily emigrants from the east seeking new land.

From the 1030s, zealous militants known as Almoravids began an overt conversion campaign that extended to the western Sahel and Sahara. This movement eventually swept into Ghana, and finally Kumbi in 1076. Farther west, the Fulbe rulers of Takrur along the Senegal became Muslim in the 1030s and propagated their new faith among their subjects.

SAHELIAN EMPIRES OF THE WESTERN AND CENTRAL SUDAN

*U*rbanization and state formation in sub-Saharan Africa did not occur only in response to trans-Saharan trade with the Islamic world, which dates largely from the end of the first millennium. Substantial states had risen in the first millennium C.E. in the Sahel regions just south of the Sahara proper (see Chapter 5). From about 1000 to 1600, four of these developed into notable and relatively long-lived empires: Ghana, Mali, and Songhai in the western Sudan, and Kanem-Bornu in the central Sudan.

GHANA

Ghana was located north of modern Ghana between and north of the inland Niger delta and the upper Senegal. It emerged as a regional power near the end of the first millennium and flourished for about two centuries. Its capital, Kumbi (or Kumbi Saleh), on the desert's edge, was well sited for the Saharan and Sahelian trade networks. Ghana's major population group were the Soninke. (*Ghana* is the Soninke term for "ruler.")

Ghanaian rulers were matrilineally descended. The king was supreme judge and held court regularly to hear grievances. Royal ceremonies were embellished with the full trappings of regal wealth and power appropriate to a king held to be divinely blessed if not semi-divine himself.

Tribute from the empire's many chieftaincies and taxes on royal lands and crops supplemented the duties levied on all incoming and outgoing trade. This trade involved a variety of goods—notably imported salt, cloth, and metal goods such as copper—probably in exchange for gold and perhaps kola nuts from the south. The regime apparently also controlled the gold (and, presumably, the slave) trade that originated in the savannah to the south and west.

Although the king and court of Ghana did not convert to Islam, they made elaborate arrangements to accommodate Muslim traders and government servants in their own settlement a few miles from the royal preserve in Kumbi Saleh. Muslim traders were prominent in the court, literate Muslims administered the government, and Muslim legists advised the ruler. In Ghana's hierarchical society, slaves were at the bottom; farmers and draftsmen above them; merchants above them; and the king, his court, and the nobility on top.

A huge, well-trained army secured royal control and enabled the kings to extend their sway in the late 10th century to the Atlantic shore and to the south as well (see Map 17–1). Ghanaian troops captured Awdaghast, the important southern terminus of the trans-Saharan trade route to Morocco, from the Berbers in 992. The empire was, however, vulnerable to attack from the desert fringe, as Almoravid Berber forces proved in 1054 when they took Awdaghast in a single raid.

Ghana's rulers may have converted to Islam soon after 1100. Ghana's empire was probably

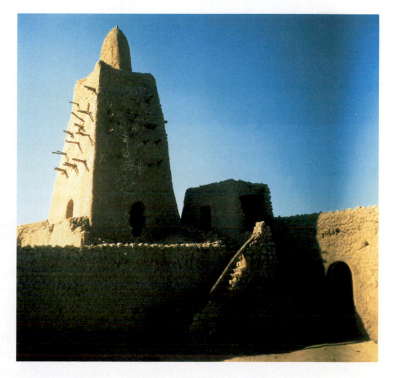

The Great Mosque in Timbuktu. This mud and wood building is typical of western Sudanese mosques. The distinctive tower of the mosque was a symbol of the presence of Islam, which came to places like Timbuktu in central and West Africa by way of overland trade routes.
Werner Forman/Art Resource, N.Y.

MAP EXPLORATION

Interactive map: To explore this map further, go to **http://www.prenhall.com/craig/map17.1**

MAP 17–1

Africa ca. 900–1500.   Shown are major cities and states referred to in the text. The main map shows the region of West Africa occupied by the empire of Ghana from ca. 990 to ca. 1180. The inset shows the region occupied by Mali between 1230 and 1450.

WHY WAS Ghana's location important for its prosperity?

destroyed in the late 12th century by the militantly anti-Muslim Soso people from the mountains southeast of Kumbi Saleh.

MALI

After the Almoravids brought their reform movement to the western Sahel at the end of the 11th century, their proselytizing zeal led to conversion of many of the region's ruling classes. It was, however, over a half-century after the breakup of

Ghana's empire before anyone in the western Sahel, Muslim or non-Muslim, could reestablish an empire of comparable extent. With Ghana's collapse and the Almoravids' failure to build a new empire below the Sahara (largely because of their focus on North Africa), the western Sudan broke up into smaller kingdoms. The former Ghanaian provinces of Mande and Takrur were already independent before 1076, and in the early 12th century Takrur's control of the Senegal valley and the gold-producing region of Galam made it briefly the strongest state in the western Sudan. Like Ghana, however, it was soon eclipsed by developments to the east, along the upper Niger—first the brief Soso ascendancy and then the rise of Mali.

In the mid-13th century, the Keita ruling clan of a Ghanaian successor kingdom, Mali, forged a new and lasting empire. The Keita kings dominated enough of the Sahel to control the flow of West African gold from the Senegal regions and the forestlands south of the Niger to the trans-Saharan trade routes, and the influx of copper and especially salt in exchange. Because they were farther south, in the fertile land along the Niger, than their Ghanaian predecessors had been, they were better placed to control all trade on the upper Niger and to add to it the Gambia and Senegal trade to the west. They were also able to use war captives for plantation labor in the Niger inland delta to produce surplus food for trade.

Agriculture and cattle farming were the primary occupations of Mali's population and, together with the gold trade, the mainstays of the economy. Rice was grown in the river valleys and millet in the drier parts of the Sahel. Together with beans, yams, and other agricultural products, this made for a plentiful food supply. Fishing flourished along the Niger and elsewhere. Animal husbandry was strongest among pastoralists of the Sahel, such as the Fulani (or Fulbe), but cattle, sheep, and goats were also plentiful in the Niger valley by the 14th century. Many of the Fulani seem to have been attracted by excellent pasturages to the riverine regions. The chief craft specialties were metalworking (iron and gold) and weaving of cotton grown within the empire.

The Malinke, a southern Mande-speaking people of the upper Niger region, formed the core population of the new state. They lived in walled urban settlements typical of the western savannah region. Each walled town was surrounded by its own agricultural land, and held perhaps 1,000 to 15,000 people.

The Keita dynasty had converted early to Islam (ca. 1100). During Mali's heyday in the 13th and 14th centuries, its kings often made the pilgrimage to Mecca. From their travels in the central Islamic lands, they brought back ideas about political and military organization. Through Muslim traders' networks, Islam also connected Mali to other areas of Africa.

Mali's imperial power was built largely by one leader, the Keita King Sundiata (or Sunjaata; r. 1230–1255). Sundiata and his successors, aided by significant population growth in the western savannah, exploited their agricultural resources and Malinke commercial skills to build an empire even more powerful than its Ghanaian predecessor. Sundiata extended his control well beyond the former domains of Ghana, west to the Atlantic coast and east beyond Timbuktu. By controlling the commercial entrepôts of Gao, Walata, and Jenne, he was able to dominate the Saharan as well as the Niger trade. He built his capital, Niani, into a major city. Niani was located on a tributary of the Niger in the savannah at the edge of the forest in a gold- and iron-rich region, well away from the lands of the Sahel nomads and well south of Ghana's capital, Kumbi. Niani had access to the forest trade products of gold, kola nuts, and palm oil; it was easily defended by virtue of its surrounding small hills; and it was easily reached by river.

QUICK REVIEW

Mali

- Keita clan forged Mali in mid-13th century
- Keita kings controlled the flow of West African gold
- Agriculture and cattle farming were primary occupations of Mali's people

11.3
Ibn Battuta in Mali

QUICK REVIEW

King Sundiata (r. 1230–1255)

- Built Mali's imperial power
- Mali's empire was more powerful than its Ghanaian predecessor
- Empire encompassed three major regions: Senegal, the central Mande states, and the peoples of the Niger in the Gao region

The Great Mosque at Jenne. Jenne was one of the important commercial centers controlled by the empire of Mali in the 13th and 14th centuries.

Ann Stalcup.

DOCUMENT
CD-ROM

11.1
Mansa Musa: The "King Who Sits on a Mountain of Gold"

Mansa Musa, King of Mali. The 14th-century Catalan Atlas shows King Mansa Musa of Mali, seated on a throne. A rider on a camel approaches him.

The Granger Collection.

The empire that Sundiata and his successors built ultimately encompassed three major regions and language groups of Sudanic West Africa: (1) the Senegal region (including Takrur), occupied by speakers of the West Atlantic Niger-Kongo language group (including Fulbe, Tukulor, Wolof, Serer); (2) the central Mande states between Senegal and Niger, occupied by the Niger-Kongo-speaking Soninke and Mandinke peoples; and (3) the peoples of the Niger in the Gao region who spoke Songhai, the only Nilo-Saharan language west of the Lake Chad basin.

Mali was less a centralized bureaucratic state than the center of a vast sphere of influence that included provinces and tribute-paying kingdoms. Many chieftaincies retained much of their independence but recognized the sovereignty of the supreme, sacred *mansa*, or "emperor," of the Malian realms.

The greatest Keita king proved to be Mansa Musa (r. 1312–1337), whose pilgrimage through Mamluk Cairo to Mecca in 1324 became famous. At home, he consolidated Mali's power, securing peace for most of his reign throughout his vast dominions. Musa's devoutness as a Muslim fostered the further spread of Islam in the empire and beyond. Under his rule, Timbuktu became known far and wide for its *madrasas* (religious schools), libraries, poets, scientists, and architects—making the city the leading intellectual center of sub-Saharan Islam as well as a major trading city of the Sahel.

Mali's dominance waned in the 15th century as the result of competition for its throne. As time went on, subject dependencies became independent, and the empire withered. After 1450, a new Songhai power in Gao to the east ended Mali's imperial authority.

SONGHAI

Gao became an imperial power in the reign of Sonni Ali (1464–1492). Sonni Ali made the Songhai Empire so powerful that it dominated the political history of the western Sudan for more than a century and was arguably the most powerful state in Africa (see Map 17–2).

Askia Muhammad al-Turi (r. 1493–1528) continued Sonni Ali's expansionist policies. Between them, Sonni Ali and Askia Muhammad built an empire that stretched from near the Atlantic into the Sahara and the central Sudan. The ancient caravan trade across the Sahara to the North African coasts provided their major source of wealth. Muhammad al-Turi was an enthusiastic Muslim. He built up the Songhai state after the model of the Islamic empire of Mali. In his reign, Muslim scholars made Timbuktu a major intellectual and legal training center for the whole Sudan. Nevertheless, his reforms failed to Islamize the empire or to ensure a strong central state under his less able successors.

The last powerful Askia leader was Askia Dawud (r. 1549–1583), under whom Songhai economic prosperity and intellectual life peaked. Still, difficulties mounted. Civil war broke out over succession to the throne in 1586, and the empire was divided. The once-great state became only one among many regional competitors in the western Sudan.

KANEM AND KANEM-BORNU

A fourth sizable Sahelian empire, Kanem, in the central Sudan, arose after 1100. Roughly contemporaneous with the Malian Empire to the west, Kanem began as a southern Saharan confederation of the black nomadic tribes known as Zaghawah. Their key leader, Mai Dunama Dibbalemi (r. ca. 1221–1259), was probably the first Kanuri leader to embrace Islam, which appears to have entrenched itself among the Kanuri ruling class during his reign. Dibbalemi used Islam to sanction his rule and provide a rationale for expansion through *jihad*, or holy "struggle" against polytheists. Dibbalemi and his successors expanded Kanuri power to control important trade routes to Libya and Egypt.

Sahelian Empires of the Western Sudan

ca. 990–ca. 1180?	Empire of Ghana
1076	Ghana loses Awdaghast to Almoravids
1180–1230	Soso clan briefly controls the old Ghanaian territories
ca. 1230–1450	Empire of Mali, founded by Sundiata
1230–1255	Reign of Sundiata
1312–1337	Reign of Mansa Musa
1374	Independent Songhai state emerges in Gao after throwing off Malian rule
ca. 1450–1600	Songhai Empire at Gao
1464–1591	Askia dynasty
1464–1492	Reign of Sonni Ali
1493–1528	Reign of Askia Muhammad al-Turi
1549–1583	Reign of Askia Dawud
1590s	Collapse of the Songhai Empire

MAP EXPLORATION

Interactive map: To explore this map further, go to **http://www.prenhall.com/craig/map17.2**

MAP 17–2

Africa ca. 1500–1800. Important towns, regions, peoples, and states are presented in the main map. The inset shows the empire of Songhai at its greatest extent in the early 16th century.

WHAT WAS Songhai's major source of wealth?

Civil strife, largely over the royal succession, weakened the Kanuri state from the later 14th century, and after 1400, the locus of power shifted from Kanem proper westward, to the land of Bornu, southwest of Lake Chad. Near the end of the 16th century, firearms and Turkish military instructors enabled the Kanuri leader Idris Alawma (r. ca. 1575–1610) to unify Kanem and Bornu. He set up an avowedly Islamic state and extended his rule even into Hausaland, between Bornu and the Niger River. The center of trading activity as well as political power and security now shifted from the Niger bend east to the territory under Kanuri control.

Deriving its prosperity from the trans-Saharan trade, Idris Alawma's regional empire survived for nearly a century, but by 1700, its power had been reduced by the Hausa states to the west.

THE EASTERN SUDAN

The Christian states of Maqurra and Alwa in the Nilotic Sudan, or Nubia, lasted for more than 600 years from their early seventh-century beginnings. Often thought of as isolated, Christian Nubia in fact maintained political, religious, and commercial contact with Egypt, the Red Sea world, and the east-central and even central Sudan. From late Fatimid times onward, both Maqurra and Alwa were subject to growing Muslim minorities. The result was a long-term intermingling of Arabic and Nubian cultures and the creation of a new Nilotic Sudanese people and culture.

Islam spread slowly with Arab immigration into the upper Nile region. A significant factor in the gradual disappearance of Christianity in Nubia was the apparently elite character of Christianity there and its association with foreign Egyptian Coptic Christianity. Maqurra became officially Muslim at the beginning of the 14th century. The Islamization of Alwa came somewhat later, under the Funj sultanate that replaced the Alwa state.

The Funj state flourished from just after 1500 until 1762. The Funj developed an Islamic society whose Arabized character was unique in sub-Saharan Africa. A much-reduced Funj state held out until an Ottoman-Egyptian invasion in 1821.

THE FORESTLANDS—COASTAL WEST AND CENTRAL AFRICA

WEST AFRICAN FOREST KINGDOMS: THE EXAMPLE OF BENIN

Many states had developed in West Africa centuries before the first Portuguese reports of their existence in 1485. Benin, the best known of these kingdoms, reflects, especially in its art, the sophistication of West African culture before 1500.

Benin State and Society   A distinct kingdom of Benin likely existed as early as the 12th century, and the power of the king, or *oba*, at this time was sharply limited by the *uzama*, an order of hereditary indigenous chiefs. Only in the 15th century, with King Ewuare, did Benin become a royal autocracy and a large state of major regional importance.

Ewuare apparently established a government in which he had sweeping authority, although he exercised it in light of the deliberations of a royal council formed from the palace uzama and the townspeople. He gave each chief specific administrative responsibilities and rank in the government hierarchy. Ewuare and his successors engaged in major wars of expansion and claimed for the office of oba an increasing ritual authority.

Central Sudanic Empires

ca. 1100–1500	Kanuri Empire of Kanem
ca. 1220s–1400	Height of Empire of Kanem
1221–1259	Reign of Mai Dunama Dibbalemi
1575–1846	Kanuri Empire of Kanem-Bornu
1575–1610	Reign of Idris Alawma, major architect of the state

WHY DID Christianity gradually disappear in Nubia?

HOW DID the arrival of Europeans affect the peoples of West and Central Africa?

oba   Title of the king of Benin.

uzama   Order of hereditary chiefs in Benin.

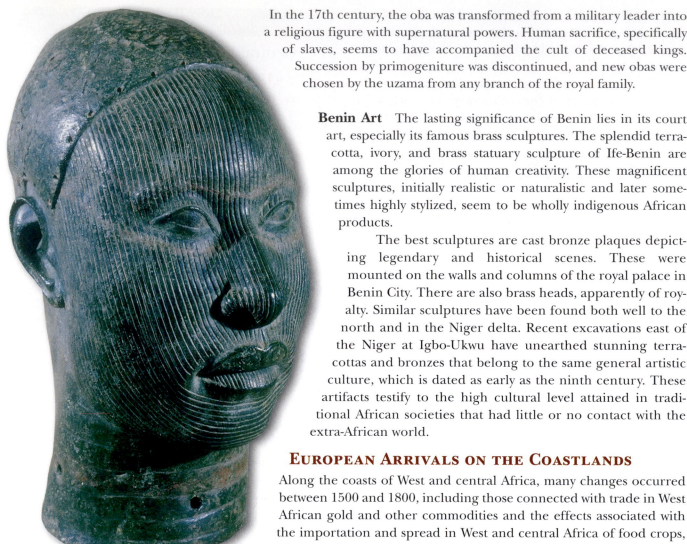

Brass head. This naturalistic brass head (29 cm high), which dates to the 13th century, conveys a serenity remarkably similar to classical Greek sculpture.

© Frank Willet.

In the 17th century, the oba was transformed from a military leader into a religious figure with supernatural powers. Human sacrifice, specifically of slaves, seems to have accompanied the cult of deceased kings. Succession by primogeniture was discontinued, and new obas were chosen by the uzama from any branch of the royal family.

Benin Art The lasting significance of Benin lies in its court art, especially its famous brass sculptures. The splendid terracotta, ivory, and brass statuary sculpture of Ife-Benin are among the glories of human creativity. These magnificent sculptures, initially realistic or naturalistic and later sometimes highly stylized, seem to be wholly indigenous African products.

The best sculptures are cast bronze plaques depicting legendary and historical scenes. These were mounted on the walls and columns of the royal palace in Benin City. There are also brass heads, apparently of royalty. Similar sculptures have been found both well to the north and in the Niger delta. Recent excavations east of the Niger at Igbo-Ukwu have unearthed stunning terracottas and bronzes that belong to the same general artistic culture, which is dated as early as the ninth century. These artifacts testify to the high cultural level attained in traditional African societies that had little or no contact with the extra-African world.

EUROPEAN ARRIVALS ON THE COASTLANDS

Along the coasts of West and central Africa, many changes occurred between 1500 and 1800, including those connected with trade in West African gold and other commodities and the effects associated with the importation and spread in West and central Africa of food crops, such as maize, peanuts, squash, sweet potatoes, cocoa, and cassava (manioc) from the Americas. The gradual involvement of Africa in the emerging global economic system paved the way for eventual colonial domination of the continent, especially its coastal regions, by the Europeans. The European names for segments of the coastline—the Grain (or Pepper) Coast, the Ivory Coast, the Gold Coast, and the Slave Coast—identify the main exports that could be extracted by ship and vividly indicate the nature of the emerging relationship.

Senegambia In West Africa, Senegambia—which takes its name from the Senegal and Gambia Rivers—was one of the earliest regions affected by European trade. Its maritime trade with European powers, like the older overland trade, was primarily in gold and products such as salt, cotton goods, hides, and copper. Senegambian states also provided perhaps a third of all African slaves exported during the 16th century. Thereafter, the focus of the slave trade shifted south and east along the coast. Over time, Portuguese-African mulattos and the British came to control the Gambia River trade, while the French won the Senegal River markets.

Benin

ca. 1100–1897	Benin state
ca. 1300	First Ife king of Benin state
1440–1475	Reign of Ewuare

The Gold Coast The Gold Coast derives its name from its importance after 1500 as the outlet for West Africa's gold fields. Here, beginning with the Portuguese at Elmina in 1481, European states and companies built coastal forts to protect their trade. The trade encouraged the growth of larger states—like the Akan forest states near the coast and the Gonja state just north of the forest—perhaps because they could better control commerce.

The intensive contact of the Gold Coast with Europeans also led to the spread of American crops, notably maize and cassava, into the region, which contributed to substantial population growth. Slaves became big business here in the late 17th century, especially in the Accra region. The economy was so disrupted by the slave trade that gold mining declined. Eventually more gold came into the Gold Coast from the sale of slaves than went out from its mines.

CENTRAL AFRICA

The vast center of the subcontinent is bounded by swamps in the north, coastal rain forests to the west, highlands to the east, and deserts in the south. Before 1500, these natural barriers impeded international contact and trade with the interior.

The coming of the Portuguese broke down this isolation, albeit slowly. The Portuguese came looking for gold and silver but found none. Instead, they exported such goods as ivory and palm cloth. Ultimately, their main export was slaves, first to the Portuguese sugar plantations on Sao Thomé island in the Gulf of Guinea, then to Brazil.

The Kongo Kingdom Kongo was the major state with which the Portuguese dealt after coming to central Africa in 1483. Dating from probably the 14th century, the Kongo kingdom was located on a fertile, well-watered plateau south of the lower Zaïre River valley, between the coast and the Kwango River in the east. Here, astride the border between forest and grassland, the Kongo kings had built a central government based on a pyramid structure of tax or tribute collection balanced by rewards for those faithful in paying their taxes. Kongo society was dominated by the king, whose authority was tied to acceptance of him as a kind of spiritual spokesman of the gods or ancestors. By 1600, Kongo was half the size of England and alongside farming boasted a high state of specialization in weaving and pottery, salt production, fishing, and metalworking.

The Portuguese brought Mediterranean goods, preeminently luxury textiles from North Africa, to trade for African goods. Such luxuries augmented the prestige and wealth of the ruler and his elites. However, slaves became the primary export that could be used to obtain foreign luxury goods. Imports, such as fine clothing, tobacco, and alcohol, did nothing to replace the labor pool lost to slavery.

At first the Portuguese put time and effort into education and Christian proselytizing, but the need for more slaves led to their concentrating on exploiting the human

Benin Bronze Plaque. From the palace of the Obas of Benin it dates to the Edo period of Benin culture, 1575–1625. It depicts two Portuguese males, perhaps a father and son, holding hands. It is likely that they represent the traders or government officials who came to the African coasts in increasing numbers from the end of the 15th century on.
Werner Forman, Art Resource, N.Y.

Central Africa

1300s	Kongo kingdom founded
1483	Portuguese come to central African coast
ca. 1506–1543	Reign of Affonso I as king of Kongo
1571	Angola becomes Portuguese proprietary colony

HISTORY'S VOICES

AFFONSO I OF KONGO WRITES TO THE KING OF PORTUGAL

I n 1526, Affonso, the Christian African king of Kongo, wrote to the Portuguese monarch ostensibly to complain about the effects of slaving on the Kongo people and economy. But the real issue was that the Portuguese were circumventing his own royal monopoly on the inland slave trade. One of the insidious effects of the massive demand of the Atlantic trade for slaves was the ever-increasing engagement in it of African monarchs, chieftains, and merchants.

HOW HAD the introduction of Portuguese merchants and European goods upset the social and political situation in Kongo? How had these goods tempted Affonso's subjects into the slave trade? How did Affonso wish to change the relationship of his people to Portugal? Was the king more worried about human rights or his economic losses?

Sir, Your Highness [of Portugal] should know how our Kingdom is being lost in so many ways that it is convenient to provide for the necessary remedy, since this is caused by the excessive freedom given by your factors and officials to the men and merchants who are allowed to come to this Kingdom to set up shops with goods and many things which have been prohibited by us, and which they spread throughout our Kingdoms and Domains in such an abundance that many of our vassals, whom we had in obedience, do not comply because they have the things in greater abundance than we ourselves; and it was with these things that we had them content and subjected under our vassalage and jurisdiction, so it is doing a great

harm not only to the service of God, but the security and peace of our Kingdoms and State as well.

And we cannot reckon how great the damage is, since the mentioned merchants are taking every day our natives, sons of the land and the sons of our noblemen and vassals and our relatives, because the thieves and men of bad conscience grab them wishing to have the things and wares of this Kingdom which they are ambitious of; they grab them and get them to be sold; and so great, Sir, is the corruption and licentiousness that our country is being completely depopulated, and Your Highness should not agree with this nor accept it as in your service. And to avoid it we need from those [your] Kingdoms no more than some priests and a few people to teach in schools, and no other goods except wine and flour for the holy sacrament. That is why we beg of Your Highness to help and assist us in this matter, commanding your factors that they should not send here either merchants or wares, because it is *our will that in these Kingdoms there should not be any trade of slaves nor outlet for them.**

Concerning what is referred above, again we beg of Your Highness to agree with it, since otherwise we cannot … remedy such an obvious damage. Pray Our Lord in His mercy to have Your Highness under His guard and let you do for ever the things of His service. I kiss your hands many times. …

From *The African Past*, trans. by J. O. Hunwick, reprinted in Basil Davidson (Grosset and Dunlap, The Universal Library), pp. 191–193. Reprinted by permission of Curtis Brown Ltd. Copyright © 1964 by Basil Davidson.

*Emphasis in the original.

resources of central Africa. Regional rulers sought to procure slaves from neighboring kingdoms, as did Portuguese traders who went inland themselves. As the demand grew, local rulers increasingly attacked neighbors to garner slaves for Portuguese traders (see Chapter 18).

The Kongo ruler Affonso I (r. ca. 1506–1543), a Christian convert, began by welcoming Jesuit missionaries and supporting conversion. But in time he broke with the Jesuits and encouraged traditional practices, even though he himself remained a Christian. Affonso had constant difficulty curbing slaving practices and provincial governors who often dealt directly with the Portuguese, undermining royal authority (see "Affonso I of Kongo Writes to the King of Portugal"). Affonso's successor restricted Portuguese activity to Mpinda harbor and the Kongo capital of Mbanza Kongo (São Salvador). A few years later, Portuguese attempts to name the Kongo royal successor caused a bloody uprising against them that led in turn to a Portuguese boycott on trade with the kingdom.

Thereafter, disastrous internal wars shattered the Kongo state. Kongo, however, enjoyed renewed vigor in the 17th century. Its kings ruled as divine-right monarchs at the apex of a complex sociopolitical pyramid that rose from district headmen through provincial governors to

East and Southeast Africa

900–1500	"Great Zimbabwe" civilization
ca. 1200–1400	Development of Bantu Kiswahili language
ca. 1300–1600	Height of Swahili culture
1698	Omani forces take Mombasa, oust Portuguese from East Africa north of the port of Mozambique
1741–1856	United sultanate of Oman and Zanzibar

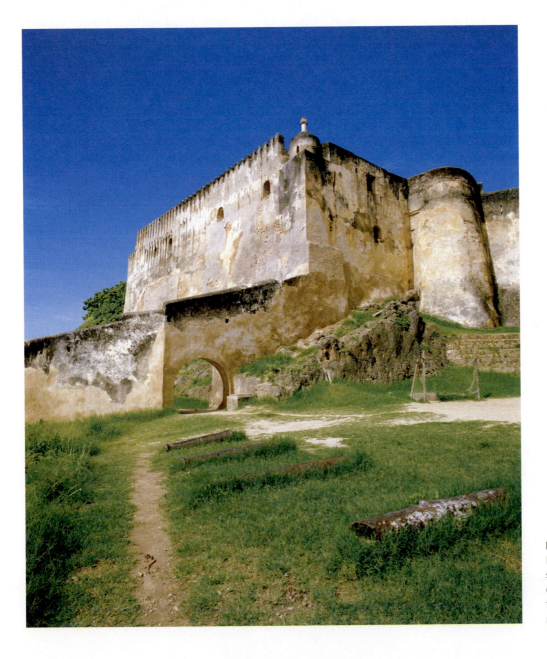

Fort Jesus, Mombasa, Kenya. Built by the Portuguese in the sixteenth century, it is the most conspicuous reminder of their former presence in East Africa.

Robert Harding World Imagery.

the court nobility and king. Royal power came to depend on a guard of musket-armed hired soldiers. The financial base of the kingdom rested on tribute from officials holding positions at the king's pleasure and on taxes and tolls on commerce. Christianity, the state religion, was accommodated to traditional beliefs. Kongo sculpture, iron and copper technology, and dance and music flourished.

Angola To the south, in Portuguese Angola, the experience was even worse than in Kongo. By 1600, Angola was exporting thousands of slaves yearly through the port of Luanda. In less than a century, the hinterland had been plundered. The Portuguese arrival had brought economic and social catastrophe.

EAST AFRICA

SWAHILI CULTURE AND COMMERCE

HOW DID Swahili language and culture develop?

The participation of East African port towns in the lucrative southern seas trade was ancient. Arabs, Indonesians, and even Indians had trafficked there for centuries. From the eighth century onward, Islam traveled with Arab and Persian sailors and merchants to these southerly trading centers. In the 13th century, Muslim traders from Arabia and Iran began to come in increased numbers and to dominate the coastal cities. Henceforward, Islamic faith and culture were often predominant along the seacoast, from Mogadishu to Kilwa.

By this time, a common language had also developed from the interaction of Bantu and Arabic speakers along the coast. This tongue is called *Swahili*, or *Kiswahili*, from the Arabic *sawahil*, "coastlands." Swahili language and culture probably developed first in the northern towns of Manda, Lamu, and Mombasa, then farther south along the coast to Kilwa. Likewise, the spread of Islam was largely limited to the coastal civilization and did not reach inland. This contrasts with lands farther north, in the Horn of Africa, where Islamic kingdoms developed in the Somali hinterland as well as on the coast.

Swahili civilization reached its apogee in the 14th and 15th centuries. The harbor trading towns were the administrative centers of the local Swahili states, and most of them were sited on coastal islands or easily defended peninsulas. To these ports came merchants from abroad and from the African hinterlands, some to settle and stay. These towns had impressive mosques, fortress-palaces, harbor fortifications, fancy residences, and commercial buildings.

Today, historians recognize that the ruling dynasties of the Swahili states were probably African in origin, with an admixture of Arab or Persian immigrant blood. Swahili coastal centers boasted an advanced, cosmopolitan level of culture. By comparison, most of the populace in the small villages lived in mud houses and sometimes stone houses and earned their livings by farming or fishing, the two basic coastal occupations besides trade. Society consisted of three principal groups: local nobility, commoners, and resident foreigners engaged in commerce. Slaves constituted a fourth class, although their local extent (as opposed to their sale) is disputed.

The flourishing trade of the coastal centers was fed mainly by export of inland ivory. Other exports included gold, slaves, turtle shells, ambergris, leopard skins, pearls, fish, sandalwood, ebony, and local cotton cloth. The chief imports were cloth, porcelain, glassware, china, glass beads, and glazed pottery. Certain exports tended to dominate particular ports: cloth, sandalwood, ebony, and ivory at Mogadishu; ivory at Manda; and gold at Kilwa. Cowrie shells were a

Swahili Language and culture that developed from the interaction of native Africans and Arabs along the East African coast.

North Africa	Sahel	Eastern Sudan	West and Central Africa	East Africa	Southern Africa
Morocco	Ghana	Maqurra	Benin	Zanzibar	"Great Zimbabwe"
Algiers	Mali	Alwa	Kongo		
Tunis	Songhai	Funj			
Tripoli	Kanem				
Egypt					

common currency in inland trade, but coins were used in the major trading centers. The gold trade itself apparently became important only in the 15th century.

THE PORTUGUESE AND THE OMANIS OF ZANZIBAR

The decline of the original Swahili civilization in the 16th century can be attributed primarily to the arrival of the Portuguese and their destruction of the old oceanic trade (in particular, the Islamic commercial monopoly) and the main Islamic city-states along the eastern coast.

In Africa, as everywhere, the Portuguese saw the "**Moors**" as implacable enemies. Many Portuguese viewed the struggle to wrest the commerce and seaports of Africa and Asia from Islamic control as a Christian crusade. The initial Portuguese victories along the African coast led to the submission of many small Islamic coastal ports and states. Still, there was no concerted effort to spread Christianity. Thus, the long-term cultural and religious consequences of the Portuguese presence were slight. After 1660, the eastern Arabian state of Oman ejected the Portuguese everywhere north of Mozambique.

The Omanis soon shifted their home base to Zanzibar, which became a major power in East Africa. Their control of the coastal ivory and slave trade fueled a substantial recovery of prosperity by the later 18th century. The domination of the east coast by Omani African sultans, descendants of the earlier invaders, continued until 1856. Thereafter, Zanzibar and its coastal holdings became independent, and then passed to the British. Still, the Islamic impact on the whole coast survives today.

SOUTHERN AFRICA

SOUTHEASTERN AFRICA: "GREAT ZIMBABWE"

At about the same time that the east-coast trading centers were beginning to flourish, a purely African civilization was enjoying its heyday inland in modern southern Zimbabwe. It was founded in the 10th or 11th century by Bantu-speaking Shona people, who still inhabit the same general area today. It seems to have become a large and prosperous state between the late 13th and the late 15th centuries. We know it only through the archaeological remains of an estimated 150 settlements in the Zambezi-Limpopo region.

QUICK REVIEW

East African Port Towns
- Part of trade with Middle East, Asia, and India
- Tied together by common language, *Swahili*
- Swahili civilization reached its peak in the 14th and 15th centuries

Moors Spanish and Portuguese term for Muslims.

HOW DID slavery affect race relations in the Cape Colony?

14.1
Kilwa, Mombasa, and the Portuguese: Realities of Empire

The most impressive of these ruins is known today as "Great Zimbabwe"—a huge, 60-odd-acre site encompassing two major building complexes. One—the so-called acropolis—is a series of stone enclosures on a high hill. It overlooks another, much larger enclosure that contains many ruins and a circular tower, all surrounded by a massive wall some 32 feet high and up to 17 feet thick. The acropolis complex may have contained a shrine, whereas the larger enclosure was apparently the royal palace and fort. The stonework reflects a wealthy and sophisticated society. Artifacts from the site include gold and copper ornaments, soapstone carvings, and imported beads, as well as china, glass, and porcelain of Chinese, Syrian, and Persian origins.

The state itself seems to have had partial control of the increasing gold trade between inland areas and the east coast. We can speculate that this large settlement was the capital city of a prosperous empire and the residence of a ruling elite. Its wider domain was made up mostly of smaller settlements whose inhabitants lived by subsistence agriculture and cattle raising and whose culture was considerably different from that of the capital. Without written or new archaeological sources, we shall likely never know exactly what allowed this impressive civilization to develop and to dominate its region for nearly 200 years.

THE PORTUGUESE IN SOUTHEASTERN AFRICA

The Portuguese destroyed Swahili control of both the inland gold trade and the overseas trade. Their chief objective was to obtain gold from the interior.

"Great Zimbabwe." The most impressive of 300 such stone ruins in modern Zimbabwe and neighboring countries. These sites give clear evidence of the advanced Iron Age mining and cattle-raising culture that flourished in this region between about 1000 and 1500 C.E. The people, thought to have been of Bantu origins, apparently had a highly developed trade in gold and copper with outsiders, including Arabs on the east coast. As yet, all too little is known about this impressive society.

Robert Aberman and Barbara Heller/
Art Resource, N.Y.

Although the Portugese derived little lasting profit from their enterprise, all along the Zambezi a lasting and destabilizing consequence of their intrusion was the creation of quasi-tribal chiefdoms led by mixed-blood Portuguese landholders, who were descended from the first Portuguese estate holders along the Zambezi. By the late 18th century, they were too strong for either the Portuguese or the regional African rulers to control. They remind us of how diverse the peoples of modern Africa are.

SOUTH AFRICA: THE CAPE COLONY

In South Africa, the Dutch planted the first European colonials almost inadvertently, yet the consequences of their action were to be ultimately as grave and far-reaching as any European incursion onto African soil. The first Cape settlement was built in 1652 by the Dutch East India Company as a resupply point and way station for Dutch vessels on their route between the Netherlands and the East Indies. The support station gradually became a settler community, the forebears of the Afrikaners of modern South Africa.

The local Khoikhoi (see Chapter 5) had neither a strong political organization nor an economic base beyond their herds. They bartered livestock freely to Dutch ships. As company employees established farms to supply the Cape station, they began to displace the Khoikhoi. Conflicts led to the consolidation of European landholdings and a breakdown of Khoikhoi society. Military success led to even greater Dutch control of the Khoikhoi by the 1670s.

The Khoikhoi became the chief source of colonial wage labor, but the colony also imported slaves. Slavery set the tone for relations between the emergent, and ostensibly "white," Afrikaner population and the "coloreds" of other races. Free or not, the latter were eventually identified with slave peoples.

After the first settlers spread out around the company station, nomadic white livestock farmers, or *Trekboers*, moved more widely afield, leaving the richer, but limited, farming lands of the coast for the drier interior tableland. There they contested still wider groups of Khoikhoi cattle herders for the best grazing lands. Again the Khoikhoi lost. By 1700, their way of life was destroyed.

The Cape society in this period was thus a diverse one. The Dutch Company officials (including Dutch Reformed ministers), the emerging Afrikaners (both settled colonists and Trekboers), the Khoikhoi, and the slaves of diverse nationalities played differing roles. Intermarriage and cohabitation of masters and slaves added to the complexity. The emergence of *Afrikaans*, a new vernacular language of the colonials, shows that the

Carving from Great Zimbabwe. This carving (steatite, 40.5 cm high) is thought to represent a mythical eagle that carries messages from man to the gods. It dates to ca. 1200–1400 C.E.

Werner Forman Archive/Art Resource, N.Y.

Trekboers White livestock farmers in Cape Colony.

Afrikaans New language, derived from Dutch, that evolved in the 17th- and 18th-century Cape Colony.

Southern Africa

1652 First Cape colony settlement of Dutch East India Company

1795 British replace Dutch as masters of Cape Colony

Cape Town, with European ships in its harbor. The colony relied on shipping for commercial links with the outside world.

National Archives of South Africa.

apartheid "Apartness," the term referring to racist policies enforced by the white-dominated regime that existed in South Africa from 1948 to 1992.

Dutch immigrants themselves were also subject to acculturation processes. By the time of English domination after 1795, the sociopolitical foundations—and the bases of the *apartheid* doctrine—of modern South Africa were firmly laid.

SUMMARY

North Africa Developments in African history from 1000 to 1800 varied from region to region. In North Africa, the key new factor was the imperial expansion of the Ottoman Empire as far west as Morocco. But regionalism soon rendered Ottoman authority in North Africa purely nominal.

Empires of the Sudan Several substantial states arose south of the Sahara: Ghana, Mali, Songhai, and Kanem. The ruling elites of these states converted to or were heavily influenced by Islam, although most of their populations clung to their older traditions. Much of the wealth of these states was tied to their control of the trans-Saharan trade routes. Farther south, in the coastal forestlands of Central Africa, another substantial kingdom arose in Benin, famous for its brass sculptures.

East Africa On the east coast, Islam influenced the development of the distinctive Swahili culture and language, and Islamic traders linked the region to India and East Asia.

The Coming of the Europeans The key development of the 15th century was the arrival of European traders, missionaries, and warships. The Portuguese and later Europeans came in search of commerce, converts to Christianity, and spheres of influence. Their arrival disrupted indigenous African culture and political relations and presaged Africa's involvement in and exploitation by a new, expanding global trading system dominated by Europeans.

IMAGE KEY

for pages 414–415

a. Moroccan Coin dating from Songhai Empire
b. Benin plaque
c. Golden rhino found at Mapungubwe
d. Thirteenth-century brass head from Benin
e. Mosque in Janne
f. Mansa Musa early medieval painting
g. The Djinquereber mosque in Timbuktu
h. Benin plaque
i. Fort Jesus, Mombasa, Kenya, Africa
j. "Great Zimbabwe," one of 300 stone ruins
k. Great Zimbabwe carving (stearite, 40.5cm high) representing a mythical eagle carrying messages to the gods.

REVIEW QUESTIONS

1. Why did Islam succeed in sub-Saharan and East Africa? How did warfare and trade affect its success?

2. What was the importance of the empires of Ghana, Mali, and Songhai to world history? Why was the control of the trans-Saharan trade so important to these kingdoms? What was the importance of Islamic culture to them? Why did each of these empires break up?

3. How did the Portuguese affect East and central Africa? How did European coastal activities affect the African interior?

4. How did the Portuguese and Dutch differ from or resemble the Arabs, Persians, and other Muslims who came as outsiders to sub-Saharan Africa?

5. Who were the Trekboers and what was their conflict with the Khoikhoi? How was the basis for apartheid formed in this period?

KEY TERMS

Afrikaans (p. 431)
apartheid (p. 432)
Moors (p. 429)

oba (p. 423)
Swahili (p. 428)

Trekboers (p. 431)
uzama (p. 423)

 For additional study resources for this chapter, go to:
www.prenhall.com/craig/chapter17

18 Conquest and Exploitation
The Development of the Transatlantic Economy

CHAPTER HIGHLIGHTS

European Conquest of the New World The contact between the native peoples of the American continents and the European explorers of the fifteenth and sixteenth centuries transformed world history. In the Americas, the native peoples had established a wide variety of civilizations, but until the European explorations, the civilizations of the Americas and Eurasia and Africa had no significant contact with each other.

Within half a century of the landing of Columbus, millions of America's native peoples had encountered Europeans intent on conquest, exploitation, and religious conversion. Because of their technology and the new diseases they brought with them, as well as internal divisions among the native Americans, the Europeans achieved a rapid conquest.

The Transatlantic Economy In both North and South America, economies of exploitation were established. From the mid-Atlantic English colonies through the Caribbean and into Brazil, slave-labor plantations forcibly imported slaves from Africa. The economies and peoples of Europe, Africa, and the Americas were thus drawn into a vast worldwide web of production based on slave labor.

Slavery The impact of slavery in the Americas was not limited to the life of the black slaves. Whites in the New World numbered about 12 million in 1820, compared to some six million blacks. However, only about two million whites had migrated there, compared to some 11 million or more Africans forcibly imported as slaves. Such numbers reveal the effects of brutal slave conditions and the high mortality and low birthrates of slave populations. None of these statistics, however, enables us to asses the role that slavery has played in the Americas or, in particular, the United States. The United States actually received only a bit more than a quarter as many slaves as did Brazil, yet the consequences of the forced migration of just over a half-million Africans remain massive. The Atlantic slave trade's impact continues to be felt at both ends of the original "trade."

Charlestown, July 24th, 1769.

TO BE SOLD,
On Thursday the third Day
of August next,
A CARGO
OF
NINETY-FOUR
PRIME, HEALTHY
NEGROES,
CONSISTING OF
Thirty-nine Men, Fifteen Boys,
Twenty-four Women, and
Sixteen Girls.
JUST ARRIVED,
In the Brigantine DEMBIA, Fran-
cis Bare, Master, from SIERRA-
LEON, by
DAVID & JOHN DEAS.

CHAPTER QUESTIONS

WHAT WAS mercantilism?

WHAT ROLES did the Roman Catholic Church play in Spanish America?

HOW WERE sugar production and slavery intertwined in colonial Brazil?

HOW WERE the economies of the French and British North American colonies integrated into the transatlantic economy?

WHY WAS the transatlantic slave trade so economically important?

CHAPTER OUTLINE

- Periods of European Overseas Expansion
- Mercantilist Theory of Economic Exploitation
- Establishment of the Spanish Empire in America
- Economies of Exploitation in the Spanish Empire
- Colonial Brazil and Slavery
- French and British Colonies in North America
- Slavery in the Americas
- Africa and the Transatlantic Slave Trade

The European encounter with the American continents in the late 15th century made the region an area where European languages, legal and political institutions, trade, and religion prevailed. These developments in the Americas gave Europe more influence over other world cultures than it would otherwise have achieved.

Within decades of the European voyages of discovery, Native Americans, Europeans, and Africans began to interact in a manner unprecedented in human history. By the end of the 16th century, Europe, the Americas, and Africa had become linked in a vast transatlantic economy that extracted wealth from the American continents largely on the basis of the nonfree labor of impressed Native Americans and imported African slaves in a plantation economy that extended from Maryland to Brazil. The slave trade connected the economy of sections of Africa to the transatlantic economy and devastated the African people and cultures involved in it, but it also enriched the Americas with African culture.

PERIODS OF EUROPEAN OVERSEAS EXPANSION

WHAT IMPACT has European expansion had on the peoples of Asia, Africa, Australia, and the Americas?

Since the late 15th century, Europe's contacts with the rest of the world have passed through four stages. The first was the discovery, exploration, conquest, and settlement of the Americas and commercial expansion elsewhere. The second was an era of trade rivalry among Spain, France, and Great Britain. During this period (to 1820) the British colonies of North America and the Spanish colonies of Mexico and Central and South America broke free from European control. The third period spanned the 19th century and was characterized by the development of European empires in Africa and Asia. Imperial ideology at this time involved theories of trade, national honor, race, religion, and military strength. The last period of European experience with empire occupied the mid-20th century and was a time of decolonization—a retreat from empire.

It was technological advantages, not innate cultural superiority, that enabled Europeans for four and a half centuries to exercise global dominance beyond the proportions of Europe's size and population. However, the legacy of European imperialism—a memory of suffering, abuse, and exploitation—survives to complicate contemporary international relations.

MERCANTILIST THEORY OF ECONOMIC EXPLOITATION

WHAT WAS mercantilism?

The European empires of the 16th through the 18th centuries were based on commerce and were established primarily to promote trade. As a result, extensive trade rivalries sprang up around the world, and competitors developed navies to protect their interests. The empires also relied largely on slave labor. Indeed, the Atlantic slave trade was a major way in which European merchants profited. That trade in turn forcibly thrust the people of Africa into the life and culture of the New World.

If any formal economic theory lay behind these empires, it was **mercantilism**, a system in which governments heavily regulate trade and commerce to increase national wealth. From beginning to end, the economic well-being of the home country was the primary concern of mercantilist writers. They believed that a nation had to gain more gold and silver bullion than its rivals and that one nation's economy could grow only at the expense of others. Governments did this by establishing colonies overseas to provide markets and natural resources for the home country, which furnished military security and

mercantilism Term used to describe close government control of the economy that sought to maximize exports and accumulate as much precious metals as possible to enable the state to defend its economic and political interests.

Batavia. The Dutch established a major trading base at Batavia in the East Indies in the 17th century. Its geographical position allowed the Dutch to dominate the spice trade. Batavia is now Djakarta, capital of modern-day Indonesia.

Bildarchiv Preussicher Kulturbesitz.

political administration for these colonies. The home country and its colonies were to trade exclusively with each other. For decades, both sides assumed that the colonies were the inferior partner in a monopolistic relationship.

Mercantilist ideas were always neater on paper than in practice. By the early 18th century, it was clear that mercantilist assumptions did not correspond with reality. Colonial and home markets did not mesh. Spain, for instance, could not produce enough goods for South America, and manufacturing in the British North American colonies challenged production in England. Colonists of different countries also wanted to trade with one another. Governments could not control all their subjects, and they could be dragged into war by clashes among their colonies. Problems associated with the mercantile empires led to conflicts around the world.

ESTABLISHMENT OF THE SPANISH EMPIRE IN AMERICA

CONQUEST OF THE AZTECS AND THE INCAS

Within 20 years of the arrival of Columbus (1451–1506), Spanish explorers in search of gold had claimed the major islands of the Caribbean and suppressed the native peoples. These actions presaged what was to occur on the continent.

In 1519, Hernan Cortés (1485–1547) landed in Mexico with about 500 men and a few horses. He opened communication with Moctezuma II (1466–1520), the Aztec emperor. Moctezuma hesitated to confront Cortés, attempting at first to appease him with gifts of gold. Cortés forged alliances with subject peoples of the Aztecs. His forces then marched on the Aztec capital of Tenochtitlán (modern Mexico City), where Moctezuma welcomed him. Cortés soon made Moctezuma a prisoner in his own capital. After Moctezuma died from unknown circumstances, the Spaniards were driven from Tenochtitlán. But they returned, and the Aztecs were defeated in late 1521. Cortés proclaimed the Aztec Empire to be New Spain.

In 1532, Francisco Pizarro (c. 1478–1541) landed on the western coast of South America to take over the Inca Empire. His force included about 200 men

WHAT ROLES did the Roman Catholic Church play in Spanish America?

QUICK REVIEW

Francisco Pizarro (c. 1478–1541)
- Invasion force landed in South America in 1532
- Forces included 200 men, horses, guns, and swords
- 1533: Executed the Inca ruler and captured Cuzco

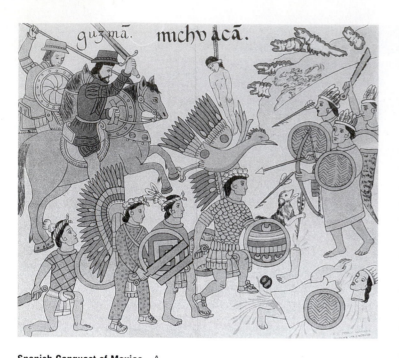

Spanish Conquest of Mexico. A 16th-century Aztec drawing depicts a battle during the Spanish conquest of Mexico. Note how the Spanish are assisted by a far greater number of Indian allies.

Corbis–Bettmann. Archivo Iconografico. S. A./Corbis.

armed with guns, swords, and horses, the military power of which the Incas did not understand. Pizarro lured the Inca ruler, Atahualpa (c. 1500–1533), into a conference, then seized him and had him garroted in 1533. The Spaniards then captured Cuzco, the Inca capital, ending the Inca Empire.

The conquests of Mexico and Peru are among the most dramatic and brutal events in modern world history. Small military forces armed with advanced weapons quickly subdued two advanced, powerful groups. European diseases, especially smallpox, aided the conquerors. Having never been explosed to European diseases, the native populations had no natural immunity to them.

Beyond the drama and bloodshed, these conquests marked a turning point. Whole civilizations with long histories and enormous social, architectural, and technological achievements were destroyed. Native American cultures endured, but European culture had the upper hand.

THE ROMAN CATHOLIC CHURCH IN SPANISH AMERICA

The Spanish conquest of the West Indies, Mexico, and South America opened these regions to the Roman Catholic faith. As it had in the Castilian reconquest of the Iberian peninsula from the Moors, religion played a central role in the conquest of the New World. In both cases, the obligation Christians felt to spread their faith was used to justify military conquest and the extension of political control

OVERVIEW   THE COLUMBIAN EXCHANGE

The same ships that carried Europeans and Africans to the Americas also transported animals, plants, and diseases that had never before appeared in the New World. There was a similar transport back to Europe and Africa. Historians call this cross-continental flow "the Columbian exchange." The overall result was an ecological transformation that continues to shape the world.

To the Americas

Animals:	cattle, chickens, goats, horses, pigs, and sheep
Plants:	almonds, apples, apricots, bananas, barley, cabbage, cherries, dandelions, grapes, lemons, mangos, melons, oats, okra, olives, onions, oranges, peaches, pears, plums, radishes, rice, sugar cane, wheat, and other green vegetables
Diseases:	bubonic plague, chicken pox, diphtheria, influenza, malaria, measles, smallpox, typhoid, and typhus

From the Americas

Animals:	turkeys
Plants:	avocados, beans, blueberries, chilis, cocoa, guavas, maize, manioc (tapioca), peanuts, pecans, pineapples, potatoes, pumpkins, squash, sweet peppers, sweet potatoes, tobacco, and tomatoes
Diseases:	syphilis

and dominance. The link between the goals of the church and the state meant that the Roman Catholic Church in the New World worked to protect the interests of the Spanish authorities.

The relationship between political authority and the propagation of religious doctrine was even closer in the New World than on the Iberian peninsula. The papacy recognized that it could not self-support such an extensive missionary effort and turned over much of the control of the church in the New World to the Spanish monarchy. A close relationship between the monarchy and the church was created. The zeal of both institutions increased in the 16th century as the papacy and the Habsburg monarchy attempted to prevent Protestantism from establishing a foothold in America. As a consequence, the Roman Catholicism that spread throughout Spanish America was the zealous faith of the Counter-Reformation.

The Roman Catholic Church, first with the aid of the Franciscans and Dominicans, and later the Jesuits, sought to convert the Native Americans and eradicate Indian religious practices. Religious conversion involved, among other things, an attempt to destroy still other aspects of Native American culture. Converts, however, did not enjoy equality with Europeans; even late in the 18th century there were few Native American Christian priests.

There were some tensions between the early Spanish conquerors and the friars. Without conquest, the church could not convert the Native Americans, but the priests often deplored the harsh treatment native peoples received from their conquerors. The most outspoken clerical critic of the Spanish conquerors was Bartolomé de Las Casas (1474–1566), a Dominican. He contended that conquest was not necessary for conversion, and after 1550 his agitation inspired the royal government to pass legislation aimed at improving conditions for the native peoples. Las Casas's writings inspired the "**Black Legend**," according to which all Spanish treatment of the Native Americans was inhumane. Although substantially true, the Black Legend exaggerated the case against Spain. Certainly the rulers of the native empires—as the Aztec demands for sacrificial victims attest—had often themselves been cruel to their subject peoples.

By the end of the 16th century, the church in Spanish America had become largely an institution upholding the colonial status quo. Although priests did defend the communal rights of Indian tribes, the colonial church prospered through its exploitation of the resources of the New World. Those who spoke for the church did not challenge Spanish domination, and the church only modestly moderated the forces exploiting human labor and material wealth. By the late 18th century, the Roman Catholic Church had become one of the most conservative forces in Latin American society.

Economies of Exploitation in the Spanish Empire

Colonial Spanish America had an economy of exploitation in two senses. First, its organization of labor involved dependent servitude or slavery. Second, resources were exploited for the economic advantage of Spain.

Varieties of Economic Activity

The early *conquistadores* ("conquerors") had been interested primarily in gold, but by the middle of the 16th century, silver mining provided the chief source of metallic wealth. Great silver mining centers were in Bolivia and northern Mexico.

15.1
The Black Legend of Spain: Bartolomé de Las Casas

Black Legend Argument that Spanish treatment of Native Americans was uniquely inhumane.

HOW WERE sugar production and slavery intertwined in colonial Brazil?

conquistadores Meaning "conquerors." Spanish conquerors of the New World.

Biological exchanges
Origin and movement of plants and animals

- from Europe
- from America
- from Asia

Diseases

- bubonic plague
- diphtheria, influenza, measles, smallpox, and whooping cough
- syphilis

MAP 18–1

Biological Exchanges, 1000–1600 C.E. Though the transfer of plants, animals, and diseases had been going on for centuries, European expansion set in motion a global movement transformed the world.

HOW DID the Columbian exchange alter environments around the world?

The Spanish crown received one fifth of all mining revenues. Silver mining for the benefit of Spaniards and the Spanish crown epitomized the extractive economy on which Latin American colonial life was based.

This extractive economy required labor, but there were too few Spanish colonists to provide it, and most of the colonists who came to the Americas did not want to work for wages. So, the Spaniards turned first to the native population for workers and then to African slaves. Indian labor dominated on the continent and African labor in the Caribbean (see Map 18–1).

Encomienda The Spanish devised a series of institutions to exploit Native American labor. The first was the *encomienda*, a formal grant by the crown of the right to the labor of a specific number of Native Americans for a particular time. The Spanish crown disliked the encomienda system. The monarchy was distressed by reports from clergy that the Native Americans were being mistreated and feared that encomienda holders were becoming a powerful nobility in the New World. Encomienda as an institution declined by the middle of the 16th century.

Repartimiento The passing of the encomienda led to the *repartimiento*, largely copied from the draft labor practices of the Incas. Repartimiento required adult male Native Americans to devote a set number of days of labor annually to

encomienda Grant by the Spanish crown to a colonist of the labor of a specific number of Indians for a set period of time.

repartimiento Labor tax in Spanish America that required adult male Native Americans to devote a set number of days a year to Spanish economic enterprises.

Spanish economic enterprises. The time limitation on repartimiento led some Spanish managers to try to maximize productivity by working teams of men to exhaustion—sometimes to death—before replacing them with the next rotation.

The Hacienda   The *hacienda*, which dominated rural and agricultural life in Spanish colonies on the continent, developed when the crown made grants of land. These grants created large landed estates for *peninsulares*, whites born in Spain, or creoles, whites born in America. This use of the resources of the New World for royal patronage did not directly burden Native Americans because the grazing that occurred on the haciendas required less labor than did the mines. But laborers on the hacienda were usually in formal servitude to the owner and had to buy goods for everyday living on credit from him. They were rarely able to repay the resulting debts and thus could not leave. This system was known as *debt peonage*. The hacienda economy produced foodstuffs for mining areas and urban centers, and haciendas became one of the most important features of Latin American life.

THE DECLINE OF THE NATIVE AMERICAN POPULATION

Conquest, exploitation, forced labor, and European diseases decimated the Indian population (see Map 18–1). Beginning in the 16th century, Native Americans began to die off in huge numbers. In New Spain (Mexico) alone, the population probably declined from approximately 25 million to fewer than 2 million within the first century after the conquest. Thereafter, the Indian population began to expand slowly, but the precipitous drop eliminated the easy supply of exploitable labor.

COMMERCIAL REGULATION AND THE FLOTA SYSTEM

Because Queen Isabella of Castile (r. 1474–1504) had commissioned Columbus, the legal link between the New World and Spain was the crown of Castile. The governing of America was assigned to the Council of the Indies, which nominated the viceroys of New Spain and Peru, the chief executives in the New World.

hacienda   Large landed estates in Spanish America.

peninsulares   Persons born in Spain who settled in the Spanish colonies.

debt peonage   Requirement that laborers remain and continue to work on a hacienda until they had paid their debts to the owner for goods bought from him on credit.

Smallpox.   Introduced by Europeans to the Americas, smallpox had a devastating effect on Native American populations. The disease swept through the Aztec capital of Tenochtitlán soon after the Spaniards arrived, contributing to the fall of the city. This illustration of the effect of the plague in the Aztec capital is from a post-conquest history known as the Florentine Codex compiled for Spanish church authorities by Aztec survivors.

Sixteenth-century drawing of smallpox victims. Atzec original codex Florentino. Courtesy President and Fellows of Harvard College. Courtesy Peabody Museum of Archeology and Ethnology, Harvard University, photograph by Hillel Burger.

Each of the viceroyalties included subordinate judicial councils known as *audiencias*. A variety of local officers presided over municipal councils. Virtually all political power flowed from the top of this political structure downward; there was little local initiative or self-government (see Map 18–2).

Colonial political structures existed largely to support the commercial goals of Spain. But the system of monopolistic trade regulation was often breached. The Casa de Contratación (House of Trade) in Seville regulated all trade with the New World and was the most influential institution of the Spanish Empire. The entire organization was geared to benefit the Spanish monarchy and privileged merchant groups.

A complicated system of trade and bullion fleets administered from Seville maintained the trade monopoly. Each year a fleet of commercial vessels controlled by Seville merchants and escorted by warships carried merchandise from Spain to specified ports in America. These included Portobello, Veracruz, and Cartagena. There were no authorized ports on the Pacific Coast. Areas such as Buenos Aires received goods only after the shipments had been unloaded at one of the authorized ports. After selling their wares, the ships were loaded with silver and gold bullion. They then usually wintered in fortified Caribbean ports before sailing back to Spain. Regulations prohibited Spanish colonists from trading directly with each other and from building their own shipping and commercial industries. Foreign merchants were also forbidden to breach the Spanish monopoly.

COLONIAL BRAZIL AND SLAVERY

In 1494, by the Treaty of Tordesillas, the pope divided the overseas empires of Spain and Portugal by drawing a line west of the Cape Verde Islands. In 1500, a Portuguese explorer landed in present-day Brazil, east of the papal line. This gave Portugal a foothold in South America. Portugal, however, had fewer resources to devote to its New World empire than did Spain. Its rulers, therefore,

Sugar Plantation. Brazil and the West Indies were a major source of the demand for slave labor. Slaves are shown here grinding sugar cane and refining sugar, which was then exported to the consumer markets in Europe.

© Hulton-Deutsch Collection/Corbis.

MAP EXPLORATION

Interactive map: To explore this map further, go to **http://www.prenhall.com/craig/map18.2**

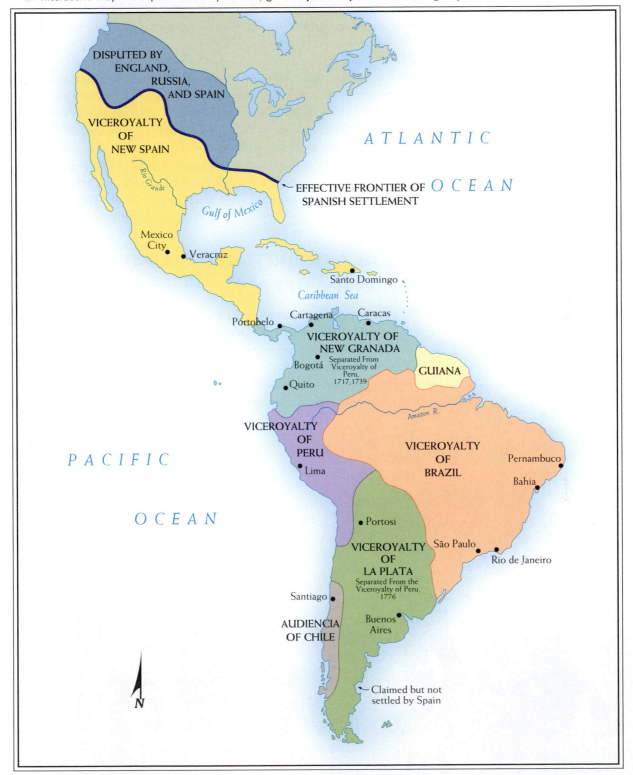

DISPUTED BY ENGLAND, RUSSIA, AND SPAIN

VICEROYALTY OF NEW SPAIN

Rio Grande

ATLANTIC

EFFECTIVE FRONTIER OF SPANISH SETTLEMENT

OCEAN

Gulf of Mexico

Mexico City

Veracruz

Santo Domingo

Caribbean Sea

Cartagena · Caracas

Portobelo

VICEROYALTY OF NEW GRANADA

Separated From Viceroyalty of Peru, 1717, 1739

Bogotá

GUIANA

Quito

Amazon R.

VICEROYALTY OF PERU

VICEROYALTY OF BRAZIL

Pernambuco

Lima

Bahia

PACIFIC

Portosi

São Paulo

OCEAN

VICEROYALTY OF LA PLATA

Separated From the Viceroyalty of Peru, 1776

Rio de Janeiro

Santiago

Buenos Aires

AUDIENCIA OF CHILE

Claimed but not settled by Spain

N

MAP 18–2

Viceroyalties in Latin America in 1780. Spain organized its vast holdings in the New World into viceroyalties, each of which had its own governor and other administrative officials.

HOW EFFECTIVE was Spain's control over its New World colonies?

left exploitation of the region to private entrepreneurs. Because the native peoples in the lands that Portugal claimed were nomadic, the Portuguese, unlike the Spanish, imported Africans as slaves rather than using the native Indian population as their work force.

By the mid-16th century, sugar production had gained preeminence in the Brazilian economy, and the dominance of sugar meant the dominance of slavery. Slavery became even more important when, in the early 18th century, gold was discovered in southern Brazil. Nowhere, except perhaps in the West Indies, was slavery so important as it was in Brazil, where it persisted until 1888.

The taxation and administration associated with gold mining brought new wealth to Portugal's monarchs that strengthened them by allowing them to rule without recourse to Cortés or the parliament for taxation. Through transatlantic trade, the diffusion of Brazilian gold also promoted the economies of all the major trading nations.

FRENCH AND BRITISH COLONIES IN NORTH AMERICA

French explorers moved down the St. Lawrence River valley in Canada during the 17th century. French fur traders and missionaries followed, with the French government sponsoring the missionary effort. By the end of the 17th century, Canada was sparsely populated by the French. Their largest settlement was Quebec, founded in 1608. It was primarily through the fur trade that French Canada functioned as part of the early transatlantic economy.

HOW WERE the economies of the French and British North American colonies integrated into the transatlantic economy?

The Fur Trade. Europeans and Indians, from an engraving of 1777.
©The Granger Collection, New York.

Beginning with the first successful settlement in Jamestown, Virginia, in 1607, English colonies spread along the eastern seaboard of the future United States. With the exception of Maryland, these colonies were Protestant. The Church of England dominated the southern colonies. In New England, varieties of Protestantism associated with or derived from Calvinism were in the ascendancy. In their religious affiliations, the English-speaking colonies manifested two important traits derived from the English experience. First, much of their religious life was organized around self-governing congregations. Second, their religious outlook derived from those forms of Protestantism that were suspicious of central political authority. In this regard, their cultural and political outlook differed sharply from the cultural and political outlook associated with the Roman Catholics of the Spanish Empire. In a sense, the ideologies of the extreme Reformation and Counter-Reformation confronted each other in the Americas.

The English colonists had complex interactions with the Native American populations. They had only modest interest in missionizing the natives and, as in South America, European diseases took a high toll on the native population. Unlike Mexico and Peru, however, North America had no large Native American cities. The Native American populations were dispersed, and intertribal animosity was intense. The English often used one tribe against another, and the Native Americans also tried to use the English or the French in their own conflicts. From the late 17th century through the American Revolution, however, the Native Americans were drawn into the Anglo-French Wars that were fought in North America as well as Europe (see Chapter 20).

The economies of the English-speaking colonies were primarily agricultural. From New England through the Middle Atlantic states, there were mostly small farms tilled by free white labor; from Virginia southward a plantation economy dependent on slavery predominated. The principal ports—Boston, Newport, New York, Philadelphia, Baltimore, and Charleston—were the chief centers through which goods moved back and forth between the colonies and England and the West Indies. The commercial economies of these cities were all related to the transatlantic slave trade.

Until the 1760s, most Americans, like their English counterparts, were monarchists who were suspicious of monarchical power. Their politics involved patronage and individual favors. Their society was hierarchical. It had an elite that functioned like an aristocracy and many ordinary people who were dependent on that aristocracy. Throughout the colonies during the 18th century, the Anglican church grew in influence and membership. The prosperity of the colonies might eventually have led them to separate from England, but in 1750 few people anticipated that break.

Roanoke. The first successful English colonies in North America in the 17th century were preceded by two failed efforts on Roanoke Island in what is now North Carolina in the late 16th century. John White accompanied both attempts, the second as governor. White was a perceptive and sensitive observer whose watercolor paintings provide invaluable information about Native American life in the coastal Carolina region at the time of contact. This painting shows the Algonquian village of Secoton. The houses were bark-covered. In the lower left is a mortuary temple. Dancers in the lower right are performing a fertility ceremony. The man sitting in the platform in the upper right is keeping birds away from the corn crop.

The Bridgeman Art Library International Ltd.

Both England and France had important sugar islands in the Caribbean, with plantations worked by African slaves. The trade and commerce of the northern British colonies were focused on meeting the needs of these islands.

SLAVERY IN THE AMERICAS

Black slavery was the final mode of forced or subservient labor in the New World. It extended throughout the Americas.

ESTABLISHMENT OF SLAVERY

As the numbers of Native Americans in South America declined, the Spanish and Portuguese turned to African slaves. By the late 1500s, in the West Indies and the cities of South America, black slaves surpassed the white population.

On much of the South American continent dominated by Spain, slavery declined during the late 17th century, but it continued to thrive in Brazil and in the Caribbean. In British North America, it began with the importation of slaves to Jamestown in 1619, and quickly became a fundamental institution.

The spread of slavery in Brazil and the West Indies was promoted by the market for sugar. Only slave labor could provide enough workers for the sugar plantations. As the production of sugar expanded, so did the demand for slaves.

By 1700, the Caribbean Islands were the world center for sugar production. As the European appetite for sugar grew, so did the slave population. By 1725, black slaves may have constituted almost 90 percent of the population of the West Indies. There and in Brazil and the southern British colonies, prosperity and slavery went hand in hand. The wealthiest colonies were those that raised consumer staples, such as sugar, rice, tobacco, or cotton, by slave labor.

THE PLANTATION ECONOMY AND TRANSATLANTIC TRADE

The **plantation economy** encompassed plantations that stretched from Maryland through the West Indies and into Brazil and formed a vast corridor of slave societies. This kind of society—defined by a total dependence on slave labor and racial difference—had not existed before the European discovery and exploitation of the Americas. The social and economic influence of plantation slavery also touched West Africa, Europe, and New England. It persisted from the 16th century through the second half of the 19th century. Every society in which it existed still contends with its effects.

The slave trade was part of the larger system of transatlantic trade that linked Europe, Africa, and the European colonies in the Americas. In this system, the Americas supplied labor-intensive raw materials (tobacco, sugar, coffee, precious metals, cotton, and indigo). Europe supplied manufactured goods (textiles, liquor, guns, metal wares, and beads) and cash. Africa supplied gold,

WHICH ECONOMIC factors led to the spread of slavery in the New World?

plantation economy Economic system stretching between Chesapeake Bay and Brazil that produced crops, especially sugar, cotton, and tobacco, using slave labor on large estates.

Slave Auction Notice. Africans who survived the voyage across the Atlantic were immediately sold into slavery in the Americas. This slave-auction notice describes a group of slaves whose ship had stopped at Charleston, South Carolina, and then landed elsewhere in the region to auction its human cargo. Notice the concern to assure potential buyers that the slaves were healthy.

Corbis-Bettmann.

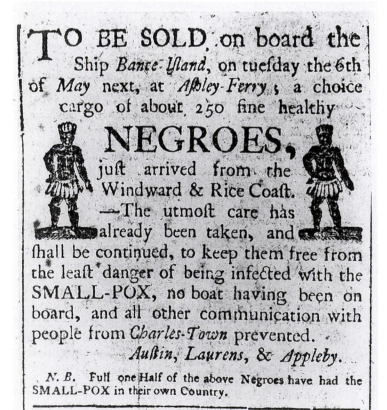

ivory, wood, palm oil, gum, and other products, as well as the slaves who provided the labor to create the American products. By the 18th century, slaves were
the predominant African export.

SLAVERY ON THE PLANTATIONS

The American plantations to which the African slaves arrived produced for an
overseas market that was part of a larger integrated transatlantic economy. In
turn, plantation owners imported virtually all the finished or manufactured
goods they consumed.

The conditions of plantation slaves differed from colony to colony. Vast
slave holdings were the exception. Black slaves living in Portuguese areas had the
fewest legal protections. In the Spanish colonies, the church provided some protection, but devoted more effort to protecting Native Americans. Slave codes in
the British and the French colonies provided only the most limited protection.
Regulations were designed to prevent slave revolts and favored the master rather
than the slave. Masters were permitted to punish slaves by harsh corporal punishment. Slaves were forbidden to gather in large groups lest they plan a rebellion.
Slave marriages were usually not recognized by law. Children of slaves were
owned by the owner of the parents, and slave families could be separated by sale
or inheritance. The death rate among slaves was high. Their lives were sacrificed
to the ongoing expansion of the plantations that made their owners wealthy and
that produced goods for consumers in Europe.

The African slaves who were transported to the Americas were converted to
Christianity: in the Spanish domains to Roman Catholicism, and in the English
colonies to Protestantism. In both cases, they were largely separated from
African religious traditions. Although slaves mixed Christianity with some
African religion, the conversion of Africans to Christianity represented another
example of the crushing of non-European cultural values in the New World.

Europeans were also prejudiced against black Africans. Many Europeans
thought Africans were savages or looked down on them because they were slaves.
These attitudes had been shared by both Christians and Muslims in the
Mediterranean world, where slavery had long existed. Furthermore, many
European cultures attached negative connotations to blackness. Although racial
thinking in regard to slavery became more important in the 19th century, the
fact that slaves were differentiated from the rest of the population by race as well
as by their status as chattel property was fundamental to the system.

AFRICA AND THE TRANSATLANTIC SLAVE TRADE

*T*he establishment of plantations demanding slave labor drew Africa into
the heart of the transatlantic economy. As Native Americans were decimated by conquest and disease or proved unsatisfactory as plantation
laborers, colonial entrepreneurs began to look elsewhere for workers. The
Portuguese first, and then the Spanish, Dutch, French, and English, turned to
Africa for slaves. The Atlantic slave trade was not overtly the result of racist
principles but of the economic needs of the colonial powers and their willingness (based on tacit racist assumptions) to exploit weaker peoples to satisfy
those needs.

The Portuguese were the principal transporters throughout most of the history of the slave trade. During the 18th century, which saw the greatest shipments,

Job Ben Solomon. Captured by
Mandingo enemies and sold to a
Maryland tobacco planter, Job Ben
Solomon accomplished the nearly
impossible feat of returning to Africa
as a free man. By demonstrating his
talents as a Muslim scholar, including
his ability to write the entire Qur'an
from memory, he astonished his owners and eventually convinced them to
let him go home.

"The Fortunate Slave," An Illustration of African
Slavery in the early 18th century by Douglas Grant
(1968). From "Some Memoirs of the Life of Job,"
by Thomas Bluett (1734). Photo by Robert D. Rubic/
Precision Chromes, Inc. The New York Public
Library, Research Libraries.

WHY WAS the transatlantic slave
trade so economically important?

15.3

Olaudah Equiano, *The Interesting Narrative of the Life of Olaudah Equiano, or Gustavus Vassa, the African*

the French and English carried almost half the total traffic. Americans were avid slavers who managed to make considerable profits even after Britain and the United States outlawed slaving in 1807 (see Map 18–3.)

Slaving was an important part of the massive new overseas trade that financed much of the European and American economic development that so changed the West during the 19th century. This trade, bought at the price of immense human suffering, helped propel Europe and some of its colonial off-shoots in the Americas to world dominance.

MAP EXPLORATION

Interactive map: To explore this map further, go to **http://www.prenhall.com/craig/map18.3**

MAP 18–3

The Slave Trade, 1400–1860. Slavery is an ancient institution and complex slave-trading routes were in existence in Africa, the Middle East, and Asia for centuries, but it was the need to supply labor for the plantations of the Americas that led to the greatest movement of peoples across the face of the earth.

WHY WAS the slave trade so economically important?

THE BACKGROUND OF SLAVERY

Slavery seems to have been a tragic fact of human societies as far back as we can trace it. Although linked to warfare, it cannot be explained by military or economic necessity.

Virtually every premodern state around the globe depended on slavery. The Mediterranean and African worlds were no exception. Slave institutions in sub-Saharan Africa were ancient. The Islamic states of southwestern Asia and North Africa increased this traffic, although they took fewer slaves from Africa than from Eastern Europe and central Asia. (Hence it is not surprising that the word *slave* is derived ultimately from *Slav.*) Both Mediterranean-Christian and Islamic peoples were using slaves—mostly Greeks, Bulgarians, Turkish prisoners of war, and Black Sea Tartars, but also Africans—before the voyages of discovery opened sub-Saharan sources of slaves for the new European colonies.

Not all forms of slavery were as dehumanizing as the chattel slavery in the Americas. Islamic law, for example, ameliorated slavery. All slavery, however, involved the forceful exploitation and degradation of human beings, the denial of basic freedoms, and the sundering of family ties.

Africa suffered immense social devastation when it was the chief supplier of slaves to the world. Societies that were built on the exploitation of African slavery also suffered enduring consequences, not the least of which is racism.

SLAVERY AND SLAVING IN AFRICA

The trade that supplied African slaves to the Islamic lands and Asia has been termed the "oriental" slave trade. The Sudan and the Horn of Africa were the two prime sources of slaves for this trade. The trade managed by Europeans is called the "occidental" slave trade. Voyages beginning in the 15th century by first the Portuguese and then other Europeans made the western coasts of Africa as far south as Angola the prime slaving areas.

Before the full development of the transatlantic slave trade (about 1650), slavery and slave trading had been no more significant in Africa than anywhere else.[1] Indigenous African slavery resembled that of other premodern societies. Estimates suggest that about 10,000 slaves per year, most of them female, were taken from sub-Saharan Africa through the oriental trade.

By about 1650, the newer occidental slave trade of the Europeans had become as large as the oriental trade and for the ensuing two centuries far surpassed it. It affected all of Africa, disrupting especially western and central African

A Slave Coffle. This 18th-century print shows bound African captives being forced to a slaving port. It was largely African middlemen who captured slaves in the interior and marched them to the coast.

North Wind Picture Archives.

15.2
"Our Kingdom is Being Lost," Nzinga Mbemba (Affonso I)

Estimated Slave Imports into the Americas and Old World by Region, 1451–1870

British North America	523,000
Spanish America	1,687,000
British Caribbean	2,443,000
French Caribbean	1,655,000
Dutch Caribbean	500,000
Danish Caribbean	50,000
Brazil (Portuguese)	4,190,000
Old World	297,000
Total	**11,345,000**

Figures as calculated by James A. Rawley, *The Transatlantic Slave Trade: A History* (New York: W. W. Norton, 1981), p. 428, based on his and other more recent revisions of the careful but older estimates of Philip D. Curtin, *The Atlantic Slave Trade: A Census* (Madison: University of Wisconsin Press, 1969), especially pp. 266, 268.

[1] The summary follows closely that of P. Manning, *Slavery and African Life: Occidental, Oriental, and African Slave Trades* (Cambridge: Cambridge University Press, 1990), pp. 127–140.

Conquest of the Americas and the Transatlantic Slave Trade

1494	The Treaty of Tordesillas divides the overseas empires of Spain and Portugal
1500	The Portuguese arrive in Brazil
1519–1521	Hernan Cortés conquers the Aztec Empire
1531–1533	Francisco Pizarro conquers the Inca Empire
1607	Jamestown, Virginia, first permanent English settlement in North America, founded
1608	The French found Quebec
1619	First African slaves brought to British North America
1650	Transatlantic slave trade becomes bigger than the older oriental slave trade
1700s	More than 6 million slaves imported from Africa to the Americas
1807	Slavery abolished in British domains
1808	The importation of slaves abolished in the United States
1874–1928	Indigenous African slavery abolished
1888	Slavery abolished in Brazil

society. As a result of the demand for young male slaves on the plantations of the Americas, West Africa experienced a sharp drain on its productive male population. Between 1640 and 1690, the number of slaves sold to European carriers doubled, indicating the increasing participation of Africans in the trade. The demand for slaves increased internal warfare in western and central Africa. Moreover, as the external trade destroyed the male-female population balance, an internal market for female slaves arose.

These developments accelerated during the 18th century when African states and slave traders were most heavily involved in the trade. The population declined sharply in the coastal and inland areas hardest hit by the ravages of the trade.

As European and American nations began to outlaw slaving and slavery in the 19th century, the oriental and internal trades increased. Slave exports from East Africa and the Sudan and Horn increased after about 1780, and indigenous African slavery also expanded. This traffic was dominated by the same figures—merchants, warlords, and rulers—who had profited from external trade.

Indigenous African slavery began a real decline only at the end of the 19th century because of the dominance of European colonial regimes and internal changes. The formal end of African indigenous slavery occurred only in 1928 in Sierra Leone.

THE AFRICAN SIDE OF THE TRANSATLANTIC TRADE

Africans were actively involved in the transatlantic slave trade. European slave traders generally obtained their human cargoes from private or government-sponsored African middlemen along the coast. This situation was the result of both the ability of Africans to control inland trade and the vulnerability of Europeans to tropical disease. Thus, it was largely African middlemen who undertook the capture or procurement of slaves and the difficult task of marching them to the coast. These middlemen were generally either wealthy merchants or the agents of African chieftaincies or kingdoms.

The media of exchange for slaves varied. At first the items were usually gold dust, firearms, or alcohol. Increasingly, they involved monetary payments. This trade drained productive resources (human beings) in return for nonproductive wealth.

The chief West and central African slaving regions provided different numbers of slaves at different times, and the total number of exported slaves varied between periods. When one area could not meet demand, the European traders shifted to other locales. Traders went where population density and African merchant or state suppliers promised the best numbers and prices.

THE EXTENT OF THE SLAVE TRADE

The slave trade fluctuated greatly from period to period. It peaked between 1701 and 1810, accounting for more than 60 percent of the total. The final half-century of slaving (ending in 1870) accounted for more than 20 percent of the total. The Portuguese transported more than a million slaves to Brazil between

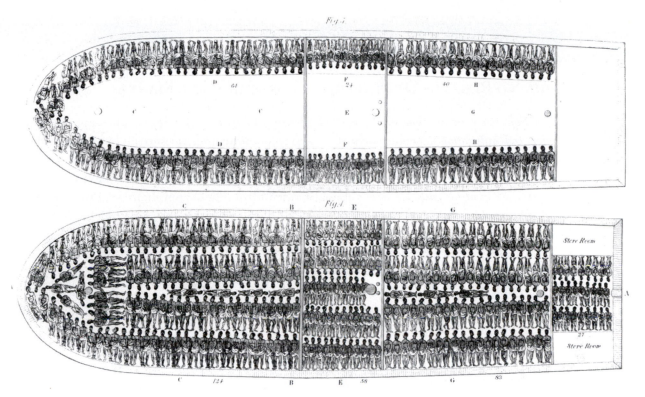

1811 and 1870. It is sobering to contemplate how long it took the "modern" occidental world to abolish the trade in African slaves.

The overall number of African slaves exported during the occidental trade—effectively, between 1451 and 1870—is still debated and must be seen in the larger context of all types of slaving in Africa in the same period. A major unknown is the number of slaves who died under the brutal conditions to which they were subjected when captured and transported overland and by sea. The most reliable estimates pertain only to those slaves who actually landed abroad. As the table on page 443 shows, just those who actually reached an American or Old World destination in the occidental trade totaled more than 11 million.

At a minimum, Africa lost some 13 million people to the Atlantic trade alone. Another 5 million or more were lost to the oriental trade. Finally, according to the estimate of one expert, an additional 15 million people were enslaved within African societies themselves.[2]

CONSEQUENCES OF THE SLAVE TRADE FOR AFRICA

Statistics hint at the massive impact slave trading had on African life, but the actual effects remain in dispute. We do not know for certain if the Atlantic trade brought net population loss or gain to specific areas of West Africa. The rapid spread of maize and cassava cultivation in forest regions after these plants were imported from the Americas may have fueled African population increases that offset regional human loss through slaving. We know, however, that slaving took away many of the strongest young men and, in the oriental-trade zones, most of the young women. Similarly, we do not know if more slaves were captured as byproducts of local wars or from pure slave raiding, but we do know they were captured and removed from their societies (see "Olaudah Equiano Recalls His Experience at the Slave Market in Barbados").

Slave Ship. Loading plan for the main decks of the 320-ton slave ship *Brookes*. The *Brookes* was only 25 feet wide and 100 feet long, but as many as 609 slaves were crammed onboard for the nightmarish passage to the Americas. The average space allowed each person was only about 78 inches by 16 inches.

Photographs and Prints Division, Schomburg Center for Research in Black Culture, The New York Public Library, Astor, Lenox, and Tilder Foundations.

[2]Ibid., pp. 37, 170–171.

HISTORY'S VOICES

OLAUDAH EQUIANO RECALLS HIS EXPERIENCE AT THE SLAVE MARKET IN BARBADOS

O*laudah Equiano composed one of the most popular and influential slave narratives of the late 18th and early 19th centuries. He also led a remarkable life. Born in West Africa in what is today Nigeria, he spent his early life among the Ibo. He was captured and sold into slavery, making the dreaded Atlantic crossing. In the passage that follows, Equiano recounts his arrival in Barbados and the experience of cultural disorientation, his sale into slavery, and seeing Africans separated from their families. His life did not end in slavery, the most destructive aspects of which he also described in vivid detail. He achieved his freedom and then had an adventuresome career sailing on various commercial and military ships plying the Caribbean, the Atlantic, and the Mediterranean. Equiano also made a trip to the Arctic Ocean. His account consequently describes not only the life of a person taken from Africa and sold into American slavery, but also the life of a person who, once free, explored the entire transatlantic world. His autobiographical narrative, which first appeared in 1789 and displayed Equiano's wide reading, served two purposes for the antislavery campaign that commenced in the second half of the 18th century. First, it provided a firsthand report of the slave experience in crossing from Africa to America. Second, his powerful rhetoric and clear arguments demonstrated that, if free, Africans could achieve real personal independence. Many defenders of slavery had denied that Africans possessed the character and intelligence to be free.*

WHAT WERE the fears of the Africans on the slave ship as they approached the port? How were older slaves in Barbados used to calm their fears? How did the sale of slaves proceed? What happened to African families in the process of the sale?

At last, we came in sight . . . of Barbados, . . . and we soon anchored . . . off Bridgetown. Many merchants and planters now came on board. . . . They put us in separate parcels, and examined us attentively. They also made us jump, and pointed to the land, signifying we were to go there. We thought by this we should be eaten by these ugly men, as they appeared to us; and when, soon after we were all put down under the deck again, there was much dread and trembling among us, and nothing but bitter cries to be heard all the night from these apprehension, insomuch that at last the white people got some old slaves from the land to pacify us. They told us we were not to be eaten, but to work, and were soon to go on land, where we should see many of our country people. This report eased us much. . . . We were conducted immediately to the merchant's yard, where we were all pent up together like so many sheep in a fold, without regard to sex or age. As every object was new to me, everything filled me with surprise . . . and indeed I thought these people were full of nothing but magical arts. . . . We were not many days in the merchant's custody before we were sold after their usual manner which was this: On a signal given (as the beat of a drum), the buyers rush at once into the yard where the slaves are confined, and make choice of that parcel they like best. The noise and clamour with which this is attended, and the eagerness visible in the countenances of the buyers, serve not a little to increase the apprehension of the terrified Africans, who may well be supposed to consider them as the ministers of that destruction to which they think themselves devoted. In this manner, without scruple, relations and friends separate, most of them never to see each other again. I remember in the vessel in which I was brought over, in the men's apartment, there were several brothers who, in the sale, were sold in different lots; and it was very moving on this occasion to see and hear their cries at parting. . . . Surely this is a new refinement in cruelty, which, while it has no advantage to atone for it, thus aggravates distress, and adds fresh horrors even to the wretchedness of slavery.

Source: *The Interesting Narrative of the Life of Olaudah Equiano or Gustavus Vassa, The African, Written by Himself* (first published 1789), as quoted in Henry Louis Gates Jr., and William L. Andrews, eds., *Pioneers of the Black Atlantic: Five Slave Narratives from the Enlightenment, 1772–1815* (Washington, DC: Counterpoint, 1998), pp. 221–223.

Nor do we know if slaving inhibited trade or stimulated it. Commerce in African products from ivory to wood and hides often accompanied that in slaves. Still, we do know that the exchange of productive human beings for money or goods that were not used to build a productive economy was ultimately a loss for African society.

Finally, because we do not yet have accurate estimates of the total population of Africa at different times over the four centuries of the Atlantic slave trade, we cannot determine with certainty its demographic impact. We can, however, make educated guesses. If, for example, tropical Africa had 50 million inhabitants in 1600, it would then have had 30 percent of the combined population of the Americas, the Middle East, Europe, and Africa. If in 1900, after the depredations of the slave trade, it had 70 million inhabitants, its population would have dropped to about 10 percent of the combined population of the same world regions. Current estimates indicate that overall African population growth suffered significantly as a result of the slave trade. Figures like these also give some idea of slavery's probable impact on Africa's ability to keep up with the modern industrializing world.[3]

Even in West and central Africa, which bore the brunt of the Atlantic trade, its impact and the response to it were varied. In a few cases, kingdoms such as Dahomey (the present Republic of Benin) seem to have derived immense economic profit by making slaving a state monopoly. Other kingdoms derived no gain from it. In many instances, including the rise of Asante power or the fall of the Yoruba Oyo Empire, increased slaving was a result as well as a cause of regional change. Increased warfare meant increased prisoners to be sold; however, whether slaving was a motive for war is still unclear.

Similarly, if it can be established, as seems evident, that a major increase in indigenous slavery was a result of the external trade to occident and orient, we have to assume major social consequences for African society. The specific consequences would, however, differ according to regional situations. For example, in West Africa more men were taken as slaves than women, whereas in the Sahelian Sudanic regions, more women than men were taken. In the west, the loss of so many men increased the pressures for polygamy and possibly the use of female slaves, whereas in the Sahelian Sudanic regions, the loss of women may have stimulated polyandry and reduced the birthrate.

Even though slavery existed previously in Africa, the scale of the Atlantic trade was unprecedented and hence had an unprecedented impact. In general, the slave trade changed patterns of life and balances of power in the main affected areas, whether by stimulating trade or warfare, by disrupting market and political structures, by increasing slavery inside Africa, or by disturbing the male-female ratio (and hence the work-force balance and birthrate patterns) and consequently the basic social institution of monogamous marriage.

[3]Ibid., pp. 126–148, 168–176.

Plantation. In the American South, the islands of the Caribbean, and in Brazil, slaves labored on sugar plantations under the authority of overseers.

The Granger Collection.

QUICK REVIEW

Difficulties in Determining Consequences of the Slave Trade

- Do not know how slave trade affected specific West African regions
- Cannot determine number of slaves captured during wars and captured during pure slave raiding
- Do not know how slave trading affected commerce in African products

The overseas slave trade at the least siphoned off indigenous energy and channeled it in counterproductive or destructive directions. This inhibited economic development. The Atlantic slave trade was one of the most tragic aspects of European involvement in Africa.

IMAGE KEY

for pages 434–435

a. Job Ben Solomon, a freed slave who returned to Africa

b. A poster for a slave auction in Charleston

c. John Singleton Copley, "Watson and the Shark," ca. 1778

d. A chunk of silver metal and rock

e. Spanish map showing the seven cities of Cibola and Baja California, 16th century

f. Dried tobacco leaves

g. Slave ship, ca. 1790

h. Samuel Scott, "Old Custom House Quay"

i. Bartolemé de Las Casas

j. Slaves grinding sugar cane and refining sugar

k. Fur traders and Indians

l. Slaves harvest sugar cane on a plantation

SUMMARY

European Conquest of the New World Contact between the native peoples of the American continents and the European explorers of the 15th and 16th centuries transformed world history. In the Americas, the native peoples had established a wide variety of civilizations. Some of their most remarkable architectural monuments and cities were constructed during the centuries when European civilizations were reeling from the collapse of Roman power. Until the European explorations, the civilizations of the Americas and Eurasia and Africa had no significant contact with one another.

Within half a century of Columbus's landing, millions of America's native peoples encountered Europe's intent on conquest, exploitation, and religious conversion. Because of their advanced weapons, navies, and the diseases they brought with them, as well as internal divisions among the Native Americans themselves, Europeans achieved a rapid conquest.

The Transatlantic Economy In both North and South America, economies of exploitation were established. In Latin America, various institutions were developed to extract native labor. From the mid-Atlantic English colonies through the Caribbean and into Brazil, slave-labor plantation systems were established. Slaves were forcibly imported from Africa and sold in America to plantation owners. The economies and peoples of Europe, Africa, and the Americas were thus drawn into a worldwide web of production based on slave labor.

Slavery The impact of slavery in the Americas was not limited to the life of the black slaves. Whites in the New World numbered about 12 million in 1820, compared to some 6 million blacks. However, only about 2 million whites had migrated there, compared to some 11 million or more Africans forcibly imported as slaves. Such numbers reveal the effects of brutal slave conditions and the high mortality and low birthrates of slave populations.

None of these statistics, however, enables us to asses the role that slavery has played in the Americas or, in particular, the United States. The United States actually received only a bit more than a quarter as many slaves as did Brazil alone or the British and French Caribbean regions together, yet the consequences of the forced migration of just over a half-million Africans remain massive. Consider just the American Civil War and the endurance of racism and inequality or, more positively, the African contribution to American industrial development, language, music, literature, and artistic culture. The Atlantic slave trade's impact continues to be felt at both ends of the original trade route.

REVIEW QUESTIONS

1. How were small groups of Spaniards able to conquer the Aztec and Inca Empires?

2. What was the the mercantilist economic theory? How accuately did it describe the relationship between the colonies and their homelands?

3. Why did forced labor and slavery develop in tropical colonies? How was slavery in the Americas different from slavery in earlier societies?

4. What was the effect of the transatlantic slave trade on African societies? What role did Africans themselves play in the slave trade?

KEY TERMS

Black Legend (p. 439)   *encomienda* (p. 440)   **peninsulares** (p. 441)
conquistadores (p. 439)   *hacienda* (p. 441)   **plantation economy** (p. 446)
debt peonage (p. 441)   **mercantilism** (p. 436)   *repartimiento* (p. 440)

  For additional study resources for this chapter, go to:
www.prenhall.com/craig/chapter18

19 East Asia in the Late Traditional Era

CHAPTER HIGHLIGHTS

China China's last two imperial dynasties were the Ming (1368–1644) and the Qing or Manchus (1644–1911). Although China could not match the dynamism of the West during these years, its society became more integrated and its government more sophisticated. The population reached 410 million, cities grew, and commerce expanded. Chinese government depended on the Confucian bureaucracy and the gentry class. Under the Manchus, China expanded to the east and annexed Taiwan. There also was growing trade with the West, especially Britain, but it was conducted under highly restricted terms by Chinese officials.

Japan After more than a century of civil war among the warrior aristocracy (the Warring States Era, 1467–1600), the Tokugawa shoguns (1600–1868) restored order. Their government controlled the aristocracy and encouraged economic growth. Christianity, which had made many converts in Japan, was driven underground, and Japan was closed to the outside world except for a small Dutch presence at Nagasaki. Japanese drama, literature, and art flourished, as did commercial life.

Korea and Vietnam China considered both Korea and Vietnam to be tributary states, and both countries adopted Chinese Confucian culture and forms of government while preserving their political independence.

CHAPTER QUESTIONS

WHY DID the Chinese accept Manchu rule?

WHAT WAS the "Warring States Era" in Japan?

HOW DID the Tokugawa control Japan?

HOW DID Chinese culture influence Korea and Vietnam?

CHAPTER OUTLINE

LATE IMPERIAL CHINA
- Ming (1368–1644) and Qing (1644–1911) Dynasties

JAPAN
- Warring States Era (1467–1600)
- Tokugawa Era (1600–1868)

KOREA AND VIETNAM
- Korea
- Vietnam
- Southeast Asia

This chapter underlines the dynamism of China and Japan during the centuries between the "medieval" and the "modern" eras. "Late traditional society" does not mean "late static society." In both countries, social structures became more integrated and the apparatus of government became more sophisticated. These advances shaped Chinese and Japanese responses to the West during the 19th century. Even Korea and Vietnam did not lack dynamism. But during these centuries the West was transformed. As we view East Asia from the perspective of Europe, it appears to have been in slow motion, but the truth was that the West was rapidly accelerating.

LATE IMPERIAL CHINA

MING (1368–1644) AND QING (1644–1911) DYNASTIES

WHY DID the Chinese accept Manchu rule?

The Ming and the Qing were China's last dynasties. The former was Chinese, the latter a foreign dynasty (Manchus) established by conquest. The two were nevertheless remarkably similar in their institutions and pattern of rule.

LAND AND PEOPLE

China's population reached about 410 million people in the mid-19th century. This population density stimulated commerce and gave new prominence to the scholar-gentry. Population growth was paralleled by an increase in the food supply.

There are many unanswered questions regarding the population growth during these six centuries. Was there a decline in the death rate and, if so, why? Or did the development of new lands and technology enable more mouths to be fed? Certainly, the Ming–Qing Era was the longest continuous period of good government in Chinese history. But by the early 19th century, the Chinese standard of living may have begun to decline. An ever-increasing population was no blessing.

CHINA'S THIRD COMMERCIAL REVOLUTION

Early Ming emperors were isolationists with an agrarian orientation. They established government monopolies that stifled enterprise and depressed the southeastern coastal region by restricting maritime trade and shipping. In the mid-16th century, commerce started to grow again, buoyed by the surge of population and agriculture and a relaxation of government controls. If the growth during the Han and Song dynasties may be called China's first and second commercial revolutions, then the expansion between 1500 and 1800 was its third. By the early 19th century, China was the most highly commercialized nonindustrial society in the world.

One stimulus to commerce was imported silver. The Chinese balance of trade was favorable. Beginning in the mid-16th century, silver from Japan entered China, and from the 1570s, Spanish galleons brought in Mexican and Peruvian silver. In the 18th century, private **Shaanxi banks** opened branches throughout China to facilitate the transfer of funds and extend credit for trade. Eventually they opened offices in Singapore, Japan, and Russia. As in Europe, the influx of silver and the overall increase in liquidity led to inflation and commercial growth in China.

Urban growth between 1500 and 1800 was mainly at the level of market towns. These towns provided the link between the local markets and the larger

Shaanxi banks Private commercial banks in China under the Manchus.

provincial capitals and cities. Commercial integration of local, intermediate, and large cities spread over China. Interregional trade also gained, but China did not develop a national economy. Seven or eight regional economies, each the size of a large European nation, were the focus for most economic activity. But a new level of trade developed among them, especially where water transport made such trade economical.

Women and the Commercial Revolution   The Confucian family ideal changed little during the Ming and Qing dynasties. A woman was expected first to obey her parents, then her husband, and finally her son—when he succeeded his father as family head. Physically, women were more restricted as footbinding spread through the upper classes and to some commoners. One exception to the rule was the Manchus. One Manchu (Qing) emperor issued an edict banning footbinding, but it was ignored by the Chinese.

As population grew and the size of the average landholding shrunk, more women worked at home, making products for commercial markets. And as their contribution to the household income grew, their voice in household decisions often became larger than Confucian doctrines would suggest.

Foot Binding.   As a young girl her arches were broken and her feet forced into iron training shoes. Later, her deformed feet were encased in silk slippers, forcing her to walk with a slow and swaying gait.

AP WideWorld Photos.

QUICK REVIEW

Women Under the Qing and Ming
- Confucian family ideals changed little during the Ming and Qing eras
- Footbinding spread among the upper classes and some commoners
- As population grew, more women worked at home

Political System   Despite these massive demographic and economic changes, political superstructure of China changed very little. Government during the Ming and Qing was much like that of the Song or Yuan, only stronger. Sources of strength of the Ming–Qing system were the spread of education, the use of Confucianism as an ideology, stronger emperors, better government finances, more competent officials, and a larger gentry class with an expanded role in local society.

Role of Confucianism   Confucian teachings were more widespread in late imperial China than ever before. There were more schools. Academies preparing candidates for the civil service examinations multiplied, and literacy outpaced population growth. The Confucian view of society was patriarchal. The family, headed by the father, was the basic unit. The emperor, the son of Heaven and the ruler-father of the empire, stood at its apex. In between were the district magistrates, the "father-mother officials." The idea of the state as the family *writ large* carried with it duties and obligations at every level.

In comparison to Europe, where religious philosophies were less involved with the state and where a revolution in science was reshaping religious and political doctrines, China had greater unity and a more integrated worldview.

Emperor   Ming–Qing emperors were more powerful than ever and made all important decisions. They wielded despotic powers at their courts. They had secret police and prisons where those who committed even minor offenses might be tortured. Even high officials might suffer humiliating and fatal punishment. The dedication and loyalty even of officials who were cruelly mistreated attest to the depth of their Confucian ethical training.

During the Qing, the life-and-death authority of emperors did not diminish, but officials were generally better treated. As foreign rulers, the Manchu emperors took care not to alienate Chinese officials.

The Forbidden Palace in Beijing was an icon of the emperor's majesty. The entire palace complex focused on the ruler. Its massive walls and vast courtyards progress to the audience hall where the emperor sat on an elevated dais above

The great Manchu emperor Qianlong (r. 1736–1795).

© Metropolitan Museum of Art, Rogers Fund, 1942 (42.141.8).

gentry In China, a largely urban, landowning class that represented local interests and functioned as quasi-bureaucrats under the magistrates.

the officials, who knelt before him. Behind the audience hall were the emperor's private chambers and his harem. By the 17th century, there were 9,000 palace ladies and perhaps as many as 70,000 eunuchs. The glory of the emperor extended to his family, whose members were awarded vast estates in North China.

Bureaucracy A second component of the Ming–Qing system was the government itself. At the top were the military, the censorate, and the administrative branch; beneath the administration were the six ministries and the web of provincial, prefectural, and district offices. Government was better financed than during earlier dynasties. As late as the 1580s, huge surpluses were accumulated at both the central and the provincial levels. Only during the last 50 years of the Ming did soaring military expenses bankrupt the government. When, in the second half of the 17th century, the Manchus reestablished a strong central government, they restored the flow of taxes to levels close to those of the Ming.

The good government of the Ming–Qing system in China was largely a product of the ethical commitment and ability of its officials. No officials in the world today approach in power or prestige those of the Ming and the Qing. When the Portuguese arrived early in the 16th century, they called these officials "mandarins." The rewards of an official career were so great that the competition to enter it was intense. As the population grew and schools increased, entrance became ever more competitive. (see "The Seven Transformations of an Examination Candidate").

After being screened at the district office, a candidate took the county examination. If he passed, he became a member of the gentry and was exempted from state labor service. This examination required years of study. About half a million passed each year. The second hurdle was the provincial examination held every third year. Only one in a hundred was successful. The final hurdle was the metropolitan examination, also held triennially. Fewer than 90 passed each year.

Gentry A final component in the Ming–Qing system was the **gentry** class. It was an intermediate layer between the elite bureaucracy above and the village below. The lowest level of bureaucratic government was the district magistrate. Although the population increased sixfold during the Ming and the Qing, the number of district magistrates increased only from 1,171 to 1,470. To prevent conflicts of interest, an outsider was appointed as district magistrate. His office compound had a large staff of secretaries and advisers, but to govern effectively, he had to obtain the cooperation of the local *literati* or gentry.

By *gentry* we do not mean a rural elite, like English squires. The Chinese gentry was largely urban, living in market towns or district seats. Socially and educationally, its members were of the same class as the magistrate—a world

The Seven Transformations of an Examination Candidate

The Chinese civil service examination was a grueling ordeal. Like a chess tournament, it required physical and mental strength. Chinese critics said, "To pass the provincial examination a man needed the spiritual strength of a dragon-horse, the physique of a donkey, the insensitivity of a wood louse, and the endurance of a camel." The following selection is by a 17th-century writer who never succeeded in passing.

Is the style of this passage overdone or effective? What is distinctively Chinese about it?

When he first enters the examination compound and walks along, panting under his heavy load of luggage, he is just like a beggar. Next, while undergoing the personal body search and being scolded by the clerks and shouted at by the soldiers, he is just like a prisoner. When he finally enters his cell and, along with the other candidates, stretches his neck to peer out, he is just like the larva of a bee. When the examination is finished at last and he leaves, his mind in a haze and his legs tottering, he is just like a sick bird that has been released from a cage. While he is wondering when the results will be announced and waiting to learn whether he passed or failed, so nervous that he is startled even by the rustling of the trees and the grass and is unable to sit or stand still, his restlessness is like that of a monkey on a leash. When at last the results are announced and he has definitely failed, he loses his vitality like one dead, rolls over on his side, and lies there without moving, like a poisoned fly. Then, when he pulls himself together and stands up, he is provoked by every sight and sound, gradually flings away everything within his reach, and complains of the illiteracy of the examiners. When he calms down at last, he finds everything in the room broken. At this time he is like a pigeon smashing its own precious eggs. These are the seven transformations of a candidate.

Source: From I. Miyazaki, *China's Examination Hell*, trans. by C. Schirokauer. Copyright © 1976 Weatherhill, pp. 57–58.

apart from clerks or village headmen. They usually owned land, which enabled them to avoid manual labor and to send their children to private academies. As absentee landlords whose lands were worked by sharecroppers, they were often exploitative. But they also acted as local leaders. They represented community interests vis-à-vis the bureaucracy. They also performed quasi-official functions on behalf of their communities: maintaining schools and Confucian temples and repairing roads, bridges, canals, and dikes. The gentry class was the matrix from which officials arose; it was the local upholder of Confucian values.

Pattern of Manchu Rule   The collapse of the Ming dynasty in 1644 and the establishment of Manchu (Qing) rule was less of a break than might be imagined. First, the transition was short. Second, the Manchus, unlike the Mongols, were already partially Sinicized. Even before entering China, they had ruled over the Chinese settled in Manchuria.

In the late 16th century, an able leader unified the Manchurian tribes, proclaimed a new dynasty, and established a Confucian government. When the Ming collapsed, the Manchus presented themselves as the conservative upholders of the Confucian order. The Chinese gentry preferred the Manchus to Chinese rebel leaders, whom they regarded as bandits. After the Manchu

Late Imperial China

Ming Dynasty 1368–1644

1368–1398	Reign of first Ming emperor; Chinese armies invade Manchuria, Mongolia, and eastern Central Asia
1402–1424	Reign of third Ming emperor; Chinese armies invade Vietnam and Mongolia
1405–1433	Voyage of Zheng He to India and Africa
1415	Grand Canal reopened
1472–1529	Wang Yang-ming, philosopher
1592–1598	Chinese army battles Japanese army in Korea

Qing (Manchu) Dynasty 1644–1911

1668	Manchuria closed to Chinese immigrants (by Willow Palisade)
1661–1722	Reign of Kangxi
1681	Suppression of revolts by Chinese generals
1683	Taiwan captured
1689	China and Russia sign Treaty of Nerchinsk
1736–1795	Reign of Qianlong
1793	Macartney mission

conquest, most officials served its new Qing dynasty. The Qing as a Chinese dynasty dates from 1644.

As a tiny fraction of the Chinese population, the Manchus adopted institutions to maintain themselves as an ethnically separate elite group. One was their military organization. Manchu garrison forces were segregated and not put under the jurisdiction of Chinese officials. They were given stipends and lands to cultivate. They were forbidden to marry Chinese, their children had to study Manchu, and they were not permitted to bind the feet of their daughters. In 1668, northern and central Manchuria were closed to Chinese immigrants.

The second institutional feature was the appointment of one Chinese and one Manchu to each key post in the central government. At the provincial level, Chinese governors were overseen by Manchu governor-generals. Most officials and all district magistrates beneath the governors were Chinese.

A particular strength of the Manchu dynasty was the long reigns of two extremely able emperors, Kangxi (1661–1722) and Qianlong (1736–1795). Kangxi was a man of great vigor. He rose at dawn to read official documents before meeting with officials. He presided over palace examinations. Well versed in the Confucian classics, he won the support of scholars.

Kangxi also displayed an interest in European science, a subject he studied with Jesuit court astronomers. He opened four ports to foreign trade and carried out public works, improving the dikes on the Huai and Yellow Rivers and dredging the Grand Canal. During his reign, he made six tours of China's southern provinces. Kangxi, in short, was a model emperor.

Qianlong began his reign in 1736. Under his rule the Qing dynasty attained its highest level of prosperity and power. Like Kangxi, he was vigorous, wise, conscientious, careful, and hard-working. He visited South China on inspection tours and patronized scholars on a grand scale.

Only in his last years did Qianlong lose his grip and permit a court favorite to practice corruption on an almost unprecedented scale. In 1796, the White Lotus Rebellion broke out. Qianlong's successor put down the rebellion, but the ample financial reserves that had existed throughout the 18th century were never reestablished. China nevertheless entered the 19th century with its government intact and with a peaceful and stable society. There were few signs of what was to come.

MING–QING FOREIGN RELATIONS

Ming   The first Ming emperor (r. 1368–1398) oversaw the expansion of China's borders. By the time he died, China controlled the northern steppe and had recovered jurisdiction over the southern tier of Chinese provinces (see Map 19–1). During the reign of the third Ming emperor (1402–1424), northern Vietnam became a Chinese province and remained so for two decades.

The Ming emperors "managed" China's frontiers using a tribute system. Ambassadors of vassal kings acted out their subordination to the universal ruler

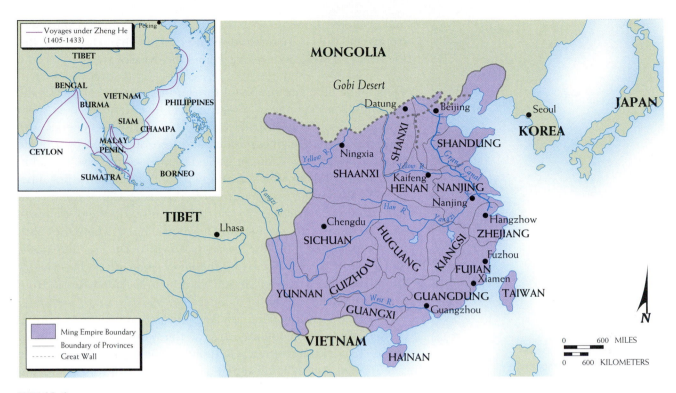

MAP 19–1
Ming Empire and the Voyages of Zheng He.   The inset map shows the voyages of Zeng He to Southeast Asia and India. Some ships of his fleet even reached East Africa. (Zheng himself did not.)

WHAT WAS the purpose of Zheng He's voyages?

of the celestial kingdom by approaching the emperor, performing the kowtow (kneeling three times and each time bowing his head to the floor three times), and presenting gifts. In return, the vassal kings were sent seals confirming their status, given permission to use the Chinese calendar and year-period names, and appointed to the Ming nobility.

The most far-ranging ventures of the third Ming emperor were the maritime expeditions that sailed to Southeast Asia, India, the Arabian Gulf, and East Africa between 1405 and 1433. They were commanded by the eunuch Zheng He, a Muslim from Yunnan (see Map 19–1). The first of these armadas had 62 major ships and carried 28,000 sailors, soldiers, and merchants. Trade was not the primary purpose. The expeditions were intended to make China's glory known to distant kingdoms and to enroll them in the tribute system.

The expeditions ended as abruptly as they had begun. They were costly at a time when the dynasty was fighting in Mongolia and building Beijing. What was remarkable about these expeditions was not that they came a half-century earlier than the Portuguese voyages of discovery, but that China had the maritime technology needed for exploration and chose not to use it. China lacked the combination of restlessness, greed, faith, and curiosity that motivated the Portuguese.

The chief threat to the Ming dynasty was the Mongols. In the 1430s, they captured the emperor, and in 1550 they overran Beijing. They were defeated by a Chinese army in the 1560s and signed a peace treaty in 1571.

A second threat came from Japan, whose pirates raided the Chinese coast in the 15th and 16th centuries. After Hideyoshi unifyied Japan, he twice invaded

16.2
Dynastic Change in China Tears a Family Apart

16.5
Letter to King George: China and Great Britain

Giraffe with Attendant. Some emperors had private zoos and gladly received exotic animals as gifts from tribute states. A painting by Shen Du (1357–1438).

Philadelphia. Museum of Art: Given by John T. Dorrance.

Western Factories in Canton (Guangzhou) c. 1800–1815. A factory was a trading post, not a manu-factory. This street scene shows many Chinese mingling with a few Westerners wearing tall hats. The factories were built on riverbanks outside the city walls. Western merchants were not allowed to bring their wives to China, they were tightly controlled by Chinese merchant guilds, and communicated with the Chinese in pidgin (business) English.

The Henry Francis du Pont Winterthur Museum, Inc.

and occupied Korea in 1592 between 1597 and 1598. China sent troops, and the Japanese withdrew after the death of Hideyoshi. But the strain on Ming finances weakened the dynasty.

Qing   The final and successful foreign threat to the Ming was the Manchus. After coming to power in 1644, the Manchu court spent decades consolidating its rule within China. Chinese generals who had helped the Manchus revolted and were supported by a pirate state on Taiwan. The emperor Kangxi suppressed the revolts, and in 1683 he took Taiwan, which became a part of China for the first time.

As always, the principal foreign threats to China came from the north and northwest. By the 1660s, Russian traders, trappers, and adventurers had reached northern Manchuria, where they built forts and traded with the eastern Mongols. During the 1680s, Kangxi drove the Russians from the lower Amur River. This victory led to the 1689 Treaty of Nerchinsk, which excluded Russia from northern Manchuria.

In the west, the situation was more complex, with a three-corner relationship among Russia, the western Mongols, and Tibet. Kangxi, and then Qianlong, campaigned against the Mongols, invaded Tibet, and in 1727 signed a new treaty with Russia. During the campaigns, the Chinese temporarily came to control millions of square miles of new territories. It is a telling comment on the Chinese concept of empire that ever since that time, even after China's borders contracted during the 19th century, the Chinese have insisted that the Manchu conquests of non-Chinese peoples define their legitimate borders. The roots of the present-day contention over borders between China and the countries of the former Soviet Union go back to these events during the 18th century, as does the Chinese claim to Tibet.

Contacts with the West   Europeans had made their way to China during the Tang and the Yuan dynasties. But only with Europe's oceanic expansion in the 16th century did they arrive in large numbers. Some came as missionaries, of whom the most successful were the Jesuits. They studied Chinese and the Confucian classics and conversed with scholars. They used their knowledge of astronomy, geography, engraving, and firearms to win entry to the court at Beijing and appointments in the bureau of astronomy.

When the Manchus came to power in 1644, the Jesuits kept their position. They appealed to the curiosity of the court with instruments such as telescopes, clocks, and clavichords. They tried to propagate Christianity. They attacked Daoism and Buddhism, but argued that Confucianism as a rational philosophy complemented Christianity, just as Aristotle's teaching complemented Christian theology in Europe. They interpreted the Confucian rites of ancestor worship as secular and nonantagonistic to Christianity. A few high court officials were converted.

Meanwhile, their Franciscan and Dominican rivals had reported to Rome that the Jesuits condoned the Confucian rites. Papal bulls in 1715 and

1742 forbade Chinese Christians to participate in the family rites of ancestor worship. Thereupon the emperor banned Christianity in China.

Other Europeans came to China to trade. The Portuguese came first in the early 16th century and were permitted to trade on a tiny peninsula at Macao. They were followed by the Dutch from the East Indies (Indonesia), by the British East India Company in 1699, and by Americans in 1784.

By the early 18th century, Westerners could trade only at Canton outside its walls along the river. They could not bring their wives to China. They were subject to Chinese law and were controlled by official merchant guilds. Nevertheless, the trade was profitable to both sides.

The British East India Company developed a triangular commerce among China, India, and Britain. For China, this trade produced an influx of specie, and the Chinese officials in charge grew immensely wealthy. Chafing under the restrictions, the British government in 1793 sent the Macartney mission to China to negotiate the opening of other ports, fixed tariffs, representation at Beijing, and so on. The emperor Qianlong permitted Lord Macartney (1736–1806) to present his gifts, which the Chinese described as tribute, but he turned down Macartney's requests. Western trade remained encapsulated at Canton.

MING–QING CULTURE

Chinese culture had begun to turn inward during the Song dynasty in reaction to Buddhism. This tendency continued into the Ming and Qing, when Chinese culture became virtually impervious to outside influences. This reflected a tradition and a social order that had stood the test of time, but it also indicated a closed system of ideas with weaknesses that would become apparent in the 19th century.

Ming and Qing Chinese highly esteemed the traditional categories of high culture: painting, calligraphy, poetry, and philosophy. Porcelains of great beauty were also produced. The pottery industry of Europe began during the 16th century to imitate these wares, and Chinese and Japanese influences have dominated Western ceramics ever since.

Chinese today see the novel as the characteristic cultural achievement of the Ming and Qing. The novel in China grew out of plot-books used by earlier storytellers. Like the stories, Chinese novels consisted of episodes strung together. As most novels were written in colloquial Chinese, which was not quite respectable in the society of scholars, their authors wrote under pseudonyms.

JAPAN

The two segments of late traditional Japan could not be more different. The Warring States Era (1467–1600), the last phase of Japan's medieval history, was marked by internal wars and anarchy. Within a century, all vestiges of the old manorial or estate system were scrapped and almost all of the Ashikaga lords were overthrown. The Tokugawa era (1600–1868) that followed saw Japan under a stronger government than ever before. During the Tokugawa era, Japanese

Ming Dynasty Ink Painting by Wu Wei (1479–1508). The seated human figure is a part of the tranquility of nature. Nature, densely concentrated at the left and lower portions of the painting, stretches off into space in the middle and upper-right portion.

Wu Wei, "Scholar Seated Under a Tree," China. Ink + traces of colour on silk. 14.7 × 8.25. Chinese and Japanese Special Fund. © 1996. All rights reserved. Courtesy of Museum of Fine Arts, Boston.

QUICK REVIEW

Chinese Contacts with the West
- Europeans arrived in China in large numbers after the 16th century
- The most successful missionaries were the Jesuits
- By the 18th century, Europeans could only trade at Canton

culture was transformed, preparing it for the challenge it would face during the mid-19th century.

WARRING STATES ERA (1467–1600)

WHAT WAS the "Warring States Era" in Japan?

*I*n 1467, a dispute arose over who would be the next Ashikaga shōgun. The dispute led to wars throughout Japan for 11 years. Most of Kyoto was destroyed in the fighting, and the authority of the Ashikaga bakufu came to an end. This first war ended in 1477, but the fighting resumed and continued for more than a century.

WAR OF ALL AGAINST ALL

Even before 1467, the Ashikaga equilibrium had been precarious. The regional **daimyo** lords had relied on their relationship to the *bakufu* to hold their stronger vassals in check, while relying on these vassals to preserve their independence against strong neighbors. The collapse of bakufu authority after 1467 left the regional lords standing alone, removing the last barrier to internecine wars. The regional lords became prey to the stronger among their vassals as well as to powerful neighboring states.

By the end of the 16th century, hundreds of little "Warring States daimyo" had emerged, each with his own warrior band. The constant wars among these men were not unlike those of the early feudal era in Europe. The most efficient in revamping their domains for military ends survived. The less ruthless, who clung to old ways, were defeated and absorbed.

As fighting continued, local states gave way to regional states until the late 16th century, all of Japan was brought under the hegemony of a single lord, Toyotomi Hideyoshi (1536–1598). But it was only with the victory of Tokugawa Ieyasu (1542–1616) at the Battle of Sekigahara in 1600 that true unification was finally achieved. Ieyasu radically transformed Japanese society.

daimyo Japanese territorial lord.

Warring States Japan and the Era of Unification (1467–1600)

1467–1568	Battles throughout Japan
1543	Portuguese arrive in Japan
1568	Oda Nobunaga takes Kyoto and partially unifies Japan
1575	Battle of Nagashino
1582	Nobunaga assassinated
1588	Hideyoshi starts sword hunt
1590	Hideyoshi completes unification
1592, 1597–1598	Hideyoshi sends armies to Korea
1597	Hideyoshi bans Christianity
1598	Hideyoshi dies, his generals battle for succession
1600	Battle of Sekigahara; Tokugawa reunifies Japan

FOOT SOLDIER REVOLUTION

During the Warring States period, the foot soldier replaced the aristocratic mounted warrior as the backbone of the military. Soldiers were still called *samurai* and were still vassals of a lord, but their numbers, social status, and techniques of warfare changed dramatically. All public lands and estates, including the emperor's, were seized and converted into fiefs, which were privately governed by the fief holder. A fief was not divided among heirs, but passed intact to the ablest son. Larger revenues made larger armies possible–in the tens of thousands. New weapons also appeared, a two-handed thrusting spear in the mid-14th century and muskets in the mid-16th century.

The society that emerged from the Warring States period might, in some sense, be described as feudal. By the late 16th century, all warriors in Japan were part of a pyramid of vassals and lords headed by a single overlord and warriors of rank held fiefs and vassals of their own. But in other respects, Japan was more like postfeudal Europe. First, most of the military class were soldiers, not aristocrats. Even though they were called samurai and were vassals, they were not given fiefs but were paid with stipends of rice. Second, unlike feudal England, where the military class was about one-quarter of 1 percent of the population, in mid-16th-century Japan the military may have reached 7 or 8 percent. It was comparable in size to European mercenary armies of the 14th or 16th centuries. Third, the recruitment of village warriors gave rise to problems. Taxes became harder to collect. Local samurai were often involved in uprisings that sometimes spread through whole provinces. Again, the parallels with postfeudal Europe seem closer. Fourth, even in a feudal society, not everything is feudal. Commercial growth continued in the Warring States Era.

DOCUMENT CD-ROM
16.7
The Laws for Military House (Buke Shohatto), 1615

FOREIGN RELATIONS AND TRADE

Japanese pirate-traders plied the seas of East Asia during the 15th and 16th centuries. To halt their depredations, the Ming emperor invited the third Ashikaga shōgun to trade with China. An agreement was reached in 1404. However, piracy stopped only after Japan was reunified at the close of the 16th century.

The content of the trade reflected the progress of Japanese crafts. Early Japanese exports to China were raw materials, but by the 16th century, manufactured goods were rising in importance. In exchange, Japan received copper cash, porcelains, paintings, books, and medicines. Then, in 1635, the imposition of a policy of national seclusion ended Japan's foreign trade. No Japanese were permitted to leave Japan, and the construction of large ships was prohibited.

Overlapping Japan's maritime expansion in the seas of East Asia was the arrival of European ships. Portuguese pirate-traders arrived in Japan in 1543. Spanish galleons came in 1587, and they were followed by the Dutch and the English after the turn of the century.

The Portuguese became important as shippers. They carried Southeast Asian goods and Japanese silver to China and Chinese silk to Japan, and they used their profits to buy spices for the European market.

Traders brought with them Jesuit missionaries, who concentrated their efforts on the samurai. Christian converts numbered about 300,000 in 1600—a higher percentage of Japanese were Christian than today. It is difficult to explain why Christianity met with greater success in Japan than in other Asian lands. When introduced, it was seen as a new Buddhist sect. There seemed little difference to the Japanese between the cosmic Buddha of Shingon and the Christian God, between the paradise of Amida and the Christian heaven, or between prayers to Kannon—the female *bodhisattva* of mercy—and to the Virgin Mary. The Japanese also noted the theological similarity between the pietism of the Pure Land sect and that of Christianity. The personal example of the Jesuits was also important.

The fortunes of Christianity began to decline in 1597, when six Spanish Franciscans and 20 Japanese converts were crucified in Nagasaki. Hideyoshi was aware of Spanish colonialism in the Philippines, and a Spanish pilot had apparently boasted that merchants

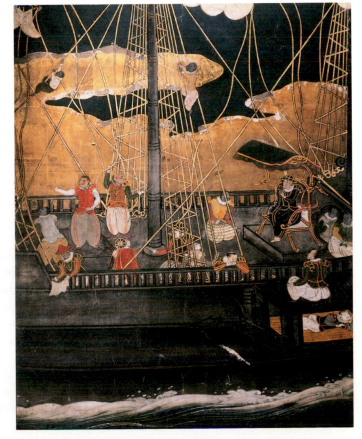

"The Arrival of the Portuguese in Japan." Portuguese merchants arrived in Japan in 1543 from India and the East Indies. Their crews were multiethnic, and they brought Jesuit priests as well.

Giraudon/Art Resource, N.Y.

and priests were preparing Japan for conquest. Sporadic persecutions continued until 1614, when Tokugawa Ieyasu formally banned the foreign religion. Some Christians recanted. More than 3,000 others were martyred. The last resistance was an uprising in 1637 and 1638 in which 37,000 Christians died. After that, Christianity survived in Japan only as a hidden religion. A few of these "hidden Christians" reemerged in the late 18th century.

HOW DID the Tokugawa control Japan?

TOKUGAWA ERA (1600–1868)

POLITICAL ENGINEERING AND ECONOMIC GROWTH DURING THE 17TH CENTURY

After the unifications of 1590 and 1600, Japan's leaders sought to create a peaceful, stable, orderly society. By the middle or late 17th century, Japan's society and political system had been radically reengineered. Vigorous economic and demographic growth had also occurred. This combination of political and economic change made the 17th century a period of great dynamism.

Hideyoshi's Rule   In the summer of 1588, Hideyoshi ordered a "sword hunt" to disarm the peasants. Once the hunt was completed, the 5 percent of the population who were still equipped as samurai used their monopoly on weapons to control the other 95 percent.

Hideyoshi next froze the social classes. Samurai were prohibited from quitting the service of their lord. Peasants were barred from abandoning their fields to become townspeople. Samurai, farmers, and townspeople tended to marry within their respective classes, and each class developed a unique cultural character.

Having disarmed the peasantry, Hideyoshi ordered surveys to define each parcel of land by location, size, soil quality, product, and cultivator's name. Hideyoshi's survey laid the foundations for a systematic land tax. Domains and fiefs were henceforth ranked in terms of their assessed yield.

Establishment of Tokugawa Rule   Hideyoshi assumed that his vassals would honor their oaths of loyalty to his heir, and he was especially trustful of his great ally Tokugawa Ieyasu. This trust, however, was misplaced. After his death in 1598, Hideyoshi's former vassals broke into two opposing camps. In 1600, they fought a great battle from which Tokugawa Ieyasu emerged victorious. Ieyasu established his headquarters in Edo (modern Tokyo), in the center of his military holdings in eastern Japan (see Map 19–2). He took the title of shōgun in 1603 and called his government the bakufu. Ieyasu then used his military power to reorganize Japan.

Ieyasu's first move was to confiscate the lands of his defeated enemies and use them to reward his vassals and allies. During the first quarter of the 17th century, the bakufu confiscated the domains of 150 daimyo and transferred 229 daimyo from one domain to another. The transfers severed long-standing ties between daimyo and their disarmed former village retainers. When a daimyo was transferred to a new fief, he took his samurai retainers with him. The rearrangement created a defensive system with the staunchest Tokugawa supporters nearest to the center of power.

The Tokugawa also established other controls. Legal codes regulated the imperial court, the temples and shrines, and the daimyo. Military houses were enjoined to use men of ability and to practice frugality. Only with bakufu consent could daimyo marry or repair their castles.

MAP EXPLORATION
Interactive map: To explore this map further, go to **http://www.prenhall.com/craig/map19.2**

MAP 19–2
Tokugawa Japan and the Korean Peninsula. The area between Edo and Osaka in central Honshu was both the political base of the Tokugawa bakufu and its rice basket. The domains that would overthrow the Tokugawa bakufu in the late 19th century were mostly in outlying areas of southwestern Japan.

WHAT CONTROLS did the Tokugawa impose to restrain the daimyo?

The Tokugawa also established a hostage system that required the wives and children of daimyo to reside permanently in Edo and the daimyo themselves to spend every second year in Edo. This transformed feudal lords into courtiers.

Another key control was the national policy of seclusion. Seclusion was no barrier to cultural imports from China and Korea. But except for small Chinese and Dutch trading contingents at Nagasaki, no foreigners were permitted to enter Japan, and on pain of death no Japanese were allowed to go abroad. Nor could oceangoing ships be built. This policy was strictly enforced until 1854. Seclusion enclosed the system of Tokugawa rule. Cut off from outside political contacts, for the Japanese, their homeland became the world.

The Commercial District of Osaka, the "kitchen" of Tokugawa Japan. Warehouses bear the crests of their merchant houses. Ships (upper right) loaded with rice, cotton goods, *sake*, and other goods are about to depart for Edo (Tokyo). Their captains vied with one another to arrive first and get the best price.

Courtesy Albert Craig.

QUICK REVIEW

The Japanese Economy
- Agricultural production doubled between 1600 and 1700
- Peace sustained economic growth
- Economic growth and national integration led to a rich and diverse urban society

Kabuki Realistic form of Japanese theater similar to English Elizabethan drama.

Nō play Highly stylized form of Japanese drama in which the chorus provides the narrative line as in classical Greek plays.

The 17th-Century Economy The political dynamism of the period from Hideyoshi through the first century of Tokugawa rule was matched by economic growth. Resources no longer needed for war were allocated to land reclamation and agriculture. This doubled food production, which led to a doubling of population from about 12 million in 1600 to 24 million in 1700.

Peace also sustained growth in commerce. Medieval guilds were abolished and Japan's central markets were freed from monopolistic restrictions. The result was a burgeoning of trade and the formation of a national market network. As this network expanded, economic functions became more differentiated and efficient.

Economic growth and the national integration of the economy led to a richness and diversity in urban life. Townsmen governed their districts. Samurai city managers watched over the city as a whole. Official services were provided by schools, police, and firefighters. But there were also servants, cooks, messengers, restaurant owners, priests, doctors, teachers, sword sharpeners, book lenders, instructors in the martial arts, prostitutes, and bathhouse attendants. In the world of popular arts, there were woodblock printers and artists, book publishers, puppeteers, acrobatic troupes, storytellers, and **Kabuki** and **Nō** actors. Merchant establishments included money changers, pawnbrokers, peddlers, small shops, single-price retail establishments like the House of Mitsui, and great wholesale merchants.

18TH AND EARLY 19TH CENTURIES

By the late 17th century, the political engineering of the Tokugawa state was complete. After that, few important changes were made in governing institutions. In the economy, too, dynamic growth gave way to slower growth within a high-level equilibrium. Yet changes of a different kind were under way.

The Forty-Seven Rōnin The 18th century began with a famous drama. In 1701, a daimyo at Edo Castle drew his sword and wounded an official who had insulted him. It was a capital crime to unsheath a sword within the castle, and the daimyo was ordered to commit *harakiri* (that is, to disembowel himself), which he promptly did. This made his retainers *rōnin*, masterless samurai. Almost two years later, they avenged their master by beheading the official whose insult had cost them their daimyo. All 47 of them then obeyed an order to kill themselves. They were widely acclaimed for the purity of their sense of duty and their loyalty to their lord, but Tokugawa society held law to be the only basis of social order. The law forbade personal vendettas, and the law could not be trumped by ethical considerations.

Cycles of Reform   Most political history of late Tokugawa Japan is written in terms of alternating cycles of laxity and reform. Even during the mid-17th century, the expenses of the bakufu and daimyo states were often greater than their income. In part, the reason was structural. Taxes were based on agriculture in an economy that was becoming commercial. It was simple mathematics. After the samurai were paid their stipends, not enough was left for the expenses of domain government and the costs of the Edo establishments. In part, it was the toll of extraordinary costs, such as a bakufu levy, the wedding of a daimyo's daughter, or the rebuilding of a castle after a fire. And finally, it was a taste for luxury among daimyo and retainers of rank.

Over the years a familiar pattern emerged. To make ends meet, domains would borrow from merchants. Then, as finances became even more difficult, a reformist clique of officials would return the domain to a more frugal and austere way of life. But since no one likes to practice frugality forever, a new round of spending would begin. The bakufu carried out three great reforms:

1716–1733	Tokugawa Yoshimune	17 years
1787–1793	Matsudaira Sadanobu	6 years
1841–1843	Mizuno Tadakuni	2 years

The first two reforms were long and successful; the third was not. Its failure set the stage for the ineffective response of the bakufu to the West in the mid-19th century.

Bureaucratization   The balance between centralization and decentralization lasted until the end of the Tokugawa era. Not a single domain ever tried to overthrow the bakufu hegemony, nor did the bakufu ever try to extend its control

Bridal Procession. The bridal procession of Yohime, the 21st daughter of the 11th Tokugawa shōgun, approaches the Edo mansion of the Kaga daimyo. The red gate (upper right), built in 1827 for this occasion, is today an entrance to the main campus of Tokyo University. The 11th shōgun had 28 sons and 27 daughters by his more than 40 concubines. Of his children, 13 sons and 12 daughters survived to maturity. This woodblock print by Kunisada is a "national treasure."
Courtesy Albert Craig.

over the domains. But bureaucracy grew steadily both within the bakufu and the domains. By 1850, all but the largest samurai fiefs were administered by district officials who collected the domain taxes and forwarded their income to the samurai. Along with the growth in bureaucracy came a proliferation of administrative codes and paperwork: records of births, adoptions, name changes, samurai ranks, fief registers, stipend registers, land and tax registers, court proceedings, and so on.

Of course, there were limits to bureaucratization. Only samurai could aspire to official posts, and decision-making posts were limited to upper-ranking samurai. But in periods of financial crises a demand arose for men of ability, and middle- or lower-middle-ranking samurai became staff assistants to bureaucrats of rank.

The Later Tokugawa Economy   By 1700, the economy approached the limit of expansion within the available technology. The population reached 26 million early in the 18th century and remained at that level into the mid-19th century, a period during which the population of China more than doubled.

After 1700, taxes were stabilized and land surveys were few. Evidence suggests little increase in grain production and only slow growth in agricultural byproducts. Some families made conscious efforts to limit their size to raise their standard of living. Contraception and abortion were commonplace, and infanticide was practiced in hard times. But periodic disease, shortages of food, and late marriages among the poor were more important factors in limiting population growth.

Some farmers remained independent cultivators, but by the mid-19th century, about a quarter of all cultivated lands were worked by tenants. Most landlords had small holdings. Though they were often village leaders, they were not at all like the Chinese gentry. The misery of the lower stratum of rural society contributed to an increase in peasant uprisings during the late 18th and early 19th centuries. Authorities had no difficulty quelling them, and no uprising in Japan approached those that erupted in late Manchu China.

Commerce grew slowly during the late Tokugawa. In the early 18th century, it was again subjected to regulation by guilds. Merchants paid set fees in return for monopoly privileges in central marketplaces. Guilds were also reestablished in the domains, and some domains created domain-run monopolies on products such as wax, paper, indigo, or sugar. The problem facing domain leaders was how to share in the profits without injuring the competitive standing of domain exports. Most late Tokugawa commercial growth was in rural industries—*sake*, soy sauce, dyes, silks, or cotton. Some were organized and financed by city merchants. Others competed with city merchants, shipping directly to the end markets to circumvent monopoly controls. The expansion of labor in rural industries may explain why the population of late Tokugawa cities declined.

The largest question about the Tokugawa economy concerns its relation to Japan's rapid industrialization in the late 19th century. Some scholars have suggested that Japan had a "running start." Others have stressed Japan's backwardness in comparison with European developers. The question is unresolved.

Tokugawa Era (1600–1868)

1600	Tokugawa Ieyasu reunifies Japan
1615	"Laws of Military Houses" issued
1639	Seclusion policy adopted
1642	Edo hostage system in place
1644–1694	Bashō, poet
1653–1724	Chikamatsu Monzaemon, dramatist
1701	The 47 rōnin avenge their lord
1853, 1854	Commodore Matthew Perry visits Japan

TOKUGAWA CULTURE

Two hundred fifty years of peace and prosperity provided a base for an ever-more complex culture and a broader popular participation in cultural life. In the villages, Buddhism became more deeply rooted, and new folk religions proliferated By the early 19th century, most well-to-do farmers could read and write. The aristocratic culture of the ranking samurai houses also remained vigorous. Nō plays continued to be staged. The medieval tradition of black ink painting was continued by the Kanō school and other artists.

The Ashikaga tradition of restraint, simplicity, and naturalness in architecture was extended. The imperial villa in Katsura outside of Kyoto, which has roots in medieval architecture, still inspires Japanese architects. The gilded and colored screen paintings that had surged in popularity during Hideyoshi's rule developed further, culminating in the powerful works of Ogata Kōrin (1658–1716).

Zen Buddhism, having declined during the Warring States period, was revitalized by the monk Hakuin (1686–1769). One of the great cultural figures of the Tokugawa era, Hakuin was also a writer, painter, calligrapher, and sculptor.

Some scholars have described Tokugawa urban culture as having two divisions. One was the work of serious, high-minded samurai, who produced a vast body of Chinese-style paintings, poetry, and philosophical treatises. The other was the product of the townspeople: low brow, irreverent, secular, satirical, and often scatological. The samurai esteemed Song-style paintings of mountains and waterfalls, often adorned with quotations from the Confucian classics or Tang poetry. The townspeople collected prints of local beauties, actors, courtesans, and scenes from everyday life. Samurai moralists saw money as the root of evil; merchants saw it as their goal in life.

Literature and Drama   Is cultural creativity more likely during periods of economic growth and political change or during periods of stability? The greatest works of literature and philosophy of Tokugawa Japan were produced between 1650 and 1725, just as the initial political transformation was being completed. The economy was still growing and the society was not yet set in its ways.

One of the major literary figures and certainly the most entertaining was Ihara Saikaku (1642–1693), who is generally credited with having re-created the Japanese novel. Saikaku was the heir to an Osaka merchant house. He was raised to be its master, but after his wife died he let the head clerk manage the business and devoted himself to poetry, the theater, and the pleasure quarters. At the age of 40, he wrote and illustrated *The Life of an Amorous Man*, the story of a modern and bawdy Prince Genji who cuts a swath through bathhouse girls, shrine maidens, courtesans, and boy actors. The success of the work led to a sequel, *The Life of an Amorous Woman*, the tale of a woman undone by passion.

A second major figure of Osaka culture at the turn of the century was the dramatist Chikamatsu Monzaemon (1653–1724). Born a samurai, Chikamatsu wrote for both the Kabuki and the puppet theater. Kabuki had begun early in the 17th century as suggestive skits and erotic dances performed by actresses. In 1629, the bakufu forbade women to perform on the stage. By the 1660s, Kabuki had evolved into a more serious drama with male actors playing both male and female roles.

The three main types of Kabuki plays were dance pieces, which were influenced by the tradition of the Nō; domestic dramas; and historical pieces. Chikamatsu wrote all three. In contrast to Saikaku's protagonists, the men and

Kabuki Theater, 1790. The male actors provide the drama—even female roles are played by men. A reprint of a three-panel woodblock print by Utagawa Toyokuni (1769–1825) from the late 1790s.

Toyokuni Utagawa. Interior of a Theater. Nineteenth Century © Musee Grimet, Paris, France. Giraudon/Art Resource, N.Y.

women in Chikamatsu's dramas struggle to fulfill the duties and obligations of their stations in life. Only when their passions become uncontrollable do the plays end in tragedy. The emotional intensity of the ending is heightened by the restraint shown by the actors before they reach their breaking point.

It is interesting to compare Kabuki and Nō drama. Nō is like early Greek drama in that the chorus provides the narrative line. In Nō, the stylization of action is extreme. In Kabuki, as in Elizabethan drama, the actors declaim their lines with the dramatic realism demanded by the commoner theatergoers of 17th-century Japan.

In the early 18th century, Kabuki was exceeded in popularity by the puppet theater (Bunraku). Many of Chikamatsu's plays were written for this genre. In the late 18th century, the puppet theater, in turn, declined, and Kabuki again blossomed as Japan's premier form of drama.

Confucian Thought   The most important change in Tokugawa intellectual life was that the ruling elite abandoned the religious worldview of Buddhism in favor of the more secular values of Confucianism, opening many avenues for further changes.

The great figures of Tokugawa Confucianism lived in the late 17th and early 18th centuries. They adapted Chinese Confucianism to fit Japanese society. One problem, for example, was that in Chinese Confucianism there was no place for a shōgun, whereas in the Japanese tradition of sun-line emperors, there was no room for the Mandate of Heaven. Most Tokugawa thinkers handled this discrepancy by saying that heaven gave the emperor its mandate and that the emperor then entrusted political authority to the shōgun. One philosopher suggested that the divine emperor acted for heaven and gave the mandate to the shōgun. Neither solution was very realistic, for, in fact, the emperor was as much a puppet as the dolls used in the Osaka theater.

Another problem was the difference between China's centralized bureaucratic government and Japan's "feudal" system of lord-vassal relationships. Samurai loyalty was clearly not that of a scholar-official to the Chinese emperor. Some Japanese Confucianists solved this problem by saying that it was China that had deviated from the feudal society of the Zhou sages, whereas in Japan, Tokugawa Ieyasu had recreated that society.

A third problem concerned the "central flowery kingdom" and the barbarians around it. No philosopher could bring himself to say that Japan was the real middle kingdom and China the barbarian, but some argued that centrality was relative, and still others suggested that China under barbarian Manchu rule had lost its claim to universality. These are just a few of a large range of issues that were debated relative to Japanese political organization, Shinto, and Japanese family practices. By the early 18th century, the difficulties had been addressed, and a revised Confucianism acceptable for use in Japan had come into being.

Japanese thought retained its intellectual vitality into the mid-19th century. Thinkers were stimulated in part by disputes among different schools of Confucianism and, perhaps, by Japan's lack of an examination system. The best energies of its samurai youth were not channeled into writing the conventional and sterile "eight-legged essay" that was required for the Chinese examination system. Official preferment—within the constraints of Japan's hereditary system—was more likely to be obtained by writing a proposal for domain reforms.

The intellectual vitality was also a result of a rapid expansion of schools, which began in the early 18th century. By the early 19th century, every domain had its own official school. Commoner schools, in which reading, writing, and the rudiments of Confucianism were taught, grew apace. In the first half of the 19th century, private academies also appeared throughout the country. By the mid-19th century, about 40 to 50 percent of the male population and 15 to 20 percent of the female population was literate—a far higher rate than in most of the world, and on a par with some late developers in Europe.

Other Developments in Thought   For Tokugawa scholars, how to deal with China was a vexing, emotional problem. They praised China as the teacher country and respected its creative tradition. They studied its history, philosophy, and literature. But they also sought to preserve a separate Japanese identity. Most scholars dealt with this problem by adapting Confucianism to fit Japan. But two schools, National Studies and Dutch Studies, criticized the Chinese influence on Japanese life and culture.

National Studies began as a philological examination of ancient Japanese texts. Sources of its inspiration were Shinto and the Neo-Confucian School of Ancient Learning. Just as the School of Ancient Learning had sought to discover the original, true meanings of the Chinese classics before they were contaminated by Song metaphysics, so the scholars in the National Studies tradition tried to find in the Japanese classics the original true character of Japan before it had been contaminated by Chinese ideas. They concluded that the early Japanese spirit was free, spontaneous, clean, lofty, and honest, in contrast to the Chinese spirit, which they characterized as rigid, cramped, and artificial. National Studies also reaffirmed Japan's imperial institution.

National Studies became influential during the late Tokugawa Era and influenced the Meiji Restoration. Its doctrines continued thereafter as one strain of Japanese ultranationalism.

A second development was **Dutch Studies**. After Christianity had been proscribed and the policy of seclusion adopted, all Western books were banned in Japan. Some knowledge of Dutch was maintained by the official interpreters who dealt with the Dutch at Nagasaki. The ban on Western books (except for those propagating Christianity) was ended in 1720 by the shōgun Tokugawa Yoshimune (r. 1716–1745).

During the 18th century, a school of "Dutch medicine" was established in Japan. Japanese pioneers recognized early that Western anatomy texts were superior to Chinese. The first Japanese dissection of a corpse occurred in 1754. By the mid-19th century, there were schools of Dutch Studies in the main cities of Japan, and instruction was available in some domains as well. Medicine was the primary occupation of those who studied Dutch. But some knowledge of Western astronomy, geography, botany, physics, chemistry, and arts also entered Japan.

Starting in the late 18th century, the Japanese began to be aware of the West, and especially of Russia, as a threat to Japan. In 1791, a concerned scholar wrote *A Discussion of the Military Problems of a Maritime Nation*, advocating strong navy and coastal defenses. During the early 19th century, such concerns mounted. A sudden expansion in Dutch Studies occurred after Commodore Matthew Perry's visits to Japan in 1853 and 1854. During the 1860s, Dutch Studies became Western Studies, as English, French, German, and Russian were added to the languages studied at the bakufu Institute for the Investigation of Barbarian Books. In sum, Dutch Studies laid a foundation on which the Japanese built quickly when the need arose for knowledge of the West.

National Studies Japanese intellectual tradition that emphasized native Japanese culture and institutions and rejected the influence of Chinese Confucianism.

HOW DID Chinese culture influence Korea and Vietnam?

KOREA AND VIETNAM

A feature of world history, as noted earlier, is the spread of heartland civilizations into their surrounding areas. In East Asia, the heartland civilization was China. The surrounding areas it transformed were Japan, Korea, and Vietnam. Like the Japanese, Koreans and Vietnamese devised writing systems using Chinese ideographs. They partially modeled their governments on those of China. They accepted Chinese Buddhism and Confucianism and with them Chinese conceptions of the universe, state, and human relationships. The Confucian definitions of the relations between ruler and minister, father and son, and husband and wife were emphasized in Korea and Vietnam as they were in China. But at the same time, Koreans and Vietnamese, who spoke non-Chinese tongues, saw themselves as separate peoples and gradually came to take pride in their independence. In Europe, Germany might be a parallel case: it became civilized by borrowing the heartland Greco-Christian culture of the Mediterranean area, but it kept its original tongue and elements from its earlier culture.

KOREA

A range of mountains along its northern rim divides the Korean peninsula from Manchuria, making it a distinct geographical unit. Mountains continue south through the eastern third of Korea, while in the west and south are coastal plains and broad river valleys. Two additional geographical factors affected Korean history: (1) the northwestern corner of Korea was only 300 miles from the northeastern corner of historical China—close enough for Korea to be vulnerable to invasions by its powerful neighbor but far enough away so that most of the time China found it easier to treat Korea as a tributary; and (2) the southern rim of Korea was just 100 miles from Japan.

EARLY HISTORY

During the first millennium B.C.E., agriculture, bronze, and iron were introduced to Korea, transforming its primitive society. But Koreans were still ruled by tribal chiefdoms in 108 B.C.E., when the Han Emperor Wudi sent an army into North Korea to menace the flank of the Hunnish (Xiongnu) Empire that had spread across the steppe to the north of China. Wudi built a Chinese city, which survived into the fourth century C.E., and established commanderies and prefectures to administer the land.

Between the fourth and seventh centuries, three archaic states emerged from earlier tribal confederations. Silla, one of the three, together with armies from Tang China, conquered the other two in the seventh century. Silla was recognized by China in 675 as an autonomous tribute state. The period of Silla rule may be likened to Nara Japan: Korea borrowed Chinese writing, established some government offices on the Chinese model, sent annual embassies to the Tang court, and took in Chinese Buddhism and Chinese arts and philosophies. Yet within the Silla government, birth mattered more than scholarship and rule by aristocrats continued, while in village Korea, the worship of nature deities was only lightly affected by the Buddhism that spread among the ruling elites.

Glazed Pot. Celadon glazes spread from China to Korea during the Koryo period (918–1392). Pots such as this late 12th- or early 13th-century ewer are prized by collectors around the world for their graceful contours and detail.

Melon-shaped Ewer, Stoneware. Koryo dynasty, ca. 12th century H. 9"Diam. 19 1/2". Korea. The Avery Brundage Collection/Asian Art Museum of San Francisco.

Silla underwent a normal end-of-dynasty decline, and in 918, a warlord general founded a new dynasty, the Koryo. The English word "Korea" is derived from this dynastic name. This was a creative period. Korean scholars advanced in their mastery of Chinese principles of government. New genres of poetry and literature appeared. Korean potters made celadon vases rivaling those of China. Printing using moveable metallic type was invented during the 13th century. But most important was the growth of Buddhism. Temples, monasteries, and nunneries were built throughout the land, and Buddhist arts flourished.

Despite cultural advances, the Koryo state was weak. Its economy was undeveloped: trade was by barter, and Chinese missions commented on the extravagance of officials in the capital and the squalor of commoners and slaves in Korea's villages. The dynasty was aristocratic, and as centuries passed, private estates and armies arose, and civil officials were replaced by military men. Frequent incursions from across Korea's northern border weakened the state. The cost of wars with the Mongols was particularly high. The Koryo court survived as long as it did by becoming in succession the tributary of the Song, Liao, Chin, and Mongol dynasties.

Korea

108 B.C.E.–4th century C.E.	Chinese rule in northern Korea
4th century C.E.–675	Three archaic states
675–918	Silla Era
918–1392	Koryo dynasty
1392–1910	Choson Era
1592, 1596	Japanese invasions of Korea
1627, 1637	Manchu invasions of Korea
1671	Famine

THE CHOSON ERA: LATE TRADITIONAL KOREA

In 1392, a Koryo general, Yi Songgye, founded a new dynasty. It lasted until 1910; its amazing longevity was directly related to the stability of Ming–Qing China.

After seizing power, Yi carried out an extensive land reform and strengthened his government by absorbing into his officialdom members of the great Koryo families. During the Yi, or Choson period, these elite families, known as *yangban*, monopolized education, official posts, and land. Beneath them were the commoners, the "good people," tax-paying free subjects of the king. Beneath the commoners and constituting perhaps one third of the population were government and private slaves. Korean scholars argue that they were not like slaves in other lands, since there were no slave auctions, and, following Confucian teachings, husbands were not separated from their wives. But Korean slaves were nonetheless property. They were often attached to land, they could be given as gifts, and their children were slaves to be used as their owners willed.

Early Choson culture showed many signs of vigor. Lyrical poetry and then prose reached new heights. The most important intellectual trend was the gradual movement of the yangban away from Buddhism and their acceptance of Neo-Confucianism.

But at mid-dynasty, invasions dealt a severe blow to the well-being of Choson society. Hideyoshi, having brought all of Japan under his control, decided to conquer China through Korea. His samurai armies devastated Korea in 1592 and 1596. The invasions ended with his death in 1598. On both occasions the Ming court sent troops to aid its tributary, but the Chinese armies devastated the land almost as badly as the Japanese. A third disaster occurred in 1627 and 1637 when Manchu troops invaded pro-Ming Korea. The result of these multiple incursions was a drop in taxable land to about a quarter of its late-16th-century level. Behind this statistic lay famine, death, and misery.

Had the late-16th-century Choson government been stronger, it might have recovered. But cliques of officials had begun to fight among themselves

yangban Elite Korean families of the Choson period.

over official positions. Many in the losing factions were executed or imprisoned. As the struggles became more fierce, the effectiveness of government declined. High officials in Seoul used their power to garner private agricultural estates and established local academies to prepare their own kinsmen for the official examinations.

From the mid-17th century on, Korea offers a mixed picture. Literacy rose and a new popular fiction of fables, romances, and novels appeared. Women writers became important for the first time. Among some yangban there was a philosophic reaction against what was perceived as the emptiness of Neo-Confucianism. Calling for "practical learning" to effect a renewal of Korean society, scholars criticized the Confucian classics and outlined plans for administrative reforms and the encouragement of commerce. Unfortunately, their recommendations were not adopted, and the society continued its decline. More Koreans died in the famine of 1671 than during Hideyoshi's invasions. Overtaxation, drought, floods, pestilence, and famine became commonplace. Robberies occurred in daytime Seoul, and bandits plagued the countryside. Disgruntled officials led peasants in revolts in 1811 and 1862. Because of the concentration of officials, wealth, and military power at Seoul and because of Manchu support for the ruling house, neither revolt toppled the dynasty, but the revolts left Korea unable to meet challenges it was soon to face.

VIETNAM

EARLY VIETNAM

Until the 15th century C.E., the Vietnamese inhabited only the northern portion of the modern country of Vietnam, the basin of the Red River (centering on Hanoi). Central Vietnam and the southeastern coast were ruled by the state of Champa. Most of the Mekong River delta in the south (centering on Saigon, or Ho Chi Minh City) was ruled by Cambodian empires (see Map 19–3).

The political history of the Vietnamese began in 208 B.C.E., when a renegade Han dynasty general formed the state of Nan Yueh. It ruled over southeastern China and the Red River basin from its capital, which was near present-day Canton. In Vietnamese, the Chinese ideograph "Yueh" is read "Viet." The name "Vietnam," literally "Viet to the south," is derived from the name of this early state. In 111 B.C.E., Han Wudi brought it under Chinese rule.

For more than a millennium after 111 B.C.E., Vietnam was ruled by China. The administrative center was a fort with a Chinese governor and Chinese troops. The governor ruled through the heads of powerful Vietnamese families. Then, in 39 C.E., the Truong sisters led a revolt against Chinese rule—the husband of one sister had been executed by the Chinese. Thereafter, more officials were sent from China and direct bureaucratic rule was instituted. Later, Vietnamese historians made the two sisters into national heroes.

During these early centuries, change was slow. Buddhism was introduced into Vietnam from China.

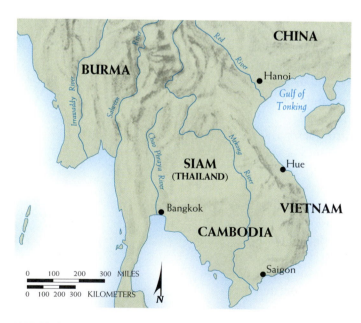

MAP 19–3
Vietnam and Neighboring Southeast Asia.

WHICH RELIGIONS intermingled in Southeast Asia?

Chinese officials and immigrants married Vietnamese women, which led to the formation of a Sino-Vietnamese political elite. The influence of Chinese higher culture was largely confined to this elite.

The pace of change increased during the Tang dynasty (618–907). Vietnam was still treated as a border region, but Chinese administration became stronger. Vietnam was divided into provinces, which the Chinese referred to as **Annam**, the "pacified south." This name was never forgotten. When the French came to Vietnam in the 19th century, they called its people the *Annamese*.

Japan and Korea reached out and took in Chinese learning during the Tang, and so in some ways did Vietnam. In all three societies, Buddhism entered, flourished in the capitals, and then percolated into local areas, where it absorbed earlier religious traditions. In all three, other aspects of China's higher culture affected mainly the elites, while an older way of life continued among villagers. But the differences were also significant. Japanese and Korean rulers wanted to imitate China's civilization and use it for their own ends. In Vietnam, the rulers were Chinese, and no such transformation occurred.

THE SECOND MILLENNIUM: POLITICS AND SOCIETY

Ten major revolts challenged Vietnam's Chinese rulers—not an unusual number for a Chinese border region with a non-Chinese population. The last revolt, in 939 when China was weak, established Vietnamese independence, and Vietnam never again became a part of China.

Several approaches have been taken to writing the history of Vietnam's second millennium. One divides it into dynastic periods:

Ly	1009–1225
Tran	1225–1400
Le	1428–1787
Nguyen	1802–1880s

As in China, dynasties began with strong military figures, who established courts, extended their control over the countryside, and collected taxes. Most founders of dynasties were members of the Sino-Vietnamese elite. Dynasties ended with the decentralization of power, the breakdown of taxation, and the rise of regional armies. But the idea of a "dynastic cycle" of slow administrative decline fits Vietnam less well than it does China. For one thing, even early in a dynasty, administrations were weaker than in China. Local magnates contested central control for longer periods. Also, each new Chinese dynasty invaded Vietnam to regain control over an area that had once been ruled by China. These invasions often reshaped dynasties. The Tran dynasty, for example, was extended for 20 more years by Ming forces. For still another, the dynastic name was sometimes kept even after its ruling house had lost power. During the 17th and 18th centuries, for example, Vietnam was divided into two states, one ruling from Hanoi and the other from Hue. In short, though the "dynasty" may be a convenient unit for dividing the second millennium into large blocks of time, it is less useful for analysis.

Another approach is to see Vietnam in relation to the Chinese state and Chinese civilization. Although Chinese invasions of Vietnam were unsuccessful, Vietnamese rulers found it easier to "manage" China than to defy it. Every Vietnamese dynasty became a "tributary" of China. Missions were sent to China bearing tribute. The head of the mission professed the Vietnamese ruler's submission to the Chinese emperor and performed the kowtow. In correspondence with

Annam Chinese term for Vietnam.

OVERVIEW   THE RELIGIONS OF SOUTHEAST ASIA

The countries of Southeast Asia, the area between India and China, have been influenced by Indian, Chinese, Muslim, and, since the 16th century, Western culture and religion. Hinduism, Buddhism, Islam, and Christianity were all brought to the area by invaders, merchants, and missionaries. Their presence is reflected in the religious makeup of the countries of Southeast Asia in the 21st century. While most of these countries are predominately Buddhist, Muslim, or Christian, most of them also include many adherents of other religions.

Predominately Buddhist	Burma
	Thailand, but with a significant Muslim minority
	Cambodia
	Laos
	Vietnam, but with a large Christian, primarily Roman Catholic, minority
	Singapore, includes Muslim, Christian, and Hindu minorities
Predominately Muslim	Indonesia, but the island of Bali is Hindu, and there is a large Christian minority
	Malaysia, but with Hindu, Buddhist, and Christian minorities
	Brunei
Predominately Christian	Philippines, but with a large Muslim minority

the Chinese "emperor," the Vietnamese rulers styled themselves as "kings," a title indicating their subordinate status. But their submission was little more than formulaic. Within Vietnam, Vietnamese rulers styled themselves as "emperors." They claimed their mandate to rule came directly from heaven, equal to the mandate of China's ruler. They denied the universality of the Chinese imperium by referring to China not as the Middle Kingdom but as the Northern Court—their own government being the Southern Court. Yet over the centuries, the imprint of Chinese culture became more pronounced. One highpoint was the reign of Le Thanh Tong (1442–1497), one of the strongest rulers in Vietnamese history. Le used Chinese culture and institutions as an advanced technology to strengthen his government. He established schools, introduced Neo-Confucianism, institutionalized an examination system, and promulgated a legal code that remained in effect through the remainder of the Le dynasty.

A third approach to Vietnamese history is to see it as a steady "march to the south" continuing from the 15th through the 18th centuries. Until the 15th century, the Vietnamese inhabited only the northern portion of modern Vietnam, the Red River basin. Central and southeastern Vietnam was Champa, the kingdom of the Chams, a Malayan people who engaged in trade and piracy. The Chams converted to Islam and for centuries waged intermittent wars with the Vietnamese. In 1357, when Tran rule was weak, a Cham army pillaged Hanoi, but Le Thanh Tong destroyed Champa.

Le Thanh Tong's successors could not hold together the lands he conquered, but settlers from the crowded Red River delta began to drift into the south, and autonomous Vietnamese states arose in the area. By 1700, a southern Vietnamese state with a capital at Hue had conquered Saigon, and by 1757 it had occupied present-day southern Vietnam. This chain of events made south

Vietnam different from the north. It was less Confucian and, as a frontier society, less educated. It included large minority populations of Muslim Chams and Cambodians, who practiced a Southeast Asian form of Buddhism. Massive emigrations of Chinese into southeast Asia also began during these centuries. Today about 1 million Chinese live in south Vietnam alone and play key roles in its economy. Such ethnic and religious diversity made the south far more difficult to govern than the more homogeneous north.

During the last half of the 18th century, Vietnam was wracked by wars. In 1802, one warlord established Vietnam's last dynasty, the Nguyen. Its capital was at Hue. In coming to power, the new emperor had been aided by French advisers, several of whom were rewarded with high posts. The Nguyen dynasty, nonetheless, became more Chinese than any previous dynasty. It adopted the law codes of Manchu China and established institutions such as the Six Boards, Hanlin Academy, Censorate, and a hierarchy of civil and military officials recruited by examinations. These initiatives were intended to placate Confucian scholars in the north, to strengthen the court, and to weaken the military figures who had helped the dynasty's rise. From the time of its second emperor, the Nguyen dynasty also became anti-French and anti-Christian.

During the first half of the 19th century, Vietnam was probably governed better than any other Southeast Asian state, but it had weaknesses. There were tensions between the north, which was overpopulated, well schooled, and furnished most of the official class, and the south, which was ethnically diverse, educationally backward, and poorly represented in government. Trade and artisanal industries were less developed than in China and Japan, only small amounts of specie circulated, and periodic markets were more common than permanent market towns. The government rested on a society characterized largely by self-sufficient villages. In sum, Vietnam entered the second half of the 19th century even less prepared than China or Japan for the challenges posed by the West.

SOUTHEAST ASIA

The historical civilizations of Southeast Asia were shaped by four movements. One was the drift of peoples and languages from north to south. Ranges of mountains rising in Tibet and southern China divide Southeast Asia into river valleys. The Mon and Burmese peoples had moved from the southeast slopes of the Tibetan plateau into the Upper Irrawaddy by 500 B.C.E. and continued south, founding the kingdom of Pagan in 847 C.E. Thai tribes moved south from China down the valley of the Chao Phraya River later, founding the kingdoms of Sukhothai (1238–1419) and Ayutthaya (1350–1767). Even today, Thai-speaking tribes are found in south China. The Vietnamese, too, arose in the north and moved into present-day central and south Vietnam only in recent historical times.

A second movement was the Indianization of Southeast Asia. Between the 1st and 15th centuries, Indian traders and missionaries established outposts throughout southeast Asia. As Hinduism and Buddhism spread through the region, Indian-type states with god-kings were established, and Indian scripts, legal codes, literature, drama, art, and music were adopted. Today, Burma, Thailand, and Cambodia retain an Indian-type of Buddhism.

A third movement was of Arab and Indian traders who sailed across the Indian Ocean to dominate trade with the Spice Islands (the Moluccas of present-day Indonesia) between the 13th and 15th centuries. They married into local ruling families and spread Islam. Local rulers who converted became sultans. Today Malaysia and Indonesia are predominantly Muslim.

The fourth movement was the Chinese **diaspora**, an emigration of Chinese to most parts of the world but especially to Southeastern Asia. It was in full tide by 1842. Initially, most Chinese were indentured laborers on plantations, but many moved to cities to become shopkeepers. China's mercantile ethos was stronger than that of the southern peoples. In most of Southeast Asia, urban economies were largely developed and controlled by Chinese. The greatest concentrations of Chinese, apart from Singapore, were in Malaysia, Indonesia, and Thailand.

diaspora Dispersion of an originally homogeneous people or culture. Among the many diasporas in world history, some of the most famous are the Jewish, the Chinese, the African, the Irish, and the Armenian.

SUMMARY

China China's last two imperial dynasties were the Ming (1368–1644) and the Qing, or Manchus (1644–1911). Although China could not match the dynamism of the West during these years, its society became more integrated and its government more sophisticated. The population reached 410 million, cities grew, and commerce expanded. Chinese government depended on the Confucian bureaucracy and the gentry class. Under the Manchus, China expanded to the east and annexed Taiwan. There also was growing trade with the West, especially Britain, but it was conducted under highly restricted terms by Chinese officials.

Japan After more than a century of civil war among the warrior aristocracy (the Warring States Era, 1467–1600), the Tokugawa shōguns (1600–1868) restored order. Their government controlled the aristocracy and encouraged economic growth. Christianity, which had made many converts in Japan, was driven underground, and Japan was closed to the outside world except for a small Dutch presence at Nagasaki. Japanese drama, literature, and art flourished, as did commercial life.

Korea and Vietnam China considered both Korea and Vietnam to be tributary states, and both countries adopted Chinese Confucian culture and forms of government while preserving their political independence.

Southest Asia Southeast Asian civilizations have been heavily influenced by the movement of peoples, religions (especially Hinduism and Buddhism), and the Chinese diaspora, which increased in the 19th century.

IMAGE KEY
for pages 456–457

a. Long grain rice
b. Kitagawa Utamaro (1753–1806), "Mother Bathing Her Son"
c. Chinese carved lacquer box
d. Karaori kimono
e. Tai Chin, "Fisherman on an Autumn River" (1390–1460)
f. Woodblock print of the commercial district of Osaka
g. Stoneware ewer from the the Koryo dynasty in Korea
h. A pile of table salt
i. Manchu emporer Ch'ien Lung
j. "The Arrival of the Portuguese in Japan."

REVIEW QUESTIONS

1. Why did the economy grow in late traditional China?

2. Did Manchu rule resemble Mongol rule, or was it different? In what regards were Kangxi and Qianlong indistinguishable from Chinese emperors?

3. How did Ming–Qing foreign relations set the stage for China's 19th-century encounter with the West?

4. How did military technology in Japan change during the 15th and 16th centuries?

5. How was Chinese culture a "technology" used by Japan, Korea, and Vietnam for state building? Why were the results in each country so different?

KEY TERMS

Annam (p. 479)   gentry (p. 460)   **National Studies** (p. 475)
daimyo (p. 466)   **Kabuki** (p. 470)   **Shaanxi banks** (p. 458)
diaspora (p. 482)   **Nō play** (p. 470)   *yangban* (p. 477)

 For additional study resources for this chapter, go to:
www.prenhall.com/craig/chapter19

20 State Building and Society in Early Modern Europe

CHAPTER HIGHLIGHTS

Models of European Political Development In the seventeenth and eighteenth centuries, five great powers emerged in Europe: France, Britain, Austria, Prussia, and Russia. Through their military strength, economic development, and in some cases colonial empires, they would affect virtually every other world civilization.

The Old Regime Eighteenth-century European society was traditional, hierarchical, corporate, and privileged–features that had characterized Europe and the world for centuries. All societies also confronted the scarce food supplies. For the eighteenth century, however, an improved food supply helped support a larger population. New agricultural techniques and the expanding population created pressures on social structures. Commerce also grew during the eighteenth century. Agriculture became more commercialized. Cities expanded.

Changes in European Society European society stood on the brink of a new era in which the social, economic, and political relationships of centuries would be destroyed. The commercial spirit and the values of the marketplace clashed with the traditions of peasants and guilds. By the early nineteenth century it led to a conception of human beings as individuals rather than as members of communities.

The expansion of the European population further stimulated change and challenge to tradition and hierarchy. New wealth meant that birth would cease to determine social relationships.

The eighteenth century furthermore witnessed the beginning of industrial production in response to the demands for consumer goods by the expanding population. Industrialization also affected Europe's relations with much of the non-European world. For the first time in history, major changes in one region of Europe left virtually no corner of the globe untouched.

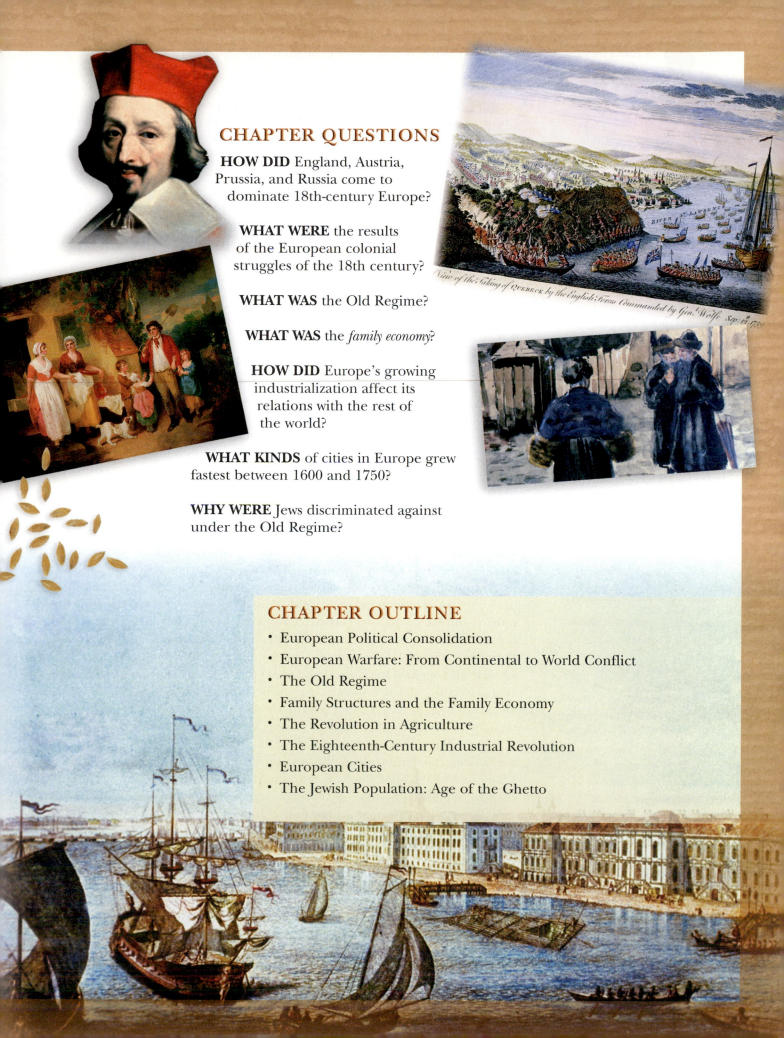

CHAPTER QUESTIONS

HOW DID England, Austria, Prussia, and Russia come to dominate 18th-century Europe?

WHAT WERE the results of the European colonial struggles of the 18th century?

WHAT WAS the Old Regime?

WHAT WAS the *family economy*?

HOW DID Europe's growing industrialization affect its relations with the rest of the world?

WHAT KINDS of cities in Europe grew fastest between 1600 and 1750?

WHY WERE Jews discriminated against under the Old Regime?

CHAPTER OUTLINE

- European Political Consolidation
- European Warfare: From Continental to World Conflict
- The Old Regime
- Family Structures and the Family Economy
- The Revolution in Agriculture
- The Eighteenth-Century Industrial Revolution
- European Cities
- The Jewish Population: Age of the Ghetto

From the early 17th century to the mid-20th century, Europe exercised unprecedented domination over other parts of the world. Two factors accounted for this situation. First, by the mid-18th century, five major states had become dominant in Europe: Great Britain, France, Austria, Prussia, and Russia. In the late 17th century these five states began to fight among themselves, first in Europe and then in their colonial empires. These conflicts had major consequences for the non-European world.

The second factor leading to Europe's dominance was a series of economic advances that laid the foundation for the social and economic transformation of the world. For the first time, Europeans developed a more or less stable food supply, and the population of Europe entered a major period of growth. New inventions, known collectively as the Industrial Revolution, gave Europe a productive capacity previously unknown in human history, and these advantages gave Europeans the power to dominate much of the world.

EUROPEAN POLITICAL CONSOLIDATION

TWO MODELS OF EUROPEAN POLITICAL DEVELOPMENT

HOW DID England, France, Austria, Prussia, and Russia come to dominate 18th-century Europe?

In the second half of the 16th century, changes in European military organization, weapons, and tactics sharply increased the cost of warfare and forced monarchs to seek new revenues. Rulers like the king of France, who established secure financial bases without the support of nobles or assemblies, exercised absolute rule. The English monarch, however, by the end of the 17th century, could govern only with Parliament. These two governmental systems—**absolutism** in France and **parliamentary monarchy** in England—shaped Europe's political evolution.

TOWARD PARLIAMENTARY GOVERNMENT IN ENGLAND

When Elizabeth I died in 1603, the English crown passed to James VI of Scotland, the son of Mary Queen of Scots, who became James I of England, the first of the Stuart dynasty. The Stuart kings aspired to absolute power, and their pursuit of an income to support it threatened the economic well-being of the nobility and the landed and commercial elites represented in Parliament. These groups invoked traditional English liberties and effectively resisted the Stuarts. **Puritans** (Calvinists), who wanted a more radical reformation of the Anglican Church, also opposed the kings. Both James I (r. 1603–1625) and his son Charles I (r. 1625–1649), who had Catholic sympathies, confronted a combined political and religious opposition to their absolutist policies.

In 1642, the conflict between Charles I and Parliament erupted into civil war, which the parliamentary and Puritan forces won in 1645. In 1649, a "rump" Parliament (one from which the opposition had been removed) beheaded Charles I and abolished the monarchy, the House of Lords, and the established church. England became a Puritan republic led by Oliver Cromwell (1599–1658), the victorious general in the civil war. After Cromwell died in 1658, disillusionment with Puritan strictness and republican mismanagement prompted restoration of the Stuart monarchy under Charles II (r. 1660–1685). His Parliament was dominated by conservative members of the Church of England, and the policies it pursued severely restricted both Protestant Non-Conformists and Roman Catholics. Parliament's Test Act established an oath as a qualification for office that no Roman Catholic could take in good conscience.

James II (r. 1685–1688), the brother who succeeded Charles in 1685, was a Roman Catholic. He decreed toleration for both Roman Catholics and Protestant Non-Conformists and imprisoned seven Anglican bishops who refused to publicize

QUICK REVIEW

Charles II (r. 1660–1685)
- England returned to the 1642 status quo when Charles assumed throne
- Charles favored religious toleration
- Issued Declaration of Indulgence in 1672 suspending all laws against non-Anglicans

absolutism Term applied to strong centralized continental monarchies that attempted to make royal power dominant over aristocracies and other regional authorities.

Parliamentary monarchy Form of limited monarchy developed in England.

Puritans English Protestants who sought to "purify" the Church of England of any vestiges of Catholicism.

his suspension of laws against Catholics. James's policy of toleration had as it goal the extension of royal authority over all English institutions.

Members of England's Parliament hoped that James would be succeeded by his eldest daughter, Mary (r. 1689–1694), a Protestant and the wife of William of Orange (1650–1702), stadtholder of the Netherlands. But on June 20, 1688, James II's Catholic second wife gave birth to a Catholic male heir to the throne. This prompted Parliament to invite William of Orange to invade England to preserve its "traditional liberties," that is, the Anglican Church and parliamentary government.

THE "GLORIOUS REVOLUTION"

William of Orange met no opposition when he landed an army in England in November 1688. James fled to France, and Parliament proclaimed William III and Mary II the new monarchs. This bloodless coup was celebrated as the **Glorious Revolution**, for the government it established limited the powers of the monarchy and guaranteed the civil liberties of the English privileged classes. Henceforth, England's monarchs would rule by the consent of Parliament, which convened every three years. Roman Catholics were declared ineligible to inherit the English throne. The Toleration Act of 1689 permitted all forms of Protestant worship but outlawed Roman Catholicism.

The Act of Settlement in 1701 ended a century of strife by bequeathing the English crown to Germany's Protestant House of Hanover if Anne (r. 1702–1714), the second daughter of James II and the heir to the childless William and Mary, died without issue. At Queen Anne's death in 1714, the Elector of Hanover became George I of England (r. 1714–1727), the third foreigner to occupy its throne in just more than a century.

During the first quarter of the 18th century, Britain enjoyed political stability and economic prosperity. Robert Walpole (1676–1745), George I's chief minister from 1721 to 1742, was adept at handling the House of Commons and exercising influence through control of government patronage. He maintained peace abroad and the status quo at home. The dominant economic interests were represented in Parliament, and their taxes funded a powerful army and navy that made Great Britain into a world power—with a commercial empire extending from New England to India.

The power of the British monarchs and their ministers were limited, and Parliament could not wholly ignore popular pressure. Many members of Parliament held independent views. Newspapers and public debate flourished. Free speech could be exercised, as could freedom of association. No standing army intimidated the populace. The English state showed how military power could coexist with political liberty, and Britain became the model for European progressives who opposed the absolutist regimes on the continent. The political ideas that emerged in the British Isles during the 17th century also took deep root in Britain's North American colonies.

Oliver Cromwell. His model army defeated the royalists in the English Civil War. After the execution of Charles I in 1649, Cromwell dominated the short-lived English republic, conquered Ireland and Scotland, and ruled as Lord Protector from 1653 until his death in 1658.

Stock Montage, Inc./Historical Pictures Collection.

Glorious Revolution Largely peaceful replacement of James II by William and Mary as English monarchs in 1688. It marked the beginning of constitutional monarchy in Britain.

DOCUMENT CD-ROM

18.2
The Ideal Absolute
State (1697): Jean Domat

divine right of kings Theory that monarchs are appointed by and answerable only to God.

Louis XIV of France (r. 1643–1715). He was the dominant European monarch in the second half of the 17th century. The powerful centralized monarchy he created established the prototype for the mode of government later termed absolutism.

Bridgemann-Giraudon/Art Resource, N.Y.

RISE OF ABSOLUTE MONARCHY IN FRANCE: THE WORLD OF LOUIS XIV

The French monarchy took a different path. During the minority of Louis XIV (r. 1643–1715), who ascended the throne at age 5, Cardinal Mazarin (1602–1661), his regent, tried to strengthen royal control. The result was a series of widespread rebellions between 1649 and 1652 called the Fronde (after the slingshot used by street urchins).

YEARS OF PERSONAL RULE

After Mazarin's death in 1661, Louis XIV assumed personal control of the government. Louis concentrated unprecedented authority in the monarchy but, with the Fronde in mind, took care not to intrude excessively on local social and political institutions. Because he governed directly, rebels could not defend themselves from a charge of treason by claiming that they opposed only bad ministers and not the king.

Louis ruled through powerful councils, whose members he chose from families long in royal service or people just beginning to advance socially. Unlike the ancient noble families, they had no power bases in the provinces and depended solely on the king for their positions.

Louis XIV was innovative in the use of the physical setting of his court to enhance his political power. The palace at Versailles, which was built between 1676 and 1708, was a temple to royalty. Its splendor proclaimed the majesty of the Sun King, as Louis was known. It housed thousands of the more important nobles, royal officials, and servants, and preoccupation with Versailles' elaborate court ceremonies kept nobles from the real business of government.

Louis owed his concept of royal authority to his devout tutor, the political theorist Bishop Jacques-Bénigne Bossuet (1627–1704). Bossuet defended what he called the "**divine right of kings**" by citing examples of Old Testament rulers divinely appointed by and answerable only to God. Medieval popes had insisted that only God could judge a pope, and Bossuet made the same claim for a king. As God's regents on Earth, kings could not be bound by nobles and parliaments, for as Louis XIV allegedly explained: "*L'état, c'est moi*" ("I am the state").

Louis insisted on religious conformity, and in October 1685 he revoked the Edict of Nantes (1598), which had protected France's Huguenots. Protestant churches and schools were closed, Protestant ministers exiled, nonconverting laity condemned as galley slaves, and Protestant children taken to be baptized by Catholic priests. More than a quarter million people fled and joined France's opponents in England, Germany, Holland, and the New World.

Louis used most of the wealth and authority he had amassed to lead France into a long series of wars (discussed later) that weakened the nation. Despite this, he established a model for strong

Versailles. As painted in 1668 by Pierre Patel the Elder (1605–1676), the central building is the hunting lodge built for Louis XIII earlier in the century. The wings that appear here were some of Louis XIV's first expansions.

Giraudon/Art Resource, N.Y.

centralized monarchy that other monarchs in central and eastern Europe copied. They saw Louis as more successful than the Stuarts of Great Britain, who could only rule through Parliament.

RUSSIA ENTERS THE EUROPEAN POLITICAL ARENA

The emergence of Russia as an active European power was a wholly new development in European politics. Previously, Russia had hardly been considered part of Europe, and prior to 1673 it maintained no permanent ambassadors in Western Europe. Hemmed in by Sweden on the Baltic and by the Ottoman Empire on the Black Sea, Russia had no warm-water ports. Its chief outlet for trade to the west was Archangel on the White Sea, which was ice-free for only part of the year.

BIRTH OF THE ROMANOV DYNASTY

The last half of the reign of Ivan IV (r. 1533–1584), or Ivan the Terrible, was a time of enormous political turmoil in Russia. An era called the Time of Troubles followed, and in 1613, an assembly of nobles tried to stabilize the situation by electing as tsar a 17-year-old boy, Michael Romanov (r. 1613–1645). He began the dynasty that ruled Russia until 1917, but his country remained weak and impoverished. The *boyars*, the old nobility, controlled its bureaucracy, and the *streltsy*, or guards of the Moscow garrison, constantly threatened mutiny.

PETER THE GREAT

In 1682, a 10-year-old boy named Peter (r. 1682–1725), the future Peter the Great, ascended the throne with the help of the streltsy, who expected to exploit

QUICK REVIEW

Versailles

- Palace of Versailles: Central element in the image of the French monarchy
- Nobles who wanted Louis's favor congregated at Versailles
- Life at Versailles governed by elaborate etiquette

boyars   Russian nobility.

streltsy   Professional troops who made up the Moscow garrison. They were suppressed by Peter the Great.

OVERVIEW   GREAT POWERS AND DECLINING POWERS IN EUROPE

In the 17th and 18th centuries, five European states—Britain, France, Austria, Prussia, and Russia—became great European powers and remained so until and, in every case except Austria, even after the end of World War I in 1918. At the same time, four other states that had been major European powers declined permanently into secondary status. The table below lists the main strengths of the rising powers and the main sources of weakness of the declining states.

Five Great Powers

State	Government	Strengths
Britain	Constitutional Monarchy	Commercial and financial resources; navy; colonial Empire; overseas trade; intellectual liberty; growing industry; religious toleration
France	Absolute Monarchy	Army; large population; cultural preeminence; colonial empire; intellectual vibrancy
Austria	Absolute Monarchy	Imperial prestige; dynastic loyalty: army
Prussia	Absolute Monarchy	Army; efficient bureaucracy
Russia	Absolute Monarchy	Army; large population; extensive natural resources; imperial control over church and state

Four Declining Powers

State	Government	Weaknesses
Spain	Absolute Monarchy	Stagnant economy; inefficient government; weak military; enforced religious and intellectual conformity
Ottoman Empire	Absolute Monarchy	Backward economy; unstable government; resistance to change; outmoded military
Sweden	Constitutional Monarchy	Small population; weak economy
Netherlands	Republic	Divided government; small population; declining economy

him. Like Louis XIV, the turmoil of his youth convinced Peter that the power of the tsar had to be made supreme over the boyars and the streltsy and that the tsar needed a strong military.

The military resources of Europe's maritime powers fascinated Peter I, and in 1697, he toured Western Europe incognito (allowing him to avoid the ceremony that would have attended an official royal visit). He spent his happiest moments inspecting shipyards, docks, and shops that produced military hardware, and he returned to Moscow determined to copy the technology he had seen abroad. He also understood that his plans for making Russia into a great nation would require him to oppose the long-standing power and traditions of the Russian nobles.

Taming the Streltsy and Boyars   In 1698, while Peter was abroad, the streltsy rebelled. On his return, Peter brutally suppressed their revolt. Approximately 1,000 of them were put to death and their corpses publicly displayed to discourage future disloyalty. Peter then built a new military that would serve him and not itself. He employed ruthless methods of conscription and over the course of his reign drafted about 300,000 men. He adopted policies for the officer corps and general military discipline patterned on those of West European armies.

Peter sustained a campaign against the boyars and their antiquated customs. He personally shaved their long beards and sheared off the hand-covering sleeves of their shirts and coats. These traditional emblems of their rank had made them the butt of jokes at the European courts. Peter skillfully played one group against another, as he set about rebuilding Russia's government and military after the pattern of the more powerful European states.

Developing a Navy   In the mid-1690s, Peter built a navy to compete in the Black Sea with the Ottoman Empire, and in 1695, he began a war with the Ottomans. He also constructed a Baltic fleet to fight the Great Northern War with Sweden (1700–1721). In 1721, the Peace of Nystad confirmed Russia's conquest of Estonia, Livonia, and part of Finland. Peter had acquired the ice-free ports that were to give Russia influence in European affairs.

Founding St. Petersburg   In 1703, Peter founded a new capital, the city of St. Petersburg, at a site on the Gulf of Finland. He compelled the boyars to construct townhouses there and joined the European monarchs who copied Louis XIV by constructing smaller versions of Versailles. However, the founding of St. Petersburg was more than the establishment of a central imperial court. It oriented Russia to the West and signaled Peter's determination to hold his position on the Baltic coast.

The Case of Peter's Son Aleksei and Reforms of Peter the Great's Final Years   Other reforms arose from Peter's family difficulties. Peter's son Aleksei had never demonstrated much intelligence or ambition, yet Peter distrusted him. Late in 1717, Peter suspected that Aleksei had become the focal point for a seditious plot, and he undertook an investigation. He personally interrogated Aleksei, who was eventually condemned to death and died under mysterious circumstances on June 26, 1718.

The interrogations surrounding Aleksei had revealed more opposition to Peter at court than he had suspected. He decided that force alone would not eliminate all his opponents, so he implemented radical administrative reforms designed to bring the nobility and the Russian Orthodox Church more closely under the authority of persons loyal to the tsar.

Administrative Colleges   In December 1717, Peter reorganized domestic administration, using the example of Swedish institutions called *colleges*—bureaus operating according to written instructions rather than departments headed by a single minister. He established eight colleges to handle such things as the collection of taxes, foreign relations, war, and economic affairs. Each college was given a foreign adviser, and by making careful appointments Peter balanced influence within these colleges between nobles and people personally loyal to himself.

England

Year	Event
1603	James VI of Scotland becomes James I of England
1625	Charles I becomes king of England
1629	Charles I dissolves Parliament and embarks on 11 years of personal rule
1640	April–May, Short Parliament; November, Long Parliament convenes
1642	Outbreak of the Civil War
1649	Charles I executed
1649–1660	Various attempts at a Puritan Commonwealth
1660	Charles II restored to the English throne
1670	Secret Treaty of Dover between France and England
1672	Parliament passes the Test Act
1685	James II becomes king of England
1688	Glorious Revolution
1689	William III and Mary II come to the throne of England
1701	Act of Settlement provides for Hanoverian Succession
1702–1714	Reign of Queen Anne, the last of the Stuarts
1714	George I of Hanover becomes king of England
1721–1742	Ascendancy of Sir Robert Walpole

Rise of Russian Power

1533–1584	Reign of Ivan the Terrible
1584–1613	Time of Troubles
1613	Michael Romanov becomes tsar
1682	Peter the Great becomes tsar as a boy
1689	Peter assumes personal rule
1697	European tour of Peter the Great
1698	Peter suppresses the streltsy
1700	The Great Northern War begins between Russia and Sweden; Russia defeated at Narva by Charles XII
1703	St. Petersburg founded
1709	Russia defeats Sweden at Poltava
1718	Death of Aleksei, son of Peter the Great
1721	Peace of Nystad ends the Great Northern War
1721	Peter establishes control over the Russian church
1722	The Table of Ranks
1725	Peter dies, leaving an uncertain succession

Table of Ranks Official hierarchy established by Peter the Great in imperial Russia that equated a person's social position and privileges with his rank in the state bureaucracy or army.

Achieving Secular Control of the Church Peter also curtailed the independence of the Russian Orthodox Church, some of whose clergy sympathized with the tsar's son. In 1721, Peter abolished the post of *patriarch* and submitted the church to a government department called the *Holy Synod*. It consisted of several bishops headed by a layman, the *procurator general*. It made sure that the church supported the tsar's secular agenda.

Table of Ranks In 1722, Peter drew the nobles into state service by means of a **Table of Ranks**. It used rank in the bureaucracy or military to determine a person's social position and privileges, not descent from the old landed families, who generally resisted his reforms. Peter made the social standing of individual boyars a function of their willingness to serve his new centralized government.

Peter took many decisive actions, but he never settled on a successor. When Peter died in 1725, he left no obvious heir to the throne. For about 30 years, soldiers and nobles decided who ruled Russia. Peter had laid the foundations of a modern Russia, but not a stable state.

THE HABSBURG EMPIRE AND THE PRAGMATIC SANCTION

In 1648, the Habsburg family established a permanent hold on the title of Holy Roman Emperor, but their power depended on eliciting cooperation from scores of political entities of various kinds. While establishing their authority over the German states, the Habsburgs also consolidated their power within their hereditary possessions outside the Holy Roman Empire: the kingdom of Bohemia (in modern Czechoslovakia), the duchies of Moravia

St. Petersburg. Peter the Great built St. Petersburg on the Gulf of Finland to provide Russia with better contact with Western Europe. He moved Russia's capital there from Moscow in 1703. This is an 18th-century view of the city.

The Granger Collection.

Vie des bords de la Neva en descendant la rivière entre le Palais d'hyver de Sa Majesté Imperiale & les batimens de l'Academie des Sciences

and Silesia, Hungary, Croatia, and Transylvania. In each of their territories, the Habsburgs needed help from local nobles, and they often had to bargain with nobles in one part of Europe to maintain their position in another.

Despite these internal weaknesses, Leopold I (r. 1658–1705) blocked the advances of the Turks into central Europe and thwarted aggression by Louis XIV. The Ottomans recognized his sovereignty over Hungary in 1699 and extended his territorial holdings over much of the Balkan Peninsula and western Romania.

In the early 18th century the Habsburg emperor Charles VI (r. 1711–1740) had no male heir, and Charles feared that after he died the Austrian Habsburg lands might fall prey to the surrounding powers. Determined to prevent that disaster, he devoted most of his reign to seeking the approval of his family, the estates of his realms, and the major foreign powers for a document called the ***Pragmatic Sanction***. This provided the legal basis for a single line of inheritance within the Habsburg dynasty through Charles VI's daughter Maria Theresa (1740–1780). When Charles VI died, he believed that he had secured legal recognition of the unity of the Habsburg Empire and the succession of his daughter. However, his failure to provide his daughter with a strong army or a full treasury left her lands vulnerable to foreign aggression. Less than two months after his death in December 1740, Frederick II of Prussia invaded the Habsburg province of Silesia, and Maria Theresa had to fight for her inheritance.

THE RISE OF PRUSSIA

Prussia expanded into a German power vacuum created by the Peace of Westphalia. It was built by the Hohenzollern family, rulers of Brandenburg since 1417. By inheritance, the Hohenzollerns acquired a series of territories, most of which were not contiguous with Brandenburg, but which, by the late 17th century, consituted a block of territory within the Holy Roman Empire second only to that of the Habsburgs. Beginning in the mid-17th century, Hohhenzollern rulers forged their geographically separated holdings into a powerful state and built an army that empowered them to rule without the approval of the local nobility.

There was, however, a political and social tradeoff between the Hohenzollerns and their nobles, the **Junkers**. In exchange for obedience to the Hohenzollerns, the Junkers received the right to total authority over the serfs on their estates. Furthermore, the heaviest taxes were imposed on the peasants and the urban classes. Junkers increasingly dominated the army officer corps, and all officials and army officers took an oath of loyalty to the Hohenzollern rulers. The army provided the state with a semblance of unity and made Prussia a desirable ally. In 1701, the Habsburg emperor repaid the Hohenzollerns for their help by granting them the title "King in Prussia."

Frederick William I (r. 1713–1740) of Prussia governed through a bureaucracy structured along military lines and mobilized his small realm to support the third or fourth largest army in Europe. Separate laws applied to soldiers and to civilians. Given that the officer corps was the highest social class, military service attracted the sons of Junkers. The army, the Junker nobility, and the monarchy fused into a single political entity. The military dominated Prussian government, society, and daily life as in no other state in Europe. Other nations had armies; the Prussian army had a nation.

Although Frederick William I built the best army in Europe, he avoided conflict. His army was a symbol of Prussian power and unity, not an instrument for foreign aggression. At his death in 1740, he passed the army to his son Frederick II (Frederick the Great, r. 1740–1786), but not the wisdom to refrain

Pragmatic Sanction Legal basis negotiated by Emperor Charles VI (r. 1711–1740) for the Habsburg succession through his daughter Maria Theresa (r. 1740–1780).

Junkers Noble landlords of Prussia.

from using it. Almost immediately, Frederick II voided the Pragmatic Sanction and invaded Silesia. This began an Austrian-Prussian competition for control of Germany that dominated central European affairs for more than a century.

EUROPEAN WARFARE: FROM CONTINENTAL TO WORLD CONFLICT

WHAT WERE the results of the European colonial struggles of the 18th century?

Whereas religious zeal had fueled the European wars of the Reformation Era, dynastic and commercial rivalry drove wars from the reign of the Louis XIV through the conclusion of the Seven Years' War in 1763. Through their conflicts with each other, the European powers developed the military weapons and naval prowess that they used against non-European peoples.

THE WARS OF LOUIS XIV

Thanks to France's consolidation under the power of its absolute king, Louis XIV could afford to raise and maintain a large and powerful army and entertain dreams of dominating Europe. In 1667, he led France into the first of four major wars designed to expand his territory, and he was soon regarded as a menace to the whole of Western Europe, Catholic and Protestant alike. In 1681, Louis's forces occupied the free city of Strasbourg, prompting defensive coalitions to form against him. One of these, the League of Augsburg, grew to include England, Spain, Sweden, the United Provinces, and the major German states, including the Habsburg emperor. Between 1689 and 1697, the League of Augsburg and France battled each other on European fronts in the Nine Years' War, while England and France also warred in North America. In 1697, the Peace of Ryswick secured Holland's borders and thwarted Louis's expansion into Germany.

18.3
The Sighs of Enslaved France (1690):
Pierre Jurieu

On November 1, 1700, Charles II of Spain (r. 1665–1700) died and bequeathed his estate to Louis's grandson, Philip of Anjou, or Philip V of Spain (r. 1700–1746). This tipped the balance of power in Europe in France's favor, and England, Holland, and the Holy Roman Empire formed the Grand Alliance as a countermeasure. The War of the Spanish Succession (1701–1714) soon enveloped Western Europe. France finally made peace with England at Utrecht in July 1713 and with Holland and the emperor at Rastadt in March 1714. Philip V retained Spain, but England got Gibraltar, a base for action in the Mediterranean. The long war left France economically and politically exhausted (see Map 20–1).

France

1649–1652	The Fronde, a revolt of nobility and townspeople against the crown
1661	Louis XIV assumes personal rule
1667	Louis XIV invades Flanders
1672	France invades the United Provinces
1678–1679	Peace of Nijmwegen
1682	Louis establishes his court at Versailles
1685	Edict of Nantes revoked
1689–1697	Nine Years' War between France and the League of Augsburg
1697	Peace of Ryswick
1701–1714	War of the Spanish Succession
1713	Treaty of Utrecht between England and France
1714	Treaty of Rastadt between the emperor and France

THE 18TH-CENTURY COLONIAL ARENA

The Treaty of Utrecht in 1713 established boundaries for the colonial empires of the first half of the 18th century. Except for Portugal's Brazil, Spain claimed all of mainland South America, Mexico, Cuba, half of Hispaniola, Florida, and California. Britain held the North Atlantic seaboard, Nova Scotia, Newfoundland, Jamaica, and Barbados as well as a few trading stations on the Indian subcontinent. The Dutch controlled Surinam (Dutch Guiana) and various trading stations in Ceylon, Bengal, and Java (modern-day Indonesia). The French claimed the St. Lawrence River valley; the Ohio and Mississippi river valleys; Saint Domingue

MAP 20–1

Europe In 1714. The War of the Spanish Succession ended a year before the death of Louis XIV. The Bourbons had secured the Spanish throne, but Spain had forfeited its possessions in Flanders and Italy.

WHICH COUNTRIES benefitted the most from the war?

(Haiti), Guadeloupe, and Martinique in the West Indies; and trading stations in India and West Africa. French and English settlers in North America clashed throughout the 18th century.

The Treaty of Utrecht gave the British a 30-year *asiento*, or contract, to furnish slaves to the Spanish Empire and the right to send one ship each year to the trading fair at Portobello. The British cheated, and when the Spanish government under the Bourbon kings decided to enforce its monopoly over trade with its empire, the stage was set for conflict.

WAR OF JENKINS'S EAR

In 1731, when a Spanish coastal patrol boarded a British vessel to search for contraband, there was a fight, and an English captain, Robert Jenkins, had his ear cut off. He preserved it in a jar of brandy and in 1738 displayed it to the British Parliament as evidence of atrocities Spain was said to inflict on British merchants in the West Indies. Late in 1739, Great Britain went to war with Spain and, in junction with Prussia's aggression on the continent, began a series of worldwide European wars.

THE WAR OF THE AUSTRIAN SUCCESSION (1740–1748)

In December 1740, Frederick II of Prussia seized the Austrian province of Silesia. Maria Theresa of Austria preserved the Habsburg Empire by sacrificing some of the power of its crown. She ensured the loyalty of the Magyars of Hungary, the most important of her domains, by granting them considerable local autonomy. The link between her war with Prussia, the War of the Austrian Succession, and the British–Spanish commercial conflict was made by France. French aristocrats pushed their government to support Prussia against Austria, France's long-standing enemy. French aid to Prussia helped consolidate a new and powerful German state, a threat that brought Great Britain into the continental war against France and Prussia. In 1744, the conflict expanded beyond the continent when France decided to support Spain against Britain in the New World. The war ended in stalemate in 1748. By the Treaty of Aix-la-Chapelle, however, Prussia retained Silesia. There was a truce but not a permanent peace.

THE SEVEN YEARS' WAR (1756–1763)

In 1756, a dramatic shift of alliances occurred. Prussia and Great Britain signed the Convention of Westminster. The Prussians and the British hoped that their alliance would dissuade Russia and France from invading Germany. When Austria countered the loss of its British ally by turning to France, the European alliances of the previous century were reversed.

In August 1756, Frederick II's invaded Saxony to head off what he thought was a conspiracy against Prussia by Saxony, Austria, and France. This began the Seven Years' War. In the spring of 1757, France and Austria formed a new alliance targeted at Prussia, and Sweden, Russia, and the smaller German states joined them. Two factors in addition to Frederick's strong leadership saved Prussia: British financial aid, and the death in 1762 of Empress Elizabeth of Russia (r. 1741–1762). Her successor, Tsar Peter III, (d. 1762), fervently admired Frederick and immediately made peace with Prussia. The Treaty of Hubertusburg of 1763 ended the Seven Years' War with no changes in borders.

More impressive than Prussia's survival were Great Britain's victories in every theater of conflict. These were the work of William Pitt the Elder (1708–1778), who was named secretary of state in charge of the war in 1757. North America, however, was Pitt's real concern. He won control of all of North America east of the Mississippi for Great Britain in what American historians call the French and Indian War. Pitt's aspirations were global. He took Quebec from the French in 1759 and Montreal a year later. The French West Indies fell to the British fleet. British forces on the Indian subcontinent, under Robert Clive (1725–1774), defeated the French in 1757 and cleared the way for the conquest of all India by the British East India Company. By the Treaty of Paris of 1763, Britain received all of Canada, the Ohio River valley, and the eastern half of

QUICK REVIEW

The Seven Years' War (1756–1763)

- Prussian invasion of Saxony sparked war
- War spread into North America
- Treaty of Paris ended war in 1763

European Conflicts of the Mid-18th Century

1739	Outbreak of War of Jenkins's Ear between England and Spain
1740	War of the Austrian Succession commences
1748	Treaty of Aix-la-Chapelle
1756	Convention of Westminster between England and Prussia
1756	Seven Years' War opens
1759	British forces capture Quebec
1763	Treaty of Hubertusburg
1763	Treaty of Paris

the Mississippi River valley. France retained footholds in India at Pondicherry and Chandernagore and regained the West Indies sugar islands of Guadeloupe and Martinique.

The mid-century wars established a new balance of power on the European continent and the high seas (see Map 20–2). Prussia became a great continental power, and Great Britain gained a world empire. France's retreat from North America opened the way for a continent dominated by the English language and

MAP 20–2

The Colonial Arena. The acquisition of overseas colonies by European powers led to intense rivalries on a global scale. Territories frequently changed hands during the 18th century.

WHY WERE colonies central to European conflicts in the 18th century?

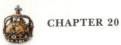

Protestantism. Latin America remained dominated by the Spanish and Portuguese languages and Roman Catholicism. On the subcontinent of Asia the foundation was laid for nearly two centuries of British dominance. The global dominance of the European powers was a function of their wars, but also of dramatic economic developments taking place on the continent.

THE OLD REGIME

WHAT WAS the Old Regime?

The period before the French Revolution's outbreak in 1789 is called the *ancien régime*, or the **Old Regime**. Politically, the age was characterized by absolute monarchies, growing bureaucracies, and aristocratically led armies. Economically, it featured the predominance of agriculture, food shortages, slow transportation, a low level of iron production, unsophisticated financial institutions, and competitive commercial overseas empires. Socially, people saw themselves less as individuals than as members of corporate bodies.

MAINTENANCE OF TRADITION

Few outside the political, commercial, and intellectual elite favored change. Nobles defended their ancient rights against intrusion by expanding monarchical bureaucracies. Peasants called for the revival or maintenance of their customary manorial rights. Except for early signs of industrial development in Britain, economies were predominantly traditional. Everything depended on the quality and quantity of the grain harvest.

HIERARCHY AND PRIVILEGE

The medieval sense of hierarchy became more rigid during the century. Some cities tried, with little success, to enforce sumptuary laws that forbade persons to dress like their social superiors, but it was the corporate nature of social relationships that was the most effective enforcer of hierarchy. Each state or society was a community composed of smaller communities. Eighteenth-century Europeans did not claim individual rights. Their rights were those of the communities of which they were a part. A "community" might be a village, a municipality, nobility, the church, a guild, a university, or a parish. Its privileges might involve exemption from taxation or degrading punishment or the right to practice a trade or craft.

ARISTOCRACY

The 18th century was the great age of the aristocracy. Nobles constituted about 1 to 5 percent of the population of any given country. They were the single wealthiest group, and land was the chief source of their income. They possessed the widest range of powers and dominated polite society. Aristocracy everywhere was a matter of birth and legal privilege, but in other respects, aristocrats differed markedly from country to country. Great Britain boasted the smallest, wealthiest, best defined, and most socially responsible aristocracy. Moving eastward across Europe, aristocrats became more numerous, not always wealthy, but possessing increasing degrees of arbitrary, repressive authority.

A European-wide *aristocratic resurgence* marked the 18th century as various nobilities sought to defend their privileges against the expanding power of monarchies and the growing wealth of commercial classes. The nobles restricted entry into their ranks and institutions. By monopolizing appointments to the officer corps of the armies, the bureaucracies, the government ministries, and the church, they tried to control the power of the monarchies. They tried to curtail royal authority by using institutions they already controlled: the British

Old Regime Term applied to the pattern of social, political, and economic relationships and institutions that existed in Europe before the French Revolution.

aristocratic resurgence Eighteenth-century aristocratic efforts to resist the expanding power of European monarchies.

Parliament, the French *parlements*, their local estates, and provincial diets. Nobles also pressed the peasantry for higher rents or long-forgotten feudal dues as a way to shore up their position and reassert traditional privileges.

THE LAND AND ITS TILLERS

Land was the economic basis of life in the 18th century. Well over three-fourths of all Europeans lived on the land and never traveled more than a few miles from their birthplaces. Most were poor, and their lives were hard.

PEASANTS AND SERFS

Most people who worked the land were subject to domination by landowners. This was true to different degrees for free peasants, such as English tenants and most French cultivators, and for the serfs of Germany, Austria, and Russia, who were bound to individual plots of land and particular lords. Landlord power increased from west to east. Most French peasants owned some land, but nearly all peasants were subject to feudal dues and to forced labor on a lord's estate for a certain number of days each year.

In Prussia and Austria, despite attempts by the monarchies to improve the lot of serfs, landlords exercised almost complete control over them. Moreover, throughout continental Europe the burden of state taxation fell on the tillers of the soil. Through various legal privileges and the ability to demand concessions from their monarchs, the landlords escaped the payment of numerous taxes. The serf's condition was worst in Russia. Russian serfs were regarded merely as economic commodities. Their services were attached to an individual lord rather than to a particular plot of land. Their landlords could demand up to six days a week of labor from them, and like Prussian and Austrian landlords, they could punish their serfs. Although serfs had little recourse against their lords, custom, tradition, and law provided a few protections. For example, the marriages of serfs, unlike those of most slaves, were legally recognized. The landlord could not disband the family of a serf (see "Russian Serfs Lament Their Condition").

QUICK REVIEW

Servants under the Old Regime
- Worked in exchange for room, board, and wages
- Usually young and not socially inferior to employer
- Work as servants allowed young people to save toward independence

parlement French regional court dominated by hereditary nobility. The most important was the Parlement of Paris, which claimed the right to register royal decrees before they could become law.

Road Work. Eighteenth-century France had some of the best roads in the world, but they were often built with forced labor. French peasants were required to work part of each year on such projects. This system, called the *corvée*, was not abolished until the French Revolution in 1789.

Joseph Vernet, "Construction of a Road." Louvre, Paris, France/Bridgemann-Giraudon/ Art Resource, N.Y.

HISTORY'S VOICES

RUSSIAN SERFS LAMENT THEIR CONDITION

As with other illiterate groups in European history, it is difficult to recapture the voices of Russian serfs. The following verses from "The Slaves' Lament," a popular ballad from the era of the Pugachev Rebellion (1773–1775), indicate that serfs were aware of how the legislation of that era, which favored the landowning classes, affected their lives. Note how the verses suggest that the tsar may be more favorable to serfs than their landowners are. Throughout this ballad, serfs present themselves as slaves.

WHAT SPECIFIC complaints about landlords are expressed in these verses? What charges indicate that serfs may believe their situation has worsened? What hope do they seem to place in the tsar? What idealized picture of the world do the serfs believe they would themselves create?

O woe to us slaves living for the masters!
We do not know how to serve their ferocity!
Service is like a sharp scythe;
And kindness is like the morning dew.
* * * * *
Brothers, how annoying it is to us
And how shameful and insulting
That another who is not worthy to be equal with us
Has so many of us in his power.
* * * * *
And if we steal from the lord one half kopeck,
The law commands us to be killed like a louse.
And if the master steals ten thousand,
Nobody will judge who should be hanged.
The injustice of the Russian sheriffs has increased:
Whoever brings a present is right beyond argument.
They have stopped putting their trust in the Creator
     for authority,
And have become accustomed to own us like cattle.
All nations rebuke us and wonder at our stupidity,
That such stupid people are born in Russia.
And indeed, stupidity was rooted in us long ago,

as each honour here has been given to vagrants.
The master can kill the servant like a gelding;
The denunciation by a slave cannot be believed.
Unjust judges have composed a decree
That we should be tyrannically whipped with a knout
     for that.
* * * * *
Better that we should agree to serve the tsar.
Better to live in dark woods
Than to be before the eyes of these tyrants;
They look on us cruelly with their eyes
And eat us as iron eats rye. No one wants to serve
     the tsar
But only to grind us down to the end.
And they try to collect unjust bribes,
And they are not frightened that people die cruelly.
* * * * *
Ah brothers, if we got our freedom,
We would not take the lands or the fields for
     ourselves.
We would go into service as soldiers, brothers,
And would be friendly among ourselves,
Would destroy all injustice
And remove the root of evil lords.
* * * * *
They [the landlords] sell all the good rye to the
     merchants,
And give us like pigs the bad.
The greedy lords eat meat at fast time,
And even when meat is allowed, the slaves
must cook meatless cabbage soup.
O brothers, it is our misfortune
always to have rye kasha.
The lords drink and make merry,
And do not allow the slaves even to burst out
     laughing.

Source: Paul Dukes, trans. and ed., *Russia under Catherine the Great: Select Documents on Government and Society* (Oriental Research Partners, 1978), pp. 115–117. Reprinted by permission of Oriental Research Partners.

Peter the Great (r. 1682–1725) gave whole villages of serfs to favored nobles, and Catherine the Great (r. 1762–1796) confirmed the authority of the nobles over their serfs in exchange for the nobility's political cooperation. The result was considerable unrest: more than 50 peasant revolts between 1762 and 1769. They culminated between 1773 and 1774 in Pugachev's rebellion, the largest peasant uprising of the 18th century. When it was finally and brutally suppressed, any discussion of liberalizing the condition of Russia's serfs was postponed for a generation. Smaller peasant revolts or disturbances occurred in Bohemia in 1775, in Transylvania in 1784, in Moravia in 1786, and in Austria in 1789. The peasants and serfs normally directed their wrath against property rather than persons, and they sought to reassert traditional or customary rights against practices they perceived as innovations. In this respect, the peasant revolts were profoundly conservative.

FAMILY STRUCTURES AND THE FAMILY ECONOMY

In preindustrial Europe, the household was the basic unit of production and consumption. In rural areas, small towns, and cities, the household mode of organization predominated: farms, artisans' workshops, and small merchants' shops. This created what is called the *family economy*.

THE FAMILY ECONOMY

Throughout Europe people saw themselves as family members working together in an interdependent rather than an independent or individualistic manner. Their goal was to sustain a family household by jointly producing or earning enough food to support its members. In the countryside, they usually farmed. In cities and towns, artisan crafts or paid employment produced their income. Almost everyone lived within a household because few could support themselves independently. Indeed, except for members of religious orders, people who were not part of a household were viewed as potentially criminal, disruptive, or a drain on the charity of others.

Every member of a family in the family economy had to work. Few peasant households in Western Europe had enough land to support themselves by farming alone. One or more of their family members had to work elsewhere and send wages home. It was not uncommon for a father to become a migrant worker and shift the burden of work on his own farm to his wife and younger children. Within the family economy, all of the goods and income produced benefitted the household, not individual family members. The need to survive poor harvests or economic slumps required everyone to work.

In the urban version of the family economy, the father was usually a chief craftsman who employed one or more servants. But he also expected his children to work in his shop. His eldest child was usually trained in the trade, and his wife

Emelyan Pugachev (1726–1775).
He led the largest peasant revolt in Russian history. In this contemporary propaganda picture, he is shown in chains. An inscription in Russian and German was printed below the picture decrying the evils of revolution and insurrection.
Bildarchiv Preussischer Kulturbesitz.

WHAT WAS the *family economy*?

family economy Basic structure of production and consumption in preindustrial Europe.

Women's Work. During the 18th century, with their employment opportunities tightly restricted, many unmarried women and widows served as governesses to children of the aristocracy and other wealthier groups in Europe.

Chardin, Jean-Baptiste-Simeon: "The Governess" (#6432), National Gallery of Canada, Ottawa.

QUICK REVIEW

Women in Preindustrial Society

- By age 7 girls contributed to household work
- Most girls left home between ages of 12 and 14
- A young woman's chief goal was to accumulate a dowry

WHY WAS land the economic basis of 18th-century life?

might sell the wares he produced or pursue another trade. The wife of a merchant also often ran her husband's business, especially when he traveled to purchase new goods. When business was poor, family members looked for other employment to help the family unit survive.

WOMEN AND THE FAMILY ECONOMY

The family economy constrained the lives of women in preindustrial society. In Western Europe, a woman's life experience was largely a function of her ability to establish and maintain a household. Marriage was an economic necessity for her, for a woman outside a household was highly vulnerable. Unless she was an aristocrat or a member of a religious order, she could probably not support herself. Consequently, much of a woman's life was devoted first to serving her parents' household and then to establishing one of her own.

By the age of 7, a girl was expected to begin to do household work. On a farm, she might look after chickens or water animals or carry food to adult men and women working the land. In an urban artisan's household, she would do some form of light work, such as cleaning, carrying, sewing, or weaving. She remained in her parents' home until they found more remunerative work for her elsewhere. An artisan's daughter might not leave home until marriage because she was learning valuable skills from her parents. Girls who grew up on farms, however, soon became of little value to their families. These girls left home, usually by the age of 12 or 14. They were likely to migrate to a nearby town or city to become household servants, but would rarely travel more than 30 miles from their parents' home.

A young woman's chief goal was to accumulate a dowry, some capital she could contribute to setting up a household with her husband. Marriage within the family economy was a joint economic undertaking. It might take a young woman 10 years or more to accumulate a dowry. This meant that marriage was usually postponed until a woman's mid- to late 20s.

A married woman's work was in many ways a function of her husband's occupation, but at all stages in life women played active, often decisive roles in the family economy. Ensuring an adequate food supply for the household was always the dominant concern, and domestic duties, childbearing, and child rearing were subordinate to economic survival. Couples practiced birth control. Young children were placed with wet nurses so that their mothers could continue to work. Wet nursing was a way for some to contribute to their households. Industriousness was a woman's lot in life.

THE REVOLUTION IN AGRICULTURE

The main goal of peasant society was to ensure the stability of the local food supply. That supply was never certain and became more uncertain the farther east one traveled. A failed harvest meant not only hardship, but also death from either outright starvation or protracted debility. Poor harvests played havoc with prices, and even small increases in the cost of food could

Farm Family.   Painted by the English artist Francis Wheatley (1747–1801) near the close of the 18th century, this scene is part of a series illustrating a day in the life of an idealized country-side farm family. Note the artist's assumptions about the division of labor by gender. Men work in the fields, women work in the home or look after the needs of men and children. As other illustrations in this chapter show, many 18th-century women in fact worked outside the home, but considerable social pressure was developing at this time to restrict them to domestic roles. This painting and the others in the series are thus more prescriptive than descriptive, intended in part to persuade their viewers that women belonged in their separate family sphere. Many, perhaps most, families living in the country could not maintain the closeness that these paintings extol. To survive, many had to send members to work on other farms or even to other regions.

squeeze peasant or artisan families. If prices increased sharply, many of those families sought help from their local government or the church. Peasants felt helplessness before the whims of nature and the marketplace, and they resisted change on the assumption that traditional cultivation practices best ensured the food supply.

During the century, bread prices, spurred by demand from a growing population, slowly but steadily rose. Prices rose faster than urban wages and brought no advantage to the small peasant producer. The beneficiaries were landlords and the wealthier peasants who had surplus grain to sell. The increasing price of grain encouraged these people to innovate in farm production and begin an *agricultural revolution.*

New Crops and New Methods   The agricultural revolution began during the 16th and 17th centuries in the Low Countries, where Dutch landlords and farmers devised better ways to build dykes and to drain land so that they could farm more extensive areas. They experimented with new crops, such as clover and turnips, that would increase the supply of animal fodder and replenish the soil.

The Dutch innovations spread to England during the early 18th century and provided the increased food production needed to support the development of an industrial society. They ensured adequate food for cities and freed surplus agricultural labor for industrial work, but the landlords' new approach to farming undermined traditional peasant life. The objective of farming ceased to be the provision of a local food supply and became the pursuit of the largest possible profit.

Enclosure Replaces Open-Field Method   Many of the agricultural innovations were incompatible with Britain's traditional modes of working the land. Small cultivators in village communities usually tilled unconnected strips, and

agricultural revolution
Innovations in farm production that began in the eighteenth century and led to a scientific and mechanized agriculture.

French peasants. Throughout the age of splendor of Louis XIV, millions of French peasants endured lives of poverty and hardship.

Source to come

enclosures Consolidation or fencing in of common lands by British landlords to increase production and achieve greater commercial profits. It also involved the reclamation of waste land and the consolidation of strips into block fields.

their traditional two- or three-field systems of rotation left much land fallow and unproductive each year. Decisions about planting were made communally. The system discouraged innovation and aimed to produce a steady, but not a growing, supply of food.

In 1700, approximately half the arable land in Britain was farmed by the open-field method. By the second half of the century, the rising price of wheat encouraged landlords to consolidate or enclose their lands to increase production. **Enclosure** involved fencing common lands, reclaiming previously untilled waste, and transforming cultivated strips into block fields. These procedures disrupted the economic and social life of the countryside and incited riots. The larger landlords resorted to parliamentary acts for help in enclosing lands. Between 1761 and 1792, almost 500,000 acres were enclosed through parliamentary acts, as compared with 75,000 acres between 1727 and 1760. In 1801, a general enclosure act streamlined the process.

Enclosures expanded farming, promoted innovation, and increased food production on larger agricultural units. They also disrupted traditional communities and forced many people off the land, but they did not depopulate the countryside. As more land was reclaimed for farming and a demand for services subsidiary to farming grew, population began to increase.

POPULATION EXPANSION

Agricultural improvement was both a cause and a result of an immense growth in the population of Europe. Exact figures are lacking, but the best estimates suggest that in 1700 Europe's population was between 100 million and 120 million people. By 1800, the figure had risen to almost 190 million, and by 1850, to 260 million. Causes of this growth are unclear. The death rate declined, thanks to fewer wars and epidemics in the 18th century. But changes in the food supply itself may have been the chief reason for sustained population growth. One contributing factor was the introduction of widespread cultivation of a New World tuber, the potato. Enough potatoes could be raised on a single acre to feed one peasant's family for an entire year.

THE 18TH-CENTURY INDUSTRIAL REVOLUTION

AN EVENT IN WORLD HISTORY

In the second half of the18th century the European economy underwent an **Industrial Revolution**. This development, more than any other change, has distinguished the West from the rest of the world. Previously, economies had been relatively static. But since the late 18th century, Europe's ecomomy has expanded at a relatively steady rate. Depressions and recessions have been temporary, and even during economic downturns the Western economy has continued to grow.

At considerable social cost and dislocation, industrialism produced more goods and services than ever before in human history and overcame the ancient economy of scarcity. New means of production demanded new kinds of skills, new discipline in work, and a large labor force. The goods produced met consumer demand and created new demand. In the long run, the poverty in which most Europeans had always lived was overcome, and industrialization gave human beings more control over the forces of nature than they had ever known. But industrialism also upset the political and social structures of the Old Regime and prompted political and social reform. The economic elite of the emerging industrial society challenged the political dominance of the aristocracy. Traditional communities declined, people were displaced, and cities grew. This occurred wherever industrialization spread during the next two centuries.

Industrialization produced a flood of consumer products for Europeans to market to the world. It encouraged international trade in which Western nations supplied finished goods in exchange for raw materials. As a consequence, other areas of the globe became economically dependent on European and American demand. This uneven commerce allowed Europeans to accumulate the wealth that allowed them to dominate world markets for almost two centuries, and it helped the West develop the military forces that ensured political dominance as well.

Much of the history of the non-Western world from the middle of the 18th century to the present can be understood in terms of how the nonindustrialized nations

HOW DID Europe's growing industrialization affect its relations with the rest of the world?

Industrial Revolution
Mechanization of the European economy that began in Britain in the second half of the 18th century.

Major Inventions in the Textile-Manufacturing Revolution

1733	John Kay's flying shuttle
1765	James Hargreaves's spinning jenny (patent 1770)
1769	James Watt's steam engine patent
1769	Richard Arkwright's water frame patent
1787	Edmund Cartwright's power loom

initially reacted to the penetration of their world by Westerners made wealthy and powerful by industrialized economies. Africa and Latin America became generally dependent economies. Japan, in the middle of the 19th century, decided it had to imitate Europe. China succumbed to indirect rule by Europeans. Southeast Asia and the Middle East were drawn into the network of resource supply to the West. The process of industrialization that commenced in small factories in 18th-century Europe has changed the world more than any other single development in the last two centuries.

INDUSTRIAL LEADERSHIP OF GREAT BRITAIN

Great Britain was the home of the Industrial Revolution. Several factors contributed to the early start of industrialization in Britain. Britain was the single largest free-trade area in Europe, with good roads and waterways without tolls or other internal trade barriers. There were rich deposits of coal and iron ore. The political structure was stable, and property rights were secure. A sound system of banking and public credit created a good investment climate. Taxation was heavy, but fairly collected. In addition to domestic consumer demand, the British economy also benefitted from the demand for goods from the North

OVERVIEW   WHY THE INDUSTRIAL REVOLUTION BEGAN IN BRITAIN

Great Britain was the home of the Industrial Revolution, and until the middle of the 19th century, it maintained the industrial leadership of Europe. Several factors contributed to the early industrialization of Britain.

Natural Resources Infrastructure	1. Britain had extensive deposits of coal and iron ore. 2. Britain had an extensive network of roads and canals that facilitated the shipment of raw materials and goods.
Society	1. The predominance of London: London was the largest city in Europe and the social, commercial, financial, and political center of Britain. It was thus both an enormous market for consumer goods and created a demand for these goods in the rest of Britain, which sought to emulate London fashions. 2. The prevalence of newspapers: Newspapers thrived in Britain, and advertisements in them increased consumer demand for goods. 3. Wealth in Britain brought status: British society was relatively mobile. Wealthy merchants and entrepreneurs could rise socially, enter the aristocracy, and enjoy political influence.
Government, Financial Institutions, and Empire	1. The rule of law: Britain had a stable government that guaranteed property rights. 2. Britain was a free trade area. No internal tolls inhibited the shipment of goods and raw materials within Britain. 3. Britain had a sound system of banking and public credit that created a stable climate for investing in commerce and industry. 4. Taxes were collected efficiently and fairly. No class was exempt from paying taxes. 5. The colonial empire: British colonies were both a market for British goods and sources of raw materials for British manufacturers.

American colonies. Finally, British society was relatively open and allowed people who had money, or who could earn it, to rise socially.

New Methods of Textile Production   Eighteenth-century European society concentrated primarily on agriculture, but small-scale household manufacturing permeated the countryside. The same peasants who tilled the land in spring and summer often spun thread or wove textiles in winter. Under the **domestic** or *putting-out system*, agents of urban textile merchants distributed wool or other fibers to the homes of peasants, who spun it into thread. The agent then transported the thread to other peasants, who wove it into cloth, and the merchant sold the final product. Sometimes spinners or weavers owned their own equipment, but more often than not the merchant capitalist provided the machinery.

By mid-century production bottlenecks had developed within the domestic system. The demand for cotton textiles exceeded production as population increased in Great Britain and its colonies The most famous inventions of the Industrial Revolution were stimulated by consumer demand for cotton textiles. John Kay's invention of the flying shuttle in the 1730s gave weavers the technical capacity to produce enough fabric to satisfy demand, but spinners could not make enough thread for the weavers. Manufacturers offered prizes for the invention of a machine to correct this imbalance, and about 1765 James Hargreaves (d. 1778) invented the **spinning jenny**.

The spinning jenny was a piece of machinery for cottage use. The invention that moved cotton textile manufacture from the home to the factory was Richard Arkwright's (1732–1792) **water frame**, patented in 1769. When Arkwright lost his patent rights, other manufacturers used his invention, and numerous factories sprang up in the countryside near streams that provided water power. By 1815, cotton composed 40 percent of the value of British domestic exports, and by 1830 just over 50 percent.

The Steam Engine   The invention that more than any other enabled industrialization to spread from one industry to another was the steam engine. For the first time in history, human beings were able to tap an unlimited source of inanimate power. Unlike engines powered by water or wind, the steam engine, fueled by coal, provided a portable, steady source of power that could be applied to many industrial and transportation uses.

The first practical engine using steam power was invented by Thomas Newcomen (1663–1729) in the early 18th century. It was large, inefficient, and practically immovable, but English mine operators used it to pump water out of coal and tin mines. During the 1760s, James Watt (1736–1819) began to experiment with a model of a Newcomen machine at the University of Glasgow. In 1769, he patented an improved design, but it required precise metalwork. Watt's partner Matthew Boulton (1728–1809), a toy manufacturer, worked with John Wilkinson (1728–1808), a cannon manufacturer, to find ways to drill the precise

Blacksmith Shop. During the 18th century, most goods were produced in small workshops, such as this English blacksmith shop shown in a painting by Joseph Wright of Derby (1734–1797), or in the homes of artisans. Not until very late in the century, with the early stages of industrialization, did a few factories appear.

Joseph Wright of Derby, "The Blacksmith's Shop," signed and dated 1771, oil on canvas, 50 1/2 × 41 in. (128.3 × 104.0 cm). Yale Center for British Art, Paul Mellon Collection.

domestic or putting-out system of textile production Method of producing textiles in which agents furnished raw materials to households whose members spun them into thread and then wove cloth, which the agents sold as finished products.

spinning jenny Machine invented in England by James Hargreaves around 1765 to mass-produce thread.

water frame Water-powered device invented by Richard Arkwright to produce a more durable cotton fabric. It led to the shift in the production of cotton textiles from households to factories.

Dress Shop. Consumption of all forms of consumer goods increased greatly in the 18th century. This engraving illustrates a shop, probably in Paris. Here women, working apparently for a woman manager, are making dresses and hats to meet the demands of the fashion trade.

Bildarchiv Preussischer Kulturbesitz.

metal cylinders required by Watt's engines. In 1776, the Watt steam engine found its first commercial application pumping water from mines. Boulton persuaded a reluctant Watt to adapt the engines for use in running cotton mills, and by the early 19th century the steam engine had become the prime mover in every industry. Applied to ships and then to wagons on iron rails, it also revolutionized transportation.

Iron Production The manufacture of high-quality iron was essential for industrial development. In the course of the 18th century, British ironmakers began to use coke (derived from coal) instead of charcoal to smelt ores, and the steam engine provided power for high temperature blast furnaces. Britain had large coal deposits, and the steam engine improved iron production while increasing demand for iron. In 1784, Henry Cort (1740–1800) introduced a new method for melting and stirring molten ore that yielded a purer iron. He also developed a rolling mill that shaped molten metal into bars, rails, or other forms. Previously, metal had to be pounded into shape. All of these innovations achieved a better, more versatile, and cheaper product, and by the early 19th century, annual British iron production amounted to more than a million tons.

EUROPEAN CITIES

PATTERNS OF PREINDUSTRIAL URBANIZATION

WHAT KINDS of cities in Europe grew fastest between 1600 and 1750?

Remarkable changes occurred in the pattern of city growth between 1500 and 1800. In 1500, there were approximately 156 cities within Europe (excluding Hungary and Russia) with a population greater than 10,000. Only Paris, Milan,

Venice, and Naples had more than 100,000 inhabitants. By 1800, approximately 363 cities had 10,000 or more inhabitants, and 17 of those had populations larger than 100,000. The percentage of the European population living in urban areas had risen from just over 5 percent to just over 9 percent. The urban concentration had also shifted from southern Mediterranean Europe to the north.

URBAN CLASSES

The Upper Classes   At the top of the urban social structure stood a generally small group of nobles, major merchants, bankers, financiers, clergy, and government officials. They usually constituted a self-appointed and self-electing oligarchy who governed the city through its corporation or city council. In a few cities on the continent, artisan guilds featured in urban governments, but most city councils were dominated by the local nobility and the commercial elite.

The Middle Class   Prosperous, but not wealthy, merchants, tradesmen, bankers, and professional people were a city's most dynamic citizens. They constituted its middle class, or *bourgeoisie*. The middle class had less wealth than most nobles, but more than urban artisans. Middle-class people lived in the cities and towns, and their sources of income had little or nothing to do with the land. They normally supported reform, change, and economic growth. They resented aristocratic privilege and social exclusiveness and wanted rational regulations for trade and commerce.

As the century passed, the bourgeoisie increasingly begrudged the aristocracy, and as the middle class grew in size and wealth and aristocratic control of political and ecclesiastical power tightened, tension increased. On the other hand, the middle class tended to fear the lower urban classes, a potentially violent element in society and a threat to property.

Artisans   The segment of the urban population that suffered most from the greed of the middle class and nobility consisted of shopkeepers, artisans, and wage earners—the largest single group in any city. They had their own culture, values, and institutions and, like the rural peasants, were conservative. Their economic position was highly vulnerable, and their lives centered on their work. They usually lived near or at their place of employment and worked in shops with fewer than a half dozen other people. They formed guilds to protect their interests, but by the 18th century these had declining influence and reinforced conservative values. Guilds were dedicated to preserving the jobs of their members, and they tried to prevent too many competitors from entering their markets.

THE JEWISH POPULATION: AGE OF THE GHETTO

There were small Jewish communities in Amsterdam and other Western European cities, but most European Jews lived in eastern Europe. In 1762, Catherine the Great of Russia specifically excluded Jews from a manifesto that welcomed foreigners to settle in Russia, although she eased this a few years later. The first partition of Poland in 1772 (see Chapter 23) gave Russia a large Jewish population and created larger Jewish communities in Prussia and Austria.

QUICK REVIEW

Urban Classes
- Upper classes: Nobles, large merchants, bankers, financiers, clergy, government officials
- Middle class: Prosperous merchants, tradesmen, bankers, professionals
- Artisans: shopkeepers, wage earners, artisans

WHY WERE Jews discriminated against under the Old Regime?

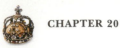

Ghetto in Cracow. During the Old Regime, European Jews were separated from non-Jews, typically in districts known as ghettos. Relegated to the least desirable section of a city or to rural villages, most lived in poverty. This watercolor painting depicts a street in Kazimlesz, the Jewish quarter of Cracow, Poland.

Judaica Collection Max Berger, Vienna Austria/©Erich Lessing/Art Resource, N.Y.

ghettos Separate communities in which Jews were required by law to live.

Jews did not have the same rights as Christians, unless such rights were specifically granted to them by a sympathetic monarch. They were resident aliens whose status could change at the whim of a government. Under the Old Regime, they lived apart from non-Jews—in cities usually in districts called *ghettos*; and in the countryside in separate villages. They were treated as a distinct people religiously and legally and often bore the burden of discriminatory legislation.

During the 17th century, a few Jews helped finance wars for major rulers. The most famous of these "court Jews" was Samuel Oppenheimer (1630–1703), who helped the Habsburgs fund the struggle against the Turks that defended Vienna. The court Jews were exceptional, for most European Jews lived in poverty and worked at the lowest occupations. Their religious beliefs, rituals, and community set them apart, and numerous issues kept them in positions of social inferiority. But under the Old Regime, the discrimination they suffered was based on religious separateness, not racial prejudices. Jews who converted to Christianity were admitted to the political and social institutions of European society.

SUMMARY

Models of European Political Development In the 17th and 18th centuries, five great powers emerged in Europe: France, Britain, Austria, Prussia, and Russia. Through their military strength, economic development, and in some cases colonial empires, they would affect virtually every other world civilization.

Britain In the 17th century, conflict between the Stuart kings and Parliament arising out of political, religious, and economic issues led to civil war, the execution of Charles I, a short-lived English republic under Oliver Cromwell, and in 1688 and 1689 the Glorious Revolution that finally limited royal authority and established the supremacy of Parliament. Although 18th-century England was not a democracy, its people had more rights and liberties than the subjects of the absolutist monarchs who ruled the other European great powers. In a series of worldwide colonial struggles with France, Britain used its commercial resources and navy to profit from France's entanglements in Europe and emerge supreme in North America and India.

France   Under Louis XIV (r. 1643–1715), France became the model of an absolute monarchy. Louis used his splendid court at Versailles to overawe the French aristocracy and promote a glittering image of French culture that impressed all of Europe. However, he was not able completely to overcome opposition from the French elites who sought to reassert their influence under his successors. His revocation of the Edict of Nantes weakened France by driving thousands of French Protestants into exile. Louis pursued an aggressive foreign policy that expanded France's borders but cost France dearly in wealth and resources and provoked strong opposition from the other European powers. In the War of the Spanish Succession, he succeeded in placing his grandson on the throne of Spain, but the war left France exhausted.

Russia   Russia became a great power under Peter the Great (r. 1682–1725). Peter curbed the power of the Russian church and aristocracy and opened Russia to Western technology and military and commercial influences. He built his new capital at St. Petersburg. He also built an efficient army and navy and established a centralized bureaucracy to collect revenue.

Central Europe   The Habsburgs remained Holy Roman Emperors, but their power rested on their hereditary domains—Austria, Hungary, Bohemia, and northern Italy. Although the Habsburgs reconquered Hungary from the Ottomans, the rise of Prussia under the Hohenzollerns challenged Habsburg dominance in Central Europe. The Hohenzollern rulers built Prussia from a collection of scattered German states into a great power by developing an efficient bureaucracy and a powerful army. Under Frederick II (r. 1740–1786), Prussia emerged from a series of wars with Austria, France, and Russia as one of the strongest European states and the rival to Habsburg power in central Europe.

The Old Regime   Eighteenth-century European society was traditional, hierarchical, corporate, and privileged—features that had characterized Europe and the world for centuries. All societies also confronted scarce food supplies. For the 18th century, however, an improved food supply helped support a larger population. New agricultural techniques and the expanding population created pressures on social structures. Commerce also grew during the 18th century. Agriculture became more commercialized, with more money payments. Cities expanded.

Changes in European Society   European society stood on the brink of a new era in which the social, economic, and political relationships of centuries

IMAGE KEY
for pages 484–485

a. F. Boucher, *The Breakfast*, 1739. Francois Boucher (1703–1770). Louvre, Paris, France. Copyright Scala/Art Resource.
b. Grains of wild einkorn.
c. Maria Theresa of Austria. Kunsthistorisches Museum, Vienna.
d. The Crown of Louis XV, 1722.
e. A long-handled churn.
f. Cardinal Richelieu.
g. The taking of Quebec by British forces in September 1759. The Granger Collection, New York.
h. Francis Wheatley's *Evening*.
i. The Jewish quarter Kazimlesz in Krakow, Poland.
j. St. Petersburg, Russia.

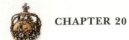

would be destroyed. The commercial spirit and the values of the marketplace clashed with the traditions of peasants and guilds. That commercial spirit brought social change; by the early 19th century it led to a conception of human beings as individuals rather than as members of communities.

The expansion of the European population further stimulated change and challenge to tradition, hierarchy, and corporateness. The traditional economic and social organization (the family economy) had presupposed a stable or declining population. A larger population created the need for new ways to solve old problems. The social hierarchy had to accommodate more people. Corporate groups, such as the guilds, had to confront an expanded labor force. New wealth meant that birth would cease to determine social relationships.

The 18th century also witnessed the beginning of industrial production in response to the demands for consumer goods by the expanding population. New inventions greatly increasing productive capacity first appeared in the English textile industry. Thereafter industrial modes of production spread to the manufacture of iron. The steam engine provided a portable source of energy, allowing factories to be moved from the countryside into cities.

Industrialization also affected Europe's relations with much of the non-European world. For the first time in history, major changes in one region of Europe left virtually no corner of the globe untouched. By the close of the 18th century, a movement toward world interconnectedness and interdependence had begun.

REVIEW QUESTIONS

1. By the end of the 17th century, what differences had emerged between the governments of England and France? Why did each nation develop as it did?

2. How and why did Russia emerge as a great power?

3. What was the *family economy*? What roles did women play in preindustrial society?

4. What caused the agricultural revolution? What caused the Industrial Revolution?

5. How did population growth affect the development of Europe in the 18th century?

6. What was the status of European Jews in the Old Regime? What were the sources of prejudice against them?

KEY TERMS

absolutism (p. 486)

agricultural revolution (p. 503)

aristocratic resurgence (p. 498)

boyars (p. 489)

divine right of kings (p. 488)

domestic or putting-out system
(p. 507)

enclosures (p. 504)

family economy (p. 501)

ghettos (p. 510)

Glorious Revolution (p. 487)

Industrial Revolution (p. 505)

Junkers (p. 493)

Old Regime (p. 498)

parliamentary monarchy (p. 486)

Pragmatic Sanction (p. 493)

Puritans (p. 486)

spinning jenny (p. 507)

streltsy (p. 489)

Table of Ranks (p. 492)

water frame (p. 507)

 For additional study resources for this chapter, go to:
www.prenhall.com/craig/chapter20

21 The Last Great Islamic Empires
1500–1800

CHAPTER HIGHLIGHTS

The Last Islamic Empires The period from 1500 to 1800, marks the cultural and political blossoming of the last Islamic empires and their sharp decline. The Islamic vitality in the first half of this period was exemplified in the Ottoman, Safavid, and Mughal Empires. All three built vast bureaucracies and arguably the greatest cities in the world of their time. They patronized the arts. Yet they were conservative societies. Economically, they remained tied to agricultural production and taxation based on land. They did not undergo the social or religio-political revolutions that rocked the West after 1500 or the sort of generative changes in material and intellectual life that the Western world experienced during the same period. There was no compelling challenge to traditional Islamic ideals, even though numerous Islamic movements of the eighteenth century did call for reform.

Decline By the latter half of this period, all these empires were in economic, political, and military decline, even if intellectual and artistic vigor held on.

Thus, it is not surprising that European expansionism impinged in these three centuries upon Africa, India, Indonesia, and the Islamic heartland, rather than the reverse. None of the Islamic states, fared well in their encounters with Europeans during this age. Their growing domination of the world's seas allowed Europeans to contain or to bypass the major Islamic lands in their quest for commercial empires.

Industrial development joined economic wealth and political stability by the late 1700s to give the West global military supremacy for the first time. Before 1800, the Europeans were able to bring only minor Islamic states under colonial administrations. However, the footholds they gained in Africa, India, and Southeast Asia laid the groundwork for rapid colonial expansion after 1800. The age of the last great Muslim empires was the beginning of the first great modern European empires.

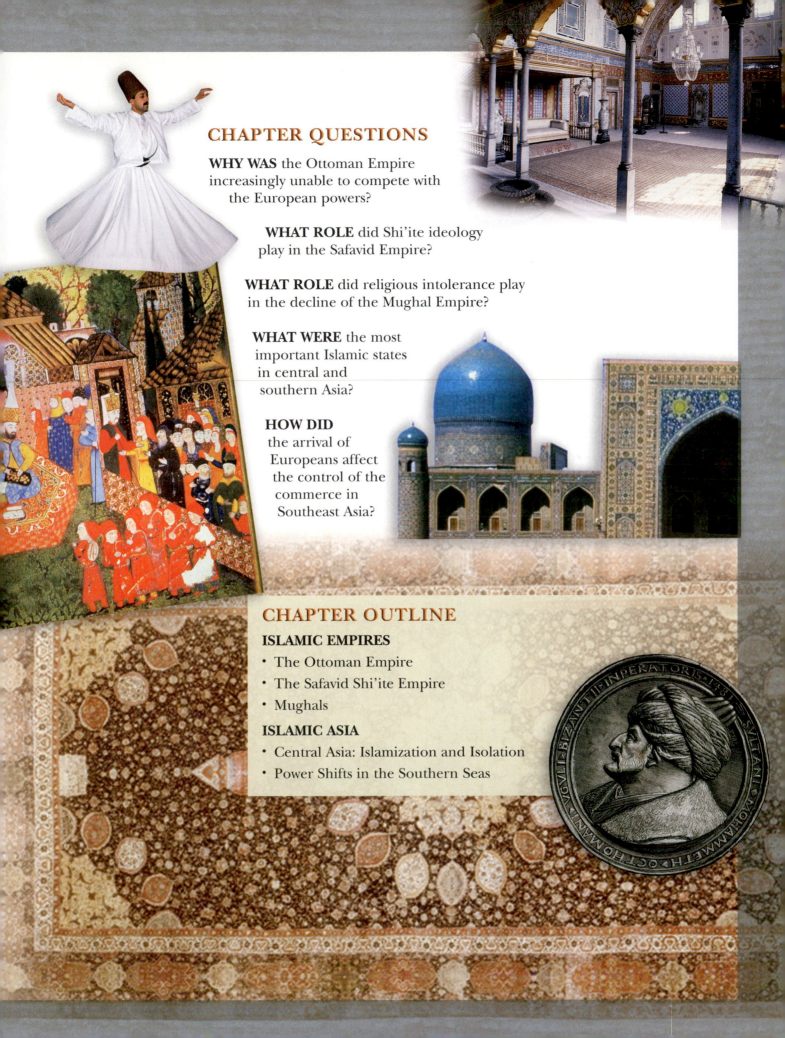

CHAPTER QUESTIONS

WHY WAS the Ottoman Empire increasingly unable to compete with the European powers?

WHAT ROLE did Shi'ite ideology play in the Safavid Empire?

WHAT ROLE did religious intolerance play in the decline of the Mughal Empire?

WHAT WERE the most important Islamic states in central and southern Asia?

HOW DID the arrival of Europeans affect the control of the commerce in Southeast Asia?

CHAPTER OUTLINE

ISLAMIC EMPIRES

- The Ottoman Empire
- The Safavid Shi'ite Empire
- Mughals

ISLAMIC ASIA

- Central Asia: Islamization and Isolation
- Power Shifts in the Southern Seas

Between 1450 and 1650, Islamic culture and statecraft blossomed. The creation of the Ottoman, Safavid, and Mughal Empires marked the global apogee of Islamic culture and power.

In 1600, Islamic civilization seemed as strong and vital as that of Western Europe, China, or Japan. Yet by the late 17th century, Islamic power was in retreat before the rising tide of Western European military and economic imperialism, even though Islamic cultural life and Muslim religion flourished. Hindus were the chief religious group the Muslims displaced (see Map 21–1).

WHY WAS the Ottoman Empire increasingly unable to compete with the European powers?

Grand Mufti Chief religious authority of the Ottoman Empire. Also called "the Shaykh of Islam."

Shari'a Islamic religious law.

Süleyman the Lawgiver (r. 1520–1566). Süleyman the Lawgiver giving advice to the Crown Prince, Mehmed Khan. From a contemporaneous Ottoman miniature.

Folio 79a of the *Talikizade Shenamesi*, Library of the Topkapi Palace Museum, A3592/Photograph courtesy of Talat Halman.

ISLAMIC EMPIRES

THE OTTOMAN EMPIRE

ORIGINS AND DEVELOPMENT OF THE OTTOMAN STATE BEFORE 1600

The Ottomans were a Turkish dynasty that reached Anatolia (Asia Minor) in the time of the Seljuks of Rum (1098–1308). In the 14th century, the Ottomans expanded into central Anatolia and west across the Dardanelles (in 1356) onto European soil. The Ottomans built a formidable army, and by 1421, Ottoman control extended as far as the Danube. Constantinople fell in 1453 to Sultan Mehmed II, "the Conqueror" (r. 1451–1481). It became the Ottoman capital and was renamed Istanbul. After hundreds of years, Byzantium, the center of eastern Christendom, was no more. Its conquest stimulated the Ottoman appetite for European territory. As the extraordinary conquests of the Ottomans continued, Christian Europe again felt threatened by Islam.

By 1512, Ottoman rule was secure in southeastern Europe. Under Selim I (r. 1512–1520) and Süleyman, "the Lawgiver" ("Süleyman the Magnificent"; r. 1520–1566), this sovereignty was greatly expanded. Selim subjugated Egypt (1517), Syria-Palestine, and most of North Africa. The Yemen and western Arabia, including Mecca and Medina, also came under his control. Süleyman added the Caucasus, Mesopotamia, and most of Hungary to the Ottoman Empire (see Map 21–1).

These conquests enabled the Ottoman ruler legitimately to claim to be the caliph for all Muslims—a claim signified by the titles "Protector of the Sacred Places [Mecca and Medina]" and "emperor" (padishah). Ottoman military might was, at this point, unmatched by any world state, except possibly China.

THE "CLASSICAL" OTTOMAN ORDER

Mehmed II was the true founder of the Ottoman political system. He replaced tribal chieftains with men loyal to him and began a tradition of formal legislation. He organized the *ulama* into a hierarchy under a "Sheikh of Islam," the **Grand Mufti**. Süleyman the Lawgiver reconciled customary law and **Shari'a**, religious law, and regularized both the law and the bureaucracy. The Ottoman state was structured as one

MAP EXPLORATION

Interactive map: To explore this map further, go to **http://www.prenhall.com/craig/map21.1**

MAP 21–1

The Islamic World ca. 1700. The three rival "gunpowder" empires—the Safavid, Mughal, and Ottoman Empires—dominated the Islamic heartlands.

BY 1700, was the Islamic world in decline?

vast military institution. All its members held military rank. The ruling class were Muslim men who pledged total allegiance to the sultan. However, some women, although concealed from public eye, played important roles. They had ceremonial functions and influence over the appointment of officers and formulation of economic policy.

Several measures helped ensure the sultan's power. Young Ottoman princes received leadership training in the provinces, allowing them to experience life outside the capital. The succession was theoretically left to God in a power struggle that ended with the strongest aspirant to the sultanate seizing the throne. Stability of succession was guaranteed by the legal requirement that the man who won the throne would execute all his brothers, a policy that continued into the late 16th century.

12.2
Süleyman "The Lawgiver" and the Advantages of Islam: Oigier de Busbecq

12.4
The Ottomans: Empire-builders at the Crossroads of Three Continents

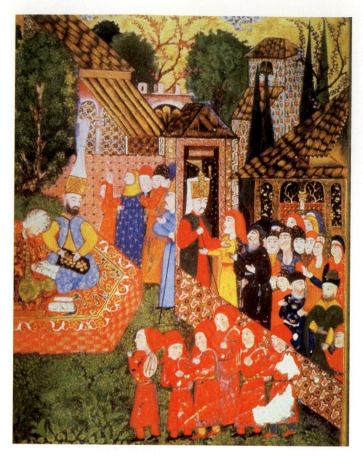

Devshirme. An Ottoman portrayal of the *devshirme*. This miniature painting from about 1558 depicts the recruiting of young Christian children (located at the bottom of the picture) for the Sultan's elite Janissary corps.

Arifi, "Suleymanname," Topkapi Palace Museum, II 1517, fol. 31b, photograph courtesy of Talat Halman.

devshirme System under the Ottoman Empire that required each province to furnish a levy of Christian boys who were raised as Muslims and became soldiers in the Ottoman army.

Janissaries Elite Ottoman troops who were recruited through the *devshirme*.

The Ottomans organized the religious scholars, or *ulama*, as a department of government. A system of courts and judges rested on a comprehensive system of educational institutions ranging from local mosque schools to four elite madrasas in Istanbul. Scholars held graded rank with the hierarchy reflecting their level of schooling. The ulama enjoyed great prestige and usually functioned as part of the state apparatus. The religious establishment upheld the *Shari'a* and the sultan recognized its authority, but the functional law of the land was the ruler's legislation, or Qanun. The *Shari'a* theoretically governed the *Qanun*, but sometimes their conformity was only a pious fiction.

Ottoman rulers kept the military loyal by checking the power of the old landed aristocracy and by using slave soldiers whose only allegiance was to the sultan. To sustain the quality of these slave troops, the Ottomans established the provincial slave levy, or *devshirme*. Christian boys were chosen from the peasantry to be raised as Muslims and trained to serve in both army and bureaucracy. The most famous slave corps was the **Janissaries**, the elite infantry of the empire. They reduced the aristocratic cavalry's preeminence and, unlike the cavalry, were equipped with firearms.

AFTER SÜLEYMAN: CHALLENGES AND CHANGE

The reign of Süleyman marked the peak of Ottoman prestige and power (see Map 21–2). Beginning with his weak son, Selim II (1566–1574), the empire was plagued by corruption, decentralization, and maritime setbacks. Agricultural failures, commercial imbalances, and inflation were hard to check. Despite the fact that the empire seesawed between decline and vitality, its cultural achievements during the 17th and 18th centuries were impressive.

Political and Military Developments The post-Süleyman era began with the loss of territory in the east to the Persian Safavids (1603). By this time the Ottoman military apparatus was weakening, partly from fighting two-front wars with the Safavids and the Habsburgs and partly because of European advances in technology. The Janissaries, once the backbone of Ottoman power, became disruptive and tried to influence decision making and even dynastic succession. Finally, the increasing employment of mercenaries resulted, whenever peace was declared, in the release of masses of unemployed armed men into the countryside. They sacked provincial towns and practiced banditry.

Economic Developments Financing the Ottoman state grew more difficult. By 1600, the increase in the Janissary corps from 12,000 to 36,000 men had drained state coffers. Fluctuations in silver caused inflation. To avoid shortages that would raise prices for domestic consumers, the Ottomans encouraged imports and discouraged exports, a policy that hurt the Ottoman economy in the long run. Unemployment increased as the population doubled in the 16th century. As central authority weakened, provincial notables (*ayan*) grew stronger until, by the 18th century, they were virtually independent.

Culture and Society   The 17th and 18th centuries were an era of vitality in artistic and intellectual life. The sultan used patronage of the arts and sciences to back the Ottoman claim to universal authority. The ulama, however, became an aristocratic and increasingly corrupt elite. Major religious posts were controlled by a handful of families and became hereditary sinecures that were often sold or leased.

Notable among the scholars of the period is Katib Chelebi (d. 1657), the most illustrious of the many polymaths who wrote histories, social commentary, geographies, and encyclopedic works. Thanks to men like the imperial master architect Sinan (d. 1578), the Ottomans developed distinctive artistic and architectural forms in the late 16th century. The first half of the 18th century saw the introduction of the printing press to the Ottoman Empire and the flourishing of the golden age of Ottoman poetry and art.

Socially, the period saw the consolidation of Ottoman society as a multi-ethnic and multireligious state. All subjects, both Muslim and non-Muslim, were organized into small communities called *millets*. These communities were responsible for their members from cradle to grave, providing education, justice, charitable aid, and liason with the sultan's government. They were usually headed by a religious leader and had considerable freedom to handle their own internal affairs. This made the empire a haven for minority groups, especially Jews. Many Jews settled in Ottoman lands following their expulsion from Spain in 1492. The large Christian population of the empire was well treated until the 17th century, when they began to suffer increasing discrimination. They then began to look to Europe and Russia for liberation.

During the 18th century, relations between Muslims and non-Muslims generally grew increasingly strained. This was, in part, a reaction to the rise in the economic and social status of non-Muslims—particularly in the rich mercantile middle class. Non-Muslims monopolized foreign trade and, in the 18th century, European countries gave many of them citizenship, which qualified them for trade privileges the sultan granted to foreign governments.

One of the characteristic social institutions of later Ottoman society, the coffeehouse, flourished from the mid-16th century on. It rapidly became a major common space for socializing, as people gathered to drink coffee, play games, read, and discuss public affairs. It stimulated the development of a common Ottoman urban culture among lower and middle classes.

millets   Small self-governing communities within the Ottoman Empire.

The Ottoman Empire

ca. 1280	Foundation of early Ottoman principality in Anatolia
1356	Ottomans cross Dardanelles into Europe
1451–1481	Rule of Sultan Mehmed II, "the Conqueror"
1453	Fall of Constantinople to Mehmed the Conqueror
1512–1520	Rule of Selim I
1517	Ottoman conquest of Egypt, assumption of claim to Abbasid caliphal succession from Mamluks
1520–1566	Rule of Süleyman, "the Lawgiver"
1578	Death of Ottoman master architect, Sinan
1683	Ottoman siege of Vienna
1699	Treaty of Karlowitz, loss of Hungarian and other European territory
1774	Loss of Crimea to Russia; tsar becomes formal protector of Ottoman Orthodox Christians
1918	End of empire

MAP 21–2

The Ottoman Empire at its Zenith, late 16th century. This large and multiethnic empire spanned three continents and lasted for more than 400 years.

WHAT WERE the strengths and weaknesses of the Ottoman Empire's geographical position?

THE DECLINE OF OTTOMAN MILITARY AND POLITICAL POWER

After the failure in 1683 of a second siege of Vienna, the Ottomans were driven out of Hungary and Belgrade and never again threatened Europe. The treaty of Karlowitz sealed the loss of Hungary to Austria (1699). Defeat by Russia cost the Ottomans the Crimea and made the tsar the protector of the Orthodox Christians within the Islamic empire (1774). The Ottoman economy had been based on conquest and control of land. Once expansion stopped, the sultans failed to adapt to the effects that European capitalism and industrialization were having on the world economy. Henceforth, the Ottomans were prey to the West. Outflanked by Russia to their north and by European sea power to the south and west, the Ottomans were also blocked in the east by Shi'ite foes in Iran. They never regained their earlier power and influence, and their empire collapsed in 1918.

THE SAFAVID SHI'ITE EMPIRE

ORIGINS

As noted in Chapter 13, Iranian history changed under the Safavid dynasty after 1500. The Safavids originated in the 14th century as hereditary Turkish spiritual leaders of a Sunni Sufi order in the northwestern Iranian province of Azerbaijan. In the 15th century, the Safavid order evolved a new, militant Shi'ite ideology. The Safavid spiritual masters (*shaykhs* and *pirs*) claimed descent from the seventh imam of the Twelver Shia (see Chapter 13), which made them the focus of Shi'ite religious allegiance.

The growing strength of the Safavids led to conflict with the dominant Sunni groups around Tabriz. The Safavids emerged victorious in 1501 under the leadership of the young Safavid master-designate Isma'il. By 1506, he had established sovereignty over the southern Caucasus, Azerbaijan, the Tigris-Euphrates valley, and western Iran. By 1512, the Safavids had taken eastern Iran from the Uzbek Turks. The Uzbeks, however, became implacable foes of the Safavids and throughout the ensuing century often forced them to fight a debilitating two-front war—Uzbeks in the east; Ottomans in the west.

Strong central rule now united Iran for the first time since the Abbasid caliphate. The regime adopted existing Persian bureaucratic institutions. Shah Isma'il enforced Shi'ite conformity on the Sunni majority, and Shi'ite conformity slowly took root across the realm—perhaps bolstered by Persian self-consciousness in the face of the Sunni Ottomans, Arabs, Uzbeks, and Mughals who surrounded Iran. He was determined to rule not merely as a leader of a Sufi religious movment but to govern as a restoration of the historic Iranian monarchy.

The Ottomans were determined that this Sufi-inspired Shi'ite monarchy not spread further into their territory. The better-armed army of Selim I defeated the Safavids in 1514, beginning a series of Ottoman-Safavid conflicts that continued for two centuries. The Ottomans took control of the Fertile Crescent and forced the Safavids to move their capital and their focus eastward to Isfahan.

SHAH ABBAS I

Tahmasp I (r. 1524–1576), Isma'il's successor, survived attacks by both Ottomans and Uzbeks. The strength of Shi'ite religious feeling and the allegiance of government bureaucrats preserved his regime. A few years later, the greatest Safavid ruler, Shah Abbas I (r. 1588–1629), pushed the Ottomans out of Azerbaijan and Iraq and turned back Uzbek invasions in Khorasan. He also sought alliances with the Ottomans' European enemies. This latter tactic, used by several Safavid rulers, reflects the division that the new militant Persian Shi'ism had brought to the Islamic world. Abbas also began to trade with the English and Dutch. The prosperity Iran enjoyed during his reign is reflected by the magnificent capital he built at Isfahan.

WHAT ROLE did Shi'ite ideology play in the Safavid Empire?

pirs Shi'ite holy men.

Worldly and Spiritual Drunkenness. This painting by the great 16th-century Safavid Iranian court painter Sultan Muhammad is from an illustrated copy of the *Diwan*, or collected works of the lyric and mystical poet Hafiz (1319–1389?). Hafiz appears himself as a drunken figure in the upper window. The entire picture plays the worldly drunkenness and debauchery of the characters in the center against the spiritual inebriation of the dancing Sufis in the garden and the angels on the roof. The angels, too, are shown drinking, a visual reference to the line of Hafiz at the top: "The angel of mercy took the cup of revelry."

Courtesy of the Metropolitan Museum of Art and Arthur M. Sackler Museum, Harvard University. Promised gift of Mr. and Mrs. Stuart Cary Welch, 1988; © 1989 Metropolitan Museum of Art.

The Safavid Empire

ca. 1500	Rise of Safavids under Shah Isma'il
1501–1512	Safavid conquest of greater Iran; Shi'ite state founded
1588–1629	Rule of Shah Abbas I
1722	Forced abdication of last Safavid ruler
1736–1747	Rule of the Sunni Afghan leader, Nadir Shah; revival of Sunni monarchy in Iran
1739	Nadir Shah sacks Delhi

12.5

The Safavid Shi'ite
Empire of Persia

The Shah's Mosque (Masjid-i Shah) in Isfahan, Iran. During its heyday as the Safavid capital, Isfahan was given the lofty epithet "half of the world." Its elegant architecture and lavish use of ceramic tiles reflects the majestic Safavid self-image.

Corbis-Bettmann.

The most enduring feature of the Safavid consolidation of power in Iran was the replacement of Sunni Islam with Shi'ite Islam as the official religion. The Safavids discouraged pilgrimages to Mecca and urged visits to Karbala or to the shrine of Husayn, the grandson of the Prophet Muhammad.

SAFAVID DECLINE

After Shah Abbas, with the exception of Abbas II (1642–1666) and Husayn I (1694–1722), the empire never again found as able a leader. This led finally to its decline and collapse, the chief causes of which were (1) continued pressure from Ottoman and Uzbek armies, (2) economic decline, and (3) the power and bigotry of the Shi'ite ulama. The conservative ulama introduced Shi'ite legalism, emphasized their own authority over that of the Safavid monarch, persecuted religious minorities, and encouraged hatred of Sunni Muslims.

Shi'ite exclusivism inspired tribal revolts among the Sunni Afghans. In 1722, an Afghan leader took Qandahar (in modern Afghanistan) and then captured Isfahan and forced the abdication of Husayn I. Safavid princes managed to retake western Iran, but the empire's greatness was past. A revived, but officially Sunni, monarchy under Nadir Shah (r. 1736–1747) restored much of Iran's lost territories. However, his military ventures, which included the conquest of Delhi, sapped the empire's finances, and his despotic reign left a legacy of instability for Iran that continued for half a century.

CULTURE AND LEARNING

The most impressive achievement of the Safavid Era, besides the conversion of Iran to Shi'ism, was a cultural renaissance during the 16th and 17th centuries. Traditions of painting, originating with the powerful miniatures of the preceding century, were cultivated and modified. Portraiture and scenes from everyday life became popular. Among the most developed crafts were ceramic tiles, porcelain, and carpets. In architecture, the magnificent public squares, parks, palaces, hospitals, caravanserais, mosques, and other buildings of Isfahan constructed in Shah Abbas's time illustrate Safavid taste. Isfahan was the quintessential expression of the faith and imperial grandeur of Iran.

The Safavid age also saw a distinctively Shi'ite piety develop. It focused on commemorating the suffering of the imams and remaining loyal to the Shi'ite ulama, who alone (through knowledge of the Qur'an and traditions descending from Muhammad and the Imams) could provide guidance until the return of the hidden imam (see Chapter 11).

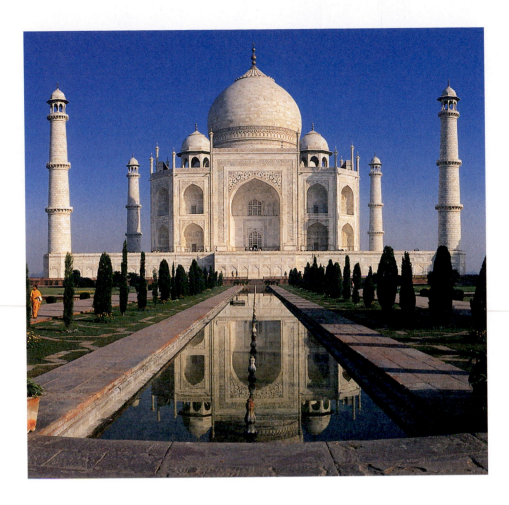

The Taj Mahal. Probably the most beautiful tomb in the world, the Taj was built from 1631 to 1653 by Shah Jahan for his beloved wife, Mumtaz Mahal. Located on the south bank of the Yamuna River at Agra, the Mughal capital, the Taj Mahal remains the jewel of Mughal architecture.

Michael Gotin.

THE MUGHALS

ORIGINS

In the early 16th century, invaders from the northwest, repeating an age-old pattern in Indian history, ended the political fragmentation that had, by 1500, reduced the Delhi sultanate to one among many Indian states. These invaders were descended from Timur (Tamerlane) and known to history as the **Mughals** (a Persianate form of *Mongol*). From 1525 to 1527, the founder of the Mughal dynasty, Babur, marched on India. By the time of his death in 1530, he ruled an empire stretching from the Himalaya to the Deccan. Akbar "the Great" (r. 1556–1605), however, was the real founder of the Mughal Empire, and the greatest Indian ruler since Ashoka (ca. 264–223 B.C.E.).

AKBAR'S REIGN

Akbar added North India and the northern Deccan to the Mughal dominions. Even more significant, however, were his governmental reforms, cultural patronage, and religious toleration. He reorganized government and rationalized the tax system. His marriages with Rajput princesses and his appointment of Hindus to power eased Muslim–Hindu tensions. So did his cancellation of the poll tax on non-Muslims (1564). Under his leadership, the Mughal Empire became a truly Indian empire.

WHAT ROLE did religious intolerance play in the decline of the Mughal Empire?

QUICK REVIEW

Akbar (r. 1556–1605)
- Added North India and the northern Deccan to Mughal Empire
- Carried out extensive governmental reforms
- Was interested in a variety of religious faiths

Mughals Descendants of the Mongols who established an Islamic empire in India in the 16th century with its capital at Delhi.

Akbar showed unusual interest in different religious traditions. He frequently brought together representatives of various faiths to discuss religion. Akbar tried to promulgate among his intimates a new monotheistic creed that subsumed Muslim, Hindu, and other viewpoints. However, his ideas died with him.

THE LAST GREAT MUGHALS

Akbar's three immediate successors were Jahangir (r. 1605–1627), Shah Jahan (r. 1628–1658), and Awrangzeb (r. 1658–1707). Although each left behind significant achievements, none matched Akbar. The problems of sustaining an Indian empire took their toll on Mughal power. The reigns of Jahangir and Shah Jahan were the golden age of Mughal culture. But the burdens imposed by military campaigns and the erosion of Akbar's administrative and tax reforms led to economic decline. Jahangir set a fateful precedent when he allowed English merchants to establish a trading post at Surat on the western coast in Gujarat. No less a burden on the treasury were Shah Jahan's elaborate building projects, the most magnificent of which was the Taj Mahal (built 1632–1653), the unparalleled tomb that he built for his beloved consort, Mumtaz.

With Shah Jahan, religious toleration began to fade, and under Awrangzeb, religious fanaticism reversed Akbar's earlier policies. The resulting disorder hastened the decline of Mughal power. Awrangzeb persecuted non-Muslims, destroying Hindu temples, reimposing the poll tax (1679), and alienating the Rajput leaders, whose forebears Akbar had cultivated. His intransigent policies coincided with the spread of the militant Sikh movement and the rise of Hindu Maratha nationalism.

SIKHS AND MARATHAS

In the late 16th and early 17th centuries, the Sikhs, who trace their origins to the teachings of Guru Nanak (d. 1538), became a distinctive religious movement. Neither Muslim nor Hindu, they had their own scripture, ritual, and ideals. Awrangzeb was angered by their rejection of Islam, and he launched a persecution that earned him their lasting enmity. The Sikhs developed into a formidable military force, and Awrangzeb and his successors had to contend with repeated Sikh uprisings.

The Hindu Marathas, led by Shivaji (d. 1680) and driven by religious and nationalistic fervor, founded their own empire about 1646. By the time of Shivaji's death, the Maratha army had become the most disciplined military in India. After Awrangzeb's death, the Marathas created a confederation of the Deccan States under their leadership. While acknowledging Mughal sovereignty, the Marathas controlled far more of India after 1740 than did the Mughals.

POLITICAL DECLINE

In addition to these wars, other factors sealed the fate of the Mughal Empire after Awrangzeb's death in 1707: the rise in the Deccan of the powerful Islamic state of Hyderabad in 1724, the Persian invasion of North India by Nadir Shah in 1739, the invasions (1748–1761) by the Afghan tribal leader Ahmad Shah Durrani (r. 1747–1773), and the British

---

QUICK REVIEW

Awrangzeb (r. 1658–1707)

- Reversed policy of religious toleration
- Persecuted non-Muslims
- Policies coincided with spread of militant Sikh movement and rise of Hindu Maratha nationalism

---

India: The Mughals and Contemporary Indian Powers

1525–1527	Rule of Babur, founder of Indian Timurid state
1538	Death of Guru Nanak, founder of Sikh religious tradition
1556–1605	Rule of Akbar "the Great"
1605–1627	Rule of Jahangir
1628–1658	Rule of Shah Jahan, builder of the Taj Mahal
1646	Founding of Maratha Empire
1658–1707	Rule of Awrangzeb
1680	Death of Maratha leader, Shivaji
1708	Death of 10th and last Sikh guru, Gobind Singh
1724	Rise of Hyderabad state
1739	Iranian invasion of North India under Nadir Shah
1757	British East India Company victory over Bengali forces at Plassey

HISTORY'S VOICES

GURU ARJUN'S FAITH

These lines are from the pen of the fifth guru of the Sikh community, Arjun (d. 1606). In them he repeated the teaching of Kabir, a 15th-century Indian saint whose teachings are included with those of Guru Nanak and other religious poets in the Sikh holy scripture, the Adi Granth. This teaching focuses on the error of clinging to a doctrinaire communalist faith, be it that of the Hindus or of the Muslims.

WHY MIGHT syncretic teachings, such as those of the Sikhs, have been appealing in 17th-century India?

I practice not fasting, nor observe the [month of] Ramazan:
I serve Him who will preserve me at the last hour.

The one Lord of the earth is my God,
Who judgeth both Hindus and Muslims.
I go not on a pilgrimage to Mecca, nor worship at Hindu places of Pilgrimage.
I serve the one God and no other.
I neither worship as the Hindus, nor pray as the Muslims.
I take the Formless God into my heart, and there make obeisance unto Him.
I am neither a Hindu nor a Muslim.
The soul and the body belong to God whether He be called Allah or Ram.
Kabir hath delivered this lecture.
When I meet a true guru or pir, I recognize my own Master.

Source: Max Arthur Macauliffe, *The Sikh Religion*, 6 vols. (Oxford: Clarendon Press, 1909), p. 422.

victories over Bengali forces at Plassey in Bengal (1757) and over the French on the southeastern coast (1740–1763). By 1819, the dominance of the British East India Company had eclipsed Indian power, but the Mughal line did not officially end until 1858.

RELIGIOUS DEVELOPMENTS

The period from about 1500 to 1650 was of major importance for Indian religious life. In the 16th century, a number of religious figures preached a piety that transcended the legalism of both the ulama and the Brahmans and rejected caste distinctions. In these ideas, we can see both Muslim Sufi and Hindu *bhakti* influences at work. Guru Nanak, the spiritual father of the Sikh movement, preached faith and devotion to one loving and merciful God. He opposed narrow allegiance to particular creeds or rites and excessive pride in external religious observance. Dadu (d. 1603) preached a similar message. He was born a Muslim but strove to get people to transcend the division between Muslim and Hindu (see "Guru Arjun's Faith").

There was also a Hindu revival epitomized by Chaitanya (d. ca. 1533), who stressed total devotion to Lord Krishna. The forebears of present-day Hare Krishna devotees, his followers spread his ecstatic public praise of God and his message of the equality of all in God's sight. Tulasidas's (d. 1623) retelling of the *Ramayana* remains among the most popular works of Indian literature. Tulasidas used the story of Rama's adventures to present *bhakti* ideas that remain alive in Hindu life.

Muslim eclectic tendencies came primarily from the Sufis. By 1500, the Chishtiya Sufi order especially had won many converts to Islam. Such Sufis were,

The great central square of the Registan, in Samarkand. The 17th-century Shir Dar Madrasa is on the right and the 15th-century Ulugh Beg Madrasa is on the left. Samarkand and other major Central Asian cities were centers of Islamic culture and learning as well as political power.

Michel Gotin/Ouzebekistan.

WHAT WERE the most important Islamic states in central and southern Asia?

however, often opposed by the ulama, many of whom were royal advisers and judges responsible for upholding the religious law. The more intolerant side of the spirit of Awrangzeb's time eventually won the day. The possibilities for Hindu–Muslim rapprochement waned, presaging the communal strife that has recently so marred southern Asian history.

ISLAMIC ASIA

CENTRAL ASIA: ISLAMIZATION AND ISOLATION

Islam established a solid footing in Central Asia in the 15th century. Even in the preceding century, as the nomadic peoples of western Central Asia began to settle, the familiar pattern of Islamic diffusion from trading and urban centers had set in. Islamization slowed only in the late 16th century when Mongolia proper converted to Buddhism. In the region between the Aral and Caspian Seas, the most important states were founded by Uzbek and Chaghatay Turks.

UZBEKS AND CHAGHATAYS

During the 15th century, a new steppe khanate had been formed by the unification in 1428 of assorted clans of Turks and Mongols known as the Uzbeks. In time, an Uzbek leader who was descended from Genghis Khan, Muhammad Shaybani (d. 1510), invaded Transoxiana (1495–1500) and founded an Uzbek Islamic empire. Muhammad's line continued Uzbek rule in Transoxiana at Bukhara into the 18th century, while another Uzbek line ruled the khanate of Khiva in western Turkestan from 1512 to 1872.

OVERVIEW   MAJOR ISLAMIC STATES, CA. 1600

From the 15th century to the 18th century was the age of the last great Islamic empires. These states dominated the Islamic world, which stretched from Morocco on the Atlantic coast of North Africa across the Near East and along the eastern coast of Africa to the southeast Asian islands that today make up the Republic of Indonesia. Despite these political divisions and the religious divide between Sunni and Shi'ite Muslims, in many respects the Islamic world formed a single cultural unit.

State	Location	Islamic Tradition
Ottoman Empire	Balkans, Anatolia, North Africa, Syria, Iraq, Arabia	Sunni
Safavid Empire	Iran, Afghanistan Caucasus	Shi'ite
Mughal Empire	India	Sunni
Uzbeks	Central Asia: Kiva, Bokhara	Sunni
Chaghatays	Central Asia: Tukistan	Sunni
Acheh	Sumatra	Sunni

Hindus were the chief religious group the Muslims displaced. Islam never ousted the Indian Buddhist cultures of Burma, Thailand, and Indochina, but it did win most of Malaysia, Sumatra, Java, and the "Spice Islands" of the Moluccas. By the end of the 15th century, Islam had also spread along the East African coast.

Of the other Central Asian Islamic states after 1500, the most significant was established by the Chaghatay Turks. A revived Chaghatay state in eastern Turkestan lasted from about 1514 to 1678.

CONSEQUENCES OF THE SHI'ITE RIFT

On the surface, the Ottoman, Mughal, Safavid, and Central Asian were Islamic states that had much in common. Yet the deep religious division between the Shi'ite Safavids and their Sunni neighbors proved stronger than their common bonds. Shi'ite-Sunni political competition was sharpened by Safavid militancy, to which the Sunni states responded in kind. Both sought alliances with non-Muslim states. Although trade continued, the international flow of Islamic commerce was hurt by a militant Shi'ite state astride the overland trade routes of the larger Islamic world. The Safavid Shi'ite schism also ruptured the cultural traditions of the "abode of Islam." The militant Shi'ism of Iran isolated Central Asia from the rest of the Muslim world after 1500. However healthy Islam remained in this region, its ties to the Islamic heartlands diminished. Contact came primarily through pilgrims, Sufis, ulama, and students. Central Asian Islam mostly developed in isolation, peripheral to the Islamic mainstream.

POWER SHIFTS IN THE SOUTHERN SEAS

SOUTHERN-SEAS TRADE

The first half of the second millennium witnessed the spread of Islamic religion and culture along the southern rim of Asia, from the Red Sea and East Africa to the South China Sea. In port cities, Islamic traders established thriving

HOW DID the arrival of Europeans affect the control of the commerce in Southeast Asia?

communities that often became the dominant influence. Typically, this first stage of conversion in cities was followed by Islam's transmission to surrounding areas and inland regions of Hindu, Buddhist, or pagan culture. In this transmission, Sufi orders played the main role. However, conquest by Muslim coastal states quickened the process in Indonesia and East Africa.

CONTROL OF THE SOUTHERN SEAS

The Portuguese reached the East African coast in 1498. In the following three centuries, the history of the lands along the trade routes of the southern Asian seas was affected not only by Islamic networks but by the increasing influence of Christian Western Europe. The key attractions of these diverse lands for Europeans were their commercial and strategic possibilities.

In the 16th century, the Europeans began to displace by force the Muslims who dominated the maritime southern rim of Asia. They owed their success to support from their homelands and their superior warships. The effectiveness of this combination was evident along the west coast of India, where the Portuguese carved out a power base in the early 16th century at the expense of Muslim traders. They did so by employing their superior naval power, exploiting indigenous rivalries, and using terror.

However, Islamization continued apace, even in the face of Christian proselytizing and European power. The Muslims rarely abandoned their faith, which proved generally attractive to new peoples they encountered. The result was usually an Islamicized, but racially mixed, population.

The upshot of these developments was that while European imperialism had considerable military and economic success, European culture and Christian missionary work made little headway against Islam. Only in the Philippines did a substantial population become Christian.

The Southern Seas: Arrival of the Portuguese

1498	Portuguese come to the East African coast and to the west coast of India
1500–1512	Portuguese establish bases on west Indian coast, replace Muslims as Indian Ocean power
early 1500s	Muslim sultanates replace Hindu states in Java, Sumatra
1524–1910	State of Acheh in northwestern Sumatra
1600s	Major increase in Islamization and connected spread of Malay language in the archipelago
1641	Dutch conquest of Malacca
ca. 1800	Dutch replace Muslim states as main archipelago power
1873–1910	War between Holland and Acheh

THE INDIES: ACHEH

The history of the Indonesian archipelago has always revolved around the international demand for the spices it produces. By the 15th century, there were coastal Islamic states on the Malay Peninsula, the north shores of Sumatra and Java, and the Moluccas (the "Spice Islands"). Several Islamic sultanates developed in the 16th and 17th centuries, even as Europeans staked claims in the region. The most powerful of these sultanates was Acheh in northwestern Sumatra (ca. 1524–1910). It provided the only counterweight to the Portuguese presence across the straits in Malacca (Malaysia). Acheh dominated the pepper trade of Sumatra and thrived until the end of the 16th century. In the first half of the 17th century, the sultanate controlled both coasts of Sumatra and parts of the Malay peninsula. Meanwhile, the Dutch replaced the Portuguese, and in the early 20th century, they finally won full control of the region—after nearly 40 years of intermittent war with Acheh (1873–1910).

MAP 21–3
European Commercial Presence in Southeast Asia. Beginning with the Portuguese and Spanish in the 16th century, and then the Dutch in the 17th century, European powers established commercial bases throughout Southeast Asia, often cooperating with local rulers.

WHAT WERE the motives for European penetration of Southeast Asia?

SUMMARY

The Last Islamic Empires The period from 1500 to 1800 marks the cultural and political blossoming of the last Islamic empires and their sharp decline. The Islamic vitality in the first half of this period was exemplified in the Ottoman, Safavid, and Mughal Empires. All three built vast bureaucracies and arguably the greatest cities of their time. They patronized the arts. Yet they were conservative societies. Economically they remained tied to agricultural production and

IMAGE KEY

for pages 514–515

a. Emperor Jahangir seated on an hourglass conversing with a Muslim mystic.

b. Riaz Abbasi, Woman with a veil ca. 1590–95.

c. The Christ Church in Dutch Square, Melaka, Malaysia.

d. A whirling Dervish.

e. Topkapi Palace, Istanbul.

f. Suleyman the Lawyer giving advice to the Crown Prince, Mehmed Khan.

g. Samarcande, Place du Reghistan.

h. Ardabil carpet from Safavid dynasty in Iran.

i. Ottoman Sultan Mehmed II on a coin.

taxation based on land. They did not undergo the social or religious-political revolutions that rocked the West after 1500 or the sort of generative changes in material and intellectual life that the Western world experienced during the same period. There was no compelling challenge to traditional Islamic ideals, even though numerous Islamic movements of the 18th century called for reform.

Decline By the latter half of this period, all these empires were in economic, political, and military decline, even if they continued intellectually and artisticly vigorous. It is not surprising, therefore, that European expansionism impinged during these three centuries on Africa, India, Indonesia, and the Islamic heartland, rather than the reverse. None of the Islamic states fared well in their encounters with Europeans during this age. Growing domination of the world's seas allowed Europeans to contain or bypass the major Islamic lands in their quest for commercial empires.

Industrial development joined economic wealth and political stability by the late 1700s to give the West global military supremacy for the first time. Before 1800, the Europeans were able to bring only minor Islamic states under colonial administrations. However, the footholds they gained in Africa, India, and Southeast Asia laid the groundwork for rapid colonial expansion after 1800. The age of the last great Muslim empires was the beginning of the first great modern European empires.

REVIEW QUESTIONS

1. What were the sources of the early Ottoman Empire's strength? What explains its later weakness?

2. What is the historical significance of the Safavid Empire in Iran?

3. What united all Islamic states? What began to divide them between 1500 and 1800?

4. What were Akbar's main policies toward the Hindu population? How did the Sikhs develop into a formidable military power?

5. How did outside powers affect the peoples of the South Seas lands?

KEY TERMS

devshirme (p. 518)   **millets** (p. 519)   *pirs* (p. 521)
Grand Mufti (p. 516)   **Mughals** (p. 523)   *Shari'a* (p. 516)
Janissaries (p. 518)

 For additional study resources for this chapter, go to:
www.prenhall.com/craig/chapter21

Visualizing The Past

The "Other" in the Early Modern Period

THE EARLY modern era (c. 1350–1750 c.e.) experienced increased trade and movements of peoples throughout the world. How did artists depict the strangers they encountered? Why do portrayals of the "other" reveal as much about the artist as the subject?

In the West, the early modern period coincides with what is often called the "Age of Discovery," when Europeans "discovered" the New World and sailed for the first time to sub-Saharan Africa and Asia. Cultures also increased their encounters with peoples from other parts of the world. During this rich period of encounter, cultural prejudices influenced the way artists depicted people they had never seen before. Aspects and features most remarkable, strange, attractive, or repulsive were often emphasized.

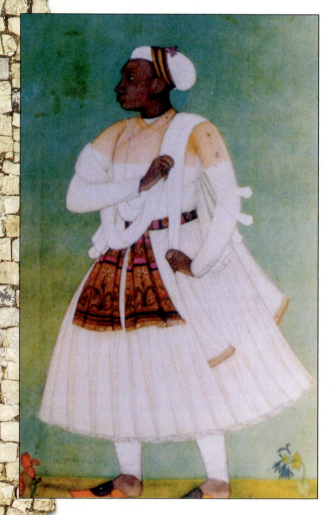

◄ **Africans as Voyagers.** This superb painting of an Indian of African origin demonstrates that Africans were voyagers to other lands and that not all Africans who went elsewhere went as slaves. The man in this image is a merchant, probably a member of the Janjeera people, originally from Ethiopia. Janjeera merchants emigrated to India in the Middle Ages. Some remained there and during the 15th century they and their descendants obtained positions of power and authority in local governments. The sumptuous dress and dignified bearing of this man suggests wealth and influence.

K. L. Kamat.

Portuguese Trade with Africa. In the 16th and 17th centuries, the Portuguese explored the coast of West Africa, where they established trading outposts and forts, and the beginnings of the Atlantic slave trade. One of Africa's most important products was ivory, which African artisans carved into exquisite objects for the luxury trade. Saltcellars like the one depicted here, carved in Nigeria at the court of Benin in the 15th or 16th century, were popular in Portugal. African artists carving for a Portuguese audience often depicted Portuguese merchants, emphasizing those aspects of the Europeans that most impressed them: the heavy beards, the cross, heavy armor, and sword.

African, Nigeria, Edo peoples, court of Benin, Saltcellar: Portuguese Figure, 15th–16th century, Ivory; H. 7-1/8 in. (18.1 cm). The Metropolitan Museum of Art, Louis V. Bell and Rogers Funds, 1972.(972.63ab) Phoytograph by Stan Reis. Photograph © 1984 The Metropolitan Museum of Art.

▲
Europeans in East Asia. This image shows a portion of a Namban screen from late 16th-century Japan. Europeans, beginning with the Portuguese, began arriving in Japan at this time. The Japanese found the strangely dressed Portuguese merchants and the African slaves, Indian pilots, and Catholic clerics who accompanied them fascinating.

De Young Memorial Museum/San Francisco/USA.

The Fall of the Aztecs. In Asia and Africa, early modern Europeans went as traders rather than as conquerors. In the New World, disease, superior weaponry, horses, and political disunity of the native peoples permitted Europeans to engage in conquest. This image from the Florentine codex depicts the fall of the Aztec capital Tenochtitlán. Note the Spanish soldiers
▼

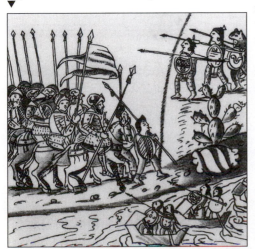

mounted on horses on the left. The Aztecs had never seen horses before they were greatly terrified by these strange creatures. The codex, produced in the 16th century by natives under the supervision of a Spaniard, Fray Bernardino de Sahagún, is the product of a blending of Spanish and Aztec culture and art styles.
Courtesy of the Library of Congress.

TIMELINE 1750–1800

PART FIVE   ENLIGHTENMENT AND REVOLUTION IN THE WEST

EUROPE

1756–1763	Seven Years' War
1762–1796	Catherine II "the Great" reigns in Russia
1763	Peace of Paris Seven Years' War
1772	First partition of Poland
1783	Peace of Paris
1789	French Revolution begins
1793 and 1795	Last partitions of Poland

Sir Isaac Newton ▶

◀ *July 14, 1789,*
Bastille prison, Paris

NEAR EAST / INDIA

1757	British victory at Plassey, in Bengal
1761	English oust French from India
1772–1784	Warren Hastings' administration in India
1772–1833	Ram Mohan Roy, Hindu reformer in India
1794–1925	Qajar shahs in Iran
1805–1849	Muhammad Ali in Egypt

▲ *Muhammad Ali*

EAST ASIA

1753–1806	Kitagawa Utamaro, Tokugawa Era artist
1787–1793	Matsudaira Sadanobu's reforms in Japan
1789	White Lotus Rebellion in China
1823–1901	Li Hung-chang, powerful Chinese governor-general

◀ *Utamaro*
woodblock print

AFRICA

1754–1817	Usman Dan Fodio, founder of Sultanate in northern and central Nigeria
1762	End of Funj Sultanate in eastern Sudanic region

THE AMERICAS

1759–1788	Spain reorganizes government of its American Empire
1776	American Declaration of Independence
1791	First 10 amendments to U.S. Constitution (Bill of Rights) ratified
1791	Negro slave revolt in French Santo Domingo
1794	Canada Constitutional Act divides the country into Upper and Lower Canada

The "Boston Massacre" on ▶
March 5, 1770, by Paul Revere

1804–1814	Napoleon's empire
1814–1815	Congress of Vienna
1830–1848	Louis Philippe reigns in France
1832	First British Reform Act
1837–1901	Queen Victoria of England
1848	Revolutions across Europe

1835	Introduction of English education in India
ca. 1839–1880	Tanzimat reforms, Ottoman Empire
1839–1897	Muslim intellectual Jamal al-Din Al-Afghani
1845–1905	Muhammad Abduh

◀ British colonial rule in India (1880)

1835–1908	Empress Dowager Cixi
1839–1842	Opium War; 1842, Treaty of Nanjing grants Hong Kong to the British and allows them to trade in China
1844	Similar treaties made between China and France and the United States

Armed Chinese junk ▶ during the Opium War

1804	Fulani Jihad into Hausa lands
1806	British take Cape Colony from the Dutch
1817–1828	Zulu chief Shaka reigns
1830–1847	French invasion of Algeria
1830s	Dutch settlers, the Boers, expand northward from Cape Colony
1848–1885	Sudanese Madhi, Muhammad Ahmad

◀ Miners excavating diamonds in South Africa

1804	Haitian independence
1808–1824	Wars of independence in Latin America
1822	Brazilian independence
1847	Mexican War

Simón Bolívar ▶

22 The Age of European Enlightenment

CHAPTER HIGHLIGHTS

The Scientific Revolution The scientific ideas of the sixteenth and seventeenth centuries changed the way Western intellectuals thought about the world and humankind. Instead of a view of nature and humanity based on Scripture and divine revelation, Western thinkers came to rely on mathematical laws, empirical data, and experimentation. Copernicus, Kepler, and Galileo overturned the ancient idea that the Earth was the center of the universe and that the sun and the planets revolved around it. Francis Bacon urged the necessity for observation and experimentation. Newton showed the effects of gravity and established an enduring basis for physics. Locke argued that human beings were masters of their own destiny.

The Enlightenment The Enlightenment *philosophes* used reason as a basis for reform and to advocate progressive social, economic, and political movements. Voltaire attacked religious intolerance and advocated strong central government. Montesquieu and other *philosophes* argued for limited, constitutional government. Rousseau wished to reform society so that it focussed on virtue rather than material happiness. The spirit of the Enlightenment continues to pervade Western society.

Enlightened Absolutism Enlightened absolutism was a form of monarchical government dedicated to the rational strengthening of central government. Many of the reforms enlightened monarchs imposed were influenced by the ideas of the *philosophes,* but the chief goal of these rulers was to increase their own authority and military strength. The most important enlightened monarchs were Frederick II of Prussia, Joseph II of Austria, and Catherine the Great of Russia.

CHAPTER QUESTIONS

WHAT WAS the Scientific Revolution?

WHY WAS the *Encyclopedia* so important?

WHY DID the *philosophes* regard the church as the chief enemy of reform and human happiness?

HOW DID the *philosophes* hope that reason would change society?

WHAT WAS enlightened absolutism?

CHAPTER OUTLINE

- The Scientific Revolution
- The Enlightenment
- The Enlightenment and Religion
- The Enlightenment and Society
- Enlightened Absolutism

*No intellectual force of the past three centuries has so transformed the world as Western science and technology. Science today dominates human life, and scientific knowledge, which yields military advantages as well as medical and economic progress, is a goal of modern states. The impact of science could make itself felt first in Europe and then elsewhere only when the conviction spread that change and reform were possible and desirable. This attitude came into its own in Europe only after 1700. The movement that fostered it is called the **Enlightenment**. It was an expression of confidence in the human mind and faith in the power of rational criticism to challenge tradition and revealed religion and discover truth. It promoted the spirit of innovation and quest for improvement that have come to characterize modern Western society. This has perhaps been Europe's most important cultural export to the rest of the world.*

Enlightenment Eighteenth-century movement led by the philosophes that held that change and reform were both desirable through the application of reason and science.

WHAT WAS the Scientific Revolution?

THE SCIENTIFIC REVOLUTION

*T*he 16th and 17th centuries witnessed a sweeping change in the way people viewed the universe. Initially being the center of the universe, the Earth came to be seen as only a planet orbiting the sun, which itself became one of millions of stars. This transformation led to a rethinking of ethics and religion as well as scientific theory, and science and the scientific method set a new standard for evaluating knowledge in the West.

The process by which this new view of scientific knowledge came to be established is termed the *Scientific Revolution*. Unlike most revolutions, it was a slow, complex movement that never involved more than a few hundred people. It entailed reappropriation of older knowledge as well as new discoveries, and it gradually achieved greater cultural authority in the Western world than any other form of intellectual activity. It has become one of the defining characteristics of modern Western civilization. Although workers in many fields contributed to it, the discipline that created the most early excitement about its potential was astronomy.

NICOLAUS COPERNICUS REJECTS AN EARTH-CENTERED UNIVERSE

17.1
The Heliocentric Statement (ca. 1520) Nicolaus Copernicus

The Ptolemaic System   Before Polish astronomer Copernicus (1473–1543) published *On the Revolutions of the Heavenly Spheres*, in which was his standard description of the Earth and the heavens, was a system proposed in Ptolemy's (ca. 90–168) *Almagest* (150 C.E.). The **Ptolemaic system** assumed that the Earth was the center of the universe. Surrounding the Earth was a series of crystalline spheres to which the heavenly bodies were attached. Aristotelian physics underlay the Ptolemaic systems. The heavy Earth provided a stable center, and the movement of the heavenly bodies was explained by their attachment to rotating crystalline spheres. The state of rest was assumed to be a natural condition and motion the exceptional thing that required explanation.

However, astronomers observed the planets moving in noncircular patterns around the Earth, and at times they appeared to go backward. The Ptolemaic system explained these strange motions by proposing the *epicycle*: a second revolution by a planet in an orbit tangent to its primary orbit around the Earth. The Ptolemaic explanations were effective as long as one accepted Aristotelian physics and the Christian belief that the Earth rested at the center of the created universe.

Scientific Revolution Sweeping change in the scientific view of the universe that occurred in the West in the 16th and 17th centuries.

Ptolemaic system Pre-Copernican explanation of the universe, which placed the Earth at the center of the universe.

Copernicus's Universe   Copernicus challenged this picture in the most conservative manner possible. He suggested that if the Earth were assumed to move about the sun in a circle, there were fewer difficulties with the Ptolemaic system. With the sun at the center of the universe, mathematical astronomy would make more sense. The epicylces became smaller, and the retrograde motion of the planets could be explained as an optical illusion arising from an observer viewing the planets from a moving Earth. Except for the modification in the position of the Earth, most of Copernicus's book was Ptolemaic. It, however, prompted others who were discontented with the Ptolemaic system to think in new ways. Copernicus's combination of mathematics, empirical data, and observation established the model for scientific thinking.

TYCHO BRAHE AND JOHANNES KEPLER

The Danish astronomer Tycho Brahe (1546–1601) advocated a different kind of Earth-centered system in which the moon and the sun revolved around the Earth, and the other planets revolved around the sun. His critique of the Copernican model was supported by unprecedentedly accurate tables of astronomical observations made with the naked eye.

When Brahe died, these tables passed to Johannes Kepler (1571–1630), a German astronomer. Kepler was a convinced Copernican, but after much work he discovered that to keep the sun at the center of things, he must abandon Copernicus's circular orbits. The mathematical relationships that emerged from Brahe's observations suggested that the orbits of the planets were elliptical. Kepler published his findings in 1609. He had solved the problems of planetary orbits by using Copernicus's sun-centered universe and Brahe's empirical data, but the available theories could not explain why the planetary orbits were elliptical. The solution to that problem awaited Sir Isaac Newton.

GALILEO GALILEI

In 1609, the Italian scientist Galileo Galilei (1564–1642) first turned a telescope to the heavens. He saw stars where none had been known to exist, mountains on the moon, spots moving across the sun, and moons orbiting Jupiter. It suddenly became clear that the heavens were far more complex than anyone had suspected and that the Ptolemaic system could not accommodate these new phenomena.

Galileo publicized his findings and arguments for the Copernican system in his *Dialogues on the Two Chief Systems of the World* (1632). It was condemned by the Roman Catholic Church, which compelled him to recant his opinions. He did so, but reputedly muttered, "It [the Earth] still moves."

Galileo articulated the concept of a universe totally subject to mathematical laws. He believed that the smallest atom operated in consort with the same mathematical principles as the largest heavenly sphere. He championed the application of mathematics to scientific investigation with the objective of developing mathematical formulae that would explain all phenomena. The English philosopher Francis Bacon advocated a different method based solely on **empiricism**, but both empirical induction and mathematical analysis proved fundamental to scientific investigation.

FRANCIS BACON: EMPIRICAL METHOD

Francis Bacon (1561–1626) attacked the scholastic belief that most truth had already been discovered, as well as the scholastic reverence for tradition and the

empiricism   Use of experiment and observation derived from sensory evidence to construct scientific theory or philosophy of knowledge.

17.4
Isaac Newton

Sir Isaac Newton. Newton discovered the mathematical and physical laws governing the force of gravity. Newton believed that religion and science were compatible and mutually supportive, and that the study of nature gave one a better understanding of the Creator. This portrait of Newton is by Sir Godfrey Kneller.

Sir Godfrey Kneller. Sir Isaac Newton. Bildarchiv Preussischer Kulturbesitz.

work of the ancients. He urged contemporaries to strike out on their own in search of a new understanding of nature.

Bacon was one of the first major European writers to champion innovation and change. Most people in Bacon's day thought that the best era of human history lay in antiquity. Bacon dissented from that view. He believed that human knowledge should produce useful results and that knowledge of nature should be used to improve the human condition. He anticipated a future of material improvement achieved through the empirical examination of nature. Although he did not make any major scientific discovery, his great achievement was to persuade others that scientific thought must proceed by means of empirical observation, not syllogistic reasoning or inference from assumptions.

ISAAC NEWTON DISCOVERS THE LAWS OF GRAVITATION

Isaac Newton (1642–1727) solved the major remaining problems of planetary motion and established a basis for physics that endured for more than two centuries. In 1687, he published *The Mathematical Principles of Natural Philosophy*, better known by its Latin title, *Principia Mathematica*. Newton was indebted to Galileo's argument that both motion and rest should be understood as givens that would continue (inertia) until something intervened to alter them. It was the cause of a change in these natural states that a scientist needed to explain. Galileo's mathematical bias also permeated Newton's thought. Newton reasoned that all physical objects exerted attractions, a force called gravity. Every object in the universe mutually attracted every other object, which explained why the planets moved in an orderly manner. Newton demonstrated the effect of gravity mathematically, but did not explain gravity itself.

Newton was a mathematical genius, but he also upheld the importance of empirical data and observation. The final test of any theory for him was whether it described what could actually be observed.

With the work of Newton, the natural universe became a realm governed by mechanistic laws. Spirits and divinities were no longer needed to explain it. This attitude helped to dispel belief in witchcraft and liberate human beings from the fear of a chaotic, inexplicable universe. Most scientists were devout and still found a place for God as the rational Creator of a rational, lawful nature. To study nature was to come to a better understanding of its Creator. Science and faith, they argued, were mutually supporting.

This approach to reconciling religion and science removed obstacles to the spread of the new physics and astronomy. Faith in a rational God also encouraged faith in the rationality of human beings and in their capacity to improve their lot. The Scientific Revolution convinced people of the desirability of change and critiquing inherited views.

WOMEN IN THE WORLD OF THE SCIENTIFIC REVOLUTION

Historians speculate about the relationship of women to the new science. Factors that had long excluded women from intellectual life continued during the Enlightenment to block their participation in the Scientific Revolution. The institutions of European intellectual life all but excluded women. With a few exceptions in Italy, women were not admitted to European universities until the end of the 19th century. Scientific academies spurned them, and there were no social spaces in which they might easily conduct scientific work.

A few isolated women—from both the nobility and the artisan class—did engage in scientific research, but only with the aid of men in their families.

Margaret Cavendish (1623-1673) had access to a circle of natural philosophers who gathered around her husband, the Duke of Newcastle. She published several books: *Observations upon Experimental Philosophy* (1666), *Grounds of Natural Philosophy* (1668), and *Descriptions of the New World, Called the Blazing World* (1666)—an introduction to science for women.

Artisan women had the advantage of always having been admitted to the crafts practiced by their families. In Germany, a number of women became astronomers by assisting astronomer fathers and husbands. Their discoveries were sometimes credited to men, and they were consistently refused posts and admission to learned academies. Although a few books were written to explain science to female readers, the dominant intellectual assumption of the 18th century was that differences between male and female minds made natural science a male vocation.

JOHN LOCKE

John Locke (1632–1704) attempted to discover laws governing the human mind similar to those which Newton had discovered as explanations for natural phenomena.

Major Publication Dates of the Enlightenment

1687	Newton's *Principia Mathematica*
1690	Locke's *Essay Concerning Human Understanding*
1733	Voltaire's *Letters on the English*
1738	Voltaire's *Elements of the Philosophy of Newton*
1748	Montesquieu's *Spirit of the Laws*
1750	Rousseau's *Discourse on the Moral Effects of the Arts and Sciences*
1751	First volume of the *Encyclopedia* edited by Diderot and d'Alembert
1755	Rousseau's *Discourse on the Origin of Inequality*
1762	Rousseau's *Social Contract*
1763	Voltaire's *Treatise on Toleration*
1776	Smith's *Wealth of Nations*
1779	Lessing's *Nathan the Wise*
1792	Wollstonecraft's *A Vindication of the Rights of Woman*

OVERVIEW   MAJOR FIGURES IN THE SCIENTIFIC REVOLUTION

The Scientific Revolution was a major turning point in Western culture. Although the Scientific Revolution never involved more than a few hundred people, the ideas they formulated and publicized gradually overturned the theological and religious modes of thought that were central to the medieval worldview. Humankind and life on Earth became the focus of Western thinking, and Western intellectuals developed more self-confidence in their capacity to shape the world and their own lives. Below is a list of the major scientific thinkers of the 16th and 17th centuries and their most important accomplishments.

Nicolaus Copernicus (1473–1543)	Argued that the Earth moved around the sun. His combination of mathematical astronomy with empirical observation and data became the model of scientific thought.
Tycho Brahe (1546–1601)	Compiled accurate tables of astronomical observations.
Johannes Kepler (1571–1630)	Used Brahe's data to argue that the orbits of the planets were elliptical.
Galileo Galilei (1564–1642)	First astronomer to use a telescope. Argued that mathematical laws governed the universe.
Francis Bacon (1561–1626)	Argued that scientific thought must conform to empirical evidence. Championed innovation and change.
Isaac Newton (1642–1727)	Explained the effect of gravity mathematically and established a theoretical basis for physics that endured until the late 19th century.
John Locke (1632–1704)	Argued that human nature was a blank slate that could be molded by modifying the environment. Human beings could thus take charge of their own destiny without divine aid.

Locke's *Essay Concerning Human Understanding* (1690) postulated that the human mind is blank at the time of birth. People, therefore, have no innate ideas. All their knowledge derives from sense experience. Each individual mind grows as it acquires information from the senses. Given that people's intellects are shaped by the interaction between their minds and the world, Locke argued that human nature can be molded by modifying the environment. Locke also rejected the Christian view that human beings were flawed by original sin. Human beings do not need to wait for divine aid; they can take charge of their own destinies.

Locke wrote *Two Treatises of Government* during the reign of Charles II (r. 1660–1685) in which he made a case against absolute monarchy. Nature's rational law, he argued, dictates that all human beings are equal and independent and that no one should harm another or disturb his property. People voluntarily relinquish some of their freedom and contract with their rulers for the protection and preservation of their natural rights. Rulers are, therefore, not absolute but bound by nature's laws. A monarch who does not comply can legitimately be overthrown. In *Letter Concerning Toleration*, Locke argued that governments existed to protect property and civil order. They should not legislate on religion, for the pursuit of salvation is the responsibility of the individual.

THE ENLIGHTENMENT

*T*he movement known as the Enlightenment included writers living at different times in various countries. Its early exponents, the **philosophes**, popularized the rationalism and scientific ideas of the 17th century. They exposed contemporary social and political abuses and argued that reform was necessary and possible. They confronted oppression and religious condemnation and by mid-century had brought enlightened ideas to the European public in a variety of formats.

VOLTAIRE

The most influential of the philosophes was François Marie Arouet, called Voltaire (1694–1778). During the 1720s, Voltaire offended the French authorities and was briefly imprisoned. In 1733, after visiting England, he published *Letters on the English*, which praised the intellectual and political freedom found in England and indirectly criticized French society. In 1738, he published *Elements of the Philosophy of Newton*, which popularized the thought of the great scientist. Both works enhanced his reputation.

Thereafter, Voltaire lived either in France or near Geneva, just across the French border where the royal authorities could not bother him. His essays, histories, plays, stories, and letters made him the literary dictator of Europe. He turned the venom of his satire against one evil after another in French and European life. In *Candide* (1759), he attacked war, religious persecution, and unwarranted optimism about the human condition. Like most philosophes, Voltaire believed that human society could and should be improved. But he was never certain that reform, if achieved, would be

---

FRANÇOIS · DE · VOLTAIRE · COPIÉ · D'APRÈS · LE TABLEAU FAIT PAR LARGILIÈRE · EN · 1718 · ÉLU · EN · 1746

permanent. Enlightenment optimism constituted a tempered hopefulness rather than a glib certainty. Pessimism can be found as an undercurrent in most Enlightenment works.

THE ENCYCLOPEDIA

The middle of the century witnessed the publication of the *Encyclopedia*, one of the greatest monuments of the Enlightenment. Under the leadership of Denis Diderot (1713–1784) and Jean le Rond d'Alembert (1717–1783), the first volume appeared in 1751. When completed in 1772, it numbered 17 volumes of text and 11 of plates. The *Encyclopedia* was the product of more than 100 authors, and its editors had solicited articles from all the major French philosophes. Attempts were made to censor it and halt its publication, but it was ultimately completed. The *Encyclopedia* made a plea for freedom of expression and set forth the most advanced critical ideas in religion, government, and philosophy. It also provided practical information in areas such as manufacturing, canal building, and agriculture.

The *Encyclopedia* had been designed to secularize learning, and the articles concentrated on humanity and its well-being. The encyclopedists looked to antiquity rather than to the Christian centuries for their inspiration, and they believed that the welfare of humankind lay not in the pursuit of revelation but in the application of reason to human relationships. The *Encyclopedia* diffused enlightened thought throughout the continent and drew German and Russian thinkers into the movement.

THE ENLIGHTENMENT AND RELIGION

In the eyes of the philosophes, the chief enemy of the improvement and happiness of humankind was the church. They were especially critical of Roman Catholicism. But all the Christian churches advocated a religious rather than a scientific view of humankind and taught the idea that human beings were sinful and in need of divine grace. Religion turned attention away from this world and the solution to its problems to the world to come. The philosophes also indicted the churches for fostering intolerance and bigotry.

DEISM

The philosophes believed that religion should conform to reason and have as its primary goal the promotion of morality. Newton had convinced many that nature was a rational system. It seemed logical, therefore, that the God who had created it must also be rational. Lockean philosophy argued that all human knowledge derived from empirical experience. This cast doubt on the possibility of divine revelation and suggested that religion ought to be totally grounded on rational arguments. The rational religion of the Enlightenment is called *deism.*

There were two major points in the deists' creed. The first was a belief that God is a rational deity, which they thought could be supported by empirical observation of the rational laws God had established for the natural phenomena He created. If God is rational, then God must have established a rational basis for human morality. Because reason dictates that good must be rewarded and evil punished—and this does not inevitably happen in this life, there must be a life after death, when justice is done.

Deism was empirical, tolerant, reasonable, and capable of encouraging virtuous living. The deists hoped that rational religion would put an end to sectarian

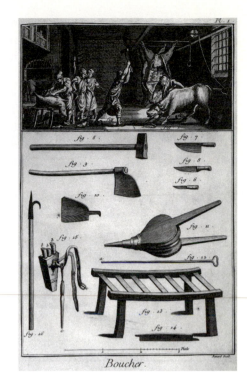

Illustration from the *Encylopedia*. The *Encyclopedia* included hundreds of illustrations of the work of skilled artisan. Here is illustrated the work of butchers in a slaugherhouse and the implements of their labors.
Corbis/Bettman.

WHY DID the *philosophes* regard the church as the chief enemy of reform and human happiness?

17.6
On Universal Toleration: Voltaire

deism Belief in a rational God who had created the universe, but then allowed it to function without his interference according to the mechanisms of nature and a belief in rewards and punishments after death for human action.

divisions, religious persecution, and fanaticism. They also anticipated the disappearance of a priestly class, for rational individuals could come to an understanding of God by themselves without the need for dogma, ritual, or sacrament.

TOLERATION

The centuries immediately preceeding the Englightenment had been characterized by bloody religious wars, and philosophes hoped that the triumph of reason and science would end denominational hatred and establish religious toleration.

Voltaire championed this cause. In 1762, the French authorities ordered the execution of a Huguenot named Jean Calas (1698–1762) for having allegedly murdered his son to prevent him from converting to Roman Catholicism. Calas was tortured but died without confessing his guilt. Voltaire made the dead man's cause his own. In 1763, he published a *Treatise on Toleration,* and he continued to hound the authorities until in 1765 the decision against Calas was reversed. For Voltaire, the case illustrated the dangers of religious fanaticism and the need for rational judicial reform. In 1779, Gotthold Lessing's (1729–1781) play about a Jew, *Nathan the Wise,* broadened the plea for toleration beyond Christian sects to include all religious faiths. All of these calls for toleration argued that secular values were more important than religious ones.

ISLAM IN ENLIGHTENMENT THOUGHT

With the exception of the Balkans, there were few Muslims in Europe in the 18th century. European merchants traded with Islamic countries, but most of the information Europeans had about Islam came from hostile sources: histories, travel diaries, and books by Christian missionaries. They dismissed Islam as a false religion, a rival to Christianity that was characterized by carnality and sexual promiscuity.

Several European universities established chairs of Arabic studies in the 17th century, but the professors who held them tended to agree with the Christian theologians and to equate Islam with religious fanaticism. In 1742, Voltaire published a tragedy with the explicit title *Fanaticism, or Mohammed the Prophet.* Charles Louis de Secondat, baron de Montesquieu, claimed that Muslim countries were the prime examples of the dangers of religious despotism. Excessive influence of religious leaders, he insisted, prevented the Ottoman Empire from adapting itself to advances in science and technology.

John Toland, a deist advocate for religious toleration, was more generous in his assessment of Islam. He shocked many of his contemporaries by contending that Islam derived from early Christian writings and was a form of Christianity. The historian, Edward Gibbon, praised Muhammad's leadership and Islam's success in building a great empire. Lady Mary Wortley Montagu (1689–1762), who lived in Istanbul with her husband, the British ambassador, found much to praise about Ottoman society. Compared to the constraints on the lives of women in England, she insisted that upper-class Turkish women were remarkably free and well treated. She lamented the misinformation about the Muslim world that circulated through Europe.

The few European voices calling for fairness and empathy for Islam had little impact. But it must be acknowledged that Muslims, for their part, showed little curiosity about the West. The *ulama* maintained that Islam had superceded Christianity as a religion and, therefore, Muslims had little to learn from Europe's Christian culture.

Map of Turkey and View of Constantinople. Few Europeans visited the Ottoman Empire. What little they know about it came from reports of travellers and from illustrations such as this view of Constantinople the empire's capital.

© Historical Picture Archive/Corbis.

THE ENLIGHTENMENT AND SOCIETY

The philosophes believed that rational analysis of social behavior would reveal laws in human relationships similar to those found in natural phenomena. The discovery of social laws, they predicted, would end inhumane conduct, a byproduct of ignorance.

HOW DID the philosophes hope that reason would change society?

MONTESQUIEU AND *THE SPIRIT OF THE LAWS*

Charles Louis de Secondat, Baron de Montesquieu's (1689–1755) *The Spirit of the Laws* (1748) was perhaps the most influential book of the century. Montesquieu took an empirical approach to the study of law, passing his conclusions on legal texts from ancient as well as modern nations. He concluded that no single set of laws could apply to all peoples at all times and in all places. Only a careful examination and evaluation of many variables could reveal what mode of government would prove most beneficial for a given people.

The French, Montesquieu believed, would be best served by a monarchy whose power was limited by intermediary institutions: the aristocracy, the towns, the *parlements*, and other corporate bodies whose liberties the monarch had to respect. Their role was to preserve the liberty of subjects by restraining the power of their ruler. Montesquieu was a political conservative, but he believed that France's oppressive and inefficient monarchy was degrading life in France and it needed reform.

One of Montesquieu's most influential insights was the concept of the division of powers. He thought that Great Britain provided an excellent example of this principle in action. It vested executive power in its monarch, legislative power in its Parliament, and judicial power in its courts, and any two of these branches of government could check the power of the other. His perception of the 18th-century British constitution was incorrect, but his analysis made a strong case for limiting the power of rulers by constitutional means and relying on legislatures, not monarchs, to make laws. Montesquieu's ideas guided the West's subsequent experiments with liberal democracies.

ADAM SMITH ON ECONOMIC GROWTH AND SOCIAL PROGRESS

The most important Enlightenment exposition of economics was Adam Smith's (1723–1790) *An Inquiry into the Nature and Causes of the Wealth of Nations* (1776). Smith urged abolition of England's mercantile system. Mercantilists claimed that economic regulation by the state was needed to preserve the wealth of a nation as well as to increase wealth by taking it away from other nations. But Smith believed that such regulation constricted wealth and production. He believed that if individuals were unleashed to pursue their self-interest, the result would be economic expansion, for the rational demands of the marketplace would guide their productive activities.

Smith saw nature as a boundless expanse of material resources to be exploited for the benefit of humankind, and this idea came to dominate life in the West. At the time when Smith was writing, the population of the world was much smaller than it is today. Its people were poorer, and the quantity of undeveloped resources per capita was much greater than it is now. For people of the 18th century, the improvement of the human condition seemed to require the uninhibited exploitation of natural resources.

Smith is usually regarded as the founder of *laissez-faire* economics, the school that advocates a very limited role for government in economic life. However, Smith was not opposed to all government participation in the economy. He believed that the state should provide schools, armies, navies, and roads and undertake commercial ventures that were desirable but too risky for private enterprise. Smith, like most of the philosophes, was less doctrinaire than any brief summary of their thought suggests.

Smith's theories helped to justify Western imperialism. Smith endorsed a model popular with other social theorists of his day: the *four-stage theory*. It divided human societies into four categories according to their economic basis: hunting and gathering, pastoral or herding, agricultural, and commercial. Movement through these stages was assumed to be progress. This meant that economic development was the indicator of where a group fell on the continuum between barbarism and civilization. Smith's theory allowed Europeans to view their society as the pinnacle of human achievement and to justify their pursuit of imperial domination of the world as a civilizing mission.

ROUSSEAU

Jean-Jacques Rousseau (1712–1778) saw things differently. His *Discourse on the Moral Effects of the Arts and Sciences* (1750) contended that civilization and enlightenment had corrupted, not elevated, human nature. In a *Discourse on the Origin of Inequality* (1755), he agreed that economic problems were at the root of evil in the world, but the problem was maldistribution of property, not production. Rousseau felt that the purpose of society should be to nurture better, not wealthier, people. His vision of reform was much more radical than that of other philosophers.

The Social Contract (1762) outlines the kind of political structure that Rousseau believed would overcome the evils of contemporary society. Most 18th-century political thinkers regarded society as a collection of independent

laissez-faire French phrase meaning "allow to do." In economics, the doctrine of minimal government interference in the working of the economy.

Printing Shops. Shops such as this were the productive centers for the book trade and newspaper publishing that spread the ideas of the Enlightenment.

The Granger Collection.

individuals pursuing selfish goals, and they advocated liberating these individuals from the undue bonds of government. Rousseau, however, claimed that society was more important than the individual, because individuals are what they are only because of their relationship to the larger community. Lone, independent human beings can achieve little, but in a community they become moral creatures capable of significant action. Rousseau, drawing on Plato and Calvin, claimed that true freedom was obedience to law—that is, rules determined by the general will. The general will, Rousseau believed, was the opinion of the majority of voting citizens who acted with adequate information and under the influence of virtuous customs and morals. This majority was always right, and to obey it was to be free. If a minority disagreed, it had (paradoxically) to be forced to be free. Radical direct democracy entailed collective action against individual citizens. Rousseau assaulted the 18th-century cult of the individual and selfishness and was at odds with the commercial spirit that was transforming his world.

ENLIGHTENED CRITICS OF EUROPEAN EMPIRE

Most of the Enlightenment's thinkers equated the expansion of Europe's empires with the spread of civilization and progress, but there were a few who disagreed. They were troubled, in particular, by the treatment of Native Americans and the enslavement of Africans. The leading critics of empire were: the philosophers Immanuel Kant (1724–1804) and Johann Gottfried Herder (1744–1803), and the encyclopedist Denis Diderot (1713–1784). They argued for a common humanity shared by all people that required recognition of their dignity and treatment of them with respect. They insisted that no single description of human nature could be exalted as an absolute standard and then used to dehumanize peoples who differed from it. Non-European cultures deserved respect and understanding and should not be destroyed on the assumption that they were inferior and, therefore, valueless. Humanity manifests itself, they believed, in different cultural forms that are too complex to be judged by a single standard. Herder went so far as to suggest that "European culture" itself was an abstraction that existed nowhere. The objections these men raised to slavery and abuse of native peoples (see "Denis Diderot Condemns European Empires") found a sympathetic hearing in some circles, but their criticisms of empire did not.

HISTORY'S VOICES

DENIS DIDEROT CONDEMNS EUROPEAN EMPIRES

Denis Diderot was one of the most prolific writers of the Enlightenment. He is most known for his role as editor of the Encyclopedia. Some of his writings were published without being directly attributed to him. Among these were his contributions to Abbé G. T. Raynal's History of the Two Indies, published in various changing editions after 1772. Diderot's contributions appear to have been made in 1780. The entire History was critical of the European colonial empires that had arisen since the Spanish encounter with the New World. Diderot was particularly concerned to condemn the inhumane treatment of the native populations of the Americas, the greed displayed by all Europeans, and the establishment of various forms of forced labor.

WHAT IS the basis for Diderot's view that Europeans have behaved tyrannically? How does he portray the behavior of Europeans once they have left their own native countries and find themselves in foreign areas? What are the specific social results he associates with European greed?

Let the European nations make their own judgment and give themselves the name they deserve . . . Their explorers arrive in a region of the New World unoccupied by anyone from the Ole World, and immediately bury a small strip of metal on which they have engraved these words: *This country belongs to us.* Any why does it belong to you? . . . You have no right to the natural products of the country where you land, and you claim a right over your fellow-men. Instead of recognizing this man as a brother you only see him as a slave, a beast of burden. Oh my fellow citizens! You think like that and you behave like that; and you have ideas of justice, a morality, a holy religion . . . in common with

whose whom you treat so tyrannically. This reproach should especially be addressed to the Spaniards.

****

Beyond the Equator a man is neither English, Dutch, French, Spanish, nor Portuguese. He retains only those principles and prejudices of his native country which justify or excuse his conduct. He crawls when he is weak; he is violent when strong; he is in a hurry to acquire, in a hurry to enjoy, and capable of every crime which will lead him most quickly to his goals. He is a domestic tiger returning to the forest; the thirst for blood takes hold of him once more. This is how all the Europeans, every one of them, indistinctly, have appeared in the countries of the New World. There they have assumed a common frenzy—the thirst for gold.

****

The Spaniard, the first to be thrown up by the waves onto the shores of the New World, thought he had no duty to people who did not share his color, customs, or religion. He saw in them only tools for his greed, and he clapped them in irons. These weak men, not used to work, soon died in the foul air of the mines, or in other occupations which were virtually as lethal. Then people called for slaves from Africa. Their number has gone up as more land has been cultivated. The Portuguese, Dutch, English, French, Danes, all the nations, free or subjected, have without remorse sought to increase their fortune in the sweat, blood and despair of these unfortunates. What a horrible system!

Source: Denis Diderot, *Political Writings*, John Hope Mason and Robert Wokler, eds., (Cambridge: Cambridge University Press, 1998), pp. 177, 178, 186.

WOMEN IN THE THOUGHT AND PRACTICE OF THE ENLIGHTENMENT

Women, especially in France, helped to promote the careers of the philosophes. In Paris, the salons of women such as Marie-Thérèse Geoffrin (1699–1777), Julie de Lespinasse (1733–1776), and Claudine de Tencin (1689–1749) gave the philosophes a receptive forum for debating and publicizing their ideas. These women were well connected to political figures, and they were able to provide protection for philosophes whom the authorities might otherwise have silenced. The Marquise de Pompadour (1721–1764), the mistress of Louis XV, for example, helped defeat efforts to censor the *Encyclopedia.*

Despite their reliance on female patrons and general enthusiasm for reform, the philosophes advocated no radical changes in the social condition of women. Montesquieu, for example, believed that women were not naturally inferior to men and that they should play a greater role in society, but he also believed that men should dominate marriage and family. Furthermore, although he supported the right of women to divorce and opposed laws that oppressed them, he exalted chastity as the primary female virtue.

The salon of Mme. Marie-Thérèse Geoffrin (1699–1777). This was one of the most important gathering spots for Enlightenment writers during the mid-18th century. Well-connected women such as Mme. Geoffrin were instrumental in helping the philosophes they patronized to bring their ideas to the attention of influential people in French society and politics.

Giraudon/Art Resource, N.Y.

The *Encyclopedia*'s articles that dealt with women emphasized their physical inferiority, usually attributing it to menstruation or childbearing. Women, it was assumed, were reared to be frivolous and unconcerned with serious issues. The encyclopedists discussed women primarily in the context of the family, considered motherhood their most important occupation, and defended a double standard of sexual behavior. Despite the impression the articles give of women's relegation to the domestic sphere, the *Encyclopedia*'s illustrations show women, many of them lower and working class, involved in economically productive activities.

Rousseau urged women to embrace their traditional roles. In his novel *Émile* (1762), he declared that women should be educated to be subordinate to men and to center their lives on bearing and rearing children. He portrayed women as weaker and inferior to men, except perhaps for their capacity for feeling and giving love. He excluded them from public affairs and confined them to the domestic sphere.

Despite these views (and his ill treatment of his many children and the women who bore them), Rousseau won a vast following among women in the 18th century. They may have responded to the stress he put on women's emotions and subjective feelings in his various writings. By portraying domestic life and the roles of wife and mother as noble vocations, he gave middle- and upper-class women confidence that their lives had purpose.

In 1792, in *A Vindication of the Rights of Woman,* Mary Wollstonecraft (1759–1797) tested Rousseau's ideas against the philosophes' standards of reason and progressive enlightenment. She accused Rousseau and others who upheld traditional roles for women of attempting to narrow women's visions and limit their experiences. She argued that to confine women to the separate domestic sphere because of their supposed physiological limitations was to make them the sensual slaves of men and prevent them from achieving moral and intellectual identities of their own. Denying them good educations impeded human progress by squandering the talents of half the human species. Wollstonecraft demanded for women the kind of intellectual liberty that male writers of the Enlightenment insisted were the rights of men.

ENLIGHTENED ABSOLUTISM

During the last third of the 18th century, several European rulers embraced many of the philosophes' reforms and experimented with a form of government called *enlightened absolutism*. Their goal was to rationalize administration by strengthening centralized government at the cost of local authorities. Frederick II of Prussia, Joseph II of Austria, and Catherine II of Russia were the major monarchs who were influenced by the Enlightenment, but they often found that political and social realities forced them to moderate the policies recommended by the philosophes with whom they corresponded or who were guests at their courts.

The relationship between these monarchs and the writers of the Enlightenment was complicated. Rulers were motivated to pursue rational economic and social integration of their realms less as an end in itself than as a means toward enhancing their military strength. They used "enlightened" reforms to pursue goals favored by the philosophes but also to further what the philosophes considered irrational militarism.

JOSEPH II OF AUSTRIA

No 18th-century ruler embodied rational, impersonal authority more than Emperor Joseph II of Austria, the son of Maria Theresa (r. 1740–1780). He prided himself on his narrow, passionless rationality, but he genuinely wanted to improve the lot of his people. However, his well-intentioned efforts prompted rebellions by both aristocrats and peasants from Hungary to the Austrian Netherlands.

The Habsburgs' empire was Europe's most diverse political entity. Its rulers never succeeded in creating a unified government or enlisting the loyalties of its various groups of aristocrats. Maria Theresa preserved the monarchy during the War of the Austrian Succession (1740–1748) by guaranteeing independence for aristocrats, especially the Hungarians. But after the conflict, she improved her position in Austria and Bohemia by imposing a more efficient system of tax collection. Even clergy and nobles were compelled to pay. She established central councils to deal with political problems. She expanded primary schooling, and she tried to redirect educational institutions to training officials for royal service. Concern for peasants and serfs (from whom she recruited her military manpower) led her to limit the services that landowners could demand from them..

Like his mother, Joseph believed that royal authority could promote prosperity and military power, but his reforms were more wide ranging than hers. His chief goal was to overcome the pluralism of the Habsburg domains by increasing the power of the central monarchy. In particular, he wanted to lessen Hungarian autonomy. He even refused to be crowned king of Hungary to avoid having to guarantee Hungarian privileges in a coronation oath. He reorganized local government in Hungary, increasing the authority of his own officials and imposing the use of German. The Magyar nobility, however, resisted, and in 1790 he rescinded most of his centralizing measures.

Joseph extended freedom of worship to Lutherans, Calvinists, and the Greek Orthodox. He gave Jews the right

Russia from Peter the Great Through Catherine the Great

1725	Death of Peter the Great
1741–1762	Elizabeth
1762	Peter III
1762	Catherine II (the Great) becomes empress
1767	Legislative Commission summoned
1768	War with Turkey
1771–1774	Pugachev's Rebellion
1772	First Partition of Poland
1774	Treaty of Kuchuk-Kainardji ends war with Turkey
1775	Reorganization of local government
1783	Russia annexes the Crimea
1785	Catherine issues the Charter of the Nobility
1793	Second Partition of Poland
1795	Third Partition of Poland
1796	Death of Catherine the Great

to worship privately and relieved them of certain taxes and signs of personal degradation. His empire was officially Roman Catholic, but he brought its church under royal control. He forbade his bishops to communication directly with the pope. He dissolved more than 600 monasteries and confiscated their lands, and he replaced traditional seminaries with eight general seminaries specializing in training men for parish duties. Joseph made Roman Catholic priests state employees and prevented the church from exercising much independent influence. His policies, known as *Josephinism*, prefigured those of the French Revolution.

Joseph believed that reducing traditional burdens would make the peasants more productive and industrious. He abolished serfdom and gave peasants more personal freedom. They were allowed to marry, engage in skilled work, and have their children trained in these skills without permission from their landlord. Manorial courts were reformed, and peasants were given right of appeal to royal officials. Joseph also encouraged landlords to change land leases so that it would be easier for peasants to inherit or transfer them.

In 1789, Joseph declared that all proprietors were to be taxed, regardless of social status. The aristocrats protested, and his death in 1790 ended attempts to put the system into effect. His policies created a legacy of turmoil for his heir, and his brother Leopold II (r. 1790–1792), although sympathetic to Joseph's goals, had to repeal many of his decrees.

CATHERINE THE GREAT OF RUSSIA

Joseph II never grasped the necessity of cultivating support for his policies, but Catherine II (r. 1762–1796) understood the fragility of her dynasty's power. After the death of Peter the Great in 1725, the court nobles and the army had chosen the heirs to Russia's throne. Peter's daughter Elizabeth (r. 1741–1762) was succeeded by Peter III, one of her nephews. He was weak and possibly insane, but his marriage in 1745 profoundly affected the future of his Romanov dynasty. His bride was the German princess, historically known as Catherine the Great. A few months into his reign, Peter III was deposed and murdered—with Catherine's approval, and she was proclaimed empress.

Catherine's familiarity with the Enlightenment and western Europe convinced her that Russia had to implement reforms if it hoped to remain a great power. Having acquired the throne by means of a palace coup, she well understood the necessity of recruiting support for whatever she tried to do. Consequently, in 1767 she summoned a Legislative Commission to advise her on reforms for Russia's government. More than 500 delegates represented all sectors of Russian life, and Catherine provided them with a set of *Instructions* drawn from the philosophes' theories. Catherine dismissed the commission before several of its key committees reported. It, however, gathered a vast amount of information about conditions in Russia, and its debates suggested that most Russians saw no alternative to an autocratic monarchy. Catherine herself had no intention of backing away from absolutism.

Catherine the Great. She ascended to the Russian throne after the murder of her husband. She tried initially to enact major reforms, but she never intended to abandon absolutism. She assured the nobility of their rights and by the end of her reign had imposed press censorship.

The Granger Collection.

Catherine carried out limited reforms on her own authority. In 1775, she reorganized local government to solve problems brought to light by the Legislative Commission. Instead of creating a royal bureaucracy, she gave most local offices to nobles. In 1785, she issued the Charter of the Nobility, which guaranteed the nobles certain rights and privileges. She issued a similar charter for townspeople. The empress had to rely on the nobles and urban classes, for she had too few educated subjects to establish an independent bureaucracy, and her treasury could not afford to sustain a professional army.

Catherine, like her predecessors, continued efforts to acquire warm-water ports. She fought the Turks from 1768 to 1774, and by the Treaty of Kuchuk-Kainardji won Russia a direct outlet on the Black Sea. In 1783, she annexed the Crimea (see Map 22–1).

MAP 22–1

Expansion of Russia, 1689–1796. The overriding territorial aim of the two most powerful Russian monarchs of the 18th century, Peter the Great (in the first quarter of the century) and Catherine the Great (in the last half of the century) was to secure navigable outlets to the sea in both the north and the south for Russia's vast empire; hence Peter's push to the Baltic Sea and Catherine's to the Black Sea. Russia also expanded into Central Asia and Siberia during this time period.

WHICH EMPIRE came into direct conflict with Russian expansion?

THE PARTITION OF POLAND

Russia's military successes made the other states of eastern Europe uneasy, but their anxieties were allayed by an agreement that led to the First Partition of Poland (see Map 22–2). Frederick the Great made a proposal to Russia and Austria that, by giving each something, would prevent conflict among them and save appearances. After complicated, secret negotiations among the three powers, the Polish state lost approximately one third of its territory. Two additional partitions of Poland in 1793 and 1795 removed Poland from the map of Europe entirely, and it was not restored until 1919. Without a strong central government, Poland's political weakness made the country ripe for plunder by the strong states that surrounded it.

MAP 22–2

Partitions of Poland, 1772, 1793, and 1795. The eradication of Poland from the map displayed 18th-century power politics at its most extreme.

WHY WAS Poland so easily destroyed in the 18th century?

IMAGE KEY

for pages 536–537

a. Astronomer Tycho Brahe from the *Atlas Major* by Joan Blaeu

b. Jean-Jacques Rousseau (1712–1778)

c. Catherine the Great as a young princess.

d. Catherine the Great after ascending to the Russian throne.

e. Voltaire (1694–1778).

f. Sir Isaac Newton (1642–1727).

g. One of Galileo's early telescopes.

h. The composing room of a print shop.

i. The salon of Mme. Marie-Therese Geoffrin

SUMMARY

The Scientific Revolution The scientific ideas of the 16th and 17th centuries changed the way Western intellectuals thought about the world and humankind. Instead of a view of nature and humanity based on Scripture and divine revelation, Western thinkers came to rely on mathematical laws, empirical data, and experimentation. Copernicus, Kepler, and Galileo overturned the ancient idea, sanctioned by the Bible, that the Earth was the center of the universe and that the sun and the planets revolved around it. Galileo maintained that the world was governed by mathematical laws. Francis Bacon urged the necessity for observation and experimentation. Newton showed the effects of gravity and established an enduring basis for physics. Locke argued that human beings were masters of their own destiny.

The Enlightenment The Enlightenment philosophes used reason as a basis for reform and to advocate progressive social, economic, and political movements. Voltaire attacked religious intolerance and advocated a strong central government to impose rational solutions to social and political problems. Montesquieu and other philosophes argued for a limited, constitutional government. Rousseau wished to reform society to focus on virtue rather than material happiness. He maintained that in the pursuit of virtue the needs of society were more important than those of the individual. The spirit of the Enlightenment continues to pervade Western society.

Enlightened Absolutism Enlightened absolutism was a form of monarchical government dedicated to the rational strengthening of central government. Many of the reforms enlightened monarchs imposed were influenced by the ideas of the philosophes, but the chief goal of these rulers was to increase their own authority and military strength, as witnessed by the fate of Poland. The most important enlightened monarchs were Frederick II of Prussia, Joseph II of Austria, and Catherine the Great of Russia.

REVIEW QUESTIONS

1. What did Copernicus, Galileo, and Newton contribute to the Scientific Revolution? Is the Scientific Revolution accurately described as a revolution?

2. How did the Enlightenment change Western attitudes toward reform, faith, and reason?

3. Why were the philosophes opposed to organized religion? What did they prefer in its place?

4. What aspects of the Enlightenment did Rousseau oppose?

5. What kind of reforms did enlightened monarchs' implement? What was their purpose?

KEY TERMS

deism (p. 543)   *laissez-faire* (p. 546)   **Ptolemaic system** (p. 538)
empiricism (p. 539)   **philosophes** (p. 542)   **Scientific Revolution** (p. 538)
Enlightenment (p. 538)

  For additional study resources for this chapter, go to:
www.prenhall.com/craig/chapter22

23 Revolutions in the Transatlantic World

CHAPTER HIGHLIGHTS

The Transatlantic Revolutions The revolutions and the crusade against slavery that occurred throughout the transatlantic world between 1776 and the 1830s transformed three continents: North America, Europe, and South America. The foundations of modern liberal democracy were laid, and the largest republic since ancient times was established in North America. In France, written constitutions and elected legislatures became essential parts of government. In Latin America, republicanism triumphed everywhere except Brazil. Never again could government be undertaken in these regions without some form of participation by the governed.

Economic and Social Liberalization The expanding forms of political liberty found their counterparts in an economic life freed from the constraints of the old colonial empires and slavery. The new American republic constituted a vast free trade zone. And for the first time since the encounter with Europe, Latin America could trade freely among its own peoples and those of the rest of the world. In France and Europe, where the Napoleonic armies had carried the doctrines of the rights of man, economic life had been rationalized and freed from the domination of local authorities. National law formed the framework for economic activity. The movement to abolish slavery fostered a wage economy of free laborers which would generate its own set of problems, but it was nonetheless an economy of free human beings.

Nationalism Finally, the age of transatlantic revolutions saw the emergence of nationalism as a political force. The Americans saw themselves as forming a new kind of nation. The French had demonstrated the power of a nation mobilized for military purposes. In turn, the aggression of France had aroused national sentiment throughout Eurrope and the New World.

These various revolutions, their political doctrines, and their social and economic departures provided examples to peoples elsewhere in the world. But even more important, the transatlantic revolutions and eventual abolition of slavery meant that new political classes and independent nations would become actors on the world scene. Europeans would have to deal with a score of new nations in the Americas. The rest of the world confronted new nations freed from the direction and authority of European powers. The political changes in Europe meant that those nations and their relationships with the rest of the world would be directed by a broader range of groups than in the past.

CHAPTER QUESTIONS

WHAT WAS the new sense of liberty that arose from the American Revolution?

HOW DID the French Revolution and Napoleon transform France's government and society?

WHY DID Latin American throw off Spanish and Portuguese rule?

WHY DID slavery become unacceptable in Western society?

CHAPTER OUTLINE

- Revolution in the British Colonies in North America
- Revolution in France
- Wars of Independence in Latin America
- Toward the Abolition of Slavery in the Transatlantic Economy

Between 1776 and 1824, a world-transforming series of revolutions occurred in France and the Americas. In a half century, the peoples of the two American continents established their independence of European political control, and in Europe, the French monarchy collapsed. The leaders of all the successful revolutions sought to establish new governments based largely on Enlightenment principles. The era also witnessed the commencement of an international crusade to abolish first the slave trade and then slavery throughout the transatlantic world.

REVOLUTION IN THE BRITISH COLONIES IN NORTH AMERICA

WHAT WAS the new sense of liberty that arose from the American Revolution?

RESISTANCE TO THE IMPERIAL SEARCH FOR REVENUE

After the Treaty of Paris in 1763 ended the Seven Years' War, the British government faced two problems. The first was the cost of defending the empire they had acquired. The second was the need to organize a vast new territory: all of North America east of the Mississippi (see Map 23–1).

The British drive for revenue began in 1764 with the Sugar Act. Britain hoped to enhance revenue from imports of sugar into the colonies by the rigorous collection of what was actually a reduced tax. Smugglers were to be tried in admiralty courts without juries. A year later, Parliament passed the Stamp Act, a tax on legal documents and other items. The British considered these taxes just because they had been approved by Parliament and because the revenue was to be spent in the colonies that paid them. The Americans, however, objected that they were not represented in Parliament and insisted that they alone had the right to tax themselves. Threatend with disorder in its American lands, Parliament repealed the Stamp Act in 1766 but asserted its right to legislate for the colonies.

AMERICAN POLITICAL IDEAS

The American colonists believed that the English Revolution of 1688 had established liberties that belonged to them as well as to the British. They claimed that George III (r. 1760–1820) and the British Parliament were dissolving the bonds of allegiance that united the two peoples by attacking those liberties. The colonists thus appealed to an argument that English aristocrats of an earlier generation had used to justify limiting the power of their king in order to support a popular revolution.

In addition to the works of John Locke (1632–1704), from which these ideas largely derived, Americans were reading British political writers called the *Commonwealthmen*. These authors held republican political ideas that stemmed from the radical branches of the Puritan revolution. They dismissed much parliamentary taxation as nothing more than a means for financing political corruption, and they feared standing armies as instruments of tyranny. The policy of Great Britain toward America after the Treaty of Paris made many colonists believe that the suspicions of the Commonwealthmen were correct.

CRISIS AND INDEPENDENCE

In May 1773, Parliament allowed the East India Company to import tea directly into the American colonies. Although the law lowered the price of tea, it levied a tax on it that was imposed without the colonists' consent. Protestors in Boston reacted by throwing a shipload of tea into the harbor, an event called the Boston Tea Party.

MAP EXPLORATION

Interactive map: To explore this map further, go to
http://www.prenhall.com/craig/map23.1

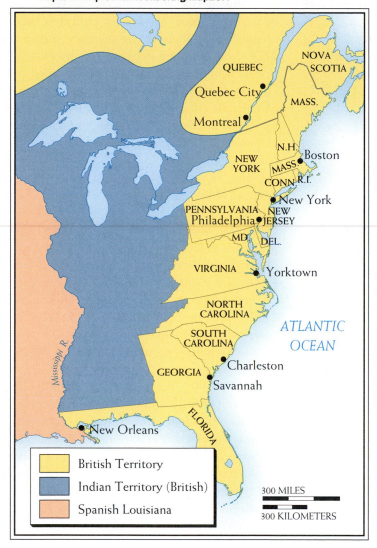

MAP 23–1

North America in 1763. In the year of the victory over France, the English colonies lay along the Atlantic seaboard. The difficulties of organizing authority over the previous French territory in Canada and west of the Appalachian Mountains would contribute to the coming of the American Revolution.

HOW DID westward expansion of the colonies lead to tensions with both the British and Indians?

The British ministry of Lord North (1732–1792) was determined to assert the authority of Parliament over the colonies. In 1774, Parliament closed the port of Boston, reorganized the government of Massachusetts, quartered troops in private homes, and transferred the trials of royal customs officials to England. Parliament also extended the boundaries of Quebec to include the Ohio River

18.4
Declaration of
Independence:
Revolutionary Declarations

The BLOODY MASSACRE perpetrated in King — Street BOSTON on March 5th 1770 by a party of the 29th REGT.

Unhappy Boston! see thy Sons deplore,
Thy hallow'd Walks besmear'd with guiltless Gore.
While faithless P—n and his savage Bands,
With murd'rous Rancour stretch their bloody Hands;
Like fierce Barbarians grinning o'er their Prey,
Approve the Carnage and enjoy the Day.

If scalding drops from Rage from Anguish Wrung
If speechless Sorrows lab'ring for a Tongue,
Or if a weeping World can ought appease
The plaintive Ghosts of Victims such as these;
The Patriot's copious Tears for each are shed,
A glorious Tribute which embalms the Dead.

But know, Fate summons to that awful Goal,
Where Justice strips the Murd'rer of his Soul:
Should venal C—ts the scandal of the Land,
Snatch the relentless Villain from her Hand.
Keen Execrations on this Plate inscrib'd,
Shall reach a Judge who never can be brib'd.

The unhappy Sufferers were Messrs. Sam! Gray, Sam! Maverick, Jam! Caldwell, Crispus Attucks & Pat! Carr
Killed. Six wounded two of them (Christ! Monk & John Clark) Mortally

Engrav'd Printed & Sold by Paul Revere Boston

"Boston Massacre." This view of the Boston Massacre of March 5, 1770 by Paul Revere owes more to propaganda than fact. There was no order to fire and the innocent citizens portrayed here were really an angry, violent mob.

The Granger Collection, New York.

The American Revolution

1760	George III becomes king
1763	Treaty of Paris concludes the Seven Years' War
1764	Sugar Act
1765	Stamp Act
1766	Stamp Act repealed and Declaratory Act passed
1770	Lord North becomes George III's chief minister
1773	Boston Tea Party
1774	First Continental Congress
1775	Second Continental Congress
1776	Declaration of Independence
1778	France enters the war on the side of America
1781	British forces surrender at Yorktown
1783	Treaty of Paris concludes War of the American Revolution

valley which the Americans regarded as an attempt to prevent them from spreading, with their political ideas, westward beyond the Appalachian Mountains.

During these years, committees of correspondence, composed of citizens critical of Britain, were established throughout the colonies, and in September 1774, these committees organized the First Continental Congress in Philadelphia. This body failed to persuade Parliament to abandon its attempt at direct supervision of colonial affairs. In 1775, the battles of Lexington, Concord, and Bunker Hill were fought, and the Second Continental Congress undertook to govern the colonies. In August 1775, George III declared the colonies in rebellion. During the winter, Thomas Paine's (1737–1809) pamphlet *Common Sense* galvanized public opinion in favor of separation from Great Britain. A colonial army and navy were organized, and on July 4, 1776, the Continental Congress adopted the Declaration of Independence. The War of the American Revolution continued until 1781, when the forces of George Washington (1732–1799) defeated those of Lord Cornwallis (1738–1805) at Yorktown. In 1778, however, the war had widened into a European conflict, for the French government supported the rebellion in the hope of weakening its traditional enemy, Great Britain. In 1779, Spain also came to the aid of the colonies. The 1783 Treaty of Paris concluded the conflict and recognized the independence of the 13 American colonies.

As the crisis with Britain unfolded, the American colonists first saw themselves as preserving traditional English liberties, but as the war went on, they developed a different understanding of what liberty meant. By the mid-1770s, they had rejected monarchy and embraced republican ideals. After the Constitution was adopted in 1788, a bill of rights was added to protect civil liberties. They rejected the aristocratic social hierarchy that had existed in the colonies and embraced democratic ideals. Although they limited the right to vote, they asserted the equality of white male citizens before the law and in social relations. They rejected social ranking based on birth and inheritance and asserted that all citizens had to have the opportunity to improve their social standing and economic lot by engaging in free commercial activity. Although the American Revolution did not free slaves or address the rights of women and Native Americans, it produced a society freer than any the world had seen—one in which political and social liberties would continue to increase. The American Revolution was a radical movement that spread its influence as Americans moved across their continent and as its success inspired other peoples to question traditional European governments. It inspired the Wars of Independence in Latin America and liberal and radical political movements in Europe.

REVOLUTION IN FRANCE

*T*he French monarchy emerged from the Seven Years' War defeated and deeply in debt, and the support it gave the American Revolution exacerbated its financial difficulties. Given France's economic vitality, the government's debt was not overly large, but the government could not enforce collection of sufficient taxes to service and repay its debt. Between 1786 and 1788, Louis XVI's (r. 1774–1792) ministers tried to persuade the aristocracy and the church to pay more taxes. The *parlement* of Paris insisted that only the Estates General could institute new taxes but failed. The Estates General had not met since 1614, but in July 1788, Louis agreed to convene it.

REVOLUTIONS OF 1789

The Estates General Becomes the National Assembly   The three "estates" that composed the Estates General were: the clergy (the First Estate), the nobility (the Second Estate), and everyone else (the **Third Estate**). The Estates General began to meet at Versailles in May 1789, and on June 1, the Third Estate, composed largely of local officials, professional men, and lawyers, invited the clergy and nobles to join it in organizing a new legislative body. A few of the lower clergy did so, and on June 17, that body declared itself the National Assembly.

Three days later, finding themselves accidentally locked out of their usual meeting place, the National Assembly moved to a nearby tennis court, where its members took the famous Tennis Court Oath. They vowed to remain in session until they had given France a constitution. Louis XVI ordered the National Assembly to desist, but this only encouraged most of the clergy and many nobles to support it. On June 27, the king capitulated, and the National Assembly reorganized as the National Constituent Assembly.

Fall of the Bastille   Two developments soon complicated the situation. First, Louis XVI tried to regain the initiative by mustering troops near Versailles and Paris. The National Constituent Assembly was beginning to demand a constitutional monarchy. Louis refused to consider their proposal and hoped that a show of military force would head off revolution.

The second development was the behavior of the people of Paris. The mustering of royal troops spread anxiety through the city, where there had already been several riots sparked by food shortages. By June, the Parisians were organizing by collecting arms and marshalling an army of their own, a citizen militia. On July 14, a crowd marched to the Bastille, a fortress in Paris that was sometimes used as a political prison, and demanded weapons for the militia. The royal troops in the Bastille fired into the crowd which then stormed the fortress, released the seven prisoners it held (none of whom was a politcal prisoner), and killed the governor. They found no weapons.

This was the first of many *journées*, or days when the populace of Paris would determine the course of the revolution. Similar disturbances took place in the provincial cities. Louis XVI came to Paris and recognized the legitimacy of its newly elected government and its National Guard.

The Great Fear and Surrender of Feudal Privileges   As disturbances erupted in various cities, the *Great Fear* swept across the French countryside. Peasants rose up to vent their anger at injustices and reclaim rights and property that they had

HOW DID the French Revolution and Napoleon transform France's government and society?

QUICK REVIEW

National Assembly
- June 17, 1789: Third Estate declares itself National Assembly
- Tennis Court Oath: Pledge to sit until France had a constitution
- June 27, 1789: King capitulates to National Assembly

 18.8
Edmund Burke: Reflections on the Revolution in France

Third Estate   Branch of the French Estates General representing all of the kingdom outside the nobility and the clergy.

Storming of the Bastille. On July 14, 1789, crowds stormed the Bastille, a prison in Paris. This event, whose only practical effect was to free a few prisoners, marked the first time the populace of Paris redirected the course of the revolution.

Anonymous, France, 18th century. "Seige of the Bastille, 14 July, 1789." Obligatory mention of the following: Musee de la Ville de Paris, Musee Carnavalet, Paris, France. Bridgeman-Giraudon/Art Resource, N.Y.

18.7
Declaration of the Rights of Man and Citizen

lost during the aristocratic resurgence of the previous quarter century. Châteaux were burned, documents were destroyed; and peasants refused to pay feudal dues.

On the night of August 4, 1789, aristocrats in the assembly attempted to halt the disorder. By prearrangement, liberal nobles and churchmen "spontaneously" surrendered their hunting and fishing rights, judicial authority, tithes, and special exemptions. They were giving up what they had already lost and what they could not have regained without civil war. Many were subsequently compensated for their losses. Nonetheless, after August 4, France's laws applied equally to all its citizens.

Declaration of the Rights of Man and Citizen   On August 27, 1789, the assembly issued the *Declaration of the Rights of Man and Citizen*. It proclaimed that all men were born free and equal with natural rights to liberty, property, and personal safety. Governments existed to protect those rights. All political sovereignty resided in the nation and its representatives. All citizens were to be equal before the law and to be equally eligible for public offices—as appropriate to their abilities and character. There was to be due process of law, and innocence was to be presumed until proof of guilt. Freedom of religion was affirmed. Taxation was to be apportioned equitably according to capacity to pay. Property rights were declared sacred.

When Louis XVI stalled before ratifying the declaration and the aristocrats' renunciation of their feudal privileges, his hesitation fanned suspicions that he might try to resort to force. Continuing bread shortages also angered the masses. On October 5, several thousand Parisian women marched to Versailles, demanding bread—one of several occasions when women played a major role in the revolution. The king agreed to sanction the decrees of the assembly, but the Parisians demanded more. They insisted that Louis and his family return to Paris. On October 6, 1789, the king and his family followed the crowd back to Paris and settled in the palace of the Tuileries. The assembly joined them. Things then remained relatively quiet until the summer of 1792.

RECONSTRUCTION OF FRANCE

The National Constituent Assembly set about reorganizing France. The assembly was determined to protect property but limit the political influence of small property owners and the unpropertied elements within the populace. While championing equality before the law, the assembly spurned social equality and extensive democracy. It thus charted a course that 19th-century liberals across Europe and in other areas of the world were to follow.

Political Reorganization   The Constitution of 1791 established a constitutional monarchy with a unicameral Legislative Assembly. The monarch could delay, but not halt, legislation. Voting was restricted to about 50,000 men. (France was home to about 26 million.)

The exclusion of women from voting and holding office did not pass unnoticed. In 1791, Olympe de Gouges (d. 1793), a butcher's daughter who became a radical in Paris, composed a *Declaration of the Rights of Woman*, which she ironically addressed to Queen Marie Antoinette (1755–1793). The document was fundamentally the *Declaration of the Rights of Man and Citizen* with the word *woman* strategically inserted. It demanded that women be regarded as citizens, not merely daughters, sisters, wives, and mothers of citizens. Olympe de Gouges further insisted that women be allowed to own property and that men be compelled

Women's March.   The women of Paris marched to Versailles on October 5, 1789. The following day the royal family was forced to return to Paris with them. Henceforth, the French government would function under the constant threat of mob violence.

Anonymous, 18th century C.E. "To Versailles, to Versailles." The Women of Paris going to Versailles, 7 October, 1789. French, Musee de la Ville de Paris, Musee Carnavalet, Paris, France. Photograph copyright Bridgeman-Giraudon/Art Resource, N.Y.

to recognize the paternity of their children. She called for equality of the sexes in marriage and improved education for women. Her demands illustrated how the public listing of rights in the *Declaration of the Rights of Man and Citizen* created expectations even among those to whom it did not apply.

The National Constituent Assembly replaced France's former provinces with 83 departments *(départements)*. The ancient judicial courts, including the *parlements,* were replaced by uniform courts with elected judges and prosecutors. Legal procedures were simplified, and the most degrading punishments abolished.

Economic Policy   The National Constituent Assembly suppressed the guilds, removed regulations on the grain trade, and established the metric system of uniform weights and measures. In 1790, it placed the burden of proof and the obligation to pay compensation on peasants who tried to rid themselves of residual feudal dues. In 1791, it enacted the Chapelier Law forbidding worker associations. This crushed efforts by urban workers to protect their wages. Peasants and laborers were to be left to the mercy of the free market.

The assembly decided to raise the money that was needed the pay the national debt by confiscating and selling the lands of the Roman Catholic Church. The assembly authorized the issuance of **assignats**, or government bonds, the value of which was guaranteed by the revenue generated from the sale of church property. When the *assignats* began to circulate as currency, the assembly succumbed to the temptation to issue larger quantities of them. This caused their value to fall, and fueled inflation that further stressed the urban poor.

Civil Constitution of the Clergy   In July 1790, the assembly issued the Civil Constitution of the Clergy, which transformed the Roman Catholic Church into a branch of the government. The number of bishoprics was reduced, and the borders of dioceses were conformed to those of the new departments. Priests and bishops were to be elected and paid salaries by the state. The assembly consulted neither the pope nor the French clergy about these changes, and the king approved them reluctantly.

The Civil Constitution of the Clergy roused immense opposition from the French clergy. The assembly demanded that all clergy take an oath to support the Civil Constitution, but only about half complied. In reprisal, the assembly designated the clergy who had not taken the oath as "refractory" and ordered them to cease performing clerical functions. Refractory priests responded by celebrating mass.

In February 1791, the pope condemned not only the Civil Constitution of the Clergy but also the *Declaration of the Rights of Man and Citizen.* That condemnation marked the start of a Roman Catholic offensive against liberalism and revolution that continued for more than a century. The pope's action meant that many French people were torn between religious devotion and revolutionary loyalty. They divided between supporters of the constitutional priests and of the refractory clergy. Louis XVI favored the latter.

Counterrevolutionary Activity   In the summer of 1791, the queen and some nobles persuaded Louis XVI to flee, but the royal family was caught and returned to Paris. The escapade had the unfortunate effect of persuading the leaders of the National Constituent Assembly that France's chief counterrevolutionary occupied its throne.

On August 27, 1791, Leopold II of Austria (r. 1790–1792), who was the brother of Marie Antoinette, and Frederick William II (r. 1786–1797) of Prussia

assignats   Government bonds based on the value of confiscated church lands issued during the early French Revolution.

further endangered the royal family by issuing the Declaration of Pillnitz. They promised to intervene in France to protect the royal family if the other major European powers agreed that they could do so. The latter provision rendered the declaration meaningless for Great Britain would not consent. It had the effect, however, of convincing France's revolutionaries that they were surrounded by aristocratic and monarchical foes.

A SECOND REVOLUTION

In September 1791, a new Legislative Assembly was elected, and it convened on October 1 in an atmosphere that was becoming increasingly radical. Since the earliest days of the revolution, clubs of politically like-minded persons had sprung up in Paris. The best organized were the *Jacobins*, who had links with similar groups in the provinces. On April 20, 1792, the Legislative Assembly, led by a group of Jacobins known as the *Girondists* (because many came from the department of the Gironde), voted to declare war on Austria.

End of the Monarchy   The war went badly, and the looming threat to France radicalized the political environment. The result was a *second revolution*, which swept away the monarchy and established a republic.

Late in July, pressure from the working-class delivered the government of Paris into the hands of a committee, or commune, consisting of representatives from the municipal wards. On August 10, 1792, a mob invaded the Tuileries. Louis XVI and Marie Antoinette sought refuge with the Legislative Assembly. Royal guards and many Parisians were killed in the process. Thereafter, the royal family was imprisoned, and the king suspended from his political functions.

The Convention and the Role of Sans-Culottes   In early September, the Paris Commune killed about 1,200 people held in the city jails. Most were common criminals whom the crowd accused of being counterrevolutionaries. The Commune then compelled the Legislative Assembly to call for the election, by universal manhood suffrage, of a new assembly to write a democratic constitution. That body, the **Convention**, met on September 21, 1792, and declared France a republic.

The second revolution had been the work of radical Jacobins and of the people of Paris known as the *sans-culottes*, meaning "without breeches." (Working men wore long trousers instead of the knee breeches favored by aristocratic courtiers.) The sans-culottes were shopkeepers, artisans, wage earners, and a few factory workers. They had no political authority under the Old Regime, and the National Constituent Assembly had left them victims of unregulated free-market economy (see "A Pamphleteer Describes a Sans-Culotte").

The sans-culottes wanted price controls for food. They resented most forms of social inequality and were hostile to the aristocracy and the original leaders of the revolution. They advocated a community of small property owners. They were antimonarchical, republican, and suspicious of government. The Jacobins, by contrast, were republicans who favored representative government and an unregulated economy. However, once the Convention began its deliberations, the more extreme Jacobins, known as the Mountain, worked with the sans-culottes to pass revolutionary reforms and win the war.

In December 1792, Louis XVI was put on trial. He was convicted of conspiring against the state and was beheaded on January 21, 1793. The killing of a king shocked Europe, and France found itself isolated and at war with virtually everyone.

Jacobins Radical republican party during the French Revolution that displaced the Girondists.

Convention French radical legislative body from 1792 to 1794.

sans-culottes Meaning "without breeches." The lower-middle classes and artisans of Paris during the French Revolution.

HISTORY'S VOICES

A Pamphleteer Describes a Sans-Culotte

his document from 1793 describes a sans-culotte as a hardworking, useful, patriotic citizen who sacrifices himself to the war effort. It contrasts those virtues with the lazy and unproductive luxury of the noble and the self-interested plottings of the politician.

WHAT SOCIAL resentments appear in this description? How could these resentments create solidarity among the sans-culottes to defend the revolution? How does this document relate civic virtue to work? Where does this document suggest that the sans-culotte may need to confront enemies of the republic?

A sans-culotte you rogues? He is someone who always goes on foot, who has no millions as you would all like to have, no chateaux, no valets to serve him, and who lives simply with his wife and children, if he has any, on a fourth or fifth story.

He is useful, because he knows how to work in the field, to forge iron, to use a saw, to use a file, to roof a house, to make shoes, and to shed his last drop of blood for the safety of the Republic.

And because he works, you are sure not to meet his person in the Café de Chartres, or in the gaming houses where others conspire and game; nor at the National theatre . . . nor in the literary clubs . . . .

In the evening he goes to his section, not powdered or perfumed, or smartly booted in the hope of catching the eye of the citizenesses in the galleries, but ready to support good proposals with all his might, and to crush those which come from the abominable faction of politicians.

Finally, a sans-culotte always has his sabre sharp, to cut off the ears of all enemies of the Revolution; sometimes he even goes out with his pike; but at the first sound of the drum he is ready to leave for the Vendée, for the army of the Alps or for the army of the North . . . .

Source: "Reply to an Impertinent Question: What Is a Sans-Culotte?" April 1793. Reprinted in Walter Markov and Albert Soboul, eds., *Die Sansculotten von Paris*, and republished trans. by Clive Emsley in Merryn Williams, ed., *Revolutions: 1775–1830* (Baltimore, MD: Penguin Books, in association with the Open University, 1971), pp. 100–101.

Civil war broke out as well. In March 1793, aristocratic officers and priests raised a royalist revolt in western France and won local popular support.

THE REIGN OF TERROR AND ITS AFTERMATH

The **Reign of Terror** is the name given to a period, from autumn 1793 through mid-summer 1794, marked by thousands of quasi-judicial executions and murders. Two factors created the environment for the outbreak of the Terror: (1) the fear created by internal and external wars, and (2) the revolutionary aspirations of the Convention and the sans-culottes.

Committee of Public Safety In April 1793, the Convention established a Committee of Public Safety and charged it with responsibility for saving the revolution from enemies at home and abroad. It eventually assumed quasi-dictatorial power and generally enjoyed a working political relationship with the sans-culottes of Paris.

In June 1793, the Parisian sans-culottes invaded the Convention, drove out the Girondists, and gave the Mountain complete control. On August 23 the Convention decreed a *levée en masse*, or general military requisition of

Reign of Terror Period between the summer of 1793 and the end of July 1794 when the French revolutionary state used extensive executions and violence to defend the Revolution and suppress its alleged internal enemies.

levée en masse French revolutionary conscription (1792) of all males into the army and the harnessing of the economy for war production.

Execution of Louis XVI. On January 21, 1793, the Convention executed Louis XVI by guillotine.

Execution of Louis XVI. Aquatint. French, 18th century. Musée de la Ville de Paris, Musée Carnavalet, Paris. France. Giraudon/ Art Resource, N.Y.

population. It conscripted males into the army and mobilized economic production for military purposes. On September 29, price controls were imposed in accordance with sans-culottes' demands. During these same months, the armies of the revolution crushed many of the counterrevolutionary disturbances in the provinces.

The Society of Revolutionary Republican Women   In May 1793, Pauline Léon and Claire Lacombe founded the Society of Revolutionary Republican Women. Its members sought stricter price controls, worked to ferret out food hoarders, and brawled with market women it considered too insufficiently revolutionary. The women of the society also demanded the right to wear the revolutionary cap that male citizens had adopted. By October 1793, the Jacobins in the Convention had begun to fear the turmoil the increasingly radical Society was causing, and it banned all women's clubs and societies.

There were other examples of repression of women in 1793. When Olympe de Gouges spoke out against the Terror, she was tried and guillotined in November 1793. Women were excluded from the French army and from entering the galleries to watch the debates of the Convention.

The Republic of Virtue   The pressures of war made it relatively easy to excuse violations of the usual rules of due process. But the Convention and the Committee of Public Safety felt morally justified in doing so, for they saw themselves as creating something new in history: a republic devoted to eradicating aristocratic and monarchical corruption and promoting civic virtue.

Revolutionary Calendar. To symbolize the beginning of a new era in human history, French revolutionary legislators established a new calendar. This calendar for Year Two (1794) proclaims the indivisible unity of the revolution and the goals of Liberty, Equality, and Fraternity.

Art Resource/Bildarchiv Preussischer Kulturbesitz.

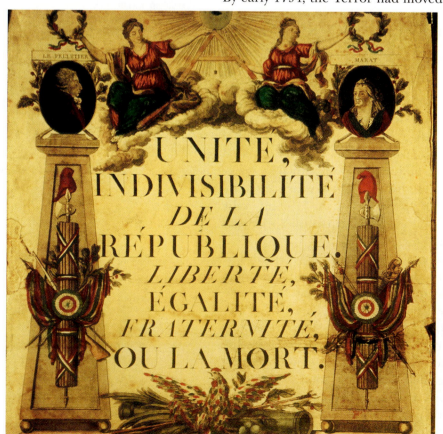

Dechristianization   The revolutionaries associated the Christian religion with the repressive policies of the Old Regime and decided to abolish traditional theism in favor of an enlightened cult of reason. In October 1793, the Convention authorized a new, rationalized calendar dating from the first day of the French Republic. It featured 12 months of 30 days with names associated with the seasons and climate. In November 1793, the Convention renamed the Cathedral of Notre Dame the Temple of Reason. The legislature then sent trusted members as "deputies-on-mission" into the provinces to enforce dechristianization by closing churches and persecuting clergy and believers. This religious policy roused much opposition and alienated the provinces from the revolutionary government in Paris.

Progress of the Terror   During late 1793 and early 1794, Maximilien Robespierre (1758–1794) emerged as the chief figure on the Committee of Public Safety. The Jacobin Club provided his base of power, and he had the support of the sans-culottes of Paris. For political reasons, he considered dechristianization to be a strategic blunder.

The Reign of Terror was the work of a series of revolutionary tribunals established by the Convention during the summer of 1793. They were instituted to try the enemies of the republic, but the definition of enemy broadened as the months passed. Marie Antoinette, other members of the royal family, and many aristocrats were executed in October 1793. They were then followed by Girondist politicians. Robespierre gradually turned the Terror against republican political figures of the left and right and exterminated leaders who might have threatened his own position. On June 10, he secured a law that permitted the revolutionary tribunal to convict suspects without evidence. By early 1794, the Terror had moved to the provinces, where the deputies-on-mission presided over the execution of thousands of people.

In May 1794, at the height of his power, Robespierre concluded that the worship of reason was too abstract for most citizens. He replaced it with the Cult of the Supreme Being, but he did not long preside over this new religion. On July 27 (the Ninth of Thermidor), his opponents staged a coup. Members of the Convention, by prearrangement, shouted him down when he rose to speak and executed him the next day.

The Reign of Terror had claimed 40,000 victims. Most were peasants and sans-culottes who had rebelled against the revolutionary government. By the late summer of 1794, provincial uprisings had been crushed and the war against foreign enemies was going well. Those factors and the feeling that the revolution had consumed enough of its own children brought the Terror to an end.

The Thermidorian Reaction: End of the Terror and Establishment of the Directory   The tempering of the revolution, a phase called the **Thermidorian Reaction**, began in July 1794, with the establishment of a new constitutional regime. The influence of wealthy middle-class and professional people replaced that of the sans-culottes. Many of the people responsible for the Terror were removed from public life, and the Jacobin Club was closed.

The Thermidorian Constitution of the Year III was a conservative document that provided for bicameral legislative government dedicated to protecting the rights of property owners. Its executive branch was a five-person Directory elected by the upper legislative house.

True to their belief in an unregulated economy, the Thermidorians repealed the ceiling on prices. Rising prices led to food riots during the winter of 1794–1795, but the Convention suppressed them in an attempt to bring an end to the era of sans-culottes *journées*. When on October 5, 1795, a Paris mob rioted, a general named Napoleon Bonaparte (1769–1821) used artilery to disperse the crowd.

THE NAPOLEONIC ERA

Napoleon Bonaparte was born in 1769 to a poor noble family in Corsica. Because France had annexed Corsica in 1768, he was able to obtain a commission as a French artillery officer. At the start of his career, he was a fiery Jacobin. In 1793, he played a leading role in recovering the port of Toulon from the British. This won him promotion to the rank of brigadier general, and his defense of the Directory in 1794 won him a command in Italy. By October 1797, he had crushed the Austrians and concluded the Treaty of Campo Formio, which took Austria out of the war and left France dominant over Italy and Switzerland.

In November 1797, the triumphant Bonaparte returned to Paris to confront France's only remaining enemy, Britain. Judging it impossible to invade England, he decided to try to capture Egypt from the Ottoman Empire and cut off Britain's communication with India. However, Admiral Horatio Nelson (1758–1805) destroyed the French fleet and stranded the French army in Egypt. The Russians, Austrians, and Ottomans then joined Britain to form the Second Coalition, and in 1799, the Russian and Austrian armies defeated the French in Italy and Switzerland and threatened to invade France.

Bonaparte abandoned his men and returned to France in October 1799. On November 10, 1799 (19 Brumaire), he overthrew the Directory, and in December 1799, he issued the Constitution of the Year VII. It established him in power with the title First Consul. The constitution received approval from the electorate in a rigged plebiscite, and a government called the **Consulate** brought the revolution to an end.

The Consulate in France (1799–1804)   Bonaparte quickly won a peace for France. Russia had already left the Second Coalition, and in 1800, a French victory at Marengo in Italy took Austria out of the war. In 1802, Britain concluded the Treaty of Amiens, and all of Europe was at peace—at least temporarily.

Bonaparte also restored peace and order at home. In an effort to suppress political opposition, Bonaparte used generosity, flattery, and bribery to win over some of his enemies; issued a general amnesty; and employed people from all political factions. He set up a centralized administration in which all departments were managed by prefects appointed by the central government in Paris. Secret police helped him uncover and stamp out royalist rebellions and plots.

Thermidorean Reaction
Reaction against the radicalism of the French Revolution that began in July 1794. Associated with the end of terror and establishment of the Directory.

Consulate   French government dominated by Napoleon from 1799 to 1804.

The French Revolution

1789

May 5	Estates General opens at Versailles
June 17	Third Estate declares itself the National Assembly
June 20	National Assembly takes the Tennis Court Oath
July 14	Fall of the Bastille
July	Great Fear spreads in the countryside
August 4	Nobles surrender their feudal rights in a meeting of the National Constituent Assembly
August 27	*Declaration of the Rights of Man and Citizen*
October 5–6	Parisian women march to Versailles and force Louis XVI and his family to return to Paris

1790

July 12	Civil Constitution of the Clergy adopted
July 14	New constitution accepted by the king

1791

June 20–24	Louis XVI and his family attempt to flee France
August 27	Declaration of Pillnitz
October 1	Legislative Assembly meets

Napoleon placated French Catholics who had been angered by revolutionary attacks on religion. In 1801, he concluded a concordat with Pope Pius VII (r. 1800–1823). Both refractory and constitutional clergy were forced to resign. Their replacements received spiritual investiture from the pope, but the state named the bishops and paid their salaries and the salary of one priest in each parish. In return, the church gave up claims to its confiscated property, the clergy swore oaths of loyalty to the state, and the Organic Articles of 1802 established the supremacy of the state over the church. Similar laws applied to Protestant and Jewish religious organizations.

In 1802, another plebiscite ratified Bonaparte's appointment as consul for life, and he set about transforming the basic laws and institutions of France on the basis of both liberal principles derived from the Enlightenment and the revolution and conservative principles going back to the Old Regime and the spirit that had triumphed at Thermidor. This was especially true of the Civil Code of 1804, usually called the Napoleonic Code. It, however, stopped far short of the full equality advocated by liberal rationalists. Fathers were granted extensive control over their children and men over their wives. Labor unions were forbidden, and the rights of workers were subordinated to those of employers.

In 1804, Bonaparte used the fear created by a failed assassination attempt to strengthen his hold on power. Another new constitution, ratified by a plebiscite, designated Napoleon Emperor of the French. Napoleon summoned the pope to Notre Dame to take part in the coronation, but at the ceremony Napoleon crowned himself.

Napoleon's Empire (1804–1814) Between his coronation as emperor and his final defeat at Waterloo (1815), Napoleon conquered most of Europe. France's victories ended the Old Regime and its feudal trappings in western Europe, and forced the eastern European states to reorganize themselves. Everywhere, opposition to Napoleon's advance unleashed the passions of nationalism.

Napoleon's military interventions led Britain to issue him an ultimatum and finally, in May 1803, to declare war. William Pitt the Younger (1759–1806) was returned to office as prime minister in 1804, and he persuaded Russia and Austria once again to try to block France's expansion. On October 21, 1805, Britain scored a major victory. Lord Nelson destroyed the French and Spanish fleets at the Battle of Trafalgar just off the Spanish coast. He was killed, but his victory guaranteed Britain control of the sea.

On land, however, between October 1805 and July 1807, Napoleon defeated the armies of Austria, Prussia, and Russia. He forced Austria to withdraw from northern Italy. He replaced the Holy Roman Empire with the Confederation of the Rhine, and Prussia and Russia were compelled to become his allies.

Napoleon could not be secure, however, until he had defeated Britain. Unable to compete with the British navy, he tried to cut off British trade with

Europe. This, he hoped, would cripple British commercial and financial power and drive the British from the war. This strategy, called the Continental System, harmed the European economies and roused opposition to Napoleon. The British economy, however, survived because of its access to the Americas and the eastern Mediterranean.

The Wars of Liberation   In 1807, a French army invaded the Iberian Peninsula to force Portugal to abandon its alliance with Britain. When a revolt broke out in Madrid in 1808, Napoleon deposed the Spanish Bourbons and placed his brother Joseph (1768–1844) on the Spanish throne. Napoleon's Spanish opponents launched a guerrilla war, and the British supported them by sending an army under Sir Arthur Wellesley (1769–1852), later the Duke of Wellington. This began a long campaign that played a critical role in Napoleon's ultimate defeat.

The Austrians renewed the war in 1809, but the French defeated them at the battle of Wagram. The resulting peace cost Austria territory containing 3.5 million subjects. Another spoil of victory was the Archduchess Marie Louise (1791–1847), Francis I's (r. 1792–1835) 18-year-old daughter. Napoleon married her in hopes of founding a dynasty. Bonaparte divorced his first empress, Josephine de Beauharnais (1763–1814), because she had borne him no children.

The Franco-Russian alliance began to falter. The Continental System had harmed the Russian economy, and Napoleon's establishment of a Polish state, the Grand Duchy of Warsaw, on Russia's doorstep angered Tsar Alexander I (r. 1800–1825). In 1810, Russia withdrew from the Continental System and began to prepare for war.

To stifle the Russian military threat, Napoleon amassed a so-called Grand Army of more than 600,000 men and invaded the country. Russia's generals decided to oppose him by retreating before his advance and stripping the countryside of supplies. Russia was too vast for Napoleon to maintain lines to supply, and his men could not live off the devastated land.

In September 1812, Russian public opinion forced the army to fight. At Borodino, the French lost 30,000 men and the Russians almost twice as many. The Russian army continued its advance, and occupied Moscow. In October, however, supply problems forced the Grand Army to begin a long, painful retreat. Perhaps only 100,000 lived to tell the tale.

In 1813, patriotic pressure and national ambition brought together the last and most powerful coalition against Napoleon. With British financing, the Russians drove westward to be joined by Prussia and Austria. From the west, Wellington marched his peninsular army into France. Napoleon waged a skillful campaign but met decisive defeat in October at Leipzig. At the end of March 1814, the allied army marched into Paris. Napoleon abdicated and went into exile on the island of Elba off the coast of Italy.

The French Revolution (continued)

1792		
	April 20	France declares war on Austria
	August 10	Tuileries palace stormed, and Louis XVI takes refuge with the Legislative Assembly
	September 2–7	September Massacres
	September 21	Convention meets, and monarchy abolished
1793		
	January 21	Louis XVI executed
	February 1	France declares war on Great Britain
	March	Counterrevolution breaks out
	April 6	Committee of Public Safety formed
	July	Robespierre enters Committee of Public Safety
	August 23	*Levée en masse* proclaimed
	September 29	Maximum prices set on food and other commodities
	October 16	Queen Marie Antoinette executed
	November 10	Cult of Reason proclaimed; revolutionary calendar
1794		
	May 7	Cult of the Supreme Being proclaimed
	July 27	Ninth of Thermidor and fall of Robespierre
	July 28	Robespierre executed
1795	August 22	Constitution of the Year III adopted, establishing the Directory

William Pitt and Napoleon. In this early 19th-century cartoon, England, personified by a caricature of William Pitt, and France, personified by a caricature of Napoleon, are carving out their areas of interest around the globe.

Cartoon by Gillray/Corbis-Bettmann.

Napoleonic Europe

1797	Napoleon concludes Treaty of Campo Formio
1799	Consulate established
1801	Concordat between France and papacy
1802	Treaty of Amiens
1803	War renewed between France and Britain
1804	Napoleonic Civil Code issued; Napoleon crowned emperor
1805	Nelson defeats French fleet at Trafalgar
1806	Continental System
1808	Beginning of Spanish resistance to Napoleonic domination
1809	Wagram; Napoleon marries Archduchess Marie Louise of Austria
1812	Invasion of Russia
1813	Leipzig (Battle of the Nations)
1814	Congress of Vienna convenes (September)
1815	Waterloo (June 18); Holy Alliance formed (September 26)
1821	Napoleon dies on Saint Helena; The Congress of Vienna and the European Settlement

THE CONGRESS OF VIENNA AND THE EUROPEAN SETTLEMENT

Once Napoleon was gone, the allies began to pursue their separate ambitions. The key leader was Viscount Castlereagh (1769–1822), the British foreign secretary. Even before the victorious allied armies entered Paris, he had negotiated the Treaty of Chaumont (March 9, 1814). It restored the Bourbons to the French throne and returned France to its 1792 frontiers. Remaining problems were left for a conference at Vienna.

The Congress of Vienna met from September 1814 until November 1815. The victors agreed that no single state should be allowed to dominate Europe. They constructed a series of states to prevent French expansion (see Map 23–2). They established the kingdom of the Netherlands in the north and added Genoa to Piedmont in the south. Prussia was given new territories in the west to deter French aggression along the Rhine River. Austria obtained control of northern Italy to prevent a repetition of Napoleon's conquests there. Most of Napoleon's arrangements in the rest of Germany were left untouched, and the Holy Roman Empire was not revived. The Congress established the rule of legitimate monarchs and rejected any compromise with the republican and democratic politics that had flowed from the French Revolution.

Eastern Europe created problems that divided the victors. Alexander I wanted Russia to govern all of Poland. Prussia wanted all of Saxony. Austria, however, refused to allow Prussia's power to grow and Russia to expand. The Polish-Saxon question gave France a chance to regain

MAP EXPLORATION

Interactive map: To explore this map further, go to **http://www.prenhall.com/craig/map23.2**

MAP 23–2
Europe 1815, after the Congress of Vienna. The Congress of Vienna achieved the post-Napoleonic territorial adjustments shown on the map. The most notable arrangements dealt with areas along France's borders (the Netherlands, Prussia, Switzerland, and Piedmont), in Poland, and northern Italy.

WHY DID the Congress of Vienna seek to place strong states on the borders of France?

influence in international affairs. The French Foreign Minister Talleyrand (1754–1838) negotiated a secret treaty with Britain and Austria. When the news leaked out, the tsar agreed to accept jurisidiction over a smaller Poland, and Prussia settled for part of Saxony. France was a major party to all future deliberations.

When Napoleon escaped from Elba and returned to France on March 1, 1815, the allies reunited and sent their armies to crush him. Wellington and the Prussians defeated him at Waterloo in Belgium on June 18, 1815. Napoleon was again exiled, this time to Saint Helena, a tiny island off the coast of Africa. He died there in 1821.

OVERVIEW THE VIENNA SETTLEMENT

The Congress of Vienna met from September 1814 to November 1815 to redraw the map of Europe after the defeat of Napoleon. With few exceptions, the borders the Congress agreed on remained in place until the 1850s. The statesmen at Vienna wanted to prevent another outbreak of the wars that had followed the French Revolution. The main principles behind their deliberations were a determination to confine France, which they saw as the home of revolution, within its traditional boundaries: legitimacy, by which they meant the restoration of Europe's traditional monarchs to their thrones; and compensation—the idea that the states that had defeated Napoleon deserved to be "compensated" for their expenditure of lives and treasure with new territory. Below is a summary of what the statesmen at Vienna achieved.

Britain	was compensated with a number of former French and Dutch colonies. It also became the dominant naval power in the Mediterranean by annexing Malta in the central Mediterranean and the Ionian Islands at the mouth of the Adriatic.
France	was reduced to its 1792 frontiers and ringed along its borders with a series of strengthened states to discourage French aggression. Thus, Prussia was given the Rhineland along France's eastern frontier; the Kingdom of the Netherlands was created to the north of France by combining Belgium and Holland; and the Kingdom of Sardinia on France's southern border was strengthened by the addition of the great port of Genoa.
Germany	The Holy Roman Empire was not revived. Instead, it was replaced by a loose Germanic confederation of mostly monarchical states under the presidency of Austria. Prussia was compensated by receiving two thirds of Saxony, which had been an ally of Napoleon.
Italy	Austria was compensated by becoming the dominant power in Italy and by being given Lombardy and Venetia. The Papal States were reconstituted, and the legitimate Italian rulers were restored to their thrones: the House of Savoy in Piedmont-Sardinia; the Bourbons in the Two Sicilies and Lucca; the Habsburgs in Tuscany, Modena, and Parma. Most of these rulers depended on Austrian support. The old republics of Venice and Genoa, which Napoleon had abolished, were not restored.
Poland	Poland was not restored as an independent state. It remained divided among Prussia, Austria, and Russia. Russia was compensated by being given the largest share of Poland.
Scandinavia	Denmark, another ally of Napoleon, had to cede Norway as compensation to Sweden, which had lost Finland to Russia.

The main outlines of the Vienna Settlement remained in place, and the alliance of England, Austria, Prussia, and Russia was renewed on November 20, 1815. It was to be a coalition for the maintenance of peace, and its existence and later operation represented an important departure in European affairs. The statesmen at Vienna, unlike their 18th-century counterparts, had seen the armies of the French Revolution change borders and overturn the political and social order of the continent. They were determined to prevent a recurrence of those upheavals. Their purpose was not to punish France but to establish a framework for future stability. The great powers, through the Vienna settlement, agreed to work together to defend the status quo and not, as in the 18th century, to use military force to change it.

The Congress of Vienna produced a long-lasting peace. Its work has been criticized for failing to recognize and provide for the great movements that would stir the 19th century—nationalism and democracy—but such criticism is unrealistic. The settlement, like all such agreements, was aimed at solving past ills, and in that it succeeded. It spared Europe a general war until 1914.

WARS OF INDEPENDENCE IN LATIN AMERICA

The French Revolution and the Napoleonic wars inspired movements for independence throughout Latin America. France was driven from Haiti, Portugal from Brazil, and Spain from all its American empire except for Cuba and Puerto Rico.

WHY DID Latin America throw off Spanish and Portuguese rule?

18TH-CENTURY DEVELOPMENTS

After Spain's defeat in the Seven Years' War in 1763, its king, Charles III (r. 1759–1788), decided that the American colonial system had to be changed. He abolished the monopolies of Seville and Cádiz, opened more South American and Caribbean ports to trade, and authorized direct trade between American ports. In 1776, he organized a fourth viceroyalty that encompassed much of present-day Argentina, Uruguay, Paraguay, and Bolivia. Charles III also tried to make tax collection more efficient and to eliminate bureaucratic corruption by appointing *intendents*, bureaucrats loyal only to the crown.

These reforms returned the empire to direct Spanish control. Many *peninsulares*, whites born in Spain, went to the New World to fill these new posts, depriving **Creoles**, whites born in America, of opportunity. Expanding trade brought more Spanish merchants to Latin America, where economic activity continued to be organized for the benefit of Spain.

peninsulares Native-born Spaniards who immigrated from Spain to settle in the Spanish colonies.

Creoles Persons of European descent who were born in the Spanish colonies.

FIRST MOVEMENTS TOWARD INDEPENDENCE

A slave revolt (1794–1804) led by Toussaint L'Ouverture (1746–1803) won Haiti independence from France. Haiti's revolution was the result of a popular uprising by a repressed social group. It proved to be the great exception in the Latin American wars for liberty from European masters. On the South American continent, it was the Creole elite who led the campaigns against Spain and Portugal. Few Indians, blacks, mestizos, mulattos, or slaves were involved or benefited from the end of Iberian rule. The Creoles were determined that political independence from Spain and Portugal should not entail the loss of their privileges. In this respect they were not unlike American revolutionaries in the southern colonies who wanted to reject British rule but keep their slaves—or the French revolutionaries who did not want to extend liberty to the French working class.

Toussaint L'Ouverture. L'Ouverture (1744–1803) began the revolt that led to Haitian independence in 1804.

Historical Pictures Collection/Stock Montage, Inc.

Creole complaints against Spain resembled those of the American colonists against Great Britain. Merchants wanted to trade more freely within their region and with North America and Europe. They wanted commercial regulations that would benefit them rather than Spain, and they resented Spanish policies and political patronage that favored peninsulares.

From the 1790s onward, Spain suffered reverses in the wars associated with the French Revolution and Napoleon. Military pressures forced the Spanish monarchy to resort to desperate measures to fill its treasury. Among these were increased taxation and the confiscation of property in the Americas that hurt the Creole elite.

Creole leaders had read the Enlightenment *philosophes* and believed that the political reforms the *philosophes* championed would benefit their region. They were also well aware of the political arguments that had justified the American

Revolution. The event that crystallized Creole discontent into revolt against Spain was Napoleon's overthow of the Portuguese monarchy in 1807 and the Spanish government in 1808. The Portuguese royal family fled to Brazil, but the Bourbon monarchy of Spain seemed vanquished. The Creole elite feared that a monarchy headed by Napoleon's brother in Spain would harm their economic and social interests and would drain the region of resources for Napoleon's wars. Creole juntas, or political committees, formed between 1808 and 1810 and claimed the right to govern regions of Latin America. Ten years of warfare ensued before Spain conceded Latin American independence.

SAN MARTÍN IN RÍO DE LA PLATA

The first region to assert its independence was the Río de la Plata, or modern Argentina. In 1810, the junta in Buenos Aires thrust off Spanish authority and sent soldiers to liberate Paraguay and Uruguay. They were defeated, but Paraguay asserted its own independence, and Brazil absorbed Uruguay.

The Buenos Aires government then attempted to liberate Peru, the greatest remaining stronghold of royalist power on the continent (see Map 23–3). In 1814, José de San Martin (1778–1850) led an army over the Andes Mountains. By early 1817, he had occupied Santiago in Chile and established Bernardo O'Higgins (1778–1842) as supreme dictator. In 1821, he drove royalist forces from Lima and assumed the title of Protector of Peru.

SIMÓN BOLÍVAR'S LIBERATION OF VENEZUELA

In 1810, Simón Bolívar (1783–1830), a firm advocate of independence and republicanism, had helped organize a liberating junta in Caracas, Venezuela. Between 1811 and 1814, civil war broke out as royalists, slaves, and cowboys challenged his republican government and drove him into exile. In 1819, with help from Haiti, he captured Bogotá, capital of New Granada (modern Colombia, Bolivia, and Ecuador) and established a base for attacking Venezuela. In 1821, his forces captured Caracas, and he was named president.

In July 1822, the armies of Bolívar and San Martín liberated the city of Quito, but the two leaders disagreed about the future political structure of Latin America. San Martín believed in monarchies; Bolívar favored republics. Shortly thereafter, San Martín retired from public life and moved to Europe. In 1823, Bolívar sent troops into Peru and on December 9, 1824, at the battle of Ayacucho, defeated the Spanish royalist forces. The battle marked the end of Spain's effort to retain its American empire.

INDEPENDENCE IN NEW SPAIN

The drive for independence in New Spain (modern Mexico, Texas, California, and the rest of the southwestern United States) illustrates how socially conservative the Latin American colonial revolutions were. As elsewhere, a local governing junta was organized. But before it had time to act, a Creole priest, Miguel Hidalgo y Costilla (1753–1811),

Simón Bolívar. Bolívar was the liberator of much of Latin America. He inclined toward a policy of political liberalism.

SuperStock Inc.

MAP 23–3
The Independence Campaigns of San Martín and Bolívar.

HOW DO the wars for independence in Latin America compare with the colonists' revolt against British rule in North America?

incited the Indians of his parish to rebel. They and other repressed groups responded to Father Hidalgo's call for social reform, and he soon had 80,000 followers. But in July 1811, he was captured and executed. Leadership of his movement then passed to José María Morelos y Pavón (1765–1815), a more radical mestizo priest. In 1815, he too was captured and executed.

In 1820, a revolution in Spain forced Ferdinand VII (r. 1813–1833) to accept a liberal constitution, and conservative Mexicans feared that a liberal Spanish monarchy would try to impose liberal reforms on Mexico. Therefore, for the most conservative of reasons, they declared Mexico independent under a government determined to resist social reform.

Great Britain supported the independence movements in Latin America, for independence opened the markets of the continent to British trade. In 1823, Britain accepted the Monroe Doctrine, the United States' insistence that there be no further intervention by European powers in America, and Britain soon recognized the Spanish colonies as independent states. Through the rest of the century, British commercial interests dominated Latin America.

The Wars of Latin American Independence

1759–1788	Charles III of Spain carries out imperial reforms
1794	Toussaint L'Ouverture leads slave revolt in Haiti
1804	Independence of Haiti
1807	Portuguese royal family flees to Brazil
1808	Spanish monarchy falls to Napoleon
1808–1810	Creole committees organized to govern much of Latin America
1810	Buenos Aires junta sends forces to liberate Paraguay and Uruguay
1811	Miguel Hidalgo y Costilla leads rebellion in New Spain and is executed
1811–1815	José María Morelos y Pavón leads rebellion in New Spain and is executed
1814	San Martín organizes army
1815	Brazil declared a kingdom
1817	San Martín occupies Santiago, Chile
1820	Revolution in Spain
1821	
February 24	New Spain declares independence
June 29	Bolívar captures Caracas, Venezuela
July 28	San Martín liberates Peru
1822	
July 26–27	San Martín goes into exile
September 7	Dom Pedro declares Brazilian independence
1824	Battle of Ayacucho—final Spanish defeat

WHY DID slavery become unacceptable in Western society?

BRAZILIAN INDEPENDENCE

Brazilian independence came relatively peacefully. As already noted, the Portuguese royal family and several thousand officials took refuge in Brazil in 1807, and their arrival transformed Rio de Janeiro into a court city. The prince regent Joao (r. 1816–1826) in 1815 declared Brazil a kingdom and no longer merely a colony of Portugal. In 1820, a revolution took place in Portugal, and its leaders offered the throne to Joao and demanded the return of Brazil to colonial status. Joao, who had become Joao VI in 1816, returned to Portugal and left his son Pedro (r. 1822–1831) as regent in Brazil. In 1822, Pedro asserted Brazil's independence and became emperor of Brazil. The country remained a monarchy until 1889.

TOWARD THE ABOLITION OF SLAVERY IN THE TRANSATLANTIC ECONOMY

In 1750, few questioned the institution of slavery, but by 1888, slavery no longer existed in the transatlantic economy. This transformation of economic and social life occurred as the result of an international effort, first to abolish the slave trade and then to abolish slavery itself. No previous society in world history had attempted to abolish slavery. Its elimination in the transatlantic world is one of the most permanent achievements of the 18th-century Enlightenment and revolutions.

The 18th-century crusade against slavery originated among writers of the Enlightenment and religious critics. The era's movements championing political and social equality were inconsistent with the radical inequality of slavery, and the case Adam Smith made in *The Wealth of Nations* for free labor and free markets undermined economic defenses of slavery. Some *philosophes* also idealized native peoples as closer to nature and objected to slavers robbing Africans of their alleged original innocence. In such a climate, slavery grew to be regarded as unacceptable.

The slave system was a transatlantic affair, and so was the crusade against it. English Quakers began the protest against slavery, and Quaker communities in America quickly joined them in the fight. During the American Revolution, small groups of reformers, usually organized by Quakers, established an antislavery network, and emancipation gradually spread among the northern states. In 1787, the Continental Congress forbade slavery in the Northwest Territory north of the Ohio River.

Despite these American efforts, Great Britain was the true center for the antislavery movement. During the early 1780s, antislavery reformers in Britain decided that the best strategy was to work toward ending the slave trade rather than slavery itself. To many, the slave trade seemed worse than the holding of slaves, and attacking slavery raised complicating issues of property rights. If the trade were ended, it seemed likely as well that planters would have to treat their remaining slaves more humanely.

While the British reformers worked for the abolition of the slave trade, some slaves took matters into their own hands. The slave revolt in Haiti was a warning to slave owners throughout the West Indies. Other slave revolts occurred in Virginia, South Carolina, and British-controlled Demarra, but these were suppressed.

For economic reasons, some British West Indies planters decided that abolition of the slave trade might be in their best interest. They were experiencing soil exhaustion and increased competition from French planters. There was a glut of sugar on the market, and the price was falling. Without new slaves, the French would lack the labor they needed to exploit their islands.

By 1807, abolition sentiment was strong enough for Parliament to prohibit slave trading from any British port. Thereafter, the suppression of this trade became a major goal of 19th-century British foreign policy. The British navy maintained a squadron off West Africa to halt slave traders.

Sentiment to abolish slavery itself increased. In 1833, following the passage of the Reform Bill in Great Britain, Parliament abolished the right of British subjects to hold slaves, and in the British West Indies, 750,000 slaves were freed.

Leaders of the Latin American wars of independence were disposed by Enlightenment ideas to disapprove of slavery, and they sought the support of slaves by promises of emancipation. The newly independent nations slowly freed their slaves to maintain good relations with Britain, from whom they needed economic support. Slavery had disappeared from Latin America by the middle of the century, with the important exception of Brazil.

The other old colonial powers in the New World were slower to abolish slavery. Portugal did nothing about slavery in Brazil, and Brazil's independent government continued slavery. Portugal ended slavery elsewhere in its American possessions in 1836; the Swedes, in 1847; the Danes, in 1848; but the Dutch did not abolish the practice until 1863. France had a significant antislavery movement, but did not abolish slavery in its West Indian possessions until 1848.

Despite opposition, during the first 30 years of the 19th century, slavery expanded in parts of the transatlantic world: the lower south of the United States (for the cultivation of cotton), Brazil (for the cultivation of coffee), and Cuba (for the cultivation of sugar). World demand for the products of these regions made the slave system economically viable. Slavery ended in the United States only after the Civil War. In Cuba it persisted until 1886, and full emancipation did not occur in Brazil until 1888 (see Chapters 25, 26, and 27).

The emancipation crusade, like slave trading itself, drew Europeans into African affairs. In 1787, the British established a colony for free blacks from Britain in Sierra Leone. The French established a smaller experiment at Libreville in Gabon. The most famous and lasting attempt to settle former black slaves in Africa was the establishment of Liberia through the efforts of the American Colonization Society after 1817. Liberia became an independent republic in 1847. These efforts to move former slaves back to Africa had only modest success, but they had a profound influence on West Africa.

Other antislavery reformers were less interested in establishing outposts for settlement of former slaves than in transforming the African economy itself. These reformers attempted to spread both Christianity and free trade to Africa, hoping to exchange British manufactured goods for tropical goods produced by Africans. These commercial efforts of the antislavery movement marked the first serious intrusions of European powers into the heart of Africa.

The American Civil War finally halted any large-scale demand for slaves from Africa. Antislavery reformers then concentrated on ending the slave trade in East Africa and the Indian Ocean. This campaign against slavery and the slave trade in Africa itself became one of the rationales for the establishment of the late-19th-century European colonial empires.

SUMMARY

The Transatlantic Revolutions The revolutions and the crusade against slavery that occurred throughout the transatlantic world between 1776 and the 1830s transformed three continents. In North America, in France and other parts of Europe, and in South America, political experiments challenged government by both monarchy and aristocracy. The foundations of modern liberal democracy were laid. The largest republic since ancient times had been established in North America. In France, written constitutions and elected legislatures remained essential parts of the government. In Latin America, republicanism triumphed everywhere except Brazil. Never again could government be undertaken in these regions without some form of participation by the governed.

Economic and Social Liberalization The expanding forms of political liberty found their counterparts in an economic life freed from the constraints of the old colonial empires and the slavery that marked their plantations. The new American republic constituted a vast free trade zone. Its commerce was open to the world. And for the first time since the encounter with Europe, Latin America could trade freely among its own peoples and those of the rest of the world. In France and Europe, where the Napoleonic armies had carried the doctrines of the rights of man, economic life had been rationalized and freed from the domination of local authorities and local weights and measures. National law formed the framework for economic activity. The movement to abolish slavery fostered a wage economy of free laborers. That kind of economy would generate its own set of problems and social dislocation, but it was nonetheless an economy of free human beings.

Nationalism Finally, the age of transatlantic revolutions saw the emergence of nationalism as a political force. All of the revolutions, because of their popular political base, had given power to the idea of nations defined by their own character and historical past rather than by dynastic rulers. The Americans saw themselves as forming a new kind of nation. The French had demonstrated the power of a nation mobilized for military purposes. In turn, the aggression of France had aroused national sentiment, especially in Great Britain, Spain, and Germany. The new nations of Latin America also sought to define themselves by their heritage and historical experience rather than by their past in the Spanish and Portuguese Empires.

These various revolutions, their political doctrines, and their social and economic departures provided examples to peoples elsewhere in the world. But

IMAGE KEY
for pages 556–557

a. The Execution of Louis XVI, on January 21, 1793.

b. Marie Antoinette.

c. Napoleon.

d. *The Third of May, 1808*, Francisco de Goya, 1814–1815.

e. Simón Bolívar.

f. Bostonians Paying the Excise Man, or tarring & feathering.

g. Marie Antoinette, sketched from life by Jacques-Louis David.

h. A poster celebrating French liberation.

i. The slave quarters of a Spanish slave ship.

j. Francois Dominique Toussaint L'Ouverture.

k. Storming of the Bastille, July 14, 1789.

even more important, the transatlantic revolutions and eventual abolition of slavery meant that new political classes and independent nations would become actors on the world scene. Europeans would have to deal with a score of new nations in the Americas. The rest of the world confronted new nations freed from the direction and authority of European powers. The political changes in Europe meant that those nations and their relationships with the rest of the world would be directed by a broader range of groups than in the past.

REVIEW QUESTIONS

1. What role did economic interests play in the American Revolution? What was the contribution of European ideas and political developments?

2. How did attempts to reform the French monarchy come to abolish it in favor of a republic?

3. What caused the Reign of Terror? Was it an inevitable outcome of the revolution or a violation of its principles?

4. How did Napoleon rise to power? What brought about his downfall? What did the Congress of Vienna achieve?

5. Did the revolutions that established the indepence of the Latin American countries differ from or follow the courses of the American and French revolutions?

6. What inspired the antislavery movement? What explains its success?

KEY TERMS

assignats (p. 564)
Consulate (p. 569)
Convention (p. 565)
Creoles (p. 575)

Jacobins (p. 565)
levée en masse (p. 566)
peninsulares (p. 575)
Reign of Terror (p. 566)

sans-culottes (p. 565)
Thermidorean Reaction (p. 569)
Third Estate (p. 561)

 For additional study resources for this chapter, go to:
www.prenhall.com/craig/chapter23

24 Political Consolidation in Nineteenth-Century Europe and North America, 1815–1880

CHAPTER HIGHLIGHTS

Nationalism Nationalism is the modern concept that people who share the same customs, culture, language, and history should also share the same government. It became the most powerful European political ideology of the nineteenth and early twentieth centuries.

Liberalism Politically, nineteenth-century liberals sought to establish constitutional governments that recognized civil liberties and made the executive responsible to a legislature elected by men of wealth and property. Economically, liberals wanted a laissez-faire economy with minimal government involvement.

Italian and German Unification With French assistance, most of the Italian peninsula was united by 1860.
German unification was achieved by Prussia between 1864 and 1871. Germany was henceforth the dominant power on the European continent.

North America In the United States, westward expansion brought vast new territories under the republic from the Mississippi River to the Pacific, but sectional conflict over economic issues and slavery led to the outbreak of the Civil War in 1861. Northern victory led to the abolition of slavery, the creation of a continent-wide free labor market, and enormous economic development that would make the United States the world's leading industrial power. Canada in these years achieved self-government from Britain and created a united Canadian federation in 1867.

Eastern Europe Nationalism created problems for the three eastern European empires: Germany, Russia, and Austria, but Habsburg Austria faced the greatest challenge from nationalism because it was a dynastic, not a national, state. Eleven different nationalities made up the Habsburg Monarchy, each with its own national aspirations. In 1867 the Habsburgs worked out the *Ausgleich*, or Compromise, with the Magyars, by which Hungary became an autonomous kingdom under the Habsburg emperor.

Racism and Anti-Semitism In the late nineteenth century, biological determinism, the concept that some peoples or races were inherently superior to others, took root in Western thought. In Germany, Austria, and France, some nationalists used the concept of race to blame the Jews for their countries' economic and political problems. Part of the Jewish response was the launching of the Zionist movement to found a separate Jewish state.

CHAPTER QUESTIONS

WHAT IS nationalism?

WHY WERE efforts to achieve
political liberalism more successful
in France and Britain than in
Russia between 1815 and 1830s?

WHAT WERE the causes of the
American Civil War?

HOW DID Canada achieve united self-government?

WHAT WERE the steps that led
to Italian and German unification?

HOW DID nationalism affect
the Habsburg Empire?

CHAPTER OUTLINE

- The Emergence of Nationalism in Europe
- Early Nineteenth-Century Political Liberalism
- Efforts to Liberalize Early Nineteenth-Century
  Political Structures
- Testing the New American Republic
- The Canadian Experience
- Midcentury Political Consolidation in Europe
- Unrest of Nationalities in Eastern Europe
- Racial Theory and Anti-Semitism

During the 19th century, two fundamental long-term developments occurred in the northern transatlantic world that would have a profound impact over the decades in every culture on the face of the Earth. First, in both Europe and North America a process of political consolidation took place that made the nation-states of that region the strongest of the period. Second, and directly contributing to that political strength, powerful, new industrial economies with a new kind of society no longer based primarily on the land emerged in Europe and North America. As a result of this political consolidation and industrialization, the nations of the northern transatlantic became the world's major military powers. By the close of the 19th century and well into the 20th, this political and military power allowed the nations of Europe and the United States to exert unprecedented political, military, and economic influence around the globe. On the basis of this power, many people in Europe and North America came to claim superiority to people dwelling in other cultures and other regions. Moreover, the manner in which Europeans and to a lesser extent Americans developed sets of ideas to explain what was happening politically and economically in their regions would later be used by people elsewhere in the world as they responded to the worldwide power that the northern transatlantic powers exerted.

This chapter will examine the process of political consolidation in the northern transatlantic world, while Chapter 25 will explore the social changes that occurred in the 19th century. Although we will consider the two processes separately, each contributed to the other.

WHAT IS nationalism?

THE EMERGENCE OF NATIONALISM IN EUROPE

Nationalism is based on the relatively modern concept that a nation is composed of people who are joined together by the bonds of common language, customs, culture, and history, and who, because of those bonds, should share the same government. That is to say, political and ethnic boundaries should coincide. This idea came into its own during the late 18th and early 19th centuries. Nationalists opposed the principle upheld at the Congress of Vienna that legitimate monarchies or dynasties should provide the basis for political unity. Nationalists rejected the concept of multinational states such as the Austrian or Russian Empires. They also objected to peoples of the same ethnic group, such as Germans and Italians, dwelling in political units smaller than that of the ethnic nation.

CREATING NATIONS

Nationalists created nations in the 19th century. During the first half of the century, writers spread *nationalistic* concepts. Many were historians who chronicled a people's past or literary scholars who established a national literature by collecting and publishing earlier writings in the people's language. In effect, they gave a people a sense of their past and a literature of their own, which schoolteachers spread.

The language to be used in schools and government was a point of contention for nationalists. In France and Italy, official versions of the national language were imposed in the schools. In eastern Europe, nationalists attempted to resurrect the national language. Often these resurrected languages were virtually invented by scholars. This process led to far more linguistic uniformity within European nations than had existed before the 19th century. Proficiency in the official language became a path to advancement. A uniform language helped to persuade people who had not thought of themselves as constituting a nation to believe that they were a nation. Yet even in 1850, less than half of the inhabitants of France, for example, spoke French.

nationalism Belief that one is part of a nation, defined as a community with its own language, traditions, customs, and history that distinguish it from other nations and make it the primary focus of a person's loyalty and sense of identity.

MEANING OF NATIONHOOD

Nationalists used a variety of arguments to express what they meant by nation-hood. Some claimed that gathering Italians, for example, into a unified Italy would promote economic and administrative efficiency. Others insisted that nations, like biological species, were distinct creations of God.

A significant difficulty for nationalism was, and is, determining which ethnic groups should be considered nations with claims to territory and political auton-omy. In theory, any of them could, but nationhood came to be associated with groups that were large enough to support an economy, that had a history of signif-icant cultural association, that possessed a cultural elite who could nourish the national language, and that could conquer other peoples to protect their own independence. Many smaller ethnic groups claimed to fulfill these criteria but could not achieve either independence or recognition. They could and did, how-ever, create unrest within the political units they inhabited. Such was the situation in Europe, and the American Civil War can be seen as having similar origins.

REGIONS OF NATIONALISTIC PRESSURE IN EUROPE

During the 19th century, nationalists challenged the political status quo in six major areas of Europe. Irish nationalists wanted independence from Britain or at least self-government. German nationalists wanted a single nation encompassing all German-speaking peoples, challenging the multinational Austrian Empire and pitting Prussia and Austria against each other. Italian nationalists sought to unify the peninsula and drive out the Austrians. Polish nationalists struggled, pri-marily against Russia, to restore Poland as an independent nation. In eastern Europe, Hungarians, Czechs, Slovenes, and others sought either autonomy or formal recognition within the Austrian Empire. Finally, in the Balkans, national groups sought independence from Ottoman and Russian control. In each area, nationalist activity ebbed and flowed. The dominant governments often thought they needed only to repress the activity or ride it out, but over the course of the century nationalists changed the map and political culture of Europe—as the Confederate States of America failed to do in the United States.

EARLY 19TH-CENTURY POLITICAL LIBERALISM

T he term *liberal* as used in present-day American political rhetoric has vir-tually no relationship to the kinds of ideologies that were described as lib-eral in the 19th century.

POLITICS

European **liberalism** derived from the Enlightenment, the example of English liberties, and the French *Declaration of the Rights of Man and Citizen*. Liberals favored legal equality, religious toleration, freedom of the press, and limits to the arbitrary power of governments. They believed that the legitimacy of govern-ment emanated from the freely given consent of the governed expressed through elected parliaments. Most important, free government required that state or crown ministers be responsible to the representatives of the nation rather than to the monarch.

These goals were limited. The people who espoused them tended to be those who were excluded from the existing political processes but whose wealth

20.3
Fustel de Coulanges, "What Is a Nation?" A Reply to Mr. Mommsen, Professor in Berlin

WHAT POLITICAL and economic goals did 19th-century liberals wish to achieve?

liberalism In the 19th century, support for representative government dominated by the propertied classes and minimal government interference in the economy.

and education made them feel that such exclusion was unjustified. Liberals were often academics, members of the learned professions, and people involved in commerce and manufacturing. They were products of career fields that admitted and rewarded people on the basis of talent. Monarchical and aristocratic regimes often failed to recognize their status and interests.

European liberals were not democrats. They despised the lower classes. Liberals transformed the 18th-century concept of aristocratic liberty into a new concept of privilege based on wealth and property. By the mid-century, this meant that throughout Europe, liberals had separated themselves from the working class. In the first half of the 19th century, political liberals generally did not support political rights for women, but liberal political principles provided women with strong arguments to use when agitating for rights.

ECONOMICS

The economic goals of the liberals furthered their separation from the working class. Liberal elements in the landed and commercial middle class, influenced by the Enlightenment and Adam Smith, wanted to be able to manufacture and sell goods freely. They favored the removal of barriers to trade and, from the 1830s onward, sought construction of rail networks for wide distribution of trade.

Economic liberals opposed the old paternalistic traditions in which governments of guilds passed legislation to fix wages and labor practices. They regarded labor simply as a commodity to be bought and sold freely. Liberals favored an open economy in which people were free to use their talents and property to enrich themselves. They contended that this would lead to more goods and services for everyone at lower prices.

The economic goals of European liberals found many followers outside Europe among groups who favored the expansion of free trade, new transport systems, and a free market in labor. In the United States, people with this outlook often attacked slavery as inefficient and paternalistic. In Latin America, political liberals sought to repeal legislation that had protected Native Americans under Spanish rule.

RELATIONSHIP OF NATIONALISM AND LIBERALISM

Liberalism and nationalism were often complementary. The idea that people should be free to pursue careers that rewarded their talents could be used to make a case for the liberation of suppressed national groups that were not free to realize their cultural or political potential. The efficient government and administration required by commerce and industry, which liberals favored, also necessitated joining small German and Italian states into larger political units. Nationalist movements could gain the sympathy of liberals by making representative government and political liberty one of the goals.

LIBERALISM AND NATIONALISM IN MODERN WORLD HISTORY

The French Revolution in Europe had demonstrated by the early 19th century that the ideals of political liberalism could easily cross dynastic borders. In time those liberal ideals as well as those of nationalism would spread around the globe. Thus, what began as a European development is also important for global history. The concept of the "rights of man and citizen" was used during the Wars of Independence in Latin America to challenge Spanish government. By the close of the 19th century, those same ideals had been turned against the colonial governments that Europeans imposed on Africa and Asia. Furthermore, the belief that people should have the right to govern themselves inspired the settlers who spread across both the United States and Canada as well as those who settled in Australia and New Zealand. Similarly, the belief that individual ethnic groups should constitute independent nations became a major political conviction that led peoples living under European colonial government during the late 19th century and, even more importantly, the 20th century to challenge the right of Europeans and later Americans to govern them or dominate their lives through economic power. Political developments in Europe during the early 19th century profoundly affected global politics during the 20th century.

A CONVENTION OF HEMMERS AND STITCHERS HELD AT LYNN, FEB. 28, FOR ADOPTING A LIST OF PRICES; MRS. E. HALL, PRESIDING.—(See page 284.)

Female Activism. Women's gatherings, like the first women's rights convention in Seneca Falls in 1848 and this meeting of strikers in Lynn in 1860, were indicators of widespread efforts to liberalize 19th-century European and American political structures.
Lynn Museum.

WHY WERE efforts to achieve political liberalism more successful in France and Britain than in Russia between 1815 and the 1830s?

EFFORTS TO LIBERALIZE EARLY 19TH-CENTURY EUROPEAN POLITICAL STRUCTURES

European nations did not move toward liberal political structures rapidly or without considerable conflict. Indeed, after the Congress of Vienna, most conservatives hoped that they had established blocks to liberal advances. The following examples indicate the kinds of situations that confronted European liberals early in the 19th century.

RUSSIA: THE DECEMBRIST REVOLT OF 1825 AND THE AUTOCRACY OF NICHOLAS I

In the process of driving Napoleon's army across Europe and then occupying defeated France, many officers in the Russian army were introduced to the ideas of the French Revolution and the Enlightenment. They realized how economically backward and politically stifled Russia was, and groups within the officer corps began to form secret societies. These societies were small and divided in their goals; they agreed only that the government of Russia must change. In 1825, they decided to stage a coup d'état the following year.

Events intervened. In late November 1825, Tsar Alexander I suddenly and unexpectedly died. His death created two crises. The first was a dynastic one: Alexander had no direct heir. His brother, Constantine, was next in line to be tsar, but Constantine, who commanded Russian forces in Poland, had renounced any claim to the throne. Secret instructions left by Alexander and made public only after his death named the tsar's younger brother, Nicholas (r. 1825–1855), his successor, but the legality of Alexander's orders was uncertain. Constantine acknowledged Nicholas as tsar, and Nicholas acknowledged Constantine. This family muddle continued for about three weeks, during which Russia actually had no ruler. Then, in early December, the army command reported to Nicholas the existence of a conspiracy among certain officers. Nicholas concluded that he could not delay and had himself declared tsar.

The second crisis now unfolded—a plot by junior officers to rally the troops under their command to compel reform. On December 26, 1825, the army was to take the oath of allegiance to Nicholas, who was less popular than Constantine and was regarded as more conservative. Nearly all of the regiments did so, but the Moscow regiment refused. Its chief officers, surprisingly, were not secret society members, but they supported Constantine and wanted a constitution. Attempts to settle the situation peacefully failed, and late in the afternoon Nicholas ordered cavalry and artillery to attack the insurgents. Five of the plotters were executed, and more than 100 other officers were exiled to Siberia.

The revolt had the effect of ending liberalism as even a moderate political influence in Russia. It also made Nicholas I the conservative policeman of Europe, ready to provide troops to suppress liberal and nationalist movements wherever they appeared. Except for a modest experiment early in the 20th century, tsarist Russia was never to know a genuinely liberal political reform.

REVOLUTION IN FRANCE (1830)

In 1824, Louis XVIII (r. 1814–1824), the Bourbon restored to the throne of France by the Congress of Vienna, died. He was succeeded by his brother, Charles X (r. 1824–1830). The new king considered himself a monarch by divine right. He wanted to restore lands that the French aristocrats had lost during the revolution and pressed other conservative measures through the Chamber of Deputies. Opposition soon developed. After elections in 1827, Charles moderated his conservatism, but French liberals pressed for a constitutional regime. Matters came to a head in 1829 when Charles abandoned efforts to accommodate liberals and appointed an ultra-royalist ministry. This backfired.

In 1830, Charles X called for new elections, and the liberals scored a stunning victory. Instead of attempting to accommodate the new Chamber of Deputies, the king and his ministers decided to attempt a royalist seizure of power. In June and July 1830, the ministry sent a naval expedition against Algeria. On July 9, reports of its victory, the start of a French empire in North Africa, reached Paris. On July 25, 1830, Charles X, euphoric in victory, issued the Four Ordinances. They restricted freedom of the press, dissolved the

Vive La France. *Liberty Leading the People* by Eugene Delacroix is a famous evocation of the Revolution of 1830.

Giraudon/Art Resource, N.Y.

recently elected Chamber of Deputies, called for new elections, and limited the franchise to the wealthiest people in the country.

Liberal newspapers immediately called on the nation to reject the monarch's actions. The laboring populace of Paris, suffering since 1827 from the effects of an economic downturn, took to the streets and erected barricades. The king called out troops, and more than 1,800 people died during the ensuing battles in the city. On August 2, Charles X abdicated and left France for exile in England. The liberals in the Chamber of Deputies named a new ministry composed of constitutional monarchists. They proclaimed Louis Philippe (r. 1830–1848), the Duke of Orléans and the head of the liberal branch of the royal family, the new monarch. In the so-called **July Monarchy**, Louis Philippe reigned as king of the French rather than of France. He had to cooperate with the Chamber of Deputies, and he could not dispense with laws on his own authority. The revolutionary tricolor replaced the white flag of the Bourbons. The Charter, or constitution, was regarded as embodying the natural rights of the people rather than a concession of privileges granted them by the monarch. Catholicism was recognized only as the religion of the majority of the people, not the official religion. Censorship was abolished. The franchise, though still restricted, was extended.

Socially, the Revolution of 1830 proved quite conservative. The landed oligarchy retained its economic, political, and social influence. Money became the path to power and influence in the government, resulting in much corruption. Most revealing, the liberal monarchy displayed scant sympathy for the lower and working classes.

THE GREAT REFORM BILL IN BRITAIN (1832)

The passage of the **Great Reform Bill**, which became law in 1832, was the result of events different from those that occurred on the continent. In Britain, the forces of conservatism and reform compromised with each other. As a result, during the century Great Britain was regarded as the exemplary liberal state not only of Europe but of the world.

English determination to maintain union with Ireland began the reform process. England's relationship to Ireland was not unlike that of Russia's to Poland or Austria's to Hungary. The Act of Union in 1800 between England and Ireland had suppressed the separate Irish parliament and seated Irish representatives in the British parliament at Westminster. Only Protestant Irishmen, however, could be elected to represent what was an overwhelmingly Catholic country.

During the 1820s, under the leadership of Daniel O'Connell (1775–1847), Irish nationalists organized the Catholic Association to agitate for **Catholic emancipation**, as the movement for legal rights for Roman Catholics was known. In 1828, O'Connell was elected to Parliament but could not legally take his seat. The British ministry of the Duke of Wellington (1769–1852) realized that henceforth Ireland might elect a predominantly Catholic delegation to Parliament, and if they were not seated, civil war might erupt. Consequently, in 1829, Wellington and Robert Peel (1788–1850) steered the Catholic Emancipation Act through Parliament. Roman Catholics could now become members of Parliament. This measure, together with the repeal in 1828 of restrictions against Protestant nonconformists, ended the monopoly held by members of the Church of England on British political life.

Catholic emancipation alienated many of Wellington's Tory supporters. In the election of 1830, many supporters of parliamentary reform were returned to

July Monarchy French regime set up after the overthrow of the Bourbons in July 1830.

Great Reform Bill (1832) Limited reform of the British House of Commons and expansion of the electorate to include a wider variety of the propertied classes. It laid the groundwork for further orderly reforms within the British constitutional system.

Catholic emancipation Grant of full political rights to Roman Catholics in Britain in 1829.

Parliament. Some Tories thought that parliamentary reform was necessary because they believed that Catholic emancipation could have been passed only by a corrupt House of Commons. The Wellington ministry soon fell. The Tories were badly divided, and King William IV (r. 1830–1837) turned to the Whigs under the leadership of Earl Grey (1764–1845) to form a government.

The Whig ministry authored a major reform bill that had two broad goals. The first was to replace "rotten" boroughs, which had few voters, with representatives for the previously unrepresented and populous manufacturing districts and cities. The second was to increase the number of voters in England and Wales. In 1831, the House of Commons narrowly defeated the bill. Grey called for a new election in which a majority in favor of the bill was returned to the Commons. The House of Commons passed the reform bill, but the House of Lords rejected it. Mass meetings were held throughout the country, and riots broke out in several cities. Finally, William IV agreed to create enough new peers to give a third reform bill a majority in the House of Lords. Under this pressure, the measure became law in 1832.

The Great Reform Act expanded the size of the English electorate, but it was not a democratic measure. The electorate was increased by more than 200,000 persons, or by almost 50 percent. The basis of voting, however, remained a property qualification, and some working-class voters actually lost the vote when their old franchise rights were abolished. New urban boroughs gave the growing cities a voice in the House of Commons. Yet the passage of the Reform Act did not, as it was once thought, constitute the triumph of the middle-class interest in England. For every new urban electoral district, a new rural district was also created. It was expected that the aristocracy would dominate the rural elections.

Although passed with much turmoil and conflict, the Great Reform Act established the foundation for long-term political stability in Britain. During the 1840s, a major working-class political movement known as **Chartism** brought the demands of industrial workers into the political process. Despite the tensions created by Chartism, British political structures survived intact. Throughout the second half of the 19th century, Great Britain continued to symbolize the confident liberal state. A large body of ideas emphasizing competition and individualism was accepted by the members of all classes. Even the leaders of trade unions during these years asked only to receive some of the fruits of prosperity and a chance to prove their social respectability. Parliament absorbed new groups and interests into the existing political processes.

The most important example of the opening of parliamentary processes was the Second Reform Act passed by a Conservative government in 1867. By increasing the number of voters from approximately 1,430,000 to 2,470,000, it advanced Britain toward democracy. Benjamin Disraeli (1804–1881), who led the conservatives in the House of Commons, thought significant portions of the working class would eventually support conservative candidates who responded to social issues. He also thought the growing suburban middle class would become more conservative.

Chartism First large-scale European working-class political movement. It sought political reforms that would favor the interests of skilled British workers in the 1830s and 1840s.

Gladstone and Disraeli   The election of 1868, which followed the Second Reform Act, dashed Disraeli's hopes. William Gladstone (1809–1898) became the new prime minister, and his ministry (1868–1874) witnessed the culmination of classical British liberalism. Gladstone introduced competitive examinations into the civil service, abolished the purchase of army officers' commissions, and introduced the secret ballot. He opened Oxford and Cambridge universities to students of all religious denominations and, by the Education Act of 1870, made the British government responsible for establishing and running elementary schools, which previously had been maintained by the various churches.

The liberal policy of creating popular support for the nation by extending political liberty and reforming abuses had its conservative counterpart in concern about social reform. Disraeli succeeded Gladstone as prime minister in 1874. Whereas Gladstone looked to individualism, free trade, and competition to solve social problems, Disraeli believed the state should protect its weaker citizens and that paternalistic legislation would alleviate class antagonism. His most important measures were the Public Health Act of 1875, which consolidated and extended previous sanitary legislation, and the Artisans Dwelling Act of 1875, through which the government became involved in providing housing for the working class.

The Irish Question   Ireland remained a major issue for the British government. From the late 1860s onward, Irish nationalists had sought to achieve home rule for Ireland, by which they meant more Irish control of local government. What they demanded from the British government resembled what Hungarians first and then Czechs demanded from the Habsburg government (discussed later in this chapter). The Irish, like the Hungarians and Czechs in the Habsburg Empire, were a profoundly disruptive force in British politics.

The leader of the Irish movement for **home rule** was Charles Stewart Parnell (1846–1891). By 1885, Parnell had organized 85 Irish members of the House of Commons into a tightly disciplined party that often voted as a bloc. After the election of 1885, the Irish Party held the balance of power in a house divided between the English liberals and conservatives. The Irish could decide which party would take office, and in December 1885, Gladstone won their votes by announcing his support for home rule for Ireland. However, the issue split Gladstone's Liberal Party. In 1886, a group known as the Liberal Unionists

William Gladstone (1809–1898)

• Became prime minister in election of 1868

• His ministry witnessed the culmination of classical British liberalism

• Carried out reforms of governmental abuses and extended political liberty

home rule Advocacy of a large measure of administrative autonomy for Ireland within the British Empire between the 1880s and 1914.

A House of Commons Debate.
William Ewart Gladstone, standing on the right, is attacking Benjamin Disraeli, who sits with legs crossed and arms folded. Gladstone served in the British Parliament from the 1830s through the 1890s. Four times the Liberal Party prime minister, he was responsible for guiding major reforms through Parliament. Disraeli, regarded as the founder of modern British conservatism, served as prime minister from 1874 to 1880.
Mary Evans Picture Library.

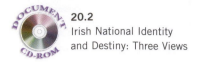

20.2
Irish National Identity
and Destiny: Three Views

joined with the conservatives to defeat Gladstone's Home Rule Bill. Gladstone called for a new election, which the liberals lost. They remained permanently divided. The new conservative ministry of Lord Salisbury (1830–1903) attempted to reconcile the Irish to the English government through public works and administrative reform, but he had only marginal success.

In 1892, Gladstone returned to power and sponsored a second Home Rule Bill that passed the House of Commons but was defeated in the House of Lords. With the failure of this bill, further action on the Irish question was suspended until a liberal ministry passed the third Home Rule Bill in the summer of 1914. However, the implementation of home rule was then suspended for the duration of World War I.

As already noted, the Irish question affected British politics much the way that the nationalities problem affected Austria. Normal British domestic issues could not be adequately addressed because of the political divisions created by Ireland. The split of the Liberal Party hurt the cause of further social and political reform. The people who could agree about reforms could not agree on Ireland, and Ireland seemed more important. Because the two traditional parties failed to deal with the social questions, by the turn of the century a newly organized Labour Party appeared to fill the vacuum.

QUICK REVIEW

Factors Leading to Revolutions
- Food shortages due to bad harvests
- Recession and widespread unemployement
- Pressure from continental liberals for change

1848: YEAR OF REVOLUTIONS IN EUROPE

In 1848, a series of liberal and nationalistic revolutions and revolts spread across Europe (see Map 24–1). No single factor caused this general revolutionary groundswell, but similar conditions existed in several countries. Severe food shortages had prevailed since 1846 due to poor harvests. The commercial and industrial economy was in recession, resulting in widespread unemployment. However, the pressure for change in 1848 originated not with the working classes but with the political liberals, who were generally drawn from the middle classes. Throughout the continent, liberals were pushing for more representative governments, civil liberty, and free and unregulated economies.

To put additional pressure on their governments, the liberals began to appeal for support from the urban working classes, even though the goals of the two groups were different. The working classes wanted more jobs and better working conditions rather than political reform for its own sake. By refusing to follow political revolution with social reform, the liberals separated themselves from their temporary working-class allies. Without potential mass support, the liberal revolutions were easy prey for the armies of reactionary governments. Consequently, the revolutions of 1848 failed to establish genuinely liberal or national states.

The revolutions of 1848 were confined to the continent, and their results were important for individual nation-states. In France, the monarchy of Louis Philippe was overthrown and briefly replaced by a republic. In 1851, the republic was in turn overthrown in a military coup led by Louis Napoleon, a nephew of Napoleon I. Thereafter, Louis Napoleon created the Second Empire and took the title of Napoleon III. In Prussia and the Austrian Empire, short-lived revolutions brought political liberals and nationalists to the fore, but in each case the revolutions were suppressed by the military. The same was true of efforts by Italian nationalists to thrust off Austrian rule of Italy.

From the standpoint of world history, the chief importance of the failed liberal and national revolutions of 1848 was the emergence on the European continent of strongly conservative governments that would dominate the scene for the next quarter century. The turmoil of 1848 through 1850 ended the era of

MAP 24-1

Centers of Revolution in 1848–1849. The revolution that toppled the July Monarchy in Paris in 1848 soon spread to Austria and many of the German and Italian states. Yet by the end of 1849, most of these uprisings had been suppressed.

WHICH REGIONS were most affected by the uprisings of 1848 and 1849?

liberal revolution that had begun in 1789. Liberals and nationalists had discovered that rational argument and local insurrections would not help them to achieve their goals. The working class also adopted new tactics and organization. The era of the riot and urban insurrection was ending. In the future, workers would turn to trade unions and political parties to achieve their political and social goals. Finally, after the revolutions of 1848, the political initiative in Europe passed for a time to the conservative political groups.

The defeat of liberal political forces in 1848 and the triumph of conservative powers also influenced the modernization of Japan. Within a few years,

Japan was to emerge from its long, self-imposed isolation. After the Meiji Restoration, the new leaders of Japan looked to Europe for examples of successful modern nations. The nation they would most clearly copy was the conservative, militaristic Germany that emerged after the defeat of the liberals of 1848.

TESTING THE NEW AMERICAN REPUBLIC

TOWARD SECTIONAL CONFLICT

WHAT WERE the causes of the American Civil War?

While the nations of Western Europe very slowly embraced political liberalism, the United States of America was continuing its bold republican political experiment. By the first quarter of the century, however, serious sectional tensions had arisen, the most important of which concerned the institution of slavery in the southern states.

The issue had come up at the Constitutional Convention of 1788, which debated what proportion of the slave population, if any, should be counted in determining how many seats the southern states would have in the House of Representatives. A compromise allowed the slave-holding states to count three-fifths of their slaves when calculating their population for representation in Congress. The Constitution also forbade any federal attempt to prevent the importation of slaves until 1808. Between 1788 and 1808, thousands of slaves were brought into the United States.

The opening of the western territories to settlement revived debates over slavery. The Ordinance of 1787, passed by Congress under the Articles of Confederation, had prohibited slavery in the Northwest Territory (the future states of Illinois, Indiana, Michigan, Ohio, and Wisconsin). Territory south of the Ohio River and beyond the Mississippi River was, however, open to slavery. By 1820, the number of slave and free states was evenly divided, and there was, therefore, an equal number of senators from slave and free states. That year, Missouri was admitted as a slave state and Maine as a free one. The Missouri Compromise temporarily ended congressional debate over slavery by decreeing that no slave states would be carved out of land north of the southern border of Missouri. However, problems loomed, for the economies of the North and the South were rapidly diverging.

Northern Economic Development The North's economy featured family farms, free labor, commerce, and early industrialization in textiles. Northern farmers tended primarily to produce foodstuffs for local markets. Their farms were relatively small and worked by family members and free hired laborers. Workers in the towns, on the ships, and in the factories of the North were also free. The political spokesmen for the North tended to favor tariffs to protect their young industries from cheaper foreign competition. Many Americans whose political views otherwise resembled European liberals differed from their European counterparts in their support for tariffs.

The North was the site of the earliest textile factories in the United States. Samuel Slater had established the first textile mill in Rhode Island in 1790. He had learned how to manufacture textiles in the new mills of industrializing Great Britain. His transfer of that technology to America illustrates how important British and European advances were transported to the United States. Much of the early industrialization of the United States depended on such technological transfers. By the second decade of the 19th century, the North had hundreds of cotton factories. These mills used cotton that was produced in the South, but most southern cotton was sold overseas, mainly to the growing British textile industry.

Textile Mill. In New England, as in Europe, textile manufacturing was the first of the highly mechanized industries. American and European textile mills closely resembled each other because those in America had been copied from European and most particularly English technology.

The Granger Collection, N.Y.

During the second quarter of the century, innovations in transportation led to the fuller integration of different parts of the Northern economy (see Map 24–2). Canals were built to link the major rivers with manufacturing and agricultural markets. The most famous was the Erie Canal, which connected the Hudson River to the Great Lakes. Other canals linked the Great Lakes to the Ohio River. Major efforts were undertaken to make the Ohio, Mississippi, and Missouri Rivers navigable so that steamboats could transport goods. But by the late 1840s, in America as in Europe, railroads were becoming the future of transportation. Most of the railways linked the Northeast and the West and fostered the commercial agriculture of the Midwest. Its products were sold in the Northeast and exported from Northern ports. The development of east–west railways weakened ties between the North and the South by undermining the older north–south river-based trade routes of the Ohio and Mississippi. The building of the early railways also aided the development of the Northern coal and iron industries. The expansion of railways at mid-century caused new sectional tensions, as it became clear that they were opening vast territories for settlement and reigniting a national debate over the future of slavery.

Rivers, canals, and railways allowed the upper Midwest to develop into a rich area for agriculture. Consequently, much of the northern economy was as rural and agricultural as the southern. What most distinguished the two regions was free versus slave labor. The southern economy depended on slavery and could expand only if slavery were allowed to spread as well (see Map 24–2).

The Southern Economy   The overwhelmingly rural economy of the American South was dependent on cotton and slavery. In this respect, the Southern economy resembled those of many Latin American countries, which used slave labor to produce a specialized crop or exploit a natural resource for export. The South had to export goods, especially raw cotton, either to the North or to Europe, primarily to Great Britain, to maintain its standard of living.

The invention of the cotton gin by Eli Whitney (1765–1825) in 1793 made cotton cultivation much more profitable because the seed no longer had to be laboriously picked out of the raw cotton by hand. The industrial revolution in textiles kept cotton prices high, and the expansion in world population kept the demand for cotton cloth steady. The South profited from growing the cotton, New England profited from shipping it, and other parts of the North profited from supplying the manufactured goods the South needed. The South had virtually no incentive to diversify its agriculture.

Slavery in the American South   Slavery had been abolished in the North by the early 19th century. This was a response to the egalitarian principles of the American Revolution and a recognition of the fact that slavery had never been fundamental to the northern economy. But in the South, the growth of a cotton-producing empire in the Mississippi Delta in the early 19th century gave slavery a new lease on life. Although most southern families never owned any slaves and relatively few slave owners possessed more than a few, the institution of slavery survived for many reasons. For one, it was economically viable, and no one could find a way that was politically or socially acceptable to white southerners to abolish it. No less important was the strong commitment to the protection of private property, which included slaves, throughout American society in both the North and the South. Perhaps the most basic reason for the endurance of slavery after the early 19th century, however, was racist thinking that saw Blacks as fundamentally inferior to Whites. Such thinking was not

Cotton fields. Slaves harvest cotton under the watchful eyes of an overseer, mid 19th-century.

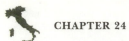

MAP EXPLORATION

Interactive map: To explore this map further, go to **http://www.prenhall.com/craig/map24.2**

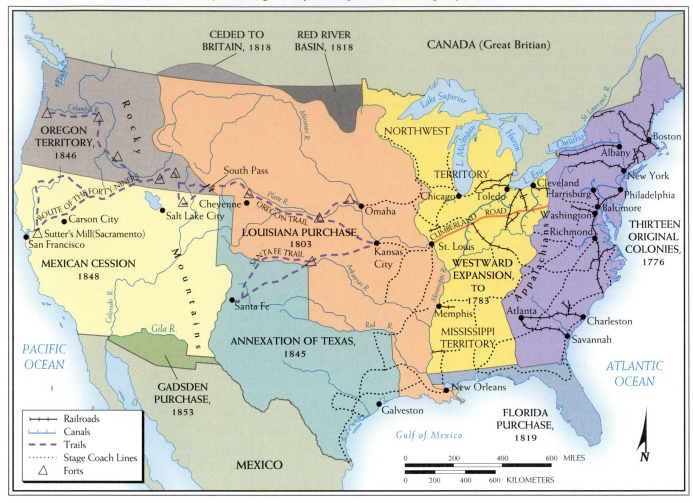

MAP 24–2

19th-Century North America. During the 19th century the United States expanded across the entire North American continent. The revolutionary settlement had provided most of the land east of the Mississippi. The single largest addition thereafter was the Louisiana Purchase of 1803. The annexation of Texas, and later the Mexican Cession following the Mexican War, added the major southwestern territories. The borders of the Oregon Territory were settled through long, difficult negotiations with Great Britain.

HOW DID the westward expansion of the United States help cause the Civil War?

peculiar to the South, but it functioned there to bolster arguments against abolishing slavery.

All American slaves were non-White, the descendants of Africans who had been forcibly captured and shipped in the most wretched of conditions to the United States (see Chapter 17). Despite much miscegenation among Africans and their White slave owners and Native Americans, the various slave codes defined as Black virtually anyone who had any African antecedents. Slaves were regarded as chattel property; that is, they could be sold, given away, or gambled away like any other piece of property. They had no recourse to law or constitutional protections and could be, and often were, treated badly by their masters. Whipping and beating were permitted. State laws protected slaves from extreme violence, but were laxly enforced; slaves had no serious protection from the law or legal authorities. Their standard of living was generally poor. Although owners wanted to see their slave investments reproduce themselves, slaves suffered from overwork and diseases associated with poor nutrition, sanitation, and housing.

Slaves worked primarily in the fields, where they plowed, hoed, and harvested cotton, rice, sugar, tobacco, or corn. They were usually organized into work gangs supervised by White overseers. This work was, like all farming, seasonal; but during planting or harvest seasons, people labored from sunrise to sunset. Children also worked in the fields. Older or more privileged slaves might be employed in their owner's house, cleaning, cooking, or taking care of his children.

Recent scholarship has emphasized how the slave communities helped to preserve family life and inner personalities of the slaves. Some elements of African culture persisted; African legends were passed on orally. Religion proved extraordinarily important. Slaves, for instance, found special meaning in the Old Testament stories of the Jews' liberation from Egypt, and they combined elements of African religion with evangelical Protestantism. Their efforts to preserve a sense of community and family had to contend with the fact that their marriages and family ties were not legally recognized. The integrity of the slave family could be violated at the master's whim or as a result of changing economic circumstances. White men often sexually exploited Black slave women. Because slaves were property, they could be sold for profit or transported when the owner moved to a different region. Consequently, families could be, and were, separated by sale or after an owner's death. Many young children were reared and cared for by other slaves to whom they were not related. In a world of White dominance, the institutions, customs, and religions of the slave community were the only means Black slaves had to protect the autonomy of their own personalities.

THE ABOLITIONIST MOVEMENT

During the 1830s, a militant antislavery movement emerged in the North. Its leaders and followers refused to accept what they regarded as the moral compromise of living in a nation that tolerated slavery. Abolitionists, such as William Lloyd Garrison, editor of *The Liberator*, condemned the Union and the Constitution as structures that perpetuated slavery. Former slaves who had escaped slavery such as Frederick Douglass and Sojourner Truth, and freeborn Black Americans such as Daniel A. Payne, also joined the cause. The antislavery movement, which was initially only one of many American reform movements, gained adherents as the question of extending slavery into the new territories came to the fore toward the end of the Mexican War (1846–1848). This military victory added significant new territory in the Southwest and California, in addition to Texas, which had been annexed in 1845. Through negotiations with Britain, the United States also acquired the vast Oregon Territory in the Northwest in 1846.

Scars of Slavery. This Louisiana slave named Gordon was photographed in 1863 after he had escaped to Union lines during the Civil War. He bears the permanent scars of the violence that lay at the heart of the slave system. Few slaves were so brutally marked, but all lived with the threat of beatings if they failed to obey.

Corbis/Bettmann.

Southerners feared that the changing climate of national feeling about slavery and the opening of territories where slavery might be prohibited would eventually make them a minority in the country and render them impotent to defend their political position and social institutions. Northerners, for their part, came to believe that proslavery factions had somehow conspired to win control of the federal government. The Compromise of 1850 temporarily restored political calm and reassured the South. But many Northerners thought that the compromise only demonstrated the strength of the slave-power conspiracy in Washington.

The introduction of the Kansas-Nebraska Bill in 1854 renewed the formal national political debate over slavery and galvanized the antislavery forces. The bill, which was introduced by Stephen A. Douglas (1813–1861), proposed popular sovereignty: Each new territory was to decide by popular vote whether slavery was to be permitted within its borders. This involved repealing the Missouri Compromise, which had prohibited slavery in most of the Louisiana Territory. It also meant that every newly organized territory would have to debate slavery. In 1854, opposition to the Kansas-Nebraska Bill inspired the formation of the new Republican Party. Some of the bill's opponents did more than debate it: John Brown went to Kansas, where armed conflict had already broken out, to wage virtual guerrilla warfare against slaveholding settlers. In 1854, civil war was already being waged in "Bleeding Kansas."

In 1857, in the Dred Scott decision, the Supreme Court effectively repealed the Missouri Compromise by declaring that Congress could not prohibit slavery in the territories. The decision further declared that slaves did not become free by living in free states and that slaves did not have rights that others were bound to respect. For radical antislavery Northerners, the decision raised the most serious questions about the morality of the Union itself, and it seemed once again to be evidence for a southern conspiracy to protect slavery. Thereafter, slavery dominated national political debate.

In 1859, John Brown seized the federal arsenal at Harpers Ferry, Virginia, as part of an effort to foment a slave rebellion. He was captured, tried, and hanged, further increasing sectional polarization. Radical Southerners feared more than ever a northern conspiracy to attack the institution of slavery, while northern radicals feared that the South would use the federal government to protect slavery. Thus the politics of both sections became radicalized.

The Republican Party had become the party that opposed slavery, although most Republicans did not favor outright abolition. In 1858, Abraham Lincoln (1809–1865) ran against Stephen Douglas for the U.S. Senate in Illinois. Lincoln lost, but he made a national reputation for himself in the debates leading up to the election. In 1860, Lincoln, the Republican candidate, was elected president. Neither he nor the Republican Party had campaigned for the abolition of slavery. Nonetheless, Southerners perceived his election as the victory of a party and a president dedicated to the eradication of slavery. In December 1860, southern states began to secede and formed the Confederate States of

Abraham Lincoln. The election of Lincoln in 1860 sparked the secession crisis that started the Civil War. This picture shows Lincoln as he was when elected, without the famous beard that he grew later.

Preston Butler/Library of Congress.

America. Attempts at political compromise to maintain the Union failed, and when Confederate forces fired on Fort Sumter in Charleston harbor in April 1861, the most destructive war in U.S. history began.

The Civil War lasted almost four years, and it transformed the nation. In 1863, Lincoln emancipated the slaves in the rebel states. The Emancipation Proclamation made the North's fight a campaign to extend liberty, not just to suppress a southern rebellion. By the time the Confederacy was defeated in 1865, the South was occupied by northern armies, its farms were often fallow, its transportation network disrupted, and many of its cities in ruins. Southern political leaders had virtually no impact on the immediate postwar decisions. The Thirteenth, Fourteenth, and Fifteenth Amendments to the Constitution largely recast the character of the Union. The Thirteenth abolished slavery, the Fourteenth granted citizenship to the former slaves, and the Fifteenth allowed them to vote. The Fourteenth Amendment also limited political activity by people who had taken up arms against the Union. These amendments resolved the issues of slavery and the relative roles of the state and federal governments.

The Civil War and the Reconstruction Era that followed overturned the antebellum social and political structures of the South. Slaves were freed and for a time participated broadly and actively in the politics of the southern states. For more than 10 years, federal troops occupied parts of the South. Many of the antebellum southern leaders abandoned politics. Attempts to bring manufacturing into the South met with limited success. Economically, the South remained largely rural and dependent on cotton, but for the first time since its earliest colonial era, its work force was free. Many of the freed slaves and poor Whites who tilled the land remained hopelessly in debt to wealthier landowners, and rampant racism hindered economic development. For the rest of the century, the South remained in a semicolonial relationship to the North. More than ever, to pay for the goods and services it needed, the South had to export raw materials or partially finished goods to the North, according to economic rules set by northern manufacturers and financiers. Poverty was the norm throughout the rural South.

Within the context of world history, the American Civil War is important for several reasons. With the exception of the Taiping Rebellion in China (1851–1864), it was the greatest war that occurred anywhere in the world between the defeat of Napoleon in 1815 and the onset of World War I in 1914. It resulted in the establishment of a continent-wide free labor market, even though freed Blacks lived in great poverty and an economic dependence not unlike that of the rural classes of Latin America. The free labor market, purged of slavery, helped to open the entire North American continent to economic development. The war also allowed American political and economic interests to develop without the distraction of the debates over states' rights and the morality of slavery. Thereafter, free labor became the American norm, and the debates over the role of industrial labor in the United States resembled those in Europe (see the next chapter).

THE CANADIAN EXPERIENCE

*U*nder the Treaty of Paris of 1763, all of Canada came under the control of Great Britain. Canada then, as now, included both an English-speaking and a French-speaking population—the latter concentrated primarily in Quebec. The Quebec Act of 1774 made the Roman Catholic Church the established church in Quebec. During the American Revolution approximately 30,000 English loyalists fled the colonies and settled in Canada. They strengthened English influences and were staunchly loyal to the British Crown.

HOW DID Canada achieve united self-government?

Tension between the French and English populations led, in part, to the Constitutional Act of 1791, which divided the colony into Upper Canada (primarily English) and Lower Canada (primarily French). Each section had its own legislature, and a governor-general presided over the two provinces on behalf of the British Crown. Cape Breton Island, New Brunswick, Newfoundland, Nova Scotia, and Prince Edward Island remained separate colonies.

In the early 19th century, relations with the United States were often tense. There were local disputes over the fur trade and fear that the United States would dominate Canada. That apprehension, along with the Anglo-French ethnic divisions, constitute two of the major themes of Canadian history.

By the late 1830s, political tensions in Canada were beginning to generate considerable internal pressure. Long-established families with powerful economic interests in both Upper and Lower Canada were at odds with new settlers seeking opportunities to prosper, and there were quarrels over the influence of the British Crown in local affairs. In 1837, rebellions occurred in both Upper and Lower Canada. Although there were relatively few casualties, Great Britain realized that the situation needed to be resolved.

ROAD TO SELF-GOVERNMENT

The British government, operating in the more liberal political climate following the first Reform Act (1832), was determined to avoid another North American revolution. Consequently, it sent the Earl of Durham (1792–1840) to Canada with extensive authority to implement reforms. In 1839, his *Report on the Affairs of British North America* advocated extensive self-government for Canada. He recommended that most Canadian affairs be left in the hands of a Canadian legislature and that only foreign policy and defense remain under British control. Durham also proposed that the two Canadian provinces be united. He thought that political unification would eventually promote English culture throughout Canada and overwhelm the French influence in Quebec. In effect, Durham wanted Canadians to govern themselves so that English culture would dominate. The Canada Act of 1840 accepted his recommendations and established a single legislature composed of two houses as Canada's government.

Durham's report established the political pattern that the British government would, to a greater or lesser extent, follow with its other English-speaking colonies during the 19th century. Britain sought to foster responsible self-government in Australia, New Zealand, and South Africa. The Canadian experience thus had a considerable impact throughout the world. But, until well into the 20th century, the British government, like other Western imperial powers, also generally believed that non-White peoples such as those of India required direct British colonial administration.

KEEPING A DISTINCTIVE CULTURE

Canadians learned to exercise self-government, but distinct English and French cultures survived to complicate that task. Within the legislature there were almost always tradeoffs between the eastern and western sections of the nation. Furthermore, during the American Civil War fears arose that the American republic might seek to invade or dominate Canada. One response to this fear was an attempt to unite the Maritime Provinces in 1862. Those discussions led to broader considerations of the desirability for a stronger federation among all the parts of Canada.

The result of those debates and discussions was the British North America Act of 1867, which created a Canadian federation. Canadians hoped to avoid what they saw as flaws in the U.S. Constitution. The Canadian system of government was to be federal, but with much less emphasis on states' rights than in the United States. Canadians established a parliamentary mode of government, but also chose to retain allegiance to the British monarchy represented by a governor-general as head of state. The person most responsible for establishing this new government and for leading it between 1867 and 1891 was John A. MacDonald (1815–1891).

MID-CENTURY POLITICAL CONSOLIDATION IN EUROPE

*W*hile the United States and Canada were establishing themselves as strong unified political entities in North America, major political consolidation occurred in Europe that would have an enormous impact on the rest of the world. As has so often been true in modern European history, war made change possible. In this case, a conflict disrupted the international balance that had prevailed since 1815 and unleashed forces that upset the internal political situation in several of the involved states. The war itself was in some respects less important than the political consequences that flowed from it during the next decade.

THE CRIMEAN WAR

The Crimean War (1854–1856), named after the Black Sea peninsula on which it was largely fought, originated from a long-standing rivalry between Russia and

WHAT WERE the steps that led to Italian and German unification?

Florence Nightingale. During the Crimean War, Florence Nightingale of Great Britain organized nursing care for the wounded.

Corbis-Bettmann Archive.

the Ottoman Empire. Russia wanted to extend its influence over the Ottoman provinces of Moldavia and Walachia (now in Romania). In 1853, Russia went to war against the Ottomans on the pretext that the Ottomans had given Roman Catholic France, instead of Orthodox Russia, the right to protect Christians and Christian shrines in the Holy Land. The next year France and Great Britain supported the Ottoman Empire to protect their interests in the eastern Mediterranean. Austria and Prussia remained neutral. The war quickly bogged down after the French and the British invaded the Crimea. In March 1856, a peace conference convened in Paris and eventually concluded a treaty highly unfavorable to Russia.

The Crimean War shattered the image of an invincible Russia that had prevailed since the close of the Napoleonic Wars. It also shattered the power of the Concert of Europe to settle international disputes on the continent. The major European powers were no longer willing to cooperate to maintain the existing borders between themselves and their neighbors. For the next 25 years, instability prevailed in European affairs, allowing a largely unchecked adventurism in foreign policy.

ITALIAN UNIFICATION

Italian nationalists had long wanted to unite the small absolutist principalities of the peninsula into a single state but could not agree on how to do it. Romantic republicans, such as Giuseppe Mazzini (1805–1872) and Giuseppe Garibaldi (1807–1882), sought to drive out the Austrians by popular military force and to establish a republic. They not only failed but also frightened more moderate Italians. The person who eventually achieved unification was Count Camillo Cavour (1810–1861), the prime minister of Piedmont.

Piedmont (the "Kingdom of Sardinia"), in northwestern Italy, was the most independent state on the peninsula (see Map 24–3). It had unsuccessfully fought against Austria in 1848 and 1849. Following the second defeat, King Charles Albert (r. 1831–1849) abdicated in favor of his son, Victor Emmanuel II (r. 1849–1878). In 1852, the new monarch chose Cavour—a moderate liberal in economics and a strong monarchist who rejected republicanism—as his prime minister.

Cavour believed that if Italians proved themselves to be efficient and economically progressive, the great powers might decide that Italy could govern itself. He worked for free trade, railway construction, credit expansion, and agricultural improvement. He also fostered the Nationalist Society, which established chapters in other Italian states to press for unification under the leadership of Piedmont. Cavour also believed that Italy could be unified only with the aid of France.

Cavour supported the French and British in the Crimean War so as to have a seat at the peace conference, where he raised the question of Italian unification. He won nothing specific, but Napoleon III (r. 1852–1870) of France expressed sympathy for his cause. In 1858, Cavour and the French emperor met to plot war with Austria.

During the winter and spring of 1859, tension grew between Austria and Piedmont as the latter mobilized its army. In late April, when war erupted, France came to Piedmont's aid. On June 4, the Austrians were defeated at Magenta, and on June 24, at Solferino in Lombardy. Fearing too extensive a Piedmontese victory, Napoleon III concluded a separate peace with Austria at Villafranca on

MAP 24–3

The Unification of Italy. Beginning with the association of Sardinia and Piedmont by the Congress of Vienna in 1815, unification was achieved through the expansion of Piedmont between 1859 and 1870. Both Cavour's statesmanship and the campaigns of ardent nationalists played large roles.

WHAT WERE the stages of Italian unification between 1815 and 1870?

July 11. Piedmont received Lombardy, but the Veneto remained under Austrian control. Cavour felt betrayed by France, but the war had at least driven Austria from most of northern Italy. Later that summer Parma, Modena, Tuscany, and the Romagna voted to unite with Piedmont.

At this point the forces of romantic republican nationalism compelled Cavour to pursue unification of northern and southern Italy. In May 1860, Garibaldi landed in Sicily with more than 1,000 troops. He captured Palermo and prepared to attack the mainland. By September, the city and kingdom of Naples, probably the most corrupt absolutist state in Italy, were under his control. To forestall a republican victory Cavour rushed troops south to confront Garibaldi. On the way Cavour's troops conquered the Papal States except for the area around Rome, which remained under the pope's direct control.

Garibaldi's nationalism won out over his republicanism, and he unhappily accepted domination by the Piedmontese. In late 1860, Naples and Sicily voted to join Piedmont's northern union. In March 1861, Victor Emmanuel II was proclaimed king of Italy. Three months later Cavour died. The new state was governed by the conservative constitution promulgated in 1848 by Charles Albert. Italy gained the Veneto in 1866 as a result of the war between Austria and Prussia, and Rome in 1870 as a result of the Franco-Prussian War.

GERMAN UNIFICATION

The unification of Germany was the single most important political development in Europe between 1848 and 1914. It was spearheaded by Prussia's conservative army, monarch, and prime minister, who outflanked the kingdom's liberals.

William I's (r. 1861–1888) primary concern was the Prussian army. In 1860, his war minister and chief of staff proposed enlarging the army and increasing the service of conscripts from two to three years, but the liberal-dominated Prussian parliament refused to approve the necessary taxes. A deadlock continued for two years.

Bismarck In September 1862, William I turned for help to the person who, more than any other single individual, determined the course of European history for the next 30 years: Otto von Bismarck (1815–1898). Bismarck came from Junker stock, and his outlook was deeply informed by the most traditional Prussian values: admiration for the monarchy, the nobility, and the army. After being appointed prime minister and foreign minister in 1862, Bismarck immediately moved against the liberal parliament. He contended that further parliamentary votes on taxes were not required, for the Prussian constitution

---

German and Italian Unification

	1854	Crimean War opens
	1855	Cavour leads Piedmont into war on side of France and England
	July 20, 1856	Treaty of Paris concludes Crimean War
	1858	Secret conference between Napoleon III and Cavour
	1859	War of Piedmont and France against Austria
	1860	Garibaldi lands his forces in Sicily and conquers southern Italy
1861		
	March 17	Death of Cavour
	June 6	Proclamation of the Kingdom of Italy;
	1862	Bismarck becomes prime minister of Prussia
	1864	Danish War
	1866	Austro-Prussian War; Veneto ceded to Italy
	1867	North German Confederation formed
1870		
	July 12	Crisis over Hohenzollern candidacy for the Spanish throne
	July 13	Bismarck publishes edited press dispatch
	July 19	France declares war on Prussia
	September 1	France defeated at Sedan and Napoleon III captured
	September 4	French Republic proclaimed
	October 2	Italian state annexes Rome
1871		
	January 18	Proclamation of the German Empire at Versailles
	March 18–May 28	Paris Commune
	May 10	Treaty of Frankfurt between France and Germany

permitted the government to function on the basis of taxes that had already been approved. The army and most of the bureaucracy backed his interpretation of the constitution, but new elections in 1863 sustained the liberal majority in the parliament. Bismarck sought a cause that would draw popular support away from the liberals and toward the monarchy and the army. His tactic was to use foreign affairs to divert public attention from domestic matters by having Prussia assume leadership of the effort to unify Germany.

Bismarck favored what was known as the *kleindeutsch*, or small German, solution to unification. It excluded Austria. To promote his plan, he fought two brief wars. In 1864, he went to war with Denmark over the status of the duchies of Schleswig and Holstein, German-speaking areas that had long been administered by the Danish monarchy (see Map 24–4). The Austrians helped defeat Denmark and joined Prussia in jointly administering the two duchies. Bismarck then concluded various alliances with France and Italy to gain their support against Austria, and in the summer of 1866, decisively defeated Austria in the Seven Weeks' War. The consequent Treaty of Prague excluded the Habsburgs from German affairs and left Prussia the only major power among the German states.

In 1867, Hanover, Hesse, Nassau, and the city of Frankfurt, all of which had supported Austria during the war, were annexed by Prussia, and their rulers deposed. Prussia and these newly incorporated territories, plus Schleswig and Holstein and the rest of the German states north of the Main River, constituted the North German Confederation. Prussia was its undisputed leader.

Creating a Nation. The proclamation of the German Empire in the Hall of Mirrors at Versailles, January 18, 1871, after the defeat of France in the Franco-Prussian War. Kaiser Wilhelm I is standing at the top of the steps under the flags; Bismarck is in the center in a white uniform.

Bildarchiv Preussicher Kulturbesitz/Original: Friedrichsruher Fassung, Bismarck-Museum.

THE FRANCO-PRUSSIAN WAR AND THE GERMAN EMPIRE

Bismarck next looked for an opportunity to bring the states of southern Germany into the confederation. It appeared during complex diplomatic negotiations surrounding the possibility that a cousin of William I of Prussia might become king of Spain. France opposed this, for it did not want a second state on its borders ruled by a Hohenzollern. Bismarck personally edited a press dispatch about these negotiations to make it appear that William I had insulted the French ambassador, even though the king had not done so. Bismarck's intention was to goad France into war, and he succeeded. On July 19, France

kleindeutsch Meaning "small German." Argument that the German-speaking portions of the Habsburg Empire should be excluded from a united Germany.

OVERVIEW   ITALIAN AND GERMAN UNIFICATION

The unifications of Italy and Germany, which took place between 1859 and 1871, were the two most important political developments that occurred in Europe between the end of the Napoleonic Wars in 1815 and the outbreak of World War I in 1914. Creation of the Kingdom of Italy in 1860 and of the German Empire in 1871 were the most significant nationalist triumphs of the 19th century. Moreover, the formation of these two states permanently changed the balance of power in Europe. Austria lost its historic role as the dominant power in Italian and German affairs, and Germany replaced France as continental Europe's most powerful nation. Below are the steps by which Italy and Germany achieved unification.

Italy	1855	Piedmont enters the Crimean War on the side of France and Britain.
	1858	Napoleon III of France and Count Cavour of Piedmont secretly discuss a war against Austria in Italy.
	1859	France and Piedmont defeat Austria. Austria cedes Lombardy to Piedmont. Tuscany, Parma, Modena and the Romagna revolt against their pro-Austrian rulers and vote to join Piedmont.
	1860	Garibaldi conquers Sicily and Naples. Cavour sends troops to occupy southern Italy and the Papal States except for Rome.
	1861	Proclamation of the Kingdom of Italy.
	1866	Italy receives Venetia in return for siding with Prussia against Austria in the Austro-Prussian War.
	1870	Italy occupies Rome when the French garrison is withdrawn to fight in the Franco-Prussian War.
Germany	1862	Otto von Bismarck becomes prime minister of Prussia.
	1864	Prussia and Austria defeat Denmark and occupy Schleswig-Holstein.
	1866	Prussia defeats Austria and forms the North German Confederation. Prussia annexes Hanover, Hesse, Nassau, and Frankfurt. The Habsburgs are excluded from German affairs.
	1870	Prussia defeats France in the Franco-Prussian War. The southern German states of Bavaria, Wurtemberg, Baden, and Hesse Darmstadt fight alongside Prussia.
	1871	Proclamation of the German Empire. France cedes Alsace-Lorraine to Germany.

declared war. Napoleon III hoped that victory would increase popular support for his regime. The states of southern Germany supported Prussia against France, and on September 1, at Sedan, the Germans defeated the French army and captured Napoleon III. By late September, Paris was besieged. It capitulated on January 28, 1871. Ten days earlier, in the Hall of Mirrors at the Palace of Versailles, the German Empire had been proclaimed. The rulers of the states of south Germany had requested William I to accept the imperial title—allowing them to retain their kingly titles and thrones.

The unification of Germany established a strong, coherent state in the middle of Europe. It had been forged by the Prussian army and monarchy and would be dominated by Prussian institutions. It possessed enormous economic resources and nationalistic ambitions. For the next 80 years, Europe had to come to grips with this new political reality both on the continent and abroad. For some, the unification of Italy and Germany implied that nationalistic aspirations could only be fulfilled by armed force. France, in the wake of its defeat by Prussia, again became a republic—the Third Republic—governed by a chamber of deputies, a senate, and a president.

MAP 24–4
Nationalities within the Habsburg Empire. The patchwork appearance reflects the unusual problem of the numerous ethnic groups that the Habsburgs could not, of course, meld into a modern national state. Only the Magyars were recognized in 1867, leaving nationalist Czechs, Slovaks, and the others chronically dissatisfied.

HOW DID the Compromise of 1867 affect the Habsburg Empire?

UNREST OF NATIONALITIES IN EASTERN EUROPE

*I*n an age increasingly characterized by national states, liberal institutions, and industrialism, the Habsburg domains remained dynastic, absolutist, and agrarian. Following the revolutions of 1848, Emperor Francis Joseph (r. 1848–1916) and his ministers attempted to impose a centralized administration on the multinational empire. The system amounted to a military and bureaucratic government dominated by German-speaking Austrians. This especially annoyed the Hungarians. The defeats in 1859 and 1866 and the exclusion of Austria from Italy and from German affairs compelled Francis Joseph to come to terms with the Hungarian nobles. The subsequent **Ausgleich**, or Compromise, of 1867 transformed the Habsburg Empire into a dual monarchy. Francis Joseph was crowned king of Hungary in Budapest. Except for the common monarch, foreign policy, and army, Austria and Hungary functioned almost as separate states (see Map 24–4).

HOW DID nationalism affect the Habsburg Empire?

ausgleich Meaning "compromise." Agreement between the Habsburg emperor and the Hungarians to give Hungary considerable administrative autonomy in 1867. It created the Dual Monarchy, or Austria-Hungary.

HISTORY'S VOICES

LORD ACTON CONDEMNS NATIONALISM

Lord Acton (1834–1902) was a major 19th-century English historian and commentator on contemporary religious and political events. In all his writings, he was deeply concerned with the character and preservation of liberty. His was one of the earliest voices to warn against the political dangers of nationalism.

WHY DOES Acton see the principle of nationality as dangerous to liberty? Why does he see nationalism as a threat to minority groups? Why does he see nationalism as a threat to democracy?

The greatest adversary of the rights of nationality is the modern theory of nationality. By making the State and the nation commensurate with each other in theory, it reduces practically to a subject condition all other nationalities that may be within the boundary. It cannot admit them to an equality with the ruling nation which constitutes the State, because the State would then cease to be national, which would be a contradiction of the principle of its existence. According, therefore, to the degree of humanity and civilization in that dominant body which claims all the rights of the community, the inferior races are exterminated, or reduced to servitude, or outlawed, or put in a condition of dependence.

If we take the establishment of liberty for the realization of moral duties to be the end of civil society, we must conclude that those states are substantially the most perfect which, like the British and Austrian Empires, include various distinct nationalities without oppressing them. Those in which no mixture of races has occurred are imperfect; and those in which its effects have disappeared are decrepit. A State which is incompetent to satisfy different races condemns itself; a State which labors to neutralize, to absorb, or to expel them, destroys its own vitality; a State which does not include them is destitute of the chief basis of self-government. The theory of nationality, therefore, is a retrograde step in history . . . .

[N]ationality does not aim either at liberty or prosperity, both of which it sacrifices to the imperative necessity of making the nation the mold and measure of the State. Its course will be marked with material as well as moral ruin, in order that a new invention may prevail over the works of God and the interests of mankind. There is no principle of change, no phrase of political speculation conceivable, more comprehensive, more subversive, or more arbitrary than this. It is a confutation of democracy, because it sets limits to the exercise of the popular will, and substitutes for it a higher principle.

Source: John Emerich Edward Dalbert-Acton, *First Baron Acton, Essays in the History of Liberty*, ed. by J. Rufus Fears (Indianapolis IN: Liberty Classics, 1985), pp. 431–433.

Many of the other national groups within the empire—including the Czechs, Ruthenians, Romanians, and Serbo-Croatians—opposed the compromise because it permitted the German-speaking Austrians and the Hungarian Magyars to dominate the other nationalities in their respective states. The Czechs of Bohemia were the most vocal group. For more than 20 years, they were conciliated by generous Austrian patronage and posts in the bureaucracy, but by the turn of the century they were becoming restive. They and German-speaking groups in the Austrian Reichsrat disrupted the Parliament rather than permit a compromise on language issues. This ended constitutional government, for the emperor ruled thereafter by imperial decree with the support of the bureaucracy. Constitutionalism survived in Hungary, but only because the Magyars used it to dominate competing national groups.

20.1
Program of the Serb
Society of National Defense
[Narodna Odbrana]

Nationalist unrest within the Habsburg Empire, in addition to causing internal political difficulties, constituted one of the major sources of political instability for all of central and eastern Europe. Virtually all the nationality problems had a foreign policy as well as a domestic political dimension. Both the Serbo-Croatians and the Poles believed they deserved a wholly independent state in union with their fellow nationals who lived outside the empire. Other national groups, such as Ukrainians, Romanians, and Bosnians, saw themselves as potentially linked to Russia, Romania, Serbia, or a larger, yet-to-be-established Slavic state. Many of these nationalities looked to Russia for protection. Out of these nationalistic tensions emerged much of the turmoil that would spark World War I. The dominant German population of Austria proper was generally loyal to the emperor. However, a significant segment of the Austrian German population was strongly nationalistic and yearned to be part of the united German state being established by Bismarck. These nationalistic Germans in the Austrian Empire often hated the non-German national groups, particularly the Jews. Such attitudes would influence Adolf Hitler (1889–1945) in his youth and would shape his political opinions.

Nationality problems touched each of the three great central and eastern European empires—the German, the Russian, and the Austrian. All had Polish populations. Each shared at least two other major national groups. Each nationality regarded its own aspirations and discontents as more important than the larger good or even survival of the empire they inhabited. The stirrings of nationalism affected the fate of all three empires from the 1860s through the outbreak of World War I. The government of each would be overturned during the war, and the Austrian Empire would disappear. These same unresolved problems of central and eastern European nationalism would then lead directly to World War II. During more recent years they have led to civil war in what was formerly Yugoslavia and to the breakup of what used to be called Czechoslovakia. (See "Lord Acton Condemns Nationalism.")

RACIAL THEORY AND ANTI-SEMITISM

*T*heories about race were a new source of late-century nationalistic unrest. Racial thinking, or **racism**, had long existed in Europe. Renaissance explorers had displayed considerable prejudice against non-Whites. Since at least the 18th century, biologists and anthropologists had classified human beings according to the color of their skin, their language, and their stage of civilization. Late 18th-century linguistic scholars, who had observed similarities between many of the European languages and Sanskrit, had postulated the existence of an ancient race called the Aryans, speakers of the original language from which the rest derived. During the Romantic period, writers had called the different cultures of Europe *races*. The debates over slavery in the European colonies and the United States had given further opportunity for the development of racial theory. And finally, in the late 19th century, the concept of race emerged as a single dominant explanation for the history and the character of large groups of people.

Arthur de Gobineau (1816–1882), a reactionary French diplomat, enunciated the first important theory of race as the major determinant of human history. In his four-volume *Essay on the Inequality of the Human Races* (1853–1854), Gobineau argued that the problems of Western civilization stemmed from the

WHY DID anti-Semitism arise in the late 19th century?

racism Pseudoscientific theory that biological features of race determine human character and worth.

Theodor Herzl. Herzl's visions of a Jewish state would eventually lead to the creation of Israel in 1948.

BBC Hulton/Corbis-Bettmann.

anti-Semitism Prejudice, hostility, or legal discrimination against Jews.

slow degeneration of its original white Aryan race. Aryans, he theorized, had unwisely intermarried with inferior yellow and Black races and diluted the greatness and ability conveyed by their blood. Gobineau saw no way to reverse their degeneration.

Gobineau's essay remained relatively obscure for years. Houston Stewart Chamberlain (1855–1927), an Englishman who settled in Germany, put racial theory on an alleged scientific basis in his widely read two-volume work, *Foundations of the Nineteenth Century* (1899). He championed the concept of biological determinism through race. Chamberlain, relying on modern genetic theory, argued, in opposition to Gobineau, that the human race could be improved and that a superior race could be developed. Furthermore, he fingered the Jews as the major obstacle to European racial regeneration. Chamberlain's book and the lesser works on which it drew aided the spread of **anti-Semitism**.

ANTI-SEMITISM AND THE BIRTH OF ZIONISM

The tragic anti-Semitic campaigns, which cast such dark shadows across the 20th century, emerged in part from the racial theorizing of the late 19th century. Religious anti-Semitism dated from at least the Middle Ages, but following the French Revolution, Western European Jews had gradually gained entry into civil society in Austria, Britain, France, and Germany. Popular anti-Semitism, which identified the Jewish community with money and banking interests, persisted. During the last third of the century, as finance capitalism changed the economic structure of Europe, people who suffered from the changes focused their anger on the Jewish community. In Austria, France, and Germany various political leaders and parties used their anti-Semitism to considerable political advantage.

To this already ugly situation, racial thought contributed the belief that no matter how well Jews assimilated to the culture and even the religions of the countries they inhabited, their Jewishness—and thus their alleged danger to the society—remained. The problem of race was not in the character of Jews, but in their blood.

An important Jewish response to the rabid outbreak of this new form of anti-Semitism was the launching in 1896 of the Zionist movement: a campaign to found a separate Jewish state in Palestine. Its founder was an Austro-Hungarian, Theodor Herzl (1860–1904). The growth of political anti-Semitism, especially in Austria and France, as well as Herzl's personal experiences with discrimination, convinced him that liberal politics and the institutions of the liberal state could not protect the Jews in Europe or ensure that they would be treated justly. In 1896, Herzl published *The Jewish State*, in which he called for a separate state in which the Jews of the world might be assured of those rights and liberties that they should be enjoying in the liberal states of Europe. Herzl followed the tactics of late-century mass democratic politics by directing his appeal in particular to the impoverished Jews who lived in the ghettos of eastern Europe and the slums of Western Europe. The original call to **Zionism** thus combined a rejection of the anti-Semitism of Europe with a desire to establish some of the ideals of both liberalism and socialism in a state outside Europe.

Racial thinking and revived anti-Semitism were part of a wider late-century aggressive nationalism. Previously, nationalism had been a literary and liberal movement. From the 1870s onward, however, nationalism became a movement with mass support, well-financed organizations, and political parties. The new nationalism tended to redefine nationality in terms of race and blood, and it opposed the internationalism of both liberalism and socialism. National loyalty was proposed as a means for overcoming divisions of class, religion, and geography. Nationalistic patriotism sometimes became a secular religion in the hands of state schoolteachers, who were replacing the clergy as the instructors of youth. Aggressive and racist, nationalism would become the most powerful ideology of the early 20th century.

Zionism Movement to create a Jewish state in Palestine (the Biblical Zion).

Summary

Nationalism Nationalism is the modern concept that people who share the same customs, culture, language, and history should also share the same government. It became the most powerful European political ideology of the 19th and early 20th centuries. Nationalists challenged both the domestic and the international order of the Vienna settlement in the decades after 1815.

Liberalism Politically, 19th-century liberals sought to establish constitutional governments that recognized civil liberties and made the executive responsible to a legislature elected by men of wealth and property. Economically, liberals wanted a laissez-faire economy with minimal government involvement. They thought that people should be free to use their talents and property to enrich themselves without the state intervening to protect the working classes or the poor. Liberals often supported nationalists' efforts to create a single national state that could function as a more efficient economic unit. Although efforts to liberalize tsarist Russia failed, liberalism largely triumphed in France after the revolution of 1830 and in Britain after the passage of the Great Reform Bill. The British were, however, unable to resolve the problem of Irish nationalism in the 19th century.

Italian and German Unification With French assistance, Piedmont and its premier Count Camillo Cavour managed to unite most of the Italian peninsula by 1860. The new Kingdom of Italy was formed from the northern Italian duchies, Austrian Lombardy, the Papal States, and the Kingdom of the Two Sicilies. Austrian Venetia was added in 1866, and Italy occupied Papal Rome in 1870.

German unification was achieved by Prussia under the leadership of Otto von Bismarck between 1864 and 1871. In three victorious wars against Denmark, Austria, and France, Bismarck forged the German states into a German Empire dominated by Prussia. Germany was henceforth the dominant power on the European continent.

IMAGE KEY
for pages 582–583

a. Transylvanian revolutionaries revolt against Russian rule, 1848.
b. A pro-slavery poster warns of "the Slave Power."
c. A Louisiana slave named Gordon after escaping to Union lines during the Civil War, 1863.
d. The leaders of Europe in debate during the Congress of Vienna.
e. Gladstone.
f. Italian Nationalist General Garibaldi.
g. John Brown and his men, trapped by U.S. Marine fire.
h. The proclamation of the German Empire in the Hall of Mirrors at Versailles, January 18, 1871.

North America   In the United States, westward expansion and war against Mexico brought vast new territories under the republic from the Mississippi River to the Pacific, but sectional conflict between North and South over economic issues and slavery culminated in the outbreak of the Civil War in 1861. Northern victory led to the abolition of slavery, the creation of a continent-wide free labor market, and enormous economic development that would make the United States the world's leading industrial power in the 20th century.

Canada achieved self-government from Britain and created a united Canadian federation in 1867. However, Canada remained part of the British Empire and retained its connection with the British monarchy.

Eastern Europe   Nationalism created problems for the three eastern European empires: Germany, Russia, and Austria, but Habsburg Austria faced the greatest challenge from nationalism because it was a dynastic, not a national, state. Eleven different nationalities made up the Habsburg monarchy, each with its own national aspirations. In 1867, the Habsburgs worked out the *Ausgleich*, or Compromise, with the Magyars, by which Hungary became an autonomous kingdom under the Habsburg emperor. Thereafter the Habsburg monarchy became known as Austria-Hungary. However, Czechs, Croats, and other Slavs in the monarchy became increasingly dissatisfied.

Racism and Anti-Semitism   In the late 19th century, biological determinism, the concept that some peoples or races were inherently superior to others, took root in Western thought. In Austria, France, and Germany, some nationalists used the concept of race to blame the Jews for their countries' economic and political problems. Part of the Jewish response was the launching of the Zionist movement to found a separate Jewish state.

REVIEW QUESTIONS

1. What is nationalism? Where did significant nationalist movements develop between 1815 and 1830? Which were successful and which were unsuccessful?

2. What were the characteristics of 19th-century liberalism? How did they differ from conservatives? What relationship did liberalism have to nationalism?

3. Why did the American North and the South diverge and become distinctively different regions? How did the debate over slavery evolve?

4. Why was it so difficult to unify Italy?

5. How was Germany unified? How did its unification affect European politics?

6. How did racial theory evolve in the modern era?

KEY TERMS

anti-Semitism (p. 610)

ausgleich (p. 607)

Catholic Emancipation (p. 589)

Chartism (p. 590)

Great Reform Bill (p. 589)

home rule (p. 591)

July Monarchy (p. 589)

kleindeutsch (p. 605)

liberalism (p. 585)

nationalism (p. 584)

racism (p. 609)

Zionism (p. 611)

 For additional study resources for this chapter, go to:
www.prenhall.com/craig/chapter24

Visualizing The Past

Imagining Women in the Eighteenth and Nineteenth Centuries

WHAT DOES the artistic depictions of women in the eighteenth and nineteenth centuries tell us about the ways in which modern societies have imagined the roles of women in society?

Although the roles of many women changed significantly in the eighteenth and nineteenth centuries, in part due to the new demands and opportunities brought about by industrialization, the themes of sexuality, spirituality, docility, and maternal caring that characterized artists' imaginations of women in earlier eras also appear in the art of this period. Since most artists until the 20th century were male, depictions of women and gender roles often derive from a male perspective on the *proper* roles of women in a society, and not necessarily on the reality of women's lives.

Suzuki Harunobu, "Geisha as Daruma Crossing the Sea." Edo period, mid-eighteenth century. In this color woodcut we see a geisha, a woman whose profession was to entertain men, in a pose mirroring that of a famous Zen Buddhist master, Daruma. Her clothing, highly feminine, with hints of her delicate body beneath it, contrast with the Zen spirituality her pose suggests.
Suzuki Harunobu, "Geisha as Daruma Crossing the Sea", Edo period, mid-18th century. Color woodcut, 10 7/8 × 8 1/4" (27.6 × 21 cm). Philadelphia Museum of Art. Gift of Mrs. Emile Geyelin, in memory of Anne Hampton Barnes.

**Eugene Delacroix, "The Women of ▶
Algiers in Their Apartment," 1834.**
Delacroix, the leading French
Romantic painter, spent six months in
North Africa in 1832. In the painting
shown here Delacroix depicts a
common theme in eighteenth and
nineteenth-century depictions of the
"Orient": the position of women in
Islamic society in general, and the
harem in particular. Western commentators often described Islamic society
as barbaric because of its perceived
marginalization and exploitation of
women. Note the passivity of the light-
skinned women in contrast to the
dominant pose of the black servant.
*Delacroix, Eugene (1798–1863). The Women of
Algiers in Their Apartment. Oil on canvas,
180 × 229 cm. Louvre, Paris, France.*

◀ **Veiled Women.** This nineteenth-century print
of a veiled woman in traditional costume from
Tartarstan in Central Asia shows another aspect
of how women were imagined. Note how the
veils and layers of clothing are used to hide
femininity in the interests of modesty. Unlike
men's clothing, the woman's costume does not
reveal any sort of professional identity. Gender,
rather than economic activities, continued to
define women's identity in the modern world.
©Dorling Kindersley

Europeans in New Zealand. This postcard from late ▶
nineteenth-century New Zealand depicts a group of people
bathing on the seaside. Here we see another recurring theme
in modern images of gender: women as wives and mothers.
The point here is that the beach and, by implication New
Zealand itself, which many Europeans still viewed as an exotic
and somewhat dangerous destination, was safe and
"family-friendly." The wilderness of New Zealand, once home
to the dangerous Maori, has now been tamed by European
gentility and domesticity, so that it has become a suitable destination even for European women and children.
©Dorling Kindersley

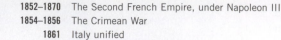
PART SIX   INTO THE MODERN WORLD

EUROPE

1852–1870	The Second French Empire, under Napoleon III
1854–1856	The Crimean War
1861	Italy unified
1861	Emancipation of Russian serfs
1866	Austro-Prussian War; creation of Dual Monarchy of Austria-Hungary in 1867
1870–1871	Franco-Prussian War; German Empire proclaimed in 1871
1873	Three Emperors League

◀ Karl Marx

▲ German Empire proclaimed

NEAR EAST/ INDIA

1857–1858	Sepoy Rebellion: India placed directly under the authority of the British government in 1858
1869	Suez Canal completed; 1875, British purchase controlling interest
1869–1948	Mohandas (Mahatma) Gandhi
1876–1949	Muhammad Ali Jinnah, "founder of Pakistan"

"Mahatma" Gandhi ▶

EAST ASIA

1850–1873	Taiping and other rebellions
1853–1854	Commodore Perry "opens" Japan to the West, ending seclusion policy
1859	French seize Saigon
1860s	Establishment of treaty ports in China
1864	French protectorate over Cambodia
1868	Meiji Restoration in Japan
1870s	Civilization and Enlightenment movement in Japan
1870s–1890s	Self-Strengthening movement in China

The empress ▶
dowager Tz'u-hsi

AFRICA

1856–1884	King Mutasa of Buganda reigns
1870	British protectorate in Zanzibar
1879–1880	Henry M. Stanley gains the Congo for Belgium
1880s	Mahdist revival and uprising in Sudan
1880	French protectorate in Tunisia and the Ivory Coast

THE AMERICAS

1854	Kansas-Nebraska Act
1856	Dred Scott Decision
1859	Raid on Harper's Ferry
1860	Abraham Lincoln elected U.S. president
1861–1865	U.S. Civil War
1862–1867	French invasion of Mexico
1863	Emancipation Proclamation in United States
1865–1877	Reconstruction
1865–1870	Paraguayan War
1879–1880	Argentinian conquest of the desert

George Caleb Bingham, "Fur Traders ▶
Descending the Missouri" ca. 1845

1882   Triple Alliance
1890   Bismarck dismissed by Kaiser Wilhelm II
1902   Entente Cordiale
1905   January 22, "Bloody Sunday"
1905   Revolution in Russia
1914   War begins in Europe

◄ *"Bloody Sunday," Russia*

1882   English occupation of Egypt
1886   India National Congress formed
1889–1964   Jawaharlal Nehru
1899   Ottoman sultan Abdulhamid II grants concession to Kaiser Wilhelm II to extend railway to Baghdad ("Berlin-to-Baghdad" Railway)
1908   "Young Turk" Revolt

1889   Meiji Constitution in Japan
1894–1895   Sino-Japanese War; Japan gets Taiwan as colony
1898–1900   Boxer Rebellion in China
1904–1905   Russo-Japanese War
1910   Japan annexes Korea
1911   Republican Revolution begins in China; Ch'ing dynasty overthrown

Promulgation ▶ of the Meiji Constitution

1884–1885   International Conference in Berlin to prepare rules for further acquisition of African territory; the Congo Free State declared
1884   German Southwest Africa
1885   British control Nigeria and British East Africa
1894   French annex Dahomey
1899   German East Africa; British in Sudan
1899–1902   Boer War
1900   Nigeria a British Crown colony
1907   Orange Free State and the Transvaal join with Natal and Cape Colony to form the Union of South Africa
1911   Liberia becomes a virtual U.S. protectorate
1914   Ethiopia the only independent state in Africa

◄ *Three carved wooden African figures of colonial officials*

1880s   Slavery eliminated in Cuba and Brazil
1898   Spanish-American War
1901   Theodore Roosevelt elected U.S. president
1910–1917   Mexican Revolution
1912   Woodrow Wilson elected U.S. president

◄ *Slavery in Brazil*

25 Northern Transatlantic Economy and Society, 1815–1914

CHAPTER HIGHLIGHTS

Workers After 1850, European workers underwent a process of proletarianization as the process of industrialization spread across the continent. To protect their interests, European workers joined trade unions and socialist parties, such as the Labour Party in Britain. The Marxist critique of modern capitalism strongly influenced European socialism when the German Social Democratic Party adopted the thought of Karl Marx. In Russia, Lenin founded the Bolsheviks as an elite Marxist party that advocated the overthrow of the tsarist regime through a revolution of workers and peasants.

Urban Reform European cities grew rapidly after 1850. The growth of industry and the influx of new workers led to slums and a host of urban health and social problems. In response, middle-class reformers redesigned cities and improved sanitation, housing, and water and sewer systems.

Women Nineteenth-century women were divided along class lines. Unlike working-class women, most women of the upper and middle classes adopted a cult of domesticity and did not work outside the home. Most jobs available to women were low paying and insecure. Women of all classes faced social, political, and legal disabilities that were only gradually improved in the late nineteenth and early twentieth centuries. Before World War I, only Norway allowed women to vote, and few women could earn university degrees or enter the professions.

Jewish Emancipation With the exception of Russia, European countries had abolished their legal restrictions on Jews by the mid-nineteenth century. Jews became more fully integrated into European political and economic life. After 1880, however, anti-Semitism increased as Jews were blamed for economic and social problems.

The United States By 1914, the United States had become the world's leading industrial power. However, despite the creation of a mass industrial work force, socialism did not take root in the United States. Under presidents Theodore Roosevelt and Woodrow Wilson, the Progressive Movement enacted a number of social and political reforms. The United States also embarked on a more aggressive foreign policy with the Spanish-American War, the acquisition of a colonial empire, interventions in Latin America, and, under Wilson, participation in World War I.

CHAPTER QUESTIONS

WHAT DOES the term *proletarianization* mean?

WHAT SOCIAL AND LEGAL disabilities did European women confront in the nineteenth century?

HOW DID emancipation affect Jewish participation in European social and political life outside of Russia?

WHY DID Marxism become so influential among European socialists?

HOW DID industrialization in the United States differ from industrialization in Europe?

CHAPTER OUTLINE

During the 19th century, northwestern Europe and the United States developed major industrial economies. These economies produced more goods and services than ever before in world history. This economic achievement undergirded the enormous international political power exerted by the industrial nations of the West from that time to the present.

The first half of the 19th century witnessed in Europe and to a lesser extent in the United States the emergence of a new kind of industrial labor force. Laborers worked in factories rather than in their homes or in small artisan workshops. More often than not the new industrial working class dwelled in cities. The presence and growth of this new labor force were the most important social developments of the century and would produce a vast influence on European and American political life. It was out of the social and political experience of this work force that the political movement known as socialism arose.

During the second half of the 19th century, European and American political, economic, and social life assumed many characteristics of our present-day world. In Europe nation-states with large electorates, political parties, centralized bureaucracies, and universal military service emerged. In the United States the politics associated with the Progressive movement brought the presidency to the center of American political life. On both sides of the North Atlantic, business adopted large-scale corporate structures, and the labor force organized itself into trade unions. The number of white-collar laborers grew as urban life became predominant throughout western Europe. But even as new vast cities arose in the United States, farming continued to spread across the central Midwest and upper Southwest. During this period, too, women began to assert new political awareness and to become politically active in both Europe and America.

During these same years Europe quietly became dependent on the resources and markets of the rest of the world. Farms in the United States, Canada, Latin America, Australia, and New Zealand supplied food to much of the world. Consequently, climate changes in Kansas, Argentina, or New Zealand might now affect the European economy. However, before World War I the dependence was concealed by Europe's industrial, military, and financial supremacy. At the time Europeans assumed their supremacy to be natural, but the 20th century would reveal it to have been temporary. Nevertheless, while it prevailed, Europeans dominated most of the other peoples of the world and displayed extreme self-confidence. Toward the close of the 19th century, the United States, having achieved the status of a major industrial power as well as an agricultural supplier, now entered the world stage as a military power, defeating Spain in the Spanish-American War in 1898. With that victory, the United States also acquired its first colonial territories.

During these same decades a number of major new ideas arose: theories of evolution in biology, relativity in physics, the irrational in philosophy, and psychoanalysis. These concepts shaped the intellectual outlook for the rest of the century.

WHAT DOES the term

proletarianization mean?

19.1
Sybil (1845)
Benjamin Disraeli

EUROPEAN FACTORY WORKERS AND URBAN ARTISANS

Although the seeds of industrial production had been sown in the 18th century, it was only in the 19th century that much of Europe headed toward a more fully industrial society. By 1830, only Great Britain had attained that status, but new factories and railways were beginning to be constructed elsewhere in Europe. However, what characterized the second quarter of the century was less the triumph of industrialism than the final gasps of those economic groups that opposed it and were displaced by it. Intellectually, the period saw the formulation of the major creeds supporting and criticizing the new society.

The specter of poor harvests haunted Europe. The worst was the failure of potato crops that produced the Irish famine from 1845 to 1847. Half a million Irish peasants starved to death; hundreds of thousands emigrated. Many moved to urban areas to find work in factories.

In much of northern Europe both artisans and factory workers underwent a process of *proletarianization*. This term indicates the entry of workers into a wage economy and their gradual loss of significant ownership of the means of production, such as tools and equipment, and of control

over the conduct of their own trades. The process occurred rapidly wherever the factory system arose. The factory owner provided the financial capital to construct the factory, purchase the machinery, and secure the raw materials. Factory workers contributed their labor for a wage. Those workers also submitted to factory discipline, which meant that work conditions became largely determined by the demands for smooth operation of the machines. Closing of factory gates to late workers, fines for lateness, dismissal for drunkenness, and public scolding of faulty laborers constituted attempts to enforce regularity on humans that would match the regularity of cables, wheels, and pistons. Factory workers had no direct say over the quality of the product or its price. For all their difficulties, factory conditions were often better than those of textile workers who resisted the factory mode of production. In particular, English hand-loom weavers, who continued to work in their homes, experienced decades of declining trade and growing poverty in their unsuccessful competition with power looms.

Urban artisans in the 19th century experienced proletarianization more slowly than factory workers, and machinery had little to do with the process. The emergence of factories in itself did not harm urban artisans. Many even prospered from the development. For example, the construction and maintenance of the new machines generated demand for metal workers, who consequently did well. The actual erection of factories and the expansion of cities benefited all craftsmen in the building trades, such as carpenters, roofers, joiners, and masons. Lower prices for machine-made textiles aided artisans involved in the making of clothing, such as tailors and hatters, by reducing the costs of their raw materials. Where the urban artisans encountered difficulty and found their skills and livelihood threatened was in the organization of production.

In the 18th century, a European town or city workplace usually consisted of a few artisans laboring for a master, first as apprentices and then as journeymen, according to established guild regulations and practices. The master owned the workshop and the larger equipment, and the apprentices and journeymen owned their tools. The journeyman could expect to become a master. This guild system had allowed considerable worker control over labor recruitment and training, production pace, product quality, and price.

Industrial Labor and Pro-Slavery Arguments. The condition of European industrial workers entered the political debates on both sides of the Atlantic. This 1841 proslavery cartoon from the United States contrasts allegedly healthy, well-cared-for African-American slaves with unemployed British factory workers living in poverty. American proslavery advocates also frequently made the comparison between supposed contented southern slaves and miserable northern "wages slaves."
Courtesy of the Library of Congress.

QUICK REVIEW

Factory Work
- Proletarianization: loss of ownership of the means of production
- Factory work demanded submission to new kind of work discipline
- Factory workers were better off than the hand-loom workers who competed with them

proletarianization Process whereby independent artisans and factory workers lose control of the means of production and of the conduct of their own trades to the owners of capital.

OVERVIEW MAJOR EUROPEAN CITIES IN 1914

Between 1850 and the outbreak of World War I, European cities from Britain to Russia grew rapidly as rural populations moved to the cities in search of jobs, stimulation, and social opportunities. The tables below show the growth of seven major European cities between 1850 and 1910 and list 14 other European cities whose populations had grown to exceed 500,000 by 1914.

Growth of Major Cities	1850	1880	1914
Berlin	419,000	1,122,000	2,071,000
Birmingham	233,000	437,000	840,000
Frankfurt	65,000	137,000	415,000
London	2,685,000	4,470,000	7,256,000
Madrid	281,000	398,000	600,000
Paris	1,053,000	2,269,000	2,888,000
Vienna	444,000	1,104,000	2,031,000

Cities with More than 500,000 People, 1914

Amsterdam	Hamburg	Munich
Barcelona	Istanbul	Naples
Brussels	Liverpool	St. Petersburg
Budapest	Manchester	Warsaw
Glasgow	Moscow	

In the 19th century, the situation of the urban artisan changed. It became increasingly difficult for artisans to exercise corporate or guild direction and control over their trades. The French Revolution had outlawed such organizations in France. Across Europe, political and economic liberals disapproved of labor and guild organizations and attempted to make them illegal.

Other destructive forces were also at work. The masters often found themselves under increased competitive pressure from larger, more heavily capitalized establishments or from the possibility of the introduction of machine production into a previously craft-dominated industry. In many workshops masters began to follow a practice, known in France as *confection*, whereby goods such as shoes, clothing, and furniture were produced in standard sizes and styles rather than by special orders for individual customers. This practice increased the division of labor in the workshop. Each artisan produced a smaller part of the uniform final product. Consequently, less skill was required of each artisan, and the particular skills possessed by a worker became less valuable. Masters also attempted to increase production and reduce their costs for piecework. Those attempts often led to work stoppages or strikes. Migrants from the countryside or small towns into the cities created, in some cases, a surplus of relatively unskilled workers who were willing to work for lower wages or under less favorable and protected conditions than traditional artisans. The dilution of skills and lower wages, caused not by machinery but by changes in the organization of artisan production, made it much more difficult for urban journeymen to become masters with their own workshops where they would be in charge. Increasingly, these artisans became lifetime wage laborers whose skills were simply bought and sold in the marketplace.

In the United States defenders of slavery frequently compared what they claimed to be the protected situation of slaves living on plantations with the plight of factory workers in Europe and the northern United States. They argued that a free market in wage labor left workers worse off than slaves. But the situation in the European labor market as in the American North was much more complicated than the defenders of slavery contended.

19TH-CENTURY EUROPEAN WOMEN

WOMEN IN THE EARLY INDUSTRIAL REVOLUTION

The industrial economy ultimately produced an immense impact on the home and the family life of women. First, it took virtually all productive work out of the home and allowed many families to live on the wages of the male spouse alone. That transformation prepared the way for a new concept of gender-determined roles in the home and in general domestic life. Women came to be associated with domestic duties such as housekeeping, food preparation, child rearing and nurturing, and household management. Men were associated almost exclusively with breadwinning. Children were reared to match these gender patterns. Previously, this domestic division of labor had prevailed only among the relatively small middle and gentry classes. During the 19th century, it came to characterize the working class as well. Second, industrialization created new modes of employment that allowed many young women to earn enough money to marry or, if necessary, to support themselves independently. Third, industrialism, although fostering more employment for women, lowered the skills required of them.

Because the Industrial Revolution had begun in textile production, women and their labor were deeply involved from the start. While both spinning and weaving were still domestic industries, women usually worked in all stages of production. Hand spinning was virtually always a woman's task. When spinning was moved into factories and involved large machines, however, men displaced women. The higher wages commanded by male cotton-factory workers allowed many women to stop working or to work only to supplement their husbands' wages.

With the next generation of machines in the 1820s, unmarried women rapidly became employed in the factories. However, their jobs tended to require less skill than most work done by men and less skill than women had previously exercised in the home production of textiles. There was thus a certain paradox in the impact of the factory on women. Many new jobs opened to them, but those jobs were less skilled than what had been available to them before. Moreover, the women in the factories were almost always young and single or widows. At marriage or perhaps at the birth of the first child, a woman usually found that her husband earned enough money for her to leave the factory. Factory owners also disliked employing married women because of the likelihood of pregnancy, the influence of husbands, and the duties of child rearing.

In Britain and elsewhere by mid-century, industrial factory work accounted for less than half of all employment for women. The largest group of employed women in France continued to work on the land. In England they were domestic servants. Domestic industries, such as lace glove and garment making and other kinds of needlework, employed many women. Their conditions of labor were almost always harsh, whether they worked in their homes or in sweated work-shops. Generally all work done by women commanded low wages and involved

WHAT SOCIAL and legal disabilities did European women confront in the 19th century?

19.3
Sadler Report: Child Labor

Working-class women. Although new opportunities opened to them in the late 19th century, many working-class women, like these women ironing in a laundry, remained in traditional occupations. As the wine bottle suggests, alcoholism was a problem for women as well as men engaged in tedious work. The painting is by Edgar Degas.

Photo R.M.N./Senice Photographique des Muses Nationaux, Paris.

low skills. They had virtually no way to protect themselves from exploitation. The cleaning lady, with mop and bucket, was a common sight across the continent and symbolized the plight of working women.

One of the most serious problems facing working women was the uncertainty of employment. Because they almost always found themselves in the least skilled jobs and trades, their employment was never secure. Much of their work was seasonal. Many working-class women feared they might be compelled to turn to prostitution. On the other hand, cities and the more complex economy did allow a greater variety of jobs. Movement to cities and entrance into the wage economy also gave women wider opportunities for marriage. Cohabitation before marriage seems to have been common. Parents did not arrange marriages as frequently as in the past. Marriage also generally meant that a woman would leave the work force to live on her husband's earnings. If all went well, that arrangement might improve her situation, but if the husband became ill or died, or deserted her, she would have to reenter the market for unskilled labor at a more advanced age.

Nonetheless, many of the traditional practices associated with the family economy survived into the industrial era. As a young woman came of age, both family needs and her desire to marry still directed what she would do with her life. The most likely early occupation for a young woman was domestic service. A girl born in the country usually migrated to a nearby town or city for such employment, often living initially with a relative. As in the past, she would attempt to earn enough in wages to give herself a dowry so that she might marry and establish her own household. If she became a factory worker, she would probably live in a supervised dormitory. By convincing parents that their daughters would be safe, these factory owners attracted young women workers. The lives of young women in the cities were more precarious than it had been earlier. There were fewer family and community ties and more available young men. These men, who worked for wages rather than in the older apprenticeship structures, were more mobile, so relationships between men and women were often fleeting. In any case, illegitimate births increased. That is to say, fewer women who became pregnant before marriage found the father willing to marry them.

Marriage in the wage industrial economy was also different. It still involved the starting of a separate household, but the structure of gender relationships within the household was different. Marriage was less an economic partnership: The husband might be able to support the entire family. The wage economy and the industrialization that separated workplace and home made it difficult for women to combine domestic duties with work. When married women worked, it was usually in the nonindustrial sector of the economy. More often than not children rather than the wife were sent to work, which may help explain the increase of fertility within marriages, since children in the wage economy tended to be an economic asset. Married women worked outside the home only when family needs or illness or the death of a spouse really required them to do so.

Within the home, the domestic duties of working-class women were an essential factor in the family wage economy. Homemaking came to the fore when a life at home had to be organized that was separate from the place of work. Wives were primarily concerned with food and cooking, but they often were also in charge of the family's finances. The role of the mother expanded when the children still living at home became wage earners. She was then providing home support for her entire wage-earning family. She created the environment

Women in Textile Factories. As textile production became increasingly automated in the 19th century, textile factories required fewer skilled workers and more unskilled attendants. To fill these unskilled positions, factory owners turned increasingly to unmarried women and widows, who worked for lower wages than men and were less likely to form labor organizations.

Bildarchiv Preussischer Kulturbesitz.

to which the family members returned after work. The longer period of home life of working children may also have strengthened the affection between those children and their hardworking, homebound mothers.

SOCIAL DISABILITIES CONFRONTED BY ALL WOMEN

During the early 19th century, virtually all European women faced social and legal disabilities in property rights, family law, and education. By the close of the century, each area had shown improvement. In this period European women, like European men, led lives that reflected their social rank. Yet within each rank, the experience of women was distinct from that of men. Women remained, generally speaking, economically dependent and legally inferior, whatever their social class. Their position thus resembled that of women around the world in that all women found their lives circumscribed by traditional social customs and expectations.

Women and Property   Until the last quarter of the century, in most European countries no married woman, whatever their social class, could own property. In effect, upon marriage women lost to their husbands' control any property they owned or that they might inherit or earn by their own labor. Their legal identities were subsumed into their husbands' and they had no independent standing before the law. The courts saw the theft of a woman's purse as a theft of her husband's property. Because European society was based on private property and wage earning, these disabilities put married women at a great disadvantage, limiting their freedom to work, save, and relocate.

Reform of women's property rights came slowly. By 1882, Great Britain allowed married women to own property in their own right. In France, however, a married woman could not even open a savings account in her own name until 1895, and not until 1907 were married women granted possession of their own wages. In 1900, Germany allowed women to take jobs without their husbands' permission, but a German husband retained control of most of his wife's property except for her wages. Similar laws prevailed elsewhere in Europe.

Family Law   European family law also worked to the disadvantage of women. Legal codes required wives to obey their husbands. The Napoleonic Code and the remnants of Roman law made women legal minors throughout Europe. Divorce was difficult for most of the century. Until 1857, divorce required an act of Parliament in England. Most nations did not permit divorce by mutual consent. French law forbade divorce between 1816 and 1884. Thereafter the chief recognized legal cause for divorce was cruelty and injury, which had to be proven in court. In Great Britain adultery was the usual cause for divorce, but a woman had to prove her husband's adultery as well as other offenses, whereas a man only had to prove his wife's adultery. In Germany only adultery or serious maltreatment was recognized as grounds for divorce. Across Europe extramarital sexual relations by husbands were more tolerated than those of wives. Everywhere, divorce required legal hearings and proof, making the process expensive and all the more difficult for women who did not control their own property.

The authority of husbands also extended to children. A husband could take children away from their mother and give them to someone else to rear. Only the husband, in most countries, could permit his daughter to marry. In some countries he could virtually force his daughter to marry the man of his

Middle-Class Family. Family was central to the middle-class conception of a stable and respectable social life. This portrait of the Bellelli family is by Degas. Notice that the husband and father sits at his desk, suggesting his association with business and the world outside the home, whereas the wife and mother stands with their children, suggesting her domestic role.

Edgar Degas (1834–1917), "The Bellelli Family" c. 1858–60. Musee d'Orsay, Paris, France. Photograph Copyright Bridgeman-Giraudon/Art Resource, N.Y.

choice. In cases of divorce and separation, the husband normally assumed authority over children no matter how he had treated them previously.

The sexual and reproductive rights of women, which have been so widely debated in recent years, could hardly be discussed in the 19th century. Both contraception and abortion were illegal. The law on rape normally worked against women. Wherever they turned—whether to physicians or lawyers—women confronted an official or legal world populated and controlled by men.

Educational Barriers   Throughout the 19th century, women had less access to education than men, and what was available to them was inferior. Not surprisingly, the percentage of illiterate women exceeded that of men. Most women were educated only enough for the domestic careers they were expected to follow.

University and professional education remained reserved for men until at least the third quarter of the century. The University of Zurich opened its doors to women in the 1860s. The University of London admitted women for degrees in 1878. Women were not awarded degrees at Oxford until 1920 or at Cambridge until 1921. They could not attend Sorbonne lectures until 1880. Just before the turn of the century, universities and medical schools in the Austrian Empire allowed women to matriculate, but Prussian universities did not until after 1900. Russian women did not attend universities before 1914, but other institutions that awarded degrees were open to them. Italian universities were more open to both women students and women instructors than similar institutions elsewhere in Europe.

The absence of a system of private or public secondary education for women prevented most of them from gaining the qualifications they needed to enter a university whether or not the university prohibited them. Considerable evidence suggests that educated, professional men feared the competition of women. Women who attended universities and medical schools were sometimes labeled political radicals.

By 1900, men in the educated elite also feared the challenge educated women posed to traditional gender roles in the home and workplace. Restricting their access to secondary and university education helped bar women from social and economic advancement. Women would benefit only marginally from the expansion of professional employment that occurred during the late 19th and early 20th centuries. Although a few women did enter the professions, especially medicine, most nations prevented women from becoming lawyers until after World War I.

Schoolteaching at the elementary level, which was seen as a female job because of its association with the nurturing of children, became a professional haven for women. Trained at institutions that were equivalent to normal schools, women schoolteachers were regarded as educated, but not as university educated. Secondary education remained largely the province of men.

The few women who pioneered in the professions and on government commissions and school boards or who dispersed birth control information faced grave social obstacles, personal humiliation, and often outright bigotry. These women and their male supporters were challenging that clear separation of life into male and female spheres that had emerged in middle-class European society during the 19th century. Women themselves often hesitated to support feminist causes or expanded opportunities for themselves because they had been so thoroughly acculturated into the recently stereotyped roles. Many women saw a real conflict between family responsibilities and feminism.

Major Dates in Late 19th-Century and Early 20th-Century Women's History

1857	Revised English divorce law
1865	University of Zurich admits women for degrees
1869	*The Subjection of Women* by John Stuart Mill and Harriet Taylor
1878	University of London admits women as candidates for degrees
1882	English Married Woman's Property Act
1894	Union of German Women's Organizations founded
1901	National Council of French Women founded
1903	British Women's Social and Political Union founded
1907	Norway permits women to vote on national issues
1910	British suffragettes adopt radical tactics
1918	Vote extended to some British women
1918	Weimar constitution allows German women to vote
1920–1921	Oxford and Cambridge Universities award degrees to women
1922	French Senate defeats bill extending vote to women
1928	Britain extends vote to women on same basis as men

NEW EMPLOYMENT PATTERNS FOR WOMEN

During the late 19th century, two major developments affected the economic lives of women. The first was an expansion in the variety of jobs available outside the better-paying learned professions. The second was a withdrawal of married women from the work force. These two seemingly contradictory developments require explanation.

Availability of New Jobs   The expansion of governmental bureaucracies, the emergence of corporations and other large-scale businesses, and the expansion of retail stores opened many new employment opportunities for women. The need for elementary schoolteachers, usually women, grew with compulsory education laws. Technological inventions and innovations, such as the typewriter and eventually the telephone, also fostered female employment. Women by the

Women Working at a Telephone Exchange.
The invention of the telephone opened new employment opportunities for women.

Mary Evans Picture Library.

thousands became secretaries and clerks for governments and private businesses. Even more became shop assistants.

Although these jobs did open new and often better employment opportunities for women, they nonetheless required low-level skills and involved minimal training. They were occupied primarily by unmarried women or widows. Few women had prominent positions.

Employers continued to pay women low wages because they assumed, often knowing better, that a woman did not need to support herself independently but could expect additional financial support from her father or husband. Consequently, a woman who did need to support herself independently could rarely find a job paying an adequate income or a position that paid as well as one held by a man who was supporting himself independently.

Withdrawal from the Labor Force Most of the women filling these new service positions were young and unmarried. After marriage, or certainly after the birth of her first child, a woman normally withdrew from the labor force. She either did not work or she worked at home. This pattern was not new, but it had become more common by the end of the 19th century. The industrial occupations that women had filled in the mid-19th century, especially textile and garment making, were shrinking. Those industries thus offered fewer jobs for either married or unmarried women. Employers in offices and retail stores preferred young, unmarried women whose family responsibilities would not interfere with their work. The decline in the number of births also meant that fewer married women were needed to look after other women's children.

The wages paid to male workers increased during this period, thus reducing families' need for a second income. Also, thanks to improving health conditions, men lived longer than before, so wives were less likely to be thrust into the work force by an emergency. Smaller families also lowered the need for supplementary wages. Working children stayed longer at home and continued to contribute to the family's wage pool.

Finally, the cultural dominance of the middle class, with its generally idle wives, established a pattern of social expectations. The more prosperous a working-class family became, the less involved in employment its women were supposed to be. Indeed, the less income-producing work a wife did, the more prosperous and stable the family was considered.

Yet behind these generalities stands the enormous variety of social and economic experience late 19th-century women actually encountered. As might be expected, social class largely determined these individual experiences.

LATE 19TH-CENTURY WORKING-CLASS WOMEN

Although less dominant than earlier in the century, the textile and garment-making industries continued to employ many women. The German clothing-making trades illustrate the kind of vulnerable economic situation that women could encounter as a result of their limited skills and the organization of the trade. The manufacture of mass-made clothes in Germany was designed to require minimal capital investment by manufacturers and to protect them from significant risk. A major manufacturer would arrange to produce clothing through a putting-out system. He would purchase the material and then put it out for tailoring. The clothing was made not in a factory but usually in independently owned, small sweatshops or by workers in their homes.

In 1896, there were more than 80,000 garment workers, mostly women, in Berlin. When business was good, employment for these women was high. If business became poor, however, less work was put out, idling many of them. In effect, the workers who actually sewed the clothing carried much of the risk of the enterprise. Some women did work in factories, but they, too, were subject to layoffs. Furthermore, women in the clothing trade were nearly always in positions less skilled than those of the male tailors or the middlemen who owned the workshops.

The expectation of separate social and economic spheres for men and women and the definition of women's chief work as pertaining to the home contributed heavily to the exploitation of women workers outside the home. Because their wages were regarded merely as supplementing their husbands', they became particularly vulnerable to the economic exploitation that characterized the German putting-out system for clothing production. Women were nearly always treated as casual workers in Europe.

THE RISE OF POLITICAL FEMINISM

As can be seen from the previous discussion, liberal society and its values neither automatically nor inevitably improved the lot of women. In particular, it did not give them the right to vote or access to political activity. Male liberals feared that granting the vote to women would benefit political conservatives because women were thought to be unduly controlled by the clergy. Consequently, anticlerical liberals often had difficulty working with feminists.

Obstacles to Achieving Equality   Women also were often reluctant to support feminist causes. Political issues relating to gender were only one of several priorities for many women. Some were sensitive to their class and economic interests. Others subordinated feminist political issues to national unity and nationalistic patriotism. Still others would not support particular feminist organizations because of differences over tactics. The various social and tactical differences among women often led to sharp divisions within the feminists' own ranks. Except in England, it was often difficult for working-class and middle-class women to cooperate. Roman Catholic feminists were uncomfortable with radical secularist feminists.

Although liberal society and law presented women with many obstacles, they also provided feminists with many of their intellectual and political tools. As early as 1792 in Britain, Mary Wollstonecraft (1759–1797), in *The Vindication of the Rights of Women*, applied the revolutionary doctrines of the rights of man to the predicament of the members of her own sex (see Chapter 22). John Stuart Mill (1806–1873), with his wife Harriet Taylor (1804–1858), applied the logic of liberal freedom to the position of women in *The Subjection of Women* (1869). The arguments for utility and efficiency so dear to middle-class liberals could be used to expose the human and social waste implicit in the inferior role assigned to women.

Furthermore, the socialist criticism of capitalist society often, though by no means always, included a harsh indictment of the social and economic position to which women had been relegated. The earliest statements of feminism arose from critics of the existing order and were often associated with people who had unorthodox opinions about sexuality, family life, and property. This hardened resistance to the feminist message, especially on the continent.

These difficulties prevented continental feminists from raising the kind of massive public support or mounting the large demonstrations that feminists in Great Britain and the United States could. Everywhere in Europe, however, including Britain, the feminist cause was badly divided over both goals and tactics.

Women's Suffrage. The creator of this poster cleverly reveals the hypocrisy and foolishness of denying the vote to women.

Private collection/Bridgeman Art Library.

Votes for Women in Britain Europe's most advanced women's movement was in Great Britain. There, Millicent Fawcett (1847–1929) led the moderate National Union of Women's Suffrage Societies. She believed Parliament would grant women the vote only when convinced that women would be respectable and responsible in their political activity. In 1908, this organization could rally almost half a million women in London. Fawcett was the wife of a former Liberal Party cabinet minister and economist. Her tactics were those of English liberals.

Emmeline Pankhurst (1858–1928) led a different and much more radical branch of British feminists. Pankhurst's husband had been active in both labor and Irish nationalist politics. Irish nationalists had developed numerous disruptive political tactics. Early labor politicians also occasionally had confrontations with police over the right to hold meetings. In 1903, Pankhurst and her daughters founded the Women's Social and Political Union. For several years they and their followers, known derisively as **suffragettes**, lobbied publicly and privately for women's suffrage. By 1910, having failed to move the government, they turned to the violent tactics of arson, window breaking, and sabotage of postal boxes. They marched en masse on Parliament. The liberal government of Herbert Asquith (1852–1928), prime minister from 1908 to 1916, imprisoned many of the demonstrators and force-fed those who went on hunger strikes in jail. The government refused to extend the franchise. Only in 1918, and then as a result of their contribution to the war effort, did some British women receive the vote.

Political Feminism on the Continent The contrast of France and Germany shows how advanced the British women's movement was. In France, when Hubertine Auclert (1848–1914) began campaigning for the vote in the 1880s, she stood virtually alone. During the 1890s, several women's organizations emerged. In 1901, the National Council of French Women (CNFF) was organized among upper-middle-class women, but it did not support the vote for women for several years. French Roman Catholic feminists, such as Marie Mauguet (1844–1928), supported the franchise. Almost all French feminists,

suffragettes British women who lobbied and agitated for the right to vote in the early 20th century.

however, rejected violence. They also were never able to organize mass rallies. The leaders of French feminism believed that the vote could be achieved through careful legalism. In 1919, the French Chamber of Deputies granted the vote to women, but in 1922 the French Senate defeated the bill. French women did not receive the right to vote until 1944, at the end of World War II.

In Germany feminist awareness and action were even more underdeveloped. German law actually forbade German women from political activity. Because no group in the German Empire enjoyed extensive political rights, women were not certain that they would benefit from demanding them. Any such demand would be regarded as subversive of both the state and society.

In 1894, the Union of German Women's Organizations (BDFK) was founded. By 1902, it was calling for the right to vote. But it was largely concerned with improving women's social conditions, their access to education, and their right to other protections. The group also worked to see women admitted to political or civic activity on the municipal level. Their work usually included education, child welfare, charity, and public health. The German Social Democratic Party supported women's suffrage, but that Socialist Party was so disdained by the German authorities and German Roman Catholics that this support only made suffrage more suspect in their eyes. Women received the vote in Germany only in 1918 under the constitution of the Weimar Republic. Before World War I, only in Norway (1907) could women vote on national issues.

JEWISH EMANCIPATION

One of the most important social changes to occur throughout Europe during the 19th century was the emancipation of European Jews from the narrow life of the ghetto into a world of equal or nearly equal citizenship and social status. This transformation represented one of the major social impacts of political liberalism on European life.

EARLY STEPS TO EQUAL CITIZENSHIP

Emancipation, slow and never fully completed, began in the late 18th century and continued throughout the 19th century. It moved at different paces in different countries. In 1782, Joseph II (r. 1765–1790), the Habsburg emperor, issued a decree that placed the Jews of his empire under more or less the same laws as Christians. In France, the National Assembly recognized Jews as French citizens in 1789. During the Napoleonic Wars, Jewish communities in Italy and Germany were allowed to mix on a generally equal footing with the Christian population.

These various steps toward political emancipation were frequently limited or partially repealed with changes in rulers or governments. Even in countries that granted them political rights, Jews could not own land and could be subject to discriminatory taxes. Nonetheless, by the first half of the 19th century, Jews in western Europe and to a much lesser extent in central and eastern Europe had begun to acquire equal or nearly equal citizenship.

In Russia, however, the traditional modes of prejudice and discrimination continued unabated until World War I. Jews were treated as aliens under Russian rule. The government undermined Jewish community life, limited publication of Jewish books, restricted areas where Jews might live, required internal passports from Jews, and banned them from many forms of state service and many institutions of higher education. The police and others were allowed to conduct **pogroms**—organized riots—against Jewish neighborhoods and villages.

HOW DID emanicipation affect Jewish participation in European social and political life outside of Russia?

pogroms Organized riots against Jews in the Russian Empire.

BROADENED OPPORTUNITIES

After the Revolutions of 1848, and especially in western Europe, the situation of European Jews improved for several decades. Throughout Germany, Italy, the Low Countries, and Scandinavia, Jews were allowed full rights of citizenship. After 1858, Jews in Great Britain could sit in Parliament. In Austria-Hungary, full legal rights were extended to Jews in 1867. From approximately 1850 to 1880, there was relatively little organized or overt prejudice toward Jews. They entered the professions and other occupations once closed to them. They participated fully in the literary and cultural life of their nations. They were active in the arts and music. They became leaders in science and education. Jews intermarried freely with non-Jews as legal prohibitions against such marriages were repealed during the last quarter of the century.

Outside of Russia, Jewish political figures served in the highest offices of the state. Politically they tended to be aligned with liberal parties because such groups had championed equal rights. Later in the century, especially in eastern Europe, many Jews became associated with the Socialist parties.

The prejudice that had been associated with religious attitudes toward Jews seemed to have dissipated, although it still appeared in rural Russia and eastern Europe. From these regions, hundreds of thousands of European Jews immigrated to the United States. Almost anywhere in Europe Jews might encounter prejudice on a personal level. But in western Europe, including England, France, Italy, Germany, and the Low Countries, the Jewish populations seem to have felt relatively secure from the old dangers of legalized persecution and discrimination.

Feelings toward Jews began to change during the last two decades of the 19th century. In the 1870s, anti-Semitic sentiments attributing the economic stagnation of the decade to Jewish bankers and financial interests began to be voiced. In the 1880s, organized anti-Semitism erupted in Germany as it did in France in the 1890s. As described in Chapter 24, those developments gave birth to Zionism, the movement to establish a Jewish state in Palestine. However, Zionism was initially a minority movement within the Jewish community. Most Jewish leaders believed the attacks on Jewish life to be temporary recurrences of older prejudice; they felt that their communities would remain safe under the legal protections that had been extended during the century. That analysis would be proved disastrously wrong during the 1930s and 1940s.

WHY DID Marxism become so influential among European socialists?

EUROPEAN LABOR, SOCIALISM, AND POLITICS TO WORLD WAR I

THE WORKING CLASSES IN THE LATE 19TH CENTURY

After 1848, European workers ceased taking to the streets and rioting to voice their grievances. They also stopped trying to revive the old paternalistic guilds. They accepted the inevitability of modern industrial production and sought a share of the benefits it produced. They looked to new organizations and ideologies to defend their interests: trade unions, democratic political parties, and socialism.

Trade Union   Trade unionism came of age as legal protections were extended to unions throughout the second half of the century. Unions became fully legal in Great Britain in 1871 and were allowed to picket in 1875. In France, the Third Republic fully legalized unions in 1884. After 1890, they could function in

Germany with little disturbance. Initially, most trade unions were slow to enter the political process directly. As long as the traditional governing classes looked after labor interests, members of the working class rarely sought office themselves.

The mid-century organizational efforts of the unions aimed to improve the wages and working conditions of skilled workers. By the close of the century, large industrial unions for unskilled workers were also being organized. They confronted extensive opposition from employers, and were often recognized only after long strikes. In the decade before 1914, strikes were common through-out Europe as unions attempted to raise wages to keep up with inflation. However, despite the advances of unions and the growth of their membership in 1910 to approximately 3 million in Britain, 2 million in Germany, and 977,000 in France, they never included a majority of the industrial labor force. Unions did represent a new collective fashion in which workers could associate to confront the economic difficulties of their lives and attain better security.

Democracy and Political Parties   The democratic franchise gave workers direct political influence, which meant they could no longer be ignored. Except for Russia, all the major European states adopted broad-based, if not perfectly democratic, electoral systems. Democracy brought new modes of popular pressure to bear on all governments. Discontented groups could now voice their grievances and advocate their programs within government rather than from outside it.

The advent of democracy witnessed the formation for the first time in Europe of organized mass political parties, such as had existed throughout the 19th century in the United States. In the liberal European states with narrow electoral bases, most voters had been men of property who understood what they had at stake in politics. Organization had been minimal. The expansion of the electorate brought into the political processes many people whose level of political consciousness and interest was low. This electorate had to be organized and taught the nature of power and influence in the liberal democratic state. The organized political party—with its workers, news-papers, offices, social life, and discipline—was the vehicle that mobilized the new voters. The largest single group in these mass electorates was the working class. The democratization of politics presented the Socialists with opportunities and required the traditional ruling class to vie with them for the support of the new voters.

MARXIST CRITIQUE OF THE INDUSTRIAL ORDER

During the 1840s, Karl Marx (1818–1883) produced the most influential of all critiques of the newly emerged industrial order. His analysis became so important because later in the century it was adopted by the leading Socialist political party in Germany, which in turn influenced most other European Socialist parties including a small group of exiled Russian Socialists led by V. I. Lenin. Marx was born in the Rhineland. His Jewish middle-class parents sent him to the University of Berlin, where he became deeply involved in radical politics. During 1842 and 1843, he edited the radical *Rhineland Gazette*. Soon the German

Major Dates in the Development of Socialism

1864	International Working Men's Association (the First International) founded
1875	German Social Democratic Party founded
1876	First International dissolved
1878	German antisocialist laws passed
1884	British Fabian Society founded
1889	Second International founded
1891	German antisocialist laws permitted to expire
1891	German Social Democratic Party's Erfurt Program
1895	French *Confédération Générale du Travail* founded
1899	Eduard Bernstein's *Evolutionary Socialism*
1902	Formation of the British Labour party
1902	Lenin's *What Is to Be Done?*
1903	Bolshevik-Menshevik split

Karl Marx. Marx's Socialist philosophy eventually triumphed over most alternative versions of socialism in Europe, but his monumental work has been subject to varying interpretations, criticisms, and revisions that continue to this day.

Bildarchiv Preussischer Kulturbesitz.

19.8
Karl Marx and
Friedrich Engels

authorities drove him into exile—first in Paris; then in Brussels; and finally, after 1849, in London.

In 1844, Marx met Friedrich Engels (1820–1895), another young middle-class German, whose father owned a textile factory in Manchester, England. The next year, Engels published *The Condition of the Working Class in England*, which presented a devastating picture of industrial life. The two men became fast friends. Late in 1847, they were asked to write a pamphlet for a newly organized and ultimately short-lived secret Communist league. *The Communist Manifesto*, published in German, appeared early in 1848. Marx, Engels, and the league had adopted the name *Communist* because the term was more self-consciously radical than *Socialist. Communism* implied the outright abolition of private property rather than some less extensive rearrangement of society. The *Manifesto* itself was a work of fewer than 50 pages. It would become the most influential political document of modern European history, but that development lay in the future. At the time it was simply one more political tract. Moreover, neither Marx nor his thought had any effect on the revolutionary events of 1848.

In *The Communist Manifesto*, Marx and Engels contended that human history must be understood rationally and as a whole. According to their analysis, history is the record of humankind's coming to grips with physical nature to produce the goods necessary for survival. That basic productive process determines the structures, values, and ideas of a society. Historically, the organization of the means of production has always involved conflict between the classes who owned and controlled the means of production and those classes who worked for them. That necessary conflict has provided the engine for historical development; it is not an accidental byproduct of mismanagement or bad intentions. Consequently, only a radical social transformation, not piecemeal reforms, can eliminate the social and economic evils inherent in the very structures of production. Such a revolution will occur as the inevitable outcome of the development of capitalism.

In Marx's and Engels's eyes, the class conflict that had characterized previous Western history had become a struggle between the bourgeoisie and the proletariat, or between the middle class and the workers in the 19th century. The character of capitalism ensured the sharpening of the struggle. Capitalist production and competition would steadily increase the size of the unpropertied proletariat. Large-scale mechanical production crushed both traditional and smaller industrial producers into the ranks of the proletariat. As the business structures grew larger and larger, smaller middle-class units would be squeezed out by the competitive pressures. Competition among the few remaining gigantic concerns would lead to more intense suffering by the proletariat. As the workers suffered increasingly from the competition among the ever-enlarging firms, they would foment revolution and finally overthrow the few remaining owners of the means of production. For a time the workers would organize the means of production through a dictatorship of the proletariat, which would eventually give way to a propertyless and classless communist society.

This proletarian revolution was inevitable, according to Marx and Engels. The structure of capitalism required competition and consolidation of enterprise.

Although the class conflict involved in the contemporary process resembled that of the past, it differed in one major respect. The struggle between the capitalistic bourgeoisie and the industrial proletariat would culminate in a wholly new society that would be free of class conflict. The victorious proletariat, by its very nature, they contended, could not be a new oppressor class: "The proletarian movement is the self-conscious, independent movement of the immense majority, in the interest of the immense majority."[1] The result of the proletarian victory would be "an association, in which the free development of each is the condition for the free development of all."[2] The victory of the proletariat over the bourgeoisie represented the culmination of human history. For the first time, one group of people would not be oppressing another. Marx's analysis was conditioned by his own economic environment. The 1840s had seen much unemployment and deprivation. Capitalism, however, did not collapse as he predicted, nor did the middle class during the rest of the century or later become proletarianized. Rather, more and more people came to benefit from the industrial system. Nonetheless, within a generation Marxism had captured the imagination of many Socialists and large segments of the working class. Its doctrines were allegedly based on the empirical evidence of hard economic fact. This much proclaimed scientific aspect of **Marxism** helped the ideology, as science became more influential during the second half of the century. Marx had made the ultimate victory of socialism seem certain. His works also suggested that the path to socialism lay with revolution rather than reform. As Marxist thought permeated the international Socialist movement during the next 75 years, it would provide the ideological basis for some of the most momentous and ultimately repressive political movements in the history of virtually the entire modern world.

GERMANY: SOCIAL DEMOCRATS AND REVISIONISM

Karl Marx's ideas ultimately came to exercise such vast influence, as they were being adopted by the German Social Democratic Party (SPD). Founded in 1875, the SPD suffered 12 years of persecution by Otto von Bismarck (1815–1898), who believed socialism would undermine German politics and society. In 1878, there was an attempt to assassinate Emperor William I (r. 1861–1888). Bismarck unfairly blamed the Socialists and steered antisocialist laws through the Reichstag, the German Parliament. These measures suppressed the organization, meetings, newspapers, and other public activities of the SPD. Nonetheless, the SPD steadily polled more votes in elections to the Reichstag.

Repression having failed, Bismarck enacted social welfare legislation to wean German workers from socialist loyalties. These measures provided health insurance, accident insurance, and old age and disability pensions. The German state itself thus organized a system of social security that did not change the system of property holding or politics.

In 1891, after forcing Bismarck's resignation, Emperor William II (r. 1888–1918) allowed the antisocialist legislation to expire. The SPD then had to decide how to operate as a legalized party. Their new direction was announced in the Erfurt Program of 1891. In good Marxist fashion, the program declared the imminent doom of capitalism and the necessity of socialist ownership of the means of production. However, these goals were to be achieved by legal political participation rather than by revolutionary activity. Since the revolution was inevitable, it was argued, the immediate task of Socialists was to improve workers'

Marxism Theory of Karl Marx (1818–1883) and Friedrich Engels (1820–1895) that history is the result of class conflict, which will end in the inevitable triumph of the industrial proletariat over the bourgeoisie and the abolition of private property and social class.

[1] Robert C. Tucker, ed., *The Marx-Engels Reader* (New York: W. W. Norton, 1972), p. 353.
[2] Ibid.

lives. In theory, the SPD was vehemently hostile to the German Empire, but in practice the party functioned within its institutions.

This situation of the SPD, however, generated the most important internal socialist challenge to the orthodox Marxist analysis of capitalism and the socialist revolution. Eduard Bernstein (1850–1932) wrote what was regarded as his socialist heresy. Bernstein, who was familiar with the British **Fabians**, questioned whether Marx and his later orthodox followers had been correct in their pessimistic appraisal of capitalism and the necessity of revolution. In *Evolutionary Socialism* (1899), Bernstein pointed to the rising standard of living in Europe, the ongoing power of the middle class, and the opening of the franchise to the working class. He argued that a humane socialist society required not revolution but more democracy and social reform. Bernstein's doctrines, known as *revisionism*, were widely debated among German Socialists and were finally condemned as theory, although the party actually pursued a peaceful, reformist program. His critics argued that evolution toward social democracy might be possible in liberal, parliamentary Britain but not in authoritarian, militaristic Germany with its basically powerless Reichstag. Therefore, the German SPD continued to advocate revolution.

The German debate over revisionism became important for the later history of Marxist socialism. The German SPD was, as noted, the most successful prewar Socialist party. Its rejection of an ideology of reform socialism in favor of revolutionary socialism influenced all Socialists who looked to the German example. Most significant, Lenin adopted this position, as did the other leaders of the Russian Revolution. Thereafter, wherever Soviet Marxism was influential, the goal of its efforts would be revolution rather than reform.

GREAT BRITAIN: THE LABOUR PARTY AND FABIANISM

No form of socialism made significant progress in Great Britain, the most advanced industrial society of the day. Members of the growing trade unions normally supported Liberal Party candidates. The "new unionism" of the late 1880s and the 1890s organized the dock workers, the gas workers, and similar unskilled groups. Employer resistance to unions heightened class antagonism. In 1892, Keir Hardie (1856–1915) became the first independent worker elected to Parliament. In 1893, the Socialist Independent Labour Party was founded, but it remained ineffective.

In 1901, however, a decision by the House of Lords (Britain's supreme court) removed the legal protection previously accorded union funds. The Trades Union Congress responded by launching the Labour Party, which sent 29 members to Parliament in the election of 1906. Their goals did not yet encompass socialism. The British labor movement also became more militant. In scores of strikes, workers fought for wages to meet the rising cost of living. The government intervened to

Fabians British Socialists in the late 19th and early 20th centuries who sought to achieve socialism through gradual, peaceful, and democratic means.

revisionism Advocacy among 19th-century German Socialists of achieving a humane socialist society through the evolution of democratic institutions, not revolution.

Trade Union Membership Certificate. Trade unions continued to grow in late-century Great Britain. The effort to curb the unions eventually led to the formation of the Labour Party. The British unions often had quite elaborate membership certificates, such as this one for the National Union of Gas Workers and General Labourers of Great Britain and Ireland.

The Granger Collection.

mediate these strikes, which in 1911 and 1912 involved the railways, the docks, and the mines.

British socialism itself remained primarily the preserve of intellectuals. The Socialists who exerted the most influence were from the Fabian Society, founded in 1884. The society took its name from Q. Fabius Maximus (d. 203 B.C.E.), the Roman general who defeated Hannibal by waiting before attacking. Its name thus indicated a gradualist approach to social reform. Its leading members were Sydney Webb (1859–1947), Beatrice Webb (1858–1943), H. G. Wells (1866–1946), and George Bernard Shaw (1856–1950). Many of the Fabians were civil servants who believed that the problems of industry, the expansion of ownership, and the state direction of production could be solved and achieved gradually, peacefully, and democratically. They sought to educate the country to the rational wisdom of socialism. They were particularly interested in collective ownership on the municipal level, or so-called gas-and-water socialism.

RUSSIA: INDUSTRIAL DEVELOPMENT AND THE BIRTH OF BOLSHEVISM

Following its defeat in the Crimean War, the tsarist government in Russia had undertaken a series of major internal reforms. The most important of these was the emancipation of the serfs in 1861. That measure was extremely complicated and in effect required serfs to pay for their land. The poverty of the emancipated serfs became a political cause for groups of urban revolutionaries in Russia who succeeded in assassinating Tsar Alexander II (r. 1855–1881) in 1881. Thereafter, the government pursued a policy of general political repression.

At the same time in the late 19th century, the tsarist government was determined to make Russia an industrial power. It favored the growth of heavy industries, such as railways, iron, and steel. A small but significant industrial proletariat arose. By 1900, Russia had approximately 3 million factory workers. Their working and living conditions were bad by any standard.

New political departures accompanied this economic development. In 1901, the Social Revolutionary Party was founded. It opposed industrialism and looked to the communal life of rural Russia as a model for the economic future. In 1903, the Constitutional Democratic Party, or Cadets, was formed. Liberal in outlook, the Cadets were drawn from people who participated in the *zemstvos* (local governments). They wanted a parliamentary regime with responsible ministries, civil liberties, and economic progress. The Cadets hoped to model themselves on the liberal parties of western Europe.

Lenin's Early Thought and Career   The situation for Russian Socialists differed radically from that in other major European countries. Russia had no representative political institutions and only a small working class. Compromises and accommodations achieved elsewhere were meaningless in Russia, where socialism in both theory and practice had to be revolutionary. The Russian Social Democratic Party had been established in 1898. It was Marxist, and its members greatly admired the German SPD, but tsarist repression meant that it had to function in exile.

The leading late-19th-century Russian Marxist was Georgii Plekhanov (1857–1918), based in Switzerland. His chief disciple was Vladimir Ilyich Ulyanov (1870–1924), who took the name of Lenin. The future leader of the communist revolution was the son of a high bureaucrat. His older brother had been executed in 1887 for participating in a plot against Alexander III (r. 1881–1894).

Marxist revolutionary Vladimir Ilyich Lenin. Lenin sits alone at a desk littered with papers and books.
Corbis/Bettman.

Bolsheviks Meaning the "majority." Term Lenin applied to his faction of the Russian Social Democratic Party. It became the Communist Party of the Soviet Union after the Russian Revolution.

Mensheviks Meaning the "minority." Term Lenin applied to the majority moderate faction of the Russian Social Democratic Party opposed to him and the Bolsheviks.

In 1893, Lenin moved to St. Petersburg, where he briefly practiced law. Soon he, too, was drawn to the revolutionary groups among the factory workers. In 1895, he was exiled to Siberia. After his release in 1900, Lenin spent most of the next 17 years in Switzerland.

In Switzerland, Lenin became deeply involved in the organizational and policy disputes of the exiled Russian Social Democrats. They all considered themselves Marxists, but quarreled about the proper nature of a Marxist revolution in primarily rural Russia and the structure of their own party. The Social Democrats were modernizers who favored further industrial development. Most believed that Russia must develop a large proletariat before the revolution could come. This same majority hoped to mold a mass political party like the German SPD.

Lenin dissented from both positions. In *What Is to Be Done?* (1902), he condemned any accommodations. He also criticized a trade unionism that settled for short-term gains rather than true revolutionary change for the working class. Lenin further rejected the concept of a mass party composed of workers. Revolutionary consciousness would not arise spontaneously from the working class. It must be carried to them by a small, elite party, "people who make revolutionary activity their profession."[3]

The guiding principle of that party should be "the strictest secrecy, the strictest selection of members, and the training of professional revolutionaries."[4]

Establishment of the Bolsheviks In 1903, at the London Congress of the Russian Social Democratic Party, Lenin split the party ranks. Although it lost most of the votes during the congress, Lenin's group mustered a slim majority near the close. Thereafter, his faction assumed the name *Bolsheviks*, meaning "majority," and the other, more moderate, democratic revolutionary faction became known as the *Mensheviks*, or "minority." There was, of course, a considerable public relations advantage to the name *Bolshevik*. (In 1912, the Bolsheviks organized separately from other Social Democrats.) In 1905, Lenin complemented his organizational theory with a program for revolution in Russia. His *Two Tactics of Social Democracy in the Bourgeois-Democratic Revolution* urged that the socialist revolution unite the proletariat and the peasants. He grasped better than any other revolutionary the profound discontent in the Russian countryside. He knew that an alliance of workers and peasants in rebellion probably could not be suppressed. Lenin's two principles of an elite party and a dual social revolution allowed the Bolsheviks, in late 1917, to capture the leadership of the Russian Revolution and to transform the political face of the modern world.

The Revolution of 1905 and Its Aftermath The quarrels among the Russian Socialists had no immediate influence within Russia itself. In 1904, Russia went to war with Japan, but the result was defeat and political crisis. The Japanese captured Port Arthur, Russia's base on the eastern coast of China, early in 1905. A few days later, on January 22, a priest named Father Gapon (1870–1906) led thousands of workers to petition the tsar for improvements in industrial conditions. As the petitioners approached the Winter Palace in Saint

[3]Quoted in Albert Fried and Ronald Sanders, eds. *Socialist Thought: A Documentary History* (Garden City, NY: Anchor Doubleday, 1964), p. 459.
[4]Ibid., p. 468.

Petersburg, troops opened fire. About 100 people were killed, and many more were wounded.

Revolutionary disturbances spread throughout Russia: Sailors mutinied, peasants revolted, and property was attacked. An uncle of the tsar was assassinated. Liberal Constitutional Democratic leaders from the *zemstvos* demanded political reform. University students went on strike. In early October 1905, strikes broke out in Saint Petersburg, and worker groups, called *soviets*, virtually controlled the city. Tsar Nicholas II (r. 1894–1917) promised Russia constitutional government.

Early in 1906, the tsar announced the election of a parliament, the **Duma**, with two chambers. However, he reserved for himself ministerial appointments, financial policy, and military and foreign affairs. Nicholas named as his chief minister P. A. Stolypin (1862–1911). Neither the tsar nor his minister was sympathetic to the Duma. It would meet, disagreements would occur, and it would be dismissed. In 1906, however, the government canceled any redemptive payments the peasants still owed from the emancipation of the serfs in 1861. Thereafter Stolypin repressed rural discontent.

After Stolypin's assassination in 1911 by a social revolutionary, the tsarist government simply muddled along. But the imperial family became surrounded by scandal over the influence of Grigori Rasputin (1871?–1916), who seemed able to heal the tsar's hemophilic son, the heir to the throne. The undue influence of this strange and uncouth man, the continued social discontent, and the conservative resistance to liberal reforms rendered the position and policy of the tsar uncertain after 1911.

EUROPEAN SOCIALISM IN WORLD HISTORY

The debates among late 19th- and early 20th-century European Socialists were complicated and in some respects obscure. They proved, however, significant not only for European politics but for political developments around the world. The impact arose for two reasons. First, Europeans who immigrated to North and South America carried many of these socialist ideas and quarrels with them. They continued to debate the issues in their new homelands. Second, by the end of the 19th century, numerous students from different parts of the European empires in Africa and Asia traveled to Europe for education. There they confronted these debates among European Socialists. Many of those students later returned home to become leaders of anticolonial political movements and carried with them the ideas and quarrels about methods, theory, and tactics they had encountered among European Socialists.

Major Dates in Turn-of-the-Century Russian History

1895	Lenin arrested and sent to Siberia
1897	Eleven-and-a-half-hour workday established
1898	Russian Social Democratic Party founded
1900	Lenin leaves Russia for western Europe
1901	Social Revolutionary Party founded
1903	Constitutional Democratic Party (Cadets) founded
1903	Bolshevik-Menshevik split
1904	Russo-Japanese War begins
1905	
January	Japan defeats Russia
January 22	Revolution breaks out in Saint Petersburg after Bloody Sunday massacre
October 20	General strike
October 26	*October Manifesto* establishes constitutional government
1906	
May 10	Meeting of first Duma
June	Stolypin appointed prime minister
July 21	Dissolution of first Duma
November	Land redemption payments canceled for peasants
1907	
March 5–June 16	Second Duma seated and dismissed
1907	Franchise changed and a third Duma elected, which sits until 1912
1911	Stolypin assassinated by a social revolutionary
1912	Fourth Duma elected
1914	World War I breaks out

soviets Workers' and soldiers' councils formed in Russia during the revolution.

Duma Russian parliament, after the revolution of 1905.

HOW DID industrialization in the United States differ from industrialization in Europe?

NORTH AMERICA AND THE NEW INDUSTRIAL ECONOMY

*T*he full industrialization of the United States followed a pattern not unlike that of 19th-century Europe. The first industry to become thoroughly mechanized was textile manufacture, followed by growth in the iron and steel industries. There were certain significant differences, however. The United States industrialized considerably later than Great Britain. Its major expansion in iron and steel took place after the Civil War and was thus approximately contemporary to the economic rise of the newly united Germany. In the United States, there had always been enormous social respect for entrepreneurial enterprise. American manufacturers and commercial developers thus encountered little of the prejudice against trade and commerce that existed among the European aristocracy. Wealthy American businessmen had considerable political influence. The United States possessed an immense internal market that functioned without trade restraints for the shipment of unprocessed goods to factories or of finished products to their markets. Much of the capital for American industrial expansion came from British bankers who saw the United States as an area of secure investment. Finally, the United States had a relative shortage of labor and consequently relatively high wages—factors that attracted so many immigrants to the industrial sector during the second half of the century.

In America as in Europe, however, the railways spurred the most intense industrial growth. The number of railway miles increased from approximately 50,000 in the mid-1860s to almost 200,000 by 1900. Much of the construction was made possible by vast European investments in the United States. The railways created enormous demand for iron, steel, coal, and lumber. They also stimulated settlement, vastly expanded markets, and helped to knit the country together.

EUROPEAN IMMIGRATION TO THE UNITED STATES

The same conditions that made American life so difficult for Blacks and Native Americans (see Chapter 23) turned the United States into a land of vast opportunity for White European immigrants. These immigrants faced religious and ethnic discrimination as well as frequent poverty in the United States; however, for many of them and their children, the social and economic structures of the United States allowed for assimilation and remarkable upward social mobility. This was especially true of those immigrants, mostly from northern and western Europe, who arrived approximately between 1840 and 1890—the great period of German, English, Welsh, Scottish, and Irish immigration. Among this group, the Irish undoubtedly encountered the most difficulties and resistance.

Toward the end of the century and well into the next—in what is sometimes known as the New Immigration—millions of people arrived from the Mediterranean, eastern Europe, and the Balkans (see Map 25–1). Most of these peoples left economically depressed areas, and financed their immigration themselves. However, some American companies did send ships to Italy for immigrants to work in American factories and mines.

These new immigrants, who generally came to work in the growing industrial cities, were perceived as fundamentally different from those who had come before them. They were seen and treated as of a lower class and inherently more difficult to assimilate than earlier immigrants. Predominately Roman Catholic, Orthodox, and Jewish, they encountered much intolerance. The same kind of racial theory that spread through Europe during these years was present in the

	Emigration from Europe
	Emigration from Japan
	Emigration from China
	Emigration from India
	Migration from European Russia

PACIFIC OCEAN

NEW ZEALAND
AND
AUSTRALIA
2 million

CALIFORNIA   ALASKA   JAPAN

UNITED
STATES
OF AMERICA
33.6 million
1821 to 1920

CANADA
2.3 million

ARCTIC
OCEAN

CHINA

WEST INDIES

SWEDEN

RUSSIA
550,000
1860 to 1900

SIAM   EAST INDIES

IRELAND   U.K.

GERMANY

INDIA

FRANCE

Odessa
2 million to USA
1890 to 1910

SPAIN   ITALY

INDIAN
OCEAN

GUIANA

MOROCCO

ALGERIA
764,000

ARABIA

Slaves
to Arabia

SOUTH
AMERICA
3.6 million

BRAZIL

Slaves

CAPE
COLONY
160,000
to 1888   NATAL

ATLANTIC
OCEAN

N

Number of Immigrants		
From Asia		700,000
Main groups		
Chinese	370,000	
Japanese	275,000	
From Canada		2,200,000
From Europe		30,000,000
Main groups		
Germans	5,000,000	
Irish	4,500,000	
Italians	4,500,000	
Poles	2,600,000	
English	2,600,000	
Jews	2,000,000	
From Latin America		900,000

MAP 25–1
Patterns of Global Migration, 1840–1900.   Emigration was a global process by the late 19th century, yet more immigrants went to the United States than to all the other nations combined.

HOW DID global migration alter societies of the late 19th century?

United States. These new immigrants were often regarded as being from less desirable racial stocks. As a result, turn-of-the-century immigrants often encountered serious prejudice and endured lives of enormous poverty. They also often settled into communities of people from their own ethnic background. What ultimately held them together were various private organizations, such as

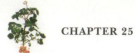

churches and synagogues, clubs, newspapers in their own languages, and social agencies they organized for themselves.

Although none of these immigrants faced the same legal discrimination as did American Blacks, the Jews encountered restricted covenants on real estate, obstacles to joining private clubs, and quotas for admission to many schools and universities. Asian immigrants to the U.S. West Coast faced harsher prejudice.

UNIONS: ORGANIZATION OF LABOR

The expansion of industrialism led to various attempts to organize labor unions. In America as in Europe, workers faced great resistance from employers and those who feared that labor unions might lead to socialism. Another difficulty arose from the social situation of the labor force itself. White laborers would not organize alongside Blacks. Different ethnic minorities would not cooperate. The ongoing flood of immigration ensured a supply of workers willing to work for low wages. Business owners more often than not could divide and conquer the sprawling, ethnically mixed labor force.

The first effort at labor organization occurred in the 1870s with the National Labor Union and railroad unions. In 1881, the American Federation of Labor (AFL) was founded. In contrast to earlier organizations and the advanced European socialist movement, such as that in Germany, it did not seek to transform the life of workers in a radical fashion but rather focused on higher wages and better working conditions. The AFL concentrated on organizing skilled

Ellis Island. In 1892, the federal government opened the immigration station on Ellis Island, located in New York City's harbor, where about 80 percent of the immigrants to the United States landed. As many as 5,000 passengers per day reported to federal immigration officers for questions about their background and for physical examinations, such as this eye exam. Only about 1 percent were quarantined or turned away for health problems.

Brown Brothers.

workers; it did not seek to organize whole industries. Among its most effective leaders was Samuel Gompers (1850–1924). Other unions, such as the United Mine Workers and the Railway Brotherhoods, organized workers by industry.

The industrialization of the United States—again, like that of Europe—saw major periods of business crisis or downturn. Serious depressions occurred in both the 1870s and the 1890s. There was no government relief. What little relief there was came from local authorities and private charities. This pattern would continue until the Great Depression of the 1930s. The economic turmoil of the 1880s and 1890s spawned violent strikes. Perhaps the most famous of these incidents was the breaking of the Pullman strike in Chicago in 1894 by federal troops. The major goal of labor thereafter was to achieve the full legal right to organize. Although the Clayton Act of 1914 moved in that direction, the clear right to organize with the protection of the federal government was achieved only through the legislation of Franklin Roosevelt's (1882–1945) New Deal in the 1930s.

Socialism was a path not taken by American labor and one not allowed to be taken. Leaders of the conservative unions worked against the Socialists, and spokesmen for business did everything possible to block their influence. Federal and state governments actively sought to repress socialist activities wherever they appeared. After the Bolshevik Revolution of 1917, virtually all American Socialists were persecuted as Bolshevists during the 1920s and beyond. The United States thus became the land where many social issues tended to be addressed by trade unions rather than by socialist parties. Furthermore, although many conservative American political and business leaders disliked them, unions were not legally attacked in the United States as they were in Britain, which led to the founding of the British Labour Party after the turn of the century.

In many European countries, socialist parties, or ministers like Bismarck who attempted to outflank the Socialists, had pressed their governments to pass legislation providing social security and other social services. As with so many other policies favorable to labor, no significant legislation of this kind was passed in the United States, at either the federal or state level, until the New Deal.

THE PROGRESSIVES

Much of the power in American politics in the decades after the Civil War, especially in cities, often lay in the hands of political bosses. This system depended on patronage at every level of government. In return for jobs, contracts, licenses, favors, and sometimes actual services, the boss expected and received political support. Government was a vehicle for distributing spoils. The point of boss politics was not merely venality; it was also a way, however crude and unattractive, of organizing the disorderly social and economic forces of the great cities. It was a way of managing cities that were growing as never before with highly diverse populations.

Toward the close of the century, reform-minded political figures began to emerge on the city and state levels. These reformers feared that people such as themselves from the White upper-middle classes might soon lose political and social influence. Deeply disturbed by the corruption of much of political life, these reformers found the urban environment with its slums an unacceptable picture of disorder. They wanted to see more efficient and less corrupt government. They also wanted the government to become a direct agent of change and reform. Pursuing these goals, they ushered in what has been called the *Progressive Era*, which lasted from approximately 1890 through 1914. Although the Progressives were reformers, they were not always liberal by later standards. For example, Progressives in the South often disenfranchised Blacks and poor Whites by imposing literacy tests and similar devices.

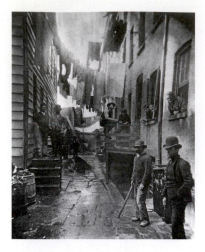

Bandits' Roost. The Progressive photographer Jacob Riis documented the squalor, poverty, and despair of New York City's slums at the turn of the century, including this famous 1888 shot of " Bandits' Roost" near Mulberry Street.

The Progressives began their reform work on the local level, especially in the cities, before they launched into national politics. The disorder and extreme disparity of wealth and poverty in the cities disturbed them. Urban reformers believed that the politics of bosses and patronage robbed cities of the money needed to make them livable places. In place of patronage, they demanded social and municipal services to clean up the cities. They repeatedly attacked special interests who blocked reform. Progressive mayors called for lower utility rates and streetcar fares and also attacked police corruption.

SOCIAL REFORM

Not only politicians joined the progressive crusade. Churches began to address the question of social reform. It was in this era that the "Social Gospel" was first preached, with its message that Christianity involved civic action. Young men and women began to work in settlement houses in the slums. The most famous was Chicago's Hull House, led by Jane Addams (1860–1935). Other young persons from the middle class became active in housing and health reform, education, and charities. They conducted extensive surveys of the poorest parts of the great cities. These people believed that the urban environment could be cleaned up and social order made to prevail. Their vision of such social order was that of the White middle class.

Beginning in the mid-1890s, progressivism began to affect state governments. There the impulse toward reform involved various attempts to protect whole classes of persons who were perceived as unable to protect themselves against exploitation, especially children and women working under unwholesome conditions for low wages. Other aspects of progressivism at the state level involved the civil-service requirements and the regulation of railways. Virtually all of these reformers partook of the cult of science that was so influential in the late 19th century. They believed that the problems of society were susceptible to scientific, rational management. The general public interest should replace special interests.

THE PROGRESSIVE PRESIDENCY

Roosevelt   Theodore Roosevelt became president in 1901 after the assassination of William McKinley (1843–1901). Roosevelt had been police commissioner of New York City and later a reforming governor of New York State. Roosevelt, in effect, created the modern American presidency. By force of personality and intelligence, he began to make the presidency the most important and powerful branch of government. As president, he began to set the agenda for national affairs and to define the problems that the federal government was to address. He surrounded himself with strong advisers and Cabinet members. He used his own knowledge of party patronage to beat the bosses at their own game.

In domestic policy, Roosevelt was determined to control the powerful business trusts. No centers of economic power should, through their organization, be stronger than the federal government. He successfully moved against some of the most powerful financiers in the country, such as J. P. Morgan and John D. Rockefeller. Through legislation associated with the term "Square Deal," Roosevelt attempted to assert the public interest over that of the various powerful special interests. He was not opposed to big business in itself, but he wanted it to operate according to rules established by the government for the public good.

In 1902, Roosevelt brought the moral power of the presidency to the aid of mine workers who were on strike. He appointed a commission to arbitrate the dispute. This was a major intrusion of the federal government into the economic system. It reversed the policies that had prevailed a decade earlier, when the government had used federal troops to break strikes. Roosevelt sought to make the presidency and the federal government the guarantor of fairness in economic relations. Thus he fostered the passage of the Pure Food and Drug Act and the Meat Packing Act in 1906, which protected the public against adulterated foodstuffs. Here again, the regulatory principle came to the fore. His conservation policies ensured that millions of acres of national forests came under the care of the federal government.

Roosevelt was associated with a vigorous, imperialistic foreign policy that had roots in the 1890s. In 1898, McKinley had led the nation into the Spanish-American War, and the United States had emerged as an imperial power with control of Cuba, Puerto Rico, Guam, and the Philippines. Roosevelt believed that the United States should be a major world power, and he sent a war fleet around the world. In Latin America, naval intervention assured the success of the Panamanian revolt of 1903 against Colombia. A treaty with the new Panamanian government allowed the United States to construct and control a canal across the Isthmus of Panama. The United States was following the model of the European great powers, which had been intervening in Africa and Asia. Like the other great powers, the imperialist policies of the United States were built on a conviction of racial superiority.

Roosevelt was succeeded in 1909 by William Howard Taft (1857–1930), his hand-picked successor. Taft disappointed Roosevelt, and in 1912 the election was a three-way contest among Taft, Roosevelt (running as a third-party candidate), and Woodrow Wilson. The Democrat Wilson won and brought a different concept of progressivism to the White House.

Wilson   Woodrow Wilson (1856–1924) was a former president of Princeton University and a reforming governor of New Jersey, where he had battled the bosses. While still an academic, he had criticized the weak presidency of the late 19th century. Wilson, like Roosevelt, accepted a modern industrialized nation. However, unlike Roosevelt, Wilson disliked big business almost in and of itself. He believed in economic competition in which the weak would receive protection from the government. Wilson termed his attitude and policy the New Freedom. Although he had pressed this idea during the campaign, in office he followed a policy of moderate regulation of business.

Wilson also had a different view of the presidency. He saw the office as responsible for leading Congress to legislative decisions. Wilson was the first American president since 1800 to deliver the State of the Union address to Congress in person. He presented Congress with a vast agenda of legislation and then worked carefully with the Democratic leadership to see that it was passed. Although Wilson appeared to be an advanced reformer, he retained many beliefs that have disappointed his later admirers. For example, he reinstated racial segregation in the federal civil service and opposed female suffrage.

Wilson had long seen his real goals in terms of domestic reform. But war broke out in Europe in August 1914. Although Wilson was reelected in 1916 on the slogan "He Kept Us Out of War," in April 1917, he led the nation into the European conflict. The expertise that he and other Progressives had brought to the task of efficient domestic government was then turned to making the nation an effective military force. These two impulses—the first toward domestic reform, the second toward a strong international role—had long marked the Progressive movement and would shape American history in the years after the war.

The American Progressives resembled political leaders of their generation in Great Britain. The Conservative Benjamin Disraeli (1804–1881) and liberals

Theodore Roosevelt. This 1905 cartoon portraying President Theodore Roosevelt, "The World's Constable," appeared in *Judge* magazine. In depicting the president as a strong but benevolent policeman bringing order in a contentious world, the artist Louis Dalrymple drew on familiar imagery from Roosevelt's earlier days as a New York City police commissioner.

The Granger Collection.

William Gladstone (1809–1898) and David Lloyd-George (1863–1945) had supported various measures of social reforms. Elsewhere in Europe political leaders in France and Germany had undertaken reforms in housing and urban life to forestall the advance of socialism and to address the problems of industrialization and urbanization. These leaders had favored unprecedented use of central government authority and the establishment of stronger governments.

THE EMERGENCE OF MODERN EUROPEAN THOUGHT

HOW DID science transform European thinking in the late 19th century?

natural selection According to Darwin, the process in nature by which only the organisms best adapted to their environment tend to survive and transmit their genes, while those less adapted tend to be eliminated.

At mid-century, learned persons viewed the world much as Newton had described it: as rational, mechanical, and dependable. Its laws could be discovered objectively through experiment and observation, and scientists could describe physical nature as it really existed. Science had become a recognized discipline at universities, and the word *scientist* was coined in the early 1830s. In the last quarter of the 19th century and the first decade of the 20th century, Western intellectuals began to portray physical reality, human nature, and society in ways different from those of the past. The vast change in thinking commenced in the realm of biology.

DARWIN'S THEORY OF NATURAL SELECTION

In 1859, Charles Darwin's (1809–1882) *On the Origin of Species* carried the mechanical interpretation of physical nature into the world of living things (see "Darwin Defends a Mechanistic View of Nature"). Darwin did not originate the concept of evolution, which had been discussed widely before he wrote the essay. What he and Alfred Russel Wallace (1823–1913) did, working independently, was to formulate the principle of natural selection, which explained how species change or evolve over time.

The two scientists contended that more living organisms come into existence than can survive in their environment. Those organisms with a marginal advantage in the struggle for existence (the "fittest") produce more surviving offspring and repopulate their species. This principle of survival of the fittest Darwin called **natural selection**. What neither Darwin nor anyone else in his day could explain was the origin of those chance variations that provided some living things with the new traits. Only after 1900, when the work on heredity of the Austrian monk Gregor Mendel (1822–1884) received public attention, did the mystery of those variations begin to be unraveled.

Darwin and Wallace's mechanistic theory removed the idea of preconceived divine purpose from organic nature. Thus it not only contradicted the biblical narrative of the Creation, but also undermined both the deistic argument for the existence of God from the design of the universe and the belief that the universe was a fixed, stable system. If the world of nature was in flux, it implied that society, values, customs, and beliefs might also be changeable.

In 1871, in *The Descent of Man*, Darwin applied the principle of evolution by natural selection to human beings. Darwin contended that humankind's moral nature and religious sentiments, as well as its physical frame, had evolved in response to the requirements of survival. Neither the origin nor the character of humankind required postulating a deity to explain their existence. Not since Copernicus had removed the Earth from the center of the universe had human pride received so sharp a blow.

Natural Selection. Theories about the evolution of humankind from the higher primates aroused enormous controversy. This caricature shows Darwin with a monkey's body holding a mirror to an apelike creature.

National History Museum, London, UK/Bridgeman Art Library.

THE REVOLUTION IN PHYSICS

By the late 1870s, many physical scientists were questioning whether mechanistic models, solid atoms, and absolute time and space truly described the real universe. In 1883, Ernst Mach (1838–1916) published *The Science of Mechanics,* in which he urged that scientists consider their concepts descriptive not of the physical world in itself, but of the sensations of the scientific observer. Similarly, the French scientist Henri Poincaré (1854–1912) urged that the theories of scientists be regarded as hypothetical constructs of the human mind rather than as true descriptions of nature. By World War I, few scientists believed they could portray the "truth" about physical reality.

X Rays and Radiation   Discoveries in the laboratory supported the view that nature was more complex than Newton had imagined. In December 1895, Wilhelm Roentgen (1845–1923) published a paper on his discovery of X rays, a form of energy that penetrated various opaque materials. Major steps in the exploration of radioactivity followed within months of the publication of his paper. In 1896, Henri Becquerel (1852–1908) discovered that uranium emitted a similar form of energy. The next year, J. J. Thomson (1856–1940), at Cambridge University, formulated the theory of the electron, and the interior world of the atom became a new realm for human exploration. In 1902, Ernest Rutherford (1871–1937) explained radiation as the disintegration of atoms of radioactive materials.

Theories of Quantum Energy, Relativity, and Uncertainty   The discovery of radioactivity and discontent with Newtonian mechanical models led to revolutionary theories in physics. In 1900, Max Planck (1858–1947) pioneered the quantum theory of energy, according to which energy is a series of discrete quantities, or packets, rather than a continuous stream. In 1905, Albert Einstein (1879–1955) published his first epoch-making papers on **relativity** in which he contended that time and space form a continuum and that measurement of time and space depends on the observer as well as on the entities being observed. In 1927, Werner Heisenberg (1901–1976) set forth his uncertainty principle. It states that the behavior of subatomic particles can only be inferred by statistical probability rather than observed as an outcome of cause and effect.

The mathematical complexity of 20th-century physics meant that science would rarely again be intelligible to the masses—although it was starting to affect daily life more than ever. Scientists from the late 19th century onward won the financial support of governments and private institutions for their work, and they have altered modern life more significantly than any other intellectuals.

FRIEDRICH NIETZSCHE AND THE REVOLT AGAINST REASON

During the second half of the century, philosophers, such as the German philosopher Friedrich Nietzsche (1844–1900), began to question the adequacy of rational thinking to address the human situation. Nietzsche was wholly at odds with the values of his era. He attacked Christianity, democracy, nationalism, rationality, science, and progress. He was less interested in changing values than in discovering their sources. He wanted to tear away the masks of respectable life and find out how human beings made such masks.

His first important work was *The Birth of Tragedy* (1872) in which he urged that the nonrational aspects of human nature are as important and noble as reason itself. He insisted that instinct and ecstasy had important functions and that to limit humankind to rational behavior was to impoverish human life. In

Marie and Pierre Curie. The Curies were two of the most important figures in the advance of physics and chemistry. Marie was born in Poland in 1869 but worked for most of her life in France. She is credited with the discovery of radium, for which she was awarded the Nobel Prize in 1911.

relativity   Theory of physics, first expounded by Albert Einstein in 1905, in which time and space exist not separately, but rather as a combined continuum.

HISTORY'S VOICES

DARWIN DEFENDS A MECHANISTIC VIEW OF NATURE

*I*n the closing paragraphs of On the Origin of Species *(1859), Charles Darwin contrasted the view of nature he championed with that of his opponents. He argued that an interpretation of organic nature based on mechanistic laws was actually nobler than an interpretation based on divine creation. In the second edition, however, Darwin added the term* Creator *to these paragraphs.*

WHY DOES Darwin believe a mechanistic creation suggests no less dignity than creation by God? How does the insertion of the term Creator change this passage? What is the grandeur that Darwin finds in his view of life?

Authors of the highest eminence seem to be fully satisfied with the view that each species has been independently created. To my mind it accords better with what we know of the laws impressed on matter by the Creator, that the production and extinction of the past and present inhabitants of the world should have been due to secondary causes, like those determining the birth and death of the individual. When I view all beings not as special creations, but as the lineal descendants of some few beings which lived long before the first bed of the Cambrian [geological] system was deposited, they seem to me to become ennobled. . . .

It is interesting to contemplate a tangled bank, clothed with many plants of many kinds, with birds singing on the bushes, with various insects flitting about, and with worms crawling through the damp earth, and to reflect that these elaborately constructed forms, so different from each other, and dependent upon each other in so complex a manner, have all been produced by laws acting around us. These laws, taken in the largest sense, being Growth with Reproduction; Inheritance which is almost implied by reproduction; Variability from the indirect and direct action of the conditions of life, and from use and disuse: a Ratio of Increase so high as to lead to a Struggle for Life, and as a consequence to Natural Selection, entailing Divergence of Character and the Extinction of less-improved forms. Thus, from the war of nature, from famine and death, the most exalted object which we are capable of conceiving, namely the production of the higher animals, directly follows. There is grandeur in this view of life, with its several powers, having been originally breathed by the Creator into a few forms or into one; and that, whilst this planet has gone cycling on according to the fixed law of gravity, from so simple a beginning endless forms most beautiful and most wonderful have been, and are being evolved.

Source: Charles Darwin, *On the Origin of Species and the Descent of Man* (New York: Modern Library, n.d.), pp. 373–374.

Nietzsche's view, the strength to live heroically and achieve great art derived from sources beyond rationality.

In later works, such as the prose poem *Thus Spake Zarathustra* (1883), Nietzsche criticized democracy and Christianity, claiming that they promoted mediocrity and sheepish behavior. He announced the death of God and proclaimed the coming of the *Overman* (Übermensch). The term was frequently interpreted as referring to a superman or superrace, but Nietzsche had in mind the kind of heroism that Homer had described and that had motivated the ancient Greeks. He thought the values of Christianity and of bourgeois morality prevented humankind from realizing its heroic potential.

In two of Nietzsche's most profound works, *Beyond Good and Evil* (1886) and *The Genealogy of Morals* (1887), he sought to uncover the social and psychological sources of judgments of good and evil. He claimed that morality was only a human convention and that when people realized this, they were freed to create new life-affirming values. Christianity and middle-class respectability could be replaced by a new moral order that glorified pride, assertiveness, and strength rather than meekness, humility, and weakness.

THE BIRTH OF PSYCHOANALYSIS

The major figures of late 19th-century science, art, and philosophy shared a determination to probe beneath surface appearances. They sought to discern the undercurrents, tensions, and complexities within atoms, families, rationality, and social relationships. This was particularly true of Sigmund Freud (1856–1939).

Development of Freud's Early Theories   In 1886, Freud, an Austrian Jew, opened a medical practice in Vienna, where he lived until driven out by the Nazis in 1938. His earliest medical interests were psychic disorders. In late 1885, he had studied in Paris with Jean-Martin Charcot (1825–1893), who used hypnosis to treat cases of hysteria.

In the mid-1890s, Freud abandoned hypnosis and began to urge his patients to talk freely and spontaneously about themselves. He found that they associated their particular neurotic symptoms with a chain of experiences going back to childhood. He also noted that sex was significant in his patients' problems. For a time, he thought that perhaps sexual incidents during childhood accounted for their illnesses. But by 1897, he had replaced that idea with a theory of infantile sexuality. He suggested that infants have sexual drives and energy and that these things do not simply emerge at puberty. He thus questioned the concept of childhood innocence and made sexuality one of the bases of mental order and disorder.

Freud's Concern with Dreams   During the same decade, Freud also examined the psychic phenomena of dreams. He believed that the seemingly irrational content of dreams must have a reasonable, scientific explanation. He concluded that dreams allow unconscious wishes, desires, and drives that had been excluded from everyday conscious life to enjoy freer play in the mind. During waking hours, the mind represses or censors certain wishes, which are as important to the individual's psychological makeup as conscious thought is. In fact, Freud argued, unconscious drives and desires contribute to conscious behavior. Freud developed these ideas in his most important book, *The Interpretation of Dreams* (1900).

Freud's Later Thought   In later books and essays, Freud developed a new model of the of the mind as an arena in which three entities struggle: the id, the superego, and the ego. The **id** consists of amoral, irrational, driving instincts for sexual gratification, aggression, and general physical and sensual pleasure. The **superego** embodies the external moral imperatives and expectations imposed on the personality by society and culture. The **ego**, by mediating between the impulses of the id and the standards of the superego, helps the personality cope with the inner and outer demands of its existence.

Freud was a realist who wanted human beings to live free of fear and illusion by rationally understanding themselves and their world. However, he understood the immense sacrifice of instinctual drives required for rational civilized behavior. It is a grave misreading of Freud to see him as urging humankind to thrust off all repression. He believed that excessive repression could lead to mental disorder, but he also believed that civilization and the survival of humankind required some repression of sexuality and aggression. Freud thought the sacrifice and struggle were worthwhile, but he was pessimistic about the future of civilization in the West.

QUICK REVIEW

Sigmund Freud (1856–1939)

- Founder of psychoanalysis
- Worked in Vienna until he was driven out by the Nazis in 1938
- Focused attention on infantile sexuality
- Emphasized the importance of what happens in the mind below the level of consciousness

id   According to Freudian psychoanalysis, the part of the mind that consists of amoral, irrational, driving instincts for sexual gratification, aggression, and physical and sensual pleasure.

superego   According to Freud, the part of the mind that embodies the external moral imperatives and expectations imposed on the personality by society and culture.

ego   According to Freudian theory, the part of the mind that mediates between the impulses of the id and the asceticism of the superego and allows the personality to cope with the inner and outer demands of its existence.

HOW DID Muslim thinkers respond to Western science?

QUICK REVIEW

Islam and the West

- European thinkers applied the same scientific critique to Islam as they did to Christianity and Islam

- European racism shaped attitudes towards Arabs

- Response to Western ideas and technology varied in the Islamic world

ISLAM AND LATE 19TH-CENTURY EUROPEAN THOUGHT

The few late 19th-century European thinkers who wrote about Islam interpreted it, consistent with the contemporary scientific outlook, as a historical phenomenon that, like the other great world religions, was only a product of a particular culture. The influential French writer Ernest Renan (1823–1892) and sociologists such as the German Max Weber, saw Muslim religion and cultures as incapable of developing science and closed to new ideas. Their views, however, were opposed by Jamal al-din Al-Afghani (1839–1897), an Egyptian intellectual, who argued that, given time, Islam (which was, afterall, 600 years younger than Christianity) would eventually produce cultures as modern as those in Europe.

European racial and cultural outlooks that denigrated non-White peoples framed concepts of the Arab world. Christian missionaries reinforced this by blaming Islam for Arab economic backwardness, for mistreating women, and for condoning slavery. Because the penalty for abjuring Islam is death, missionaries made few converts among Muslims. So they turned their efforts to founding schools and hospitals, hoping these Christian foundations would eventually lead some Muslims to Christianity. Few Muslims converted, but these institutions taught young Arabs Western science and medicine, and many of their students became leaders in the Middle East.

Within the Islamic world, political leaders who championed Western scientific education and technology confronted a variety of responses from religious thinkers. Some of these thinkers (the Salafi or the salafiyya movement, for example) believed there was no inherent contradiction between science and Islam. They believed that Muhammad had addressed the issues of his day and that similarly a reformed Islamic faith could modernize itself without imitating the West. This outlook, which had originally sought to reconcile Islam with the modern world, eventually led many Muslims in the 20th century to oppose Western influence.

Other Islamic religious leaders simply rejected the West and modern thought. They included the Mahdist movement in Sudan, the Sanussiya in Libya, and the Wahhabi movement in the Arabian peninsula (see Chapter 27). Religiously based opposition was strongest in those portions of the Middle East where the European presence was least direct—outside of Algeria, Egypt, Morocco, and Tunisia (which for all intents and purposes were under the control of Western powers by 1900), and Turkey, where Ottoman leaders had long been deeply involved with the West.

SUMMARY

Workers During the course of the 19th century, European workers underwent a process of proletarianization as the process of industrialization spread across the continent. To protect their interests, European workers joined trade unions and socialist parties, such as the Labour Party in Britain. The Marxist critique of modern capitalism strongly influenced European socialism when the German Social Democratic Party adopted the thought of Karl Marx. In Russia, Lenin founded the Bolsheviks as an elite Marxist party that advocated the overthrow of the tsarist regime through a revolution of workers and peasants.

Women In the 19th century, women were divided along class lines. Unlike working-class women, most women of the upper and middle classes adopted a cult of domesticity and did not work outside the home. Most jobs available to women were low paying and insecure. Women of all classes faced social, political, and legal disabilities that were only gradually improved in the late 19th and early 20th centuries.

Jewish Emancipation With the exception of Russia, European countries had abolished their legal restrictions on Jews by the mid-19th century. After 1880, however, anti-Semitism increased as Jews were blamed for economic and social problems.

The United States By 1914, the United States had become the world's leading industrial power. Despite the creation of a mass industrial work force, socialism did not take root in the United States. The United States also embarked on a more aggressive foreign policy.

Modern European Thought By the first decades of the 20th century, philosophers, scientists, psychologists, and artists began to portray physical reality, human nature, and society in ways that seem familiar to us today. Physicists probed the mysteries of the atom. Theories of evolutionary biology contended that human nature is part of the order of nature, traditional morality and the primacy of reason were challenged by Nietzsche and Freud. Within the Islamic world, modern European thought produced a variety of often conflicting responses.

REVIEW QUESTIONS

1. What accounts for the proletarianization of the European labor force?

2. How did industrialization affect working-class women? What were the social factors that limited the opportunities of women?

3. How did the ideas of Karl Marx come to dominate so much late 19th-century European socialism? Why did socialism not emerge as a major political force in the United States?

4. What caused the rise of trade unions and mass political parties?

5. Why were the debates of "opportunism" and "revisionism" important to the socialist parties? Why were there so many disputes among Socialists?

6. What were the major changes in science in the late 19th century?

IMAGE KEY

for pages 618–619

a. A Bull Moose Party campaign button.
b. Women laundry workers in the late 19th century, as painted by Edgar Degas (1834–1917).
c. *A Sunday on La Grande Jatte–1884*, by George Seurat (1859–1891).
d. Workmen repairing a sewer of London.
e. A crowd of Italian socialists depicted by Giuseppe Pellizza da Volpedo, *Il Quatro Stato*, 1901.
f. The Great Railroad Strike of 1877.
g. Jean Juares.
h. Textile production.
i. Factories spewing smoke over the English landscape.
j. Women working as operators at a telephone exchange.

KEY TERMS

Bolsheviks (p. 638)
Duma (p. 639)
ego (p. 649)
Fabians (p. 636)
id (p. 649)

Marxism (p. 635)
Mensheviks (p. 638)
natural selection (p. 646)
pogroms (p. 631)
proletarianization (p. 621)

relativity (p. 647)
revisionism (p. 636)
soviets (p. 639)
suffragettes (p. 630)
superego (p. 649)

  For additional study resources for this chapter, go to:
www.prenhall.com/craig/chapter25

26 Latin America from Independence to the 1940s

LEAL INTERPRETE
DE LOS "DESCAMISADOS"

CHAPTER HIGHLIGHTS

Economic Dependence In the 1820s, Latin America threw off Spanish and Portuguese rule. But the traditional elites remained in control. A series of strongmen called *caudillos* dominated most Latin American republics. Nor did independence bring economic prosperity. Because Latin American economies remained dependent on producing agricultural commodities for export, foreign nations dominated Latin American economic life. When commodity prices collapsed during the Great Depression, Latin American economies were devastated.

Argentina After independence, Buenos Aires came to dominate Argentina economically and politically. Agricultural exports, the growth of industry, and large-scale European immigration contributed to a strong export economy. However, urban social discontent and the growth of nationalism in the 1930s led to military intervention in politics and the dictatorship of Juan Perón from 1946 to 1956.

Mexico In the first decades after independence, Mexico was politically and economically unstable. Mexico lost half its territory to the United States, and it was invaded by France in the 1860s. The long-lasting dictatorship of Porfirio Díaz brought political stability but led to increasing discontent. The Mexican Revolution that began in 1911 produced cautious social and economic reform under the one-party rule of the PRI, the Institutional Revolutionary Party, which remained in power until the end of the century.

Brazil Brazil was a stable constitutional monarchy after independence until 1889. It also retained slavery until 1888. The establishment of a republic did not change Brazil's economic dependence on coffee exports, however, and the collapse of coffee prices in 1929 led to the dictatorship of Getulio Vargas. Although politically repressive, Vargas instituted social reforms and promoted industrial development, which continued to expand in the decade after his death in 1954.

CHAPTER QUESTIONS

HOW DID the absence of a social revolution affect Latin America after independence?

WHAT WAS the economy of dependence?

WHO WERE the *caudillos*?

WHY WAS the history of Brazil after independence different from that of Argentina and Mexico?

CHAPTER OUTLINE

· Independence Without Revolution

· Economy of Dependence

· Search for Political Stability

· Three National Histories

By the mid-1820s, Latin Americans had driven out their colonial rulers and broken the colonial trade monopolies. Although rich in natural resources, the region did not achieve widespread prosperity and political stability for more than a century after independence.

The explanations for why Latin America has been less stable and prosperous than Europe and North America lie in the role it played in the integrated global economic system that began to develop when it achieved political independence. This system prevented Latin Americans from achieving economic independence. The region's leaders thought their nations could prosper by providing raw materials to the world economy. Most Latin American nations developed export economies devoted to raw materials or semifinished goods. This decision made their export products vulnerable to worldwide fluctuations in demand. They were also susceptible to influence from foreign business interests and interference by U.S. and European governments.

Latin America had much in common with Africa and Asia during the 19th and early 20th centuries. In all three regions, areas would specialize by filling a niche to supply a particular raw product to the increasingly integrated world economy. While this economic strategy might bring initial prosperity, it provided too narrow a base for sustained economic well-being. In contrast, the economic advance of the United States and Europe was largely due to their ability to dominate and exploit niche economies around the globe.

INDEPENDENCE WITHOUT REVOLUTION

HOW DID the absence of a social revolution affect Latin America after independence?

IMMEDIATE CONSEQUENCES OF LATIN AMERICAN INDEPENDENCE

The wars of independence liberated Latin America from direct European control but left it economically exhausted and politically unstable (see Map 26–1). Only Brazil tended to prosper immediately after independence. In contrast, the new republics of the former Spanish Empire felt themselves vulnerable. Because the wars of independence had been civil wars, the new governments realized that many of their populations might welcome their collapse. Economic life contracted: In 1830, overall production was lower than in 1800. Rugged terrain over vast distances made interregional trade difficult. The old patterns of overseas trade had been disrupted. There was an absence of funds for investment. Many wealthy *peninsulares* departed. Consequently, Latin American governments and businesses looked to Britain for protection, markets, and investment.

Independence also created new sources of discontent. There was much disagreement about the character of the future government. Institutions, such as the Roman Catholic Church, sought to maintain their privileges. Indian communities found themselves subject to new exploitation. Quarrels arose between the **Creole** elites of different regions of the new nations. The agricultural hinterlands resented the predominance of the port cities. Investors or merchants from one Latin American nation found themselves in conflict with those of others over tariffs or mining regulations. Civilians became rivals of the military.

ABSENCE OF SOCIAL CHANGE

Yet all the elites opposed social reform. The Creole victors in the wars of independence granted equal rights to all persons and, except for Brazil, had abolished slavery by 1855. However, the right to vote depended on a property qualification, and peasants remained subservient to their landlords. Colonial racial codes disappeared, but not racial prejudice. Persons of white or nearly white complexion tended to constitute the elite of Latin America. Most important, there were no major changes in landholding; the ruling classes protected the interests of landholders.

Creole A person of European descent born in Latin America or the Caribbean.

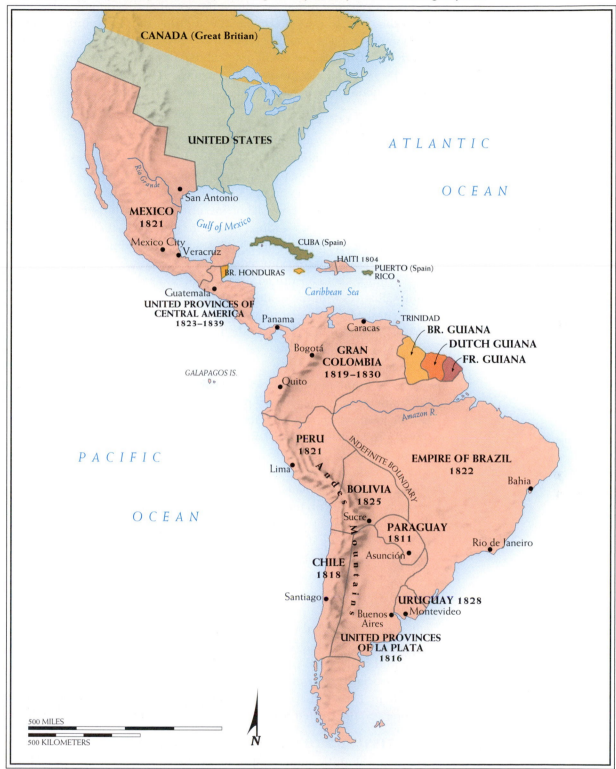

MAP 26–1

Latin America In 1830.   By 1830 most of Latin America had been liberated from Europe. This map shows the initial borders of the states of the region with the dates of their independence. The United Provinces of La Plata formed the nucleus of what later became Argentina.

HOW DID Brazil become a monarchy after independence?

Except for Mexico in 1910, no Latin American nation until the 1950s experienced a revolution that overthrew the social and economic structures dating from the colonial period. The absence of such social revolution is perhaps the most important factor in Latin American history during the first century of independence. The rise and fall of political regimes represented quarrels among the elite. Everyday life for most of the population did not change. Throughout the social structure, there was no mutual trust or allegiance to the political system.

CONTROL OF THE LAND

Most Latin Americans during the 19th century lived in the countryside. Agriculture was dominated by large *haciendas*, or plantations. The landowners ruled these estates as small domains. The *latifundia* (the large rural estates) grew larger during the 19th century from confiscated church lands and conquered Indian territories. Work was labor intensive because little machinery was available. For some products—salted meats, for example—there was a limited manufacturing stage in Latin America. Most crops, including grains, tobacco, sugar, coffee, and cacao, were exported.

Landowners constituted a society of their own. They sometimes formed family alliances with the wealthy urban classes who were involved in export commerce or the law. Younger sons might enter the army or the church. Landowners served in the national parliaments. Their wealth, literacy, and social connections made them the rulers of the countryside, and the army would protect them from any social uprising.

The rural work force was socially and economically dependent on the landowners. In Brazil, slavery persisted until 1888. In other rural areas, many people lived as virtual slaves. **Debt peonage** was widespread and often tied a peasant to the land like a serf. Later in the 19th century, the new lands that were opened were generally organized as large holdings with tenants rather than as small land holdings with independent farmers. This was different from both the United States and Canada. Poor transportation made internal travel difficult and kept many people on the land. Little effort was made to provide education, leaving Latin American peasants ignorant, lacking technological skills, and incapable of improving their condition.

The second half of the 19th century witnessed a remarkable growth in Latin American urban life. There was some movement from the countryside to the city and an influx of European and even Asian immigrants. Throughout this period there arose a political and social trade-off between the urban and rural elites. Each permitted the other to pursue its economic self-interest and repress discontent. Nonetheless, the growth of the urban centers shifted political influence to the cities and gave rise to an urban working class and the social discontents associated with many poor people working in difficult situations. Urban growth in Latin America created difficulties not unlike those that arose in Europe and the United States at about the same time.

SUBMISSIVE POLITICAL PHILOSOPHIES

The political philosophies embraced by the Creole elites also discouraged challenges to the social order. The political ideas associated with European liberalism, which flourished in Latin America after independence, supported republican government but limited the franchise to property holders. Thus in Latin America, as in Europe, liberalism protected property and tended to ignore the social problems of the poor. The Creole elite also exhibited racial prejudice toward non-Whites.

debt peonage System that forces agricultural laborers (peons) to work and live on large estates until they repaid their debts to the estate's owner.

Economic liberalism and the need for British investment led to free trade. After independence, Latin America exported less than it had under colonial rule and achieved a trade balance only by exporting precious metals. The general economic view was that Latin America would produce raw materials for export in exchange for manufactured goods imported from Europe, especially from Britain.

For most of the 19th century, the landed sector of the economy dominated because cheap imports and a shortage of local capital discouraged indigenous industrialism. Latin American liberals championed the great landed estates and the social dependence associated with them. The produce of the new land could contribute export goods to pay for the import of finished goods. Liberals thus favored confiscating land owned by the church and the Indians, because they did not exploit their lands in a progressive manner, according to the liberals.

During the second half of the century, **positivism**, the ideas of French philosopher Auguste Comte (1798–1857), swept across Latin America. Comte and his followers had advocated the cult of technological progress. This undemocratic outlook suggested that either technocrats or authoritarians could best achieve modernization. It was popular among military officers and influenced the ongoing Latin American struggle between civilian and military elites. The great slogan of Latin American positivism, emblazoned on the flag of the Brazilian republic, was "Order and Progress." Groups that challenged the existing social order were viewed as unprogressive.

Toward the close of the century, the officer corps was often the most important educated elite in a country. Their education and attachment to the army gave them influence, generally conservative.

Finally, European theories of "scientific" racism were used to preserve the Latin American social status quo. Racial theory could attribute the economic backwardness of the region to its vast non-white or mixed-blood population. This explanation shifted responsibility for the economic difficulties of Latin America away from the mostly white governing elites toward Indians, blacks, **mestizos**, and **mulattos**, who had long been exploited or repressed.

This conservative intellectual heritage affected 20th-century political thought. First, it can be seen in the tendency of military groups in Latin America to view themselves as the guarantors of order. They were ready to seize control from civilians to thwart social change. Second, it can be seen in the way the political elites of Latin America opposed communism after the Russian Revolution. Governments used the fear of communism to resist political movements—communist or not—that advocated social reform or questioned property arrangements. Communism would become an even more powerful issue after the Cuban Revolution of 1957 installed a communist state in Latin America.

A Chilean Cattle Estate. The great landowners of Latin America ruled their huge estates as small domains.

Sergio Larrain/Magnum Photos Inc.

positivism Philosophy of Auguste Comte that science is the final, or positive, stage of human intellectual development because it involves exact descriptions of phenomena, without recourse to unobservable operative principles, such as gods or spirits.

mestizos Persons of mixed Native American and European descent.

mulattos Persons of mixed African and European descent.

ECONOMY OF DEPENDENCE

*T*he wars of independence destroyed the colonial trade monopolies. But Latin America remained dependent on non-Latin American economies. Trade was free and the nations were independent, but other nations continued to shape Latin American economic life.

One of the chief reasons for this dependence was the absence of large internal markets. Trade after independence flowed in the same direction that it had flowed before independence because Europe remained the source of imports of finished goods. Furthermore, then as now, geographical barriers

WHAT WAS the economy of dependence?

hindered internal trade, and European and American investments in railways facilitated exports.

NEW EXPLOITATION OF RESOURCES

The wars of independence disrupted the Latin American economy. Mines were flooded; machinery was in disrepair; labor was dispersed. Agricultural production was also disrupted. To restore old industries such as mining, and gain access to steamships and railroads, Latin Americans had to turn to Europe and North America. For decades, Britain economically dominated Latin America. The desire to pour manufactured goods into Latin America led Britain and other nations to discourage the development of manufacturing industries there.

To pay for foreign imports, Latin American nations produced agricultural commodities. Production for the export market led governments to expand into unsettled territory and to confiscate the lands of the church.

After 1850, the Latin American republics became relatively more prosperous. Chile exported copper and nitrates as well as wheat. Peru exported guano for fertilizer. Coffee was becoming king in Venezuela, Brazil, Colombia, and Central America. Sugar continued to be produced in the West Indies and Cuba, which remained under Spanish control. Argentina supplied hides and tallow. But this limited prosperity was based on the export of agricultural commodities or raw materials and the importation of finished goods. Yet the export economy seemed to foster genuine economic growth.

Both the trading patterns for these goods and internal improvements in Latin American production linked the economy of the region to Europe and, after 1900, to the United States. Europeans and North Americans provided capital and the technological skills to build bridges, roads, railroads, steam lines, and mines. But whenever the economy of Europe or the United States floundered, Latin America was hurt. The region could not control its own economic destiny.

INCREASED FOREIGN OWNERSHIP AND INFLUENCE

During the late 19th century, the relative prosperity of the export sector increased the degree of dependence. The growing European demand gave Latin Americans a false sense of security. The vast profits to be made through mining and agricultural exports discouraged investment in local industry. Foreigners saw no reason to capitalize local industry that might replace imported goods. By late in the century, the wealthy in Latin America had, in effect, lost control of valuable sectors of their economy. For example, in 1901 British and other foreign investors owned approximately 80 percent of the Chilean nitrate industry.

Foreign powers also used their political and military influence to protect their economic interests. Britain, as the dominant power until the turn of the century, was frequently involved in the political affairs of the Latin American nations. From the Spanish-American War of 1898 onward, the United States began

20.7
Francisco Garcia
Calderón, "The North
American Peril"

Brazilian Coffee. This photograph shows Brazilian coffee being loaded onto a British ship. Most Latin American countries developed an export economy based on the exchange of agricultural products, raw materials, and semifinished goods for finished goods and services from abroad. Until recently, the coffee industry dominated both the political and economic life of Brazil.
Corbis-Bettmann.

to exercise more direct influence in the region. In 1903, to facilitate its plans to build a canal across Panama, the United States participated in the rebellion that allowed Panama to separate from Colombia. The U.S. military intervened in the Caribbean and Central America. By the 1920s, the United States had replaced Britain as the dominant trading partner of Latin America.

U.S. interventions were one cost of Latin America's dependent economy. More significant costs, however, arose from fundamental shifts in world trade that were brought on by World War I and continued through the 1920s. First, the amount of trade carried on by European countries decreased. Second, during the 1920s, world prices of agricultural commodities dropped. Latin American nations had to produce more goods to pay for their imports. Third, synthetic products manufactured in Europe or North America replaced the natural products supplied by Latin America. Finally, petroleum began to replace other natural products as an absolute percentage of world trade. This shift meant that petroleum-exporting countries, such as Mexico, gained a greater share of export income.

United States and Latin America. U.S. influence and investments in Latin America grew rapidly after 1900 and surpassed those of Britain by the 1920s. As this cartoon illustrates, the United States tended to regard its southern neighbors as at best junior and dependent partners.

Corbis-Bettmann.

ECONOMIC CRISES AND NEW DIRECTIONS

The Great Depression produced a crisis in this **neocolonial economy**. Commodity prices collapsed. The republics of Latin America could not repay their debts to foreign banks. The Depression led to the beginning of a new economic era in Latin America after the conclusion of World War II. It was marked by economic nationalism and a determination to create national economies that were not wholly dependent on foreign events and wealth.

With the Depression, it became necessary to substitute domestic manufactured goods for those imported from abroad. Various nations pursued policies called **import substitution**, and by the mid-1940s there were three varieties of manufacturing in Latin America. First, there were industries that, as in the past, transformed raw materials for export, such as food processing, mining, and petroleum refining. Second, there were industries addressing local demands, such as power plants and machine shops. Third, there were industries, basically assembly plants, that transformed imported materials to take advantage of cheap labor. None of this manufacturing involved heavy industry.

neocolonial economy
Economic relationship between a former colonial state and countries with more developed economies in which the former colony exports raw materials to and imports manufactured goods from the more developed nations.

import substitution
Replacement of imported goods with those manufactured domestically.

SEARCH FOR POLITICAL STABILITY

*T*he new states of independent Latin America had no experience in self-government. The Spanish Empire had been ruled directly by the monarchy and by Spanish-born bureaucrats. This monarchical or paternalistic heritage survived in the proclivity of the Latin American political elites to tolerate or support strong executives. The early republic constitutions were frequently suspended or rewritten, so that a strong leader could consolidate his power. Such figures were called *caudillos*. They usually came from the officer corps or enjoyed strong ties to the army. The real basis of their rule was force. Caudillos might support conservative causes, such as protection of the church or

WHO WERE the *caudillos*?

caudillo Latin American strongman, or dictator, usually with close ties to the military.

strong central government, or they might pursue liberal policies, such as the confiscation of church land, the extension of landed estates, and the development of education.

Even when caudillos were forced from office and parliamentary government was restored, the regimes that replaced them were neither genuinely liberal nor democratic. Parliamentary governments usually ruled by courtesy of the military and in the interest of the elites. No matter who ruled, the lives of most of the population changed little. Except for the Mexican Revolution of 1910, Latin American politics was run by and for the elite.

THREE NATIONAL HISTORIES

WHY WAS the history of Brazil after independence different from that of Argentina and Mexico?

*A*rgentina, Mexico, and Brazil possess more than 50 percent of the land, people, and wealth of the region. Their histories illustrate the general themes of Latin American history.

ARGENTINA

Argentine history from independence to World War II can be divided into three eras. From the rebellion against Spain in 1810 until mid-century, the question of which region of the nation would be dominant was foremost. From 1853 until 1916, Argentina experienced economic expansion and large-scale immigration from Europe, which transformed its society and its world position. From 1916 to 1943, Argentines failed to establish a democratic state and struggled with an economy they did not control.

Buenos Aires versus the Provinces In 1810, the junta in Buenos Aires overturned Spanish government. However, the other regions of the viceroyalty of Río de la Plata refused to accept its leadership. Paraguay, Uruguay, and Bolivia went their separate ways. Conflicts between Buenos Aires and the remaining provinces dominated the first 70 years of Argentine history. Eventually, Buenos Aires established its primacy because it dominated trade on the Río de la Plata.

A commercial treaty in 1823 established Great Britain as a dominant trading partner. Thus began a deep intermeshing of trade and finance between the two nations that would continue for more than a century. In 1831, the caudillo of the province of Buenos Aires, Juan Manuel de Rosas (1793–1877), negotiated the Pact of the Littoral, whereby Buenos Aires was put in charge of foreign relations and trade while the other provinces ran their own internal affairs. Within Buenos Aires, Rosas set up dictatorial rule. His major policies were expansion of trade and agriculture, suppression of the Indians, and nationalism.

Expansion and Growth of the Republic Rosas's success in strengthening Buenos Aires bred resentment in other provinces. In 1852, Rosas was overthrown. The next year a federal constitution was promulgated for the Argentine Republic, but Buenos Aires remained economically and politically dominant.

The Argentine economy was agricultural, the chief exports at mid-century being animal products. Internal

Argentina

1810	Junta in Buenos Aires overthrows Spanish government
1827–1852	Era of Rosas's dictatorial government
1876	Ship refrigeration makes possible export of beef around the world
1879–1880	Conquest of the Desert against the Indian population
1914–1918	Argentina remains neutral in World War I
1930s	Period of strong influence of nationalist military
1943–1956	Era of Juan and Eva Perón

transportation was poor and the country was sparsely populated. Technological advances changed this situation during the last quarter of the century. In 1876, the first refrigerator ship steamed into Buenos Aires. Henceforth, it would be possible to transport Argentine beef to Europe. Furthermore, it became clear that wheat could be farmed throughout the pampas. In 1879 and 1880, the army carried out a major campaign against the Indian population. The British soon began to construct and manage railways to carry wheat to the coast, where it would be loaded on British and other foreign steamships. Government policy made the purchase of land by wealthy Argentines simple and cheap. The owners, in turn, rented the land to tenants. The predominance both of large landowners and of foreign business interests thus continued throughout the most significant economic transformation in Argentine history.

The vastly increased production of beef and wheat made Argentina one of the wealthiest nations of Latin America and an agricultural rival of the United States. The opening of land, even if only for tenant farming and not ownership, encouraged many Europeans, particularly from Spain and Italy, to emigrate to Argentina. The immigrants also provided workers for the food-processing, service, and transportation industries in Buenos Aires. By 1900, Argentina had become much more urbanized and industrialized. More people had reason to be politically discontent. Moreover, the children of the immigrants often became the strongest Argentine nationalists during the 20th century.

Prosperity quieted political opposition for a time. The conservative landed oligarchy governed under presidents who perpetuated a strong export economy. Like similar groups elsewhere, they ignored the social questions raised by urbanization and industrialization.

However, the urban middle and professional classes wanted a greater share in political life and an end to corruption. In 1890, these groups founded the Radical Party. Its leader, Hipólito Irigoyen (1850–1933), was elected president in 1916. Without significant support in the legislature, his presidency brought few changes. In World War I, Argentina traded with both sides. Nonetheless, the war put pressure on the economy, and labor agitation resulted. Irigoyen used troops against strikers. Thereafter, the Radical Party pursued policies that benefited landowners and urban business interests. This was possible because of the close relationship between agricultural producers and processors and because both the landed and the middle classes resisted concessions to the working classes.

The Military in Ascendence   By the end of the 1920s, the Radical Party had become corrupt and directionless. The worldwide commodity depression hurt exports. In 1930, the military staged a coup. The officers returned power to conservative civilians, and Argentina remained dependent on the British export market.

In the 1930s, a right-wing nationalistic movement, *nacionalismo*, arose among writers, journalists, and a few politicians. It resembled the fascist political movements then active in Europe. Its supporters equated British and American domination of the economy with imperialism. They rejected liberalism, detested communism, were anti-Semitic, and supported the Roman Catholic Church. Nacionalismo advocated social reforms that recognized the needs of workers and the poor, but that also sought to promote social harmony rather than communist revolution or socialist reconstruction of the economy. In effect, these groups were anti-imperialistic, socially concerned, authoritarian, and sympathetic to the

nacionalismo Right-wing Argentine nationalist movement that arose in the 1930s and resembled European fascism.

Eva and Juan Perón. Eva was as influential as her husband during his years in power in the late 1940s and early 1950s. She was especially effective in attracting popular support for his government. They are shown here in a reception line in 1951.

Corbis-Bettmann.

Perónism Authoritarian, nationalist movement founded in Argentina in the 1940s by the dictator Juan Perón.

La Reforma The 19th-century Mexican liberal reform movement that opposed Santa Ana's dictatorship and sought to foster economic progress, civilian rule, and political stability. It was strongly anticlerical.

rule of a modern caudillo. World War II gave these attitudes and their supporters new influence.

The war closed most of Europe to Argentine exports, creating an economic crisis. In 1943, the military again seized control. Many of the officers were fiercely nationalistic children of immigrants. Some had become impressed by the fascist and Nazi movements and were hostile to Britain. They contended that the government must address social questions, industrialize the country, and liberate it from foreign economic control. In these respects, they echoed the *nacionalistas*.

Between 1943 and 1946, Juan Perón (1895–1974), one of the colonels involved in the 1943 coup, forged this social discontent and authoritarianism into a political movement known as **Perónism**. It was authoritarian, anticommunist, and socially progressive. Perón understood that political power could be exerted by appeals to the Argentine working class. He gained the support of the trade unions that were opposed to communism. In 1946, he made himself the voice of working-class democracy, even though he created an authoritarian regime that only marginally addressed industrial problems. He was aided by his wife, the former actress Eva Duarte (1919–1952), who enjoyed charismatic support among the working class.

Perón was the supreme 20th-century embodiment of the caudillo. His power and appeal were rooted in the antiliberal attitudes that had been fostered by the corruption and aimlessness of Argentine politics during the Depression. He was ousted in 1956, but stability would continue to elude Argentine politics.

Mexico

For the first century of Mexican independence, conservative forces held sway, but in 1910, the Mexican people launched the most far-reaching revolution in Latin American history.

Turmoil Follows Independence   The years from 1820 to 1876 were a time of turmoil, economic floundering, and humiliation. Independent Mexico attempted no liberal political experiments. Its first ruler was Agustín de Iturbide (1783–1824), who ruled until 1823 as an emperor. Thereafter, Mexico was governed by a succession of caudillo presidents, who depended on the army for support. The strongest of these figures was Antonio López de Santa Anna (1795–1863), a general and political opportunist who was finally exiled in 1855.

The mid-century movement against Santa Anna's autocracy was called *La Reforma*. In theory, its supporters were liberal, but Mexican liberalism was associated with anticlericalism, confiscation of church lands, and opposition to military influence on national life and politics. La Reforma aimed to produce political stability and civilian rule and attract foreign capital and immigrants. Its attack on the church led to further civil war. In January 1861, Benito Juárez (1806–1872) entered Mexico City as the temporary victor.

Political instability was matched by economic stagnation. The mines that had produced Mexico's colonial wealth were in poor condition, and the country could not repair them. The hacienda system left farming in a backward condition. Cheap imports of manufactured goods stifled domestic industries. Transportation was primitive. The government's remedy was massive foreign borrowing; as a result, interest payments consumed the national budget.

Foreign Intervention   Political weakness and economic disarray invited foreign intervention. The territorial ambitions of the United States led to war with Mexico in 1846 and the U. S. Army occupation of Mexico City. Mexico lost a vast portion of its territory, including what is now New Mexico, Arizona, and California.

Further foreign intervention occurred as a result of Juárez's liberal victory in 1861. Mexican conservatives and clerics invited the Austrian Archduke Maximilian (1832–1867) to become the emperor of Mexico. Napoleon III (r. 1852–1870) of France, who portrayed himself as a defender of the Roman Catholic Church, provided support for this venture. In May 1862, French troops invaded Mexico. Maximilian became emperor, but was unable to gain support from much of the population. In 1867, Juárez captured the unhappy emperor and executed him.

Díaz and Dictatorship   The liberal leaders continued their measures against the church but also failed to rally popular support. In 1876, Porfirio Díaz (1830–1915), a liberal general, seized power and retained it until 1911. He maintained one of the most successful dictatorships in Latin American history by giving almost every political sector something it wanted. He allowed landowners to purchase public land cheaply; he cultivated the army; and he made peace with the church. He used repression against opponents and bribery to cement the loyalty of his supporters. Wealthy Mexicans grew even richer, and Mexico became a respectable member of the international financial community. Foreign capital, especially from the United States, flooded the nation.

Yet problems remained. The peasants wanted land. Many Mexicans were malnourished. Labor unrest afflicted the textile and mining industries. Real wages for the working class declined. The Panic of 1907 in the United States disrupted the Mexican economy. By 1910, the *Pax Porfiriana* was unravelling.

Revolution   In 1911, Francisco Madero (d. 1913), a wealthy landowner and moderate liberal, led an insurrection that drove Díaz into exile. Shortly thereafter, Madero was elected president. He recognized the right of unions to strike, but was unwilling to undertake agrarian reform that might have changed the pattern of landholding. More radical leaders called for social change. Pancho Villa (1874–1923) in the north and Emiliano Zapata (1879–1919) in the south rallied mass followings of peasants who demanded fundamental changes in rural landholding. In late 1911,

Benito Juarez. Juarez led *La Reforma*, a mid-19th-century movement opposed to the autocracy of Santa Anna. He is portrayed with the tools of an engineer in front of a background of railway building to suggest his dedication to economic progress and modernization in Mexico.

Portrait of Benito Juarez. Oil on canvas, 1941. Presidential collection of portraits of Mexican Presidents. Corbis-Bettmann.

Mexico

1820–1823	Agustín de Iturbide rules as emperor
1833–1855	Santa Anna dominates Mexican political scene
1846–1848	Mexico defeated by United States and loses considerable territory
1861	Victory of liberal forces under Juárez
1862–1867	French troops led by Archduke Maximilian of Austria invade Mexico
1876–1911	Era of Porfirio Díaz
1911	Beginning of Mexican Revolution Zapata proclaims Plan of Ayala
1917	Forces of Carranza proclaim constitution
1929	Institutional Revolutionary Party (PRI) organized

The Mexican Revolution. The forces of Emiliano Zapata march on Xochimilco in 1914. Women fought alongside men and played other prominent roles during the Mexican Revolution.

UPI/Corbis-Bettman.

Zapata proclaimed his Plan of Ayala, which set forth a program of large-scale peasant confiscation of land. Much of the struggle during the next 10 years would be between supporters and opponents of such agrarian reform. (See Document: Emiliano Zapata Issues the Plan of Ayala.)

Madero was squeezed between conservatives and the radical peasant revolutionaries. No one trusted him. In early 1913, he was overthrown by General Victoriano Huerta (1854–1916), who had help from the United States. In the meantime, Venustiano Carranza (1859–1920), a wealthy landowner, put himself at the head of a large army that initially received the support of both Zapata and Villa. On August 15, 1914, Carranza's forces entered Mexico City. Thereafter, disputes between Carranza, Villa, and Zapata arose both from political rivalry and from Carranza's refusal to embrace radical agrarian reform. Carranza eventually won out.

Carranza's political skills helped him build a broad base and edge out Villa and Zapata as the chief leader of the revolution. He separated the concerns of urban industrial workers from the land hunger of rural peasants, and thus doomed the effort to implement an agrarian revolution.

In early 1915, Carranza's army attacked Villa and Zapata. The peasant leaders still commanded regional support but could not win control of the nation. During 1916, Carranza confronted U.S. military intervention along the border that continued until early 1917, when the United States became

HISTORY'S VOICES

EMILIANO ZAPATA ISSUES THE PLAN OF AYALA

By November 1911, the Díaz regime had fallen in Mexico, and Francisco Madero was attempting to establish a moderately liberal government. He was confronted by a major popular peasant revolution led in the valley of Morelos by Emiliano Zapata. On November 28, the rebel leader set forth his opposition to Madero and announced sweeping goals of land reform. Zapata never took dominant control of the Mexican Revolution, but the radical economic demands of his Plan of Ayala would influence the course of Mexican social development for the next 30 years.

WHY DID Zapata place so much emphasis on collective ownership of natural resources? What is Zapata's vision of future economic life? Who would be the winners and losers from his proposed policies?

. . . be it known: that the lands, woods, and water usurped by the *hacendados* [great landowners] . . . henceforth belong to the towns or citizens in possession of the deeds concerning these properties of which they were despoiled through the devious action of our oppressors. The possession of said properties shall be kept at all costs, arms in hand. The usurpers who think they have right to said goods may state their claims before special tribunals to be established upon the triumph of the Revolution.

. . . the immense majority of Mexico's villages and citizens own only the ground on which they stand. They suffer the horrors of poverty without being able to better their social status in any respect, or without being able to dedicate themselves to industry or agriculture due to the fact that the lands, woods, and water are monopolized by a few. For this reason, through prior compensation, one-third of such monopolies will be expropriated from their powerful owners in order that the villages and citizens of Mexico may obtain *ejidos* [agricultural communities], colonies, town sites, and rural properties for sowing or tilling, and in order that the welfare and prosperity of the Mexican people will be promoted in every way.

The property of those *hacendados* . . . who directly or indirectly oppose the present plan shall be nationalized, and two-thirds of their remaining property shall be designated for war indemnities—pensions for the widows and orphans of the victims that succumb in the struggle for this plan.

Source: James W. Wilkie and Albert L. Michaels, eds., *Revolution in Mexico: Years of Upheaval, 1910–1940.* Copyright © 1969 by Alfred A. Knopf, p. 46.

involved in World War I in Europe. Throughout the turmoil in Mexico, the U.S. government attempted to protect American interests through diplomacy and military intervention.

By 1917, after years of civil war, Carranza's forces wrote a constitution. Although the Constitution of 1917 set forth a program for ongoing social revolution—and political reform, it was never pursued with vigor. Years would pass before all the provisions of the constitution could be enforced, but it provided the goals and ideals toward which Mexican governments were expected to strive.

Carranza and his subordinates recognized the agrarian problem but were cautious about addressing it. They admired the economic development they had seen in California and were determined to modernize Mexican political life and attract capital investment; Mexican leaders would share these goals from that time onward. Thus, despite the radical rhetoric and the upheaval among peasants that the revolution involved, the Mexican revolution saw the victory of a middle-class elite who would attempt to govern through enlightened paternalism.

The decade after 1917 witnessed both confusion and consolidation. In 1919, Zapata was killed. Carranza was assassinated in 1920; Villa in 1923. In this turmoil, Carranza's generals provided stability. During the 1920s, they served as presidents. They moved cautiously and hesitated to press land redistribution but were opposed by the Roman Catholic Church. In 1929, Plutarco Elías Calles (1877–1945) organized the **PRI**, the Institutional Revolutionary Party, which remained in power for the rest of the century.

In 1934, Lázaro Cárdenas (1895–1970) was elected president and moved to fulfill the promises of 1917. He turned tens of millions of acres of land over to peasant villages and nationalized the oil industry.

With the election of Manuel Ávila Camacho (1897–1955) in 1940, the era of revolutionary politics ended. Thereafter, the major issues in Mexico were those associated with postwar economic development. But unlike other Latin American nations, Mexico, because of its revolution, could confront those issues with a democratic perspective and a sense of social responsibility.

BRAZIL

Postcolonial Brazil differed from other newly independent nations in the region. Its language and heritage were Portuguese, not Spanish. For the first 67 years of its independence, it had a stable monarchical government. And it retained slavery until 1888.

Brazil became an independent empire in 1822. The first emperor, Pedro I (r. 1822–1831), while serving as regent for his father, the king of Portugal, had put himself at the head of the independence movement. Although he granted Brazil a constitution in 1823, Pedro's high-handed rule led to his abdication in 1831. Brazilians then took hold of their own destinies.

His 15-year-old son, Pedro II (r. 1831–1889), assumed power in 1840 and governed Brazil until 1889. Pedro II established a reputation as a constitutional monarch by asking leaders of both the conservative and the liberal political parties to form ministries. Consequently, Brazil enjoyed political stability.

The Slavery Issue   The great divisive issue in Brazil was slavery. Sugar production remained the mainstay of the economy until the 1850s, when coffee cultivation began to dominate Brazilian agriculture. Like sugar planters, coffee producers also used slave labor, but their profits were much larger than those of the sugar producers, so a transition to free labor would have been easier for them. Coffee planters also tended to see themselves as economic progressives. Hence, people investing in coffee were more open to emancipation than those who had invested in sugar, which depended on slave labor to be profitable.

By 1850, Brazil had virtually ceased importing slaves. The end of slave imports doomed the institution of slavery because the slave population could not reproduce itself. It was nonetheless one issue to face this inevitability and another to abolish slavery.

The Paraguayan War of 1865–1870 postponed consideration of the slave question. This conflict pitted Brazil, Argentina, and Uruguay against Paraguay. The dictator of Paraguay, Francisco Solano López (1827–1870), fought a war

PRI   The Institutional Revolutionary Party, which emerged from the Mexican revolution of 1911 and governed Mexico until the end of the 20th century.

Antislavery Print.   Slavery lasted longer in Brazil than in any other nation in North or South America. Antislavery groups circulated prints such as this one published in France to illustrate the brutality of slave life in Brazil.

The Granger Collection, N.Y.

of attrition. His death in battle ended the war, but only after more than half of the adult male population of Paraguay had been killed.

The end of the war returned slavery to the forefront of Brazilian politics. Brazil and the Spanish colonies of Puerto Rico and Cuba were now the only slaveholding countries in the hemisphere. The emperor favored gradual emancipation. A law in 1871 freed slaves owned by the crown and decreed legal freedom for future children of slaves, but it required them to work on plantations until the age of 21. However, throughout the 1870s and 1880s, the abolition movement grew in Brazil. In 1888, Pedro II was in Europe and his daughter was regent. She favored abolition and signed a law abolishing slavery without compensation to the slave owners. Thus ended slavery in Brazil.

A Republic Replaces Monarchy   The law that abolished slavery also brought to a head other issues that in 1889 ended the monarchy. Planters who received no financial compensation for their slaves were resentful. Roman Catholic clerics were disaffected by disputes with the emperor over education. Pedro II was unwell; his daughter, the heir to the throne, was unpopular. The officer corps of the army wanted more political influence. In November 1889, the army sent Pedro II into exile.

The Brazilian republic lasted from 1891 to 1930. Like the monarchy, it was dominated by a small group of wealthy persons. The political arrangement that allowed the republic to function smoothly was an agreement among the state governors. The president was to be chosen alternately from the states of São Paulo and Minas Gerais. In turn, the other 18 governors had local political control. Fixed elections and patronage kept the system going. Literacy tests left few people qualified to vote. There was little organized opposition.

From the 1890s onward, the coffee industry dominated the nation. Around 1900, Brazil was producing more than three-fourths of the world's coffee. The crop's success led to overproduction. To meet this problem, the government subsidized prices with loans from foreign banks and taxes on the rest of the economy, which felt exploited by the coffee interests. Throughout the life of the republic, Brazil produced essentially a single product for export and few goods for internal consumption.

Economic Problems and Military Coups   The end of slavery, the expansion of coffee production, and the beginning of urban industry attracted foreign immigrants. They tended to settle in the cities and constituted the core of the early industrial labor force. In Brazil, as elsewhere, World War I caused major economic disruption. Urban labor discontent appeared. The failure to address urban and industrial social problems and the political corruption led to attempted military coups. The revolts demonstrated that segments of the military wanted a modern nation that was not dependent on a single exportable product and a political system that recognized interests besides those of the coffee planters.

Brazil

1822	Brazil becomes an independent empire
1840	Pedro II assumes personal rule
1840s and 1850s	Spread of coffee cultivation
1865–1870	Paraguayan War
1871	First law curbing slavery
1888	Slavery abolished
1889	Fall of the monarchy
1929	Collapse of coffee prices
1930–1945	Vargas Era
1957	Construction of Brasília begins
1964	Military takes control of the government

QUICK REVIEW

The Brazilian Republic
- 1889: Pedro III sent into exile
- Brazilian republic (1891–1930) controlled by small group of wealthy persons
- Coffee production dominated the Brazilian economy

Coffee had ruled as the economic "king" of the Brazilian republic, and its collapse brought the republic down with it. In 1929, coffee prices hit record lows, and the economic structure of the republic lay in shambles. In October 1930, a military coup installed Getulio Vargas (1883–1954) in the presidency. Vargas governed Brazil until 1945.

The Vargas years represent a major turning point in Brazilian history. Vargas was initially supported by the reform elements in the military, middle-class groups, and urban workers. In office, he was a pragmatist who wanted to hold on to power and modernize Brazil. Vargas recognized the new social and economic groups shaping Brazilian political life. First with constitutionalism and then with dictatorship, he attempted to allow the government to act on behalf of those groups without allowing them to influence or direct the government in a democratic manner. However, he did not form his own political party or movement as Perón would later do in Argentina. Vargas rather attempted to function like a ringmaster directing the various forces in Brazilian life. His failure to establish a genuinely stable institutional political framework for a Brazil that included many interest groups besides the coffee planters still influences Brazil.

Vargas and his supporters sought to lessen dependence on coffee by fostering industries that would produce domestically goods that had previously been imported from abroad. The policy succeeded, and by the mid-1930s, domestic manufacturing was increasing. Vargas also established a legal framework for labor relations that included an eight-hour work day and a minimum wage.

In the Brazilian context, these measures appeared reformist, if not necessarily liberal. However, in the late 1930s, Vargas confronted major political opposition and assumed dictatorial power in 1937. His regime thereafter was repressive. He claimed to have established an ***Estado Novo*** ("new state"). He presented himself as the protector of national stability against factions that would foster instability and of the national interest against international opponents.

Like the European dictators of the same era, Vargas used censorship, secret police, and torture. He also diversified and modernized the economy. In 1940, a five-year plan provided more state direction for the economy. His government favored the production of goods from heavy industry that would be used in Brazil itself. To maintain the support of trade unions, the state issued a progressive labor code. Siding with the Allies in World War II, Brazil built up large reserves of foreign currency through the export of foodstuffs. This economic activity and imposed political stability allowed the government to secure foreign loans for further economic development. By the end of the war, Brazil was becoming the major Latin American industrial power.

Participation in World War II on the side of the Allies had led many in Brazil to believe that they should not remain under a dictatorship. This attitude was widespread in the military, which had fought in Europe and established close contact with the United States. In 1945, the military carried out a coup, and Vargas retired temporarily from political life.

The new regime, which was democratic, continued the policy of economic development through foreign-financed industrialization. When in 1950 Vargas was elected president, his return to office was anticlimactic. He was elderly and past his prime. When a member of his staff became involved in the assassination of a journalist, the military demanded that Vargas resign. Instead, he took his own life in 1954.

In the decade after Vargas's death, Brazil remained a democracy, although an unstable one. The government began to undertake vast projects such as the

---

QUICK REVIEW

Getulio Vargas (1883–1954)

- October 1930: Vargas comes to power in military coup
- Vargas sought to represent a wider spectrum of Brazilian society without giving up personal power
- Assumed dictatorial power in 1937

Estado Novo "New state" based on political stability and economic and social progress supposedly established by the dictator Getulio Vargas after 1937.

OVERVIEW   LATIN AMERICA'S DEPENDENT ECONOMY

After independence, most Latin American nations relied on export economies that sold raw materials or semifinished goods, such as animal hides and leather, to the world's economy. Most manufactured goods were imported, primarily from Britain. This created a dependent economy in which Latin American prosperity depended on other nations to pay high prices for its raw materials. What made this dependence even more precarious was that most Latin American nations relied on one or two products for their export earnings. When prices for these products fell or collapsed, as they did during the Great Depression of the 1930s, Latin America had little else to trade, and its prosperity plummeted. The table below shows the main products of the principal Latin American countries between the 1820s and 1930.

Argentina	animal products (meat, leather, wool), grain
Bolivia	tin, silver
Brazil	coffee, sugar, rubber
Chile	copper
Colombia	coffee, cattle
Ecuador	bananas
Mexico	silver, cattle, oil
Peru	nitrates, silver
Uruguay	animal products (meat, leather)
Venezuela	coffee, cattle

costly construction of the new capital of Brasília, begun in 1957. The rapid growth of cities and the expansion of a working class radicalized political life. The political system could not readily accommodate itself to the concerns of workers and the urban poor. Poverty and illiteracy plagued both the cities and the countryside.

By the early 1960s, when President João Goulert (1918–1977) took office, Brazilian political life was in turmoil. Goulert's predecessors, including Vargas, had attempted to balance interests and political forces. However, Goulert committed himself to the left. In 1964, he announced his support for land reform, which was anathema to conservatives. Goulert also questioned the authority of the military hierarchy. In March 1964, the military, claiming to protect Brazil from communism, seized control of the government, ending its post–World War II experiment with democracy.

SUMMARY

Economic Dependence In the 1820s, Latin America threw off Spanish and Portuguese rule. But the traditional elites—landowners, military officers, the church—remained in control. A series of strongmen called caudillos dominated most Latin American republics. Nor did independence bring economic prosperity. Because Latin American economies remained dependent on producing agricultural commodities for export, foreign nations, particularly

IMAGE KEY
for pages 652–653

a. A Mexican felt hat.
b. Eva Perón
c. Coffee beans.
d. *Orgy-Night of the Rich*, 1926, by Diego Rivera.
e. El Toro, a black bull.
f. Juan and Eva Perón in 1951.
g. *De Indio y Mestiza Nace Coyote*; South American painting.
h. General Juan Manuel de Rosas.
i. Porters carrying bags of coffee beans.
j. Mexico's civil war leader Emiliano Zapata's forces are seen here marching to Xochimico.

Britain, dominated Latin American economic life. When commodity prices collapsed during the Great Depression, Latin American economies were devastated. The crisis did, however, lead to the beginnings of manufacturing in many Latin American countries in an effort to avoid dependence on imports.

Argentina After independence, Buenos Aires came to dominate Argentina economically and politically. Agricultural exports, the growth of industry, and large-scale European immigration contributed to a strong export economy. However, urban social discontent and the growth of nationalism in the 1930s led to military intervention in politics and the corporatist dictatorship of Juan Perón from 1946 to 1956.

Mexico In the first decades after independence, Mexico was politically and economically unstable. Mexico lost half its territory to the United States and was invaded by France in the 1860s. The long-lasting dictatorship of Porfirio Díaz brought political stability but led to increasing discontent. The Mexican Revolution that began in 1911 produced cautious social and economic reform under the one-party rule of the PRI, the Institutional Revolutionary Party.

Brazil Brazil was a stable constitutional monarchy after independence until 1889. It also retained slavery until 1888. The establishment of a republic did not change Brazil's economic dependence on coffee exports, however, and the collapse of coffee prices in 1929 led to the dictatorship of Getulio Vargas. Although politically repressive, Vargas instituted social reforms and promoted industrial development.

REVIEW QUESTIONS

1. What was the condition of the Latin American economies after independence? What role did their economies play in the worldwide economy that developed in the 19th century?

2. Did the structure of Latin American societies change after independence? What role did the traditional elites play in the economic and political life of their nations? What was the condition of the mass of the population?

3. How did European and U.S. investments affect Latin America?

4. Why did Latin American nations find it difficult to develop stable regimes? What role did the military play?

5. How did European immigration affect Argentina? Why was Juan Perón able to hold power?

6. How did the Vargas regime change the Brazilian economy? Why did Brazilian democracy end in a military coup in 1964?

KEY TERMS

caudillo (p. 659)

Creole (p. 654)

debt peonage (p. 656)

Estado Novo (p. 668)

import substitution (p. 659)

La Reforma (p. 662)

mestizos (p. 657)

mulattos (p. 657)

nacionalismo (p. 661)

neo-colonial economy (p. 659)

Perónism (p. 662)

positivism (p. 657)

PRI (p. 666)

 For additional study resources for this chapter, go to:
www.prenhall.com/craig/chapter26

27 India, the Islamic Heartlands, and Africa
The Challenge of Modernity (1800–1945)

CHAPTER HIGHLIGHTS

Western Encroachment   The century and a half following the French Revolution was a bleak one for the Indian subcontinent, Africa, and the Islamic societies. For centuries there had been a rough balance among the major cultural regions of the world. Suddenly, over the span of 150 years, Europe came to dominate the globe.

The Middle East, Africa, Iran, Central Asia, India, and Indonesia-Malaysia, along with Central and South America—what is today referred to as "the Third World" of "developing nations"—were most drastically affected by European imperialism and colonialism. Regardless of indigenous developments in these regions, the decisive development of this era was unprecedented domination by the west.

Reactions of Native Peoples   The vitality of so many of the cultures and traditions that bore the brunt of the Western onslaught has been striking. Arab, Iranian, Indian, African, and other encounters with Western material and intellectual domination produced different responses and initiatives. These have borne full fruit in political, economic, and intellectual independence only since 1945; however, most began much earlier, some even well before 1800. The imperial-colonial experiences of the Third World nations may well prove to have been not only ones of misery and reversal, but also of transition to positive development and resurgence, despite the looming economic, educational, and demographic problems that plague many of them.

K. ATA TURK

Congo. No. 63. Caravane d'Ivoire à vendre.

CHAPTER QUESTIONS

HOW DID British rule affect India?

WHAT ROLE did Gandhi play in ending British rule in India?

WHY DID Islamic reform movements arise during the eighteenth century?

WHAT WERE the three typical Islamic reactions to Western encroachment?

WHAT WERE the main Islamic reform movements in nineteenth-century Africa?

HOW DID Africans react to European colonialism?

CHAPTER OUTLINE

THE INDIAN EXPERIENCE

- British Dominance and Colonial Rule
- From the Raj to Independence

THE ISLAMIC EXPERIENCE

- Islamic Responses to Declining Power and Independence
- Western Political and Economic Encroachment
- The Western Impact
- Islamic Responses to Foreign Encroachment

THE AFRICAN EXPERIENCE

- New States and Power Centers
- Islamic Reform Movements
- Increasing European Involvement
- African Resistance to Colonialism: The Rise of Nationalism

The encroachment of the European nations on the rest of the world from the late 15th century onward brought radical changes. In the West itself, spiritual and material disruption accompanied the Renaissance, the Reformation, the Enlightenment, and the Industrial and Scientific revolutions. The effects of these watershed European developments on the Indian, Asian, and African worlds came more rapidly, in greater concentration, and with less preparation than they had in the West.

*To call these complex processes of "modernization" does not reflect the acute differences between the relatively lengthy and gradual processes of change in Western Europe and the more rapid and disruptive changes that European imperialism and colonialism brought to other parts of the world. The very concept of "modernity" has been appropriated by the West. Western dominance has led it to a specific and novel notion of modernity: namely, as a special set of ideas and institutions that evolved in Europe between the Renaissance and the early 20th century and was then gradually exported to, or imposed on, other societies. The expression "**the impact of modernity**" refers to how the introduction of "modern" Western civilization affected traditional cultures.*

The consequences of the spread of Western culture have been so massive that today non-Western peoples are often merely its passive recipients. The American or European view of the world often portrays the West as the active, creative, dominant force in recent history, as though the rest of the world were some monolithic, archaic entity.

As parochial as such chauvinistic generalizations are, the impingement of the West has been a major element in the recent history of African, Asian, and Indian civilizations. Yet in all of these "Third World" areas, Western modernity entered cultures that had ancient and highly developed traditions of their own. These traditions did not simply melt away on the arrival of the Westerners. Rather, a profound transformation took place that sought to balance the challenges of modernity with tradition.

impact of modernity Effect of western political, economic, and social ideas and institutions on traditional societies.

HOW DID British rule affect India?

THE INDIAN EXPERIENCE

BRITISH DOMINANCE AND COLONIAL RULE

*I*n the 18th century, Britain became the dominant naval and commercial power in the southern seas. In India by the early 19th century, the British had built the largest European colonial empire in the Afro-Asian world. India was the "jewel in the crown" of that empire.

BUILDING THE EMPIRE: THE FIRST HALF OF THE 19TH CENTURY

It was no simple undertaking for Britain to penetrate multiethnic, multilingual, multiconfessional India. To do so, the British had to convince various stratas of Indian society and various ethnic groups that cooperation with Britain's imperial enterprise was in their best interests.

A half century before the British Crown asserted direct rule over India in 1858, the British wielded effective imperial control through the East India Company. Those areas not annexed were recognized as independent princely states. They retained their status only so long as they remained faithful to Britain. The India that resulted was a polyglot mixture of tributary states and provinces that the British administered directly.

The economic impact of company rule was extensive. The need for ever higher revenues squeezed peasants. In addition, demand for Indian indigo, cotton, and opium in the China and British trade also decreased in the 1830s, and famines brought widespread suffering.

Company rule also affected the physical face of India. Company policies encouraged settled agriculture and small commodity production at the expense of the nomadic and pastoralist cultures of North and central India. British "pacification" involved the clearing of land to deny natural cover to military enemies and the often-forced settlement of peasants in new regions. Early in the 19th century, European loggers caused extensive deforestation as, after 1840, did the tracts leveled for tea and coffee plantations in Assam and the Bengal hills. This ecological destruction was part of the transformation of India into a more homogeneous peasant farming society that provided a better base for colonial administration.

The Indians were by no means passive in the face of this exploitation. The first half of the 19th century saw almost constant revolt in one place or another. The revolts included peasant movements of noncooperation, Muslim farm workers' attacks on British and Hindu estate owners, grain riots, tribal revolts, and other actions. They culminated in the Indian Revolt of 1857.

The immediate trigger of the Indian Revolt was the concern among Bengal troops that animal grease on newly issued rifles exposed them to ritual pollution, a violation of the rules of their religion. Behind this issue, however, lay other grievances, including the addition of Sikhs, Gurkhas, and lower-caste soldiers to the army; deteriorating economic conditions; outrage at excessive tax rates; and anger at the 1856 British annexation of the princely state of Awadh. Another contributing factor to the revolt was the desire to rebuild a pre-British political order in North India. The revolt was not an all-India affair. It centered on Delhi, where the last Mughal emperor joined in the rebel cause.

The British eventually won the day. With their forces augmented by Sikhs from the Panjab and Gurkhas from Bengal, they overcame the divided Indian opposition. By the end of 1857, the revolt was broken, often with great brutality. In 1858, the East India Company was dissolved, and India came under direct rule of the British Crown.

The "Mutiny" of 1857 was not a nationalist revolution, but a series of antiforeigner, anti-British spontaneous uprisings. Still, it highlighted resentment of the burdens of foreign domination that were to grow increasingly oppressive for Indians of all regions and religions during the ensuing 90 years of crown rule, known as the **raj**.

BRITISH–INDIAN RELATIONS

The overall impact of British presence on the Indian masses was brutal but impersonal and largely economic. India was effectively integrated into Britain's economy, becoming a market for British goods, providing Britain with raw materials and other products, and helping Britain maintain a healthy balance of trade.

British cultural imperialism was never a major nor even an official policy of the East India Company. Nonetheless, the British–Indian relationship had a paternalistic and patronizing dimension, both before and after the events of 1857. The ethos of the British rulers included the understanding that they had the task of governing an inferior "race" that could not handle the job by itself. Even Indians whose university degrees or army training were impeccable by British standards were never accepted as equals. From army to civil-service ranks, the upper echelon of command was British.

Despite this unequal relationship, British ideas influenced a small but powerful Indian elite in both their business and political life and their manners and

20.4
Lord William Bentinck, Comments on Ritual Murder and the Limits of Religious Toleration

raj The years from 1858 to 1947 during which India was governed directly by the British Crown.

The Indian Mutiny of 1857. The mutinous Sepoy cavalry attacking a British infantry division at the 1857 battle of Cawpore. Although the uprising was suppressed, it was not easily forgotten. In its aftermath the British reorganized the government of India.

The Granger Collection, New York.

customs. Conversion to Christianity was rare, but Christian and secular values associated with the European Enlightenment influenced Hindu and Muslim educated classes.

In the 19th century, probably the most influential member of the Indian elite to engage the British on their own ground was Ram Mohan Roy (1772–1833). Roy, a Bengali Hindu, rose to the top of the native ranks of East India Company service and became a strong voice for reform, both of Hindu life and of British colonial policy. Roy was a modernist who wanted to meld the best of European-Christian morality and thought with the best of Hindu piety and thought. He opposed autocratic and unfair British legal and commercial practices and campaigned in India and England to reform the company's India policies. He studied the Christian scriptures and the great thinkers of European civilization and drew on these sources in his Hindu reform efforts. His public campaigns for education, political involvement, and social progress against the "backward" practices and ideas of many of his Hindu compatriots alienated most of the leading Hindu thinkers of his age, but 20th-century Indians have often seen him as a visionary.

While many Indians sought to acquire British ways and join the British in business and administration, many more resented their subordinate status. The antiimperial sentiment that blossomed into the nationalist movement at the end of the 19th century extended to the grass-roots level—among tribal groups, peasant farmers, and workers. Whatever their status, the distrust and animosity most Indians felt continued to grow.

FROM THE RAJ TO INDEPENDENCE

THE BURDEN OF CROWN RULE

The Revolt of 1857 had numerous consequences beyond the transfer of the administration of India to the British Crown. The bloody conflict exacerbated mutual fear and hatred. Before the revolt, the British had maintained a largely native army under British officers. After the revolt, they tried to maintain a ratio of at least one British to three Indian soldiers. The army was financed by Indian, not British, revenues. This imposed a huge economic burden on India, diverting one third of its annual revenues to pay for its own occupation.

British economic policies and accelerating population growth put great strains on India's poor. Cheap British goods were exchanged for Indian raw materials and the products of its home industries, harming Indian craft industries and forcing multitudes into poverty or onto the land. Industrialization, which might have provided work for India's unemployed masses, was avoided. Finally, many peasants lost their hereditary lands because of other British policies, forcing thousands to emigrate to Britain's dominions in South Africa, where they worked as indentured servants.

The Revolt of 1857 also created a poisonous distrust of Indians within the British colonial administration. **Cantonments** segregating White masters from natives became the rule in Indian cities. Despite the intentions expressed in royal statements and the opening of the civil service to Indian candidates, at least nominally, the raj discouraged equality between Indian and Britisher.

INDIAN RESISTANCE

Indians soon took up political activism. Late in the 19th century, they founded the institutions that would help overcome regionalism, build national feeling, and end colonial rule. In 1885, Indian modernists formed the Indian National Congress. The Muslim league developed as a counterbalance to the Hindu-dominated Congress. The league ultimately worked for, and gained, a separate independent Muslim state, Pakistan. Erratic British policies strengthened the desire for independence.

Besides the British themselves, Indian internal divisions were the major obstacle to independence. These divisions included the many language groups and subject princely states of the subcontinent. These, however, were not even the most critical divisions. For much of British rule, every Indian politician was first a representative of his own region or state and second an Indian nationalist. Furthermore, the Indian elite had little in common with the masses beyond antagonism to foreign rule, making unified resistance difficult. Conflict among Hindus, Muslims, Sikhs, and Jains also impeded concerted political action.

Yet a nationalist movement took root. Three principal elements within the independence movement led to the creation of India and Pakistan in 1947.

WHAT ROLE did Gandhi play in ending British rule in India?

 27.2 Gandhi and Nehru: "Two Utterly Different Standpoints": Jawaharal Nehru

cantonments Segregation of areas in which Europeans lived in British-ruled India from those areas inhabited by native Indians.

Faces of the Raj. A tennis party at the Residency, Kapurkala, Punjab, ca. 1894.

Hulton/Corbis-Bettman.

India

1772–1833	Ram Mohan Roy, Hindu reformer
1857–1858	Indian Revolt of 1857, followed by direct crown rule as a British colony
1885	Indian National Congress formed
1869–1948	Mohandas K. Gandhi
1873–1938	Muhammad Iqbal
1876–1949	Muhammad Ali Jinnah
1889–1964	Jawaharlal Nehru
1947	Independence and partition

"Mahatma" Mohandas K. Gandhi. Also known as the "Great Soul," Gandhi is honored as the father of the modern state of India.

UPI/Corbis-Corbis-Bettmann.

The first element consisted of those in the National Congress who sought gradual reform and progress toward Indian self-governance, or *svarāj*. This position did not preclude opposition to the British, but it did mean trying to change the system from within. Among the proponents of this approach were the spiritual and political genius Mohandas K. Gandhi (1869–1948) and his follower Jawaharlal Nehru (1889–1964). Nehru became the first prime minister of India. Gandhi was the principal Indian leader after World War I and directed the all-India drive that finally forced out the British. An English-trained lawyer, Gandhi drew not only on his own Hindu (and Jain and Buddhist) heritage, but also on the ideas of Western liberal and Christian thinkers. In the end, Gandhi became a world figure.

The second element consisted of the militant Hindu nationalists, whose leader, the extremist B. G. Tilak (1856–1920), stressed the use of Indian languages and a revival of Hindu culture and learning. Tilak also subscribed to an anti-Muslim, Hindu communalist vision of Indian self-governance. The Hindu extremists looked to a return to traditional Indian values and self-sufficiency. Their ideas still influence Indian political life, as the resurgence of Hindu extremist groups in recent years and communal strife, especially with Muslims, are unhappy testimony.

Muslims made up the third element. The subcontinent held many divergent regional and sectarian Muslim constituencies. Their leaders could be brought to make common cause only by the fear that, as a minority, Muslims stood to lose what power they had in a Hindu-majority, all-India state. Muslims had been slower than the Hindus to take up British ideas and education and thus lagged behind the Hindu intelligentsia in numbers and influence with the British or other Indians.

HINDU–MUSLIM FRICTION ON THE ROAD TO INDEPENDENCE

In the 20th century, the rift between Muslims and Hindus in the subcontinent grew wider. In the end, the great Indo-Muslim poet and thinker, Muhammad Iqbal (1873–1938), and the "founder of Pakistan," Muhammad Ali Jinnah (1876–1949), helped move Muslims to separatism.

The independence of India and Pakistan from Western domination was only achieved with violence. Blood was spilled in the long battle with the British, in communal violence between Hindus and Muslims that accompanied partition in 1947, and in the ongoing dispute over Kashmir between India and Pakistan. Still, the victory of 1947 gave the people of the subcontinent, Indians and Pakistanis, at last a sense of participation in the world of nations on their own terms instead of on those dictated by a foreign power. The British left a legacy of unity and egalitarian and democratic ideals that Indian nationalists turned to their own uses.

THE ISLAMIC EXPERIENCE

ISLAMIC RESPONSES TO DECLINING POWER AND INDEPENDENCE

*T*he 18th century saw the weakening of the great Muslim empires and the increasing ascendancy of the West. The diverse Islamic peoples and states were thrust into a struggle for survival. The decline of Islamic preeminence was also the result of internal problems.

By the 18th century, the largest Muslim empires had declined from their heydays in the 16th and 17th centuries. They had grown decentralized, were less stable economically and politically, and were increasingly dominated by entrenched hereditary elites. For millennia, the Middle East had prospered by providing the trade link between Europe and Asia, but modern sea routes made the region more peripheral to a world economy centered on Western Europe. The Middle East, however, became enmeshed in the European imperial competition for its industrial resources, particularly oil. As the Western powers asserted dominance over the region, conflict ensured. But Muslim intellectuals also began to study the basis for European ascendancy and to question whether European values, education, and technology could be used to revitalize the Islamic world without totally secularizing it.

During the 18th century, reform movements sought to revive Islam as a comprehensive guide for living and to purify it from the more stultifying developments in Islamic societies during the preceding centuries. In major urban areas, reformers sought to reenginer the armies, institutions and soceities of the Middle East to conform to the reality of European domination. As they sought to adapt to contemporary society, they emphasized the malleability of Islam. However, in rural areas less touched by European influence, reformers rejected the more flexible forms of Islam and Western models.

The most famous of these movements was that of the **Wahhabis**, the followers of Ibn Abd al-Wahhab (1703–1792) in Arabia. It sought to combat excesses of popular and Sufi piety to break the stranglehold of the *ulama*'s conformist interpretations of legal and religious issues. The only authorities were to be the Qur'an and the traditions of the Prophet. Allied with a local Arab prince, Sa'ud, the Wahhabi movement swept much of the Arabian peninsula. It was crushed in the early 19th century by the Ottomans. It finally saw victory under a descendant of Sa'ud at the onset of the 20th century and has become the guiding ideology of Saudi Arabia.

Other Muslim reform movements reflected similar revivalist and even militantly pietist responses to Islamic decadence and decline. This call continues to rally movements from Africa to Indonesia. In Islamic societies everywhere in recent times, it has provided a response to the challenge of Western-style "modernity" and a model for cultural and religious life.

WHY DID Islamic reform movements arise during the 18th century?

The Founding Father of Pakistan. Muhammad Ali Jinnah was the president of India's Muslim League. In the 1930s, he advanced the "two nations" theory and made the first formal demand for a separate Muslim homeland. His ideas led to the establishment of Pakistan.

AP Wide World Photos.

Linking Asia and Europe. The opening of the Suez Canal in 1869 was a major engineering achievement. It also became a major international waterway benefiting all maritime states, reducing the distance from London to Bombay by half.

Index Stock Imagery, Inc.

WHY WAS it easy for Western powers to encroach on the Islamic world during the 19th century?

WESTERN POLITICAL AND ECONOMIC ENCROACHMENT

From the late 1700s until World War II, the political fortunes of Islamic states were increasingly dictated by Western powers. Western governments extracted capitulations favorable to their own interests from indigenous governments in exchange for promises of military protection or other considerations. These capitulations took the form of treaty clauses granting commercial concessions, special protection, and "extraterritorial" legal status to European merchant enclaves. Such concessions had originally been reciprocal and had served the commercial purposes of Muslim rulers and some merchants as well as Western traders. However, they eventually provided Western powers with pretexts for direct intervention in Ottoman, Iranian, Indian, and African affairs. The Ottoman Empire suffered from internal disunity; its provincial rulers, or *pashas*, were virtually independent. This, combined with the economic problems facing all the agrarian societies of Asia and Africa, made it easy for the Western powers—with their industrializing economies and militaries—to take control. Repeated Ottoman diplomatic and military defeats made that once great imperial power "the sick man of Europe" after 1800; similar weaknesses allowed Westerners to control Indian and Iranian states.

Napoleon Bonaparte's (1769–1821) unsuccessful invasion of Egypt in 1798 heralded a new era of European imperialism and colonialism in the region. By this date, the British had already wrested control over India and the Persian Gulf from the French; they now became the preeminent European power in the eastern Mediterranean as well. The Russians presented the most serious 19th-century challenge to Britain's colonial empire. Russia sought to gain as much territory and influence in the Iranian and Central Asian regions as possible. Afghanistan, an independent kingdom established by Ahmad Shah Durrani (r. 1737–1773), acted as a buffer that prevented Russia from penetrating southwestward into British India. In the Iranian and Ottoman regions, however, Russia and Britain—with French involvement—struggled with each other for supremacy. The Crimean War of 1854–1856 (see Chapter 24) was one result of this conflict.

HOW DID Iran react to the West during the 19th century?

THE WESTERN IMPACT

Beyond the overt political and commercial impact of the West, Western political ideology, culture, and technology proved critical factors for change in Islamic societies. Outside of India, this effect was most strongly felt in Egypt, Lebanon, North Africa, and Turkey. The Islamic states least and last affected by Western "modernity" were Iran, Afghanistan, and the Central Asian khanates.

Iran The rulers of Iran from 1794 to 1925 were the Qajar shahs, whose absolutist reign was not unlike that of the Safavids. However, the Qajars did not claim, as had the Safavids, to descent from the Shi'ite *imams*. Under Qajar rule, the *ulama* of the Shi'ite community became less strongly connected with the state apparatus. This period also saw the emergence of a Shi'ite traditionalist doctrine that encouraged all Shi'ites to choose a ***mujtahid***—a qualified scholarly guide—from among the *ulama* and follow his religious/legal interpretations. As a result, the *ulama* were often the chief critics of the government (not least for attempts to admit Western influences) and exponents of the people's grievances.

mujtahid Shi'ite religious-legal scholar.

A demonstration of *ulama* power occurred in 1890 when the Qajar Shah granted a 50-year monopoly on tobacco sales to the British. In 1891, the *ulama* decreed a tobacco boycott to protest the concession. This popular action was supported by modernist-nationalist opponents of the Qajar regime who had strong connections to Iran's commercial, or ***bazaari***, middle classes. The Shah was forced to rescind the concession, resulting in a stunning victory for opponents of the spread of Western commercial interests. Ironically, though, it only made Iran more dependent on Western capital. The government was forced to pay exorbitant compensation to British interests, and it incurred its first foreign debt.

Subject as it was to the machinations of outsiders, such as Russia, Britain, and France, Iran felt the impact of Western ideas, especially in the latter half of the century, when younger Iranian intellectuals began to warm to Western liberalism. As in other Islamic countries, the seeds of secular nationalism were being sown where religious sentiments had held sway. It worked with a desire among larger sectors of the populace for a voice in government. An uneasy alliance of Iranian modernists with conservative *ulama* proved, on occasion, an effective counterforce to Qajar absolutism, as in the tobacco boycott and in the early stages of the effort to force the Qajars to accept a constitution in 1906–1911. Yet such alliances did not bridge the inherent ideological divisions of the two groups.

ISLAMIC RESPONSES TO FOREIGN ENCROACHMENT

As the Iranian case shows, Western impingement on the Islamic world in the 19th and 20th centuries elicited varied responses. Every people or state had a different experience. Yet we can point to at least three typical styles of reaction: (1) a tendency to emulate and adopt Western ideas and institutions; (2) the attempt to join Western innovations with traditional Islamic institutions; and (3) a traditionalist rejection of Western influence in favor of either the status quo or return to a purified Islamic community.

EMULATION OF THE WEST

A strategy of emulation is exemplified in the career of the virtually independent Ottoman viceroy Muhammad Ali (ca. 1769–1849), pasha of Egypt from 1805 to 1849. He set out to rejuvenate Egypt's agriculture, to introduce modern industry, to modernize the army with European help, and to introduce European education and culture in government schools. Although he did not bring Egypt to a position of power equal to the European states, and his successors' financial and political catastrophes led the British to occupy Egypt (1882–1922), Muhammad Ali did set his country on the path to becoming a modern national state. Hence he is rightly called "the father of modern Egypt."

Efforts to appropriate Western experience and success were made by several Ottoman sultans and viziers after the defeat of the Turks by Russia in 1774. Most notable were the reforms of Selim III (r. 1762–1808), Mahmud II (r. 1808–1839), and the so-called Tanzimat, or beneficial "legislation" era from about 1839 to 1880. Selim made serious attempts at economic as well as

bazaari Iranian commercial middle class.

WHAT WERE the three typical Islamic reactions to Western encroachment?

Islamic Lands

1703–1792	Ibn Abd al-Wahhab
1737–1773	Rule of Ahmad Shah Durrani, founder of modern Afghanistan
1794–1925	Qajar shahs of Iran
1798	Invasion of Egypt by Napoleon Bonaparte
1805–1849	Rule of Muhammad Ali in Egypt
ca. 1839–1880	Era of the Tanzimat reforms of the Ottoman Empire
1839–1897	Jamal al-Din al-Afghani
1845–1905	Muhammad Abduh
1882–1922	British occupation of Egypt
1908	"Young Turk" revolution
1922–1938	Mustafa Kemal, "Atatürk" in power

Kemal Atatürk. This 1928 photograph shows Atatürk (right) giving instruction in the Latin alphabet. It reflects the personal engagement of Mustafa Kemal in the many reform efforts he instituted.

Historical Pictures Collection/Stock Montage Inc.

administrative and military reform. Mahmud's reforms were much like those of Muhammad Ali. Most important were his destruction of the Janissary corps, his tax and bureaucratic reforms, and his encouragement of Western military and educational methods. Like Muhammad Ali, he was less interested in promoting European enlightenment ideas about citizen rights and equity and more interested in building a stronger, more modern government.

The Tanzimat reforms, introduced by several liberal Ottoman ministers of state, continued the efforts of Selim and Mahmud. They were intended to bring the Ottoman state into line with ideals espoused by the European states, to give European powers less cause to intervene in Ottoman affairs, and to regenerate confidence in the state.

The 19th-century Ottoman reforms failed to save the empire. Nevertheless, they paved the way for the rise of Turkish nationalism, the "Young Turk" revolution of 1908, and the nationalist revolution of the 1920s that produced modern Turkey.

The creation of the Turkish republic out of the ashes of the Ottoman state after World War I is probably the most extreme example of an effort to modernize and nationalize an Islamic state on a Western model. This state was largely the child of Mustafa Kemal (1881–1938), known as "Atatürk" ("father of the Turks"), its first president (1922–1938). Atatürk's major reforms ranged from the introduction of a European-style code of civil law to the abolition of the caliphate, Sufi orders, Arabic script, and the Arabic call to prayer. These changes constituted a radical attempt to secularize an Islamic state and to separate religious from political and social institutions. Nothing quite like it has ever been repeated. Despite some adjustments and even reversals of Atatürk's measures, Turkey has maintained its independence, reaffirmed its commitment to democratic government, and emerged with a unique but still distinctly Islamic identity.

INTEGRATION OF WESTERN AND ISLAMIC IDEAS

The attempt to join modernization with traditional Islamic institutions and ideas is exemplified in the thought of famous Muslim intellectuals, such as Jamal al-Din al-Afghani (1839–1897), and Muhammad Abduh (1845–1905). These thinkers argued for a progressive Islam rather than a materialist Western secularism as the best answer to life in the modern world.

Afghani is best known for his emphasis on the unity of the Islamic world, or **pan-Islamism**, and on a populist, constitutionalist approach to political order.

WOMEN AND REFORM IN THE MIDDLE EAST

Though the discussion of reform, religion, and modernity in the Middle East was dominated by men, some of the region's women raised the issue of woman's role in modern society. Most important were those women who demanded political rights. Some Iranian women confronted their fathers and brothers in the Iranian Parliament in December 1911, concerned that the men might capitulate to the Russian-British demands to remove the American reforming administrator,

pan-Islamism Movement that advocates that the entire Muslim world should form a unified political and cultural entity.

Morgan Schuster. The wives of some Egyptian diplomats, after returning from Paris in 1919, discarded the veil. In 1929, some Palestinian women convened a Women's Congress of Palestine to address the political issues that ensued after the Wailing Wall riots of the same year. In the late 19th and early 20th centuries, a number of journals and magazines devoted to women's concerns appeared. These mainly focused on traditional issues such as cooking, parenting, and fashion, but some stressed that women were an essential part of society and should not be excluded from participation in commerce and politics. The Egyptian Feminist Union was founded in 1923 by Huda Sha'rawi (1879–1947) to fight for women's suffrage, reform of marriage laws, and equal access to education. In a well-publicized gesture, Sha'rawi and her colleague Saize Nabrawi removed their veils in the midst of the crowd at Cairo's train station. For them the veil symbolized the inadequate public status of women in Middle Eastern countries. Many Middle Eastern feminists stress, however, that women's inequality is rooted in wide-ranging cultural, political, and economicial structures that need to be addressed long before the issue of the veil.

PURIFICATION AND REVIVAL OF ISLAM

A third Muslim reaction to Western domination has focused on recourse to Islamic values and ideals to the exclusion of "outside" forces. This approach includes reformist revivalism like Wahhabism and the kind of conservatism often associated with Sunni or Shi'ite "establishment" *ulama*, as in Iran since 1979. The conservative spirit has often been the target of revivalist reformers who see in it the worst legacy of medieval Islam. Still, both conservative and revivalist Muslim thinkers look for answers to the questions facing Muslims in the modern world within, not outside, the Islamic tradition.

NATIONALISM

Nationalism is a product of modern history. Nationalist movements in the Islamic world have been either stimulated by Western models or produced in reaction to Western exploitation and colonial occupation. During the late 19th century, many intellectuals in Asia or Africa grappled with the question of identity and whether their ethnic or linguistic group constituted a distinct nation or whether they were part of a larger whole. The often arbitrary or artificial division of the colonial world by European administrators demanded an answer to this question in Asia and Africa. In the European capitals, new "nations" were drawn on the map to reflect the realities and interests of imperialism rather than the facts on the ground. In due time, these borders took on an aura of legitimacy. However, forging nations from artificial parameters has proven to be a difficult and sometimes violent process.

THE AFRICAN EXPERIENCE

Between 1800 and 1945, virtually every part of Africa changed, but nowhere more than sub-Saharan Africa. With the exception of South Africa below the Transvaal, tropical and southern Africa came under major influence and finally colonial control from outside only after

Southern Africa

ca. 1800–1818	Dingiswayo, Nguni Zulu king, forms new military state
1800–1825	The *mfecane* among the Bantu of southeastern Africa
1795	British take Cape Colony from the Dutch
ca. 1818–1828	Shaka's reign as head of the Nguni state; major warfare, destruction, and expansion
ca. 1825–1870	Sotho kingdom of King Mosheshwe in Lesotho region
1835–1843	Great Trek of Boers into Natal and north onto the high veld beyond the Orange River
1843	British annexation of Natal province
1852–1860	Creation of the Orange Free State and the South African Republic

1880. Before then, internal developments—demographic and power shifts and then the rise of Islamic reform movements—overshadowed the European presence in the continent.

NEW STATES AND POWER CENTERS

SOUTHERN AFRICA

WHAT NEW states arose in Africa during the early 19th century?

In the south, below the Limpopo River, the first quarter of the 19th century saw devastating internal warfare, depopulation, and forced migrations of many Bantu peoples in what is known as the *mfecane*, or "crushing" era. Likely brought on by a population explosion and economic competition, the mfecane was marked by the rise of military states among the northern Nguni-speaking Bantu. Its result was a period of warfare and chaos; depopulation; and the creation of multitribal, multilingual Bantu states in modern Malawi, Mozambique, Tanzania, Zambia, and Zimbabwe.

The Nguni warrior-king Dingiswayo formed the first of the new military states between about 1800 and 1818. The most important state was formed by his successor, Shaka, leader of the Nguni-speaking Zulu nation and kingdom (ca. 1818–1828). Shaka's brutal military tactics led to the Zulu conquest of a vast dominion in southeastern Africa and the depopulation of some 15,000 square miles. Refugees fled north into Sotho-speaking Bantu territory or south to put increasing pressure on the southern Nguni peoples. Chaos ensued north and south of Zululand and even in the high veld above the Orange River.

mfecane Period of widespread warfare and chaos among Bantu peoples in east-central Africa during the early 19th century.

Great Trek Migration between 1835 and 1847 of Boer pioneers (called *voortrekkers*) north from British-ruled Cape Colony to establish their own independent republics.

The Kingdom of Lesotho. Mosheshwe, king and founder of Lesotho. Not all of the Bantu peoples followed the militaristic example of Shaka. Mosheshwe, prince of a subtribe of the Sotho Bantus, fought off Zulu attacks and led his people to a mountain stronghold in southern Africa, where, through diplomacy and determination, he founded a small nation that has endured to the present. The kingdom became the British protectorate of Basutoland in 1868. In 1966 it achieved independence as the kingdom of Lesotho under Mosheshwe's great-grandson, King Mosheshwe II.

Courtesy of the Library of Congress.

The net result was the creation of diverse states. Some people tried to imitate the military state of Shaka; others fled to the mountains; others even went west into the Kalahari. The most famous of these was Lesotho, the Sotho kingdom of King Mosheshwe, which survived as long as he lived (from the 1820s until 1870). Mosheshwe defended his people from the Zulu and held off the Afrikaners, missionaries, and British. After his death, the latter groups became Lesotho's chief predators.

The new state-building spawned by the mfecane was nullified by Boer expansion and British annexation of the Natal province (1843). These developments stemmed from the **Great Trek** of Boer *voortrekers*, which took place between 1835 and 1843. This migration brought about 6,000 Afrikaners from the eastern Cape Colony northeastward into the more fertile regions of southern Africa, Natal, and the high veld above the Orange River. It resulted in the creation after 1850 of two Afrikaner republics: the Orange Free State between the Orange and Vaal Rivers and the South African Republic north of the Vaal.

EAST AND CENTRAL AFRICA

In East and east-central Africa, external trade resulted in the formation of strong states. In the Lakes region, peoples such as the Nyamwezi to the east of Lake Tanganyika and the Baganda west of Lake Victoria gained regional power from as early as the late 18th century through trade with the Arab-Swahili eastern coast and the eastern Congo to the west. This east–west commerce involved slaves; ivory; copper; and, from the outside, Indian cloth, firearms, and manufactured goods.

WEST AFRICA

In West Africa, the slave trade was replaced by European demand for palm oil and gum arabic by the 1820s. In the first half of the century, *jihad* (holy struggle) movements of the Fulbe (or Fulani) and others shattered the stability of the western savannah and forest regions from modern Senegal and Ghana through southern Nigeria. Wars and dislocation resulted in the rise of regional kingdoms, such as those of Asante and Dahomey (modern Benin). These eventually succumbed to internal dissension and the colonial activities of Britain and France later in the century.

ISLAMIC REFORM MOVEMENTS

The vitality of Islam was a significant agent of change in sub-Saharan Africa before the European rush for colonies in the 1880s. It is still a factor. In 1800, Islam was already well established from West Africa across the Sudan to the Red Sea and along the East African coast. Islam was the law of the land in states such as the sultanate of Zanzibar on the eastern coast and the waning Funj sultanate on the Blue Nile in the eastern Sudan. But in many African "Islamic" states, the rural populace were still partly, if not wholly, pagan, and even the urban elites were only nominally Muslim.

The 19th century is notable for the militant Islamic revivalist and reform movements of jihad, which fixed and spread Islam as a lasting part of the African scene. The most important jihad movement was led by a Fulbe Muslim scholar from Hausa territory in the central Sahel. Usman Dan Fodio (1754–1817) was influenced by the reformist ideas that spread throughout the Muslim world in the 18th century. Shortly after 1804, he gathered an army and conquered most of the Hausa lands of northern and central Nigeria, bringing an explicitly Islamic order to the area. Dan Fodio left behind a sultanate centered on the new capital of Sokoto and governed by one of his sons, Muhammad Bello, until 1837. The Fulbe became the ruling class in the Hausa regions, and Islam spread into the countryside, where it still predominates (see "Usman Dan Fodio on Evil and Good Government").

Other 19th-century reform movements had similar success in spreading a revivalist, reformist Islamic message among the masses. Most notable were the Sanusi of Libya and the eastern Sahara (after about 1840) and the Mahdist uprising of the eastern Sudan (1880s and 1890s). The Libyan movement provided the focus for resistance to the Italian invasion of 1911. The Sudanese Muhammad Ahmad (1848–1885) condemned the corruption of basic Muslim ideals and declared himself the awaited deliverer, or Mahdi, in 1881. He led the northern Sudan in rebellion against Ottoman-Egyptian control. His successor governed the Sudan until the British destroyed the young Islamic state in 1899. In the Caucasus, Islamic reform movements merged into resistance against Russian expansion.

INCREASING EUROPEAN INVOLVEMENT

Muslim reform movements were not the only important developments in Africa during the 19th century. Another was the growing involvement of Europe, which led to European domination of the continent. Before the mid-1800s, the penetration of White outsiders had been limited largely to coastal areas, although their slave trade had had significant effects inland (see Chapter 17 and Map 27–1). This changed as trading companies, explorers, missionaries, and then colonial troops and governments moved into Africa. Ironically, the elimination of the slave trade (primarily through Britain's efforts) was accompanied by increased European exploration and Christian missionizing, which ushered in imperial and colonial ventures that were to have even more disastrous consequences than slaving.

Challenging Russia. A Muslin separatist movement led by Imam Shamil established an independent state in 1834 that lasted for 25 years in the Caucasus region of Dagestan.

Getty Images Inc. – Hulton Archive Photos.

WHAT WERE the main Islamic reform movements in 19th-century Africa?

WHAT WAS the "scramble for Africa?"

HISTORY'S VOICES

USMAN DAN FODIO ON EVIL AND GOOD GOVERNMENT

Following in the tradition of the Wahhabis in Arabia and virtually all previous Islamic reform movements, Dan Fodio (1754–1817) stressed adherence to Muslim norms as expressed in the Shari'a, the Divine Law. In the two excerpts that follow, he enumerated some of the evils of the previous Hausa rulers and their "law," and then listed five principles of proper Islamic government.

WHAT DOES the first principle of good government, that "authority shall not be given to one who seeks it," mean? What abuses by government listed by Dan Fodio might be most appalling to the average Muslim? Why?

One of the ways of their government [that is, of the Hausa or Habe kings] is succession to the emirate by hereditary right and by force to the exclusion of consultation. And one of the ways of their government is the building of their sovereignty upon three things: the people's persons, their honour, and their possessions; and whomsoever they wish to kill or exile or violate his honour or devour his wealth they do so in pursuit of their lusts, without any right in the Shari'a. One of the ways of their government is their imposing on the people monies not laid down by the Shari'a, being those which they call janghali and kurdin ghari and kurdin salla. One of the ways of their governments is their intentionally eating whatever food they wish, whether it is religiously permitted or forbidden, and wearing whatever clothes they wish, whether religiously permitted or forbidden, and drinking what beverages [ta'am] they wish, whether religiously permitted or forbidden, and riding whatever riding beasts they wish, whether religiously permitted or forbidden, and taking what women they wish without marriage contract, and living in decorated palaces, whether religiously permitted or forbidden, and spreading soft (decorated) carpets as they wish, whether religiously permitted or forbidden. . . .

And I say—and help is with God—the foundations of government are five things: the first is that authority shall not be given to one who seeks it. The second is the necessity for consultation. The third is the abandoning of harshness. The fourth is justice. The fifth is good works. And as for its ministers, they are four. (The First) is a trustworthy wazir to wake the ruler if he sleeps, to make him see if he is blind, and to remind him if he forgets, and the greatest misfortune for the government and the subjects is that they should be denied honest wazirs. And among the conditions pertaining to the wazir is that he should be steadfast in compassion to the people, and merciful towards them. The second of the ministers of government is a judge whom the blame of a blamer cannot overtake concerning the affairs of God. The third is a chief of police who shall obtain justice for the weak from the strong. The fourth is a tax collector who shall discharge his duties and not oppress the subjects. . . .

From translation of Usman Dan Fodio's *Kitab al-Farq* by M. Hiskett, *Bulletin of the School of Oriental and African Studies*, London, 1960, Part 3, p. 558. Reprinted by permission of Oxford University Press, Oxford, Great Britain.

EXPLORATION

The 19th-century European explorers—mostly English, French, and German—uncovered for Westerners the "secrets" of Africa: sources and courses of the Niger, Nile, Zambezi, and Congo Rivers; natural wonders such as Mount Kilimanjaro and Lake Tanganyika; and fabled places like Timbuktu, the once, great Berber trading gateway and center of Islamic learning. The history of European exploration is one of fortune hunting, self-promotion, violence, and mistakes, but also of patience and perseverance, bravery and dedication.

MAP EXPLORATION

Interactive map: To explore this map further, go to **http://www.prenhall.com/craig/map27.1**

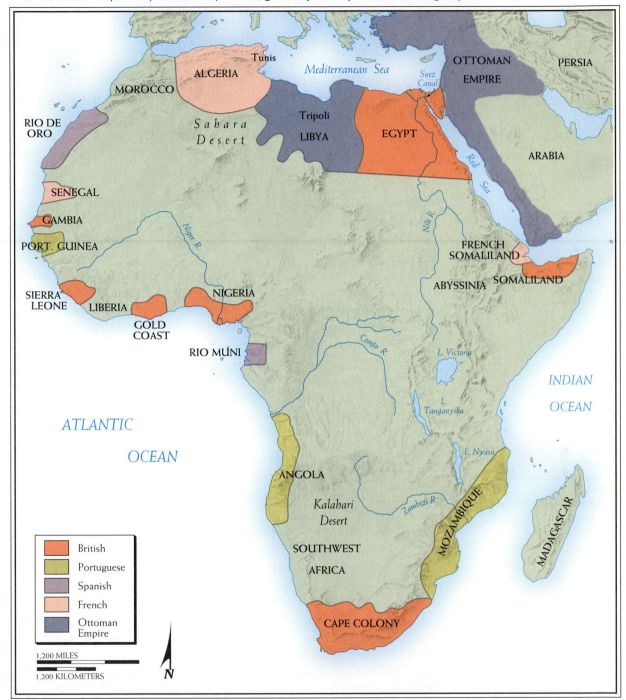

MAP 27–1

Imperial Expansion in Africa up to 1880. Until the 1880s, only a few European countries held colonies in Africa, mostly on the fringes of the continent. A comparison of this map with Map 27–2 shows how rapidly the situation changed.

WHICH EUROPEAN country held the most African possessions at this time?

Central Africa

1754–1817	Usman Dan Fodio, Fulbe leader of major Islamic jihad
1810	Dan Fodio founds Islamic sultanate in lands of former Hausa states of northern and central Nigeria
1817–1837	Reign at Sokoto of Muhammad Bello, son of Dan Fodio

The explorers stimulated European interest and opened the way for traders, missionaries, and finally soldiers and governors from the Christian West. One of the greatest explorers was Dr. David Livingstone (1813–1873), who was a missionary dedicated to Africa and its peoples as few other Westerners have been.

CHRISTIAN MISSIONS

The late 19th century saw an influx of Christian missionaries, both Protestant and Catholic (by 1900, perhaps as many as 10,000). The missionaries came to know the African peoples far better than did the explorers. Their accounts of Africa contained chauvinistic and misleading descriptions of the "degraded" state of African culture and religion, but they brought real knowledge of and interest in Africa to Europe. Their schools also brought some alphabetic culture and literacy to the African tribal world. Although their settlements, often in remote areas, provided European governments with convenient pretexts for intervention, the missionaries themselves were more often idealists than opportunists. Many who went into the tropical regions succumbed to diseases, such as malaria, yellow fever, and sleeping sickness. If they were often paternalistic and instruments of the imperialism of their home countries, they also sought to provide Africans with medicine and education. Through the ideals of their faith, the missionaries provided Africans—sometimes inadvertently—with a weapon of principle to use against their European exploiters. African Christian churches, for example, played a leading role in resisting apartheid in South Africa, despite White Christian oppression and collusion with racism in that country and elsewhere in Africa (see Chapter 35). The role of Africans in the European domination of Africa was neither simple nor wholly positive.

THE COLONIAL "SCRAMBLE FOR AFRICA"

Before 1850, the only significant European attempts to take African territory were in South Africa and Algeria. In South Africa, as we have noted, the Boers came into conflict with Bantu tribes on their Great Trek. The French invaded Algeria in 1830, settled Europeans on choice farmlands, and waged war on native resistance fighters (1830–1847). Over most of the continent, however, the European presence was felt with real force only from the 1880s. Yet by World War I, all of Africa except Ethiopia and Liberia was divided arbitrarily into a patchwork of European colonial administrations (see Map 27–2).

This takeover was supported by mounting European popular and commercial interests fueled by the publicity given African exploration and missionary work. The European desire for the markets and resources of Africa, together with intra-European competition for power and prestige, pushed one European state after another to lay claim to whatever segments of Africa they could.

This wholesale takeover was made possible by the superior power the West commanded. In particular, European technical expertise opened up the interior of the continent. Except for the Nile and the Niger, the great African rivers have impassible waterfalls near the sea. Steamboats above the falls and railroads around them provided access to the African interior and opened its riches to exploitation.

Britain and France were the colonial vanguards. The British had the largest involvement. On one axis, it ranged from their South African holdings (begun

A Missionary Visit to a Zulu Kraal. The 19th-century European and American enthusiasm for working toward "the evangelization of the world in our time" found one of its major outlets in missionary efforts in Africa, such as the one depicted here in the southern part of the continent.

Courtesy of the Library of Congress.

when they took the Cape Colony from the Dutch in 1795) to their protectorate in Egypt (from 1882). On another axis, it extended from trading interests in West Africa to colonies such as Sierra Leone and Gambia, to protectorate rule, as in the Niger districts after 1885, and to a Zanzibar-based sphere of influence in East Africa.

The British preferred "indirect" to "direct" colonial administration. Their rule was only slightly more enlightened than that of the French, who carved out a colonial empire under their direct control. The French had long had government-supported trading outposts in West Africa. Tunisia and the Ivory Coast became French protectorates in the 1880s; Dahomey was bloodily annexed in 1894; and the colony of French Equatorial Africa was proclaimed in 1910.

Beginning in the mid-1880s, the European powers began to seek mutual agreement to their claims on segments of Africa. Leopold II of Belgium (r. 1865–1909) and Otto von Bismarck (1815–1898) in Germany established their claims to parts of South, Central, and East Africa. France and England set about consolidating their African interests. Italy took African colonial territory in Eritrea, Somaliland, and Libya. But the Italian design on Ethiopia was thwarted when Ethiopia defeated an Italian invasion in 1896. The Italians eventually conquered Ethiopia in 1935. The **"scramble for Africa"** was over by the outbreak of World War I. In the aftermath of the war, Germany lost its African possessions to other colonial powers. Europe's colonies in Africa did not gain independence (see Chapters 33 and 35) until after World War II in the 1950s.

European colonial rule in Africa is one of the uglier chapters of modern history. The paternalistic attitudes of late-19th-century Europe and America amounted to racism when applied in Africa. The regions with large-scale White settlement produced the worst exploitation at

20.6
Rudyard Kipling

scramble for Africa Late 19th-century takeover of most of Africa by European powers.

Colonial Africa

1830	French invasion of Algeria
1890	British protectorate in Zanzibar
ca. 1880	French protectorate in Tunisia and Ivory Coast
1880s–1890s	Mahdist uprising in eastern Sudan
1882	British protectorate in Egypt
1894	French annexation of Dahomey
1910	French colony of Equatorial Africa

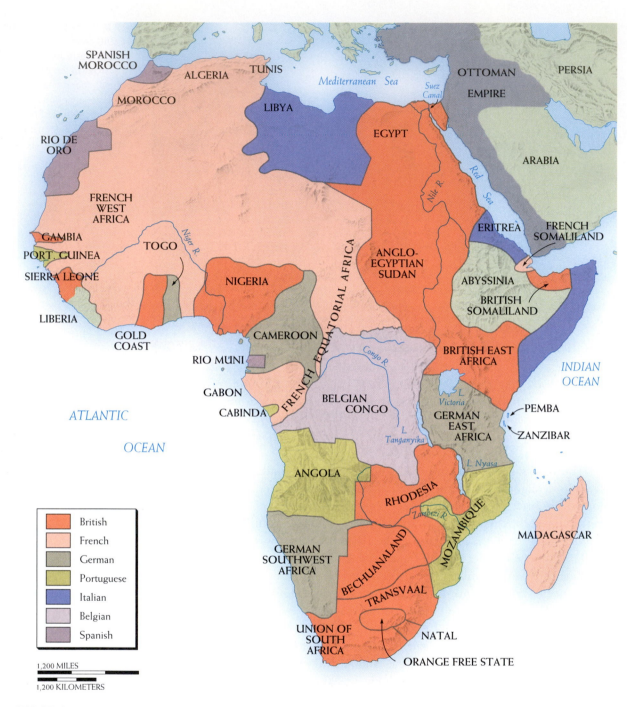

MAP 27–2
Partition of Africa, 1880–1914.   By 1914, the only countries in Africa that remained independent were Liberia and Abyssinia (Ethiopia). The occupying powers included most large European states.

COMPARE THIS map to Map 27–1. Which new European countries have entered the "scramble for Africa"?

the expense of vastly greater native populations. The worst legacy of the European presence was the White racist state of modern South Africa, which only ended in 1994. No Western nation can have a clear conscience about its involvement in Africa.

OVERVIEW   COLONIALISM, 1815–1914

Between the end of the Napoleonic Wars and the outbreak of World War I, European powers, the United States, and Japan extended their rule over much of the Near East, Africa, Asia, and the Pacific. The imposition of foreign rule was often the result of conquest, but it also occurred through purchase or the imposition of a "protectorate" in which a local ruler kept his title but ceded real power, especially over foreign affairs, defense, and finances, to colonial advisors or officials. By 1914, except for the Latin American republics, only Liberia and Abyssinia (Ethiopia) in Africa, the Ottoman Empire in the Near East, and Iran, Afghanistan, Thailand, and China had escaped some form of colonial rule. The table below lists the countries and territories that the Western powers and Japan acquired or dominated as protectorates (in which a local ruler keeps his title but cedes real power to a foreign country) between 1815 and 1914. In addition, older possessions, such as British India and the Portuguese colonies of Angola and Mozambique, were also increased during these hundred years.

NEAR EAST AND NORTH AFRICA

Britain	Aden (in Yemen), Bahrain, Cyprus, Egypt, Kuwait, Oman, Qatar, United Emirates
France	Algeria, Morocco, Tunisia
Italy	Libya, Rhodes

AFRICA

Belgium	Congo (Zaire)
Britain	Botswana, Ghana, Kenya, Lesotho, Malawi, Nigeria, Somaliland, Sudan, Swaziland, Uganda, Zambia, Zanzibar, Zimbabwe, Zululand (in South Africa)
France	Benin, Burkina Faso, Central African Republic, Chad, Congo, Djibouti, Ivory Coast, Madagascar, Mali, Mauretania, Niger
Germany	Burundi, Cameroons, Namibia, Rwanda, Tanganyika (Tanzania), Togo
Italy	Eritrea, Somalia

ASIA

Britain	Brunei, Hong Kong, Malaysia, Myanmar (Burma), Nepal, Papua, Singapore
France	Cambodia, Laos, Vietnam
Germany	New Guiana, Tientsin (in China)
Japan	Korea, Okinawa, Taiwan
Netherlands	Acheh
Russia	Amur Territories (from China), Central Asia, Chechnya
United States	Philippines

PACIFIC

Britain	Fiji, Tonga, Solomons
France	New Caledonia, Tahiti
Germany	Carolines, Marianas
United States	Guam, Hawaii, Midway, Wake

AFRICAN RESISTANCE TO COLONIALISM: THE RISE OF NATIONALISM

Mutesa of Bugand and His Court. Noted for his cunning and diplomatic skill and for his autocratic and often cruel conduct, Mutesa was one of the few African rulers who was able to maintain a powerful and successful army and court, which enabled him to deal effectively with Egyptian and British efforts to encroach on his sphere of influence.

Brown Brothers.

African states were not, however, passive objects of European manipulation. Astute native rulers sought to use the European presence to their own advantage. Some, like the Bagandan king Mutesa in the 1870s (in what is today Uganda), succeeded for some time. Direct armed resistance was doomed (even Ethiopia's) because of European technological superiority. Nevertheless, such resistance was widespread. In the end, however, other factors brought an end to most foreign rule on African soil.

The most prominent factor was the rise of nationalism across Africa, especially after World War I. However little the colonial partition of Africa reflected native divisions, it still influenced nationalist movements and the eventual shape of African states. The "national" consciousness of the diverse peoples of a given colonial unit was fueled by common opposition to foreign rule, use of a common European tongue, and the assimilation of European thought and culture by an educated native elite. These elites were educated in mission schools and foreign universities. Their ranks increased in the early 20th century. From them came the leaders of Africa's nationalist movements between the two world wars and of Africa's independent nations after World War II.

The severest indigenous critiques of the Western treatment of Africa often drew on Western religious and political ideals. The process culminated in the creation of more than 40 self-governing African nations after 1945. African independence movements were based on modern nationalist models from Europe and America rather than ancient ones derived from native tradition. The nationalist and independence movements sought to eject the colonial intruders, not to return to an earlier status quo. Their aim was to take over and run for themselves the Western institutions that colonialism had introduced. This legacy from the West is still visible today.

SUMMARY

Western Encroachment The century and a half following the French Revolution was a bleak one for the Indian subcontinent, Africa, and the Islamic societies. For centuries there had been a rough balance in material and intellectual culture, commerce, and political stability among the major cultural regions of the world. Suddenly, during the course of 150 years, the European sector of the global community came to dominate the rest of the world.

The Middle East, Africa, Iran, Central Asia, India, and Indonesia-Malaysia, along with Central and South America—what is today referred to as the "Third World" of "developing nations"—were most drastically affected by European imperialism and colonialism. Regardless of indigenous developments in these regions, the decisive development of this era was unprecedented domination by a single segment of the global community. Western dominance, sometimes positive, often sordid and ugly, was by no means synonymous with "progress," as Westerners have often liked to think.

Indigenous Reactions   The vitality of so many of the cultures and traditions that bore the brunt of the Western onslaught has been striking. Arab, Iranian, Indian, African, and other encounters with Western material and intellectual domination produced different responses and initiatives. These have borne full fruit in political, economic, and intellectual independence only since 1945; however, most began much earlier, some even well before 1800.

One result of the imperial-colonial experience almost everywhere has been the sharpening of cultural self-consciousness and self-confidence among those peoples most negatively affected by Western dominance. The imperial-colonial experiences of the Third World nations may well prove to have been not only ones of misery and reversal, but also of transition to positive development and resurgence, despite the looming economic, educational, and demographic problems that plague many of them.

REVIEW QUESTIONS

1. What kind of policies did the British follow in India? What were the kinds of political activism against British rule were there in India after 1800?

2. How was the Islamic world internally divided after 1800? How did those divisions influence the coming of European powers?

3. How did nationalism affect European control in south Asia, Africa, and the Middle East?

4. What was the role of African nationalism in resisting foreign control?

IMAGE KEY

for pages 672–673

a. A fez.
b. Kemal Ataturk.
c. ivory for sale, congo.
d. An Imperial procession, or *durbar*.
e. Mahatma Ghandi.
f. Bungandan Kabaka Mutesa I and members of his court.
g. A page from a 19th-century Moroccan Koran.
h. Imam Shamil of Dagestan.
i. Sepoy cavalry attacking British infantry at the Battle of Cawpore in 1857.

KEY TERMS

bazaari (p. 681)
cantonments (p. 677)
Great Trek (p. 684)

mfecane (p. 684)
mujtahid (p. 680)
pan-Islamism (p. 682)

raj (p. 675)
scramble for Africa (p. 689)
Wahhabis (p. 679)

 For additional study resources for this chapter, go to:
www.prenhall.com/craig/chapter27

ISLAM

The Islamic tradition is one of the youngest major world religions. Since its inception during the lifetime of the Prophet Muhammad (632 B.C.E.) it has grown, like the Christian and Buddhist traditions, into a worldwide community not limited by national boundaries or defined in racial or ethnic terms. It began among the Arabs but spread widely. Islam's historical heartlands are those Arabic-, Turkic-, and Persian-speaking lands of the Near East between Egypt and Afghanistan. However, today more than half of its faithful live in Asia east of Karachi, Pakistan; and more Muslims live in sub-Saharan Africa than in all of the other Arab lands. There are also growing Muslim minorities in the United States and Europe.

The central vision of Islam is a just and peaceful society where people can freely worship God. It focuses on a human community of worshippers who recognize the absolute sovereignty and oneness of God and strive to do God's will. Muslims believe that divine will is found first in his revealed word, the Qur'an; then as elaborated and specified in the actions and words of his final prophet, Muhammad; and finally as interpreted and extended in the scriptural exegesis and legal traditions of the Muslim community during the past 13½ centuries.

Muslim vision thus centers on one God who has guided humankind throughout history by means of prophets or apostles and repeated revelations. God is the Creator of all, and in the end all will return to God. God's majesty would seem to make him a distant, threatening deity of absolute justice; there is such an element in the Muslim understanding of the wide chasm between the human and the Divine. Still, there is an immanent as well as a transcendent side to the Divine in the Muslim view. Indeed, Muslims have given us some of the greatest images of God's closeness to his faithful worshipper, images that have a special place in the thought of the Muslim mystics, who are known as *Sufis* (taken originally from *suf*, "wool," because of the early Muslim ascetics' use of simple wool dress).

Muslims understand God's word in the Qur'an and the elaboration of that word by tradition to be a complete prescription for human life. Thus Islamic law is not law in the Western sense of civil, criminal, or international systems. Rather, it is a comprehensive set of standards for the moral, ritual, social, political, economic, aesthetic, and even hygienic and dietary dimensions of life. By being faithful to God's law, the Muslim hopes to gain salvation on the Last Day, when human history shall end and all of God's creatures who have ever lived will be resurrected and called to account for their thoughts and actions during their lives on earth. Some will be saved, but others will be eternally damned.

Thus *Islam*, which means "submission [to God]," has been given as a name to the religiously defined system of life that Muslims have sought to institute wherever they have lived. Muslims have striven to organize their societies and political realities around the ideals represented in the traditional picture of the Prophet's community in Medina and Mecca. This approach necessitated compromise in which power was given to temporal rulers and accepted by Muslim religious

Muhammad and Ali. This 16th-century Persian miniature shows the prophet Muhammad and his kinsman Ali purifying the Ka'ba in Mecca of pagan idols. The Ka'ba is the geographical point toward which all Muslims face when performing ritual prayer.

Art Resource/Bildarchiv Preussischer Kulturbesitz.

Friday Congregational Worship. Every Friday at the noon hour of daily worship, Muslims are enjoined to gather in as large a congregation as possible to worship together and listen to a weekly preaching in the major mosque in their town or city. Here at a mosque in Jakarta, Indonesian Muslims are seen in the midst of worship rites. More Muslims live in Indonesia than in any other country.

Getty Images, Inc. — Photodisc.

leaders as long as those rulers protected God's Law, the *Shari'ah*. The ideal of a single international Muslim community, or *Umma*, has never fully been realized politically, but it remains an ideal.

Many movements of reform over the centuries have called for greater adherence to rigorist interpretations of Islamic law and greater dominance of piety and religious values in sociopolitical as well as individual life. The most famous of these movements, that of the Wahhabis in 18th-century Arabia, remains influential in much of the Muslim world, including Saudi Arabia. The Wahhabis' puritanical zeal in fighting what they consider "innovations" in many regional Islamic contexts, such as Shi'ism, Sufi traditions, and all more liberal forms of Islamic practice, continues to the present day. Wahhabism has had considerable success in the past half century and was apparently the spawning ground of the extremist views of Osama bin Laden's al-Qaeda terrorist movement, which is largely Arab in its ethnic makeup and has turned

from fighting Muslim states it regards as un-Islamic to opposing what it considers the U.S. intrusion into the Arab Islamic world and its unpopular foreign policy in the region. While mainstream Muslims everywhere reject bin Laden's extremism, Wahhabi zealotry has adherents on the fringes of Islamic communities around the world. In this respect, Islam is not unlike Christianity, Judaism, Hinduism, or other major religions, each of which has over its history spawned literalists, zealots, and extremists, who have urged violence in the name of their version of their parent faith.

The major sectarian, or minority, groups among Muslims are those of the Shi'ites, who have held out for an ideal of a temporal ruler who is also the spiritual heir of Muhammad and God's designated deputy on earth. Most Shi'ites, notably those of Iran, hold that after 11 designated blood descendants of the prophets had each failed to be recognized by the majority of Muslims as the rightful leader, or *Imam*, the 12th disappeared and remains to this day physically absent from the world, although not dead. He will come again at the end of time to vindicate his faithful followers.

Muslim piety takes many forms. Common duties of Muslims are central for Muslims everywhere: faith in God and trust in his Prophet; regular performance of ritual worship (*Salat*); fasting during daylight hours for 30 days in Ramadan (the ninth month of the lunar year); giving one's wealth to the needy (*zakat*); and at least once in a lifetime, if able, making the pilgrimage to Mecca and its environs (*Hajj*). Other more regional or popular, but ubiquitous, practices are also important. Celebration of the Prophet's birthday indicates the exalted popular status of Muhammad, even though any divine status for him is strongly rejected theologically. Recitation of the Qur'an permeates all Muslim practice, from daily worship to celebrations of all kinds. Visitation of saints' tombs is a prominent form of popular devotion. Sufi chanting or even ecstatic dancing are also practiced by Muslims around the world.

Muslims vary enormously in their physical environment, language, ethnic background, and cultural allegiances. What binds them now as in the past are not political allegiances but religious affinities and a shared heritage of religious faith and culture. How these allegiances and sensibilities will fare in the face of global challenges will be an important factor in shaping the world of the 21st century.

- How has the ideal of a single, international Muslim community influenced Islamic history? World history?
- What impact have reform movements had on Islam since its inception? What impact do they have today?

28 Modern East Asia

CHAPTER HIGHLIGHTS

China: the Nineteenth Century For 2000 years, the only threats to China had come from beyond its frontiers. The Opium War of 1839–1842, and other wars with European powers, were seen as "coastal incursions," which posed little threat to the Qing heartland. Far more serious were the Taiping and other rebellions, which seized villages, threatened gentry control of local society, and attacked officials at both district and provincial levels. For China, the important story of the nineteenth century was the success of gentry armies in suppressing these rebellions, a success using Western weapons but based on traditional values. Not until the very end of the century did the Chinese begin substantial Westernizing reforms—and by then it was too late.

China: the Twentieth Century After the Qing fell in 1912, China was ruled for a decade and a half by regional warlords, a pattern not unlike the aftermaths of previous dynasties. But the ferment of the newly entering flood of Western ideas fed a growing nationalism, which eventually led to the Communists defeating the Guomindang in a civil war that wracked China between 1945 and 1949.

The Transformation of Japan In contrast to China, the Tokugawa regime collapsed quickly—only 15 years after the arrival of Perry in 1853. The new Meiji government began sweeping Westernizing reforms in every field. Economic growth went hand in hand with universal education. The emperor became the unifying symbol for traditional and conservative thinkers. The Diet (Japan's parliament) became the focus for progressives and liberals. Parliamentary democracy made gains up until the 1920s. But then the Great Depression and a crisis in Manchuria opened the way for the rise of militarism in the 1930s.

CHAPTER QUESTIONS

WHAT WERE the most serious threats to Manchu rule in the nineteenth century?

WHO WERE the key figures in the revolution of 1911?

WHY DID the communists win the Chinese Civil War?

WHAT ROLE did the Chōshū and Satsuma play in the overthrow of Tokugawa rule?

WHAT POWERS did the Meiji Constitution give to the emperor?

WHY DID Japan set out to build a modern economy?

CHAPTER OUTLINE

MODERN CHINA (1839–1949)

- Close of Manchu Rule
- From Dynasty to Warlordism (1895–1926)
- Cultural and Ideological Ferment: The May Fourth Movement
- Nationalist China

MODERN JAPAN (1853–1945)

- Overthrow of the Tokugawa Bakufu (1853–1868)
- Building the Meiji State (1868–1890)
- Growth of a Modern Economy
- The Politics of Imperial Japan (1890–1945)
- Japanese Militarism and German Nazism

In the mid-19th century, the West was the expanding, aggressive, imperialistic force in world history; it was the trigger for change throughout the world. But the response to the Western impact depended on internal forces in each country. Japan and China were both relatively successful in their responses, for neither became a colony.

The two countries' governing elites were educated in Confucianism, which was just secular enough to crumble in the face of the more powerful secularism of 19th-century science and the doctrines associated with it. In both countries, one of the "breakdown products" of the Confucian sociopolitical identity was a strong new nationalism.

But in most other respects, modern Japan and China could hardly be more different. The coming of Commodore Matthew Perry (1794–1858) in 1853 and 1854 precipitated rapid change in Japan. The old Tokugawa regime collapsed, and the Japanese built a modern state. Economic growth followed. By 1900, Japan had defeated China and was about to defeat Russia. After the Great Depression, Japan, like Italy and Germany, became an aggressive and militarized state and was defeated in World War II. But after the war, Japan reemerged more stable and productive, and with a stronger parliamentary government than ever before.

In contrast, the hold of tradition in China was remarkable. But in one sense, its strength was China's weakness, for only after the overthrow of Manchu rule in 1911 was China willing to begin the modernization that Japan had started in 1868. Even then it was unsuccessful. Along with warlordism, new ills arose from the rending of the very fabric of the dynastic pattern. That China "failed" during this modern century is the view held by the Chinese themselves.

MODERN CHINA (1839–1949)

China's modern century was not the century in which it became modern, but the one in which it encountered the modern West. Its first phase, from the Opium War to the fall of the Qing or Manchu dynasty (1911), was little affected by Western impact. Only during the decade before 1911 did the Confucian tradition begin to be discarded in favor of new ideas from the West. The second phase, from 1911 to the establishment of a communist state in 1949, was a time of turmoil: decades of warlord rule, war with Japan, and then four years of civil war.

CLOSE OF MANCHU RULE

THE OPIUM WAR

The 18th-century three-country trade—British goods to India, Indian cotton to China, and Chinese tea to Britain—was in China's favor. Then the British replaced cotton with Indian opium, and by the 1820s, the balance of trade was reversed.

To check the evil of opium and the outflow of silver, the Chinese government banned opium in 1836. In 1839, the government sent Lin Zexu (1785–1850) to Guangzhou (Canton) to superintend the ban. He destroyed a six-month supply of opium belonging to foreign merchants, leading to a confrontation with the British.

War broke out in November 1839. For the next two years, the British fought battles and attempted negotiations. The Chinese troops were ineffective. The war was finally ended in August 1842 by the Treaty of Nanjing, the first of the **"unequal treaties."**

The treaty gave Britain the island of Hong Kong and a huge indemnity. It also opened five ports: Fuzhou, Guangzhou, Ningpo, Shanghai, and Xiamen

---

WHAT WERE the most serious threats to Manchu rule in the 19th century?

"unequal treaties"
Agreements imposed on China in the 19th century by European powers, the United States, and Japan that granted their citizens special legal and economic privileges on Chinese soil.

(Amoy). British merchants and their families could reside in the ports and engage in trade; Britain could appoint a consul for each city; and British residents within China were subject to British, not Chinese, law. In 1844, similar treaties followed with the United States and France.

After the signing of the British treaty, Chinese imports of opium increased, but other kinds of trade did not grow as much as had been hoped. Western merchants blamed the lack of growth on Chinese officials. They also complained that Guangzhou remained closed to trade. Chinese authorities were incensed by the export of coolies to work in Cuba and Peru. A second war broke out in 1856, and the British captured Beijing in 1860. New treaties provided for indemnities, the opening of 11 new ports, the stationing of foreign diplomats in Beijing, the propagation of Christianity anywhere in China, and the legalization of the opium trade.

Meanwhile, the Russians were encroaching on China's northern frontier. In 1858, China ceded the north bank of the Amur to Russia, and in 1860, China gave Russia the Maritime Province between the Ussuri River and the Pacific.

REBELLIONS AGAINST THE MANCHU

More serious threats to Manchu rule were the Nian, Muslim, and **Taiping rebellions** that convulsed China between 1850 and 1873. The torment and suffering caused by these events were unparalleled in world history. China's population dropped by 60 million.

The Taipings were begun by Hong Xiuquan (1814–1864), a schoolteacher from the southern province of Kwangtung. Influenced by Protestant tracts, Hong announced that he was the younger brother of Jesus and that God had told him to rid China of Manchus, Confucians, Daoists, and Buddhists. Like earlier rebels, the Taipings combined moral reform, religious fervor, and a vision of egalitarian society. The Taipings were soon joined by peasants, miners, and workers. Fighting spread until the Taipings controlled most of the Yangzi basin and had entered 16 of the 18 Chinese provinces. Their army numbered close to a million.

The other rebellions were of lesser note. The Nian were located north of the Taipings along the Huai River. They were organized in secret societies and raided the countryside. Eventually they built an army, collected taxes, and ruled 100,000 square miles. A longer revolt was of Muslims against Chinese in the southwest and the northwest. These rebellions took advantage of the weakened state of the dynasty and occurred in areas that had few officials and no Qing military units.

Against the rebellions, the imperial forces proved helpless: In 1852, the court sent Zeng Guofan (1811–1872) to south-central China to organize a local army. Zeng, a product of the Confucian examination system, saw the Manchu government, of which he was an elite member, as the upholder of morality and the social order, and Chinese rebels as would-be destroyers of that order. He recruited members of the gentry as officers. They were Confucian, and as landlords had the most to lose from rebel rule. They recruited soldiers from their local areas and stopped the Taipings' advance.

In 1860, when the British and French occupied Beijing, a reform government began internal changes, adopted a policy of cooperation with Western powers, and put Zeng in charge of suppressing all the rebellions. Zeng appointed able officials to raise regional armies. Foreigners and Shanghai merchants gave their support. The Taipings collapsed when Nanjing was captured in 1864. The Nian were suppressed by 1868 and the Muslim rebellion was put down five years later. Scholar-officials, relying on local gentry, had saved the dynasty.

21.1
Lin Tse-hsu [Lin Zexu], Letter of Moral Admonition to Queen Victoria

QUICK REVIEW

Rebellions
- Taiping: Led by Hung Hsiu-ch'uan (1814–1864), the Taiping assembled an army of close to a million men
- Nien: Located along the Huai River, the Nien came to control a 100,000-square-mile area
- Muslim rebellions: Muslim revolt against Chinese in southwest and northwest, areas where China had few officials and little military presence

Taiping rebellion A 19th-century revolt against China's Manchu dynasty that was inspired by quasi-Christian ideas and that led to enormous suffering and destruction before its collapse in 1868.

Empress Dowager. Tz'u-hsi, the empress dowager (1835–1908), manipulated the levers of power at the Manchu court in Peking.

Hulton Picture Library/Corbis-Bettmann.

SELF-STRENGTHENING AND DECLINE (1874–1895)

In view of the dynasty's advanced stage of administrative decentralization, the Chinese resiliency and capacity to rebuild in the two decades after the suppression of the rebellions were impressive. But if we ask how effective China's response was to the West, or if we compare China's progress with that of Japan, then China during the same decades looks almost moribund. Historians often call these years the period of "self-strengthening," yet China was relatively weaker at the end of the period than at the start.

The Court at Beijing China's inability to act effectively is explained partly by the situation at the court. Prince Gong (1833–1898) and the empress dowager (1835–1908) were coregents for the young emperor. Prince Gong was a man of ideas. In 1861, he established a new office to handle the court's relations with foreign diplomats in Beijing. The following year, he established a school to train Chinese in foreign languages. However, outmaneuvered by the empress dowager, he was ousted in 1884.

The empress dowager had produced the only male child of the former emperor. She had no conception of how to reform China; her single goal was power. She acquired it by forging a political machine of conservative bureaucrats, military commanders, and eunuchs, and by maintaining a balance between the court and the regional governor-generals. The result was a court just able to survive but too weak to govern effectively.

Regional Governments The most vital figures during these decades were a handful of able governors-general. Each had an army and was in charge of two or three provinces. They were loyal to the dynasty that they had restored in the face of almost certain collapse and were allowed great autonomy.

Their first task was reconstruction. Millions were hungry or homeless. The leaders' response was massive and effective. Just as they had mobilized the gentry to suppress the rebellions, now they obtained their cooperation in rebuilding. They set up refugee centers, reduced taxes in the devastated Yangzi valley, reclaimed lands gone to waste, began water-control projects, and built granaries. By the early 1890s, well-being had been restored to Chinese society.

Their second task was self-strengthening—the adoption of Western arms and technology. The Chinese built arsenals and shipyards, a telegraph company, railways, and cotton mills. The formula applied in running these enterprises was "official supervision and merchant operation." Major decisions were made by scholar-officials, but day-to-day operations were left to the merchants.

Treaty Ports The **treaty ports**, of which there were 14 by the 1860s, were little islands of privilege and security, under the rule of foreign consuls, where capital was safe from confiscation, trade was free, and "squeeze" (extortion by officials) was the exception. Foreign companies naturally located in the ports, as did Chinese merchants who were also attracted by these conditions. Well into the 20th century, the foreign concessions (treaty-port lands leased in perpetuity by foreigners) remained the vital sector of China's modern economy.

treaty ports Chinese ports ruled by foreign consuls where foreigners enjoyed commercial privileges and immunity from Chinese laws.

The effects of the treaty ports and of Western imperialism on China were largely negative. Under the low tariffs mandated by the treaties, Chinese industries had little protection from imports. Native cotton spinning was almost destroyed by imports of yarn. Chinese tea lost ground to Indian tea and Chinese silk to Japanese silk. China found few products to export. The level of foreign trade stayed low, and China's interior markets were affected only slightly.

By the 1870s, foreign powers had reached an accommodation with China. They counted on the court to uphold the treaties; in return, they became a prop for the dynasty. By 1900, for example, the court's revenues from customs fees were larger than those from any other source. The fees were collected by the Maritime Customs Service, an efficient and honest treaty-port institution headed by an Irishman. In 1895, the Maritime Customs Service had 700 Western and 3,500 Chinese employees.

THE BORDERLANDS: THE NORTHWEST, VIETNAM, AND KOREA

China's other foreign relations were with fringe lands that China claimed by right of past conquest or as tributaries. The tributaries were the mirrors in which China saw reflected its own self-image as a universal empire. During the late 19th century, this image was strengthened in the northwest but dealt a fatal blow in Vietnam and Korea.

The Northwest   In the northwest, China confronted imperial Russia. Caught between them, the independent nomadic tribes were rendered impotent. By 1878, China had reconquered Chinese Turkestan, which was renamed Xinjang, or the "New Territories." A treaty signed with Russia in 1881 restored most of the Ili region in western Mongolia to Chinese control. The victories strengthened court conservatives who wished to take a stronger stance toward the West.

Vietnam   Vietnam, which had retained its independence from China since 935, saw itself as an independent state but used the Chinese writing system, modeled its laws and government on those of China, and traded with China. China simply saw Vietnam as a tributary.

During the 1840s, the second emperor of the Nguyen dynasty, which had begun in 1802, moved to reduce French influences and suppress Christianity. Thousands were killed, including French and Vietnamese priests. The French responded by seizing Saigon and Cochin China in 1859, establishing a protectorate over Cambodia in 1864, and taking Hanoi in 1882. China in 1883 sent troops to aid its tributary, but after a two-year war with France, in 1885 China was forced to abandon its claims to Vietnam. By 1893, France had brought together Vietnam, Cambodia, and Laos to form the Federation of Indochina, which remained a French colony until 1940.

Korea   Unlike Vietnam, Korea saw itself as a tributary of China on Chinese terms. The Korean ruler styled himself as a king and not an emperor.

During the last decades of the long (1392–1910) Choson dynasty, the Korean state was weak. It hung on to power in part by enforcing a policy of seclusion almost as total as that of Tokugawa Japan, winning it the name of the Hermit Kingdom. Its only foreign ties were with China and Japan. In 1876, Japan "opened" Korea to international relations, using much the same tactics that Perry had used against Japan. Japan then contended with China for influence in Korea.

QUICK REVIEW

Korea in the Late 19th Century
- Tributary of China
- The Korean state was weak in the last decades of the 19th century
- After 1876, Japan contended with China for influence in Korea

In 1893, a popular religious sect unleashed a rebellion against the Seoul government. When the government requested Chinese help to suppress the rebellion, China sent troops, but Japan sent more, and in 1894, war broke out between China and Japan. Taiwan became Japan's first colony. The defeat convinced many in China that basic changes were inevitable.

FROM DYNASTY TO WARLORDISM (1895–1926)

China was ruled by officials who had mastered the Confucian classics. This intellectual formation was resistant to change. For most officials living in China's interior, the foreign crises of the 19th century were "coastal phenomena," soon forgotten. Few officials realized the magnitude of the foreign threat.

China's defeat by Japan in 1895 came as a shock. The response within China was a new wave of reform proposals. The most influential thinker was Kang Youwei (1858–1927), who described China as "enfeebled" and blamed the "conservatives." They did not understand, Kang argued, that Confucius himself had been a reformer who had invented the idea of a golden age to persuade the rulers of his own age to adopt his ideas. History was evolutionary—a march forward from absolute monarchy to constitutional monarchy to democracy. Kang's reinterpretation of Confucianism removed a major barrier to the entry of Western ideas into China.

In 1898, the emperor himself became sympathetic to Kang's ideas and launched "one hundred days of reform." He took as his models Peter the Great (r. 1682–1725) and the Japanese Meiji Emperor (r. 1867–1912). Edicts were issued to reform China's schools, railroads, police, laws, military, bureaucracy, post offices, and examination system. But conservative resistance was nationwide. At court, the empress dowager regained control and ended the reforms. Kang fled to Japan. One reformer was executed.

The response of the Western powers to China's 1895 defeat was to define spheres of interest, which usually consisted of a leasehold along with railway rights and commercial privileges. Russia gained a leasehold at Port Arthur; Germany acquired one in Shandung. Britain got the New Territories adjoining Jiulong (Kowloon) at Hong Kong. New ports and cities were opened to foreign trade. The United States was in a weaker position, so it enunciated an "open-door" policy: equal commercial opportunities for all powers and the preservation of the territorial integrity of China.

At this time there was a religious society in China known as the **Boxers** (in Chinese, literally the "Righteous and Harmonius Fists"). They rebelled first in Shandung in 1898, and, gaining court support, entered Beijing in 1900. There followed a two-month siege of the foreign legation quarter. The rebellion was fueled by pent-up resentments against decades of foreign encroachments. Eventually an international force captured Beijing, and the Russians occupied Manchuria.

WHO WERE the key figures in the revolution of 1911?

Boxers Nationalistic Chinese religious society that attacked foreigners and their encroachments on China in the late 19th century.

"Open Door" Cartoon. An American view of the "open door." The combination of high self-esteem and negative attitudes toward foreigners at the turn of the century was not a Chinese monopoly.

Corbis-Bettmann.

The defeat of the Boxers convinced even conservative Chinese leaders of the futility of clinging to old ways. A more powerful reform movement began, with the empress dowager in its vanguard. But the dynasty could not control the movement and eventually was bypassed.

Educational reforms began in 1901. Women were admitted to newly formed schools. In place of Confucianism, instructors taught science, mathematics, geography, and an antiimperialist version of Chinese history. Western doctrines, such as classical economics, liberalism, socialism, anarchism, and social Darwinism, were introduced into China. By 1906, there were 8,000 Chinese students in Japan, which became a hotbed of Chinese reformist and revolutionary societies.

Military reforms were begun by Yuan Shikai (1859–1916), whose New Army drew on Japanese and Western models. Young men from gentry families, spurred by patriotism, joined the New Army as officers. Their loyalty was to their commanders and their country, not to the dynasty.

In 1905, the examination system was abolished; officials were to be recruited directly from the schools and those who had studied abroad. Provincial assemblies were formed in 1909, and a consultative assembly was established in Beijing in 1910.

These changes sparked the 1911 revolution. It began with an uprising in Sichuan province against a government plan to nationalize the main railways. The key figures were:

1. Gentry who stood to lose their investments in the railways.

2. Qing military commanders, who declared their provinces independent.

3. Sun Zhongshan (or Sun Yat-sen) (1866–1925), a republican revolutionary. He organized the Revolutionary Alliance in Tokyo in 1905 and was associated with the Nationalist Party (Guomindang) formed in 1912.

4. Yuan Shikai, who arranged for the last child emperor to abdicate, for Sun to step aside, and for himself to become president of the new Republic of China.

The nationalists won an election called in 1913, but Yuan routed them and proclaimed a new dynasty with himself as emperor. The idea of another dynasty, however, met opposition from all quarters. Yuan died in June 1916. China then fell into the hands of warlord armies. The years until the late 1920s were a time of agony for the Chinese people. Yet they were also in a time of intense intellectual ferment.

Execution of Boxers. The rebels, arms bound behind, lie headless. Chinese soldiers watch. In the 1900 siege of the foreign legations in Bejing, 76 foreigners were killed by the Boxers. Twelve years later, the dynasty fell.

Neg./Transparency no. 336289. (Photo Copied by P. Goldberg). Courtesy Dept. of Library Services, American Museum of Natural History.

Cultural and Ideological Ferment: The May Fourth Movement

A period of freedom and vigorous experimentation with new doctrines began in 1914 and extended into the 1920s. It is called the May Fourth Movement after an incident in Beijing in 1919 in which thousands of students protested the settlement at Versailles that awarded former German possessions in Shandung to Japan. The nationalist fervor that led the

WHAT WAS the May Fourth Movement?

students to demonstrate in the streets changed the complexion of Chinese thought. Leading thinkers began to judge ideas in terms of their value in solving China's problems.

During the May Fourth era, the center of advanced thought was Beijing. Ideas propounded there quickly spread to the rest of China, especially to its urban centers. Protest demonstrations against imperialist privilege broke out in Guangzhou, Shanghai, and Wuhan, as they had in the capital. Nationalism and antiimperialist sentiment were stronger than liberalism, although most thinkers spoke of democracy. Only members of an older generation of reformers, appalled by the slaughter of World War I and what they saw as Western materialism, advocated a return to traditional philosophies.

After the Russian Revolution of 1917, Marxism-Leninism entered China. The Leninist definition of imperialism as the last crisis stage of capitalism put the blame for China's ills on the West and offered "feudal" China the possibility of leapfrogging over capitalism to socialism. Marxist study groups formed in Beijing and other cities. In 1919, a student from Hunan, Mao Zedong, who had worked in the Beijing University library, returned to Changsha to form a study group. The Chinese Communist Party was formed in Shanghai in 1921; Zhou Enlai (1898–1976) formed a similar group in Paris the same year.

NATIONALIST CHINA

GUOMINDANG UNIFICATION OF CHINA AND THE NANJING DECADE (1927–1937)

WHY DID the communists win the Chinese Civil War?

Sun Zhongshan had fled to Japan during the 1913–1916 rule by Yuan Shikai. He returned to Guangzhou in 1916, but he was a poor organizer, and his **Guomindang (GMD)**—or Nationalist Party—made little headway. From 1923, Sun began to receive Soviet support. He reorganized his party on the Leninist model, with an executive committee on top of a national party congress, provincial and county organizations, and local party cells.

Since 1905, Sun had enunciated his "three principles of the people": nationality, livelihood, and rights. Sun's nationalism was now directed against Western imperialism. The principle of people's livelihood was defined in terms of equalizing land holdings and nationalizing major industries. By "people's rights" Sun meant democracy, although he argued that it must be preceded by a preparatory period of single-party dictatorship. Sun sent his loyal lieutenant Jiang Jieshi (Chiang Kai-shek) (1887–1975) to the Soviet Union for study. Jiang returned after four months with a cadre of Russian advisers and established a military academy at Huangpu south of Guangzhou in 1924. Sun died in 1925. By 1926, the Huangpu Academy had graduated several thousand officers, and the GMD army numbered almost 100,000. The GMD had become the major political force in China.

The growth of the party was spurred by changes within Chinese society. Industries arose in the cities. Labor unions were organized. New ventures were begun outside the treaty ports. A politically conscious middle class developed.

The quicksilver element in cities was the several million students. In May 1925, students demonstrated in Shanghai. Police in the international settlement fired on the demonstrators. The incident inflamed national and antiimperialist feelings. Strikes and boycotts of foreign goods were called throughout China.

Under these conditions the Chinese Communist Party (CCP) also grew and was influential in student organizations, labor unions, and even within the GMD. Sun had permitted CCP members to join the GMD as individuals, but had

Guomindang (GMT) China's Nationalist Party, founded by Sun Zhongshan.

enjoined them from organizing CCP cells within it. Moscow approved of this policy. It felt that the CCP was too small to accomplish anything on its own.

By 1926, Jiang Jieshi felt ready to march against the warlords. He worried about the growing communist strength, however, and before setting off he ousted the Soviet advisers and CCP members from the GMD offices in Guangzhou. The march north began in July. By the spring of 1927, Jiang's army had reached the Yangzi, defeating warlord armies as it advanced.

After entering Shanghai in April 1927, Jiang carried out a sweeping purge of the CCP. Many were killed. The surviving CCP members fled to the mountainous border region of Hunan and Jiangxi to the southwest and established the "Jiangxi Soviet." Jiang's army took Beijing and gained the nominal submission of most northern Chinese warlords during 1928. Most foreign powers recognized the GMD regime as the government of China.

Jiang Jieshi was the key figure in the government. He believed in military force. He was unimaginative, strict, and incorruptible. Jiang venerated Sun Zhongshan and his three "people's principles." But where Sun was a revolutionary, Jiang was conservative and, though a Methodist, often appealed to Confucian values. The New Life Movement begun by Jiang in 1934 was an attempt to revitalize these values.

Jiang's power rested on the army, the party, and the bureaucracy. The army was dominated by the Huangpu clique, which was loyal to Jiang, and by officers trained in Japan. After 1927, German advisers reorganized Jiang's army along German lines with a general staff system. The larger part of GMD revenues went to the military, which was expanded into a modernized force of 300,000. Huangpu graduates also controlled the secret military police and used it against communists and any others who opposed the government. The GMD was a dictatorship under a central committee. Jiang became president of the party in 1938.

The densely populated central and lower Yangzi provinces were the area of GMD strength. The party, however, was unable to control the outlying areas occupied by warlords, communists, and the Japanese. Warlords ruled some areas until 1949. In 1931, Jiang attacked the Jiangxi Soviet. In 1934, the communists were forced to flee to the southwest and then to Shaanxi province in northwestern China in the epic "**Long March.**" During this march Mao Zedong wrested control of the CCP from the Moscow-trained, urban-oriented leaders and established his unorthodox view that a Leninist party could base itself on the peasantry.

The Japanese had held special rights in Manchuria since the Russo-Japanese War of 1905. When Jiang's march north and Chinese nationalism threatened the Japanese position, Japan's army engineered a military coup in 1931, and in 1932 it established a puppet state and proclaimed the independence of Manchuria. In the years that followed, Japanese forces moved south as far as the Great Wall. Chinese nationalism demanded that Jiang resist. Jiang, well aware of the disparity between his

Long March Flight of the Chinese communists from their nationalist foes to northwest China in 1934.

Modern China

1839–1842	Opium War
1850–1873	Taiping and other rebellions
1870s–1880s	Self-strengthening movement
1894–1895	Sino-Japanese War
1898	One hundred days of reform
1898–1900	Boxer Rebellion
1911	Republican revolution overthrows Qing dynasty
1912–1916	Yuan Shikai president of Republic of China
1916–1928	Warlord era
1919	May Fourth incident
1924	Founding of Huangpu Military Academy
1926–1928	March north and Guomindang reunification of China
1934–1935	Chinese Communists' Long March to Yan'an
1937–1945	War with Japan
1945–1949	Civil war and the establishment of the People's Republic of China

armies and those of Japan, said that the internal unification of China must take precedence. In 1937, however, a full-scale war with Japan broke out, and China's situation changed.

WAR AND REVOLUTION (1937–1949)

The war with Japan began in July 1937 as an unplanned clash at Beijing and then quickly spread. Beijing and Tianjin fell to Japan within a month, Shanghai was attacked in August, and Nanjing fell in December. During the following year, the Japanese took Guangzhou and set up puppet regimes in Beijing and Nanjing. In 1940, the leader of the left wing of the GMD and many of his associates joined the Japanese puppet government. Japan proclaimed its "New Order in East Asia." It expected Jiang to submit. Instead, in 1938 he relocated his capital to Chongqing, far to the west, and was joined by thousands of Chinese.

Jiang's stubborn resistance won admiration from all sides. But the withdrawal to Chongqing cut the GMD off from most of the Chinese population; programs for modernization ended; and the GMD's former tax revenues were lost. Inflation increased geometrically and exacerbated the already widespread corruption.

The United States sent advisers and military equipment to strengthen Jiang's forces after the start of the Pacific War. However, Jiang wanted not to fight the Japanese but to husband his forces for a postwar confrontation with the communists. Within his own army a gap appeared between officers and men. Conditions in the camps were primitive, food poor, and medical supplies inadequate. The young saw conscription almost as a death sentence. Jiang's unwillingness to commit his troops against the Japanese also meant that the surge of anti-Japanese patriotism was not converted to popular support for the GMD.

For the communists, the Japanese occupation was an opportunity. Headquartered at Yan'an, they began campaigns to promote literacy and self-sufficiency. Soldiers farmed so as not to burden the peasants. The CCP abandoned its earlier policy of expropriating lands in favor of reductions in rents and interest. They took only those offices needed to ensure their control and shared the rest with the GMD and other parties. They expanded village councils to include tenants. But they also strengthened their party internally.

Party membership expanded from 40,000 in 1937 to 1.2 million in 1945. Schools were established in Yan'an to train party cadres. Orthodoxy was maintained by a rectification campaign. Those tainted by impure tendencies were made to repent at public meetings. Mao's thought was supreme. To the Chinese at large, Mao represented himself as the successor to Sun Zhongshan, but within the Communist Party he presented himself as a theoretician in the line of Marx (1818–1883), Engels (1820–1895), Lenin (1870–1924), and Stalin (1879–1953).

The communists learned to operate at the grass-roots level. They infiltrated Japanese-controlled areas and GMD organizations and military units. CCP armies were built up from 90,000 in 1937 to 900,000 in 1945. These armies were supplemented by

Mao Zedong. Photographed at his cave headquarters in Shaanxi province during World War II, Mao Zedong (1893–1976) wears a padded winter jacket and writes with a Chinese brush.

Getty Images, Inc. – Taxi.

a rural people's militia and by guerrilla forces. The Yan'an leadership and its party, army, and mass organizations possessed cohesion, determination, and morale that were lacking in Chongqing.

But the strength of the Chinese communists as of 1945 should not be overstated. When the war in the Pacific ended in 1945, China's future was unclear. Even the Soviet Union recognized the GMD as the government of China and expected it to win the postwar struggle. The Allies directed Japanese armies to surrender to the GMD forces in 1945. The United States flew Jiang's troops to key eastern cities. His armies were by then three times the size of the communists' and far better equipped.

A civil war broke out immediately. Efforts by U.S. General George Marshall (1880–1959) to mediate were futile. Until the summer of 1947, GMD armies were victorious—even capturing Yan'an. But the tide turned in July as CCP armies went on the offensive in north China. In January 1949, Beijing and Tianjin fell. A few months later all of China was in communist hands. Many Chinese fled with Jiang to Taiwan or escaped to Hong Kong. In China, apprehension was mixed with anticipation. The feeling was widespread that the future of China was once again in the hands of the Chinese.

MODERN JAPAN (1853–1945)

OVERTHROW OF THE TOKUGAWA BAKUFU (1853–1868)

From the 17th century into the 19th century, the natural isolation of the islands of Japan was augmented by the country's policy of seclusion, making Japan into a little world of its own. The 260-odd domains were the states of this world, the bakufu in Edo was its hegemon, and the imperial court in Kyoto provided a religious sanction for the bakufu-domain system. Then at mid-century, the American ships of Commodore Perry came and forced Japan to sign a treaty, opening it to foreign intercourse. Fourteen years later, the entire bakufu-domain system collapsed, and a group of talented leaders seized power. Seclusion, like the case of a watch, had been necessary to preserve the Tokugawa political mechanism. With the case removed, the inner workings flew apart.

Little changed during the first four years after Perry. The break came in 1858 when the bakufu, ignoring the imperial court's disapproval, was persuaded to sign a commercial treaty with the United States. Some daimyo, who wanted a voice in national policy, criticized the treaty as contravening the hallowed policy of seclusion. Younger samurai, frustrated by their exclusion from office, started a movement to "honor the emperor." The bakufu, in turn, responded with a purge. But in 1860, the head of the bakufu council was assassinated by extremist samurai. His successors lacked the nerve to continue his tough policies.

In 1861, two domains, Chōshū and Satsuma, emerged to heal the breach between the bakufu and the court. First, Chōshū officials proposed a policy that favored the bakufu but made concessions to the court. Next, Satsuma advocated a policy that made further concessions and ousted Chōshū as "the friend of the court." In response, the moderate reformist government of Chōshū adopted the proemperor policy of its extremist faction and, in turn, ousted Satsuma. Satsuma then seized the court in 1863 in a military coup.

24.6
"From the Countryside to the City" (May 1949): Mao Zedong

WHAT ROLE did the Chōshū and Satsuma play in the overthrow of Tokugawa rule?

Several points are of note about the 1861–1863 diplomatic phase of domain action:

1. Even after 250 years of bakufu rule, several domains could still act when the opportunity occurred.
2. The two domains that acted first and most of the others that followed had many samurai and substantial financial resources.
3. Both Satsuma and Chōshū had fought against the Tokugawa in 1600 and remembered an earlier independence.
4. By 1861–1863, the new politics had opened decision making to middle-ranking samurai officials in a way that would have been impossible before 1853.

The 1863 Satsuma coup at the Kyoto court initiated a military phase of politics in which battles would determine every turning point. As long as Satsuma and Chōshū remained enemies, politics stalemated and the bakufu continued as hegemon. But when the two domains became allies in 1866, the bakufu was overthrown in less than two years.

One factor contributing to this process was the movement for a "union of court and camp"; daimyo campaigned for a new conciliar rule in which they

Commodore Matthew Perry Meeting Japanese Officials at Kurigahama in 1853. At the right are two emissaries of the bakufu; at the left is Perry's Chinese translator, who speaks English and communicates with the Japanese in written Chinese. Perry's ships are visible in the background, along with smaller Japanese craft.

U.S. Naval Academy Museum.

HISTORY'S VOICES

A JAPANESE VIEW OF THE INVENTIVENESS OF THE WEST

Serious Japanese thinkers reacted to their country's weakness with proposals to adopt Western science and industry. But the "Civilization and Enlightenment Movement" of the 1870s had its lighter side as well. In 1871, the novelist Kanagaki Robun wrote a satire about a man with an umbrella, a watch, and eau de cologne on his hair, eating with a friend in a new beef restaurant. Before the Restoration, Buddhism had banned beef eating as a defilement. The comic hero, however, wonders "why we in Japan haven't eaten such a clean thing before." He then goes on to rhapsodize about Western inventions.

WHAT DO pickled onions have to do with the marvels of Western technology?

In the West they're free of superstitions. There it's the custom to do everything scientifically, and that's why they've invented amazing things like the steamship and the steam engine. Did you know that they engrave the plates for printing newspapers with telegraphic needles? And that they bring down wind from the sky with balloons? Aren't they wonderful inventions! Of course, there are good reasons behind these inventions. If you look at a map of the world you'll see some countries marked "tropical," which means that's where the sun shines closest. The people in those countries are all burnt black by the sun. The king of that part of the world tried all kinds of schemes before he hit on what is called a balloon. That's a big round bag they fill with air high up in the sky. They bring the bag down and open it, causing the cooling air inside the bag to spread out all over the country. That's a great invention. On the other hand, in Russia, which is a cold country where the snow falls even in summer and the ice is so thick that people can't move, they invented the steam engine. You've got to admire them for it. I understand that they modeled the steam engine after the flaming chariot of hell, but anyway, what they do is to load a crowd of people on a wagon and light a fire in a pipe underneath. They keep feeding the fire inside the pipe with coal, so that the people riding on top can travel a great distance completely oblivious to the cold. Those people in the West can think up inventions like that, one after the other . . . You say you must be going? Well, good-bye. Waitress! Another small bottle of *sake*. And some pickled onions to go with it!

Source: *Modern Japanese Literature*, D. Keene, ed. and trans. pp. 32–33. Copyright © 1956 Grove Press. Reprinted by permission of Grove/Atlantic, Inc.

would participate together with the emperor and withdrew support from the bakufu. A second feature of the years between 1863 and 1868 was anti-foreignism. Extremists assassinated foreigners as well as bakufu officials; one of their slogans was "expel the barbarians." A third was the formation of new rifle units, commanded mostly by lower samurai. These units transformed political power in Japan. A fourth development during 1867 and 1868 was a cultural shift in the way Japanese saw themselves. During the Tokugawa era, the Japanese saw themselves as civilized Confucians and much of the rest of the world as barbarians. But in the face of Western gunboats, this view seemed hollow. Turning the traditional view on its head, the West, with its technology, science, and humane laws, was now seen as "civilized and enlightened;" China, Japan, and countries like Turkey were seen as half civilized; and other areas were dismissed as barbarian. Moreover, influential scholars claimed that technology was not detachable, but grew out of the Western legal, political, economic, and educational stysems (see "A Japanese View of the Inventiveness of the West").

WHAT POWERS did the Meiji Constitution give to the emperor?

BUILDING THE MEIJI STATE (1868–1890)

*T*he idea of a "developing nation" did not exist in the mid-19th century. Yet Japan, after the 1868 **Meiji restoration**, was just such a nation. (The years from 1868 to 1912 are referred to as the Meiji period, after the name of the emperor.) It was committed to progress, which meant achieving wealth and power of the kind possessed by Western industrial nations. There was no blueprint for progress. The government advanced by trial and error. It also demanded that the Japanese people make sacrifices for the sake of the future.

The announcement of the restoration of rule by an emperor was made on January 3, 1868. In the battles that followed, Chōshū and Satsuma troops defeated those of the bakufu. Edo surrendered and was renamed Tokyo, the "eastern capital." Edo castle became the imperial palace. A year later, the last bakufu holdouts surrendered. At the start the Meiji government was made up of only a small group of samurai leaders from Chōshū, Satsuma, and a few other domains. They have been described, only half humorously, as 12 bureaucrats in search of a bureaucracy. But their vision defined the goals of the new government.

CENTRALIZATION OF POWER

Their immediate goal was to centralize political power. By 1871, the young leaders had replaced the domains with prefectures controlled from Tokyo. To ensure a break with the past, each new prefectural governor was chosen from samurai of other regions.

Having centralized political authority, about half of the most important Meiji leaders went abroad for a year and a half to study the West. On their return to Japan in 1872, they discovered that officials were planning war with Korea. They quashed the plan, insisting that priority be given to domestic development.

The second goal or task of the Meiji leaders was to stabilize government revenues that, because the land tax was collected mostly in grain, fluctuated with the price of rice. The government converted the grain tax to a money tax. But a third of the revenues still went to pay for samurai stipends, so in 1873 the government raised a conscript army and abolished the samurai class. The samurai were paid off in government bonds; but as the bonds fell during the inflation of the 1870s, most former samurai became impoverished. What had begun as a reform of government finance ended as a social revolution.

Some samurai rebelled. The last and greatest uprising was in 1877. When it was suppressed in 1878, the Meiji government became militarily secure.

POLITICAL PARTIES

Other samurai opposed the government by forming political parties and campaigning for popular rights, elections, and a constitution. They drew heavily on liberal Western models. National assemblies, they argued, were the means used by advanced societies to tap the energies of their peoples. Parties in a national assembly would unite the emperor and the people, thereby curbing the Satsuma-Chōshū clique. Samurai were the mainstay of the early party movement, despite its doctrines proclaiming all classes to be equal. In 1881, the government promised a constitution and a national assembly within 10 years. As the date for national elections approached, the parties gained strength, and the ties between party notables and local men of influence grew closer.

Meiji restoration Overthrow of the Tokugawa *bakufu* in Japan in 1868 and the transfer, or "restoration," of power to the imperial government under the Emperor Meiji.

THE CONSTITUTION

The government viewed the party movement with distaste but was not sure how to counter it. Itō Hirobumi (1841–1909), originally from Chōshū, went abroad to shop for a constitution that would serve the needs of the Meiji government. He brought home a German jurist to help adapt the conservative Prussian constitution of 1850 to Japanese uses. As promulgated in 1889, the Meiji constitution granted extensive powers to the emperor and severely limited the powers of the lower house in the **Diet** (the English term for Japan's bicameral national assembly).

The emperor was sovereign. According to the constitution, he was "sacred and inviolable," and in Itō's commentaries this was defined in Shinto terms. The emperor was given direct command of the armed forces. Yamagata Aritomo (1838–1922) had set up a German-type general staff system in 1878. The emperor had the right to name the prime minister and to appoint the cabinet. He could dissolve the lower house of the Diet and issue imperial ordinances when the Diet was not in session. The Imperial Household Ministry, which was outside the cabinet, administered the great wealth given to the imperial family during the 1880s—so that the emperor would never have to ask the Diet for funds. It was understood that the Meiji leaders would act for the emperor in all of these matters. Finally, the constitution itself was presented as a gift from the emperor to his subjects.

The lower house of the Diet was given the authority only to approve budgets and pass laws, and both of these powers were hedged. The previous year's budget would remain in effect if a new budget was not approved. The appointive House of Peers, the upper house of the Diet, had to approve any bill to become law. Furthermore, the vote was given only to adult males paying 15 yen or more in taxes. In 1890, this was about 5 percent of the adult male population. In sum, Itō's intention was to create not a parliamentary system, but a constitutional system that included a parliament as one of its parts.

Diet Bicameral Japanese parliament.

The Promulgation of the Meiji Constitution in 1889. The emperor standing under the canopy, was declared "sacred and inviolable." Seated on the throne, at the left, is the empress.

Shosai Ginko (Japanese, act. 1874–1897). View of the Issuance of the State Constitution in the State Chamber of the New Imperial Palace, March 2, 1889 (Meiji 22), Ink and color on paper, 14 1/8 × 28 3/8 in. "The Metropolitan Museum of Art, Gift of Lincoln Kirstein, 1959 (JP3233-3235) Photograph © The Metropolitan Museum of Art.

WHY DID Japan set out to build a modern economy?

During the 1880s, the government also created institutions to limit the future influence of the political parties. In 1884, it created a new nobility with which to stock the future House of Peers. The nobility was composed of ex-nobles and the Meiji leaders themselves. Itō, born a lowly foot soldier, ended as a prince. In 1885, he established a cabinet system and became the first prime minister. In 1887, Itō established a Privy Council, with himself as its head, to approve the constitution he had written. In 1888, laws were passed and civil service examinations instituted to insulate the imperial bureaucracy from the tawdry concerns of politicians.

GROWTH OF A MODERN ECONOMY

The late Tokugawa economy was not markedly different from the economies of other East Asian countries. Almost 80 percent of the population lived in the countryside at close to a subsistence level. Taxes were high, and two-thirds of the land tax was paid in kind. Money had only partially penetrated the rural economy. Japan had not developed factory production with machinery, steam power, or large accumulations of capital.

Early Meiji reforms unshackled the late Tokugawa economy. Occupations were freed, which meant that farmers could trade and samurai could farm. Barriers on roads were abolished, as were the monopolistic guilds. The abolition of domains threw open regional economies and a groundswell of new commercial ventures and traditional, agriculturally based industries followed.

Silk was the wonder crop. The government introduced mechanical reeling, enabling Japan to win markets previously held by the hand-reeled silk of China. Silk production rose from 2.3 million pounds in the post-Restoration era to 93 million pounds in 1929.

A parallel unshackling occurred on the land. The land tax reform of the 1870s created an incentive for growth by giving farmers a clear title to their land and by fixing the tax in money. The freedom to buy and sell land led to a rise in tenancy from perhaps 25 percent in 1868 to about 44 percent at the turn of the century. Progressive landlords bought fertilizer and farm equipment. Rice production rose from 149 million bushels a year during 1880–1884 to 316 million during 1935–1937. More food, combined with a drop in the death rate—the result of better hygiene—led to population growth: from about 30 million in 1868 to 45 million in 1900 to 73 million in 1940. Because the farm population remained constant, the extra hands were available for factory and other urban jobs.

FIRST PHASE: MODEL INDUSTRIES

The modern sector of the economy was the government's greatest concern. It developed in four phases. The first was the era of model industries, which lasted until 1881. With military strength as a major goal, the Meiji government expanded arsenals and shipyards, built telegraph lines, made a start on railroads, developed mines, and established factories. The quantitative output of these early industries was insignificant, however. They were pilot-plant operations that doubled as "schools" for technologists and labor.

Just as important to economic development were banks, post offices, ports, roads, commercial laws, a system of primary and secondary schools, a government university, and so on. They were patterned after European and American examples.

A Model Industry. A silk factory, late 1800s. Note the male foreman, whose western-style dress contrasts with the traditional attire of the female workers.

SECOND PHASE: 1880S–1890S

More substantial growth in the modern sector took place during the 1880s and 1890s. It was marked by the appearance of what would later become the great industrial combines known as *zaibatsu*. One of the first industries to benefit was cotton textiles. By 1896, the production of yarn had reached 17 million pounds, and by 1913 it was more than 10 times that amount. Production of cotton cloth rose from 22 million square yards in 1900 to 2.7 billion in 1936.

Another area of growth was railroads. Railroads gave Japan an internal circulatory system, opening up hitherto isolated regions. In 1872, Japan had 18 miles of track; in 1894, 2,100 miles; and by 1934, 14,500 miles.

Cotton textiles and railroads were followed during the 1890s by cement, bricks, matches, glass, beer, chemicals, and other private industries. The government created a favorable climate for growth: The society and the polity were stable, the yen was sound, capital was safe, and taxes on industry were low. In every respect, the conditions enjoyed by Japan's budding entrepreneurs differed from those of China.

THIRD PHASE: 1905–1929

Economic growth spurted ahead during World War I. But an economic slump followed the war, and the economy grew slowly during the 1920s. One factor was renewed competition from a Europe at peace; another was the earthquake that destroyed Tokyo in 1923. Agricultural productivity also leveled off during the 1920s: It became cheaper to import food from the colonies than to invest in new agricultural technology at home.

By the 1920s, Japanese society, especially in the cities, was becoming modern. The Japanese were healthier and lived longer. Personal savings rose with the standard of living. Even factory workers drank beer, went to movies, and read newspapers. By 1925, primary school education was universal. Japan had done what no other non-Western nation had even attempted: It had achieved universal literacy. Nevertheless, an immense cultural and social gap remained between the majority who had only a primary school education and the 3 percent who attended university. This gap was a basic weakness in the political democracy of the 1920s.

The costs of growth were sometimes high. Because textiles played a large role in the early phase of Japan's modern economic growth, well into the 20th century more than half of the industrial labor force was women. They went to the mills after leaving primary school and returned to their villages before marrying. Their working hours were long, their dormitories crowded, and their movements restricted. Some contracted tuberculosis, the plague of late-19th- and early-20th-century Japan, and were sent back to their villages to die.

FOURTH PHASE: DEPRESSION AND RECOVERY

A Japanese bank crisis in 1927, followed by the worldwide Great Depression in 1929, plunged Japan into unemployment and suffering. The political consequences were enormous. Yet most of Japan recovered by 1933, more rapidly than any other industrial nation.

The recovery was fueled by an export boom and military procurements. During the 1930s, the production of pig iron, raw steel, and chemicals doubled. By 1937, Japan had a merchant fleet of 4.5 million tons, the third largest and the newest in the world. The quality of Japan's manufacturers also rose. The outcry in the West against Japanese exports at this time was not so much

---

QUICK REVIEW

Development of the Japanese Economy

- First Phase (–1881): Development of model industries
- Second Phase (1880s–1890s): Emergence of the zaibatsu and growth of the railroads
- Third Phase (1905–1929): Slow economic growth and modernization of Japanese society
- Fourth Phase (1929–1937): Depression and recovery

zaibatsu Large industrial combines that came to dominate Japanese industry in the late 19th century.

because of volume—a modest 3.6 percent of world exports in 1936—but because Japanese products had become competitive in terms of quality.

THE POLITICS OF IMPERIAL JAPAN (1890–1945)

WHY DID Japan join the imperialist scramble for colonies?

Parliaments began in the West and have worked better there than in the rest of the world. Even so cautious a constitution as that of Meiji had no precedent outside the West at the time. How are we then to view the Japanese political experience after 1890?

One view is that because Japanese society was not ready for constitutional government, the militarism of the 1930s was inevitable. From the perspective of an ideal democracy, Japanese society had many weaknesses: a small middle class, weak trade unions, an independent military under the emperor, a strong emperor-centered nationalism, and so on. But these weaknesses did not prevent the Diet from growing in importance, nor did they block the transfer of power from the bureaucratic Meiji leaders to the political party leaders. The transfer fell short of full parliamentary government. However, had it not been derailed by the Great Depression and other events, the advance toward parliamentary government might well have continued.

FROM CONFRONTATION TO THE FOUNDING OF THE SEIYŪKAI (1890–1900)

In 1890, the Meiji leaders—sometimes called *oligarchs*, the few who rule—were concerned with nation building, not politics. They saw the cabinet as serving the emperor and nation above the ruck of partisan interests. They viewed the political parties as ineffective and irresponsible. They saw the lower house of the Diet as a place to let off steam without interfering in the government's work of building a new Japan. But the oligarchs had miscalculated: The authority of the lower house to approve or turn down the budget made it more powerful than they had intended. This involved the oligarchs, willy-nilly, in the political struggles.

The first act of the parties in the new 1890 Diet was to slash the government's budget. Prime Minister Yamagata had to make concessions to get part of the cut restored. This pattern continued for 10 years. Rising costs meant that the previous year's budget was never enough. The government tried to intimidate and bribe the parties, but failed. Opposing political parties maintained their control of the lower house. They also had the support of the voters, mostly well-to-do landowners, who opposed the government's heavy land tax.

In 1900, Itō Hirobumi formed a new party, called the Rikken Seiyūkai, or "Friends of Constitutional Government." It was composed of ex-bureaucrats associated with Itō and of politicians from the Liberal Party that Itagaki Taisuke (1837–1919) had formed in 1881. For most of the next 20 years, it was the most important party in Japan, providing parliamentary support for successive governments through its control of the lower house. This arrangement was satisfactory to both sides: Prime ministers got the Diet support necessary for the government to function smoothly, and party politicians got cabinet posts and pork barrel legislation with which to reward their supporters.

THE GOLDEN YEARS OF MEIJI

The years before and after the turn of the century represented the culmination of what the government had striven for since 1868. Economic development was under way. Japan got rid of extraterritoriality in 1899 and regained control of its own tariffs in 1911. However, it was international events that won Japan recognition as a world power.

The first event was a war with China in 1894–1895 over Korea. From its victory, Japan secured Taiwan, the Pescadores Islands, the Kwantung Peninsula in southern Manchuria, an indemnity, and a treaty giving it the same privileges in China as those enjoyed by the Western powers (see Map 28–1.). Russia, however, with French and German support, forced Japan to give up the Kwantung Peninsula, which included Port Arthur. Three years later, Russia took Kwantung for itself.

The second event was Japan's participation in 1900 in the international force that relieved the Boxers' siege of the foreign legations in Beijing. A third

24.2
Japanese Imperialism

MAP 28–1

Formation of the Japanese Empire. The Japanese Empire grew in three stages: the Sino-Japanese War of 1894–1895, the Russo-Japanese War of 1904–1905, and Japanese conquests in Manchuria and nothern China after 1931.

WHAT WERE the reasons behind Japan's desire for an empire on the Asian mainland?

Russo-Japanese War. Japanese soldiers with flag and bayonets charge across a smoky field to engage Russian troops in the 1904–1905 Russo-Japanese War. Victory over Russia gave Korea to Japan and a new international standing. The popularity of postcards, such as this one, reflected the new nationalism of Japan.

Corbis-Bettmann.

development was the Anglo-Japanese Alliance of 1902. For Britain, this alliance ensured Japanese support for its East Asian interests and warded off the likelihood of a Russian-Japanese agreement over spheres of influence in Northeast Asia. For Japan, the alliance meant it could fight Russia without fear of intervention by a third party.

The fourth event was the war with Russia that began in 1904. Japanese armies drove the Russians from their railway zones in Manchuria and seized Mukden in March 1905. The Russians sent their Baltic fleet to join the battle, but it was annihilated by Admiral Tōgō (1847–1934) at the Straits of Tsushima. After months of war, both countries were worn out, and Russia was plagued by revolution. President Theodore Roosevelt (1858–1919) proposed a peace conference in Portsmouth, New Hampshire. The resulting treaty gave Japan the Russian lease in the Liaotung Peninsula, the Russian railway in south Manchuria, the southern half of Sakhalin, and a recognition of Japan's "paramount interest" in Korea, which was annexed in 1910.

Japan joined the imperialist scramble for colonies because it wanted equality with the great Western powers, and military power and colonies were the best credentials. Enthusiasm for empire was shared by political party leaders, most liberal thinkers, and conservative leaders alike.

RISE OF THE PARTIES TO POWER

The founding of the Seiyū kai by Itō in 1900 ended a decade of confrontation between the Diet and the government. The aging oligarch Itō found it intolerable to deal with party politicians, who, unlike the bureaucrats, neither obeyed him nor paid him the respect that he thought was his due. In 1903, he relinquished the presidency of the party to Saionji Kinmochi (1849–1940), who passed the post to Hara Takashi (1856–1921) in 1914. With Hara, the office found the man.

Hara was an outsider. Born a generation after the founding fathers of the Meiji state, he helped Itō to found the Seiyū kai and was the most able politician in Japan. His goals for Japan centered on the expansion of national wealth and power and were no different from those of Itō or Yamagata. But he felt that they should be achieved by party government, not oligarchic rule, and worked to expand the power of his party. The years between 1905 and 1921 were marked by the struggle between these two alternative conceptions of government.

The struggle can be represented as a rising curve of party strength and a descending curve of oligarchic influence. The rising curve had two vectors: a buildup of the Seiyū kai party machine that enabled it to win elections and maintain itself as the majority (or plurality) party in the Diet, and the strengthening of the Diet vis-á-vis other elites within the government in Tokyo. For the former, Hara obtained campaign funds from moneyed interests. He also promoted pork barrel legislation. Constituencies that supported Seiyū kai candidates got new schools, bridges, dams, roads, or even railroad lines. Hara was even willing to call on the police and local officials to aid Seiyū kai election campaigns.

In co-opting other governmental elites, the Seiyū kai had mixed success. The party increased its representation in the cabinet and gained some patronage appointments in the bureaucracy, although most bureaucrats remained professionals and resisted the intrusion of political appointees. The House of Peers and the Privy Council, which ratified treaties, remained independent bodies. The Seiyū kai had no success in penetrating the military services.

The descending curve of weakening oligarchic control reflected the aging of the "men of Meiji." In 1900, Itō was the last oligarch to become prime minister. From 1901 to 1912, Katsura Tarō (1847–1913), a Chōshū general and Yamagata's protégé, and Saionji, Itō's protégé, took turns in the post. Both had Seiyū kai support. The oligarchs were also weakened by changes within the elites. A younger generation of officers in the military services chafed at the continuing domination by the old cliques. In the civil bureaucracy, younger officials who had graduated from the Law Faculty of Tokyo Imperial University were achieving positions of responsibility. They saw the bureaucracy as an independent service and resisted oligarchic control almost as much as they resisted that of the parties.

The oligarchs maintained their power to act for the emperor in appointing prime ministers. With the deaths of Itō in 1909 and Yamagata in 1922, this vital function was taken over by Saionji and, later, by ex-prime ministers.

As the rising and descending curves approached each other, the political parties advanced. Several turning points were critical. One came in 1912. When the army's demands for a larger budget were refused, it withdrew its minister, causing Saionji's cabinet to collapse. Katsura tried to govern using imperial decrees in place of Diet support. This infuriated the parties, and even the Seiyū kai withdrew its support. Massive popular demonstrations broke out. Katsura was forced to resign in 1913. The lower house had defeated an oligarchic prime minister.

The curves finally crossed in 1918 when Hara became prime minister. It was the first time a politician who was not a Meiji founding father or a protégé of one had obtained the post. He enacted reforms but did nothing to remedy the parliamentary shortcomings of the Meiji constitution.

A third development was the wave of liberalism that began during World War I and culminated in the period of party governments from 1924 to 1932. Joining the Allies in World War I, Japan had been influenced by democratic thought from England and America. Scholars discussed revising the Meiji constitution. Labor unions were organized, at first liberal and often Christian, and later Marxist. A social movement was launched to improve conditions in Japan's industrial slums and to pass social and labor legislation. Japan's second political party, the Kenseikai, which had been out of power since 1916, steadily grew more liberal and adopted several of the new social causes as its own, such as universal manhood suffrage. When Hara cut the tax qualification for voting from 10 to 3 yen—a considerable extension of the franchise—the Kenseikai criticized the change as insufficient.

In 1924, the Kenseikai and the Seiyū kai formed a coalition government. For the next eight years, the presidents of one or the other of the two major parties were appointed as prime ministers.

The cabinets (1924–1926) of Katō Kōmei are considered the peak of parliamentarianism in prewar Japan. Blunt, cold, and haughty, Katō was respected, if not liked. He was an Anglophile who advocated a British model of government. His ministry passed universal manhood suffrage, increased academic appointments to the House of Peers, and cut the military budget. He also enacted social and labor legislation. In effect, he legalized the moderate socialist movement and outlawed revolutionary socialism. Katō's cabinet brought Japan close to a true parliamentary government.

MILITARISM AND WAR (1927–1945)

The future of Japan's parliamentary coalition seemed assured during the mid-1920s. The economy was growing, society was stable, and the party leaders were experienced. Japan's international position was secure. By a decade later, however, the party leaders had lost the gains of 35 years. By 1945, Japan had been defeated in a devastating war and was occupied by foreign troops for the first time in its history. How did this come about?

Simply put, a small shift in the balance of power among the governmental elites established by the Meiji constitution had produced a major change in Japan's foreign policy. The parties had been the obstreperous elite between 1890 and 1926 and had advanced by forcing the other elites to compromise. From the late 1920s, the military became the obstreperous elite and did the same. Beginning in 1932, military men replaced party presidents as prime ministers. In 1937, Japan went to war with China; and by the end of 1941, Japan was allied with Germany and Italy and had gone to war with the United States.

From their inception, the military services in Japan had been constructed on different principles from Japan's civilian society. Soldiers were not samurai. Universal conscription had put the new military on a changed footing. But the armed services had their own schools, which inculcated the values of discipline, bravery, loyalty, and obedience. The military saw themselves as the heirs of those who had founded the modern Japanese state and the guardians of Japanese tradition. They contrasted their loyalty to the emperor and their concern for all Japanese with the pandering to special interests by the political parties.

They resented their diminished national stature during the 1920s, when military budgets were cut and the prestige of a military career declined. But even during the liberal 1920s there had been no change in the constitutional position of the services. The general staffs remained directly responsible to the emperor. With the passing of the Meiji oligarchs, this meant they were responsible to no one but themselves.

A Crisis in Manchuria   The new multilateral treaties (the 1924 Washington Conference and the 1930 London Conference) that replaced the earlier system of bilateral treaties (such as the Anglo-Japanese Alliance) recognized the existing colonies of the victors in World War I but opposed new colonial ventures.

Japan's position in Manchuria was ambiguous. Because Japan maintained its rule through a tame Chinese warlord, Manchuria was not, strictly speaking, a colony. But because Japan had gained its special position in Manchuria at the cost of 100,000 lives in the 1905 Russo-Japanese War, it saw its claim to Manchuria as similar to that of Western nations to their colonies.

From the late 1920s, the Guomindang unification of China and the blossoming of Chinese nationalism threatened Japan's special position. Japanese army units tried to block the march north and murdered the Manchurian warlord when he showed signs of independence. In this crisis, the party government in Tokyo equivocated, hoping to preserve a status quo that was crumbling before its eyes. The army saw Manchuria as a buffer between the Soviet Union and the Japanese colony of Korea. In 1931, the army provoked a crisis, took over Manchuria, and proclaimed it an independent state in 1932. When the League of Nations condemned this action, Japan withdrew from the league in 1933.

The Great Depression Japan's government acted effectively to counter the Great Depression, as noted earlier, but the recovery came too late to help the political parties. By 1936, political trends that had begun during the worst years of the depression had become irreversible.

The depression galvanized the political left and right. The political left was composed mainly of socialist moderates, who won 8 Diet seats in 1928 and 37 in 1937. Supported by unionists and white-collar workers, they would reemerge as an even stronger force after World War II. The radical left consisted of many little Marxist parties led by intellectuals and of the Japanese Communist Party. Although small and subject to governmental repression, the radical parties were influential in intellectual and literary circles during the 1920s and 1930s.

The Radical Right and the Military The political right in pre–World War II Japan is difficult to define. Most Japanese, even socialists, were imbued with an emperor-centered nationalism. During the 1930s, however, a new array of right-wing organizations went beyond the usual nationalism to challenge the status quo. Civilian ultranationalists used Shinto myths and Confucian values to attack Western liberalism in Japan's urban society. Some bureaucrats looked to the example of Nazi Germany and argued for the exclusion of party politicians from government. Military officers envisioned a "defense state" guided by themselves. They argued for military expansion and an autarchic colonial empire insulated from the uncertainties of the world economy. Young officers of the revolutionary right advocated "direct action" against the elites of the parliamentary coalition. They called for a second restoration of imperial power.

Modern Japan

Overthrow of Tokugawa Bakufu

1853–1854	Perry obtains Treaty of Friendship
1858	Bakufu signs commercial treaty
1861–1863	Chōshū and Satsuma mediate
1866	Chōshū defeats bakufu army
1868	Meiji restoration

Nation Building

1868–1871	Shaping a new state
1873–1878	Social revolution from above
1877–1878	Satsuma rebellion
1889	Meiji Constitution promulgated
1890	First Diet session

Imperial Japan

1894–1895	Sino-Japanese War
1900	Seiyū kai formed
1904–1905	Russo-Japanese War
1910	Korea annexed

Era of Party Government

1918	Hara becomes prime minister
1924	Katō becomes prime minister, universal manhood suffrage passed

Militarism

1931	Japan takes Manchuria
1937	War with China
1941	Japan attacks Pearl Harbor
1945	Japan surrenders

Tōjō Hideki. Prime minister at the time of the attack on Pearl Harbor in 1941, Tōjō Hideki (1884–1948) was one of the chief figures in the rise of Japanese militarism.

Corbis-Bettmann.

The last group precipitated political change. On May 15, 1932, junior army and navy officers attacked the Seiyū kai offices, the Bank of Japan, and the Tokyo police headquarters, and murdered Prime Minister Inukai. The attack occurred at the peak of right-wing agitation and the pit of the depression. Saionji decided that it would be unwise to appoint another party president as the new prime minister; and chose instead a moderate admiral. For the next four years, cabinets were led by moderate military men, but with party participation. These cabinets satisfied neither the parties nor the radical young officers.

During 1936 and 1937, Japanese politics continued to drift to the right. In the election of February 1936, the opposition overturned the Seiyū kai-dominated Diet with the slogan, "What shall it be, parliamentary government or Fascism?" A week later, young officers attempted a coup in Tokyo. They killed cabinet ministers and occupied the Diet and other government buildings. They wanted their army superiors to form a new government. Saionji and other men about the emperor stood firm; the navy opposed the rebellion; and within three days it was suppressed. It was the last "direct action" by the radical right in prewar Japan. The ringleaders were tried and executed, and generals sympathetic to them were retired. The officers in charge of the purge within the army were tough-minded elitist technocrats. They included General Tōjō Hideki (1884–1948), who would lead Japan into World War II.

But the services interfered more than ever in the formation of cabinets. From 1936 on, moderate prime ministers gave way to more outspokenly militaristic figures.

Opposition to militarism remained substantial nonetheless. In the 1937 election, the two major centrist parties, which had joined in opposition to the government, won 354 Diet seats. The Japanese people were more level-headed than their leaders. But the centrists' victory proved hollow. The Diet could not oppose a government in wartime, and by summer, Japan was at war in China.

The Road to Pearl Harbor   Three critical junctures occurred between the outbreak of the war with China and World War II in the Pacific. The first was the decision in January 1938 to strike a knockout blow at the Nationalist Party (GMD) government. The war had begun as an unplanned skirmish between Chinese and Japanese troops in the Beijing area but had quickly spread. The Japanese army's leaders disagreed on whether to continue. Many held that the only threat to Japanese interests in Korea and Manchuria was the Soviet Union, and that a long war in China was foolish. But as the Japanese armies advanced, the general staff argued that the only way to end the war was to convince the nationalists that fighting was hopeless. The army occupied most of the cities and railroads of eastern China, but Jiang Jieshi refused to give in. A stalemate ensued that lasted until 1945. China was never a major theater of the war in the Pacific.

The second critical decision was the signing of the **Tripartite Pact** with Germany and Italy in September 1940. Japan had long admired Germany. In

Tripartite Pact Alliance between Japan and Nazi Germany and Fascist Italy that was signed in 1940.

1936, it had joined Germany in the Anti-Comintern Pact directed against international communism. It also wanted an alliance with Germany against the Soviet Union. Germany insisted, however, that any alliance would also have to be directed against the United States and Britain. The Japanese disagreed. The Japanese navy saw the American Pacific fleet as its only potential enemy and was not willing to risk being dragged into a German war. When Japanese troops battled Russian troops in an undeclared mini-war from May to September 1939 on the Mongolian border, sentiment rose in favor of an alliance with Germany, but then Germany "betrayed" Japan by signing a nonaggression pact with the Soviet Union. For a time Japan decided to improve its relations with the United States, but America insisted that Japan get out of China. By the late spring of 1940, German victories in Europe—the fall of Britain appeared imminent—again led military leaders in Japan to favor an alliance with Germany.

When Japan signed the Tripartite Pact, it had three objectives: to isolate the United States, to inherit the Southeast Asian colonies of the countries defeated by Germany in Europe, and to improve its relations with the Soviet Union through the good offices of Germany. The last objective was reached when Japan signed a neutrality pact with the Soviet Union in April 1941. Two months later, Germany attacked the Soviet Union without consulting its ally, Japan. It compounded this second "betrayal" by asking Japan to attack the Soviet Union in the east. Japan waited and watched. When the German advance was stopped short of Moscow, Japan decided to honor the neutrality pact and turn south. This decision marked, in effect, the end of Japan's participation in the Axis. Thereafter, it fought its own war in Asia. Yet instead of deflecting American criticism as intended, the pact, by linking Japan to Germany, led to a hardening of America's position on China.

The third and fatal decision was to go to war with the United States. In June 1940, following Germany's defeat of France, Japanese troops had moved into northern French Indochina. The United States retaliated by limiting strategic exports to Japan. When Japanese troops took southern Indochina in July 1941, the United States embargoed all exports to Japan; this cut Japanese oil imports by 90 percent. The navy's general staff argued that oil reserves would last only two years; after that the navy would lose its capability to fight. Its general staff pressed for the capture of the oil-rich Dutch East Indies. But it was too dangerous to move against Dutch and British colonies in Southeast Asia with the United States on its flank in the Philippines. The navy, therefore, planned a preemptive strike against the United States, and on December 7, 1941, it bombed Pearl Harbor. The Japanese decision for war wagered Japan's land-based air power, shorter supply lines, and what it saw as greater will power against American productivity. The navy's chief of staff compared the war with the United States to a dangerous operation that might save the life of a critically ill patient. In the end, the war left Japan defeated and in ruins.

JAPANESE MILITARISM AND GERMAN NAZISM

The growths of militarism in Japan and Nazi German had some similarities. Both countries were late developers with elitist, academic bureaucracies and strong military traditions. Both had patriarchal family traditions and relatively new parliamentary systems. Both tried to solve the economic problems created by the Great Depression with territorial expansion. Both persecuted socialists and liberals. Both had modernized their military services, schools,

WHAT ARE the differences and similarities between the rise of militarism in Japan and Germany?

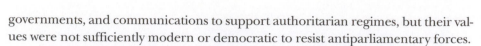

governments, and communications to support authoritarian regimes, but their values were not sufficiently modern or democratic to resist antiparliamentary forces.

There were differences between the two countries. Japan was more homogeneous than Germany. It had no Catholic-Protestant split, no *Junker* class, and no significant socialist movement. In Germany, parliament ruled, and the Nazis had to win an election to come to power. Japan's Diet was weaker. Control of the government was taken away from the Seiyūkai and Minseitō even while they continued to win elections.

The process by which the two countries went to war was also different. The Nazis created a mass party and a totalitarian state and then declared war. In Japan, there was neither a mass party nor a single group of leaders in continuous control of the government. It was not the totalitarian state that made war as much as it was war that made the state totalitarian—creating a nationalism so intense that university students became suicide *(kamikaze)* pilots after the outbreak of hostilities.

The Allies compared General Tōjō, Japan's prime minister, with Hitler. However, while Nazi authority survived until Hitler died in a Berlin bunker, General Tōjō was removed from office when American planes began to bomb Japan in 1944. The military continued to prosecute the war. But when the Imperial Conference on August 14, 1945, divided three-to-three over the Allied ultimatum demanding unconditional surrender, the emperor broke the deadlock, saying that the unendurable must be endured. It was the only important decision that he had ever been allowed to make.

SUMMARY

China: The 19th Century   China's bureaucracy centered on the imperial court in Beijing. The court was concerned about governing China and, then, to protecting its land frontiers. For 2,000 years, the only threats to China had come from beyond those frontiers. The expansion of imperial Russia reinforced this orientation. In the east, China was protected by the ocean. Even the Sino-Japanese pirates of the 16th century had been more a nuisance than a serious threat, and Europeans were initially viewed in the same light. The Opium War was fought in 1839–1842, and other wars with European powers thereafter, but these were seen as "coastal incursions," which posed little threat to the Qing heartland. Far more serious were the Taiping and other rebellions, which seized villages, threatened gentry control of local society, and attacked officials at both district and provincial levels. For China, the important story of the 19th century was the success of gentry armies in suppressing these rebellions, a success using Western weapons but based on traditional values. Not until the very end of the century after Japan's defeat of China in 1895 and its defeat of Russia in 1905 did the Chinese begin substantial Westernizing reforms—and by then it was too late for the dynasty.

China: The 20th Century   After the Qing fell in 1912, China was ruled for a decade and a half by regional warlords, a pattern not unlike the aftermaths of previous dynasties. But the ferment of the newly entering flood of Western ideas fed a growing nationalism. This nationalism permeated the Huangpu Military Academy that trained the officers of the Guomindang (or Nationalist) army; it lent legitimacy to the army's march north and to the establishment of the Nanjing government. By 1934, the Guomindang was winning; communists were forced to abandon bases in south China and flee to the arid northwest. But then

Japan invaded and occupied just those areas on which the Guomindang had depended. The communists built up their army, extended their influence into "occupied China," and won the civil war that wracked China between 1945 and 1949.

The Transformation of Japan In contrast to China, the Tokugawa regime collapsed quickly—only 15 years after the arrival of Perry in 1853. With its collapse, an elaborate structure of vested interests was destroyed. Leon Trotsky once spoke of dislocations in history produced by modern weapons in countries with less advanced technologies. Traditional vested interests in Japan—represented by samurai rebellions using old-fashioned weapons—attempted to fight against the new reformist government in the decade after 1868, but they lost every battle. The new Meiji government began sweeping Westernizing reforms in every field. Economic growth went hand in hand with universal education. The emperor became the unifying symbol for traditional and conservative thinkers. The Diet (Japan's parliament) became the focus for progressives and liberals. A shifting balance between conservatives and liberals ensued, with parliamentary democracy making gains into the 1920s. But then the Great Depression and a crisis in Manchuria opened the way for the rise of militarism in the 1930s. One thing led to another and Japan went to war with the United States in 1941.

IMAGE KEY

for pages 696–697

a. Chinese president Sun Yat Sen.
b. A duotype of Field Marshall Oyama's infantrymen confront Russian troops.
c. Japan's first foreign mission headed by Prince Iwakura.
d. Shoes designed for bound feet.
e. The dowager empress Tz'u-hsi.
f. Picture of steam engine traffic at Shiodome, 1872.
g. The Comodore Perry expedition to Japan.
h. Imperial Japanese national flag.

REVIEW QUESTIONS

1. Which had the greater impact on China, the Opium War or the Taiping rebellions?

2. How did the Qing (or Manchu) dynasty recover from the Taiping rebellions? Why did the recovery not prevent the overthrow of the dynasty in 1911?

3. Did the May Fourth Movement prepare the way for the nationalist revolution and communist revolutions?

4. After the Meiji restoration, what steps did Japan's leaders take to achieve their goal of "wealth and power"?

5. What were the strengths and weaknesses of Japan's prewar parliamentary institutions? What led to the sudden rise of militarism during the 1930s?

KEY TERMS

Boxers (p. 702)
Diet (p. 711)
Guomindang (GMD) (p. 704)
Long March (p. 705)

Meiji restoration (p. 710)
Taiping rebellions (p. 699)
treaty ports (p. 700)

Tripartite Pact (p. 720)
unequal treaties (p. 698)
zaibat (p. 713)

 For additional study resources for this chapter, go to:
www.prenhall.com/craig/chapter28

Visualizing The Past...

Industrialization

HOW DID the advent of industrialization in the 19th and early 20th centuries shape the art of those countries that industrialized? Did artists view industrialization as a negative or a positive force?

The Industrial Revolution began in Britain in the 18th century. By the mid-19th century factories, coal-fired machines, and railroads had spread throughout Western Europe, and also the eastern portion of the United States. By the later 19th-century industrialization and railroad building advanced in the United States, and also in Japan, which had become the most industrialized non-Western power in the world by the 1930s. Industry was understood to be about power, not only the power machines generated and artists celebrated, but also the power of political and military domination.

◄ **Power Loom Weaving of cotton cloth in a textile mill; colored engraving, 1834.** Industrialization began in the cloth industry because cloth was the most important manufactured product in the world from ancient times to the dawn of the modern era. Early factory owners often employed women, whose labor came cheaper than that of men. Factory women worked long hours and were subject to close supervision designed to ensure that their morals would not suffer in the factory setting.
The Granger Collection.

Shōsai Ikkei, "Picture of Steam Engine Traffic at Shiodome," 1872. In stark contrast to China, Japan's strategy for dealing with Western imperialism in 19th-century Asia was to compete with it head on as an industrial power. To do this, Japan imported, copied, and ultimately improved on Western technology. In this image we see in the foreground the great symbol of 19th-century technology, the railroad, as well as modern, Western-style buildings and, in the distance, steamships in the harbor.

Courtesy of the Library of Congress. Gift of Mrs E. Crane Chadbourne; 1930.

Diego Rivera, "Detroit Industry," Mural, North Wall, 1933. As industrialization spread from the cloth industry to all forms of manufacture, it became increasingly dominated by men, both because it became a mainstay of male employment in the West but also because its association with power and war meant that it was imagined as largely masculine. In this image we see strong, upright American men at work manufacturing the premier symbol of American industry—the automobile.

Diego Rivera (1886–1957). "Detroit Industry". North Wall, 1933. © 2003 Banco de Mexico Diego Rivera & Frida Kahlo Museums Trust. Av. Cinco de Mayo No. 2, Col. Centro, Del. Cuauhtemoc 06059, Mexico, D.F. Reproduction authorized by the Instituto Nacional de Bellas Artes y Literatura. Photograph © 2001 The Detroit Institute of Art/Bridgeman Art Library.

▼

Kazimir Malevich, "The Knife Grinder," 1912. To those who experienced industrialization, technology seemed to speed up life to a dizzying rate. Although some found the new emphasis on speed and motion disorienting, many celebrated it—none more than the futurists, a group of painters active in the first decades of the twentieth century. In the painting shown here, the distinction between the knife grinder and his work dissolves into a dizzying blur of geometric shapes.

725

PART SEVEN   GLOBAL CONFLICT AND CHANGE

EUROPE

1914–1918	World War I
1917	Bolsheviks seize power, Russia
1919	Versailles Settlement
1922	Mussolini seizes power, Italy
1925	Locarno Pact
1933	Hitler comes to power
1936	Spanish Civil War begins
1938	Munich Conference
1939	World War II begins

▲ *American World War II poster*

1944	D-Day
1945	World War II ends
1948	Berlin blockade and airlift
1949	NATO treaty; Russia detonates atomic bomb
1953	Death of Stalin
1955	Warsaw Pact
1956	Soviets crush Hungarian revolt
1957	EEC founded
1958	Charles de Gaulle comes to power in France

◄ Guernica, *Pablo Picasso, 1937*

NEAR EAST / INDIA

1922	British leave Egypt
1922–1938	Mustafa Kemal first president of Turkey
1928	The Muslim Brotherhood founded by Hasan Al-Banna

1947	Indian Independence; creation of Pakistan
1948	Assassination of Mahatma Gandhi
1949	State of Israel founded
1953	Mosaddeq overthrown in Iran
1954–1970	Abdel Nasser leads Egypt
1956	Suez Crisis

Mao Zedong ▶ with Nikita Khrushchev

EAST ASIA

1916–1928	Warlord Era in China
1919	May 4th Movement in China
1925	Universal male suffrage in Japan
1928–1937	Nationalist government in China at Nanking
1931	Japan occupies Manchuria
1937–1945	Japan at war with China

1941	Japan attacks Pearl Harbor
1945	Japan surrenders after U.S. atomic bombs
1945–1949	Civil War in China; People's Republic founded
1950	N. Korea invades S. Korea
1952	U.S. ends occupation of Japan
1953–1972	Double-digit growth in Japan
1955	Liberal-Democratic Party formed in Japan
1959–1960	Sino-Soviet split

AFRICA

1919	W.E.B. DuBois holds first Pan-African Congress in Paris
1935	Mussolini invades Ethiopia

1942–1945	World War II engulfs North Africa
1955–1962	Wars of independence in French Algeria
1956	Sudan gains independence from Britain and Egypt
1956	Morocco and Tunisia gain independence from France
1957	Ghana an independent state under Kwame Nkrumah

THE AMERICAS

1917	U.S. enters World War I
1929	Wall Street crash; the Great Depression begins
1930–1945	Vargas dictatorship in Brazil
1932	F.D. Roosevelt elected U.S. president
1938	Mexico nationalizes oil

1941	U.S. enters World War II
1945	Death of F.D. Roosevelt
1946	Perón elected president in Argentina
1954	U.S. Supreme Court outlaws segregation
1955	Perón overthrown
1956	Montgomery bus boycott
1959	Fidel Castro comes to power in Cuba

◄ *Fidel Castro*

1960	Paris Summit Conference collapses after U-2 incident
1961	Berlin Wall erected
1964	Khrushchev replaced as Soviet prime minister by Kosygin; replaced as party secretary by Brezhnev
1968	Soviets invade Czechoslovakia
1972	British Impose direct rule on Northern Ireland
1972	Israeli Olympic athletes killed by Arab terrorists
1974	End of military rule in Greece
1974	Portuguese dictatorship deposed; democratic reforms begin

1977	Brezhnev president of USSR
1979	Margaret Thatcher becomes British prime minister
1980	Solidarity Movement in Poland
1981	Crackdown against Solidarity
1984–1985	Bitter strikes by miners in England
1984	Mikhail Gorbachev introduces *glasnost* in USSR

▲ *Opening of the Berlin Wall, 1989*

1989	Berlin Wall demolished
1990	Germany unified
1991	Failed coup in Soviet Union; Yeltsin emerges as leader of Russia
1991	Major replaces Thatcher as England's prime minister
1993	Czechoslovakia divides into two republics
1995	Dayton Peace Accords end war in Bosnia
1999	NATO military campaign against Serbia
2000	Putin elected president of Russia; overthrow of Milŏsevic in Yugoslavia

1966	Indira Gandhi becomes prime minister of India
1967	Israeli-Arab June War
1969	Golda Meir becomes prime minister of Israel
1969	Arafat elected P.L.O. chairman
1971	India-USSR friendship treaty
1973	Arab-Israeli October War
1972	Independence for Bangladesh
1973	OPEC oil embargo

1977	Menachem Begin becomes prime minister of Israel
1978	Iranian revolution under Khomeini's leadership
1979	Egyptian-Israeli Peace Treaty
1979	Iran takes U.S. hostages
1979	Soviets invade Afghanistan
1980–1988	Iran-Iraq War
1981	Hostages released in Iran
1981	Egypt's Sadat assassinated; succeeded by Hosni Mubarak
1982	Israel invades Lebanon
1984	Indira Gandhi assassinated

1989	Soviets leave Afghanistan
1989	Death of Khomeini
1990	Central Asian States become independent on fall of USSR
1990–1991	Gulf War
1991	Indian prime minister Rajiv Ghandi assassinated

Oil wells left burning ▶
by Iraqi troops in Kuwait

1959–1975	Vietnam War
1965–1976	Cultural Revolution devastates China
1968	Death of Ho Chi Minh, president of North Vietnam
1971	Lin Piao killed in China
1972	President Nixon visits China
1973	Economic growth slows in Japan

▲ *The Cultural Revolution, China*

1976	Death of Mao Tse-tung
1978–1989	New Economic policies of Teng Hsiao-p'ing in China
1978–1989	Vietnam occupies Cambodia
1980s	Double-digit economic growth in South Korea and Taiwan

Tienanmen Square ▶

1988	Japan's GNP second in world
1989	Vietnam pledges to withdraw from Cambodia
1989	China crushes pro-democracy demonstrations in Beijing
1991–1992	Political scandals and plummeting stock market in Japan
1992	Kim Young Sam, civilian party leader, elected S. Korean president

1960	Belgian Congo granted independence as Zaire
1963	Kenya becomes an independent republic
1964	Zanzibar, the Congo, and Northern Rhodesia (Zambia) become independent republics
1965	Revolution in Kenya
1967–1970	Nigerian Civil War
1974	Drought and famine in Africa
1974	Emperor Haile Selassie of Ethiopia is deposed
1974–1975	Portugal grants independence to Guinea, Angola, Mozambique, Cape Verde

1980	Southern Rhodesia (Zimbabwe) gains independence from Britain
1984	Bishop Desmond Tutu awarded Nobel Peace Prize
1985	U.S. economic sanctions against South Africa result in more repression

1989	Conservative Botha government resigns in South Africa; DeKlerk becomes president
1992	Nelson Mandela freed from prison in South Africa
1994	Nelson Mandela elected president of South Africa

Nelson Mandela ▶

1960	Kennedy elected president
1962	Cuban Missile Crisis
1963	Kennedy assassinated
1964	Passage of Civil Rights Act
1965	U.S. expands Vietnam commitment
1968	Martin Luther King and Robert Kennedy assassinated; campus unrest
1968	Nixon elected
1970	Allende elected in Chile
1972	Nixon visits China and USSR; is reelected president
1973	Watergate scandal breaks
1973	Perón reelected, Argentina
1973	Chile's Allende overthrown
1974	Nixon resigns presidency

1979	Revolution in Nicaragua and El Salvador
1980	Iran hostage crisis
1980	Reagan elected president
1982	War between Argentina and Great Britain over Islas Malvinas (Falkland Islands)
1983	Argentine military government overthrown; elected government restored
1983	End of Mexican oil boom
1988	Major arms agreement between U.S. and USSR

1991	Gulf War
1992	Clinton elected president
1994	Revolt in Chiapas, Mexico
1998	Pope visits Cuba
2001	Terrorists attacks on the World Trade Center in New York City and the Pentagon in Washington, D.C.

29 Imperialism and World War I

CHAPTER HIGHLIGHTS

The New Imperialism European imperialism in the last part of the nineteenth century brought the Western countries into contact with most of the world. By 1914, European nations had divided Africa among themselves and controlled large parts of Asia and the islands of the Pacific. Much of the Middle East was under the nominal control of the Ottoman Empire, which was in its death throes and under European influence. The Monroe Doctrine made Latin America a protectorate of the United States. Japan had become an imperial power at the expense of China and Korea.

World War I The emergence of a new, powerful German state at the center of Europe upset the old balance of power. The German emperor, William II, sought more power and influence for his country. The result was a system of alliances that divided Europe into two armed camps. What began as yet another Balkan War involving the European powers became a world war that influenced the rest of the world. As the terrible war of 1914–1918 dragged on, the real motives that had driven the European powers to fight gave way to public affirmations of the principles of nationalism and self-determination.

The Peace Settlement The peoples under colonial rule took these statements seriously and sought to win their own independence and nationhood. For the most part they were disappointed by the peace settlement. However, the old imperial nations, especially Britain and France, had paid an enormous price in lives, money, and will for their victory in the war. Colonial peoples pressed for the rights that were proclaimed as universal by the West but denied to their colonies. Tension between colonies and their ruling nations was a cause of instability in the world created by the Paris treaties of 1919.

CHAPTER QUESTIONS

WHAT WAS the New Imperialism?

WHAT WERE the two alliance systems that faced each other in Europe before 1914?

WHAT CAUSED the outbreak of World War I in 1914?

WHY WERE the Bolsheviks able to seize power in Russia ?

WHY DID the Versailles settlement leave Germany bitter?

CHAPTER OUTLINE

- Expansion of European Power and the "New Imperialism"
- Emergence of the German Empire
- World War I
- The Russian Revolution
- End of World War I

During the second half of the 19th century, Europe exercised unprecedented control over the rest of the world. The Americas, Australia, and New Zealand almost became part of the European world as streams of European immigrants populated these areas. Africa was divided among European nations (see Chapter 27), and Europe imposed its power across Asia (see Map 29–1 and Chapter 28). By 1900, European dominance had brought every part of the globe into a single world economy.

But these developments helped to foster competition and hostility among the great powers of Europe and to bring on a terrible war. The frenzy for imperial expansion that seized Europeans in the late 19th century did much to destroy its peace, prosperity, and dominant place in the world.

EXPANSION OF EUROPEAN POWER AND THE "NEW IMPERIALISM"

WHAT WAS the
New Imperialism?

Explosive developments in 19th-century science, technology, industry, agriculture, transportation, communication, and military weapons enabled a few Europeans (and Americans) to impose their will on other peoples many times their number. Westerners had institutional as well as material advantages—particularly the mobilizing power of national states and a belief in the superiority of their civilization.

By the mid-19th century, only Great Britain retained extensive overseas holdings, and there was general hostility to territorial expansion. The dominant doctrine of free trade opposed political interference in other lands. But after 1870, European states swiftly exerted control over about a fifth of the world's land area and a tenth of its population in a movement called the **New Imperialism** (see Map 29–1).

THE NEW IMPERIALISM

Imperialism can be defined as extending a nation's influence by some form of power over foreign peoples. The usual pattern of the New Imperialism was for the European nation to invest capital in the "backward" country and thereby to transform its economy and culture. To guarantee their investments, European states would establish different degrees of political control ranging from full annexation as a colony, to protectorate status (whereby the local ruler was controlled by the dominant European state), to "spheres-of-influence" status (whereby the European state received special privileges without direct political involvement).

MOTIVES FOR THE NEW IMPERIALISM: ECONOMIC INTERPRETATION

There is still no agreement about the motives for the New Imperialism. The most widespread interpretation has been economic. Lenin saw imperialism as the final stage in capitalism's development—the pursuit of monopoly. He claimed that as capitalists exhausted opportunities of investment in their home countries, they persuaded their governments to acquire colonies. The facts, however, do not support this thesis. Only a small part of European investments overseas went to the colonies acquired by the new imperialism. Most of it went to older, established areas like the United States, Canada, and Australia. Colonies were not usually important markets for the great imperial nations, and

New Imperialism Extension in the late 19th and early 20th centuries of Western political and economic dominance to Asia, the Middle East, and Africa.

MAP 29–1

Asia 1880–1914. As in Africa (see Maps 27–1 and 27–2), the late 19th century saw imperialism spread widely and rapidly in Asia. Two new powers, Japan and the United States, joined the British, French, and Dutch in extending control throughout south and southeast Asia and in exploiting an enfeebled China.

HOW DID the new Japanese empire affect the balance of power in Asia?

THE DEVILFISH IN EGYPTIAN WATERS.

John Bull. An American cartoonist in 1888 depicted John Bull (England) as the octopus of imperialism, grabbing land on every continent. Notice the hand at the left poised to grab Egypt.

The Granger Collection, N.Y.

it is not even clear that control of the new colonies was particularly profitable.

CULTURAL, RELIGIOUS, AND SOCIAL INTERPRETATIONS

Some advocates of imperialism argued that the European nations had a responsibility to bring the benefits of their superior civilization and Christianity to the people of "backward" lands, but few people were influenced by such arrogant arguments, although many shared the assumptions behind them (see "Social Darwinism and Imperialism"). Politicians suggested that imperial expansion might solve domestic social problems by deflecting public attention from problems at home or providing an outlet for surplus population. The new colonies, however, attracted few European emigrants. Most went to the Americas and Australia.

STRATEGIC AND POLITICAL INTERPRETATIONS: THE SCRAMBLE FOR AFRICA

Strategic and prestige considerations seem to have been more important in bringing on the New Imperialism. The completion of the Suez Canal in 1869 made Egypt vital to the British because it sat astride the shortest route to India. When Egypt's stability was threatened in the 1880s, the British established a protectorate. Then, to protect Egypt, they advanced into the Sudan.

Other European nations equated status (Britain was the model) with the possession of colonies and sought colonies as evidence of their own importance. This explains much of the scramble for Africa (see Chapter 27). France became involved in North Africa in 1830, when it sent a naval expedition to Algeria to suppress piracy. By 1882, the French controlled Algeria and Tunisia. Soon lesser states like Belgium, Portugal, Spain, and Italy were seeking African colonies. In 1884 and 1885, Germany declared protectorates over southwestern Africa, Togoland, the Cameroons, and East Africa—despite the fact that these places had no particular strategic importance.

THE IRRATIONAL ELEMENT

Germany's annexations started a wild scramble by other European powers, and by 1890, almost all of Africa was parceled out. In Asia, Japan exerted claims on China and Korea that frightened the other powers with interests in China. Russia, France, and Germany applied diplomatic pressure to contain Japan, and all pressed feverishly for concessions in China. In 1899, the United States proposed the "open door policy," which opposed annexations in China and allowed all nations to trade there on equal terms. Victory in the Spanish-American War of 1898 had won the United States control over Cuba and Puerto Rico, and the Americans then purchased the Philippines and Guam from Spain. In 1898, the United States annexed Hawaii. By 1900, most of the world had come under the control of the industrialized West.

HISTORY'S VOICES

SOCIAL DARWINISM AND IMPERIALISM

One of the intellectual foundations of the New Imperialism was the doctrine of social Darwinism, a pseudoscientific application of Darwin's ideas about biology to nations and races. The impact of social Darwinism was substantial. In the selection that follows, an Englishman, Karl Pearson (1857–1936), attempts to connect concepts from evolutionary theory—the struggle for survival and the survival of the fittest—to the development of human societies.

HOW DOES the author connect Darwin's ideas to the concept of human progress? Is it reasonable to equate biological species with human societies, races, or nations? How do the author's ideas justify imperial expansion? What arguments can you make against the author's assertions?

History shows me one way, and one way only, in which a state of civilisation has been produced, namely, the struggle of race with race, and the survival of the physically and mentally fitter race. This dependence of progress on the survival of the fitter race, terribly black as it may seem to some of you, gives the struggle for existence its redeeming features; it is the fiery crucible out of which comes the finer metal. You may hope for a time when the sword shall be turned into the ploughshare, when American and German and English traders shall no longer compete in the markets of the world for raw materials, for their food supply, when the white man and the dark shall share the soil between them, and each till it as he lists. But, believe me, when that day comes mankind will no longer progress; there will be nothing to check the fertility of inferior stock; the relentless law of heredity will not be controlled and guided by natural selection. Man will stagnate. . . . The path of progress is strewn with the wreck of nations; traces are everywhere to be seen of the hecatombs of inferior races, and of victims who found not the narrow way to the greater perfection. Yet these dead peoples are, in very truth, the stepping stones on which mankind has arisen to the higher intellectual and deeper emotional life of today.

Source: Karl Pearson, *National Life from the Standpoint of Science*, 2nd ed. (Cambridge, UK: Cambridge University Press, 1907), pp. 21, 26–27, 64.

EMERGENCE OF THE GERMAN EMPIRE

FORMATION OF THE TRIPLE ALLIANCE (1873–1890)

Prussia's victories over Austria and France and its creation of the German Empire in 1871 revolutionized European diplomacy. The sudden appearance of a powerful new state posed problems.

The balance of power created at the Congress of Vienna was altered radically. Britain and Russia retained their position. Austria, however, had lost ground and was threatened by nationalism within the Austro-Hungarian Empire. French power and prestige were badly damaged by the Franco-Prussian War and the German annexation of Alsace-Lorraine. The French were both afraid of Germany and resentful of their loss of territory and of France's traditional dominance in western Europe.

BISMARCK'S LEADERSHIP (1873–1890)

Until 1890, Otto von Bismarck (1815–1898) continued to guide German policy. He insisted after 1871 that Germany wanted no further territorial gains, and he

WHAT WERE the two alliance systems that faced each other in Europe before 1914?

QUICK REVIEW

Bismarck's Goals
- No additional German territorial expansion
- Tried to cultivate friendship with France
- Sought to prevent alliance between France and any other European power that would threaten Germany on two fronts

meant it. He wanted to avoid a war that might undo his achievement. He tried to assuage France by cultivating friendly relations and supporting its colonial aspirations. He also prepared for the worst. If France could not be conciliated, it must be isolated. Bismarck sought to prevent an alliance between France and any European power—especially Austria or Russia—that would threaten Germany with a war on two fronts.

War in the Balkans Bismarck's first move was to establish the Three Emperors' League in 1873. The league brought together the three great conservative empires of Germany, Austria, and Russia. It collapsed when Russia went to war with Turkey in 1877. The tottering Ottoman Empire was preserved chiefly by the competing aims of those powers who awaited its demise. Ottoman weakness encouraged its Slavic subjects in the Balkans to rebel.

When Russia entered the fray, it created an international crisis. The Russians hoped to gain control of Constantinople. Russian intervention also reflected the influence of the **Pan-Slavic movement**, which sought to bring all the Slavs, even those under Austrian or Ottoman rule, under the protection of Holy Mother Russia.

The Ottoman Empire was forced to sue for peace. The Treaty of San Stefano of March 1878 was a Russian triumph. The Slavic states in the Balkans were freed of Ottoman rule, and Russia obtained territory and an indemnity. But the terms of the Russian victory alarmed the other great powers. Austria feared that the new Slav states and the increase in Russian influence would threaten its own Balkan provinces. The British were alarmed by the possible Russian control of Constantinople. Disraeli (1804–1881) was determined to resist, and British public opinion supported him.

Pan-Slavic movement Effort to create a nation or federation that would embrace all the Slavic peoples of Eastern Europe.

Congress of Berlin Disraeli sent a fleet to Constantinople, and Britain and Austria forced Russia to agree to an international conference at which the provisions of San Stefano would be reviewed by the other great powers. The resulting Congress of Berlin met in June and July of 1878 under the presidency of Bismarck.

The decisions of the Congress were a blow to Russian ambitions. Bulgaria lost two thirds of its territory. Austria-Hungary was given Bosnia and Herzegovina to "occupy and administer" under formal Ottoman rule. Britain received Cyprus, and France gained permission to occupy Tunisia. These were compensations for the gains that Russia was permitted to keep. Germany asked for nothing, but the Russians were angry. The Three Emperors' League was dead.

The south Slavic states of Serbia and Montenegro resented the Austrian occupation of Bosnia and Herzegovina. The south Slavic question, no less than the estrangement between Russia and Germany, was a threat to the peace of Europe.

Bismarck and the young Kaiser William II meet in 1888. The two disagreed over many issues, and in 1890 William dismissed the aged chancellor.

German Information Center.

German Alliances with Russia and Austria Bismarck could ignore the Balkans, but not Russia. He concluded a secret treaty with Austria in 1879. This Dual Alliance provided that if either Germany or Austria were attacked by Russia, the ally would help the attacked party. If either was attacked by another country, each promised at least to maintain neutrality. The treaty was renewed every five years until 1918.

Bismarck never allowed the alliance to drag Germany into Austria's Balkan quarrels. He made it clear to the Austrians that Germany would never attack Russia. Bismarck expected the Austro-German negotiations to frighten Russia into seeking closer relations with Germany, and he was right. By 1881, he had renewed the Three Emperors' League on a firmer basis.

The Triple Alliance   In 1882, Italy, annoyed by the French preemption of Tunisia, asked to join the Dual Alliance. Bismarck was now allied with three of the great powers and friendly with Great Britain, which held aloof from all alliances. France was isolated. Although the Three Emperors' League was allowed to lapse, the Triple Alliance (Germany, Austria, and Italy) was renewed for another five years in 1887. To restore German relations with Russia, Bismarck negotiated the Reinsurance Treaty that same year, in which both powers promised to remain neutral if either was attacked. However, a change in the German monarchy overturned Bismarck's system.

In 1888, William II (r. 1888–1918) came to the German throne. Like many Germans of his generation, he was filled with a sense of Germany's destiny as the leading power of Europe. To achieve a "place in the sun," he wanted a navy and colonies like Britain's. These aims, of course, ran counter to Bismarck's policy. In 1890, William dismissed Bismarck.

During Bismarck's time, Germany was a force for European peace. This position would not have been possible without its great military power. But it also required a statesman who could exercise restraint and understand what his country needed and what was possible.

FORGING THE TRIPLE ENTENTE (1890–1907)

Franco-Russian Alliance   After Bismarck's retirement, his system of alliances collapsed. General Leo von Caprivi refused the Russian request to renew the Reinsurance Treaty, which he considered incompatible with the Austrian alliance. Political isolation and the need for foreign capital drove the Russians toward France. The French, who were even more isolated, were glad to pour capital into Russia if it would help produce security against Germany. In 1894, the Franco-Russian alliance was signed.

Britain and Germany   Britain now became the key to the international situation. Colonial rivalries pitted the British against the Russians in Central Asia and against the French in Africa. Traditionally, Britain had also opposed Russian control of Constantinople and French control of the Low Countries. There was no reason to think that Britain would soon become friendly to its traditional rivals or abandon its friendliness toward the Germans. Yet within a decade of William II's accession, Germany had become the enemy in the minds of the British. The problem lay in Germany's foreign and naval policies.

At first Germany tried to win over the British to the Triple Alliance, but when Britain clung to "splendid isolation," Germany sought to demonstrate its worth as an ally by making trouble for Britain. The Germans began to exert pressure against Britain in Africa by barring British attempts to build a railroad from Capetown to Cairo. They also openly sympathized with the Boers of South Africa in their resistance to British expansion.

In 1898, William's dream of a German navy began to achieve reality with the passage of a naval law providing for 19 battleships. In 1900, a second law doubled that figure. The architect of the new navy, Admiral Alfred von Tirpitz (1849–1930), proclaimed that Germany's naval policy was aimed at Britain. As the German navy grew and German policies seemed more threatening, the British abandoned their traditional policies.

Entente Cordiale   In 1902, Britain concluded an alliance with Japan to help defend British interests in the Far East against Russia. Next, Britain in 1904 made a series of agreements with the French, collectively called the Entente Cordiale. It was not a formal treaty and had no military provisions, but it settled all outstanding colonial differences between the two nations. The Entente Cordiale went far toward aligning the British with Germany's great potential enemy.

First Moroccan Crisis   In March 1905, William II landed at Tangier and challenged the French predominance there in a speech in favor of Moroccan independence. Germany's chancellor, Prince Bernhard von Bülow (1849–1929), intended to show France how weak it was and how little it could expect from Britain; he also hoped to gain colonial concessions.

The Germans might have achieved their aims, but they demanded an international conference to exhibit their power. The conference met in 1906 at Algeciras in Spain. Austria sided with its German ally, but Spain, Italy, and the United States voted with Britain and France. The French were confirmed in their position in Morocco, and German bullying had driven Britain and France closer together. Sir Edward Grey (1862–1933), the British foreign secretary, without making a firm commitment, authorized conversations between the British and French general staffs. By 1914, French and British military and naval plans were so mutually dependent that the two countries were effectively, if not formally, allies.

British Agreement with Russia   Hardly anyone believed that Britain and Russia could ever be allies. The Russo-Japanese War of 1904–1905 made such a development seem even less likely because Britain was allied with Russia's enemy. But defeat and the Russian Revolution of 1905 left Russia weak and reduced British apprehensions. The British were also concerned that Russia might drift into the German orbit.

With French support, in 1907 an agreement settled Russo-British quarrels in Central Asia and Persia and opened the door for wider cooperation. The Triple Entente, an informal but powerful association of Britain, France, and Russia, was now ranged against the Triple Alliance. Because Italy was unreliable, Germany and Austria-Hungary stood surrounded by two great land powers and Great Britain.

William II and his ministers had turned Bismarck's nightmare of the prospect of a two-front war with France and Russia into a reality and had added Britain to the hostile coalition. Bismarck's alliance system had been intended to maintain peace, but the new one increased the risk of war and made the Balkans, where Austrian and Russian ambitions clashed, a likely spot for it.

WORLD WAR I
THE ROAD TO WAR (1908–1914)

Except for the Greeks and the Romanians, most of the inhabitants of the Balkans were Slavs and felt a kinship with one another and with Russia. For centuries they had been ruled by Austrians, Hungarians, or Turks, and the nationalism that characterized late-19th-century Europe made many Slavs eager for liberty or at least autonomy. The more radical among them longed for a union of the south Slavic, or Yugoslav, peoples in a single nation led by independent Serbia. They hoped to detach all the Slavic provinces (especially Bosnia, which bordered on Serbia) from Austria. Serbia was to unite the Slavs at the expense of Austria, as Piedmont had united the Italians and Prussia the Germans.

The Bosnian Crisis   In 1908, modernizing reformers called the Young Turks overthrew the Ottoman government. This threatened to revive the empire and

QUICK REVIEW

First Moroccan Crisis
- March 1905: William II implies Germany has a role in furthering Moroccan independence
- Germany hoped to weaken relationship between France and Great Britain
- 1906: Conference in Algeciras confirms France's claims in Morocco

WHAT CAUSED the outbreak of World War I in 1914?

precipitated a series of Balkan crises that would lead to world war. Austria and Russia decided to act before Turkey became stronger. They agreed to call an international conference in which each of them would support the other's demands. Russia would agree to the Austrian annexation of Bosnia and Herzegovina, and Austria would support Russia's request to open the Dardanelles to Russian warships.

Austria, however, declared the annexation unilaterally before any conference was called. The British, concerned about their own position in the Mediterranean, rejected the Russian demand. The Russians were furious. The Serbs were enraged by the annexation of Bosnia. The Russians were too weak to do anything but accept the new situation. The Germans were unhappy because Austria's action threatened their relations with Russia. But Germany felt so dependent on the Dual Alliance that it assured Austria of its support. To an extent, German policy was being made in Vienna. It was a dangerous precedent. At the same time, the failure of Britain and France to support Russia strained the Triple Entente and made it harder for them to oppose Russian interests again if they wanted to retain Russian friendship.

Second Moroccan Crisis   The second Moroccan crisis, in 1911, emphasized the French and British need for mutual support. When France sent an army to Morocco to put down a rebellion, Germany took the opportunity to extort colonial concessions in the French Congo by sending the gunboat *Panther* to the port of Agadir in Morocco, allegedly to protect German citizens there. As in 1905, the Germans went too far.

Anglo-German relations had already been deteriorating, chiefly because of the naval race. The British now mistakenly believed that the Germans meant to turn Agadir into a naval base on the Atlantic. The crisis passed when France yielded bits of the Congo and Germany withdrew from Morocco. The main result was to draw Britain closer to France. Plans were formulated for a British expeditionary force to help defend France against German attack, and the British and French navies agreed to cooperate.

The Balkan Wars   After the second Moroccan crisis, Italy feared that France would move into Ottoman Libya. Consequently, in 1911 Italy attacked the Ottoman Empire to forestall the French, and obtained Libya and the Dodecanese Islands in the Aegean. The Italian victory encouraged the Balkan states to try their luck. In 1912, Bulgaria, Greece, Montenegro, and Serbia attacked the Ottoman Empire and won easily. The Serbs and the Bulgarians then quarreled about the division of Macedonia, and in 1913, Turkey and Romania joined Greece and Serbia against Bulgaria, which lost much of what it had gained since 1878.

The Austrians were determined to limit Serbian gains and prevent the Serbs from obtaining a port in Albania on the Adriatic. An international conference sponsored by Britain in early 1913 resolved the matter in Austria's favor and called for an independent kingdom of Albania. But Austria felt humiliated by the public airing of Serbian demands and in October unilaterally forced Serbia to withdraw from Albania. Russia again let Austria have its way.

The lessons learned from this affair influenced behavior in the final crisis of 1914. The Russians had, as in 1908, been embarrassed by their passivity, and their allies were now more reluctant to restrain them. The Austrians were determined not to accept an international conference again. They and their German allies had seen that better results might be obtained from a threat of force.

SARAJEVO AND THE OUTBREAK OF WAR (JUNE–AUGUST 1914)

The Assassination   On June 28, 1914, a Bosnian nationalist killed the Austrian Archduke Francis Ferdinand (1863–1914), heir to the throne, and his wife in the Bosnian capital of Sarajevo. The assassin was a member of a conspiracy hatched by a political terrorist society. The chief of intelligence of the Serbian army had helped plan the crime. Even though his role was unknown at the time, it was generally believed that Serbian officials were involved.

Germany and Austria's Response   The assassination was condemned throughout Europe. To those Austrians who had long favored an attack on Serbia as a solution to the empire's Slavic problem, the opportunity seemed irresistible. But Count Stefan Tisza (1861–1918), speaking for Hungary, resisted. Count Leopold Berchtold (1863–1942), the Austro-Hungarian foreign minister, knew that German support would be required if Russia should decide to protect Serbia and to persuade the Hungarians to accept a war. The question of peace or war, therefore, had to be answered in Berlin.

William II and Chancellor Theobald von Bethmann-Hollweg (1856–1921) promised German support for an attack on Serbia. They urged the Austrians to move swiftly, while the other powers were still angry at Serbia. They also indicated that a failure to act would be evidence of Austria-Hungary's uselessness as an ally. Therefore, the Austrians planned to attack Serbia. They hoped, with the protection of Germany, to avoid a general European conflict, but were prepared to risk one. The Germans also knew that they risked a general war, but hoped to "localize" the fight between Austria and Serbia.

These calculations proved to be incorrect. Bethmann-Hollweg hoped that the Austrians would strike while the outrage of the assassination was still fresh. He also hoped that German support would deter Russian involvement. Failing that, he was prepared for a continental war that would bring rapid victory over France and allow a full-scale attack on the Russians, who were always slow to bring their strength into action. The German chancellor convinced himself that the British would stand aloof.

However, the Austrians were slow to act. They did not even deliver their deliberately unacceptable ultimatum to Serbia until July 24, when the general hostility toward Serbia had begun to subside. Serbia returned a conciliatory answer, but the Austrians were determined not to turn back. On July 28, they declared war on Serbia, even though they could not field an army until mid-August.

The Triple Entente's Response   The Russians responded angrily to the Austrian demands on

Assassination of the Archduke.

Above: The Austrian Archduke Franz Ferdinand and his wife in Sarajevo on June 28, 1914. Later in the day the royal couple were assassinated by young revolutionaries trained and supplied in Serbia, igniting the crisis that led to World War I. Below: Moments after the assassination the Austrian police captured one of the assassins.

Brown Brothers.

Serbia. The government ordered partial mobilization to pressure Austria to hold back its attack on Serbia.

Mobilization of any kind, however, was generally understood to be equivalent to an act of war. It was especially alarming to General Helmuth von Moltke (1848–1916), head of the German general staff. Russian mobilization could upset the delicate timing of Germany's battle plan—the **Schlieffen Plan**, which required an attack on France first—and would endanger Germany. From this point on, Moltke pressed for war. The pressure of military necessity became irresistible.

The western European powers were not eager for war. But the French gave the Russians the same assurances that Germany had given its ally. The British worked hard for another conference of the powers, but Austria would not hear of it. The Germans privately supported the Austrians but were publicly conciliatory in the hope of keeping the British neutral.

When Bethmann-Hollweg realized that if Germany attacked France, Britain would fight, he tried to persuade the Austrians to negotiate, but the Austrians could not retreat without losing their own self-respect and that of the Germans. On July 30, Austria ordered mobilization against Russia. Russia and Germany then ordered general mobilization. The Schlieffen Plan went into effect. The Germans invaded Belgium on August 3, which violated the treaty of 1839, in which the British had guaranteed Belgian neutrality. This undermined sentiment in Britain for neutrality and united the nation against Germany. Germany then invaded France. On August 4, Britain declared war on Germany. Europe would never be the same.

STRATEGIES AND STALEMATE (1914–1917)

Throughout Europe jubilation greeted the outbreak of war. No general war had been fought since Napoleon, and the horrors of modern warfare were not yet understood. The dominant memory was of Bismarck's swift and decisive campaigns, in which costs and casualties were light and the rewards great.

Both sides expected to take the offensive and win a quick victory. The Triple Entente powers—or the Allies, as they came to be called—had superior numbers and financial resources as well as command of the sea. Germany and Austria, the Central Powers, had the advantages of internal lines of communication and of having launched their attack first.

The War in the West   After 1905, Germany's war plan was the one developed by Count Alfred von Schlieffen (1833–1913), chief of the German general staff from 1891 to 1906. It aimed to sweep through Belgium to the English Channel, then wheel to the south and east to envelop the French and crush them against the German fortresses in Lorraine. In the east, the Germans planned to stand on the defensive against Russia until France had been beaten, a task they thought would take only six weeks.

Coming of World War I

1871	End of the Franco-Prussian War; creation of the German Empire; German annexation of Alsace-Lorraine
1873	Three Emperors' League (Germany, Russia, and Austria-Hungary)
1877	Russo-Turkish War
1878	Congress of Berlin
1879	Dual Alliance between Germany and Austria
1881	Three Emperors' League is renewed
1882	Italy joins Germany and Austria in Triple Alliance
1888	William II becomes German emperor
1890	Bismarck dismissed
1894	Franco-Russian alliance
1898	Germany begins to build battleship navy
1902	British alliance with Japan
1904	Entente Cordiale between Britain and France
1904–1905	Russo-Japanese War
1905	First Moroccan crisis
1907	British agreement with Russia
1908–1909	Bosnian crisis
1911	Second Moroccan crisis; Italy attacks Turkey
1912–1913	First and Second Balkan wars
1914	Outbreak of World War I

22.4
The Perversion of Technology: War in "No Man's Land"

Schlieffen Plan   Germany's plan for achieving a quick victory in the West at the outbreak of World War I by invading France through Belgium and Luxembourg.

The Western Front. French troops advancing on the Western Front. This picture of trench warfare characterizes the 20th century's first great international conflict. Trenches were protected by barbed wire and machine guns, which gave defenders the advantage.

Hulton/Corbis-Bettmann.

Italia Irredenta Meaning "unredeemed Italy." Italian-speaking areas that had been left under Austrian rule at the time of the unification of Italy.

Women Munitions Workers in England. The World War I demanded more from the civilian populations than had previous wars, resulting in important social changes. Demands of the munitions industries and a shortage of men (so many of whom were in uniform) brought many women out of traditional roles at home and into factories and other war work.

Hulton Getty Picture Collection/Tony Stone Images.

The execution of his plan, however, was left to Helmuth von Moltke, a gloomy and nervous man, who made enough tactical mistakes to cause it to fail by a narrow margin. As a result, the French and British were able to stop the Germans at the Battle of the Marne in September 1914. Thereafter, the war in the West became one of position. Both sides dug in behind a wall of trenches protected by barbed wire that stretched from the North Sea to Switzerland. Machine-gun nests made assaults dangerous. Both sides, nonetheless, attempted massive attacks initiated by artillery bombardments of unprecedented force and duration. Still, the defense always prevented a breakthrough.

The War in the East In the East, the Russians advanced into Austrian territory and inflicted heavy casualties, but Russian incompetence and German energy soon reversed the situation. General Erich Ludendorff (1865–1937), under the command of the elderly Paul von Hindenburg (1847–1934), destroyed or captured an entire Russian army at the Battle of Tannenberg. In 1915, the Central Powers drove into the Baltic states and western Russia, inflicting more than 2 million casualties. Russian confidence was shaken (see Map 29–2).

Both sides sought new allies. Turkey and Bulgaria joined the Central Powers. Italy joined the Allies in 1915, after they agreed to give it *Italia Irredenta* (i.e., the Trentino, the South Tyrol, Trieste, and some of the Dalmatian Islands) from Austria after victory. Romania joined the Allies in 1916 but was quickly defeated and driven from the war. In the Far East, Japan honored its alliance with Britain and overran the German colonies in China and the Pacific.

In 1915, the Allies undertook to break the deadlock in the fighting by going around it. The idea came chiefly from Winston Churchill (1874–1965), First Lord of the British Admiralty. He proposed to attack the Dardanelles and capture Constantinople. This policy would knock Turkey from the war and ease communication with Russia. Success depended on daring leadership, but the attack was inept. Before the campaign was abandoned, the Allies lost almost 150,000 men.

Return to the West Both sides turned back to the West in 1916. Erich von Falkenhayn (1861–1922), who had succeeded Moltke in September 1914, sought success by an attack on the French stronghold of Verdun. It failed. The Allies, in turn, launched a major offensive along the River Somme in July, resulting in enormous casualties on both sides (see Map 29–3).

The War at Sea As the war continued, control of the sea became more important. The British imposed a strict blockade to starve out the enemy, regardless of international law. The Germans responded with submarine warfare to destroy British shipping and starve the British. They declared the waters around the British Isles a war zone, where

FARTHEST GERMAN ADVANCE, SUMMER, 1918

SUMMER, 1918

Rostov

Moscow

Sea of Azov

Black Sea

Angora

OTTOMAN EMPIRE

CYPRUS

Kharkov

Poltava

CRIMEA

UKRAINE

Gomel

Dnieper R.

Kiev

Odessa

Galatz

FARTHEST GERMAN ADVANCE, DEC., 1917

Constantsa

Constantinople

Petrograd (St. Petersburg)

Jassy

DEC., 1917

Varna

Dardanelles

SUMMER, 1918

Minsk

Pinsk

RUSSIAN FRONT

BRUSILOV'S OFFENSIVE AUG., 1916

ROMANIA

Bucharest

Sofia

Strumitsa

Gallipoli, 1915-1916

Revel

ESTONIA

LATVIA

DEC., 1917

Vilna

RUSSIA

Brest Litovsk

Lemberg

Gorlice

FEB., 1915

Debrecen

TRANSYLVANIA

Hermanstadt

Belgrade

Nish

SERBIA

MONTE-NEGRO

Skopje

1915

1916

GREECE

1917-18

FINLAND

Kaunas

Suwalki

1914

Warsaw

Cracow

MAY, 1915

SLOVAKIA

Budapest

AUSTRIA-HUNGARY

Sarajevo

ALBANIA

BALKAN FRONT

Baltic Sea

Memel

EAST PRUSSIA

FARTHEST RUSSIAN ADVANCE, 1914

FEB., 1915

Danzig

Breslau

SILESIA

Oder R.

MORAVIA

BOHEMIA

Vienna

Klagenfurt

TYROL

Trieste

Agram

Fiume

Caporetto

Adriatic Sea

Taranto

Naples

Stockholm

Göteborg

SWEDEN

Copenhagen

Hamburg

Berlin

Leipzig

Dresden

Prague

GERMAN EMPIRE

Elbe R.

Munich

AUG., 1917

MARCH, 1918

Venice

ITALIAN FRONT

ITALY

Rome

Genoa

Christiania

NORWAY

DENMARK

NETH.

Kiel Canal

Bremen

Essen

Cologne

Frankfurt

Nuremberg

Strasbourg

Berne

SWITZ.

Milan

Turin

CORSICA

SARDINIA

Mediterranean Sea

SICILY

North Sea

Amsterdam

Brussels

Liège

BELG.

LUX.

Metz

Mainz

Koblenz

Rhine

Sedan

Verdun

Toul

Belfort

Geneva

Lyons

Rhône R.

Marseilles

FRANCE

WESTERN FRONT

Compiègne

Versailles

Paris

Clermont-Ferrand

Aberdeen

Edinburgh

Hull

Yarmouth

London

Dover

UNITED KINGDOM

Le Havre

Ypres

Arras

ATLANTIC OCEAN

SPAIN

Leningrad

Koblenz

Leipzig

400 MILES

400 KILOMETERS

N

Triple Entente

Allies of the Triple Entente

Central Powers

Allies of the Central Powers

Neutral

Battle Lines

MAP 29–2

World War I in Europe. Despite the importance of military action in Asia, in the Middle East, and at sea, the main theaters of activity in World War I were in the European areas shown here.

WHICH REGIONS were most affected by military action?

MAP EXPLORATION

Interactive map: To explore this map further, go to
http://www.prenhall.com/craig/map29.3

1 Farthest German Advance, Sept., 1914
2 Nivelle's Offensive, Spring, 1917
3 Hindenburg Line (Stabilized Line) 1917–1918
4 German Gains, March–July, 1918
5 Major American Drives, Nov. 11, 1918
6 Armistice Line, Nov. 11, 1918

MAP 29–3

The Western Front 1914–1918. This map shows the crucial Western Front in detail.

IF THE Germans had captured Paris, what effect would this have had on the war?

WHY WERE the Bolsheviks able to seize power in Russia?

23.1 The Bolshevik Seizure of Power (November–December 1917)

even neutral ships would not be safe. Both policies were unwelcome to neutrals, especially the United States. But the sinking of neutral ships by German submarines was both more dramatic and offensive than Britain's blockade.

In 1915, the British liner *Lusitania* was torpedoed by a German submarine. Among the 1,200 drowned were 118 Americans. President Woodrow Wilson (1856–1924) protested, and the Germans desisted rather than further anger the United States. This development gave the Allies a considerable advantage. The German fleet that had cost so much money and had caused so much trouble played no significant part in the war.

America Enters the War In December 1916, President Wilson attempted to bring about a negotiated peace. But neither side would give up its hopes for total victory. The war seemed likely to continue until one or both sides reached exhaustion. Two events early in 1917 changed the situation. On February 1, the Germans announced the resumption of unrestricted submarine warfare, which led the United States to declare war on Germany on April 6.

One of the deterrents to an earlier American intervention had been the presence of autocratic tsarist Russia among the Allies. Wilson could conceive of the war only as an idealistic crusade "to make the world safe for democracy." That problem was resolved in March 1917 by a revolution in Russia that overthrew the tsarist government.

THE RUSSIAN REVOLUTION

The March Revolution in Russia was neither planned nor led by political faction. It was the result of the collapse of the monarchy's ability to govern. Military and domestic failures produced massive casualties, hunger, strikes, and disorganization. All political factions were discontented.

In early March 1917, strikes and demonstrations erupted in Petrograd, as Saint Petersburg had been renamed. The ill-disciplined troops in the city refused to fire on the demonstrators, and the tsar abdicated on March 15. The Duma formed a provisional government composed chiefly of Constitutional Democrats with Western sympathies. Various socialists also began to organize the workers into councils called *soviets*. They became estranged as the Constitutional Democratics failed to control the army or purge "reactionaries" from the government.

The provisional government decided to continue the war against Germany, but a new offensive in the summer of 1917 collapsed. Disillusionment with the war, shortages of food and other necessities, and the demand for land reform undermined the government, even after its leadership had been taken over by the moderate socialist Alexander Kerensky (1881–1970).

Since April the Bolsheviks had been working against the provisional government. The Germans had rushed V. I. Lenin (1870–1924) in a sealed train from his exile in Switzerland to Petrograd in the hope that he would cause trouble for the revolutionary government. The Bolsheviks demanded that all political power go to the soviets, which they controlled. They attempted a coup, but it failed. Lenin fled to Finland, and his chief collaborator, Leon Trotsky (1877–1940), was imprisoned.

An abortive right-wing counter-coup gave the Bolsheviks another chance. Trotsky, released from prison, led the powerful Petrograd Soviet. Lenin returned in October and insisted that the time was ripe to take power. On November 6, the Bolsheviks seized power.

The victors moved to fulfill their promises and to assure their own security. The provisional government had decreed an election for late November to select a Constituent Assembly. The Social Revolutionaries won a large majority over the Bolsheviks. When the assembly gathered in January, the Red Army, controlled by the Bolsheviks, dispersed it. All other political parties ceased to function in any meaningful fashion. The Bolshevik government nationalized the land and turned it over to its peasant proprietors. Factory workers were put in charge of their plants. Banks were seized for the state, and the debt of the tsarist government was repudiated. The property of the church was also seized.

The Bolsheviks signed an armistice with Germany in December 1917. On March 3, 1918, they accepted the Treaty of Brest-Litovsk, by which Russia yielded Finland, Poland, the Baltic states, and the Ukraine. Some territory in the Transcaucasus region went to Turkey. The Bolsheviks also agreed to pay an indemnity. These terms were a high price to pay for peace, but the Bolsheviks needed time to impose their rule on Russia.

Until 1921, the Bolsheviks confronted massive domestic resistance. A civil war erupted between the "Red" Russians supporting the revolution and the **"White" Russians**, who opposed the Bolsheviks and received aid from the Allies. In the summer of 1918, the tsar and his family were murdered. However, led by Trotsky, the Red Army overcame the opposition. By, 1921, Lenin and his supporters were in firm control.

Petrograd Munitions Workers Demonstrating in 1917. The barely-legible slogan at the top of the banner reads, "Victory to the Petrograd Workers!"

Rla-Novosti/Sovfoto/Eastfoto.

White Russians Russians who opposed the Bolsheviks (the "Reds") in the Russian Civil War of 1918–1921.

END OF WORLD WAR I

MILITARY RESOLUTION

The Treaty of Brest-Litovsk brought Germany to the peak of its success. In 1918, it decided to gamble everything on a last offensive. But the German army could not get beyond the Marne. Germany was exhausted. The Allies, on the other hand, were bolstered by the arrival of American troops in ever-increasing numbers. They launched a counteroffensive that was irresistible. As the Austrian fronts in the Balkans and Italy collapsed, the German high command knew that the end was imminent but wanted peace to be made before the army could be thoroughly defeated in the field, so that the responsibility should fall on civilians.

WHY DID the Versailles settlement leave Germany bitter?

The army therefore allowed a new government to be established on democratic principles to seek peace. The new government, under Prince Max of Baden (1867–1928), asked for peace on the basis of the **Fourteen Points** that President Wilson had declared as the American war aims. These were idealistic principles, but Wilson insisted that he would deal only with a democratic German government that spoke for the German people.

The disintegration of the German army forced William II to abdicate on November 9, 1918. The Social Democratic Party proclaimed a republic to prevent the establishment of a soviet government under the control of its Leninist wing. Two days later this republican, socialist-led government signed an armistice and accepted German defeat. The German people were, in general, unaware that their army had been defeated. No foreign soldier stood on German soil. Many Germans expected a mild settlement. The real peace embittered the German people, many of whom came to believe that Germany had been stabbed in the back by republicans and socialists at home.

Casualties on all sides came to about 10 million dead and twice as many wounded. The financial resources of the European states were badly strained. The victorious Allies, formerly creditors to the world, became debtors to the new American colossus.

22.6
The Balfour Declaration

The old international order, moreover, was dead. Russia was ruled by a Bolshevik dictatorship that preached world revolution. Germany was in chaos. Austria-Hungary had disintegrated. These changes stirred the colonial empires ruled by the European powers; they would never again be as secure as they had seemed before the war. Europe was no longer the center of the world, free to interfere when it wished or to ignore the outer regions if it chose. Its easy confidence in progress was shattered by four years of horrible war. The memory of that war shook the nerve of the victorious Western powers in the postwar world.

SETTLEMENT AT PARIS

The Peacemakers Representatives of the victorious states gathered at Versailles and other Parisian suburbs in the first half of 1919. Wilson speaking for the United States, David Lloyd George (1863–1945) for Britain, Georges Clemenceau (1841–1929) for France, and Vittorio Emanuele Orlando (1860–1952) for Italy made up the Big Four. Japan also had an important part in the discussions.

Wilson's idealism came into conflict with the war aims of the victorious powers and with the secret treaties that had been made before and during the war. The British and French people had been told that Germany would be made to pay for the war. Romania had been promised Transylvania at the expense of Hungary. Italy and Serbia had competing claims in the Adriatic. During the war, the British had encouraged Arab hopes of an independent Arab state carved out of the Ottoman Empire; those plans conflicted with the Balfour Declaration (1917), in which the British also seemed to accept Zionism and to promise the Jews a national home in Palestine. Both of these plans conflicted with an Anglo-French agreement to divide the Near East between themselves.

The national goals of the victors presented further obstacles to an idealistic "peace without victors." France was eager to achieve a settlement that would permanently weaken Germany and preserve French political and military superiority. Italy sought to acquire *Italia Irredenta*; Britain looked to its imperial interests; Japan pursued its own advantage in Asia; and the United States insisted on

Fourteen Points President Woodrow Wilson's (1856–1924) idealistic war aims.

OVERVIEW   CASUALTIES OF THE MAJOR BELLIGERENTS IN WORLD WAR 1

Country	Killed	Wounded	Total Killed as Percentage of Population
Austria-Hungary	1.1 million	3.62 million	1.9%
Belgium	38,000	44,000	0.5%
Britain	723,000	1.16 million	1.6%
Bulgaria	88,000	152,000	1.9%
France	1.4 million	2 million	3.4%
Germany	2 million	4.2 million	3.0%
Italy	578,000	947,000	1.6%
Romania	250,000	120,000	3.3%
Russia	1.8 million	1.45 million	1.1%
Serbia	278,000	138,000	5.7%
Turkey	804,000	400,000	3.7%
United States	114,000	205,000	0.1%

freedom of the seas, which favored American commerce, and on its right to maintain the Monroe Doctrine.

Finally, the peacemakers of 1919 faced a world in turmoil. The greatest immediate threat appeared to be Bolshevism. While Lenin and his colleagues were distracted by civil war, the Allies landed small armies in Russia to help overthrow the Bolshevik regime. Communist governments were established in Bavaria and Hungary. Berlin also experienced an abortive communist uprising. The Allies were so worried that they supported the suppression of these communist movements by right-wing forces. They even permitted an army of German volunteers to fight the Bolsheviks in the Baltic states. But fear of Germany remained the chief concern for France, and traditional interests governed the policies of the other Allies.

The Peace   The Paris settlement consisted of five separate treaties between the victors and the defeated powers. The Soviet Union (as Russia was now called) and Germany were excluded from the peace conference. The Germans were simply presented with a treaty and compelled to accept it. The principle of national self-determination was violated often, as it was unavoidable. The undeserved adulation accorded Wilson on his arrival turned into equally undeserved scorn. He had not abandoned his ideals but had given way to the irresistible force of reality.

The League of Nations   Wilson put great faith in the new **League of Nations**. Its covenant was an essential part of the peace treaty. The league was not intended as an international government but as a body of sovereign states that agreed to pursue common policies. If war threatened, the members promised to submit the matter to an international court or the League Council. Refusal to abide by this

League of Nations Association of sovereign states set up after World War I to pursue common policies and avert international aggression.

Peacemakers. The Allies promoted Arab efforts to secure independence from Turkey in an effort to remove Turkey from the war. Delegates to the peace conference of 1919 in Paris included British Colonel T. E. Lawrence, who helped lead the rebellion against Turkey, and representatives from the Middle East. Prince Feisal, the third son of King Hussein, stands in the foreground of this picture; Lawrence is in the middle row, second from the right; and Brigadier General Nuri Pasha Said of Baghdad is second from the left.

Corbis-Bettmann.

agreement would justify league intervention in the form of economic or military sanctions.

But the league was to have no armed forces. Action would require the unanimous consent of its council, which was to consist of Britain, France, Italy, the United States, Japan, and four other states with temporary seats. The league was generally seen as a device to ensure the security of the victorious powers, and the exclusion of Germany and the Soviet Union undermined the league's claim to evenhandedness.

Provisions of the covenant that dealt with colonial areas and disarmament were ineffective. Members of the league remained fully sovereign and pursued their national interests.

Germany   In the West, the main territorial issue was the fate of Germany. The French would have liked to set up the Rhineland as a buffer state, but Lloyd George and Wilson would not permit that. But France did receive Alsace-Lorraine and the right to work the coal mines of the Saar for 15 years. Germany west of the Rhine, and 50 kilometers east of it, was to be a demilitarized zone; Allied troops could stay on the west bank for 15 years. The treaty also provided that Britain and the United States would guarantee to aid France if it were attacked by Germany. Such an attack was made more unlikely by the permanent disarmament of Germany. Its army was limited to 100,000 men; its fleet was all but eliminated; and it was forbidden to have war planes, submarines, tanks, heavy artillery, or poison gas. As long as these provisions were observed, France would be safe (see Map 29–4).

The East   The settlement in the East ratified the collapse of the empires that had ruled it for centuries. Germany lost part of Silesia, and East Prussia was cut off from the rest of Germany by a corridor carved out to give the revived state of Poland access to the sea. The Austro-Hungarian Empire disappeared. Most of its German-speaking people in the small Republic of Austria were forbidden to unite with Germany. The Magyars occupied the much-reduced kingdom of Hungary.

The Czechs of Bohemia and Moravia joined with the Slovaks and Ruthenians to form Czechoslovakia, which also included several million unhappy Germans. The southern Slavs were united in the kingdom of Serbs, Croats, and Slovenes, or Yugoslavia. Italy gained the Trentino and Trieste. Romania gained Transylvania from Hungary and Bessarabia from Russia. Bulgaria lost territory to Greece and Yugoslavia. Finland, Estonia, Latvia, and Lithuania became independent states, and much of Poland was carved out of formerly Russian soil. In the Caucasus, the new nations of Georgia, Armenia, and Azerbajan took advantage of the turmoil following the Russian revolution to enjoy a period of independence (1918–1921). Ukraine and Russia were also autonomous during this brief period.

Map legend:

- Autonomous states, 1920–1940
- Austria-Hungary, 1914
- Germany, 1914
- Areas lost by Germany in 1919
- Areas lost by Bulgaria
- Areas lost by Russia
- Areas lost by The Ottoman Empire

MAP 29–4

World War I Peace Settlement in Europe and the Middle East.   The map of central and eastern Europe, as well as that of the Middle East, underwent drastic revision after World War I. The enormous territorial losses suffered by Germany, Austria-Hungary, the Ottoman Empire, Bulgaria, and Russia were the other side of the coin represented by gains for France, Italy, Greece, and Romania and by the appearance, or reappearance, of at least eight new independent states from Finland in the north to Yugoslavia in the south, to Georgia in the east. The mandate system for former Ottoman territories outside Turkey proper laid foundations for several new, mostly Arab, states in the Middle East.

HOW DID the creation of new countries in central and eastern Europe set the stage for future conflicts?

The old Ottoman Empire also disappeared. The new republic of Turkey was limited to little more than Constantinople and Asia Minor. Palestine and Iraq came under British control and Syria and Lebanon under French control as mandates under the purely theoretical authority of the League of Nations. Germany's former colonies in Africa and the Pacific were divided among the victors.

Reparations Before the armistice, the Germans promised to pay compensation "for all damages done to the civilian population of the Allies and their property." However, France and Britain were eager to have Germany pay the full cost of the war. No sum was fixed at the conference. Germany was to pay $5 billion annually until 1921, when a final figure would be set, which Germany would have to pay within 30 years. The French calculated that either Germany would be bled into impotence or refuse to pay and justify French intervention.

To justify these huge reparation payments, the Allies inserted the notorious **war guilt clause** into the treaty, which placed the responsibility for the war solely on Germany. The Germans bitterly resented the charges but had to accept the treaty as it was written by the victors without negotiation. The German government led by the Social Democrats and the Catholic Center Party signed the treaty. These parties formed the backbone of the German Republic, but they never overcame the stigma of accepting the treaty.

EVALUATION OF THE PEACE

Few peace settlements have been more attacked than the Treaty of Versailles, but many of the attacks on it are unjustified. Germany was neither dismembered nor ruined. Reparations were scaled down, and until the Great Depression of the 1930s, the German economy recovered. The attempt at achieving self-determination for nationalities was less than perfect, but it was the best Europe had ever accomplished.

The peace, nevertheless, was unsatisfactory. The elimination of the Austro-Hungarian Empire, however inevitable, created serious problems. Economically it was disastrous, for it separated raw materials from manufacturing areas and producers from their markets. Poland and especially Czechoslovakia contained unhappy German minorities. Disputes over territories in eastern Europe promoted further tension. The peace also rested on a defeat that Germany did not admit. The Germans believed they had been cheated, not defeated.

Finally, the peace failed to accept reality. Germany and Russia must inevitably play an important part in European affairs, yet they were excluded from the settlement and from the League of Nations. Given the many discontented parties, the peace was not self-enforcing; yet no satisfactory machinery for enforcing it was established. The league was never a serious force for this purpose. It was left to France, with no guarantee of support from Britain and no hope of help from the United States, to defend the new arrangements. France was simply not strong enough for the task if Germany were to rearm. The Treaty of Versailles was neither conciliatory enough to remove the desire for change, nor harsh enough to make another war impossible.

war guilt clause Clause of the Versailles Treaty, which assigned responsibility for World War I solely to Germany.

SUMMARY

The New Imperialism European imperialism in the last part of the 19th century brought the Western countries into contact with most of the world. By 1914, European nations had divided Africa among themselves and controlled large parts of Asia and the islands of the Pacific. Much of the Middle East was under the nominal control of the Ottoman Empire, which was in its death throes and under European influence. The Monroe Doctrine made Latin America a protectorate of the United States. Japan had become an imperial power at the expense of China and Korea.

World War I   The emergence of a new, powerful German state at the center of Europe upset the old balance of power. Bismarck, however, preserved the peace for as long as he remained in power. The new German emperor, William II, abandoned the policy of restraint and sought more power and influence for his country. The result was a system of alliances that divided Europe into two armed camps. What began as yet another Balkan War involving the European powers became a global war. As the terrible war of 1914–1918 dragged on, the motives that had driven the European powers to fight gave way to public affirmations of the principles of nationalism and self-determination.

The Peace Settlement   The peoples under colonial rule took these statements seriously and sought to win their own independence and nationhood. For the most part they were disappointed by the peace settlement. The British and French Empires were larger than ever. The United States added to the islands it controlled in the Pacific. Japan was rewarded at the expense of China.

However, the old imperial nations, especially Britain and France, had paid an enormous price in lives, money, and will for their victory in the war. Colonial peoples pressed for the rights that were proclaimed as universal by the West but denied to their colonies; influential minorities in the countries that ruled them sympathized with colonial aspirations for independence. Tension between colonies and their ruling nations would be a cause of world instability.

REVIEW QUESTIONS

1. What was the New Imperialism?

2. What role did Bismarck expect the new Germany to play after 1871? Was he wise to tie Germany to Austria-Hungary?

3. Why did Britain abandon "splendid isolation"?

4. How did developments in the Balkans lead to the outbreak of World War I? Did Germany want a general war?

5. Why did Germany lose World War I? Was Versailles too harsh or too conciliatory? How might it have been improved?

6. Why was Lenin successful in establishing Bolshevik rule in Russia? Was it wise policy for him to take Russia out of the war?

IMAGE KEY

for pages 728–729

a. Dice showing the flags of Russia, Japan, Belgium, and the United Kingdom.

b. *The New York Times* announces the sinking of the Lusitania, May 8, 1915.

c. A map of the British empire in 1886.

d. Shells containing poison gas.

e. Lenin at the Tribune, 1930, by Alexander Gerasimov.

f. A red triplane with the German Iron Cross.

g. A British biplane.

h. American cartoon, 1882, depicting John Bull (England) as the octopus of imperialism.

i. A Renault tank, 1917.

j. English and Belgian uniform styles.

KEY TERMS

Fourteen Points (p. 744)

Italia Irredenta (p. 740)

League of Nations (p. 745)

New Imperialism (p. 730)

Pan-Slavic movement (p. 734)

Schlieffen Plan (p. 739)

war guilt clause (p. 748)

White Russians (p. 743)

 For additional study resources for this chapter, go to:
www.prenhall.com/craig/chapter29

30 Depression, European Dictators, and the American New Deal

CHAPTER HIGHLIGHTS

Postwar Problems The Versailles settlement left much of Europe dissatisfied. In the 1920s there were endless wrangles over reparations between Germany and the Allied powers. After World War I, Europe never recovered its prewar prosperity or stability. The onset of the Great Depression in 1929 caused severe problems in both Europe and the United States and led to the Nazi seizure of power in Germany and FDR's New Deal in the United States.

The Soviet Union The Bolsheviks had expected communist revolutions to break out across Europe. When that did not happen, they were forced to consolidate their regime within Russia. Lenin's New Economic Policy gave the state control over heavy industry, transportation, and international commerce but allowed for small-scale private enterprise and peasant farms. Stalin abandoned this policy to push for rapid industrialization. He abolished private enterprise, collectivized agriculture, and eliminated his opponents in a series of purges.

Fascist Italy Benito Mussolini came to power in Italy in 1922, promising order and a strong state. Although he achieved power by legal means, he soon transformed Italy into a single-party dictatorship.

Nazi Germany The postwar Weimar Republic in Germany was buffeted by social, political, and financial instability. Rampant inflation destroyed the savings of the middle class. The Great Depression brought financial collapse and massive unemployment. Many Germans looked to Adolf Hitler and the Nazi Party for solutions. Once Hitler came to power in 1933, he quickly established a one-party dictatorship based on police terror, propaganda, and the cult of himself as supreme leader. The Jews, in particular, were persecuted. Hitler also formed an alliance with the German army and began a program of rapid rearmament.

The United States The United States emerged from World War I as a world power, but retreated into isolation during the 1920s. The prosperity of the 1920s ended in the Great Depression. Franklin Delano Roosevelt's New Deal greatly expanded the power of the federal government in social and economic affairs and preserved capitalism in a democratic setting.

CHAPTER QUESTIONS

WHAT FACTORS made the Great Depression so severe and longlasting?

HOW DID Stalin gain and keep power in the Soviet Union?

WHY DID the Fascists achieve power in Italy?

WHAT ROLE did terror play in Nazi Germany?

HOW DID FDR's policies affect the role of the federal government?

CHAPTER OUTLINE

- After Versailles: Demands for Revision and Enforcement
- Toward the Great Depression in Europe
- The Soviet Experiment
- The Fascist Experiment in Italy
- German Democracy and Dictatorship
- The Great Depression and the New Deal in the United States

In the two decades that followed the Paris settlement, the Western world saw a number of experiments in politics and economic life. Two broad factors accounted for these experiments. First, the war, the Russian Revolution, and the peace treaty had transformed the political face of Europe. The new regimes that emerged in the wake of the collapse of the monarchies of Germany, Austria-Hungary, and Russia faced economic dislocation and nationalistic resentments.

Second, the Great Depression caused political instability and economic crisis. In Europe this often produced authoritarian regimes. In the United States it led to an increased role for the federal government.

AFTER VERSAILLES: DEMANDS FOR REVISION AND ENFORCEMENT

The Paris settlement fostered resentments that counted among the chief political factors in Europe for the next two decades. The arrangements for reparations led to endless haggling. National groups in eastern Europe felt that injustice had been done to them and demanded border adjustments. The victorious powers, especially France, often believed that the treaty was being inadequately enforced. Too many political figures were willing to fish in these troubled international waters for domestic votes.

TOWARD THE GREAT DEPRESSION IN EUROPE

Three factors combined to bring about the severity and the extended length of the **Great Depression**. First, a financial crisis stemmed directly from the war and the peace settlement. In addition, a crisis erupted in the production and distribution of goods in the world market. Finally, these difficulties were exacerbated because no major western European country or the United States provided responsible economic leadership.

FINANCIAL TAILSPIN

France was determined to collect reparations from Germany. The United States was no less determined that its allies repay the wartime loans it had extended to them. German reparations were to provide the means of repaying these debts.

The quest for payment of German reparations caused one of the major diplomatic crises of the 1920s; the crisis itself resulted in further economic upheaval. In early 1923, the Allies—and France in particular—declared Germany to be in default of its reparation payments. On January 11, French troops occupied the Ruhr mining and manufacturing district. The **Weimar Republic** ordered passive resistance. Confronted with this tactic, the French ran the German mines and railroads. The Germans paid, but Britain became more sympathetic to Germany. The cost of the Ruhr occupation, moreover, damaged the French economy.

The political and economic turmoil of the Ruhr invasion led to international attempts to ease German payment of reparations. The most famous were the Dawes Plan of 1924 and the Young Plan of 1929, both devised by Americans. At the same time, American investment capital was pouring into Europe. However, the crash of Wall Street in October 1929—the result of unregulated speculation—saw the loss of large amounts of money. Thereafter, little American capital was available for investment in Europe.

WHAT FACTORS made the Great Depression so severe and longlasting?

Great Depression Prolonged worldwide economic downturn that began in 1929 with the collapse of the New York Stock Exchange.

Weimar Republic German democratic regime that existed between the end of World War I and Hitler's coming to power in 1933.

In May 1931, the Kreditanstalt—a primary lending institution for much of central and eastern Europe—collapsed. The German banking system then came under severe pressure. As German difficulties increased, U.S. President Herbert Hoover (1874–1964) announced in June 1931 a one-year moratorium on all payments of international debts. The Hoover moratorium was a prelude to the end of reparations. In the summer of 1932, the Lausanne Conference, in effect, ended the era of reparations.

PROBLEMS IN AGRICULTURAL COMMODITIES

The 1920s witnessed a contraction in the market demand for European goods. The difficulty arose from agriculture. Better methods of farming and more extensive transport facilities all over the globe vastly increased the quantity of grain. Wheat prices fell to record lows, decreasing the income of European farmers, while increasing the cost of the industrial goods they used. Consequently, farmers had great difficulty paying off their debts. These problems were especially acute in central and eastern Europe and abetted farmers' disillusionment with liberal politics.

Outside Europe similar problems affected wheat, sugar, coffee, rubber, wool, and lard producers. The people who produced these goods in under-developed nations could no longer make enough money to buy finished goods from industrial Europe. Commodity production had outstripped world demand.

The result was stagnation and depression for European industry. Coal, iron, and textiles had depended largely on international markets. Unemployment spread from these industries to those producing consumer goods. Unemployment in Britain and Germany during the 1920s had created "soft" domestic markets. The policies of reduced spending, with which the governments confronted the depression, further weakened domestic demand. By the early 1930s, the depression was feeding on itself.

DEPRESSION AND GOVERNMENT POLICY

The depression did not mean absolute economic decline or total unemployment. However, the economic downturn made people insecure. Even the employed often seemed to make no progress, and their anxieties created discontent.

Governments of the late 1920s and the early 1930s were not well suited to confront these problems. The electorates demanded action. Government response depended largely on the severity of the depression in a particular country and on the self-confidence of its political system.

Great Britain and France undertook moderate political experiments. In 1924, the Labour Party in Great Britain established itself as a viable governing entity. Under the pressure of the depression, Labour prime minister Ramsay MacDonald (1866–1937) organized a National Government, which was a coalition of the Labour, Conservative, and Liberal parties. It remained in power until 1935, when a Conservative ministry led by Stanley Baldwin (1867–1947) replaced it.

The most important French political experiment was the **Popular Front** Ministry, which came to office in 1936. This government was composed of socialists,

Human Casualties. One of the last American soldiers killed on the Western Front in November 1918. The carnage of World War I was one of the main causes of European weakness and instability in the 1920s and 1930s.
American Stock/Archive Photos.

Popular Front Government of all left-wing parties that took power in France in 1936 to enact social and economic reforms.

radicals, and communists—the first time that socialists and communists had cooperated in a ministry. The Popular Front addressed major labor problems in the French economy, but by 1938 it was at an end.

The political experiments of the 1920s and 1930s that reshaped world history involved a Soviet government in Russia, a Fascist regime in Italy, and a Nazi dictatorship in Germany.

THE SOVIET EXPERIMENT

The Bolshevik Revolution in Russia led to the most durable of all 20th-century authoritarian governments. The Communist Party of the Soviet Union retained power from 1917 until the end of 1991, and it influenced the history of much of the world like no other single factor. Unlike the Italian Fascists or the German National Socialists, the Bolsheviks seized power violently through revolution. Their leaders long felt insecure about their hold on the country. The Communist Party was not a mass party nor a nationalistic one. The Bolsheviks confronted a much less industrialized economy than that in Italy or Germany. They believed in and practiced the collectivization of economic life attacked by right-wing dictatorships. The Marxist-Leninist ideology was broader than the nationalism of the Fascists and the racism of the Nazis. Communism was an exportable commodity. Communists regarded their government and their revolution as epoch-making events in the development of humanity. Fear of communism and determination to stop its spread were leading political forces in Western Europe and the United States for most of the rest of the century and would influence their relationships to much of the rest of the world.

WAR COMMUNISM

Within months of the revolution, a new secret police, known as *Cheka*, appeared. Throughout the Russian civil war Lenin had declared that the Bolshevik Party, as the vanguard of the revolution, was imposing the dictatorship of the proletariat. Under the economic policy of "**War Communism**," the revolutionary government confiscated banks, transport facilities, and heavy industry. The state also requisitioned grain and shipped it from the countryside to feed the army and the cities.

War Communism helped the Red Army defeat its opponents. The revolution had survived and triumphed. The policy, however, generated domestic opposition. Many Russians were no longer willing to make the sacrifices demanded by central party bureaucrats. In 1920 and 1921, strikes occurred. Peasants resisted the requisition of grain. In March 1921, the navy mutinied. Each of these incidents suggested that the proletariat itself was opposing the dictatorship of the proletariat. Also, by late 1920, it had become clear that revolution would not sweep across the rest of Europe. The Soviet Union was a vast island of revolutionary socialism in a sea of worldwide capitalism.

War Communism Economic policy adopted by the Bolsheviks during the Russian civil war to seize the banks, heavy industry, railroads, and grain.

New Economic Policy (NEP) Limited revival of capitalism, especially in light industry and agriculture, introduced by Lenin in 1921 to repair the damage inflicted on the Russian economy by the civil war and War Communism.

THE NEW ECONOMIC POLICY

Lenin made a strategic retreat. In March 1921, he outlined the **New Economic Policy**, or NEP. Apart from "the commanding heights" of banking, heavy industry, transportation, and international commerce, private economic enterprise was allowed and peasants could farm for a profit. The countryside became more stable, and a secure food supply seemed assured for the cities. Similar free enterprise flourished within light industry and retail trade. The revolution seemed to have transformed Russia into a land of small farms and private shops and businesses.

STALIN VERSUS TROTSKY

The NEP had caused sharp disputes within the Politburo, the highest governing committee of the Communist Party. These frictions increased when Lenin suffered a stroke in 1922 and died in 1924. An intense struggle for leadership of the party commenced. Two factions emerged. One was led by Trotsky; the other by Joseph Stalin (1879–1953), who had become general secretary of the party in 1922.

The power struggle was fought over the question of Russia's path toward industrialization and the future of the Communist revolutionary movement. Trotsky, speaking for what became known as the left wing, urged rapid industrialization and looked to voluntary collectivization of farming by poor peasants as a means of increasing agricultural production. Trotsky further argued that the revolution in Russia could succeed only if new revolutions took place elsewhere.

A right-wing faction manipulated by Stalin opposed Trotsky. This group pressed for the continuation of Lenin's NEP. Stalin was the ultimate victor. His power lay in his command of bureaucratic and administrative methods. He mastered the crucial details of party structure, including admission and promotion. He had the support of the lower levels of the party when he clashed with other leaders.

In 1924, Stalin enunciated, in opposition to Trotsky, the doctrine of "socialism in one country." Russian success did not depend on the fate of the revolution elsewhere. Stalin thus nationalized the previously international scope of the Marxist revolution. By 1927, Trotsky had been ousted from the party. In 1929, he was expelled from Russia and was eventually murdered in 1940 by one of Stalin's agents. With the removal of Trotsky, Stalin was firmly in control of the Soviet state.

DECISION FOR RAPID INDUSTRIALIZATION

During the depression, the Soviet Union registered tremendous industrial advance. As usual in Russia, the direction and impetus came from the top. Stalin far exceeded the tsars in the coercion and terror he brought to the task. Russia achieved its economic growth during the 1930s only at the cost of millions of human lives.

Through 1928, Lenin's NEP steered Soviet economic development. A few farmers, the *kulaks*, became prosperous. During 1928 and 1929, the kulaks and other farmers withheld grain from the market because prices were too low. Food shortages in the cities caused unrest. Stalin came to a momentous decision. Russia must industrialize rapidly to match the power of the West. Agriculture must be collectivized to produce sufficient grain for food and export and to free peasant labor for the factories. This program, which basically embraced Trotsky's earlier economic position, unleashed a second Russian revolution.

Agricultural Policy   In 1929, Stalin ordered party agents to confiscate hoarded wheat. As part of the general plan to collectivize farming, the government undertook to eliminate the kulaks as a class. A kulak, however, soon came to mean any peasant who opposed Stalin's policy. In the countryside, peasants at all levels of wealth resisted stubbornly. They wreaked their vengeance on the policy of **collectivization** by slaughtering more than 100 million horses and cattle between 1929 and 1933. The situation in the countryside amounted to open warfare.

As many as 10 million peasants were killed, and millions of others were sent to labor camps. Because of the turmoil, famine persisted in 1932 and 1933. Yet Stalin persevered. Peasants had their lands incorporated into large collective farms. The state controlled the machinery for these units.

Lenin. Anxiety over the spread of the Bolshevik Revolution was a fundamental factor of European politics during the 1920s and 1930s. Images like this Soviet portrait of Lenin as a heroic revolutionary conjured fears among people in the rest of Europe of a political force determined to overturn their social, political, and economic institutions.

Gemalde von A. M. Gerassimow, "Lenin as Agitator"/Bildarchiv Preussischer Kulturbesitz.

QUICK REVIEW

Stalin's Rise to Power
- Sided with the opposition to Trotsky in the 1920s
- Used control of the Central Committee to marginalize Trotsky and his supporters
- Emerged from struggle with Trotsky with unchallenged control of the Soviet state

collectivization   Bedrock of Stalinist agriculture, which forced Russian peasants to give up their private farms and work as members of collectives, large agricultural units controlled by the state.

Soviet Communist Party Meeting. By the mid-1930s Stalin's purges had eliminated many leaders and other members from the Soviet Communist Party. This photograph of a meeting of a party congress in 1936 shows a number of the surviving leaders with Stalin, who sits fourth from the right in the front row. To his left is Vyacheslav Molotov, long-time foreign minister. The first person on the left in the front row is Nikita Khrushchev, who headed the Soviet Union in the late 1950s and early 1960s.

Itar-Tass/Sovfoto/Eastfoto.

The government now had primary direction over the food supply. Peasants could no longer determine whether there would be stability or unrest in the cities. Stalin and the Communist Party had won the battle of the wheat fields, but the problem of producing enough grain still plagues the former Soviet Union.

Five-Year Plans The revolution in agriculture had been undertaken for the sake of industrialization. The increased grain supply was to feed the labor force and provide exports to finance the imports required for industrial development. The industrial achievement of the Soviet Union between 1928 and World War II was one of the most striking accomplishments of the 20th century. Russia made a more rapid advance toward economic growth than any other nation in the Western world has ever achieved during a similar period of time. Soviet industrial production rose approximately 400 percent between 1928 and 1940. Few consumer goods were produced. Labor for this development was supplied internally. Capital was raised from the export of grain, even at the cost of internal shortage. Technology was borrowed from industrialized nations.

The organizational vehicle for industrialization was a series of five-year plans that began in 1928. The State Planning Commission, or Gosplan, set goals of production and organized the economy to meet them. Coordinating all facets of production was difficult and complicated. A vast program of propaganda was undertaken to sell the five-year plans to the Russian people. The industrial labor force became subject to regimentation similar to that being imposed on the peasants. The accomplishment of the three five-year plans probably allowed the Soviet Union to survive the German invasion.

Many non-Russian contemporaries looked at the Soviet economic experiment uncritically. While the capitalist world lay in the throes of the depression, the Soviet economy had grown at an unprecedented pace. These observers seemed to have had little idea of the social cost of the Soviet achievement. Millions had been killed or uprooted. The suffering and human loss during those years will probably never be known; it far exceeded anything described by Marx and Engels in relation to 19th-century industrialization in Western Europe.

THE PURGES

Stalin's decisions to industrialize rapidly and to move against the peasants aroused internal political opposition because they were departures from the policies of Lenin. In 1933, Stalin began to fear that he would lose control over the party apparatus. These fears were probably paranoid. Nevertheless, they resulted in the **Great Purges**, among the most mysterious and horrendous political events of this century.

On December 1, 1934, Sergei Kirov (1888–1934), the popular party chief of Leningrad (formerly Saint Petersburg), was assassinated. In the wake of the shooting, thousands of people were arrested, and still more were expelled from the party and sent to labor camps. It now seems certain that Stalin himself authorized Kirov's assassination to forestall any threat from him.

Great Purges Imprisonment and execution of millions of Soviet citizens by Stalin between 1934 and 1939.

The purges after Kirov's death were just the beginning. Between 1936 and 1938, spectacular show trials were held in Moscow. Previous high Soviet leaders publicly confessed political crimes and were executed. Their confessions were palpably false. Other leaders and party members were tried in private and shot. Thousands of people received no trial at all. It is inexplicable why some were executed, others sent to labor camps, and still others left unmolested. After the civilian party members had been purged, important officers, including heroes of the civil war, were killed. The exact numbers of executions and imprisonments are unknown but ran into the millions.

The scale of the political turmoil was unprecedented. The Russians themselves did not comprehend what was occurring. The only rational explanation is found in Stalin's concern for his own power. The purges created a new party structure absolutely loyal to him.

Despite the violence and repression, the Soviet experiment found many sympathizers. The Soviet Union after the Bolshevik seizure of power had fostered Communist parties subservient to Moscow throughout the world. Others who were not members of these parties sympathized with what they believed were the goals of the Soviet Union. During at least the first 50 years of its existence, the Soviet Union managed to capture the imagination of some intellectuals around the globe who hoped for a utopian egalitarian transformation of society. During much of the 1930s, the Soviet Union also appeared as an enemy to the fascist experiments in Italy and Germany. The Marxist ideology championed by the Soviet Union appeared to many people living in the European colonial empires as a vehicle for freeing themselves. The Soviet Union welcomed and trained many such anti-colonial leaders. With what is now known about Soviet repression, it is difficult to understand the power its presence exercised over many people's political imaginations, but that attraction was a factor in world politics from the 1920s through at least the early 1970s.

23.4
Nadezhda Mandelstam,
Hope Against Hope

THE FASCIST EXPERIMENT IN ITALY

The first authoritarian political experiment in western Europe that arose in part from fears of the spread of bolshevism occurred in Italy. The general term *fascist*, which has been used to describe the various right-wing dictatorships that arose between the wars, was derived from the Italian fascist movement of Benito Mussolini (1883–1945).

Governments regarded as fascist were antidemocratic, anti-Marxist, antiparliamentary, and frequently anti-Semitic. They hoped to hold back the spread of Bolshevism, which seemed a real threat at the time. They sought a world that would be safe for the middle class and small farmers. **Fascism** rejected the political ideas of the French Revolution and of liberalism. Facist adherents believed that parliamentary politics and parties sacrificed national greatness to petty party disputes. They wanted to overcome the class conflict of Marxism and the party conflict of liberalism by consolidating all classes within the nation for great national purposes. Fascist governments were usually single-party dictatorships rooted in mass political parties and characterized by terrorism and police surveillance.

RISE OF MUSSOLINI

The Italian *Fasci di Combattimento* ("Band of Combat") was founded in 1919 in Milan. Most of its members were veterans who felt that the sacrifices of World War I had been in vain. They resented Italy's failure to gain the city of Fiume at the Paris conference. They feared socialism, inflation, and labor unrest.

WHY DID the Fascists achieve power in Italy?

fascism Political movements that tend to be antidemocratic, anti-Marxist, antiparliamentary, and often anti-Semitic. Fascists were invariably nationalists and exhalted the nation over the individual. They supported the interests of the middle class and rejected the ideas of the French Revolution and 19th-century liberalism. The first fascist regime was founded by Benito Mussolini (1883–1945) in Italy in the 1920s.

Mussolini and the Black Shirts.
Mussolini poses with supporters the day after the Black Shirt March on Rome intimidated the king of Italy into making him prime minister.

Bildarchiv Preussischer Kutturbesitz.

Their leader, or *Duce*, Benito Mussolini, had been active in Italian socialist politics but broke with the socialists in 1914 and supported Italian entry into the war. He then established his own paper, *Il Popolo d'Italia*, and was wounded in the army. As a politician, Mussolini was an opportunist. He could change his ideas and principles to suit any occasion. Action for him was always more important than thought. His goal was political survival.

Many Italians were dissatisfied with the parliamentary system. They felt that Italy had not been treated as a great power at the peace conference and had not received the territories it deserved. The main spokesman for this discontent was the extreme nationalist writer Gabriele D'Annunzio (1863–1938). In 1919, he captured Fiume with a force of patriotic Italians. The Italian army drove him out, but this made the parliamentary ministry seem unpatriotic.

Between 1919 and 1921, Italy was also wracked by social turmoil. Numerous strikes occurred, and workers occupied factories. Peasants seized land. Parliamentary government seemed incapable of dealing with this unrest. Many Italians believed that a Communist revolution might break out.

Mussolini first supported the factory occupations and land seizures, but soon reversed himself. He had discovered that many upper- and middle-class Italians who were pressured by inflation and feared property loss had no sympathy for the workers or peasants. They wanted order. Consequently, Mussolini and his Fascists took direct action in the face of the government inaction. They terrorized Socialist supporters, attacked strikers and farm workers, and protected strikebreakers. Conservative land and factory owners were grateful. The government ignored these crimes. By early 1922, the Fascists controlled the local government in much of northern Italy.

In 1921, Mussolini and 34 of his followers had been elected to the Chamber of Deputies. The Fascist movement now had hundreds of thousands of supporters. In October 1922, the Fascists, dressed in their characteristic black shirts, began a march on Rome. King Victor Emmanuel III (r. 1900–1946) refused to authorize using the army against them, which ensured a Fascist seizure of power. The cabinet resigned. On October 29, the king telegraphed Mussolini in Milan and asked him to become prime minister. The next day Mussolini arrived in Rome by train and, as head of the government, greeted his followers when they entered the city.

Technically, Mussolini had come into office by legal means. The monarch had the power to appoint the prime minister. Mussolini, however, had no majority in the Chamber of Deputies. Behind the legal facade lay the months of terrorist intimidation and the threat of the Fascists' October march.

THE FASCISTS IN POWER

Duce Meaning "leader." Mussolini's title as head of the Fascist Party.

Mussolini, who had not expected to be appointed prime minister, succeeded because of the impotence of his rivals, his use of his office, his power over the masses, and his ruthlessness. On November 23, 1922, the king and Parliament granted Mussolini dictatorial authority for one year to restore order. Wherever possible, Mussolini appointed Fascists to office. In 1924, Parliament changed the election law so that the party that gained the largest popular vote (with at least 25 percent) received two-thirds of the seats in the chamber. Coalition government, with all its compromises and hesitations, would no longer be necessary. In the election of 1924, the Fascists won complete control of the Chamber of Deputies. They used that majority to end legitimate parliamentary life. Laws permitted Mussolini to rule by decree. In 1926, Italy was transformed into a single-party, dictatorial state.

One domestic initiative brought Mussolini significant political dividends and respectability. Through the Lateran Accord of February 1929, the Roman Catholic Church and the Italian state made peace with each other. The agreement recognized the pope as the temporal ruler of Vatican City. The Italian government agreed to pay an indemnity to the papacy for confiscated land. The state also recognized Catholicism as the religion of the nation, exempted church property from taxes, and allowed church law to govern marriage.

23.5
The Rise of Benito Mussolini

GERMAN DEMOCRACY AND DICTATORSHIP
THE WEIMAR REPUBLIC

The Weimar Republic was born from the defeat of the imperial army, the revolution of 1918, and the hopes of German Liberals and Social Democrats. Its name derived from the city of Weimar where its constitution was written in August 1919. While the constitution was being debated, the republic, headed by the Social Democrats, accepted the hated Versailles Treaty. Although its officials had signed only under duress, the republic was permanently associated with the national disgrace. Throughout the 1920s, the government was required to fulfill the economic and military provisions imposed by the Paris settlement. Nationalists and military figures whose policies had brought on the tragedy and defeat of the war blamed the young republic and the socialists for its results. In Germany, the desire to revise the treaty was related to a desire to change the form of government.

The Weimar Constitution was an enlightened document. It guaranteed civil liberties and provided for direct election, by universal suffrage, of the **Reichstag** and the president. It also, however, contained structural flaws that eventually allowed it to be overthrown. A complicated system of proportional representation made it relatively easy for small political parties to gain seats in the Reichstag, which resulted in instability. The president appointed and removed the chancellor, the head of the cabinet. Article 48 allowed the president, in an emergency, to rule by decree. This permitted a possible presidential dictatorship.

In March 1920, a right-wing putsch, or armed insurrection, erupted in Berlin. It failed, but only after government officials had fled the city. In the same month, strikes took place in the Ruhr, and the government sent in troops. Such extremism from both the left and the right would haunt the republic. In May 1921, the Allies presented a reparations bill for 132 billion gold marks. The German government accepted this preposterous demand only after new Allied threats. Throughout the early 1920s, there were assassinations or attempted assassinations of republican leaders. Violence was the hallmark of the first five years of the republic.

Invasion of the Ruhr and Inflation   Inflation brought on the major crisis of this period. The war and postwar deficit spending generated an immense rise in prices. The value of German currency fell. By early 1921, the German mark traded against

WHAT ROLE did terror play in Nazi Germany?

Reichstag German parliament, which existed in various forms, until 1945.

DOCUMENT CD-ROM

23.6
Adolf Hitler, *Mein Kampf*

Major Political Events of the 1920s and 1930s

1919

August	Constitution of the Weimar Republic promulgated	
1920	Putsch in Berlin	

1921

March	Lenin initiates his New Economic Policy

1922

October	Fascist march on Rome leads to Mussolini's assumption of power

1923

January	France invades the Ruhr
November	Hitler's Beer Hall Putsch
1924	Death of Lenin
1925	Locamo Agreements
1928	Kellogg-Briand Pact; first five-year plan launched in USSR

1929

January	Trotsky expelled from USSR
February	Lateran Accord between the Vatican and the Italian state
October	New York stock market crash
November	Stalin's power affirmed

the American dollar at a ratio of 64 to 1, compared with a ratio of 4.2 to 1 in 1914. The German financial community contended that the mark could not be stabilized until the reparations issue had been solved. Meanwhile, the government kept issuing paper money, which it used to redeem government bonds.

The French invasion of the Ruhr in January 1923, to secure the payment of reparations, and the German response of passive economic resistance produced cataclysmic inflation. Unemployment spread, creating a drain on the treasury and reducing tax revenues. The printing presses had difficulty providing enough paper currency to keep up with the daily rise in prices. Money was literally not worth the paper it was printed on. Stores were unwilling to exchange goods for the worthless currency, and farmers hoarded produce.

The values of thrift and prudence were undermined. Middle-class savings, pensions, insurance policies, and investments in government bonds were wiped out. Debts and mortgages could not be paid off. Speculators made fortunes, but to the middle and lower-middle classes, inflation was another trauma coming hard on the heels of military defeat and the peace treaty. This social and economic upheaval was behind the later German desire for order and security at almost any cost.

Hitler's Early Career　In 1923, Adolf Hitler (1889–1945) made his first significant appearance on the German political scene. The son of a minor Austrian customs official, his hopes of becoming an artist had been dashed in Vienna. Hitler absorbed the rabid German nationalism and extreme anti-Semitism that flourished there. He came to hate Marxism, which he associated with Jews. During World War I, Hitler fought in the German army, was wounded, rose to the rank of corporal, and won the Iron Cross for bravery. The war gave him his first sense of purpose.

After the conflict, Hitler settled in Munich and became associated with a small nationalistic, anti-Semitic party that in 1920 adopted the name of National Socialist German Workers Party, better known as the Nazis. The group paraded under a red banner with a black swastika. Its program called for the repudiation of the Versailles Treaty, the unification of Austria and Germany, the exclusion of Jews from German citizenship, agrarian reform, the prohibition of land speculation, the confiscation of war profits, state administration of the giant cartels, and the replacement of department stores with small retail shops.

The "socialism" that Hitler and the Nazis had in mind had nothing to do with traditional German socialism. It meant not state ownership of the means of production but the subordination of all economic enterprise to the welfare of the nation. It often implied protection for small economic enterprises. The Nazis discovered that their social appeal was to the lower-middle class, which found itself squeezed between big business and socialist labor unions. The Nazis tailored their message to this troubled economic group.

Nazi stormtroopers, or SA *(Sturm Abteilung)*, were organized under the leadership of Captain Ernst Roehm (1887–1934). The stormtroopers were the chief Nazi instrument for terror and intimidation before the party controlled the government. The existence of such a private party army was a sign of the potential for violence in the Weimar Republic and of contempt for the republic.

The social and economic turmoil following the French occupation of the Ruhr and the German inflation gave the Nazis an opportunity for direct action against the Weimar Republic. By this time, Hitler dominated the Nazi Party. On November 9, 1923, Hitler and a band of followers, accompanied by General Erich Ludendorff (1865–1937), attempted an unsuccessful putsch at a beer hall in Munich. Local authorities crushed the rising, and 16 Nazis were killed. Hitler and Ludendorff were tried for treason. The general was acquitted. Hitler made himself into a national figure. In his defense, he condemned the republic, the Versailles Treaty, and the Jews. He was sentenced to five years in prison but spent only a few months in jail before being paroled. During this time, he dictated *Mein Kampf* ("My Struggle"). Another result of the brief imprisonment was his decision to seize political power by legal methods.

The Stresemann Years Gustav Stresemann (1878–1929) was primarily responsible for the reconstruction of the republic and its achievement of a sense of self-confidence. Stresemann abandoned the policy of passive resistance in the Ruhr. With the aid of banker Hjalmar Schacht (1877–1970), he introduced a new German currency. The rate of exchange was 1 trillion of the old German marks for one new Rentenmark. Stresemann also moved against challenges from both the left and the right. He supported the crushing of both Hitler's abortive putsch and smaller communist disturbances. In late November 1923, after four months as chancellor, he became foreign minister, a post he held until his death in 1929.

In 1924, the Weimar Republic and the Allies renegotiated the reparation payments. French troops left the Ruhr in 1925. The same year, Field Marshal Paul von Hindenburg (1847–1934), a military hero and a conservative monarchist, was elected president and governed in strict accordance with the constitution. The prosperity of the latter 1920s seemed to reconcile conservative Germans to the republic. Foreign capital flowed into Germany, and employment improved smartly. Giant industrial combines spread.

In foreign affairs, Stresemann pursued a conciliatory course. He fulfilled the provisions of the Versailles Treaty but attempted to revise it by diplomacy. He accepted the settlement in the west but aimed to recover German-speaking territories lost to Poland and Czechoslovakia and possibly to unite with Austria, chiefly by diplomatic means.

Locarno These developments gave rise to the Locarno Agreements of October 1925. Foreign ministers Austen Chamberlain (1863–1937) for Britain and Aristide Briand (1862–1932) for France accepted Stresemann's proposal for a fresh start. France and Germany accepted the western

Major Political Events of the 1920s and 1930s (*continued*)

1930		
March	Brüning government begins in Germany	
September	Nazis capture 107 seats in German Reichstag	
1931		
August	National Government formed in Britain	
1932		
March 13	Hindenberg defeats Hitler for German presidency	
May 31	Franz von Papen forms German cabinet	
July 31	German Reichstag election	
November 6	German Reichstag election	
December 2	Kurt von Schleicher forms German cabinet	
1933		
January 30	Hitler made German chancellor	
February 27	Reichstag Fire	
March 5	Reichstag election	
March 23	Enabling Act consolidates Nazi power	
1934		
June 30	Blood purge of the Nazi Party	
August 2	Death of Hindenburg	
December 1	Assassination of Kirov leads to the beginning of Stalin's purges	
1936		
May	Popular Front government in France	
July–August	Most famous of public purge trials in Russia	

frontier established at Versailles. Britain and Italy agreed to intervene against the aggressor if either side violated the frontier or if Germany sent troops into the demilitarized Rhineland. No such agreement was made about Germany's eastern frontier, but the Germans made arbitration treaties with Poland and Czechoslovakia, and France strengthened its alliances with those countries. France supported German membership in the League of Nations and agreed to withdraw its occupation troops from the Rhineland in 1930, five years earlier than specified at Versailles.

The Locarno Agreements brought new hope to Europe. Chamberlain, Briand, and Stresemann received the Nobel Peace Prize. The spirit of Locarno was carried even further when the leading European states, Japan, and the United States signed the Kellogg-Briand Pact in 1928, renouncing "war as an instrument of national policy." The joy and optimism were not justified. France had merely recognized its inability to coerce Germany without help. Britain had shown its unwillingness to uphold the settlement in the east. Germany was not reconciled to the eastern settlement.

In both France and Germany, moreover, the conciliatory politicians represented only a part of the nation. In Germany especially, most people continued to reject Versailles and regarded Locarno as only an extension of it. Despite these problems, war was by no means inevitable. Europe, aided by American loans, was returning to prosperity. German leaders like Stresemann would certainly have continued to press for change, but not through force, much less a general war. Continued prosperity and diplomatic success might have won the loyalty of the German people for the Weimar Republic and moderate revisionism, but the Great Depression of the 1930s brought new forces to power.

DEPRESSION AND POLITICAL DEADLOCK

The outflow of foreign, and especially American, capital from Germany that began in 1928 undermined the prosperity of the Weimar Republic. The resulting economic crisis brought parliamentary government to a halt. In 1928, a coalition of center parties and the Social Democrats governed. When the depression struck, the coalition partners differed sharply on economic policy, and the coalition dissolved in March 1930. President von Hindenburg appointed Heinrich Brüning (1885–1970) as chancellor. Lacking a majority in the Reichstag, the new chancellor governed through emergency presidential decrees. The Weimar Republic had become a presidential dictatorship.

German unemployment rose from 2,258,000 in March 1930 to more than 6,000,000 in March 1932. The economic downturn and the parliamentary deadlock worked to the advantage of extremists. In the election of 1928, the Nazis had won only 12 seats in the Reichstag and the Communists won 54. In the election of 1930, the Nazis won 107 seats and the Communists won 77.

The power of the Nazis in the streets also rose. Unemployment fed thousands of men into the stormtroopers, which had almost 1 million members in 1933. The SA attacked Communists and Social Democrats. For the Nazis, politics meant the capture of power through terror and intimidation as well as through elections. Decency and civility in political life vanished. Nazi rallies resembled religious revivals. They paraded through the streets and the countryside. They gained powerful supporters in the business, military, and newspaper communities. Some intellectuals were also sympathetic. The Nazis transformed this discipline and enthusiasm born of economic despair and nationalistic frustration into electoral results.

European Turmoil. In this painting, which reflects the mood of social and political disillusionment that prevailed in much of Europe in the 1920s, George Grosz satirized conservative and right-wing groups in Weimar Germany, including the army, the courts, the newspapers, and the Nazi Party.

Bildarchiv Preussischer Kulturbesitz.

HITLER COMES TO POWER

For two years, Brüning governed with the confidence of Hindenburg. The economy did not improve, and the political situation deteriorated. In 1932, the 83-year-old president stood for reelection. Hitler ran against him and Hindenburg won. But Hitler got 36.8 percent of the final vote. The vote convinced Hindenburg that Brüning had lost the confidence of conservative Germans. In May 1932, he appointed Franz von Papen (1878–1969) chancellor. Papen was one of a small group of extremely conservative advisers on whom Hindenburg had become dependent. With the continued paralysis in the Reichstag, the advisers' influence over the president amounted to control of the government.

Hitler. Hitler's mastery of the techniques of mass politics and propaganda—including huge staged rallies like this one in 1938—was an important factor in his rise to power.

Bildarchlv Preussischer Kulturbesitz.

Papen and the circle around the president wanted to draw the Nazis into cooperation with them without giving Hitler effective power. The government needed the popular support on the right that only the Nazis seemed able to generate. The Hindenburg circle decided to convince Hitler that the Nazis could not come to power on their own. Papen removed the ban on Nazi meetings that Brüning had imposed and called a Reichstag election for July 1932. The Nazis won 230 seats and polled 37.2 percent of the vote. Hitler would only enter the cabinet if he were made chancellor. Hindenburg refused. Another election was called in November. The Nazis gained only 196 seats, and their percentage of the popular vote dipped to 33.1 percent.

In early December 1932, Papen resigned, and General Kurt von Schleicher (1882–1934) became chancellor. People were now afraid of civil war between the extreme left and the far right. Schleicher tried to fashion a coalition of conservatives and trade unionists. The Hindenburg circle did not trust Schleicher's motives, which have never been clear. They persuaded Hindenburg to appoint Hitler chancellor. To control him, Papen was named vice chancellor, and other traditional conservatives were appointed to the cabinet. On January 30, 1933, Adolf Hitler became the chancellor of Germany.

Hitler had come into office by legal means. The proper procedures had been observed. This permitted the civil service, courts, and other government agencies to support him in good conscience. He had forged a rigidly disciplined party structure and had mastered the techniques of mass politics and propaganda. His support appears to have come from across the social spectrum. Pockets of resistance appeared among Roman Catholic voters in the country and small towns. Otherwise, support for Hitler was strong among farmers, veterans, and the young, who had suffered from the insecurity of the 1920s and the depression. Hitler promised them security, effective government in place of petty politics, and a strong, restored Germany.

There is little evidence that business contributions made any crucial difference to the Nazis' success. Hitler's supporters were frequently suspicious of business and

Anti-Jewish Policies. Soon after seizing power, the Nazi government began harassing German Jewish businesses. Non-Jewish German citizens were urged not to buy merchandise from shops owned by Jews.

Bildarchiv Preussischer Kulturbesitz.

Führer Meaning "leader." Title taken by Hitler when he became dictator of Germany.

giant capitalism. They wanted a simpler world in which small property would be safe from both socialism and large-scale capitalist consolidation. These people looked to Hitler and the Nazis rather than to the Social Democrats because the latter never appeared sufficiently nationalistic. The Nazis won out over other conservative nationalistic parties because, unlike those conservatives, the Nazis addressed the problem of social insecurities.

HITLER'S CONSOLIDATION OF POWER

Once in office, Hitler moved swiftly to consolidate his control. This process had three facets: the capture of full legal authority, the crushing of alternative political groups, and the purging of rivals within the Nazi Party itself. On February 27, 1933, a mentally ill Dutch Communist set fire to the Reichstag building in Berlin. The Nazis turned the incident to their own advantage by claiming that the fire proved the existence of a Communist threat to the government. To the public, this seemed plausible. Under Article 48, Hitler suspended civil liberties and arrested Communists or alleged Communists. This decree was not revoked for as long as Hitler ruled Germany.

In early March, another Reichstag election took place. The Nazis still received only 43.9 percent of the vote. However, the arrest of Communist deputies and the fear aroused by the fire meant that Hitler could control the Reichstag. On March 23, 1933, the Reichstag passed an Enabling Act, which permitted Hitler to rule by decree. Thereafter, there were no legal limits on his power. The Weimar Constitution was never formally repealed.

Hitler understood that he and his party had come to power because his potential opponents had stood divided between 1929 and 1933. To prevent them from regrouping, Hitler outlawed or undermined any German institutions that might have served as rallying points for opposition. By the close of 1933, all major institutions of potential opposition—trade unions, other political parties, the federal state governments—had been eliminated.

The final element in Hitler's personal consolidation of power involved the Nazi Party itself. Ernst Roehm, the commander of the SA, was a possible rival to Hitler. The German officer corps, whom Hitler needed to rebuild the army, were jealous of the SA. To protect his own position and to shore up support with the army, Hitler ordered the murder of key SA officers, including Roehm. Between June 30 and July 2, 1934, more than 800 people were killed, including the former chancellor Kurt von Schleicher and his wife. The German army, which might have prevented the murders, did nothing. On August 2, 1934, President Hindenburg died, and the offices of chancellor and president were combined. Hitler was now the sole ruler, or *Führer*, of Germany and of the Nazi Party.

THE POLICE STATE

Terror and intimidation had helped propel the Nazis to office. As Hitler consolidated his power, he oversaw the organization of a police state. The chief vehicle of police surveillance was the SS (*Schutzstaffel*), or security units, commanded by Heinrich Himmler (1900–1945). This group was a more elite paramilitary organization than the larger SA. In 1933, the SS had approximately 52,000 members. It was the instrument that carried out the blood purges of the party in 1934. By 1936, Himmler had become head of all police matters in Germany.

The police character of the Nazi regime was all-pervasive, but the people who most consistently experienced its terror were the Jews. Anti-Semitism had been a key plank of the Nazi program—anti-Semitism based on biological racial theories stemming from late-19th-century thought rather than from religious discrimination. Before World War II, the Nazi attack on the Jews went through three stages. In 1933, the Nazis excluded Jews from the civil service and attempted to enforce boycotts of Jewish businesses. The boycotts won little public support. In 1935, the Nuremberg Laws robbed German Jews of their citizenship. All persons with at least one Jewish grandparent were defined as Jews. The professions and major occupations were closed to Jews. Marriage and sexual intercourse between Jews and non-Jews were prohibited. Legal exclusion and humiliation of the Jews became the norm (see "The Nazis Pass Their Racial Legislation").

The persecution of the Jews increased again in 1938. In November, under orders from the Nazi Party, thousands of Jewish stores and synagogues were destroyed. The Jewish community itself had to pay for the damage that occurred on this **Kristallnacht** because the government confiscated the insurance money. In both large and petty ways, the German Jews were harassed. This persecution allowed the Nazis to inculcate the rest of the population with the concept of a master race of pure German "Aryans" and also to display their own contempt for civil liberties.

After the war broke out, Hitler decided in 1942 to destroy the Jews in Europe. It is thought that more than 6 million Jews, mostly from eastern Europe, died as a result of that decision, unprecedented in its scope and implementation.

WOMEN IN NAZI GERMANY

The Nazis believed in separate social spheres for men and women. Men belonged in the world of action, women in the home. The two spheres should not mix. Respect for women should arise from their function as wives and mothers.

These attitudes conflicted with the social changes that German women, like women elsewhere in Europe, had experienced during the first three decades of

Kristallnacht Meaning "crystal night" because of the broken glass that littered German streets after the looting and destruction of Jewish homes, businesses, and synagogues across Germany on the orders of the Nazi Party in November 1938.

OVERVIEW   POLITICAL TYRANNY OF THE 1920S AND 1930S

Although political tyranny was not new to Europe, several factors in the 1920s and 1930s combined to give dictators of the right and the left unique power. The regimes set up by Mussolini in Italy, Stalin in Russia, and Hitler in Germany shared the following characteristics:

1. Well-organized political parties

2. Nationalism

3. Programs that promised to cure social, political, and economic frustrations and end the pettiness of everyday politics

4. A monopoly over mass communications and propaganda

5. Highly effective instruments of terror and police power

6. Real or imagined national, class, or racial enemies who could be demonized to whip up mass support

7. Command over modern technology and its capacity for immense destruction

HISTORY'S VOICES

THE NAZIS PASS THEIR RACIAL LEGISLATION

nti-Semitism was a fundamental tenet of the Nazi Party and became a major policy of the Nazi government. This comprehensive legislation of September 15, 1935, carried anti-Semitism into all areas of public life and into some of the most personal areas of private life as well. It was characteristically titled the Law for the Protection of German Blood and Honor. Hardly any aspect of Nazi thought and action shocked the non-German world as much as this policy toward the Jews.

HOW WOULD this legislation have affected the normal daily interaction between Jews and non-Jews in Germany? Why are there specific prohibitions against mixed marriages and sexual relations between Jews and non-Jews? How does this legislation separate German Jews from the symbols of German national life?

Imbued with the knowledge that the purity of German blood is the necessary prerequisite for the existence of the German nation, and inspired by an inflexible will to maintain the existence of the German nation for all future times, the Reichstag has unanimously adopted the following law, which is now enacted:

Article I: (1) Any marriages between Jews and citizens of German or kindred blood are herewith forbidden. Marriages entered into despite this law are invalid, even if they are arranged abroad as a means of circumventing this law.

(2) Annulment proceedings for marriages may be initiated only by the Public Prosecutor.

Article II: Extramarital relations between Jews and citizens of German or kindred blood are herewith forbidden.

Article III: Jews are forbidden to employ as servants to their households female subjects of German or kindred blood who are under the age of forty-five years.

Article IV: (1) Jews are prohibited from displaying the Reich and national flag and from showing the national colors.

(2) However, they may display the Jewish colors. The exercise of this right is under state protection.

Article V: (1) Anyone who acts contrary to the prohibition noted in Article I renders himself liable to penal servitude.

(2) The man who acts contrary to the prohibition of Article II will be punished by sentence to either a jail or penitentiary.

(3) Anyone who acts contrary to the provisions of Articles III or IV will be punished with a jail sentence up to a year and with a fine, or with one of these penalties.

Article VI: The Reich Minister of Interior, in conjunction with the Deputy to the Führer and the Reich Minister of Justice, will issue the required legal and administrative decrees for the implementation and amplification of this law.

Article VII: This law shall go into effect on the day following its promulgation, with the exception of Article III, which shall go into effect on January 1, 1936.

Source: *Documents of German History*, Louis L. Snyder, ed. and trans. Copyright © 1938 Rutgers the State University, pp. 427–428. Reprinted by permission of Rutgers University Press.

the 20th century. German women had become much more active and assertive. They worked in factories or were independently employed, and had begun to enter the professions. Under the Weimar Constitution, they voted. Throughout the Weimar period, there was also a lively discussion of women's emancipation. For the Nazis, these developments were signs of cultural weakness.

The Nazis' point of view was supported by women of a conservative outlook and women who followed traditional roles as housewives. In a period of high unemployment, the Nazi attitude also appealed to many men because it discouraged women from competing with them in the workplace. Such competition had begun during World War I, and many Nazis considered it symptomatic of the social confusion that had followed the German defeat.

The Nazi discussion of the role of women was also rooted in Nazi racism. It was the special task of German mothers to preserve racial purity. Hitler championed this view of women. They were to breed strong sons and daughters for the German nation. Nazi journalists often compared the role of women in childbirth to that of men in battle. Each served the state in particular gender roles. In both cases, the good of the nation was superior to that of the individual.

The Nazis also attacked feminist outlooks. Women were encouraged to bear many children, because the Nazis believed the declining German birth rate was the result of emancipated women who had spurned their natural roles as mothers. The Nazis sponsored schools that taught women how to rear children.

The Nazis also saw women as educators of the young and thus the protectors of German cultural values. Through cooking, dress, music, and stories, mothers were to instill a love for the nation. As consumers for the home, women were to buy German goods and avoid Jewish merchants.

The Nazis realized that in the midst of the depression many women would need to work, but the party urged them to pursue employment that the Nazis considered natural to their character. These tasks included agriculture, teaching, nursing, social work, and domestic service. Nonetheless, the percentage of women employed in Germany changed little from the Weimar to the Hitler years: 37 percent in 1928 and in 1939. Thereafter, because of the war, many more women were recruited into the German work force.

THE GREAT DEPRESSION AND THE NEW DEAL IN THE UNITED STATES

HOW DID FDR's policies affect the role of the federal government?

The United States emerged from World War I as a world power. However, it retreated from that role when the Senate refused to ratify the Versailles Treaty and failed to join the League of Nations. In 1920, Warren Harding (1865–1923) became president and urged a return to what he termed "normalcy," which meant minimal involvement abroad and conservative economic policies at home. Business interests remained in the ascendent, and the federal government took a relatively inactive role in national life, especially under Harding's successor, Calvin Coolidge (1872–1933).

The first seven or eight years of the decade witnessed remarkable American prosperity. New electrical appliances such as the radio, phonograph, washing machine, and vacuum cleaner appeared on the market. Real wages rose for many workers. Industry grew at a robust rate. Automobile manufacturers assumed a major role in national economic life. Factories became mechanized. Engineers and efficiency experts were the heroes of the business world. The stock market boomed. This activity stood in marked contrast to the economic dislocations of Europe.

The material prosperity appeared, however, in a divided society. Segregation remained a basic fact of life for Black Americans. The Ku Klux Klan, which sought to terrorize Blacks, Roman Catholics, and Jews, enjoyed a resurgence. The Prohibition Amendment of 1919 (repealed in 1933) forbade the manufacture and transport of alcoholic beverages. In the wake of this divisive national policy, major criminal operations arose to supply liquor and disrupt civic life. Many immigrants came from Mexico and Puerto Rico. They

Assembly line. Ford Motor Company assembly-line workers on the job in 1928 in Dearborn, Michigan.
© Hulton Getty/Archive Photos.

settled in cities where their labor was desired but where they were often not welcomed or assimilated. Finally, the wealth of the nation was concentrated in too few hands.

ECONOMIC COLLAPSE

In March 1929, Herbert Hoover became president, the third Republican in as many elections. On October 29, 1929, the New York Stock Exchange crashed. Other financial markets also went into a tailspin. During the next year the stock market continued to fall. Banks that had loaned people money with which to speculate in the market suffered great losses.

The financial collapse of 1929 triggered the Great Depression in America, although there were other underlying domestic causes. Manufacturing firms had not made sufficient capital investment. The disproportionate amount of profits going to about 5 percent of the U.S. population undermined the purchasing power of other consumers. Agriculture was in trouble. Finally, the economic difficulties in Europe and Latin America, which predated those in the United States, meant foreigners were less able to purchase American products.

The most pervasive problem of the Great Depression was unemployment. Joblessness hit unskilled workers first but then worked its way up the job ladder to touch factory and white-collar workers. As unemployment spread, small retail businesses suffered. In the major American manufacturing cities, hundreds of thousands of workers could not find jobs. The price of corn fell so low in some areas that it was not profitable to harvest it. By the early 1930s, banks began to fail, and people lost their savings.

The federal government was not equipped to address the emergency. There was no tradition of federal action to alleviate economic distress. President Hoover organized economic conferences and encouraged the Federal Reserve to make borrowing easier. He supported the ill-advised Hawley-Smoot Tariff Act of 1930, which hoped to protect American industry by a high tariff barrier. Hoover believed relief was a matter for local government and voluntary organizations; however, many local relief agencies had run out of money by 1931.

NEW ROLE FOR GOVERNMENT

The election of 1932 was one of the most crucial in American history. The Democratic Party's candidate, Franklin Delano Roosevelt (1882–1945), promised "a new deal for the American people." He overwhelmingly defeated Hoover, and quickly redirected federal policy toward the depression.

Roosevelt had been born into a moderately wealthy New York family and was a distant cousin of Theodore Roosevelt (1858–1919). After serving in World War I as Assistant Secretary of the Navy, in 1920 he ran as the Democratic vice presidential candidate. The next year, however, he was struck with polio and his legs became paralyzed, but he went on to be elected governor of New York in 1928. As president, he attempted to convey to the nation the same kind of optimistic spirit that had informed his own struggle of the 1920s.

Roosevelt's first goal was to give the nation a sense that the federal government was meeting the economic challenge. The first hundred days of his administration became legendary. He immediately closed all the banks and permitted only sound institutions to reopen. Congress rapidly passed a new banking act and then enacted the Agricultural Adjustment Act and the Farm Credit Act to aid farmers. To provide jobs, Roosevelt sponsored the Civilian

Conservation Corps. The Federal Emergency Relief Act funded state and local relief agencies. To restore confidence, Roosevelt began making speeches, known as "fireside chats," to the American people.

Roosevelt's most ambitious program was the National Industrial Recovery Act (NIRA), which established the National Recovery Administration (NRA). This agency attempted to foster codes written by various industries to regulate wages and prices to monitor competition and thus protect jobs and assure production.

The NIRA and other New Deal legislation, such as the Wagner Act of 1935, which established the National Labor Relations Board and the Fair Labor Standards Act of 1938, provided a larger role in the American economy for organized labor. It became easier for unions to organize. Union membership grew, and American unionism took on a new character. Most unions had been organized by craft and were affiliated with the American Federation of Labor (AFL). In the 1930s, however, whole industries composed of workers in various crafts were organized in a single union. The most important of these organizations were the United Mine Workers and United Automobile Workers. These new unions organized themselves into the Congress of Industrial Organizations (CIO). The CIO and the AFL merged in the 1950s. These strong industrial labor organizations introduced a new force into the American economic scene.

In 1935, the U.S. Supreme Court declared the NRA unconstitutional. Thereafter, Roosevelt deemphasized centralized economic planning. The number of federal agencies increased, but they operated in general independence from each other.

Through New Deal legislation, the federal government was far more active in the economy than it had ever been. The government itself attempted to provide relief for the unemployed in the industrial sector. The major institution of the relief effort was the **Works Progress Administration**. Created in 1935, the WPA began a massive program of public works.

Programs of the New Deal years also involved the federal government directly in economic development rather than turning such development over to private enterprise. Through the Tennessee Valley Authority (TVA), the government became directly involved in the economy of the four states of the Tennessee River valley. The TVA built dams and then produced and sold hydroelectricity. Never had the government undertaken so extensive an economic role. Another major new function for the government was providing security for the elderly, through the establishment of the Social Security Administration in 1935.

In one area of American life after another, it was decided that the government must provide personal economic security. These actions established a mixed economy in the United States—one in which the federal government would play an active role alongside the private sector.

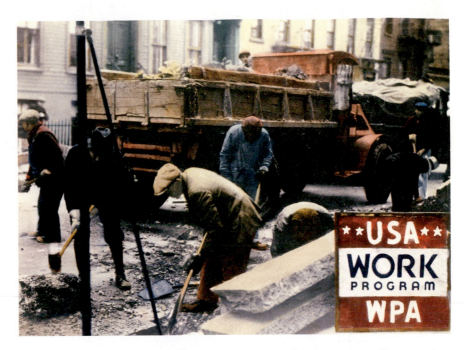

The Works Progress Administration. This economic relief effort agency was one of the chief New Deal organizations designed to create public works projects that would generate employment, as with this group repairing a street.

Corbis/Bettmann.

Works Progress Administration New Deal program created by the Roosevelt administration in 1935 that provided relief for the unemployed in the industrial sector during the Great Depression in the United States.

Yet the New Deal did not solve the unemployment problem. In the late 1930s, the economy began to falter again. Only the entry of the nation into World War II brought the U.S. economy to full employment.

The experience of the United States under the New Deal stood in marked contrast to the economic and political experiments in Europe. Many businesspeople found Roosevelt too liberal and his policies too activist. Nonetheless, the New Deal preserved capitalism in a democratic setting, where, again in contrast to Europe, there was free political debate—much of it critical of the administration. The United States had demonstrated that a nation with a vast industrial economy could confront its gravest economic crisis and still preserve democracy.

IMAGE KEY

for pages 750–751

a. Poster glorifying work, Soviet Union, 1930s.

b. Hitler salutes from an open car at a rally in 1938.

c. A Works Progress Administration (WPA) poster.

d. Il Duce, Benito Mussolini.

e. A George Grosz painting satirizing conservative and right-wing groups in Weimar Germany.

f. Works Progress Administration (WPA) workers.

g. A Soviet propaganda poster.

h. A Volkswagen on a German Reich postage stamp, 1939.

i. Unemployed workers outside the Municipal Lodging House in New York City during the Great Depression, 1930.

SUMMARY

Postwar Problems   The Versailles settlement left much of Europe dissatisfied. The 1920s saw endless wrangles over reparations between Germany and the Allied powers. After World War I, Europe never recovered its prewar prosperity or stability. The onset of the Great Depression in 1929 caused severe problems in both Europe and the United States and led to the Nazi seizure of power in Germany and Roosevelt's New Deal in the United States.

The Soviet Union   The Bolsheviks had expected Communist revolutions to break out across Europe. When that did not happen, they were forced to consolidate their regime within Russia. Lenin's New Economic Policy gave the state control over heavy industry, transportation, and international commerce but allowed for small-scale private enterprise and peasant farms. Stalin abandoned this policy. He abolished private enterprise, collectivized agriculture, and eliminated his opponents in a series of purges. Despite this, Marxist parties around the world were subservient to the Soviet Union as the world's only Communist state and the enemy of fascism.

Fascist Italy   Benito Mussolini came to power in Italy in 1922. Many Italians were dissatisfied with the terms of the Versailles Treaty and frightened by the social unrest that followed World War I. Mussolini promised order and a strong state. Although he achieved power by legal means, he soon transformed Italy into a single-party dictatorship. In 1929, he came to terms with the Catholic Church by negotiating the Lateran Accord, which recognized the pope as the independent ruler of Vatican City.

Nazi Germany   The postwar Weimar Republic in Germany was buffeted by social, political, and financial instability. Many Germans refused to accept Germany's defeat in World War I or the terms of the Versailles Treaty. Rampant inflation destroyed the savings of the middle class. The Great Depression brought financial collapse and massive unemployment. Many Germans looked to Adolf Hitler and the Nazi Party for solutions. Once Hitler came to power in 1933, he quickly established a one-party dictatorship based on police terror, propaganda, and the cult of himself as supreme leader. The Jews, in particular, were persecuted.

The United States The United States emerged from World War I as a world power, but retreated into isolation during the 1920s. The shallow prosperity of the 1920s ended in the Great Depression. Franklin Delano Roosevelt's New Deal greatly expanded the power of the federal government in social and economic affairs and preserved capitalism in a democratic setting.

REVIEW QUESTIONS

1. How did Stalin achieve supreme power in the Soviet Union? Why did he decide that Russia had to industrialize rapidly and collectivize agriculture? Did these policies succeed? How did they affect the Russian people? What were the causes of the Great Purges?

2. How did Mussolini achieve power? What were the characteristics of the Fascist state?

3. Why did Weimar Republic collapse? How did Hitler come to power?

4. Why did the U.S. economy collapse in 1929? How did Roosevelt combat the depression?

KEY TERMS

collectivization (p. 755)

Duce (p. 758)

fascism (p. 757)

Führer (p. 764)

Great Depression (p. 752)

Great Purges (p. 756)

Kristallnacht (p. 765)

Mein Kampf (p. 761)

New Economic Policy
  (NEP) (p. 754)

Popular Front (p. 753)

Reichstag (p. 759)

War Communism (p. 754)

Weimar Republic (p. 752)

Works Progress
  Administration (p. 769)

 For additional study resources for this chapter, go to:
www.prenhall.com/craig/chapter30

31

World War II

CHAPTER HIGHLIGHTS

The Coming of War The second great war of the twentieth century (1939–1945) grew out of the unsatisfactory resolution of the first war. Whatever the flaws of the treaties of Paris, the world suffered an even more terrible war than the first as a result of failures of judgment and will on the part of the victorious democratic powers. The United States disarmed almost entirely and withdrew into foolish isolation; it could play no important part in restraining the ambitious dictators who would bring on the war. Britain and France refused to face the threat posed by the Axis powers until the most deadly war in history was required to put it down.

World War II The second war itself was plainly a world war. The Japanese occupation of Manchuria in 1931 was a precursor. Italy attacked Ethiopia in 1935. Italy, Germany, and the Soviet Union intervened in the Spanish Civil War (1936–1939). Japan attacked China in 1937. The formation of the Axis among Germany, Italy, and Japan guaranteed that the war would be fought around the world. The use of atomic weapons brought the struggle to a close, but what are called conventional weapons did almost all the damage. The survival of civilization was threatened even without the use of nuclear devices.

The world quickly split into two unfriendly camps: the Western, led by the United States, and the Eastern, led by the Soviet Union. This division hastened the liberation of former colonial territories.

CHAPTER QUESTIONS

WHAT WERE the main events between 1933 and 1939 that led to World War II?

WHY WAS 1943 the turning point in World War II?

HOW DID war affect civilians in Germany, France, Britain, and the Soviet Union?

WHY DID cooperation between the Soviet Union and the Western powers break down in 1945?

CHAPTER OUTLINE

- Again the Road to War (1933–1939)
- World War II
- The Domestic Fronts
- Preparations for Peace

The more idealistic survivors of World War I, especially in the United States and Britain, thought of it as "the war to end all wars" and "a war to make the world safe for democracy." Only thus could they justify the slaughter, expense, and upheaval. Yet only 20 years after the peace treaties, a second great war broke out that was more global than the first. In this war, the democracies would be fighting for their lives against militaristic, nationalistic, authoritarian, and totalitarian states in Europe and Asia. Britain and the United States would be allied with the Communist Soviet Union. The defeat of the militarists and dictators would lead to a Cold War in which the European states became second-class powers, subordinate to the Soviet Union and the United States.

AGAIN THE ROAD TO WAR (1933–1939)

WHAT WERE the mains events between 1933 and 1939 that led to World War II?

In light of the world depression of the 1930s, the Versailles Treaty that ended World War I took on a special meaning for Germans. The reparations demanded by the Allies had contributed to ruinous inflation in Germany, and many Germans blamed their economic troubles on the treaty. Adolf Hitler and the Nazi Party had long denounced the treaty as the source of Germany's problems, and the economic woes of the the early 1930s seemed to bear them out. This, in addition to Nazi party discipline and a message of fervent nationalism, helped Hitler overthrow the Weimar Republic and take control of Germany.

HITLER'S GOALS

The Nazi destruction of political opposition meant that German foreign policy lay in Hitler's hands. From first to last, Hitler's racial theories and goals were central in his thought. He intended to bring the entire German people (*Volk*), understood as a racial group, together into a single nation. The new Germany would include all the Germanic parts of the old Habsburg Empire, including Austria. This virile nation would need more space to live (*Lebensraum*), which would be taken from the Slavs, a lesser race. The new Germany would be purified by the removal of the Jews, the most inferior race in Nazi theory. The plan required the conquest of Poland and the Ukraine to settle Germans and provide badly needed food. However, neither *Mein Kampf* nor later statements of policy were blueprints for action. Hitler exploited opportunities as they arose. But he never lost sight of his goals, which would almost certainly require a major war (see "Hitler Describes His Goals").

DESTRUCTION OF VERSAILLES

When Hitler came to power, Germany was weak. The first problem was to shake off the fetters of Versailles and make Germany a formidable military power. In October 1933, Germany withdrew from an international disarmament conference and from the League of Nations. These acts were merely symbolic, but in March 1935, Hitler renounced the disarmament provisions of the Versailles Treaty with the formation of a German air force. Soon he reinstated conscription, which aimed at an army of half a million men.

His path was made easier because the League of Nations was ineffective. In September 1931, Japan occupied Manchuria. China appealed to the league, which condemned the Japanese for resorting to force. But the powers would not impose sanctions. Japan withdrew from the league and kept Manchuria.

The league condemned Hitler's decision to rearm Germany, but took no steps to prevent it. France and Britain met with Mussolini in June 1935 to form the so-called Stresa Front and agreed to maintain the status quo in Europe by force if

Lebensraum "Living space," Nazi plan to colonize and exploit eastern Europe.

HISTORY'S VOICES

HITLER DESCRIBES HIS GOALS

From his early career, Hitler had certain long-term general views and goals. They were set forth in his Mein Kampf, which appeared in 1925, and included consolidation of the German Volk ("people"), provision of more land for the Germans, and contempt for such "races" as Slavs and Jews. Here are some of Hitler's views.

WHAT IS the basic principle on which Hitler's policy is founded? How does he justify his plans for expansion? What reasons does he give for hostility to France and Russia? What is the basis for Hitler's claim of a right of every man to own farmland? Was that a practical goal for Germany in the 1930s? Was there any way for Hitler to achieve his goals without a major war?

The National Socialist movement must strive to eliminate the disproportion between our population and our area—viewing this latter as a source of food as well as a basis for power politics—between our historical past and the hopelessness of our present impotence. . . .

The demand for restoration of the frontiers of 1914 is a political absurdity of such proportions and consequences as to make it seem a crime. Quite aside from the fact that the Reich's frontiers in 1914 were anything but logical. For in reality they were neither complete in the sense of embracing the people of German nationality, nor sensible with regard to geo-military expediency. . . .

As opposed to this, we National Socialists must hold unflinchingly to our aim in foreign policy, namely, to secure for the German people the land and soil to which they are entitled on this earth. . . .

. . . The soil on which some day German generations of peasants can beget powerful sons will sanction the investment of the sons of today, and will some day acquit the responsible statesmen of blood-guilt and sacrifice of the people, even if they are persecuted by their contemporaries. . . .

Much as all of us today recognize the necessity of a reckoning with France, it would remain ineffectual in the long run if it represented the whole of our aim in foreign policy. It can and will achieve meaning only if it offers the rear cover for an enlargement of our people's living space in Europe. . . .

If we speak of soil in Europe today, we can primarily have in mind only Russia and her vassal border states. . . .

. . . See to it that the strength of our nation is founded, not on colonies, but on the soil of our European homeland. Never regard the Reich as secure unless for centuries to come it can give every scion of our people his own parcel of soil. Never forget that the most sacred right on this earth is a man's right to have earth to till with his own hands, and the most sacred sacrifice the blood that a man sheds for this earth.

necessary. But Britain was desperate to maintain superiority at sea. Contrary to the Stresa accords, Britain soon made a separate naval agreement with Hitler, allowing him to rebuild the German fleet to 35 percent of the British navy.

ITALY ATTACKS ETHIOPIA

The Italian attack on Ethiopia in October 1935 made the impotence of the League of Nations and the timidity of the Allies even clearer. Using a border incident as an excuse, Mussolini's intent was to avenge a humiliating defeat that the Italians had suffered in 1896 and perhaps to divert Italians from Fascist corruption and Italy's economic troubles.

The League of Nations voted economic sanctions and imposed an arms embargo. But Britain and France were afraid of alienating Mussolini, so they refused to place an embargo on oil, the one economic sanction that could have prevented Italian victory. Nor did the British prevent the movement of Italian troops and munitions through the Suez Canal. This wavering policy was disastrous. The League of Nations and collective security were discredited, and Mussolini turned to Germany.

REMILITARIZATION OF THE RHINELAND

On March 7, 1936, Hitler took his greatest risk yet, sending a small armed force into the demilitarized Rhineland. This was a breach of the Versailles Treaty and of the Locarno Agreements. It also removed an important element of French security. Yet Britain and France made only a feeble protest.

A Germany that was rapidly rearming and had a defensible western frontier presented a new problem to the Western powers. Their response was the policy of **appeasement**. It was based on the assumption that Germany had real grievances, that Hitler's goals were limited, and that the wise thing to do was to make concessions before a crisis could lead to war. Behind this approach was the horror of another war. As Germany armed, the French huddled behind their defensive wall, the Maginot Line, and the British hoped for the best.

THE SPANISH CIVIL WAR

The new European alignment that found the Western democracies on one side and the Fascist states on the other was made clearer by the Spanish Civil War, which broke out in July 1936. In 1931, the Spaniards had established a republic. Elections in February 1936 brought to power a government of the left. The defeated groups, especially the Falangists, the Spanish version of Fascists, would not accept defeat at the polls. In July, General Francisco Franco (1892–1975) led an army against the republic.

Thus began a civil war that lasted almost three years. Germany and Italy aided Franco with troops and supplies. The Soviet Union sent equipment and advisers to the republicans. Leftists from Europe and America volunteered to fight against fascism.

The civil war, fought on ideological lines, brought Germany and Italy closer together, leading to the Rome-Berlin **Axis** Pact in 1936. They were joined in the same year by Japan in the Anti-Comintern Pact, ostensibly against communism. In western Europe, the appeasement mentality reigned. By early 1939, the Fascists had won control of Spain.

AUSTRIA AND CZECHOSLOVAKIA

In 1934, Mussolini, not yet allied with Hitler, frustrated a Nazi coup in Austria by threatening military intervention. In March 1938, the new diplomatic situation encouraged Hitler to try again. Mussolini made no objection, and Hitler marched into Vienna to the cheers of his Austrian sympathizers.

The *Anschluss*, or union of Germany and Austria, had great strategic significance. Czechoslovakia was now surrounded by Germany on three sides. It was allied both to France and the Soviet Union but contained about 3.5 million ethnic Germans who lived in the Sudetenland, a portion of Czechoslovakia near the German border. Supported by Hitler, they agitated for privileges and autonomy within the Czech state. The Czechs made concessions; but Hitler's true intent was to destroy Czechoslovakia.

appeasement Anglo-French policy of making concessions to Germany in the 1930s to avoid a crisis that would lead to war. It assumed that Germany had real grievances and Hitler's aims were limited and ultimately acceptable.

Axis Alliance between Nazi Germany and Fascist Italy. Also called the Pact of Steel.

Anschluss Meaning "union." Annexation of Austria by Germany in March 1938.

The French, as usual, deferred to British leadership. The British prime minister Neville Chamberlain (1869–1940) was determined not to allow Britain to go to war again. In September 1938, German intervention seemed imminent. Chamberlain sought to appease Hitler by compelling the Czechs to grant the Sudetenland separate status. But Hitler then increased his demands and insisted on immediate German military occupation of the Sudetenland (see Map 31–1).

MUNICH

France and Britain prepared for war. At the last moment, Mussolini proposed a conference of Germany, Italy, France, and Britain. The group met on September 29 at Munich. Hitler received almost everything he had demanded. The Sudetenland became part of Germany, thus depriving the Czechs of any chance of self-defense. In return, the rest of Czechoslovakia was spared. Hitler promised, "I have no more territorial demands to make in Europe." Chamberlain told a cheering crowd, "I believe it is peace for our time."

 MAP EXPLORATION

Interactive map: To explore this map further, go to **http://www.prenhall.com/craig/map31.1**

MAP 31–1

Partitions of Czechoslovakia and Poland, 1938–1939. The immediate background of World War II is found in the complex international drama unfolding on Germany's eastern frontier in 1938 and 1939. Germany's expansion inevitably meant the victimization of Austria, Czechoslovakia, and Poland. With the failure of the Western powers' appeasement policy and the signing of a German-Soviet pact, the stage for the war was set.

HOW DID the failure of appeasement lead to war?

Agreement at Munich. On September 29–30, 1938, Hitler met with the leaders of Britain and France at Munich to decide the fate of Czechoslovakia. Allied leaders abandoned the small democratic nation in a vain attempt to appease Hitler and avoid war. Hitler sits in the center of the picture. To his right is British Prime Minister Neville Chamberlain.

Ullstein Bilderdienst.

25.1
Adolf Hitler, The Obersalzberg Speech

WHY WAS 1943 the turning point in World War II?

Soon, however, Poland and Hungary tore bits of territory from Czechoslovakia, and the Slovaks demanded autonomy. Finally, on March 15, 1939, Hitler broke his promise and occupied Prague, putting an end to Czech independence. Munich remains an example of short-sighted policy that helped bring on a war in disadvantageous circumstances as a result of the very fear of war and the failure to prepare for it.

Hitler's occupation of Prague discredited appeasement in Britain. Poland was the next target of German expansion. In the spring of 1939, the Germans put pressure on Poland to restore the formerly German city of Danzig and allow a railroad and a highway through the Polish corridor to connect East Prussia with the rest of Germany. When the Poles would not yield, the pressure mounted. On March 31, Chamberlain announced a Franco-British guarantee of Polish independence. Hitler did not take the guarantee seriously. He knew that both countries were unprepared for war and that much of their populations opposed war for Poland.

Moreover, France and Britain could not get effective help to the Poles. The only way to defend Poland was to bring Russia into the alliance against Hitler, but a Russian alliance posed problems. Each side was suspicious of the other. The French and British were hostile to communism, and since Stalin's (1879-1953) purge of the officer corps of the Red Army, they questioned Russia's military abilities. Besides, both Poland and Romania were suspicious of Russian intentions—with good reason. As a result, Western negotiations with Russia were slow and cautious.

THE NAZI-SOVIET PACT

The Russians resented being left out of the Munich agreement and were annoyed by the low priority that the West seemed to give to negotiations with Russia. They feared, rightly, that the Western powers meant for them to bear the burden of the war against Germany. As a result, they opened negotiations with Hitler, and on August 23, 1939, the world was shocked to learn of a Nazi-Soviet nonaggression pact. Its secret provisions divided Poland between them and allowed Russia to annex the Baltic states and take Bessarabia from Romania. Communist parties in the West changed their line overnight from advocating resistance to Hitler to a policy of peace and quiet.

The Nazi-Soviet Pact sealed the fate of Poland. On September 1, 1939, the Germans invaded Poland. Two days later, Britain and France declared war on Germany. World War II had begun.

WORLD WAR II (1939–1945)

GERMAN CONQUEST OF EUROPE

The speed of the German victory over Poland astonished everyone, and the Russians hastened to collect their share of the booty before Hitler could deprive them of it. On September 17, Russia invaded Poland from the east, dividing the country with the Germans. The Russians then absorbed Estonia, Latvia, and Lithuania. In November 1940, the Russians invaded Finland, but the Finns fought back and retained their independence.

Meanwhile, the western front was quiet. The French remained behind the Maginot Line. Britain imposed the traditional naval blockade. Cynics in the west called it the phony war, but in April 1940, the Germans invaded Denmark and Norway. A month later, a combined land and air attack struck the Low Countries. The Dutch surrendered in a few days, and the Belgians less than two weeks later. British and French armies in Belgium were forced to flee to the English Channel to seek escape from the beaches of Dunkirk. More than 200,000 British and 100,000 French soldiers were saved, but valuable equipment was abandoned.

The Maginot Line ran from Switzerland to the Belgian frontier. Hitler's swift advance through Belgium therefore circumvented France's main line of defense. The French army, poorly led, collapsed. Mussolini attacked France on June 10, though without success. Less than a week later, the French government, under the ancient hero of Verdun, Henri Philippe Pétain (1856–1951), asked for an armistice.

The terms of the armistice, signed on June 22, 1940, allowed the Germans to occupy more than half of France, including the Atlantic and English Channel coasts. To prevent the French from fleeing to North Africa to continue the fight, Hitler left southern France unoccupied. Pétain set up a dictatorial regime at the resort city of Vichy and collaborated with the Germans to preserve as much autonomy as possible. The French were too stunned to resist. Many thought that Hitler's victory was certain and saw no alternative to collaboration. A few, notably General Charles de Gaulle (1890–1969), fled to Britain and organized the French National Committee of Liberation, or "Free French." As expectations of a quick German victory faded, French resistance arose.

BATTLE OF BRITAIN

Hitler expected the British to come to terms. Any chance that the British would consider terms disappeared when Winston Churchill (1874–1965) replaced Chamberlain as prime minister in May 1940.

Churchill established a close relationship with the U.S. President Franklin D. Roosevelt. In 1940 and 1941, before the United States was at war, America sent military supplies and even convoyed ships across the Atlantic to help the British survive.

As Britain remained defiant, Hitler was forced to contemplate an invasion, which required control of the air. The German air force (**Luftwaffe**) destroyed much of London, and about 15,000 people were killed. But the Royal Air Force (RAF), aided by the newly developed technology of radar, inflicted heavy losses on the *Luftwaffe*. Hitler was forced to abandon his plans for invasion.

GERMAN ATTACK ON RUSSIA

Operation Barbarossa, the code name for the invasion of Russia, was aimed at knocking Russia out of the war before winter could set in. Success depended in

Coming of World War II

1919 June	Versailles Treaty
1923 January	France occupies the Ruhr
1925 October	Locarno Agreements
1931 Spring	Onset of Great Depression in Europe
1933 January	Hitler comes to power
October	Germany withdraws from League of Nations
1935 March	Hitler renounces disarmament, starts an air force, and begins conscription
October	Mussolini attacks Ethiopia
1936 March	Germany reoccupies and remilitarizes the Rhineland
July	Outbreak of Spanish Civil War
October	Formation of the Rome-Berlin Axis
1938 March	Anschluss with Austria
September	Munich Conference and partition of Czechoslovakia
1939 March	Hitler occupies Prague; France and Great Britain guarantee Polish independence
August	Nazi-Soviet pact
September 1	Germany invades Poland
September 3	Britain and France declare war on Germany

Luftwaffe German air force in World War II.

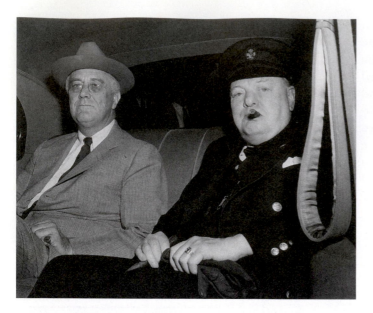

Churchill and Roosevelt. The close cooperation between Prime Minister Winston Churchill of Britain and President Franklin Roosevelt of the United States helped to assure the effective alliance of their two countries in World War II.

UPI/Corbis-Bettmann.

QUICK REVIEW

Operation Barbarossa

- June 22, 1941: Surprise invasion of Soviet Union by Germany (Operation Barbarossa) launched
- Germany advanced rapidly in the early stages of the campaign
- German failure to deliver a decisive blow delayed victory until winter set in, turning the tide in the Soviet's favor

---

Blitzkrieg Meaning "war by lightening strokes." German tactic early in World War II of employing fast-moving, massed armored columns supported by air power to overwhelm the enemy.

---

part on an early start, but here Hitler's Italian alliance proved costly. Mussolini had launched an attack against the British in Egypt and also invaded Greece. But in North Africa the British counterattacked and drove into Libya, and the Greeks repulsed the Italians. In March 1941, the British sent help to the Greeks, and Hitler was forced to divert his attention to the Balkans and to Africa. General Erwin Rommel (1891–1944) soon drove the British back into Egypt. In the Balkans, the German army occupied Yugoslavia and crushed Greek resistance, but the price was a delay of six weeks for Barbarossa. This proved to be costly the following winter.

Operation Barbarossa was launched against Russia on June 22, 1941, and it almost succeeded. Stalin panicked. By November, the German army stood at the gates of Leningrad, on the outskirts of Moscow, and on the Don River. Of the 4.5 million troops with which the Russians had begun the fighting, they had lost 2.5 million; of their 15,000 tanks, only 700 were left.

A German victory seemed imminent, but Hitler at that point diverted significant forces to the south. By the time he decided to march on Moscow, winter was setting in. The German army lacked appropriate equipment, and Stalin had reorganized, fortified the city, and brought in troops from Siberia. In November and December, the Russians counterattacked. Hitler's *Blitzkrieg* ("war by lightening strokes") turned into a war of attrition.

HITLER'S EUROPE

The demands of war and Hitler's defeat prevented him from fully carrying out his plans, so no one can be sure precisely what he intended. But the measures he took before his death suggest a regime unmatched in history for planned terror and inhumanity. Hitler regarded the conquered lands merely as a source of plunder and slave labor. He stripped them of entire industries and their peoples of basic necessities. He intended ultimately to displace their inhabitants and appropriate their lands to provide Lebensraum for Germans. Regions such as Scandinavia and the Low Lands, inhabited by people racially akin to the Germans, were to be absorbed into Germany.

RACISM AND THE HOLOCAUST

The most horrible aspect of the Nazi rule in Europe arose from the inhumanity inherent in Hitler's racial doctrines. He considered the Slavs *Untermenschen*, subhuman creatures like beasts. In Poland, the upper and professional classes were jailed, deported, or killed, and harsh living conditions were imposed. In Russia, the situation was even worse. Hitler spoke of his Russian campaign as a war of extermination. The SS formed extermination squads to eliminate 30 million Slavs to make room for the Germans. Some 6 million Russian prisoners of war and civilians may have died under Nazi rule.

Hitler meant to make Europe *Judenrein* ("free of Jews"). Eventually he decided on the "final solution of the Jewish problem": extermination. The Nazis built extermination camps in Germany and Poland and killed millions of men, women, and children just because they were Jews (see Map 31–2). Before the war was over, 6 million Jews had died in what is called the **Holocaust**. Only about a million survived, mostly in pitiable condition.

THE ROAD TO PEARL HARBOR

The war took on truly global proportions in December 1941. In January 1938, Japan had invaded China to overthrow the Chinese Nationalist Party government in Nanjing. They occupied most of the cities and railroads of eastern China, killing more than 300,000 people and brutally raping 7,000 women. Jiang Jieshi (Chiang Kai-shek) refused to surrender, however, and a stalemate ensued until the end of the global conflict in 1945.

In September 1940, Japan signed the Tripartite Pact with Germany and Italy. Germany's European victories in late spring 1940 seemed a prelude to German victory, and Japan hoped that the pact would help it achieve three objectives: to isolate the United States (which was demanding that Japan withdraw from China); to take over the Southeast Asian colonies of Britain, France, and the Netherlands; and to improve its relations with the Soviet Union with Germany's help. Japan remained neutral when Germany attacked the Soviet Union and ceased at that point to work with the Axis powers. But its association with them hardened America's demands that it leave China.

In June 1941, when Japan occupied northern French Indochina, the United States retaliated by limiting strategic exports to Japan, and when Japanese troops took southern Indochina a month later, the United States embargoed all exports to Japan, cutting Japanese oil imports by 90 percent. The Japanese navy urged seizure of the oil-rich Dutch East Indies, but this was dangerous so long as the United States held the Philippines. Japan's navy, therefore, planned a preemptive strike against the United States.

AMERICA'S ENTRY INTO THE WAR

On Sunday morning, December 7, 1941, even while Japanese representatives were negotiating in Washington, Japan launched an air attack on Pearl Harbor, Hawaii, the chief American naval base in the Pacific. The next day, the United

MAP 31–2

The Holocaust. The Nazi policy of ethnic cleansing—targeting Jews, gypsies, political dissidents, and "social deviants"—began with imprisoning them in concentration camps, but by 1943 the *Endlösung*, or Final Solution, called for the systematic extermination of "undersirables."

WHICH COUNTRIES were most severely affected by the Holocaust?

Holocaust Nazi extermination of millions of European Jews between 1940 and 1945. Also called the "final solution to the Jewish problem."

MAP 31–3

Axis Europe 1941.   On the eve of the German invasion of the Soviet Union, the Germany-Italy Axis bestrode most of Western Europe by annexation, occupation, or alliance—from Norway and Finland in the north to Greece in the south and from Poland to France. Britain, the Soviets, a number of insurgent groups, and, finally, the United States had before them the long struggle of conquering this Axis "fortress Europe."

WHAT WERE the strengths and weaknesses of Germany's territorial position in 1941?

States and Britain declared war on Japan. Three days later, Germany and Italy declared war on the United States.

THE TIDE TURNS

Although its potential power was enormous, America was ill-prepared for war. The U.S. Army was tiny, inexperienced, and poorly supplied. American industry was not ready for war. By the summer of 1942, the Japanese Empire stretched

Pearl Harbor. The successful Japanese attack on the American base at Pearl Harbor in Hawaii on December 7, 1941, together with simultaneous attacks on other Pacific bases, brought the United States into war against the Axis powers. For Japan, it was the opening phase of a campaign to capture European and American colonies in Southeast Asia.

U.S. Army Photograph.

from the Aleutian Islands south almost to Australia, and from Burma east to the Gilbert Islands in the mid-Pacific (see Map 31–4).

In the same year, the Germans almost reached the Caspian Sea. In Africa, Rommel drove the British back toward the Suez Canal. Relations between the democracies and their Soviet ally were not close; German submarines were threatening British supplies.

The tide turned at the Battle of Midway in June 1942. American planes destroyed four Japanese aircraft carriers. Soon U.S. Marines landed on Guadalcanal in the Solomon Islands and began to reverse the momentum of the war. Japan was checked sufficiently to allow the Allies to concentrate their efforts first in the West.

Allied Landings in Africa, Sicily, and Italy   In November 1942, an Allied force landed in French North Africa. Even before that landing, the British Field Marshal Bernard Montgomery (1887–1976), after stopping Rommel at El Alamein, had begun a drive to the west. The American general Dwight D. Eisenhower (1890–1969) pushed eastward through Morocco and Algeria. The German army was trapped in Tunisia and crushed. In July and August 1943, the Allies took Sicily. Mussolini was driven from power, the Allies landed in Italy, and Marshal Pietro Badoglio (1871–1956), leader of the new Italian government, declared war on Germany. German resistance in Italy was tough and determined, but the need to defend it further strained the Germans' energy and resources.

Battle of Stalingrad   The Russian campaign became especially demanding. In the summer of 1942, the Germans resumed the offensive. Their goal was the oil fields near the Caspian Sea, and they got as far as Stalingrad on the Volga. Hitler was determined to take the city and Stalin to hold it. The Battle of Stalingrad

MAP 31–4

The War in the Pacific.   As in Europe, the Allies initially had trouble recapturing areas that the Japanese had quickly seized early in the war. The map shows the initial expansion of the Japanese and the long struggle of the Allies to push them back to their homeland and defeat them.

WHAT WAS the American strategy for defeating Japan in World War II?

raged for months. The Russians lost more men than the Americans lost in combat during the entire war, but their defenses prevailed. Hitler overruled his generals and would not allow a retreat. An entire German army was lost.

Stalingrad marked the turning point of the Russian campaign. Thereafter, as German resources dwindled, the Russians advanced westward inexorably.

Strategic Bombing   In 1943, the Allies also gained ground in production and logistics. The industrial might of the United States came into play. New technology and tactics began eliminating the submarine menace. In the same year, the American and British air forces began massive bombardments of Germany by night and day. In 1944, the Americans introduced long-range fighters that could protect the bombers and allow accurate missions by day. By 1945, the Allies could bomb at will.

DEFEAT OF NAZI GERMANY

On June 6, 1944 (D-Day), Allied troops landed in Normandy (see Map 31–5). By September, France had been liberated. In December, the Germans launched a counterattack called the Battle of the Bulge through the Forest of Ardennes. It was their last gasp. The Allies recovered and crossed the Rhine in March 1945. German resistance crumbled. There could be no doubt that the Germans had lost the war on the battlefield.

In the east, the Russians were within reach of Berlin by March 1945. Because the Allies insisted on unconditional surrender, the Germans fought until May. Hitler committed suicide in an underground hideaway in Berlin on May 1, 1945. The Russians occupied Berlin. The Third Reich had lasted only a dozen years.

MAP 31–5

Defeat of the Axis in Europe, 1942–1945. Here we see some major steps in the progress toward Allied victory against Axis Europe. From the south through Italy, the west through France, and the east through Russia, the Allies gradually conquered the continent to bring the war in Europe to a close.

WHY WAS it important for the Allies to force the Germans to fight on more than one front?

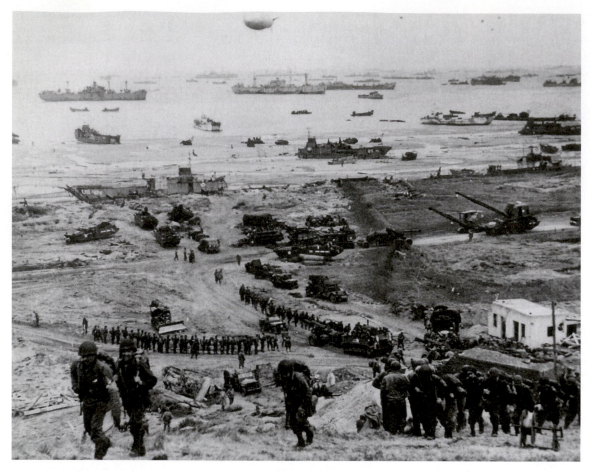

D-Day. Allied troops landed in Normandy on D-Day, June 6, 1944. This photograph, taken two days later, shows long lines of men and equipment moving inland from the beach to reinforce the troops leading the invasion.

Archive Photos.

 25.4
Hiroshima and Nagasaki

FALL OF THE JAPANESE EMPIRE

The war in Europe ended on May 8, 1945. By then victory over Japan was in sight. The Japanese attack on the United States had been a calculated risk. The longer the war lasted, the greater the impact of American superiority in industry and human resources. Beginning in 1943, American forces began a campaign of "island hopping," selecting places strategically located along the enemy supply line. Relentlessly, they moved northeast toward the Japanese homeland. American bombers destroyed Japanese industry and disabled the Japanese navy. But the Japanese government, dominated by a military clique, refused to surrender.

The Americans made plans for an assault on the Japanese homeland, which, they calculated, would cost huge casualties. At this point, science and technology presented the Americans with another choice. Since early in the war a secret program group had been working to use atomic energy for military purposes.

On August 6, 1945, an American plane dropped an atomic bomb on the city of Hiroshima. More than 70,000 of its 200,000 residents were killed. Two days later, the Soviet Union declared war on Japan and invaded Manchuria. The next day, a second atomic bomb fell on Nagasaki. The Japanese were still prepared to face an invasion, but Emperor Hirohito (r. 1926–1989) forced the government to surrender on August 14. Even then, the U.S. cabinet made the condition that Japan could keep its emperor. President Harry S. Truman

(1884–1972), who had come to office on April 12, 1945, on the death of Franklin D. Roosevelt, accepted the condition. Peace was formally signed on September 2, 1945.

THE COST OF WAR

World War II was the most terrible war in history. Military deaths are estimated at 15 million, and at least as many civilians were killed. If deaths linked indirectly to the war are included, 40 million people may have died. Most of Europe and parts of Asia were devastated. Yet the end of the war brought little opportunity for relaxation. The dawn of the Atomic Age made people conscious that another major war might destroy humanity. Everything depended on the conclusion of a stable peace, but the victors soon quarreled.

Hiroshima. This photo, taken a few days after the atomic bomb was dropped, poignantly captures the total devastation wreaked on the city. Corbis-Bettmann.

HOW DID war affect civilians in Germany, France, Britain, and the Soviet Union?

THE DOMESTIC FRONTS

World War II represented an effort of total war by all the belligerents. One result was the carnage that occurred in the fighting. Another was an unprecedented organization of civilians on the various home fronts. Each domestic effort and experience was different, but few escaped the impact of the conflict. Shortages, propaganda, and new political developments were ubiquitous.

GERMANY: FROM APPARENT VICTORY TO DEFEAT

Hitler had expected the strategy of *Blitzkrieg* to win the war so quickly that Germany's society and economy would not be adversely affected. During the first two years of the war, Hitler demanded few sacrifices from the German people. Spending on domestic projects continued; food was plentiful; the economy was not on a full wartime footing. Failure to knock out the Soviet Union changed everything. Germany had to mobilize for total war, and the government demanded major sacrifices.

A great expansion of army and military production began in 1942. Albert Speer (1905–1981) guided the economy, and Germany met its military needs instead of making consumer goods. German businesses aided the growth of wartime production. Between 1942 and late 1944, the output of military products tripled; but as the war went on, the army absorbed more men from industry, hurting the production of even military goods.

Beginning in 1942, everyday products became scarce. The standard of living fell. Food rationing began in April 1942, and shortages were severe until the Nazi government seized food from occupied Europe. To preserve their own home front, the Nazis passed on the suffering to their defeated neighbors.

By 1943, there were serious labor shortages. The Nazis required German teenagers and the elderly to work in the factories, and many women joined them. To achieve total mobilization, the Germans closed retail businesses, made more women do compulsory service, shifted non-German domestic workers to wartime industry, moved artists and entertainers into military service, closed theaters, and reduced basic public services. Finally, the Nazis forced thousands of people from conquered lands to labor in Germany.

Hitler assigned women a special place in the war effort. The celebration of motherhood continued, with an emphasis on the mothers of military figures. Films portrayed ordinary women who became brave and patriotic during the war and remained faithful to their soldier husbands. Government portrayed other wartime activities of women as the natural fulfillment of their maternal roles. As air raid wardens, they protected their families; as workers in munitions plants, they aided their sons on the front lines. Women working on farms were feeding their soldier sons and husbands; as housewives they were helping to win the war by managing their households frugally. Finally, by their faithful chastity, German women were protecting racial purity.

The war years also saw an intensification of political propaganda. The Nazis believed that weak domestic support had led to Germany's defeat in World War I, and they were determined that this would not happen again. Propaganda Minister Josef Goebbels (1897–1945) used radio and films to boost the Nazi cause. Movies demonstrated German military might. As the German armies were checked on the battlefield, especially in Russia, propaganda became a substitute for victory. The propaganda also aimed to frighten the German population about the consequences of defeat.

After May 1943, when the Allies began their major bombing offensive over Germany, one German city after another endured bombing, fires, and destruction. But the bombing did not undermine German morale—on the contrary, it may have confirmed the fear of defeat by such savage opponents and increased German resistance.

World War II brought increased power to the Nazi Party. Every area of the economy and society came under its influence or control. The Nazis were determined that they, rather than the German officer corps, would profit from the new authority flowing to the central government because of the war effort. Throughout the war years there was little serious opposition to Hitler or his ministers. In 1944, a small group of army officers attempted to assassinate Hitler; they failed, and had no significant popular support.

The war brought great changes to Germany, but what transformed the country afterward was the experience of defeat accompanied by destruction, invasion, and occupation. A new state with new political structures emerged.

FRANCE: DEFEAT, COLLABORATION AND RESISTANCE

In France, the Vichy government cooperated with the Germans for a variety of reasons. Some collaborators believed that the Germans were sure to win. A few sympathized with the ideas and plans of the Nazis. Many conservatives regarded the French defeat as a judgment on what they saw as the corrupt Third Republic. But most of the French were not active collaborators and remained demoralized by defeat.

Youth rally. Members of the Nazi German Women's Youth Movement perform calisthenics.

Getty Images Inc. – Hulton Archive Photos.

Many conservatives and extreme rightists saw the Vichy government as a device to reshape the French national character and halt the decadence they associated with liberalism. The Roman Catholic clergy gained status under Vichy. The church supported Pétain; his government supported religious education. Vichy adopted the church's views of the importance of family and spiritual values. Divorce was made difficult; large families were rewarded.

The Vichy regime embraced a chauvinistic nationalism. It persecuted foreigners who were not regarded as genuinely French. The chief victims were French Jews. Anti-Semitism was not new in France. Even before Germany undertook Hitler's "final solution" in 1942, the French had begun to remove Jews from government, education, and publishing. In 1941, the Germans began to intern Jews living in occupied France. In 1942, they began deporting Jews, ultimately more than 60,000, to extermination camps. The Vichy government made no protest, and its own anti-Semitic policies facilitated the process.

Serious internal resistance to the German occupiers and the Vichy government developed only late in 1942. The Germans attempted to force young French people to work in German factories; some fled and joined the Resistance, but the total number of resisters was small. Many were deterred by fear. Some disliked the violence that resistance entailed. So long as it appeared that the Germans would win the war, moreover, resistance seemed imprudent and futile. In all, less than 5 percent of the adult French population appear to have been involved.

By early 1944, an Allied victory appeared inevitable, and the Vichy government was clearly doomed. Only then did an active resistance assert itself. From Algiers on August 9, 1944, the Committee of National Liberation declared the authority of Vichy illegitimate. French soldiers joined in the liberation of Paris and established a government for Free France. On October 21, 1945, France voted to adopt a new constitution as the basis of the Fourth Republic.

GREAT BRITAIN: ORGANIZATION FOR VICTORY

On May 22, 1940, Parliament gave the government emergency powers. The government could institute compulsory military service, food rationing, and economic controls.

Churchill and the British war cabinet mobilized the nation. By the end of 1941, British production had already surpassed Germany's. Factory hours were extended, and women were brought into the work force in great numbers. Unemployment disappeared, and the working classes had more money to spend than they had enjoyed for many years.

The bombing "blitz" conducted by the *Luftwaffe* against British cities from 1940 to 1941 was the most immediate and dramatic experience of the war for the British people. Many homes were destroyed; families removed their children to the countryside; more than 30,000 people were killed. This toll was much smaller than the number of Germans killed by Allied bombing. In England as in Germany, however, the bombing seems to have made the people more determined.

Churchill cheered and encouraged the British people. They had to make many sacrifices: Transportation facilities were strained; food, clothing, and gasoline for civilians were in short supply.

The British established their own propaganda machine. The British Broadcasting Company (BBC) sent programs to every country in Europe to encourage resistance. At home the government used the radio to unify the nation. Soldiers heard the same programs as their families.

We Can Do It! A World War II poster encourages American women to show their strength and go to work for the war effort.

For most of the population the standard of living actually improved during the war, as did the general health of the nation. These gains should not be exaggerated, but many connected them with the active involvement of the government in the economy and the lives of the citizens. This wartime experience may have contributed to the Labour Party's victory in 1945; many feared that conservative rule would revive the economic misery of the 1930s.

THE UNITED STATES: AMERICAN WOMEN AND AFRICAN AMERICANS IN THE WAR EFFORT

The induction of millions of American men into the armed forces created a demand for workers that was filled, in part, by women. The Great Depression had already increased the numbers of female workers, despite lingering and widespread hostility to the idea of women working outside their homes. America's entry into the war changed that quickly. The need for vast amounts of equipment to wage the war opened the way to employment for them and another disadvantaged group—African Americans. Blacks from the South migrated to northern and western cities to seek well-paying jobs. Popular songs celebrated the woman "behind the man behind the gun" as well as "Rosie the Riveter," a young woman building aircraft to protect her boyfriend in the Marines.

THE SOVIET UNION: "THE GREAT PATRIOTIC WAR"

No nation suffered more deaths or destruction during World War II than the Soviet Union. Perhaps 16 million people were killed. Hundreds of cities and towns and more than half of the industrial and transportation facilities of the country were devastated.

In the decade before the war, Stalin had already made the Soviet Union a highly centralized nation. The country was on what amounted to a wartime footing long before the conflict erupted, and the induction of millions of citizens into the army did not increase the military's influence at the expense of the Communist Party—that is, Stalin.

Soviet propaganda differed from that of other nations. Because the Soviet government distrusted the loyalty of its citizens, it confiscated radios. Instead, loudspeakers broadcast to the people. Soviet propaganda emphasized Russian patriotism: The struggle was called "The Great Patriotic War."

Stalin even made peace with the Russian Orthodox Church. He hoped that this would give him more support at home and make the Soviet Union more popular in eastern Europe where the Orthodox church predominated.

Within occupied portions of the Soviet Union, resistance arose against the Germans. The swiftness of the German invasion had stranded thousands of Soviet troops, some of whom escaped and carried on irregular warfare behind enemy lines. Stalin supported partisan forces for two reasons: He wanted to cause difficulty for the Germans; and the Soviet-sponsored resistance reminded the peasants in the conquered regions that the Soviet government had not disappeared. Stalin feared that the peasants' hatred of the Communist government might lead them to collaborate with the invaders.

As the Soviet armies reclaimed the occupied areas and then moved across eastern and central Europe, the Soviet Union established itself as a world power second only to the United States. Stalin had been a reluctant belligerent, but he emerged a major victor. The war and the extraordinary patriotic effort and sacrifice it generated consolidated the power of Stalin and the party more effectively than had the political and social policies of the 1930s.

PREPARATIONS FOR PEACE

WHY DID cooperation between the Soviet Union and the Western powers break down in 1945?

The split that followed the war between the Soviet Union and its wartime allies should cause no surprise. As the self-proclaimed center of world communism, the Soviet Union was dedicated to the overthrow of the capitalist nations. The Western allies were no less open about their hostility to communism and its chief purveyor, the Soviet Union.

Although cooperation against a common enemy and strenuous propaganda helped improve Western feeling toward the Soviet ally, Stalin remained suspicious and critical of the Western war effort. Likewise, Churchill never ceased planning to contain the Soviet advance into Europe. Roosevelt seems to have hoped that the Allies could continue to work together after the war. But even he was losing faith by 1945. Differences in historical development and ideology, as well as traditional conflicts over power and influence, dashed hopes of a satisfactory peace settlement and continued cooperation.

THE ATLANTIC CHARTER

In August 1941, even before America entered the war, Roosevelt and Churchill agreed to the Atlantic Charter. A broad set of principles in the spirit of Wilson's Fourteen Points, it provided a theoretical basis for the peace they sought. When Russia and the United States joined Britain in the war, the three powers entered a military alliance, leaving political questions aside. In Moscow in October 1943, their foreign ministers reaffirmed earlier agreements to fight on until the enemy surrendered unconditionally and to continue cooperating after the war in a united-nations organization.

TEHRAN

The first meeting of the three leaders took place at Tehran, the capital of Iran, in 1943. Western promises to open a second front in France the next summer (1944) and Stalin's agreement to join in the war against Japan (when Germany was defeated) created an atmosphere of goodwill in which to discuss a postwar settlement. Stalin wanted to retain what he had gained in his pact with Hitler and to dismember Germany. Roosevelt and Churchill made no firm commitments. The most important decision was for the Western allies to attack Germany from Europe's west coast. This decision meant, in retrospect, that Soviet forces would occupy eastern Europe and control its destiny. At Tehran in 1943, the Western allies did not foresee this clearly, for the Russians were still fighting deep within their own frontiers.

But by August 1944, Soviet armies were in sight of Warsaw, which had risen in expectation of liberation. But the Russians allowed the Polish rebels to be annihilated. The Russians also gained control of Romania and Hungary. Alarmed by these developments, Churchill went to Moscow and met with Stalin in October. They agreed to share power in the Balkans on the basis of Soviet predominance in Romania and Bulgaria, western predominance in Greece, and equality of influence in Yugoslavia and Hungary. But the Americans were hostile to such un-Wilsonian devices as "spheres of influence."

The three powers agreed on Germany's disarmament and denazification and on its division into four zones of occupation by France and the Big Three (the USSR, Britain, and the United States). Churchill, however, began to balk at Stalin's plan to dismember Germany and to his demands for $20 billion in reparations and forced labor. These matters caused dissension in the future.

Eastern Europe remained a problem. Everyone agreed that the Soviet Union deserved neighboring governments that were friendly, but the West

Big Three at Potsdam. This photograph shows the "Big Three" at Potsdam. By the summer of 1945 only Stalin remained of the original leaders of the major Allies. Roosevelt and Churchill had been replaced by Harry Truman and Clement Attlee, respectively.

Corbis-Bettmann.

25.6
The Charter of the United Nations

insisted that they also be independent and democratic. However, Stalin knew that freely elected governments in Poland and Romania would not be safely friendly to Russia. He had already established a subservient government in Poland. Under pressure, Stalin agreed to include some Poles friendly to the West. He also promised self-determination and free democratic elections. He probably thought it worth endorsing some meaningless principles as the price of continued harmony. In any case, he soon violated these agreements.

YALTA

The next meeting of the Big Three was at Yalta in the Crimea in February 1945. The Western armies had not yet crossed the Rhine. The war with Japan continued, and no atomic explosion had yet taken place. Roosevelt, faced with an invasion of Japan and heavy losses, was eager to bring the Russians into the Pacific war.

As a true Wilsonian, Roosevelt also suspected Churchill's determination to maintain the British Empire. The Americans thought that Churchill's plan to set up British spheres of influence in Europe would encourage the Russians to do the same and lead to another war. To encourage Russian participation in the war against Japan, Roosevelt and Churchill made extensive concessions to Russia in Asia. Again in the tradition of Wilson, Roosevelt wanted a United Nations. Soviet agreement on these points seemed well worth concessions elsewhere.

POTSDAM

The Big Three met for the last time in the Berlin suburb of Potsdam in July 1945. Much had changed. Germany was defeated, and news of a successful atomic weapon reached the American president during the meetings. President Truman had replaced Roosevelt; and Clement Attlee (1883–1967), leader of the Labour Party, replaced Churchill during the conference. Progress on undecided questions was slow.

Russia's western frontier was moved far into what had been Poland and German East Prussia. In compensation, Poland was moved about a hundred miles west, at the expense of Germany. The Allies agreed that Germany would be divided into occupation zones until the final peace treaty was signed, and the country remained divided until the end of the Cold War more than 40 years later.

A Council of Foreign Ministers was established to draft peace treaties for Germany's allies. Disagreements made the job difficult, and it was not until February 1947 that Bulgaria, Finland, Hungary, Italy, and Romania signed treaties. The Russians signed their own agreements with the Japanese in 1956.

SUMMARY

The Coming of War The second great war of the 20th century (1939–1945) grew out of the unsatisfactory resolution of the first. In retrospect, the two wars appear to some people to be one continuous conflict, with the two main periods of fighting separated by an uneasy truce. To others, that point of view distorts the situation by implying that the second war was the inevitable result of the first and its inadequate peace treaties.

The latter opinion seems more sound. Whatever the flaws of the treaties of Paris, the world suffered an even more terrible war than the first as a result of failures of judgment and will on the part of the victorious democratic powers. The United States, which had become the wealthiest and potentially the strongest nation in the world, disarmed almost entirely and withdrew into foolish isolation; it could play no important part in restraining the ambitious dictators who would bring on the war. Britain and France refused to face the threat posed by the Axis powers until the most deadly war in history was required to put it down. If the victorious democracies had remained strong, responsible, and realistic, they could have remedied whatever injustices or mistakes arose from the treaties without endangering the peace.

World War II The second war itself was plainly a world war. The Japanese occupation of Manchuria in 1931 was a precursor. Italy attacked Ethiopia in 1935. Italy, Germany, and the Soviet Union intervened in the Spanish Civil War (1936–1939). Japan attacked China in 1937. These developments revealed that aggressive forces were on the march across the globe and that the defenders of the world order lacked the will to stop them. The formation of the Axis among Germany, Italy, and Japan guaranteed that the war would be fought around the world. There was fighting and suffering in Asia, Africa, the islands of the Pacific, and Europe. The use of atomic weapons brought the struggle to a close, but conventional weapons did almost all the damage. The survival of civilization was threatened even without the use of nuclear devices.

This was ended not with unsatisfactory peace treaties but with no treaty at all in the European area where it had begun. The world quickly split into two unfriendly camps: the West led by the United States, and the East led by the Soviet Union. This division hastened the liberation of former colonial territories.

IMAGE KEY
for pages 772–773

a. An Allied war poster, World War II.

b. Jews were rounded up in Warsaw for deportation to concentration "death" camps.

c. A Nazi party membership book, with a photograph of the member.

d. The Big Three Conference— Winston Churchill, Franklin Delano Roosevelt, and Josef Stalin.

e. An American propaganda poster, World War II.

f. An atomic bomb explosion like that in Hiroshima, Japan.

g. A refugee Jewish girl.

h. An Imperial Japanese war bond.

REVIEW QUESTIONS

1. What were Hitler's foreign policy aims?

2. Why did Britain and France adopt a policy of appeasement in the 1930s? Strategically, was the policy a good or bad move?

3. Why did Hitler invade Russia? Why did the invasion fail?

4. What were Hitler's racial beliefs? What policies did they inspire?

5. How did America become involved in the war? What was the significance of its intervention? Why did it drop atomic bombs on Japan?

KEY TERMS

Anschluss (p. 776)
appeasement (p. 776)
Axis (p. 776)

Blitzkrieg (p. 780)
Holocaust (p. 781)

Lebensraum (p. 774)
Luftwaffe (p. 779)

 For additional study resources for this chapter, go to:
www.prenhall.com/craig/chapter31

32 The West Since World War II

CHAPTER HIGHLIGHTS

The Cold War U.S.–Soviet cooperation did not survive World War II. After 1945 Europe was divided into a Soviet-dominated zone in the East (the Warsaw Pact) and a U.S.-led zone in the West (NATO). U.S.–Soviet rivalry played itself out around the world from the 1950s to the 1980s, although gradually a spirit of détente arose between the two powers, especially under President Ronald Reagan and Soviet leader Mikhail Gorbachev. The Cold War ended with the collapse of Communist rule in Eastern Europe in 1989 and the disappearance of the Soviet Union in 1991.

Postwar European Society Since World War II, European society has been marked by a rise in prosperity and consumerism, more rights and opportunities for women, moves toward political and economic unification symbolized by the adoption of a common currency, the euro, in 2002 and the publication of a draft constitution for a united Europe in 2003.

The United States The major themes in postwar American history were opposition to Communism at home and abroad, the expansion of civil rights to African Americans, and economic prosperity. Politically, the relatively liberal years from the late 1950s through the 1970s were succeeded by a growing conservatism especially under the presidencies of Ronald Reagan, George Bush, and George W. Bush. Even the Democratic President Bill Clinton was more a centrist than a liberal. After the terrorist attacks of September 11, 2001, the United States embarked on a war on terrorism that led to wars in Afghanistan and Iraq.

Eastern Europe The failure of the Communist regimes in Eastern Europe and the Soviet Union to produce economic prosperity or political liberalization led to their growing unpopularity. Soviet economic difficulties led Mikhail Gorbachev to institute liberal reforms that led to the collapse of the communist rule first in Eastern Europe, then in the Soviet Union itself. The disappearance of the Soviet Union led to independence for much of the former Soviet empire. Russia itself has experienced social, economic, and political turmoil under presidents Boris Yeltsin and Vladimir Putin.

In the former Yugoslavia, the end of Communist rule led to disintegration and civil war. In the 1990s the NATO powers, led by the United States, intervened to halt the fighting and end a pattern of ethnic atrocities.

CHAPTER QUESTIONS

WHAT WERE the causes of the Cold War?

WHAT MAJOR trends have marked European society since World War II?

WHAT ARE the main themes that have characterized postwar America?

WHY DID communist regimes collapse so easily in Eastern Europe in 1989?

HOW DID the West respond to the collapse of Yugoslavia?

WHAT PROBLEMS has Europe faced since the fall of Communism?

Since the conclusion of World War II, Europe's influence on the world has been transformed. The destruction of the war itself left Europe incapable of exercising the kind of power it had formerly exerted. The **Cold War** *between the United States and the Soviet Union made Europe a divided and contested territory. Furthermore, Europeans soon began to lose control of their overseas empires.*

The decision by the United States to take an activist role in world affairs touched every aspect of the postwar world. American domestic politics and foreign policy became intertwined as in no previous period of American history.

Like virtually every other part of the world, Europe experienced the impact of American culture through military alliances, trade, tourism, and popular entertainment. Europeans also began to build structures for greater economic cooperation.

While Western Europe enjoyed increased democratization and unprecedented prosperity, Eastern Europe experienced economic stagnation and Soviet domination. Yet from the late 1970s onward, there were political stirrings in the East. These culminated in 1989 with revolutions throughout Eastern Europe and in 1991 with the collapse of Communist government in the Soviet Union itself. Since then, Europeans have sought new political direction. The movement toward unification, particularly economic, continues in Western Europe. Political confusion and economic stagnation afflict some of the nations that emerged from the Soviet Union, and the attacks of September 11, 2001, on the United States led to events that have challenged the post-World War II Western alliance.

THE COLD WAR ERA

INITIAL CAUSES

The tense relationship between the United States and the Soviet Union that dominated world history during the second half of the 20th century originated in the closing months of World War II.

The split arose from basic differences of ideology and interest. The Soviet Union's attempt to extend its control westward into Europe and southward into the Middle East was a continuation of the policy of tsarist Russia. It had been Britain's traditional role to restrain Russian expansion into these areas; the United States inherited that task as Britain's power waned. The alternative was to permit a major increase in power by a huge, traditionally hostile state. That state, dedicated in its official ideology to the overthrow of nations like the United States, was governed by Stalin (1879–1953), an absolute dictator with a proven record for horrible cruelties. Few nations would take such risks.

However, the United States made no attempt to roll back Soviet power where it already existed, even though American military forces were the greatest in its history, American industrial power was unmatched, and America had a monopoly on atomic weapons. In less than a year from the war's end, the United States reduced its forces in Europe from 3.5 million to half a million. The speedy withdrawal was in accord with America's peacetime goals. These goals included support for self-determination, autonomy, and democracy in the political sphere; and free trade, freedom of the seas, no barriers to investment, and the Open Door in the economic sphere. As the strongest, richest nation in the world, the United States would benefit from an international order based on such goals.

However, the Soviets saw American resistance to its expansion as a threat to its security and legitimate aims. American objections over Poland and other states were seen as attempts to undermine regimes friendly to Russia and encircle the Soviet Union with hostile neighbors.

WHAT WERE the causes of the Cold War?

26.1
The Soviet Victory: Capitalism versus Communism (February 1946): Joseph Stalin

Cold War Ideological and geographical struggle between the United States and its allies and the USSR and its allies that began after World War II and lasted until the dissolution of the USSR in 1989.

The growth in France and Italy of Communist parties taking orders from Moscow led the Americans to believe that Stalin was engaged in a worldwide plot to subvert capitalism and democracy. We do not know for certain if these suspicions were justified, but most people in the West considered them plausible.

AREAS OF EARLY COLD WAR CONFLICT

The new mood of hostility among the former allies appeared quickly. In February 1946, both Stalin and his foreign minister, Vyacheslav Molotov (1890–1986), publicly spoke of the Western democracies as enemies. A month later, Churchill (1874–1965) delivered a speech in Fulton, Missouri, in which he spoke of an Iron Curtain dividing a free and democratic West from an East under totalitarian rule. In this atmosphere, difficulties grew.

26.2
"An Iron Curtain Has Descended Across the Continent" (March 1946): Sir Winston Churchill

The attempt to deal cooperatively with the problem of atomic energy was an early victim of the Cold War. The United States continued to develop its own atomic weapons in secrecy, and the Russians did the same. By 1949, the Soviet Union had exploded its own atomic bomb, and the race for nuclear weapons was on.

The resistance of Westerners to what they perceived as Soviet intransigence and Communist subversion took clearer form in 1947. Since 1944, civil war had been raging in Greece between the royalist government restored by Britain and insurgents supported by the Communist countries. In 1947, Britain informed the United States that it was financially no longer able to support the Greeks. On March 12, President Truman (1884–1972) asked Congress to provide funds to support Greece and Turkey, which was also under Soviet pressure. Congress complied. In what became known as the Truman Doctrine, the American president advocated a policy of supporting "free people who are resisting attempted subjugation by armed minorities or by outside pressures," by implication anywhere in the world.

For Western Europe, where the menacing growth of Communist parties was fueled by postwar poverty and hunger, the Americans devised the European Recovery Program. Named the **Marshall Plan** after George C. Marshall (1880–1959), the secretary of state who introduced it, this program provided broad economic aid to European states only on condition that they work together. The Soviet Union forbade its satellites to take part.

Marshall Plan U.S. program, named after Secretary of State George C. Marshall, that provided economic aid to Europe after World War II.

The Berlin Airlift. Every day for almost a year Western planes supplied the city until Stalin lifted the Berlin blockade in May 1949.

Bildarchiv Preussischer Kulturbesitz.

The Marshall Plan helped restore prosperity to Western Europe and set the stage for its unprecedented economic growth. The plan also led to the establishment there of solid democratic regimes.

Stalin's answer was to replace all multiparty governments behind the Iron Curtain with thoroughly Communist regimes under his control. He also organized in 1947 the Communist Information Bureau (Cominform), dedicated to spreading revolutionary communism throughout the world.

In February 1948, a brutal display of Stalin's policy took place in Prague. The Communists expelled the democratic members of what had been a coalition government and murdered the foreign minister. Czechoslovakia was brought fully under Soviet rule.

These Soviet actions increased America's determination to make its own arrangements in Germany. The Russians dismantled German industry in the eastern zone, but the Americans tried to make Germany self-sufficient, which meant restoring its industrial capacity. To the Soviets the restoration of a powerful industrial Germany was unacceptable.

When the Western powers agreed to go forward with a separate constitution for the western sectors of Germany in February 1948, the Soviets walked out of the joint Allied Control Commission. Berlin, although well within the Soviet zone, was governed by all four powers. The Soviets sealed off the city by closing all railroads and highways to West Germany. Their purpose was to drive the Western powers out of Berlin.

The Western allies responded to the Berlin Blockade with an airlift of supplies that lasted almost a year. In May 1949, the Russians were forced to reopen access to Berlin. The incident hastened the separation of Germany into two states, which prevailed for 40 years. West Germany became the German Federal Republic in September 1949, and the eastern region became the German Democratic Republic a month later.

NATO AND THE WARSAW PACT

Meanwhile, Western Europe was coming closer together. The Marshall Plan encouraged international cooperation. In April 1949, Belgium, Britain, Denmark, France, Iceland, Italy, Luxembourg, the Netherlands, Norway, and Portugal signed a treaty with Canada and the United States that formed the North Atlantic Treaty Organization (NATO) for mutual assistance in case of attack. NATO formed the West into a bloc. A few years later Greece, Turkey, and West Germany joined the alliance (see Map 32–1).

Unlike the NATO states, the states of Eastern Europe were under direct Soviet domination through local Communist parties controlled from Moscow and overawed by the Red Army. The Warsaw Pact of May 1955, which included Albania, Bulgaria, Czechoslovakia, East Germany, Hungary, Poland, Romania, and the Soviet Union, merely gave formal recognition to a system that already existed. Europe stood divided into two unfriendly blocs.

CRISES OF 1956

The events of 1956 had considerable significance both for the Cold War and for what they implied about the realities of European power in the postwar era.

Suez In July 1956, President Gamal Abdel Nasser (1918–1970) of Egypt nationalized the Suez Canal. Britain and France feared that this action would imperil their supplies of oil in the Persian Gulf. In October 1956, war broke out between Egypt and Israel. The British and French intervened; however, the United States refused to support them. The Soviet Union protested vehemently. The Anglo-French forces had to be withdrawn, and control of the canal remained with Egypt. The Suez intervention proved that without the support of the United States, the nations of Western Europe could no longer impose their will on the rest of the world.

Poland Developments in Eastern Europe demonstrated similar limitations on independent action among the Soviet bloc nations. When the prime minister of Poland died, the Polish Communist Party refused to choose a successor

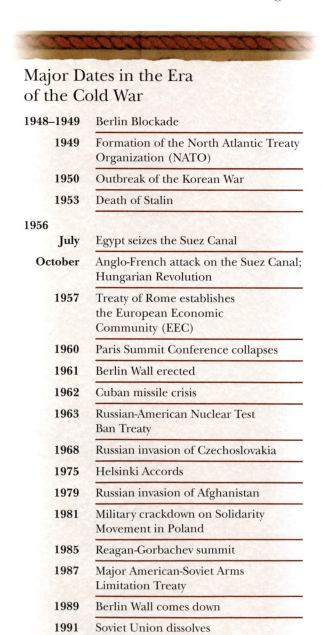

Major Dates in the Era of the Cold War

1948–1949	Berlin Blockade
1949	Formation of the North Atlantic Treaty Organization (NATO)
1950	Outbreak of the Korean War
1953	Death of Stalin
1956	
July	Egypt seizes the Suez Canal
October	Anglo-French attack on the Suez Canal; Hungarian Revolution
1957	Treaty of Rome establishes the European Economic Community (EEC)
1960	Paris Summit Conference collapses
1961	Berlin Wall erected
1962	Cuban missile crisis
1963	Russian-American Nuclear Test Ban Treaty
1968	Russian invasion of Czechoslovakia
1975	Helsinki Accords
1979	Russian invasion of Afghanistan
1981	Military crackdown on Solidarity Movement in Poland
1985	Reagan-Gorbachev summit
1987	Major American-Soviet Arms Limitation Treaty
1989	Berlin Wall comes down
1991	Soviet Union dissolves

MAP 32–1

Major Cold War European Alliance Systems. The North Atlantic Treaty Organization, which includes both Canada and the United States, stretches as far east as Turkey. By contrast, the Warsaw Pact nations were the contiguous Communist states of Eastern Europe, with the Soviet Union as the dominant member.

WHY DID NATO and the Warsaw Pact emerge and become rivals after World War II?

selected by Moscow. Considerable tension developed. In the end, Wladyslaw Gomulka (1905–1982) emerged as the new communist leader of Poland. He proved acceptable to the Soviets because he promised to keep Poland in the Warsaw Pact. However, he halted the collectivization of Polish agriculture and improved relations with the Polish Roman Catholic Church.

Uprising in Hungary Hungary provided the second trouble spot for the Soviet Union. In late October, fighting erupted in Budapest. A new ministry headed by Imre Nagy (1896–1958) was installed. Nagy was a Communist who sought an independent position for Hungary. Unlike Gomulka, he called for Hungarian withdrawal from the Warsaw Pact. Soviet troops deposed Nagy, who was later executed, and imposed Janos Kadar (1912–1989) as premier.

THE COLD WAR INTENSIFIED

The events of 1956 ended the era of fully autonomous action by the European nation-states. The two superpowers had demonstrated the new political realities. After 1956, the Soviet Union began to talk about "peaceful coexistence" with the United States. In 1959, tensions relaxed sufficiently for Soviet Premier Nikita

Soviet Invasion of Czechoslovakia. In the summer of 1968 Soviet tanks rolled into Czechoslovakia, ending that country's experiment in liberalized communism, known as the Prague spring. This picture shows defiant, flag-waving Czechs passing a Soviet tank in the immediate aftermath of the invasion.

Hulton Archive Photos/Getty Images, Inc.

Khrushchev (1894–1971) to tour the United States. A summit meeting was scheduled for May 1960 in Paris, and American President Dwight D. Eisenhower (1890–1969) was to go to Moscow.

Just before the gathering, the Soviet Union shot down an American U-2 aircraft that was flying reconnaissance over Soviet territory. Khrushchev refused to take part in the summit conference, and Eisenhower's trip to the Soviet Union was canceled.

In fact, the Soviets had long been aware of the American flights. They chose to protest at this time for two reasons. Khrushchev had hoped that the leaders of Britain, France, and the United States would be so divided over the future of Germany that a united Allied front would be impossible. The divisions did not arise, so the conference would have been of little use to him. Second, by 1960 the Communist world had become split between the Soviets and the Chinese, who accused the Russians of lacking revolutionary zeal. Khrushchev's action was an attempt to show the hard-line attitude of the Soviet Union toward the capitalist world.

The abortive Paris conference opened the most difficult period of the Cold War. Throughout 1961, thousands of refugees from East Germany had fled to West Berlin. To stop this outflow, in August 1961 the East Germans erected a concrete wall along the border between East and West Berlin that remained until November 1989.

A year later, the Cuban missile crisis brought the most dangerous days of the Cold War. The Soviet Union placed missiles in Cuba, a nation friendly to Soviet aims. The missiles were placed less than a hundred miles from the United States. The United States blockaded Cuba, halted the shipment of new missiles, and demanded the removal of existing installations. After a tense week, the Soviets backed down and the crisis ended.

DÉTENTE AND AFTERWARD

In 1963, the two powers concluded a Nuclear Test Ban Treaty. This agreement marked the start of a detente, or lessening in tensions, between the United States and the Soviet Union that intensified during the presidency of Richard Nixon (1913–1994). This policy involved trade agreements and mutual reduction of strategic armaments. But the Soviet invasion of Afghanistan in 1979 hardened relations between Washington and Moscow, and the U.S. Senate refused to ratify the Strategic Arms Limitation Treaty of 1979.

However, President Ronald Reagan (b. 1911) and Soviet leader Mikhail S. Gorbachev (b. 1931) held a friendly summit meeting in 1985, the first East–West summit in six years. Other meetings followed. In December 1987, the United States and the Soviet Union agreed to dismantle more than 2,000 medium- and shorter-range missiles. The treaty provided for mutual inspection. This action represented the most significant agreement since World War II between the two superpowers.

Thereafter, the political upheavals in Eastern Europe and the Soviet Union overwhelmed the issues of the Cold War. The Soviet Union abandoned its support for Communist governments in Eastern Europe. By the close of 1991, the Soviet Union itself had collapsed. The Cold War was over.

EUROPEAN SOCIETY IN THE SECOND HALF OF THE 20TH CENTURY AND BEYOND

*T*he sharp division of Europe into a democratic West and Communist East for most of the second half of the 20th century makes generalizations about social and economic developments difficult. Prosperity in the West contrasted with shortages in the Eastern economies, which were managed to benefit the Soviet Union. Most of the developments discussed in this chapter have taken place in Western Europe.

TOWARD WESTERN EUROPEAN UNIFICATION

Since 1945, the nations of Western Europe have taken unprecedented steps toward economic cooperation. The process is not completed. The collapse of the Soviet Union and the emergence of new free governments in Eastern Europe have further complicated the process.

The Marshall Plan and NATO gave the involved countries new experience in working with each other and demonstrated the gains from cooperative action. In 1950, Belgium, France, Italy, Luxembourg, the Netherlands, and West Germany organized the European Coal and Steel Community. Its success reduced suspicions about the concept of coordination and economic integration.

In 1957, through the Treaty of Rome, the six members of the Coal and Steel Community agreed to form a new organization: the **European Economic Community (EEC)**, or Common Market. The members sought to achieve the eventual elimination of tariffs, a free flow of capital and labor, and similar wage and social benefits in all the participating countries. The chief institution of the EEC was a High Commission composed of technocrats.

The Common Market was a stunning success. By 1968, all tariffs among the six members had been abolished. Trade and labor migration among the members grew steadily. Moreover, nonmember states began to seek membership. In 1973, Denmark, Great Britain, and Ireland became members, and Austria, Finland, Greece, Portugal, Spain, and Sweden were eventually admitted.

In 1988, the leaders of the EEC decided to create a virtual free-trade zone throughout the member community. In 1991, the Treaty of Maastricht called for a unified currency and a strong central bank. The European Community was renamed the **European Union (EU)**.

However, as the prospect of unity becomes imminent, the people of Europe have begun to raise issues about the democratic nature of the emerging political entity they are being asked to join. They are clearly in favor of closer cooperation, but they are unwilling to see it set forth only by politicians and bureaucrats. They want a wider European market to be genuinely free and not overregulated.

The most striking element of the expanding momentum of economic cooperation is the common currency, called the **euro**. In 1999, the currencies of Austria, Belgium, Finland, France, Germany, Ireland, Italy, Luxembourg, the Netherlands, Portugal, and Spain were fixed according to the value of the euro. In 2002, their

WHAT MAJOR trends have marked European society since World War II?

European Economic Community Economic association formed by France, Germany, Italy, Belgium, the Netherlands, and Luxembourg in 1957. Also known as the Common Market.

European Union New name given to the EEC in 1993. It included most of the states of Western Europe.

euro Common currency created by the EEC in the late 1990s.

President Ronald Reagan and Premier Mikhail Gorbachev. The two world leaders confer at a summit meeting in December 1989.
AP/Wide World Photos.

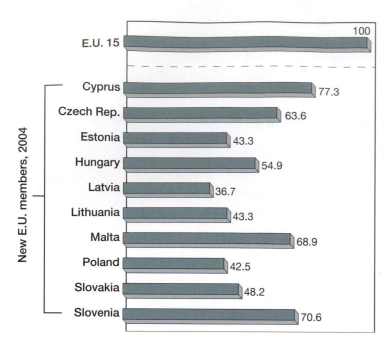

New E.U. members, 2004

E.U. 15 — 100
Cyprus — 77.3
Czech Rep. — 63.6
Estonia — 43.3
Hungary — 54.9
Latvia — 36.7
Lithuania — 43.3
Malta — 68.9
Poland — 42.5
Slovakia — 48.2
Slovenia — 70.6

Figure 32–1. Gross National Product of Existing EU Members Compared to New Member States, 2004. The cost of absorbing new EU members, many of which have standards of living that are far lower, is high but the economic potential is great.

national currencies and that of Greece were replaced by new coins and notes denominated in the euro. Such a widespread common currency is unprecedented in European history.

In 2004, the EU accepted 10 new members. This expansion poses enormous challenges, because the economies of the new members (mostly former states from the Eastern Soviet bloc) are much less developed than those of the former members.

STUDENTS AND POPULAR MUSIC

Nothing so characterized both student and youth culture in the second half of the 20th century as rock music, which first emerged in the 1950s. The lyrics of the Beatles, the British rock group that became wildly popular on both sides of the Atlantic in the 1960s, may have become the most widely dispersed poetry in history. Rock appealed across national and cultural borders and did much to create a more uniform European culture.

It also offered a critique of contemporary society. Many lyrics emphasized the need for love, the anguish of isolation, a desire for sexual liberation, and hopes for community and peace. During the 1960s, rock music in the West promoted antiwar movements, student rebellions that rocked both Europe and the United States, and discontent with the older generation. In the 1970s and 1980s, rock music emerged as a major vehicle for cultural and political protest in Eastern Europe and the Soviet Union.

THE MOVEMENT OF PEOPLES

Many people have migrated from, to, and within Europe during the past half century.

External Migration In the decade and a half after 1945, approximately a half million Europeans each year settled elsewhere in the world. Many of these migrants were educated city dwellers.

Decolonization in the postwar period contributed to an inward flow of European colonials and non-European inhabitants of the former colonies to Europe. This influx has caused social tension and conflict. In Great Britain, for example, during the 1980s clashes arose between the police and non-European immigrants. France has had similar difficulties. Moreover, large Islamic populations now exist in several European nations and have become political factors in France and Germany.

Internal Migration The major motivation for internal migration from the late 1950s onward was economic opportunity. The prosperous nations of northern and Western Europe offered jobs that paid good wages and provided excellent benefits. Thus, there was a flow of workers from the poorer countries of Greece, Italy, Portugal, Spain, Turkey, and Yugoslavia into the wealthier countries of the Benelux nations, France, Switzerland, and West Germany. The establishment of the EEC in 1957 facilitated this movement.

The migration of workers into northern Europe snowballed after 1960. Several hundred thousand workers would enter France and Germany each year. They were usually welcomed during years of prosperity, and resented when economies began to slow in the mid-1980s. In Germany during the early 1990s, they were attacked.

In the late 1980s, politics again became a major factor in European migration. With the collapse of the Communist governments of Eastern Europe in 1988 and 1989, people from all over Eastern Europe have migrated to the West. The civil war in the former Yugoslavia has also created many refugees. However, the new migrants are generating resentment. Several nations have taken steps to restrict migration.

THE NEW MUSLIM POPULATION

Well into the 20th century, Europeans encountered Muslims, if at all, as subjects in their colonies. With the exception of a few minority communities in the Balkans and the former Soviet Empire, Europeans saw themselves and their national cultures as Christian or secular.

European indifference to Islam began to change in the 1960s as a sizable Muslim population settled in Europe. Two factors encouraged Muslim emigration to Western Europe: Europe's economic growth and decolonization. As Western economies recovered in the wake of World War II, a labor shortage developed in Europe, and laborers ("guest workers"), many of whom came from Muslim nations, were imported to fill it. The aftermath of decolonization and the quest for a better life led Muslims from East Africa and the Indian subcontinent to Great Britain and others from North Africa to France. Smaller but significant numbers settled in Denmark, Italy, the Netherlands, Spain, and Sweden—nations that had always had homogeneous populations.

These Muslim immigrant communities share some characteristics. Many Muslims came to Europe expecting eventually to return to their homelands, an expectation their host countries shared. Unlike the United States, few European countries had any experience in dealing with large-scale immigration, and the various Muslim communities have largely remained unassimilated. Most of the Muslim immigrants to Europe were neither highly skilled nor professionally educated, and many of the unskilled jobs that they originally filled have disappeared. As European economic growth has slowed, Muslims have become a target blamed for a host of problems from crime to unemployment.

The radicalization of parts of the Islamic world has also affected Europe's Muslim communities. Muslims in both Germany and Great Britain have been involved in radical Islamic groups, and some belonged to organizations involved in the September 11, 2001, attack on the United States. The French government has exerted more control over its Muslim community. Despite the fact that Europe's Muslims are not a homogeneous group, their communities are often plagued by poverty and unemployment and are a major concern for Europeans, who disagree on how to deal with them.

NEW PATTERNS IN THE WORK AND EXPECTATIONS OF WOMEN

Since World War II, the work patterns and social expectations of women have changed markedly. In all social ranks, women have begun to assume larger economic and political roles. They have entered the professions and are filling major managerial positions.

Feminism   Enormous gains were made during the second half of the 20th century, but gender inequality remained a major characteristic of European societies at the start of the 21st century. After World War II, European feminism developed a

Muslim Women Wearing Headscarves, France. The presence of foreign-born Muslims whose labor is necessary for the prosperity of the European economy is a major issue in contemporary Europe. Many of these Muslims, such as these women, live in self-contained communities.

Figaro Magazine/Torregano/Getty Images, Inc.

HISTORY'S VOICES

SIMONE DE BEAUVOIR URGES ECONOMIC FREEDOM FOR WOMEN

Simone de Beauvoir was the single most important feminist voice of mid-20th-century Europe. In The Second Sex, *published in France in 1949, she explored the experience of women coming of age in a world of ideas, institutions, and social expectations shaped historically by men. Much of the book discusses the psychological strategies that modern European women had developed to deal with their status as "the second sex." Toward the end of her book, de Beauvoir argues strongly that economic freedom and advancement for women are fundamental to their personal fulfillment.*

WHY DOES de Beauvoir argue that the achievement of civic rights must be accompanied by economic freedom for women? Why does the example of the small number of professional women illustrate issues for European women in general? How does de Beauvoir indicate that even professional women must overcome a culture in which the experience of women is fundamentally different from that of men? Do her comments seem relevant for women at the opening of the 21st century?

According to French law, obedience is no longer included among the duties of a wife, and each woman citizen has the right to vote; but these civil liberties remain theoretical as long as they are unaccompanied by economic freedom. . . . It is through gainful employment that woman has traversed most of the distance that separated her from the male; and nothing else can guarantee her liberty in practice. Once she ceases to be a parasite, the system based on her dependence crumbles; between her and the universe there is no longer any need for a masculine mediator. . . .

When she is productive, active, she regains her transcendence; in her projects she concretely affirms her status as subject; in connection with the aims she pursues, with the money and the rights she takes possession of, she makes trial of and senses her responsibility. . . .

There are . . . a fairly large number of privileged women who find in their professions a means of economic and social autonomy. These come to mind when one considers woman's possibilities and her future . . . [E]ven though they constitute as yet only a minority; they continue to be the subject of debate between feminists and antifeminists. The latter assert that the emancipated women of today succeed in doing nothing of importance in the world and that furthermore they have difficulty in achieving their own inner equilibrium. The former exaggerate the results obtained by professional women and are blind to their inner confusion. There is no good reason . . . to say they are on the wrong road; and still it is certain that they are not tranquilly installed in their new realm: as yet they are only halfway there. The woman who is economically emancipated from man is not for all that in a moral, social, and psychological situation identical with that of man. The way she carried on her profession and her devotion to it depends on the context supplied by the total pattern of her life. For when she begins her adult life she does not have behind her the same past as does a boy; she is not viewed by society in the same way; the universe presents itself to her in a different perspective. The fact of being a woman today poses peculiar problems for an independent human individual.

Source: Simone de Beauvoir, *The Second Sex*, trans. by H. M. Parshley. Copyright 1952 and renewed 1980 by Alfred A. Knopf, Inc. Reprinted by permission of Alfred A. Knopf, a division of Random House Inc.

new agenda. Simone de Beauvoir's (1908-1986) book, *The Second Sex* (1949), was a major influence (see "Simone de Beauvoir Urges Economic Freedom for Women"). She and other feminists documented the social, legal, and economic disadvantages of their gender, challenged discrimination against women in family law, and called attention to social problems such as spousal abuse.

More Married Women in the Work Force   Both middle- and working-class women have increasingly sought employment outside the home, and the number of married women in the work force has risen sharply. Some employers adjust hours to accommodate them, and consumer conveniences and child care made it easier for them to work. Given that 20th-century children were compelled to spend much of their time in school, they are no longer expected to contribute to the support of their families. If additional income is needed, their mothers work outside the home. But even when there is no financial necessity, both parents are now likely to pursue careers.

New Work Patterns   In the late 20th century, the work pattern of European women displayed much more continuity than it did in the 19th century. Single women enter the work force after their schooling and continue to work after marriage. The number of married women in the work force has risen sharply. Both middle- and working-class married women have sought jobs outside the home. They might withdraw from the work force to care for young children but return when the children begin school.

Several factors created this new pattern, but women's increasing life expectancy is one of the most important. The lengthening life span has meant that child rearing occupies much less of women's lives. Women throughout the Western world have new concerns about how they will spend those years when they are not rearing children. The age at which women have decided to bear children has risen. In urban areas, childbearing occurs later and the birthrate is lower than elsewhere.

Many women have begun to limit the number of children they bear or to forgo childbearing altogether. Both men and women continue to expect to marry. But the new careers open to women and the desire of couples for a higher standard of living have contributed to a declining birthrate.

Women in the New Eastern Europe   Many paradoxes surround the situation of women in Eastern Europe now that it is no longer governed by Communists. Under communism women generally enjoyed social equality as well as a broad spectrum of government benefits. Well over 50 percent of women worked in these societies both because they could and because it was expected of them. There were, however, no significant women's movements since they, like all independent associations, were frowned on.

The new governments of the region are free, but have shown little concern toward women's issues. Economic difficulties may endanger the funding of various health and welfare programs that benefit women and children, like the extensive maternity benefits they used to enjoy. Moreover, the high proportion of women in the work force could leave them more vulnerable than men to the region's economic troubles.

AMERICAN DOMESTIC SCENE SINCE WORLD WAR II

Three major themes have characterized the postwar American experience—opposition to the spread of communism, expansion of civil rights to Blacks and other minorities at home, and a determination to achieve economic growth.

Simone de Beauvoir.   Depicted here with her companion, philosopher Jean Paul Sartre, de Beauvoir was the major feminist writer in postwar Europe.

Getty Images Inc./Hulton Archive Photos.

WHAT ARE the main themes that have characterized postwar America?

TRUMAN AND EISENHOWER ADMINISTRATIONS

The foreign policy of President Harry Truman was directed against Communist expansion in Europe and East Asia. Domestically, the Truman administration tried to continue the New Deal. However, Truman encountered opposition from conservative Republicans, who in 1947 passed the Taft-Hartley Act, which limited labor-union activity. Truman won the 1948 election against great odds. Through policies he termed the Fair Deal, he sought to extend economic security.

Those efforts, however, were frustrated by fears of a domestic Communist menace fanned by Senator Joseph McCarthy (1909–1957) of Wisconsin. That development, a frustration with the war in Korea, and perhaps the natural weariness of the electorate after 20 years of Democratic Party government, led to the election of war hero Dwight Eisenhower in 1952.

The Eisenhower years now seem a period of calm. Eisenhower ended the Korean War. The country was generally prosperous. The president was less activist than either Roosevelt or Truman had been.

Beneath the apparent quiet, however, stirred forces that would lead to the disruptions of the 1960s.

CIVIL RIGHTS

In 1954, the U.S. Supreme Court, in *Brown v. Board of Education of Topeka,* declared racial segregation unconstitutional. Shortly thereafter, the court ordered the desegregation of schools. In 1957, President Eisenhower had to send troops into Little Rock, Arkansas, to integrate the schools, and for the next 10 years, the struggle over school integration and civil rights for Black Americans stirred the nation. Southern states attempted to resist desegregation. American Blacks began to protest it. In 1955, Reverend Martin Luther King, Jr. (1929–1968) organized a boycott in Montgomery, Alabama, against segregated buses that marked the beginning of the use of civil disobedience to fight racial discrimination in the United States. The civil rights struggle continued well into the 1960s. The greatest achievements of the movement were the Civil Rights Act of 1964, which desegregated public accommodations, and the Voting Rights Act of 1965, which cleared the way for Blacks to vote. Black citizens were brought nearer to the mainstream of American life than they had ever been.

However, much remained undone. In 1967, race riots occurred in American cities. Those riots, followed by the assassination of Martin Luther King, Jr., in 1968, weakened the civil rights movement. Not until the late 1980s did a new leader emerge in the person of the Reverend Jesse Jackson (b. 1941). He spearheaded a move to register Black voters, but progress on race relations has been slow. In 1992, a court decision involving treatment of Black Americans by police sparked one of the most destructive riots in American history in Los Angeles. Furthermore, as other groups, particularly Latino Americans, began to raise issues on behalf of their own communities, racial relations became more complicated. Black Americans and other minorities continue to lag behind White Americans economically.

NEW SOCIAL PROGRAMS

The advance of the civil rights movement in the late 1950s and early 1960s represented the cutting edge of a new advance of political liberalism. In 1960, John F. Kennedy (1917–1963) narrowly won the presidential election. He attempted unsuccessfully to expand medical care under the Social Security program, but the reaction to his assassination in 1963 allowed his successor, Lyndon Johnson

(1908–1973), to press for activist legislation. Johnson's domestic program, known as the War on Poverty, established major federal programs to create jobs and provide job training. It also added new entitlements to the Social Security program, including Medicare, which provides medical services for the elderly and disabled. Johnson's drive for what he termed the Great Society ended the era of major federal initiatives that had begun under Franklin Roosevelt. By the late 1960s, the electorate had become more conservative.

THE VIETNAM WAR AND DOMESTIC TURMOIL

Johnson's activist domestic vision was overshadowed by the U.S. involvement in Vietnam (see Chapter 33). By 1965, Johnson had decided to send American troops to Vietnam. This policy led to the longest of American wars. At home, the war and the military draft provoked large-scale protests on the streets and on college campuses. The Vietnam War divided the nation as had no conflict since the Civil War.

Lyndon Johnson decided not to seek reelection in 1968. Richard Nixon led the Republicans to victory. His election marked the beginning of an era of American politics dominated by conservative policies. Perhaps the most important act of his administration was to establish diplomatic relations with the People's Republic of China. Although half of the casualties in the Vietnam War occurred under Nixon's administration, he concluded the war in 1972. That same year he was reelected, but the Watergate scandal began to erode his administration.

THE WATERGATE SCANDAL

On the surface, the Watergate scandal involved only the burglary of the Democratic Party national headquarters by White House operatives in 1972. The deeper issues related to presidential authority and the right of the government to intrude into the lives of citizens. In 1973, Congress established a committee to investigate the scandal. Testimony revealed that President Nixon had recorded conversations in the White House. In the summer of 1974, the newly released tapes showed that Nixon had ordered federal agencies to try to cover up White House participation in the burglary. After this revelation, Nixon resigned, becoming the first American president to resign from office.

The Watergate scandal further shook public confidence in the government. It was also a distraction from the major problems facing the country, especially inflation, which had resulted from fighting the war in Vietnam while expanding federal domestic expenditures. The administrations of Gerald Ford (1974–1977; b. 1913) and Jimmy Carter (1977–1981; b. 1924) battled inflation and high interest rates without success.

THE TRIUMPH OF POLITICAL CONSERVATISM

In 1980, Ronald Reagan was elected president by a large majority and reelected four years later. Reagan was the first fully ideological conservative to be elected in the postwar era. He sought to reduce the role of the federal government in

Kent State Protest. The clash between protesting students and the Ohio National Guard at Kent State University was the most violent moment in the protests against the U.S. involvement in Vietnam.

AP/Wide World Photos.

Farewell. President Richard M. Nixon flashes his trademark "V" gesture one last time before boarding a helicopter after his resignation.

American life through major tax cuts. This plus vastly increased defense spending produced the largest fiscal deficit in American history, but inflation was controlled, and the economy expanded.

In 1988, George H. W. Bush (b. 1924) was elected to succeed Reagan. In the summer of 1990, in response to the invasion of Kuwait by Iraq, he initiated the largest mobilization of American troops since the Vietnam War and forged a worldwide coalition, which forced Iraq out of Kuwait in 1991.

But Bush stumbled in the face of serious economic problems. In 1992, the Democratic nominee, Governor William (Bill) Clinton (b. 1946) of Arkansas, won the election.

In 1994, the Republic Party won majorities in both houses of Congress in an election that marked a major conservative departure in American political life. This Congress continued the conservative redirection of federal policy that had begun under Reagan.

President Clinton and a Republican-dominated Congress were reelected in 1996, but scandals plagued both parties. Because of a personal sexual scandal and allegations of perjury, President Clinton was impeached in 1998 but acquitted in early 1999 by the Senate. In terms of policy, Clinton was seen as moving the Democractic Party into a more conservative stance.

The presidential election of 2000 between Texas governor George W. Bush (son of the former president) and Vice President Al Gore was the closest in modern American history. Gore won a majority of the popular vote, but failed to win a majority in the electoral college. The pivotal electoral votes depended on which candidate carried Florida, where the final vote count was disputed for more than a month after the November election. After complicated legal disputes over how, or indeed whether, to recount the Florida vote, the U.S. Supreme Court voted 5 to 4 to halt the recount, which resulted in Bush being declared the winner in Florida and thus in the presidential election as well.

On September 11, 2001, surprise terrorist attacks on New York City and Washington, D.C., transformed the political life of the United States. In October 2001, the United States began a war against terrorism. U.S. forces overran the forces of the extremist Islamic Taliban regime in Afghanistan, which had tolerated the presence of Islamic terrorists. In 2003, as a second step in the response to the terrorist threat, the United States invaded Iraq (see Chapter 34).

In 2004, President Bush overcame Democratic challenger John Kerry and was reelected, this time with a popular and electoral college majority vote. This strengthened his hand in pursuing his conservative legislative agenda and foreign policy.

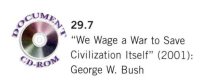

29.7

"We Wage a War to Save Civilization Itself" (2001): George W. Bush

WHY DID Gorbachev seek to change the Soviet Union?

The Soviet Union to 1989

*T*he major themes of Soviet history after 1945 were the rivalry with the United States for world leadership, the rivalry with China for leadership of Communist nations, the effort to sustain Soviet domination of Eastern Europe, and a series of unsuccessful attempts to reform the Stalinist state, which ended in 1991 with the collapse of the Soviet Union.

The Soviet Union emerged from World War II as a major world power, but Stalin did not modify the repressive regime he had fostered. The central bureaucracy grew. Heavy industry was still favored at the expense of consumer goods. Agriculture remained troubled. Stalin's authority was unchallenged. He solidified Soviet control over Eastern Europe.

THE KHRUSHCHEV YEARS

Stalin died on March 6, 1953. No single leader immediately replaced him, but by 1956, Nikita Khrushchev (1894–1971) became premier, but without the extraordinary powers of Stalin.

In 1956, at the Twentieth Congress of the Communist Party, Khrushchev denounced Stalin and his crimes. The speech shocked party circles and opened the way for limited internal criticism of the Soviet government. Under Khrushchev, intellectuals were somewhat freer to express their opinions. In economic policy, Khrushchev made moderate efforts to decentralize economic planning, but the consumer sector improved only marginally. The ever-growing defense budget and the space program made major demands on the nation's productive resources.

Khrushchev redirected Stalin's agricultural policy. The Soviet Union could not feed its own people. Khrushchev removed the most restrictive regulations on private cultivation, but the agricultural problem continued to grow.

By 1964, Communist Party leaders had concluded that Khrushchev had tried to do too much too soon and had done it poorly. His foreign policy, culminating in the backdown over the Cuban missile crisis, appeared a failure. On October 16, 1964, Khrushchev was forced to resign. Leonid Brezhnev (1906–1982) emerged as his successor.

BREZHNEV

The Soviet government became more repressive after 1964. Intellectuals enjoyed less freedom, and Jewish citizens were harassed. The internal repression gave rise to a dissident movement. A few Soviet citizens dared to criticize the regime for violating the human rights provisions of the 1975 Helsinki Accords. The dissidents included the Nobel Prize–winning physicist Andrei Sakharov (1921–1989). The Soviet government responded with more repression.

In foreign policy, the Brezhnev years witnessed attempts both to reach accommodation with the United States and to continue to expand Soviet influence and maintain Soviet leadership of the Communist movement. Growing spending on defense sqeezed the consumer side of the economy.

In December 1979, the Soviet Union invaded Afghanistan for reasons that still remain unclear. The Afghanistan invasion exacerbated tensions with the United States and tied the hands of the Soviet government in Eastern Europe. Soviet hesitation to react to events in Poland during the 1980s stemmed in part from the military committment in Afghanistan and from the condemnation the invasion provoked from Western European Communists and from many governments. The Soviet government also lost support at home as its army became bogged down and suffered steady losses.

COMMUNISM AND SOLIDARITY IN POLAND

In July 1980, the Polish government raised meat prices. The result was strikes across the country. In August, a strike at the Lenin shipyard at Gdansk spread to other shipyards, transport facilities, and factories. The strikers, led by Lech Walesa (b. 1944), refused to negotiate through the government-controlled unions. The Gdansk strike ended on August 31 after the government promised the workers the right to organize an independent union, Solidarity. Less than a week later the Polish Communist head of state was replaced.

In the summer of 1981, for the first time in any European Communist state, secret elections for the Polish party congress permitted real choices among the

Mujahidin. Muslim guerrilla warriors are pictured here with a captured Soviet armored vehicle in January 1980 near Afghanistan's border with Pakistan. The Soviet invasion of Afghanistan in 1979 met with fierce resistance and sparked a sharp response from the United States, which halted sales of wheat to the Soviet Union and boycotted the Olympic Games held in Moscow in 1980.

C. Spengler/Sygma.

candidates. Poland remained a Communist state, but real debate was temporarily permitted within the party congress. This experiment ended in December 1981. General Wojciech Jaruzelski (b.1923) became head of the party, and martial law was declared.

GORBACHEV ATTEMPTS TO REDIRECT THE SOVIET UNION

By the time of Brezhnev's death in 1982, the Soviet system seemed incapable of meeting the needs of its people or pursuing a successful foreign policy. But no observers expected rapid change in the Soviet Union or its satellites.

However, in 1985, Mikhail S. Gorbachev (b. 1931) came to power and immediately set about making the most remarkable changes that the Soviet Union had witnessed since the 1920s. His reforms unleashed forces that within seven years would force him to retire and end both Communist rule and the Soviet Union itself.

Initially, Gorbachev and his supporters challenged the way the party and bureaucracy managed the Soviet government and economy. Under the policy of *perestroika*, or restructuring, they proposed major economic and political reforms. The centralized economic ministries were streamlined. By early 1990, Gorbachev had even begun to advocate private ownership of property. He and his advisers considered policies to move the economy rapidly toward a free market. However, the Soviet economy, instead of growing, stagnated and even declined. Shortages of food, consumer goods, and housing became chronic. Old-fashioned Communists blamed these results on the abandonment of centralized planning, while democratic critics blamed them on overly slow reform.

Gorbachev also allowed public criticism of Soviet history and Soviet Communist Party policy. This development was termed *glasnost*, or openness. In factories, workers were permitted to criticize party officials and the economic plans of the party and the government. Censorship was relaxed and free expression encouraged. Dissidents were released from prison. In 1988, a new constitution permitted contested elections. After real political campaigning, the Congress of People's Deputies was elected in 1989 and then formally elected Gorbachev as president.

The Soviet Union was a vast empire of diverse nationalities. Some had been conquered under the tsars; others had been seized by Stalin. Glasnost quickly brought to the fore the discontents of all such peoples. Gorbachev proved inept in addressing these ethnic complaints.

perestroika Meaning "restructuring." Attempt in the 1980s to reform the Soviet government and economy.

glasnost Meaning "openness." Policy initiated by Mikhail Gorbachev in the 1980s of permitting open criticism of the policies of the Soviet Communist Party.

WHY DID communist regimes collapse so easily in Eastern Europe in 1989?

1989: YEAR OF REVOLUTIONS IN EASTERN EUROPE

In 1989, Soviet domination and Communist rule in Eastern Europe ended. None of these revolutions could have taken place without the refusal of the Soviet Union to intervene militarily as it had done in 1956 and 1968. For the first time since the end of World War II, the peoples of Eastern Europe could shape their own political destiny. Once they realized the Soviets would stand back, thousands of citizens denounced Communist Party domination and asserted their desire for democracy.

The generally peaceful character of most of these revolutions was not inevitable. It may have resulted from the shock with which the world responded to the violent repression of prodemocracy protesters in Beijing's Tiananmen Square in May 1989. The Communist Party officials of Eastern Europe and the

Soviet Union clearly decided that they could not offend world opinion with a similar attack.

SOLIDARITY REEMERGES IN POLAND

During the mid-1980s, Poland's government relaxed martial law. By 1984, leaders of Solidarity began again to work for free trade unions and democratic government. New dissenting organizations emerged. Poland's economy continued to deteriorate. In 1988, new strikes occurred. This time the communist government failed to reimpose control. Solidarity was legalized.

Jaruzelski, with the tacit consent of the Soviet Union, promised free elections to parliament. When elections were held in 1989, the Communists lost overwhelmingly to Solidarity candidates. On August 24, 1989, after negotiating with Lech Walesa, Jaruzelski named Tadeusz Mazowiecki (b. 1927) the first non-Communist prime minister of Poland since 1945. The appointment was made with the express approval of Gorbachev.

HUNGARY MOVES TOWARD INDEPENDENCE

Hungary had for some time shown the greatest national economic independence of the Soviet Union in Eastern Europe. The Hungarian government had emphasized the production of food and consumer goods. In early 1989, as events unfolded in Poland, the Hungarian Communist government permitted independent political parties and free travel between Hungary and Austria, opening the first breach in the Iron Curtain. Thousands of East Germans then moved through Hungary and Austria to West Germany.

In May 1989, Premier Janos Kadar (1912–1989) was voted from office by the parliament. In October, Hungary promised free elections. By 1990, a coalition of democratic parties governed the country.

THE BREACH OF THE BERLIN WALL AND GERMAN REUNIFICATION

In the autumn of 1989, demonstrations erupted in East German cities. The streets filled with people demanding an end to Communist Party rule.

Gorbachev told the leaders of the East German Communist Party that the Soviet Union would no longer support them. They resigned, making way for a younger generation of Communist Party leaders who promised reforms. They convinced few East Germans, however. In November 1989, the government of East Germany ordered the opening of the Berlin Wall, and thousands of East Berliners crossed into West Berlin. By early 1990, the Communist government of East Germany had been swept away.

The citizens of the two Germanies were determined to reunify. By February 1990, reunification had become a foregone conclusion, accepted by France, Great Britain, the Soviet Union, and the United States.

THE VELVET REVOLUTION IN CZECHOSLOVAKIA

Late in 1989, in "the velvet revolution," Communist rule in Czechoslovakia unraveled. In November, under popular pressure from street demonstrations and well-organized political opposition, the Communist Party began to retreat from office. The patterns were similar to those occurring elsewhere: Old leadership

The Fall of the Berlin Wall. The most dramatic moment in the weeks of the collapse of Communist regimes in Eastern Europe occurred in November 1989 when crowds destroyed the Berlin Wall, the most prominent symbol of the Cold War divisions in Europe.

A.Avarkian/Time Life Pictures/Getty Images, Inc.

29.1
A United Germany in a United Europe (June 5, 1990): Helmut Kohl

resigned, and younger Communists replaced them. The changes they offered were inadequate.

The popular new Czech leader was Václav Havel (b. 1936), a playwright of international standing whom the government had imprisoned. Havel and his group, which called itself Civic Forum, negotiated changes with the government that included an end to the political dominance of the Communist Party and the inclusion of non-Communists in the government. In late December 1989, Havel was elected president.

VIOLENT REVOLUTION IN ROMANIA

The most violent upheaval of 1989 occurred in Romania, where President Nicolae Ceausescu (1918–1989) had governed without opposition for almost a quarter century. Romania was a corrupt, one-party state with total centralized economic planning. Ceausescu, who had long been at odds with the Soviet government, maintained his Stalinist regime in the face of Gorbachev's reforms. He was supported by a loyal security force.

On December 15, troubles erupted in the city of Timisoara in western Romania. The security forces fired on demonstrators, and casualties ran into the hundreds. By December 22, Bucharest was in full revolt. Fighting broke out between the army, which supported the revolution, and the security forces. Ceausescu and his wife attempted to flee the country but were captured and executed on December 25. His death ended the fighting. The provisional government in Bucharest announced the first free elections since the end of World War II.

THE COLLAPSE OF THE SOVIET UNION

WHY DID the Soviet Union collapse?

Gorbachev believed that the Soviet Union could no longer afford to support Communist governments in Eastern Europe. He was beginning to realize that the Communist Party within the Soviet Union was also losing power.

RENUNCIATION OF COMMUNIST POLITICAL MONOPOLY

In early 1990, Gorbachev formally proposed that the Soviet Communist Party abandon its monopoly of power. After intense debate, the Central Committee abandoned the Leninist position that only a single elite party could act as the vanguard of the revolution and forge a new Soviet society.

Gorbachev confronted challenges from three major political forces by 1990. One group—considered conservative in the Soviet context—wanted to maintain the influence of the Communist Party and the Soviet army. They were disturbed by the country's economic stagnation and disorder. They appeared to have significant support. During late 1990 and early 1991, Gorbachev, who himself seems to have been disturbed by the nation's turmoil, began to appoint members of this group to government posts. In other words, Gorbachev seemed to be making a strategic retreat. He apparently believed that these more conservative forces could give him the support he needed against opposition from a second group, led by Boris Yeltsin (b. 1931), who wanted to move quickly to a market economy and a more democratic government. In 1990, Yeltsin was elected president of the Russian Republic, the most important of the Soviet Union's constituent republics. That position gave him a firm political base from which to challenge Gorbachev's authority and increase his own.

The third force was regional unrest, especially from the three Baltic republics of Estonia, Latvia, and Lithuania. During 1989 and 1990, the parliaments of the Baltic republics tried to increase their independence, and Lithuania actually declared itself independent. Discontent also arose in the Soviet Islamic republics in Central Asia. Gorbachev sought to negotiate new constitutional arrangements between the republics and the central government but failed. This may have been the most important reason for the rapid collapse of the Soviet Union.

THE AUGUST 1991 COUP

The turning point came in August 1991 when the conservative forces that Gorbachev had brought into the government attempted a coup. Armed forces occupied Moscow, and Gorbachev himself was placed under house arrest in the Crimea. Yeltsin denounced the coup and asked the world for help.

Within two days the coup collapsed. Gorbachev returned to Moscow, but in humiliation, having been victimized by the groups he had turned to for support. From that point on, Yeltsin steadily became the dominant political figure in the nation. The Communist Party, compromised by its participation in the coup, collapsed. On December 25, 1991, the Soviet Union ceased to exist, Gorbachev left office, and the Commonwealth of Independent States came into being (see Map 32–2).

MAP 32–2

The Commonwealth of Independent States.   In December 1991, the Soviet Union broke up into its 15 constituent republics. Eleven of these were loosely joined in the Commonwealth of Independent States. Also shown is the autonomous region of Chechnya, which has waged two bloody wars with Russia in the last decade.

WHAT DOES the breakup of the Soviet Union say about the importance of nationalism in the modern world?

THE YELTSIN YEARS

As president of Russia, Yeltsin was head of the largest and most powerful of the new states, but by 1993 he faced serious problems. Opposition to Yeltsin personally and to his economic and political reforms grew in the Russian Parliament. Its members were mostly former Communists who wanted to slow or halt the movement toward reform. In September 1993, Yeltsin suspended Parliament, which responded by deposing him. The military, however, backed Yeltsin and surrounded the Parliament building. On October 4, 1993, after pro-Parliament rioters rampaged through Moscow, Yeltsin ordered tanks to attack the Parliament building, crushing the revolt.

These actions consolidated Yeltsin's position and authority. The major Western powers supported him. The crushing of Parliament left Yeltsin far more dependent on the military. And the country's continuing economic problems bred unrest. In the December 1993 parlimentary elections, radical nationalists made an uncomfortably strong showing. In 1994 and again after 1999, the central government has found itself at war in the province of Chechnya. In December 1999, Yeltsin, who suffered from poor health, resigned and was succeeded as president by Vladimir Putin. Putin was elected to a full term in April 2000, promising strong leadership.

Putin renewed the war against the rebels in Chechnya, which has resulted in heavy casualties and enormous destruction there, but has also strengthened Putin's political support in Russia itself. After the terrorist attacks on the United States, Putin extended cooperation with the American assault on Afghanistan largely because the Russian government was afraid that Islamic extremism would spread beyond Chechnya to other regions in Russia and to the largely Muslim nations that bordered Russia in Central Asia and the Caucasus.

The Chechen war spawned a major terrorist act. In September 2004, a group of Chechens captured an elementary school in Beslan (in the north Caucasus) and held 1,200 students, teachers, and parents hostage for several days. When government troops stormed the school, approximately 330 hostages were killed. In the wake of this event, Putin has pursued policies of strong governmental centralization that cast doubt on the future of democratic processes in Russia.

THE COLLAPSE OF YUGOSLAVIA AND CIVIL WAR

HOW DID the West respond to the collapse of Yugoslavia?

Yugoslavia was created after World War I. Its borders included six major national groups—Serbs, Croats, Slovenes, Montenegrins, Macedonians, and Bosnians (Muslims)—among whom there have been ethnic disputes for centuries. The Croats and Slovenes are Roman Catholic and use the Latin alphabet. The Serbs, Montenegrins, and Macedonians are Eastern Orthodox and use the Cyrillic alphabet. The Bosnians are Islamic. Most members of each group reside in a region with which they are associated historically—Serbia, Croatia, Slovenia, Montenegro, Macedonia, and Bosnia-Herzegovina—and these regions constituted individual republics within Yugoslavia. Many Serbs, however, lived outside Serbia proper.

Yugoslavia's first Communist leader, Marshal Tito (1892–1980), had acted independently of Stalin in the late 1940s and pursued his own foreign policy. He muted ethnic differences by encouraging a cult of personality around himself and by complex power sharing. After his death, economic difficulties undermined the central government, and Yugoslavia dissolved into civil war.

In the late 1980s, the old ethnic differences came to the fore again in Yugoslav politics. Nationalist leaders—most notably Slobodan Milošević (b. 1941) in Serbia and Franjo Tudjman (1922–1999) in Croatia—gained authority. The Serbs contended that Serbia did not exercise sufficient influence in Yugoslavia and that Serbs living in Yugoslavia but outside Serbia encountered discrimination, especially from Croats. Ethnic tension and violence soon resulted. During the summer of 1991, in the wake of the changes in the former Soviet bloc nations, Slovenia and Croatia declared independence from the central Yugoslav government and were recognized by the European community.

From this point on, violence escalated. By June 1991, full-fledged war had erupted between Serbia and Croatia. At its core, however, the conflict was ethnic; as such, it highlights the potential for violent ethnic conflict within the former Soviet Union.

The conflict took a new turn in 1992 as Croatian and Serbian forces determined to divide Bosnia-Herzegovina. The Muslims in Bosnia—who had lived alongside Serbs and Croats for generations—soon became crushed between the opposing forces. The Serbs in particular, pursuing a policy called "ethnic cleansing," a euphemism redolent of some of the worst horrors of World War II, killed or forcibly moved many Bosnian Muslims.

The United Nations attempted unsuccessfully to mediate the conflict and imposed sanctions, which had little influence. But in 1995, NATO forces carried out strategic air strikes. Later that year, under the leadership of the United States, the leaders of the warring forces completed a peace agreement in Dayton, Ohio, which recognized an independent Bosnia. The terms of the agreement were enforced by the presence of NATO troops.

The situation in the former Yugoslavia remained dangerous and deadly. During 1997 and 1998, Serbia moved against ethnic Albanians living in its province of Kosovo. In 1999, NATO again undertook air strikes against Serbian forces, and forced Serbia to withdraw from Kosovo. In 2000, a popular revolution swept the nondemocratic government of Yugoslavia. In 2003, the two remaining Yugoslav republics, Serbia and Montenegro, each become autonomous.

MAP EXPLORATION

Interactive map: To explore this map further, go to
http://www.prenhall.com/craig/map32.3

MAP 32–3
Ethnic Composition in the Former Yugoslavia. The rapid changes in Eastern Europe during the close of the 1980s intensified long-standing ethnic tensions in the former Yugoslavia. This map shows where Yugoslavia's ethnic population lived in 1991, before internal conflicts escalated.

HOW DOES the Balkans conflict illustrate the importance of ethnic identity in the modern world?

CHALLENGES TO THE ATLANTIC ALLIANCE

After the collapse of the Soviet Union, NATO not only decided to continue, but it expanded its membership to include the Czech Republic, Hungary, and Poland. Its purpose, however, is now ill-defined. Having reluctantly undertaken to settle the civil war in the former Yugoslavia, NATO

WHAT PROBLEMS has Europe faced since the fall of Communism?

Terrorist Bombing, Madrid. Police search for clues from the debris of one of the trains destroyed in the terrorist attack of March 11, 2004.

AP/Wide World photos.

tried to become Europe's internal peacekeeper, but not all its members or the European public supported its assumption of this role.

NATO's uncertain mission and continental Europe's inward looking-tendency shaped reactions to the September 11, 2001, attack by al-Qaeda on the United States. Initially, Europeans deeply sympathized with Americans, but a significant split soon developed over President George W. Bush's response to the terrorist assault.

The September 11 attacks transformed American foreign policy, turning it into what Bush termed "a war on terrorism." In late 2001, the United States attacked and rapidly overthrew the Taliban government of Afghanistan. This destroyed some of al-Qaeda's bases, but not its leadership.

Following the Afghan campaign, the Bush administration asserted a policy of preemptive strikes to deal with potential enemies of the United States. The administration argued that the possibility that weapons of mass destruction (allegedly being developed in Iraq and elsewhere) might fall into the hands of terrorist organizations posed so severe a danger to the United States that it could not wait to respond to an attack but had to take strike first. This was a major departure from previous U.S. foreign policy, and it aroused considerable debate when the Bush administration acted on it by invading Iraq in 2003 (see Chapter 34). Some European governments (notably Bulgaria, Italy, Poland, Spain, and the United Kingdom) supported the move, but other traditional European allies of the United States (particularly, France and Germany) were opposed—as was most of the European public.

Terrorists have struck in Europe and have shown how al-Qaeda-sponsored attacks can influence European politics. On March 11, 2004, at least 190 people were killed in commuter train bombings in Madrid, Spain, and on July 7, 2005, more than fifty were killed by a similar attack in London. The Spanish attack occurred just before a general election. The Spanish government, which had supported the American invasion of Iraq, was voted from office and replaced by one that announced that it would withdraw troops from the conflict.

Profound divisions now exist between the United States and many of its historic postwar allies. Their future relationship will no doubt be determined by more than the issue of the Iraq war. The wider conflict between the West and radical political Islam may will be the factor that shapes the future of the Atlantic alliance, as was the division between a democractic West and a Communist Eastern block in the past.

SUMMARY

The Cold War U.S.–Soviet cooperation did not survive World War II. After 1945, Europe was divided into a Soviet-dominated zone in the East (the Warsaw Pact) and a U.S.-led zone in the West (NATO). U.S.–Soviet rivalry played itself out around the world from the 1950s to the 1980s, although gradually a spirit of détente arose between the two powers, especially under President Ronald Reagan and Soviet leader Mikhail Gorbachev. The Cold War ended with the collapse of Communist rule in Eastern Europe in 1989 and the disappearance of the Soviet Union in 1991.

Postwar European Society Since World War II, European society has been marked by a rise in prosperity and consumerism, more rights and opportunities for women, and moves toward political and economic unification symbolized by the adoption of a common currency, the euro, in 2002 and the publication of a draft constitution for a united Europe in 2003.

The United States The major themes in postwar American history were opposition to communism at home and abroad, the expansion of civil rights to African Americans, and economic prosperity. Politically, the relatively liberal years from the late 1950s through the 1970s were succeeded by a growing conservatism, especially under the presidencies of Ronald Reagan, George Bush, and George W. Bush. Even the Democratic President Bill Clinton was more a centrist than a liberal. After the terrorist attacks of September 11, 2001, the United States embarked on a war on terrorism that led to wars in Afghanistan and Iraq.

Eastern Europe The failure of the Communist regimes in Eastern Europe and the Soviet Union to produce economic prosperity or political liberalization led to their growing unpopularity. Soviet economic difficulties led Mikhail Gorbachev to institute liberal reforms that led to the collapse of the Communist rule first in Eastern Europe, then in the Soviet Union itself. The disappearance of the Soviet Union opened the way for independence in much of the former Soviet Empire. Russia itself has experienced social, economic, and political turmoil under presidents Boris Yeltsin and Vladimir Putin.

In the former Yugoslavia, the end of Communist rule led to dismemberment and civil war. In the 1990s, the NATO powers, led by the United States, intervened to halt the fighting and end a pattern of ethnic atrocities.

IMAGE KEY
for pages 794–795

a. A jazz record by Coleman Hawkins with an explicit civil rights message.

b. A Cuban missile site.

c. A huge euro symbol in a park in Frankfurt's banking district in Germany.

d. A teenager holds a Czech flag and a poster of president Vaclav Havel.

e. A piece of the Berlin Wall.

f. A construction worker building the Berlin Wall in 1961.

g. The European Union Headquarters in Brussels, Belgium.

h. Dr. Martin Luther King, Jr.

i. A toppled statue of Vladimir Lenin in the former Soviet Union.

j. A demonstration in Prague, Czechoslovakia.

REVIEW QUESTIONS

1. What were the causes of the Cold War? What was its effect on the foreign policies of the United States and the Soviet Union?

2. How did the outcome of World War II affect Europe's position in the world? What were the factors behind the movement toward European unification?

3. What were the most important developments in the domestic history of the United states in the last half of the 20th century?

4. What were the causes for the collapse of the Soviet Union? What problems has the collapse of Communist rule led to in Eastern Europe and elsewhere?

5. Why did the old Yugoslavia break apart and slide into civil war? How did the West respond to this crisis?

6. How did the American response to the attacks of September 11, 2001, affect relations with European allies? Why is the behavior of America's allies different now than it was during the Cold War?

KEY TERMS

Cold War (p. 796)
euro (p. 801)
European Economic Community (p. 801)

European Union (p. 801)
glasnost (p. 810)

Marshall Plan (p. 797)
perestroika (p. 810)

 For additional study resources for this chapter, go to:
www.prenhall.com/craig/chapter32

33 East Asia
The Recent Decades

CHAPTER HIGHLIGHTS

Japan The U.S.-led occupation after World War II established a democratic government and set Japan on the way to its remarkable postwar prosperity. By the twenty-first century, Japan had the second largest economy in the world. Politically, the conservative Liberal Democratic Party has remained dominant, despite occasional electoral losses. Socially Japan has remained stable with the world's highest longevity rate.

China Communist rule was established in 1949. Until his death in 1976, Mao Zedong remained in control of China. Mao broke with the Soviet Union in the 1950s and launched the disastrous Cultural Revolution in 1965. After his death, China opened its economy to free-market reforms. The result has been surging economic growth and rising prosperity. Politically, however, the Communist Party has blocked democratic reform, even using force in 1989 to crush prodemocratic demonstrations.

Taiwan The Nationalist Party set up a separate state in Taiwan under U.S. protection after their defeat in the Chinese civil war in 1949. Since then Taiwan has evolved into a prosperous democratic state. The Chinese government, however, insists that Taiwan is an integral part of China. The status of Taiwan could lead to conflict between the United States and China.

Korea The postwar occupation of Korea by the Soviets and the United States led to its division into the Communist state of North Korea and the pro-Western South Korea. This division survived the Korean War of 1950–1953. The prosperity of democratic South Korea contrasts with the poverty and hunger of North Korea. Although contacts between the two Koreas have increased, the North remains a closed society.

Vietnam From the end of World War II until the 1970s, Vietnam was almost continuously involved in war, first against the reimposition of French colonial rule, then against the United States and its South Vietnamese allies. North Vietnam's victory over the South in 1975 reunified the country, but Vietnam remains relatively poor, only slowly moving toward economic liberalization.

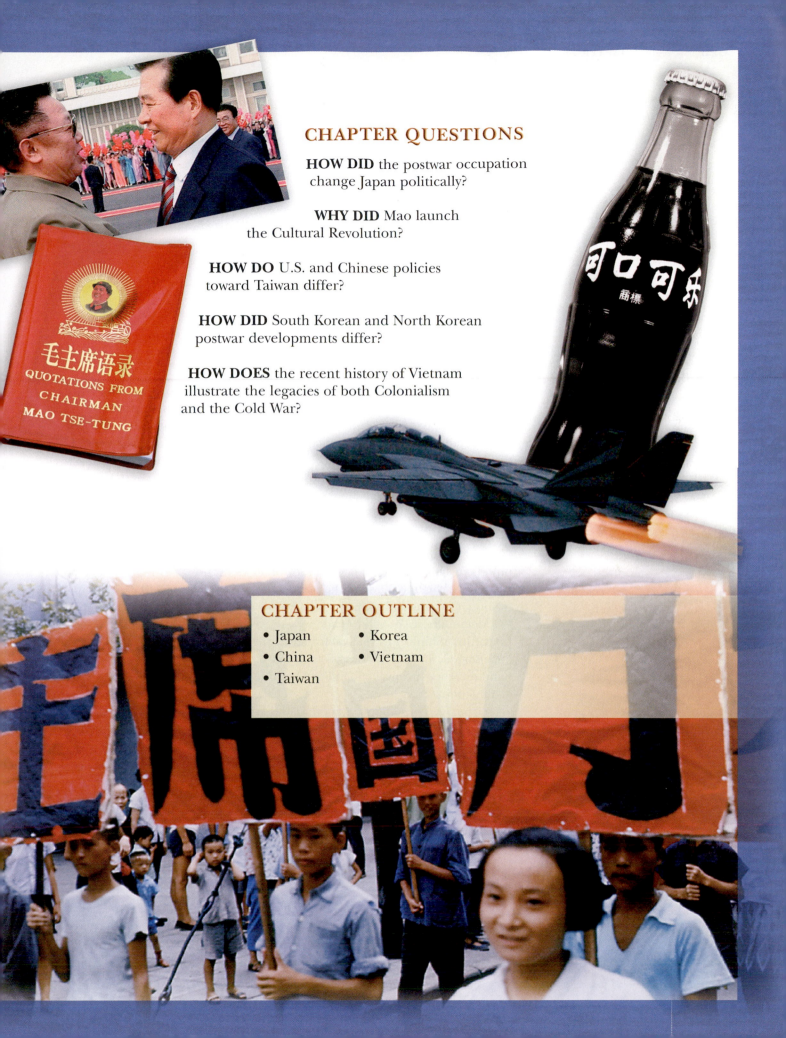

CHAPTER QUESTIONS

HOW DID the postwar occupation change Japan politically?

WHY DID Mao launch the Cultural Revolution?

HOW DO U.S. and Chinese policies toward Taiwan differ?

HOW DID South Korean and North Korean postwar developments differ?

HOW DOES the recent history of Vietnam illustrate the legacies of both Colonialism and the Cold War?

毛主席语录
QUOTATIONS FROM
CHAIRMAN
MAO TSE-TUNG

可口可乐
商標

CHAPTER OUTLINE

- Japan
- China
- Taiwan
- Korea
- Vietnam

The history of East Asia since the end of World War II can be divided into two phases (see Map 33–1). In the first phase, from 1945 to 1980, several East Asian nations became Communist but achieved only a small improvement in the conditions of their peoples. In stark contrast, the nations that used a mixture of state guidance and market-oriented economies made the region as a whole the most dynamic in the postwar world.

The second phase of postwar East Asian history began in the 1980s and continues to the present. During the 1980s, those nations that had prospered continued to grow. But during the 1990s, a recession rippled through East Asia and growth halted or slowed.

The most remarkable positive changes occurred in China, which, even while maintaining a Communist dictatorship, introduced many features of a market economy. The result was explosive growth and social change. Vietnam adopted a weaker version of the same policies. Only North Korea resisted the changes sweeping the rest of the Communist world, and as its entered the 21st century, its people suffered hunger and misery.

Japan

HOW DID the postwar occupation change Japan politically?

By early 1945, most Japanese were poor, hungry, and ill-clothed. Cities were burnt out, factories scarred by bombings; ships had been sunk, railways were dilapidated, and trucks and cars were scarce. On August 15, 1945, the emperor broadcast Japan's surrender to the Japanese people. They expected a harsh and vindictive occupation, but when they found it constructive, their receptivity to new democratic ideas and their repudiation of militarism led one Japanese writer to label the era "the second opening of Japan."

THE OCCUPATION

General Douglas MacArthur was the Supreme Commander for the Allied powers in Japan, and the occupation forces were mostly American. The chief concern of the first phase of the occupation was demilitarization and democratization. Civilians and soldiers abroad were returned to Japan and the military was demobilized. Wartime leaders were brought to trial for "crimes against humanity." Shinto was disestablished as the state religion, labor unions were encouraged, and the holding companies of **zaibatsu** combines were dissolved. Land reform expropriated landlord holdings and sold them to landless tenants at a fractional cost.

The new constitution, written by MacArthur's headquarters and passed into law by the Japanese Diet, fundamentally changed Japan's polity in five respects:

1. A British-style parliamentary state was established along with an American-style independent judiciary and a federal system of prefectures with elected governors.

2. Women were given the right to vote.

3. The rights to life, liberty, the pursuit of happiness, a free press, and free assembly were guaranteed.

4. Article 9, the no-war clause, stipulated, "The Japanese people forever renounce war as a sovereign right of the nation."

5. The constitution defined a new role for the emperor as "the symbol of the state deriving his position from the will of the people with whom resides sovereign power."

The Japanese people accepted the new constitution and embraced democracy with uncritical enthusiasm. To create a climate in which the new democracy

zaibatsu Groups of Japanese companies, or "trusts," that had a common ownership and dominated the economy of prewar Japan.

MAP 33–1
Contemporary Asia.

WHICH NATIONS in East Asia are Communist today?

could flourish, the occupation in its second phase turned to Japan's economic recovery. It dropped plans to deconcentrate big business further, encouraged the Japanese government to curb inflation, and cracked down on Communist unions. The United States also gave Japan $2 billion in economic aid.

The outbreak of the Korean War in 1950 diverted American military attention away from Japan, and the Japanese cabinet and Diet began to assume more responsibility for the country. When Japan regained its sovereignty in April 1952, the changeover was hardly noticeable in the daily life of the Japanese people. On the same day as the peace treaty, Japan signed a security treaty with the United

Japan Since 1945

1945	Japan surrenders
1946	Peace and security treaties
1948–1954	Yoshida ministries
1950–1953	Korean War
1955	Liberal and Democratic Parties merge
1955–1973	Double-digit economic growth
1972	Japan recognizes the People's Republic of China
1973–1989	Economic growth continues at slower pace
1991	Bubble bursts and recession begins
1991	Socialists lose Diet seats
1994–1996	Non-LDP coalitions govern; LDP-led coalitions reestablished
2001	Koizumi Junichir becomes prime minister
2003	Japan sends troops to Iraq

States, which became the cornerstone of Japan's minimalist defense policy.

PARLIAMENTARY POLITICS

Japan's postwar politics can be divided into three periods. The first, from 1945 to 1955, was the continuation of prewar party politics as modified to fit the new political environment. Two conservative parties, the Liberals and the Democrats, and the Japanese Socialist Party emerged. For most of this first decade, the Liberals held power.

In the long second period from 1955 to 1993, the Liberal Democratic Party (**LDP**), which was formed by a merger of the two conservative parties, held power and the Japanese Socialist Party was the permanent opposition.

The LDP became identified as the party that was rebuilding Japan and maintaining Japan's security through close ties with the United States. Despite the cozy relationships that developed between the LDP and business, periodic scandals, and a widespread distrust of politicians, the Japanese people voted to keep it in power. Rule by a single party for such a long period provided an unusual continuity in government policies.

A third era of politics began with the 1993 election. The notable feature of this era was the decline and fall of the left. The end of the Cold War and the worldwide rejection of Marxism contributed to the demise of socialism in Japan, and the Communist Party also slumped. The collapse of the left inaugurated an era of multiparty conservative politics, but the LDP remains the largest party. Japanese politics were plagued by scandals and factional strife during the 1990s, but the major issue was the economy. Concern for the economy has strengthened opposition to the LDP and raised the posibility that a two-party system might emerge as Japan's future.

ECONOMIC GROWTH

The extraordinary story of the economic rise of East Asia after World War II began with Japan. Several factors explain this growth. An infrastructure of banking, marketing, and manufacturing skills had carried over from prewar Japan. The international situation was also favorable: oil was cheap, access to raw materials and export markets was easy, and American sponsorship gained Japan early entry into international financing organizations. A tradition of frugality created a rate of savings close to 20 percent, which helped reinvestment.

A revolution in education contributed as well. By the early 1980s, almost all middle-school graduates went on to high school, and a rising percentage went on to higher education. By the early 1980s, Japan was graduating more engineers than the United States. (The annual output of law schools in the United States equals the total number of lawyers in Japan.) This upgrading of human capital and channeling of its best minds into productive careers let Japan tap the huge backlog of technology that had developed in the United States during and after the war years. After "improvement engineering," Japan sold its products to the world.

Another factor was an abundance of high-quality, cheap labor provided by a postwar baby boom. Workers quickly moved from agriculture to industry, and labor organizations proved no bar to economic growth. (In 2005, only about

LDP Liberal Democratic Party. A conservative party that has dominated postwar Japanese politics.

one-fifth of the labor force belonged to unions.) The government also aided manufacturers with tariff protection, foreign exchange, and special depreciation allowances. Industries engaged in advanced technologies benefited from cheap loans, subsidies, and research products of government laboratories. Critics who spoke of "Japan Inc." as though Japan were a single gigantic corporation overstated the case, but government was more supportive of business than it was regulative.

By 1973, the Japanese economy had become "mature." Double-digit growth gave way to 4 percent growth. Smokestack industries declined while service industries, pharmaceuticals, specialty chemicals, scientific equipment, computers, and robots grew. Japan's trade began to generate huge surpluses. The surpluses were generated mainly by the appetite of world markets for Japanese products, but they were also a result of protectionist policies that the United States and Europe insisted be abolished.

Even slower growth, or no growth at all, characterized the 1990s. Japanese had bid up the price of corporate shares and land to unrealistic levels, and in 1991, the "bubble" burst. As banks and individuals retrenched, the economy slowed. Unemployment rose from the usual 1.5 to more than 5 or 6 percent, and hidden unemployment was higher. Newspapers accused the government of inaction, but the scale of the problem was enormous. The Japanese were unwilling to shoulder new taxes and preferred instead to increase their savings. No political party dared propose new taxes or a bailout of the banks.

Some saw the recession as a necessary correction of speculative excesses and believed that Japan could export its way out of recession. While domestic consumption sank, exports rose, and Japan's favorable balance of trade grew. The Japanese excelled in quality and efficiency of production, and in 2002 an export-led recovery began. It was linked with the soaring Chinese economy.

At the start of the third millennium, Japan's economy was second only to the United States—slightly larger than the economies of the rest of Asia combined. Japan has achieved a European level of affluence through the peaceful development of human resources in a free society (see Figure 33–1).

Society and Culture

The triple engines of change in postwar Japan were occupation reforms, economic growth, and a rapid expansion of higher education. Together, they produced deep cultural strains and social dislocations. In 1945, almost half of the population lived in villages rooted in the past; half a century later most Japanese lived in cities, and a tiny portion of the population raised the food that fed the rest. In 1945, arranged marriages and three-generation extended families were common. Now, nuclear families and "love matches" are the rule. Consumerism increased, and the status of women rose. Reforms imposed during the American occupation gave women the right to vote, legal equality, and equal inheritance rights. As women were admitted to prestigious universities and embarked on careers, the average age of marriage rose and more wives worked outside the home. Divorce rates also tripled. Prospering in the new Japan

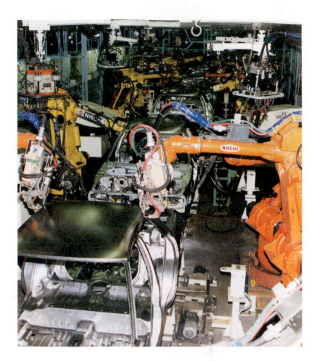

Nissan Motors Assembly Line. An almost completely automated assembly line at Nissan Motors' Zama factory is shown here. The high cost of labor in Japan makes such robot-intensive production economical.

Reuters/Susumu Takahashi/Archive Photos.

Figure 33-1

A Comparison of Japan with Germany and France in the Year 2005 (IMF Estimates)			
	GDP (in billions)	Population (in millions)	Per Capita GDP
Germany	$2,769	83	$33,575
France	$2,052	64	$33,111
Total	$4,821	147	$32,796 (average)
Japan	$4,759	127	$37,241

depended on education, and a rigorous system of examinations determined admission at every level. The enormous prewar gap between the tiny educated elite and the masses disappeared as 90 percent of Japanese came to see themselves as middle class. This fostered democracy and a new respect for personal autonomy helped diminish some traditional ethnic prejudices. The highly disciplined lifestyle encouraged by the educational system and corporate culture, however, created a phenomenon called *karoshi*, or death from overwork.

The most serious social problem facing Japan today is the aging of its population. By 2010, there will be fewer than two workers for every retired person. A recurring question is how the old will be supported and how they will vote in elections. All developed nations have experienced a comparable shift in demographics, but the imbalance is particularly severe in Germany, Italy, and Japan. Japan is crowded, and some see its current low birthrate as an opportunity to reduce population. Many illegal immigrants, however, come from other parts of Asia to take lowly jobs that the Japanese despise.

The cultural strains produced by Japan's rapid transformation have dislocated some people and created followings for new religions. One aberrant apocalyptic cult released nerve gas in a Tokyo subway in 1995. Yet traditions of lifetime employment, a low crime rate, stable families, and a flourishing artistic culture (which excels at Western as well as traditional Japanese arts) testify to Japan's remarkable success at recovering from the devastation of World War II.

JAPAN AND THE WORLD

Japan has three sets of critical international relationships. The first is with the world. On this front it defends the free trade on which its economy depends, but also excels as a donor of foreign aid. Its second relationship is with its neighbors in East Asia. For reasons of history and proximity, it is particularly sensitive to developments in China, Korea, the Russian Far East, and Taiwan. China's growing military strength is a concern. Japan's third critical relationship is with the United States. The two nations are major trading partners, and the security treaty concluded between them in 1952 is the cornerstone of Japan's defense planning. Japan, however, feels increasingly vulnerable in light of the nuclear arsenals of its neighbors, and should its trust in the U.S. "nuclear umbrella" waver, it would quickly become a nuclear power.

WHY DID Mao launch the Cultural Revolution?

CHINA

The story of China after 1949 is rooted in theories about economics and population. Marx rejected the Malthusian hypothesis that population growth tends to outstrip food production as a myth of capitalist societies, and Mao Zedong agreed and closed down the population studies institutes at China's universities. From 1949 until 1981, China's population increased from 550 million to nearly 1 billion. Growth in the Chinese economy was eaten up by all the new mouths, and in 1981 China adopted a policy of one child per family. Thereafter the increase slowed, but population exceeded 1.3 billion in 2005.

SOVIET PERIOD (1950–1960)

Civil war in China ended in 1949 as the last troops of Chiang Kai-shek (Jiang Jieshi) fled to Taiwan. The People's Republic of China was proclaimed in October. In the decade that followed, the Soviet model was adopted for the government, the army, the economy, and higher education.

Areas inhabited by Tibetans, Uighur Turks, Mongols, and other minorities were occupied by the Chinese army and settled by Chinese immigrants. Political consolidation then followed. The Communist Party held the key levers of power in the government, army, and security forces. Mao was chairman of the party and head of state. He ruled through the Politboro and a system of regional, provincial, and district committees with party cells in every village, factory, school, and government office. Party members were exhorted to enforce the local enactment of government policies. Economic reconstruction was attempted on a massive scale, with the help of the Soviet Union, which sent financial aid as well as engineers and planners.

Rural society underwent two fundamental changes: land redistribution and then collectivization. In the early 1950s, hundreds of thousands of landlords were killed and their holdings redistributed to the landless. Subsequently, all lands were seized by the state and collectivized.

During the early 1950s, intellectuals and universities also became a target for "thought reform," brainwashing. This involved study and indoctrination in Marxism, group pressures to produce an atmosphere of insecurity and fear, followed by confession, repentance, and reacceptance by society. The indoctrination was intended to strengthen party control and mobilize human energies on behalf of the state.

By the late 1950s, Mao was disappointed with the results of collectivization, and in 1958, he resorted to mass mobilization to unleash the productive energies of the people, a policy called the **Great Leap Forward**. Campaigns were organized to accomplish vast projects, and village-based collective farms gave way to communes of 30,000 persons or more. The results were disastrous. Between 1958 and 1962, 20 to 30 million Chinese reportedly starved to death. Policies were modified, but agricultural production continued to fall, plagued by the ills of low incentives and collective responsibility.

Sino-Soviet relations also deteriorated. Disputes arose over borders. China was dissatisfied with Soviet aid. The Soviet Union condemned the Great Leap Forward as "leftist fanaticism" and resented Mao's view of himself, after Stalin's death, as the foremost exponent of world communism. In 1960, the Soviet Union halted economic aid and withdrew its engineers from China. Each country deployed about a million troops along their mutual border. The Sino-Soviet split was arguably the single most important development in postwar international politics.

The years between 1960 and 1965 saw conflicting trends. The failure of the Great Leap Forward led some Chinese leaders to turn away from Mao's reckless radicalism toward more moderate policies. Mao remained head of the party but had to give up his post as head of state. Yet even as the government moved toward realistic goals and stable bureaucratic management, a new mass movement was begun to promote ideological indoctrination.

THE GREAT PROLETARIAN CULTURAL REVOLUTION (1965–1976)

In 1965, Mao again emerged to dominate Chinese politics. He feared that the Chinese revolution—his revolution—would end up as a Soviet-style bureaucratic

China Since 1949

1949	Communist victory; People's Republic of China
1950	Sino-Soviet alliance; China invaded Tibet
1953	First Five-Year Plan
1958	Great Leap Forward
1960–1963	Sino-Soviet split
1965–1976	Cultural Revolution
1972	Nixon visit to Beijing
1976	Mao Zedong dies
1978	Deng Xiaoping in power
1989	Tienanmen Square incident
1997	Deng Xiaoping dies
1998–2001	China's economy grows while rest of Asia in recession

Great Leap Forward Mao's disastrous attempt to modernize the Chinese economy in 1958.

Cultural Revolution. Participants in this march hold a banner of Mao Zedong.
Archive Photos.

Cultural Revolution Movement launched by Mao between 1965 and 1976 against the Soviet-style bureaucracy that had taken hold in China. It involved widespread disorder and violence.

communism run for the benefit of officials. So he called for a new revolution to create a truly egalitarian culture.

Obtaining army support, Mao urged students and teenagers to form bands of Red Guards to carry out a new **Cultural Revolution**. Mao's sayings, the "Little Red Book," assumed the status of scripture. Universities were shut down as student factions fought. Teachers were beaten, imprisoned, and humiliated. Books were burned and art destroyed. Homes were ransacked for foreign books and Chinese who had studied abroad were persecuted. Red Guards beat to death those viewed as reactionaries. High officials were purged. Chinese today recall these events as a species of mass hysteria that defies understanding.

Eventually Mao tired of the violence and near anarchy. In 1968 and 1969 he called in the army. Millions of students and intellectuals were sent to the countryside to work on farms. Worsening relations with the Soviet Union also made China's leaders desire greater stability at home. When President Richard Nixon proposed a renewal of ties, China responded. Nixon visited Beijing in 1972, opening a new era of diplomatic relations.

The second phase of the Cultural Revolution between 1969 and 1976 was moderate only in comparison with what had gone before. On farms and in factories, ideology was still substituted for economic incentives. Universities reopened, but students were admitted by class background, not examination. In 1971, the so-called Gang of Four, which included Mao's wife and was abetted by the aging Mao, came to power.

CHINA AFTER MAO

Political Developments   Mao's death in 1976 brought immediate changes. The Gang of Four and their radical supporters were arrested. In their place, Deng Xiaoping (1904–1997) emerged as the dominant figure in Chinese politics. Deng ousted his enemies, rehabilitated those purged during the Cultural Revolution, and put his supporters in power. After the lunacy of the Cultural Revolution, a "normal" Communist Party dictatorship was a relief. The people could now enjoy a measure of security and material improvement. There continued, however, a tension between the determination of the ruling party to maintain its grip on power and its desire to obtain the benefits of liberalization.

Universities returned to normal in 1977. Entrance examinations were reinstituted, purged teachers returned to their classrooms, and scholars were sent to study in Japan and the West. Students began to demand still greater freedoms with the hope that they would lead to political democracy.

The new spirit came to a head in April and May of 1989, when hundreds of thousands of students, workers, and people from all walks of life demonstrated for democracy in Tienanmen Square in Beijing and in dozens of other cities. The government sent in tanks and troops. Hundreds of students were killed, and leaders who did not escape abroad were jailed. The event defined the political climate in China for the decade that followed: freedom was allowed in most areas of life, but no challenge to Communist Party rule was tolerated.

Economic Growth In the economic sphere, China's leaders repudiated the policies of Mao. Deng's great achievement in the years after 1978 was to demonstrate in China the superiority of market incentives to central planning.

In China's villages, as the farm household became the basic unit of production, grain production rose. But when farmers living near cities found it more profitable to abandon grains in favor of speciality crops, the government worried about growing dependence on imported grains. In 2003, it established subsidies to promote grain production.

State-operated enterprises, which often ran at a loss and employed twice the labor needed to run them efficiently, were a constant drain on China's state-owned banks. As the free market sector grew faster, their share of production declined. Finally, the government announced that "state ownership" would give way to "public ownership." The costs of such privatization would be high—defaulted loans, bankruptcies, unemployed workers, and a sudden rise in pensioners, but the drain on the state budget would end. The contribution of state-owned enterprises to total industrial production declined from 40 to 31 percent from 1997 to 2003, but much of this was due to rapid growth in the market sector of the economy.

The main driver of the new economy was the free market sector. After 1980, the Chinese economy grew faster than any other Asian economy. Exports skyrocketed. New enterprises surged in special economic zones along the coasts, and the tide of enterprise swept inland. Yet in the hinterlands large regions lagged behind. To achieve growth, the government was willing to tolerate personal and regional inequities.

The factors that fueled this growth were clear: China used tariffs to shield its markets while making use of cheap labor to flood foreign markets with goods and build up its currency reserves–which in 2003 were second only to those of Japan. China joined the World Trade Organization in 2001; since then its protectionism has become less blatant.

Social Change During the Mao years, farmers had been tied to their collective or village. Cities were closed to those without residence permits. City dwellers were members of "units" that provided their members with jobs, housing, food, child care, medical services, and pensions. Party cadres exercised near total control over the unit's members. Block organizations reported any infractions of "socialist morality" to the authorities.

Under Deng, controls were loosened. The "unit" diminished in importance as food became widely available in free markets and apartments were sold to their inhabitants on easy terms. As workers with higher salaries began to provide for their own needs, life became freer and more enjoyable. The market economy placed a premium on individual decisions and initiatives.

The new prosperity and changing mores became increasingly evident. By the 1990s, Chinese designers were holding fashion shows in Shanghai and

Goddess of Democracy and Freedom. Student activists construct a "Goddess of Democracy and Freedom," taking the Statue of Liberty as their model. The goddess was in place in Tienanmen Square shortly before tanks drove students from the square in June 1989.

Reuters/Ed Nachtrieb/Archive Photos.

29.4
Deng Xiaoping, A Market Economy for Socialist Goals

Shanghai Street Scene. Bikers and cars move in separate lanes. New highrise buildings are in the background. Note the three-wheel bike transporting lumber in the foreground.

Jeff Greenberg/PhotoEdit.

Beijing. Young people associated freely. The "household treasures" of the 1960s, radios and bicycles, gave way to stoves and refrigerators, washing machines and color televisions. Motorbikes and privately owned cars competed in crowded streets with the flow of bicycles. Private restaurants opened, and travel for pleasure became commonplace. The awareness of most Chinese that their living standard has improved sharply over the past two decades shapes their attitudes.

But the new wealth was unevenly distributed. The more successful entrepreneurs bought houses, cars, microwaves, computers, and cell phones. They traveled abroad and sent their children to private schools. But many barely scraped by, and in the hinterlands, poverty and hardship remained the rule.

China and the World From the 1950s to the 1970s, China isolated itself from the rest of the world. The Sino-Soviet split defined its relations to the north, and the Cold War defined its relations with Japan, South Korea, Taiwan and the United States. It aided North Vietnam during America's Vietnam War, but then briefly invaded Vietnam. During the 1980s, trade ties with the non-Communist world led China to look outward and adopt more moderate policies. In the 1990s, foreign relations improved across the board. Relations with Russia became amicable, and China welcomed investment from Taiwan and South Korea. China also worked to improve ties with Southeast Asia.

China's relations with the United States were difficult. U.S. military alliances with Japan, South Korea, Taiwan, and the non-Communist nations of Southeast Asia were the main countervailing force to Chinese hegemony in the region, and China resented the U.S. presence in what it considered its sphere of influence. A new relationship began to be forged when President Nixon visited China in 1972. In 1979, the United States extended diplomatic recognition to China.

From the 1980s, trade with the United States was vital to China's economic growth, and it became more so during the 1990s as the rest of East Asia slipped into recession. Imbalance of trade between the two nations displeases the United States, as does Chinese piracy of U.S. movies, computer software, and CDs. The United States is also critical of Chinese human rights abuses, nuclear testing, and arms sales. Nonetheless, the United States hopes that a deeper Chinese engagement with the United States and the rest of the world will lead to better relations. A generational change in Chinese leadership took place when Hu Jintao became premier in 2003, but apart from a slightly more open style of governance, it is not clear what the change will mean (see "U.S. Foreign Policy: A Chinese Dissident's View").

HOW DO U.S. and Chinese policies toward Taiwan differ?

TAIWAN

Taiwan is a mountainous island less than a hundred miles off the coast of central China. A little larger than Massachusetts, it has a population of 22 million. Originally a remote and backward part of the Qing Empire, Taiwan became a Japanese colony in 1895. The Japanese colonial government suppressed opium and bandits, eradicated epidemic diseases, built roads and railroads, reformed the land system, and improved agriculture. It also introduced mass education and light industries.

HISTORY'S VOICES

U.S. FOREIGN POLICY: A CHINESE DISSIDENT'S VIEW

ei Jingsheng, a Chinese advocate of democratic rights, was deported to the United States in late 1997. A year later, in The New York Times *op-ed page essay, he criticized U.S. policy as pandering to Chinese tyranny.*

SHOULD U.S. foreign policy be used to promote human rights even in poor countries with cultural traditions different from the West? Or should the United States avoid interference in the domestic politics of other nations and aim primarily at furthering American economic and security goals? What can foreign policy achieve? Where should the balance be struck?

CHINA'S DIVERSIONARY TACTICS

One year ago, after 18 years in a Chinese prison, I was "released" and sent here. A Chinese official said that if I ever set foot in China again, I would immediately be returned to prison. . . .

The State Department, in a report last January, used my forced exile as evidence that China was taking "positive steps in human rights" and that "Chinese society continued to become more open." These "positive steps" led the United States and its allies to oppose condemnation of China at a meeting of the United Nations Commission on Human Rights in April. In the months that followed, President Clinton and other Western leaders traveled to China, trumpeting increased economic ties and muting criticism on human rights.

Thus, without fear of sanction, the Chinese Government intensified its repression in 1998. Once the leaders achieved their diplomatic victories, they turned to their main objective: the preservation of tyrannical power. This year, about 70 people are known to have been arrested. . . .

Li Peng, the speaker of the National People's Party Congress, declared recently, "If an organization's purpose is to promote a multiparty system in China and to negate the leadership prerogatives of the Chinese Communist Party, then it will not be permitted to exist."

This statement clearly shows that the Communist Party's primary objective is to sustain its tyranny, and to do so it must deny the people basic rights and freedoms. We must measure the leaders' progress on human rights not by the "release" of individuals but by the people's ability to speak, worship and assemble without official interference and persecution.

Source: Wei Jingsheng, *The New York Times*, 24 December 1998. Copyright © 1998 by *The New York Times*. Reprinted by permission.

Anticolonial feelings rose slowly, but the Taiwanese were happy to see the Japanese leave in 1945. Kuomintang (Guomindang) officials, however, looted the economy and ruled harshly. By the time Jiang Jieshi and 2 million other military and civilian mainlanders fled to the island in 1949, its economy and society were in disarray. Taiwanese hated their new rulers and even compared them unfavorably to the Japanese.

In the mid-1950s, order was restored, and rapid economic growth followed. By the late 1990s, Taiwan had the healthiest economy in recession-ridden Asia.

Taiwan's politics was authoritarian until Jiang Jieshi died in 1976. Taiwan then moved toward representative government. In 1987, martial law ended and opposition parties were permitted.

In 1996, Li Denghui, a native Taiwanese, was elected president in what was, as he put it, "the first free election in 5,000 years of Chinese history."

Since 1949, the Communist government in Beijing had claimed that Taiwan was a province of China controlled by a "bandit" government. It did not rule out taking Taiwan by force and refused diplomatic relations with any nation maintaining such ties with Taiwan. From the outbreak of the Korean War in 1950 until 1979, Taiwan was a protégé of the United States. In 1979, however, the United States broke off relations with Taipei and recognized Beijing as the sole government of a China that included Taiwan. But the United States continued to trade with Taiwan and to sell it arms, and curiously, it was during the years of diplomatic limbo after the 1979 break that Taiwan's economy grew and its society became democratic.

Both China and the United States are, at the start of the 21st century, apprehensive about Taiwan. China fears that a prosperous, democratic Taiwan would have legitimacy in the eyes of the world and no wish to rejoin the mainland. The United States fears that an increasingly powerful China might try to use military force to retake the island. Many in the U.S. Congress believe that the United States could not stand by and allow that to happen.

KOREA

*K*orea was annexed by Japan in 1910. The imposition of colonialism on a people with a high indigenous culture and a strong sense of national identity engendered a powerful anticolonial nationalism. After World War II, Korea was divided into a Communist north and a non-Communist south. When a civil war ensued, the United States entered the conflict to stem the spread of communism.

KOREA AS A JAPANESE COLONY

Japan introduced measures designed to make Korea into a model colony. A land survey and land tax reform clarified land ownership. Infectious diseases dropped, and the population grew from 14 million in 1910 to 24 million in 1940. Attendance at schools became widespread. New money was issued and banks established. A huge investment was made in roads, railways, telegraph lines, hydroelectric power, nitrogenous fertilizer plants, and mining. Koreans who studied at Japanese universities brought new knowledge back to Korea. By the 1930s a modern culture was forming in Korea's cities.

Being a Japanese colony was a hard road to modernity, for the colonial government was authoritarian. The government's goal was to make Korea a subordinate part of imperial Japan. Any benefits to the Koreans were incidental. Education was given in Japanese. In government, banking, or industry, Koreans were relegated to the lower echelons. The colonial regime suppressed all nationalist movements and political opposition. The police were brutal. Koreans were pressured to adopt Japanese names, drafted to fight in Japan's wars, and sent to labor in Japan. "Comfort women" were recruited, sometimes forcibly, to service Japanese troops. Only in recent years has this bitter colonial legacy begun to subside.

NORTH AND SOUTH

With Japan's defeat in 1945, U.S. forces occupied Korea south of the 38th parallel and Soviet troops occupied the north. Two separate states developed. In the south, the United States settled for the anti-Communist government of Syngman Rhee (1875–1965), a long-term nationalist leader whose party won the May 1948 election. Many of Rhee's officials and officers had served the Japanese. His government was strongly supported by conservative Koreans and those who had fled the north.

In the north, the Russians established a Communist government under Kim Il-Sung (1912–1994) in 1948 and withdrew its troops from North Korea—now the

HOW DID South Korean and North Korean postwar developments differ?

QUICK REVIEW

Two Koreas

- After defeat of Japan in 1945, U.S. troops occupied the south and Soviet troops occupied the north
- U.S. supported government of Syngman Rhee in south
- Soviets supported government of Kim Il-Sung in north

26.6
General Douglas MacArthur, Report to Congress, April 19, 1951: "Old Soldiers Never Die"

Democratic People's Republic of Korea. During 1949 and early 1950, the United States also withdrew most of its troops from the south, part of a general disengagement from continental Asia that followed the Communist victory in China.

CIVIL WAR AND U.S. INVOLVEMENT

On June 25, 1950, North Korea invaded the south. The North Korean leader had received Stalin's permission for the invasion and a promise from Mao to send Chinese troops if the United States entered the war. His plan was for a quick victory, but the United States saw the invasion as an act of aggression by world communism. It rushed troops from Japan to South Korea and obtained U.N. backing.

During the first months of the war, the unprepared American and South Korean forces were driven southward into a small area around Pusan (see Map 33–2). But then, amphibious units landed at Inchon and drove deep into North Korea. American policy shifted from containment of communism to a roll-back. China then sent in "volunteers" to rescue the beleaguered North Koreans and pushed the overextended U.N. forces back to a line close to the 38th parallel. The war ended with an armistice on July 27, 1953. Thereafter, the two Koreas maintained a hostile peace. The 142,000 American casualties made the war the fourth largest in U.S. history.

RECENT DEVELOPMENTS

North Korea remained a closed, authoritarian state with a planned economy. It stressed heavy industry, organized its farmers in collectives, and controlled education and the media. Shortages of food, clothing, and other necessities were chronic. The cult of personality surrounding "the great leader" Kim Il-Sung developed beyond that of even Stalin or Mao. His son, "the beloved leader" Kim Jong-il (b. 1942), succeeded his father in 1994—the only hereditary succession in a Communist state.

In South Korea, Rhee was forced to retire in 1960. There followed 27 years of rule by two generals, Park Chung-hee and Chun Doo-hwan. Their rule was semi-authoritarian: Opposition parties were legal and active but their leaders were often jailed. Park and Chun promoted economic growth. They supported business and expanded higher education, emphasizing science and technology. Labor was disciplined, hardworking, and cheap. The United States gave large amounts of aid and provided an open market for Korean exports. These factors produced double-digit growth. By the 1990s, South Korea had moved into the ranks of developed nations, and by 2005 it had become the world's 11th largest economy.

Industrialization and urbanization produced an affluent and educated middle class that resented authoritarian rule. In 1987, Chun's term ended, and a free election was held. Despite the fact that Chun's hand-picked successor, Roh Tae-woo, became president, most Koreans saw the election as an opening to democracy. This was confirmed four years later when Kim Young-sam, a moderate politician, was elected president, purged the generals who had supported Park and Chun, and launched investigations into his predecessors' finances. In 1995, Chun and Roh were sent to prison, but later released. Kim Dae-jung was elected

MAP 33–2
Korea, 1950–1953. This map indicates the major developments in the bitter three-year struggle that followed the North Korean invasion of South Korea in 1950.

WHY DID the Korean War end in stalemate?

The Two Kims. South Korean President Kim Dae-jung traveled to Pyongyong in June 2000 to promote his "sunshine policy." As he departs he hugs Kim Jong-il, the North Korean leader. But when the North Korean leader failed to respond with a visit to Seoul or with an easing of tensions, sunshine turned to rain, and Kim Dae-jung's popularity sagged.

Koren Pool/Yonhap/AP/Wide World Photos.

HOW DOES the recent history of Vietnam illustrate the legacies of both Colonialism and the Cold War?

27.7
Views of a Viet Cong Official
27.8
An American Prisoner of War

Viet Minh Communist-dominated popular front organization formed by Ho Chi Minh to establish an independent Vietnamese republic.

president in 1997, the first successful opposition candidate. He took office with high hopes but encountered insurmountable difficulties. As the economy sagged, the public became unsettled. Kim adoped a "sunshine policy" of openness, reconciliation, and material aid toward North Korea, an initiative that won him a Nobel Peace Prize in 1998. When North Korea failed to reciprocate, however, Kim's popularity declined.

In 2002, another opposition politician, Roh Moohyun, became president. In March 2004, the conservative majority party in the National Assembly voted to impeach him, but the public showed its disapproval in the April elections by giving Roh's party a majority of the assembly's seats. Returned to office, Roh was critical of the United States and open to closer relations with China and North Korea.

Since the Korean War, South Korea had been allied with the United States, which guaranteed its defense. North Korea was backed by the Soviet Union and China. But after the collapse of the Soviet Union, Russia lost interest in its ally, and China was drawn closer to South Korea for economic reasons.

North Korea, increasingly isolated, has a poor record. Its economy is in shambles, and its government has engaged in assassinations, conterfeiting, drug smuggling, and kidnapping. A Pakistan connection has enabled it to begin to develop nuclear weapons. China, Japan, South Korea, and the United States have tried to persuade North Korea to renounce nuclear arms, but as of 2004, the futures of negotiations and the North Korean state were unclear.

VIETNAM

THE COLONIAL BACKDROP

The Nguyen dynasty that reunited Vietnam in 1802 proved no match for France. France completed its conquest of Vietnam and Cambodia by 1883 and added Laos in 1893.

In many ways, Indochina was a classic case of colonialism: people of one race and culture, for the sake of economic benefits and national glory, controlling and exploiting a people of another race and culture in a far-off land. To obtain access to the country's natural resources, the French built harbors, roads, and a railway. They established rubber and tea plantations, introduced modern mining technology to extract coal, and built breweries, rice and paper mills, and glass and cement factories. Native workers were paid low wages. In the south, 3 percent of landowners owned 45 percent of the land and received 60 percent of the crop. Rice consumption by peasants declined. More than 80 percent of the population was illiterate.

Under the French, only clandestine opposition parties survived. The most skilled organizer of such parties was Ho Chi Minh (1892–1969), who founded the Indochinese Communist Party in 1930. Shortly before the outbreak of the Pacific War, the Japanese occupied Vietnam. Ho, who in 1941 had formed the **Viet Minh** (League for the Independence of Vietnam) as a popular front organization to resist the Japanese, proclaimed the Democratic Republic of Vietnam in 1945. Since then, the history of Vietnam can be seen in terms of three cycles of war followed by two decades of peace.

THE ANTICOLONIAL WAR

The first war lasted from 1946 to 1954. On one side was the Viet Minh, led by Ho. It was controlled by Communists but also included representatives of nationalist parties. On the other side were the French and their conservative Vietnamese allies. The French lost a major battle at Dien Bien Phu in 1954 and departed in defeat.

A conference at Geneva divided the country into a Communist north and a non-Communist south. In the south, Ngo Dinh Diem, a non-Communist nationalist, established the Republic of Vietnam.

THE VIETNAM WAR

The second cycle of war was from 1959 to 1975 and involved the United States. During the 1940s, the United States, which opposed colonialism, urged the French to reach an accommodation with Ho Chi Minh. But after the rise of Communist China, the United States came to see French actions in Vietnam as an attempt to stem the tide of communism. When the French withdrew, it supported Diem.

Fighting began with guerrilla warfare in the south and eventually became a full-scale war between the north and the south (see Map 33–3). The north received material aid from the Soviet Union and China. The south was supported by the United States, whose forces increased to more than half a million in 1969. Despite such massive assistance, South Vietnam—and the United States—lost the war. In January 1973, a ceasefire was arranged in Paris, and two months later the last U.S. troops left. Fighting then broke out anew between north and south; the South Vietnamese forces collapsed in 1975, and the country was reunited under the Hanoi government in the north. Saigon was renamed Ho Chi Minh City. Thousands of South Vietnamese were sent to labor camps or fled their homeland.

Many explanations have been offered for the loss of the war: South Vietnam was ethnically and religiously diverse and difficult to govern; its governments were often corrupt and enjoyed minimal support from their people; some Vietnamese viewed the United States, like France, as a colonial occupier; South Vietnam's armies did not fight as well as their opponents; and the jungle terrain of Vietnam blunted the technological edge of the American forces.

WAR WITH CAMBODIA

Vietnam's third cycle of war was with its neighbor, Cambodia. Pol Pot (1926–1998) and the Communist **Khmer Rouge** ("Red Cambodia") had come to power in 1975. His government evacuated cities and towns, abolished money and trade, banned Buddhism, and killed an estimated 1 million people, roughly 15 percent of the total population.

Clashes occurred between Khmer Rouge troops and Vietnamese troops along their common border. Historically, Vietnam was Cambodia's traditional enemy, as China was Vietnam's. In 1978, Vietnam occupied much of Cambodia, and the next year, Vietnam set up a puppet government. Most Cambodians

MAP EXPLORATION

Interactive map: To explore this map further, go to
http://www.prenhall.com/craig/map33.3

MAP 33–3

Vietnam and its Southeast Asian Neighbors. The map identifies important locations associated with the war in Vietnam.

WHICH NEIGHBORING countries were most affected by the Vietnam War?

Khmer Rouge Meaning "Red Cambodia." Radical Communist movement that ruled Cambodia from 1975 to 1978.

Genocide. A worker cleans a skull excavated from a mass grave in Cambodia. The Khmer Rouge, under Pol Pot, murdered about one-sixth of the Cambodian population. Doctors, teachers, and other educated people were especially targeted.

AP Wide World Photos.

accepted Vietnamese rule, for they feared Pol Pot more than they hated Vietnam. But Cambodia failed to completely suppress Pol Pot's guerilla forces.

In its international relations, the unified Vietnam of 1975 became an ally of the Soviet Union. Relations with China, never good, worsened. In 1979, China invaded four northern provinces. Vietnamese troops repelled the invaders, but losses were heavy on both sides. Border shellings and attacks continued for years thereafter.

RECENT DEVELOPMENTS

The collapse of the Soviet Union destroyed Vietnam's primary international relationship. Vietnam's leaders also became aware that victories in wars were hollow so long as their people remained destitute.

In 1989, Vietnam withdrew from its costly occupation of Cambodia. A United Nations–sponsored government representing contending Cambodian factions took charge. In 1997, a pro-Vietnamese Communist leader, Hun Sen, staged a coup and took over. His position was strengthened when Pol Pot died in 1998 and the Khmer Rouge collapsed.

By the mid-1990s, Vietnam's relations with China had improved. In 1995, Vietnam joined ASEAN (Association of Southeast Asian Nations), reestablished diplomatic relations with the United States, and moved toward "normal" relations with the rest of the world.

At home, the Communist Party-dominated government monopolized political power, controlled the army, police, and media, and supported a large sector of state-run industries. But it also encouraged the growth of a market economy, and the production of consumer goods grew. Between 1991 and 1996, the economy achieved an average growth of more than 8 percent and received more offers of foreign investment than it could absorb. By 1996, shops in Vietnam were full of food and goods, when only 10 years earlier there had been famine in some areas. Much of the credit for this belongs to the liberal, pluralistic, cosmopolitan south.

But all was not rosy. The economy grew, but so did population. With 82 million people, Vietnam is one of the world's most densely populated nations. A high percentage of labor was agricultural, and in the countryside barter was not uncommon. The gap in the standard of living between urban and rural Vietnamese also increased. Foreign investors were drawn to Vietnam by cheap labor but were put off by the shortages, delays, red tape, and financial bottlenecks they encountered.

SUMMARY

Japan The U.S.-led occupation after World War II established a democratic government and set Japan on the way to its remarkable postwar prosperity. By the 21st century, Japan had the second largest economy in the world. Socially, Japan has remained stable and healthy with the world's highest longevity rate.

China Communist rule was established in 1949. Until his death in 1976, Mao Zedong remained in control of China. Mao broke with the Soviet Union in the 1950s and launched the disastrous Cultural Revolution in 1965. After his death, China opened its economy to free-market reforms. The result has been surging economic growth and rising prosperity. Politically, however, the Communist Party has blocked democratic reform, even using force in 1989 to crush pro-democratic demonstrations.

Taiwan The Nationalist Chinese set up a separate state in Taiwan under U.S. protection after their defeat in the Chinese civil war in 1949. Since then Taiwan has evolved into a prosperous democratic state. The Chinese government, however, insists that Taiwan is an integral part of China. The future of Taiwan could lead to conflict between the United States and China.

Korea The postwar occupation of Korea by the Soviets and the United States led to its division into the Communist state of North Korea and the pro-Western South Korea. This division survived the Korean War of 1950–1953. The prosperity of democratic South Korea contrasts with the poverty and hunger of North Korea. Although contacts between the two Koreas have increased, the North remains suspicious and largely closed to the world.

Vietnam From the end of World War II until the 1970s, Vietnam was almost continuously involved in war, first against the reimposition of French colonial rule, then against the United States and its South Vietnamese allies. North Vietnam's victory over South Vietnam in 1975 reunified the country, but Vietnam remains poor and the communist government has resisted political or economic liberalization.

IMAGE KEY
for pages 818–819

a. Cover of a Japanese comic book.

b. A highway interchange and bridge over the Huangpu River in Shanghai, China.

c. A North Korean national meeting to commemorate the 91st birthday of late-president Kim Il-Sung.

d. South Korean president Kim Dae-jung, right, and North Korean leader Kim Jong Il.

e. Mao Zedong's little red book.

f. A prototype of a bottle for selling Coca-Cola in China.

g. An American-built F-14 Tomcat.

h. Young Chinese children march in the streets while carrying red banners during the Cultural Revolution.

REVIEW QUESTIONS

1. Is postwar Japan better understood in terms of a return to the liberalism of the 1920s, or as a fresh start based on occupation reforms? Why did the occupation of Japan go so smoothly and the recent American occupation of Iraq so poorly?

2. Is China after 1949 better understood as an outgrowth of its earlier history or in the context of a comparison with the Soviet Union and other Communist states?

3. What background factors shaped Korea and Vietnam in the period after World War II? How did the Cold War affect these countries?

KEY TERMS

Cultural Revolution (p. 826)   **Khmer Rouge** (p. 833)   **Viet Minh** (p. 832)
Great Leap Forward (p. 825)   **LDP** (p. 822)   *zaibatsu* (p. 820)

 For additional study resources for this chapter, go to:
www.prenhall.com/craig/chapter33

34 Postcolonialism and Beyond: Latin America, Africa, Asia, and the Middle East

CHAPTER HIGHLIGHTS

The Postcolonial World Since 1945 the European colonial empires have disappeared from Africa and Asia and have been replaced by a multitude of independent states. These states have had to adjust their political and economic relations first to one or other of the superpowers during the Cold War and then, since the disappearance of the Soviet Union, to the West.

Latin America Most Latin American countries remain politically and economically dependent on the United States. Except in Cuba, no revolutionary movement has been able to overturn the traditional structure of Latin American society. Despite social and economic problems, Argentina and Brazil have managed to move from military rule to stable, democratic, civilian government.

Africa Independent Africa has faced severe problems: overpopulation, poverty, the absence of an educated middle class, tribal and class conflict, arbitrary boundaries, disease, economic dependence, and political instability. The challenge for Africa as a whole is to build a truly civil society and achieve economic health and political stability.

The Middle East Oil and the Muslim reaction to the creation of the state of Israel have dominated the history of the Middle East since the 1940s. While the possession of vast deposits of oil has made some Middle Eastern governments wealthy, it has not led to the creation of prosperous democratic societies. The existence of Israel has inflamed the Middle East for more than five decades. Although peace efforts have made some progress, the cycle of terror and retaliatory violence has persisted, and it is unclear whether a viable Palestinian state can be created.

Political Islamism, although not a monolithic movement, has proved increasingly disruptive to the region and the entire world.

In the wake of the terrorist attacks of September 11, 2001, the United States finds itself increasingly embroiled in a chaotic and unstable region of the world.

CHAPTER QUESTIONS

WHAT ARE the two main developments that have occurred in the postcolonial world since 1945?

WHERE IN Latin America did the major attempts to establish revolutionary governments occur?

WHAT ARE the most serious problems that Africa faces in the twenty-first century?

HOW DID the creation of the state of Israel affect the history of the modern Middle East?

HOW HAS the growth of Hindu nationalism affected Indian politics?

CHAPTER OUTLINE

- Beyond the Postcolonial Era
- Latin America Since 1945
- Postcolonial Africa
- Central, South, and Southeast Asia
- The Postcolonial Middle East

The last half of the 20th century saw Europe eclipsed by the rise of the two superpowers—the United States and the Soviet Union—and then witnessed the collapse of the latter (see Chapter 32). The same era witnessed the end of the age of Western colonialism, challenges to European and superpower imperialism, and the emergence of new nations in Africa and Asia.

Two developments in non-Western regions have major implications for the future. East Asia, Japan, and China have emerged as major political and economic powers. Radical Islamic movements present a political and military challenge across much of the globe. The period of colonialism that began in earnest in the 17th century was a relatively brief episode in world history. The last significant colonial holdings were given their independence in the 1960s, but the legacies of colonialism—positive as well as negative—continue to have major impacts.

BEYOND THE POSTCOLONIAL ERA

It could be argued that with the passing of **apartheid** in South Africa, the postcolonial era has also ended. What we shall witness in the future are waves of economic growth, such as that of the early 1990s in much of East Asia; the forging of dramatic new political alignments, both regional and transregional; internal struggles in country after country to build political systems that allow the development of civil society and limit the destructive domination of oligarchic or dictatorial regimes; and, most dramatically, the determination of radical Islam to confront Western and, in particular, American influences.

Since 1945, two distinct developments have occurred in the postcolonial world. The first—in a process that is generally termed *decolonization*—was the emergence of the various parts of Africa and Asia from the direct administration of foreign powers (see Map 34–1). The second was the organization of those previous colonial dependencies as independent states with greater or lesser degrees of stability.

The latter phase has gone through four stages: the influence of Cold War rivalries on the new states, the economic effects of **globalization**, progress in the spread of the ideals of civil society and participatory government, and finally a resurgence of cultural and religious traditions. This may lead to a **clash of civilizations**, a bloody assertion of ethnic and cultural chauvinism, or the discovery of common values and concerns that leads to the emergence of a more nuanced view of the world as a domain in which diverse peoples learn to get along.

LATIN AMERICA SINCE 1945

During the last half century, the nations of Latin America have experienced divergent paths of political and economic change. Their leaders have tried to alleviate their people's dependence on the more developed nations. At best, these efforts have had mixed results; at worst, they have led to repression and tragedy.

Before World War II, the states of Latin America had been economically dependent on the United States and Western Europe. Beginning in the 1950s, Latin America became an arena for confrontations between the United States and the Soviet Union.

During this era attempts were made to expand the industrial base and agricultural production of the various national economies.

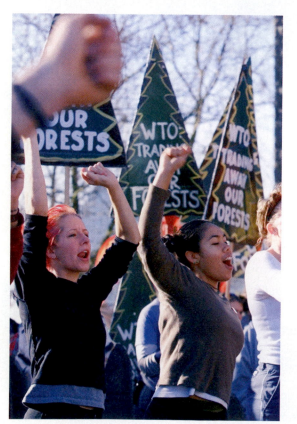

WHAT ARE the two main developments that have occurred in the postcolonial world since 1945?

Protest. The globalization of the world economy has sparked hostile political reaction. Numerous groups demonstrate at the World Trade Organization meetings to protest the development of previously untouched parts of the world, which they claim causes environmental damage and expanded wealth for the developed nations and unemployment and poverty elsewhere.
AP Wide World Photos.

MAP EXPLORATION

Interactive map: To explore this map further, go to **http://www.prenhall.com/craig/map34.1**

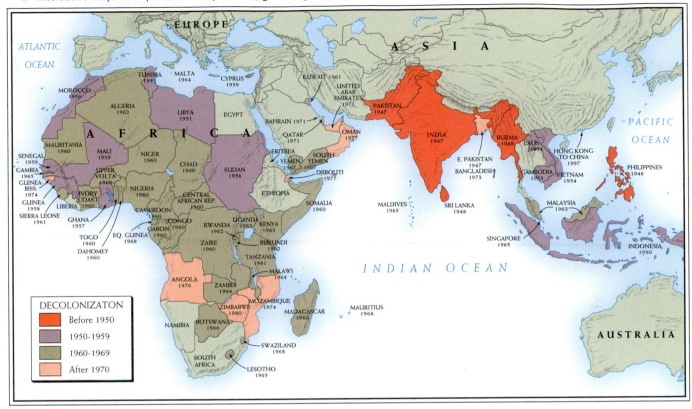

MAP 34–1
Decolonization Since World War II.   The Western powers' rapid retreat from imperialism after World War II is graphically shown on this outline map covering half the globe, from West Africa to the Southwest Pacific.

HOW ARE the effects of colonialism still present in Africa and Asia today?

Financing came from U.S. and Western European banks or from Soviet subsidies. Enormous debts were contracted that made Latin American economies virtual prisoners to the fluctuations of world interest rates and international banks or to Soviet subsidies. These new relationships, however, did not alter the underlying character of most Latin American economies, which remain exporters of agricultural commodities and mineral resources. Since the 1970s, Latin America has also shipped massive amounts of cocaine to the United States and Europe. This has led to political turmoil and civil war in Columbia.

A culture of poverty continues to be the most dominant social characteristic of the area. Migration into the cities from the countryside has caused urban overcrowding and slums inhabited by the desperately poor. The standards of health and nutrition have often fallen. The growth of service industries in the cities has also fostered the emergence of a professional, educated middle class that often wants to imitate the lifestyle of their social counterparts in the United States and Western Europe. This new professional middle class has displayed little taste for radical politics, social reform, or revolution. They and the more traditional elites were willing, especially during the 1960s and 1970s, to support military governments pledged to maintain the status quo.

Political events in Latin America led to the establishment of authoritarian governments of both the left and the right and to a retreat from the model of

WHERE IN Latin America did the major attempts to establish revolutionary governments occur?

apartheid "Apartness." Term referring to racist policies enforced by the White-dominated regime that existed in South Africa from 1948 to 1992.

globalization Term used to describe the increasing economic and cultural interdependence of societies around the world.

clash of civilizations Political theory, most often identified with Harvard political scientist Samuel P. Huntington, which contends that conflict between the world's religio-cultural traditions or "civilizations" increasingly dominates world affairs.

parliamentary democracy. Only Mexico, Colombia, Venezuela, and Costa Rica remained parliamentary states throughout this period. Elsewhere, two paths of political development were followed. In Cuba and Nicaragua, and briefly in Chile, revolutionary Socialist governments with close ties to the Soviet Union were established. Elsewhere, often in response to the fear of revolution or communism, military governments held power, sometimes punctuated with brief interludes of civilian rule. Such were the situations in Argentina, Bolivia, Brazil, Chile, Peru, and Uruguay. Governments of both the left and the right engaged in political repression.

These political changes fostered new roles for the military and the Roman Catholic Church. Latin American armies have played key political roles since the wars of independence. But since World War II, they have frequently assumed the direct government of nations rather than using indirect influence. Many Roman Catholic priests and bishops have protested inequalities and attacked political repression. Certain Roman Catholic theologians have combined traditional Christian concern for the poor with Marxist ideology to formulate what is called a **liberation theology**. This Latin American theological initiative has been attacked by the Vatican.

Since the 1980s, Latin America has changed significantly. Several nations have moved toward democratization and free-market economies. This marks a sharp departure from the 1930s and 1940s, when the state itself was seen as largely responsible for economic development. Yet in most nations, the military keeps a watchful eye on democratic developments and possible disorder. The end of the Cold War brought to a close one source of external political challenge, but the internal social problems of these nations continue to raise difficulties for their governments. In several nations, drug-producing cartels have challenged the authority of governments themselves.

REVOLUTIONARY CHALLENGES

There were four major attempts among the nations of Latin America to establish revolutionary governments pursuing major social and economic change. They occurred in Cuba in 1959, in Chile in 1970, in Nicaragua in 1979, and in Peru in the 1980s. Each involved a Marxist political organization, and each, with the exception of the Shining Path revolutionary movement in Peru, sought a close relationship with the Soviet Union. The establishment of these governments provoked active resistance by the United States and opposition to social and political change from traditional elites across Latin America.

The Cuban Revolution   Cuba had remained a colony until the Spanish-American War of 1898. Thereafter, it achieved independence within a sphere of U.S. influence that took the form of economic domination and military intervention. The governments of the island were ineffective and corrupt. During the 1950s, Fulgencio Batista (1901–1973), a dictator supported by the United States, ruled Cuba.

Historically, Cuba had been politically restive. On July 26, 1953, Fidel Castro Ruz (b. 1926), the son of a wealthy landowner, his close associate, Ernesto Che Guevara, and others attacked a government army barracks. The revolutionary movement that he thereafter came to lead in exile took its name from that date: the Twenty-Sixth of July Movement. In 1956, Castro and a handful of followers landed in Cuba. They took refuge in the Sierra Maestra mountains and attacked Batista's forces. Batista fled Cuba on New Year's Day in 1959. In January, Castro arrived in Havana as the revolutionary victor.

liberation theology Effort by certain Roman Catholic theologians to combine Marxism with traditional Christian concern for the poor.

Castro undertook the most extensive political, economic, and social reconstruction seen in recent Latin American history. He rejected parliamentary democracy and governed Cuba in an authoritarian manner. The revolutionary government carried out major land redistribution. Both small landowners and large state farms were established.

The Cuban Revolution spurned an industrial economic model and concentrated on the agricultural sector. Sugar preserved its leading role, and the Cuban economy remained monocultural. The sugar industry depended on large Soviet subsidies and on the Soviet-bloc nations for its market. In that respect, the Cuban economy did not escape the cycle of external dependence.

In foreign affairs, the Cuban Revolution was characterized by a sharp break with the United States and a close relationship with the Soviet Union. Castro aligned himself with the Cuban Communist Party and with the Soviet bloc. The United States was hostile toward Castro and toward the presence of a Communist state less than a hundred miles from Florida. In 1961, the United States and Cuban exiles launched the unsuccessful Bay of Pigs invasion. The close Cuban relationship to the Soviet Union led to the missile crisis of 1962, the most dangerous incident of the Cold War. In the late 1970s and the 1980s, a dialogue of sorts was undertaken between Cuba and the United States, but mutual distrust continues.

Fidel Castro. The Cuban dictator is shown here waving to cheering crowds acknowledging his triumph over the Batista regime on January 1, 1959.
UPI/Corbls-Bettmann.

With the collapse of the Soviet Union and the end of the Cold War, the future of Castro's Cuba has become uncertain. Cuba remains the only state closely associated with the former Soviet bloc that has not experienced political or economic reform. Subsidies that flowed from the Soviet Union to support the Cuban economy, however, have ended, creating a shortage of consumer goods. The Marxist political and economic ideology stands discredited throughout the world, but the aging Castro's leadership remains intact. Cuba must confront the need for a successor to Castro. It also must confront the need for economic reform and find a new role in a Latin American order in which the issues of the Cold War are no longer relevant. One hint of new direction came in 1998 when the Castro government permitted a highly publicized visit from Pope John Paul II.

Throughout the Cold War, Cuba assumed an importance far greater than its size might suggest. After 1959, it served as a center for the export of Communist revolution and it sent troops to Angola in the late 1970s. The U.S. government sought to prevent the establishment of a second Cuba in Latin America. That goal led to intervention in other revolutionary situations and to support for authoritarian governments in Latin America.

Chile   Until the 1970s, Chile was the most enduring model of parliamentary democracy in Latin America. During the 1960s, however, Chilean politics became polarized. Unemployment rose at an alarmic rate. There was labor unrest and popular resentment of the economic domination of Chile by large U.S. corporations.

The situation came to a head in 1970 when Salvador Allende (1908–1973), the candidate of the left-wing political coalition and a Marxist, was elected president. His coalition did not control the Chilean congress, nor did it have the support of the military. The center and right-wing political groups took a watch-and-wait attitude. Allende nationalized some businesses. Other policies were blocked in the congress, and Allende had to govern by decree. By this device he began to expropriate foreign property, much of which belonged to U.S. corporations. This policy frightened the Chilean owners of small and medium-sized businesses, but did not satisfy workers. Inflation ballooned. Harvests were poor.

In the autumn of 1973, Allende found himself governing a nation in turmoil without significant domestic political support and with many foreign enemies. He proved unwilling to make political compromises or to change his policies. The army became hostile. The government of the United States was disturbed by the prospect of a Marxist nation on the western coast of South America. The Nixon administration supported the discontent within the Chilean army. In mid-September 1973, an army coup overthrew Allende, who was killed in the presidential palace.

Thereafter, for 15 years Chile was governed by a military junta under General Augusto Pinochet (b. 1915). The military government pursued a close relationship with the United States and resisted Marxism in the hemisphere. It established a state-directed free-market economy and reversed the expropriations of the Allende years. There was also harsh political repression.

In a referendum held in late 1988, Chileans rejected Pinochet's bid for another term as president. Democratization was relatively smooth. Civilian rule has included efforts to investigate the political repression of the Pinochet years. Thousands of cases of torture and murder have been revealed. The Chilean government itself moved slowly, not wishing to revisit the most controversial era of the nation's history. In 1999, while Pinochet was visiting Great Britain, Spain indicted him and sought his extradition to stand trial for the disappearance of Spanish citizens under his rule. He was arrested, but ultimately returned to Chile, where he was judged too sick to stand trial.

The Sandinista Revolution in Nicaragua In the summer of 1979, a Marxist guerrilla force, the **Sandinistas**, overthrew the corrupt dictatorship of the Somoza family in Nicaragua. The Somozas had governed Nicaragua as their personal preserve since the 1930s with support from the United States. The Sandinistas established a collective government that pursued social and economic reform and reconstruction. The movement—with Roman Catholic priests on its leadership council—epitomized the new political and social forces in Latin America. However, the revolutionary government confronted significant domestic political opposition and military challenge from the contra guerrilla movement.

The government of the United States, particularly under the Reagan administration (1981–1989), was hostile toward the Sandinistas. America provided both direct and indirect aid to the opposition guerrillas. The U.S. government feared the spread of Marxist revolutionary activity in Central America, a fear reinforced by the close ties between the revolutionary government and the Soviet Union. For the United States, the Sandinista government represented in Central America a problem analogous to that of Cuba a generation earlier.

Sandinista rule came to a relatively quick end. In early 1990, after a negotiated peace settlement with the contras, they lost the presidential election to an opposition coalition and relinquished power peacefully.

PURSUIT OF STABILITY UNDER THREAT OF REVOLUTION

Argentina In 1955, the Argentine army revolted against the Perón dictatorship and Juan Perón (1895–1974) went into exile. Two decades of economic stagnation and social unrest followed. In 1973, Perón was recalled from exile in a desperate attempt to restore stability, but died about a year later.

Sandinistas Marxist guerrilla force that overthrew the Somoza dictatorship in Nicaragua in 1979.

By 1976, the army had undertaken direct rule. There was widespread repression; thousands of citizens disappeared, never to be heard of again. In April 1982, General Leopoldo Galtieri (b. 1926) launched a disastrous invasion of the Islas Malvinas (Falkland Islands). Argentina was defeated by Britain, and the military junta discredited.

In 1983 civilian rule was restored, and Argentina set out on the road to democratization. Under President Raul Alfonsín (b. 1927), many of the former military figures responsible for the years of repression received prison sentences. Alfonsín also sought more real political authority for the Argentine congress. Argentina has provided the most extensive example in Latin America of the restoration of democratic practices after military rule. Peaceful elections and transitions of governments have occurred for two decades despite serious economic difficulties. In 2001, however, it became clear that Argentina would be unable to repay its foreign debts, and rising unemployment, a currency devaluation, and drastic cuts in basic government services have subsequently led to political turmoil.

Brazil   In 1964, the military assumed the direct government of Brazil and did not fully relinquish it until the mid-1980s. The military government stressed order and used repression to maintain it. The army itself, however, was divided. Many officers were concerned that the corruption of everyday politics would undermine the army's reputation and esprit de corps. Consequently, within the army itself, certain forces sought to restore a more democratic government. In 1985, civilian government returned under the military's watchful eye.

The military government fostered denationalized industrial development. Non-Brazilian corporations were invited to spearhead the drive toward industrialization. Brazil opted for an industrialism guided and dominated from the outside. One result was a massive foreign debt, the servicing and repayment of which have become perhaps Brazil's most important national problem. Brazil also became the major industrialized nation in Latin America. Its industrialization, however, was guided and dominated from outside and led to the accumulation of a massive foreign debt that now constitutes Brazil's most important national problem. Industrialization has also had a huge impact on the Brazilian rain forest. By 1998, large landowners, encouraged by subsidies and tax incentives, had cleared 12 percent of Brazil's rain forest.

The question now is how the social changes wrought by industrialism, such as growing urbanization, will receive political accommodation. In Brazil, as in Argentina, economic and social pressures have spawned conditions ripe for political agitation. It was just that possibility that led both the traditional and the new professional elites to support authoritarian government in the past.

In 1990, Fernando Collor de Mello was elected president. He advocated privatization and allowing market forces to stimulate growth. In 1992, however, he was impeached on charges of corruption. In 1995, Fernando Henrique Cardoso won the presidency and pursued economic policies devised by technocrats, who hoped to achieve economic growth with stability. By 2003, however, Brazil's economy had slowed sharply, and in that year Luiz Inácio Lula da Silva became the first person from a working-class background to be elected Brazil's president. He has attempted to combine socialist concern for social services with an austere economic policy.

Mexico   Institutionally, Mexico has undergone few political changes since World War II. In theory, the government continued to pursue the goals of the revolution. Power remained in the control of the Partido Revolucionario Institucional (PRI).

Zapatistas. Named after the revolutionary hero Emiliano Zapata (depicted on the banner), the Zapatistas demanded rights for the impoverished Native American population of Mexico, especially in the southern state of Chiapas where this photograph was taken in 1997.

AP/Wide World Photos.

Yet shifts had occurred under this apparently stable surface. The government retreated from some of the aims of the revolution and appeared conservative when compared to Marxist states. In the early 1950s, certain large landowners were exempted from the expropriation and redistribution of land. The Mexican government maintained relations with Cuba and the other revolutionary regimes of Latin America but also resisted Marxist doctrines in Mexico. When necessary, it arrested malcontents.

Mexico experienced an oil boom from 1977 to 1983, but the world oil glut burst that bubble. The aftermath revealed the absence of stable growth. Like so many other states in the region, Mexico amassed large foreign debts and thus surrendered real economic independence.

In 1988, the PRI encountered a challenge at the polls. Opposition candidates received much of the vote in a hotly contested election. The PRI remained in power but with the knowledge that it would not be able to dominate the political scene as it had done. Thereafter, the leadership began to decentralize the party. President Carlos Salinas moved to privatize economic enterprise. He also favored free-trade agreements. The most important of these was the North American Free Trade Agreement (NAFTA), which created a vast free-trade area including Mexico, Canada, and the United States. In 1991, Salinas made new accommodations with the Roman Catholic Church, thus moving away from the traditional anticlericalism of Mexican politics. By 1991, the PRI appeared to have regained its former political ascendancy.

However, in 1994 Mexico underwent political shocks. Troops had to quell armed rebellion in Chiapas. During the election that year, the leading candidate was assassinated and party members were charged with complicity in the deed. Party corruption received increased publicity. Early in 1995, Mexico suffered a major economic downturn, and only loans from the United States saved the economy. Ernesto Zedillo, elected president in 1994, blamed Salinas and his family for the situation, and the corruption of the Salinas government became public. The government faced further unrest in Chiapas, growing power among drug lords, and turmoil within the governing party itself. In 2000, the PRI lost the election for the presidency, though it has remained the most powerful party in the Mexican legislature.

CONTINUITY AND CHANGE IN RECENT LATIN AMERICAN HISTORY

The most striking feature about the history of the past four decades in Latin America is its tragic continuity with the region's previous history. Revolution has brought moderate social change, but at the price of authoritarian government, economic stagnation, and dependence on foreign powers. Real independence has not been achieved. Throughout the region for much of the period, parliamentary democracy has been fragile; it was the first element of national life to be sacrificed to the conflicting goals of socialism, economic growth, or resistance to revolution.

Recent trends toward democratization and market economics may, however, mark a break in that pattern. The region could enjoy healthy economic growth if inflation can be contained and investment fostered. The challenge will be to see that the fruits of any new prosperity are shared in a way that prevents resentment and turmoil. Furthermore, as in the past, economic turmoil far from Latin America may harm it. Each time such turmoil has occurred, the governments of Latin America, like the current government of Mexico, have found themselves economically dependent on either the United States or Europe.

POSTCOLONIAL AFRICA

owhere is the dramatic continuity between often arbitrary colonial territories and emergent independent states clearer than in Africa. Most of its modern nations are direct inheritors of their colonial predecessors' boundaries, and the former colonial capitals have become the new national capitals, even though the colonial frontiers had little to do with the boundaries of traditional tribal territories or indigenous states. If nationalism was a European export to the rest of the world, Africa provides striking examples of how attractive it can be as a motive for supratribal and transregional state formation.

African nationalism can be dated generally to the period between the two world wars, when regional opposition to colonial occupation began to be replaced by large-scale movements. World War II proved a catalyst for African nationalism, both among Africans themselves and for Europe, which was largely disposed to give up its colonial empires after the war.

THE TRANSITION TO INDEPENDENCE

In 1950, apart from Egypt, only Liberia, Ethiopia, and White-controlled South Africa were sovereign states. By 1980, no African state (with the exception of two tiny Spanish holdings on the Moroccan coast) was ruled by a European state, although South Africa and Namibia continued to be dominated by Whites. Native sons, such as Patrice Lumumba (1925-1961) in the Congo became symbols of African self-determination and freedom from foreign domination (see "The Pan-African Congress Demands Independence").

The actual transition from colonial administrative territories to independent national states was less fraught with conflict and bloodshed than one might have expected. The most protracted and bloody wars of independence from European overlords were the guerrilla struggles fought in French Algeria from 1955 to 1962; in Portuguese Angola and Mozambique from 1961 to 1975; and in Zaire (formerly the Belgian Congo), Zambia (formerly Northern Rhodesia), and Zimbabwe (formerly Southern Rhodesia) from 1960 to 1980. Usually, however, the transfer of power was relatively peaceable.

The same cannot be said of the internal conflicts that often arose after colonial withdrawal. Much of the instability in emergent African states has been a legacy of both the colonial powers' minimal efforts to prepare their subjects for self-government and the haphazard 19th-century

WHAT ARE the most serious problems that Africa faces in the 21st century?

27.4
Kwame Nkrumah, I Speak of Freedom: A Statement of African Ideology

Ethnic Conflict. Rwandan refugees carry their belongings as they stream out of the Mugunga refugee camp in Zaire (Congo) toward Rwanda in one of the many ethnic conflicts that tore apart central Africa in the 1990s.
David Guttenfelder/AP Wide World Photos.

HISTORY'S VOICES

THE PAN-AFRICAN CONGRESS DEMANDS INDEPENDENCE

For more than two centuries before World War II, European powers had dominated or directly ruled large parts of Africa. Before World War II, nationalist political movements came to the fore in a number of these colonial empires. After the war, nationalist movements burgeoned throughout most of the colonial world.

The costs of fighting World War II meant the European powers had less wealth with which to govern their colonies. In addition, the principles of the victorious Allies in Europe were inconsistent with colonialism, as was the foreign policy of the United States, now the dominant Western power.

In the following passage, representatives to the 1945 Fifth Pan-African Congress meeting in Manchester, England, set forth their demand for freedom.

WHAT ARE the social and political goals these African leaders demanded? How did World War II help to allow such goals to be voiced? Why did these leaders believe they deserved to resort to force?

DECLARATION TO THE COLONIAL POWERS

The delegates believe in peace. How could it be otherwise, when for centuries the African peoples have been the victims of violence and slavery? Yet if the Western world is still determined to rule mankind by force, then Africans, as a last resort, may have to appeal to force in the effort to achieve freedom, even if force destroys them and the world.

We are determined to be free. We want education. We want the right to earn a decent living; the right to express our thoughts and emotions, to adopt and create forms of beauty. We demand for Black Africa autonomy and independence so far and no further than it is possible in this One World for groups and peoples to rule themselves subject to inevitable world unity and federation.

We are not ashamed to have been an age-long patient people. We continue willingly to sacrifice and strive. But we are unwilling to starve any longer while doing the world's drudgery, in order to support by our poverty and ignorance a false aristocracy and a discarded imperialism.

We condemn the monopoly of capital and the rule of private wealth and industry for private profit alone. We welcome economic democracy as the only real democracy.

Therefore, we shall complain, appeal and arraign. We will make the world listen to the fact of our condition. We will fight in every way we can for freedom, democracy, and social betterment.

Source: Molefi Kete Asante and Abus S. Abarry, *African Intellectual Heritage: A Book of Sources* (Philadelphia: Temple University Press, 1996), pp. 520–521.

QUICK REVIEW

African Independence
- By 1980, no African state was ruled by a European state
- Transition to independent states was less bloody than expected
- Internal conflicts since independence have led to instability and violence

division of the continent into often arbitrary colonial units. The establishment of new African governments often succeeded only after substantial civil strife.

Few African states had the numbers of educated and experienced native citizens that were needed to staff the apparatuses of a sovereign country, and this alone made for difficult times after independence. Corruption and military coups were rife; the attempt to implement planned economies on a socialist model often brought economic catastrophe; and tribal and regional revolts at times led to civil war.

Most dangerous and costly were the separatist struggles, civil wars, and border clashes between new states that grew out of the independence struggles. The Nigerian civil war of 1967–1970, in which more than 1 million people died, was a bloody example. However, these conflicts tended to ratify the postcolonial state divisions that had almost always kept to the old colonial boundaries (instead of regional or tribal/linguistic divisions within these units).

Every African state has had a different history in the half century since World War II; here we shall look at two cases: Nigeria and South Africa.

Nigeria   Nigeria is the most populous state in Africa, with about 100 million inhabitants. It was formed when the British joined their protectorates of Northern and Southern Nigeria in 1914. Nigeria achieved independence in 1960 and ratified a republican constitution in 1964 that federated the three major provincial regions—the Eastern, Western, and Northern—under a national government based in Lagos, the former British administrative capital. Nigeria's largest ethnic and linguistic groups are the major ones of the same three regions or provinces: Igbo (Ibo) in the Eastern, Yoruba in the Western, and Hausa and Fulani in the Northern. Nigeria's official language is English.

Nowhere was the aftermath of independence bloodier than in Nigeria, which was, at its inception, the most potentially successful state in independent Africa. The three-province federation soon proved to be unworkable, and a 1966 coup brought a military government into power. Its leader, an Ibo, was assassinated within seven months, and Lt. Colonel Yakubo Gawon (b. 1934) took over amid ethnic unrest that ended in massacres in the fall of 1966. Gawon's government subdivided the three provinces into states, but in May 1967, the Eastern Province's assembly empowered its leader, Lt. Colonel Odumegwu Ojukwu (b. 1933), to form the independent state of Biafra out of the three states of the Eastern Province. Ojukwu was an Ibo nationalist but aspired to control lands beyond those of the Ibos—especially the off-shore oil reserves of the Eastern Province. The new Biafran state gained recognition from several African states; and arms and support from France, South Africa, and Portugal. Worldwide propaganda depicted Biafra as a small, brave, mostly Christian country fighting for its survival.

The ensuing two and one-half years saw a bloody civil war. The larger federal forces slowly chipped away at first the non-Ibo regions, then the Ibo heartland of the Biafran state. Famine was a major cause of casualties, and the estimated death toll soared above a million by the time the Biafrans surrendered in January 1970. Out of this brutal conflict, however, came a sense of Nigerian unity, along with a major role for the military in Nigerian politics. The struggle also contributed to the development of African diplomacy and of international aid efforts in Africa.

Gawon was overthrown by another commander in 1975. In the ensuing 25 years, Nigeria has been plagued by political instability, with its leadership passing usually from one military ruler to another. The regime of General Sani Abacha (1993–1998) was especially brutal.

Abacha died in June 1998. Civilian rule was restored in 1999, and a civilian government and elected president ratified and implemented a new constitution. Elections again took place in 2003. There is considerable hope that democratic rule will continue, despite enduring religious communal animosities and ethnic divisions.

South Africa   One of the most tragic chapters in the history of modern Africa has finally been closed: that of White-minority rule in South Africa, with its radical separation of White from non-White peoples in all areas of life as official government policy for nearly 50 years. In the rest of East and southern Africa, minority White-settler governments tried in vain in the postwar period to put down African independence movements. Only in South Africa did they manage, until the 1990s, to sustain a White supremacist state.

From the time the Afrikaner-led National Party (NP) came to power in 1948, the Union of South Africa was governed according to the racist policy of

Nelson Mandela. On May 10, 1994, Nelson Mandela was sworn in as president of South Africa, bringing an end to the apartheid, White minority government that had imprisoned him for 27 years.

David Brauchli/AP/Wide World Photos.

28.2
"The Struggle Is My Life" (1961): Nelson Mandela

apartheid ("apartness"). Until the dismantling of this policy after 1991, the country's White minority (in 1991, 5.4 million persons) ran the country. Its 31 million Blacks, 3.7 million "coloreds" (of mixed blood), and 1 million Indians were kept strictly segregated—treated, at best, as second-class citizens or, in the case of Blacks, as noncitizens or even nonhumans. This system was maintained by repression, to quell dissent and enforce apartheid laws.

The history of apartheid and its passing is a bloody but triumphant one. In part, as a result of worldwide opposition, South Africa saw itself become isolated from the 1960s onward. Meanwhile, the rest of Africa—including other White-run states like Rhodesia (now Zimbabwe)—progressed to majority, African rule. In 1961, South Africa withdrew from the British Commonwealth of Nations. In the 1960s and 1970s, the government created three tiny "independent homelands" for Blacks inside the country, allowing the White minority to treat Blacks as immigrant "foreigners" in the parts of South Africa where most had to work. The international community refused to recognize the homelands, or "Bantustans." South Africa's isolation was further dramatized when two antiapartheid Black leaders, the Zulu chief Albert Luthuli in 1960 and the Anglican archbishop Desmond Tutu in 1984, were awarded the Nobel Prize for their work against apartheid.

By 1978, when Pieter Botha (b. 1916) came to power, apartheid was failing: The homelands were economic and political catastrophes; the country was in a recession; skilled Whites were emigrating; and South Africa was becoming an international pariah. In the 1980s, internal opposition to apartheid grew.

Beginning in 1986, many nations imposed economic sanctions against the government. Antiapartheid movements in the United States and elsewhere had convinced companies and individuals to divest themselves of investments in South Africa. Strikes by Black workers in 1987 led the government to give virtually unlimited power to its security forces, but the violence created support in the West for a trade embargo of South Africa.

In June 1988, more than 2 million Black workers went on strike to protest new repressive labor laws and a ban on political activity by trade unions and antiapartheid groups. President Botha resigned in August 1989. His replacement, F. W. de Klerk (b. 1936) (also of the NP, but younger and more ready for accommodation), began to dismantle White-only rule and the official structures of apartheid. In February 1990, de Klerk announced radical changes, and a series of landmark government actions followed: lifting of the ban on the African National Congress (ANC), the main antiapartheid organization; release of ANC leader Nelson Mandela after 27 years of imprisonment; and repeal of the Separate Amenities Act, the legal basis for segregation in public places. In 1991, the race registration law was repealed. In March 1992, a Whites-only referendum voted to grant constitutional equality to all races. The NP government under de Klerk's leadership also negotiated with the ANC leader Mandela, and despite terrorist attempts from both Black and White extremists to derail the talks, the two leaders brought their own and 18 other parties of both sides to endorse an interim constitution, which was to be implemented once national elections could be held in which all citizens of South Africa would be enfranchised. (Mandela and de Klerk shared the Nobel Peace Prize for 1993.)

Elections were held in April 1994. The ANC won 63 percent of the vote, and the NP 20 percent, thus relegating apartheid to the slag heap of history. The nonracial constitution of December 1996 offers a new basis for the future, but the new state faces huge problems: one of the world's most extreme income inequalities; insufficient education and economic infrastructure; rampant Black poverty; high unemployment; militant extremist groups; inadequate public services in much of the country; potentially severe water supply and water quality problems; and difficulties in attracting foreign investment. The obstacles will, however, no longer include a state system that holds the majority of the population in bondage.

While the new independent states of Africa have been anything but models, nevertheless Africa did not revert to tiny tribal and regional political units. However, some struggles—such as those in the Sudan, Somalia, Rwanda, Sierra Leone, Congo, and Liberia—are still ongoing, their human consequences catastrophic, and their ultimate outcomes not clear.

THE AFRICAN FUTURE

Most African states have not achieved peace and prosperity. On the other hand, the last 50 years have seen radical change and development. The prospects for government stability are not entirely bleak. Economic problems loom large, but even here progress is being made. In any case, every African state is different; each faces unique problems and must draw on its unique resources. Probably the most serious problems are those with which almost all of Africa's new nations have to contend: overpopulation, poverty, disease, famine, lack of professional and technical expertise, and general economic underdevelopment. In particular, the explosive growth of new urban centers at the expense of rural areas has brought disruptive changes in the continent's traditionally agrarian-based societies, age-old family and tribal allegiances, religious values, and sociopolitical systems. The challenge for African nations in the 21st century is to build a truly civil society and achieve economic health and political stability in the face of internal divisions, exploding population growth, and world-market competition.

CENTRAL, SOUTH, AND SOUTHEAST ASIA— THE ISLAMIC HEARTLAND

*T*he lands today dominated or significantly marked by Islamic culture and containing either Muslim majority populations or major Muslim minority numbers stretch from North and West Africa to the Philippines. The various nations of this huge region of Central, South, and Southeast Asia illustrate the many different ways in which Islamic faith and practice may manifest themselves and affect political life.

HOW DID the creation of the state of Israel affect the history of the modern Middle East?

TURKEY

In Turkey, a non-Arab country, civil society and a democratically elected government has become the norm, despite struggles over the place of religion in society and lapses into military rule. Economically, Turkey has had difficulties, but it and Israel are the most economically advanced countries in the Middle East. With the creation of new Turkic-language-speaking states in Central Asia after the breakup of the Soviet Union, Turkey is making a bid to strengthen its ties with this underdeveloped part of the world.

Geographically and culturally Turkey is part of both Europe and Asia. Istanbul, its main commerical and cultural center, is located in continental Europe. In recent years, Turkey, already a member of NATO, has sought admission to the European Union. Turkey participates in European cultural events, such as soccer competitions and other contests, but the issue of its membership in the EU is controversial. Many Europeans are skeptical about admitting an overwhelmingly Muslim nation ino the union. Turkey's human rights record (particularly with respect to its Kurdish minority), imprisonment of journalists, suppression of freedom of speech, and serious indebtedness to the International Money Fund are also problems. The emergence of various Islamist parties further complicate the political landscape. It remains to be seen with which region Turkey ultimately will align itself.

IRAN AND ITS ISLAMIC REVOLUTION

Iran was ruled from 1925 to 1941 as a monarchy by a former army commander, Reza Khan, who had come to power by military takeover and governed under the old Persian title Shah Reza Pahlavi. Like his contemporary in Turkey, Atatürk (1881–1938), he attempted to introduce modernist economic, educational, and governmental reforms (but, unlike Turkey, favoring monarchy). By the time Russian and British forces deposed Reza in 1941 and installed his son, Muhammad Reza, as shah, the power of the Shi'ite religious leaders, or *ulama*, had been muted and a strong, centralized state established. The son continued his father's secularist state building from the end of World War II until 1978, with one interruption. In 1951, a nationalist revolution established Muhammad Mosaddeq (1881–1967) in control. But in 1953, a counterrevolution, covertly supported by America and Britain, restored the shah. Memory of this continues to make Iranians suspicious of American motives.

In the 1960s, Muhammad Reza Shah was forced to institute land reform and various socialist or populist programs. However, his violent repression of the leftist and especially the religious opposition alienated the Iranian masses, as did his failure to narrow the gap between the wealthy elites and the poor. In 1978, religious leaders and secularist revolutionaries joined forces to overthrow the shah in an uprising fueled by Shi'ite Islamic feeling and symbolism. In 1979, the constitution of a new Islamic republic was adapted under the guidance of the Shi'ite religious leader, or **ayatollah**, Ruhollah Khomeini (1902–1989). A protracted war with Iraq (1980–1988) followed, and the new regime instituted repressive measures against its enemies not unlike those of the shah. Still, the new state—with religious leaders exercising a degree of political power not seen since the 16th century—has survived. Khomeini and his successors, Hashemi Rafsanjani (b. 1934) and Ali Khameini (b. 1939), struggled to combine Muslim values with 20th-century *realpolitik,* a challenge that remains for their successors.

In 1997, a resounding majority in the first real national election since the 1979 revolution brought Mohammad Khatami to the presidency. Khatami, a moderate cleric and former minister of culture, has tried to steer a moderate, more liberal course for Iran. Many think his administration marks progress toward a more stable, more internationally engaged government in Iran, but the wide-ranging reforms that people expected have failed to materialize. There have been sporadic, unsuccessful student protests against the

ayatollah Major Shi'ite religious leader.

Khomeini. The bearded ayatollah waves to a cheering throng in Tehran, Iran in February 1979.

Reuters/Corbs-Bettmann.

clerical government, and in 2003, Shirin Ebadi, an Iranian lawyer, won the Nobel Peace Prize for her efforts to improve the status of women in Iran.

AFGHANISTAN AND THE FORMER SOVIET REPUBLICS

North of Iran, 40 million Central Asian Muslims predominate in the broad region that stretches across the south-central reaches of the former USSR between the Crimea and China, and 30 million or more Muslims live in Chinese Central Asia. These people have sustained their religious and intellectual traditions in the face of Russian and Chinese imperialism, and when the Soviet Union collapsed in 1990, they established many separate, independent nations. They are loosely connected through the Commonwealth of Independent States (CIS), which contains Kazakhstan, Kyrgyzstan, Tajikistan, Turkmenistan, Uzbekistan, Azerbaijan, Georgia, and Moldova. These Central Asian Islamic republics had little time or infrastructure to manage their transition to independence. It remains to be seen whether they can avoid economic collapse and ethnic or regional conflict to become politically viable.

Afghan Women. Shortly after the Taliban was driven out of Kabul in November 2001, several Afghan women, one unveiled, venture out in the street.

Reuters/Corbis-Bettmann.

The Soviet invasion of Afghanistan in 1979 (see Chapter 32) drew thousands of fundamentalist Muslims to Afghanistan to fight for the eviction of the Russians, whom they regarded as Western imperialists. Conservative Arab states, which wanted to divert the energies of their religious extremists, and the United States, which saw this in the context of the Cold War, supported them, and they succeeded by the late 1980s. The Soviets' withdrawal created a power vacuum that had been filled by 1998 by the *Taliban*. They imposed a version of Islamic law, which mandated strict regimentation of women and public executions and mutilations for criminal offenses. They also allowed Muslim terrorists known as *al-Qaeda* ("Base") to establish training camps in their country. These camps produced the terrorists who attacked the United States on September 11, 2001. A U.S. response to those attacks was a military campaign that overthrew the Taliban's regime.

INDIA

India, a largely Hindu state, and Pakistan, a largely Muslim state, gained independence in 1947 after the British agreed to divide the subcontinent. Hindu-Muslim communal violence and disputes over Kashmir and other areas have plagued the two states ever since. The displacement of Muslims from the new India as well as Hindus and Sikhs from the new Pakistan—about 8 million people in each case—was a tragedy with lingering consequences. Five underground nuclear tests carried out by India in mid-May 1998, were followed by Pakistani tests two weeks later. The crises that continue to flare between the two nations now involve the threat of a nuclear exchange.

Mohandas Gandhi's (1869–1948) Congress Party has dominated Indian politics since his assassination in 1948. Jawaharlal Nehru (1889–1964) kept India neutral during the era of the Cold War and saw India through the critical period of reorganization as an independent state. He reduced the communal hatreds, religious zealotry, and regional tensions that followed partition, and he promoted the economic development of his overpopulated new nation. Hindi and English were set as the national languages, and Nehru's resolute opposition to caste privilege helped increase equality of citizenship.

Nehru's successor, Lal Bahadur Shastri (1904–1966), saw India through a war and standoff with Pakistan in 1965. His successor, Nehru's daughter, Indira Gandhi (1917–1984; no relation to Mohandas Gandhi), continued her father's policies. In 1971, she guided India to a victory over Pakistan that led to the creation of Bangladesh in place of East Pakistan. This war, and the subsequent development of an atomic bomb with Russian help, made India the major power in South Asia, but Gandhi's failure to improve India's general economic health undermined her popularity. In 1977, she and the Congress Party were ousted by the voters. Three years later, she was reelected and served as prime minister until efforts to quell Sikh separatism led to her assassination in 1984 by two Sikhs from her own guard.

Rajiv Gandhi (1944–1991), Indira's son, succeeded her. He managed the thorny Sikh issue and worked to resolve problems with Pakistan, but charges of corruption led to the fall of his government. V.P. Singh (b. 1931) succeeded him as prime minister, and when Singh resigned, Gandhi again ran for office. During the campaign, he was assassinated by a Sri Lankan Tamil suicide bomber. The leader of the Congress Party, P. V. Narasimha Rao, was then asked to form a government. He made substantial economic progress and dealt successfully with a wide variety of communal and separatist problems. In 1997, Vice President K. R. Narayanan assumed the presidency, and he and his party were displaced in 2004 by an unexpected Congress Party victory.

India, the world's largest functioning democracy, faces major problems: mass poverty and disease, separatist movements, and runaway population growth—to mention only a few. The growing strength of militant Hindu nationalists and fundamentalists and new outbreaks of communal violence between Hindus and India's large Muslim minority pose serious threats to the country's political stability.

PAKISTAN AND BANGLADESH

The architect and first president of Pakistan, Muhammad Ali Jinnah (1876–1948), oversaw the creation of a Muslim state that then consisted of widely separated East and West Pakistan, the two predominantly Muslim areas of northwest India and East Bengal. In 1971, East Pakistan seceded to form a new Islamic nation, Bangladesh. Indian and Bangladeshi relations are troubled, but the main political division in the subcontinent remains that between India and Pakistan.

Pakistan's efforts to balance religious and secular ideologies and solve massive economic problems have been hampered by bloodshed, military coups, and periodic lapses into dictatorship. The most recent brought Zia ul-Haqq (1924–1988) to power in 1977. The elections of November 1988, following his death in a suspicious air crash, restored parliamentary government. This government was headed by the first female leader of a modern Islamic state, Benazir Bhutto (b. 1953), the daughter of the man whom Zia ul-Haqq overthrew and executed. The president dismissed her government in August 1990. Benazir returned to the prime ministership, only to be deposed by the president on charges of corruption in 1996 and convicted in 1999. In 1999, General Parviz Musharraf, Chief of Army Staff, took over as chief executive, and he and his country are confronting direct challenges from radical Islam.

INDONESIA AND MALAYSIA

The new East Indies state of Indonesia came into being in 1949 as a nominal republic. It succeeded the long Dutch and brief Japanese domination of the East Indies. The much smaller territory of Malaya, a federation under a rotating monarch, received its independence from British colonial rule in 1957. It was later joined by the states of Sarawak and Sabah in northern Borneo, forming the federation of Malaysia.

Indonesia is the largest Muslim country in the world and must reach a consensus among its disparate and scattered parts on how its religious faith is to be reconciled with secularist government. The overriding problem for Malaysia is the cleft between the largely Chinese and partly Indian non-Muslim minority on the one hand and the largely Muslim majority of Malay and other indigenous peoples on the other.

THE POSTCOLONIAL MIDDLE EAST

 o other part of the postcolonial world so dominates international concern and conflict as the Middle East. The issues have arisen as a result of the new nations established in the region since World War I.

HOW HAS the growth of Hindu nationalism affected Indian politics?

NEW NATIONS IN THE MIDDLE EAST

The modern Middle East arose from the fall of the Ottoman Empire and the intervention in the region by Western powers, which carved out new nations and protectorates. Egypt, Iraq, and Saudi Arabia became sovereign states after World War I; Lebanon and Syria were given independence by France during World War II. In 1948, Great Britain abandoned its protectorate over Palestine, and the United Nations recognized the state of Israel. Subsequently, other Arab states gained independence: Jordan, 1946; Libya, 1951; Morocco and Tunisia, 1956; Algeria, 1962; and, by 1971, Yemen, Oman, and the small Arabian Gulf states (see Map 34–2).

These states all share the classical Arabic written language (*fusha*), but the spoken colloquial language (*'amiyya*) varies from place to place. Attempts to create pan-Arab alliances or federations have failed primarily because of regional differences and political interests, but appeals to Arab nationalism remain powerful.

In the wake of World War II, many proponents of Arab nationalism, such as Gamal Abdul Nasser of Egypt (1918–1970), were sympathetic to socialism or the Soviet Union. But because socialism and communism were Western ideologies, the orientation of left-leaning Arab nationalists was no less Western than that of Arabs friendly to the United States. The overt atheism of Soviet communism was equally offensive to devout Arab Muslims.

Not all the new states were on the same footing. Oil, for instance, made Saudi Arabia wealthy and powerful and the Gulf states, such as Kuwait, rich, but not powerful. States that lacked oil, such as Egypt, Jordan, and Syria, were burdened by large impoverished populations. All the Arab governments, however, worked out arrangements with local Muslim authorities. The Saudi royal family modernized Arabia's infrastructure, but turned its educational system over to a rigorist, puritanical form of Islam called *Wahhabism*. The Egyptian government played different Islamic groups against one another. These governments retained the support of prosperous, devout middle-class Muslims while doing little about the plight of the poor.

MAP 34–2

The Modern Middle East and the Distribution of Major Religious Communities. The inset map shows Israel and the occupied territories.

HOW HAS religion shaped the Arab-Israeli conflict?

THE ARAB-ISRAELI CONFLICT

Nowhere have the effects of the West's interventions in the Middle East been more sharply felt than in the creation of the state of Israel in the former British mandate territory of Palestine (1948). The British Balfour Declaration of 1917 supported establishment of a national homeland for the Jews in Palestine, but by 1920 there were only about 60,000 Jews (one-tenth the number of Arabs) in Palestine.

The interwar years saw increasing Jewish settlement and growing communal conflict. Immigration of Jews, largely from Eastern Europe, increased in the

27.5
Israel's Proclamation of
Independence

1920s and 1930s. Britain's efforts to restrict it in 1936 tragically prevented many Jews from escaping the Nazi Holocaust. After the war, the Zionist movement received a tremendous boost from Jews worldwide and the Allied nations, which felt the need to atone for the Holocaust by securing a refuge for Jews. The dream of return to the Holy Land had a long history in Judaism.

Under the Ottomans, the Holy Land had been the home of Arabic-speaking Palestinians, primarily Muslims, but also Christians and Jews. None of these had a hand in determing the fate of their land. The Palestinians understandably do not to see why they should be displaced, either because of another people's historic religious attachment to the land or as reparation for Europe's sins against the Jews. Jews, however, felt a desperate need for a homeland where they might be safe from future persecutions and persistent anti-Semitism.

By 1945, Britain was beset in Palestine by Jews seeking to settle there and by Jewish underground and terrorist organizations aiming to oust the British. In 1947, the British turned the problem over to the United Nations. The U.N. called for partition of the mandate territory into a Jewish and an Arab state. The Arab states refused to accept the U.N. resolution, but in May 1948, Jews in Palestine proclaimed the independent state of Israel. Egypt, Iraq, Jordan, Lebanon, Saudi Arabia, and Syria promptly attacked Israel but lost to the better-armed, better trained, and more resolute Israelis. The Israeli-Arab war of 1948–1949 won the Jews not only the U.N.-proposed territory, but also a substantial portion of that proposed for a Palestinian state. The creation of Israel subjected some Palestinians to Israeli rule or occupation and produced a massive Palestinian refugee problem. Another war in 1967 and the aftermaths of two subsequent *intifadahs* further swelled refugee ranks.

The Arab nations and the Palestinian people have generally not accepted Israel's right to exist as a state, and Israel (supported by the United States) has aggressively sought to ensure its survival, often by means that defy world opinion and international laws applying to **occupied territories**. The most serious military confrontations have been: the Suez Crisis of 1956, when Israel (and briefly France and England) invaded the Sinai; the 1967 June war (the "Six Day War"), when Israel occupied the Sinai, the Golan Heights, and the West Bank (of the Jordan River); the October (Yom Kippur) war of 1973, when the Egyptians and Syrians staged a surprise attack on Israel; and the Israeli invasions of Lebanon in 1978 and 1982 to extricate anti-Israeli terrorist refuges. Since the fall of 2000, the region has spiraled into an abyss of violence with repeated Israeli military assaults on towns and refugee camps in the West Bank and Gaza and regular Palestinian extremist suicide attacks on mainly civilian targets. The highly provocative construction by Israel of a massive "separation wall" through the West Bank is currently (2004) impinging on more Palestinian territory as an effort to protect Israelis from suicide bombings.

Israel has responded to extremist terrorist attacks and civilian resistance such as the *intifadah* ("uprising," or literally, "shaking"), in the occupied territories with air and commando raids on Arab states thought to support Palestinian terrorism; with repressive, measures against the Palestinian populations in the occupied territories, and a hard-line stance against negotiation over the status of

intifadah Literally, "shaking." Uprisings by the Palestinians against Israeli occupation.

occupied territories Land occupied by Israel as a result of wars with its Arab neighbors in 1948–1949, 1967, and 1973.

Confrontation. An Israeli settler in prayer shawl carries his American M16 assault rifle past a group of Palestinians in Hebron, who sit in front of a shuttered shop where a large Star of David has been painted.
Kevin Lamarque/Getty Images, Inc./Hulton Archive Photos.

Intifadah. A Palestinian boy hurls a slingshot in the Gaza strip. Though Israel withdrew its forces from Gaza in the summer of 2005, the future for Palestinians is rife with fear and uncertainty.

the territories seized in 1967. The United States has pulled back from serious efforts to mediate.

Arab and some non-Arab states have have supported guerrilla groups attacking Israel and have refused until recently to deal directly with Israel. However, in the late 1970s, Gamal Abdel Nasser's successor, Egyptian President Anwar Sadat (1918–1981), broke ranks and, through the mediation of U.S. President Jimmy Carter (b. 1924), dealt directly with Israel's prime minister Menachem Begin (1913–1994). The Camp David Accords (1978 and 1979) formally concluded peace between the two countries, but in 1981, Sadat was assassinated by Egyptian Muslim extremists. His successor, Husni Mubarak (b. 1928), continued to honor the treaty.

Recent Israeli military actions in the occupied territories were provoked by, but in turn have brought on, more Palestinian terrorist bombings in Israel and abroad. Arabs and many Muslims outside the Arab world have come to view Jews, without distinction, as oppressors and enemies, and many Jews around the world have similarly vilified all Arabs and Muslims.

Some events of recent years gave at least brief hope for resolution of the conflict. In 1991, in the wake of the Gulf War that followed Iraq's invasion of Kuwait, the parties to the Arab-Israeli conflict began peace negotiations. The result was the 1993 Middle East Peace Agreement, or the Oslo Agreement, which promised a negotiated settlement and the creation of an independent Palestinian state alongside Israel. But there has been little substantive progress made in the 11 years since the 1993 agreement. Jordan and Egypt agreed in 1994 to a peace treaty with Israel, but some other Arab states remain unwilling to negotiate. Israel, for its part, has continued actions that preclude formation of a viable state on contiguous territory, and extremists on both sides pose obstacles to the success of the peace initiative. In November 1995, a Jewish Israeli extremist assassinated Prime Minister Yitzhak Rabin for trying to make peace. Then, in the run-up to the Israeli elections of May 29, 1996, Palestinian extremists carried out a series of savage bombings on buses and in crowded shopping areas. This helped a Likud conservative hard-liner, Benjamin Netanyahu (b. 1949), win over Rabin's Labor successor, Shimon Peres, by a margin of less than 1 percent and cast more uncertainty on peace prospects. The Netanyahu regime repeatedly took rigid stands and provocative actions involving settlements and territorial claims. The Palestinian Authority, which was created by the 1993 peace agreement, did not behave any better. Under Yasser Arafat (1929–2004), it grew steadily more corrupt, ineffective, and out of touch with its constituencies. Despite the efforts of both Palestinian and Israeli security forces, Palestinian guerrillas of the extremist wing of the resistance organization Hamas have slaughtered Israeli civilians in a sustained effort to torpedo the **peace process**. These terrorist attacks have exacerbated the already dire plight of thousands of Palestinian families, keeping them in the poverty that recruits new volunteers for the extremist resistance groups.

In March 2000, Ariel Sharon, a former army general, became prime minister. His administration has been marked by an escalation of violence on both sides, but he has proposed that Israel withdraw from Gaza and close Israeli settlements in that region. His government has also begun to erect a fence separating Israeli and Palestinian territory. Arafat's death in late 2004 may present a new opportunity for negotiations with the new Palestinian president, Mahmoud Abbas.

MIDDLE EASTERN OIL

peace process Efforts, chiefly led by the United States, to broker a peace between the state of Israel and the PLO.

Oil, or black gold, has been a blessing and a curse for the Middle East. Since its discovery in Iran in 1908 and the beginning of its production in Saudi Arabia in 1939, the world demand for oil has surged. The Arab and other oil-rich Third

World states—such as Indonesia, Iran, Nigeria, and Venezuela—have used oil to their advantage in international diplomacy since the mid-1970s. Oil has given peripheral and virtually unknown countries of the Sahara or the Arabian deserts major influence over the world of international banking and finance. Middle Eastern oil supplies are so important that the United States and European nations were willing, in partnership with some Arab countries, to go to war to reverse Iraq's invasion of Kuwait in 1990.

The economic benefits of oil are obvious, but they have not inevitably conferred political benefits on the people in the Middle East. The Middle East has been subject to considerable foreign involvement in its affairs from Europe, the United States, and the former Soviet Union, which has sometimes been detrimental to its political development.

THE RISE OF POLITICAL ISLAMISM

The increase in the global importance of the oil-producing states of the Middle East has coincided with a surging movement there and elsewhere for the revival of pristine Muslim values and reformation of Muslim societies. Many Muslims have sought to return to the "fundamentals" of Islam, which they see as a means for rejuvenating societies corrupted by Western secularist and materialist values. A major new element in Muslim revivalism is a consciousness of being a viable response to the destructive influence of Western-style "modernity."

Much of the appeal of Islamist groups everywhere is their willingness and ability to address the needs of the underclasses in Middle Eastern, North African, and Asian cities and countries. Where governments of Muslim-majority countries have failed to provide social services such as housing, medical care, education, and jobs, the Islamist groups have succeeded. While the world press reports only on the relatively small fringe groups of Islamist extremists, Muslims at the grass-roots level have watched while the major Islamist groups in the dictatorships or military regimes under which most of them live provide services for which the state has long abdicated responsibility.

Such Muslim fundamentalism—or more correctly, "Islamist reformism"—motivated the overthrow of the the shah of Iran in 1978, the Muslim Brethren movement in Egypt and elsewhere, the Welfare Party in Turkey, and many other groups, from Morocco to the Persian Gulf and beyond the Middle East. All such Islamist groups see themselves as traditionalist, as true to basic Muslim values and norms. Whether these movements will bring lasting change to Islamic societies is an open issue, but there is no question about their current attraction and influence.

European expansion over much of the globe brought far more social and political change than religious or even cultural change to the Islamic world. Globally it promoted European-style nationalism and the idea of the nation-state, post-Enlightenment ideals of individual liberties and rights and representative government, and the concept of religious faith as a private matter separate from citizenship. Such ideas proved revolutionary in the Islamic world, especially in this century.

Parts of the Islamic world in the 20th century have a checkered history of autocratic governments that were as far removed from their citizenries as any medieval or premodern dynasty. Experiments with European-style parliamentary government have only rarely taken hold; nor have either liberal democratic or Marxist-socialist ideals proven viable for the long term. Until recently, however, little of the political discourse in Islamic lands has given serious thought to *Islamic* alternatives.

The postcolonial independence of many national states divorced politics from Islamic religious traditions and norms. Where leaders had previously claimed Muslim faith and allegiance, some espoused secular ideologies and ignored religion except to use it as a political weapon. In the late 20th and early 21st centuries, Islamic religious allegiance has commonly been invoked to bolster a ruler's claim to legitimacy and to cloak mundane objectives and programs in pious garb. In short, the recent past has seen no realization of an "ideal" Islamic state in which religious and political authority are conjoined. Even in the postrevolutionary Islamic Republic of Iran a clear division exists between political realities and religious standards. However, sincerely the latter are claimed as the basis of state policy, no one can miss the frequent stretching of norms to justify pragmatic political decisions. When we look at the Islamist movements of recent decades, we find that the calls for a congruence of religion and politics in the Islamic world trace less to some kind of ideal model of a religious state or so-called **theocracy** than to a sorely felt need for simple social and political justice. The cries for a "jihad" of Muslims are aimed less often outward than inward, less at foreign "devils" and more at domestic tyrants, corruption, and social and economic injustice. The most international and widely influential of all contemporary Islamic revivalist or reform movements, the Tabligh-i Jama'at, is explicitly apolitical. It aims to convert the individual to true submission *(islam)* not lip service on the principle that reform of the world begins with oneself.

As for those reform movements that are avowedly political, be they activist but nonviolent (the majority) or extremist and violent (the minority), they feed on the deep sense of socioeconomic and political injustice that citizens of most Islamic countries rightfully feel. When such feelings go over the edge, the result is extremism and terrorism. Osama bin Laden, the disposessed Saudi millionare who founded and has led al-Qaeda, from the 1990s to the present, stunned the world by using U.S. civilian airliners to destroy the World Trade Center towers and part of the Pentagon building on September 11, 2001. His motive was revenge for the American military presence in Saudi Arabia, the American-led blockade of Iraq, and the American support of Israel against the Palestinians.

These carefully executed and massively destructive attacks have involved the U.S. military ever more deeply in the Middle East and Central Asia. In October 2001, the United States attacked the Taliban government of Afghanistan, rapidly overthrew it, and dispersed, but did not destroy, al-Qaeda's organization. Whether this military response to the threat of terrorism will be successful remains to be seen. Further U.S. intervention followed in 2003 with the invasion of Iraq.

IRAQ AND U.S. INTERVENTION

The modern nation of Iraq was established after World War I. Iraq as such had never been a distinct political unit and until 1921 was primarily a geographic term, referring to today's southern Iraq. Postwar imperial concern and the potential of oil under Iraqi soil motivated the British government to oversee the creation of an Iraq that they felt would best protect their interests in the region. Given the disparate ethnic and religious groups in the country, the British could not find a suitable native leader. Therefore, they imported a politician from Arabia, Faysal ibn Husayn, crowned him first king of the Hashemite monarchy. The dynasty ruled until 1958, with the help of British advisers, soldiers, and a

theocracy State ruled by religious leaders who claim to govern by divine authority.

British-dominated consortium of oil companies.

Iraqis developed a sense of national identity that led them to resent the foreign presence in their country, and in 1958, a bloody coup, led by Abd al-Karim Qasem, terminated the monarchy. By 1979, the Ba'ath party had become the dominant force in Iraq politics, bringing Saddam Hussein to the start of his tyrannical reign. Following a long, bloody, and unsuccessful war with Iraq (1980–1988), Saddam Hussein invaded and occupied Kuwait (1990). After an international military coalition under the leadership of the United States (in Operation Desert Storm) expelled the Iraqi army from Kuwait, Iraq became an international pariah. It was subject to economic sanctions monitored by the United Nations until 1998, when the Iraqi government expelled the U.N. inspectors.

Terrorist Attack. On September 11, 2001 a terrorist attack targeted the World Trade Center Towers in New York City. In this photograph the first of the twin towers is in flames as the second plane heads directly toward the second tower. In a very brief time both towers collapsed with the loss of nearly 3,000 lives.

Masatomo Kuriya, Corbis/Sygma.

The U.S. government adopted a policy of regime change in Iraq during the last years of the Clinton administration, though it did little to carry out that policy. In the wake of the September 11, 2001, terrorist attacks, however, the Bush administration decided that Saddam Hussein had to be overthrown to remove the threat of Iraqi weapons of mass destruction. During late 2002 and early 2003, the U.S. and British governments sought to obtain passage of the U.N. Security Council resolutions that would require Iraq to disarm on its own or to face disarmament by military force. When opposition from France and Russia blocked the resolution, Australia, Great Britain, and the United States, with more then 40 other nations (the "Coalition of the Willing") invaded Iraq. After three weeks of fighting that began in mid-March 2003, the Coalition removed Saddam Hussein from power.

The invasion of Iraq occasioned considerable international opposition, most notably from France, Germany and Russia, and provoked large antiwar demonstrations in the United States and other parts of the world. The war has created strains within the European Union and NATO and begun a new era in international relations.

Currently, it is immensely difficult to ensure peace and stability in Iraq. Many Iraqis have resisted occupation by foreign forces and historical factors militate against formation of a new unified government. The unpreparedness of the Americans and their allies to deal with the chaos of postwar Iraq has exacerbated matters, and the failure to find weapons of mass destruction in Iraq led to wide questioning of the rationale for the war. Throughout Iraq an insurgency has been launched

Traffic Cop. A U.S. Marine directs Iraqi civilians in the northern city of Kirkuk in April 2003.

Sebastian Bolesch/Das Fotoarchiv/ Peter Arnold, Inc.

against the Coalition forces and against Iraqis who cooperate with the coalition and the recently installed Iraqi government. However, President George W. Bush, who was reelected in 2004, has vowed to continue to pursue his existing policies in the Middle East. In late January 2005, an election was held in Iraq under conditions of insurgent attacks to elect the assembly that wrote a new constitution, in October 2005 the constitution was ratified. The challenge of securing general internal support for the construction of democratic processes now confronts the Iraqi government and American policy makers.

SUMMARY

The Postcolonial World Since 1945, the European colonial empires have disappeared from Africa and Asia and have been replaced by a multitude of independent states. These states had to adjust their political and economic relations to one or the other of the superpowers during the Cold War and then, since the disappearance of the Soviet Union, to the West.

Latin America Most Latin American countries remain politically and economically dependent on the United States. Except in Cuba, no revolutionary movement has been able to overturn the traditional structure of Latin American society. Despite social and economic problems, Argentina and Brazil have managed to move from military rule to stable democratic, civilian government. In Mexico, the long dominance of the PRI ended in 2000.

Africa Independent Africa has faced severe problems: overpopulation, poverty, the absence of an educated middle class, tribal and class conflict, arbitrary boundaries, disease, economic dependence, and political instability. The challenge for Africa as a whole is to build a truly civil society and achieve economic health and political stability.

The Middle East Oil and Muslim reaction to the creation of the state of Israel have dominated the history of the Middle East since the 1940s. While the possession of vast deposits of oil has made some Middle Eastern governments wealthy, it has not led to the creation of prosperous democratic societies. Although efforts by the United States to sponsor an Arab-Israeli peace have made some progress, the cycle of terror and retaliatory violence has persisted.

Political Islamism, although not a monolithic movement, has proved increasingly disruptive to the region and the entire Islamic world.

In the wake of the terrorist attacks of September 11, 2001, the United States finds itself increasingly embroiled in a chaotic and unstable region of the world.

IMAGE KEY

for pages 836–837

a. A fifty-gallon oil drum.

b. A statue of deposed Iraqi leader Saddam Hussein is toppled by American forces in April, 2003.

c. Bangladeshi women with a cellular phone.

d. Former South African president Nelson Mandela.

e. Zapatistas demonstrate in Mexico.

f. Ernesto "Che" Guevera.

g. Late Palestinian leader Yasser Arafat.

h. Rwandan refugees.

i. As Tower One burns, another hijacked airliner aims for Tower Two of the World Trade Center, September 11, 2001.

REVIEW QUESTIONS

1. How did the superpower rivalry of the Cold War affect Latin America? How successful has the worldwide trend toward democratization been in Latin America?

2. What factors contributed to the spread of decolonization in sub-Saharan Africa? Why were the newly independent states so fragile? What was the apartheid regime in South Africa? How was it dismantled, and what problems does the new South Africa face?

3. What roles does Islam play in Iran, Pakistan, Malaysia, and Turkey? What does the influence of Islam in these regions suggest about the power of religious tradition in modern politics and society?

4. How have interventions by European powers and the United States affected the modern Middle East? How did the Arab-Israeli conflict begin? How has it developed?

5. What is political Islamism? Why has it taken so radical a course? Why has the United States become its primary target? How did the United States respond to the attacks of September 11, 2001?

KEY TERMS

apartheid (p. 839)
ayatollah (p. 850)
clash of civilizations (p. 839)
globalization (p. 839)

intifadah (p. 855)
liberation theology (p. 840)
occupied territories (p. 855)

peace process (p. 856)
Sandinistas (p. 842)
theocracy (p. 857)

For additional study resources for this chapter, go to:
www.prenhall.com/craig/chapter34

Visualizing The Past

Imperialism and Race in Modern Art

HOW HAVE the experiences of imperialism and race influenced modern and contemporary art in both style and technique?

The second half of the 19th century witnessed the "second wave" of European imperialism. The United States and Japan also participated in the frenzy of the industrialized powers to obtain the labor and natural resources of other regions. Colonizers focused their attention on regions such as China, the African interior, and the Pacific Islands, which were not yet firmly ensconced in older colonial empires.

The colonial experience has been an important legacy in Western and non-Western art alike, in terms of providing artistic themes, but also in the influence of Western techniques in painting and sculpture on indigenous artists. The result has been an original and imaginative blending of styles and techniques that in turn have greatly influenced Western artists.

Paul Gauguin, "Where do we come from? What are we? Where are we going?" (1897), Oil on canvas. Gauguin was one of the last French impressionist painters of the late 19th century. Like colonists, he imagined the people of French Tahiti as a kind of "noble savage" among whom he would find the primitive, spiritually pure lifestyle he sought. Race thus is central to his depiction of the Tahitians, but always in an idealized vision of peace and simplicity.

Museum of Fine Arts, Boston, Mass./A.K.G., Berlin/Super Stock.

▼

As in the image of Cortés, the naked female form, signifying the violated body of the colonized people, is at the heart of Penny Siopis's conception of the experience of South African Blacks under White rule. Siopis's figure literally embodies the suffering of all Black South Africans, but also their dignity and patience, in stark contrast to the decadent, voyeuristic whites presumably viewing the painting.

José Clemente Orozco, "Cortés y Malinzin," (1926), fresco.
Orozco, in his fresco of the great Spanish conquistador Hernan Cortés and Cortés' Indian translator and concubine, Malinzin (Malinche), deals with themes of race, conquest, and gender in a much less idealized way than Gauguin. Both the style and theme of this work reflect the often uneasy but creative mixing of Western and Indian genes and culture that characterizes Mexico's *mestizo* society.

Taguchi Beisaku, "Strange-looking Manchurian Horsemen on an Expedition to Observe the Japanese Camp in the Distance near Sauhoku (Sokako)" 1894.
Japan also entered the race for colonial possessions in the last decade of the 19th century. Two wars, one with China (1894–1895) and the other with Russia (1904–1905), resulted in the 1905 Treaty of Portsmouth that earned Japan control of Manchuria, hegemony over Korea, and outright annexation of Sakhalin Island. In this Japanese painting from the period, we see two Manchurian horsemen portrayed as barbaric and ghoulish.

The World in Transition

1500 – 1600	1600 – 1700	1700 – 1800

EUROPE

1500 – 1600	1600 – 1700	1700 – 1800
1517–1555 Protestant Reformation **1533–1584** Ivan the Terrible of Russia reigns **1540** Jesuit Order founded by Ignatius Loyola **1543–1727** Scientific Revolution **1556–1598** Philip II of Spain reigns **1558–1603** Elizabeth I of England reigns **1562–1598** French Wars of Religion **1581** The Netherlands declares its independence from Spain **1588** Defeat of the Spanish Armada **1589–1610** Henry IV, founds Bourbon dynasty, France	**618–1648** Thirty Years' War **1640–1688** Frederick William, the Great Elector, reigns in Brandenburg-Prussia **1642–1646** Puritan Revolution in England **1643–1715** Louis XIV of France reigns **1682–1725** Peter the Great of Russia reigns **1688** Glorious Revolution in England **1690** *Second Treatise of Civil Government* by John Locke	**1701** Act of Settlement provides for Protestant succession to English throne **1702–1713** War of Spanish Succession **1740–1748** War of Austrian Succession **1756–1763** Seven Years' War **ca. 1750** Industrial Revolution begins in England **1772** First partition of Poland **1789** First French Revolution **1793 and 1795** Last two partitions of Poland

NEAR EAST/ASIA

1500 – 1600	1600 – 1700	1700 – 1800
500–1722 Safavid Shi'ite rule in Iran **1512–1520** Ottoman ruler Selim I **1520–1566** Ottoman ruler Suleiman the Magnificent **1525–1527** Babur founds Mughai dynasty in India **1540** Hungary under Ottoman rule **1556–1605** Akbar the Great of India reigns **1571** Battle of Lepanto; Ottomans defeated **ca. 1571–1640** Safavid philosopher-writer Mullah Sadra **1588–1629** Shah Abbas I of Iran reigns	**1628–1657** Shah Jahan reigns; builds Taj Mahal as mausoleum for his beloved wife **1646** Founding of Maratha Empire **1648** Delhi becomes the capital of Mughal Empire **1658–1707** Shah Aurangzeb, the "World Conqueror," reigns in India **1669–1683** Last military expansion by Ottomans: 1669, seize Crete; 1670s, the Ukraine; 1683, Vienna	**1700** Sikhs and Marathas bring down Mughal Imperial Power **1708** British East India Company and New East India Company merge **1722** Last Safavid ruler forced to abdicate **1724** Rise in the Deccan of the Islamic state of Hyderabad **1725** Nadir Shah of Afganhistan becomes ruler of Persia **1739** Persian invasion of northern India, by Nadir Shah **1748–1761** Ahmad Shah Durrani of Afghanistan invades India **1757** British victory at Plassey, in Bengal

EAST ASIA

1500 – 1600	1600 – 1700	1700 – 1800
1500–1800 Commercial revolution in Ming-Ch'ing China; trade with Europe; flourishing of the novel **1543** Portuguese arrive in Japan **1568–1600** Era of unification follows end of Warring States Era, Japan **1587** Spanish arrive in Japan **1588** Hideyoshi's sword hunt in Japan **1592–1598** Ming troops battle Hideyoshi's army in Korea	**1600** Tokugawa Ieyasu wins battle of Sekigahara, completes unification of Japan **1600–1868** Tokugawa shogunate in Edo **1630s** Seclusion adopted as national policy in Japan **1644–1694** Bashō Japanese poet **1644–1911** Ch'ing (Manchu) dynasty in China **1661–1722** K'ang Hsi reign in China **1673–1681** Revolt of southern generals in China **1699** British East India Company arrives in China	**1701** Forty-seven ro-nin incident in Japan **1716–1733** Reforms of Tokugawa Yoshimune in Japan **1737–1795** Reign of Ch'ien Lung in China **1742** Christianity banned in China **1784** American traders arrive in China **1787–1793** Matsudaira Sadanobu's reforms in Japan **1798** White Lotus Rebellion in China

AFRICA

1500 – 1600	1600 – 1700	1700 – 1800
1506 East coast of Africa under Portuguese domination **1507** Mozambique founded by Portuguese **1517** Spanish crown authorizes slave trade to its South American colonies; rapid increase in importation of slaves to the New World **1554–1659** Sa'did Sultanate in Morocco **1575** Union of Bornu and Kanem by Idris Alawma **1591** Songhai Empire collapses	**1600s** English, Dutch, and French enter the slave trade **1619** First African slaves in North America land in Virginia **1652** First Cape Colony settlement of Dutch East India Company **1660–1856** Omani domination of East Africa	**1702** Asiento Guinea Trade Company founded for slave trade between Africa and the Americas **1700s** Transatlantic slave trade at its height **1741–1856** United Sultanate of Oman and Zanzibar **1754–1817** Usman Dan Fodio, founder of sultanate in northern and central Nigeria **1762** End of Funj Sultanate in eastern Sudanic region

THE AMERICAS

1500 – 1600	1600 – 1700	1700 – 1800
1519 Conquest of the Aztecs by Cortes **1533** Pizarro begins his conquest of the Incas **1536** Spanish under Mendoza arrive in Argentina **1544** Lima becomes capital of the viceroyalty of Peru **1584** Sir Walter Raleigh sends expedition to Roanoke Island (North Carolina)	**1607** The London Company establishes Jamestown Colony **1608** Champlain founds Quebec **1619** Slave labor introduced at Jamestown (Virginia)	**1733** Georgia founded as last English colony in North America **1739–1763** Era of trade wars in Americas between Great Britain and the French and Spanish **1763** Peace of Paris establishes British government in Canada **1776–1781** American Revolution **1783–1830** Simón Bolívar, Latin American soldier, statesman **1789** U.S. Constitution **1791** Negro slave revolt in French Santo Domingo **1791** Canada Constitution Act divides the country into Upper and Lower Canada

Consolidation and Interaction of World Civilizations

500 C.E – 800	800 – 1100	1100 –1300	1300 –1500

EUROPE

500 C.E – 800	800 – 1100	1100 –1300	1300 –1500
511 Death of Clovis, Frankish ruler of Gaul **529** Benedict of Nursia founds Benedictine Order **590–604** Pontificate of Gregory I, "The Great" **768–814** Charlemagne	**ca. 800–1000** Invasions of England and the Carolingian Empire (Vikings, Magyars, and Muslims) **843** Treaty of Verdun **910** Cluny Monastery founded **1019–1054** Yaroslav the Wise reigns; peak of Kievan Russia **1054** Schism between Latin and Greek churches **1066** Norman Conquest of England **1073–1085** Investiture controversy **1096–1270** The Crusades	**1154–115** Frederick Barbarosa invades Italy **1182–1226** St. Francis of Assisi **1198–1216** Pontificate of Innocent III **ca. 1100–1300** Growth of trade and towns **1215** Magna Carta granted **ca. 1225–1274** St. Thomas Aquinas **265–1321** Dante Alighieri	**1337** Hundred Years' War begins **ca. 1340–1400** Geoffrey Chaucer **1347–1349** The Black Death **1375–1527** The Italian Renaissance **1485** Battle of Bosworth Field; accession of Henry Tudor to the throne of England **1492** Columbus's first voyage to the New World

NEAR EAST/ASIA

500 C.E – 800	800 – 1100	1100 –1300	1300 –1500
527–565 Justinian's reign **531–579** Reign of Chosroes Anosharvian in Iran **ca. 570–632** Muhammad **622** The Hijra **616–657** Reign of Harsha **651** Death of last Sasanid ruler **661–750** Umayyad dynasty **680** Death of Al-Husayn at Karbala **ca. 710** First Muslim invasion of India **750–1258** Abbasid dynasty **786–809** Caliph Harun Al-Rashid reigns	**800–120** Period of feudal overlordship in India **900–1100** Golden age of Muslim learning **909–1171** Fatimids in North Africa and Egypt **945–1055** Buyid rule in Baghdad **994–1186** Ghaznavid rule in northwestern India, Afghanistan, and Iran **1055–1194** Seljuk rule in Baghdad **1071** Seljuk Turks capture Jerusalem **1081–1118** Byzantine emperor Alexius Comnenus reigns **ca. 1000–1300** Turko-Afghan raids into India	**1174–1193** Saladin reigns **1192** Muslim conquerors end Buddhism in India **1206–1526** Delhi Sultanate in India **ca. 1220** Mongol invasions of Iran, Iraq, Syria, India **1258** Hulagu Khan, Mongol leader, conquers Baghdad **1260–1335** Il-Khans rule Iran	**1250–1517** Mamluk rule in Egypt **1366–1405** Timur (Tamerlane) reigns **1405–1494** Timurids rule in Transoxiana and Iran **1453** Byzantine Empire falls to the Ottoman Turks

EAST ASIA

500 C.E – 800	800 – 1100	1100 –1300	1300 –1500
589–618 Sui dynasty reunifies China **607** Japan begins embassies to China **618–907** Tang dynasty in China **701–762** Li Po, Tang poet **710–784** Nara court, Japan's first permanent capital **712** Records of Ancient Matters, in Japan **713–756** Emperor Hsuan Tsung reigns in China **755** An Lu-shan rebellion in China **794–1185** Heian (Kyoto) court in Japan	**856–1086** Fujiwara dominate Heian court **960–1279** Sung dynasty in China **ca. 1000** *Pillow Book* by Shohōnagon and *Tale of Genji* by Murasaki Shikibu **1037–1101** Su Tung-p'o, Sung poet	**1130–1200** Chu Hsi, Song philosopher **1167–1227** Genghis Khan, founder of Mongol Empire **1185–1333** Kamakura shogunate in Japan **1274–1281** Mongol invasions of Japan **1279–1368** Mongol (Yuan) dynasty in China	**1336–1467** Ashikaga shogunate in Kyoto **1368–1644** Ming dynasty in China **1405–1433** Voyages of Cheng Ho **1467–1568** Warring States era in Japan **1472–1529** Wang Yang-ming, Ming philosopher

AFRICA

500 C.E – 800	800 – 1100	1100 –1300	1300 –1500
ca. 500 States of Takrur and Ghana founded **ca. 500–700** Political and commercial ascendancy of Aksum (Ethiopia) **ca. 600–1500** Extensive slave trade from sub-Saharan Africa to Mediterranean **ca. 700–800** Ghanians begin to supply gold to Mediterranean **ca. 700–900** States of Gao and Kanem **ca. 800** Appearance of the Kanur people around Lake Chad	**ca. 800–900** Decline of Aksum **ca. 900–1100** Kingdom of Ghana; capital city, Kumbi Saleh **ca. 1000–1100** Islam penetrates sub-Saharan Africa **1000–1500** "Great Zimbabwe" center of Bantu Kingdom in southeastern Africa	**ca. 1100–1897** Kingdom of Benin in tropical rain forest region **1194–1221** Kanem Empire achieves greatest expansion **1203** Kingdom of Ghana falls to Sosso people **1230–1255** King Sundiata, first ruler of Mali Empire **ca. 1230–1450** Kingdom of Mali Empire	**1307–1332** Mansa Musa, greatest king of Mali **1490s** Europeans establish trading posts on western African coast **mid-1400s** Decline of Mali Empire; creation of Songhai Empire **1468** Sonni Ali captures Timbuktu **1476–1507** Reign of King Mai Ali of Bornu in central Sudan **1493–1528** Songhai ruler Askia Muhammed reigns; consolidates Songhai Empire

THE AMERICAS

500 C.E – 800	800 – 1100	1100 –1300	1300 –1500
ca. 150–900 Classic period. Dominance of Teotihuacán in central Mexico, Tikal in southern Yucatán	**ca. 600–1000** Middle (Huari/Tiwanaku) Horizon in Andean South America	**ca. 800–1400** Chimu Empire on north coast of Peru	**1325** Founding of Aztec capital **1428–1519** Period of Aztec expansion **1492** European encounter with America **1519** Cortes conquers Aztec Empire **ca. 1350–1533** Inca Empire in Peru **1533** Pizarro executes Inca ruler Atahualpa

Empires and Cultures of the Ancient World

3000 B.C.E	1500 B.C.E	500 B.C.E	300 B.C.E	1 C.E.

EUROPE

3000 B.C.E	1500 B.C.E	500 B.C.E	300 B.C.E	1 C.E.
ca. 2500–1100 Minoan civilization ca. 1600–1100 Mycenaean civilization on Greek mainland	ca. 1100–800 Greek "dark ages" 800 Etruscan civilization begins in Italy ca. 750–550 Rise of the polis 594 Solon's legislation at Athens 509 Foundation of the Roman Republic 508 Democracy established in Athens	480–479 Persian invasion of Greece 478 Foundation of Delian League/Athenian Empire 431–404 Peloponnesian Wars 338 Battle of Chaeronia; Macedonian conquest of Greece 336–323 Career of Alexander the Great	264 Rome rules all of Italy 146 Rome destroys Carthage; rules all of western Mediterranean 44–31 Civil wars destroy Roman Republic 31 Rome rules Mediterranean 31 b.c.e.–14 c.e. Principate of Augustus	96–180 The good emperors rule Rome 180–284 Breakdown of the Pax Romana 306–337 Constantine regins 313 Edict of Milan 325 Council of Nicaea 391 Theodosius makes Christianity the official imperial religion ca. 400–500 The Germanic invasions 426 The City of God, by Augustine 476 The last Western emperor is deposed

NEAR EAST/ASIA

3000 B.C.E	1500 B.C.E	500 B.C.E	300 B.C.E	1 C.E.
ca. 3500–3000 Emergence of Sumerian city–states ca. 3000 Emergence of civilization along the Nile River ca. 2300 Emergence of Harappan civilization in Indus valley 2276–2221 Sargon of Akkad creates the first Mesopotamian Empire ca. 2000 Epic of Gilgamesh 1750 Hammurabi's code	ca. 1500 Aryan peoples migrate into northwestern India 960–933 Rule of Hebrew king Solomon ca. 628–551 Life of Zarathushtra ca. 537–486 Siddhartha Gautama 559–529 Cyrus the Great creates the Persian Empire	ca. 540–468 Vardhamana Mahavira, founder of Jain tradition 334 Alexander begins conquest of the Near East; invades India in 327 321–181 Mauryan Empire in India	ca. 300 Founding of Seleucid dynasty in Anatolia, Syria, and Mesopotamia; Ptolemaic dynasty in Egypt 269–232 Mauryan emperor Ashoka patronizes Buddhism 247 b.c.e.–224 c.e. Parthian dynasty controls Persia 180 b.c.e.–320 c.e. India politically divided	30 Crucifixion of Jesus 70 Romans destroy the Temple at Jerusalem 216–277 Mani ca. 224 Fall of Parthians, rise of Sasanids, in Persia ca. 320–500 Gupta dynasty, India ca. 400 Chandra Gupta conquers western India ca. 450 The Huns invade India

EAST ASIA

3000 B.C.E	1500 B.C.E	500 B.C.E	300 B.C.E	1 C.E.
ca. 4000 Neolithic cultures in China ca. 8000–300 Jōmon culture in Japan ca. 1766–1050 Hang dynasty in China with city–states and writing	1027–771 Western Chou dynasty, China 771–256 Eastern Chou dynasty in China ca. 771 Iron Age territoria states in China 551–479 Confucius in China	ca. 500–200 Rise of Mohist, Taoist, and Legalist schools of thought in China 401–256 Period of the Warring States in China ca. 300 Old Stone Age Jōmon culture in Japan replaced by Yayoi culture	256–206 Ch'in dynasty in China 221 Ch'in emperor unites all of China 206 b.c.e.–8 c.e. Former Han dynasty in China 179–104 Han philosopher Tung Chung-shu 145–90 Han historian Ssu-ma Chien 141–187 Emperor Wu Ti of China reigns	25–220 The Later Han dynasty, China 220–590 Spread of Buddhism in China 220–589 Six Dynasties period in China ca. 300–500 Barbarian invasions of China ca. 300–680 Archaic Yamato state in Japan

AFRICA

3000 B.C.E	1500 B.C.E	500 B.C.E	300 B.C.E	1 C.E.
ca. 3000 Practice of agriculture spreads from Nile river valley to the Sudan ca. 2000 Ivory and gold trade between Kush (Nubia) and Egypt ca. 1500 Practice of agriculture spreads from the Sudan to Abyssinia and the savanna region	750 Kushite king Kashta conquers Upper Egypt ca. 720 Kushite king Piankhy completes conquest of Egypt ca. 600 Meroitic period of Kushan civilization begins		25 Romans sack Kushite capital of Napata 00 b.c.e.–1 c.e. Probable first Indonesian migrations to east African coast	ca. 200 Camel first used for trans-Saharan transport ca. 200–900 Expansion of Bantu people ca. 250 Aksum (Ethiopia) controls the Red Sea trade ca. 300–400 Rise of kingdom of Ghana a. 350 Kush ceases to exist

THE AMERICAS

3000 B.C.E	1500 B.C.E	500 B.C.E	300 B.C.E	1 C.E.
ca. 4000 Maize already domesticated in Mexico	ca. 1500–800 Olmec civilization in Mesoamerica a. 800–200 Chavín (Early) Horizon in Andean South America	ca. 500–20 Founding of Monte Alban		ca. 200–600 Early Intermediate period in Andean South America; Moche and Nazca cultures ca. 150–900 Classic period. Dominance of Teotihuacán in central Mexico, Tikal in southern Yucatán

STUDY IN TIME

A Chronological Survey of World History

Enlightenment, Revolution, and Modernity

1750 – 1850

1850 – 1914

EUROPE

1750–1850	1850–1914
1756–1763 Seven Years' War	**1854–1856** The Crimean War
1783 Peace of Paris, ending American Revolution	**1861** Italy unified
1789 French Revolution begins	**1861** Emancipation of Russian serfs
1804–1814 Napoleon's empire	**1866** Austro-Prussian War; creation of Dual Monarchy of Austria-Hungary in 1867
1814–1815 Congress of Vienna	**1870–1871** Franco-Prussian War; German Empire proclaimed in 1871
1832 First British Reform Act	**1882** Triple Alliance
1837–1901 Queen Victoria of England	**1905** Revolution in Russia
1848 Revolutions across Europe	**1914** World War I begins in Europe

NEAR EAST/ASIA

1750–1850	1850–1914
1757 British victory at Plassey, in Bengal	**1857–1858** Sepoy Rebellion, India
1772–1833 Ram Mohan Roy, Hindu reformer in India	**1869** Suez Canal completed
1794–1925 Qajar shahs in Iran	**1869–1948** Mohandas (Mahatma) Gandhi
1805–1849 Muhammad Ali in Egypt	**1876–1949** Muhammad Ali Jinnah, "founder of Pakistan"
ca. 1839–1880 Tanzimat reforms, Ottoman Empire	**1882** English occupation of Egypt
1839–1897 Muslim intellectual Jamal al-Din Al-Afghani	**1886** India National Congress formed
	1889–1964 Jawaharlal Nehru
	1899 Ottoman sultan grants concession to Germany to extend railway to Baghdad
	1908 "Young Turk" Revolt, Turkey

EAST ASIA

1750–1850	1850–1914
1787–1793 Matsudaira Sadanobu's reforms in Japan	**1850–1873** Taiping and other rebellions, China
1789 White Lotus Rebellion in China	**1853–1854** Commodore Perry "opens" Japan to the West
1835–1908 Empress Dowager Tz'u-hsi	**1860s** Establishment of treaty ports in China
1839–1842 Opium War	**1870s–1890s** Self-Strengthening movement in China
	1889 Meiji Constitution in Japan
	1894–1895 Sino-Japanese War
	1898–1900 Boxer Rebellion in China
	1904–1905 Russo-Japanese War
	1910 Japan annexes Korea
	1911 Republican Revolution begins in China

AFRICA

1750–1850	1850–1914
1754–1817 Usman Dan Fodio, founder of Sultanate in northern and central Nigeria	**1856–1884** King Mutasa of Buganda reigns
1762 End of Funj sultanate in eastern Sudanic region	**1880s** Mahdist revival and uprising in Sudan
1806 British take Cape Colony from the Dutch	**1880** French protectorate in Tunisia and the Ivory Coast
1817–1828 Zulu chief Shaka reigns	**1885** British control Nigeria and British East Africa
1830–1847 French invasion of Algeria	**1894** French annex Dahomey
1830s Dutch settlers, the Boers, expand northward from Cape Colony	**1899** German East Africa; British in Sudan
1848–1885 Sudanese Madhi, Muhammad Ahmad	**1899–1902** Boer War
	1900 Nigeria a British Crown colony
	1907 Union of South Africa formed
	1911 Liberia becomes a virtual U.S. protectorate
	1914 Ethiopia the only independent state in Africa

THE AMERICAS

1750–1850	1850–1914
1776 American Declaration of Independence	**1854** Kansas-Nebraska Act
1791 First ten amendments to U.S. Constitution (Bill of Rights) ratified	**1856** Dred Scott Decision
1791 Negro slave revolt in French Santo Domingo	**1859** Raid on Harper's Ferry
1804 Haitian independence	**1860** Abraham Lincoln elected U.S. president
1808–1824 Wars of independence in Latin America	**1861–1865** U.S. Civil War
1822 Brazilian independence	**1862–1867** French invasion of Mexico
1847 Mexican War	**1863** Emancipation Proclamation in United States
	1865–1877 Reconstruction
	1880s Slavery eliminated in Cuba and Brazil
	1898 Spanish-American War
	1901 Theodore Roosevelt elected U.S. president
	1910–1917 Mexican Revolution
	1912 Woodrow Wilson elected U.S. president

The Birth of Civilization

8000 B.C.E	3500 B.C.E	1500 B.C.E	1000 B.C.E	500 B.C.

EUROPE

8000 B.C.E	3500 B.C.E	1500 B.C.E	1000 B.C.E	500 B.C.
End of Paleolithic introduction of farming	Copper Age	Bronze Age	**624–545** Thales of Miletus **ca. 611–546** Anaximander **ca. 546** Anaximenes	**469–399** Socrates **429–347** Plato **384–322** Aristotle **435–404** Great Peloponnesian War **ca. 460–400** Thucydides **ca. 400** Hippocrates of Cos **384–322** Demosthenes

NEAR EAST/ASIA

8000 B.C.E	3500 B.C.E	1500 B.C.E	1000 B.C.E	500 B.C.
ca. 8000 Neolithic Revolution, Mesopotamia	**ca. 3500** Development of Sumerian Cities **ca. 3000** Development of Writing in Mesopotamia **ca. 2800–2370** Early Dynastic period of Sumerian city–states **ca. 2370** Sargon establishes Akkadian dynasty and empire **ca. 2250–1750** Indus (Harappan) civilization; writing first appears in India **ca. 2125–2027** Third dynasty of Ur **ca. 2000–1800** Establishment of Amorites in Mesopotamia **ca. 1800–1500** Aryan peoples invade northwestern India **ca. 1792–1750** Reign of Hammurabi **ca. 1550** Establishment of Kassite dynasty at Babylon	**ca. 1500–1000** Rig-Vedic period, India **ca. 1400–1200** Hittite Empire **ca. 1100** Rise of Assyrian Power	**ca. 1000–961** Reign of King David **ca. 961–922** Reign of King Solomon **ca. 1000–500** Late Vedic period, India **ca. 1000–800/600** Composition of Brahmanas **ca. 800–500** Composition of major Upanishads **ca. 700–500** Probable reintroduction of writing **732–722** Assyrian conquest of Syria-Palestine **722** Assyrian conquest of Israel (Northern Kingdom) **612** Destruction of Assyrian capital at Nineveh **612–539** Neo-Babylonian (Chaldean) Empire **586** Destruction of Jerusalem fall of Judah (southern kingdom); Babylonian captivity **539** Restoration of Temple; return of exiles **540–ca. 468** Mahavira **ca. 566–ca. 486** Siddhartha Gautama, the Buddha	**ca. 400 b.c.e.–200 c.e.** Composition of great epics, the *Mahabharata* and *Ramayana*

EAST ASIA

8000 B.C.E	3500 B.C.E	1500 B.C.E	1000 B.C.E	500 B.C.
4000 b.c.e. Neolithic Revolution	**2205–1766** Xia dynasty **1766** Bronze Age city–states **1766–1050** Shang dynasty	**1050–256** Zhou dynasty	**771** Iron Age territorial states **551–479** Confucius	**500** Age of philosophers **370–290** Mencius **Fourth century** Laozi **221** China is unified under the Qin

AFRICA

8000 B.C.E	3500 B.C.E	1500 B.C.E	1000 B.C.E	500 B.C.
	3100–2700 Early Dynastic period, Egypt **ca. 3000** Writing first appears in Egypt **2700–2200** Old Kingdom (III–VI) **2200–2025** First Intermediate period **2025–1630** Middle Kingdom **1630–1550** Second Intermediate period **1550–1075** New Kindom		**671** Assyrian conquest of Egypt	

THE AMERICAS

8000 B.C.E	3500 B.C.E	1500 B.C.E	1000 B.C.E	500 B.C.
ca. 4000 Neolithic revolution in Mexico	**ca. 2750** Monumental architecture at Aspero	**1500–400** The Olmec	**800 b.c.e.–200 c.e.** Chavin (Early) Horizon	**200 b.c.e.–750 c.e.** The Classic period in central Mexico **150 b.c.e.–900 c.e.** The Classic period of Mayan civilization in the Yucatán and Guatemala

Global Conflict and Change

1914 – 1970   1970 – 2005

EUROPE

1914 – 1970	1970 – 2005
1917 Bolsheviks seize power, Russia	1972 British Impose direct rule on N. Ireland
1919 Versailles Settlement	1972 Israeli Olympic athletes killed by Arab terrorists
1922 Mussolini seizes power, Italy	1974 Portuguese dictatorship deposed
1933 Hitler comes to power	1977 Brezhnev president of USSR
1936 Spanish Civil War begins	1979 Margaret Thatcher becomes British prime minister
1939 World War II begins	1980 Solidarity Movement in Poland
1945 World War II ends	1984 Mikhail Gorbachev introduces *glasnost* in USSR
1948 Berlin blockade and airlift	1989 Berlin Wall demolished
1949 NATO treaty; Russia detonates atomic bomb	1990 Germany unified
1955 Warsaw Pact	1991 Failed coup in Soviet Union; Yeltsin emerges as leader of Russia
1956 Soviets crush Hungarian revolt	1993 Czechoslovakia divides into two republics
1957 EEC founded	1995 Dayton Peace Accords end war in Bosnia
1958 Charles de Gaulle comes to power in France	2000 Putin elected president of Russia
1961 Berlin Wall erected	2005 Angela Merkl becomes chancellor of Germany
1968 Soviets invade Czechoslovakia	

NEAR EAST/ASIA

1914 – 1970	1970 – 2005
1922 British leave Egypt	1973 Arab-Israeli October War
\1922–1938 Mustafa Kemal first president of Turkey	1973 OPEC oil embargo
1928 The Muslim Brotherhood founded	1978 Iranian revolution
1947 Indian Independence; creation of Pakistan	1979 Egyptian-Israeli Peace Treaty
1949 State of Israel founded	1979 Iran takes U.S. hostages
1953 Mosaddeq overthrown in Iran	1979 Soviets invade Afghanistan
1954–1970 Abdel Nasser leads Egypt	1980–1988 Iran-Iraq War
1956 Suez Crisis	1981 Egypt's Sadat assassinated
1966 Indira Gandhi becomes prime minister of India	1982 Israel invades Lebanon
1967 Israeli-Arab June War	1989 Soviets leave Afghanistan
	1990–1991 Gulf War

EAST ASIA

1914 – 1970	1970 – 2005
1919 May 4th Movement in China	1959–1975 Vietnam War
1925 Universal male suffrage in Japan	1965–1976 Cultural Revolution devastates China
1928–1937 Nationalist government in China	1972 President Nixon visits China
1931 Japan occupies Manchuria	1976 Death of Mao Zedong
1937–1945 Japan at war with China	1978–1989 New Economic policies of Deng Xiaoping in China
1941 Japan attacks Pearl Harbor	1988 Japan's GNP second in world
1945 Japan surrenders	1989 China crushes pro-democracy demonstrations in Beijing
1949 People's Republic of China founded	1991–1992 Political scandals and plummeting stock market in Japan
1950 N. Korea invades S. Korea	2004 Tsunami strikes Indian Ocean
1952 U.S. ends occupation of Japan	
1959–1960 Sino-Soviet split	

AFRICA

1914 – 1970	1970 – 2005
1919 Pan-African Congress in Paris	1967–1970 Nigerian Civil War
1935 Mussolini invades Ethiopia	1974 Drought and famine in Africa
1942–1945 World War II engulfs North Africa	1974 Emperor Haile Selassie of Ethiopia is deposed
1955–1962 Wars of independence in French Algeria	1974–1975 Portugal grants independence to Guinea, Angola, Mozambique, Cape Verde
1956 Sudan gains independenc	1980 Southern Rhodesia (Zimbabwe) gains independence from Britain
1956 Morocco and Tunisia gain independence	1984 Bishop Desmond Tutu awarded Nobel Peace Prize
1957 Ghana an independent state	1985 U.S. economic sanctions against South Africa
1960 Belgian Congo granted independence	1992 Nelson Mandela freed from prison in South Africa
1963 Kenya becomes an independent republic	1994 Nelson Mandela elected president of South Africa
1965 Revolution in Kenya	2004 Ellen Johnson–Sirleaf becomes woman president of Liberia

THE AMERICAS

1914 – 1970	1970 – 2005
1917 U.S. enters World War I	1970 Allende elected in Chile
1930–1945 Vargas dictatorship in Brazil	1972 Nixon visits China and USSR
1932 FDR U.S. president	1973 Watergate scandal breaks
1938 Mexico nationalizes oil industry	1973 Perón reelected, Argentina
1941 U.S. enters World War II	1973 Chile's Allende overthrown
1945 Death of FDR	1979 Revolution in Nicaragua and El Salvador
1946 Perón elected president in Argentina	1980 Reagan elected president
1954 U.S. Supreme Court outlaws segregation	1983 Argentine military government overthrown
1955 Perón overthrown	1983 End of Mexican oil boom
1956 Montgomery bus boycott	1988 Major arms agreement between U.S. and USSR
1959 Fidel Castro comes to power in Cuba	1991 Gulf War
1962 Cuban Missile Crisis	1992 Clinton elected president
1964 Passage of Civil Rights Act	1994 Revolt in Chiapas, Mexico
1965 U.S. expands Vietnam commitment	1998 Pope visits Cuba
1968 Martin Luther King and Robert Kennedy assassinated	2001 Terrorists attack the U. S.
	2005 New Orleans devastated by Hurricane Katrina

GLOSSARY

absolutism Term applied to strong centralized continental monarchies that attempted to make royal power dominant over aristocracies and other regional authorities.

Acropolis Religious and civic center of Athens. It is the site of the Parthenon.

Afrikaans New language, derived from Dutch, that evolved in the 17th- and 18th-century Cape Colony.

agape Meaning "love feast." A common meal that was part of the central ritual of early Christian worship.

agora Greek marketplace and civic center. It was the heart of the social life of the polis.

agricultural revolution Innovations in farm production that began in the eighteenth century and led to a scientific and mechanized agriculture.

amir/emir Islamic military commander.

Amitabha Buddha Buddhist Lord of the Western Paradise, or Pure Land.

Annam Chinese term for Vietnam.

Anschluss Meaning "union." Annexation of Austria by Germany in March 1938.

anti-Semitism Prejudice, hostility, or legal discrimination against Jews.

apartheid "Apartness," the term referring to racist policies enforced by the White-dominated regime that existed in South Africa from 1948 to 1992.

apostolic primacy Doctrine that the popes are the direct successors to the Apostle Peter and as such heads of the church.

appeasement Anglo-French policy of making concessions to Germany in the 1930s to avoid a crisis that would lead to war. It assumed that Germany had real grievances and Hitler's aims were limited and ultimately acceptable.

Areopagus Governing council of Athens, originally open only to the nobility. Named after the hill on which it met.

Arianism Belief formulated by Arius of Alexandria (ca. 280–336 C.E.) that Jesus was a created being, neither fully man nor fully God, but something in between.

aristocratic resurgence Eighteenth-century aristocratic efforts to resist the expanding power of European monarchies.

Aryans Indo-European people who invaded India and Iran in the second and first millenia B.C.E.

assignats Government bonds based on the value of confiscated church lands issued during the early French Revolution.

Atman-Brahman The unchanging, infinite principle of reality in Indian religion.

Atomists School of ancient Greek philosophy founded in the fifth century B.C.E. by Leucippus of Miletus and Democritus of Abdera. It held that the world consists of innumerable, tiny, solid, indivisible, and unchangeable particles called atoms.

Augustus Title given to Octavian in 27 B.C.E. and borne thereafter by all Roman emperors.

ausgleich Meaning "compromise." Agreement between the Habsburg emperor and the Hungarians to give Hungary considerable administrative autonomy in 1867. It created the Dual Monarchy, or Austria-Hungary.

Axis Alliance between Nazi Germany and Fascist Italy. Also called the Pact of Steel.

ayatollah Major Shi'ite religious leader.

bakufu "Tent government." Military regime that governed Japan under the shoguns.

bazaari Iranian commercial middle class.

bhakti Hindu devotional movements.

Black Death Bubonic plague that killed millions of Europeans in the 14th century.

Black Legend Argument that Spanish treatment of Native Americans was uniquely inhumane.

Blitzkrieg Meaning "war by lightening strokes." German tactic early in World War II of employing fast-moving, massed armored columns supported by air power to overwhelm the enemy.

bodhisattva A "Buddha to be" who postpones his own nirvana until he has helped all other beings become enlightened.

Bolsheviks Meaning the "majority." Term Lenin applied to his faction of the Russian Social Democratic Party. It became the Communist Party of the Soviet Union after the Russian Revolution.

Boxers Nationalistic Chinese religious society that attacked foreigners and their encroachments on China in the late 19th century.

boyars Russian nobility.

Brahmanas Texts dealing with the ritual application of the Vedas.

Bronze Age The name given to the earliest civilized era, ca. 4000 to 1000 B.C.E. The term reflects the importance of the metal bronze for the people of this age in making weapons and tools.

caliphate Spiritual and temporal rule of the Muslim community.

calpulli Wards into which the Aztec capital, Tenochtitlan, was divided.

cantonments Segregation of areas in which Europeans lived in British-ruled India from those areas inhabited by native Indians.

Catholic emancipation Grant of full political rights to Roman Catholics in Britain in 1829.

Catholic Meaning "universal." The body of belief held by most Christians enshrined within the church.

caudillo Latin American strongman, or dictator, usually with close ties to the military.

Censorate Branch of the imperial Chinese government that acted as a watchdog, reporting instances of misgovernment directly to the emperor and remonstrating when it considered the emperor's behavior improper.

censor Official of the Roman republic charged with conducting the census and compiling the lists of citizens and members of the Senate.

Chartism First large-scale European working-class political movement. It sought political reforms that would favor the interests of skilled British workers in the 1830s and 1840s.

chiaroscuro Use of shading to enhance naturalness in painting and drawing.

chicha Maize beer brewed by the mamakuna for the Inca elite.

chun-tzu The Confucian term for a person who behaves ethically, in harmony with the cosmic order.

civilization A form of human culture marked by urbanism, metallurgy, and writing.

clash of civilizations Political theory, most often identified with Harvard political scientist Samuel P. Huntington, which contends that conflict between the world's religio-cultural traditions or "civilizations" increasingly dominates world affairs.

Cold War Ideological and geographical struggle between the United States and its allies and the USSR and its allies that began after World War II and lasted until the dissolution of the USSR in 1989.

collectivization Bedrock of Stalinist agriculture, which forced Russian peasants to give up their private farms and work as members of collectives, large agricultural units controlled by the state.

conquistadores Meaning "conquerors." Spanish conquerors of the New World.

Consulate French government dominated by Napoleon from 1799 to 1804.

Convention French radical legislative body from 1792 to 1794.

Council of Nicaea Council of Christian bishops at Nicaea in 325 C.E. that formulated the Nicene Creed, a statement of Christian belief that rejected Arianism in favor of the doctrine that Christ is both fully human and fully divine.

Counter-Reformation Sixteenth-century reform movement in the Roman Catholic Church in reaction to the Protestant Reformation.

Creole A person of European descent born in Latin America or the Caribbean.

Crusades Religious wars directed by the church against infidels and heretics.

Cultural Revolution Movement launched by Mao between 1965 and 1976 against the Soviet-style bureaucracy that had taken hold in China. It involved widespread disorder and violence.

culture The ways of living built up by a group and passed on from one generation to another.

cuneiform A writing system invented by the Sumerians that used a wedge-shaped stylus, or pointed tool, to write on wet clay tablets that were then baked or dried (*cuneus* means "wedge" in Latin). The writing was also cut into stone.

Curia Papal government.

daimyo Japanese territorial lord.

Daoism A Chinese philosophy that teaches that wisdom lies in becoming one with the *Dao*, the "way," which is the creative principle of the universe.

debt peonage Requirement that laborers remain and continue to work on a hacienda until they had paid their debts to the owner for goods bought from him on credit.

deism Belief in a rational God who had created the universe, but then allowed it to function without his interference according to the mechanisms of nature and a belief in rewards and punishments after death for human action.

Delian League Alliance of Greek states under the leadership of Athens that was formed in 478–477 B.C.E. to resist the Persians.

demesne Part of a manor that was cultivated directly for the lord of the manor.

devshirme System under the Ottoman Empire that required each province to furnish a levy of Christian boys who were raised as Muslims and became soldiers in the Ottoman army.

dharma Moral law or duty.

diaspora Dispersion of an originally homogeneous people or culture. Among the many diasporas in world history, some of the most famous are the Jewish, the Chinese, the African, the Irish, and the Armenian.

Diet of Worms Meeting of the representatives (diet) of the Holy Roman Empire, presided over by the Emperor Charles V at the German city of Worms in 1521, at which Martin Luther was ordered to recant his ninety-five theses. Luther refused and was declared an outlaw although he was protected by the Elector of Saxony and other German princes.

Diet Bicameral Japanese parliament.

divine right of kings Theory that monarchs are appointed by and answerable only to God.

domestic or putting-out system of textile production Method of producing textiles in which agents furnished raw materials to households whose members spun them into thread and then wove cloth, which the agents sold as finished products.

Duce Meaning "leader." Mussolini's title as head of the Fascist Party.

Duma Russian parliament, after the revolution of 1905.

dynastic cycle Term used to describe the rise, decline, and fall of China's imperial dynasties.

ego According to Freudian theory, the part of the mind that mediates between the impulses of the id and the asceticism of the superego and allows the personality to cope with the inner and outer demands of its existence.

empiricism Use of experiment and observation derived from sensory evidence to construct scientific theory or philosophy of knowledge.

enclosures Consolidation or fencing in of common lands by British landlords to increase production and achieve greater commercial profits. It also involved the reclamation of waste land and the consolidation of strips into block fields.

encomienda Grant by the Spanish crown to a colonist of the labor of a specific number of Indians for a set period of time.

Enlightenment Eighteenth-century movement led by the philosophes that held that change and reform were both desirable through the application of reason and science.

Epicureans School of philosophy founded by Epicurus of Athens (342–271 B.C.E.). It sought to liberate people from fear of death and the supernatural by teaching that the gods took no interest in human affairs and that true happiness consisted in pleasure, which was defined as the absence of pain.

equestrians Literally "cavalrymen" or "knights." In the earliest years of the Roman republic, those who could afford to serve as mounted warriors.

Estado Novo "New state" based on political stability and economic and social progress supposedly established by the dictator Getulio Vargas after 1937.

Etruscans A people of central Italy who exerted the most powerful external influence on the early Romans.

Eucharist Meaning "thanksgiving." Celebration of the Lord's Supper. Considered the central ritual of worship by most Christians. Also called Holy Communion.

euro Common currency created by the EEC in the late 1990s.

European Economic Community Economic association formed by France, Germany, Italy, Belgium, the Netherlands, and Luxembourg in 1957. Also known as the Common Market.

European Union New name given to the EEC in 1993. It included most of the states of Western Europe.

Fabians British Socialists in the late 19th and early 20th centuries who sought to achieve socialism through gradual, peaceful, and democratic means.

family economy Basic structure of production and consumption in preindustrial Europe.

fascism Political movements that tend to be antidemocratic, anti-Marxist, antiparliamentary, and often anti-Semitic. Fascists were invariably nationalists and exhalted the nation over the individual. They supported the interests of the middle class and rejected the ideas of the French Revolution and 19th-century liberalism. The first fascist regime was founded by Benito Mussolini (1883–1945) in Italy in the 1920s.

fealty Oath of loyalty by a vassal to a lord, promising to perform specified services.

feudal society Social, political, military, and economic system that prevailed in the Middle Ages and beyond in some parts of Europe.

fief Land granted to a vassal in exchange for services, usually military.

Fourteen Points President Woodrow Wilson's (1856–1924) idealistic war aims.

Führer Meaning "leader." Title taken by Hitler when he became dictator of Germany.

gentry In China, a largely urban, landowning class that represented local interests and functioned as quasi-bureaucrats under the magistrates.

ghazis Warriors who carried Islam by force of arms to pagan groups.

ghettos Separate communities in which Jews were required by law to live.

glasnost Meaning "openness." Policy initiated by Mikhail Gorbachev in the 1980s of permitting open criticism of the policies of the Soviet Communist Party.

globalization Term used to describe the increasing economic and cultural interdependence of societies around the world.

Glorious Revolution Largely peaceful replacement of James II by William and Mary as English monarchs in 1688. It marked the beginning of constitutional monarchy in Britain.

Golden Horde Name given to the Mongol rulers of Russia from 1240 to 1480.

Grand Mufti Chief religious authority of the Ottoman Empire. Also called "the Shaykh of Islam."

Great Depression Prolonged worldwide economic downturn that began in 1929 with the collapse of the New York Stock Exchange.

Great Leap Forward Mao's disastrous attempt to modernize the Chinese economy in 1958.

Great Purges Imprisonment and execution of millions of Soviet citizens by Stalin between 1934 and 1939.

Great Reform Bill (1832) Limited reform of the British House of Commons and expansion of the electorate to include a wider variety of the propertied classes. It laid the groundwork for further orderly reforms within the British constitutional system.

Great Schism Appearance of two and at times three rival popes between 1378 and 1415.

Great Trek Migration between 1835 and 1847 of Boer pioneers (called *voortrekkers*) north from British-ruled Cape Colony to establish their own independent republics.

guild Association of merchants or craftsmen that offered protection to its members and set rules for their work and products.

Guomindang (GMT) China's Nationalist Party, founded by Sun Zhongshan.

hacienda Large landed estates in Spanish America.

hadith Saying or action ascribed to Muhammad.

Hajj Pilgrimage to Mecca that all Muslims are enjoined to perform at least once in their lifetime.

Harappan Term used to describe the first civilization of the Indus Valley.

Hegira Flight of Muhammad and his followers from Mecca to Medina in 622 C.E. It marks the beginning of the Islamic calendar.

heliocentric theory The theory, now universally accepted, that the Earth and the other planets revolve around the sun. First proposed by Aristarchos of Samos (310–230 B.C.E.).

Helots Hereditary Spartan serfs.

heretics Persons whose religious beliefs differ from the official doctrines of their faith.

hieroglyphics The complicated writing script of ancient Egypt. It combined picture writing with pictographs and sound signs. Hieroglyph means "sacred carvings" in Greek.

Hindu Term applied to the diverse social, racial, linguistic, and religious groups of India.

Holocaust Nazi extermination of millions of European Jews between 1940 and 1945. Also called the "final solution to the Jewish problem."

Holy Roman Empire Revival of the old Roman Empire, based mainly in Germany and northern Italy, that endured from 870 to 1806.

home rule Advocacy of a large measure of administrative autonomy for Ireland within the British Empire between the 1880s and 1914.

hoplite phalanx Basic unit of Greek warfare in which infantrymen fought in close order, shield to shield, usually eight ranks deep.

Huguenots French Calvinists.

humanism Study of the Latin and Greek classics and of the Church Fathers both for their own sake and to promote a rebirth of ancient norms and values.

humanitas Roman name for a liberal arts education.

id According to Freudian psychoanalysis, the part of the mind that consists of amoral, irrational, driving instincts for sexual gratification, aggression, and physical and sensual pleasure.

imam Islamic prayer leader.

impact of modernity Effect of western political, economic, and social ideas and institutions on traditional societies.

imperator Under the Roman republic, the title given to a victorious general. Under Augustus and his successors, it became the title of the ruler of Rome, meaning "emperor."

imperium In ancient Rome, the right to issue commands and to enforce them by fines, arrests, and even corporal and capital punishment.

import substitution Replacement of imported goods with those manufactured domestically.

Indo-European A widely distributed language group that includes most of the languages spoken in Europe, Persian, Sanskrit, and their derivatives.

Indo-Greeks Bactrian rulers who broke away from the Seleucid Empire to found a state that combined elements of Greek and Indian civilizations.

indulgences Remission of the temporal penalty of punishment in purgatory that remained after sins had been forgiven.

Industrial Revolution Mechanization of the European economy that began in Britain in the second half of the 18th century.

intifadah Literally, "shaking." Uprisings by the Palestinians against Israeli occupation.

Islam "Submission." Religion founded by the prophet Muhammad.

Italia Irredenta Meaning "unredeemed Italy." Italian-speaking areas that had been left under Austrian rule at the time of the unification of Italy.

Jacobins Radical republican party during the French Revolution that displaced the Girondists.

Jains Indian religious community that teaches compassion for all beings.

Janissaries Elite Ottoman troops who were recruited through the *devshirme*.

jatis The many subgroups that make up the Hindu caste system.

jihad "Struggle in the path of God." Although not necessarily implying violence, it is often interpreted to mean holy war in the name of Islam.

July Monarchy French regime set up after the overthrow of the Bourbons in July 1830.

Junkers Noble landlords of Prussia.

Ka'ba A black meteorite in the city of Mecca that became Islam's holiest shrine.

Kabuki Realistic form of Japanese theater similar to English Elizabethan drama.

Kalahari A large desert in southwestern Africa that partially isolates southern Africa from the rest of the continent.

kamikaze "Divine winds" that sank a portion of the invading Mongol fleet in Japan in 1281.

karma Indian belief that every action has an inevitable effect. Good deeds bring good results; evil deeds have evil consequences.

Khmer Rouge Meaning "Red Cambodia." Radical Communist movement that ruled Cambodia from 1975 to 1978.

kleindeutsch Meaning "small German." Argument that the German-speaking portions of the Habsburg Empire should be excluded from a united Germany.

Kristallnacht Meaning "crystal night" because of the broken glass that littered German streets after the looting and destruction of Jewish homes, businesses, and synagogues across Germany on the orders of the Nazi Party in November 1938.

La Reforma The 19th-century Mexican liberal reform movement that opposed Santa Ana's dictatorship and sought to foster economic progress, civilian rule, and political stability. It was strongly anticlerical.

laissez-faire French phrase meaning "allow to do." In economics, the doctrine of minimal government interference in the working of the economy.

latifundia Large plantations for growing cash crops owned by wealthy Romans.

LDP Liberal Democratic Party. A conservative party that has dominated postwar Japanese politics.

League of Nations Association of sovereign states set up after World War I to pursue common policies and avert international aggression.

Lebensraum "Living space," Nazi plan to colonize and exploit eastern Europe.

Legalism Chinese philosophical school that argued that a strong state was necessary to have a good society.

levée en masse French revolutionary conscription (1792) of all males into the army and the harnessing of the economy for war production.

liberalism In the 19th century, support for representative government dominated by the propertied classes and minimal government interference in the economy.

liberation theology Effort by certain Roman Catholic theologians to combine Marxism with traditional Christian concern for the poor.

logos Divine reason, or fire, which according to the Stoics, was the guiding principle in nature.

Long Count Mayan calendar that dated from a fixed point in the past.

Long March Flight of the Chinese communists from their nationalist foes to northwest China in 1934.

Luftwaffe German air force in World War II.

madrasa Islamic college of higher learning.

Magna Carta The "Great Charter" limiting royal power, which the English nobility forced King John to sign in 1215.

Magna Graecia Meaning "Great Greece" in Latin. The name given by the Romans to southern Italy and Sicily because there were so many Greek colonies in the region.

Magyars Majority ethnic group in Hungary.

Mahabharata and Ramayana Two classical Indian epics.

Mahayana The "Great Vehicle" for salvation in Buddhism. It emphasized the Buddha's infinite compassion for all beings.

mamakuna Inca women who lived privileged but celibate lives and had important economic and cultural roles.

Mandate of Heaven The Chinese belief that heaven entrusts or withdraws a ruler's or a dynasty's right to govern.

Manichaeism A dualistic and moralistic view of reality in which good and evil, spirit and matter warred with each other.

mannerism A style of art in the mid to late 16th century that permitted artists to express their own "manner" or feelings in contrast to the symmetry and simplicity of the art of the High Renaissance.

manors Village farms owned by a lord.

Marshall Plan U.S. program, named after Secretary of State George C. Marshall, that provided economic aid to Europe after World War II.

Marxism Theory of Karl Marx (1818–1883) and Friedrich Engels (1820–1895) that history is the result of class conflict, which will end in the inevitable triumph of the industrial proletariat over the bourgeoisie and the abolition of private property and social class.

Meiji restoration Overthrow of the Tokugawa *bakufu* in Japan in 1868 and the transfer, or "restoration," of power to the imperial government under the Emperor Meiji.

Mein Kampf Meaning "My Struggle." Hitler's statement of his political program, published in 1924.

Mensheviks Meaning the "minority." Term Lenin applied to the majority moderate faction of the Russian Social Democratic Party opposed to him and the Bolsheviks.

mercantilism Term used to describe close government control of the economy that sought to maximize exports and accumulate as much precious metals as possible to enable the state to defend its economic and political interests.

Mesoamerica Region of North America that extends from the central part of modern Mexico to Central America.

Mesopotamia Modern Iraq. The land between the Tigris and Euphrates Rivers.

Messiah The redeemer whose coming, Jews believed, would establish the kingdom of God on earth. Christians considered Jesus to be the Messiah (Christ means Messiah in Greek).

mestizos Persons of mixed Native American and European descent.

Mexica Aztecs' name for themselves.

mfecane Period of widespread warfare and chaos among Bantu peoples in east-central Africa during the early 19th century.

millets Small self-governing communities within the Ottoman Empire.

Minoan Bronze Age civilization that arose in Crete in the third and second millennia B.C.E.

mita Inca system of forced labor in return for gifts and ritual entertainments.

Mitimaqs Communities whom the Incas forced to settle in designated regions for strategic purposes.

monotheism The worship of one universal God.

Moors Spanish and Portuguese term for Muslims.

Mughals Descendants of the Mongols who established an Islamic empire in India in the 16th century with its capital at Delhi.

mujtahid Shi'ite religious-legal scholar.

mulattos Persons of mixed African and European descent.

Mycenaean Bronze Age civilization of mainland Greece that was centered at Mycenae.

"mystery" religions Cults of Isis, Mithra, and Osiris, which promised salvation to those initiated into the secret or "mystery" of their rites.

nacionalismo Right-wing Argentine nationalist movement that arose in the 1930s and resembled European fascism.

National Studies Japanese intellectual tradition that emphasized native Japanese culture and institutions and rejected the influence of Chinese Confucianism.

nationalism Belief that one is part of a nation, defined as a community with its own language, traditions, customs, and history that distinguish it from other nations and make it the primary focus of a person's loyalty and sense of identity.

natural selection According to Darwin, the process in nature by which only the organisms best adapted to their environment tend to survive and transmit their genes, while those less adapted tend to be eliminated.

neocolonial economy Economic relationship between a former colonial state and countries with more developed economies in which the former colony exports raw materials to and imports manufactured goods from the more developed nations.

Neo-Daoism A revival of Daoist "mysterious learning" that flourished as a reaction against Confucianism during the Han dynasty.

Neolithic Revolution The shift beginning 10,000 years ago from hunter-gatherer societies to settled communities.

New Economic Policy (NEP) Limited revival of capitalism, especially in light industry and agriculture, introduced by Lenin in 1921 to repair the damage inflicted on the Russian economy by the civil war and War Communism.

New Imperialism Extension in the late 19th and early 20th centuries of Western political and economic dominance to Asia, the Middle East, and Africa.

Nicene Creed A declaration of faith that the Council of Nicaea hoped would be endorsed by all Christians.

Nilotic Africa The lands along the Nile River.

ninety-five theses Document posted on the door of Castle Church in Wittenberg, Germany on October 31, 1517 by Martin Luther protesting, among other things, the selling of indulgences.

nirvana In Buddhism the attainment of release from the wheel of karma.

Nō play Highly stylized form of Japanese drama in which the chorus provides the narrative line as in classical Greek plays.

oba Title of the king of Benin.

obsidian Hard volcanic glass that was widely used in Mesoamerica.

occupied territories Land occupied by Israel as a result of wars with its Arab neighbors in 1948–1949, 1967, and 1973.

Old Regime Term applied to the pattern of social, political, and economic relationships and institutions that existed in Europe before the French Revolution.

orthodox Meaning "holding the right opinions." Applied to the doctrines of the Catholic Church.

orthopraxy Correct practice of a religion.

Paleolithic Age The earliest period when stone tools were used, from about 1,000,000 to 10,000 B.C.E. From the Greek meaning "old stone."

Panhellenic Meaning "all-Greek." The sense of cultural identity that all Greeks felt in common with each other.

pan-Islamism Movement that advocates that the entire Muslim world should form a unified political and cultural entity.

Pan-Slavic movement Effort to create a nation or federation that would embrace all the Slavic peoples of Eastern Europe.

Papal States Territory in central Italy ruled by the pope until 1870.

parlement French regional court dominated by hereditary nobility. The most important was the Parlement of Paris, which claimed the right to register royal decrees before they could become law.

Parliamentary monarchy Form of limited monarchy developed in England.

patricians Hereditary upper class of early republican Rome.

peace process Efforts, chiefly led by the United States, to broker a peace between the state of Israel and the PLO.

Peloponnesian Wars Protracted struggle between Athens and Sparta to dominate Greece between 465 and Athens' final defeat in 404 B.C.E.

peninsulares Native-born Spaniards who immigrated from Spain to settle in the Spanish colonies.

perestroika Meaning "restructuring." Attempt in the 1980s to reform the Soviet government and economy.

Perónism Authoritarian, nationalist movement founded in Argentina in the 1940s by the dictator Juan Perón.

pharaoh The god-kings of ancient Egypt. The term originally meant "great house" or palace.

Pharisees Group that was most strict in its adherence to Jewish law.

philosophes Eighteenth-century writers and critics who forged the new attitudes favorable to change. They sought to apply reason and common sense to the institutions and societies of their day.

pipiltin Aztec bureaucrats and priests.

pirs Shi'ite holy men.

plantation economy Economic system stretching between Chesapeake Bay and Brazil that produced crops, especially sugar, cotton, and tobacco, using slave labor on large estates.

plebeians Hereditary lower class of early republican Rome.

plenitude of power Teaching that the popes have power over all other bishops of the church.

pochteca Aztec merchants.

pogroms Organized riots against Jews in the Russian Empire.

polis The basic Greek political unit. Usually, but incompletely, translated as "city-state," the Greeks thought of the polis as a community of citizens theoretically descended from a common ancestor.

polytheism The worship of many gods.

Popular Front Government of all left-wing parties that took power in France in 1936 to enact social and economic reforms.

populares Roman politicians who sought to pursue a political career based on the support of the people rather than just the aristocracy.

positivism Philosophy of Auguste Comte that science is the final, or positive, stage of human intellectual development because it involves exact descriptions of phenomena, without recourse to unobservable operative principles, such as gods or spirits.

Pragmatic Sanction Legal basis negotiated by Emperor Charles VI (r. 1711–1740) for the Habsburg succession through his daughter Maria Theresa (r. 1740–1780).

PRI The Institutional Revolutionary Party, which emerged from the Mexican revolution of 1911 and governed Mexico until the end of the 20th century.

proletarianization Process whereby independent artisans and factory workers lose control of the means of production and of the conduct of their own trades to the owners of capital.

Ptolemaic system Pre-Copernican explanation of the universe, which placed the Earth at the center of the universe.

Punic Wars Three wars between Rome and Carthage for dominance of the western Mediterranean that were fought from 264 B.C.E. to 146 B.C.E.

Pure Land Buddhism Variety of Japanese Buddhism that maintained that only faith was necessary for salvation.

Puritans English Protestants who sought to "purify" the Church of England of any vestiges of Catholicism.

Quechua Inca language.

quipu Knotted string used by Andean peoples for recordkeeping.

Qur'an "A reciting." Islamic bible, which Muslims believe God revealed to the prophet Muhammad.

racism Pseudoscientific theory that biological features of race determine human character and worth.

raja An Indian king.

raj The years from 1858 to 1947 during which India was governed directly by the British Crown.

Ramadan Month when Muslims must fast during daylight hours.

Reconquista Christian reconquest of Spain from the Muslims from 1000 to 1492.

Reformation Sixteenth-century religious movement that sought to reform the Roman Catholic Church and led to the establishment of Protestantism.

regular clergy Monks and nuns who belong to religious orders.

Reichstag German parliament, which existed in various forms, until 1945.

Reign of Terror Period between the summer of 1793 and the end of July 1794 when the French revolutionary state used extensive executions and violence to defend the Revolution and suppress its alleged internal enemies.

relativity Theory of physics, first expounded by Albert Einstein in 1905, in which time and space exist not separately, but rather as a combined continuum.

Renaissance Revival of ancient learning and the supplanting of traditional religious beliefs by new secular and scientific values that began in Italy in the 14th and 15th centuries.

repartimiento Labor tax in Spanish America that required adult male Native Americans to devote a set number of days a year to Spanish economic enterprises.

revisionism Advocacy among 19th-century German Socialists of achieving a humane socialist society through the evolution of democratic institutions, not revolution.

Sahara The world's largest desert. It extends across Africa from the Atlantic to the eastern Sudan. Historically, the Sahara has hindered contact between the Mediterranean and sub-Saharan Africa.

Sahel An area of steppe and semi-desert that borders the Sahara.

samsara The endless cycle of existence, of birth, and rebirth.

samurai Professional Japanese warriors.

Sandinistas Marxist guerrilla force that overthrew the Somoza dictatorship in Nicaragua in 1979.

sans-culottes Meaning "without breeches." The lower-middle classes and artisans of Paris during the French Revolution.

satraps Governors of provinces in the Persian Empire.

savannah An area of open woodlands and grassy plains.

Schlieffen Plan Germany's plan for achieving a quick victory in the West at the outbreak of World War I by invading France through Belgium and Luxembourg.

Scholasticism Method of study based on logic and dialectic that dominated the medieval schools. It assumed that truth already existed; students had only to organize, elucidate, and defend knowledge learned from authoritative texts, especially those of Aristotle and the Church Fathers.

Scientific Revolution Sweeping change in the scientific view of the universe that occurred in the West in the 16th and 17th centuries.

scramble for Africa Late 19th century takeover of most of Africa by European powers.

secular clergy Parish clergy who did not belong to a religious order.

serfs Peasants tied to the land they tilled.

Shaanxi banks Private commercial banks in China under the Manchus.

Shahanshah "King of kings," the title of the Persian ruler.

Shari'a Islamic religious law.

Shi'a Muslims who trace their beliefs to the caliph Ali, who was assassinated in 661 C.E.

Shintō "The way of the gods." The animistic worship of the forces of nature that is the indigenous religion of Japan.

shōgun Military official who was the actual ruler of Japan in the emperor's name from the late 1100s until the mid-19th century.

Silk Road Trade route from China to the West that stretched across Central Asia.

Sophists Professional teachers who emerged in Greece in the mid-fifth century B.C.E. who were paid to teach techniques of rhetoric, dialectic, and argumentation.

soviets Workers' and soldiers' councils formed in Russia during the revolution.

spinning jenny Machine invented in England by James Hargreaves around 1765 to mass-produce thread.

Stele (also Stela) An upright stone or slab within inscribed surface, used as a monument or as a commemorative tablet.

steppe peoples Nomadic tribespeople who dwelled on the Eurasian plains from eastern Europe to the borders of China and Iran. They frequently traded with or invaded more settled cultures.

Stoics Philosophical school founded by Zeno of Citium (335–263 B.C.E.) that taught that humans could only be happy with natural law.

streltsy Professional troops who made up the Moscow garrison. They were suppressed by Peter the Great.

studia humanitatis During the Renaissance, a liberal arts program of study that embraced grammar, rhetoric, poetry, history, philosophy, and politics.

stupa A Buddhist shrine.

suffragettes British women who lobbied and agitated for the right to vote in the early 20th century.

Sufi Movement within Islam that emphasizes the spiritual and mystical.

sultan Muslim royal title that means "authority."

Sunna "Tradition." Dominant Islamic group.

superego According to Freud, the part of the mind that embodies the external moral imperatives and expectations imposed on the personality by society and culture.

Swahili Language and culture that developed from the interaction of native Africans and Arabs along the East African coast.

symposion Carefully organized drinking party that was the center of Greek aristocratic social life. It featured games, songs, poetry, and even philosophical disputation.

syncretism In religion, the equating or combining of deities.

Table of Ranks Official hierarchy established by Peter the Great in imperial Russia that equated a person's social position and privileges with his rank in the state bureaucracy or army.

taille Direct tax on the French peasantry.

Taiping rebellion A 19th-century revolt against China's Manchu dynasty that was inspired by quasi-Christian ideas and that led to enormous suffering and destruction before its collapse in 1868.

tennō "Heavenly emperor." The official title of the emperor of Japan.

tetcutin Subordinate Aztec lords.

tetrarchy Diocletian's (r. 306–337 C.E.) system for ruling the Roman Empire by four men with power divided territorially.

The *Iliad* and the *Odyssey* Epic poems by Homer about the "Dark Age" heroes of Greece who fought at Troy. The poems were written down in the eighth century B.C.E. after centuries of being sung by bards.

theocracy State ruled by religious leaders who claim to govern by divine authority.

Theravada The "Way of the Elders." A school of Buddhism that emphasized the monastic ideal.

Thermidorean Reaction Reaction against the radicalism of the French Revolution that began in July 1794. Associated with the end of terror and establishment of the Directory.

Third Estate Branch of the French Estates General representing all of the kingdom outside the nobility and the clergy.

three-field system Medieval innovation that increased the amount of land under cultivation by leaving only one-third fallow in a given year.

tlatoani An Aztec ruler.

transubstantiation Doctrine that the entire substances of the bread and wine are changed in the Eucharist into the body and blood of Christ.

treaty ports Chinese ports ruled by foreign consuls where foreigners enjoyed commercial privileges and immunity from Chinese laws.

Trekboers White livestock farmers in Cape Colony.

tribunes Roman officials who had to be plebeians and were elected by the plebeian assembly to protect plebeians from the arbitrary power of the magistrates.

Tripartite Pact Alliance between Japan and Nazi Germany and Fascist Italy that was signed in 1940.

ulama "Persons with correct knowledge." Islamic scholarly elite who served a social function similar to the Christian clergy.

Umma Islamic community.

"unequal treaties" Agreements imposed on China in the 19th century by European powers, the United States, and Japan that granted their citizens special legal and economic privileges on Chinese soil.

Upanishads Vedic texts most concerned with speculation about the universe.

Urdu-Hindi Language that combines Persian-Arabic and native Indian elements. Urdu is the Muslim version of the language; Hindi is the Hindu version.

uzama Order of hereditary chiefs in Benin.

varnas The four main classes that form the basis for Hindu caste relations.

vassal Person granted an estate or cash payments in return for accepting the obligation to render services to a lord.

Vedas Sacred texts of the ancient Aryan invaders of India. The Rig Veda is the oldest material in the Vedas.

vernacular Everyday language spoken by the people as opposed to Latin.

Viet Minh Communist-dominated popular front organization formed by Ho Chi Minh to establish an independent Vietnamese republic.

War Communism Economic policy adopted by the Bolsheviks during the Russian civil war to seize the banks, heavy industry, railroads, and grain.

war guilt clause Clause of the Versailles Treaty, which assigned responsibility for World War I solely to Germany.

water frame Water-powered device invented by Richard Arkwright to produce a more durable cotton fabric. It led to the shift in the production of cotton textiles from households to factories.

Weimar Republic German democratic regime that existed between the end of World War I and Hitler's coming to power in 1933.

White Russians Russians who opposed the Bolsheviks (the "Reds") in the Russian Civil War of 1918–1921.

Works Progress Administration New Deal program created by the Roosevelt administration in 1935 that provided relief for the unemployed in the industrial sector during the Great Depression in the United States.

yangban Elite Korean families of the Choson period.

zaibatsu Groups of Japanese companies, or "trusts," that had a common ownership and dominated the economy of prewar Japan.

Zen A form of Buddhism, which taught that Buddha was only a man and exhorted each person to attain enlightenment by his or her own efforts.

Zionism Movement to create a Jewish state in Palestine (the Biblical Zion).

Zoroastrianism A quasi-monotheistic Iranian religion founded by Zoroaster (ca. 628–551 B.C.E.) who preached a message of moral reform and exhorted his followers to worship only Ahura Mazda, the Wise Lord.

CHAPTER 1

General Prehistory

P. BOGUCKI, *The Origins of Human Society* (1999). An excellent summary of recent scholarship on the earliest origins of human societies.

F. BRAY, *The Rice Economies: Technology and Development in Asian Societies* (1986). Still the best authority on the origins of rice cultivation and its effect on the development of ancient Asia.

M. EHRENBERG, *Women in Prehistory* (1989). An account of the role of women in early times.

C. FREEMAN, *Egypt, Greece and Rome: Civilizations of the Ancient Mediterranean* (2004). Good comparative study of Egypt with Greece and Rome.

D. C. JOHNSON and M. R. EDEY, *Lucy: The Beginning of Mankind* (1981). An account of the African origins of humans.

S. M. NELSON, ed., *Ancient Queens: Archaeological Explorations* (2003). Reassesses women rulers and female power in the ancient world.

S. M. NELSON and M. ROSEN-AYALON, *In Pursuit of Gender: Worldwide Archaeological Approaches* (2002). Essays on gender and the archaeology of the ancient world.

D. L. NICHOLS and T. H. CHARLTON, eds., *The Archaeology of CityStates: Cross-cultural Approaches* (1997). One of a growing body of books and essay collections employing cross-cultural and comparative approaches to world history and archaeology.

M. OLIPHANT, *The Atlas of the Ancient World: Charting the Great Civilizations of the Past* (1992). An excellent comprehensive atlas of the ancient world.

P. L. SHINNIE, *Ancient Nubia* (1996). A study of the African state most influenced by Egyptian culture.

Near East

M. E. AUBER, *The Phoenicians and the West* (1996). A new study of an important sea-going people who served as a conduit between East and West.

BEN-TOR, ed., *The Archaeology of Ancient Israel* (1992). A useful and up-to-date survey.

J. BOTTÉRO, *Everyday Life in Ancient Mesopotamia* (2001). Interesting vignettes of ancient Mesopotamian life.

H. CRAWFORD, *Sumer and the Sumerians* (1991). A discussion of the oldest Mesopotamian civilization.

I. FINKELSTEIN and N. A. SILBERMAN, *The Bible Unearthed: Archaeology's New Vision of Ancient Israel and the Origin of its Sacred Texts* (2001). An interesting discussion of the insights of recent archaeological finds on the history of the Bible and ancient Israel.

G. LEICK, *Mesopotamia: The Invention of the City* (2002). Good discussion of the urban history of ancient Mesopotamia.

J. N. POSTGATE, *Early Mesopotamia* (1992). An excellent study of Mesopotamian economy and society from the earliest times to about 1500 B.C.E., helpfully illustrated with drawings, photos, and translated documents.

D. B. REDFORD, *Akhenaten* (1987). A study of the controversial religious reformer.

W. F. SAGGS, *The Might That Was Assyria* (1984). A history of the northern Mesopotamian Empire and a worthy companion to the author's account of the Babylonian Empire in the south.

M. VAN DE MIEROOP, *A History of the Ancient Near East, ca. 3000–323 B.C.* (2004). An up-to-date comprehensive survey of ancient Near Eastern history.

India

D. P. AGRAWAL, *The Archaeology of India* (1982). A fine survey of the problems and data. Detailed, but with excellent summaries and brief discussions of major issues.

C. CHAKRABORTY, *Common Life in the Rigveda and Atharvaveda—An Account of the Folklore in the Vedic Period* (1977). An interesting attempt to reconstruct everyday life in the Vedic period from the principal Vedic texts.

J. R. MCINTOSH, *A Peaceful Realm: The Rise and Fall of the Indus Civilization* (2002). Discusses what archaeologists have managed to unearth so far regarding Harrapan civilization.

W. D. O'FLAHERTY, *The Rig Veda: An Anthology* (1981). An excellent selection of Vedic texts in prosaic but very careful translation, with helpful notes on the texts.

J. E. SCHWARTZBERG, ed., *A Historical Atlas of South Asia* (1978). The definitive reference work for historical geography. Includes chronological tables and substantive essays.

R. THAPAR, *Early India: From the Origins to A.D. 1300* (2003). A comprehensive introduction to the early history of India.

China

M. LOEWE and E. SHAUGHNESSY eds., *The Cambridge History of Ancient China: From the Origins of Civilization to 221 B.C.* (1999). A comprehensive and authoritative history of ancient China.

K. C. CHANG, *The Archeology of Ancient China*, 4th ed. (1986). The standard work on the subject.

K. C. CHANG, *Art, Myth, and Ritual, The Path to Political Authority in Ancient China* (1984). A study of the relation between shamans, gods, agricultural production, and political authority during the Shang and Zhou dynasties.

N. DI COSMO, *Ancient China and its Enemies: The Rise of Nomadic Power in East Asian History* (2002). An excellent study of the relationship between China and nomadic peoples that was a powerful force in shaping Chinese and Central Asian history.

C. Y. HSU, *Western Chou Civilization* (1988).

D. N. KEIGHTLEY, *The Origins of Chinese Civilization* (1983).

M. E. LEWIS, *Sanctioned Violence in Early China* (1990).

X. Q. LI, *Eastern Zhou and Qin Civilizations* (1986). This work includes fresh interpretations based on archaeological finds.

Americas

R. L. BURGER, *Chavín and the Origins of Andean Civilization* (1992). A lucid and detailed account of the rise of civilization in the Andes.

M. D. COE and R. KOONTZ, *Mexico: From the Olmecs to the Aztecs* (2002). Good survey of ancient Mexico.

D. DREW, *The Lost Chronicles of the Maya Kings* (1999). Fine introduction to the history of Maya civilization.

V. W. FITZHUGH and A. CROWELL, *Crossroads of Continents: Cultures of Siberia and Alaska* (1988). Covers the area where the immigration from Eurasia to the Americas began.

R. FORD, ed., *Prehistoric Food Production in North America* (1985). Examines the origins of agriculture in the Americas.

P. D. HUNT, *Indian Agriculture in America: Prehistory to the Present* (1987). Includes a discussion of preconquest agriculture.

A. KNIGHT, *Mexico: From the Beginning to the Spanish Conquest* (2002). First of a three-volume comprehensive history of Mexico.

C. MORRIS and A. VON HAGEN, *The Inka Empire and Its Andean Origins* (1993). An overview of Andean civilization with excellent illustrations.

M. MOSELEY, *The Incas and Their Ancestors: The Archaeology of Ancient Peru* (1992). An overview of Peruvian archaeology.

J. A. SABLOFF, *The New Archaeology and the Ancient Maya* (1990). A lively account of recent research in Maya archaeology.

I. SILVERBLATT, *Moon, Sun, and Witches: Gender Ideologies and Class in Inca and Colonial Peru* (1987). A controversial but thought-provoking discussion of Incan ideas about gender.

CHAPTER 2

China

R. BERSTEIN, *Ultimate Journey: Retracing the Path of an Ancient Buddhist Monk who Crossed Asia in Search of Enlightenment* (2001). Discusses the diffusion of Buddhism from India to China.

H. G. CREEL, *What Is Taoism? And Other Studies in Chinese Cultural History* (1970).

W. T. DE BARY et al., *Sources of Chinese Tradition* (1960). A reader in China's philosophical and historical literature. It should be consulted for the later periods as well as for the Zhou.

H. FINGARETE, *Confucius—The Secular as Sacred* (1998).

Y. L. FUNG, *A Short History of Chinese Philosophy*, ed. by D. Bodde (1948). A survey of Chinese philosophy from its origins down to recent times.

A. GRAHAM, *Disputers of the Tao* (1989).

D. HAWKES, *Ch'u Tz'u: The Songs of the South* (1985).

D. C. LAU, trans., *Lao-tzu, Tao Te Ching* (1963).

D. C. LAU, trans., *Confucius, The Analects* (1979).

C. LI, ED., *The Sage and the Second Sex: Confucianism, Ethics, and Gender* (2000). A good introduction to gender and ethics in Confucian thought.

B. I. SCHWARTZ, *The World of Thought in Ancient China* (1985).

A. WALEY, *Three Ways of Thought in Ancient China* (1956). An easy yet sound introduction to Confucianism, Daoism, and Legalism.

A. WALEY, *The Book of Songs* (1960).

B. WATSON, trans., *Basic Writings of Mo Tzu, Hsun Tzu, and Han Fei Tzu* (1963).

B. WATSON, trans., *The Complete Works of Chuang Tzu* (1968).

H. WELCH, *Taoism, The Parting of the Way* (1967).

India

A. L. BASHAM, *The Wonder That Was India*, rev. ed. (1963). Still unsurpassed by more recent works. Chapter VII, "Religion," is a superb introduction to the Vedic Aryan, Brahmanic, Hindu, Jain, and Buddhist traditions of thought.

W. N. BROWN, *Man in the Universe: Some Continuities in Indian Thought* (1970). A penetrating yet brief reflective summary of major patterns in Indian thinking.

W. T. DE BARY ET AL., *Sources of Indian Tradition* (1958). 2 vols. Vol. I, *From the Beginning to 1800*, ed. and rev. by Ainslie T. Embree (1988). Excellent selections from a variety of Indian texts, with good introductions to chapters and individual selections.

P. HARVEY, *An Introduction to Buddhism* (1990). Chapters 1–3 provide an excellent historical introduction.

T. J. HOPKINS, *The Hindu Religious Tradition* (1971). A first-rate, thoughtful introduction to Hindu religious ideas and practice.

K. KLOSTERMAIER, *Hinduism: A Short History* (2000). A relatively compact survey of the history of Hinduism.

J. M. KOLLER, *The Indian Way* (1982). A useful, wide-ranging handbook of Indian thought and religion.

R. H. ROBINSON and W. L. JOHNSON, *The Buddhist Religion*, 3rd ed. (1982). An excellent first text on the Buddhist tradition, its thought and development.

R. C. ZAEHNER, *Hinduism* (1966). One of the best general introductions to central Indian religious and philosophical ideas.

Israel

A. BACH, ed., *Women in the Hebrew Bible: A Reader* (1999). Excellent introduction to the ways in which biblical scholars are exploring the role of women in the Bible.

BRIGHT, *A History of Israel* (1968), 2nd ed. (1972). One of the standard scholarly introductions to biblical history and literature.

W. D. DAVIES and L. FINKELSTEIN, eds., *The Cambridge History of Judaism*. Vol. I, *Introduction: The Persian Period* (1984). Excellent essays on diverse aspects of the exilic period and later.

J. NEUSNER, *The Way of Torah: An Introduction to Judaism* (1979). A sensitive introduction to the Judaic tradition and faith.

The Oxford History of the Biblical World, M. D. Coogan, ed. (1998).

Greece

The Cambridge Companion to Greek and Roman Philosophy, D. SEDLEY ed., (2003).

G. B. KERFERD, *The Sophistic Movement* (1981). An excellent description and analysis.

J. LEAR, *Aristotle: The Desire to Understand* (1988). A brilliant yet comprehensible introduction to the work of the philosopher.

T. E. RIHIL, *Greek Science* (1999). Good survey of Greek science incorporating recent reseach on the topic.

J. M. ROBINSON, *An Introduction to Early Greek Philosophy* (1968). A valuable collection of the main fragments and ancient testimony to the works of the early philosophers, with excellent commentary.

G. VLASTOS, *The Philosophy of Socrates* (1971). A splendid collection of essays illuminating the problems presented by this remarkable man.

G. VLASTOS, *Platonic Studies*, 2nd ed. (1981). A similar collection on the philosophy of Plato.

G. VLASTOS, *Socrates, Ironist and Moral Philosopher* (1991). The results of a lifetime of study by the leading interpreter of Socrates in our time.

Comparative Studies

(Increasingly world historians are looking at ancient civilizations in relationship to each other rather than as isolated entities to try to understand commonalities and differences in social and cultural development.)

W. DONIGER, *Splitting the Difference: Gender and Myth in Ancient Greece and India* (1999).

G. E. R. LLOYD, *The Ambitions of Curiosity: Understanding the World in Ancient Greece and China* (2002).

G. E. R. LLOYD, *The Way and the Word: Science and Medicine in Early China and Greece* (2002).

T. McEVILLEY, *The Shape of Ancient Thought: Comparative Studies of Greek and Indian Philosopies* (2002).

CHAPTER 3

The Rise of Greek Civilization

P. CARTLEDGE, *The Spartans* (2003). A readable account of this enigmatic people.

J. CHADWICK, *The Mycenaean World* (1976). A readable account by a man who helped decipher Mycenaean writing.

R. DREWS, *The Coming of the Greeks* (1988). A fine discussion of the Greeks' arrival as part of the movements of the Indo-European peoples.

J. V. FINE, *The Ancient Greeks* (1983). An excellent survey that discusses historical problems and the evidence that gives rise to them.

M. I. FINLEY, *World of Odysseus*, rev. ed. (1965). A fascinating attempt to reconstruct Homeric society.

P. GREEN, *Xerxes at Salamis* (1970). A lively and stimulating history of the Persian War.

D. HAMEL, *Trying Neaira* (2003). A lively account of the events surrounding a famous jury trial that sheds interesting light on Athenian society in the fourth century B.C.E.

V. D. HANSON, *The Western Way of War* (1989). A brilliant and lively discussion of the rise and character of the hoplite phalanx and its influence on Greek society.

V. D. HANSON, *The Other Greeks* (1995). A revolutionary account of the Greek invention of the family farm and its centrality for the shaping of the *polis*.

D. KAGAN, *The Great Dialogue: A History of Greek Political Thought from Homer to Polybius* (1965). A discussion of the relationship between the Greek historical experience and political theory.

W. K. LACEY, *The Family in Ancient Greece* (1984).

J. F. LAZENBY, *The Defense of Greece, 490–479 B.C.* (1993). A new and valuable study of the Persian Wars.

J. F. McGLEW, *Tyranny and Political Culture in Ancient Greece* (1993). A recent account of political developments in the Archaic period.

O. MURRAY, *Early Greece* (1980). A lively and imaginative account of the early history of Greece to the end of the Persian War.

A. M. SNODGRASS, *The Dark Age of Greece* (1972). A good examination of the archaeological evidence.

B. S. STRAUSS, *The Battle of Salamis: The Naval Encounter That Saved Greece and Western Civilization* (2004). A lively account of the major naval battle of the Persian Wars and its setting.

A. G. WOODHEAD, *Greeks in the West* (1962). An account of the Greek settlements in Italy and Sicily.

W. J. WOODHOUSE, *Solon the Liberator* (1965). A discussion of the great Athenian reformer.

S. G. MILLER, *Ancient Greek Athletics* (2004). The most complete and most useful account of the subject.

Classical and Hellenistic Greece

W. BURKERT, *Greek Religion* (1987). An excellent study by an outstanding student of the subject.

J. R. LANE FOX, *Alexander the Great* (1973). An imaginative account that does more than the usual justice to the Persian side of the problem.

Y. GARLAN, *Slavery in Ancient Greece* (1988). An up-to-date survey.

P. GREEN, *Alexander to Actium: The Historical Evolution of the Hellenistic Age* (1990). A remarkable synthesis of political and cultural history.

C. D. HAMILTON, *Agesilaus and the Failure of Spartan Hegemony* (1991). An excellent biography of the king who was the central figure in Sparta during its domination in the fourth century B.C.E.

N. G. L. HAMMOND, *Philip of Macedon* (1994). A new biography of the founder of the Macedonian Empire.

N. G. L. HAMMOND AND G. T. GRIFFITH, *A History of Macedonia*, Vol. 2, *550–336 B.C.* (1979). A thorough account of Macedonian history that focuses on the careers of Philip and Alexander.

R. JUST, *Women in Athenian Law and Life* (1988). An account of women's place in Athenian society.

D. KAGAN, *The Peloponnesian War* (2003). A narrative history of the war.

B. M. W. KNOX, *The Heroic Temper: Studies in Sophoclean Tragedy* (1964). A brilliant analysis of tragic heroism.

D. M. LEWIS, *Sparta and Persia* (1977). A valuable discussion of relations between Sparta and Persia in the fifth and fourth centuries B.C.E.

A. A. LONG, *Hellenistic Philosophy: Stoics, Epicureans, Sceptics* (1974). An account of Greek science in the Hellenistic and Roman periods.

R. MEIGGS, *The Athenian Empire* (1972). A fine study of the rise and fall of the empire, making excellent use of inscriptions.

J. J. POLLITT, *Art and Experience in Classical Greece* (1972). A scholarly and entertaining study of the relationship between art and history in classical Greece, with excellent illustrations.

J. J. POLLITT, *Art in the Hellenistic Age* (1986). An extraordinary analysis that places the art in its historical and intellectual context.

E. W. ROBINSON, *Ancient Greek Democracy* (2004). A stimulating collection of ancient sources and modern interpretations.

D. M. SCHAPS, *Economic Rights of Women in Ancient Greece* (1981).

B. S. STRAUSS, *Athens After the Peloponnesian War* (1987). An excellent discussion of Athens' recovery and of the nature of Athenian society and politics in the fourth century B.C.E.

B. S. STRAUSS, *Fathers and Sons in Athens* (1993). An unusual synthesis of social, political, and intellectual history.

V. TCHERIKOVER, *Hellenistic Civilization and the Jews* (1970). A fine study of the impact of Hellenism on the Jews.

G. VLASTOS, *Socrates, Ironist and Moral Philosopher* (1991). The results of a lifetime of study by the leading interpreter of Socrates in our time.

CHAPTER 4

Iran

M. BOYCE, *Zoroastrians: Their Religious Beliefs and Practices* (1979). The most recent survey, organized historically and based on extensive research.

M. BOYCE, ed. and trans., *Textual Sources for the Study of Zoroastrianism* (1984). Well-translated selections from a broad range of ancient Iranian materials.

J. M. COOK, *The Persian Empire* (1983). Survey of the Achaemenid period.

J. CURTIS, *Ancient Persia* (1989). Excellent portfolio of photographs of artifacts and sites, with a clear historical survey of the arts and culture of ancient Iran.

W. D. DAVIES AND L. FINKLESTEIN, ed., *The Cambridge History of Judaism*, Vol. 1, Introduction; "The Persian Period". Good articles on Iran and Iranian religion as well as Judaism.

J. DUCHESNE-GUILLEMIN, trans., *The Hymns of Zarathushtra*, trans. by M. Henning (1952, 1963). The best short introduction to the original texts of the Zoroastrian hymns.

R. N. FRYE, *The Heritage of Persia* (1963, 1966). A first-rate survey of Iranian history to Islamic times: readable but scholarly.

R. GHIRSHMAN, *Iran* (1954). Good material on culture, society, and economy as well as politics and history.

W. W. MALANDRA, trans. and ed., *An Introduction to Ancient Iranian Religion: Readings from the Avesta and Achaemenid Inscriptions* (1983). Helpful especially for texts of inscriptions relevant to religion.

India

A. L. BASHAM, *The Wonder That Was India*, rev. ed. (1963). Excellent material on Mauryan religion, society, culture, and history.

A. L. BASHAM, ed., *A Cultural History of India* (1975). A fine collection of historical-survey essays by a variety of scholars. See Part I, "The Ancient Heritage" (Chapters 2–16).

N. N. BHATTACHARYYA, *Ancient Indian History and Civilization: Trends and Perspectives* (1988). Covers Mauryan and Gupta times as well as earlier periods, with chapters on political systems, cities and villages, ideology and religion, and art.

W. T. DE BARY et al., COMP., *Sources of Indian Tradition*, 2nd ed. (1958). Vol. I: *From the Beginning to 1800*, ed. and rev. by Ainslie T. Embree (1988). Excellent selections from a wide variety of Indian texts, with good introductions to chapters and selections.

B. ROWLAND, *The Art and Architecture of India: Buddhist/Hindu/Jain*, 3rd rev. ed. (1970). The standard work, lucid and easy to read. Note Part Three, "Romano-Indian Art in North-West India and Central Asia."

V. A. SMITH, ed., *The Oxford History of India*, 4th rev. ed. by Percival Spear et al. (1981), pp. 71–163. A dry, occasionally dated historical survey. Includes useful reference chronologies.

R. THAPAR, *Ashoka and the Decline of the Mauryans* (1973). The standard treatment of Ashoka's reign.

R. THAPAR, *A History of India, Part I* (1966), pp. 50–108. Three chapters that provide a basic survey of the period.

S. WOLPERT, *A New History of India*, 2nd ed. (1982). A basic survey history. Chapters 5 and 6 cover the Mauryans, Guptas, and Kushans.

Greek and Asian Dynasties

A. K. NARAIN, *The Indo-Greeks* (1957. Reprinted with corrections, 1962). The most comprehensive account of the complex history of the various kings and kingdoms.

F. E. PETERS, *The Harvest of Hellenism* (1970), pp. 222–308. Helpful chapters on Greek rulers of the Eastern world from Seleucus to the last Indo-Greeks.

J. W. SEDLAR, *India and the Greek World: A Study in the Transmission of Culture* (1980). A basic work that provides a good overview.

D. SINOR, ed., *The Cambridge History of Early Inner Asia* (1990). See especially Chapters 6 and 7.

CHAPTER 5

P. BOHANNAN AND P. CURTIN, *Africa and Africans*, rev. ed. (1971). An enjoyable and enlightening discussion of African history and prehistory and of major African institutions (e.g., arts, family life, religion).

R. BULLIET, *The Camel and the Wheel* (1990). Explains why the camel was chosen over the wheel as a means of transport in the Sahara.

P. CURTIN, S. FEIERMANN, L. THOMPSON, AND J. VANSINA, *African History* (1978). Probably the best survey history. The relevant portions are chapters 1, 2, 4, 8, and 9.

T. R. H. DAVENPORT, *South Africa: A Modern History*, 3rd rev. ed. (1987). Chapter 1 gives excellent summary coverage of prehistoric southern Africa, the Khoisan peoples, and the Bantu migrations.

B. DAVIDSON, *The African Past* (1967). A combination of primary-source selections and brief secondary discussions trace sympathetically the history of the diverse parts of Africa.

P. GARLAKE, *The Kingdoms of Africa* (1978). A lavishly illustrated set of photographic essays that provide a helpful introduction to the various historically important areas of precolonial Africa.

E. GILBERT AND J. REYNOLDS, *Africa in World History* (2004). The best new survey of African history, placing it in a global context.

R. W. JULY, *Precolonial Africa: An Economic and Social History* (1975). A very readable, topically arranged study. See especially "The Savannah Farmer," "The Bantu," "Cattlemen," and "The Traders" chapters.

H. LOTH, *Woman in Ancient Africa*, trans. by S. Marnie (1987). An interesting survey of legal, familial, cultural, and other aspects of women's roles.

R. OLIVER, *The African Experience* (1991). A masterly, balanced, and engaging sweep through African history. The chapters on prehistory and early history are outstanding summaries of the results and implications of recent research.

I. VAN SERTIMA, *Black Women in Antiquity* (1984, 1988). Studies of queens, goddesses, matriarchy, and other aspects of the role and status of women in Egyptian, Ethiopian, and other African societies of the past.

CHAPTER 6

From Republic to Empire

R. BAUMANN, *Women and Politics in Ancient Rome* (1995). A Study of the role of women in roman public life.

A. H. BERNSTEIN, *Tiberius Sempronius Gracchus: Tradition and Apostasy* (1978). A new interpretation of Tiberius's place in Roman politics.

T. J. CORNELL, *The Beginnings of Rome: Italy and Rome from the Bronze Age to the Punic Wars, c. 1000–264 B.C.* (1995). A consideration of the royal and early republican periods of Roman history.

T. CORNELL AND J. MATTHEWS, *Atlas of the Roman World* (1982). Much more than the title indicates, this book presents a comprehensive view of the Roman world in its physical and cultural setting.

J-M. DAVID, *The Roman Conquest of Italy* (1997). A good analysis of how Rome united Italy.

A. GOLDSWORTHY, *Roman Warfare* (2002). A good military history of Rome.

A. GOLDSWORTHY, *In the Name of Rome: The Men Who Won the Roman Empire* (2004). The story of Rome's greatest generals in the republican and imperial periods.

E. S. GRUEN, *Diaspora: Jews Amidst Greeks and Romans* (2002). A fine study of Jews in the Hellenistic and Roman world.

E. S. GRUEN, *The Hellenistic World and the Coming of Rome* (1984). A new interpretation of Rome's conquest of the eastern Mediterranean.

W. V. HARRIS, *War and Imperialism in Republican Rome, 327–70 B.C.* (1975). An analysis of Roman attitudes and intentions concerning imperial expansion and war.

A. KEAVENEY, *Rome and the Unification of Italy* (1988). The story of how Rome organized her defeated opponents.

S. LANCEL, *Carthage, A History* (1995). Includes a good account of Rome's dealings with Carthage.

J. F. LAZENBY, *Hannibal's War: A Military History of the Second Punic War* (1978). A careful and thorough account.

F.G.B. MILLAR, *The Crowd in Rome in the Late Republic* (1999). A challenge to the view that only aristocrats counted in the late republic.

M. PALLOTTINO, *The Etruscans*, 6th ed. (1974). Makes especially good use of archaeological evidence.

H. H. SCULLARD, *A History of the Roman World 753–146 B.C.*, 4th ed. (1980). An unusually fine narrative history with useful critical notes.

G. WILLIAMS, *The Nature of Roman Poetry* (1970). An unusually graceful and perceptive literary study.

Imperial Rome

W. BALL, *Rome in the East: The Transformation of an Empire* (2001). A thorough account of the influence of the East on Roman history.

T. BARNES, *The New Empire of Diocletian and Constantine* (1982).

K. R. BRADLEY, *Slavery and Society at Rome* (1994). A study of the role of slaves in Roman life.

P. BROWN, *The Rise of Western Christendom: Triumph and Diversity, 200–1000* (1996). A vivid picture of the spread of Christianity by a master of the field.

A. FERRILL, *The Fall of the Roman Empire, The Military Explanation* (1986). An interpretation that emphasizes the decline in the quality of the Roman army.

K. GALINSKY, *Augustan Culture* (1996). A work that integrates art, literature, and politics.

A. H. M. JONES, *The Later Roman Empire*, 3 vols. (1964). A comprehensive study of the period.

D. KAGAN, ed., *The End of the Roman Empire: Decline or Transformation?* 3rd ed. (1992). A collection of essays discussing the problem of the decline and fall of the Roman Empire.

J. E. LENDON, *Empire of Honor, The Art of Government in the Roman World* (1997). An original and path-breaking interpretation.

E. N. LUTTWAK, *The Grand Strategy of the Roman Empire* (1976). An original and fascinating analysis by a keen student of modern strategy.

R. MACMULLEN, *Roman Social Relations, 50 B.C. to A.D. 284* (1981).

R. MACMULLEN, *Corruption and the Decline of Rome* (1988). A study that examines the importance of changes in ethical ideas and behavior.

R. W. MATHISON, *Roman Aristocrats in Barbarian Gaul: Strategies for Survival* (1993). An unusual slant on the late empire.

J.F. MATTHEWS, *Laying Down the Law: A Study of the Theodosian Code* (2000). A study of the importance of Roman law as a source for the understanding of Roman history and civilization.

W. A. MEEKS, *The Origins of Christian Morality: The First Two Centuries*. An account of the shaping of Christianity in the Roman Empire.

F. MILLAR, *The Emperor in the Roman World, 31 B.C.–A.D. 337* (1977). A study of Roman imperial government.

F. MILLAR, *The Roman Empire and Its Neighbors*, 2nd ed. (1981).

H. M. D. PARKER, *A History of the Roman World from A.D. 138 to 337* (1969). A good survey.

M. I. ROSTOVTZEFF, *Social and Economic History of the Roman Empire*, 2nd ed. (1957). A masterpiece whose main thesis has been much disputed.

V. RUDICH, *Political Dissidence Under Nero, The Price of Dissimulation* (1993). A brilliant exposition of the lives and thoughts of political dissidents in the early empire.

E. T. SALMON, *A History of the Roman World, 30 B.C. to A.D. 138* (1968). A good survey.

R. SYME, *The Roman Revolution* (1960). A brilliant study of Augustus, his supporters, and their rise to power.

R. SYME, *The Augustan Aristocracy* (1985). An examination of the new ruling class shaped by Augustus.

L. A. THOMPSON, *Romans and Blacks* (1989).

CHAPTER 7

D. BODDE, *China's First Unifier* (1938). A study of the Qin unification of China, viewed through the Legalist philosopher and statesman LiSi.

T. T. CH'U, *Law and Society in Traditional China* (1961). Treats the sweep of Chinese history from 202 B.C.E. to 1911 C.E.

T. T. CH'U, *Han Social Structure* (1972).

A. COTTERELL, *The First Emperor of China* (1981). A study of the first Qin emperor.

R. COULBORN, *Feudalism in History* (1965). One chapter interestingly compares the quasi feudalism of the Zhou with that of the Six Dynasties period.

J. K. FAIRBANK, E. O. REISCHAUER, AND A. M. CRAIG, *East Asia: Tradition and Transformation* (1989). A fairly detailed single-volume history covering China, Japan, and other countries in East Asia from antiquity to recent times.

J. GERNET, *A History of Chinese Civilization* (1982). A survey of Chinese history.

D.A. GRAFF AND R. HIGHAM, *A Military History of China* (2002).

C. Y. HSU, *Ancient China in Transition* (1965). On social mobility during the Eastern Zhou era.

C. Y. HSU, *Han Agriculture* (1980). A study of the agrarian economy of China during the Han dynasty.

J. LEVI, *The Chinese Emperor* (1987). A novel about the first Qin emperor based on scholarly sources.

M. LOEWE, *Everyday Life in Early Imperial China* (1968). A social history of the Han dynasty.

J. NEEDHAM, *The Shorter Science and Civilization in China* (1978). An abridgment of the multivolume work on the same subject with the same title—minus Shorter—by the same author.

S. OWEN, ed. and Trans., *An Anthology of Chinese Literature: Beginnings to 1911* (1996).

I. ROBINET, *Taoism: Growth of a Religion* (1987).

M. SULLIVAN, *The Arts of China* (1967). An excellent survey history of Chinese art.

D. TWITCHETT AND M. LOEWE, eds., *The Ch'in and Han Empires, 221 B.C.E.–C.E. 220* (1986). Vol. 1 of *The Cambridge History of China*.

Z. S. WANG, *Han Civilization* (1982).

B. WATSON, *Ssu-ma Ch'ien, Grand Historian of China* (1958). A study of China's premier historian.

B. WATSON, *Records of the Grand Historian of China*, Vols. 1 and 2 (1961). Selections from the *Shiji* by Sima Qian.

B. WATSON, *The Columbia Book of Chinese Poetry* (1986).

F. WOOD, *The Silk Road: Two Thousand Years in the Heart of Asia* (2003). A lively narrative combined with photographs and paintings.

A. WRIGHT, *Buddhism in Chinese History* (1959).

Y. S. YU, *Trade and Expansion in Han China* (1967). A study of economic relations between the Chinese and their neighbors.

CHAPTER 8

General

P. BOL, *This Culture of Ours* (1992). An insightful intellectual history of the Tang through the Song dynasties.

J. CAHILL, *Chinese Painting* (1960). An excellent survey.

J. K. FAIRBANK AND M. GOLDMAN, *China: A New History* (1998). The summation of a lifetime engagement with Chinese history.

F. A. KIERMAN JR., AND J. K. FAIRBANK, eds., *Chinese Ways in Warfare* (1974). Chapters by different authors on the Chinese military experience from the Zhou to the Ming.

Sui and Tang

P. B. EBREY, *The Aristocratic Families of Early Imperial China* (1978).

D. MCMULLEN, *State and Scholars in T'ang China* (1988).

S. OWEN, *The Great Age of Chinese Poetry: The High T'ang* (1980).

S. OWEN, trans. and ed., *An Anthology of Chinese Literature: Beginnings to 1911* (1996).

E. G. PULLEYBLANK, *The Background of the Rebellion of An Lu-shan* (1955). A study of the 755 rebellion that weakened the central authority of the Tang dynasty.

E. O. REISCHAUER, *Ennin's Travels in T'ang China* (1955). China as seen through the eyes of a ninth-century Japanese Marco Polo.

E. H. SCHAFER, *The Golden Peaches of Samarkand* (1963). A study of Tang imagery.

SO. TEISER, *The Ghost Festival in Medieval China* (1988). On Tang popular religion.

D. TWITCHETT, ed., *The Cambridge History of China*, Vol. III: *Sui and T'ang China, 589–906 Part 1*, (1979).

G. W. WANG, *The Structure of Power in North China During the Five Dynasties* (1963). A study of the interim period between the Tang and the Song dynasties.

A. F. WRIGHT, *The Sui Dynasty* (1978).

Song

B. BIRGE, *Women, Property, and Confucian Reaction in Song and Yuan China (960–1366)* (2002). The rights of women to property—whether in the form of dowries or inheritances—were considerable during the Song but declined thereafter.

C. S. CHANG AND J. SMYTHE, *South China in the Twelfth Century* (1981). China as seen through the eyes of a twelfth-century Chinese poet, historian, and statesman.

E. L. DAVIS, *Society and the Supernatural in Song China* (2001).

J. W. HAEGER, ed., *Crisis and Prosperity in Song China* (1975).

R. HYMES, *Statesmen and Gentlemen* (1987). On the transformation of officials into a local gentry elite during the twelfth and thirteenth centuries.

R. HYMES, *Way and Byway: Taoism, Local Religion, and Models of Divinity in Sung and Modern China* (2002).

M. ROSSABI, *China Among Equals* (1983). A study of the Liao, Qin, and Song Empires and their relations.

W. M. TU, *Confucian Thought, Selfhood as Creative Transformation* (1985).

K. YOSHIKAWA, *An Introduction to Song Poetry*, trans. by B. Watson (1967).

Yuan

T. T. ALLSEN, *Mongol Imperialism* (1987).

J. W. DARDESS, *Conquerors and Confucians: Aspects of Political Change in Late Yuan China* (1973).

DE RACHEWILTZ, trans., *The Secret History of the Mongols: A Mongolian Epic Chronicle of the Thirteenth Century* (2003). A new translation of a key historical work on the life of Genghis.

H. FRANKE AND D. TWITCHETT, eds., *The Cambridge History of China*, Vol. VI: *Alien Regimes and Border States, 710–1368* (1994).

J. D. LANGLOIS, *China Under Mongol Rule* (1981).

R. LATHAM, trans., *Travels of Marco Polo* (1958).

H. D. MARTIN, *The Rise of Chingis Khan and His Conquest of North China* (1981).

D. MORGAN, *The Mongol Empire and its Legacy* (1999). Genghis, the several khanates, and the aftermath of empire.

P. RATCHNEVSKY, *Genghis Khan, His Life and Legacy* (1992). The rise to power of the Mongol leader, with a critical consideration of historical sources.

CHAPTER 9

M. ADOLPHSON, *The Gates of Power: Monks, Courtiers, and Warriors in Premodern Japan* (2000). A new interpretation stressing the importance of temples in the political life of Heian and Kamakura Japan.

B.L. BATTEN, *To the Ends of Japan: Premodern Frontiers, Boundaries, and Interactions.* (2003). An interesting treatment of Heian Japan, topic by topic.

C. BLACKER, *The Catalpa Bow* (1975). An insightful study of folk Shinto.

R. BORGEN, *Sugawara no Michizane and the Early Heian Court* (1986). A study of a famous courtier and poet.

D. M. BROWN, ed., *The Cambridge History of Japan: Ancient Japan* (1993). This series of six volumes sums up several decades of research on Japan.

D. BROWN AND E. ISHIDA, eds., *The Future and the Past* (1979). A translation of a history of Japan written in 1219.

The Cambridge History of Japan, D.M. BROWN, ed.; Vol. 1, *Ancient Japan*, W. McCullough and D. H. Shively eds; Vol. 2, *Heian Japan*, K. Yamamura, ed. Vol. 3, *Medieval Japan*. Fine multi-author works.

M. COLLCUTT, *Five Mountains* (1980). A study of the monastic organization of medieval Zen.

T.D. CONLON, *State of War: The Violent Order of Fourteenth Century Japan* (2003). Compare Conlon's account with those of Souyri and Friday.

P. DUUS, *Feudalism in Japan* (1969). An easy survey of the subject.

W. W. FARRIS, *Population, Disease, and Land in Early Japan, 645–900* (1985). An innovative reinterpretation of early history.

W. W. FARRIS, *Heavenly Warriors: The Evolution of Japan's Military, 500–1300* (1992).

W. W. FARRIS, *Sacred Texts and Buried Treasures* (1998). Studies of Japan's prehistory and early history, based on recent Japanese research.

K. F. FRIDAY, *Samurai, Warfare and the State in Early Medieval Japan* (2004). Weapons and warfare in Japan from the tenth to fourteenth centuries.

A. E. GOBLE, *Gō Daigo's Revolution* (1996). A provoking account of the 1331 revolt by an emperor who thought emperors should rule.

J. W. HALL, *Government and Local Power in Japan, 500–1700: A Study Based on Bizen Province* (1966). A splendid and insightful book.

J. W. HALL AND T. TOYODA, *Japan in the Muromachi Age* (1977). Another collection of essays.

D. KEENE, ed., *Anthology of Japanese Literature from the Earliest Era to the Mid-Nineteenth Century* (1955).

D. KEENE, ed., *Twenty Plays of the Nō Theatre* (1970).

T. LAMARRE, *Uncovering Heian Japan: An Archeology of Sensation and Inscription* (2000). The "archeology" in the title refers to digging into literature.

I. H. LEVY, *The Ten Thousand Leaves* (1981). A fine translation of Japan's earliest collection of poetry.

J. P. MASS AND W. HAUSER, eds., *The Bakufu in Japanese History* (1985). Topics in *bakufu* history from the twelfth to the nineteenth centuries.

I. MORRIS, trans., *The Pillow Book of Sei Shōnagon* (1967). Observations about the Heian court life by the Jane Austen of ancient Japan.

S. MURASAKI, *The Tale of Genji*, trans. by A. Waley (1952). A comparison of this translation with that of Seidensticker is instructive.

S. MURASAKI, *The Tale of Genji*, trans. by E. G. Seidensticker (1976). The world's first novel and the greatest work of Japanese fiction.

R. J. PEARSON et al., eds., *Windows on the Japanese Past: Studies in Archaeology and Prehistory* (1986).

D. L. PHILIPPI, trans., *Kojiki* (1968). Japan's ancient myths.

J. PIGGOT, *The Emergence of Japanese Kingship* (1997).

E. O. REISCHAUER, *Ennin's Diary, the Record of a Pilgrimage to China in Search of the Law and Ennin's Travels in T'ang China* (1955).

E. O. REISCHAUER AND A. M. CRAIG, *Japan: Tradition and Transformation* (1989). A more detailed work covering the sweep of Japanese history from the early beginnings through the 1980s.

H. SATO, *Legends of the Samurai* (1995). Excerpts from various tales and writings.

D. H. SHIVELY and W. H. McCULLOUGH, eds., *The Cambridge History of Japan: Heian Japan* (1999).

D. T. SUZUKI, *Zen and Japanese Culture* (1959).

H. TONOMURA, *Community and Commerce in Late Medieval Japan* (1992).

R. TSUNODA, W. T. DE BARY, AND D. KEENE, comps., *Sources of the Japanese Tradition* (1958). A collection of original religious, political, and philosophical writings from each period of Japanese history. The best reader. A new edition should be out soon.

H. P. VARLEY, *Imperial Restoration in Medieval Japan* (1971). A study of the 1331 attempt by an emperor to restore imperial power.

A. WALEY, trans., *The Nō Plays of Japan* (1957). Medieval dramas.

K. YAMAMURA, ed., *Cambridge History of Japan: Medieval Japan* (1990).

CHAPTER 10

Iran

M. BOYCE, *Zoroastrians: Their Religious Beliefs and Practices* (1979). A detailed survey by the current authority on Zoroastrian religious history. See Chapters 7–9.

M. BOYCE, ed. and trans., *Textual Sources for the Study of Zoroastrianism* (1984). A valuable anthology with an important introduction that includes Boyce's arguments for a revision of the dates of Zoroaster's life (to between 1400 and 1200 B.C.E.).

R. N. FRYE, *The Heritage of Persia* (1963). Still one of the best surveys, Chapter 6 deals with the Sasanid era.

R. GHIRSHMAN, *Iran* (1954 [orig. ed. 1951]). An introductory survey of similar extent to Frye, but with differing material also.

R. GHIRSHMAN, *Persian Art: The Parthian and Sasanid Dynasties* (1962). Superb photographs, and a very helpful glossary of places and names. The text is minimal.

GEO WIDENGRAN, *Mani and Manichaeism* (1965). Still the standard introduction to Mani's life and the later spread and development of Manichaeism.

India

A. L. BASHAM, *The Wonder That Was India* (1963). The best survey of classical Indian religion, society, literature, art, and politics.

W. T. DE BARY et al., comp., *Sources of Indian Tradition*, 2nd ed. (1958), Vol. I, *From the Beginning to 1800*, ed. and rev. by Ainslie T. Embree (1988). Excellent selections from a wide variety of Indian texts, with good introductions to the text selections.

S. DUTT, *Buddhist Monks and Monasteries of India* (1962). The standard work. See especially Chapters 3 ("Bhakti") and 4 ("Monasteries Under the Gupta Kings").

D. G. MANDELBAUM, *Society in India* (1972). 2 vols. The first two chapters in Volume I of this study of caste, family, and village relations are a good introduction to the caste system.

B. ROWLAND, *The Art and Architecture of India: Buddhist/Hindu/Jain*, 3rd rev. ed. (1970). See the excellent chapters on Sungan, Andhran, and other early Buddhist art (6–8, 14), the Gupta period (15), and the Hindu Renaissance (17–19).

V. A. SMITH, *The Oxford History of India*, 4th rev. ed. (1981). See especially pages 164–229 (the Gupta period and following era to the Muslim invasions).

R. THAPAR, *A History of India, Part I* (1966), pp. 109–193. Three chapters covering the rise of mercantilism, the Gupta "classical pattern," and the southern dynasties to ca. 900 C.E..

P. YOUNGER, *Introduction to Indian Religious Thought* (1972). A sensitive attempt to delineate classical concerns of Indian religious thought and culture.

CHAPTER 11

O. GRABAR, *The Formation of Islamic Art* (1973). A critical and creative interpretation of major themes in the development of distinctively Islamic forms of art and architecture.

A. HOURANI, *A History of the Arab Peoples* (1991). A masterly survey of the Arabs down through the centuries and a clear picture of many aspects of Islamic history and culture that extend beyond the Arab world.

H. KENNEDY, *The Prophet and the Age of the Caliphates: The Islamic Near East from the Sixth to the Eleventh Century* (1986). The best survey of early Islamic history.

I. LAPIDUS, *A History of Islamic Societies* (1988). A comprehensive overview of the rise and development of Islam all over the world.

F. E. PETERS, *Muhammad and the Origins of Islam* (1994). A balanced analysis of the life of Muhammad.

F. RAHMAN, *Major Themes of the Qur'an* (1980). The best introduction to the basic ideas of the Qur'an and Islam, seen through the eyes of a perceptive Muslim modernist scholar.

F. SCHUON, *Understanding Islam* (1994). Compares the Islamic worldview with Catholic Christianity. A dense, but intellectually stimulating, discussion.

M. SELLS, *Approaching the Qur'an. The Early Revelations* (1999). A fine introduction and new translations of some of the more common earlier Qur'anic revelations.

B. STOWASSER, *Women in the Qur'an, Traditions and Interpretation* (1994). An outstanding systematic study of statements regarding women in the Qur'an.

CHAPTER 12

K. ARMSTRONG, *Muhammad: A Biography of the Prophet* (1992). Strong on religion.

R. BARTLETT, *The Making of Europe, 950–1350* (1992). A study of the way immigration and colonial conquest shaped the Europe we know.

M. BLOCH, *Feudal Society*, Vols. 1 and 2, trans. by L. A. Manyon (1971). A classic on the topic and as an example of historical study.

P. BROWN, *Augustine of Hippo: A Biography* (1967). Late antiquity seen through the biography of its greatest Christian thinker.

J. H. BURNS, *The Cambridge History of Medieval Political Thought c. 350–c. 1450* (1991). The best scan.

R. H. C. DAVIS, *A History of Medieval Europe: From Constantine to St. Louis* (1972). Unsurpassed in clarity.

R. FLETCHER, *The Barbarian Conversion: From Paganism to Christianity* (1998). Up-to-date survey.

J. B. GLUBB, *The Great Arab Conquests* (1995). Jihadists.

G. GUGLIELMO, ed., *The Byzantines* (1997). Updates key issues.

D. GUTAS, *Greek Thought, Arabic Culture* (1998). A comparative intellectual history.

G. HOLMES, Ed., *The Oxford History of Medieval Europe* (1992). Overviews of Roman and northern Europe during the "Dark Ages."

B. LEWIS, *The Middle East: A Brief History of the Last 2,000 Years* (1995)

C. MANGO, *Byzantium: The Empire of New Rome* (1980).

J. MARTIN, *Medieval Russia 980–1584* (1995). A concise narrative history.

R. MCKITTERICK, ed., *Carolingian Culture: Emulation and Innovation* (1994). Fresh essays.

J.J. NORWICH, *Byzantium: The Decline and Fall* (1995).

J.J. NORWICH, *Byzantium: The Apogee* (1997). The whole story in two volulmes.

R.I. PAGE, *Chronicles of the Vikings: Records, Memorials, and Myths* (1995). Sources galore.

F. ROBINSON, ed., *The Cambridge Illustrated History of the Islamic World* (1996). Spectacular.

S. RUNCIMAN, *Byzantine Civilization* (1970). Succinct, comprehensive account by a master.

P. SAWYER, *The Age of the Vikings* (1962). Old but solid account.

C. STEPHENSON, *Medieval Feudalism* (1969). Excellent short summary and introduction.

L. WHITE JR., *Medieval Technology and Social Change* (1962). Often fascinating account of how primitive technology changed life.

H. WOLFRAM, *The Roman Empire and Its Germanic Peoples* (1997). Challenging, but most rewarding.

CHAPTER 13

The Islamic Heartlands

L. AHMED, *Women and Gender in Islam. Historical Roots of a Modern Debate* (1992). A good historical survey of the status of women in Middle Eastern societies.

J. BERKEY, *The Formation of Islam. Religion and Society in the Near East 600–1800* (2002). An interesting new synthesis foducing on political and religious trends.

C. E. BOSWORTH, *The Islamic Dynasties: A Chronological and Genealogical Handbook* (1967). A handy reference work for dynasties and families important to Islamic history in all periods and places.

M. A. COOK, *Commanding Right and Forbidding Wrong in Islamic Thought* (2001). A masterful anaylsis of the development of Islamic law.

P. K. HITTI, *History of the Arabs*, 8th ed. (1964). Still a useful English resource, largely for factual detail. See especially Part IV, "The Arabs in Europe: Spain and Sicily."

A. HOURANI, *A History of the Arab Peoples* (1991). The newest survey history and the best, at least for the Arab Islamic world.

S. K. JAYYUSI, ed., *The Legacy of Muslim Spain*, 2 vols. (1994). A comprehensive survey of the arts, politics, literature, and society by experts in various fields.

B. LEWIS, ed., *Islam and the Arab World* (1976). A large-format, heavily illustrated volume with many excellent articles on diverse aspects of Islamic (not simply Arab, as the misleading title indicates) civilization through the premodern period.

D. MORGAN, *The Mongols* (1986). A recent and readable survey history.

J. J. SAUNDERS, *A History of Medieval Islam* (1965). A brief and simple, if sketchy, introductory survey of Islamic history to the Mongol invasions.

India

W. T. DE BARY et al., comp., *Sources of Indian Tradition*, 2nd ed. (1958), Vol. I, *From the Beginning to 1800*, ed. and rev. by Ainslie T. Embree (1988). Excellent selections from a wide variety of Indian texts, with good introductions to chapters and individual selections.

S. M. IKRAM, *Muslim Civilization in India* (1964). The best short survey history, covering the period 711 to 1857.

R. C. MAJUMDAR, gen. ed., *The History and Culture of the Indian People*, Vol. VI, *The Delhi Sultanate*, 3rd ed. (1980). A comprehensive political and cultural account of the period in India.

F. ROBINSON, ed., *The Cambridge History of India, Pakistan, Bangladesh, Sri Lanka, Nepal, Bhutan, and the Maldives* (1989). A very helpful quick reference source with brief but well-done survey essays on a wide range of topics relevant to South Asian history down to the present.

A. WINK, *Al-Hind: The Making of the Indo-Islamic World*, Vol. 1 (1991). The first of five promising volumes to be devoted to the Indo-Islamic world's history. This volume treats the seventh to eleventh centuries.

Southeast Asia

L. ANDAYA, *The World of Maluku: Eastern Indonesia in the Early Modern Period* (1993). A comprehensive view of the formation of what is now Indonesia.

B. W. ANDAYA AND L. ANDAYA, *A History of Malaysia* (1982). A good overivew of Indonesia's smaller but critical northern neighbor.

J. SIEGEL, *Shadow and Sound: The Historical Thought of a Sumatran People* (1979). An excellent analysis tracing the relation between foreign influences and local practice.

CHAPTER 14

B. S. BAUER, *The Development of the Inca State* (1992). An important new work that emphasizes archaeological evidence over the Spanish chronicles in accounting for the emergence of the Inca Empire.

F. F. BERDAN, *The Aztecs of Central Mexico: An Imperial Society* (1982). An excellent introduction to the Aztecs.

R. E. BLANTON, S. A. KOWALEWSKI, G. FEINMAN, AND J. APPEL, *Ancient Mesoamerica: A Comparison of Change in Three Regions* (1981). Concentrates on ancient Mexico.

K. O. BRUHNS, *Ancient South America* (1994). A clear discussion of the archaeology and civilization of the region with emphasis on the Andes.

R. L. BURGER, *Chavín and the Origins of Andean Civilization* (1992). A detailed study of early Andean prehistory by one of the leading authorities on Chavín.

R. M. CARMACK, J. GASCO, AND G. H. GOSSEN, *The Legacy of Mesoamerica: History and Culture of a Native American Civilization* (1996). A survey of Mesoamerica from its origins to the present.

I. CLENDINNEN, *Aztecs: An Interpretation* (1995). A fascinating attempt to reconstruct the Aztec world.

M. D. COE, *Breaking the Maya Code* (1992). The story of the remarkable achievement of deciphering the ancient Maya language.

M. D. COE, *The Maya* (1993). The best introduction.

M. D. COE, *Mexico from the Olmecs to the Aztecs* (1994). A wide-ranging introductory discussion.

G. CONRAD AND A. A. DEMAREST, *Religion and Empire: The Dynamics of Aztec and Inca Expansionism* (1984). An interesting comparative study.

S. D. GILLESPIE, *The Aztec Kings* (1989).

R. HASSIG, *Aztec Warfare.*

J. HYSLOP, *Inka Settlement Planning* (1990). A detailed study.

M. LEÓN-PORTILLA, *Fifteen Poets of the Aztec World* (1992). An anthology of translations of Aztec poetry.

M. E. MILLER, *The Art of Mesoamerica from Olmec to Aztec* (1986). A well-illustrated introduction.

C. MORRIS AND A. VON HAGEN, *The Inka Empire and Its Andean Origins* (1993). A clear overview of Andean prehistory by a leading authority. Beautifully illustrated.

M. E. MOSELY, *The Incas and Their Ancestors: The Archaeology of Peru* (1992). Readable and thorough.

J. A. SABLOFF, *The Cities of Ancient Mexico* (1989). Capsule summaries of ancient Mesoamerican cultures.

J. A. SABLOFF, *Archaeology and the Maya* (1990). A look at changing views of the ancient Maya.

L. SCHELE and M. E. MILLER, *The Blood of Kings* (1986). A rich and beautifully illustrated study of ancient Maya art and society.

R. S. SHARER, *The Ancient Maya*, 5th ed. (1994). A classic. Readable, authoritative, and thorough.

M. P. WEAVER, *The Aztecs, Maya, and Their Predecessors* (1993). A classic textbook.

CHAPTER 15

L. B. ALBERTI, *The Family in Renaissance Florence*, trans. by R. N. Watkins (1962). A contemporary humanist, who never married, explains how a family should behave.

E. AMT, ed., *Women's Lives in Medieval Europe: A Source-book* (1992). Outstanding collection of sources.

H. BARON, *The Crisis of the Early Italian Renaissance*, Vols. 1 and 2 (1996). New edition of an old, major work, setting forth the civic dimension of Italian humanism.

G. BARRACLOUGH, *The Origins of Modern Germany* (1963). Penetrating political narrative.

S. BRAMLY, *Discovering the Life of Leonard da Vinci* (1991). The man and the genius.

G. BRUCKER, *Renaissance Florence* (1983). Still one of the best introductions.

G. BULL, *Michelangelo: A Biography* (1995). Recent life in full.

J. BURCKHARDT, *The Civilization of the Renaissance in Italy* (1867). The famous classic that still has as many defenders as detractors.

S. FLANAGAN, *Hildegard of Bingen, 1098–1179: A Visionary Life* (1995). A most interesting German woman.

E. HALLAM, ed., *Chronicles of the Crusades* (1989). All nine!

D. HERLIHY, *Medieval Households* (1985). Survey of Middle Ages that defends the medieval family against modern caricatures.

D. HERLIHY AND C. KLAPISCH-ZUBER, *Tuscans and Their Families* (1985). Important work based on unique demographic data that gives the reader an appreciation of quantitative history.

G. HOLMES, *Renaissance* (1996). An expert's take on the subject.

J. C. HOLT, *Magna Carta*, 2nd ed. (1992). The famous document and its interpretation by succeeding generations.

J. HUIZINGA, *The Waning of the Middle Ages: A Study of the Forms of Life, Thought, and Art in France and the Netherlands in the Dawn of the Renaissance* (1924). A classic study of "mentality" at the end of the Middle Ages.

L. JARDINE, *Worldly Goods: A New History of the Renaissance* (1996). The material side of the Renaissance.

M. KING, *Women of the Renaissance* (1991). Women's presence and creativity.

W. H. MCNEILL, *Plagues and Peoples* (1976). The Black Death in a broader context.

R. I. MOORE, *The Formation of a Persecuting Society: Power and Deviance in Western Europe, 950–1250* (1987). A sympathetic look at heresy and dissent.

T. NOONAN, *Contraception: A History of Its Treatment by the Catholic Theologians and Canonists* (1967). A fascinating account of medieval theological attitudes toward sexuality and sex-related problems.

J. RILEY-SMITH, ed., *Oxford Illustrated History of the Crusades* (1995) Lucid, gorgeous, and up-to-date.

J. WEISHEIPL, *Friar Thomas* (1980). Biography of Saint Thomas Aquinas, both the man and the theologian.

CHAPTER 16

M. BRECHT, *Martin Luther: His Road to Reformation, 1483–1521* (1985). Best on young Luther.

C. BROWN, et al., *Rembrandt: The Master and His Workshop* (1991) A great master's art and influence.

R. BRIGGS, *Witches and Neighbors: A History of European Witchcraft* (1996). A readable introduction.

E. DUFFY, *The Stripping of the Altars* (1992). Strongest argument yet that there was no deep reformation in England.

H. O. EVENNETT, *The Spirit of the Counter Reformation* (1968). The continuity and independence of Catholic reform.

HANS-JÜRGEN GOERTZ, *The Anabaptists* (1996). Best treatment of minority Protestants.

O. P. GRELL AND A. CUNNINGHAM, *Health Care and Poor Relief in Protestant Europe* (1997) The civic side of the Reformation.

M. HOLT, *The French Wars of Religion, 1562–1629* (1995). Scholarly appreciation of religious side of the story.

J. C. HUTCHISON, *Albrecht Durer* (1990). The life behind the art.

H. JEDIN, *A History of the Council of Trent*, Vols. 1, 2 (1957–1961). Comprehensive, detailed, and authoritative.

M. KITCHEN, *The Cambridge Illustrated History of Germany* (1996). Comprehensive and accessible.

A. KORS AND E. PETERS, eds., *European Witchcraft, 1100–1700* (1972). Classics of witch belief.

W. MACCAFFREY, *Elizabeth I* (1993). Magisterial study.

G. MATTINGLY, *The Armada* (1959). A masterpiece, novel-like in style.

D. MCCOLLOCH, *The Reformation* (2004). No stone unturned, with English emphasis.

H. A. OBERMAN, *Luther: Man Between God and Devil* (1989). Authoritative biography

J. W. O'MALLEY, *The First Jesuits* (1993). Extremely detailed account of the creation of the Society of Jesus and its original purposes.

S. OZMENT, *The Age of Reform 1250–1550: An Intellectual and Religious History of Late Medieval and Reformation Europe* (1980). Broad, lucid survey.

S. OZMENT, *When Fathers Ruled: Family Life in Reformation Europe* (1983). Effort to portray the constructive side of Protestant thinking about family relationships.

S. OZMENT, *The Bürgermeister's Daughter: Scandal in a Sixteenth Century German Town* (1996). What a woman could do at law in the sixteenth century.

G. PARKER, *The Thirty Years' War* (1984). Large, lucid survey.

J. H. PARRY, *The Age of Reconnaissance* (1964). A comprehensive account of explorations from 1450 to 1650.

W. PRINZ, *Durer* (1998). Latest biography of Germany's greatest painter.

J. J. SCARISBRICK, *Henry VIII* (1968). The best account of Henry's reign.

G. STRAUSS, ed. and trans., *Manifestations of Discontent in Germany on the Eve of the Reformation* (1971). A rich collection of sources for both rural and urban scenes.

H. WUNDER, *He Is the Sun, She Is the Moon: Women in Early Modern Germany* (1998). Best study of early modern women.

CHAPTER 17

J. ABUN-NASR, *A History of the Maghrib in the Islamic Period* (1987). The most recent North African survey. Pages 59–247 are relevant to this chapter.

D. BIRMINHAM, *Central Africa to 1870* (1981). Chapters from the *Cambridge History of Africa* that give a brief, lucid overview of developments in this region.

P. BOHANNAN AND P. CURTIN, *Africa and Africans*, rev. ed. (1971). Accessible, topical approach to African history, culture, society, politics, and economics.

P. D. CURTIN, S. FEIERMANN, L. THOMPSON, AND J. VANSINA, *African History* (1978). An older, but masterly survey. The relevant portions are Chapters 6–9.

R. ELPHICK, *Kraal and Castle: Khoikhoi and the Founding of White South Africa* (1977). An incisive, informative interpretation of the history of the Khoikhoi and their fateful interaction with European colonization.

R. ELPHICK AND H. GILIOMEE, *The Shaping of South African Society, 1652–1820* (1979). A superb, synthetic history of this crucial period.

J. D. FAGE, *A History of Africa* (1978). Still a readable survey history.

M. HISKETT, *The Development of Islam in West Africa* (1984). The standard survey study of the subject. Of the relevant sections (Chapters 1–10, 12, 15), that on Hausaland, which is treated only in passing in this text, is noteworthy.

R. W. JULY, *Precolonial Africa: An Economic and Social History* (1975). Chapter 10 gives an interesting overall picture of slaving in African history.

R. W. JULY, *A History of the African People*, 3rd ed. (1980). Chapters 3–6 treat Africa before about 1800 area by area; Chapter 7 deals with "The Coming of Europe."

I. M. LEWIS, Ed., *Islam in Tropical Africa* (1966), pp. 4–96. Lewis's introduction is one of the best brief summaries of the role of Islam in West Africa and the Sudan.

D. T. NIANI, ed., *Africa from the Twelfth to the Sixteenth Century*, UNESCO General History of Africa, Vol. IV (1984). Many survey articles cover the various regions and major states of Africa in the centuries noted in the title.

R. OLIVER, *The African Experience* (1991). A masterly, balanced, and engaging survey, with outstanding syntheses and summaries of recent research.

J. A. RAWLEY, *The Transatlantic Slave Trade: A History* (1981). Impressively documented, detailed, and well-presented survey history of the Atlantic trade; little focus on African dimensions.

A. F. C. RYDER, *Benin and the Europeans: 1485–1897* (1969). A basic study.

JOHN K. THORNTON, *The Kingdom of Kongo: Civil War and Transition, 1641–1718* (1983). A detailed and perceptive analysis for those who wish to delve into Kongo state and society in the seventeenth century.

M. WILSON AND L. THOMPSON, eds., *The Oxford History of South Africa*, Vol. I., *South Africa to 1870* (1969). Relatively detailed, if occasionally dated, treatment.

CHAPTER 18

I. BERLIN, *Many Thousands Gone: The First Two Centuries of Slavery in North America* (1998); *Generations of Captivity: A History of African American Slaves* (2003). Two volumes representing the most extensive and important recent treatment of slavery in North America.

R. BLACKBURN, *The Making of New World Slavery from the Baroque to the Modern 1492–1800* (1997). An extraordinary work.

B. COBO, *History of the Inca Empire* (1979). A major discussion.

N. D. COOK, *Born to Die: Disease and New World Conquest, 1492–1650* (1998) A survey of the devastating impact of previously unknown diseases on the native populations of the Americas.

P. D. CURTIN, *The Atlantic Slave Trade: A Census* (1969). Remains a basic work.

D. B. DAVIS, *The Problem of Slavery in Western Culture* (1966). A brilliant and far-ranging discussion.

H. L. GATES JR. AND W. L. ANDREWS, eds., *Pioneers of the Black Atlantic: Five Slave Narratives from the Enlightenment 1772–1815* (1998). An anthology of autobiographical accounts.

S. GRUZINSKI, *The Conquest of Mexico: The Incorporation of Indian Societies into the Western World, 16th–18th Centuries* (1993). Interprets the experience of Native Americans, from their own point of view, during the time of the Spanish conquest.

L. HANKE, *Bartolomé de Las Casas: An Interpretation of His Life and Writings* (1951). A classic work.

R. HARMS, *The Diligent: A Voyage through the Worlds of the Slave Trade* (2002). A powerful narrative of the voyage of a French slave trader.

J. HEMMING, *The Conquest of the Incas,* (1970). A lucid account of the conquest of the Inca Empire and its aftermath.

J. HEMMING, *Red Gold: The Conquest of the Brazilian Native Americans, 1500–1760* (1978). A careful account with excellent bibliography.

H. KLEIN, *The Middle Passage: Comparative Studies in the African Slave Trade* (1978). A far-ranging overview of the movement of slaves from Africa to the Americas.

M. LEON-PORTILLA, ed., *The Broken Spears: The Aztec Account of the Conquest of Mexico* (1961). A collection of documents recounting the experience of the Aztecs from their own point of view.

P. MANNING, *Slavery and African Life: Occidental, Oriental, and African Slave Trades* (1990). An admirably concise economic-historical synthesis of the evidence, with multiple tables and statistics to supplement the magisterial analysis.

A. PAGDEN, *Lords of All the World: Ideologies of Empire in Spain, Britain, and France* c. 1500–c. 1800 (1995). An effort to explain the imperial thinking of the major European powers.

S. B. SCHWARTZ, *Sugar Plantations in the Formation of Brazilian Society: Bahia, 1550–1835* (1985). A broad-ranging study of the emergence of the plantation economy.

I. K. STEELE, *The English Atlantic, 1675–1740s: An Exploration of Communication and Community* (1986). An exploration of culture and commerce in the transatlantic world.

S. J. STEIN, *Peru's Indian Peoples and the Challenge of Spanish Conquest: Huamanga to 1640* (1983). A work that examines the impact of the conquest of the Inca empire over the scope of a century.

H. THOMAS, *Conquest: Montezuma, Cortés, and the Fall of Old Mexico* (1993). A splendid modern narrative of the event with careful attention to the character of the participants.

H. THOMAS, *The Slave Trade: The Story of the Atlantic Slave Trade: 1440–1870* (1999). A sweeping narrative overview.

J. THORNTON, *Africa and Africans in the Making of the Atlantic World, 1400–1680* (1992). A discussion of the role of Africans in the emergence of the transatlantic economy.

N. WACHTEL, *The Vision of the Vanquished: The Spanish Conquest of Peru Through Indian Eyes, 1530–1570* (1977). A presentation of Incan experience of conquest.

CHAPTER 19

China

D. BODDE AND C. MORRIS, *Law in Imperial China* (1967). Focuses on the Qing dynasty (1644–1911).

T. BROOK, *The Confusions of Pleasure: Commerce and Culture in Ming China* (1988).

C. S. CHANG AND S. L. H. CHANG, *Crisis and Transformation in Seventeenth Century China: Society, Culture, and Modernity* (1992).

P. CROSSLEY, *Translucent Mirror: History and Identity in Qing Imperial Ideology* (1999).

W. T. DE BARY, *Learning for One's Self: Essays on the Individual in Neo-Confucian Thought* (1991). A useful corrective to the view that Confucianism is simply a social ideology.

M. C. ELLIOTT, *The Manchu Way: The Eight Banners and Ethnic Identity in Late Imperial China* (2001). The latest word; compare to Crossley above.

M. ELVIN, *The Pattern of the Chinese Past: A Social and Economic Interpretation* (1973). A controversial but stimulating interpretation of Chinese economic history in terms of technology. It brings in earlier periods as well as the Ming, Qing, and modern China.

J. K. FAIRBANK, ed., *The Chinese World Order: Traditional China's Foreign Relations* (1968). An examination of the Chinese tribute system and its varying applications.

H. L. KAHN, *Monarchy in the Emperor's Eyes: Image and Reality in the Ch'ien-lung Reign* (1971). A study of the Chinese court during the mid-Qing period.

P. KUHN, *Soulstealers: The Chinese Sorcery Scare of 1768* (1990).

LI YU, *The Carnal Prayer Mat*, trans. by P. Hanan (1990).

F. MOTE AND D. TWITCHETT, eds., *The Cambridge History of China: The Ming Dynasty 1368–1644*, Vols. VI (1988) and VII (1998).

S. NAQUIN, *Peking Temples and City Life, 1400–1900* (2000).

S. NAQUIN AND E. S. RAWSKI, *Chinese Society in the Eighteenth Century* (1987).

J. B. PARSONS, *The Peasant Rebellions of the Late Ming Dynasty* (1970).

P. C. PERDUE, *Exhausting the Earth, State and Peasant in Hunan, 1500–1850* (1987).

D. H. PERKINS, *Agricultural Development in China, 1368–1968* (1969).

E. RAWSKI, *The Last Emperors: A Social History of Qing Imperial Institutions* (1998).

M. RICCI, *China in the Sixteenth Century: The Journals of Matthew Ricci, 1583–1610* (1953).

W. ROWE, *Hankow* (1984). A study of a city in late imperial China.

G. W. SKINNER, *The City in Late Imperial China* (1977).

J. D. SPENCE, *Ts'ao Yin and the K'ang-hsi Emperor: Bondservant and Master* (1966). An excellent study of the early Qing court.

J. D. SPENCE, *Emperor of China: A Self-Portrait of K'ang-hsi* (1974). The title of this readable book does not adequately convey the extent of the author's contribution to the study of the early Qing emperor.

J. D. SPENCE, *Treason by the Book* (2001). An account of the legal workings of the authoritarian Qing state that reads like a detective story.

L. A. STRUVE, trans. and ed., *Voices from the Ming-Qing Cataclysm* (1993). A reader with translations of Chinese sources.

F. WAKEMAN, *The Great Enterprise* (1985). On the founding of the Manchu dynasty.

Japan

M. E. BERRY, *Hideyoshi* (1982). A study of the sixteenth-century unifier of Japan.

M. E. BERRY, *The Culture of Civil War in Kyoto* (1994). On the Warring States era.

H. BOLITHO, *Treasures Among Men: The Fudai Daimyo in Tokugawa Japan* (1974). A study in depth.

H. BOLITHO, *Bereavement and Consolation: Testimonies from Tokugawa Japan* (2003). Instances of how Tokugawa Japanese handled the death of a child.

C. R. BOXER, *The Christian Century in Japan, 1549–1650* (1951).

The Cambridge History of Japan; Vol. 4 J.W. Hall (ed.), *Early Modern Japan* (1991). A multi-author work.

M. CHIKAMATSU, *Major Plays of Chikamatsu*, trans. by D. Keene (1961).

R. P. DORE, *Education in Tokugawa Japan* (1965).

G. S. ELISON, *Deus Destroyed: The Image of Christianity in Early Modern Japan* (1973). A brilliant study of the persecutions of Christianity during the early Tokugawa period.

J. W. HALL AND M. JANSEN, eds., *Studies in the Institutional History of Early Modern Japan* (1968). A collection of articles on Tokugawa institutions.

J. W. HALL, K. NAGAHARA, AND K. YAMAMURA, eds., *Japan Before Tokugawa* (1981).

S. HANLEY, *Everyday Things in Premodern Japan: The Hidden Legacy of Material Culture* (1997).

H. S. HIBBETT, *The Floating World in Japanese Fiction* (1959). An eminently readable study of early Tokugawa literature.

M. JANSEN, ed., *The Nineteenth Century*, Vol. 5 in *The Cambridge History of Japan* (1989).

K. KATSU, *Musui's Story* (1988). The life and adventures of a boisterous, no-good samurai of the early nineteenth century. Eminently readable.

D. KEENE, trans., *Chushingura, the Treasury of Loyal Retainers* (1971). The puppet play about the forty-seven rōnin who took revenge on the enemy of their former lord.

O.G. LIDIN, *Tanegashima: The Arrival of Europe in Japan* (2002). The impact of the musket and Europeans on sixteenth-century Japan.

M. MARUYAMA, *Studies in the Intellectual History of Tokugawa Japan*, trans. by M. Hane (1974). A seminal work in this field by one of modern Japan's greatest scholars.

J.L. McCLAIN, et. al., *Edo and Paris: Urban Life and the State in the Early Modern Era* (1994). Comparison of city life and government role in capitals of Tokugawa Japan and France.

K. W. NAKAI, *Shogunal Politics* (1988). A brilliant study of Arai Hakuseki's conceptualization of Tokugawa government.

P. NOSCO, ed., *Confucianism and Tokugawa Culture* (1984). A lively collection of essays.

H. OOMS, *Tokugawa Village Practice: Class, Status, Power, Law* (1996).

A. RAVINA, *Land and Lordship in Early Modern Japan* (1999). A sociopolitical study of three Tokugawa domains.

I. SAIKAKU, *The Japanese Family Storehouse*, trans. by G. W. Sargent (1959). A lively novel about merchant life in seventeenth-century Japan.

G. B. SANSOM, *The Western World and Japan* (1950).

J. A. SAWADA, *Confucian Values and Popular Zen* (1993). A study of *Shingaku*, a popular Tokugawa religious sect.

C. D. SHELDON, *The Rise of the Merchant Class in Tokugawa Japan* (1958).

T. C. SMITH, *The Agrarian Origins of Modern Japan* (1959). On the evolution of farming and rural social organization in Tokugawa Japan.

P. F. SOUYRI, *The World Turned Upside Down: Medieval Japanese Society* (2001). After a running start from the late Heian period, an analysis of the overthrow of lords by their vassals.

R. P. TOBY, *State and Diplomacy in Early Modern Japan: Asia in the Development of the Tokugawa Bakufu* (1984).

C. TOTMAN, *Tokugawa Ieyasu: Shōgun* (1983).

C. TOTMAN, *Green Archipelago, Forestry in Preindustrial Japan* (1989).

H. P. VARLEY, *The Ō'nin War: History of Its Origins and Background with a Selective Translation of the Chronicle of Ō'nin* (1967).

K. YAMAMURA AND S. B. HANLEY, *Economic and Demographic Change in Preindustrial Japan, 1600–1868* (1977).

Korea

T. HATADA, *A History of Korea* (1969).

W. E. HENTHORN, *A History of Korea* (1971).

KI-BAIK LEE, *A New History of Korea* (1984).

P. LEE, *Sourcebook of Korean Civilization*, Vol. I (1993).

Vietnam

J. BUTTINGER, *A Dragon Defiant, a Short History of Vietnam* (1972).

NGUYEN DU, *The Tale of Kieu* (1983).

N. TARLING, ed., *The Cambridge History of Southeast Asia* (1992).

K. TAYLOR, *The Birth of Vietnam* (1983).

A. B. WOODSIDE, *Vietnam and the Chinese Model* (1988).

CHAPTER 20

F. ANDERSON, *The Crucible of War: The Seven Years' War and the Fate of Empire in British North America, 1754–1766* (2000) A splendid narrative and analysis.

J. BLUM, *Lord and Peasant in Russia from the Ninth to the Nineteenth Century* (1961). Remains a thorough and wide-ranging discussion.

P. BURKE, *The Fabrication of Louis XIV* (1992). Examines the manner in which the public image of Louis XIV was forged in art.

P. BUSHKOVITCH, *Peter the Great: The Struggle for Power, 1671–1725* (2001). Replaces previous studies.

L. COLLEY, *Britons: Forging the Nation, 1707–1837* (1992) A major study of the making of British nationhood.

P. DEANE, *The First Industrial Revolution*, (1999). A well-balanced and systematic treatment.

J. DE VRIES, *European Urbanization 1500–1800* (1984). The most important and far-ranging of recent treatments of the subject.

W. DOYLE, *The Old European Order, 1660–1800* (1992). The most thoughtful treatment of the subject.

R. J. W. EVANS, *The Making of the Habsburg Monarchy, 1550–1700: An Interpretation* (1979). Places much emphasis on intellectual factors and the role of religion.

D. FRASER, *Frederick the Great: King of Prussia* (2001) Excellent on both Frederick and eighteenth-century Prussia.

E. HOBSBAWM, *Industry and Empire: The Birth of the Industrial Revolution* (1999). A survey by a major historian of the subject.

K. HONEYMAN, *Women, Gender and Industrialization in England, 1700–1850* (2000). Emphasizes how certain work or economic roles became associated with either men or women.

O. H. HUFTON, *The Poor of Eighteenth-Century France, 1750–1789* (1975). A brilliant study of poverty and the family economy.

L. HUGHES, *Russia in the Age of Peter the Great* (1998). An excellent account.

D. I. KERTZER AND M. BARBAGLI, *The History of the European Family: Family Life in Early Modern Times, 1500–1709* (2001). A series of broad-ranging essays covering the entire Continent.

S. KING AND G. TIMMONS, *Making Sense of the Industrial Revolution: English Economy and Society, 1700–1850* (2001). Examines the Industrial Revolution through the social institutions that brought it about and were changed by it.

M. KISHLANSKY, *A Monarchy Transformed: Britain 1603–1714* (1996) An excellent synthesis.

P. LANGFORD, *A Polite and Commercial People: England 1717–1783* (1989). An excellent survey of mid-eighteenth-century Britain covering social history as well as politics, the overseas wars, and the American Revolution.

A. LOSSKY, *Louis XIV and the French Monarchy* (1994). The most recent major analysis.

F. E. MANUEL, *The Broken Staff: Judaism Through Christian Eyes* (1992). An important discussion of Christian interpretations of Judaism.

M. A. MEYER, *The Origins of the Modern Jew: Jewish Identity and European Culture in Germany, 1749–1824* (1967). A general introduction organized around individual case studies.

D. UNDERDOWN, *Fire from Heaven: Life in an English Town in the Seventeenth Century* (1992). A lively account of how a single English town experienced the religious and political turmoil of the century.

D. VALENZE, *The First Industrial Woman* (1995). An elegant work exploring the manner in which industrialization transformed the work of women.

J. WEST, *Gunpower, Government, and War in the Mid–Eighteenth Century* (1991). A study of how warfare touched much government of the day.

CHAPTER 21

S. S. BLAIR AND J. BLOOM, *The Art and Architecture of Islam, 1250–1800* (1994). A fine survey of the period for all parts of the Islamic world.

R. CANFIELD, ed., *Turko-Persia in Historical Perspctive* (1991). A good general collection of essays.

K. CHELEBI, *The Balance of Truth* (1957). A marvelous volume of essays and reflections by probably the major intellectual of Ottoman times.

W. T. DE BARY et al., comp., *Sources of Indian Tradition*, 2nd ed. (1958),Vol. I, *From the Beginning to 1800,* ed. and rev. by Ainslie T. Embree (1988). Excellent selections from a wide variety of Indian texts, with good introductions to chapters and individual selections.

S. FAROQI, *Towns and Townsmen of Ottoman Anatolia* (1984). Examines the changing balances of economic power between the urban and rural areas.

C. H. FLEISCHER, *Bureaucrat and Intellectual in the Ottoman Empire: The Historian Mustafa Ali (1541–1600)* (1986). A major study of Ottoman intellectual history.

G. HAMBLY, *Central Asia* (1966). Excellent survey chapters (9–13) on the Chaghatay and Uzbek (Shaybanid) Turks.

R. S. HATTOX, *Coffee and Coffee-Houses: The Origins of a Social Beverage in the Medieval Near East* (1985). A fascinating piece of social history.

M. G. S. HODGSON, *The Gunpowder Empires and Modern Times*, Vol. 3 of *The Venture of Islam*, 3 vols. (1974). Less ample than Vols. 1 and 2 of Hodgson's monumental history, but a thoughtful survey of the great post-1500 empires.

S. M. IKRAM, *Muslim Civilization in India* (1964). Still the best short survey history, covering the period from 711 to 1857.

H. INALCIK, *The Ottoman Empire: The Classical Age 1300–1600* (1973). An excellent, if dated, survey with solid treatment of Ottoman social, religious, and political institutions.

H. INALCIK, *An Economic and Social History of the Ottoman Empire, 1300–1914* (1994). A masterly survey by the dean of Ottoman studies today.

C. KAFADAR, *Between Two Worlds: The Construction of the Ottoman State* (1995). A readable analysis of theories of Ottoman origins and early development.

N. R. KEDDIE, ed., *Scholars, Saints, and Sufis: Muslim Religious Institutions in the Middle East Since 1500* (1972). A collection of interesting articles well worth reading.

M. MUJEEB, *The Indian Muslims* (1967). The best cultural study of Islamic civilization in India as a whole, from its origins onward.

G. NECIPOGLU, *Architecture, Ceremonial, and Power: The Topkapi Palace in the Fifteenth and Sixteenth Centuries* (1991). A superb analysis of the symbolism of Ottoman power and authority.

L. PIERCE, *The Imperial Harem: Women and Sex in the Ottoman Empire* (1993). Ground-breaking study on the role of women in the Ottoman Empire.

D. QUATARERT, *An Economic and Social history of the Ottoman Empire 1300–1914* (1994). The authoritative account of Ottoman economy and society.

J. RICHARDS, *The Mughal Empire*, Vol. 5 of *The New Cambridge History of India* (1993). A impressive synthesis of the varying interpretations of the Mughal India.

S. A. A. RIZVI, *The Wonder That Was India*, Vol. II (1987). A sequel to Basham's original *The Wonder That Was India*; treats Mughal life, culture, and history from 1200 to 1700.

F. ROBINSON, *Atlas of the Islamic World Since 1500* (1982). Brief, excellent historical essays, color illustrations with detailed accompanying text, and chronological tables, as well as precise maps, make this a refreshing general reference work.

R. SAVORY, *Iran Under the Safavids* (1980). A solid and readable survey.

S. J. SHAW, *Empire of the Gazis: The Rise and Decline of the Ottoman Empire, 1280–1808*, Vol. I of *History of the Ottoman Empire and Modern Turkey* (1976). A solid historical survey with excellent bibliographic essays for each chapter and a good index.

CHAPTER 22

D. BEALES, *Joseph II: In the Shadow of Maria Theresa, 1741–1780* (1987). The best treatment in English of the early political life of Joseph II.

M. BIAGIOLI, *Galileo Courtier: The Practice of Science in the Culture of Absolutism* (1993). A major revisionist work that emphasizes the role of the political setting on Galileo's career and thought.

D. D. BIEN, *The Calas Affair: Persecution, Toleration, and Heresy in Eighteenth-Century Toulouse* (1960). Classic treatment of the famous case.

T. C. W. BLANNING, *The Culture of Power and the Power of Culture: Old Regime Europe 1660–1789* (2002). The strongest treatment of the relationship of eighteenth-century cultural changes and politics.

R. DARNTON, *The Literary Underground of the Old Regime* (1982). Classic essays on the world of printers, publishers, and booksellers.

P. DEAR, *Revolutionizing the Sciences: European Knowledge and Its Ambitions, 1500–1700* (2001). A broad-ranging study of both the ideas and institutions of the new science.

I. DE MADARIAGA, *Catherine the Great: A Short History* (1990). A good brief biography.

S. GAUKROGER, *Francis Bacon and the Transformation of Early-Modern Philosophy* (2001). An excellent, accessible introduction.

J. GLEIXK, *Isaac Newton* (2003) The best brief biography.

D. GOODMAN, *The Republic of Letters: A Cultural History of the French Enlightenment* (1994). Concentrates on the role of salons.

I. HARRIS, *The Mind of John Locke: A Study of Political Theory in Its Intellectual Setting* (1994). The most comprehensive recent treatment.

J. L. HEILBRON, *The Sun in the Church: Cathedrals as Solar Observatories* (2000). A remarkable study of the manner in which Roman Catholic cathedrals were used to make astronomical observations and calculations.

K. J. HOWELL, *God's TwoBooks: Copernican Cosmology and Biblical Interpretqation in Early Modern Science* (2003) Best introduction to early modern issues of science and religion.

J. MELTON, *The Rise of the Public in Enlightenmen Europe* (2001). A superb overview of the emergence of new institutions which made the expression of a broad public opinion possible in Europe.

T. MUNCK, *The Enlightenment: A Comparative Social History 1721–1794* (2000). A clear introduction to the social background making possible the spread of Enlightenment thought.

S. MUTHU, *Enlightenment against Empire* (2003) A study of philosophes who criticized the European empires of their day.

D. OUTRAM, *The Enlightenment* (1995). An excellent brief introduction.

R. PORTER, *The Creation of the Modern World: The Untold Story of the British Enlightenment* (2001) A superb, lively overview.

P. RILEY, *The Cambridge Companion to Rousseau* (2001). Excellent accessible essays by major scholars.

E. ROTHCHILD, *Economic Sentiments: Adam Smith, Condorcet, and the Enlightenment* (2001). A sensitive account of Smith's thought and its relationship to the social questions of the day.

S. SHAPIN, *The Scientific Revolution* (1996). An important revisionist survey emphasizing social factors.

L. STEINBRÜGGE, *The Moral Sex: Woman's Nature in the French Enlightenment* (1995). Emphasizes the conservative nature of Enlightenment thought on women.

P. ZAGORIN, *How the Idea of Religious Toleration Came to the West* (2003) An excellent exploration of the rise of toleration.

CHAPTER 23

R. ANSTEY, *The Atlantic Slave Trade and British Abolition, 1760–1810* (1975). A standard overview that emphasizes the role of religious factors.

B. BAILYN, *The Ideological Origins of the American Revolution* (1967). An important work illustrating the role of English radical thought in the perceptions of the American colonists.

K. M. BAKER, *Inventing the French Revolution: Essays on French Political Culture in the Eighteenth Century* (1990). Important essays on political thought before and during the revolution.

K. M. BAKER AND C. LUCAS, eds., *The French Revolution and the Creation of Modern Political Culture*, 3 vols. (1987). A splendid collection of important original articles on all aspects of politics during the revolution.

R. J. BARMAN, *Brazil: The Forging of a Nation, 1798–1852* (1988). The best coverage of this period.

C. BECKER, *The Declaration of Independence: A Study in the History of Political Ideas* (1922). Remains an important examination of the political and imperial theory of the Declaration.

J. F. BERNARD, *Talleyrand: A Biography* (1973). A useful account.

L. BETHELL, *The Cambridge History of Latin America*, Vol. 3 (1985). Contains an extensive treatment of independence.

R. BLACKBURN, *The Overthrow of Colonial Slavery, 1776–1848* (1988). A major discussion quite skeptical of the humanitarian interpretation.

T. C. W. BLANNING, ed., *The Rise and Fall of the French Revolution* (1996). A wide-ranging collection of essays illustrating the debates over the French Revolution.

J. BROOKE, *King George III* (1972). The best biography.

R. COBB, *The People's Armies* (1987). The major treatment in English of the revolutionary army.

O. CONNELLY, *Napoleon's Satellite Kingdoms* (1965). The rule of Napoleon and his family in Europe.

E. V. DA COSTA, *The Brazilian Empire* (1985). Excellent coverage of the entire nineteenth-century experience of Brazil.

D. B. DAVIS, *The Problem of Slavery in the Age of Revolution, 1770–1823* (1975). A transatlantic perspective on the issue.

F. FEHÉR, *The French Revolution and the Birth of Modernity* (1990). A wide-ranging collection of essays on political and cultural facets of the revolution.

A. FORREST, *The French Revolution and the Poor* (1981). A study that expands consideration of the revolution beyond the standard social boundaries.

M. GLOVER, *The Peninsular War, 1807–1814: A Concise Military History* (1974). An interesting account of the military campaign that so drained Napoleon's resources in western Europe.

J. GODECHOT, *The Counter-Revolution: Doctrine and Action, 1789–1804* (1971). An examination of opposition to the revolution.

A. GOODWIN, *The Friends of Liberty: The English Democratic Movement in the Age of the French Revolution* (1979). A major work that explores the impact of the French Revolution on English radicalism.

L. HUNT, *Politics, Culture, and Class in the French Revolution* (1986). A series of essays that focus on the modes of expression of the revolutionary values and political ideas.

W. W. KAUFMANN, *British Policy and the Independence of Latin America, 1802–1828* (1951). A standard discussion of an important relationship.

E. KENNEDY, *A Cultural History of the French Revolution* (1989). An important examination of the role of the arts, schools, clubs, and intellectual institutions.

M. KENNEDY, *The Jacobin Clubs in the French Revolution: The First Years* (1982). A careful scrutiny of the organizations chiefly responsible for the radicalizing of the revolution.

M. KENNEDY, *The Jacobin Clubs in the French Revolution: The Middle Years* (1988). A continuation of the previously listed study.

H. KISSINGER, *A World Restored: Metternich, Castlereagh and the Problems of Peace, 1812–1822* (1957). A provocative study by an author who became an American secretary of state.

G. LEFEBVRE, *The Coming of the French Revolution* (trans. 1947). A classic examination of the crisis of the French monarchy and the events of 1789.

G. LEFEBVRE, *Napoleon*, 2 vols., trans. by H. Stockhold (1969). The fullest and finest biography.

J. LYNCH, *The Spanish American Revolutions, 1808–1826* (1986). An excellent one-volume treatment.

P. MAIER, *American Scripture: Making the Declaration of Independence* (1997). Stands as a major revision of our understanding of the Declaration.

G. MASUR, *Simón Bolívar* (1969). The standard biography in English.

S. E. MELZER AND L. W. RABINE, eds., *Rebel Daughters: Women and the French Revolution* (1992). A collection of essays exploring various aspects of the role and image of women in the French Revolution.

M. MORRIS, *The British Monarchy and the French Revolution* (1998). Explores the manner in which the British monarchy saved itself from possible revolution.

R. MUIR, *Tactics and the Experience of Battle in the Age of Napoleon* (1998). Examines the wars from the standpoint of the soldiers in combat.

H. NICOLSON, *The Congress of Vienna* (1946). A good, readable account.

T. O. OTT, *The Haitian Revolution, 1789–1804* (1973). An account that clearly relates the events in Haiti to those in France.

R. R. PALMER, *Twelve Who Ruled: The Committee of Public Safety During the Terror* (1941). A clear narrative and analysis of the policies and problems of the committee.

R. R. PALMER, *The Age of the Democratic Revolution: A Political History of Europe and America, 1760–1800*, 2 vols. (1959, 1964). An impressive survey of the political turmoil in the transatlantic world.

C. PROCTOR, *Women, Equality, and the French Revolution* (1990). An examination of how the ideas of the Enlightenment and the attitudes of revolutionaries affected the legal status of women.

A. J. RUSSELL-WOOD, ed., *From Colony to Nation: Essays on the Independence of Brazil* (1975). A series of important essays.

P. SCHROEDER, *The Transformation of European Politics, 1763–1848* (1994). A fundamental treatment of the diplomacy of the era.

T. E. SKIDMORE AND P. H. SMITH, *Modern Latin America*, 4th ed. (1997). A very useful survey.

A. SOBOUL, *The Parisian Sans-Culottes and the French Revolution, 1793–94* (1964). The best work on the subject.

A. SOBOUL, *The French Revolution* (trans. 1975). An important work by a Marxist scholar.

D. G. SUTHERLAND, *France, 1789–1825: Revolution and Counterrevolution* (1986). A major synthesis based on recent scholarship in social history.

T. TACKETT, *Religion, Revolution, and Regional Culture in Eighteenth-Century France: The Ecclesiastical Oath of 1791* (1986). The most important study of this topic.

T. TACKETT, *Becoming a Revolutionary: The Deputies of the French National Assembly and the Emergence of a Revolutionary Culture (1789–1790)* (1996). The best study of the early months of the revolution.

J. M. THOMPSON, *Robespierre*, 2 vols. (1935). The best biography.

D. K. VAN KEY, *The Religious Origins of the French Revolution: From Calvin to the Civil Constitution, 1560–1791* (1996). Examines the manner in which debates within French Catholicism influenced the coming of the revolution.

M. WALZER, ed., *Regicide and Revolution: Speeches at the Trial of Louis XVI* (1974). An important and exceedingly interesting collection of documents with a useful introduction.

I. WOLOCH, *The New Regime: Transformations of the French Civic Order, 1789–1820s* (1994). An important overview of just what had and had not changed in France after the quarter century of revolution and war.

G. WOOD, *The Radicalism of the American Revolution* (1991). A major interpretation.

CHAPTER 24

I. BERLIN, *Generations of Captivity: A History of African-American Slaves* (2003) A major work.

D. BLACKBOURN, *The Long Nineteenth Century: A History of Germany, 1780–1918* (1998). An outstanding survey.

D. G. CREIGHTON, *John A. MacDonald* (1952, 1955). A major biography of the first Canadian prime minister.

D. DONALD, *Lincoln* (1995). Now the standard biography.

R. B. EDGERTON, *Death or Glory: The Legacy of the Crimean War* (2000). Multifaceted study of a badly mismanaged war that transformed many aspects of European domestic politics.

M. HOLT, *The Rise and Fall of the American Whig Party: Jacksonian Politics and the Onset of the Civil War* (2003) An extensive survey of the Jacksonian era.

R. KEE, *The Green Flag: A History of Irish Nationalism* (2001). A vast survey.

W. LACQUER, *A History of Zionism* (1989). The most extensive one-volume treatment.

M. B. LEVINGER, *Enlightened Nationalism: The Transformation of Prussian Political Culture, 1806–1848* (2002). A major work based on the most recent scholarship.

J. M. MCPHERSON, *The Battle Cry of Freedom: The Civil War Era* (1988). An excellent one-volume treatment.

D. MORTON, *A Short History of Canada* (2001). Useful popular history.

J. P. PARRY, *The Rise and Fall of Liberal Government in Victorian Britain* (1994). An outstanding study.

A. PLESSIS, *The Rise and Fall of the Second Empire, 1852–1871* (1985). A useful survey of France under Napoleon III.

D. M. POTTER, *The Impending Crisis, 1848–1861* (1976) A penetrating study of the coming of the American Civil War.

A. SKED, *Decline and Fall of the Habsburg Empire 1815–1918* (2001). A major, accessible survey of a difficult subject.

D. M. SMITH, *Cavour* (1984). An excellent biography.

C. P. STACEY, *Canada and the Age of Conflict* (1977, 1981). A study of Canadian foreign relations.

D. WETZEL, *A Duel of Giants: Bismarck, Napoleon III, and the Origins of the Franco-Prussian War* (2001). Broad study based on most recent scholarship.

CHAPTER 25

M. ADAS, *Machines as the Measure of Men: Science, Technology, and Ideologies of Western Dominance* (1989). The best single volume on racial thinking and technological advances as forming ideologies of European colonial dominance.

A. ASCHER AND P. A. STOLYPIN, *The Search for Stability in Late Imperial Russia* (2000). A broad-ranging biography based on extensive research.

I. BERLIN, *Karl Marx: His Life and Environment*, 4th ed. (1996). A classics volume that remains an excellent introduction.

JANET BROWNE, *Charles Darwin*, 2 vols. (2002) An eloquent, accessible biography.

J. BURROW, *The Crisis of Reason: European Thought, 1848–1914* (2000). The best overview available.

A. D. CHANDLER JR., *The Visible Hand: Managerial Revolution in American Business* (1977). Remains the best discussion of the innovative role of American business.

A. CLARKE, *The Struggle for the Breeches: Gender and the Making of the British Working Class* (1995). An examination of the manner in which industrialization made problematical the relationships between men and women.

W. CRONIN, *Nature's Metropolis: Chicago and the Great West, 1848–1893* (1991) The best examination of any major American nineteenth-century city.

P. GAY, *Freud: A Life for Our Time* (1988). The new standard biography.

R. F. HAMILTON, *Marxism, Revisionism, and Leninism: Explication, Assessment, and Commentary* (2000). A contribution from the perspective of a historically minded sociologist.

S. HAHN, *A Nation under Our Feet: Black Political Struggles in the Rural South from Slavey to the Great Migration* (2003). A major synthesis.

A. HOURANI, *Arab Thought in the Liberal Age 1789–1939* (1967). A classic account, clearly written and accessible to the nonspecialist.

D. I. KERTZER AND M. BARBAGLI, eds., *Family Life in the Long Nineteenth Century, 1789–1913: The History of the European Family* (2002). Wide-ranging collection of essays.

J. T. KLOPPENBERG, *Uncertain Victory: Social Democracy and Progressivism in European and American Thought* (1986). An extremely important comparative study.

J. KÖHLER, *Zarathustra's Secret: The Interior Life of Friedrich Nietzsche* (2002). A controversial new biography.

L. KOLAKOWSKI, *Main Currents of Marxism: Its Rise, Growth, and Dissolution*, 3 vols. (1978). Especially good on the last years of the nineteenth century and the early years of the twentieth.

P. KRAUSE, *The Battle for Homestead, 1880–1892* (1992). Examines labor relations in the steel industry.

D. LANDES, *The Wealth and Poverty of Nations: Why Some Are So Rich and Some So Poor* (1998). A major international discussion of the subject.

M. MCGERR, *A Fierce Discontent: The Rise and Fall of the Progressive Moevement in America l870–1920* (2003). The best recent synthesis.

E. MORRIS, *Theodore Rex* (2002). Major survey of Theodore Roosevelt's presidency and personality.

A. PAIS, *Subtle Is the Lord: The Science and Life of Albert Einstein* (l983). Remains the most accessible scientific biography.

J. RENDALL, *The Origins of Modern Feminism: Women in Britain, France and the United States, 1780–1860* (1985). A well-informed introduction.

R. SERVICE, *Lenin: A Biography* (2002). Based on new sources and will no doubt become the standard biography.

R. M. UTLEY, *The Indian Frontier and the American West, 1846–1890* (1984). A broad survey of the pressures of white civilization against Native Americans.

D. VITAL, *A People Apart: The Jews In Modern Europe, l789–1939* (1999). A deeply informed survey.

CHAPTER 26

S. ARROM, *The Women of Mexico City, 1790–1857* (1985). A pioneering study.

E. BERMAN, ed., *Women, Culture, and Politics in Latin America* (1990). Useful essays.

L. BETHELL, ed., *The Cambridge History of Latin America*, 8 vols. (1992). The single most authoritative coverage, with extensive bibliographical essays.

V. BULMER-THOMAS, *The Economic History of Latin America Since Independence* (1994). A major study in every respect.

E. B. BURNS, *The Poverty of Progress: Latin America in the Nineteenth Century* (1980). Argues that the elites suppressed alternative modes of cultural and economic development.

E. B. BURNS, *A History of Brazil* (1993). The most useful one-volume treatment.

D. BUSHNELL AND N. MACAULAY, *The Emergence of Latin America in the Nineteenth Century* (1994). A survey that examines the internal development of Latin America during the period.

R. CONRAD, *The Destruction of Brazilian Slavery, 1850–1889* (1971). A good survey of the most important problem in Brazil in the second half of the nineteenth century.

R. CONRAD, *World of Sorrow: The African Slave Trade to Brazil* (1986). An excellent survey of the subject.

E. V. DA COSTA, *The Brazilian Empire: Myths and Histories* (1985). Essays that provide a thorough introduction to Brazil during the period of empire.

H. S. FERNS, *Britain and Argentina in the Nineteenth Century* (1968). Explains clearly the intermeshing of the two economies.

M. FONT, *Coffee, Contention, and Change in the Making of Modern Brazil* (1990). Extensive discussion of the problems of a single-commodity economy.

R. GRAHAM, *Britain and the Onset of Modernization in Brazil* (1968). Another study of British economic dominance.

S. H. HABER, *Industry and Underdevelopment: The Industrialization of Mexico, 1890–1940* (1989). Examines the problem of industrialization before and after the revolution.

G. HAHNER, *Emancipating the Female Sex: The Struggle for Women's Rights in Brazil, 1850–1940* (1990). An extensive examination of a relatively understudied issue in Latin America.

C. H. HARING, *Empire in Brazil: A New World Experiment with Monarchy* (1958). Remains a useful overview.

J. HEMMING, *Amazon Frontier: The Defeat of the Brazilian Indians* (1987). A brilliant survey of the experience of Native Americans in modern Brazil.

R. A. HUMPHREYS, *Latin America and the Second World War*, 2 vols. (1981–1982). The standard work on the topic.

F. KATZ, ed., *Riot, Rebellion, and Revolution in Mexico: Social Base of Agrarian Violence, 1750–1940* (1988). Essays that put the violence of the revolution in a longer context.

A. KNIGHT, *The Mexican Revolution*, 2 vols. (1986). The best treatment of the subject.

S. MAINWARING, *The Catholic Church and Politics in Brazil, 1916–1985* (1986). An examination of a key institution in Brazilian life.

M. C. MEYER AND W. L. SHERMAN, *The Course of Mexican History* (1995). An excellent survey.

M. MORNER, *Adventurers and Proletarians: The Story of Migrants in Latin America* (1985). Examines immigration to Latin America and migration within it.

J. PAGE, *Perón: A Biography* (1983). The standard English treatment.

D. ROCK, *Politics in Argentina, 1890–1930: The Rise and Fall of Radicalism* (1975). The major discussion of the Argentine Radical Party.

D. ROCK, *Argentina, 1516–1987: From Spanish Colonization to Alfonsin* (1987). Now the standard survey.

D. ROCK, ed., *Latin America in the 1940s: War and Postwar Transitions* (1994). Essays examining a very difficult decade for the continent.

R. M. SCHNEIDER, *"Order and Progress": A Political History of Brazil* (1991). A straightforward narrative with helpful notes for further reading.

T. E. SKIDMORE, *Black into White: Race and Nationality in Brazilian Thought* (1993). Examines the role of racial theory in Brazil.

P. H. SMITH, *Argentina and the Failure of Democracy: Conflict Among Political Elites. 1904–1955* (1974). An examination of one of the major political puzzles of Latin American history.

S. J. STEIN AND B. H. STEIN, *The Colonial Heritage of Latin America: Essays on Economic Dependence in Perspective* (1970). A major statement of the dependence interpretation.

D. TAMARIN, *The Argentine Labor Movement, 1930–1945: A Study in the Origins of Perónism* (1985). A useful introduction to a complex subject.

H. J. WIARDA, *Politics and Social Change in Latin America: The Distinct Tradition* (1974). Excellent essays that stress the ongoing role of Iberian traditions.

J. D. WIRTH, ed., *Latin American Oil Companies and the Politics of Energy* (1985). A series of case studies.

J. WOLFE, *Working Women, Working Men: São Paulo and the Rise of Brazil's Industrial Working Class, 1900–1955* (1993). Pays particular attention to the role of women.

J. WOMACK, *Zapata and the Mexican Revolution* (1968). A classic study.

CHAPTER 27

General Works

S. COOK, *Colonial Encounters in the Age of High Imperialism* (1996). A good introduction to the imperial enterprise in Africa and Asia.

D. K. FIELDHOUSE, *The West and the Third World. Trade, Colonialism, Depedence and Development* (1999). Addresses whether colonialism was detrimental or beneficial to colonized peoples.

P. HOPKIRK, *The Great Game: The Struggle for Empire in Central Asia* (1992). Focuses on the political and economic rivalries of the imperial powers.

India

A. AHMAD, *Islamic Modernism in India and Pakistan, 1857–1964* (1967). The standard survey of Muslim thinkers and movements in India during the period.

C. A. BAYLY, *Indian Society and the Making of the British Empire, The New Cambridge History of India*, II. 1 (1988). One of several major contributions of this author to the ongoing revision of our picture of modern Indian history since the eighteenth century.

A. GHOSH, *In an Antique Land. History in the Guise of a Traveler's Tale* (1992). An anthropologist traces the footsteps of a premodern slave traveling with his master from North Africa to India. A gripping tale of premodern life in the India Ocean basin and also of contemporary Egypt.

R. GUHA, ed., *Subaltern Studies: Writings on South Asian History and Society* (1982). Essays on the colonial period that focus on the social, political, and economic history of "subaltern" groups and classes (hill tribes, peasants, etc.) rather than only the elites of India.

S. N. HAY, ed., "Modern India and Pakistan," Part VI of Wm. Theodore de Bary et al., eds., *Sources of Indian Tradition*, 2nd ed. (1988). A superb selection of primary-source documents with brief introductions and helpful notes.

F. ROBINSON, ed., *The Cambridge Encyclopedia of India, Pakistan, Bangladesh, Sri Lanka, Nepal, Bhutan, and the*

Maldives (1989). A fine collection of survey articles by various scholars, organized into topical chapters ranging from "Economies" to "Cultures."

Central Islamic Lands

J. J. DONAHUE AND J. L. ESPOSITO, eds., *Islam in Transition: Muslim Perspectives* (1982). An interesting selection of primary-source materials on Islamic thinking in this century.

W. CLEVELAND, *A History of the Modern Middle East*, 3rd ed. (2004). A balanced and well-organized overview of modern Middle Eastern history.

A. DAWISHA, *Arab Nationalism in the Twentieth Century. From Triumph to Despair* (2003). A good overview of the development of Arab nationalism.

S. DERINGIL, *The Well-Protected Domains: Ideology and the Legitimation of Power in the Ottoman Empire, 1876–1909* (1998). An impressive study on nationalism and reform in the Ottoman Empire.

D. F. EICKELMAN, *Knowledge and Power in Morocco: The Education of a Twentieth-Century Notable* (1985). A fascinating study of traditional Islamic education and society in the twentieth century through a social biography of a Moroccan religious scholar and judge.

A. HOURANI, *Arabic Thought in the Liberal Age, 1798–1939* (1967). The standard work, by which all subsequent scholarship on the topic is to be judged.

N. R. KEDDIE, *An Islamic Response to Imperialism* (1968). A brief study of al-Afghani, the great Muslim reformer, with translations of a number of his writings.

B. LEWIS, *The Emergence of Modern Turkey*, 2nd ed. (1968). A concise but thorough history of the creation of the Turkish state, including nineteenth-century background.

J. O. VOLL, *Islam: Continuity and Change in the Modern World* (1982). Chapters 1–6. An interpretive survey of the Islamic world since the eighteenth century. Its emphasis on eighteenth-century reform movements is especially noteworthy.

Africa

A. A. BOAHEN, *Africa Under Colonial Domination, 1880–1935* (1985). Vol. VII of the *UNESCO General History of Africa*. Excellent chapters on various regions of Africa in the period. Chapters 3–10 detail African resistance to European colonial intrusion in diverse regions.

W. CARTEY AND M. KILSON, eds., *The Africa Reader: Colonial Africa* (1970). Original source materials give a vivid picture of African resistance to colonial powers, adaptation to foreign rule, and the emergence of the African masses as a political force.

P. CURTIN, S. FEIERMANN, L. THOMPSON, AND J. VANSINA, *African History* (1978). The relevant portions are Chapters 10–20.

B. DAVIDSON, *Modern Africa: A Social and Political History* (1989). A very useful survey of African history.

J. D. FAGE, *A History of Africa* (1978). The relevant chapters, which give a particularly clear overview of the colonial period, are 12–16.

B. FREUND, *The Making of Contemporary Africa: The Development of African Society Since 1800* (1984). A refreshingly direct synthetic discussion and survey that take an avowedly, but not reductive, materialist approach to interpretation.

T. PAKENHAM, *The Scramble for Africa* (1991). An excellent analysis of the imperialist age in Africa.

A. D. ROBERTS, ed., *The Colonial Moment in Africa: Essays on the Movement of Minds and Materials, 1900–1940* (1986). Chapters from *The Cambridge History of Africa* treating various aspects of the colonial period in Africa, including economics, politics, and religion.

CHAPTER 28

China

P. M. COBLE, *The Shanghai Capitalists and the Nationalist Government, 1927–1937* (1980).

L. E. EASTMAN, *The Abortive Revolution: China Under Nationalist Rule, 1927–1937* (1974).

L. E. EASTMAN, *Seeds of Destruction: Nationalist China in War and Revolution, 1937–1949* (1984).

M. ELVIN AND G. W. SKINNER, *The Chinese City Between Two Worlds* (1974). A study of the late Qing and Republican eras.

J. W. ESHERICK, *The Origins of the Boxer Rebellion* (1987).

S. ETŌ, *China's Republican Revolution* (1994).

J. K. FAIRBANK AND M. GOLDMAN, *China, a New History* (1998). A survey of the entire sweep of Chinese history; especially strong on the modern period.

J. K. FAIRBANK AND D. TWITCHETT, eds., *The Cambridge History of China*. Like the premodern volumes in the same series, the volumes on modern China represent a survey of what is known. Volumes 10–15, which cover the history from the late Qing to the People's Republic, have been published, and the others will be available soon. The series is substantial. Each volume contains a comprehensive bibliography.

J. FITZGERALD, *Awakening China: Politics, Culture, and Class in the Nationalist Revolution* (1996).

C. HAO, *Chinese Intellectuals in Crisis: Search for Order and Meaning, 1890–1911* (1987).

W. C. KIRBY, ed., *State and Economy in Republican China* (2001).

P. A. KUHN, *Rebellion and Its Enemies in Late Imperial China: Militarization and Social Structure, 1796–1864* (1980). A study of how the Confucian gentry saved the Manchu dynasty after the Taiping Rebellion.

P. KUHN, Origins of the Modern Chinese State (2002).

J. LEVENSON, *Liang Ch'i-ch'ao and the Mind of Modern China* (1953). A classic study of a major Chinese reformer and thinker.

LU XUN, *Selected Works* (1960). Novels, stories, and other writings by modern China's greatest writer.

S. NAQUIN, *Peking: Temples and City Life, 1400–1900* (2000).

E. O. REISCHAUER, J. K. FAIRBANK, AND A. M. CRAIG, *East Asia: Tradition and Transformation* (1989). A detailed text on East Asian history. Contains ample chapters on Japan and China and shorter chapters on Korea and Vietnam.

H. Z. SCHIFFRIN, *Sun Yat-sen, Reluctant Revolutionary* (1980). A biography.

B. I. SCHWARTZ, *Chinese Communism and the Rise of Mao* (1951). A classic study of Mao, his thought, and the Chinese Communist Party before 1949.

B. I. SCHWARTZ, *In Search of Wealth and Power: Yen Fu and the West* (1964). A fine study of a late-nineteenth-century thinker who introduced Western ideas into China.

J. D. SPENCE, *The Gate of Heavenly Peace: The Chinese and Their Revolution, 1895–1980* (1981). Historical reflections on twentieth-century China.

J. D. SPENCE, *The Search for Modern China* (1990). A thick text but well written.

M. SZONYI, *Practicing Kinship: Lineage and Descent in Late Imperial China* (2002).

S. Y. TENG AND J. K. FAIRBANK, *China's Response to the West* (1954). A superb collection of translations from Chinese thinkers and political figures, with commentaries.

T. H. WHITE AND A. JACOBY, *Thunder Out of China* (1946). A view of China during World War II by two who were there.

Japan

G. AKITA, *Foundations of Constitutional Government in Modern Japan* (1967). A study of Itō Hirobumi in the political process leading to the Meiji constitution.

G. C. ALLEN, *A Short Economic History of Modern Japan* (1958).

A. E. BARSHAY, *The Social Sciences in Modern Japan: the Marxian and Modernist Traditions* (2004). Different interpretations of history.

J. R. BARTHOLOMEW, *The Formation of Science in Japan* (1989). The pioneering English-language work on the subject.

W. G. BEASLEY, *Japanese Imperialism, 1894–1945* (1987). Excellent short book on subject.

G. M. BERGER, *Parties Out of Power in Japan, 1931–1941* (1977). An analysis of the condition of political parties during the militarist era.

G.L. BERNSTEIN, *Recreating Japanese Women, 1600–1945* (1991).

The Cambridge History of Japan, The Nineteenth Century, M.B. Jansen, ed. (1989); *The Twentieth Century*, P. Duus, ed. (1988). Multi-author works.

A. M. CRAIG, *Chōshū in the Meiji Restoration* (2000). A study of the Chōshū domain, a Prussia of Japan, during the period 1840–1868.

A. M. CRAIG AND D. H. SHIVELY, eds., *Personality in Japanese History* (1970). An attempt to gauge the role of individuals and their personalities as factors explaining history.

P. DUUS, *Party Rivalry and Political Change in Taisho Japan* (1968). A study of political change in Japan during the 1910s and 1920s.

P. DUUS, *The Abacus and the Sword, the Japanese Penetration of Korea, 1895–1910* (1995). A thoughtful analysis.

S. ERICSON, *The Sound of the Whistle: Railroads and the State in Meiji Japan* (1996). An economic and social history of railroads, an engine of growth and popular symbol.

Y. FUKUZAWA, *Autobiography* (1966). Japan's leading nineteenth-century thinker tells of his life and of the birth of modern Japan.

A. GARON, *The State and Labor in Modern Japan* (1987). A fine study of the subject.

C. N. GLUCK, *Japan's Modern Myths: Ideology in the Late Meiji Period* (1988). A brilliant study of the complex weave of late Meiji thought.

A. GORDON, *The Evolution of Labor Relations in Japan: Heavy Industry, 1853–1955* (1985). A seminal work.

B. R. HACKETT, *Yamagata Aritomo in the Rise of Modern Japan, 1932–1922* (1973). History as seen through the biography of a central figure.

I. HALL, *Mori Arinori* (1973). A biography of Japan's first minister of education.

T. R. H. HAVENS, *The Valley of Darkness: The Japanese People and World War II* (1978). Wartime society.

C. IRIYE, *After Imperialism: The Search for a New Order in the Far East, 1921–1931* (1965). (Also see other studies by this author.)

D. M. B. JANSEN AND G. ROZMAN, eds., *Japan in Transition from Tokugawa to Meiji* (1986). Contains fine essays.

W. JOHNSTON, *The Modern Epidemic: A History of Tuberculosis in Japan* (1995). A social history of a disease.

E. KEENE, Ed., *Modern Japanese Literature, An Anthology* (1960). A collection of modern Japanese short stories and excerpts from novels.

F. Y.T. MATSUSAKA, *The Making of Japanese Manchuria, 1904–1932* (2001). On railroad strategies in empire building.

J. W. MORLEY, ed., *The China Quagmire* (1983). A study of Japan's expansion on the continent between 1933 and 1941. (For diplomatic history, see also the many other works by this author.)

R. H. MYERS AND M. R. PEATTIE, eds., *The Japanese Colonial Empire, 1895–1945* (1984).

T. NAJITA, *Hara Kei in the Politics of Compromise, 1905–1915* (1967). A study of one of Japan's greatest party leaders.

K. OHKAWA AND H. ROSOVSKY, *Japanese Economic Growth: Trend Acceleration in the Twentieth Century* (1973).

M. RAVINA, *The Last Samurai: The Life and Battles of Saigo Takamori* (2004). Unlike the movie, this account of the Satsuma uprising is historical.

G. SHIBA, *Remembering Aizu* (1999). A stirring autobiographical account of a samurai youth whose domain lost in the Meiji Restoration.

K. SMITH, *A Time of Crisis: The Great Depression and Rural Revitalization* (2001). An intellectual history of village movements during the 1930s.

J. J. STEPHAN, *Hawaii Under the Rising Sun* (1984). Japan's plans for rule in Hawaii.

R. H. SPECTOR, *Eagle Against the Sun: The American War with Japan* (1985). A narrative of World War II in the Pacific.

E. P. TSURUMI, *Factory Girls: Women in the Thread Mills of Meiji Japan* (1990). A sympathetic analysis of the key component of the Meiji labor force.

W. WRAY, *Mitsubishi and the N. Y. K., 1870–1914* (1984). The growth of a shipping *zaibatsu*, with analysis of business strategies, the role of government and imperialist involvements.

CHAPTER 29

L. ALBERTINI, *The Origins of the War of 1914*, 3 vols. (1952, 1957). Discursive but invaluable.

V. R. BERGHAHN, *Germany and the Approach of War in 1914* (1973). A work similar in spirit to both of Fischer's (see below) but stressing the importance of Germany's naval program.

R. BOSWORTH, *Italy and the Approach of the First World War* (1983). A fine analysis of Italian policy.

S. B. FAY, *The Origins of the World War*, 2 vols. (1928). The most influential of the revisionist accounts.

F. FISCHER, *Germany's Aims in the First World War* (1967). An influential interpretation that stirred a great controversy in Germany and around the world by emphasizing Germany's role in bringing on the war.

F. FISCHER, *War of Illusions* (1975). A long and diffuse book that tries to connect German responsibility for the war with internal social, economic, and political developments.

D. FROMKIN, *Europe's Last Summer: Who Started the Great War in 1914?* (2004). A lively account that fixes on the final crisis in July 1914.

J. N. HORNE, *Labour at War: France and Britain, 1914–1918* (1991). An examination of a major issue on the home fronts.

J. JOLL, *The Origins of the First World War* (1984). A brief but thoughtful analysis.

P. KENNEDY, *The Rise of the Anglo-German Antagonism 1860–1914* (1980). An unusual and thorough analysis of the political, economic, and cultural roots of important diplomatic developments.

W. L. LANGER, *European Alliances and Alignments*, 2nd ed. (1966). A splendid diplomatic history of the years 1871–1890.

W. L. LANGER, *The Diplomacy of Imperialism* (1935). A continuation of the previous study for the years 1890–1902.

D. C. B. LIEVEN, *Russia and the Origins of the First World War* (1983). A good account of the forces that shaped Russian policy.

A. MOMBAUER, *The Origins of the First World War. Controversies and Consensus* (2002). A fascinating survey of the debate over the decades and the current state of the question.

R. PIPES, *A Concise History of the Russian Revolution* (1996). A one-volume version of a scholarly masterpiece.

Z. STEINER, *Britain and the Origins of the First World War* (1977). A perceptive and informed account of the way British foreign policy was made in the years before the war.

H. STRACHAN, *The First World War* (2004). A fine one-volume account of the war.

A. J. P. TAYLOR, *The Struggle for Mastery in Europe, 1848–1918* (1954). Clever but controversial.

S. R. WILLIAMSON, JR., *Austria-Hungary and the Origins of the First World War* (1991). A valuable study of a complex subject.

CHAPTER 30

W. S. ALLEN, *The Nazi Seizure of Power: The Experience of a Single German Town, 1930–1935*, rev. ed. (1984). A classic treatment of Nazism in a microcosmic setting.

J. BARNARD, *Walter Reuther and the Rise of the Auto Workers* (1983). A major introduction to the new American unions of the 1930s.

K. D. BRACHER, *The German Dictatorship* (1970). A comprehensive treatment of both the origins and the functioning of the Nazi movement and government.

A. BULLOCK, *Hitler: A Study in Tyranny*, rev. ed. (1964). The best biography.

M. BURLEIGH AND W. WIPPERMAN, *The Racial State: Germany 1933–1945* (1991). Emphasizes the manner in which racial theory influenced numerous areas of policy.

R. CONQUEST, *The Great Terror: Stalin's Purges of the Thirties* (1968). The best treatment of the subject to this date.

G. CRAIG, *Germany, 1866–1945* (1978). A major survey.

I. DEUTSCHER, *The Prophet Armed* (1954), *The Prophet Unarmed* (1959), and *The Prophet Outcast* (1963). Remains the major biography of Trotsky.

I. DEUTSCHER, *Stalin: A Political Biography*, 2nd ed. (1967). The best biography in English.

B. EICHENGREEN, *Golden Fetters: The Gold Standard and the Great Depression, 1919–1939* (1992). A remarkable study of the role of the gold standard in the economic policies of the interwar years.

E. EYCK, *A History of the Weimar Republic*, 2 vols. (trans. 1963). The story as narrated by a liberal.

M. S. FAUSOLD, *The Presidency of Herbert Hoover* (1985). An important treatment.

G. FELDMAN, *The Great Disorder: Politics, Economics, and Society in the German Inflation, 1914–1924* (1993). The best work on the subject.

S. FITZPATRICK, *Stalin's Peasants: Resistance and Survival in the Russian Village After Collectivization* (1994). A pioneering study.

P. FUSSELL, *The Great War and Modern Memory* (1975). A brilliant account of the literature arising from World War I during the 1920s.

J. K. GALBRAITH, *The Great Crash* (1979). A well-known account by a leading economist.

R. GELLATELY, *The Gestapo and German Society: Enforcing Racial Policy, 1933–1945* (1990). A discussion of how the police state supported Nazi racial policies.

H. J. GORDON, *Hitler and the Beer Hall Putsch* (1972). An excellent account of the event and the political situation in the early Weimar Republic.

R. HAMILTON, *Who Voted for Hitler?* (1982). An examination of voting patterns and sources of Nazi support.

J. HELD, ed., *The Columbia History of Eastern Europe in the Twentieth Century* (1992). Individual essays on each country.

P. KENEZ, *The Birth of the Propaganda State: Soviet Methods of Mass Mobilization, 1917–1929* (1985). An examination of the manner in which the Communist government inculcated popular support.

B. KENT, *The Spoils of War: The Politics, Economics, and Diplomacy of Reparations, 1918–1932* (1993). A comprehensive account of the intricacies of the reparations problem of the 1920s.

D. LANDES, *The Unbound Prometheus: Technological Change and Industrial Development in Western Europe from 1750 to the Present* (1969). Includes an excellent analysis of both the Great Depression and the few areas of economic growth.

B. LINCOLN, *Red Victory: A History of the Russian Civil War* (1989). An excellent narrative account.

M. MCAULEY, *Bread and Justice: State and Society in Petrograd, 1917–1922* (1991). A study that examines the impact of the Russian Revolution and Leninist policies on a major Russian city.

D. J. K. PEUKERT, *Inside Nazi Germany: Conformity, Opposition, and Racism in Everyday Life* (1987). An excellent discussion of life under Nazi rule.

R. PIPES, *The Unknown Lenin: From the Secret Archives* (1996). A collection of previously unpublished documents that indicated the repressive character of Lenin's government.

P. PULZER, *Jews and the German State: The Political History of a Minority, 1848–1933* (1992). A detailed history by a major historian of European minorities.

L. J. RUPP, *Mobilizing Women for War: German and America Propaganda, 1939–1945* (1978). Although concentrating on a later period, it includes an excellent discussion of general Nazi attitudes toward women.

A. M. SCHLESINGER, JR., *The Age of Roosevelt*, 3 vols. (1957–1960). The most important overview.

D. M. SMITH, *Mussolini's Roman Empire* (1976). A general description of the Fascist regime in Italy.

D. M. SMITH, *Italy and Its Monarchy* (1989). A major treatment of an important neglected subject.

A. SOLZHENITSYN, *The Gulag Archipelago*, 3 vols. (1974–1979). A major examination of the labor camps under Stalin by one of the most important contemporary Russian writers.

R. J. SONTAG, *A Broken World, 1919–1939* (1971). An exceptionally thoughtful and well-organized survey.

A. J. P. TAYLOR, *English History, 1914–1945* (1965). Lively and opinionated.

H. A. TURNER JR., *German Big Business and the Rise of Hitler* (1985). An important major study of the subject.

H. A. TURNER JR., *Hitler's Thirty Days to Power* (1996). A narrative of the events leading directly to the Nazi seizure of power.

L. YAHIL, *The Holocaust: The Fate of European Jewry, 1932–1945* (1990). A major study of this fundamental subject in twentieth-century history.

CHAPTER 31

A. ADAMTHWAITE, *France and the Coming of the Second World War,* 1936–1939 (1977). A careful account making good use of the French archives.

E. R. BECK, *Under the Bombs: The German Home Front,* 1942–1945 (1986). An interesting examination of a generally unstudied subject.

R. S. BOTWINICK, *A History of the Holocaust,* 2nd ed., 2002. A brief but broad and useful account of the causes, character and results of the Holocaust.

A. BULLOCK, *Hitler: A Study in Tyranny,* rev. ed. (1964). A brilliant biography.

W. S. CHURCHILL, *The Second World War,* 6 vols. (1948–1954). The memoirs of the great British leader.

A. CROZIER, *The Causes of the Second World War,* 1997. An examination of what brought on the war.

R. B. FRANK, *Downfall: The End of the Imperial Japanese Empire,* 1998. A thorough, well-documented account of the last months of the Japanese empire and the reasons for its surrender.

J. L. GADDIS, *We Now Know: Rethinking Cold War History* (1998). A fine account of the early years of the Cold War making use of new evidence emerging since the collapse of the Soviet Union.

J. L. GADDIS, P. H. GORDON, E. MAY, eds., *Cold War Statesmen Confront the Bomb: Nuclear diplomacy Since 1945* (1999). A collection of essays discussing the effect of atomic and nuclear weapons on diplomacy since WW II.

M. GILBERT, *The Holocaust: A History of the Jews of Europe During the Second World War* (1985). The best and most comprehensive treatment.

A. IRIYE, *Pearl Harbor and the Coming of the Pacific War* (1999). Essays on how the Pacific war came about, including a selection of documents.

J. KEEGAN, *The Second World War* (1990). A lively and penetrating account by a master military historian.

I. KERSHAW, *Hitler: 1889–1936: Hubris* (1999) and *Hitler: 1936–1945: Nemesis* (2001). An outstanding two-volume biography.

W. F. KIMBALL, *Forged in War: Roosevelt, Churchill, and the Second World War,* (1998). A study of the collaboration between the two great leaders of the West based on a thorough knowledge of their correspondence.

W. MURRAY AND A. R. MILLETT, *A War to be Won: Fighting the Second World War,* (2000). A splendid account of the military operations in the war.

R. OVERY, *Why the Allies Won* (1997). An anlysis of the reasons for the victory of the Allies with special emphasis on technology.

N. RICH, *Hitler War Aims,* 2 vols. (1973–1974). The best study of the subject in English.

H. THOMAS, *The Spanish Civil War,* 3rd ed. (1986). The best account in English.

P. WANDYCZ, *The Twilight of French Eastern Alliances,* 1926–1936 (1988). A well-documented account of the diplomacy of central and eastern Europe in a crucial period.

G. L. WEINBERG, *A World at Arms: A Global History of World War II* (1994). A thorough and excellent narrative account.

CHAPTER 32

B. S. ANDERSON AND J. P. PINSSER, *A History of Their Own: Women in Europe from Prehistory to the Present,* Vol. 2 (1988). A broad-ranging survey.

R. BERNSTEIN, *Out of the Blue: The Story of September 11, 2001 from Jihad to Ground Zero* (2002). An excellent account by a gifted journalist.

A. BROWN, *The Gorbachev Factor* (1996). An important commentary by an English observer.

D. CALLEO, *Rethinking Europe's Future* (2003) A daring book by an experienced commentator.

J. L. GADDIS, *What We Know Now* (1997). Examines the Cold War in light of newly released documents.

D. J. GARROW, *Bearing the Cross: Martin Luther King, Jr. and the Southern Leadership Conference 1955–1968* (1986). The best work on the subject.

W. HITCHCOCK, *Struggle for Europe: The Turbulent History of a Divided Continent, 1945–2002* (2003). The best overall narrative now available

D. KEARNS, *Lyndon Johnson and the American Dream* (1976). A useful biography.

J. KEEP, *The Last of the Empires: A History of the Soviet Union, 1956–1991* (1995). A clear narrative.

M. MANDELBAUM, *The Ideas That Conquered the World: Peace, Democracy, and Free Markets* (2002). An important analysis by a major commentator on international affairs.

J. MANN, *The Rise of the Vulcans: The History of Bush's War Cabinet* (2004). An account of the major foreign policy advisors behind the invasion of Iraq.

R. MANN, *A Grand Delusion: America's Descent into Vietnam* (2001). The best recent narrative.

J. McCORMICK, *Understanding the European Union: A Concise Introduction* (2002) Outlines the major features.

N. NAIMARK, *Fires of Hatred: Ethnic Cleansing in Twentieth-Century Europe* (2002). A remarkably sensitive treatment of a tragic subject.

R. SAWKA AND ANNE STEVENS, eds., *Contemporary Europe* (2000). A collection of essays on major topics.

G. STOKES, ed., *From Stalinism to Pluralism: A Documentary History of Eastern Europe Since 1945* (1996). An important collection of documents that are not easily accessible elsewhere.

M. WALKER, *The Cold War and the Making of the Modern World* (1994). A major survey.

CHAPTER 33

China

R. BAUM, *Burying Mao: Chinese Politics in the Age of Deng Xiaoping* (1996).

A. CHAN, R. MADSEN, J. UNGER, *Chen Village under Mao and Deng* (1992).

J. CHANG, *Wild Swans: Three Daughters of China* (1991). An intimate look at recent Chinese society through three generations of women. Immensely readable.

J. FENG, *Ten Years of Madness: Oral Histories of China's Cultural Revolution* (1996).

J. FEWSMITH, *China Since Tiananmen: The Politics of Transition* (2001). Focus is on the rise to power of Jiang Zemin and Chinese politics during the nineties.

B. M. FROLIC, *Mao's People: Sixteen Portraits of Life in Revolutionary China* (1987).

T. GOLD, *State and Society in the Taiwan Miracle* (1986). The story of economic growth in postwar Taiwan.

M. GOLDMAN, *Sowing the Seeds of Democracy in China: Political Reform in the Deng Xiaoping Era* (1994).

A. IRIYE, *China and Japan in the Global Setting* (1992).

D. M. LAMPTON, *Same Bed, Different Dreams: Managing U.S.–China Relations, 1989–2000* (2001).

H. LIANG, *Son of the Revolution* (1983). An autobiographical account of a young man growing up in Mao's China.

K. LIEBERTHAL, *Governing China, from Revolution Through Reform* (2004).

B. LIU, *People or Monsters? and Other Stories and Reportage from China After Mao* (1983). Literary reflections on China.

R. MACFARQUHAR AND J. K. FAIRBANK, eds., *The Cambridge History of China*, Vol. 14, *Emergence of Revolutionary China* (1987), and Vol. 15, *Revolutions Within the Chinese Revolution, 1966–1982* (1991).

L. PAN, *Sons of the Yellow Emperor: A History of the Chinese Diaspora* (1990). A pioneer study that treats not only Southeast Asia but the rest of the world as well.

M. R. RISTAINO, *Port of Last Resort: The Diaspora Communities of Shanghai* (2001).

T. SAICH, *Governance and Politics of China* (2004).

H. WANG, *China's New Order* (2003). Translation of a work by a Qinghua University professor, a liberal within the boundaries of what is permissable in China.

G. WHITE, ed., *In Search of Civil Society: Market Reform and Social Change in Contemporary China* (1996).

M. WOLF, *Revolution Postponed: Women in Contemporary China* (1985).

ZHANG X. AND SANG Y., *Chinese Lives: An Oral History of Contemporary China* (1987).

Japan

G. L. BERNSTEIN, *Haruko's World: A Japanese Farm Woman and Her Community* (1983). A study of the changing life of a village woman in postwar Japan.

T. BESTOR, *Neighborhood Tokyo* (1989). A portrait of contemporary urban life in Japan.

G. L. CURTIS, *The Logic of Japanese Politics: Leaders, Institutions, and the Limits of Change* (1999).

G. L. CURTIS, *Policymaking in Japan: Defining the Role of Politicians* (2002).

M. H. CUSUMANO, *The Japanese Automobile Industry* (1985). A neat study of the postwar business strategies of Toyota and Nissan.

R. P. DORE, *City Life in Japan* (1999). A classic, reissued.

R. P. DORE, *Land Reform in Japan* (1959). Another classic.

S. GARON, *Molding Japanese Minds: The State in Everyday Life* (1997).

S. M. GARON, *The Evolution of Civil Society from Meiji to Heisei* (2002). That is to say, from the mid–nineteenth century to the present day.

A. GORDON, ed., *Postwar Japan as History* (1993).

H. HIBBETT, ed., *Contemporary Japanese Literature: An Anthology of Fiction, Film, and Other Writing Since 1945* (1977). Translations of postwar short stories.

Y. KAWABATA, *The Sound of the Mountain* (1970). Sensitive, moving novel by Nobel author.

J. NATHAN, *Sony, the Private Life* (1999). A lively account of the human side of growth in the Sony Corporation.

D. OKIMOTO, *Between MITI and the Market* (1989). A discussion of the respective roles of government and private enterprise in Japan's postwar growth.

S. PHARR, *Losing Face: Status Politics in Japan* (1996).

E. F. VOGEL, *Japan as Number One: Lessons for America* (1979). While dated and somewhat sanguine, this remains an insightful classic.

Korea and Vietnam

B. Cumings, *Korea, The Unknown War* (1988).

B. Cumings, *The Origins of the Korean War* (Vol. 1, 1981; Vol. 2, 1991).

B. Cumings, *The Two Koreas: On the Road to Reunification?* (1990).

C. J. Eckert, *Korea Old and New, A History* (1990). The best short history of Korea, with extensive coverage of the postwar era.

C. J. Eckert, *Offspring of Empire: The Koch'ang Kims and the Colonial Origins of Korean Capitalism, 1876–1945* (1991).

G. M. T. Kahin, *Intervention: How America Became Involved in Vietnam* (1986).

S. Karnow, *Vietnam: A History*. rev. ed. (1996).

L. Kendall, *Shamans, Housewives, and Other Restless Spirits: Women in Korean Ritual and Life* (1985).

K. B. Lee, *A New History of Korea* (1984). A translation by E. Wagner and others of an outstanding Korean work covering the full sweep of Korean history.

T. Li, *Nguyen Cochinchina: South Vietnam in the Seventeenth and Eighteenth Centuries* (1998).

D. Marr, *Vietnam 1945: The Quest for Power* (1995).

C. W. Sorensen, *Over the Mountains Are Mountains* (1988). How peasant households in Korea adapted to rapid industrialization.

A. Woodside, *Vietnam and the Chinese Model* (1988). Provides the background for Vietnam's relationship to China.

CHAPTER 34
Latin America

P. Bakewell, *A History of Latin America: c. 1450 to the Present* (2003). An up-to-date survey.

A. Chomsky et al., *The Cuba Reader: History, Culture, Politics* (2004). Very useful, broad-ranging anthology.

J. Dominguez and M. Shifter, *Contructing Democratic Governance in Latin America* (2003). Contains individual country studies.

G. Joseph et al. , *The Mexico Reader: History, Culture, Politics*(2003). Excellent introduction to major issues.

P. Lowden, *Moral Opposition to Authoritarian Rule in Chile* (1996). A discussion of Chilean politics from the standpoint of human rights.

J. Preston and S. Dillon, *Opening Mexico: The Making of a Democracy* (2004). Excellent analysis of recent developments in Mexico.

H. Wirarda, *Democracy and Its Discontents: Development, Interdependence, and U.S. Policy in Latin America* (1995). A useful overview.

Africa

B. Davidson, *Let Freedom Come* (1978). Remains a thought commentary of African independence.

R. W. July, *A History of the African People,* 5th ed. (1995). Provides a careful and clear survey of post–World War I history and consideration of nationalism.

J. Herbst, *States and Power in Africa* (2000). Relates current issues of African state-building to those before to the colonial era.

J. H. Latham, *Africa, Asia, and South America Since 1800: A Bibliographic Guide* (1995). A valuable tool for finding materials on the topics in this chapter.

N. Mandela, *Long Walk to Freedom: The Autobiography of Nelson Mandela* (1995). Autobiography of the African leader who transformed South Africa.

L. Thompson, *A History of South Africa* (2001). The best survey.

N. Van de Walle, *African Economies and the Politics of Perm anent Crisis, 1979–1999* (2001). Exploration of difficulties of African economic development.

India and Pakistan

O. B. Jones, *Pakistan: Eye of the Storm* (2003). Best recent introduction.

R. Rashid, *Taliban: Militant Islam, Oil and Fundamentalism in Central Asia* (2001). Analysis of radical Isalmist regime in Afghanistan.

R. W. Stern, *Changing India: Bourgeois Revolution on the Subcontinent* (2003). Overview of forces now changing Indian society.

S. Wolpert, *A New History of India* (2003). The closing chapters of this fine survey history are particularly helpful in orienting the reader in postwar Indian history until the mid-1980s.

Islam and the Middle East

A. Ahmed, *Discovering Islam. Making Sense of Muslim Hisotry and Society*, rev. ed. (2003). An excellent and readable overiew of Islamic– Western relations.

J. Esposito, *The Islamic Threat: Myth or Reality*, 2nd ed. (1992). A useful corrective to some of the polemics against Islam and Muslims today.

J. J. Esposito, ed., *The Oxford Encyclopedia of Islam* (1999). A thematic survey of Islamic history, particularly strong in the Modern Era.

D. FROMKIN, *A Peace to End All Peace: The Fall of the Ottoman Empire and the Creation of the Modern Middle East* (2001). Very good on the impact of World War I on the region.

G. FULLER, *The Future of Political Islam* (2003). A very good overview of Islamist ideology by a former CIA staff member.

J. KEAY, *Sowing the Wind: The Seeds of Conflict in theMiddle East* (2003). A balanced account.

N. R. KEDDIE, *Modern Iran. Roots and Results of Revolution* (2003). Chapters 6–12 focus on Iran from 1941 through the first years of the 1978 revolution and provide a solid overview of history in this era.

G. KEPEL, *Jihad: The Trail of Political Islam* (2002). An extensive treatment by a leading French scholar of the subject.

Bronze equestrian statuette of Charlemagne, from Metz Cathedral, 9th–10th c. 3/4 view. Louvre, Paris, France. Copyright Bridgeman-Giraudon/Art Resource, NY; William haranguing his troups for combat with the English army. Detail from the Bayeux tapestry, scene 51. Musee de la Tapisserie, Bayeux, France. Photograph copyright Bridgeman-Giraudon/Art Resource, NY; Ewer with carved flower sprays. China; Yaozhou, Shaanxi province. Northern Song dynasty (960–1127). Porcelain with carved decoration under celadon glaze. H. 9 5/8 in × W. 5 1/4 in × D. 7 3/4 in, H. 24.5 cm × W. 13.4 cm × D. 19.7 cm. Museum purchase, B66P12 © Asian Art Museum of San Francisco. Used by permission; A leaf from a Manichaean Book, Kocho, Temple K (MIK III 6368), 8th–9th century, manuscript painting, 17.2 × 11.2 cm. Museum fur Indische Kunst, Staatliche Museen Preussischer Kulturbesitz, Berlin; Copyright Werner Forman/Art Resource, NY; Odyssey Productions, Inc

Part 3, Timeline, top to bottom, left to right: Art Resource, NY; The Nelson-Atkins Museum of Art, Kansas City, Missouri. (Purchase: Nelson Trust) 50-20; The Granger Collection, NY; Albert Craig; Werner Forman/Art Resource, NY; Templo Mayor CoyoIxauhqui. Aztec Moon Goddess Stone. Aztec, 15th century. Stone, diameter 11'6" (3.5 m).

Chapter 8 a. Corbis/Bettmann; c. CORBIS-NY; d. CORBIS-NY; e. Gift of the Asian Art Museum of San Francisco. The Avery Brundage Collection, B66P12; f. Worcester Art Museum; g. Dorling Kindersley Media Library.

Chapter 9 a. Corbis/Bettmann; c. Araldo de Luca/Corbis/ Bettmann; d. Corbis/Bettmann; e. Tokyo National Museum; f. Corbis/Bettmann; g. "Fan-Shaped Sutra" Tokyo National Museum. Image: TNM Image Archives. Source: **http://TnmArchives.jp/**; h. "Scroll w/depictions of the Night Attach on the Sanjo Palace" from Heiji monogatari emaki, 2nd half of the 13th c. Unknown. Japanese, Kamakura Period. Handscroll; ink & colors on paper. 41.3 × 699.7 cm. Fenollosa-Weld C. Courtesy of Museum of Fine Arts, Boston; i. PPS/Pacific Press Service.

Chapter 10 a. Corbis/Bettmann b. Art Resource, NY; c. J. Kershaw/Dorling Kindersley Media Library; d. J. Kershaw/ Dorling Kindersley Media Library; e. Corbis/Bettmann; f. © Hulton-Deutsch Collection/CORBIS; g. Sassanid Art. Bottom of a silver bowl with Sassanid relief work. Leningrad Museum. Corbis-Bettmann; h. Borromeo; Art Resource, NY; i. The Nelson-Atkins Museum of Art, Kansas City, Missouri. (Purchase: Nelson Trust) 50-20; j. Paul Almasy; Corbis/ Bettmann; k. J. Kershaw; Dorling Kindersley Media Library.

Chapter 11 a. Courtesy of Freer Gallery of Art, Smithsonian Institution, Washington, DC; b. Bowl. Unidentified. 10th Century, Earthenware painted under glaze H 11.2 × Diam. 39.3 cm. Iran. freer Gallery of Art, Smithsonian Institution, Washington, D.C.: Purchase, F1957.24; c. Mehmet Biber/ Photo Researchers, Inc.; d. Dorling Kindersley Media Library; e. Arabic Manuscript: 30.60 Page from a Koran, 8th–9th century. Kufic script. H: 23.8 × W: 35.5 cm. Courtesy of the Freer Gallery of Art, Smithsonian Institution, Washington, D.C.; f. Werner Forman Archive; Art Resource, NY; g. Library of Congress; h. Scala/Art Resource, NY; i. Adam Lubroth, Art Resource, NY.

Chapter 12 a. Trinity College, Dublin, Ireland/Rev. Raymond Schoder/SuperStock; c. Book of Kells: St. Matthew, Chi Rho initial. Ca. 800 C.E.. Trinity College, Dublin, Ireland, © Art Resource, NY; d. © Werner Forman/Art Resource, NY; e. Scala/Art Resource, NY; f. Bodleian Library, University of Oxford; g. Giraudon/Art Resource; h. Bronze equestrian statuette of Charlemagne, from Metz Cathedral, 9th–10th c. 3/4 view. Louvre, Paris, France. Copyright Giraudon/Art Resource, NY; i. Giraudon/Art Resource, NY; j. Giraudon/Art Resource, NY; k. Kunsthistorisches Museum, Vienna.

Chapter 13 a. "Khusraw at the castle of Shirin" Folio from a manuscript by Nizami. Iran, early 15th century. Opaque watercolor, ink, and gold on paper; 25.7 × 18.4 cm. Courtesy of the Freer Gallery of Art, Smithsonian Institution, Washington DC, Purchase F1931.36. b. Bowl. Iran, late 12th century. Stone-paste painted over glaze with luster; 7.8 × 17.3 cm. Arthur M. Sackler Gallery, Smithsonian Institution, Washington, D.C. Gift of Osborne and Gratia Hauge, S1997.113; c. Adam Woolfitt; Corbis/Bettmann; d. Giraudon/Art Resource, NY; Robert Harding World Imagery; e. Geoff Dann; Dorling Kindersley Media Library; f. Clare Arni; Dorling Kindersley Media Library; g. By permission of the British Library.

Chapter 14 a. Lowell Georgia/NGS Image Collection; b. Siede Preis; Getty Images, Inc.-Photodisc; c. © CONACULTA-INAH-MEX. Authorized reproduction by the Instituto Nacional de Antropologia e Historia; e. Getty Images Inc./Photodisc; f. ©Erich Lessing/Art Resource, NY; g. Robert Frerck/Odyssey Productions, Inc.; h. Sexto Sol/Getty Images Inc. - Photodisc; i. © CONACULTA-INAH-MEX. Authorized reproduction by the Instituto Nacional de Antropologia e Historia; j Robert and Linda Mitchell Photography; k. Robert Frerk/Odyssey Productions; l. © Bettmann/CORBIS.

Chapter 15 a. Dorling Kindersley/The Wallace Collection; b. Cliché des Musees Nationaux, Paris; c. Museo Civico, Bologna, Italy; d. Giraudon/Art Resource, NY; e. Scala/Art Resource, NY; f. Scala/Art Resource, NY; g. Scala/Art Resource, NY; h. Scala/Art Resource, NY; i. Photograph © Erich Lessing/Art Resource, NY; j. Reunion des Musees Nationaux/Art Reesource, NY.

Part 4 Timeline, top to bottom, left to right: Elizabeth I (1558–1603) standing on a map of England in 1592. An astute politician in both foreign and domestic policy, Elizabeth was perhaps the most successful ruler of the sixteenth century. By courtesy of the National Portrait Gallery, London; Sultan Muhammad (active ca. 1501–1545), "Allegory of Worldly and Otherworldly Drunkenness". Leaf from a manuscript of a "Divan" by Hafiz, folio 137r. Opaque watercolor, ink and gold on paper. 11 3/8 × 8 1/2 in. (28.9 × 21.6 cm). Promised Gift of Mr. and Mrs. Stuart Cary Welch, Jr. in honor of the students of Harvard University and Radcliffe College. Partially owned by The Metropolitan Museum of Art and The Arthur M. Sackler Museum, Harvard University, 1988. Copyright 1989, Metropolitan Museum of Art; Library of Congress; The Bridgeman Art Library International Ltd; © Archivo Iconografico, S. A./Corbis.

Part 4 Timeline, top to bottom, left to right: Bridgeman-Giraudon/Art Resource, NY; Francis Wheatley (RA) (1747–1801) "Evening", signed and dated 1799, oil on canvas, 17 1/2 × 21 1/2 in.

WORLD HISTORY DOCUMENTS CD-ROM

SINGLE PC LICENSE AGREEMENT AND LIMITED WARRANTY

READ THIS LICENSE CAREFULLY BEFORE OPENING THIS PACKAGE. BY OPENING THIS PACKAGE, YOU ARE AGREEING TO THE TERMS AND CONDITIONS OF THIS LICENSE. IF YOU DO NOT AGREE, DO NOT OPEN THE PACKAGE. PROMPTLY RETURN THE UNOPENED PACKAGE AND ALL ACCOMPANYING ITEMS TO THE PLACE YOU OBTAINED THEM.

1. **GRANT OF LICENSE AND OWNERSHIP:** THE ENCLOSED COMPUTER PROGRAMS <<AND DATA>> ("SOFTWARE") ARE LICENSED, NOT SOLD, TO YOU BY PEARSON EDUCATION, INC. PUBLISHING AS PEARSON PRENTICE HALL ("WE" OR THE "COMPANY") AND IN CONSIDERATION OF YOUR PURCHASE OR ADOPTION OF THE ACCOMPANYING COMPANY TEXTBOOKS AND/OR OTHER MATERIALS, AND YOUR AGREEMENT TO THESE TERMS. WE RESERVE ANY RIGHTS NOT GRANTED TO YOU. YOU OWN ONLY THE DISK(S) BUT WE AND/OR OUR LICENSORS OWN THE SOFTWARE ITSELF. THIS LICENSE ALLOWS YOU TO USE AND DISPLAY YOUR COPY OF THE SOFTWARE ON A SIN-GLE COMPUTER (I.E., WITH A SINGLE CPU) AT A SINGLE LOCATION FOR ACADEMIC USE ONLY, SO LONG AS YOU COMPLY WITH THE TERMS OF THIS AGREEMENT. YOU MAY MAKE ONE COPY FOR BACK UP, OR TRANSFER YOUR COPY TO ANOTHER CPU, PROVIDED THAT THE SOFTWARE IS USABLE ON ONLY ONE COMPUTER.

2. **RESTRICTIONS:** YOU MAY NOT TRANSFER OR DISTRIBUTE THE SOFTWARE OR DOCUMENTATION TO ANY-ONE ELSE. EXCEPT FOR BACKUP, YOU MAY NOT COPY THE DOCUMENTATION OR THE SOFTWARE. YOU MAY NOT NETWORK THE SOFTWARE OR OTHERWISE USE IT ON MORE THAN ONE COMPUTER OR COMPUTER TER-MINAL AT THE SAME TIME. YOU MAY NOT REVERSE ENGINEER, DISASSEMBLE, DECOMPILE, MODIFY, ADAPT, TRANSLATE, OR CREATE DERIVATIVE WORKS BASED ON THE SOFTWARE OR THE DOCUMENTATION. YOU MAY BE HELD LEGALLY RESPONSIBLE FOR ANY COPYING OR COPYRIGHT INFRINGEMENT THAT IS CAUSED BY YOUR FAILURE TO ABIDE BY THE TERMS OF THESE RESTRICTIONS.

3. **TERMINATION:** THIS LICENSE IS EFFECTIVE UNTIL TERMINATED. THIS LICENSE WILL TERMINATE AUTO-MATICALLY WITHOUT NOTICE FROM THE COMPANY IF YOU FAIL TO COMPLY WITH ANY PROVISIONS OR LIMI-TATIONS OF THIS LICENSE. UPON TERMINATION, YOU SHALL DESTROY THE DOCUMENTATION AND ALL COPIES OF THE SOFTWARE. ALL PROVISIONS OF THIS AGREEMENT AS TO LIMITATION AND DISCLAIMER OF WARRANTIES, LIMITATION OF LIABILITY, REMEDIES OR DAMAGES, AND OUR OWNERSHIP RIGHTS SHALL SUR-VIVE TERMINATION.

4. **LIMITED WARRANTY AND DISCLAIMER OF WARRANTY:** COMPANY WARRANTS THAT FOR A PERIOD OF 60 DAYS FROM THE DATE YOU PURCHASE THIS SOFTWARE (OR PURCHASE OR ADOPT THE ACCOMPANYING TEXT-BOOK), THE SOFTWARE, WHEN PROPERLY INSTALLED AND USED IN ACCORDANCE WITH THE DOCUMENTATION, WILL OPERATE IN SUBSTANTIAL CONFORMITY WITH THE DESCRIPTION OF THE SOFTWARE SET FORTH IN THE DOCUMENTATION, AND THAT FOR A PERIOD OF 30 DAYS THE DISK(S) ON WHICH THE SOFTWARE IS DELIVERED SHALL BE FREE FROM DEFECTS IN MATERIALS AND WORKMANSHIP UNDER NORMAL USE. THE COMPANY DOES NOT WARRANT THAT THE SOFTWARE WILL MEET YOUR REQUIREMENTS OR THAT THE OPERATION OF THE SOFTWARE WILL BE UNINTERRUPTED OR ERROR-FREE. YOUR ONLY REMEDY AND THE COMPANY'S ONLY OBLIGATION UNDER THESE LIMITED WARRANTIES IS, AT THE COMPANY'S OPTION, RETURN OF THE DISK FOR A REFUND OF ANY AMOUNTS PAID FOR IT BY YOU OR REPLACEMENT OF THE DISK. THIS LIMITED WARRANTY IS THE ONLY WARRANTY PROVIDED BY THE COMPANY AND ITS LICENSORS, AND THE COMPANY AND ITS LICENSORS DISCLAIM ALL OTHER WARRANTIES, EXPRESS OR IMPLIED, INCLUDING WITH-OUT LIMITATION, THE IMPLIED WARRANTIES OF MERCHANTABILITY AND FITNESS FOR A PARTICULAR PUR-POSE. THE COMPANY DOES NOT WARRANT, GUARANTEE OR MAKE ANY REPRESENTATION REGARDING THE ACCURACY, RELIABILITY, CURRENTNESS, USE, OR RESULTS OF USE, OF THE SOFTWARE.

5. **LIMITATION OF REMEDIES AND DAMAGES:** IN NO EVENT, SHALL THE COMPANY OR ITS EMPLOYEES, AGENTS, LICENSORS, OR CONTRACTORS BE LIABLE FOR ANY INCIDENTAL, INDIRECT, SPECIAL, OR CONSE-QUENTIAL DAMAGES ARISING OUT OF OR IN CONNECTION WITH THIS LICENSE OR THE SOFTWARE, INCLUD-ING FOR LOSS OF USE, LOSS OF DATA, LOSS OF INCOME OR PROFIT, OR OTHER LOSSES, SUSTAINED AS A RESULT OF INJURY TO ANY PERSON, OR LOSS OF OR DAMAGE TO PROPERTY, OR CLAIMS OF THIRD PARTIES, EVEN IF THE COMPANY OR AN AUTHORIZED REPRESENTATIVE OF THE COMPANY HAS BEEN ADVISED OF THE POSSIBILITY OF SUCH DAMAGES. IN NO EVENT SHALL THE LIABILITY OF THE COMPANY FOR DAMAGES WITH RESPECT TO THE SOFTWARE EXCEED THE AMOUNTS ACTUALLY PAID BY YOU, IF ANY, FOR THE SOFTWARE OR THE ACCOMPANYING TEXTBOOK. BECAUSE SOME JURISDICTIONS DO NOT ALLOW THE LIMITATION OF LIA-BILITY IN CERTAIN CIRCUMSTANCES, THE ABOVE LIMITATIONS MAY NOT ALWAYS APPLY TO YOU.

6. **GENERAL:** THIS AGREEMENT SHALL BE CONSTRUED IN ACCORDANCE WITH THE LAWS OF THE UNITED STATES OF AMERICA AND THE STATE OF NEW YORK, APPLICABLE TO CONTRACTS MADE IN NEW YORK, EXCLUDING THE STATE'S LAWS AND POLICIES ON CONFLICTS OF LAW, AND SHALL BENEFIT THE COMPANY, ITS AFFILIATES AND ASSIGNEES. THIS AGREEMENT IS THE COMPLETE AND EXCLUSIVE STATEMENT OF THE AGREEMENT BETWEEN YOU AND THE COMPANY AND SUPERSEDES ALL PROPOSALS OR PRIOR AGREEMENTS, ORAL, OR WRITTEN, AND ANY OTHER COMMUNICATIONS BETWEEN YOU AND THE COMPANY OR ANY REPRE-SENTATIVE OF THE COMPANY RELATING TO THE SUBJECT MATTER OF THIS AGREEMENT. IF YOU ARE A U.S. GOVERNMENT USER, THIS SOFTWARE IS LICENSED WITH "RESTRICTED RIGHTS" AS SET FORTH IN SUBPARA-GRAPHS (A)-(D) OF THE COMMERCIAL COMPUTER-RESTRICTED RIGHTS CLAUSE AT FAR 52.227-19 OR IN SUB-PARAGRAPHS (C)(1)(II) OF THE RIGHTS IN TECHNICAL DATA AND COMPUTER SOFTWARE CLAUSE AT DFARS 252.227-7013, AND SIMILAR CLAUSES, AS APPLICABLE.

SHOULD YOU HAVE ANY QUESTIONS CONCERNING THIS AGREEMENT OR IF YOU WISH TO CONTACT THE COMPANY FOR ANY REASON, PLEASE CONTACT IN WRITING: LEGAL DEPARTMENT, PRENTICE HALL, 1 LAKE STREET, UPPER SADDLE RIVER, NJ 07450 OR CALL PEARSON EDUCATION PRODUCT SUPPORT AT 1-800-677-6337.